Political Philosophy
3rd Edition

Ted M. Preston, Ph.D.
Rio Hondo College

A Local Source Textbook™ Company

Political Philosophy

Preface to the 3rd Edition

The third edition of this text corrects minor errors from the second. This edition also includes an entirely new chapter. This is the first of several planned new chapters addressing "special topics" of contemporary political interest. This new chapter addresses the rising influence of "white nationalism," and explores the philosophical assumptions (and errors) that inform it. These changes are the product of the "living laboratory" provided by my students, for whom I am grateful.

Acknowledgments

To attempt to distill "the most important" Western political ideas over the past couple thousand years into an accessible and reasonably-sized text is a daunting task, and I blush at the thought of some of the important figures that I have left out. Any omissions, such as that of Rousseau or Marx, for example, should not be interpreted as a lack of importance so much as a need for focus.

Although this book is presented primarily as a historical survey of some of the major political theorists and their ideas, my hope is that the themes and ideas addressed within will appear as timeless and relevant to the reader as they seem to me.

I would (once again) like to thank my colleague Dr. Adam Wetsman for his vision of Gnutext, and his promotion of these books that I write with pleasure.

Finally, I would be remiss if I did not thank my students, for whom I write. My desire to create affordable and reader-friendly books for *you* is what makes this book, and the others, a reality.

Table of Contents

Introduction

With the possible exception of religion, is there any subject matter more volatile than "politics?" Any topic more prone to heated disagreement and less amenable to reason and proper argumentation?

Rest assured that this book is not some partisan diatribe. It emulates neither Fox News nor MSNBC. Indeed, it is not until the very last chapter of the book that contemporary politics and political parties are even addressed in any significant detail.

Instead, this book is a historical survey of some of the major philosophers who have contributed to political theory in Western culture. Once we have completed this survey, we can attempt to discern to what extent (if at all!) contemporary politics and politicians have been informed by the great minds of the philosophical tradition.

We will begin with a brief primer on critical thinking, before considering any of the actual philosophers and their arguments. We will then launch our journey at a starting-point that technically precedes the birth of philosophy by considering political themes that arise in *Antigone*. Having paid homage to the poets, we will then turn to the philosophers.

As might be appropriate, the first philosopher we will consider is Socrates himself, followed soon thereafter by the massive and comprehensive contributions of his most famous student, Plato, and then Plato's most famous student, Aristotle. We will then shift from Greece to Rome, and delve into the ideas of Cicero, and stoicism more generally.

Just as the Roman Empire gave way to a Christian Europe, so too will our investigation turn to Christian political thought via St. Augustine and St. Aquinas. The tone will shift dramatically once again when we reach the birth of "modern" politics in the works of Machiavelli and Hobbes. Their "realism" will then, itself, give way to the more optimistic theories of the Enlightenment, as exemplified by Locke.

On the heels of Locke, we will then consider the philosophy behind the founding of the American political system, and lurking in the Declaration of Independence, U.S. Constitution, and the Federalist Papers. .

We will then consider the intimate relationship between politics and economics as initially developed by Adam Smith, and then amplified by Ayn Rand.

Our last "historical" chapter will consider the application of utilitarianism to politics, including, specifically, with regard to libertarianism. Then, our journey will catch up to the present day when we consider the issue of political pluralism via John Rawls, and his influence on President Barack Obama.

Finally, our last chapter deviates from the pattern of all that came before it. It will consider contemporary political decision-making not through the lens of political theory, but through conceptual metaphors, and propose that the deep disagreements between our major political parties is not due to the influence of different philosophers, but due to profoundly different family models.

I have provided several comprehension questions at the beginning of each chapter to help students focus on key elements, vocabulary, and themes. Nearly every chapter ends with a selection (at times lengthy) of primary source materials pertaining to the philosopher (or philosophers) discussed in that chapter. These are excerpts from some of the larger works of some of the finest minds from the history of Western philosophy, spanning over two thousand years.

Although I like to think that my own summaries and introductions are illuminating, engaging primary source materials is an essential part of studying philosophy. You will discover that I have not provided summaries or explanations of the entirety of the primary source selections at the ends of the chapters (though I have summarized explained certain ideas found therin). There is a reason for the limits of my explanation, and a reason that goes beyond trying to control the length of this book. Engaging the readings *yourself*, grappling with the arguments, and coming to your own understanding (even if initially hesitant) is one of the primary tasks of philosophy. Your instructor will undoubtedly offer assistance along the way, but it's important to meet with these thinkers, your mind to their minds, and participate in the great conversation that we call philosophy. It's also important to remember that we all stand on the shoulders of those who came before us. To remain ignorant of their ideas and achievements, and to attempt to "reinvent the wheel" ourselves, is inefficient at best, and intellectually dishonest and disrespectful, at worst.

Chapter 1: Critical Thinking & Politics

Comprehension questions you should be able to answer after reading this chapter:

1. What is "epistemology?"

2. What is the definition of "knowledge?"

3. What is a "claim?" What does it mean to say that a claim has a "truth-value?"

4. What is an argument (in philosophy)?

5. What is meant by a "relevance-relationship" between premises and a conclusion? What does it mean for a deductive argument to be "valid?"

6. What does it mean for a deductive argument to be "sound?"

7. Why is the soundness of arguments often difficult to establish?

8. What is the principle of charity?

9. What is a "worldview?" What do we usually do (in general) when a claim fits with our worldview? What about when it conflicts with it? If a claim that conflicts with our worldview is proven to be true, what should we do with our worldview?

10. What are the four conditions under which it is reasonable to accept an unsupported claim as true?

11. What are the ways in which we establish the expertise of sources?

12. What are the two justification questions we ask when presented with a new piece of information?

13. What are different meanings of "fake news?" Why is "fake news" a problem?

14. When should we suspend judgment concerning the truth or falsity of a claim?

15. How is "truth" understood by epistemic relativism and by the correspondence theory?

Argument

When one thinks of "politics," the word "argument" probably comes to mind—though probably for the wrong reason! It's an old cliché that one doesn't talk about politics or religion at parties, that if you want to start an "argument" at a family dinner, you should bring up either politics or religion. That is not usually, however, what an "argument" means in the context of philosophy.

Before delving into the nuances of arguments, though, we need to back up and develop a basic understanding of epistemology, so that we *know* what we're talking about.

Epistemology, the focus of this chapter, is the study of knowledge. Believe it or not, there's some pretty serious debate concerning how best to understand "knowledge." Some, for example, believe that we can never possess knowledge. Classical skeptics fit this description. Others believe that "knowledge" is never more than personal perspective.

Despite the plurality of views, there is a generally accepted definition of knowledge that seems to work for most people, in most cases. There are some complications, of course, and some disagreements here and there, but, for the most part, Plato's understanding of knowledge is pretty good. In his dialogue, the *Theaetetus*, Plato has the character Socrates (his real life mentor and friend) explore the proper definition of knowledge. The most promising candidate that emerges is that knowledge is "justified, true belief." Or, as Plato puts it, "true belief with an account."

Why should we accept Plato's definition? Plato is a giant in Western Philosophy, to say the least. A student of Socrates himself, Plato (428/427 BCE—348/347 BCE) founded the first institution of higher education (an "Academy") in the Western world. He also developed very impressive accounts of virtually every major topic of philosophical interest. Indeed, the 20th century philosopher Alfred North Whitehead said of Plato and Philosophy:

> The safest general characterization of the European philosophical tradition is that it consists of a series of footnotes to Plato. I do not mean the systematic scheme of thought which scholars have doubtfully extracted from his writings. I allude to the wealth of general ideas scattered through them....[1]

Still, just because a definition comes from Plato doesn't *automatically* make it correct. To assume so is a fallacy—an "appeal to authority." The *reason* why (most of us) use this definition is because it seems like a pretty good one! You'll soon see why.

Knowledge: justified, true belief

Plato's definition has three components, each of which requires a little bit of explanation.

1. Belief

It is generally accepted that in order to know something, one must also believe it. It seems odd to say that I know Donald Trump is the current U.S. President, but that I don't believe that he is.

Note that the reverse is not also true. We are quite comfortable with the idea that someone can believe something without also knowing it. For example, at the moment I'm writing this sentence, I believe my mother is at her home, but I wouldn't claim to *know* that she is. It's entirely possible that I'm not remembering her schedule accurately, and that she's volunteering somewhere. Or, perhaps she's on an errand? As we can see, to know something, one must also believe it, but one can believe without knowing.

An easy way to think of the relationship between belief and knowledge, in this sense, is with the language of a "promotion." We believe all kinds of things, but some of the things we believe have a special quality to them. These beliefs earn a "promotion," and a new title: knowledge. What is this quality that earns the belief a promotion to knowledge? As it turns out, this quality concerns the other two parts of our definition of knowledge: justification, and truth.

Before delving into justification, we'll spend a little more time on belief and complicate matters by asking what a belief *is*. A good chunk of my doctoral dissertation was devoted to just that question, but, once again, that level of analysis and expertise is not needed for our own purposes right now. At the minimum, we can simply talk about what form beliefs take in our language, so that we may easily identify them in speech and writing.

Very simply, beliefs appear in the form of "claims." *Claims* are statements, assertions, or propositions (different terms meaning *roughly* the same thing, in most cases). Claims have what is called a "*truth-value.*" To say that a claim has a truth-value is simply to say that it must be either true or false (if true, then its truth-value is true; if false, then its truth-value is false). Note that we do not need to know *which* truth-value applies to a claim to know that it is a claim. Consider the examples below.

---

[1] Alfred North Whitehead, *Process and Reality*, Free Press, 1979. p. 39.

Claims
- You are reading this sentence right now.

- Donald Trump is the current U.S. president.

- There is intelligent life elsewhere in the universe.

Remember, a claim is a statement that has to be either true or false (even if we're not sure which it is). You either are, or you are not, reading this book right now. Donald Trump either is, or is not, the current U.S. President. You're probably pretty confident about those two. What about life elsewhere in the universe? Well, you might not be certain either way. But (and this is the important part), we know that there either is, or there is not, intelligent life elsewhere in the universe. In other words, that claim has a truth-value, even though we don't know (for sure, right now) if that value is "true" or if it is "false."

Now, consider the other column of examples. What time is it? True or false? You probably had to reread those sentences just now, and my question probably still doesn't make any sense. There's a reason for that. "What time is it?" is not the sort of thing that can be either true or false. Neither is "Please shut the door." Neither is "ouch." None of those has a truth-value, because none is a claim, and therefore none is a belief. Why does this matter? Because claims are the building blocks of arguments, and arguments form the core of what we study and what we do in philosophy.

An argument is an attempt to establish the truth of a claim (the conclusion) by offering evidence (premises) in support of that claim. No name-calling, no chair-throwing, no raised voices—not even any presumption of disagreement. In a philosophical context, an argument is not a fight, but simply an attempt to make a point, using evidence, and following certain rules of reason.

Although we don't usually encounter arguments in the following format (except in philosophy courses), all arguments (at least implicitly) have the same general form:

Premise₁

Not Claims
- What time is it?

- Please shut the door.

- Ouch.

Premise₂
Conclusion

Please note that we have not yet specified any particular content for that argument. That is because arguments can be about *anything*. Any time you try to persuade someone to believe anything at all, on the basis of some kind of reason/evidence, you are offering an argument. Also note that although there were two premises in the generic argument above, there is nothing special about that number. You might have only a single premise (piece of evidence), or you might have a hundred premises, or any other number whatsoever. So long as you have at least one piece of evidence, at least one reason to believe that the conclusion is true, you have provided an argument.

Every philosophical essay that you read in this book (or any other) is an argument, or at least contains arguments. What all arguments have in common is that they are attempts to prove that a claim (the conclusion) is true, by offering other claims (premises) as evidence. Note that both the conclusion of an argument and all the premises in an argument, are *claims*. This is not a trivial observation! Every (proper) piece of every argument is a claim. Therefore, every (proper) piece of every argument has a truth-value—which is what makes argument evaluation possible.

However, although some professional philosophers will sometimes write out their arguments in obvious "premise₁, premise₂, therefore conclusion" format, most philosophical readings are not so blatantly reader-friendly. Philosophical arguments will be made in the context of paragraphs, essays, chapters, or even entire books. As we read, then, our job is to identify the main point the author seems to be trying to make. This is the conclusion. Then, we must try to identify all of the supporting points the author provides in defense of that conclusion. These are the premises. Once we have identified the conclusion and premises, we are prepared to evaluate the argument.

I hope it's obvious that not all arguments are created equal. Just because you have offered a reason to believe something is true doesn't mean you have provided a *good* reason, or even a relevant one. Consider the following example:

Argument (A)
1. Egg yolks are high in cholesterol.
2. High cholesterol is associated with increased risk of heart disease.
3. Therefore, abortion is morally wrong.

Argument (A) is laughably bad, and I'm sure you realize that, but it's important to recognize *why*. It doesn't take much reflection, or any fancy vocabulary, to describe what's going "wrong" with that argument: the premises don't have anything to do with the conclusion! You might rightfully be wondering what the heck eggs and cholesterol have to do with abortion. Clearly, the premises aren't *relevant* to the conclusion.

Relevance-relationships are an important initial way to evaluate the quality of an argument. In general, if the premises aren't "relevant," then we would say that little (if any) support has been provided for the conclusion—and that doesn't make for a very good argument! One specific example of this relevance relationship occurs with deductive arguments

Deductive arguments are constructed with the intent to provide for the certainty of the conclusion, on the assumption that the premises are true. Such arguments are (generally) evaluated in terms of their validity, and soundness. Both of those words (valid, sound) have specific meaning in the context of argument, and both (especially validity) have different uses in everyday speech. For example, you might hear someone say "that's a valid point." What that person means is that you have made a good point. In that usage, valid means something like "good," or "apt," or "true." That is not what "valid" means for our purposes, though.

Validity

A deductive argument is <u>valid</u> if the conclusion necessarily follows (logically) from the premises. Another way of putting that idea is that an argument is valid when, *if* the premises are true, the conclusion must also be true. Or, an argument is valid if it's impossible for the conclusion to be false, *if* all the premises are true. To repeat: validity indicates the right kind of "relevance-relationship" between the premises and the conclusion.

You might have noticed that I italicized the word "if" in a couple of places in the previous paragraph. There's a good reason for that. When we assess an argument's validity, it's a hypothetical exercise. We're not making any claim that the premises are, in fact, true—we're just asking what would happen *if* the premises are true. Consider the following:

1. All humans are mortal.
2. Preston is a human.
3. Therefore, Preston is mortal.

Is this argument "valid," according to our definition? To find out if it is, ask yourself the following: *if* all the premises are true, must the conclusion also be true? *If* it's true that all humans are mortal, and *if* it's true that Preston is a human, then, must it also be true that Preston is mortal? The answer, of course, is "yes." Therefore, this is a valid argument. This indicates that there is the right kind of logical relationship between the premises and conclusion, there is a relationship of relevance between them. We haven't yet established that the premises are, in fact, true (that's a later step), but we have established that *if* they are true, the conclusion is as well. That is very important. Let's reconsider example (A) from above:

Argument (A)
1. Egg yolks are high in cholesterol.
2. High cholesterol is associated with increased risk of heart disease.
3. Therefore, abortion is morally wrong.

Just a few paragraphs ago, we articulated the "badness" of this argument using ordinary language. Presumably, you recognized that eggs, cholesterol, and heart disease risks have nothing to do with whether or not abortion is morally wrong! There isn't the right kind of relationship between those premises, and the conclusion. If we consider this in terms of validity, the problem becomes clear.

Is it possible for it to be true that egg yolks are high in cholesterol, and true that high cholesterol is associated with increased risk of heart disease, and yet for it to be false that abortion is morally wrong? Of course that's possible! So, if, for some weird reason, you try to prove the moral wrongness of abortion by appealing to the cholesterol content of eggs, you will fail in grand, embarrassing fashion. Even if all your evidence is proven to be true, you still will not have proven that your conclusion ("abortion is morally wrong") is true.

Soundness

If validity appeals to the hypothetical truth of the premises, soundness refers to their actual truth. *A deductive argument is "sound" when it is both valid and all its premises are, in fact, true.* Notice that in order for an argument to be sound, it must first already be valid. You can imagine an implicit checklist for argument evaluation:

☐ Is the argument valid?
☐ Is the argument sound?

Only if we can "check the first box" do we bother to consider whether the argument is sound. Let's go back to one of our earlier examples:

1. All humans are mortal.
2. Preston is a human.
3. Therefore, Preston is mortal.

Is the argument valid? Yes, it is (as established above).

✓ Is the argument valid?
☐ Is the argument sound?

Since it's valid, we can now move on to consider its soundness. Are all of the premises, in fact, true? To be honest, the question of "truth" opens Pandora's proverbial box.

What does "truth" mean? What does it take for something to be true, let alone known to be true? You could spend an entire career as a philosophy professor focusing solely on the concept of "truth," and still have plenty of questions remaining. We will not spend entire careers on the concept of truth, but we will spend some time later in this chapter on two different interpretations of what it means for a claim to be true. For now, however, let's set aside the murky notion of "truth" and assume (for the sake of argument) that we know what it means for a claim to be true. Even so, how can we tell if a particular claim is, in fact, true?

Obviously, not all claims will be easily verifiable as true. While we might be fairly confident that it is true that egg yolks are high in cholesterol, some truth-values (unfortunately, probably the ones we tend to care the most about—truth-values for claims about morality, religion, politics, etc.), might be especially difficult to establish.

Do aliens exist, or not? Hard to say, since we haven't explored the entire universe just yet. Is abortion immoral? Hard to say, since there's so much disagreement, and so many compelling arguments that can be given on both sides. Does God exist? Hard to say, since there are compelling arguments on both sides of the debate, and legitimate debate as to what does or could count as evidence for God's existence in the first place. And so forth. . . .

Recognizing that some claims will be difficult to establish, let us return to a relatively easy argument just to complete our discussion of "soundness."

1. All humans are mortal.
2. Preston is a human.
3. Therefore, Preston is mortal.

In order for this argument to be sound, it has to be valid, and all of its premises must be true. We've already established that it's valid. Are its premises, in fact, true? Does the claim that "all humans are mortal" seem to be true? If we interpret "mortal" in its usual sense ("liable or subject to death"), then it does, in fact, appear to be true. That all humans are subject to death seems to be true, like it or not. What about the second premise? Is it, in fact, true that Preston (the author of this book) is a human? Again, if we're assuming the usual sense of "human" ("a member of the genus *Homo* and especially of the species *H. sapiens*"), then it would appear that Preston being human is true as well. Given that both premises are, in fact, true, we have established that the argument is not only valid, but sound.

✓   Is the argument valid?
✓   Is the argument sound?

If you have established that an argument is sound, you have proven that the conclusion is true. It doesn't get any better than that! Unfortunately, whenever we're dealing with serious, important arguments, it's usually pretty challenging to establish that the argument is sound. Consider another argument for the wrongness of abortion:

Argument (B)
1. Murder is morally wrong.
2. Abortion is murder.
3. Therefore, abortion is morally wrong.

You should know the routine by now:

☐   Is the argument valid?
☐   Is the argument sound?

If it's true that murder is morally wrong, and it's also true that abortion is murder, must it also be true that abortion is morally wrong? Yes, this is a valid argument. Is it sound? Perhaps, but this

is far from obvious. Murder, by its usual definition, is the unjustified killing of an innocent person, so I suspect *most* people would agree that premise 1 is true.[2] Premise 2 is going to be much more controversial, though. Is abortion the unjustified killing of an innocent person? People who argue that abortion is (at least sometimes) morally acceptable will usually argue either that the fetus is not a "person," or that the killing is justified (or both). Such persons would not grant the truth of premise 2, and would not recognize the argument as sound, even though it is valid.

Let's take a moment to summarize the ground we've covered so far. An argument is an attempt to prove some point by appealing to reasons that support that point. In order for an argument to be a good argument, the premises need to be relevant (valid, in the case of deductive arguments), and preferably true as well.

Some of you might have wondered about that last sentence. Only "preferably" true? Ideally, of course, good arguments will exhibit both relevance between premises and the conclusion, and contain premises that are, in fact, true. But, if we insist that an argument have only premises known to be true in order to be "good," we might be setting the bar so high that few, if any, arguments are "good." This is because, as we have already seen, the actual truth of premises can be difficult and controversial to establish. Consider one more argument:

Argument (C)
1. If God does not exist, objective moral values and duties do not exist.
2. Objective moral values and duties do exist.
3. Therefore, God exists.

This is actually one of the more famous arguments for God's existence known as the "moral argument." For our purposes, though, let's just consider our checklist:

---

[2] In fairness, there might even be disagreement as to the truth of *this* premise!

☐   Is the argument valid?
☐   Is the argument sound?

If both premises are true, must the conclusion also be true? Yes—and this shouldn't be surprising. Any of the "major" arguments for God's existence, the arguments that have withstood the test of time (often centuries, if not millennia), are presumably going to be valid—otherwise they would have been abandoned long ago.

✓   Is the argument valid?
☐   Is the argument sound?

Now that we know it's valid, is it sound? Is it, in fact, true that if God does not exist, objective moral values and duties do not exist? Is it, in fact, true that objective moral values and duties do exist? Those who use the moral argument for God's existence will offer reasons to accept both premises as true. If you find those reasons compelling, you will presumably conclude that both premises are, in fact, true—in which case you will conclude that the argument is sound. But, if you think the reasons are not compelling, you will instead conclude that the premises are not true—in which case you will conclude that the argument is not sound. Or, perhaps some of you, even after serious consideration, will come to the honest conclusion that you're just *not sure* if those premises are true—in which case you will conclude that you don't know whether the argument is sound.

✓   Is the argument valid?
?   Is the argument sound?

That the soundness of this (or any other of the major arguments for, *or against*, God's existence) is in question should not be surprising. Remember: if an argument is sound, its conclusion *is, in fact, true*. So, if an argument for God's existence can be shown to be sound, that would mean that it is, in fact, true that God exists—and that this has been proven! Conversely, if an argument against God's existence were shown to be sound, it would mean

that God has been proven not to exist. Had either of these events occurred, you probably would have heard about it!

Similarly, if the soundness of various arguments concerning moral or political issues could be easily established, you would think that there would no longer be any debate about things like abortion, eating meat, the death penalty, the value of democracy, etc. The fact that people still passionately debate these issues should tell us something about the difficulty in establishing the soundness of those sorts of arguments.

Don't be discouraged, though. Just because it's difficult to establish the soundness of these sorts of arguments doesn't mean that there's no point in evaluating them, nor does it mean that we will be unable to say anything evaluative or interesting about them. Even if we're not *sure* if argument B is sound, it's clearly a better argument for the wrongness of abortion than the one referencing the risks of high cholesterol (argument A)!

To summarize thus far: when someone is trying to convince you of something, the first thing to ask is whether or not any support is being offered. If the answer is "no," then that person is just making a statement, and we will consider how to evaluate unsupported claims a little later in this chapter. If, however, support is being offered, then you have been presented with an *argument*.

If someone is presenting you with an argument, you need to determine whether that support is relevant to the conclusion. With deductive arguments, this is a question of *validity*—but generally speaking you can just ask whether the premises are "relevant." If they are not relevant, that doesn't mean their conclusion is false, but it does mean their evidence doesn't really count as support, and you should treat the conclusion as an unsupported claim. If the premises are relevant, then the next step is to determine if they are true.

When relevant premises are not actually true, then they don't properly support their conclusion, and you should treat the conclusion as an unsupported claim. If the premises are true, however, then the argument is in pretty good shape. After all, we already determined they were relevant, and now we've determined they're also true! With deductive arguments, that means the argument is *sound*, and the conclusion has been *proven* to be true. Even if the argument isn't deductive, though, there is still probably some very impressive support for the conclusion such that it's at least likely to be true. In that case, you should consider how well that newly-proven conclusion fits with your worldview.

We will discuss worldviews in greater detail later in this chapter, but, for now, just know that your worldview is your basic understanding of the world and how it works. When claims fit with our worldview, they don't tend to surprise us, and we usually presume they are true (even though they might not be). When they conflict with our worldviews, however, we tend to be skeptical and presume they are false (even though they might be true). When a conclusion has been proven to be true, though, that should make a difference to your worldview.

If, for example, my current worldview includes a general skepticism about the existence of aliens, but I then see live footage of an alien spacecraft on every major news network, and I am personally abducted by aliens and experimented upon, you better believe that I will revise my worldview to now include the existence of aliens!

Whatever the content of the argument, and perhaps especially when the conclusion conflicts with our own worldview, we need to be self-aware when we are evaluating it. One important element of (honest) argument evaluation is what's known as the *"principle of charity."* Basically, we want to be "charitable" when evaluating arguments—especially if we're inclined to disagree with them.

It's all too easy to develop a "straw man" interpretation of someone else's position, and then dismiss it as foolish, fallacious, or misguided. This is perhaps especially the case when dealing with politics.

The fact of the matter is that people don't tend to view their own arguments as foolish. This doesn't mean they aren't, but in order to perform an honest evaluation of an argument, we need to

present it in its best possible light. We must put ourselves in the position of the person who presented the argument, consider the argument in the strongest possible way (given the original author's intentions), and then evaluate the argument, so charitably constructed. This is a good approach to evaluating arguments, in general, but it's especially apt in the context of considering formal philosophical arguments in a book like this one.

The sorts of arguments and theories we will consider have stood the test of time. They're considered in this book for a reason. No matter what your personal views happen to be, it's uncharitable to casually dismiss "the other side" as fools offering lousy arguments. You might well conclude that "their" arguments fail, but to be justified in that conclusion you need to consider those arguments charitably, in their best light.

2. Justification

Having just spent a lot of time on arguments, and determining the relevance-relationship and truth of their premises, let us now turn to (perhaps) the most critical component of argument evaluation: justification.

Justification is probably the most critical aspect of this process because it is the process by which we attempt to determine whether claims (e.g., premises or conclusions) are (in fact) true, and therefore whether arguments are *good* arguments, and therefore whether or not we can "know" whether the conclusion of an argument is true. Justification is crucially involved in determining the truth of the premises in argument (once relevance has been established), and in evaluating the truth of an unsupported claim when no proper argument is present at all.

Justification is also probably the most controversial element of our definition of knowledge, primarily because we can bicker over what, exactly, counts as sufficient justification. Again, this is a very complicated subject, but this is not an extended treatment of epistemology, so we can get by with a basic understanding of the key ideas.

To say that knowledge requires justification is simply to say that you can only "know" something on the basis of good reasons. If I present you with a jar filled with marbles, and you guess there are 457 marbles in the jar (just pulling a number "out of the air," at random), and, with a startled look on my face, I tell you that there are, in fact, 457 marbles in the jar, we wouldn't want to say that you *knew* the number of marbles in the jar at the time you guessed. We call it a guess for a reason! You didn't know, but you took a shot at it, and happened to get lucky. That's not knowledge; it's a lucky guess.

Sometimes, we like to distinguish "believing" from "knowing" by making explicit appeals to how much justification we have for the belief in question. I claimed to believe that my mother was at home, because I have reason to think that she is. However, my confidence in those reasons is pretty low, so I don't think I have sufficient justification to claim to *know* that she's at home.

As I mentioned, justification can be a thorny issue. How can we tell when we have enough justification to claim that we know something, as opposed to merely believing it? As with many questions in philosophy, there's no obvious, uncontroversial answer to that question. We can, however, talk about ways in which our beliefs are justified, and the degree to which our beliefs are supported by evidence.

When we are presented with an unsupported claim (including the premises of most arguments), our three basic options are to accept it as true, reject it as false, or to suspend judgment because we're not sure either way. How do we know which one of those three options is the right one to exercise?

Generally speaking, it is reasonable to *accept* an *unsupported* claim if the claim:

1. Does not conflict with our own observations
2. Does not conflict with other credible claims
3. Comes from a credible source that offers us no compelling reason to expect bias
4. Does not conflict with our background information/worldview

1) The Claim does not Conflict with our own Observations

We are justifiably skeptical about claims that directly contradict what we have personally observed! If you're texting with a friend, and he is telling you that he's in his car and on the way to meet you at Starbuck's, but you are personally observing him (in secret), right then and there, standing outside the Apple Store talking to your girlfriend, then either your friend is saying something false or you are hallucinating (or something else equally unlikely). Not surprisingly, in such a case you would be inclined to reject his claim as false. On the other hand, if you just came in from the rain and are shaking off your umbrella, and your friend calls and tells you he's running late because it's raining out, you're probably going to accept his claim as true. After all, you personally witnessed the rain too.

2) The Claim does not Conflict with other Credible Claims

In courtroom settings, one of the best ways for an attorney to undermine the evidence offered by a witness or expert is to provide another witness or expert who will contradict that evidence. This is often very successful in creating "reasonable doubt" in jurors. So, for example, if one blood-splatter expert testifies that the spray patterns suggest the killer was at least six feet tall (which is bad news for the 6-foot-tall defendant), that claim is undermined if another, equally respectable, blood splatter expert says the patterns are inconclusive. In the context of philosophy, this is a notorious experience for philosophy students. One philosopher offers a compelling case that we have no free will, but then another equally impressive philosopher says the opposite. In such cases, we often must suspend judgment, even if we don't outright reject the original claim. If, on the other hand, there is no such conflict, if the claim is not being contradicted by other (credible) claims— let alone if there is consensus from a variety of sources—then we are likely to accept the claim as true.

3) The Claim comes from a Credible Source that Offers Us no Compelling Reason to Expect Bias

This criterion actually has two elements: bias, and credibility. "Bias" is an issue when the person making the claim is suspected to have an ulterior motive. For example, if someone is trying to sell you their used car, they have a personal incentive for you to buy it, and they might be inclined to be less than completely honest about the condition of the vehicle. This doesn't mean they're automatically lying, of course, but careful car buyers will inspect the vehicle, and even enlist the help of someone who knows a thing or two about cars (e.g., an automotive mechanic) to confirm the car really is in good condition. Similarly, when the Tobacco industry spent decades denying the link between smoking and cancer, a clear case can be made that they had an ulterior motive to make that claim.[3] After all, if they admitted smoking caused cancer, it might reduce the number of people who smoke, and therefore their profits. Similarly, we might be reasonably skeptical when the petroleum industry funds lobbying groups denying the link between automobile emissions and climate change.[4] The possibility of bias doesn't demonstrate the *falsity* of the claim, of course. To presume so would actually be an example of what is called the "genetic fallacy"—denying (or accepting) the truth of a claim *solely* because of its source. However, while a possibly-biased source doesn't necessarily indicate their claim is false, it should inspire us to be especially vigilant when evaluating the evidence (if any) that they provide in support of their claim.

Setting aside issues of bias, we can now turn to credibility. Unless one is a radical epistemic relativist, we recognize that not all sources are equally credible. When evaluating a claim, the source matters—especially if the subject matter is significant or if the claim conflicts with our own worldview. I should hope that you trust the

testimony of your medical doctor more than you trust the testimony of your neighbor when it comes to your health—unless of course your neighbor also happens to be a medical doctor!

If someone is especially knowledgeable about a particular topic, we tend to give extra "weight" to their claims made about that topic. Sometimes, we consider such persons "experts."

We establish expertise, generally, by considering the following criteria:

1) Education
2) Experience
3) Accomplishments

Education is just what you think it is. Generally speaking, the more educated someone is on a topic, the more likely we are to (reasonably) take him or her to be an expert on that topic. Someone who majored in chemistry as an undergraduate probably knows a lot more about chemistry than someone who majored in something else—let alone someone who has never studied chemistry at all. Someone who has a Master's degree (M.S.) in chemistry probably knows even more, and someone with a doctorate (Ph.D.) probably knows even more than that. To be skeptical of this would require you to be profoundly skeptical of the effectiveness of our education system, in general! Keep in mind, of course, that expertise based on education is limited to the focus of one's education. That Ph.D. in chemistry doesn't mean the chemist is also an expert on criminal law.

Experience is also just what you think it is. While education is terribly valuable, relevant experience is valuable as well. *All else being equal*, a medical doctor who has been in practice for 20 years is probably more knowledgeable than a first-year M.D. Once again, we have to be careful of relevance. The fact that I have been a philosophy professor for fifteen years doesn't mean that I "know better" than a first year lawyer when it comes to *legal* issues. Despite the fact that President Donald Trump has been an ostensively

---

[3] http://www.who.int/tobacco/media/en/TobaccoExplained.pdf

[4] https://www.theguardian.com/environment/2015/jul/15/exxon-mobil-gave-millions-climate-denying-lawmakers

successful business man for decades, his claim that he "knows more about ISIS than the generals" is dubious on its surface.[5] For all his business acumen, and despite his clear mastery of the media, then-candidate Trump had literally *no* experience relevant to ISIS, in contrast to "the Generals" and their combined decades of military experience, including years of recent experience specifically opposing ISIS.

Accomplishments often (though not always) come from education and experience, as well as merit. If a cancer researcher, for example, has won a Nobel Prize for her research, that scientist is probably pretty knowledgeable! Sometimes, some awards or "achievements" are questionable, and serve primarily to stoke the vanity of their recipients. For example, I get solicitations every year to be an "invited speaker" at a conference called the Oxford Round Table. It is held at the very prestigious Oxford University, and being able to put "invited speaker" on your résumé is usually a respectable achievement, for a professor like myself. However, the Oxford Round Table has no affiliation with Oxford University at all (they just rent space!), "invited speakers" (or their campuses) must *pay* several thousand dollars for the privilege to attend, and whether or not one is invited seems to be much more about whether you're on their email list than actual achievements or status in the field. In other words, this conference is largely a scam designed to make money for the organizers of the event. Today, with the increasing influence of social media, we have to be careful not to confuse "notoriety" with being "accomplished." As of 2017, Katy Perry has over 95 *million* twitter followers compared to only 45 million for CNN. It would be absurd to think that somehow Katy Perry is a more credible source of information, however, based solely on her superior popularity.

Putting all these ideas together, we can consider a "real-life" example of two experts.

Richard Dawkins:
- BA, Ph.D.: Oxford University Professor (emeritus) Oxford
- Specialization: evolutionary biology
- Achievements: numerous awards and publications

William Lane Craig:
- BA (Wheaton College),
- MA Phil of Religion & History of Christian Thought (Trinity Evangelical Divinity School), Ph.D. in PHIL (University of Birmingham),
- Ph.D. in Theology (University of Munich).
- Professor: Trinity Evangelical school and Talbot School of Theology
- Specialization: Philosophy of religion & Christian doctrine
- Achievements: numerous awards and publications

A legitimate evaluation of these two scholars recognizes that they are both very well educated and accomplished in their respective fields. Both are undoubtedly intelligent persons who deserve respect. This doesn't mean they are always correct, of course—but it does mean we should take them seriously when they offer claims concerning their areas of expertise.

An interesting application that applies to these two, specifically, is that they are considered "rivals." Craig is an outspoken Christian who debates prominent atheists around the world, trying to demonstrate the rationality of Christian faith. Dawkins, on the other hand, is a notorious critic of religion, and the author of such books as "The God Delusion."

While both men are credible experts, even legitimate experts can be guilty of stepping outside their areas of genuine expertise. Dawkins, for example, while one of the finest scholars on evolution living today, is *not* an expert on Western philosophy—let alone the philosophy of religion. Not surprisingly, when he writes a book

---

[5] https://www.youtube.com/watch?v=kul340_yMLs

like "The God Delusion" that deals with philosophy, rather than evolution, his credibility is strained. His critiques of the most famous arguments for God's existence in the Western tradition are undeniably outdated, and rely heavily on the criticisms offered by David Hume—written some two and a half centuries ago. What's worse is that what he calls his "central argument" is demonstrably invalid (according to the very standards we have addressed earlier in this chapter). Indeed, Craig has described the argument as "the worst atheistic argument in the history of Western thought."[6] In fairness, Craig should be equally cautious about extending his own expertise into the realm of biology. . . .

4) The Claim does not Conflict with our own Worldview

We each have, at our disposal, what we may call our "background knowledge," or "background information, or our "worldview." Whatever we want to call it, it is that vast collection of everything we have heard, seen, read, and otherwise learned, throughout our lives. This collection is everything we know (or think we know) about the world and how it works. It includes your understanding of hugely important questions such as whether or not God (somehow conceived) exists, to your understanding of human psychology, world history, economics, State capitals, and even sports statistics. If you have learned about it, it is part of your worldview.

When presented with a claim, we all immediately evaluate that claim not only in terms of evidence, source, and our own observations, but also with respect to how well it "fits" with our worldview. We can summarize and simplify this process by asking two general questions about that claim.

1. To what extent is the belief supported by good reasons and compelling evidence from reliable sources?

Is the belief in question supported by your own first-hand observations? Or, is it in conflict with your own observations? If you're receiving your evidence from another source, how reliable is that source? How credible is the source? Does the source have any relevant expertise? Is there any reason to be biased?

2. To what extent is the belief consistent with my worldview?

Every time we are confronted with a piece of information, we automatically and instantly evaluate it against our background knowledge. If the new information seems to "fit" with our background knowledge, we're likely to accept it as true. If it does not fit, however, if the claim is surprising to us, we're likely to hesitate and to demand more justification before accepting it as true.

For example, if I were to claim that I drove home on the Southbound 605 freeway at 5 PM on a Thursday afternoon, and the freeway was wide open, with hardly any cars on it at all, anyone living in Southern California (that is, anyone for whom the 605 freeway, on a weekday, at 5 PM, is part of their background knowledge/worldview) would immediately doubt what I'm saying. Why? Because her understanding of the world and how it works is that Southern California freeways are jammed at that time of day.

When it comes to justification, then, we'll want to know if the belief is consistent with other things that we know about the world and how it works. If the belief is consistent, so far, so good. If it is not, then we'll naturally be skeptical, and we'll require further evidence before accepting the belief.

We always need to be aware, however, that our own background knowledge can be flawed. For example, it used to be part of most people's

---

[6] http://www.reasonablefaith.org/dawkins-delusion

worldview that the Sun revolved around the Earth. Now, it's part of our worldview that it's the Earth that moves relative to the Sun. Background knowledge is subject to revision. So, the mere fact that a piece of information conflicts with your understanding of the world does not automatically mean that the claim is false. It's possible that it's true, and that it's your worldview that needs revision.

Whenever you get presented with a claim (including the conclusion of an argument) that conflicts with your worldview, but for which you're confident it's true, the reasonable thing to do is to revise your worldview accordingly. Obviously, the more you know, the better equipped you are to evaluate claims, and to be accurate in your evaluations.

It is also important to be honest about the threat of bias posed by our worldviews when evaluating information—a bias that we are *all* subject to. Thus far, I have casually commented on our tendency to accept claims that fit with our worldview, and to be skeptical of those that clash with it. This is a well-known and studied psychological tendency known as the "confirmation bias." What makes the confirmation bias dangerous, though, is that it distorts our ability to honestly and objectively evaluate claims. This is not merely some anecdotal complaint about the state of debate today. There is scientific evidence to suggest that our brains are "wired" to be resistant to change with respect to "firmly held beliefs."

A study published in 2016 showed, via neuroimaging, that when subjects were presented with arguments that contradicted their strongly held political views, they experienced "increased activity in the default mode network—a set of interconnected structures associated with self-representation and disengagement from the external world."[7] The default mode network is normally shown to active during such states as daydreaming and mind-wandering. It is labeled "default" because the network activates "by default" when the person is not engaged in a task requiring attention. This is fascinating, if true! It suggests that when our firmly-held political beliefs are challenged, our brains "check out" in ways analogous to daydreaming. How responsive to evidence and argument are we likely to be if our brains are in a "day-dreaming" state when evidence contrary to our firmly held beliefs is presented?

In the final speech President Obama gave as President, he warned against our increasing tendency to operate within our own ideological "bubbles."

> For too many of us, it's become safer to retreat into our own bubbles, whether in our neighborhoods or college campuses or places of worship or our social media feeds, surrounded by people who look like us and share the same political outlook and never challenge our assumptions. The rise of naked partisanship, increasing economic and regional stratification, the splintering of our media into a channel for every taste – all this makes this great sorting seem natural, even inevitable. And increasingly, we become so secure in our bubbles that we accept only information, whether true or not, that fits our opinions, instead of basing our opinions on the evidence that's out there.[8]

This isn't merely some anecdotal cautionary tale about liberals only watching MSNBC and conservatives only watching Fox News. A study published in the Proceedings of the National Academy of Sciences of the United States of America concluded that "selective exposure to

---

[7] Kaplan, J. T. et al. Neural correlates of maintaining one's political beliefs in the face of counterevidence. Sci. Rep. 6, 39589; doi: 10.1038/srep39589 (2016). Available at http://www.nature.com/articles/srep39589

[8] http://www.latimes.com/politics/la-pol-obama-farewell-speech-transcript-20170110-story.html

content is the primary driver of content diffusion and generates the formation of homogeneous clusters, i.e., 'echo chambers.' Indeed, homogeneity appears to be the primary driver for the diffusion of contents and each echo chamber has its own cascade dynamics."[9]

In other words, people on Facebook mostly share news that they already agree with, that is consistent with their worldview, and they don't share information that challenges it. As the researchers put it, "users show a tendency to search for, interpret, and recall information that confirm their pre-existing beliefs."

Combine this tendency with the fact that Facebook has nearly 2 billion users (out of roughly 7 billion people on the planet), and reaches 67% of U.S. adults, and that 62% of Americans get their news mainly from social media sites such as Facebook and Twitter.[10] A majority of Americans get their news primarily from social media, and research confirms the application of the confirmation bias to social media platforms. It should go without saying that these trends seriously compromise our ability to think critically, and to responsibly accept or reject claims.

A recent and ominous development of this trend has inspired me to add an entire subsection to this chapter for the first time: "Fake News."

"Fake News"

As of 2017, "Fake News" has entered into the American vocabulary, initially and specifically in the realm of politics—though the phrase is likely to "trend" and apply to other contexts as well. Initially used by liberals to describe right-wing "conspiracy theories," the phrase expanded in

use just as did the frequency of fake news itself. Conservatives then adopted the phrase themselves, and the phrase now gets used to describe multiple, significantly different things. This is where philosophy has a chance to shine, considering the experience philosophers have with conceptual analysis. The primary meanings of "fake news," as it is used, seems to be the following:

- *A work of fiction, known to be so by the author, but presented as real/true for personal, political, or financial motives.* This is the original meaning of fake news, and all other meanings are a departure from this. Another word to describe this kind of fake news is a "lie." A clear illustration of this kind of fake news is the example of Cameron Harris. As reported in an interview with Harris by the New York Times, he admitted to writing multiple completely fabricated stories that he thought would be effective "click-bait" for Trump supporters.[11] He claimed to have done so for financial reasons, citing that he made $22,000 in ad-revenue from his stories, though it was later revealed that he also worked as an aide to a Maryland Republican lawmaker.[12] Eight of his fake news stories were popular enough to attract the attention of (and debunking by) Snopes.com.[13] His most "effective" story claimed "Tens of thousands of fraudulent Clinton votes found in Ohio warehouse." By his own admission, he invented an imaginary electrical worker and named him "Randall Prince." He

[9] http://www.pnas.org/content/113/3/554.full
[10] http://www.journalism.org/2016/05/26/news-use-across-social-media-platforms-2016/?utm_content=bufferae870&utm_medium=social&utm_source=twitter.com&utm_campaign=buffer
[11] https://www.nytimes.com/2017/01/18/us/fake-news-hillary-clinton-cameron-harris.html?_r=0

[12] http://www.inquisitr.com/3901102/cameron-harris-fake-news-writer-bought-christian-times-newspaper-for-5-made-22000-and-got-fired/
[13] http://www.snopes.com/tag/christian-times-newspaper/

copied and pasted a screen shot of a man standing in front of ballot boxes using a google image search. He also identified the motive for the imaginary ballot-tampering: "the Clinton campaign's likely goal was to slip the fake ballot boxes in with the real ballot boxes when they went to official election judges on November 8th." The fact that the story was a complete *lie* did nothing to stop it from being shared with 6 million people. The fake news story went sufficiently viral that the Franklin County (Ohio) board of elections was forced to investigate—after which they confirmed the story had no basis in reality.[14]

- *Satire: while also a work of fiction (and known to be so by the author), the work is presented as fiction for the sake of entertainment or to make a point.* Satire is a long-practiced means of both entertainment and persuasion. "The Onion" is perhaps the most famous satirical website today, and it makes no pretense that its stories are true. When The Onion runs the headline, "Trump Calms Nerves Before Inaugural Address By Reminding Himself He's The Only Person Who Actually Exists," it is presumed that the reader will know that The Onion is only trying to be funny.[15] Similarly, when Jonathan Swift famously argued that a solution to Irish poverty was for Irish parents to sell their children as food to wealthy Englishmen, he wasn't being serious! Despite eating children being presented as his "Modest Proposal," his *actual* proposals were much more serious (and sincere):

> *Therefore let no man talk to me of other expedients: Of taxing our absentees at five shillings a pound:*

> *Of using neither clothes, nor household furniture, except what is of our own growth and manufacture: Of utterly rejecting the materials and instruments that promote foreign luxury: Of curing the expensiveness of pride, vanity, idleness, and gaming in our women: Of introducing a vein of parsimony, prudence and temperance: . . . Of teaching landlords to have at least one degree of mercy towards their tenants. Lastly, of putting a spirit of honesty, industry, and skill into our shop-keepers, who, if a resolution could now be taken to buy only our native goods, would immediately unite to cheat and exact upon us in the price, the measure, and the goodness, nor could ever yet be brought to make one fair proposal of just dealing, though often and earnestly invited to it.*

Satire is "fake news" in the sense that it is not *real*, but nor is it intended to be—and that is a significant difference from the original meaning of "fake news."

- *A work thought to be true and intended to be true by the author, but mistaken in one or more significant details.* In another words, a mistake. An example of a mistake in reporting that was, nevertheless, denounced as "fake news" occurred on the day Donald Trump was inaugurated as President. A White House pool reporter tweeted that a bust of Martin Luther King Jr. had been

[14] http://files.constantcontact.com/b01249ec501/58eeb35a-7d61-4807-b168-765d27ca11cf.pdf

[15] http://www.theonion.com/article/trump-calms-nerves-inaugural-address-reminding-him-55095

removed from the Oval Office.[16] In fact, the bust had simply been moved to a different part of the office, and the reporter hadn't seen it—something the reporter later acknowledged and for which he apologized. Nevertheless, the initial report was called "fake news" by detractors all the same.[17] At the risk of editorializing: honest mistakes, while bad, are not properly "fake news." A relevant indicator of intent is whether or not the person who made the initial claim is willing to admit (and correct) the mistake, and apologize.

- *A news story deemed "irrelevant," or unimportant, or distracting from "real" news* (according to the person making the claim). An example of this might be when reporters comment on the fashion choices of a politician, rather than the substance of her policies. As another example, when Senator Jeff Sessions was nominated to be U.S. Attorney General by President Trump, some reporters (and Democratic politicians) pointed to allegations of racism from his past as a potential disqualifier for confirmation. This was labeled by some as "fake news."[18]

- *A news story disliked by the reader.* This is perhaps the most disturbing usage of "fake news" of them all, in my opinion. This usage occurs when information is dismissed as "fake" simply because it conflicts with the reader's worldview, or because it would be distressing, if accepted as true. To be blunt: not liking a piece of information doesn't mean that it's false. If your medical doctor tells you that you have cancer, dismissing it as "fake news" is of no help.

The problem with the varied and inconsistent usage of the phrase "fake news" isn't just an issue of conceptual fussiness from overly-picky philosophers. Words have meaning. When President Trump refused to take questions from a CNN reporter, and dismissed the network as "fake news," it's likely that what he really meant is something like "I don't like CNN, and how CNN is reporting on my presidency."[19] However, people who listen to and respect President Trump might take his words to mean that CNN intentionally prints stories they know to be false for ulterior motives, and thereby lose confidence in the network as a reliable news source.

This isn't just bad news for CNN's ratings or profit margins. If confidence in mainstream media sources is undermined, people will retreat even *further* into their ideological bubbles, and their critical thinking skills will be even further compromised. President Trump later again labeled major media sources (viz., the New York Times, NBC, ABC, CBS, and CNN) as "fake news," but went further by denouncing them as the "enemy of the American People."

---

[16] https://twitter.com/philipindc/status/822603029950173187

[17] http://www.thegatewaypundit.com/2017/01/fakenews-media-falsely-reports-trump-removed-mlk-bust-oval-office/

[18] http://eaglerising.com/38617/cnn-fake-news-story-jeff-sessions-is-a-racist/

[19] http://www.cnn.com/videos/politics/2017/01/11/donald-trump-jim-acosta-cnn-fake-news.cnn

Cognitive linguist George Lakoff, who will be the focus of the final chapter of this book, finds this strategy to be both intentional and dangerous. The adjective "fake" modifies the function of "news." The primary purpose of "news" is to pass along factual information in service to the public good. If "news" is modified with the term "fake," it implies that the basic function of "news" has been compromised.

> It is done to serve interests at odds with the public good. It also undermines the credibility of real news sources, that is, the press. Therefore it makes it harder for the press to serve the public good by revealing truths. And it threatens democracy, which requires that the press function to reveal real truths.[20]

Perhaps we would be better and more accurately served by refraining from using the phrase "fake news" entirely? When Hillary Clinton claimed in 2008 to have run from sniper fire in Bosnia, and her claim was proven to be false, the best-case scenario is that her memory was "mistaken," and the worst-case is that she intentionally lied for some reason.[21] Why bother

calling it "fake news" when a "lie" or "mistake" more accurately conveys what occurred?

When President Trump's press secretary, Sean Spicer, in his very first press briefing, not only claimed that President Trump's inauguration audience was the largest ever, but also condemned journalists for writing "fake news" downplaying the size of the crowds, several troubling things occurred. For one, his claim about viewership was demonstrably false. President Trump's Nielson television ratings were only the fifth highest since President Richard Nixon—lower than President Obama's first inauguration, for example, but higher than the inaugurations of both Presidents Clinton and George W. Bush.[22] It's likely that President Trump and his staff would have liked it if their inauguration attendance and Nielson ratings had been the highest, but that preference doesn't mean that reporters who provide the factual numbers, in contrast, are disseminating "fake news." To suggest that they are is, again, to undermine confidence in the press, in general. It also seems unlikely to be helpful when President Trump's counselor, Kellyanne Conway described Spicer's actions in the following way: "You're saying it's a falsehood, and they're giving- Sean

---

[20]http://www.npr.org/2017/02/17/515630467/with-fake-news-trump-moves-from-alternative-facts-to-alternative-language
[21]https://www.washingtonpost.com/news/fact-checker/wp/2016/05/23/recalling-hillary-

clintons-claim-of-landing-under-sniper-fire-in-bosnia/?utm_term=.e6222cd61035
[22]

http://www.washingtonexaminer.com/trump-inaugurations-nielsen-ratings-fourth-highest-since-nixon/article/2612602

Spicer, our press secretary, gave alternative facts to that."[23]

For the sake of conceptual clarity: facts are objective, and are, by definition, true. An "alternative fact," therefore, is a clever term for something that is false—either a mistake, or a lie.

If it is a fact that 2+2 = 4, it is silly to label 2+2 = 5 as an "alternative fact." If it is a fact that Donald Trump is the 45th President of the United States, to claim that Bernie Sanders is the 45th President is not to offer an "alternative fact," but is simply to claim something that *is not true*. That President Trump's Nielson ratings for his inauguration were *not* the highest ever is a *fact*. To assert otherwise is not to provide an "alternative fact," but is simply to be either mistaken, or lying.

If you agree that "fake news" is troubling, and if you are motivated to be a good critical thinker, what can *you* do to be more wary when it comes to the news stories you accept or reject? The good news is that you have already learned how, earlier in this chapter! All of our previous discussion of justification, and how we should evaluate claims, is directly relevant to discerning whether a claim is "fake news," a lie, a mistake, or just simply true or false.

First of all, is the claim supported by evidence? In other words, is it an argument? Press Secretary Spicer didn't offer any evidence in support of his claim about the inauguration Nielson ratings—he just made an assertion. If he had offered an argument, you could try to determine whether his premises were relevant to the conclusion, and ultimately whether they were true. Had he cited Nielson numbers, you could easily fact-them—probably on your smart phone!

Don't forget the general process of evaluating unsupported claims. Recall that it's generally reasonable to accept an unsupported claim if it:

1. Does not conflict with our own observations
2. Does not conflict with other credible claims

3. Comes from a credible source that offers us no compelling reason to expect bias
4. Does not conflict with our background information/worldview

While it might not always be practical for you to investigate the source, at the very least you can try to be aware of the influence of your own worldview. If you know you are firm Trump supporter, then be aware that you are especially vulnerable to believing negative stories about Hillary Clinton—just as Hillary supporters would be especially vulnerable to believing negative stories about President Trump. Before getting indignant (and retweeting or sharing) an incendiary piece of news, try taking a few moments to carefully reflect on the claims being made, and maybe even do some fact-checking before taking a stance. Snopes.com is as very helpful resource in this regard.

Another very simple tip is to be initially skeptical about any stories riddled with spelling or grammar problems, or that use lots of CAPS or exclamation marks!!! Actual, serious journalists are usually pretty good writers, and poor writing can be a sign of an amateur blogger or internet troll.

Having completed our treatment of "fake news," we can now resume our discussion of processing claims, in general.

Thus far, we've only seriously addressed the conditions under which we accept or reject a claim, but there is a third alternative that requires some attention as well: *suspending judgment*. Basically, to *accept* a claim means you think it's true, to reject it means you think it's false, and to *suspend judgment* means you're just not sure either way.

It is OK to suspend judgment.

Let me repeat that: it is OK to suspend judgment. You certainly don't want to spend your whole life shrugging your shoulders and pleading ignorance, but nor should you pretend to know the truth value of a claim if you honestly don't. Far too often, people accept or reject claims, and take

[23] http://time.com/4642689/kellyanne-conway-sean-spicer-donald-trump-alternative-facts/

stances on issues, when they know little, if anything, about the subject in question. Pardon my coarse language, but when people do so they are engaging in "bullshit."

Believe it not, "bullshit" is officially a philosophical term, thanks to the philosopher Harry Frankfurt. Is his aptly title book, "On Bullshit," he discusses this tendency in human behavior, and distinguishes it from lying. According to Frankfurt, "bullshit" occurs when "a person's obligations or opportunities to speak about some topic exceed his or her knowledge of the facts that are relevant to the topic."[24]

In other words, if you ask me what I think about President Trump's choice for Secretary of the Interior, and I have no idea who that is (or even what he or she does), and instead of admitting "I don't know," I say that I don't approve of the choice, I have engaged in some "bullshit."[25] The claim I have made exceeds the relevant knowledge I actually have on that topic.

It's clear, I hope, that the proper thing to do in a situation like that is to suspend judgment. Yet, all kinds of people "bullshit" all the time. Why? According to Frankfurt: "Closely related instances arise from the widespread conviction that it is the responsibility of a citizen in democracy to have opinions about everything, or at least everything that pertains to the conduct of his country's affairs."[26]

In other words, there is a perceived social expectation that everyone is supposed to have (and be ready to provide) an opinion about everything. When this is combined with a crude presumption of epistemic relativism,[27] then we get an especially troubling situation: everyone feels obliged to opine about everything, and no matter how uninformed they might be, somehow their own opinion is just as good as anyone else's, and therefore worth sharing.

An intellectually honest alternative to "bullshitting," and one that, frankly, requires both self-awareness and some courage, is to be willing to suspend judgment if you honestly don't know whether a claim is true or false.

To put this "justification" process to the test, we can apply our understanding by evaluating the following two claims.

1. "I believe that, someday, my body will die."
   - Question: To what extent is the belief supported by good reasons and compelling evidence from reliable sources?
   - Answer: Ample evidence is supplied every day, every time someone dies. Obituaries, news stories about deaths, and personal experiences and memories of people (and every other animal on Earth) dying all serve as evidence.
   - Question: To what extent is the belief consistent with my worldview?
   - Answer: The claim is consistent with the complex web of our beliefs involving the natural sciences. Biology and history both inform our worldview, and our worldview certainly includes bodily death.

2. "I believe that I will win the Powerball jackpot this week."
   - Question: To what extent is the belief supported by good reasons and compelling evidence from reliable sources?
   - Answer: Excluding the possibility of

[24] Harry Frankfurt, *On Bullshit*. Princeton University Press, 2005. p. 63.
[25] In case you are curious, President Trump's Secretary of the Interior is Ryan Zinke (as of the time of this writing), and the Secretary's job is to manage the Department of the Interior, which is the government department that oversees federal land, natural resources, and the administration of programs relating to Native Americans, Alaskans, and Hawaiians.
[26] Harry Frankfurt, On Bullshit. Princeton University Press, 2005. p. 63.
[27] A view according to which all opinions are equally legitimate—and one we will consider later in this chapter.

cheating, there is no compelling evidence to indicate I will win. Indeed, it's unclear what could possibly count as evidence of this in the first place.

- Question: To what extent is the belief consistent with other my worldview?
- Answer: The claim that I will win the Powerball jackpot conflicts with our understanding of probability in general, and with our experience of lotteries, in particular. For example, the odds of winning the Powerball grand prize are 1 in 292,201,338. To win a million dollars has odds of 1 in 11,688,053.[28] In comparison, the odds of being struck by lightning *twice* in your lifetime are 1 in 9,000,000—something much more likely than being made a millionaire by the lottery![29]

When we compare these examples, we can detect a sharp contrast. In both cases, you probably (rightfully) think you do not have to suspend judgment, but can actually take a stance. The first claim (concerning bodily death) is so strongly justified that you probably not only accept it as true, but with sufficient justification to constitute knowledge. If you disagree with this, and deny that you *know* that your body will die someday, you probably think it's impossible to know *anything*.[30]

The second example (me winning the lottery) is so poorly justified as to be little better than wishful thinking—certainly *not* knowledge. In fairness, the lottery claim is about the future, and many epistemologists would say that future-indexed claims have an indeterminate truth-value, since they haven't happened yet. For that reason, you might be inclined to suspend

judgment-and that is a fair position to take. However, even if you're suspending judgment for that reason, you probably think the claim is very likely to turn out to be false.

3. Truth

As a reminder: "knowledge" is defined as "justified, true belief." We have already discussed both belies and justification, and may now turn to truth.

It is generally accepted that one can't know something that is false. I can't know (as of 2017) that George Washington is the current U.S. President—because he isn't!

Note that we can *think* that we know all kinds of things, and then discover that we were mistaken. In those cases, we never *really* knew what we believed we knew at all. This is complicated, but only a very basic understanding is needed for our purposes. In summary, if we really do know something, it must be something that is true.

What does it *mean* for something to be true? Once again, this is a complicated issue, but, once again, we can avoid needless complications by focusing just on some key concepts. Though there are several ways of understanding truth, we will focus on just two: epistemic relativism and correspondence theory.

Epistemic Relativism

Epistemic relativism claims that truth is "relative" to the observer. Truth is a matter of perspective. Truth depends on one's point of view. Several ancient Sophists were known to hold this perspective, including Protagoras who allegedly claimed that "man is the measure of all things."[31]

---

[28] http://www.powerball.com/powerball/pb_prizes.asp

[29] http://wncn.com/2016/01/12/odds-of-winning-powerball-jackpot-less-than-being-hit-by-lightning-twice/

[30] That's not necessarily a bad thing. There is a respectable and ancient school of thought called

"Skepticism" that regards knowledge as impossible to obtain.

[31] Strictly speaking, he is reported to have said "Of all things the measure is man, of the things that are, that [or "how"] they are, and of things that are not, that [or "how"] they are not." Hermann Diels and Kranz Walther. *Die Fragmente der*

Now, at a certain level, there is something obvious and unobjectionable about this idea. Most everyone would agree that there are certain kinds of claims we can make, certain kinds of judgments, which are merely expressions of personal opinion, or personal taste. One's favorite color, or whether or not one likes a band, or whether or not one likes spicy food—all such things seem to be matters of perspective. I like spicy food. My mother doesn't. She's not "wrong" or "mistaken" about spicy food—she just has different taste preferences. I really like the band "Switchfoot." I'm sure some people couldn't bear them (as hard as that is for me to believe). Again, no one is in error over such matters.

We call these sorts of claims "subjective claims." When we're dealing with subjective claims, there is no one "correct" point of view. There is no single correct answer to questions involving subjective claims. In cases of disagreement, it's not the case that someone must be wrong. Also, in cases of disagreement, there's little that can be accomplished from debate. I can sing the praises of spicy food for hours, but my mother will never be convinced of the truth of my claims and change her mind. This isn't because she's stubborn, it's because she just doesn't like spicy food! Her opinion on this matter is no better, or worse, than my own. It's just different.

Think about this, briefly, in the context of politics. To apply epistemic relativism to politics would mean believing that claims about political matters are simply matters of opinion. Such claims that would be opinions (as opposed to facts) might include the following:

- Abortion should be safe, legal, and uncommon.
- There is a Constitutional right to abortion.
- The 2nd Amendment right to bear arms means that private citizens should be able to purchase fully-automatic assault weapons.

- Same-sex marriage is something that each State should decide for itself.
- Democracy is superior to Monarchy.

So far, there's nothing terribly interesting or controversial about epistemic relativism. Where epistemic relativism does become controversial, however, is when we realize that the theory claims that *all* truths are relative; that all claims are subjective, and that none are objective.

If you stop to reflect on that for a moment, you can start to see how extraordinary that view really is (whether true, or not). If all "truths" are matters of perspective, and if no perspective is inherently any more privileged than any other, then everyone is always "right" about everything.

You believe the Earth is a sphere. I believe it's flat (I don't, really). Assuming each claim represents our own respective opinions, why would your opinion be any more "right" than mine? In a sense, we're both right—even though we're making mutually exclusive claims.

I think George W. Bush is the current U.S. President (I don't believe that either). That's my opinion, and I'm entitled to it, and your opinion isn't any more accurate than mine. "But," you might counter, "no one else shares your opinion, while lots of people share mine." Fine. That just means your opinion is more popular—it doesn't mean it's more accurate.

If all truth is subjective, then all truth is like my taste in music. If 99% of the world population couldn't stand Country music, but I loved it, my opinion that Country music is great would be no less legitimate than the nearly seven billion who disagree—it would just be a lot less popular.

To make matters even more interesting, consider this: "all truth is relative" is a claim. That means it's either true, or it's false. If it's false, then we obviously have no good reason to entertain it any further. If, on the other hand, it's true that all truth is relative, then that very claim is itself only relatively true. That is, it's just a matter of opinion, a matter of perspective. In that case, if I

Vorsokratiker. Zurich: Weidmann, 1985. DK80b1. More "recently," and perhaps more famously, the character Obi Wan Kenobi implied this view in

the film Return of the Jedi. "Luke, you're going to find that many of the truths we cling to depend greatly on our own point of view."

disagree, then my opinion is no worse, no less correct, than that of those who embrace epistemic relativism.

To sum this up, either "all truth is relative" is a relative truth, or it's not-relative. If it's relative, then it's merely an opinion that is no "more true" than an opposing opinion. If it's not-relative, then not all truth is relative, and the claim refutes itself.

There is something seemingly self-refuting, or internally inconsistent, with epistemic relativism. Since all opinions are equally true, it is simultaneously and equally true that epistemic relativism is, itself, both true and false.

Beyond this conceptual puzzle, a figure no less prominent than Socrates himself points out that we do not, in fact, regard all opinions as equally true. Consider the following examples:

Subject	Expert
Medicine	Medical Doctor
Nutrition	Nutritionist
Carpentry	Carpenter
Botany	Botanist
Chemistry	Chemist
Physics	Physicist
Philosophy	Philosopher

I'll start with a deeply personal example. If you don't believe that my understanding of philosophy, on the basis of my several degrees (B.A., M.A., and Ph.D.), years of experience (more than 20 years at the time of this writing), and "accolades" (e.g., being a tenured professor, and having published multiple articles and textbooks, etc.), is any more informed than your own, why on Earth are you bothering to read this book, or take my class? What is the point of education, in general, if every student is equally informed as his or her teacher?

Let's make it more absurd. Why bother going to the doctor when you are sick and injured? If all opinions are equal, your own opinion about your medical condition is just as good as that doctor's!

Those astrophysicists who have spent decades studying the universe and who are debating whether or not this universe is situated within a broader multiverse? Their views are no better informed than a random person who has never studied that stuff a day in his or her life. Does that seem true to you? That they are equally true opinions?

You almost certainly don't believe that, I'll wager—and that is the critic's point. In actual practice, we don't really believe that "all opinions are equal," but instead recognize that some people know what they're talking about, and others don't. If we recognize that this sort of relativism is rife with problems in non-moral contexts,[32] why should we entertain the notion in political contexts?

Does it seem plausible that every person's perspective is equally informed and "true" as any other person's when it comes to the various systems of government? To interpreting the Constitution? To various economic policies and how different systems of taxation will impact the Gross Domestic Product? To when and whether war is morally justifiable?

The question we must now consider is whether political claims concern a matter of possible expertise ("politics"), in which case we would presumably recognize that some people are better informed than others, and that not all views are equally good. Or, if we reject that, then we are presumably treating political claims as mere indicators of personal taste.

I might recognize that some people might be experts at "baking," and are certainly better informed than I am when it comes to how best to bake a cake, but I don't recognize that anyone else is somehow more informed than I am about what sort of cake *I* like! If you've gone to culinary school, your understanding of how to bake a red velvet cake is probably better informed than my own, but it makes no sense to suggest that you know better than I do regarding whether or not I *like* red velvet cake. Is politics more like baking,

---

[32] For example, think about what it would mean for it to be "just a matter of opinion" that humans require oxygen to survive.

or more like the kind of cake you like?

Using cake as our guide, consider the following examples and inferences:

Two people taste the same chocolate cake. One thinks it's overly sweet. The other thinks it could stand to be sweeter. Therefore, the sweetness of the chocolate is merely a matter of individual perspective. There is no "Truth" regarding its sweetness.

I look at a flower and perceive it to be yellow. A bee looks at the same flower and perceives it to be blue with a red center. Therefore, the appearance of the flower is a matter of individual perspective. There is no "Truth" regarding the appearance of the flower.

Such common sense differences in perspective *seem* to suggest that epistemic relativism might be the correct way to understand truth. However, if one considers carefully these examples, it will soon be clear that these examples do *not* imply that "*all* truth is relative"—indeed they presuppose something very different.

Epistemic relativism is driven by the force of the relativity of acts of perception. That is, because it is such a common experience for people to perceive "the same thing" in very different ways, it's easy to conclude that truth is relative. Be careful, though! The relativity of perception, even if true, doesn't imply that *all* truth is relative. In fact, some truths must be held to be objective in order for the relativity of other truths to make any sense.

Reconsider the chocolate cake. Two people taste the same cake with different results. Therefore, perception is relative. What is *not* thought to be relative in this example is the existence of the cake, the tasters, and the world in which both cake and tasters exist! The same sorts of presuppositions apply to the flower example.

The bee and I perceive the flower with different results, but what is *not* thought to be relative is the existence of the flower itself, the bee, myself, and the reality in which all three of us reside.

In order to even make sense of the relativity of perception, one must presuppose that it is "True" that observers exist, and that a reality exists that may be perceived differently. The commonsense observation that initially gives rise to relativism is that the "real world" exists, that perceivers (such as you, me, and the bee) exist, but that we experience the "real world" in different ways.

Much more relevant to the subject of politics, even the all-too-common claim that politicians "lie" presupposes that there is such a thing as "truth."

The 2016 U.S. Presidential election was contentious, to say the least. Both Republicans and Democrats demonized their opposition by claiming that they were liars. Trump supporters condemned Hillary Clinton for lying about emails, and "Benghazi," and countless other things. Hillary supporters condemned Donald Trump for lying about his taxes, charitable donations, his treatment of women, and various other statements made and stances taken. Politifact affirmed that they *both* lied about a variety of things, with Trump having lied more often.[33]

To use just one example, consider that on September 26th, 2016, at one of the televised President debates, Hillary Clinton said that Donald Trump had claimed climate change was a hoax. He interjected, "I did not, I did not, . . . I do not say that."[34] However, there is documentation of multiple instances of him saying precisely that, including a Tweet from November 6th, 2012, in which he said "The concept of global warming was created by and for the Chinese in order to make U.S. manufacturing non-competitive."[35]

---

[33] http://www.politifact.com/ truth-o-meter/lists/people/comparing-hillary-clinton-donald-trump-truth-o-met/
[34] https://www.youtube.com/watch?time_continue=1&v=Pll5l41Hpww

[35] https://twitter.com/realDonaldTrump/status/265895292191248385?ref_src=twsrc%5Etfw

Donald J. Trump ✔
@realDonaldTrump

The concept of global warming was created by and for the Chinese in order to make U.S. manufacturing non-competitive.

RETWEETS LIKES
104,666 67,138

11:16 AM - 6 Nov 2012

This is not about Hillary Clinton, Donald Trump, or global warming. It is, however, about whether or not there is a notion of truth that goes beyond personal opinion. If you think that lies are possible, and that either Trump or Clinton lied about something, what do you *mean* by that, if not that there is some *fact* (e.g., Trump said global warming is a hoax), but the person in question knowingly made a claim that contradicts that fact (e.g., "I did not say that.")? If Hillary Clinton lied about her use of a private email server during her tenure as Secretary of State, that implies that there is some independent truth of the matter, and that her claims don't match up to that truth. This common sense assumption about lies not "matching up" brings us to our alternative to epistemic relativism: correspondence theory.

Correspondence Theory

Consider the following statements:

- The claim that George W. Bush is the current U.S. President is true if and only if he really is the current U.S. President.
- The claim that there are exactly 457 marbles in the jar is true if and only if there really are exactly 457 marbles in the jar.
- The claim that there was life on Mars is true if and only if there really was life on Mars.

Are these statements reasonable? If you think so, you're probably sympathetic to what is known as the correspondence theory of truth.

According to correspondence theory, a claim is true if it "corresponds" to the way things "really are" in the world, if the claim "matches up" with reality, if it "maps on" to how the world actually is. This theory claims that there is a way that the universe "really is," and our claims are true, or not, depending on whether they match up with the world. This is the approach implicitly employed by most people, whether they realize it or not.

Imagine that you intercept a fellow student on the way to class, and she tells you that the class has been cancelled. Has she told you the truth? What would you need to know in order to make that assessment? Simply this: you would need to know if the class really had been cancelled. If it had, her statement was true. If it had not, her statement was false. Her claim either "corresponded" to the world, or it didn't.

Obviously, not all of our claims will be so easily verifiable. Some truth claims, including, unfortunately, the ones we tend to care the most about (i.e., claims about morality, religion, politics, etc.), might be especially difficult to establish because we might not know how "the world is" concerning that particular subject.

Do aliens exist, or not? Hard to say, since we haven't explored the entire universe just yet. Is abortion immoral? Hard to say, since there's so much disagreement, and so many compelling arguments that can be given on both sides. Should governments promote a strong middle class, primarily promote the interests of the working class, or sit back and let "the Market" decide? Hard to say, since there's so much disagreement, and so many compelling arguments that can be given on both sides. . . .

What correspondence theorists *will* claim is that even if we're not sure what the answers to some of these difficult questions are, we nevertheless can be confident that there *are* answers, and not merely equally legitimate opinions, out there for us to discover.

Conclusion

The purpose of this introductory chapter is to provide a basic overview of arguments as understood in philosophy, provide a few key vocabulary terms (e.g., validity, soundness, claim, premise, etc.), and provide a framework within which to understood how we evaluate arguments. This will serve us for the remainder of this book.

Every chapter that follows this one will be offering one or more perspectives from across the history of Western political philosophical thought. Each of these famous philosophers will be offering *arguments*—which is just to say that they will be defending their positions, offering reasons for what they believe. Your task going forward will be the following:

1. Using the Principle of Charity, identity the main points (conclusions) being made by these philosophers.
2. Using the Principle of Charity, identity the reasons/evidence (premises) being offered in support of those main points.
3. As best you can, and when possible, determine whether their premises are relevant. In some cases, this will be an indicator as to whether the argument is "valid."
4. As best you can, and when possible, use the process of justification discussed in this chapter (i.e., considering evidence, source, and fit with your worldview) to determine whether the premises are also true—and if this entails that their conclusion is true.
5. Determine your own degree of agreement or disagreement with these various philosophers and their ideas. Presumably, if you have concluded that

their arguments are "sound," you should agree! Conversely, if you still disagree, that should indicate that their arguments are somehow flawed.

Chapter 2: Politics before Philosophy

> *Comprehension questions you should be able to answer after reading this chapter:*
>
> 1. Who were the Sophists, and what were the cultural conditions that made them possible?
> 2. What did Protagoras mean when he said that "man is the measure of all things?"
> 3. What is the difference between *physis* and *nomos*?
> 4. Why did Antigone disobey Creon's law?
> 5. Why is it difficult to know what Socrates' actually believed?
> 6. What are the features of the "Socratic method?"
> 7. Why was Socrates' death inspirational to so many?

It seems reasonable to suppose that for as long as humans have been able to think, some people have had "deep thoughts." It's presumptuous to think that the first "deep thoughts" arose in the ancient Mediterranean region, however, we do have an historical record for this time and region that does reveal a remarkable shift in the way people understood their world and its operations, and we can call this the birth of "philosophy"—at least in the West.

In Greece, specifically, prior to philosophy, intellectual and moral authority was associated with celebrated poets, such as Homer or Hesiod (for both of whom, the dates of their lives are fuzzy, at best—*very* roughly 750-650 BCE). Poets and poems (e.g., The Odyssey, the Illiad, Achilles, Ulysses, etc.) served a variety of functions far beyond entertainment. They were the communities' source for history, "science," religion, and morality. Poets were no ordinary people. They were inspired by the Muses (goddesses of inspiration) in a fashion akin to divine inspiration. They spoke, therefore, with a special authority. Poets provided models of virtue and vice to be emulated or shunned (e.g., Achilles), and they explained the nature and operations of the world through myths. *These myths tried to explain the unfamiliar by appealing to the familiar.* For example, that strange glowing ball that seems to travel across the sky? A fiery chariot driven each day by the god Apollo. Unexpected events, such as natural disasters or

diseases, were the outcome of the gods' fickle and changing tempers.

The problem, though, of appealing to gods and spirits to explain all the operations of nature and events that transpired, is that these explanations didn't seem to really explain all that much. "The gods did it" doesn't really provide much more understanding of an event than the event offered by itself. Moreover, the inconsistency observed in the world, when the only explanation was "the will of the gods," was a source of confusion and frustration. To remedy this, some poets placed even the gods under the power of the "Fates." *The Fates represented an implicit, objective ordering principle, a source of "justice," as it were, to which even the gods were subject.*

Having now taken the fateful cultural step of supposing that there is some "larger" principle than the anthropomorphic, all-too-human gods with which to interpret reality, the task now shifted to figuring out just what that larger underlying and ordering principle *is*.

Many individuals came forward to offer their answers. They include Thales, Anaximander, Pythagoras, Xenophenes, Heraclitus, Parmenides, Zeno, and Democritus, among others. The pre-Socratic philosophers are a fascinating group of thinkers, and not merely for the sake of history and trivia. In a meaningful way, they changed the way the (Western) world would think for millennia to come. Their inquiries into Nature created both philosophy and, ultimately, science.

Their emphasis on reason and rigorous argumentation became a distinguishing feature of philosophy, in particular, and scholarship more generally. Their insights, while not often accepted as-is by many today, nevertheless left traces in other, later philosophers' systems (e.g., Platonism, Aristotelianism, Epicureanism, Stoicism). And, they created the cultural and intellectual climate ripe for the one to come, the one from whom they would (retroactively) receive their designation: Socrates. Before turning to Socrates, however, we will consider his "rivals," the Sophists.

From a socio-historical perspective, we might consider several possible contributors to the rise of sophistry. Ancient Greece had grown more cosmopolitan, and came into ever greater contact with other cultures and traditions. The rise of democracy meant an increased number of voices that not only were heard, but that asserted an equal claim to be heard. Even among the philosophers there was a dizzying diversity of opinions.

"Reality is water."

"No, it's fire."

"Actually, it's 'apeiron.'"

"What the heck is 'apeiron?' Never mind. Regardless, permanence is an illusion."

"On the contrary, it is change that is the illusion."

To make things more maddening, these contradictory positions were being presented via rigorous argumentation. An interesting and compelling case could be made for each. In sum, the ancient Greek world found itself flooded with, and grappling with, pluralism: a diversity of different ideas and values. Given such a cultural and intellectual backdrop, perhaps it should come as no surprise that some thinkers gave up on the search for The Truth.

The **Sophists**, to use a possibly uncomfortable analogy, were what we might expect if a stereotypical university philosophy professor today mated with an equally stereotypical lawyer. We can imagine the offspring to be a very intelligent person, capable of arguing any and every side of a debate, and focused primarily on "victory" as opposed to truth. Such were the Sophists. Among the most famous of them were Protagoras, Gorgias, and Thrasymachus. If you read much Plato, you'll encounter these names as characters in his dialogues. Indeed, both Protagoras and Gorgias have entire dialogues named after them. Of course, these Sophists always appeared as the antagonists, doing (ill-fated) intellectual battle with the hero, Socrates.

What Sophists had in common with modern day philosophy professors is that they taught in exchange for money. One account of their "curriculum" is as follows: "That learning consists of good judgement in his own affairs, showing how best to order his own home; and in the affairs of his city, showing how he may have most influence on public affairs both in speech and in action."[36] There was, therefore, a presumed political component to their instruction; their students (generally the male children of aristocratic families) were expected to participate in the life of their *polis* (political community). Then, as now, political participation involved debate, and required rhetorical skills—areas in which the sophists excelled.

What Sophists had in common with (stereotypical) modern day lawyers is that they were (generally) willing to take any side in a debate, or court case, if the price was right.

In their defense, *many Sophists were either skeptics or epistemic relativists.* That is, they either believed that "the truth" was unknowable, or else that truth is a matter of perspective. In either case, there is no (knowable) "right" answer to our deep questions, nor any (knowable) "right" outcome to a lawsuit. If "Truth" could not be the arbiter of such things, then we must default to persuasiveness instead. Rhetoric might be more important than reason, if there is no "Truth" to be discovered. Victory, not accuracy, is the only outcome to be pursued and obtained.

---

[36] Plato, *Protagoras*, 318e-319a.

Why come to such (possibly depressing) conclusions? Remember the foundation already laid by the pre-Socratics: the distinction between appearance and reality emphasized by those such as Heraclitus, Parmenides, and Zeno make skepticism not only possible, but compelling. If we have no clear access to "reality," and must operate solely by "appearances," and if the world appears differently on the basis of who is making the perception, then perhaps the sensible approach to take is that "truth" is simply a matter of perception.

One notable Sophist, Protagoras (490-420 BCE) is credited with the claim that "man is the measure of all things." By this, he meant that *perception is relative to the individual doing the perceiving*, and therefore any contact with reality is unique to that individual. Since perception is our only contact with the world, "reality" is relative to the individual who perceives it. Values are also relative. There is no Nature (*physis*), objective and independent of human traditions, perceptions, and decisions, out there for us to discover. Instead, such things are a matter of convention (*nomos*) or custom. Morality is subjective, but there is a pragmatic value to adhering to shared social conventions for the sake of peace and order.

This distinction between Nature (*physis*) and custom (*nomos*) is critically important for political philosophy, then, as now. There are certain aspects of human life that are obviously "natural." That we speak is natural—but the particular language we speak is a matter of custom. A central and enduring political question is whether politics a function of nature, or convention? Is there a *natural* norm of justice, or is justice "merely" conventional (*nomos*)? Is there a natural law, against which human laws may be evaluated as just or unjust, or are all laws merely matters of convention? Must governments conform to Nature in order to be good and just governments, or are political systems matters of convention instead?

Such questions arise in the story of Antigone, by Sophocles. Sophocles lived from 496 BCE to 406 BCE. He is one of only 3 Ancient Greek tragic playwrights whose works have survived (the other two were Aeschylus and Euripedes). For almost 50 years, Sophocles was the most-awarded playwright in the dramatic competitions of the city-state of Athens, Sophocles competed in around 30 competition, winning as many as 24 and never placing lower than second place.

He wrote 123 plays, but only 7 survive in complete form: *Ajax*, *Antigone*, *Trachinian Women*, *Oedipus the King*, *Electra*, *Philoctetes* and *Oedipus at Colonus*. Our focus will be *Antigone*.

What follows is a brief excerpt from the full play.

The Oedipus Trilogy, by Sophocles[37]
ANTIGONE

[Backstory: Oedipus sired several children with his wife/mother Jocasta. Their two daughters were Antigone and Ismene, and their two sons were Eteocles and Polyneices. After Oedipus realized he had killed his father and married his mother, in an improbable fulfillment of prophecy, Jocasta committed suicide, and Oedpidus blinded himself before begging to be exiled by his brother, Creon. Eteocles and Polyneices go to war with each other in a dispute over succession, and Polyneices enlists the aid of foreign armies in an attack against their home State of Thebes. Both brothers kill each other in battle. Their uncle Creon, who is now the king, orders Eteocles buried with proper rites, and Polyneices to remain unburied—condemning his spirit to a state of unrest forever, as a result. Creon declares it to be a capital offense, should anyone bury Polyneices, contrary to his order. Antigone finds herself in conflict between her sense of duty towards her brother, and her uncle's commands.]

. . .

[37] http://www.gutenberg.org/cache/epub /31/pg31.txt

ANTIGONE
Ismene, sister of my blood and heart,
See'st thou how Zeus would in our lives fulfill
The world of Oedipus, a world of woes!
For what of pain, affliction, outrage, shame,
Is lacking in our fortunes, thine and mine?
And now this proclamation of today
Made by our Captain-General to the State,
What can its purport be? Didst hear and heed,
Or art thou deaf when friends are banned as foes?

ISMENE
To me, Antigone, no word of friends
Has come, or glad or grievous, since we twain
Were reft of our two brethren in one day
By double fratricide; and since i' the night
Our Argive leaguers fled, no later news
Has reached me, to inspirit or deject.

ANTIGONE
I know 'twas so, and therefore summoned thee
Beyond the gates to breathe it in thine ear.

ISMENE
What is it? Some dark secret stirs thy breast.

ANTIGONE
What but the thought of our two brothers dead,
The one by Creon graced with funeral rites,
The other disappointed? Eteocles
He hath consigned to earth (as fame reports)
With obsequies that use and wont ordain,
So gracing him among the dead below.
But Polyneices, a dishonored corpse,
(So by report the royal edict runs)
No man may bury him or make lament--
Must leave him tombless and unwept, a feast
For kites to scent afar and swoop upon.
Such is the edict (if report speak true)
Of Creon, our most noble Creon, aimed
At thee and me, aye me too; and anon
He will be here to promulgate, for such
As have not heard, his mandate; 'tis in sooth
No passing humor, for the edict says
Whoe'er transgresses shall be stoned to death.
So stands it with us; now 'tis thine to show
If thou art worthy of thy blood or base.

ISMENE
But how, my rash, fond sister, in such case
Can I do anything to make or mar?

ANTIGONE
Say, wilt thou aid me and abet? Decide.

ISMENE
In what bold venture? What is in thy thought?

ANTIGONE
Lend me a hand to bear the corpse away.

ISMENE
What, bury him despite the interdict?

ANTIGONE
My brother, and, though thou deny him, thine
No man shall say that _I_ betrayed a brother.

ISMENE
Wilt thou persist, though Creon has forbid?

ANTIGONE
What right has he to keep me from my own?

ISMENE
Bethink thee, sister, of our father's fate,
Abhorred, dishonored, self-convinced of sin,
Blinded, himself his executioner.
Think of his mother-wife (ill sorted names)
Done by a noose herself had twined to death
And last, our hapless brethren in one day,
Both in a mutual destiny involved,
Self-slaughtered, both the slayer and the slain.
Bethink thee, sister, we are left alone;
Shall we not perish wretchedest of all,
If in defiance of the law we cross
A monarch's will?--weak women, think of that,
Not framed by nature to contend with men.
Remember this too that the stronger rules;
We must obey his orders, these or worse.
Therefore I plead compulsion and entreat
The dead to pardon. I perforce obey
The powers that be. 'Tis foolishness, I ween,
To overstep in aught the golden mean.

ANTIGONE
I urge no more; nay, wert thou willing still,
I would not welcome such a fellowship.
Go thine own way; myself will bury him.
How sweet to die in such employ, to rest,--
Sister and brother linked in love's embrace--
A sinless sinner, banned awhile on earth,
But by the dead commended; and with them
I shall abide for ever. As for thee,
Scorn, if thou wilt, the eternal laws of Heaven. . . .

[Enter   CREON—addressing   guards   and
counselors]

CREON
Elders, the gods have righted one again
Our storm-tossed ship of state, now safe in port.
But you by special summons I convened
As my most trusted councilors; first, because
I knew you loyal to Laius of old;
Again, when Oedipus restored our State,
Both while he ruled and when his rule was o'er,
Ye still were constant to the royal line.
Now that his two sons perished in one day,
Brother by brother murderously slain,
By right of kinship to the Princes dead,
I claim and hold the throne and sovereignty.
Yet 'tis no easy matter to discern
The temper of a man, his mind and will,
Till he be proved by exercise of power;
And in my case, if one who reigns supreme
Swerve from the highest policy, tongue-tied
By fear of consequence, that man I hold,
And ever held, the basest of the base.
And I condemn the man who sets his friend
Before his country. For myself, I call
To witness Zeus, whose eyes are everywhere,
If I perceive some mischievous design
To sap the State, I will not hold my tongue;
Nor would I reckon as my private friend
A public foe, well knowing that the State
Is the good ship that holds our fortunes all:
Farewell to friendship, if she suffers wreck.
Such is the policy by which I seek
To serve the Commons and conformably
I have proclaimed an edict as concerns
The sons of Oedipus; Eteocles
Who in his country's battle fought and fell,

The foremost champion--duly bury him
With all observances and ceremonies
That are the guerdon of the heroic dead.
But for the miscreant exile who returned
Minded in flames and ashes to blot out
His father's city and his father's gods,
And glut his vengeance with his kinsmen's blood,
Or drag them captive at his chariot wheels--
For Polyneices 'tis ordained that none
Shall give him burial or make mourn for him,
But leave his corpse unburied, to be meat
For dogs and carrion crows, a ghastly sight.
So am I purposed; never by my will
Shall miscreants take precedence of true men,
But all good patriots, alive or dead,
Shall be by me preferred and honored. . . .

[Creon is informed that the body has been buried
anyway, contrary to his orders.]

CREON
O cease, you vex me with your babblement;
I am like to think you dote in your old age.
Is it not arrant folly to pretend
That gods would have a thought for this dead
man?
Did they forsooth award him special grace,
And as some benefactor bury him,
Who came to fire their hallowed sanctuaries,
To sack their shrines, to desolate their land,
And scout their ordinances? Or perchance
The gods bestow their favors on the bad.
No! no! I have long noted malcontents
Who wagged their heads, and kicked against the
yoke,
Misliking these my orders, and my rule.
'Tis they, I warrant, who suborned my guards
By bribes. Of evils current upon earth
The worst is money. Money 'tis that sacks
Cities, and drives men forth from hearth and
home;
Warps and seduces native innocence,
And breeds a habit of dishonesty.
But they who sold themselves shall find their
greed
Out-shot the mark, and rue it soon or late.
Yea, as I still revere the dread of Zeus,
By Zeus I swear, except ye find and bring

Before my presence here the very man
Who carried out this lawless burial,
Death for your punishment shall not suffice.
Hanged on a cross, alive ye first shall make
Confession of this outrage. This will teach you
What practices are like to serve your turn.
There are some villainies that bring no gain.
For by dishonesty the few may thrive,
The many come to ruin and disgrace. . . .

[After the guards expose the body to the elements
again, Antigone is caught burying it a second time.
She is arrested and brought before the king.]

CREON
Speak, girl, with head bent low and downcast
eyes,
Does thou plead guilty or deny the deed?

ANTIGONE
Guilty. I did it, I deny it not.

CREON (to GUARD)
Sirrah, begone whither thou wilt, and thank
Thy luck that thou hast 'scaped a heavy charge.
(To ANTIGONE)
Now answer this plain question, yes or no,
Wast thou acquainted with the interdict?

ANTIGONE
I knew, all knew; how should I fail to know?

CREON
And yet wert bold enough to break the law?

ANTIGONE
Yea, for these laws were not ordained of Zeus,
And she who sits enthroned with gods below,
Justice, enacted not these human laws.
Nor did I deem that thou, a mortal man,
Could'st by a breath annul and override
The immutable unwritten laws of Heaven.
They were not born today nor yesterday;
They die not; and none knoweth whence they
sprang.
I was not like, who feared no mortal's frown,
To disobey these laws and so provoke
The wrath of Heaven. I knew that I must die,

E'en hadst thou not proclaimed it; and if death
Is thereby hastened, I shall count it gain.
For death is gain to him whose life, like mine,
Is full of misery. Thus my lot appears
Not sad, but blissful; for had I endured
To leave my mother's son unburied there,
I should have grieved with reason, but not now.
And if in this thou judgest me a fool,
Methinks the judge of folly's not acquit.

CHORUS
A stubborn daughter of a stubborn sire,
This ill-starred maiden kicks against the pricks.

CREON
Well, let her know the stubbornest of wills
Are soonest bended, as the hardest iron,
O'er-heated in the fire to brittleness,
Flies soonest into fragments, shivered through.
A snaffle curbs the fieriest steed, and he
Who in subjection lives must needs be meek.
But this proud girl, in insolence well-schooled,
First overstepped the established law, and then--
A second and worse act of insolence--
She boasts and glories in her wickedness.
Now if she thus can flout authority
Unpunished, I am woman, she the man.
But though she be my sister's child or nearer
Of kin than all who worship at my hearth,
Nor she nor yet her sister shall escape
The utmost penalty, for both I hold,
As arch-conspirators, of equal guilt.
Bring forth the older; even now I saw her
Within the palace, frenzied and distraught.
The workings of the mind discover oft
Dark deeds in darkness schemed, before the act.
More hateful still the miscreant who seeks
When caught, to make a virtue of a crime. . . .

There is a fundamental point of disagreement between Creon and Antigone that is indicative of our previously mentioned distinction between convention (*nomos*) and "natural" Law (*physis*).

Antigone knowingly violated the law! "I knew, of course I knew. The word was plain."

However, she justifies her actions by appealing to the "eternal laws of Heaven."

> Yea, for these laws were not ordained of Zeus,
> And she who sits enthroned with gods below,
> Justice, enacted not these human laws.
> Nor did I deem that thou, a mortal man,
> Could'st by a breath annul and override
> The immutable unwritten laws of Heaven.
> They were not born today nor yesterday;
> They die not; and none knoweth whence they sprang

In other words, Creon's "law" is not consistent with the Laws of the gods, and no matter how powerful a monarch Creon might be, he has no authority to override the "immutable" laws of "Heaven."

As for Creon, he emphasizes the practical importance of preserving the State, and consistency in the application of its laws. To be lenient to a family member (e.g., his nephew Polyneices, who "betrayed" Thebes by not only contesting rulership but especially by allying with foreign powers, or his niece Antigone who disobeyed his command), would be to set "friend before his country." If Creon were to show leniency, then consistency would require the spread of that leniency. "If I allow disorder in my house I'd surely have to license it abroad."

Creon thinks that the duty of the ruler is to "hold to the best plans of all," to count no friend greater than his own "fatherland." In his own mind, at least, he forbade the burial of Polyneices in order to promote the public good, for the sake of public safety, and to serve as a lesson to others. Creon regards the State as "the good ship that holds our fortunes all." In other words, the State is more important than individual interests or familial obligations. Creon simply does not recognize that there is a "higher" law that can somehow supersede his commands—his "just"

commands that he makes for the good of the community. By violating the law and appealing to her "conscience," Antigone has placed herself above the laws of her land, and then tries to make a virtue of her criminality.

> But this proud girl, in insolence well-schooled,
> First overstepped the established law, and then--
> A second and worse act of insolence--
> She boasts and glories in her wickedness.
> . . .
> More hateful still the miscreant who seeks
> When caught, to make a virtue of a crime.
> . . .

This tension is not antiquated, but deeply relevant today. Ask yourself, what would be an example of current or historical (possible) conflicts between *personal* morality, and *public* (legal) obligation? Or, to put it differently, a situation in which one's personal moral values are in conflict with the law?

Each of the following statements were made by former Arkansas Governor and current (as of 2015) Republican Presidential Candidate Mike Huckabee:

> I have opponents in this race who do not want to change the Constitution. But I believe it's a lot easier to change the Constitution than it would be to change the word of the living God. And that's what we need to do is amend the Constitution so it's in God's standards rather than trying to change God's standards so it lines up with some contemporary view of how we treat each other and how we treat the family.[38]

And:

---

[38] Mike Huckabee, 1-14-2008: http://thinkprogress.org/politics/2008/01/15/

18870/huckabee-amend-the-constitution-to-gods-standards/

The Court created a national right to same-sex marriage that doesn't exist in our Constitution, it hijacked the democratic process, subverting the will of Americans in more than 30 states who voted to protect traditional marriage, and trampling on America's most fundamental right — religious liberty....

Can the Supreme Court "decide" this? They cannot. Under our Constitution, we have three, co-equal branches of government. The courts can interpret law but cannot create it. The ruling still requires congressional funding and executive branch enforcement. The Supreme Court is not the "Supreme Branch," and it is certainly not the Supreme Being. If they can unilaterally make law, and just do whatever they want, then we have judicial tyranny.

Throughout our nation's history, the court has abused its power and delivered morally unconscionable rulings. They have rationalized the destruction of innocent human life, defined African Americans as property and justified Japanese-American internment camps. U.S. presidents, including Abraham Lincoln, Andrew Jackson, and Franklin Delano Roosevelt, ignored Supreme Court rulings, rejecting the notion that the Supreme Court can circumvent the Constitution and "make law." ...

No man — and certainly no un-elected judge — has the right to redefine the laws of nature or of nature's God. Government is not God. The purpose of marriage is to socially and biologically unite a man and a woman to create the next generation and to train the next generation to become their replacements. Marriage is a sacred covenant, not just another social contract....[39]

Antigone showcases the tension between the view that morality and justice are matters of convention, and the view that there is a "higher" morality in "Nature" against which our conventions may be compared. The Sophists were often the implicit, if not explicit spokespersons on behalf of convention. Socrates, on the other hand, spoke on behalf of "Nature."

Socrates

Socrates (470-399 BCE) is the iconic "philosopher" in the West, and even the first "political philosopher," specifically. He was a husband and father of three children. He was an itinerant teacher who seemed to rely on the support of his wealthier friends, as he charged nothing to those he "instructed." He served in the military, and his courage in war was recognized. Finally, he was put on trial for atheism and corrupting the youth of Athens. After being convicted and sentenced to death, he drank hemlock and died.

Socrates presents an interpretation problem. He never wrote anything himself. All we think we know about him come from the writing of others, most notably Plato, but also Aristophanes and Xenophon.

He is lampooned in Aristophanes' *Clouds*, and presented as a serious philosopher by both Xenophon and Plato. Our greatest source for all things Socrates is his student Plato, but Plato was roughly 45 years younger than Socrates, and was only 25 when Socrates was tried and executed. Plato was only a young child when most of the events and conversations reported in his dialogues could have actually taken place. It's unlikely that a five year old Plato was not only present for all these conversations, but memorized them precisely that he might write them down some decades later.

---

[39] http://www.usatoday.com/story/opinion/2015/06/25/supreme-court-obamacare- religious-freedom-huckabee-column/29175727/

We have, then, *"the problem of Socrates:"* *what did Socrates himself really believe and teach and say*? How much of Plato's "Socrates" is actually Socrates, and not just Plato wearing a "Socrates" mask? We can't know for sure. What we can know, however, is that Socrates (whatever he said!) was a hugely influential and revered figure for ancient philosophers, as nearly all the philosophical schools to come after him either traced themselves back to Socrates himself, or at least claimed that Socrates was an embodiment of their ideals.

Socrates is most well-known for the "*Socratic method.*" Socrates, himself, claimed to know nothing (and from this it is easy to see the lineage the Skeptics traced back to him), and also claimed to be seeking it from those with whom he spoke. Socrates starts from the position of (alleged) ignorance, all due to a fateful prophesy he received:

> You must have known Chaerephon; he was early a friend of mine, and also a friend of yours, for he shared in the recent exile of the people, and returned with you. Well, Chaerephon, as you know, was very impetuous in all his doings, and he went to Delphi and boldly asked the oracle to tell him whether -- as I was saying, I must beg you not to interrupt -- he asked the oracle to tell him whether anyone was wiser than I was, and the Pythian prophetess answered, that there was no man wiser. Chaerephon is dead himself; but his brother, who is in court, will confirm the truth of what I am saying.

> Why do I mention this? Because I am going to explain to you why I have such an evil name. When I heard the answer, I said to myself, What can the god mean? and what is the interpretation of his riddle? for I know that I have no wisdom, small or great. What then can he mean when he says that I am the wisest of men? And yet he is a god, and cannot lie; that would be

against his nature. After long consideration, I thought of a method of trying the question. I reflected that if I could only find a man wiser than myself, then I might go to the god with a refutation in my hand. I should say to him, 'Here is a man who is wiser than I am; but you said that I was the wisest.' Accordingly I went to one who had the reputation of wisdom, and observed him -- his name I need not mention; he was a politician whom I selected for examination -- and the result was as follows: When I began to talk with him, I could not help thinking that he was not really wise, although he was thought wise by many, and still wiser by himself; and thereupon I tried to explain to him that he thought himself wise, but was not really wise; and the consequence was that he hated me, and his enmity was shared by several who were present and heard me. So I left him, saying to myself, as I went away: Well, although I do not suppose that either of us knows anything really beautiful and good, I am better off than he is, -- for he knows nothing, and thinks that he knows; I neither know nor think that I know. In this latter particular, then, I seem to have slightly the advantage of him.[40]

Being proclaimed the wisest of all, Socrates sought a counter-example—someone who would prove wiser than he. So, he spoke with all sorts of prominent people, people who claimed to be wise, in an effort to confirm their wisdom. The result was always the same: by virtue of his interrogation, they were revealed to be lacking in wisdom after all. His method was notorious:

1. Ask a question concerning an important issue (all while claiming not to have an answer himself)
2. Attack whatever answers (often definitions) are provided by identifying

---

[40] Plato's *Apology.*

logical flaws (e.g., circularity, definition by example, etc.).

3. Employ a *reductio ad absurdum* argument to reveal further flaws, and/or use counter-examples to the same effect.
4. Thereby cause his sparring partner to cede defeat.

Consider the following example from the *Apology*:

But still I should like to know, Meletus, in what I am affirmed to corrupt the young. I suppose you mean, as I infer from your indictment, that I teach them not to acknowledge the gods which the state acknowledges, but some other new divinities or spiritual agencies in their stead. These are the lessons by which I corrupt the youth, as you say.

Yes, that I say emphatically.

Then, by the gods, Meletus, of whom we are speaking, tell me and the court, in somewhat plainer terms, what you mean! for I do not as yet understand whether you affirm that I teach other men to acknowledge some gods, and therefore that I do believe in gods, and am not an entire atheist -- this you do not lay to my charge, -- but only you say that they are not the same gods which the city recognizes -- the charge is that they are different gods. Or, do you mean that I am an atheist simply, and a teacher of atheism?

I mean the latter -- that you are a complete atheist.

What an extraordinary statement! Why do you think so, Meletus? Do you mean that I do not believe in the godhead of the sun or moon, like other men?

I assure you, judges, that he does not: for he says that the sun is stone, and the moon earth.

Friend Meletus, you think that you are accusing Anaxagoras: and you have but a bad opinion of the judges, if you fancy them illiterate to such a degree as not to know that these doctrines are found in the books of Anaxagoras the Clazomenian, which are full of them. And so, forsooth, the youth are said to be taught them by Socrates, when there are not unfrequently exhibitions of them at the theatre (Probably in allusion to Aristophanes who caricatured, and to Euripides who borrowed the notions of Anaxagoras, as well as to other dramatic poets.) (price of admission one drachma at the most); and they might pay their money, and laugh at Socrates if he pretends to father these extraordinary views. And so, Meletus, you really think that I do not believe in any god?

I swear by Zeus that you believe absolutely in none at all.

Nobody will believe you, Meletus, and I am pretty sure that you do not believe yourself. I cannot help thinking, men of Athens, that Meletus is reckless and impudent, and that he has written this indictment in a spirit of mere wantonness and youthful bravado. Has he not compounded a riddle, thinking to try me? He said to himself: -- I shall see whether the wise Socrates will discover my facetious contradiction, or whether I shall be able to deceive him and the rest of them. For he certainly does appear to me to contradict himself in the indictment as much as if he said that Socrates is guilty of not believing in the gods, and yet of believing in them -- but this is not like a person who is in earnest.

I should like you, O men of Athens, to join me in examining what I conceive to be his inconsistency; and do you, Meletus, answer. And I must remind the audience of my request that they would not make a disturbance if I speak in my accustomed manner:

Did ever man, Meletus, believe in the existence of human things, and not of human beings?...I wish, men of Athens, that he would answer, and not be always trying to get up an interruption. Did ever any man believe in horsemanship, and not in horses? or in flute-playing, and not in flute- players? No, my friend; I will answer to you and to the court, as you refuse to answer for yourself. There is no man who ever did. But now please to answer the next question: Can a man believe in spiritual and divine agencies, and not in spirits or demigods?

He cannot.

How lucky I am to have extracted that answer, by the assistance of the court! But then you swear in the indictment that I teach and believe in divine or spiritual agencies (new or old, no matter for that); at any rate, I believe in spiritual agencies, -- so you say and swear in the affidavit; and yet if I believe in divine beings, how can I help believing in spirits or demigods; -- must I not? To be sure I must; and therefore I may assume that your silence gives consent. Now what are spirits or demigods? Are they not either gods or the sons of gods?

Certainly they are.

But this is what I call the facetious riddle invented by you: the demigods or spirits are gods, and you say first that I do not believe in gods, and then again that I do believe in gods; that is, if I believe in demigods. For if the demigods are the illegitimate sons of gods, whether by the nymphs or by any other mothers, of whom they are said to be the sons -- what human being will ever believe that there are no gods if they are the sons of gods? You might as well affirm the existence of mules, and deny that of horses and asses. Such nonsense, Meletus, could only have been intended by you to make trial of me. You have put this into the indictment because you had nothing real of which to accuse me. But no one who has a particle of understanding will ever be convinced by you that the same men can believe in divine and superhuman things, and yet not believe that there are gods and demigods and heroes.

At this point, Meletus already looks ridiculous, given that he has been reduced to the absurd position that although Socrates believes in no gods at all, he nevertheless believes in the offspring of gods! This process will continue until it becomes obvious to any impartial observer that Socrates is not guilty of the charges brought against him—not that it helped him in that case.

There are various ways to interpret his argumentative approach, with the least charitable being that Socrates was some sort of bully who preferred clever arguments over fists. If Plato's account of Socrates (especially in the *Apology*) is remotely accurate, Socrates saw himself to be on a divine mission.

And so I go about the world, obedient to the god, and search and make enquiry into the wisdom of any one, whether citizen or stranger, who appears to be wise; and if he is not wise, then in vindication of the oracle I show him that he is not wise; and my occupation quite absorbs me, and I have no time to give either to any public matter of interest or to any concern of my own, but I am in utter poverty by reason of my devotion to the god.

He also saw himself in service to Athens, and believed that his confrontations and interrogations were efforts to improve the very souls of those with whom he spoke.

Men of Athens, I honour and love you; but I shall obey God rather than you, and while I have life and strength I shall never cease from the practice and teaching of philosophy, exhorting any one whom I meet and saying to him after my manner: You, my friend, -- a citizen of the great and mighty and wise city of Athens, -- are you not ashamed of heaping up the greatest amount of money and honour and reputation, and caring so little about wisdom and truth and the greatest improvement of the soul, which you never regard or heed at all? And if the person with whom I am arguing, says: Yes, but I do care; then I do not leave him or let him go at once; but I proceed to interrogate and examine and cross-examine him, and if I think that he has no virtue in him, but only says that he has, I reproach him with undervaluing the greater, and overvaluing the less. And I shall repeat the same words to every one whom I meet, young and old, citizen and alien, but especially to the citizens, inasmuch as they are my brethren. For know that this is the command of God; and I believe that no greater good has ever happened in the state than my service to the God. For I do nothing but go about persuading you all, old and young alike, not to take thought for your persons or your properties, but first and chiefly to care about the greatest improvement of the soul. I tell you that virtue is not given by money, but that from virtue comes money and every other good of man, public as well as private.

Although it is impossible to know, with certainty, what Socrates himself affirmed (not only because of the difficulty of sorting him out from Plato, but also because he claimed to know

nothing himself!), we can infer (via Plato) *that he seems to have believed that knowledge is innately within us, and is remembered rather than discovered*, as is evident in his conversation with Meno (found in the dialogue of that same name).

... So with virtue now. I don't know what it is. You may have known before you came into contact with me, but now you look as if you don't. Nevertheless I am ready to carry out, together with you, a joint investigation and inquiry into what it is.

But how will you look for something when you don't in the least know what it is? How on earth are you going to set up something you don't know as the object of your search? To put it another way, even if you come right up against it, how will you know that what you have found is the thing you didn't know?

I know what you mean. Do you realize that what you are bringing up is the trick argument that a man cannot try to discover either what he knows or what he does not know? He would not seek what he knows, for since he knows it there is no need of the inquiry, nor what he does not know, for in that case he does not even know what he is to look for.

Well, do you think it a good argument?

No.

Can you explain how it fails?

I can. I have heard from men and women who understand the truths of religion . . .

Pindar speaks of it too, and many another of the poets who are divinely inspired. What they say is this--see whether you think they are speaking the truth. They say that the soul of man is immortal. At one time it comes to an end--that which is called death--and at another is born again, but is never finally exterminated... . Thus the soul, since it is immortal and has been born many times, and has seen all things both here and in the other world, has learned everything that is. So we need not be surprised if it can recall the knowledge of virtue or anything else which, as we see, it once possessed. All nature is akin, and the soul has learned everything, so that when a man has recalled a single piece of knowledge--learned it, in ordinary language--there is no reason why he should not find out all the rest, if he keeps a stout heart and does not grow weary of the search, for seeking and learning are in fact nothing but recollection.[41]

This view of knowledge as recollection of things already known explains why rather than *telling* people things, informing them as to the true nature of justice, goodness, etc., he would *question* them so that they could "recall" the truth of matters themselves.

Because people already *know* the truth, including moral truths (but have just forgotten), *he believed that vice was always due to error.* No one chooses to do evil willingly, just as no one would willingly choose sickness over health. Instead, people do bad things because they just don't know ("remember") any better. If evil-doers could be properly educated, they would change their ways. Unjust actions are the result of ignorance, unjust laws are the product of poorly informed rulers, and bad political institutions are also the result of error. Presumably, this interpretation would have applied to the jurors who convicted him of atheism and corrupting the youth—they simply didn't understand what they were doing. Notice, too, that if we "remember" truths about justice, morality, etc., from our time in the "other world," there is something about those things that *transcends* the particular conventions of particular communities.

The powers-that-be in Athens condemned Socrates' beliefs and actions. He persisted, though it cost him his own life, because he believed them to be *mistaken*. Justice and goodness are not merely what some Athenian jurists proclaim it to be, but something that exists by Nature, and against which those jurists and their rulings may themselves be judged.

It seems suitable to end our brief treatment of Socrates with his death. Despite his superior arguments, Socrates was convicted on the charges brought against him. When given an opportunity to propose his own punishment, he first suggested that his "punishment" be free public meals for the rest of his life! At the urging of Plato and others present, he then suggested a modest fine. He refused to cower and plead for mercy, confident in his own righteousness. When the sentence of death was pronounced, he did not cower then either. Instead, he offered an argument for why death is not a bad thing.

Let us reflect in another way, and we shall see that there is great reason to hope that death is a good; for one of two things -- either death is a state of nothingness and utter unconsciousness, or, as men say, there is a change and migration of the soul from this world to another. Now if you suppose that there is no consciousness, but a sleep like the sleep of him who is undisturbed even by dreams, death will be an unspeakable gain. For if a person were to select the night in which his sleep was undisturbed even by dreams, and were to compare with this the other days and nights of his life, and then were to tell us how many days and nights he had passed in the course of his life better and more pleasantly than this one, I think that any man, I will not say a private man, but even the great king will not find many such days or nights, when compared with the others. Now if death be of such a nature, I say that to die is gain; for eternity is then only a single night. But if death is

---

[41] Plato, *Meno* 80c-81e.

the journey to another place, and there, as men say, all the dead abide, what good, O my friends and judges, can be greater than this? If indeed when the pilgrim arrives in the world below, he is delivered from the professors of justice in this world, and finds the true judges who are said to give judgment there, . . . Above all, I shall then be able to continue my search into true and false knowledge; as in this world, so also in the next; and I shall find out who is wise, and who pretends to be wise, and is not. What would not a man give, O judges, to be able to examine the leader of the great Trojan expedition; or Odysseus or Sisyphus, or numberless others, men and women too! What infinite delight would there be in conversing with them and asking them questions! In another world they do not put a man to death for asking questions: assuredly not. For besides being happier than we are, they will be immortal, if what is said is true.

Perhaps more important and impressive than his words, were his deeds. In another dialogue written by Plato (*Crito*), one of Socrates' friends visits him in prison prior to his execution with plans for his escape. Rather than seizing the opportunity to save his own life, Socrates seizes one last opportunity to offer moral instruction. He demonstrates that it is not life that is to be valued, but a good and just life. Socrates imagines himself being interrogated by the laws of Athens themselves should he escape.

Consider, Socrates, if this is true, that in your present attempt you are going to do us wrong. For, after having brought you into the world, and nurtured and educated you, and given you and every other citizen a share in every good that we had to give, we further proclaim and give the right to every Athenian, that if he does not like us when he has come of age and has seen the ways of the city, and made our acquaintance, he may go where

he pleases and take his goods with him; and none of us laws will forbid him or interfere with him. Any of you who does not like us and the city, and who wants to go to a colony or to any other city, may go where he likes, and take his goods with him. But he who has experience of the manner in which we order justice and administer the State, and still remains, has entered into an implied contract that he will do as we command him. And he who disobeys us is, as we maintain, thrice wrong: first, because in disobeying us he is disobeying his parents; secondly, because we are the authors of his education; thirdly, because he has made an agreement with us that he will duly obey our commands; and he neither obeys them nor convinces us that our commands are wrong; and we do not rudely impose them, but give him the alternative of obeying or convincing us; that is what we offer and he does neither. These are the sort of accusations to which, as we were saying, you, Socrates, will be exposed if you accomplish your intentions; you, above all other Athenians." Suppose I ask, why is this? they will justly retort upon me that I above all other men have acknowledged the agreement. "There is clear proof," they will say, "Socrates, that we and the city were not displeasing to you. Of all Athenians you have been the most constant resident in the city, which, as you never leave, you may be supposed to love. For you never went out of the city either to see the games, except once when you went to the Isthmus, or to any other place unless when you were on military service; nor did you travel as other men do. Nor had you any curiosity to know other States or their laws: your affections did not go beyond us and our State; we were your especial favorites, and you acquiesced in our government of you; and this is the State in which you begat your children, which is a proof of your satisfaction. Moreover, you might, if you had liked, have fixed the penalty at banishment in the course of the trial-the State which refuses to let you go now would have let you go then. But you pretended that you preferred death to exile, and that you were not grieved at death. And now you have forgotten these fine sentiments, and pay no respect to us, the laws, of whom you are the destroyer; and are doing what only a miserable slave would do, running away and turning your back upon the compacts and agreements which you made as a citizen. And first of all answer this very question: Are we right in saying that you agreed to be governed according to us in deed, and not in word only? Is that true or not?[42]

If Socrates were to escape from his sentence, he would not only violate the laws of his city-State, he would reveal himself to be a fraud. He had long claimed that death was not a bad thing, and that *nothing in life or death could truly harm a virtuous person*. If he were to flee death, his actions would contradict his words. Deeds, not mere words. In his death, Socrates' philosophy and status as a philosopher is arguably most evident.

It is one thing to be clever and gifted in speech. The Sophists could all be described so. A true philosopher, on the other hand *lives* his (or her) philosophy. Or, in Socrates' case, dies for it. Socrates was the first (recorded) philosopher to provide a living (and dying) testimony to how philosophy can transform one's life. Small wonder that nearly every philosophical school to come would point to him as either founder or inspiration.

---

[42] Plato, *Crito*, 51c-52d.

Plato (424 BCE – 328 BCE) is a very well-known ancient Greek philosopher and student of the possibly more well-known Socrates. Because Socrates wrote nothing himself, most of what we think we know about Socrates comes from the writings of others, most notably Plato. Socrates appears as the main character in numerous Platonic dialogues, including the Apology. Not to be confused with apologizing, the "Apology" comes from the Greek word "apologia," meaning to give a "reasoned defense." Here, Socrates is giving a "reasoned defense" of his teachings and activities. Although ultimately condemned by the laws and jurors of Athens, he remains steadfast in his devotion to his "higher" calling.

Plato's *Apology*

From The Dialogues of Plato – Jowett Public Domain Translation
[http://ancienthistory.about.com/library/bl/bl_text_plato_apology2.htm]

How you, O Athenians, have been affected by my accusers, I cannot tell; but I know that they almost made me forget who I was -- so persuasively did they speak; and yet they have hardly uttered a word of truth. But of the many falsehoods told by them, there was one which quite amazed me; -- I mean when they said that you should be upon your guard and not allow yourselves to be deceived by the force of my eloquence. To say this, when they were certain to be detected as soon as I opened my lips and proved myself to be anything but a great speaker, did indeed appear to me most shameless -- unless by the force of eloquence they mean the force of truth; for is such is their meaning, I admit that I am eloquent. But in how different a way from theirs! Well, as I was saying, they have scarcely spoken the truth at all; but from me you shall hear the whole truth: not, however, delivered after their manner in a set oration duly ornamented with words and phrases. No, by heaven! but I shall use the words and arguments which occur to me at the moment; for I am confident in the justice of my cause (Or, I am certain that I am right in taking this course.): at my time of life I ought not to be appearing before you, O men of Athens, in the character of a juvenile orator -- let no one expect it of me. And I must beg of you to grant me a favour: -- If I defend myself in my accustomed manner, and you hear me using the words which I have been in the habit of using in the agora, at the tables of the money-changers, or anywhere else, I would ask you not to be

surprised, and not to interrupt me on this account. For I am more than seventy years of age, and appearing now for the first time in a court of law, I am quite a stranger to the language of the place; and therefore I would have you regard me as if I were really a stranger, whom you would excuse if he spoke in his native tongue, and after the fashion of his country: -- Am I making an unfair request of you? Never mind the manner, which may or may not be good; but think only of the truth of my words, and give heed to that: let the speaker speak truly and the judge decide justly.

And first, I have to reply to the older charges and to my first accusers, and then I will go on to the later ones. For of old I have had many accusers, who have accused me falsely to you during many years; and I am more afraid of them than of Anytus and his associates, who are dangerous, too, in their own way. But far more dangerous are the others, who began when you were children, and took possession of your minds with their falsehoods, telling of one Socrates, a wise man, who speculated about the heaven above, and searched into the earth beneath, and made the worse appear the better cause. The disseminators of this tale are the accusers whom I dread; for their hearers are apt to fancy that such enquirers do not believe in the existence of the gods. And they are many, and their charges against me are of ancient date, and they were made by them in the days when you were more impressible than you are now -- in childhood, or it may have been in youth -- and the cause when heard went by default, for there was none to answer. And hardest of all, I do not know and cannot tell the names of my accusers; unless in the chance case of a Comic poet. All who from envy and malice have persuaded you -- some of them having first convinced themselves -- all this class of men are most difficult to deal with; for I cannot have them up here, and cross-examine them, and therefore I must simply fight with shadows in my own defence, and argue when there is no one who answers. I will ask you then to assume with me, as I was saying, that my opponents are of two kinds; one recent, the other ancient: and I hope that you will see the propriety of my answering the latter first, for these accusations you heard long before the others, and much oftener.

Well, then, I must make my defence, and endeavour to clear away in a short time, a slander which has lasted a long time. May I succeed, if to succeed be for my good and yours, or likely to avail me in my cause! The task is not an easy one; I quite understand the nature of it. And so leaving the event with God, in obedience to the law I will now make my defence.

I will begin at the beginning, and ask what is the accusation which has given rise to the slander of me, and in fact has encouraged Meletus to proof this charge against me. Well, what do the slanderers say? They shall be my prosecutors, and I will sum up their words in an affidavit: 'Socrates is an evil-doer, and a curious person, who searches into things under the earth and in heaven, and he makes the worse appear the better cause; and he teaches the aforesaid doctrines to others.' Such is the nature of the accusation: it is just what you have yourselves seen in the comedy of Aristophanes (Aristoph., Clouds.), who has introduced a man whom he calls Socrates, going about and saying that he walks in air, and talking a deal of nonsense concerning matters of which I do not pretend to know either much or little -- not that I mean to speak disparagingly of any one who is a student of natural philosophy. I should be very sorry if Meletus could bring so grave a charge against me. But the simple truth is, O Athenians, that I have nothing to do with physical speculations. Very many of those here present are witnesses to the truth of this, and to them I appeal. Speak then, you who have heard me, and tell your neighbours whether any of you have ever known me hold forth in few words or in many upon such matters...You hear their answer. And from what they say of this part of the charge you will be able to judge of the truth of the rest.

As little foundation is there for the report that I am a teacher, and take money; this accusation has no more truth in it than the other. Although, if a man were really able to instruct mankind, to receive money for giving instruction would, in my opinion, be an honour to him. There is Gorgias of Leontium, and Prodicus of Ceos, and Hippias of Elis, who go the round of the cities, and are able to persuade the young men to leave their own citizens by whom they might be taught for nothing, and come to them whom they not only pay, but are thankful if they may be allowed to pay them. There is at this time a Parian philosopher residing in Athens, of whom I have heard; and I came to hear of him in this way: -- I came across a man who has spent a world of money on the Sophists, Callias, the son of Hipponicus, and knowing that he had sons, I asked him: 'Callias,' I said, 'if your two sons were foals or calves, there would be no difficulty in finding some one to put over them; we should hire a trainer of horses, or a farmer probably, who would improve and perfect them in their own proper virtue and excellence; but as they are human beings, whom are you thinking of placing over them? Is there any one who understands human and political virtue? You must have thought about the matter, for you have sons; is there any one?' 'There is,' he said. 'Who is he?' said I; 'and of what country? and what does he charge?' 'Evenus the Parian,' he replied; 'he is the man, and his charge is five minae.' Happy is Evenus, I said to myself, if he really has this wisdom, and teaches at such a moderate charge. Had I the same, I should have been very proud and conceited; but the truth is that I have no knowledge of the kind.

I dare say, Athenians, that some one among you will reply, 'Yes, Socrates, but what is the origin of these accusations which are brought against you; there must have been something strange which you have been doing? All these rumours and this talk about you would never have arisen if you had been like other men: tell us, then, what is the cause of them, for we should be sorry to judge hastily of you.' Now I regard this as a fair challenge, and I will endeavour to explain to you the reason why I am called wise and have such an evil fame. Please to attend then. And although some of you may think that I am joking, I declare that I will tell you the entire truth. Men of Athens, this reputation of mine has come of a certain sort of wisdom which I possess. If you ask me what kind of wisdom, I reply, wisdom such as may perhaps be attained by man, for to that extent I am inclined to believe that I am wise; whereas the persons of whom I was speaking have a superhuman wisdom which I may fail to describe, because I have it not myself; and he who says that I have, speaks falsely, and is taking away my character. And here, O men of Athens, I must beg you not to interrupt me, even if I seem to say something extravagant. For the word which I will speak is not mine. I will refer you to a witness who is worthy of credit; that witness shall be the God of Delphi -- he will tell you about my wisdom, if I have any, and of what sort it is. You must have known Chaerephon; he was early a friend of mine, and also a friend of yours, for he shared in the recent exile of the people, and returned with you. Well, Chaerephon, as you know, was very impetuous in all his doings, and he went to Delphi and boldly asked the oracle to tell him whether -- as I was saying, I must beg you not to interrupt -- he asked the oracle to tell him whether anyone was wiser than I was, and the Pythian prophetess answered, that there was no man wiser. Chaerephon is dead himself; but his brother, who is in court, will confirm the truth of what I am saying.

Why do I mention this? Because I am going to explain to you why I have such an evil name. When I heard the answer, I said to myself, What can the god mean? and what is the interpretation of his riddle? for I know that I have no wisdom, small or great. What then can he mean when he says that I am the wisest of men? And yet he is a god, and cannot lie; that would be against his nature. After long consideration, I thought of a method of trying the question. I reflected that if I could only find a man wiser than myself, then I might go to the god with a refutation in my hand. I should say to him, 'Here is a man who is wiser than I am; but you said that I was the wisest.' Accordingly I went to one who had the reputation of wisdom, and observed him -- his name I need not mention; he was a politician whom I selected for examination -- and the result was as follows: When I began to talk with him, I could not help thinking that he was not really wise, although he was thought wise by many, and still wiser by himself; and thereupon I tried to explain to him that he thought himself wise, but was not really wise; and the consequence was that he hated me, and his enmity was shared by several who were present and heard me. So I left him, saying to myself, as I went away: Well, although I do not suppose that either of us knows anything really beautiful and good, I am better off than he is, -- for he knows nothing, and thinks that he knows; I neither know nor think that I know. In this latter particular, then, I seem to have slightly the advantage of him. Then I went to another who had still higher pretensions to wisdom, and my conclusion was exactly the same. Whereupon I made another enemy of him, and of many others besides him.

Then I went to one man after another, being not unconscious of the enmity which I provoked, and I lamented and feared this: but necessity was laid upon me, -- the word of God, I thought, ought to be considered first. And I said to myself, Go I must to all who appear to know, and find out the meaning of the oracle. And I swear to you, Athenians, by the dog I swear! -- for I must tell you the truth -- the result of my mission was just this: I found that the men most in repute were all but the most foolish; and that others less esteemed were really wiser and better. I will tell you the tale of my wanderings and of the 'Herculean' labours, as I may call them, which I endured only to find at last the oracle irrefutable. After the politicians, I went to the poets; tragic, dithyrambic, and all sorts. And there, I said to myself, you will be instantly detected; now you will find out that you are more ignorant than they are. Accordingly, I took them some of the most elaborate passages in their own writings, and asked what was the meaning of them -- thinking that they would teach me something. Will you believe me? I am almost ashamed to confess the truth, but I must say that there is hardly a person present who would not have talked better about their poetry than they did themselves. Then I knew that not by wisdom do poets write poetry, but by a sort of genius and inspiration; they are like diviners or soothsayers who also say many fine things, but do not understand the meaning of them. The poets appeared to me to be much in the same case; and I further observed that upon the strength of their poetry they believed themselves to be the wisest of men in other things in which they were not wise. So I departed, conceiving myself to be superior to them for the same reason that I was superior to the politicians.

At last I went to the artisans. I was conscious that I knew nothing at all, as I may say, and I was sure that they knew many fine things; and here I was not mistaken, for they did know many things of which I was ignorant, and in this they certainly were wiser than I was. But I observed that even the good artisans fell into the same error as the poets; -- because they were good workmen they thought that they also knew all sorts of high matters, and this defect in them overshadowed their wisdom; and therefore I asked myself on behalf of the oracle, whether I would like to be as I was, neither having their knowledge nor their ignorance, or like them in both; and I made answer to myself and to the oracle that I was better off as I was.

This inquisition has led to my having many enemies of the worst and most dangerous kind, and has given occasion also to many calumnies. And I am called wise, for my hearers always imagine that I myself possess the wisdom which I find wanting in others: but the truth is, O men of Athens, that God only is wise; and by his answer he intends to show that the wisdom of men is worth little or nothing; he is not speaking of Socrates, he is only using my name by way of illustration, as if he said, He, O men, is the wisest, who, like Socrates, knows that his wisdom is in

truth worth nothing. And so I go about the world, obedient to the god, and search and make enquiry into the wisdom of any one, whether citizen or stranger, who appears to be wise; and if he is not wise, then in vindication of the oracle I show him that he is not wise; and my occupation quite absorbs me, and I have no time to give either to any public matter of interest or to any concern of my own, but I am in utter poverty by reason of my devotion to the god.

There is another thing: -- young men of the richer classes, who have not much to do, come about me of their own accord; they like to hear the pretenders examined, and they often imitate me, and proceed to examine others; there are plenty of persons, as they quickly discover, who think that they know something, but really know little or nothing; and then those who are examined by them instead of being angry with themselves are angry with me: This confounded Socrates, they say; this villainous misleader of youth! -- and then if somebody asks them, Why, what evil does he practise or teach? they do not know, and cannot tell; but in order that they may not appear to be at a loss, they repeat the ready-made charges which are used against all philosophers about teaching things up in the clouds and under the earth, and having no gods, and making the worse appear the better cause; for they do not like to confess that their pretence of knowledge has been detected -- which is the truth; and as they are numerous and ambitious and energetic, and are drawn up in battle array and have persuasive tongues, they have filled your ears with their loud and inveterate calumnies. And this is the reason why my three accusers, Meletus and Anytus and Lycon, have set upon me; Meletus, who has a quarrel with me on behalf of the poets; Anytus, on behalf of the craftsmen and politicians; Lycon, on behalf of the rhetoricians: and as I said at the beginning, I cannot expect to get rid of such a mass of calumny all in a moment. And this, O men of Athens, is the truth and the whole truth; I have concealed nothing, I have dissembled nothing. And yet, I know that my plainness of speech makes them hate me, and what is their hatred but a proof that I am speaking the truth? -- Hence has arisen the prejudice against me; and this is the reason of it, as you will find out either in this or in any future enquiry.

I have said enough in my defence against the first class of my accusers; I turn to the second class. They are headed by Meletus, that good man and true lover of his country, as he calls himself. Against these, too, I must try to make a defence: -- Let their affidavit be read: it contains something of this kind: It says that Socrates is a doer of evil, who corrupts the youth; and who does not believe in the gods of the state, but has other new divinities of his own. Such is the charge; and now let us examine the particular counts. He says that I am a doer of evil, and corrupt the youth; but I say, O men of Athens, that Meletus is a doer of evil, in that he pretends to be in earnest when he is only in jest, and is so eager to bring men to trial from a pretended zeal and interest about matters in which he really never had the smallest interest. And the truth of this I will endeavour to prove to you.

Come hither, Meletus, and let me ask a question of you. You think a great deal about the improvement of youth?

Yes, I do.

Tell the judges, then, who is their improver; for you must know, as you have taken the pains to discover their corrupter, and are citing and accusing me before them. Speak, then, and tell the judges who their improver is. -- Observe, Meletus, that you are silent, and have nothing to say. But is not this rather disgraceful, and a very considerable proof of what I was saying, that you have no interest in the matter? Speak up, friend, and tell us who their improver is.

The laws.

But that, my good sir, is not my meaning. I want to know who the person is, who, in the first place, knows the laws.

The judges, Socrates, who are present in court.

What, do you mean to say, Meletus, that they are able to instruct and improve youth?

Certainly they are.

What, all of them, or some only and not others?

All of them.

By the goddess Here, that is good news! There are plenty of improvers, then. And what do you say of the audience, -- do they improve them?

Yes, they do.

And the senators?

Yes, the senators improve them.

But perhaps the members of the assembly corrupt them? -- or do they too improve them?

They improve them.

Then every Athenian improves and elevates them; all with the exception of myself; and I alone am their corrupter? Is that what you affirm?

That is what I stoutly affirm.

I am very unfortunate if you are right. But suppose I ask you a question: How about horses? Does one man do them harm and all the world good? Is not the exact opposite the truth? One man is able to do them good, or at least not many; -- the trainer of horses, that is to say, does them good, and others who have to do with them rather injure them? Is not that true, Meletus, of horses, or of any other animals? Most assuredly it is; whether you and Anytus say yes or no. Happy indeed would be the condition of youth if they had one corrupter only, and all the rest of the world were their improvers. But you, Meletus, have sufficiently shown that you never had a thought about the young: your carelessness is seen in your not caring about the very things which you bring against me.

And now, Meletus, I will ask you another question -- by Zeus I will: Which is better, to live among bad citizens, or among good ones? Answer, friend, I say; the question is one which may be easily answered. Do not the good do their neighbours good, and the bad do them evil?

Certainly.

And is there anyone who would rather be injured than benefited by those who live with him? Answer, my good friend, the law requires you to answer -- does any one like to be injured?

Certainly not.

And when you accuse me of corrupting and deteriorating the youth, do you allege that I corrupt them intentionally or unintentionally?

Intentionally, I say.

But you have just admitted that the good do their neighbours good, and the evil do them evil.

Now, is that a truth which your superior wisdom has recognized thus early in life, and am I, at my age, in such darkness and ignorance as not to know that if a man with whom I have to live is corrupted by me, I am very likely to be harmed by him; and yet I corrupt him, and intentionally, too -- so you say, although neither I nor any other human being is ever likely to be convinced by you. But either I do not corrupt them, or I corrupt them unintentionally; and on either view of the case you lie. If my offence is unintentional, the law has no cognizance of unintentional offences: you ought to have taken me privately, and warned and admonished me; for if I had been better advised, I should have left off doing what I only did unintentionally -- no doubt I should; but you would have nothing to say to me and refused to teach me. And now you bring me up in this court, which is a place not of instruction, but of punishment.

It will be very clear to you, Athenians, as I was saying, that Meletus has no care at all, great or small, about the matter. But still I should like to know, Meletus, in what I am affirmed to corrupt the young. I suppose you mean, as I infer from your indictment, that I teach them not to acknowledge the gods which the state acknowledges, but some other new divinities or spiritual agencies in their stead. These are the lessons by which I corrupt the youth, as you say.

Yes, that I say emphatically.

Then, by the gods, Meletus, of whom we are speaking, tell me and the court, in somewhat plainer terms, what you mean! for I do not as yet understand whether you affirm that I teach other men to acknowledge some gods, and therefore that I do believe in gods, and am not an entire atheist -- this you do not lay to my charge, -- but only you say that they are not the same gods which the city recognizes -- the charge is that they are different gods. Or, do you mean that I am an atheist simply, and a teacher of atheism?

I mean the latter -- that you are a complete atheist.

What an extraordinary statement! Why do you think so, Meletus? Do you mean that I do not believe in the godhead of the sun or moon, like other men?

I assure you, judges, that he does not: for he says that the sun is stone, and the moon earth.

Friend Meletus, you think that you are accusing Anaxagoras: and you have but a bad opinion of the judges, if you fancy them illiterate to such a degree as not to know that these doctrines are found in the books of Anaxagoras the Clazomenian, which are full of them. And so, forsooth, the youth are said to be taught them by Socrates, when there are not unfrequently exhibitions of them at the theatre (Probably in allusion to Aristophanes who caricatured, and to Euripides who borrowed the notions of Anaxagoras, as well as to other dramatic poets.) (price of admission one drachma at the most); and they might pay their money, and laugh at Socrates if he pretends to father these extraordinary views. And so, Meletus, you really think that I do not believe in any god?

I swear by Zeus that you believe absolutely in none at all.

Nobody will believe you, Meletus, and I am pretty sure that you do not believe yourself. I cannot help thinking, men of Athens, that Meletus is reckless and impudent, and that he has written this indictment in a spirit of mere wantonness and youthful bravado. Has he not compounded a riddle, thinking to try me? He said to himself: -- I shall see whether the wise Socrates will discover my facetious contradiction, or whether I shall be able to deceive him and the rest of them. For he certainly does appear to me to contradict himself in the indictment as much as if he said that Socrates is guilty of not believing in the gods, and yet of believing in them -- but this is not like a person who is in earnest.

I should like you, O men of Athens, to join me in examining what I conceive to be his inconsistency; and do you, Meletus, answer. And I must remind the audience of my request that they would not make a disturbance if I speak in my accustomed manner:

Did ever man, Meletus, believe in the existence of human things, and not of human beings?...I wish, men of Athens, that he would answer, and not be always trying to get up an interruption. Did ever any man believe in horsemanship, and not in horses? or in flute-playing, and not in flute- players? No, my friend; I will answer to you and to the court, as you refuse to answer for yourself. There is no man who ever did. But now please to answer the next question: Can a man believe in spiritual and divine agencies, and not in spirits or demigods?

He cannot.

How lucky I am to have extracted that answer, by the assistance of the court! But then you swear in the indictment that I teach and believe in divine or spiritual agencies (new or old, no matter for that); at any rate, I believe in spiritual agencies, -- so you say and swear in the affidavit; and yet if I believe in divine beings, how can I help believing in spirits or demigods; -- must I not? To be sure I must; and therefore I may assume that your silence gives consent. Now what are spirits or demigods? Are they not either gods or the sons of gods?

Certainly they are.

But this is what I call the facetious riddle invented by you: the demigods or spirits are gods, and you say first that I do not believe in gods, and then again that I do believe in gods; that is, if I believe in demigods. For if the demigods are the illegitimate sons of gods, whether by the nymphs or by any other mothers, of whom they are said to be the sons -- what human being will ever believe that there are no gods if they are the sons of gods? You might as well affirm the existence of mules, and deny that of horses and asses. Such nonsense, Meletus, could only have been intended by you to make trial of me. You have put this into the indictment because you had nothing real of which to accuse me. But no one who has a particle of understanding will ever be convinced by you that the same men can believe in divine and superhuman things, and yet not believe that there are gods and demigods and heroes.

I have said enough in answer to the charge of Meletus: any elaborate defence is unnecessary, but I know only too well how many are the enmities which I have incurred, and this is what will be my destruction if I am destroyed; -- not Meletus, nor yet Anytus, but the envy and detraction of the world, which has been the death of many good men, and will probably be the death of many more; there is no danger of my being the last of them.

Some one will say: And are you not ashamed, Socrates, of a course of life which is likely to bring you to an untimely end? To him I may fairly answer: There you are mistaken: a man who is good for anything ought not to calculate the chance of living or dying; he ought only to consider whether in doing anything he is doing right or wrong -- acting the part of a good man or of a bad. Whereas, upon your view, the heroes who fell at Troy were not good for much, and the son of Thetis above all, who altogether despised danger in comparison with disgrace; and when he was so eager to slay Hector, his goddess mother said to him, that if he avenged his companion Patroclus, and slew Hector, he would die himself -- 'Fate,' she said, in these or the like words, 'waits for you next after Hector;' he, receiving this warning, utterly despised danger and death, and instead of fearing them, feared rather to live in dishonour, and not to avenge his friend. 'Let me die forthwith,' he replies, 'and be avenged of my enemy, rather than abide here by the beaked ships, a laughing-stock and a burden of the earth.' Had Achilles any thought of death and danger? For wherever a man's place is, whether the place which he has chosen or that in which he has been placed by a commander, there he ought to remain in the hour of danger; he should not think of death or of anything but of disgrace. And this, O men of Athens, is a true saying.

Strange, indeed, would be my conduct, O men of Athens, if I who, when I was ordered by the generals whom you chose to command me at Potidaea and Amphipolis and Delium, remained where they placed me, like any other man, facing death -- if now, when, as I conceive and imagine, God orders me to fulfil the philosopher's mission of searching into myself and other men, I were to desert my post through fear of death, or any other fear; that would indeed be strange, and I might justly be arraigned in court for denying the existence of the gods, if I disobeyed the oracle because I was afraid of death, fancying that I was wise when I was not wise. For the fear of death is indeed the pretence of wisdom, and not real wisdom, being a pretence of knowing the unknown; and no one knows whether death, which men in their fear apprehend to be the greatest evil, may not be the greatest good. Is not this ignorance of a disgraceful sort, the ignorance which is the conceit that a man knows what he does not know? And in this respect only I believe myself to differ from men in general, and may perhaps claim to be wiser than they are: -- that whereas I know but little of the world below, I do not suppose that I know: but I do know that injustice and disobedience to a better, whether God or man, is evil and dishonourable, and I will never fear or avoid a possible good rather than a certain evil. And therefore if you let me go now, and are not convinced by Anytus, who said that since I had been prosecuted I must be put to death; (or if not that I ought never to have been prosecuted at all); and that if I escape now, your sons will all be utterly ruined by listening to my words -- if you say to me, Socrates, this time we will not mind Anytus, and you shall be let off, but upon one condition, that you are not to enquire and speculate in this way any more, and that if you are caught doing so again you shall die; -- if this was the condition on which you let me go, I should reply: Men of Athens, I honour and love you; but I shall obey God rather than you, and while I have life and strength I shall never cease from the practice and teaching of philosophy, exhorting any one whom I meet and saying to him after my manner: You, my friend, -- a citizen of the great and mighty and wise city of Athens, -- are you not ashamed of heaping up the greatest amount of money and honour and reputation, and caring so little about wisdom and truth and the greatest improvement of the soul, which you never regard or heed at all? And if the person with whom I am arguing, says: Yes, but I do care; then I do not leave him or let him go at once; but I proceed to interrogate and examine and cross-examine him, and if I think that he has no virtue in him, but only says that he has, I reproach him with undervaluing the greater, and overvaluing the less. And I shall repeat the same words to every one whom I meet, young and old, citizen and alien, but especially to the citizens, inasmuch as they are my brethren. For know that this is the command of God; and I believe that no greater good has ever happened in the state than my

service to the God. For I do nothing but go about persuading you all, old and young alike, not to take thought for your persons or your properties, but first and chiefly to care about the greatest improvement of the soul. I tell you that virtue is not given by money, but that from virtue comes money and every other good of man, public as well as private. This is my teaching, and if this is the doctrine which corrupts the youth, I am a mischievous person. But if any one says that this is not my teaching, he is speaking an untruth. Wherefore, O men of Athens, I say to you, do as Anytus bids or not as Anytus bids, and either acquit me or not; but whichever you do, understand that I shall never alter my ways, not even if I have to die many times.

Men of Athens, do not interrupt, but hear me; there was an understanding between us that you should hear me to the end: I have something more to say, at which you may be inclined to cry out; but I believe that to hear me will be good for you, and therefore I beg that you will not cry out. I would have you know, that if you kill such an one as I am, you will injure yourselves more than you will injure me. Nothing will injure me, not Meletus nor yet Anytus -- they cannot, for a bad man is not permitted to injure a better than himself. I do not deny that Anytus may, perhaps, kill him, or drive him into exile, or deprive him of civil rights; and he may imagine, and others may imagine, that he is inflicting a great injury upon him: but there I do not agree. For the evil of doing as he is doing -- the evil of unjustly taking away the life of another -- is greater far.

And now, Athenians, I am not going to argue for my own sake, as you may think, but for yours, that you may not sin against the God by condemning me, who am his gift to you. For if you kill me you will not easily find a successor to me, who, if I may use such a ludicrous figure of speech, am a sort of gadfly, given to the state by God; and the state is a great and noble steed who is tardy in his motions owing to his very size, and requires to be stirred into life. I am that gadfly which God has attached to the state, and all day long and in all places am always fastening upon you, arousing and persuading and reproaching you. You will not easily find another like me, and therefore I would advise you to spare me. I dare say that you may feel out of temper (like a person who is suddenly awakened from sleep), and you think that you might easily strike me dead as Anytus advises, and then you would sleep on for the remainder of your lives, unless God in his care of you sent you another gadfly. When I say that I am given to you by God, the proof of my mission is this: -- if I had been like other men, I should not have neglected all my own concerns or patiently seen the neglect of them during all these years, and have been doing yours, coming to you individually like a father or elder brother, exhorting you to regard virtue; such conduct, I say, would be unlike human nature. If I had gained anything, or if my exhortations had been paid, there would have been some sense in my doing so; but now, as you will perceive, not even the impudence of my accusers dares to say that I have ever exacted or sought pay of any one; of that they have no witness. And I have a sufficient witness to the truth of what I say -- my poverty.

Some one may wonder why I go about in private giving advice and busying myself with the concerns of others, but do not venture to come forward in public and advise the state. I will tell you why. You have heard me speak at sundry times and in divers places of an oracle or sign which comes to me, and is the divinity which Meletus ridicules in the indictment. This sign, which is a kind of voice, first began to come to me when I was a child; it always forbids but never commands me to do anything which I am going to do. This is what deters me from being a politician. And rightly, as I think. For I am certain, O men of Athens, that if I had engaged in politics, I should have perished long ago, and done no good either to you or to myself. And do not be offended at my telling you the truth: for the truth is, that no man who goes to war with you or any other multitude, honestly striving against the many lawless and unrighteous deeds which are done in a state, will save his life; he who will fight for the right, if he would live even for a brief space, must have a private station and not a public one.

I can give you convincing evidence of what I say, not words only, but what you value far more--actions. Let me relate to you a passage of my own

life which will prove to you that I should never have yielded to injustice from any fear of death, and that 'as I should have refused to yield' I must have died at once. I will tell you a tale of the courts, not very interesting perhaps, but nevertheless true. The only office of state which I ever held, O men of Athens, was that of senator: the tribe Antiochis, which is my tribe, had the presidency at the trial of the generals who had not taken up the bodies of the slain after the battle of Arginusae; and you proposed to try them in a body, contrary to law, as you all thought afterwards; but at the time I was the only one of the Prytanes who was opposed to the illegality, and I gave my vote against you; and when the orators threatened to impeach and arrest me, and you called and shouted, I made up my mind that I would run the risk, having law and justice with me, rather than take part in your injustice because I feared imprisonment and death. This happened in the days of the democracy. But when the oligarchy of the Thirty was in power, they sent for me and four others into the rotunda, and bade us bring Leon the Salaminian from Salamis, as they wanted to put him to death. This was a specimen of the sort of commands which they were always giving with the view of implicating as many as possible in their crimes; and then I showed, not in word only but in deed, that, if I may be allowed to use such an expression, I cared not a straw for death, and that my great and only care was lest I should do an unrighteous or unholy thing. For the strong arm of that oppressive power did not frighten me into doing wrong; and when we came out of the rotunda the other four went to Salamis and fetched Leon, but I went quietly home. For which I might have lost my life, had not the power of the Thirty shortly afterwards come to an end. And many will witness to my words.

Now do you really imagine that I could have survived all these years, if I had led a public life, supposing that like a good man I had always maintained the right and had made justice, as I ought, the first thing? No indeed, men of Athens, neither I nor any other man. But I have been always the same in all my actions, public as well as private, and never have I yielded any base compliance to those who are slanderously termed my disciples, or to any other. Not that I have any regular disciples. But if any one likes to come and hear me while I am pursuing my mission, whether he be young or old, he is not excluded. Nor do I converse only with those who pay; but any one, whether he be rich or poor, may ask and answer me and listen to my words; and whether he turns out to be a bad man or a good one, neither result can be justly imputed to me; for I never taught or professed to teach him anything. And if any one says that he has ever learned or heard anything from me in private which all the world has not heard, let me tell you that he is lying.

But I shall be asked, Why do people delight in continually conversing with you? I have told you already, Athenians, the whole truth about this matter: they like to hear the cross-examination of the pretenders to wisdom; there is amusement in it. Now this duty of cross-examining other men has been imposed upon me by God; and has been signified to me by oracles, visions, and in every way in which the will of divine power was ever intimated to any one. This is true, O Athenians, or, if not true, would be soon refuted. If I am or have been corrupting the youth, those of them who are now grown up and have become sensible that I gave them bad advice in the days of their youth should come forward as accusers, and take their revenge; or if they do not like to come themselves, some of their relatives, fathers, brothers, or other kinsmen, should say what evil their families have suffered at my hands. Now is their time. Many of them I see in the court. There is Crito, who is of the same age and of the same deme with myself, and there is Critobulus his son, whom I also see. Then again there is Lysanias of Sphettus, who is the father of Aeschines -- he is present; and also there is Antiphon of Cephisus, who is the father of Epigenes; and there are the brothers of several who have associated with me. There is Nicostratus the son of Theosdotides, and the brother of Theodotus (now Theodotus himself is dead, and therefore he, at any rate, will not seek to stop him); and there is Paralus the son of Demodocus, who had a brother Theages; and Adeimantus the son of Ariston, whose brother

Plato is present; and Aeantodorus, who is the brother of Apollodorus, whom I also see. I might mention a great many others, some of whom Meletus should have produced as witnesses in the course of his speech; and let him still produce them, if he has forgotten -- I will make way for him. And let him say, if he has any testimony of the sort which he can produce. Nay, Athenians, the very opposite is the truth. For all these are ready to witness on behalf of the corrupter, of the injurer of their kindred, as Meletus and Anytus call me; not the corrupted youth only -- there might have been a motive for that -- but their uncorrupted elder relatives. Why should they too support me with their testimony? Why, indeed, except for the sake of truth and justice, and because they know that I am speaking the truth, and that Meletus is a liar.

Well, Athenians, this and the like of this is all the defence which I have to offer. Yet a word more. Perhaps there may be some one who is offended at me, when he calls to mind how he himself on a similar, or even a less serious occasion, prayed and entreated the judges with many tears, and how he produced his children in court, which was a moving spectacle, together with a host of relations and friends; whereas I, who am probably in danger of my life, will do none of these things. The contrast may occur to his mind, and he may be set against me, and vote in anger because he is displeased at me on this account. Now if there be such a person among you, -- mind, I do not say that there is, -- to him I may fairly reply: My friend, I am a man, and like other men, a creature of flesh and blood, and not 'of wood or stone,' as Homer says; and I have a family, yes, and sons, O Athenians, three in number, one almost a man, and two others who are still young; and yet I will not bring any of them hither in order to petition you for an acquittal. And why not? Not from any self-assertion or want of respect for you. Whether I am or am not afraid of death is another question, of which I will not now speak. But, having regard to public opinion, I feel that such conduct would be discreditable to myself, and to you, and to the whole state. One who has reached my years, and who has a name for wisdom, ought not to demean himself.

Whether this opinion of me be deserved or not, at any rate the world has decided that Socrates is in some way superior to other men. And if those among you who are said to be superior in wisdom and courage, and any other virtue, demean themselves in this way, how shameful is their conduct! I have seen men of reputation, when they have been condemned, behaving in the strangest manner: they seemed to fancy that they were going to suffer something dreadful if they died, and that they could be immortal if you only allowed them to live; and I think that such are a dishonour to the state, and that any stranger coming in would have said of them that the most eminent men of Athens, to whom the Athenians themselves give honour and command, are no better than women. And I say that these things ought not to be done by those of us who have a reputation; and if they are done, you ought not to permit them; you ought rather to show that you are far more disposed to condemn the man who gets up a doleful scene and makes the city ridiculous, than him who holds his peace.

But, setting aside the question of public opinion, there seems to be something wrong in asking a favour of a judge, and thus procuring an acquittal, instead of informing and convincing him. For his duty is, not to make a present of justice, but to give judgment; and he has sworn that he will judge according to the laws, and not according to his own good pleasure; and we ought not to encourage you, nor should you allow yourselves to be encouraged, in this habit of perjury -- there can be no piety in that. Do not then require me to do what I consider dishonourable and impious and wrong, especially now, when I am being tried for impiety on the indictment of Meletus. For if, O men of Athens, by force of persuasion and entreaty I could overpower your oaths, then I should be teaching you to believe that there are no gods, and in defending should simply convict myself of the charge of not believing in them. But that is not so -- far otherwise. For I do believe that there are gods, and in a sense higher than that in which any of my accusers believe in them. And to you and to God I commit my cause, to be determined by you as is best for you and me.

...

There are many reasons why I am not grieved, O men of Athens, at the vote of condemnation. I expected it, and am only surprised that the votes are so nearly equal; for I had thought that the majority against me would have been far larger; but now, had thirty votes gone over to the other side, I should have been acquitted. And I may say, I think, that I have escaped Meletus. I may say more; for without the assistance of Anytus and Lycon, any one may see that he would not have had a fifth part of the votes, as the law requires, in which case he would have incurred a fine of a thousand drachmae.

And so he proposes death as the penalty. And what shall I propose on my part, O men of Athens? Clearly that which is my due. And what is my due? What return shall be made to the man who has never had the wit to be idle during his whole life; but has been careless of what the many care for -- wealth, and family interests, and military offices, and speaking in the assembly, and magistracies, and plots, and parties. Reflecting that I was really too honest a man to be a politician and live, I did not go where I could do no good to you or to myself; but where I could do the greatest good privately to every one of you, thither I went, and sought to persuade every man among you that he must look to himself, and seek virtue and wisdom before he looks to his private interests, and look to the state before he looks to the interests of the state; and that this should be the order which he observes in all his actions. What shall be done to such an one? Doubtless some good thing, O men of Athens, if he has his reward; and the good should be of a kind suitable to him. What would be a reward suitable to a poor man who is your benefactor, and who desires leisure that he may instruct you? There can be no reward so fitting as maintenance in the Prytaneum, O men of Athens, a reward which he deserves far more than the citizen who has won the prize at Olympia in the horse or chariot race, whether the chariots were drawn by two horses or by many. For I am in want, and he has enough; and he only gives you the appearance of happiness, and I give you the reality. And if I am to estimate the penalty fairly, I should say that maintenance in the Prytaneum is the just return.

Perhaps you think that I am braving you in what I am saying now, as in what I said before about the tears and prayers. But this is not so. I speak rather because I am convinced that I never intentionally wronged any one, although I cannot convince you -- the time has been too short; if there were a law at Athens, as there is in other cities, that a capital cause should not be decided in one day, then I believe that I should have convinced you. But I cannot in a moment refute great slanders; and, as I am convinced that I never wronged another, I will assuredly not wrong myself. I will not say of myself that I deserve any evil, or propose any penalty. Why should I? because I am afraid of the penalty of death which Meletus proposes? When I do not know whether death is a good or an evil, why should I propose a penalty which would certainly be an evil? Shall I say imprisonment? And why should I live in prison, and be the slave of the magistrates of the year -- of the Eleven? Or shall the penalty be a fine, and imprisonment until the fine is paid? There is the same objection. I should have to lie in prison, for money I have none, and cannot pay. And if I say exile (and this may possibly be the penalty which you will affix), I must indeed be blinded by the love of life, if I am so irrational as to expect that when you, who are my own citizens, cannot endure my discourses and words, and have found them so grievous and odious that you will have no more of them, others are likely to endure me. No indeed, men of Athens, that is not very likely. And what a life should I lead, at my age, wandering from city to city, ever changing my place of exile, and always being driven out! For I am quite sure that wherever I go, there, as here, the young men will flock to me; and if I drive them away, their elders will drive me out at their request; and if I let them come, their fathers and friends will drive me out for their sakes.

Some one will say: Yes, Socrates, but cannot you hold your tongue, and then you may go into a foreign city, and no one will interfere with you? Now I have great difficulty in making you understand my answer to this. For if I tell you that to do as you say would be a disobedience to the God, and therefore that I cannot hold my tongue,

you will not believe that I am serious; and if I say again that daily to discourse about virtue, and of those other things about which you hear me examining myself and others, is the greatest good of man, and that the unexamined life is not worth living, you are still less likely to believe me. Yet I say what is true, although a thing of which it is hard for me to persuade you. Also, I have never been accustomed to think that I deserve to suffer any harm. Had I money I might have estimated the offence at what I was able to pay, and not have been much the worse. But I have none, and therefore I must ask you to proportion the fine to my means. Well, perhaps I could afford a mina, and therefore I propose that penalty: Plato, Crito, Critobulus, and Apollodorus, my friends here, bid me say thirty minae, and they will be the sureties. Let thirty minae be the penalty; for which sum they will be ample security to you.

...

Not much time will be gained, O Athenians, in return for the evil name which you will get from the detractors of the city, who will say that you killed Socrates, a wise man; for they will call me wise, even although I am not wise, when they want to reproach you. If you had waited a little while, your desire would have been fulfilled in the course of nature. For I am far advanced in years, as you may perceive, and not far from death. I am speaking now not to all of you, but only to those who have condemned me to death. And I have another thing to say to them: you think that I was convicted because I had no words of the sort which would have procured my acquittal -- I mean, if I had thought fit to leave nothing undone or unsaid. Not so; the deficiency which led to my conviction was not of words -- certainly not. But I had not the boldness or impudence or inclination to address you as you would have liked me to do, weeping and wailing and lamenting, and saying and doing many things which you have been accustomed to hear from others, and which, as I maintain, are unworthy of me. I thought at the time that I ought not to do anything common or mean when in danger: nor do I now repent of the style of my defence; I would rather die having spoken after my manner, than speak in your manner and live. For neither in war nor yet at law ought I or any man to use every way of escaping death. Often in battle there can be no doubt that if a man will throw away his arms, and fall on his knees before his pursuers, he may escape death; and in other dangers there are other ways of escaping death, if a man is willing to say and do anything. The difficulty, my friends, is not to avoid death, but to avoid unrighteousness; for that runs faster than death. I am old and move slowly, and the slower runner has overtaken me, and my accusers are keen and quick, and the faster runner, who is unrighteousness, has overtaken them. And now I depart hence condemned by you to suffer the penalty of death, -- they too go their ways condemned by the truth to suffer the penalty of villainy and wrong; and I must abide by my award -- let them abide by theirs. I suppose that these things may be regarded as fated, -- and I think that they are well.

And now, O men who have condemned me, I would fain prophesy to you; for I am about to die, and in the hour of death men are gifted with prophetic power. And I prophesy to you who are my murderers, that immediately after my departure punishment far heavier than you have inflicted on me will surely await you. Me you have killed because you wanted to escape the accuser, and not to give an account of your lives. But that will not be as you suppose: far otherwise. For I say that there will be more accusers of you than there are now; accusers whom hitherto I have restrained: and as they are younger they will be more inconsiderate with you, and you will be more offended at them. If you think that by killing men you can prevent some one from censuring your evil lives, you are mistaken; that is not a way of escape which is either possible or honourable; the easiest and the noblest way is not to be disabling others, but to be improving yourselves. This is the prophecy which I utter before my departure to the judges who have condemned me.

Friends, who would have acquitted me, I would like also to talk with you about the thing which has come to pass, while the magistrates are busy, and before I go to the place at which I must die. Stay then a little, for we may as well talk with one another while there is time. You are my

friends, and I should like to show you the meaning of this event which has happened to me. O my judges -- for you I may truly call judges -- I should like to tell you of a wonderful circumstance. Hitherto the divine faculty of which the internal oracle is the source has constantly been in the habit of opposing me even about trifles, if I was going to make a slip or error in any matter; and now as you see there has come upon me that which may be thought, and is generally believed to be, the last and worst evil. But the oracle made no sign of opposition, either when I was leaving my house in the morning, or when I was on my way to the court, or while I was speaking, at anything which I was going to say; and yet I have often been stopped in the middle of a speech, but now in nothing I either said or did touching the matter in hand has the oracle opposed me. What do I take to be the explanation of this silence? I will tell you. It is an intimation that what has happened to me is a good, and that those of us who think that death is an evil are in error. For the customary sign would surely have opposed me had I been going to evil and not to good.

Let us reflect in another way, and we shall see that there is great reason to hope that death is a good; for one of two things -- either death is a state of nothingness and utter unconsciousness, or, as men say, there is a change and migration of the soul from this world to another. Now if you suppose that there is no consciousness, but a sleep like the sleep of him who is undisturbed even by dreams, death will be an unspeakable gain. For if a person were to select the night in which his sleep was undisturbed even by dreams, and were to compare with this the other days and nights of his life, and then were to tell us how many days and nights he had passed in the course of his life better and more pleasantly than this one, I think that any man, I will not say a private man, but even the great king will not find many such days or nights, when compared with the others. Now if death be of such a nature, I say that to die is gain; for eternity is then only a single night. But if death is the journey to another place, and there, as men say, all the dead abide, what good, O my friends and judges, can be greater than this? If indeed when the pilgrim arrives in the world below, he is delivered from the professors of justice in this world, and finds the true judges who are said to give judgment there, Minos and Rhadamanthus and Aeacus and Triptolemus, and other sons of God who were righteous in their own life, that pilgrimage will be worth making. What would not a man give if he might converse with Orpheus and Musaeus and Hesiod and Homer? Nay, if this be true, let me die again and again. I myself, too, shall have a wonderful interest in there meeting and conversing with Palamedes, and Ajax the son of Telamon, and any other ancient hero who has suffered death through an unjust judgment; and there will be no small pleasure, as I think, in comparing my own sufferings with theirs. Above all, I shall then be able to continue my search into true and false knowledge; as in this world, so also in the next; and I shall find out who is wise, and who pretends to be wise, and is not. What would not a man give, O judges, to be able to examine the leader of the great Trojan expedition; or Odysseus or Sisyphus, or numberless others, men and women too! What infinite delight would there be in conversing with them and asking them questions! In another world they do not put a man to death for asking questions: assuredly not. For besides being happier than we are, they will be immortal, if what is said is true.

Wherefore, O judges, be of good cheer about death, and know of a certainty, that no evil can happen to a good man, either in life or after death. He and his are not neglected by the gods; nor has my own approaching end happened by mere chance. But I see clearly that the time had arrived when it was better for me to die and be released from trouble; wherefore the oracle gave no sign. For which reason, also, I am not angry with my condemners, or with my accusers; they have done me no harm, although they did not mean to do me any good; and for this I may gently blame them.

Still I have a favour to ask of them. When my sons are grown up, I would ask you, O my friends, to punish them; and I would have you trouble them, as I have troubled you, if they seem to care about riches, or anything, more than about virtue; or if they pretend to be something when they are

really nothing, -- then reprove them, as I have reproved you, for not caring about that for which they ought to care, and thinking that they are something when they are really nothing. And if you do this, both I and my sons will have received justice at your hands.

The hour of departure has arrived, and we go our ways -- I to die, and you to live. Which is better God only knows.

Chapter 3: Plato & Politics

Comprehension questions you should be able to answer after reading this chapter:

1. Why did Thrasymachus believe that justice is "the will of the stronger," and how does Socrates attempt to refute this position?

2. What did Glaucon think justice is, and how does the Myth of Gyges' Ring reinforce his point?

3. What is the point of Socrates' extended political analogy, in the Republic?

4. What is the "principle of specialization," and why is it important?

5. What are the three classes in the *Republic*? What are the three parts of the soul? What do they have to do with each other?

6. Describe the lifestyle of the Guardians. What restrictions do they face, and what is the justification for this?

7. What is the "noble lie," and what is its purpose?

8. Why does Plato (as Socrates) think epistemic relativism is false?

9. What are the "Forms," and what is their relationship to particular objects?

10. What is the point of the "allegory of the cave?"

11. Why is it that only philosophers have "knowledge?"

12. What is "justice" in the *Republic*? What is "justice" in the soul?

13. What are some of the differences between the city-state proposed in the Republic and that proposed in the Laws?

We already discussed Plato a little bit in the previous chapter in the context of his friend and mentor, Socrates. Now we turn to Plato himself, where he will continue the tradition of Socrates in seeking the Truth with regard to goodness, justice, etc.

Plato is undeniably a giant in the history of Western philosophy. Perhaps humorously, "Plato" was actually his nickname, meaning "broad-shouldered"—so it seems his physical stature rivaled his intellectual stature. He lived from 428-348 BCE and was the son of a wealthy, aristocratic family. He initially studied philosophy under a Heraclitean philosopher, but at around the age of twenty began to study with Socrates. After Socrates' execution, he traveled and became influenced by Pythagorean philosophy in what is now Italy. He was summoned by Dionysius the Elder ("the tyrant of Syracuse") to promote philosophy at his court, but his efforts were not well-received, and he returned to Athens. He started his own school on a site sacred to the hero Academus, thus explaining how his school became known as the "Academy." It's worth pointing out that our contemporary use of "academy" as synonymous with a place of learning traces back to Plato's own school. This Academy is generally regarded as the first "university" in the Western world.

Plato was a prolific philosopher and writer, and we are fortunate that so many of his works survived the passage and trials of time. He was a systematic and comprehensive philosopher, writing on virtually every topic of the time.

Indeed, one well-known approach to teaching introduction to philosophy courses is to teach just the *Republic*, with the idea being that it contains everything a new philosopher needs to experience. Alfred North Whitehead went so far as to say that "the safest general characterization of the European philosophical tradition is that it consists of a series of footnotes to Plato." High praise, indeed.

Known mostly for his dialogues, his work can be divided into three periods: early, middle, and late. The "early" dialogues (where there is the most confidence that Socrates is being presented authentically) include: *Apology, Crito, Euthyphro, Laches, Charmides, Ion, Hippias Minor, Lysis, Euthydemus, Protagoras*, and *Gorgias*. The middle dialogues (for which Socrates' authentic representation is less certain) include: *Meno, Hippias Major, Cratylus, Phaedo, Symposium*, and the *Republic*. The later dialogues (in which most believe Plato has found his own voice, and uses Socrates more as a mouthpiece, if at all) include: *Parmenides, Phaedrus, Theatetus, Sophist, Statesman, Timaeus, Philebus*, and the *Laws*.

No book of this kind should even pretend to offer a thorough and systemic presentation of Plato's thought, and I have no such pretensions. Instead, in what follows, I will offer a brief overview of some of Plato's central ideas, primarily as presented in the *Republic*, with a clear emphasis on his account of justice, and those other ideas that are important with regard to understanding his account of justice. It must be noted that his views changed over time, and were not always presented in the same way. His prescriptions for government and rulership, for

example, change somewhat from the *Republic* to the *Laws*. In the *Republic*, enlightened Philosopher Kings rule with the aim of promoting harmony and preventing strife and factionalism (*Republic* 462a-b), but in the *Laws* this function is assumed by good and just laws instead (*Laws* 715c-d)—though the central focus of preventing "disharmony" is the same in both cases. Keeping in mind such adjustments to his thoughts, the *Republic* offers a fine introduction to Plato's system, as well as to philosophy in general. It even makes for an enjoyable read!

The Republic[43]

The very first line of the *Republic* inspires controversy for those paying attention.

> I went down yesterday to the Piraeus with Glaucon the son of Ariston, that I might offer up my prayers to the goddess (Bendis, the Thracian Artemis.); and also because I wanted to see in what manner they would celebrate the festival, which was a new thing. (327a)

> [A note on pagination: the reference above is an instance of what is known as "Stephanus pagination." The *Republic* is an ancient text that was been translated numerous times and edited into countless editions. Page numbers will vary, of course, based on things like paper and font size, as well as the inclusion of notes or explanatory essays. To make sure that everyone reading Plato will be able to find

---

[43] Quotations from the *Republic* that follow are from a public domain translation. I use that translation in this book so as to keep the cost of this book low. I have not, however, included the full text of that version in this book as a primary source reading, unlike several other texts. In my own classes, I will sometimes instead require my students to purchase a hard copy of the *Republic*. The reason why is simple: the free public domain version doesn't use the "Stephanus" pagination that I explain in the next footnote. When I quote

from it, I am forced to cross-reference it with another translation in order to provide that pagination. It would be far too much work to do so for the entire text, and the Stephanus pagination is useful enough that I judge it to be worth the $10 (roughly) for the hardcopy. For those who would like the free version anyway, it may be found at the following URL: http://www.gutenberg.org/ files/1497/1497-h/1497-h.htm the correct reference, regardless of which translation or edition one has, scholars make use of the "Stephanus pagination" found in the margins in nearly every edition of any of Plato's works. In this way, we can all make sure we're referring to the same sections, no matter which version of the *Republic* we have. It's a wonderfully convenient convention that I will use throughout this book.]

The opening scene of the *Republic* has Socrates returning from a celebration in honor of Athens' recognition of a new god: Bendis. Why is this controversial? If you recall the *Apology*, one of the charges leveled against Socrates involved the introduction of "new gods" as one of the means by which he corrupted the youth of Athens.

> I suppose you mean, as I infer from your indictment, that I teach them not to acknowledge the gods which the state acknowledges, but some other new divinities or spiritual agencies in their stead. These are the lessons by which I corrupt the youth, as you say.

Granted, Socrates later twists his accuser into mental pretzels by getting him to claim that Socrates both believes in new gods and demigods, in addition to being a complete atheist, but the ironic point remains for those interested in seeing it: Socrates was brought up on charges for (among other things) "introducing new gods," and the very first line of the *Republic* shows a formal, official celebration of a new god in Athens! Clearly introducing new gods is only a serious offense when it's (allegedly) done by Socrates!

The *Republic* is filled with gems like this, if only one reads slowly and carefully. I will not focus on many more of them, and will instead emphasize the general arguments, but I encourage you to allow yourself to enjoy the *Republic* as you might enjoy a good meal. Savor

each bite rather than finishing it as quickly as possible (let alone skipping the meal altogether).

One final bit of irony: although the theme of the *Apology*[44] is clearly to vindicate Socrates and reveal that the charges brought against him were unjustifiable, the *Republic* actually reveals that Socrates does, in fact, introduce "new gods" to Athens. Though he is vindicated by virtue of his devotion to "The Good," this understanding of goodness and morality is, in a fact, a sharp and radical departure from the vision of the local gods revered in Athens at the time. While not an atheist, Socrates vision of "God" as presented in the *Republic* certainly is "new."

Socrates is returning from this celebration with Glaucon (Plato's half-brother) when he is spotted by Polemarchus, the son of Cephalus. Polemarchus sends his slave to detain Socrates, and then insists that Socrates and Glaucon join him at his house where numerous others await. There is something a bit disturbing about the encounter, as Polemarchus (playfully?) seems to be forcing Socrates to join him.

> Polemarchus said to me: I perceive, Socrates, that you and your companion are already on your way to the city.
>
> You are not far wrong, I said.
>
> But do you see, he rejoined, how many we are?
>
> Of course.
>
> And are you stronger than all these? for if not, you will have to remain where you are. (327a)

In perhaps another reference to the *Apology*, Socrates suggests that he might persuade them to let him (and Glaucon) go, but Polemarchus retorts that they will refuse to listen to him, and therefore be incapable of persuasion—much like

---

[44] Don't be confused by the word. "Apology" in this sense doesn't to apologize for something, but rather is derived from the Greek word *apologia*, which means a reasoned defense.

the jurors were not persuaded by Socrates defense of himself at his trial.

Whether playful or serious, Socrates goes with them and finds himself brought into their lengthy and lofty discussions of the nature of justice. Before Socrates takes center stage and offers his massive account of justice, several others give it a try. They are Cephalus, Polemarchus, Thrasymachus, Glaucon, and Adeimantus.[45] We will consider each in turn.

Cephalus

Plato is clever in how he introduces justice as a topic of conversation. It might well have seemed forced if he had Socrates walk into the home and then immediately be asked by some other toga-wearing gentleman, "what is justice?" Instead, Cephalus, who is an elderly man, chides Socrates for not visiting more often, and claims that his "declining interest in physical pleasures is exactly matched by increasing desire for and enjoyment of conversation."

Socrates is polite and respectful of his elder, so he asks how he is doing and what he thinks of old age. Cephalus points out that many of his fellow senior citizens, when they get together, just complain about their families and grumble about being old, but he, himself, finds old age to be no burden—so long as one is disciplined and good-tempered (and it doesn't hurt, either, if one is rich, as he was).

Socrates seizes on this mention of wealth, and asks Cephalus what he thinks the greatest benefit of that wealth is to him. Cephalus answers by first pointing out that as one grows older, thoughts of death and what might await beyond death come more frequently, and with greater anxiety. He quotes Pindar as saying, in effect, that knowledge that one has been morally good is a comfort in old age. In this context, the benefit of his wealth has been that he can be more confident that he will not leave life with unpaid debts, including various sacrificial offerings to the gods.[46]

In what might well be an uncharitable maneuver, Socrates takes this to be a definition of goodness (justice[47]) itself: discharging one's debts and obligations. In the same breath, Socrates criticizes this definition in his usual style: by providing a counter-example. Suppose one had borrowed a weapon from a friend, and that friend then went insane and came asking for his weapon. Surely it would not be good (just) to pay him back what he is owed, in that case.

Cephalus, who had never sought an argument about justice in the first place, hasn't acquired any new interest in the face of Socrates' refutation. He immediately excuses himself to go attend yet another religious ceremony (to discharge another debt?), and leaves his son, Polemarchus, to deal with Socrates.

Polemarchus

Taking over for his father (who never sought the debate in the first place), Polemarchus defends a variation of his father's claim by appealing to the poet, Simonides, to whom he attributes the following interpretation of justice: "friends owe friends good deeds, not bad ones (332a)." This is later clarified to mean that we should do good for friends, and bad for enemies. More generally, give to each their due.

---

[45] Adeimantus was also one of Plato's brothers.
[46] The readers of the *Republic*, when it was written, would have been aware of what actually happened to Cephalus and his family, and it is likely that Plato relies on this. After Athens was conquered, Cephalus' family fortune was lost, and his son, Polemarchus, was executed. Plato's first readers would have known, in their own time, that what Cephalus seemed to think most important were all contingent, fleeting, and easily lost.

[47] Although "good" and "just" often have distinct meanings today, in the context of the *Republic* they mean essentially the same thing. For the remainder of this chapter, please understand the word justice also means moral goodness, and vice versa.

Socrates' immediately begins his usual strategy of developing a counter-example (334c-e).

> And so, you and Homer and Simonides are agreed that justice is an art of theft; to be practised however 'for the good of friends and for the harm of enemies,'—that was what you were saying?
>
> No, certainly not that, though I do not now know what I did say; but I still stand by the latter words.
>
> Well, there is another question: By friends and enemies do we mean those who are so really, or only in seeming?
>
> Surely, he said, a man may be expected to love those whom he thinks good, and to hate those whom he thinks evil.
>
> Yes, but do not persons often err about good and evil: many who are not good seem to be so, and conversely?
>
> That is true.
>
> Then to them the good will be enemies and the evil will be their friends?
>
> True.
>
> And in that case they will be right in doing good to the evil and evil to the good?
>
> Clearly.
>
> But the good are just and would not do an injustice?
>
> True.
>
> Then according to your argument it is just to injure those who do no wrong?
>
> Nay, Socrates; the doctrine is immoral.

> Then I suppose that we ought to do good to the just and harm to the unjust?
>
> I like that better.
>
> But see the consequence:—Many a man who is ignorant of human nature has friends who are bad friends, and in that case he ought to do harm to them; and he has good enemies whom he ought to benefit; but, if so, we shall be saying the very opposite of that which we affirmed to be the meaning of Simonides.

Socrates' criticism of this particular interpretation of justice is probably less important than the assumption and strategy that now appears for the first time in the *Republic*, but upon which he will rely throughout the remainder of the work: *justice is an "art" with a single focus, analogous to other arts.* Justice, therefore, is like cooking, or carpentry, or medicine, in that it has a focus and persons are evaluated in terms of their skill in this art by virtue of how well they achieve its end. Someone who produces bad-tasting food is not a good cook, and someone who can cure no disease is a poor doctor.

The context in which this analogy arises is that Polemarchus seeks to revise his definition in response to Socrates' counter-example. Justice, now, requires that one do good to those who are truly friends, and harm those who are truly enemies. Socrates' continues his assault (335b-e):

> When horses are injured, are they improved or deteriorated?
>
> The latter.
>
> Deteriorated, that is to say, in the good qualities of horses, not of dogs?
>
> Yes, of horses.
>
> And dogs are deteriorated in the good qualities of dogs, and not of horses?

Of course.

And will not men who are injured be deteriorated in that which is the proper virtue of man?

Certainly.

And that human virtue is justice?

To be sure.

Then men who are injured are of necessity made unjust?

That is the result.

But can the musician by his art make men unmusical?

Certainly not.

Or the horseman by his art make them bad horsemen?

Impossible.

And can the just by justice make men unjust, or speaking generally, can the good by virtue make them bad?

Assuredly not.

Any more than heat can produce cold?

It cannot.

Or drought moisture?

Clearly not.

Nor can the good harm any one?

Impossible.

And the just is the good?

Certainly.

Then to injure a friend or any one else is not the act of a just man, but of the opposite, who is the unjust?

I think that what you say is quite true, Socrates.

Then if a man says that justice consists in the repayment of debts, and that good is the debt which a just man owes to his friends, and evil the debt which he owes to his enemies,—to say this is not wise; for it is not true, if, as has been clearly shown, the injuring of another can be in no case just.

At this point, Socrates has done two very important things: he has declared (or at least assumed that) justice is a skill, and he has claimed that it is never just or right to harm another. A just person is one who improves others, who helps others. Justice, like medicine, is for the sake of the patient. At this point in the conversation, the most notorious (and famous) of Socrates' sparring partners in the *Republic* bursts into the conversation.

Thrasymachus

Several times in the course of the discussion Thrasymachus had made an attempt to get the argument into his own hands, and had been put down by the rest of the company, who wanted to hear the end. But when Polemarchus and I had done speaking and there was a pause, he could no longer hold his peace; and, gathering himself up, he came at us like a wild beast, seeking to devour us. We were quite panic-stricken at the sight of him (336b).

Socrates claims to be terrified as Thrasymachus (a well-known sophist) berates him for doing that for which Socrates was most well-known: asking questions and refuting everyone else's answers without ever offering up any of his own. Despite this (accurate) observation, within just a few paragraphs Thrasymachus is already offering his own view of justice for Socrates to critique anyway, and Socrates remains in his usual role of asking questions and refuting answers.

Perhaps to remind us all that Thrasymachus was a Sophist, Plato has him demand some sort of payment for the instruction he is about to offer, and Glaucon offers to compensate him, along with others, given that Socrates is perpetually poor. Thrasymachus relents and offers his infamous claim that "morality is nothing other than the advantage of the stronger party (338c)." He then, literally, asks why they have not applauded him.

According to Thrasymachus, justice (morality) is nothing other than the will of the stronger. Might makes right. "Justice" is simply a pretty label that we attach to the preferences and values of the ruling party (whether individual, as in a king or dictator, or group, as in an oligarchy or democracy). Whoever is in charge, wherever they might be, promote their own interests and call that "justice." When someone else takes over, they do the same thing.

In response, to Thrasymachus' position, Socrates begins his predictable line of attack. He first gets Thrasymachus to acknowledge that those in power sometimes make mistakes about what is to their advantage, and that subjects are to obey those laws anyway—and that it is right for them to do so. Accordingly, even though "justice" is defined as the advantage of the stronger, it is nevertheless "just" to do things which are actually to their disadvantage.

Socrates continues by once again making reference to justice as a skill and begins with analogy. Medicine considers the welfare of the body, not the welfare of medicine. In other words, a doctor, when she is practicing medicine, is not aimed at wealth or prestige, but at healing the sick. Also, medicine is for the advantage of the "weaker" party. It serves the patient (the one who is sick), not the doctor (the one who is well).

By analogy, *Socrates claims, rulers, when they practice the craft of ruling, consider not their own welfare, but that of their subjects*. Justice, then, is not concerned with the advantage of the stronger (i.e., the ruler), but, if anyone at all, of the weaker (i.e., the ruled).

Thrasymachus immediately offers an analogy of his own: shepherds are indeed concerned with their welfare of their flock, but only so that they can sell or eat them later! Thrasymachus then does something unusual: he seems to shift his usage of "moral" and "immoral." Though he has defined morality (justice) as the advantage of the stronger party, he now begins to claim that "immorality" is beneficial—and by "immorality" it is clear that he means specific things like theft, fraud, deceit, etc. The corrupt politician who embezzles and takes bribes is benefitted, while the honest politician loses out on those benefits. He claims that everyone recognizes that immorality is advantageous, but we publicly denounce it out of fear of being the victim of it.

Socrates proceeds to attack both points. First, with regard to the shepherd analogy, Socrates claims that different skills are at work. Medical doctors, for example, are concerned with the success of their practice. However, a *different* skill is employed when the doctor is considering and working on the financial success of her practice. When she is doing *medicine*, her craft focuses on healing the body. Similarly, the shepherd, when acting as a shepherd, is focused on the well-being of the flock. When the shepherd turns his attention to making a profit, a different skill is employed. Socrates suggests that something like "money-making" is this overarching (different) skill that conjoins with every other craft. Carpentry concerns working with wood, but to be a financially successful carpenter requires the skill of "money-making." When working with the wood, though, the skill is carpentry, not money-making. Rulers, *qua* rulers, are not working to their own benefit. When they do, they are exercising a different skill.

> Then now, Thrasymachus, there is no longer any doubt that neither arts nor governments provide for their own interests; but, as we were before saying, they rule and provide for the interests of

their subjects who are the weaker and not the stronger—to their good they attend and not to the good of the superior. And this is the reason, my dear Thrasymachus, why, as I was just now saying, no one is willing to govern; because no one likes to take in hand the reformation of evils which are not his concern without remuneration. For, in the execution of his work, and in giving his orders to another, the true artist does not regard his own interest, but always that of his subjects; and therefore in order that rulers may be willing to rule, they must be paid in one of three modes of payment, money, or honour, or a penalty for refusing (346e-347a).

Moving to Thraymachus' second point, that immorality is more beneficial to the individual than morality, Socrates once again resorts to analogy. After all, if something is like something else in one respect, it might be like it in another as well. He considers a band of pirates or thieves, and gets Thrasymachus to acknowledge that if the members were to wrong one another, they would be less successful as a group "because immorality makes for mutual conflict, hatred, and antagonism, while moral behavior makes for concord and friendship (351d)." Analogously, *when immorality arises in a single individual, it will generate internal division*, conflict, and discord. In addition to generating internal hostility, immorality will generate hostility between the immoral person and moral persons. If we acknowledge that the gods are moral, then this would mean conflict with the gods as well.

And we have admitted that justice is the excellence of the soul, and injustice the defect of the soul?

That has been admitted.

Then the just soul and the just man will live well, and the unjust man will live ill?

That is what your argument proves.

And he who lives well is blessed and happy, and he who lives ill the reverse of happy?

Certainly.

Then the just is happy, and the unjust miserable?

So be it.

But happiness and not misery is profitable.

Of course.

Then, my blessed Thrasymachus, injustice can never be more profitable than justice.

At this point, it would seem that Socrates has refuted Thrasymachus' position and has demonstrated that injustice is not more profitable than justice, and that true rulership looks not to the advantage of the ruler, but of the ruled (the "weaker party"). Moreover, Socrates has reiterated his notion of justice (goodness, morality) as a skill, and has introduced his notion of virtue as a healthy, integrated soul. Both of these ideas will continue to be prominent throughout the rest of the *Republic*.

Glaucon & Adeimantus

Thrasymachus, despite his fearsome entrance into the conversation, now wants only to done with it. In fact, he tries several times to get up and leave, only to be prevented by others. It might seem that Socrates is victorious, but some disagree. Socrates, for one, acknowledges that, thus far, he hasn't actually learned what justice *is*—only what it is *not*. Others, such as Glaucon (Plato's half-brother), believe that Thrasymachus gave up the fight too quickly.

Thrasymachus seems to me, like a snake, to have been charmed by your voice sooner than he ought to have been; but to my mind the nature of justice and injustice have not yet been made clear. Setting aside their rewards and results, I want to know what they are in themselves, and how they inwardly work in the soul. If you, please, then, I will revive the argument of Thrasymachus. And first I will speak of the nature and origin of justice according to the common view of them. Secondly, I will show that all men who practise justice do so against their will, of necessity, but not as a good. And thirdly, I will argue that there is reason in this view, for the life of the unjust is after all better far than the life of the just—if what they say is true, Socrates, since I myself am not of their opinion. But still I acknowledge that I am perplexed when I hear the voices of Thrasymachus and myriads of others dinning in my ears; and, on the other hand, I have never yet heard the superiority of justice to injustice maintained by any one in a satisfactory way. I want to hear justice praised in respect of itself; then I shall be satisfied, and you are the person from whom I think that I am most likely to hear this; and therefore I will praise the unjust life to the utmost of my power, and my manner of speaking will indicate the manner in which I desire to hear you too praising justice and censuring injustice (358b-c).

Glaucon appears to be in the awkward position of believing that a view of justice similar to Thrasymachus' might well be true, but hopes that it is not. So, he proposes to revive (a variation of) Thrasymachus' view in hopes that Socrates will demonstrate, once and for all, that justice is something more noble.

Glaucon distinguishes three different ways in which something can be perceived as good. Some things are good for their own sake, and not for their consequences (e.g., simple pleasures). Other things are good both for their own sake as well as for their consequences (e.g., health). Finally,

some things are good only for their consequences (e.g., a polio vaccine). Glaucon wonders into which of these categories should justice be placed?

His own proposal is that it falls into the third: justice is good only for its consequences. His brother Adeimantus will second this and claim that justice is valuable only for its external rewards, and what would be best is to have the *reputation* of being just, while actually being unjust. In such a case, one would reap the award of being unjust, while also reaping the rewards of being seen as just.

To support this notion of justice, Glaucon offers a very early (as in, Ancient) presentation of the **"social contract"** theory in political philosophy, while presupposing what appears to be the "psychological egoist" interpretation of human nature.

They say that to do injustice is, by nature, good; to suffer injustice, evil; but that the evil is greater than the good. And so when men have both done and suffered injustice and have had experience of both, not being able to avoid the one and obtain the other, they think that they had better agree among themselves to have neither; hence there arise laws and mutual covenants; and that which is ordained by law is termed by them lawful and just. This they affirm to be the origin and nature of justice;—it is a mean or compromise, between the best of all, which is to do injustice and not be punished, and the worst of all, which is to suffer injustice without the power of retaliation; and justice, being at a middle point between the two, is tolerated not as a good, but as the lesser evil, and honoured by reason of the inability of men to do injustice. For no man who is worthy to be called a man would ever submit to such an agreement if he were able to resist; he would be mad if he did. Such is the received account, Socrates, of the nature and origin of justice (358e-359b).

In other words, we "play nicely" with each other because it's necessary; it's in our own best interest to do so. Although we would all like to have sufficient power to do whatever we want, whenever we want, without anyone having the power to stop us, that just isn't possible. In addition, we fear being the victim of just that sort of powerful person, of being unable to protect ourselves and retaliate against those who would try to take advantage of us. As a compromise, we settle at a mid-point between these two extremes by means of a series of promises. I won't kill you, so long as you don't kill me. I won't take your stuff so long as you don't take mine. We enact, in effect, a "social contract" for the sake of safety, stability, and security—and we honor the contract not because we want to, but because we have to, because we lack the power to defy it.

To reinforce his argument, Glaucon appeals to the Myth of Gyges' ring, and invites us to consider the thought experiment that follows.

Now that those who practise justice do so involuntarily and because they have not the power to be unjust will best appear if we imagine something of this kind: having given both to the just and the unjust power to do what they will, let us watch and see whither desire will lead them; then we shall discover in the very act the just and unjust man to be proceeding along the same road, following their interest, which all natures deem to be their good, and are only diverted into the path of justice by the force of law. The liberty which we are supposing may be most completely given to them in the form of such a power as is said to have been possessed by Gyges, the ancestor of Croesus the Lydian. According to the tradition, Gyges was a shepherd in the service of the king of Lydia; there was a great storm, and an earthquake made an opening in the earth at the place where he was feeding his flock. Amazed at the sight, he descended into the opening, where, among other marvels, he beheld a hollow brazen horse, having doors, at which he stooping and looking in saw a dead body of stature, as appeared to him, more than human, and having nothing on but a gold ring; this he took from the finger of the dead and reascended. Now the shepherds met together, according to custom, that they might send their monthly report about the flocks to the king; into their assembly he came having the ring on his finger, and as he was sitting among them he chanced to turn the collet of the ring inside his hand, when instantly he became invisible to the rest of the company and they began to speak of him as if he were no longer present. He was astonished at this, and again touching the ring he turned the collet outwards and reappeared; he made several trials of the ring, and always with the same result— when he turned the collet inwards he became invisible, when outwards he reappeared. Whereupon he contrived to be chosen one of the messengers who were sent to the court; whereas soon as he arrived he seduced the queen, and with her help conspired against the king and slew him, and took the kingdom. Suppose now that there were two such magic rings, and the just put on one of them and the unjust the other; no man can be imagined to be of such an iron nature that he would stand fast in justice. No man would keep his hands off what was not his own when he could safely take what he liked out of the market, or go into houses and lie with any one at his pleasure, or kill or release from prison whom he would, and in all respects be like a God among men. Then the actions of the just would be as the actions of the unjust; they would both come at last to the same point. And this we may truly affirm to be a great proof that a man is just, not willingly or because he thinks that justice is any good to him individually, but of necessity, for wherever any one thinks that he can safely be unjust, there he is unjust. For all men believe in their hearts that injustice is far more profitable to the individual than justice, and he who argues as I have been supposing, will say that they are right. If you could imagine any one obtaining this power of becoming invisible, and never doing any wrong or touching what was another's, he would be thought by the lookers-on to be a most wretched idiot, although they would praise him to one another's faces, and keep up appearances with one another from a fear that they too might suffer injustice. Enough of this (359d-360d).

Before we come to any harsh judgments against Gyges, remember that Glaucon recommends a thought experiment. Imagine there are two such magic rings, each of which renders the wearer invisible. These days, we might need to get a little more sophisticated. Perhaps you suppose that even invisible persons might still leave behind fingerprints, or hair samples, or other means by which a clever forensic investigator could identify a perpetrator. They're magic rings. We can make them do whatever we want! Suppose the rings render the wearer invisible, magically cloaks any heat signatures, erases fingerprints, eliminates DNA evidence, etc. Now, give one of the two rings to someone whom you regard as tremendously virtuous and just. Give the other to someone quite the opposite: a vicious and unjust jerk. What, do you suppose, each would do with the ring? Glaucon believes that both the "just" and the "unjust" would come "at last to the same point." That is, they would each, eventually, do the same thing: whatever it is that each wanted. To make matters more interesting, give yourself one of the rings.

The outcome of Glaucon's thought experiment provides a particular insight into human nature. If it is true that any one of us would ultimately and inevitably abuse the power

of Gyges' ring, then the reason why most of us usually obey the rules and "play nice" with one another is fear. Although we would like to be able to do whatever we want, to whomever we want, whenever we want, we recognize that just isn't possible. None of us is Superman. However powerful a given individual might be, she isn't bulletproof (to put it bluntly). No matter how wealthy, how powerful, how well-connected, each one of us is all-too-human, and all-too-vulnerable. Realizing that, and wishing to minimize the risk we face from others, we make mutual promises to "play nice." I won't rob you so long as you don't rob me. I won't kill you, so long as you don't kill me. We surrender some of our own power, and our own freedom, when we make those promises, but in exchange for that we gain security. We behave ourselves because it is in our self-interest to do so. If it were no longer necessary, no longer in our self-interest (e.g., if we had Gyges' ring), we would no longer be inclined to "play nice." All of this is meant to demonstrate that justice is valued not for its own sake, but because of the beneficial consequences it generates. In the context of the "nature" v. "convention" debate, Glaucon seems to be arguing in favor of convention as regards justice: laws exist merely as a necessary compromise due to our inability to fulfill our true heart's desires.[48]

The final challenge thrown at Socrates' feet will produce the answer that occupies the rest of the *Republic*.

> And therefore, I say, not only prove to us that justice is better than injustice, but show what they either of them do to the possessor of them, which makes the one to be a good and the other an evil, whether seen or unseen by gods and men (367e).

---

[48] This possibly pessimistic (or possibly accurate) interpretation of human nature as that of desire-satisfying individuals who can only be entrusted to live cooperatively if provided the threat of punishment and the force of law will find voice in such later political philosophers as Hobbes and Machiavelli.

Socrates

Thus far, I have presented the first two books of the *Republic* in considerable detail. That strategy is about to change. Most of the rest of the *Republic* is the development of an extended analogy between the soul and the State for the purpose of identifying and understanding justice. Rather than proceed through this argument book by book (let alone line by line), I am going to present the analogy itself, in as clear a fashion as I can manage. This will involve skipping over large chunks of the *Republic*, and addressing some ideas out of order. I believe, though, that the end result will be a clearer and more precise presentation of the key material.

I have already mentioned an extended analogy. Socrates claims that the analogy will assist in understanding the nature of justice.

Glaucon and the rest entreated me by all means not to let the question drop, but to proceed in the investigation. They wanted to arrive at the truth, first, about the nature of justice and injustice, and secondly, about their relative advantages. I told them, what I really thought, that the enquiry would be of a serious nature, and would require very good eyes. Seeing then, I said, that we are no great wits, I think that we had better adopt a method which I may illustrate thus; suppose that a short-sighted person had been asked by some one to read small letters from a distance; and it occurred to some one else that they might be found in another place which was larger and in which the letters were larger—if they were the same and he could read the larger letters first, and then proceed to the lesser—this would have been thought a rare piece of good fortune.

Very true, said Adeimantus; but how does the illustration apply to our enquiry?

I will tell you, I replied; justice, which is the subject of our enquiry, is, as you know, sometimes spoken of as the virtue of an individual, and sometimes as the virtue of a State.

True, he replied.

And is not a State larger than an individual?

It is.

Then in the larger the quantity of justice is likely to be larger and more easily discernible. I propose therefore that we enquire into the nature of justice and injustice, first as they appear in the State, and secondly in the individual, proceeding from the greater to the lesser and comparing them (368d-369a).

Socrates proposes to spend a significant amount of time and energy developing a vision of an ideal State on the assumption that there is a meaningful analogy between the State and the individual. If true, then what we learn about justice in the case of this ideal State can be applied to our understanding of justice for the individual soul.

Before delving into the analogy itself, I want to say a few things about how to interpret what Socrates is doing. Some interpreters of the *Republic* take the political philosophy very seriously, believe that Plato (via Socrates) is presenting a serious attempt at State-building, and then (usually) critique that vision as either hopelessly utopian, or fascist. Other interpreters claim that no serious political philosophy is intended, and that all of the discussion of the State, its policies and structures and so on, is solely for the sake of the analogy. Therefore, we are not to take seriously anything Socrates says about politics except in regards to how it motivates the analogy with the individual soul. Within the *Republic* itself, Plato has Socrates acknowledge the ideal/utopian nature of the project.

you mean the city whose establishment we have described, the city whose home is in the ideal; for I think that it can be found nowhere on earth." "Well," said I, "perhaps there is a pattern of it laid up in heaven for him who wishes to contemplate it and so beholding to constitute himself its citizen. But it makes no difference whether it exists now or ever will come into being . . . (Republic, 592a-b).

The ideal Republic is found nowhere on Earth, and might never exist, for that matter—but there might, nevertheless, be an ideal "form" of government, against which all actual governments may be evaluated. In that sense, some actual statecraft might be intended.

My own view as to how seriously we are to take the political philosophy in the *Republic* is unsettled, but that unsettled-ness mirrors, in my opinion, the condition of the debate. My own opinion is that it's clear that he intends the analogy (he says so, explicitly!), so we must interpret most of the *Republic* with that analogy in mind. However, in some places he goes into political detail that would be unnecessary if his *sole* purpose was to develop an analogy. So, my own sense is that the primary purpose of this lengthy section of the *Republic* is (ultimately) to understand justice in the soul, but that there might well be some sincere effort at political philosophy as well. Having built it up so much by now, let's finally get into the analogy itself.

After describing how a community might develop with regard to its needs and division of labor, *Socrates ultimately divides his ideal community into three classes:*

1. Guardians
2. Auxiliaries
3. Producers

The Guardians are the ruling class, drawn from the Auxiliaries by virtue of having demonstrated the proper traits. Auxiliaries are warriors, in effect both military and police in one. The Producers are everyone else. It's easy to think of Producers as only "blue collar," working class types such as factory workers, farmers, etc. However, lawyers and bankers are also "Producers" in this framework. Basically, anyone who isn't an Auxiliary or Guardian is a Producer, by default.

The Principle of Specialization

These divisions are not arbitrary, nor is the selection process by which one is placed into his or her class. Selection is driven by what we might call the "principle of specialization." This principle plays a very important (and persistent) role in Socrates' argument. The first indicator of this principle in the text is found at 370b-c:

> ...we are not all alike; there are diversities of natures among us which are adapted to different occupations. . . . And if so, we must infer that all things are produced more plentifully and easily and of a better quality when one man does one thing which is natural to him and does it at the right time, and leaves other things.

Different people are best-suited for different roles in society. Some people are "natural" leaders. Others lack leadership ability, but are courageous and strong and would excel at military work. Still others lack either, but are skilled at some trade or craft. For the good of the community, individuals should do that for which they are best suited. If someone who is not suitable for leadership aspires to, and acquires, a leadership position anyway, the community suffers. The community suffers if cowards become soldiers. Natural leaders "waste" their talents when they become doctors instead. On the assumption that the good of the whole (the community) is more important than the good of the individual, individuals should be put to use in the way that best serves their community.

Remember, though, that the basic point of all this political talk is to develop an analogy by which to understand the individual soul. *Socrates claims that the soul is likewise divisible into three parts that just so happen to correspond to the three divisions in society.*[49] These three parts of the soul are as follows:

1. Reason
2. Spirit (or passion)
3. Appetite (or desire)

This tripartite understanding of the soul is employed not only in the *Republic*, but in another of Plato's works as well: *Phaedrus*. There, he employs a different analogy. The soul is like a chariot with two horses and one charioteer. One of the horses represents the appetitive/desirous part of the soul, and is the source of our instinctive desires. The other horse represents the spirited part of the soul, and is the source of our motivation and desire for personal glory. The charioteer represents the rational part of the soul, and the source of understanding and wisdom, and our desire for one's overall good.

In case it wasn't obvious, the Guardians in the community correspond to Reason in the soul. The Auxiliaries correspond to the spirited/passionate part of the soul. The Producers correspond to the appetitive/desirous part of the soul.

1. Guardians   Reason
2. Auxiliaries   Spirit/Passion
3. Producers   Appetite/desire

Despite the fact that the point of the society-building exercise is supposed to be to develop an analogy with the soul, Socrates proceeds to develop this ideal society in exhausting detail—which makes it difficult to dismiss his efforts as being aimed *solely* at developing the analogy.

Life in the *Republic*

His ideal society, to the extent that we take it seriously, might seem shockingly totalitarian to our delicate, democratic sensibilities. Although the Producers are largely free to live as they please (subject to their basic class restrictions, of

course), the lives of the Auxiliaries and Guardians are thoroughly regulated. I will offer a brief description in what follows, and you should assume that these policies apply to both the Guardians and Auxiliaries unless I specifically indicate otherwise.

They will live "spartan" lives. In Plato's own time, this expression had a more poignant meaning, of course, as Sparta had recently warred with, and defeated, Athens. However, the contemporary usage of the term is accurate. They will have no private possessions, nor private homes (416a-417b, 462c). They will live together, in barracks, and all of their possessions will be provided to them by the State. These possessions will be the basic necessities of life and of their profession. For example, Auxiliaries will be supplied armor and weapons in addition to basic daily needs. These items technically belong to the State, and have merely been "checked out" for use, in much the same way that a soldier in the U.S. military doesn't own "his" firearm. The purpose of limiting their personal possessions is to prevent them from being motivated by greed. After all, in real life leaders have a tendency to use their power to promote themselves, to acquire personal wealth and connections—and warriors might allow their personal ambition to inspire them to seize leadership (and the wealth and power it offers) by means of a military coup. If these two classes have been raised without personal possessions, they will (presumably) lack those temptations.

> Then now let us consider what will be their way of life, if they are to realize our idea of them. In the first place, none of them should have any property of his own beyond what is absolutely necessary; neither should they have a private house or store closed against any one who has a mind to enter; their provisions should be only such as are required by trained warriors, who are men of temperance and

---

[49] An argument for this tripartite model of the soul may be found on 439c-441b, for those who are interested.

courage; they should agree to receive from the citizens a fixed rate of pay, enough to meet the expenses of the year and no more; and they will go to mess and live together like soldiers in a camp. Gold and silver we will tell them that they have from God; the diviner metal is within them, and they have therefore no need of the dross which is current among men, and ought not to pollute the divine by any such earthly admixture; for that commoner metal has been the source of many unholy deeds, but their own is undefiled. And they alone of all the citizens may not touch or handle silver or gold, or be under the same roof with them, or wear them, or drink from them. And this will be their salvation, and they will be the saviours of the State. But should they ever acquire homes or lands or moneys of their own, they will become housekeepers and husbandmen instead of guardians, enemies and tyrants instead of allies of the other citizens; hating and being hated, plotting and being plotted against, they will pass their whole life in much greater terror of internal than of external enemies, and the hour of ruin, both to themselves and to the rest of the State, will be at hand (416e).

Just as they will have no private possessions, nor will they have private relationships. By virtue of what can only be described as a eugenics program, they will have non-exclusive "marriages" selected by Guardians on the basis of what will produce the best offspring. These pairings will not be permanent or exclusive, so as to prevent jealousies and possessiveness from developing. This line of reasoning extends to the offspring of those pairings as well. Those children will be raised in common, with no knowledge of the identity of their biological parents (nor will those parents know which child is their own—so as to prevent thoughts of "their own" from arising at all)(457d). Perhaps disturbingly, this system aimed at what is best for the community will also weed out some children as unfit. "Inferior"

offspring will not be "brought up." They will be "hidden away in some secret and secluded spot." This includes not only offspring resulting from unsuitable pairings, but also children with disabilities resulting from proper pairings (459e, 460c). To be clear, what we're talking about is killing "unfit" babies—though the actual process probably would have been more passive, merely leaving them out to die of exposure. All this would be done secretly, of course, to avoid disturbing the populace.

Oddly enough, the rulers (Guardians) and warriors (Auxiliaries) of this "ideal" State seem to have the least freedom and least luxuries of anyone in their community. Plato/Socrates was aware of this:

> Here Adeimantus interposed a question: How would you answer, Socrates, said he, if a person were to say that you are making these people miserable, and that they are the cause of their own unhappiness; the city in fact belongs to them, but they are none the better for it; whereas other men acquire lands, and build large and handsome houses, and have everything handsome about them, offering sacrifices to the gods on their own account, and practising hospitality; moreover, as you were saying just now, they have gold and silver, and all that is usual among the favourites of fortune; but our poor citizens are no better than mercenaries who are quartered in the city and are always mounting guard?

> Yes, I said; and you may add that they are only fed, and not paid in addition to their food, like other men; and therefore they cannot, if they would, take a journey of pleasure; they have no money to spend on a mistress or any other luxurious fancy, which, as the world goes, is thought to be happiness; and many other accusations of the same nature might be added....

> If we proceed along the old path, my belief, I said, is that we shall find the

answer. And our answer will be that, even as they are, our guardians may very likely be the happiest of men; but that our aim in founding the State was not the disproportionate happiness of any one class, but the greatest happiness of the whole;... (419a-420c)

I assume that the typical reader of this text is an American, or at least living in the United States of America. We are accustomed to a cultural norm of individualism, according to which we tend to focus on the individual, first and foremost, and then consider the needs of the broader community as something "extra," something to be promoted so long as it's not overly much at the expense of the individual. This would have been an utterly alien concept to the Greeks of Plato's time. There was much more emphasis on the group, whether it be the larger community (city state) or family. Given our own contemporary sensibilities, this claim that the aim of this ideal State is the happiness of the whole, not of any one class or individual, and that it's acceptable to impose burdens on some for the sake of the many, might sound disturbingly totalitarian—and the Guardians and Auxiliaries are subject to even more controls than these.

For example, their lives will be subject to vigorous training with regard to physical exercise, music, culture, and philosophy. The very best persons will excel in all of these, and these persons are naturally suited to be Guardians (412a-b). Training will aim at avoiding extremes. Exclusive focus on physical exercise produces brutality (411c-e), while exclusive focus on cultural studies produces "shamefully soft" characters (410d).

Training will be coeducational. The *Republic* is surprisingly "progressive" with regard to gender equality.

Let us further suppose the birth and education of our women to be subject to similar or nearly similar regulations; then we shall see whether the result accords with our design.

What do you mean?

What I mean may be put into the form of a question, I said: Are dogs divided into hes and shes, or do they both share equally in hunting and in keeping watch and in the other duties of dogs? or do we entrust to the males the entire and exclusive care of the flocks, while we leave the females at home, under the idea that the bearing and suckling their puppies is labour enough for them?

No, he said, they share alike; the only difference between them is that the males are stronger and the females weaker.

But can you use different animals for the same purpose, unless they are bred and fed in the same way?

You cannot.

Then, if women are to have the same duties as men, they must have the same nurture and education?

Yes....

Then let us put a speech into the mouths of our opponents. They will say: 'Socrates and Glaucon, no adversary need convict you, for you yourselves, at the first foundation of the State, admitted the principle that everybody was to do the one work suited to his own nature.' And certainly, if I am not mistaken, such an admission was made by us. 'And do not the natures of men and women differ very much indeed?' And we shall reply: Of course they do. Then we shall be asked, 'Whether the tasks assigned to men and to women should not be different, and such as are agreeable to their different natures?' Certainly they should. 'But if so, have you not fallen into a serious inconsistency in saying that men and women, whose natures are so entirely different, ought to perform the same actions?'—What defence will you make for us, my good Sir, against any one who offers these objections? . . .

And if, I said, the male and female sex appear to differ in their fitness for any art or pursuit, we should say that such pursuit or art ought to be assigned to one or the other of them; but if the difference consists only in women bearing and men begetting children, this does not amount to a proof that a woman differs from a man in respect of the sort of education she should receive; and we shall therefore continue to maintain that our guardians and their wives ought to have the same pursuits. . . .

And if so, my friend, I said, there is no special faculty of administration in a state which a woman has because she is a woman, or which a man has by virtue of his sex, but the gifts of nature are alike diffused in both; all the pursuits of men are the pursuits of women also, but in all of them a woman is inferior to a man (451d-455e).

Because what is relevant to the class divisions (and therefore to the training and education received by each class) are the traits suitable to each class, and because reproductive organs are relevant only to the task of conceiving and bearing children, there should be no difference, on the basis of sex or gender alone, with regard to class or training. Instead, we should recognize that some females are suitable for being Guardians, and some are not, in just the same way that some men are and some are not.

Although Plato's Socrates might seem quite the progressive or feminist in this sense, he's quite the "totalitarian" in others. For example, Socrates argues that young people are impressionable, and that it's important to control the messages they hear. If you suspect he's talking about censorship, you are correct.

You know also that the beginning is the most important part of any work, especially in the case of a young and tender thing; for that is the time at which the character is being formed and the desired impression is more readily taken.

Quite true.

And shall we just carelessly allow children to hear any casual tales which may be devised by casual persons, and to receive into their minds ideas for the most part the very opposite of those which we should wish them to have when they are grown up?

We cannot.

Then the first thing will be to establish a censorship of the writers of fiction, and let the censors receive any tale of fiction which is good, and reject the bad; and we will desire mothers and nurses to tell their children the authorised ones only (377b-c).

In one of the lengthier tangents of the *Republic*, Socrates offers a sustained critique of the poets (a primary rival to philosophers with regard to moral influence). The poets, including legends such as Hesiod and Homer, were, in effect, professional liars—and their lies produce harmful effects in the populace. For example, the poets tell stories of the gods, such as Zeus, engaging in all kinds of scandalous and immoral behavior. What a terrible example this offers to young people!

First of all, I said, there was that greatest of all lies in high places, which the poet told about Uranus, and which was a bad lie too,—I mean what Hesiod says that Uranus did, and how Cronus retaliated on him. The doings of Cronus, and the sufferings which in turn his son inflicted upon him, even if they were true, ought certainly not to be lightly told to young and thoughtless persons; if possible, they had better be buried in silence. . . . Yes, Adeimantus, they are stories not to be repeated in our State; the young man should not be told that in committing the worst of crimes he is far from doing anything outrageous; and that even if he chastises his father when he does wrong, in whatever manner, he will only be following the example of the first and greatest among the gods (378a-b).

Even should the story be true, some truths are better left not communicated—especially to the young who are so easily influenced. We must admit that this view is not so outrageous or ancient. After all, many people today are concerned about the effect that violent video games or violent (or sexually explicit) lyrics in music has on children. Is it so outlandish to suspect that if a young person continuously listens to music that glorifies the "gangster" lifestyle that he or she might be influenced to emulate it?

Of course, if young people are so impressionable, they are bound to be "impressed" by *something*. This is why the ideal State in the *Republic* doesn't merely ban certain stories, but will actively promote others. Such stories should inspire courage and remove fear of death (386b), remove the "horror of Hades" (387d), remove embarrassing stories of eminent men (387d, 389a, 389e), encourage discipline (390d), and discourage mercenary or greedy natures (390e). In addition, in order to promote a deep sense of community, Plato has Socrates offer the "*noble lie.*"

A lie? But hasn't Socrates criticized the poets for lying? Yes, but the State is a special case.

Then if any one at all is to have the privilege of lying, the rulers of the State should be the persons; and they, in their dealings either with enemies or with their own citizens, may be allowed to lie for the public good (389c).

What sort of lie does Socrates have in mind? One that will attempt (at least over time) to erase personal ambitions and replace them with a sense of solidarity and common purpose, and one which will reinforce the rigid class structure of the *Republic*.

How then may we devise one of those needful falsehoods of which we lately spoke—just one royal lie which may deceive the rulers, if that be possible, and at any rate the rest of the city?...

Speak, he said, and fear not.

Well then, I will speak, although I really know not how to look you in the face, or in what words to utter the audacious fiction, which I propose to communicate gradually, first to the rulers, then to the soldiers, and lastly to the people. They are to be told that their youth was a dream, and the education and training which they received from us, an appearance only; in reality during all that time they were being formed and fed in the womb of the earth, where they themselves and their arms and appurtenances were manufactured; when they were completed, the earth, their mother, sent them up; and so, their country being their mother and also their nurse, they are bound to advise for her good, and to defend her against attacks, and her citizens they are to regard as children of the earth and their own brothers.

You had good reason, he said, to be ashamed of the lie which you were going to tell.

True, I replied, but there is more coming; I have only told you half. Citizens, we shall say to them in our tale, you are brothers, yet God has framed you differently. Some of you have the power of command, and in the composition of these he has mingled gold, wherefore also they have the greatest honour; others he has made of silver, to be auxiliaries; others again who are to be husbandmen and craftsmen he has composed of brass and iron; and the species will generally be preserved in the children. But as all are of the same original stock, a golden parent will sometimes have a silver son, or a silver parent a golden son. And God proclaims as a first principle to the rulers, and above all else, that there is nothing which they should so anxiously guard, or of which they are to be such good guardians, as of the purity of the race. They should observe what elements mingle in their offspring; for if the son of a golden or silver parent has an admixture of brass and iron, then nature orders a transposition of ranks, and the eye of the ruler must not be pitiful towards the child because he has to descend in the scale and become a husbandman or artisan, just as there may be sons of artisans who having an admixture of gold or silver in them are raised to honour, and become guardians or auxiliaries. For an oracle says that when a man of brass or iron guards the State, it will be destroyed. Such is the tale; is there any possibility of making our citizens believe in it?

Not in the present generation, he replied; there is no way of accomplishing this; but their sons may be made to believe in the tale, and their sons' sons, and posterity after them.

I see the difficulty, I replied; yet the fostering of such a belief will make them care more for the city and for one another. (414c-415d)

While Socrates acknowledges the practical difficulty of getting the present generation to accept such a fantastic story, later generations will simply grow up hearing it as the true origin of their community—and all of this serves the greater good of their community.

Remember: a key principle motivating this entire discussion is the "principle of specialization," according to which persons are best-suited for certain roles in the community, and the community is best served by people knowing and fulfilling their respective roles. This theme is reinforced continuously in the *Republic* (370a-c, 374a, 375a, 406c, 421c, 423d, 433a).

If the goal is to produce the ideal State, and to organize it for the good of the community, then it's obvious that the issue of who should run this State will be very important. Perhaps not surprisingly, Socrates claims that only philosophers are qualified for this task.

> Unless communities have philosophers as kings, or the people who are currently called kings and rulers practice philosophy with enough integrity,...there can be no end to political troubles (473d).

What is so special about philosophers that would make them suitable Guardians? *Socrates claims that only philosophers have knowledge, while everyone else makes do with mere belief.* Moreover, he argues that only philosophers will be capable of being virtuous and expert rulers. First, he claims that philosophers love every kind of learning (474c-475c), and that no one else does (475c-480a). Then, he claims that the love of *every* kind of learning produces knowledge of ethical matters, and therefore virtue (485a-486e). Therefore, the love of every kind of learning makes one a virtuous and expert ruler. Accordingly, one is a virtuous and expert ruler if and only if one is a philosopher.

Among their many other excellent qualities, philosophers have a passion for wisdom. This reduces other passions (485d-e), and produces courage (486b) and temperance (485e). Still, Socrates has to admit that this is not the common view of philosophers. Indeed, they are often scorned and rejected by the public.[50]

> For any one of us might say, that although in words he is not able to meet you at each step of the argument, he sees as a fact that the votaries of philosophy, when they carry on the study, not only in youth as a part of education, but as the pursuit of their maturer years, most of them become strange monsters, not to say utter rogues, and that those who may be considered the best of them are made useless to the world by the very study which you extol (487c-d).

In other words, philosophers have the reputation of being weird and useless—or worse! In defense of philosophers, Socrates argues by way of analogy.

> I perceive, I said, that you are vastly amused at having plunged me into such a hopeless discussion; but now hear the parable, and then you will be still more amused at the meagreness of my imagination: for the manner in which the best men are treated in their own States is so grievous that no single thing on earth is comparable to it; and therefore, if I am to plead their cause, I must have recourse to fiction, and put together a figure made up of many things, like the fabulous unions of goats and stags which are found in pictures. Imagine then a fleet or a ship in which there is a captain who is taller and stronger than any of the crew, but he is a little deaf and has a similar infirmity in sight, and his knowledge of navigation is not much better. The sailors are quarrelling with one another about the steering—every one is of opinion that he has a right to steer, though he has never learned the art of navigation and cannot tell who taught him or when he learned,

and will further assert that it cannot be taught, and they are ready to cut in pieces any one who says the contrary. They throng about the captain, begging and praying him to commit the helm to them; and if at any time they do not prevail, but others are preferred to them, they kill the others or throw them overboard, and having first chained up the noble captain's senses with drink or some narcotic drug, they mutiny and take possession of the ship and make free with the stores; thus, eating and drinking, they proceed on their voyage in such manner as might be expected of them. Him who is their partisan and cleverly aids them in their plot for getting the ship out of the captain's hands into their own whether by force or persuasion, they compliment with the name of sailor, pilot, able seaman, and abuse the other sort of man, whom they call a good-for-nothing; but that the true pilot must pay attention to the year and seasons and sky and stars and winds, and whatever else belongs to his art, if he intends to be really qualified for the command of a ship, and that he must and will be the steerer, whether other people like or not—the possibility of this union of authority with the steerer's art has never seriously entered into their thoughts or been made part of their calling. Now in vessels which are in a state of mutiny and by sailors who are mutineers, how will the true pilot be regarded? Will he not be called by them a prater, a star-gazer, a good-for-nothing?

Of course, said Adeimantus.

Then you will hardly need, I said, to hear the interpretation of the figure, which describes the true philosopher in his relation to the State; for you understand already (488a-489b).

---

[50] It's hard not to think of Socrates' own trial and execution at this point.

In a corrupt community, amidst corrupt and blinded people, a truly wise person who be perceived as and treated as a fool. At this point, one might think Socrates is merely engaging in some special pleading, or even some sort of *ad hominem* attack. Philosophers are poorly regarded because everyone else is a fool? To shore up his position, Socrates needs to demonstrate that philosophers, as philosophers, really are people who have knowledge, and that not everyone is equally qualified with regard to knowledge, or rulership.

Among other things, this is going to require a rejection of epistemic relativism. If "all truth is relative," as many of the Sophists claimed, then it would appear to be the case that no one person is any more qualified with regard to knowledge than is anyone else. All perspectives are equal. Socrates dismisses this view, however, as absurd on its surface. In another Platonic dialogue (*Theaetetus*), Socrates considers the relativism of the Sophist, Protagoras.

> Protagoras, for his part, admitting as he does that everybody's opinion is true, must acknowledge the truth of his opponent's belief about his own belief, where they think he is wrong….That is to say, he would acknowledge his own belief to be false, if he admits that the belief of those who think him wrong is true (171a-b).

There is something seemingly self-refuting, or internally inconsistent, with epistemic relativism. Since all opinions are equally true, it is simultaneously and equally true that epistemic relativism is, itself, both true and false. Beyond this conceptual puzzle, Socrates points out that we do not, in fact, regard all opinions as equally true. If you are not a medical doctor and you think you are healthy, but a medical doctor tells you that you have cancer, do you really regard your respective opinions as equally true? Don't we recognize legitimate expertise in a great many areas of inquiry? If our subject is Plato's philosophy, do we really believe that each person's position is equally true regarding that

philosophical system? The opinions of the physicist who has specialized in string theory and the opinion of the philosopher who has specialized in Plato are equally true with regard to Plato? I think a tiger looks friendly, but a trained animal handler warns me that the tiger is about to rip my face off. Equally true opinions? Presumably not. If we acknowledge that different people have different degrees of expertise with regard to different skills, then it would stand to reason that not all people are equally equipped to rule a community (i.e., be a Guardian), and that not all people are even equally equipped to discuss and identify knowledge itself. If "philosophers" are those best equipped to perceive the Truth of things, then it is they who should lead rather than some popularly elected politician. Truth is not up to a majority vote!

This relativism is even more egregious when the issue at stake is morality itself. Socrates seizes the opportunity to take another shot at his Sophist rivals.

> Why, that all those mercenary individuals, whom the many call Sophists and whom they deem to be their adversaries, do, in fact, teach nothing but the opinion of the many, that is to say, the opinions of their assemblies; and this is their wisdom. I might compare them to a man who should study the tempers and desires of a mighty strong beast who is fed by him—he would learn how to approach and handle him, also at what times and from what causes he is dangerous or the reverse, and what is the meaning of his several cries, and by what sounds, when another utters them, he is soothed or infuriated; and you may suppose further, that when, by continually attending upon him, he has become perfect in all this, he calls his knowledge wisdom, and makes of it a system or art, which he proceeds to teach, although he has no real notion of what he means by the principles or passions of which he is speaking, but calls this honourable and that dishonourable, or

good or evil, or just or unjust, all in accordance with the tastes and tempers of the great brute. Good he pronounces to be that in which the beast delights and evil to be that which he dislikes; and he can give no other account of them except that the just and noble are the necessary, having never himself seen, and having no power of explaining to others the nature of either, or the difference between them, which is immense (493a-c).

These intellectual mercenaries know nothing of good or evil, justice or injustice. Instead, they merely observe what actually happens in the world, what people like and dislike, and proclaim those things to be good or bad, just or unjust. They perceive cultural and individual differences in practices and values, and conclude something like moral subjectivism or cultural relativism. Socrates, however, disagrees with the strategy of identifying what is just or unjust with the events of this constantly changing world—and this is a problem not merely with respect to moral knowledge.

One of the problems with recognizing "The Truth" (aside from lack of training and qualification) is that the world we experience is constantly in flux, and insufficiently stable so as to provide for knowledge. Plato, ultimately, rejects sense experience as a means of knowledge, because the senses show us only the world of change, and our perceptions are relative to the perceiver. For example, consider hot coffee. Whether or not it is hot depends not only on when the measurement is taken, but also on who is making the determination. My former father-in-law would literally heat his coffee in the microwave until it boiled. Only then did he consider it sufficiently hot. I, on the other hand, consider that to be an example of coffee that is scalding, rather than "hot." Which one of us is right, and when would we have been right?

It might sound like we're backsliding into epistemic relativism again, or into skepticism. Plato does not intend that outcome, though. Knowledge, he claims, is objective, universal, unchanging, grounded in Reason, and is

ultimately unavailable to the senses. *Knowledge will not pertain to the particular, constantly changing "things" we experience in the world of the senses, but instead to unchanging universal concepts that inform our understanding of particular things in the first place.* What we are now delving into is Plato's theory of the Forms.

The Forms

We encounter all kinds of circles in daily life. There is a mirror on my desk that I'm looking at right now. It's in the shape of a circle. The lid of my coffee cup is a circle. Doughnuts are circles, as are tires, as are wedding rings. What each one of these particular objects has in common (among other things) is that they are circular. We have a concept, an ideal, of a circle, and because each of these objects matches up (to an extent) with that concept, we recognize them as circular. None of those objects is itself a perfect circle, but each one approximates a circle—or else we never would have described it as circular.

This notion is clear from Socrates basic line of inquiry in most of the dialogues. He always seems to seek the "universal" behind the "particular." Consider, for example, his famous investigation of piety in *Euthyphro*.

And what is piety, and what is impiety?

Piety is doing as I am doing; that is to say, prosecuting any one who is guilty of murder, sacrilege, or of any similar crime-whether he be your father or mother, or whoever he may be-that makes no difference; and not to prosecute them is impiety. . . .

I dare say; and you shall tell me them at some other time when I have leisure. But just at present I would rather hear from you a more precise answer, which you have not as yet given, my friend, to the question, What is "piety"? When asked, you only replied, Doing as you do, charging your father with murder.

And what I said was true, Socrates.

No doubt, Euthyphro; but you would admit that there are many other pious acts?

There are.

Remember that I did not ask you to give me two or three examples of piety, but to explain the general idea which makes all pious things to be pious. Do you not recollect that there was one idea which made the impious impious, and the pious pious?

I remember.

Tell me what is the nature of this idea, and then I shall have a standard to which I may look, and by which I may measure actions, whether yours or those of any one else, and then I shall be able to say that such and such an action is pious, such another impious.

Socrates is assuming that there is some property of "piety" that manifests in any number of acts. It is not identical to any particular of those acts, but those acts simply are "pious" to the extent that they exemplify that quality of piety. An individual act may be pious, or impious depending on circumstances. I might be pious one moment, but impious the next. Piety itself, however, is unchanging.

Plato suggests that our concepts, not only of piety or circles, but of all sorts of other things: human, chair, Christmas tree, greeting card, television set, onion ring, etc., *are "universals" that are exemplified (to varying degrees) by particular things* (e.g., actual onion rings, or chairs). He refers to these ideals, these concepts, as "Forms."

According to this theory, there is a Form of a chair. This is what allows us to recognize objects as chairs. Particular objects are related to their Forms in a variety of ways. Particular things (e.g., the chair I am sitting on at this moment) resemble the Form of a chair (otherwise I'd call it something else!). In a very abstract sort of way Plato claims that Forms cause particulars in the sort of way that a statue causes its shadow. Particulars "participate" in their Forms to varying degrees, and this is the means by which we evaluate them. For example, at dog shows various particular dogs are judged by how well they exemplify their breed. Those that "participate" very well in their breed would be regarded as excellent examples of that breed, whereas a "mutt" wouldn't "participate" well at all. Finally, Forms are what make particulars intelligible to us at all. In that Forms are concepts, they are make thought and speech possible. Try to describe an object (e.g., a chair, a doughnut, a human being, etc.) without appealing to concepts. What could you possibly say? The thing I am sitting on is a chair. Oops. I'm not allowed to say chair. OK, it's a piece of furniture. Oops. I can't appeal to "furniture." It's underneath me. Oops. "Underneath" is a concept too. It's supportive. Oops. Gray. Oops. Etc.

At this point, we could simply understand Forms as concepts, and not have anything too controversial on our hands—but Plato does not avoid controversy. Plato doesn't merely claim that the Forms are concepts, in the sense of universal ideas; he argues that they exist, independently of our thoughts, in another realm of existence distinct from the physical world. The physical world is the one we encounter by sense experience. It is constantly changing, and doesn't permit knowledge to be acquired. This is where Plato honors Heraclitus. The intelligible world, on the other hand, is non-physical, eternal, unchanging, and intelligible to Reason. This is where Plato honors Parmenides. Parmenides and Heraclitus represented two opposite camps, one of which claiming that everything is in flux and the other claiming that there is no change at all. Plato thinks they were both on to something, but also both incorrect. Heraclitus was right about the physical world of sense experience. Parmenides was right about the mental world of the Forms. The correct view is the one that combines both into a single vision of a dualistic reality.

What does any of this have to do with philosophers, and their being the only people who have knowledge? We're getting there! Consider yet another of Plato's allegories—perhaps his most famous: the *allegory of the cave*. It is worth quoting at length.

And now, I said, let me show in a figure how far our nature is enlightened or unenlightened:—Behold! human beings living in a underground den, which has a mouth open towards the light and reaching all along the den; here they have been from their childhood, and have their legs and necks chained so that they cannot move, and can only see before them, being prevented by the chains from turning round their heads. Above and behind them a fire is blazing at a distance, and between the fire and the prisoners there is a raised way; and you will see, if you look, a low wall built along the way, like the screen which marionette players have in front of them, over which they show the puppets.

I see.

And do you see, I said, men passing along the wall carrying all sorts of vessels, and statues and figures of animals made of wood and stone and various materials, which appear over the wall? Some of them are talking, others silent.

You have shown me a strange image, and they are strange prisoners.

Like ourselves, I replied; and they see only their own shadows, or the shadows of one another, which the fire throws on the opposite wall of the cave?

True, he said; how could they see anything but the shadows if they were never allowed to move their heads?

And of the objects which are being carried in like manner they would only see the shadows?

Yes, he said.

And if they were able to converse with one another, would they not suppose that they were naming what was actually before them?

Very true.

And suppose further that the prison had an echo which came from the other side, would they not be sure to fancy when one of the passers-by spoke that the voice which they heard came from the passing shadow?

No question, he replied.

To them, I said, the truth would be literally nothing but the shadows of the images.

That is certain.

And now look again, and see what will naturally follow if the prisoners are released and disabused of their error. At first, when any of them is liberated and compelled suddenly to stand up and turn his neck round and walk and look towards the light, he will suffer sharp pains; the glare will distress him, and he will be unable to see the realities of which in his former state he had seen the shadows; and then conceive some one saying to him, that what he saw before was an illusion, but that now, when he is approaching nearer to being and his eye is turned towards more real existence, he has a clearer vision,—what will be his reply? And you may further imagine that his instructor is pointing to the objects as they pass and requiring him to name them,—will he not be perplexed? Will he not fancy that the shadows which he formerly saw are truer than the objects which are now shown to him?

Far truer.

And if he is compelled to look straight at the light, will he not have a pain in his eyes which will make him turn away to take refuge in the objects of vision which he can see, and which he will conceive to be in reality clearer than the things which are now being shown to him?

True, he said.

And suppose once more, that he is reluctantly dragged up a steep and rugged ascent, and held fast until he is forced into the presence of the sun himself, is he not likely to be pained and irritated? When he approaches the light his eyes will be dazzled, and he will not be able to see anything at all of what are now called realities.

Not all in a moment, he said.

He will require to grow accustomed to the sight of the upper world. And first he will see the shadows best, next the reflections of men and other objects in the water, and then the objects themselves; then he will gaze upon the light of the moon and the stars and the spangled heaven; and he will see the sky and the stars by night better than the sun or the light of the sun by day?

Certainly.

Last of all he will be able to see the sun, and not mere reflections of him in the water, but he will see him in his own proper place, and not in another; and he will contemplate him as he is.

Certainly.

He will then proceed to argue that this is he who gives the season and the years, and is the guardian of all that is in the visible world, and in a certain way the cause of all things which he and his fellows have been accustomed to behold?

Clearly, he said, he would first see the sun and then reason about him.

And when he remembered his old habitation, and the wisdom of the den and his fellow-prisoners, do you not suppose that he would felicitate himself on the change, and pity them?

Certainly, he would.

And if they were in the habit of conferring honours among themselves on those who were quickest to observe the passing shadows and to remark which of them went before, and which followed after, and which were together; and who were therefore best able to draw conclusions as to the future, do you think that he would care for such honours and glories, or envy the possessors of them? Would he not say with Homer,

'Better to be the poor servant of a poor master,' and to endure anything, rather than think as they do and live after their manner?

Yes, he said, I think that he would rather suffer anything than entertain these false notions and live in this miserable manner.

Imagine once more, I said, such an one coming suddenly out of the sun to be replaced in his old situation; would he not be certain to have his eyes full of darkness?

To be sure, he said.

And if there were a contest, and he had to compete in measuring the shadows with the prisoners who had never moved out of the den, while his sight was still weak, and before his eyes had become steady (and the time which would be needed to acquire this new habit of sight might be very considerable), would he not be ridiculous? Men would say of him that up he went and down he came without his eyes; and that it was better not even to think of ascending; and if any one tried to loose another and lead him up to the light, let them only catch the offender, and they would put him to death (514a-517a).

It is impossible not to recall the trial and death of Socrates yet again. This allegory attempts to depict the plight of humanity. The vast majority of us are the prisoners in the cave. What we think is knowledge is just the shadowy reflections of copies of real things, symbolic of the mere opinions taught to us by those in positions of power and influence. The objects from which the shadows are cast still only copies of the real objects as they exist outside the cave. The shadows we see, then, are just copies of copies, at least two steps removed from truth. Those who parade these objects and cast the shadows before us are symbolic of illegitimate rulers. The philosopher is the prisoner who manages to break free, who ascends from the cave to behold things are they really are (i.e., who perceives the "Forms," and, who thereby alone has knowledge). Finally, the sun which illuminates those objects is the Form of the Good itself (to be discussed later). Not surprisingly, if the philosopher returns to the cave to explain things to the rest of the prisoners, he's going to sound "crazy," and will be persecuted—just as Socrates was. Also notice that the philosopher doesn't bring light to the cave, but tries to bring prisoners upward into the light.

Compelling as this allegory might be, we still don't have an explanation (beyond metaphor) as to why the philosopher really does have knowledge while the rest of us have mere opinion. This brings us back to the Forms. *Only

the Forms provide knowledge*. Particulars are those imperfect, temporary, changing copies of the Forms that we experience in the sensory world. In the allegory of the cave, particulars are represented by the shadows cast on the walls. The Forms are represented by the original, "real" objects found on the surface. Only the philosopher gets past the shadows to the real thing, only the philosopher gets a glimpse of the forms (by means of Reason, not sight, of course). Therefore, only the philosopher can acquire knowledge.

Another way to represent this is by means of his "*Divided Line*" (also worth quoting at length).

You have to imagine, then, that there are two ruling powers, and that one of them is set over the intellectual world, the other over the visible. I do not say heaven, lest you should fancy that I am playing upon the name ('ourhanoz, orhatoz'). May I suppose that you have this distinction of the visible and intelligible fixed in your mind?

I have.

Now take a line which has been cut into two unequal parts, and divide each of them again in the same proportion, and suppose the two main divisions to answer, one to the visible and the other to the intelligible, and then compare the subdivisions in respect of their clearness and want of clearness, and you will find that the first section in the sphere of the visible consists of images. And by images I mean, in the first place, shadows, and in the second place, reflections in water and in solid, smooth and polished bodies and the like: Do you understand?

Yes, I understand.

Imagine, now, the other section, of which this is only the resemblance, to include the animals which we see, and everything that grows or is made.

Very good.

Would you not admit that both the sections of this division have different degrees of truth, and that the copy is to the original as the sphere of opinion is to the sphere of knowledge?

Most undoubtedly.

Next proceed to consider the manner in which the sphere of the intellectual is to be divided.

In what manner?

Thus:—There are two subdivisions, in the lower of which the soul uses the figures given by the former division as images; the enquiry can only be hypothetical, and instead of going upwards to a principle descends to the other end; in the higher of the two, the soul passes out of hypotheses, and goes up to a principle which is above hypotheses, making no use of images as in the former case, but proceeding only in and through the ideas themselves.

I do not quite understand your meaning, he said.

Then I will try again; you will understand me better when I have made some preliminary remarks. You are aware that students of geometry, arithmetic, and the kindred sciences assume the odd and the even and the figures and three kinds of angles and the like in their several branches of science; these are their hypotheses, which they and every body are supposed to know, and therefore they do not deign to give any account of them either to themselves or others; but they begin with them, and go on until they arrive at last, and in a consistent manner, at their conclusion?

Yes, he said, I know.

And do you not know also that although they make use of the visible forms and reason about them, they are thinking not of these, but of the ideals which they resemble; not of the figures which they draw, but of the absolute square and the absolute diameter, and so on—the forms which they draw or make, and which have shadows and reflections in water of their own, are converted by them into images, but they are really seeking to behold the things themselves, which can only be seen with the eye of the mind?

That is true.

And of this kind I spoke as the intelligible, although in the search after it the soul is compelled to use hypotheses; not ascending to a first principle, because she is unable to rise above the region of hypothesis, but employing the objects of which the shadows below are resemblances in their turn as images, they having in relation to the shadows and reflections of them a greater distinctness, and therefore a higher value (509d-511a).

The Divided Line

Objects of Cognition	Kinds of Cognition
The Form of the Good	Direct Intuition
(Intelligible World)	*(Knowledge)*
The Forms	Intellection
Mathematical Objects	Thought
Visible Objects	Common Sense Belief
(Sensible World)	*(Opinions)*
Images	Imagination

On the left side of the line, we are dealing with metaphysics, the nature of reality. The "higher" up one goes, the more "real" something is. On the right side of the line, we are dealing with epistemology. The higher up one goes, the closer one is to knowledge. The upper portion of the figure represents the intelligible world (the world of the Forms), while the lower portion represents the physical world (the world of the senses). Starting with the metaphysical side, at the very bottom we have mere images. These would include shadows, reflections, dreams, mirages, etc. They have some "reality," but are faint copies of other, more real, things. Above images, but still part of the physical world, we have all visible things—the objects we encounter by means of our senses. A statue is "more real" than its shadow, in this sense.

As we continue to ascend, we go beyond the physical world and enter the world of ideas, the Forms. We encounter mathematical objects, which are not physical, but are "real," and that provide the structure and reality to their physical counterparts. Above mathematical objects are the Forms themselves, our concepts of all the things we encounter in the physical world. *At the very peak of reality is the Form of the Good itself, that which gives reality and understanding to everything "beneath" it.*

On the right side of the line, we are dealing with epistemology, the nature of belief and knowledge. At the very bottom we have imagining, conjecture, and general ignorance. Above mere conjecture we have common sense beliefs, beliefs for which we are confident and that might even be true. As we continue to ascend we go beyond the world of the senses and enter the intelligible realm. We encounter abstract reasoning, and then finally reach direct intuition (pure "perception") of the Forms. Knowledge.

The ascent up the divided line mirrors the ascent out of the cave. In each case, the "higher" one goes, the more "real" are the things one encounters, and the closer one gets to knowledge. The philosopher is the one who has managed to climb out of the cave, who has moved beyond mere appearances and "common sense" and glimpsed the Forms, including the Form of the Good itself.

The Form of the Good is, well, a bit weird. The Form of the Good is represented by the Sun (507c-509b). The Sun is what the philosopher sees when he has emerged from the cave. It illuminates all the other objects (Forms), and is "higher" than them. Just what the Form of the Good *is* though is probably not altogether clear. Using our everyday sense of "good" in a moral context, it might be confused with other forms, such as justice, or piety, or generosity. But, if all such traits have their own Forms, what is left over for the Form of the Good itself?

A Form is the universal that gives unity to particulars. "Piety," for example, is the property which all pious acts or persons share in. The Form of piety is the absolute best with regards to piousness, because it is the yardstick against which all pious acts are measured, and that which gives meaning to piety in the first place. Procedurally, we observe many things that we call pious, and then we identify their common feature in order to intuit the Form of piety itself. With regard to the Forms, we observe many things (Form of piety, Form of circularity, etc.) that we call Forms. They appear to have something in common—namely, their "Form-ness." *The Form of the Good is, for lack of a better expression, the Form of Form-ness itself.* But, because Forms are the "best" of whatever they represent, the Form of Form-ness is the property of being best—the Form of "The Good."

This is, admittedly, an unusual use of the term "good." Later thinkers, such as Plotinus, would make the Form of the Good into a divine principle, and Christian theologians (such as St. Augustine) would claim that what Plato calls the Form of the Good is actually God. Plato himself, though, had no such anthropomorphic vision in mind. The Form of the Good is not a person, but an abstract entity—the Form of Form-ness (best-ness, Good-ness) itself.

Those who "see" the Form of the Good are those who have attained the highest level of philosophical abstraction. If it's impressive to ascend from the "shadows" or mere imaginings and opinion to knowledge of things are they really are (Forms), how much more impressive to have ascended higher still (the highest, in fact), to understand the Form that informs all the other Forms? Philosophers have glimpsed the "highest" degrees of both reality and knowledge, at this point—but it's no wonder that when they return to the cave to tell the rest of the prisoners about it, they're regarded as crazy. . . .

"Craziness" aside, imagine that the Republic (or a close approximation) to it, could be founded. Plato imagines and explains how such a State could decline through various inferior forms of government, and in so doing possibly provides clues as to how to prevent such a decline.

The ideal Republic is a sort of aristocratic meritocracy in which an elite, superior, wise, and virtuous few rule for the sake of the common good, and maintain social harmony. To continue with the state-individual analogy, a corresponding individual is one who is ruled by reason, and whose inner life is harmonious and well-regulated, much as the life of the Republic is disciplined and well-regulated, with each class following the principle of specialization.

Should the principle of specialization not be followed, however, there will be widespread societal ramifications [Although the analogy between the State and the individual implies that there is a corresponding "degeneration" for types of individuals, as well as for States, given the emphasis of this book, we will focus only on the types of governments, and their degeneration].

Society	Mental Trait	Reason for Decline
Aristocratic Meritocracy	"regal," reason, moral, harmonious	Conflict, envy, loss of PS (547b-548b)
Timocracy	"timarchic," competitive, passionate	Greed, wealth (550d-551b)
Oligarchy/ Plutocracy	"oligarchic," thrifty, ascetic	Corruption, envious revolution (555c-557a)
Democracy	"democratic," ruled by unnecessary desires	Corrupt "champion of the people" (565d-567d)
Dictatorship	"dictatorial," frenzied, maniacal	

As stated, the ideal Republic is an aristocratic meritocracy in which people are sorted into their proper class by adhering to the principle of specialization, and harmony is maintained so long as each class performs its proper function. Should the PS be abandoned, or be insufficiently enforced, the Republic will degenerate into a lower form of State.

How does this happen? Any meritocracy has the innate tendency to cease to be a meritocracy within a single generation.

Imagine a utopia in which only the very best, most-suitable and talented people become leaders in politics and business. The very best and brightest among us become wealthy and powerful as a result, and, arguably, they deserve it. And then they have children….

The children of these wealthy, powerful, best and brightest, will start out life with an undeniable advantage over their peers. There is no guarantee, however, that those qualities that made their parents the "best and brightest," will be inherited by those children. For example, the hotel magnate Conrad Hilton (1887–1979) was arguably a skilled and hard-working businessman. His children and their descendants (literally) inherited the wealth and influence he acquired by virtue of his skills and character. His great grand-daughter is Paris Hilton, known more for her scandals and her "famous-for-being-famous" antics than much else—and his great grand-son (Conrad Hughes Hilton—named after him, no less!) was arrested by the FBI for disrupting a British Airways flight in 2014. He (allegedly) threatened flight attendants, saying "I could get you all fired in five minutes. I know your boss. My father will pay this out, he has done it before. Dad paid $300,000 last time."[51] He also vowed to "own anyone on this flight" and referred to the passengers as "peasants."

The point of this is not to disparage any particular person or family, but merely to point out there is no magical guarantee that "greatness" is automatically transmitted to one's

---

[51]http://www.latimes.com/local/lanow/la-me-ln-paris-hilton-conrad-hilton-charged-20150203-story.html

descendants. In order to maintain a genuine meritocracy, there must a constant sorting, filtering, and redistributing to make sure that only the "best" remain at the "top," and that each person performs the task to which they are best-suited—no matter who their mother or father happened to be.

This is precisely what is *supposed* to happen in the *Republic*, of course. But, the human beings living within and (in some cases) ruling the Republic are human beings, after all. It might be overly tempting to a Guardian to make sure his or her own child be raised up a Guardian as well, even if that child properly should be placed in the Producer class. It's possible that some Producers or Auxiliaries might covet the power that Guardians wield, and maneuver to somehow change their station—or perhaps facilitate their children doing so. Perhaps either Guardians or Auxiliaries will come to covet the greater wealth (and personal possessions!) allowed to the Producers, and will desire to have a nice (private) home, and the ability to throw parties too.

For any of these reasons the POS might cease to be followed, and some of the *wrong* people start ruling the society. Because they aren't *properly* Guardians, they are motivated not solely (or even primarily) by the public good, but are motivated instead by wealth or power, they begin to change the laws and policies of the Republic—by allowing Guardians to acquire wealth and property, for example. This new kind of society rewards ambition and "spiritedness," and it is those previously sorted into the Auxiliary class who come to power. The result is no longer an aristocratic meritocracy, but a "timocracy."

A timocracy (of which Sparta was an example) is a government ruled by the warrior class, and, not surprisingly, emphasizing "warrior" traits. He supposes that Auxiliaries (now rulers) will look down on Producers, and mistrust Guardians. They will also desire to accumulate wealth to accompany their power. While they might have courage in abundance, these new rulers lack wisdom and moderation.

Because of the pleasure derived from accumulating and spending wealth, money comes to be valued more than virtue, and laws and customs are changed once again to favor the accumulation of wealth—but specifically in ways that favor their own class, and that restrict political power to the wealthy only. When this happens, the timocracy degenerates into an oligarchy.

An oligarchy (or plutocracy) is the rule of a wealthy elite. A report released in 2014 by researchers from Princeton and Northwestern Universities concluded that, on the basis of objective measures, the United States is not actually a democracy, but an oligarchy. "The central point that emerges from our research is that economic elites and organised groups representing business interests have substantial independent impacts on US government policy, while mass-based interest groups and average citizens have little or no independent influence."[52] Laws and policies do not generally reflect the will of the "people" so much as the will of wealthy corporate interests and other influential groups. "When a majority of citizens disagrees with economic elites and/or with organized interests, they generally lose. Moreover, because of the strong status quo bias built into the US political system, even when fairly large majorities of Americans favour policy change, they generally do not get it."

Setting aside the proper classification of the United States, Plato's critique of oligarchies, in general, is consistent with his emphasis on the POS, in general. When the poor are excluded from rulership, regardless of merit, people who should rule, don't. When the rich are empowered to rule, regardless of merit, people who shouldn't rule, do.

As of 2012, the median net worth for lawmakers in the U.S. House and Senate was just

---

[52] http://journals.cambridge.org/download.php?file=%2FPPS%2FPPS12_03%2FS15375927

14001595a.pdf&code=a7337ff4942bb8b23f42f347c677729f

over $1 million.[53] Incoming Congressional "freshmen" had a net worth that was exactly $1 million *more* than the average American household.[54] While it is possible that wealth and fitness for rulership correlate, this is by no means an obvious truth—and a system that reserves rulership exclusively for the wealthy makes precisely that controversial assumption.

Plato predicts that the increasing gap between the wealthy and the rest of the society will produce class divisions and tension. As of 2012, conflict between the rich and the poor surpassed conflict on the basis of race or immigration status as being the greatest source of tension in American society.[55] The poor, Plato predicts, increasingly desperate and resentful, will develop a revolutionary spirit that will threaten the internal stability of the society. Should a revolution actually occur, and the poor overthrow the rich (probably seizing and dividing their property, as was the case in the French Revolution and numerous Communist revolutions), a "democracy" is established."

In Plato's ranking, democracy is the second-worst form of government, second only to a dictatorship. "What could be so bad about democracy?" you might wonder.

Plato has several "problems" with democracy. For one, democracy seems to presuppose that we are all equally suited to govern, and this flies in the face of the basic idea behind the principle of specialization. According to the POS, we are *not* all equally suited to do *anything*. Just as some people are better suited for combat, and others better suited for trades, so too are some of us better suited to rule. If rulership is a skill like another, it is just plain false that we are all qualified to participate in rulership. Given the incredibly high stakes of rulership (i.e., the very well-being of the community itself!), Plato would think it both misguided and dangerous to set aside the POS.

In addition, it's important to note that Plato's usage of "democracy" might be different from your own. He is not referring to some sort of idealistic system in which each person freely and equally participates in political decision-making in the mutual pursuit of life, liberty, and happiness (though he would have reservations about that, as well, given his emphasis on the POS). Instead, the "democracy" to which Plato refers is more like anarchic mob rule. Plato thought that democracy led to the pursuit of excessive freedom, and this ultimately resulted in anarchy.

"Freedom" is the supreme value in this system, but this freedom is unchecked by virtue or even laws. People wantonly pursue their own desires and self-interests. When we are all "equal" (i.e., where each is thought to have both an equal right and an equal capacity to rule), the result is that we pursue power and personal benefit, rather than the public good. In other words, democracy lends itself to corruption. The resulting lack of discipline causes society to descend deeper and deeper into chaos, until a powerful individual seizes power in the name of order and security. A dictatorship is born.

The lowest form of government, a dictatorship is the tyrannical rule of a single individual who originally claimed power in the name of the "people," but quickly rules for his own benefit instead.

History has provided us real-world candidates for each of the government types Plato proposes. The primary difference between them lies in who is ruling, and for whom (and for what) they are ruling. This method of classification will be revived by Plato's most famous student, Aristotle, in a later chapter. For Plato, however, the Republic represents not only the ideal society, but the ideal type of person—the only types, in each case, where justice is fully actualized.

---

[53] http://www.nytimes.com/2014/01/10/us/politics/more-than-half-the-members-of-congress-are-millionaires-analysis-finds.html?_r=0

[54] http://www.usnews.com/news/articles/2013/01/18/the-five-poorest-us-senators
[55] http://www.nytimes.com/2012/01/12/us/more-conflict-seen-between-rich-and-poor-survey-finds.html

Justice

Much more detail is possible with regard to the account of the ideal State (and various supporting ideas) in the *Republic*, but for our purposes the current detail is sufficient, and we shall finally begin to connect this attempt at political philosophy to the basic analogy with the human soul which is supposed to have inspired all this State-building in the first place.

> But in reality justice was such as we were describing, being concerned however, not with the outward man, but with the inward, which is the true self and concernment of man: for the just man does not permit the several elements within him to interfere with one another, or any of them to do the work of others,— he sets in order his own inner life, and is his own master and his own law, and at peace with himself; and when he has bound together the three principles within him, which may be compared to the higher, lower, and middle notes of the scale, and the intermediate intervals— when he has bound all these together, and is no longer many, but has become one entirely temperate and perfectly adjusted nature, then he proceeds to act, if he has to act, whether in a matter of property, or in the treatment of the body, or in some affair of politics or private business; always thinking and calling that which preserves and co-operates with this harmonious condition, just and good action, and the knowledge which presides over it, wisdom, and that which at any time impairs this condition, he will call unjust action, and the opinion which presides over it ignorance.

> You have said the exact truth, Socrates.

> Very good; and if we were to affirm that we had discovered the just man and the just State, and the nature of justice in each

> of them, we should not be telling a falsehood?

> Most certainly not.

> May we say so, then?

> Let us say so.

> And now, I said, injustice has to be considered.

> Clearly.

> Must not injustice be a strife which arises among the three principles—a meddlesomeness, and interference, and rising up of a part of the soul against the whole, an assertion of unlawful authority, which is made by a rebellious subject against a true prince, of whom he is the natural vassal,—what is all this confusion and delusion but injustice, and intemperance and cowardice and ignorance, and every form of vice (443d-444b)?

Remember that, in the community, there are three classes and people are assigned to the class for which they are properly suited. For the good of the community, Producers should not perform the tasks of Guardians, nor vice versa. *A "just" State is one in which each class is successfully fulfilling its proper function.* Socrates is advancing a view of justice, then, that translates to something like "internal harmony." An unjust State, by contrast, is one that lacks such harmonious integration. Justice (internal harmony) is a virtue in the State because the proper arrangement of its parts makes its citizens good (to the extent such is possible).

We can say the same of the individual soul. *A just soul is one whose parts are in harmony.* Each class has a role to fulfill, just as each part of the soul has a role to fulfill. Each class has a virtue that corresponds to its own proper functioning, just as each part of the soul has its own virtue. Justice, for both the community and the individual, is when each part is virtuous and fulfilling its proper function.

Virtue	Part of the Soul	Manifestation in the Community
Wisdom	Reason	Thoughtful/resourceful care by the Guardians (428d)
Courage	Spirit/Passion	Lawful bravery of the Auxiliaries (429d)
Temperance	Appetite/Desire	Obedience of the Producers (431a-c)
Justice	Proper harmony among three parts	Following the principle of specialization

Justice in the individual soul is understood as internal harmony. This organization makes a person good because it emphasizes and exercises reason (paradigmatically, when contemplating the Forms). When reason rules the soul, based on its knowledge of the Forms—particularly the Form of the Good—the individual's life is arranged so as to promote reason and the Good. When we understand justice (morality) as "harmony," in this sense, one of the most basic and important questions of ethics has an answer. The question is "why be moral?" The answer is as obvious as is the answer to the question "why be healthy?"

Still our old question of the comparative advantage of justice and injustice has not been answered: Which is the more profitable, to be just and act justly and practise virtue, whether seen or unseen of gods and men, or to be unjust and act unjustly, if only unpunished and unreformed?

In my judgment, Socrates, the question has now become ridiculous. We know that, when the bodily constitution is gone, life is no longer endurable, though pampered with all kinds of meats and drinks, and having all wealth and all power; and shall we be told that when the very essence of the vital principle is undermined and corrupted, life is still worth having to a man, if only he be allowed to do whatever he likes with the single exception that he is not to acquire justice and virtue, or to escape from injustice and vice; assuming them both to be such as we have described (445a-b)?

Justice is a sort of health for the soul. Injustice is a sort of sickness. When we act rightly, we nurture the rational part of our soul (589b). When we act immorally, we feed the appetitive part of the soul, which Socrates likens to a many-headed monster (589a). In the State, the role of education and law is to provide external constraints on the "monster," if necessary (590d-591b).

That a healthy soul is preferable to an unhealthy one should be as apparent as a healthy body being preferable to an unhealthy body. The practical value of philosophy is evident: philosophy is the means by which we "ascend" out of the "cave," acquire knowledge, and achieve harmony in our soul. The challenge that Glaucon (and Adeimantus) had set before Socrates was to demonstrate not only the nature of justice, but also why justice is to be preferred for its own sake, and over injustice. This is Socrates' answer to that challenge, as presented by Plato.

The Laws

The entirety of this chapter, thus far, has focused on the account of justice and vision of political philosophy that Plato articulates in the *Republic*. As mentioned at the beginning of the chapter, however, the *Republic* was not Plato's only contribution to political philosophy, nor was it his last. Indeed, the *Laws* was written later, and was considered unfinished at the time of Plato's death.

We will not consider the *Laws* in detail or at length. Instead, we will consider a very brief overview of some basic ideas, focusing primarily on how the *Laws* relates to the *Republic*.

Although there remains some scholarly debate, the generally predominant view amongst Plato scholars is that while the *Republic* is a statement of the ideally best State, the *Laws* is a more practical concession to what is best among what is actually feasible. The radical assumptions and demands made by the *Republic* were recognized as possibly unrealistic even within the text of the *Republic* itself. As an example, in the *Republic*, the Guardians and Auxiliaries have no personal property, nor do they even have their own spouses or children.

> That State and polity come first, and those laws are best, where there is observed as carefully as possible throughout the whole State the old saying that "friends have all things really in common." As to this condition,—whether it anywhere exists now, or ever will exist,—in which there is community of wives, children, and all chattels, and all that is called "private" is everywhere and by every means rooted out of our life, and so far as

possible it is contrived that even things naturally "private" have become in a way "communized"...[56]

This describes what is actually promoted in the *Republic*, suggesting that the model in the *Republic* is the "best." Within the *Laws*, though, second and even third best options are offered, and the details of the city-state as regards private property aligns with the "second best" option. This lends itself to the very reasonable interpretation that the city-state sketched out in the *Laws* is presented as a more modest (though still idealistic!), and therefore more realistic, alternative.[57]

As was the case with the *Republic*, the *Laws* is written as a dialogue—although Socrates no longer appears as the protagonist but has been replaced by the "Athenian Stranger" (thought to represent Plato himself). The other two participants are Kleinias (from Crete) and Megillus (from Sparta). Kleinias is to found a new colony, and the conversation between the three concerns how best to structure the government and laws of this new city-state.

The central goal of the *Republic* was internal harmony (achieved via the Principle of Specialization), and a similar unity of purpose is desired and pursued in the *Laws*. "That is to say, we should state that he enacted laws with an eye not to some one fraction, and that the most paltry, of goodness, but to goodness as a whole"[58]

Although the city-state will be brand-new, there is no pretense that the citizens can be convinced of a "noble lie" (as was proposed in the *Republic*). No invented mythology will offer reason for their union and camaraderie, and it is presumed that they will arrive at their new city-state with both memories and material

---

[56] *Laws*, Book 5, 739b-c.

[57] Another interpretation of the "second-best" label attached to the *Laws* is that, in the *Republic*, there are no codified laws, per se. Instead, philosopher kings (Guardians) rule by enlightened fiat. In the *Laws*, however, the "eternal" laws of the "Forms" come down to Earth, and are recorded as legislation to be

followed. The only "philosophy" that takes place occurs in the public "preludes" meant as arguments in favor of the laws. This demotion of philosophizing to a supporting role for laws is "second-best," according to some scholars, such as Ernest Baker.

[58] *Laws*, Book 1, 630e.

possessions intact.

The land of this new city-state will be divided into 5,040 equal plots, and given (permanently) to each colonist and his heirs. The owners will not be permitted to either sell off all (or any portion) of their land, nor acquire any additional land. In this way, some measure of equality will be maintained, and massive differences in wealth will be prevented since no family will be allowed to accumulate more land, and none can be without their family plot. Indeed, there is a strict cap on accumulated wealth in that no citizen will be allowed to acquire any more than four times the natural wealth of his land. Any wealth generated beyond that will be placed into a common fund. Although, technically, this plot is allotted to the family in question, it is officially still the common-property of the city-state itself, and all members will be expected to contribute from their land to the common good (and will be supported by their community, as needed).

The ostensive point of this strict regulation of wealth and property is to prevent class divisions, envy, and conflict. This is not to say that there will be difference amongst persons, nor any classes within the city-state, however. There will be four classes of citizens, based on their wealth. The first class has wealth worth between 3 and 4 times the value of their plot of land. The second class has wealth worth between 2 and 3 times the value of their plot. The third class has wealth worth between 1 and 2 times the value of their plot—with the lowest class having wealth equal to their plot. There is general equality between men and women (as was the case in the *Republic*), and marriages are to be arranged in the interest of the common good (rather than personal preference—also like the *Republic*).

In addition to the 5,040 families/citizens, there will be many resident-foreigners allowed to live and work within the city-state. They will not be allowed to own land, nor participate in politics, but will instead work in trade and other money-making endeavors. A large population of slaves (considered property, not citizens) will do most of the physical/menial labor, allowing the citizens to have as much leisure time as possible, that they might attend to the important affairs of the city-state, and participate in political activities.

A notable difference between the *Laws* and the *Republic* is the greater role allowed to (and greater demands placed upon) each citizen. Recall that in the *Republic*, only the Guardian class had only political decision-making power (or responsibility). Everyone else was either a soldier (Auxiliary), or Producer. As of the *Laws*, however, each citizen (theoretically) has the right and responsibility to participate in the political process, to some degree. The result is that rather than a "meritocratic aristocracy" advocated in the *Republic*, we have a mix of aristocracy and democracy. The political structure of the fledgling city-state will include the following:

- The General Assembly: consisting of all citizens who are serving (or who have served) in the military. They elect most of the city's officers and magistrates, as well as judging public offenses and giving rewards of merit.

- The Guardians of the Laws: an elite group of 37 citizens who must be at least fifty years old when elected, and serve from the time of their election until the age of seventy. These Guardians supervise magistrates, exercise control over citizens in the form of fines for those who spend excessively, and by overseeing foreign travel requests. They exercise judicial authority over "difficult" or especially important trials. Finally, and perhaps most importantly, they are tasked with revising and supplementing the initial founding laws, as needed.

- The Council: 360 citizens, composed of 90 citizens elected from each of the four social classes to serve one-year terms. They are responsible for supervising elections, calling and dissolving the Assembly, and receiving foreign ambassadors.

- Miscellaneous selected Officials: Generals, Judges, Priests, and Regulators who fulfill various other functions.

- The Nocturnal Council: perhaps ominous-sounding, the "Nocturnal Council" (so-called because they will meet in the hour before dawn) is a group of the ten oldest Guardians, their selected "interns" (who must be at least 30 years or older), and a handful of especially distinguished/decorated citizens, and is responsible for making sure that the city-state and its laws consistently aims at virtue.[59]

The "Athenian" (i.e., Plato) claims that virtue (i.e., courage, moderation, wisdom, and justice) ought to be the goal of the lawgivers. Indeed, "every legislator who is worth his salt will most assuredly legislate always with a single eye to the highest goodness and to that alone"[60] Laws are only *true* laws when they have the *eudaimonia* (flourishing) of their citizens as their goal.[61] Quite *consistent* with the *Republic* is the notion, presented in the *Laws*, that there is an ideal against which the actual may be evaluated. "Ideally," the best ruler a city-state could have is a god. In actuality, it's unlikely that Apollo or Zeus will personally rule this newly founded city-state, but, fortunately, Reason is presented as the immortal/godly element within us all. Therefore, a city-state ruled by Reason is the next best thing to being ruled by a god. Laws consistent with Reason, then, are the only laws worthy of being called laws. There is no mistaking this: Reason provides the *physis* (nature) against which laws will be judged. In the nature v. convention debate, Plato once again comes down firmly on the side of nature.

Conclusion

It is difficult to overstate Plato's significance in the history of Western philosophy. In a very

real sense he "did it all," and, in a meaningful sense, much of philosophy since Plato has been a reaction to what he produced whether as elaboration or rejection and criticism. Plato's dualistic understanding of reality ("physical" v. "spiritual," "body v. "soul") as well as his clear hierarchy ("spiritual" over "physical," "soul" over "body") exerted profound influence on Christian thought once St. Augustine had "Christianized" Plato. His thorough treatment of epistemology, his quest for enlightenment depicted throughout his dialogues, and his discussion of the individual v. the collective, among others, have continued to be characteristic of philosophy ever since.

Plato's political philosophy is based off a premise that factionalism and division are the greatest dangers to the city-state—more dangerous even than war and foreign threats. He argued that genuine social harmony and political stability can't be achieved by one class or faction subduing others and "winning" for the sake of their own cause, but instead that lasting peace is better achieved through genuine cooperation and friendship of all factions within the city-state.[62] To promote internal harmony, he offers enlightened rule by philosopher kings in the *Republic*, but as of the *Laws* he tries to achieve that same harmony by turning to a more traditional polity, consisting of a mixed constitution including elements of oligarchy, aristocracy, and democracy. This sort of mixed polity is precisely what will be advocated by Plato's student, Aristotle, as we will see in our next chapter.

---

[59] The precise role and scope of power of this Nocturnal Council is subject to debate, ranging from interpretations according to which they are the true wielders of power, serving the same role as the Philosopher Kings in the Republic, to a more modest interpretation according to which they are merely wise and respected advisors.

[60] *Laws*, Book 1, 630c.
[61] Ibid., 631b.
[62] See, for example, *Republic* 462a-b and *Laws* 628a-b. This concern with internal stability will be a recurring theme over the next couple millennia, and will be revisited in a much later chapter when we turn to the work of John Rawls

Chapter 4: Aristotle & Politics

Comprehension questions you should be able to answer after reading this chapter:

1. What are Aristotle's four kinds of "cause," and what is an example for each?

2. What does each of the following mean? *Telos, areté, eudaimonia.*

3. How does one become virtuous, according to Aristotle? Be sure to include a discussion of the Golden Mean.

4. What is "*phronesis*," and what is its relationship to the Golden Mean?

5. What does it mean to say that the *Politics* is part of the same project as the *Nicomachean Ethics*?

6. What is a "*polis*," and how is it different from a mere "State?"

7. What does Aristotle mean when he says humans are "naturally" political?

8. Why would the United States (arguably) not be considered a *polis*?

9. How do the four kinds of "causes" identified in #1 above apply to the *polis*?

10. Explain Aristotle's defense of "natural slavery."

11. In what ways do both oligarchies and democracies have mistaken understandings of the proper *telos* of the *polis*?

12. What is a polity/mixed-constitution, and how is it a "second-best" constitution?

12. Explain Aristotle's favoring of the middle-class, in a polity.

If all philosophy is a "footnote to Plato," something equally clever should be coined for his most celebrated student, Aristotle. Aristotle was so revered as a philosopher that St. Thomas Aquinas referred to him simply as "The Philosopher" within his own works. Indeed, Aquinas' efforts at "Christianizing" Aristotle revolutionized Christian theology and brought about a renaissance of interest in Aristotle.

Aristotle lived from 384 BCE to 323 BCE. At around the age of 18, he began studying under Plato. He studied and taught at Plato's Academy until the time of Plato's death, when curriculum disagreements between Aristotle and Plato's successor to head the Academy (Plato's own nephew, Speussipus) inspired Aristotle to split from the Academy. There might also have been a bit of resentment involved, as Aristotle had been a strong candidate for the position as well.

Aristotle took on the job of tutor to no less a youth than Alexander the Great. He eventually opened his own school (the *Lyceum*) and his followers became known as "Peripatetics," due to their habit of walking the gardens (*peripatoi* = covered walk) while having their deep philosophical conversations.

Aristotle favored an empirical approach to knowledge (in contrast to his mentor, Plato). That is, the source of knowledge will be data collected from sense experience. Correctly interpreted, this will provide theoretical as well as scientific knowledge. As an example of his dedication to this method, he spent several years studying marine organisms, in effect inventing what we now know as the discipline of marine biology.

He was confident that from observations of particular things, we could gain insight into universal concepts. For example, to gain insight into politics, in general, he studied the particular constitutions of 158 existing states. As another example, we thought that we could learn about morality, in general, by studying actual people and how they behave.

It is no coincidence that I mention ethics and political philosophy at the same time, with regard to Aristotle: he saw them as parts of the same exploration of moral theory. Indeed, the content of the *Politics* was seen, by Aristotle, as a continuation of the *Nicomachean Ethics*. For that reason, we will spend what might seem like a surprising amount of time (for a book on political philosophy) building the ethical foundations offered in the *Nicomachean Ethics*, before moving on to "official" political theory. This is not merely for the sake of trivia, but is necessary in order to properly understand the stance Aristotle takes with regards to political institutions.

Aristotle did not limit himself to ethics, politics, and marine biology. If it existed as a subject of inquiry, he pursued it. A "renaissance man" a millennia and a half before the Renaissance, Aristotle studied and wrote about physics, "metaphysics," poetry, theater and music, logic and rhetoric and linguistics, politics and government, ethics, biology, and zoology.

Given the specific focus of this book, we will spend little time on Aristotle's metaphysics, except with respect to some ideas that will be directly relevant to our understanding of his political/ethical theory, beginning with his concept of "causation." Aristotle provides us with *four* different notions of "cause."

1. Material cause
2. Efficient cause
3. Formal cause
4. Final cause

A thing's Material cause is its matter, the raw materials of which it is made. Using the example of a statue, its Material cause is marble (or whatever kind of stone the sculptor used).

An Efficient cause is a thing's origin—the process responsible for it being what it is. In the case of the statue, its Efficient cause is the sculptor and her tools.

The Formal cause is a thing's essence, the governing idea giving it its structure and form. For the statue, its Formal cause is the vision of the completed sculpture entertained by the sculptor.

Finally, we have the Final cause. The Final cause is the end or purpose ("telos") that the thing is to fulfill. With the statue, perhaps its Final cause is to depict the likeness of Aristotle.

Two terms mentioned just now deserve a bit more explanation: Form/essence and Matter.

The "matter" of a substance is the material of which it is composed, and that which distinguishes one particular thing from another (even if they share the same essence). For example, two different cats are both understood in terms of their "catness" (essence), but what makes them two different cats is they don't share the same matter. Putting the metaphysical vocabulary aside, this is a pretty simple idea. Form and matter are each indispensable aspects of any and every thing. You can't separate them. There is no such thing (for Aristotle) as a form without matter (some sort of disembodied, abstract essence), nor is there any such thing as formless matter.

The "form" of a substance is its essence, that which makes it what it is, and not something else. Each substance must be understood in terms of its essence. We understand tables in terms of their "tableness," dogs in terms of their "dogness," and people in terms of their "humanness." A dog's essence is what makes it a dog rather than a cat. Alter a thing's essence, and it is no longer that same thing, but something else.

The essence of each kind of substance includes its "inner drive" to develop in a certain kind of way, to actualize its potential. For example, part of the essence of an acorn is its *telos* (Final cause)—namely, to become an oak tree. All things have a "*telos*" relating to their essence. The *telos* of an acorn is to become an oak tree, the *telos* of a knife is to cut. Human beings also have an essence, and a potential to actualize.

To understand the essence of humans, and our *telos*, we have to understand Aristotle's different categories of soul (I know, we're diverting into quite a lot of ancient philosophy, but trust me—his ethics will make much more sense thanks to these details).

Don't think that Aristotle is getting religious when he discusses souls. As a biologist, his understanding of "souls" was naturalistic. A soul was not some sort of spirit that flies away and goes to Heaven when the body dies. Instead, for living things, the soul just was the "essence" (form) of that kind of living thing. Because there is no such thing as form apart from matter, Aristotle's notion of the soul is not anything that could somehow survive the death of the body. That would literally make no sense to him.

There are three basic kinds of souls: vegetative, animal, and rational. Vegetative souls (sometimes called nutritive souls) are the essences of different kinds of plants. Vegetative souls make possible growth and nourishment. Anything capable of growth, therefore, can be understood in terms of a vegetative soul. Some living things are capable of more than growth, though.

Animals, unlike plants, are also capable of perception, motion, and expression. An animal soul, then, is the kind of essence that makes such things possible. Animals, therefore, are to be understood in terms of both animal and vegetative souls, whereas plants are understood only in terms of vegetative souls.

Finally, some living things (e.g., humans) are capable of more than growth, motion, perception, and expression. We are also capable of thinking, judging, and belief-formation—in short, Reason. Rational souls make this possible. Humans, then, (exclusively, according to Aristotle) have aspects of all three types.

Since a thing's potential is determined by its essence, and a thing's *telos* is determined by its potential, our own *telos* (our Final cause) is likewise determined by our essence, by the kind of thing that we are. Since that which makes humans distinctly human, and different from every other living thing, is our capacity for Reason, it should come as no surprise that Reason will play a significant role in our *telos.* Once again, the practical benefit of philosophy is clear: philosophical contemplation is not only the means by which we can understand our *telos,* but,

as the highest use of Reason, is the clearest expression of a fully actualized human being.

In addition to each thing having a *telos* (an end, a purpose), each thing has an "excellence" (in Greek, *"areté")* that serves that *telos.* Just like the *telos,* a thing's *areté* is likewise based on its essence, and is that by which we evaluate the quality of the thing with regard to its *telos.* That might sound complicated, but it's really fairly simple. A knife's *telos* is to cut. Its *areté* will be that which makes it excellent with regard to cutting. "Sharpness" seems like a pretty good candidate for its *areté*! The *telos* of an eyeball is to see. An eyeball's *areté*, then, will be that which makes it excellent with regard to seeing. An ophthalmologist could surely discuss this better than I, but I would assume that the overall shape of the eye, the transparency of its lens (e.g., not having any cataracts), and other such things would constitute the *areté* of an eyeball. The example that will matter to us, of course, is that of a human being. What is our *telos*? What is our *areté*?

Aristotle, like many ancient philosophers, believed that the ultimate "end" in life, life's ultimate goal and purpose, was *"eudaimonia."* This is sometimes translated as happiness, but that's misleading. To render it "happiness" suggests that *eudaimonia* is a feeling, or, worse yet, that's it's just a fancy Greek word for pleasure. Not so. *Eudaimonia* is better translated as *"flourishing."* It refers to an overall quality of one's life. Thus, one is not "*eudaimon*" on Monday, but not so much on Tuesday. It is one's whole life that is either "*eudaimon*," or not.

There are several ways to try to capture the meaning of a life that is "*eudaimon*." Some of them have become cliché's, but they'll suffice. Realizing your potential. Being fully alive. Thriving. Success (as a person). Being all you can be. Exemplifying what it is to be human.

Why is *eudaimonia* our *telos*? Because all other "ends" have only instrumental value. That is, we pursue them for the sake of something else. Success, for its own sake? Wealth, for its own sake? A good reputation, for its own sake? Education, for its own sake? All these things are valuable, to be sure, and certainly worthy of attainment, but for each of them there is an implicit "because." Wealth is desirable because it enables one to live comfortably, and to pursue the things important to her. Education is valuable because it better allows us to understand ourselves, and the world.

But what about *eudaimonia*? This rich notion of "happiness" involving one's entire being, culminating in a truly excellent life? Because? Just because, it seems. Aristotle thought that eudaimonia was intrinsically valuable, pursued for its own sake—the ultimate "end" to which all other worthy ends point.

Assuming Aristotle is right about that, what it means for a human to flourish will be defined by a human's essence. Reason is uniquely human, so our flourishing must involve Reason, a life in which our behavior and our character is determined and governed by Reason rather than our appetites. For Aristotle, this is what it means to be virtuous.

Virtue will be the most important ingredient in a life that is *eudaimon*. Without it, *eudaimonia* will be impossible. With it, *eudaimonia* is not guaranteed, but virtue is the most reliable means to a life that is *eudaimon*. Aristotle recognized that other factors, admittedly often beyond our control, influence our ability to flourish. For Aristotle, these other factors included political stability, wealth, beauty, reputation, having a good family, having good friends, and other similar "goods."

For many of us, some of the elements of this list seem unfair, or even outrageous—but on reflection I don't think Aristotle's claim are all that controversial. Being wealthy certainly doesn't guarantee an excellent character (and, in fact, it can be an obstacle to it for some people), but being desperately poor probably doesn't help either! Sick people can certainly have excellent character, and illness can often be a means to developing courage, patience, and other virtues. However, a life wracked with pain and suffering can hardly be called an *excellent* life. Beauty? Let's face it: attractive people have an easier time in life. That might be unfair, but it seems to be true. If you are considered attractive, you reap numerous benefits that others do not. Studies indicate that those perceived as being attractive have an easier time getting jobs (and better jobs), are promoted more often, receive better treatment from the police and the legal system, have more choices in romantic partners, and are even perceived as being more intelligent and morally better! All Aristotle is recognizing here is that the recipe for an excellent life includes several ingredients. Virtue is the most important, by far—but it's not the only ingredient.

Given that the most important ingredient is also the one over which we have the most control, it makes sense for us to focus on having a good character. Those with good character possess the virtues among their character traits. Virtues are simply dispositions (habits) to behave in certain ways. The virtues are positive dispositions, such as honesty, respectfulness, generosity, courage, etc. There are also negative dispositions (vices) such as disloyalty, cowardice, greediness, etc. Generally speaking, we want to display the virtues, and not the vices.

Aristotle had a particular understanding of the virtues. First, he thought there were two kinds: intellectual, and moral.

Intellectual virtues are based on excellence in reasoning, and can be taught. Prudence is an example of an intellectual virtue. The moral virtues, on the other hand, can't be taught (not directly, at least), but must be lived and practiced in order for one to acquire them. You could read a very well-written book on courage, for example, without it making you one bit more courageous. The way we acquire those sorts of virtues is by practicing them.

We become courageous by putting ourselves in fearsome situations, and then overcoming that fear. We become honest by telling the truth. Aristotle says, "It is right, then, to say that by doing what is just a man becomes just, and temperate by doing what is temperate, while without doing thus he has no chance of ever becoming good. But most men, instead of doing thus, fly to theories, and fancy that they are philosophizing and that this will make them good, like a sick man who listens attentively to what the doctor says and then disobeys all his orders. This sort of philosophizing will no more produce a healthy habit of mind than this sort of treatment will produce a healthy habit of body."[63]

When I lie, I am training myself to be a liar. When I steal, I am training myself to be a thief. When I act without compassion, I am training myself to be cold and cruel. If those are all traits I would like to avoid, I had better practice their opposites! Practice, then, is essential in acquiring the virtues—and they are not *our* virtues until they become habitual. To say that it is habitual means that in order to qualify as generous, for example, you have to be generous most of the time. Being generous one time in your life doesn't earn you the right to be labeled generous!

Habit covers one part of Aristotle's particular understanding of virtue. Another part refers to the "mean." For Aristotle, a virtue is a character trait that hits the "mean" and is manifested in habitual action, or what he called "habituation."

This doctrine of the "mean" is often referred to as "the Golden Mean." According to this doctrine, we should choose the "mean" over the extremes of excess and deficiency. The extremes of excess and deficiency occur when we're ruled by desires or emotions and not Reason. This reminds us of the central role of reason in human excellence. Virtue serves to correct these disorders by helping us to resist our impulses and desires that interfere with us living the good life.

For example, the virtue of courage corrects for inappropriate fear. The virtue of temperance corrects our impulses to overindulge or to seek immediate and harmful pleasures. The mean shows us a rational course of action by choosing between the two competing desire extremes (e.g., fear and wrath), letting neither desire have complete control.

That virtue is seen as a "mean" is interesting, and unusual. Most people see virtue as the opposite of a vice. Aristotle sees virtue as the mean between two vices, one of excess, and one of deficiency. The following is a list of virtues offered by Aristotle.

Issue	Vice (Deficiency)	Virtue (Mean)	Vice (Excess)
Fear	Cowardice	Courage	Foolhardiness
Pleasure/Pain	Inhibition	Temperance	Overindulgence
Spending	Miserliness	Liberality	Extravagance
Spending (major)	Shabbiness	Magnificence	Vulgarity
Ambition	Lack of ambition	Proper ambition	Over-Ambition
Self-esteem	Meekness	Magnanimity	Vanity
Anger	Timidity	Righteous Indignation	Hot-temperedness
Conversation	Boorishness	Wittiness	Buffoonery
Social Conduct	Crankiness	Friendliness	Obsequiousness

Notice, for example, that courage is not the opposite of cowardice, but rather the mean between cowardice (excessive fear) and foolhardiness (bravado). Being temperate doesn't mean that you never indulge any desires, but that you enjoy sensual delights appropriately (at the right times, and in the right amounts).

The mean is the "perfect" thing for a particular person to do in a specific situation. Note the relativity of this. Courage is different for different people. Someone with agoraphobia

---

[63] *Nicomachean Ethics*, Book 2, chapter 4

shows courage simply by stepping outside. A very sociable person, on the other hand, must take a very different sort of risk in order to display courage. What might count as a generous donation from you or me is probably quite different from what would qualify as a generous donation from a billionaire like Bill Gates.

A morally admirable person is one who has learned (over time, and with experience) what it means to be virtuous, and how to apply that understanding in ever-changing circumstances, reliably finding "just the right way" to behave, so much so that it is habitual—a reliable feature of her very character.

Although the Golden Mean sounds mathematical, it falls short of providing us a formula, or even any concrete list of "thou shalt nots." In fairness to Aristotle, he thought ethics could not be understood in that way. Ethics is not like math. If any analogy is to be made, the ancients (including Aristotle) preferred the analogy to medicine. Indeed, philosophy was often referred to as "medicine for the soul."

There is a science to medicine, to be sure, but a good doctor isn't one who has memorized all the I.C.D. codes, nor is the good psychiatrist the one who has memorized the DSM-IVTR. What makes medicine so interesting (and challenging) is those darn patients! Each one is subtly different, though their symptoms might be quite similar. Excellent doctors are the ones that can synthesize their theoretical understanding with the practical information and context before them. Martha Nussbaum, a contemporary philosopher and expert on Aristotle put it this way: "Excellent ethical choice cannot be captured completely in general rules because-like medicine-it is a matter of fitting one's choice to the complex requirements of a concrete situation, taking all of its contextual features into account."[64] The virtue necessary for this kind of skill is wisdom.

Wisdom (understood as "practical wisdom," *phronesis*) was regarded by Aristotle as the "master" virtue. Without it, none of the other virtues enjoy guidance, and we won't know how to implement them. For example, the "Golden Mean" is the virtuous avoidance of two extremes (vices). Too much "courage" becomes recklessness, and too little becomes cowardice. How much is enough, though? We need *phronesis* to discern the answer to that question.

Similarly, virtues often come into conflict with each other. Kindness is a virtue, but so is honesty. Imagine you have a friend who is going out for the evening, and she asks you how she looks. You think her outfit is unflattering. The "honest" answer might not be kind, but the "kind" answer might not be honest. Which virtue should prevail, in such a situation of conflict? Once again, *phronesis* is needed to resolve that dilemma— and no simple, formulaic answer is possible. To know the right thing to do will require that you know your friend very well. Is she very sensitive? Will an honest answer crush her self-esteem? Will it ruin the friendship? Will she be grateful for the honest feedback? Also, you would need to know the situation. How important are her plans? Is it just an average night out, with nothing at stake? Is she on a first date? Is she interviewing for a job? Does she have other options? If you tell her the outfit is unflattering, is there anything else she could wear instead, that would be appropriate and more flattering? An understanding of all these things (and probably more) is needed, in order to discern the right course of action, for that person, in that situation. Someone who can reliably discern that right thing to do, is wise.

Returning to the example of courage, Aristotle can urge us to be courageous, but that's going to sound pretty hollow until we have a context in which to understand courage. What it means to be courageous will vary from one person to the next, from one circumstance to the next—and that's why we can't get specific "rules" from virtue approaches, like "always rush into

---

[64] Martha Nussbaum, *The Therapy of Desire: Theory and Practice in Hellenistic Ethics.* Princeton University Press, 1994. p. 67.

battle." Sometimes it might be courageous to rush into battle, but other times that will be stupidity.

Towards the end of the 2003 film, The Last Samurai, all of the samurai from the last holdout clan resisting "reform" enter battle knowing it will be their last, knowing they will die. This might well be courage, as they are overcoming fear of death for the sake of their principles. However, after much success in the battle, they end their fight with a cavalry charge into a line of Gatling guns. They are cut down with only one character (the main one) managing to survive. It's questionable whether that final charge was "courageous," as a case could certainly be made that it was more foolhardy. After all, courage doesn't require one to abandon sound tactics. Was their charge courageous, or reckless? No obvious and indisputable answer is available, as virtue is a subtle thing.

This is not to say that Aristotle (and virtue ethicists, in general) provides no moral guidance. For Aristotle, guidance was everywhere. Look around Athens and take note of those who are esteemed, and those who are held in disgrace. There are already people deemed virtuous. Be like those people!

We all have moral role-models in our lives, whether they are friends, family members, teachers or priests or mentors, historical figures, or even fictional characters. Each one of us is capable of thinking of a person (perhaps several) of whom we would say, "That person is an excellent human being. I wish I were more like him (or her)." Even the "What Would Jesus Do" (WWJD) movement expresses this theme. By modeling our behavior on those who have already achieved a level of personal excellence, we can practice and pursue that excellence ourselves. This is not unlike a golfer trying to model her swing after Tiger Wood's, or a pianist studying the technique of Little Richard. Perhaps looking for "human virtues" is to overreach, but to seek after what it means to be an admirable person within your own community is not so difficult.

Speaking of community, it would be a mistake to think that Aristotle's understanding of ethics is somehow focused exclusively on the self in isolation. Aristotle was especially and overtly sensitive to the demands of community.

> The complete good is thought to be self-sufficient. Now by self-sufficient we do not mean that which is sufficient for a man all by himself, for one who lives a solitary life, but also for parents, children, wife, and in general for friends and fellow citizens, since, a human being by nature is a political animal.[65]

Aristotle even ties the flourishing of the individual to the flourishing of his greater society. As such, one cannot be happy unless a similar happiness is realized in the greater society. Since our *eudaimonia* is affected by life circumstances (e.g., health, political stability, wealth, etc.), a "bad" society will interfere with personal flourishing. One can be virtuous in spite of bad circumstances, but one would be impaired in the practice of one's virtue.

The virtue approach encourages individual greatness—but not solely for our own sake, as if there is some forced choice between self and society. Instead, this approach recognizes that we are social creatures, and must understand ourselves as part of a community. Our flourishing is tied to others. Excellent individuals make for excellent communities, and excellent communities facilitate excellent individuals.

Having shifted to discussion about the relationship between the individual and the community, it is finally time to officially turn our attention to Aristotle's *Politics*. As mentioned briefly at the beginning of this chapter, the *Politics* was intended as a continuation of the same project begun in the *Nicomachean Ethics*.

Recall that the theme of the *Nicomachean Ethics* discussed above was *eudaimonia*, and how best to achieve and live that sort of life. Because we are, by our very nature, social animals, according to Aristotle, this flourishing can't be

---

[65] *Nicomachean Ethics*, 1097b.

achieved in isolation, but can only take place within a community. His agenda in the *Politics*, then, is to determine what *kind* of political community will best serve that end. Indeed, this is foreshadowed in the *Nicomachean Ethics* when, in the last ("practical application") chapters of the work, Aristotle focuses not on individuals' opportunities for moral self-improvement, but on opportunities for legislators to craft institutions and laws that will promote virtue.

Already, we have a significant contrast between Aristotle's understanding of politics and that assumed by most "modern" political philosophers (i.e., from roughly the Renaissance until today). One of the most central questions for modern and contemporary political philosophers is "what justifies the State?" This assumes that the State is something artificial, constructed by persons for some purpose, and that the purpose must outweigh the "inconvenience" of submitting to the authority of that State and its laws.

For Aristotle, though, politics is not (ideally) about control or power, but involves free and equal citizens "ruling and being ruled in turn." Indeed, the use of force by one party to exert control over another within the same community was, for Aristotle, a sign that the State was *failing*. Tyranny, though a possible (and often actual) form of government, is not properly "politics" in Aristotle's usage. The State is not a "contract" for the sake of security (whether personal or property), but is a self-sufficient community of persons with a shared set of core values. When citizens resort to force to pursue their vision of the good life, it is obvious that there is no longer a *collective* vision of the good life in operation.

For Aristotle, the paradigm isn't one of obligation and justification, but one of flourishing—and the consequent question of which type of government (and laws) best promote that flourishing. The legislator's task is to frame a society that will make the good life possible for its citizens. Indeed, Aristotle claims that a State comes into being for the sake of life (i.e., survival), but it exists with the aim/goal (*telos*) of a *good* life.[66]

Recall from much earlier this chapter we understood a thing's *telos* as its aim, goal, or purpose. This is one kind of cause/explanation described by Aristotle: the Final Cause. We can now fruitfully apply his four kinds of cause/explanation to the *polis*.

The Material Cause of the *polis* is the individual citizens and the natural resources of the community. The Formal Cause is the (legal) constitution of the *polis*, understood not merely as a written document, but as the organizing principle of the community, analogous to the soul's relationship to the body (as understood by Aristotle). The Efficient Cause of the State is the ruler himself or herself, including, possibly, the very founder of the constitution of that *polis*. Lastly, as already mentioned, the Final Cause of the *polis* is the promotion/cultivation of virtue in its citizens.

Once our basic physical (survival) needs are met, the *polis* exists for the sake of acquiring virtue and living an excellent life. Because we are rational animals, the exercise of reason is necessary for a complete (good) life. This includes rational deliberation about goodness and justice, among other things. But, we need a *community* in order to discuss and deliberate over such things.

In future chapters, we will see how philosophers like Hobbes and Machiavelli will start with a particular understanding of human nature (e.g., that we are "naturally" egoistic), and then develop their visions of the State and of laws to account for this. Aristotle's claims about human nature, however, refer back to our previous discussion of potentiality and our *telos*. To say that we are "naturally" political and rational is to claim that it is part of our *telos* to develop our reasoning faculty and to participate in a political community. We are *potentially* rational and political in that sense, but of course there is no guarantee that we will fulfill our *telos*! Indeed, an important function of the *polis* is to help us to do exactly that.

Recall that virtue was thought necessary for flourishing, but note that many of the particular

---

[66] *Politics*, 1252b.

virtues require interaction with others. An excellent life will be one in which one has an opportunity to exhibit (and does, in fact, exhibit) various virtues such as justice, generosity, etc.

How can anyone be generous without others with whom to be generous? How can each be given their due ("justice") in a society consisting of just one person? From Aristotle's perspective, we not only naturally desire the (good) company of others, such as friends, but we *need* the company of others, within a community, just to live a complete and virtuous life.

Granted, the "need" Aristotle had in mind is much more specific than merely living in community with others. Not just any sort of community will suffice to promote flourishing. Specifically, we need to live in a "*polis*." A *polis*, technically, just means something like a "city-state," or "political community," but in practice Aristotle intends "*polis*" to refer to a political community that aims at the virtue and flourishing of its citizens, and this will require the community to have certain features.

Aristotle envisions much more than just a loose confederation of people cooperating for the sake of mutual self-interest. Friendship is the "glue" that will bind the *polis* together as a community. In a political context, friendship is harmonious agreement amongst citizens concerning their shared values and how best to govern for the sake of those values. A "friendship" based on mere (perceived) usefulness or necessity is too vulnerable to slipping into conflict and factionalism. Genuine friendship between citizens is so important that Aristotle thinks legislators should actively cultivate it by means of laws and activities, in an effort to transform potentially competing individuals into a moral *community*.

Since the good life is a life of moral and intellectual virtue, an individual must be free and autonomous so as to direct his or her life by practical reason (*phronesis*). However, the best exercise of practical reason (according to Aristotle) is the application of wisdom to the common good within a community: "to deliberate well about what is good and advantageous for oneself, not in particular areas such as what promotes health or strength, but with a view to living well overall."[67]

In other words, active political participation is part of an excellent life. This should not be confused with mere "voting." Obviously, someone who is banned from any political participation at all, such as a subject of a dictator or monarch, is being deprived of an important aspect of an excellent life, but it's also not enough just to vote for a candidate who will then represent your interests (or not!) from then on. A representative democracy like the United States is not a "*polis*" (using Aristotle's understanding) for a variety of reasons.

In the first place, considering just Presidential elections, the voter turnout among eligible voters was only 51.8% in 2012. The Midterm election of 2014 saw a participation rate of 33.24%.[68] Even the historic and controversial campaign 2016 election between Donald Trump and Hillary Clinton saw only a 55.4% voter turnout.[69] Participation in State and Local elections is notoriously worse. Although (most) American citizens *may* vote, only a slim majority of us bother to, in the best of circumstances.

Even when we do vote, there is no guarantee that we do so on the basis of "deliberation." How many voters truly understand the "issues" when they vote, and can offer a reasoned defense for their vote? How many simply vote for their party's candidate, come what may? How many of those candidates have even offered clear, reasoned presentations of their views in the first place?

Even when we do vote, and even when we do have good reasons to support our vote, given a representative system such as that of the United States, we are merely electing someone to do the deliberation on our behalf. Under the most ideal interpretation, our elected officials will reason

---

[67] *Nicomachean Ethics*, 1140a25-28.
[68] http://www.idea.int/vt/countryview.cfm?CountryCode=US

[69] http://www.cnn.com/2016/11/11/politics/popular-vote-turnout-2016/

carefully, deliberate, and then make political decisions—but in that case only the representatives are exercising their practical reason in the way Aristotle prescribes. The rest of us do not.

The United States is not a *polis* because of its size and plurality of values, as well. The assumption for Aristotle (and many other Ancient political theorists too) was that the city-state they envisioned would be quite small by our standards—one in which the citizens (generally) know one another, and in which all can be recruited for a town meeting by a single herald.

All the citizens could gather together in one location and be addressed by speakers for the sake of political decision-making. Whether deliberating on laws, or issuing judgments in trials, the premise is that the citizens are all familiar with the details of the issues or case, and even know the history and character of the persons in question—something that is difficult in large communities. "Both in order to give decisions in matters of disputed rights, and to distribute the offices of government according to the merit of candidates, the citizens of a state must know one another's characters."[70]

Perhaps a close analogy to this is "Small Town America," where we can envision a local city council meeting in which all the citizens of that town gather to speak their minds on some local city ordinance, where voters all know the candidates for local office, or in which a local criminal trial includes jurors who all know the defendant and witnesses. Such is certainly not the case when we climb to State or National politics! Electing representatives seems to lack the sort of direct participation Aristotle had in mind, but perhaps this can be supplemented by participating in campaigns, in activity on behalf of political parties (e.g., "phone banking"), by participating in and contributing to "interest groups," by focusing on local elections and political processes, etc.

Aside from participation issues, a key feature of the *polis* is a common set of values that guides the political vision of the community, and given the plurality of worldviews and value systems found in the United States (and other large, cosmopolitan States), it is far from obvious that we are all guided by the same vision. "[A] city is excellent, at any rate, by its citizens' - those sharing in the regime – being excellent; and in our case all the citizens share in the regime."[71] That is, a *polis* is a "partnership" amongst persons with similar values, who get together to reflect upon those values, and deliberate upon which policies will best promote them.

Once again, we can imagine a hypothetical town in "Small Town America," where, for better, or for worse, "everyone" shares in common some basic, core values. The community is presumably homogenous with respect to religion and culture (generally conceived), and even if they disagree as to how best implement their values, the values themselves are a "given." Also once again, that certainly ceases to be the case once we start to think of larger political communities such as the State of California—let alone the Nation, as a whole.

Perhaps interestingly, those who advocate for "State's rights" or "local control" with regard to politics are drawing upon an Aristotelian legacy, whether they realize it or not. Those who claim that local officials and citizens are better equipped to make political decisions for their own citizens (as opposed to "Big Government" bureaucrats in Washington, for example), and those who argue that local communities (at least individual States) should be allowed to express their own values in their own (local) laws, even when those laws and values might be different in other States, are making claims consistent with Aristotle's vision the *polis*.

An easy application of this would be those who advocate that "social issues," such as same-sex marriage, abortion, the legal status of marijuana, physician-assisted suicide, or even racial segregation, should be left to each State to decide for itself, based on their own values.[72] Should residents find those laws objectionable,

---

[70] *Politics*, 1326a-b
[71] *Politics*, 1332a34.

[72] Infamous desegregation opponent Governor George Wallace of Alabama is known for having

they are free to move to another State that is more to their own liking. . . .

In the spirit of fairness, an appeal to "State's rights" is not merely (or always) some sort of political "dog whistle" to reference racism, segregation, discrimination against gays, etc.— and this is so not merely because the appeal can refer to "liberal" issues such as marijuana legalization as well. More charitably, an appeal to State's rights can be an appeal to the idea that political communities *should* be communities with shared values, and a one-size-fits-all, top-down approach might ignore that. Perhaps some communities, like Portland, Oregon, are ones in which mandatory recycling, extensive accommodations to bicycle riders, and legalized marijuana cultivation "works," but perhaps those same values (and the laws that promote or protect them) don't fit in Dallas, Texas?[73]

If you think that the political community should be guided by shared values, and that the laws should promote those values, then it's clear that there must be agreement on what those values are—and this is probably implausible given larger communities where a variety of values is likely to be found.

There is no pretense of value-neutrality with regard to the government and laws of the *polis*. The function of the *polis* is moral perfection. It must, necessarily, aim at moral education. Laws are intended to shape character, and good legislators will enact laws that aim to make citizens virtuous by habituating them to good acts.

For better or for worse, the United States is a pluralistic society with a variety of competing visions of the good life. It would be difficult to pinpoint a singular "common good" towards which we all aim, and for the sake of which we all partner. The preceding analysis of the U.S. society

is not meant as a criticism, but rather as an argument that the vision of the *polis* espoused by Aristotle is something different than what we experience in the United States—and in some cases, as we will soon see, that is probably a good thing!

As we have seen, political communities can fail to qualify as a *polis* for a variety of reasons, including size, lack of shared values, and inadequate levels of political participation. There is another way in which a community fails to qualify as a *polis*, though. Not every political organization serves to fulfill our *telos*. Aristotle distinguishes several different kinds of State based on who rules, and for what purpose.

---

declared "Segregation now! Segregation tomorrow! Segregation forever!" in a 1963 address, but later remarked that he should have said, "States' rights now! States' rights tomorrow! States' rights forever!" (Carter, Dan T. *From George Wallace to Newt Gingrich: Race in the Conservative Counterrevolution*, 1963-1994. p. 1.)

[73] Please note that these are intentionally non-controversial examples. Clearly, the stakes are much higher when the difference in community standards isn't concerning recycling, but about which human beings have basic rights!

State	Who rules?	For what purpose?
Tyranny	one person	self-interest
Kingship	one person	collective interest
Oligarchy	a wealthy minority	self-interest
Aristocracy	a virtuous minority	collective interest
Populist democracy	many (usually poor)	self-interest
Polity	many	collective interest

Aristotle recognizes that all six of those types of State exist (with numerous variations), but believes that only some of them are legitimate, with the rest being deviant or corrupted versions of "proper" government types. All of the "good" constitutions (i.e., kingship, aristocracy, and polity) exhibit justice (in some sense) and promote friendship (harmony) because of their emphasis on the common good.

When one person rules for the common good, that is kingship or monarchy. When the one person rules in his own interests, however, we have a tyranny. When a minority of the population rule for the common good, and when that minority rules because of their virtue and merit, we have an aristocracy; but, when the minority rules for their own interests, and they rule because of their wealth rather than their virtue or merit, we have an oligarchy. Finally, when the "many" rule for the sake of the common good, we have a polity—the system that Aristotle seems to be advocating (despite the fact that a majority of his own population, being slaves and resident aliens, don't seem to count towards this "many!"). But, when the "many" is a mere majority ruling for their own good (e.g., the poor ruling for the sake of the poor), we have a (populist) democracy instead.

To contemporary (American) ears, the claim that "democracy" is a degenerate form of government might sound shocking. Isn't democracy the "best" form of government, the hope of the free world? Why would Aristotle have a problem with democracy?

In some respects, Aristotle's concerns about democracy echo those of his teacher, Plato. Plato condemned democracy because, among other things, it is a system that fails to recognize that rulership is a skill that requires expertise, like any other—and democracy falsely claims that all persons are equally qualified to exercise that skill.

For Aristotle (and Plato), the State exists to promote and cultivate virtue in its citizens. Laws are to mold and shape us into being better people, according to the standards of our shared community values. Such laws are necessary since most citizens are not already "virtuous" by means of their own efforts.

Most of us think of happiness in terms of desire-satisfaction, and seek a life of pleasure. In Plato's *Republic*, Plato has Socrates make the potentially surprising claim that neither the "sophists," nor any individual citizen, can "corrupt" the youth and turn them away from civic virtue.[74] This power lies in the hands of the

---

[74] The irony here is tangible. Recall that Socrates was executed for, among other things, "corrupting the youth"—a power that Plato denies Socrates (or anyone) could have. "Or are you too one of the multitude who believe that there are young men who are corrupted by the sophists, and that there are sophists in private life who corrupt to any extent worth mentioning, and that it is not rather the very men who talk in this

strain who are the chief sophists and educate most effectively and mould to their own heart's desire young and old, men and women?' 'When?' said he. 'Why, when,' I said, 'the multitude are seated together in assemblies or in court-rooms or theaters or camps or any other public gathering of a crowd, and with loud uproar censure some of the things that are said and done and approve others, both in excess, with full-

"multitude," instead. Both Plato and Aristotle seem to think that the mass of public opinion is too powerful for any individual to subvert—which means that public moral values have to be steered and firmly established from the start, by means of good (enlightened) legislation and educational programs.

Since most of us aren't professional philosophers who have already discerned the good life, we need to be steered by laws and the threat of punishment to make good choices. Of course, those who *make* these laws will need to be virtuous, in order to make sure that the laws are correctly formed and implemented. This means that legislators must be virtuous, well-educated, and wise. Not everyone is going to be equally virtuous, well-educated, and wise! Therefore, not everyone is well-suited to be legislators.

A problem with both oligarchy and democracy is that they have a mistaken vision of the proper *telos* of the *polis*, which in turns results in a mistaken application of distributive justice. The State should distribute "awards" in proportion to the contribution one makes to the State, and we evaluate contributions by appealing to the *telos* of the State: cultivating virtue.

Oligarchs mistakenly view the purpose of the State as maximizing wealth.[75] However, someone who donates the most amount of money to public accounts does not deserve the greatest "award" (or political influence) because "revenue" is not the *telos* of the State.

Where democracy errs is in thinking that the *telos* of the *polis* is to promote and maximize liberty and equality, and therefore that all persons should have equal status and privileges—but this is just as misguided, in its

own way, as was the vision promoted by the oligarchs.

Where a democracy gets it "wrong" is in taking one measure in which people are equal (i.e., all citizens are equally free), and using it as the basis for another equal distribution: political decision-making. But, just because people are equal in one respect doesn't entail that they should be equal in another, nor does being "superior" in one respect (e.g., wealth) entail that one is superior in others (e.g., virtue).

Worse, when "freedom" is taken as the relevant measure and qualification for political decision-making, freedom becomes the *telos*, the "end" towards which political decisions are oriented. Freedom then, according to Aristotle's vision, becomes interpreted as the absence of control, the freedom to do whatever one desires—but this is the abandonment of moral discipline, and amounts to anarchy.[76] If everyone pursues their own vision of "the good," and is left to their own devices to do so, the *polis* has literally ceased to exist.

Instead, the greatest awards should go to those who most contribute to virtue—and it is for this reason that Aristotle is sympathetic to the idea of an enlightened aristocracy (*aristoi*—literally, "best persons") ruling the *polis*. For a genuine, *polis*, however, Aristotle claims that "it is clear that the best constitution is that organization by which everyone, whoever he is, would do the best things and live a blessed life."[77] In order for a person to cultivate virtue and exercise practical reason so as to live that blessed life, they must have the leisure time and resources necessary to develop those traits—and here we start to run into some potentially uncomfortable "tensions" in his proposed *polis*.

---

throated clamor and clapping of hands, and thereto the rocks and the region round about re-echoing redouble the din of the censure and the praise (*Republic* 492a-c).'"

[75] Think of how the current Republican political party exalts "job creators" and, at times, literally describe the wealthiest as the "best" of us.

[76] For the sake of historical accuracy, neither contemporary democracy, nor even the democracies of Aristotle's own history, amounted to "anarchy." The liberty to pursue one's own values, while indeed anathema to a *polis*, will become quite desirable centuries later with the birth of classical liberalism.

[77] Aristotle, *Politics*, 1324a23-25.

Citizenship in the *polis*, for Aristotle, will be confined to males of "leisure" who are capable of rationally deliberating on the proper "end" (*telos*) of life. In order to have the leisure time necessary to develop virtue and to deliberate about and participate in political affairs, one can't have a "day job." Perhaps not coincidentally, Aristotle is advocating the lifestyle of his own aristocratic social class—a life of "gentlemanly leisure" that affords people like Aristotle the opportunity to study philosophy under teachers like Plato, because household slaves tend to the mundane needs of his estate!

The preceding statement was not merely an exaggeration meant to provoke you. Aristotle is serious about that aspect of the *polis*. In the previous chapter, we saw how Plato recommended in the *Laws* a small city state in which slaves and resident-aliens did all the physical labor and attended to most of the economic activities of the community so that the elite, leisured class of citizens could cultivate their virtue and participate in governing. Aristotle makes a similar proposal: all necessary economic functions will be completed by slaves and resident aliens (both being non-citizens, of course) so that citizens (specifically, *males*) have sufficient leisure time to participate in the pursuit of their common good.[78]

As it turns out, the *polis* is only "that organization by which everyone, whoever he is, would do the best things and live a blessed life" if, by "everyone" we understand only a tiny, privileged minority of the total population. These aristocrats are at liberty to be virtuous and "live a blessed life" because the majority are *not*.

Perhaps ironically, Aristotle criticizes Plato for doing essentially the same thing. "He makes one body of persons the permanent rulers of his state [thus rejecting the principle of 'ruling and being ruled in turn']. This is a system which must breed discontent and dissension . . . ."[79] This criticism applies both the Guardians in the

Republic as well as the leisured citizens (buttressed by their slaves and resident alien workers) in the *Laws*—but why wouldn't this apply equally to Aristotle's own *polis* for the very same reasons?

Slavery?

Having discussed slavery, without commentary thus far, in the context of both Plato's *Laws* and now Aristotle's *Politics*, it is time to offer a brief account (and critique) of Aristotle's defense of slavery. With very little effort, I think it can easily be shown to be incoherent, and is revealed to be an unfortunate, all-too-human "blind spot" to which even brilliant philosophers such as Aristotle are subject.

Aristotle described slaves as "animate property."[80] He holds that there are "natural slaves," and he contrasts this with those who become slaves by convention (law). It is always the "natural slave" that he has in mind when defending slavery. A "natural slave" is described as follows:

1. "anybody who by his nature is not his own man, but another's"
2. "anybody who, being a man, is an article of property"[81]

This is embarrassingly circular, of course, if offered as an argument for what makes someone a natural slave. A natural slave is someone who is another man's property? There is nothing yet "natural" about this, since anyone could be captured and placed into a condition of slavery, thereby making a person a "natural slave," by these standards! This is not what Aristotle meant, and in his defense he recognizes the need to establish whether any such persons as "natural slaves" even exist.

As it turns out, Aristotle claims that makes a human a natural slave is that he (or she) "is entirely without the faculty of deliberation."[82] For

---

[78] Ibid., 1329a24-26.
[79] Ibid.,1264b25.
[80] Ibid., 1253b2.

[81] Ibid., 1254a6.
[82] *Politics*, 1260a7. He also claims that women have a form of deliberative faculty which is

such humans, "the condition of slavery is both beneficial and just."[83] Apparently, a natural slave is some sort of mentally disabled human who is *entirely without* the ability to deliberate.

There are, of course, some people who, as a result of serious developmental delays or mental disorders, are arguably incapable of deliberating on their own behalf. In the vast majority of cases, such persons are in the care of others, wards of the State, supervised in board-and-care facilities, etc.

The problem, of course, is that such persons constitute a tiny fraction of the adult population of the adult community, whereas the slave population Aristotle has in mind is larger than the population of free citizens! Moreover, such "natural slaves," even if they were numerous, would clearly be incapable of performing all the labor (both skilled and unskilled) needed to maintain the community and homes within the *polis*—due to the very cognitive deficiencies that make them "natural slaves" in the first place!

Lamentably, his rationalization of slavery on the basis of the existence of "natural slaves" found new traction nearly two thousand years later in the context of the American slavery.

> There is one strong argument in favor of negro slavery over all other slavery: that he, being unfitted for the mechanic arts, for trade, and all skillful pursuits, leaves those pursuits to be carried on by the whites; and does not bring all industry into disrepute, as in Greece and Rome, where the slaves were not only the artists and mechanics, but also the merchants.

> Whilst, as a general and abstract question, negro slavery has no other claims over

other forms of slavery, except that from inferiority, or rather peculiarity, of race, almost all negroes require masters, whilst only the children, the women, the very weak, poor, and ignorant, &c., among the whites, need some protective and governing relation of this kind. . . .[84]

Modern (utilitarian) philosopher, John Stuart Mill, acknowledges this unfortunate philosophical "kinship."

> There was a time when the division of mankind into two classes, a small one of masters and a numerous one of slaves, appeared, even to the most cultivated minds, to be a natural, and the only natural, condition of the human race. No less an intellect, and one which contributed no less to the progress of human thought, than Aristotle, held this opinion without doubt or misgiving. . . . But why need I go back to Aristotle? Did not the slaveowners of the Southern United States maintain the same doctrine, with all the fanaticism with which men cling to the theories that justify their passions and legitimate their personal interests? Did they not call heaven and earth to witness that the dominion of the white man over the black is natural, that the black race is by nature incapable of freedom, and marked out for slavery? some even going so far as to say that the freedom of manual labourers is an unnatural order of things anywhere.[85]

Aristotle's defense of slavery is, to be blunt, indefensible.

"inconclusive"—a claim that supports, of course, his claim that males are the natural rulers of females, and that females are generally incapable of the feats of reason that males can perform—a claim that contemporary Aristotle expert and philosopher Martha Nussbaum capably refutes by both *her* standing in the philosophical

community as well as the profundity of *her* many books.

[83] Ibid., 1255a.

[84] George Fitzhugh, *Cannibals All! Or, Slaves Without Masters*: Electronic Edition (1806 - 1881), p.297.

[85] John Stuart Mill, *The Subjugation of Women* (1869), paragraph 1.9.

It is an unfortunate (and unmistakable) conceit of his classism and ethnocentrism that he could rationalize the subjugation of a multitude of people who clearly don't satisfy even his own definition of a "natural slave," for the sake of the "good life" for the elite, ruling minority.

While it might be tempting to simply forgive Aristotle's "blind spot" with regard to slavery, and try to work with his political vision without the slaves, this is more easily said than done. After all, for a community to properly be a *polis*, the citizens must collectively participate in politics for the common good, and individually cultivate their own virtue. If we eliminate the slave working class, and consider everyone a citizen and a participant in the pursuit of the good life, who is performing all the "day jobs" needed to keep the society operating? Perhaps some sort of system of shared labor could be implemented, so that everyone has a "day job" but also enough leisure time to develop their virtue and participate in politics in an informed way. This is certainly possible, but would presumably require a pretty intrusive and ambitious system of work requirements and redistribution of wealth in order to facilitate every citizen having a chance to meaningfully participate in the life of the *polis*. This is not an objection, mind you—but merely a recognition of an issue of distributive justice that would need to be addressed in order to have a *polis* without slavery (or its equivalent).

In fairness, one could argue that a critique (and the inevitable demise) of Aristotle's breathtakingly elitist vision of citizenship is contained within his own text. He does hold up aristocracy as an ideal, in which case comes the probably offensive package of "natural slaves," and a majority of residents (e.g., women, slaves, resident aliens, and artisans), who have no participation in governing, and for whom, therefore, the fulfillment of their own potential (as rational, political animals) is denied.

But, he also admits that "ruling and being ruled in turn" is an essential feature of a good

constitution—and this, of course, is an alternative to aristocracy. At times, he holds up the *telos* of the *polis* to be exclusively the attainment of virtue (favoring aristocracy), but at other times he holds up a more "complex" *telos* that includes not only virtue, but also wealth and equality—and this will favor a so-called "mixed constitution" (even if it is "second best").

The mixed constitution is so-called because it is a mix of aristocratic, oligarchic, and democratic themes. It is born from a recognition of seemingly inevitable factionalism and class division in any actual State. Ideally, no such divisions would exist, but, in the "real world," they inevitably arise. The task, then, is to forge a State that can manage those factions and remain just and stable. Essential to the success and stability of a mixed constitution is the existence of a large middle class.

The Middle Class

Presumably less offensive than the adaptation of Aristotle in the defense of American slavery is the adaptation of his appreciation of the middle class. In the United States, both major political parties angle to present themselves as the true supporters of the middle class, and both tend to emphasize the value and importance of the middle class in terms of the American economy and society, overall.[86] Today's Democrats and Republicans are hardly the first to voice appreciation of the middle class, however. Aristotle's discussion of the middle-class is worth quoting at length:

> In all states therefore there exist three divisions of the state, the very rich, the very poor, and thirdly those who are between the two. Since then it is admitted that what is moderate or in the middle is best, it is manifest that the middle amount of all of the good things of fortune is the best amount to possess. For this degree of

---

[86] The American middle class shrank from 61% to 51% from 1971 to 2011—though it remains the (slim) majority.

http://money.cnn.com/2012/08/22/news/economy/middle-class-pew/index.html?iid=EL

wealth is the readiest to obey reason, whereas for a person who is exceedingly beautiful or strong or nobly born or rich, or the opposite—exceedingly poor or weak or of very mean station, it is difficult to follow the bidding of reason; for the former turn more to insolence and grand wickedness, and the latter overmuch to malice and petty wickedness, and the motive of all wrongdoing is either insolence or malice. And moreover the middle class are the least inclined to shun office and to covet office, and both these tendencies are injurious to states. And in addition to these points, those who have an excess of fortune's goods, strength, wealth, friends and the like, are not willing to be governed and do not know how to be and they have acquired this quality even in their boyhood from their homelife, which was so luxurious that they have not got used to submitting to authority even in school, while those who are excessively in need of these things are too humble. Hence the latter class do not know how to govern but know how to submit to government of a servile kind, while the former class do not know how to submit to any government, and only know how to govern in the manner of a master. The result is a state consisting of slaves and masters, not of free men, and of one class envious and another contemptuous of their fellows. This condition of affairs is very far removed from friendliness, and from political partnership—for friendliness is an element of partnership, since men are not willing to be partners with their enemies even on a journey. But surely the ideal of the state is to consist as much as possible of persons that are equal and alike, and this similarity is most found in the middle classes; therefore the middle-class state will necessarily be best constituted in respect of those elements of which we say that the state is by nature composed. And also this class of citizens have the greatest

security in the states; for they do not themselves covet other men's goods as do the poor, nor do the other classes covet their substance as the poor covet that of the rich; and because they are neither plotted against nor plotting they live free from danger. Because of this it was a good prayer of Phocylides— "In many things the middle have the best; Be mine a middle station."

It is clear therefore also that the political community administered by the middle class is the best, and that it is possible for those states to be well governed that are of the kind in which the middle class is numerous, and preferably stronger than both the other two classes, or at all events than one of them, for by throwing in its weight it sways the balance and prevents the opposite extremes from coming into existence. Hence it is the greatest good fortune if the men that have political power possess a moderate and sufficient substance, since where some own a very great deal of property and others none there comes about either an extreme democracy or an unmixed oligarchy, or a tyranny may result from both of the two extremes, for tyranny springs from both democracy and oligarchy of the most unbridled kind, but much less often from the middle forms of constitution and those near to them. The cause of this we will speak of later in our treatment of political revolutions. That the middle form of constitution is the best is evident; for it alone is free from faction, since where the middle class is numerous, factions and party divisions among the citizens are least likely to occur. And the great states are more free from faction for the same reason, because the middle class is numerous, whereas in the small states it is easy to divide the whole people into two parties leaving nothing in between, and also almost everybody is needy or wealthy. Also democracies are more secure and more long-lived than oligarchies owing to the citizens of the middle class (for they are more numerous and have a larger share of the honors in democracies than in oligarchies, since when the poor are in a majority without the middle class, adversity sets in and they are soon ruined.[87]

A summary of the merits of the middle class, as described by Aristotle, is as follows:

- They are the most ready to listen to reason
- They suffer the least from ambition and envy
- They are more obedient than other social classes
- They are (relatively) equal peers
- They enjoy greater security/stability than do other social classes
- They neither plot nor are plotted against

While the middle-class might lack some of the "aristocratic" virtues like "magnificence,"[88] they are capable of justice and other virtues, and, by preventing extreme factionalism between the rich and poor, present a stabilizing influence for their society. Indeed, we find an echo of the Golden Mean in Aristotle's appreciation of the middle class. If the very rich is one extreme, and the very poor is the other, then the middle class will be the mean between those two extremes.

Communities are well-served when they "hit the mean." The middle class will be able to act as the mediator between the rich and the poor. In contrast, when the middle class is small and politically weak, economic inequalities will tend to grow more severe, and the community is likely to slide into corrupt rule either by oligarchs or by the "mob."

Even with a mixed-constitution/polity, Aristotle still advocates the cultivation of shared values. Although allowing political contributions from all social classes might mean that it not exclusively the virtuous aristocrats who make political decisions, this promotion of greater equality could result in greater friendship and harmony across the classes, and maybe even the overall promotion of virtue after all.

Conclusion

Aristotle's impact on philosophy, like that of his teacher, Plato, is hard to overstate. A systematic and empirically-minded thinker, Aristotle's prominence would be rivaled only by Plato for centuries after his death. His domination of physics would not end until Galileo supplanted him some two *thousand* years later. His contributions to logic, epistemology, metaphysics, and ethics provide a model for enquiry, and fodder for critique and commentary, to this day. His understanding of causation informs contemporary cosmological arguments for God's existence (for example), and his emphasis on virtue has borne fruit in the currently flourishing field of virtue ethics. Logic students still learn "Aristotle's laws" and construct "squares of opposition."

In the field of Politics (our current focus), Aristotle has been a source of inspiration for literally thousands of years. Today, he is the philosophical inspiration for contemporary conservative philosophers like Leo Strauss (and his neo-conservative heirs) as well as (classically) liberal philosophers such as Martha Nussbaum. His emphasis on a community of shared values, and the government as having a role in actively promoting certain values over others finds him at odds with contemporary libertarianism.

During the Medieval period, St. Thomas Aquinas leaned heavily on Aristotle in the

---

[87] *Politics*, 1295b4-15.

[88] This is just to say that it takes a lot of disposable income to be "magnificent" with your resources. Someone like Bill Gates can fund global

philanthropic organizations, but a typical high school teacher, while capable of generosity (relative to her own resources), could never do anything so "grand."

formulation of his own system, including his political theory. Aquinas was provided with a Latin translation of the *Politics*. He arguably fused the insights of that work with those of St. Augustine's *City of God* into what remains the core substance of Catholic political theory to this day.

Before turning to medieval political theory, however, we will finish our treatment of Ancient political thought by traveling from Greece to Rome, with Cicero as our guide.

Just as Plato was Socrates' student, Aristotle (384 BCE – 322 BCE) was Plato's student. Aristotle is also tremendously important in the history of Western philosophy, and is often understood as a practical, empirical contrast to his idealist teacher. Aristotle seemed to study and be an expert on virtually everything, ranging from physics to poetry, to marine biology, to logic, and to ethics (to name just a few). Aristotle's thought shaped much of medieval philosophy and was so respected that Aquinas refers to him simply as "the philosopher." In the first excerpt from his Nicomachean Ethics, Aristotle argues that happiness (eudaimonia) is the ultimate aim of all our actions. Given that we are rational and social animals, this fulfillment of our "end" (telos) will require a life of reason and relationships. Virtue (arete) is the most important ingredient in living an excellent life (i.e,. one that achieves eudaimonia). Intellectual virtues might be taught, but moral virtues must be practiced and trained. One means of training is to pursue the "golden mean" in our actions. In the second set of excerpts from the Politics (in the provided text, the title is translated as "A Treatise on Government"), we have samples of Aristotle criticizing Plato's versions of the ideal state, Aristotle's discussion of the major types of constitutions and their features, his controversial treatment of slavery, and his own vision for the best (achievable) political community.

The Nichomachean Ethics of Aristotle

trans. F.H. Peters, M.A. 5th edition (London: Kegan Paul, Trench, Truebner & Co., 1893).
[http://oll.libertyfund.org/index.php?option=com_staticxt&staticfile=show.php%3Ftitle=903&layout=html#chapter_70611]

BOOK I.
THE END.

In all he does man seeks same good as end or means.

Every art and every kind of inquiry, and likewise every act and purpose, seems to aim at some good: and so it has been well said that the good is that at which everything aims.

But a difference is observable among these aims or ends. What is aimed at is sometimes the exercise of a faculty, sometimes a certain result beyond that exercise. And where there is an end beyond the act, there the result is better than the exercise of the faculty.

Now since there are many kinds of actions and many arts and sciences, it follows that there are many ends also; *e.g.* health is the end of medicine, ships of shipbuilding, victory of the art of war, and wealth of economy.

But when several of these are subordinated to some one art or science,—as the making of bridles and other trappings to the art of horsemanship, and this in turn, along with all else that the soldier does, to the art of war, and so on,*—then the end of the master-art is always more desired than the ends of the subordinate arts,

since these are pursued for its sake. And this is equally true whether the end in view be the mere exercise of a faculty or something beyond that, as in the above instances.

2.

THE end is THE *good; our subject is this and its science Politics.*

If then in what we do there be some end which we wish for on its own account, choosing all the others as means to this, but not every end without exception as a means to something else (for so we should go on *ad infinitum,* and desire would be left void and objectless),—this evidently will be the good or the best of all things. And surely from a practical point of view it much concerns us to know this good; for then, like archers shooting at a definite mark, we shall be more likely to attain what we want.

If this be so, we must try to indicate roughly what it is, and first of all to which of the arts or sciences it belongs.

It would seem to belong to the supreme art or science, that one which most of all deserves the name of master-art or master-science.

Now Politics‡ seems to answer to this description. For it prescribes which of the sciences a state needs, and which each man shall study, and up to what point; and to it we see subordinated even the highest arts, such as economy, rhetoric, and the art of war.

Since then it makes use of the other practical sciences, and since it further ordains what men are to do and from what to refrain, its end must include the ends of the others, and must be the proper good of man.

For though this good is the same for the individual and the state, yet the good of the state seems a grander and more perfect thing both to attain and to secure; and glad as one would be to do this service for a single individual, to do it for a people and for a number of states is nobler and more divine.

This then is the aim of the present inquiry, which is a sort of political inquiry.*

3.

Exactness not permitted by subject nor to be expected by student, who needs experience and training.

We must be content if we can attain to so much precision in our statement as the subject before us admits of; for the same degree of accuracy is no more to be expected in all kinds of reasoning than in all kinds of handicraft.

Now the things that are noble and just (with which Politics deals) are so various and so uncertain, that some think these are merely conventional and not natural distinctions.

There is a similar uncertainty also about what is good, because good things often do people harm: men have before now been ruined by wealth, and have lost their lives through courage.

Our subject, then, and our data being of this nature, we must be content if we can indicate the truth roughly and in outline, and if, in dealing with matters that are not amenable to immutable laws, and reasoning from premises that are but probable, we can arrive at probable conclusions.*

The reader, on his part, should take each of my statements in the same spirit; for it is the mark of an educated man to require, in each kind of inquiry, just so much exactness as the subject admits of: it is equally absurd to accept probable reasoning from a mathematician, and to demand scientific proof from an orator.

But each man can form a judgment about what he knows, and is called "a good judge" of that—of any special matter when he has received a special education therein, "a good judge" (without any qualifying epithet) when he has received a universal education. And hence a young man is not qualified to be a student of Politics; for he lacks experience of the affairs of life, which form the data and the subject-matter of Politics.

Further, since he is apt to be swayed by his feelings, he will derive no benefit from a study whose aim is not speculative but practical.

But in this respect young in character counts the same as young in years; for the young man's disqualification is not a matter of time, but is due to the fact that feeling rules his life and directs all his desires. Men of this character turn the knowledge they get to no account in practice, as we see with those we call incontinent; but those who direct their desires and actions by reason will gain much profit from the knowledge of these matters.

So much then by way of preface as to the student, and the spirit in which he must accept what we say, and the object which we propose to ourselves.

4.

Men agree that the good is happiness, but differ as to what this is.

4. Since—to resume—all knowledge and all purpose aims at some good, what is this which we say is the aim of Politics; or, in other words, what is the highest of all realizable goods?

As to its name, I suppose nearly all men are agreed; for the masses and the men of culture alike declare that it is happiness, and hold that to "live well" or to "do well" is the same as to be "happy."

But they differ as to what this happiness is, and the masses do not give the same account of it as the philosophers.

The former take it to be something palpable and plain, as pleasure or wealth or fame; one man holds it to be this, and another that, and often the same man is of different minds at different times,—after sickness it is health, and in poverty it is wealth; while when they are impressed with the consciousness of their ignorance, they admire most those who say grand things that are above their comprehension.

Some philosophers, on the other hand, have thought that, beside these several good things, there is an "absolute" good which is the cause of their goodness.

As it would hardly be worth while to review all the opinions that have been held, we will confine ourselves to those which are most popular, or which seem to have some foundation in reason.

We must reason from facts accepted without question by the man of trained character.

But we must not omit to notice the distinction that is drawn between the method of proceeding from your starting-points or principles, and the method of working up to them. Plato used with fitness to raise this question, and to ask whether the right way is from or to your starting-points, as in the race-course you may run from the judges to the boundary, or *vice versâ*.

Well, we must start from what is known.

But "what is known" may mean two things: "what is known to us," which is one thing, or "what is known" simply, which is another.

I think it is safe to say that *we* must start from what is known to *us.*

And on this account nothing but a good moral training can qualify a man to study what is noble and just—in a word, to study questions of Politics. For the undemonstrated fact is here the starting-point, and if this undemonstrated fact be sufficiently evident to a man, he will not require a "reason why." Now the man who has had a good moral training either has already arrived at starting-points or principles of action, or will easily accept them when pointed out. But he who neither has them nor will accept them may hear what Hesiod says* —

"The best is he who of himself doth know;
Good too is he who listens to the wise;
But he who neither knows himself nor heeds
The words of others, is a useless man."

5.

The good cannot be pleasure, nor honour, nor virtue.

Let us now take up the discussion at the point from which we digressed.

It seems that men not unreasonably take their notions of the good or happiness from the lives actually led, and that the masses who are the least refined suppose it to be pleasure, which is the reason why they aim at nothing higher than the life of enjoyment.

For the most conspicuous kinds of life are three: this life of enjoyment, the life of the statesman, and, thirdly, the contemplative life.

The mass of men show themselves utterly slavish in their preference for the life of brute beasts, but their views receive consideration because many of those in high places have the tastes of Sardanapalus.

Men of refinement with a practical turn prefer honour; for I suppose we may say that honour is the aim of the statesman's life.

But this seems too superficial to be the good we are seeking: for it appears to depend upon those who give rather than upon those who receive it; while we have a presentiment that the good is something that is peculiarly a man's own and can scarce be taken away from him.

Moreover, these men seem to pursue honour in order that they may be assured of their own excellence,—at least, they wish to be honoured by men of sense, and by those who know them, and on the ground of their virtue or excellence. It is plain, then, that in their view, at any rate, virtue or excellence is better than honour; and perhaps we should take this to be the end of the statesman's life, rather than honour.

But virtue or excellence also appears too incomplete to be what we want; for it seems that a man might have virtue and yet be asleep or be inactive all his life, and, moreover, might meet with the greatest disasters and misfortunes; and no one would maintain that such a man is happy, except for argument's sake. But we will not dwell on these matters now, for they are sufficiently discussed in the popular treatises.

The third kind of life is the life of contemplation: we will treat of it further on.*

As for the money-making life, it is something quite contrary to nature; and wealth evidently is not the good of which we are in search, for it is merely useful as a means to something else. So we might rather take pleasure and virtue or excellence to be ends than wealth; for they are chosen on their own account. But it seems that not even they are the end, though much breath has been wasted in attempts to show that they are.

6.

Various arguments to show against the Platonists that there cannot be one universal good.

Dismissing these views, then, we have now to consider the "universal good," and to state the difficulties which it presents; though such an inquiry is not a pleasant task in view of our friendship for the authors of the doctrine of ideas. But we venture to think that this is the right course, and that in the interests of truth we ought to sacrifice even what is nearest to us, especially as we call ourselves philosophers. Both are dear to us, but it is a sacred duty to give the preference to truth.

In the first place, the authors of this theory themselves did not assert a common idea in the case of things of which one is prior to the other; and for this reason they did not hold one common idea of numbers. Now the predicate good is applied to substances and also to qualities and relations. But that which has independent existence, what we call "substance," is logically prior to that which is relative; for the latter is an offshoot as it were, or [in logical language] an accident of a thing or substance. So [by their own showing] there cannot be one common idea of these goods.

Secondly, the term good is used in as many different ways as the term "is" or "being:" we apply the term to substances or independent existences, as God, reason; to qualities, as the virtues; to quantity, as the moderate or due amount; to relatives, as the useful; to time, as opportunity; to place, as habitation, and so on. It is evident, therefore, that the word good cannot stand for one and the same notion in all these various applications; for if it did, the term could not be applied in all the categories, but in one only.

Thirdly, if the notion were one, since there is but one science of all the things that come under one idea, there would be but one science of all goods; but as it is, there are many sciences even of the goods that come under one category; as, for instance, the science which deals with opportunity in war is strategy, but in disease is medicine; and the science of the due amount in the matter of food is medicine, but in the matter of exercise is the science of gymnastic.

Fourthly, one might ask what they mean by the "absolute:" in "absolute man" and "man" the word "man" has one and the same sense; for in respect of manhood there will be no difference between them; and if so, neither will there be any difference in respect of goodness between "absolute good" and "good."

Fifthly, they do not make the good any more good by making it eternal; a white thing that lasts a long while is no whiter than what lasts but a day.

There seems to be more plausibility in the doctrine of the Pythagoreans, who [in their table of opposites] place the one on the same side with the good things [instead of reducing all goods to unity]; and even Speusippus* seems to follow them in this.

However, these points may be reserved for another occasion; but objection may be taken to what I have said on the ground that the Platonists do not speak in this way of all goods indiscriminately, but hold that those that are pursued and welcomed on their own account are called good by reference to one common form or type, while those things that tend to produce or preserve these goods, or to prevent their opposites, are called good only as means to these, and in a different sense.

It is evident that there will thus be two classes of goods: one good in themselves, the other good as means to the former. Let us separate then from the things that are merely useful those that are good in themselves, and inquire if they are called good by reference to one common idea or type.

Now what kind of things would one call "good in themselves"?

Surely those things that we pursue even apart from their consequences, such as wisdom and sight and certain pleasures and certain honours; for although we sometimes pursue these things as means, no one could refuse to rank them among the things that are good in themselves.

If these be excluded, nothing is good in itself except the idea; and then the type or form will be meaningless.*

If however, these are ranked among the things that are good in themselves, then it must be shown that the goodness of all of them can be defined in the same terms, as white has the same meaning when applied to snow and to white lead.

But, in fact, we have to give a separate and different account of the goodness of honour and wisdom and pleasure.

Good, then, is not a term that is applied to all these things alike in the same sense or with reference to one common idea or form.

But how then do these things come to be called good? for they do not appear to have received the same name by chance merely. Perhaps it is because they all proceed from one source, or all conduce to one end; or perhaps it is rather in virtue of some analogy, just as we call the reason the eye of the soul because it bears the same relation to the soul that the eye does to the body, and so on.

But we may dismiss these questions at present; for to discuss them in detail belongs more properly to another branch of philosophy.

Even if there were, it would not help us here.

And for the same reason we may dismiss the further consideration of the idea; for even granting that this term good, which is applied to all these different things, has one and the same meaning throughout, or that there is an absolute good apart from these particulars, it is evident that this good will not be anything that man can realize or attain: but it is a good of this kind that we are now seeking.

It might, perhaps, be thought that it would nevertheless be well to make ourselves acquainted with this universal good, with a view to the goods that are attainable and realizable. With this for a pattern, it may be said, we shall more readily discern our own good, and discerning achieve it.

There certainly is some plausibility in this argument, but it seems to be at variance with the existing sciences; for though they are all aiming at some good and striving to make up their deficiencies, they neglect to inquire about this universal good. And yet it is scarce likely that the professors of the several arts and sciences should not know, nor even look for, what would help them so much.

And indeed I am at a loss to know how the weaver or the carpenter would be furthered in his art by a knowledge of this absolute good, or how a man would be rendered more able to heal the sick or to command an army by contemplation of the pure form or idea. For it seems to me that the physician does not even seek for health in this abstract way, but seeks for the health of man, or rather of some particular man, for it is individuals that he has to heal.

7.

The good is the final end, and happiness is this.

Leaving these matters, then, let us return once more to the question, what this good can be of which we are in search.

It seems to be different in different kinds of action and in different arts,—one thing in medicine and another in war, and so on. What then is the good in each of these cases? Surely that for the sake of which all else is done. And that in medicine is health, in war is victory, in building is a house,—a different thing in each different case, but always, in whatever we do and in whatever we choose, the end. For it is always for the sake of the end that all else is done.

If then there be one end of all that man does, this end will be the realizable good,—or these ends, if there be more than one.

By this generalization our argument is brought to the same point as before.* This point we must try to explain more clearly.

We see that there are many ends. But some of these are chosen only as means, as wealth, flutes, and the whole class of instruments. And so it is plain that not all ends are final.

But the best of all things must, we conceive, be something final.

If then there be only one final end, this will be what we are seeking,—or if there be more than one, then the most final of them.

Now that which is pursued as an end in itself is more final than that which is pursued as means to something else, and that which is never chosen as means than that which is chosen both as an end in itself and as means, and that is strictly final which is always chosen as an end in itself and never as means.

Happiness seems more than anything else to answer to this description: for we always choose it for itself, and never for the sake of something else; while honour and pleasure and reason, and all virtue or excellence, we choose partly indeed for themselves (for, apart from any result, we should choose each of them), but partly also for the sake of happiness, supposing that they will help to make us happy. But no one chooses happiness for the sake of these things, or as a means to anything else at all.

We seem to be led to the same conclusion when we start from the notion of self-sufficiency.

The final good is thought to be self-suffing [or all-suffing]. In applying this term we do not regard a man as an individual leading a solitary life, but we also take account of parents, children, wife, and, in short, friends and fellow-citizens generally, since man is naturally a social being. Some limit must indeed be set to this; for if you go on to parents and descendants and friends of friends, you will never come to a stop. But this we will consider further on: for the present we will take self-suffing to mean what by itself makes life desirable and in want of nothing. And happiness is believed to answer to this description.

And further, happiness is believed to be the most desirable thing in the world, and that not merely as one among other good things: if it were merely one among other good things [so that other things could be added to it], it is plain that the addition of the least of other goods must make it more desirable; for the addition becomes a surplus of good, and of two goods the greater is always more desirable.

Thus it seems that happiness is something final and self-suffing, and is the end of all that man does.

To find it we ask, What is man's junction?

But perhaps the reader thinks that though no one will dispute the statement that happiness is the best thing in the world, yet a still more precise definition of it is needed.

This will best be gained, I think, by asking, What is the function of man? For as the goodness and the excellence of a piper or a sculptor, or the practiser of any art, and generally of those who have any function or business to do, lies in that function, so man's good would seem to lie in his function, if he has one.

But can we suppose that, while a carpenter and a cobbler has a function and a business of his own, man has no business and no function assigned him by nature? Nay, surely as his several members, eye and hand and foot, plainly have each his own function, so we must suppose that man also has some function over and above all these.

What then is it?

Life evidently he has in common even with the plants, but we want that which is peculiar to him. We must exclude, therefore, the life of mere nutrition and growth.

Next to this comes the life of sense; but this too he plainly shares with horses and cattle and all kinds of animals.

There remains then the life whereby he acts—the life of his rational nature,* with its two sides or divisions, one rational as obeying reason, the other rational as having and exercising reason.

But as this expression is ambiguous,‡ we must be understood to mean thereby the life that consists in the exercise of the faculties; for this seems to be more properly entitled to the name.

The function of man, then, is exercise of his vital faculties [or soul] on one side in obedience to reason, and on the other side with reason.

But what is called the function of a man of any profession and the function of a man who is good in that profession are generically the same, *e.g.* of a harper and of a good harper; and this holds in all cases without exception, only that in the case of the latter his superior excellence at his work is added; for we say a harper's function is to harp, and a good harper's to harp well.

(Man's function then being, as we say, a kind of life—that is to say, exercise of his faculties and action of various kinds with reason—the good man's function is to do this well and beautifully [or nobly]. But the function of anything is done well when it is done in accordance with the proper excellence of that thing.)‡

Resulting definition of happiness.

If this be so the result is that the good of man is exercise of his faculties in accordance with excellence or virtue, or, if there be more than one, in accordance with the best and most complete virtue.*

But there must also be a full term of years for this exercise;† for one swallow or one fine day does not make a spring, nor does one day or any small space of time make a blessed or happy man.

This, then, may be taken as a rough outline of the good; for this, I think, is the proper method,—first to sketch the outline, and then to fill in the details. But it would seem that, the outline once fairly drawn, any one can carry on the work and fit in the several items which time reveals to us or helps us to find. And this indeed is the way in which the arts and sciences have grown; for it requires no extraordinary genius to fill up the gaps.

We must bear in mind, however, what was said above, and not demand the same degree of accuracy in all branches of study, but in each case so much as the subject-matter admits of and as is proper to that kind of inquiry. The carpenter and the geometer both look for the right angle, but in different ways: the former only wants such an approximation to it as his work requires, but the latter wants to know what constitutes a right angle, or what is its special quality; his aim is to find out the truth. And so in other cases we must follow the same course, lest we spend more time on what is immaterial than on the real business in hand.

Nor must we in all cases alike demand the reason why; sometimes it is enough if the undemonstrated fact be fairly pointed out, as in the case of the starting-points or principles of a science. Undemonstrated facts always form the first step or starting-point of a science; and these starting-points or principles are arrived at some in one way, some in another—some by induction, others by perception, others again by some kind of training. But in each case we must try to apprehend them in the proper way, and do our best to define them clearly; for they have great influence upon the subsequent course of an inquiry. A good start is more than half the race, I think, and our starting-point or principle, once found, clears up a number of our difficulties.

8.

This view harmonizes various current views.

We must not be satisfied, then, with examining this starting-point or principle of ours as a conclusion from our data, but must also view it in its relation to current opinions on the subject; for all experience harmonizes with a true principle, but a false one is soon found to be incompatible with the facts.

Now, good things have been divided into three classes, external goods on the one hand, and on the other goods of the soul and goods of the body; and the goods of the soul are commonly said to be goods in the fullest sense, and more good than any other.

But "actions and exercises of the vital faculties or soul" may be said to be "of the soul." So our account is confirmed by this opinion, which is both of long standing and approved by all who busy themselves with philosophy.

But, indeed, we secure the support of this opinion by the mere statement that certain actions and exercises are the end; for this implies that it is to be ranked among the goods of the soul, and not among external goods.

Our account, again, is in harmony with the common saying that the happy man lives well and does well; for we may say that happiness, according to us, is a living well and doing well.

And, indeed, all the characteristics that men expect to find in happiness seem to belong to happiness as we define it.

Some hold it to be virtue or excellence, some prudence, others a kind of wisdom; others, again, hold it to be all or some of these, with the addition of pleasure, either as an ingredient or as a necessary accompaniment; and some even include external prosperity in their account of it.

Now, some of these views have the support of many voices and of old authority; others have few voices, but those of weight; but it is probable that neither the one side nor the other is entirely wrong, but that in some one point at least, if not in most, they are both right.

First, then, the view that happiness is excellence or a kind of excellence harmonizes with our account; for "exercise of faculties in accordance with excellence" belongs to excellence.

But I think we may say that it makes no small difference whether the good be conceived as the mere possession of something, or as its use—as a mere habit or trained faculty, or as the exercise of that faculty. For the habit or faculty may be present, and yet issue in no good result, as when a man is asleep, or in any other way hindered from his function; but with its exercise this is not possible, for it must show itself in acts and in good acts. And as at the Olympic games it is not the fairest and strongest who receive the crown, but those who contend (for among these are the victors), so in life, too, the winners are those who not only have all the excellences, but manifest these in deed.

And, further, the life of these men is in itself pleasant. For pleasure is an affection of the soul, and each man takes pleasure in that which he is said to love,—he who loves horses in horses, he who loves sight-seeing in sight-seeing, and in the same way he who loves justice in acts of justice, and generally the lover of excellence or virtue in virtuous acts or the manifestation of excellence.

And while with most men there is a perpetual conflict between the several things in which they find pleasure, since these are not naturally pleasant, those who love what is noble take pleasure in that which is naturally pleasant. For the manifestations of excellence are naturally pleasant, so that they are both pleasant to them and pleasant in themselves.

Their life, then, does not need pleasure to be added to it as an appendage, but contains pleasure in itself.

Indeed, in addition to what we have said, a man is not good at all unless he takes pleasure in noble deeds. No one would call a man just who did not take pleasure in doing justice, nor generous who took no pleasure in acts of generosity, and so on.

If this be so, the manifestations of excellence will be pleasant in themselves. But they are also both good and noble, and that in the highest degree—at least, if the good man's judgment about them is right, for this is his judgment.

Happiness, then, is at once the best and noblest and pleasantest thing in the world, and these are not separated, as the Delian inscription would have them to be:—

"What is most just is noblest, health is best,
Pleasantest is to get your heart's desire."

For all these characteristics are united in the best exercises of our faculties; and these, or some one of them that is better than all the others, we identify with happiness.

But nevertheless happiness plainly requires external goods too, as we said; for it is impossible, or at least not easy, to act nobly without some furniture of fortune. There are many things that can only be done through instruments, so to speak, such as friends and wealth and political influence: and there are some things whose absence takes the bloom off our happiness, as good birth, the blessing of children, personal beauty; for a man is not very likely to be happy if he is very ugly in person, or of low birth, or alone in the world, or childless, and perhaps still less if he has worthless children or friends, or has lost good ones that he had.

As we said, then, happiness seems to stand in need of this kind of prosperity; and so some identify it with good fortune, just as others identify it with excellence.

...

13.

Division of the faculties and resulting division of the virtues.

Since happiness is an exercise of the vital faculties in accordance with perfect virtue or excellence, we will now inquire about virtue or excellence; for this will probably help us in our inquiry about happiness.

And indeed the true statesman seems to be especially concerned with virtue, for he wishes to make the citizens good and obedient to the laws. Of this we have an example in the Cretan and the Lacedæmonian lawgivers, and any others who have resembled them. But if the inquiry belongs to Politics or the science of the state, it is plain that it will be in accordance with our original purpose to pursue it.

The virtue or excellence that we are to consider is, of course, the excellence of man; for it is the good of man and the happiness of man that we started to seek. And by the excellence of man I mean excellence not of body, but of soul; for happiness we take to be an activity of the soul.

If this be so, then it is evident that the statesman must have some knowledge of the soul, just as the man who is to heal the eye or the whole body must have some knowledge of them, and that the more in proportion as the science of the state is higher and better than medicine. But all educated physicians take much pains to know about the body.

As statesmen [or students of Politics], then, we must inquire into the nature of the soul, but in so doing we must keep our special purpose in view and go only so far as that requires; for to go into minuter detail would be too laborious for the present undertaking.

Now, there are certain doctrines about the soul which are stated elsewhere with sufficient precision, and these we will adopt.

Two parts of the soul are distinguished, an irrational and a rational part.

Whether these are separated as are the parts of the body or any divisible thing, or whether they are only distinguishable in thought but in fact inseparable, like concave and convex in the circumference of a circle, makes no difference for our present purpose.

Of the irrational part, again, one division seems to be common to all things that live, and to be possessed by plants—I mean that which causes nutrition and growth; for we must assume that all things that take nourishment have a faculty of this kind, even when they are embryos, and have the same faculty when they are full grown; at least, this is more reasonable than to suppose that they then have a different one.

The excellence of this faculty, then, is plainly one that man shares with other beings, and not specifically human.

And this is confirmed by the fact that in sleep this part of the soul, or this faculty, is thought to be most active, while the good and the bad man are undistinguishable when they are asleep (whence the saying that for half their lives there is no difference between the happy and the miserable; which indeed is what we should expect; for sleep is the cessation of the soul from those functions in respect of which it is called good or bad), except that they are to some slight extent roused by what goes on in their bodies, with the result that the dreams of the good man are better than those of ordinary people.

However, we need not pursue this further, and may dismiss the nutritive principle, since it has no place in the excellence of man.

But there seems to be another vital principle that is irrational, and yet in some way partakes of reason. In the case of the continent and of the incontinent man alike we praise the reason or the rational part, for it exhorts them rightly and urges them to do what is best; but there is plainly present in them another principle besides the rational one, which fights and struggles against the reason. For just as a paralyzed limb, when you will to move it to the right, moves on the contrary to the left, so is it with the soul; the incontinent man's impulses run counter to his reason. Only whereas we see the refractory member in the case of the body, we do not see it in the case of the soul. But we must nevertheless, I think, hold that in the soul too there is something beside the reason, which opposes and runs counter to it (though in what sense it is distinct from the reason does not matter here).

It seems, however, to partake of reason also, as we said: at least, in the continent man it submits to the reason; while in the temperate and courageous man we may say it is still more obedient; for in him it is altogether in harmony with the reason.

The irrational part, then, it appears, is twofold. There is the vegetative faculty, which has no share of reason; and the faculty of appetite or of desire in general, which in a manner partakes of reason or is rational as listening to reason and submitting to its sway,—rational in the sense in which we speak of rational obedience to father or friends, not in the sense in which we speak of rational apprehension of mathematical truths. But all advice and all rebuke and exhortation testify that the irrational part is in some way amenable to reason.

If then we like to say that this part, too, has a share of reason, the rational part also will have two divisions: one rational in the strict sense as possessing reason in itself, the other rational as listening to reason as a man listens to his father.

Now, on this division of the faculties is based the division of excellence; for we speak of intellectual excellences and of moral excellences; wisdom and understanding and prudence we call intellectual, liberality and temperance we call moral virtues or excellences. When we are speaking of a man's moral character we do not say that he is wise or intelligent, but that he is gentle or temperate. But we praise the wise man, too, for his habit of mind or trained faculty; and a habit or trained faculty that is praiseworthy is what we call an excellence or virtue.

BOOK II.
MORAL VIRTUE.
1.

Moral virtue is acquired by the repetition of the corresponding acts.

Excellence, then, being of these two kinds, intellectual and moral intellectual excellence owes its birth and growth mainly to instruction, and so requires time and experience, while moral excellence is the result of habit or custom (ἔθος), and has accordingly in our language received a name formed by a slight change from ἔθος.*

From this it is plain that none of the moral excellences or virtues is implanted in us by nature; for that which is by nature cannot be altered by training. For instance, a stone naturally tends to fall downwards, and you could not train it to rise upwards, though you tried to do so by throwing it up ten thousand times, nor could you train fire to move downwards, nor accustom

anything which naturally behaves in one way to behave in any other way.

The virtues,‡ then, come neither by nature nor against nature, but nature gives the capacity for acquiring them, and this is developed by training.

Again, where we do things by nature we get the power first, and put this power forth in act afterwards: as we plainly see in the case of the senses; for it is not by constantly seeing and hearing that we acquire those faculties, but, on the contrary, we had the power first and then used it, instead of acquiring the power by the use. But the virtues we acquire by doing the acts, as is the case with the arts too. We learn an art by doing that which we wish to do when we have learned it; we become builders by building, and harpers by harping. And so by doing just acts we become just, and by doing acts of temperance and courage we become temperate and courageous.

This is attested, too, by what occurs in states; for the legislators make their citizens good by training; *i.e.* this is the wish of all legislators, and those who do not succeed in this miss their aim, and it is this that distinguishes a good from a bad constitution.

Again, both the moral virtues and the corresponding vices result from and are formed by the same acts; and this is the case with the arts also. It is by harping that good harpers and bad harpers alike are produced: and so with builders and the rest; by building well they will become good builders, and bad builders by building badly. Indeed, if it were not so, they would not want anybody to teach them, but would all be born either good or bad at their trades. And it is just the same with the virtues also. It is by our conduct in our intercourse with other men that we become just or unjust, and by acting in circumstances of danger, and training ourselves to feel fear or confidence, that we become courageous or cowardly. So, too, with our animal appetites and the passion of anger; for by behaving in this way or in that on the occasions with which these passions are concerned, some become temperate and gentle, and others profligate and ill-tempered. In a word, acts of any kind produce habits or characters of the same kind.

Hence we ought to make sure that our acts be of a certain kind; for the resulting character varies as they vary. It makes no small difference, therefore, whether a man be trained from his youth up in this way or in that, but a great difference, or rather all the difference.

2.

These acts must be such as reason prescribes; they can't be defined exactly, but must be neither too much nor too little.

But our present inquiry has not, like the rest, a merely speculative aim; we are not inquiring merely in order to know what excellence or virtue is, but in order to become good; for otherwise it would profit us nothing. We must ask therefore about these acts, and see of what kind they are to be; for, as we said, it is they that determine our habits or character.

First of all, then, that they must be in accordance with right reason is a common characteristic of them, which we shall here take for granted, reserving for future discussion* the question what this right reason is, and how it is related to the other excellences.

But let it be understood, before we go on, that all reasoning on matters of practice must be in outline merely, and not scientifically exact: for, as we said at starting, the kind of reasoning to be demanded varies with the subject in hand; and in practical matters and questions of expediency there are no invariable laws, any more than in questions of health.

And if our general conclusions are thus inexact, still more inexact is all reasoning about particular cases; for these fall under no system of scientifically established rules or traditional maxims, but the agent must always consider for himself what the special occasion requires, just as in medicine or navigation.

But though this is the case we must try to render what help we can.

First of all, then, we must observe that, in matters of this sort, to fall short and to exceed are alike fatal. This is plain (to illustrate what we cannot see by what we can see) in the case of strength and health. Too much and too little

exercise alike destroy strength, and to take too much meat and drink, or to take too little, is equally ruinous to health, but the fitting amount produces and increases and preserves them. Just so, then, is it with temperance also, and courage, and the other virtues. The man who shuns and fears everything and never makes a stand, becomes a coward; while the man who fears nothing at all, but will face anything, becomes foolhardy. So, too, the man who takes his fill of any kind of pleasure, and abstains from none, is a profligate, but the man who shuns all (like him whom we call a "boor") is devoid of sensibility.* Thus temperance and courage are destroyed both by excess and defect, but preserved by moderation.

But habits or types of character are not only produced and preserved and destroyed by the same occasions and the same means, but they will also manifest themselves in the same circumstances. This is the case with palpable things like strength. Strength is produced by taking plenty of nourishment and doing plenty of hard work, and the strong man, in turn, has the greatest capacity for these. And the case is the same with the virtues: by abstaining from pleasure we become temperate, and when we have become temperate we are best able to abstain. And so with courage: by habituating ourselves to despise danger, and to face it, we become courageous; and when we have become courageous, we are best able to face danger.

3.

Virtue is in various ways concerned with pleasure and pain.

The pleasure or pain that accompanies the acts must be taken as a test of the formed habit or character.

He who abstains from the pleasures of the body and rejoices in the abstinence is temperate, while he who is vexed at having to abstain is profligate; and again, he who faces danger with pleasure, or, at any rate, without pain, is courageous, but he to whom this is painful is a coward.

For moral virtue or excellence is closely concerned with pleasure and pain. It is pleasure that moves us to do what is base, and pain that moves us to refrain from what is noble. And therefore, as Plato says, man needs to be so trained from his youth up as to find pleasure and pain in the right objects. This is what sound education means.

Another reason why virtue has to do with pleasure and pain, is that it has to do with actions and passions or affections; but every affection and every act is accompanied by pleasure or pain.

The fact is further attested by the employment of pleasure and pain in correction; they have a kind of curative property, and a cure is effected by administering the opposite of the disease.

Again, as we said before, every type of character [or habit or formed faculty] is essentially relative to, and concerned with, those things that form it for good or for ill; but it is through pleasure and pain that bad characters are formed—that is to say, through pursuing and avoiding the wrong pleasures and pains, or pursuing and avoiding them at the wrong time, or in the wrong manner, or in any other of the various ways of going wrong that may be distinguished.

And hence some people go so far as to define the virtues as a kind of impassive or neutral state of mind. But they err in stating this absolutely, instead of qualifying it by the addition of the right and wrong manner, time, etc.

We may lay down, therefore, that this kind of excellence [*i.e.* moral excellence] makes us do what is best in matters of pleasure and pain, while vice or badness has the contrary effect. But the following considerations will throw additional light on the point.*

There are three kinds of things that move us to choose, and three that move us to avoid them: on the one hand, the beautiful or noble, the advantageous, the pleasant; on the other hand, the ugly or base, the hurtful, the painful. Now, the good man is apt to go right, and the bad man to go wrong, about them all, but especially about pleasure: for pleasure is not only common to man with animals, but also accompanies all pursuit or choice; since the noble, and the advantageous also, are pleasant in idea.

Again, the feeling of pleasure has been fostered in us all from our infancy by our training, and has thus become so engrained in our life that it can scarce be washed out.* And, indeed, we all more or less make pleasure our test in judging of actions. For this reason too, then, our whole inquiry must be concerned with these matters; since to be pleased and pained in the right or the wrong way has great influence on our actions.

Again, to fight with pleasure is harder than to fight with wrath (which Heraclitus says is hard), and virtue, like art, is always more concerned with what is harder; for the harder the task the better is success. For this reason also, then, both [moral] virtue or excellence and the science of the state must always be concerned with pleasures and pains; for he that behaves rightly with regard to them will be good, and he that behaves badly will be bad.

We will take it as established, then, that [moral] excellence or virtue has to do with pleasures and pains; and that the acts which produce it develop it, and also, when differently done, destroy it; and that it manifests itself in the same acts which produced it.

4.

The conditions of virtuous action as distinct from artistic production.

But here we may be asked what we mean by saying that men can become just and temperate only by doing what is just and temperate: surely, it may be said, if their acts are just and temperate, they themselves are already just and temperate, as they are grammarians and musicians if they do what is grammatical and musical.

We may answer, I think, firstly, that this is not quite the case even with the arts. A man may do something grammatical [or write something correctly] by chance, or at the prompting of another person: he will not be grammatical till he not only does something grammatical, but also does it grammatically [or like a grammatical person], *i.e.* in virtue of his own knowledge of grammar.

But, secondly, the virtues are not in this point analogous to the arts. The products of art have their excellence in themselves, and so it is enough if when produced they are of a certain quality; but in the case of the virtues, a man is not said to act justly or temperately [or like a just or temperate man] if what he does merely be of a certain sort— he must also be in a certain state of mind when he does it; *i.e.,* first of all, he must know what he is doing; secondly, he must choose it, and choose it for itself; and, thirdly, his act must be the expression of a formed and stable character. Now, of these conditions, only one, the knowledge, is necessary for the possession of any art; but for the possession of the virtues knowledge is of little or no avail, while the other conditions that result from repeatedly doing what is just and temperate are not a little important, but all-important.

The thing that is done, therefore, is called just or temperate when it is such as the just or temperate man would do; but the man who does it is not just or temperate, unless he also does it in the spirit of the just or the temperate man.

It is right, then, to say that by doing what is just a man becomes just, and temperate by doing what is temperate, while without doing thus he has no chance of ever becoming good.

But most men, instead of doing thus, fly to theories, and fancy that they are philosophizing and that this will make them good, like a sick man who listens attentively to what the doctor says and then disobeys all his orders. This sort of philosophizing will no more produce a healthy habit of mind than this sort of treatment will produce a healthy habit of body.

5.
Virtue not an emotion, nor a faculty, but a trained faculty or habit.

We have next to inquire what excellence or virtue is.

A quality of the soul is either (1) a passion or emotion, or (2) a power or faculty, or (3) a habit or trained faculty; and so virtue must be one of these three. By (1) a passion or emotion we mean appetite, anger, fear, confidence, envy, joy, love, hate, longing, emulation, pity, or generally that which is accompanied by pleasure or pain; (2) a power or faculty is that in respect of which we are said to be capable of being affected in any of these ways, as, for instance, that in respect of which we are able to be angered or pained or to pity; and (3) a habit or trained faculty is that in respect of

which we are well or ill regulated or disposed in the matter of our affections; as, for instance, in the matter of being angered, we are ill regulated if we are too violent or too slack, but if we are moderate in our anger we are well regulated. And so with the rest.

Now, the virtues are not emotions, nor are the vices—(1) because we are not called good or bad in respect of our emotions, but are called so in respect of our virtues or vices; (2) because we are neither praised nor blamed in respect of our emotions (a man is not praised for being afraid or angry, nor blamed for being angry simply, but for being angry in a particular way), but we are praised or blamed in respect of our virtues or vices; (3) because we may be angered or frightened without deliberate choice, but the virtues are a kind of deliberate choice, or at least are impossible without it; and (4) because in respect of our emotions we are said to be moved, but in respect of our virtues and vices we are not said to be moved, but to be regulated or disposed in this way or in that.

For these same reasons also they are not powers or faculties; for we are not called either good or bad for being merely capable of emotion, nor are we either praised or blamed for this. And further, while nature gives us our powers or faculties, she does not make us either good or bad. (This point, however, we have already treated.)

If, then, the virtues be neither emotions nor faculties, it only remains for them to be habits or trained faculties.

6.
viz., the habit of choosing the mean.

We have thus found the genus to which virtue belongs; but we want to know, not only that it is a trained faculty, but also what species of trained faculty it is.

We may safely assert that the virtue or excellence of a thing causes that thing both to be itself in good condition and to perform its function well. The excellence of the eye, for instance, makes both the eye and its work good; for it is by the excellence of the eye that we see well. So the proper excellence of the horse makes a horse what he should be, and makes him good at running, and carrying his rider, and standing a charge.

If, then, this holds good in all cases, the proper excellence or virtue of man will be the habit or trained faculty that makes a man good and makes him perform his function well.

How this is to be done we have already said, but we may exhibit the same conclusion in another way, by inquiring what the nature of this virtue is.

Now, if we have any quantity, whether continuous or discrete,* it is possible to take either a larger [or too large], or a smaller [or too small], or an equal [or fair] amount, and that either absolutely or relatively to our own needs.

By an equal or fair amount I understand a mean amount, or one that lies between excess and deficiency.

By the absolute mean, or mean relatively to the thing itself, I understand that which is equidistant from both extremes, and this is one and the same for all.

By the mean relatively to us I understand that which is neither too much nor too little for us; and this is not one and the same for all.

For instance, if ten be larger [or too large] and two be smaller [or too small], if we take six we take the mean relatively to the thing itself [or the arithmetical mean]; for it exceeds one extreme by the same amount by which it is exceeded by the other extreme: and this is the mean in arithmetical proportion.

But the mean relatively to us cannot be found in this way. If ten pounds of food is too much for a given man to eat, and two pounds too little, it does not follow that the trainer will order him six pounds: for that also may perhaps be too much for the man in question, or too little; too little for Milo, too much for the beginner. The same holds true in running and wrestling.

And so we may say generally that a master in any art avoids what is too much and what is too little, and seeks for the mean and chooses it—not the absolute but the relative mean.

If, then, every art or science perfects its work in this way, looking to the mean and bringing its work up to this standard (so that people are wont to say of a good work that nothing could be taken from it or added to it, implying that excellence is destroyed by excess or deficiency, but secured by observing the mean; and good artists, as we say, do in fact keep their eyes fixed on this in all that they do), and if virtue, like nature, is more exact and better than any art, it follows that virtue also must aim at the mean—virtue of course meaning moral virtue or excellence; for it has to do with passions and actions, and it is these that admit of excess and deficiency and the mean. For instance, it is possible to feel fear, confidence, desire, anger, pity, and generally to be affected pleasantly and painfully, either too much or too little, in either case wrongly; but to be thus affected at the right times, and on the right occasions, and towards the right persons, and with the right object, and in the right fashion, is the mean course and the best course, and these are characteristics of virtue. And in the same way our outward acts also admit of excess and deficiency, and the mean or due amount.

Virtue, then, has to deal with feelings or passions and with outward acts, in which excess is wrong and deficiency also is blamed, but the mean amount is praised and is right—both of which are characteristics of virtue.

Virtue, then, is a kind of moderation (μεσότης τις),* inasmuch as it aims at the mean or moderate amount (τὸ μέσον).

Again, there are many ways of going wrong (for evil is infinite in nature, to use a Pythagorean figure, while good is finite), but only one way of going right; so that the one is easy and the other hard—easy to miss the mark and hard to hit. On this account also, then, excess and deficiency are characteristic of vice, hitting the mean is characteristic of virtue:

"Goodness is simple, ill takes any shape."

Virtue, then, is a habit or trained faculty of choice, the characteristic of which lies in moderation or observance of the mean relatively to the persons concerned, as determined by reason, *i.e.* by the reason by which the prudent man would determine it. And it is a moderation, firstly, inasmuch as it comes in the middle or mean between two vices, one on the side of excess, the other on the side of defect; and, secondly, inasmuch as, while these vices fall short of or exceed the due measure in feeling and in action, it finds and chooses the mean, middling, or moderate amount.

Regarded in its essence, therefore, or according to the definition of its nature, virtue is a moderation or middle state, but viewed in its relation to what is best and right it is the extreme of perfection.

But it is not all actions nor all passions that admit of moderation; there are some whose very names imply badness, as malevolence, shamelessness, envy, and, among acts, adultery, theft, murder. These and all other like things are blamed as being bad in themselves, and not merely in their excess or deficiency. It is impossible therefore to go right in them; they are always wrong: rightness and wrongness in such things (*e.g.* in adultery) does not depend upon whether it is the right person and occasion and manner, but the mere doing of any one of them is wrong.

It would be equally absurd to look for moderation or excess or deficiency in unjust cowardly or profligate conduct; for then there would be moderation in excess or deficiency, and excess in excess, and deficiency in deficiency.

The fact is that just as there can be no excess or deficiency in temperance or courage because the mean or moderate amount is, in a sense, an extreme, so in these kinds of conduct also there can be no moderation or excess or deficiency, but the acts are wrong however they be done. For, to put it generally, there cannot be moderation in excess or deficiency, nor excess or deficiency in moderation.

7.

This must be applied to the several virtues.

But it is not enough to make these general statements [about virtue and vice]: we must go on and apply them to particulars [*i.e.* to the several virtues and vices]. For in reasoning about matters of conduct general statements are too vague,* and do not convey so much truth as particular propositions. It is with particulars that conduct is concerned:‡ our statements, therefore, when applied to these particulars, should be found to hold good.

These particulars then [*i.e.* the several virtues and vices and the several acts and affections with which they deal], we will take from the following table.‡

Moderation in the feelings of fear and confidence is courage: of those that exceed, he that exceeds in fearlessness has no name (as often happens), but he that exceeds in confidence is foolhardy, while he that exceeds in fear, but is deficient in confidence, is cowardly.

Moderation in respect of certain pleasures and also (though to a less extent) certain pains is temperance, while excess is profligacy. But defectiveness in the matter of these pleasures is hardly ever found, and so this sort of people also have as yet received no name: let us put them down as "void of sensibility."

In the matter of giving and taking money, moderation is liberality, excess and deficiency are prodigality and illiberality. But both vices exceed and fall short in giving and taking in contrary ways: the prodigal exceeds in spending, but falls short in taking; while the illiberal man exceeds in taking, but falls short in spending. (For the present we are but giving an outline or summary, and aim at nothing more; we shall afterwards treat these points in greater detail.)

But, besides these, there are other dispositions in the matter of money: there is a moderation which is called magnificence (for the magnificent is not the same as the liberal man: the former deals with large sums, the latter with small), and an excess which is called bad taste or vulgarity, and a deficiency which is called meanness; and these vices differ from those which are opposed to liberality: how they differ will be explained later.

With respect to honour and disgrace, there is a moderation which is high-mindedness, an excess which may be called vanity, and a deficiency which is little-mindedness.

But just as we said that liberality is related to magnificence, differing only in that it deals with small sums, so here there is a virtue related to high-mindedness, and differing only in that it is concerned with small instead of great honours. A man may have a due desire for honour, and also more or less than a due desire: he that carries this desire to excess is called ambitious, he that has not enough of it is called unambitious, but he that has the due amount has no name. There are also no abstract names for the characters, except "ambition," corresponding to ambitious. And on this account those who occupy the extremes lay claim to the middle place. And in common parlance, too, the moderate man is sometimes called ambitious and sometimes unambitious, and sometimes the ambitious man is praised and sometimes the unambitious. Why this is we will explain afterwards; for the present we will follow out our plan and enumerate the other types of character.

In the matter of anger also we find excess and deficiency and moderation. The characters themselves hardly have recognized names, but as the moderate man is here called gentle, we will call his character gentleness; of those who go into extremes, we may take the term wrathful for him who exceeds, with wrathfulness for the vice, and wrathless for him who is deficient, with wrathlessness for his character.

Besides these, there are three kinds of moderation, bearing some resemblance to one another, and yet different. They all have to do with intercourse in speech and action, but they differ in that one has to do with the truthfulness of this intercourse, while the other two have to do with its pleasantness—one of the two with pleasantness in matters of amusement, the other with pleasantness in all the relations of life. We must therefore speak of these qualities also in order that we may the more plainly see how, in all cases, moderation is praiseworthy, while the extreme courses are neither right nor praiseworthy, but blamable.

In these cases also names are for the most part wanting, but we must try, here as elsewhere, to coin names ourselves, in order to make our argument clear and easy to follow.

In the matter of truth, then, let us call him who observes the mean a true [or truthful] person, and observance of the mean truth [or truthfulness]: pretence, when it exaggerates, may be called boasting, and the person a boaster; when it understates, let the names be irony and ironical.

With regard to pleasantness in amusement, he who observes the mean may be called witty, and his character wittiness; excess may be called buffoonery, and the man a buffoon; while boorish may stand for the person who is deficient, and boorishness for his character.

With regard to pleasantness in the other affairs of life, he who makes himself properly pleasant may be called friendly, and his moderation friendliness; he that exceeds may be called obsequious if he have no ulterior motive, but a flatterer if he has an eye to his own advantage; he that is deficient in this respect, and always makes himself disagreeable, may be called a quarrelsome or peevish fellow.

Moreover, in mere emotions* and in our conduct with regard to them, there are ways of observing the mean; for instance, shame (αἰδώς), is not a virtue, but yet the modest (αἰδήμων) man is praised. For in these matters also we speak of this man as observing the mean, of that man as going beyond it (as the shame-faced man whom the least thing makes shy), while he who is deficient in the feeling, or lacks it altogether, is called shameless; but the term modest (αἰδήμων) is applied to him who observes the mean.

Righteous indignation, again, hits the mean between envy and malevolence. These have to do with feelings of pleasure and pain at what happens to our neighbours. A man is called righteously indignant when he feels pain at the sight of undeserved prosperity, but your envious man goes beyond him and is pained by the sight of any one in prosperity, while the malevolent man is so far from being pained that he actually exults in the misfortunes of his neighbours.

But we shall have another opportunity of discussing these matters.

As for justice, the term is used in more senses than one; we will, therefore, after disposing of the above questions, distinguish these various senses, and show how each of these kinds of justice is a kind of moderation.

And then we will treat of the intellectual virtues in the same way.

8.

The two vicious extremes are opposed to one another and to the intermediate virtue.

There are, as we said, three classes of disposition, viz. two kinds of vice, one marked by excess, the other by deficiency, and one kind of virtue, the observance of the mean. Now, each is in a way opposed to each, for the extreme dispositions are opposed both to the mean or moderate disposition and to one another, while the moderate disposition is opposed to both the extremes. Just as a quantity which is equal to a given quantity is also greater when compared with a less, and less when compared with a greater quantity, so the mean or moderate dispositions exceed as compared with the defective dispositions, and fall short as compared with the excessive dispositions, both in feeling and in action; *e.g.* the courageous man seems foolhardy as compared with the coward, and cowardly as compared with the foolhardy; and similarly the temperate man appears profligate in comparison with the insensible, and insensible in comparison with the profligate man; and the liberal man appears prodigal by the side of the illiberal man, and illiberal by the side of the prodigal man.

And so the extreme characters try to displace the mean or moderate character, and each represents him as falling into the opposite extreme, the coward calling the courageous man foolhardy, the foolhardy calling him coward, and so on in other cases.

But while the mean and the extremes are thus opposed to one another, the extremes are strictly contrary to each other rather than to the mean; for they are further removed from one another than from the mean, as that which is greater than a given magnitude is further from that which is less, and that which is less is further from that which is greater, than either the greater or the less is from that which is equal to the given magnitude.

Sometimes, again, an extreme, when compared with the mean, has a sort of resemblance to it, as foolhardiness to courage, or prodigality to liberality; but there is the greatest possible dissimilarity between the extremes.

Again, "things that are as far as possible removed from each other" is the accepted definition of contraries, so that the further things are removed from each other the more contrary they are.

In comparison with the mean, however, it is sometimes the deficiency that is the more opposed, and sometimes the excess; *e.g.* foolhardiness, which is excess, is not so much opposed to courage as cowardice, which is deficiency; but insensibility, which is lack of feeling, is not so much opposed to temperance as profligacy, which is excess.

The reasons for this are two. One is the reason derived from the nature of the matter itself: since one extreme is, in fact, nearer and more similar to the mean, we naturally do not oppose it to the mean so strongly as the other; *e.g.* as foolhardiness seems more similar to courage and nearer to it, and cowardice more dissimilar, we speak of cowardice as the opposite rather than the other: for that which is further removed from the mean seems to be more opposed to it.

This, then, is one reason, derived from the nature of the thing itself. Another reason lies in ourselves: and it is this—those things to which we happen to be more prone by nature appear to be more opposed to the mean: *e.g.* our natural inclination is rather towards indulgence in pleasure, and so we more easily fall into profligate than into regular habits: those courses, then, in which we are more apt to run to great lengths are spoken of as more opposed to the mean; and thus profligacy, which is an excess, is more opposed to temperance than the deficiency is.

9.

The mean hard to hit, and is a matter of perception, not of reasoning.

We have sufficiently explained, then, that moral virtue is moderation or observance of the mean, and in what sense, viz. (1) as holding a middle position between two vices, one on the side of excess, and the other on the side of deficiency, and (2) as aiming at the mean or moderate amount both in feeling and in action.

And on this account it is a hard thing to be good; for finding the middle or the mean in each case is a hard thing, just as finding the middle or centre of a circle is a thing that is not within the power of everybody, but only of him who has the requisite knowledge.

Thus any one can be angry—that is quite easy; any one can give money away or spend it: but to do these things to the right person, to the right extent, at the right time, with the right object, and in the right manner, is not what everybody can do, and is by no means easy; and that is the reason why right doing is rare and praiseworthy and noble.

He that aims at the mean, then, should first of all strive to avoid that extreme which is more opposed to it, as Calypso* bids Ulysses—

"Clear of these smoking breakers keep thy ship."

For of the extremes one is more dangerous, the other less. Since then it is hard to hit the mean precisely, we must "row when we cannot sail," as the proverb has it, and choose the least of two evils; and that will be best effected in the way we have described.

And secondly we must consider, each for himself, what we are most prone to—for different natures are inclined to different things—which we may learn by the pleasure or pain we feel. And then we must bend ourselves in the opposite direction; for by keeping well away from error we shall fall into the middle course, as we straighten a bent stick by bending it the other way.

But in all cases we must be especially on our guard against pleasant things, and against pleasure; for we can scarce judge her impartially. And so, in our behaviour towards her, we should imitate the behaviour of the old counsellors towards Helen,* and in all cases repeat their saying: if we dismiss her we shall be less likely to go wrong.

This then, in outline, is the course by which we shall best be able to hit the mean.

But it is a hard task, we must admit, especially in a particular case. It is not easy to determine, for instance, how and with whom one ought to be angry, and upon what grounds, and for how long; for public opinion sometimes praises those who fall short, and calls them gentle, and sometimes applies the term manly to those who show a harsh temper.

In fact, a slight error, whether on the side of excess or deficiency, is not blamed, but only a considerable error; for then there can be no mistake. But it is hardly possible to determine by reasoning how far or to what extent a man must err in order to incur blame; and indeed matters that fall within the scope of perception never can be so determined. Such matters lie within the region of particulars, and can only be determined by perception.

So much then is plain, that the middle character is in all cases to be praised, but that we ought to incline sometimes towards excess, sometimes towards deficiency; for in this way we shall most easily hit the mean and attain to right doing. . . .

A Treatise on Government

Translated From The Greek Of Aristotle By William Ellis, A.M.
London &.Toronto Published By J M Dent & Sons Ltd. &.In New York By E. P. Dutton &. Co
First Issue Of This Edition 1912 Reprinted 1919, 1923, 1928
[http://www.gutenberg.org/ebooks/6762]

BOOK I

CHAPTER I

As we see that every city is a society, and every society Ed. is established for some good purpose; for an apparent [Bekker 1252a] good is the spring of all human actions; it is evident that this is the principle upon which they are every one founded, and this is more especially true of that which has for its object the best possible, and is itself the most excellent, and comprehends all the rest. Now this is called a city, and the society thereof a political society; for those who think that the principles of a political, a regal, a family, and a herile government are the same are mistaken, while they suppose that each of these differ in the numbers to whom their power extends, but not in their constitution: so that with them a herile government is one composed of a very few, a domestic of more, a civil and a regal of still more, as if there was no difference between a large family and a small city, or that a regal government and a political one are the same, only that in the one a single person is continually at the head of public affairs; in the other, that each member of the state has in his turn a share in the government, and is at one time a magistrate, at another a private person, according to the rules of political science. But now this is not true, as will be evident to any one who will consider this question in the most approved method. As, in an inquiry into every other subject, it is necessary to separate the different parts of which it is compounded, till we arrive at their first elements, which are the most minute parts thereof; so by the same proceeding we shall acquire a knowledge of the primary parts of a city and see wherein they differ from each other, and whether the rules of art will give us any assistance in examining into each of these things which are mentioned.

CHAPTER II

Now if in this particular science any one would attend to its original seeds, and their first shoot, he would then as in others have the subject perfectly before him; and perceive, in the first place, that it is requisite that those should be joined together whose species cannot exist without each other, as the male and the female, for the business of propagation; and this not through choice, but by that natural impulse which acts both upon plants and animals also, for the purpose of their leaving behind them others like themselves. It is also from natural causes that some beings command and others obey, that each may obtain their mutual safety; for a being who is endowed with a mind capable of reflection and forethought is by nature the superior and governor, whereas he whose excellence is merely corporeal is formed to be a slave; whence it follows that the different state of master [1252b] and slave is equally advantageous to both. But there is a natural difference between a female and a slave: for nature is not like the artists who make the Delphic swords for the use of the poor, but for every particular purpose she has her separate instruments, and thus her ends are most complete, for whatsoever is employed on one subject only, brings that one to much greater perfection than when employed on many; and yet among the barbarians, a female and a slave are upon a level in the community, the reason for which is, that amongst them there are none qualified by nature to govern, therefore their society can be nothing but between slaves of different sexes. For which reason the poets say, it is proper for the Greeks to govern the barbarians, as if a barbarian and a slave were by nature one. Now of these two societies the domestic is the first, and Hesiod is right when he says, "First a house, then a wife, then an ox for the plough," for the poor man has always an ox before a household slave. That society then which nature has established for daily support is the domestic, and those who compose it are called by Charondas *homosipuoi*, and by Epimenides the Cretan *homokapnoi*; but the society of many families, which was first instituted for their lasting, mutual advantage, is called a village, and a village is most naturally composed of the descendants of one family, whom some persons call homogalaktes, the children and the children's children thereof: for which reason cities were originally governed by kings, as the barbarian states now are, which are composed of those who had before submitted to kingly government; for every family is governed by the elder, as are the branches thereof, on account of their relationship thereunto, which is what Homer says, "Each one ruled his wife and child;" and in this scattered manner they formerly lived. And the opinion which universally prevails, that the gods themselves are subject to kingly government, arises from hence, that all men formerly were, and many are so now; and as they imagined themselves to be made in the likeness of the gods, so they supposed their manner of life must needs be the same. And when many villages so entirely join themselves together as in every respect to form but one society, that society is a city, and contains in itself, if I may so speak, the end and perfection of government: first founded that we might live, but continued that we may live happily. For which reason every city must be allowed to be the work of nature, if we admit that the original society between male and female is; for to this as their end all subordinate societies tend, and the end of everything is the nature of it. For what every being is in its most perfect state, that certainly is the nature of that being, whether it be a man, a horse, or a house: besides, whatsoever produces the final cause and the end which we [1253a] desire, must be best; but a government complete in itself is that final cause and what is best. Hence it is evident that a city is

a natural production, and that man is naturally a political animal, and that whosoever is naturally and not accidentally unfit for society, must be either inferior or superior to man: thus the man in Homer, who is reviled for being "without society, without law, without family." Such a one must naturally be of a quarrelsome disposition, and as solitary as the birds. The gift of speech also evidently proves that man is a more social animal than the bees, or any of the herding cattle: for nature, as we say, does nothing in vain, and man is the only animal who enjoys it. Voice indeed, as being the token of pleasure and pain, is imparted to others also, and thus much their nature is capable of, to perceive pleasure and pain, and to impart these sensations to others; but it is by speech that we are enabled to express what is useful for us, and what is hurtful, and of course what is just and what is unjust: for in this particular man differs from other animals, that he alone has a perception of good and evil, of just and unjust, and it is a participation of these common sentiments which forms a family and a city. Besides, the notion of a city naturally precedes that of a family or an individual, for the whole must necessarily be prior to the parts, for if you take away the whole man, you cannot say a foot or a hand remains, unless by equivocation, as supposing a hand of stone to be made, but that would only be a dead one; but everything is understood to be this or that by its energic qualities and powers, so that when these no longer remain, neither can that be said to be the same, but something of the same name. That a city then precedes an individual is plain, for if an individual is not in himself sufficient to compose a perfect government, he is to a city as other parts are to a whole; but he that is incapable of society, or so complete in himself as not to want it, makes no part of a city, as a beast or a god. There is then in all persons a natural impetus to associate with each other in this manner, and he who first founded civil society was the cause of the greatest good; for as by the completion of it man is the most excellent of all living beings, so without law and justice he would be the worst of all, for nothing is so difficult to subdue as injustice in arms: but these arms man is born with, namely, prudence and valour, which he may apply to the most opposite purposes, for he who abuses them will be the most wicked, the most cruel, the most lustful, and most gluttonous being imaginable; for justice is a political virtue, by the rules of it the state is regulated, and these rules are the criterion of what is right.

CHAPTER III

SINCE it is now evident of what parts a city is composed, it will be necessary to treat first of family government, for every city is made up of families, and every family [1253b] has again its separate parts of which it is composed. When a family is complete, it consists of freemen and slaves; but as in every subject we should begin with examining into the smallest parts of which it consists, and as the first and smallest parts of a family are the master and slave, the husband and wife, the father and child, let us first inquire into these three, what each of them may be, and what they ought to be; that is to say, the herile, the nuptial, and the paternal. Let these then be considered as the three distinct parts of a family: some think that the providing what is necessary for the family is something different from the government of it, others that this is the greatest part of it; it shall be considered separately; but we will first speak of a master and a slave, that we may both understand the nature of those things which are absolutely necessary, and also try if we can learn anything better on this subject than what is already known. Some persons have thought that the power of the master over his slave originates from his superior knowledge, and that this knowledge is the same in the master, the magistrate, and the king, as we have already said; but others think that herile government is contrary to nature, and that it is the law which makes one man a slave and another free, but that in nature there is no difference; for which reason that power cannot be founded in justice, but in force.

CHAPTER IV

Since then a subsistence is necessary in every family, the means of procuring it certainly makes up part of the management of a family, for without necessaries it is impossible to live, and to live well. As in all arts which are brought to perfection it is necessary that they should have their proper instruments if they would complete their works, so is it in the art of managing a family: now of instruments some of them are alive, others inanimate; thus with respect to the pilot of the ship, the tiller is without life, the sailor is alive; for a servant is as an instrument in many arts. Thus property is as an instrument to living; an estate is a multitude of instruments; so a slave is an animated instrument, but every one that can minister of himself is more valuable than any other instrument; for if every instrument, at command, or from a preconception of its master's will, could accomplish its work (as the story goes of the statues of Daedalus; or what the poet tells us of the tripods of Vulcan, "that they moved of their own accord into the assembly of the gods "), the shuttle would then weave, and the lyre play of itself; nor would the architect want servants, or the [1254a] master slaves. Now what are generally called instruments are the efficients of something else, but possessions are what we simply use: thus with a shuttle we make something else for our use; but we only use a coat, or a bed: since then making and using differ from each other in species, and they both require their instruments, it is necessary that these should be different from each other. Now life is itself what we use, and not what we employ as the efficient of something else; for which reason the services of a slave are for use. A possession may be considered in the same nature as a part of anything; now a part is not only a part of something, but also is nothing else; so is a possession; therefore a master is only the master of the slave, but no part of him; but the slave is not only the slave of the master, but nothing else but that. This fully explains what is the nature of a slave, and what are his capacities; for that being who by nature is nothing of himself, but totally another's, and is a man, is a slave by nature; and that man who is the property of another, is his mere chattel, though he continues a man; but a chattel is an instrument for use, separate from the body.

CHAPTER V

But whether any person is such by nature, and whether it is advantageous and just for any one to be a slave or no, or whether all slavery is contrary to nature, shall be considered hereafter; not that it is difficult to determine it upon general principles, or to understand it from matters of fact; for that some should govern, and others be governed, is not only necessary but useful, and from the hour of their birth some are marked out for those purposes, and others for the other, and there are many species of both sorts. And the better those are who are governed the better also is the government, as for instance of man, rather than the brute creation: for the more excellent the materials are with which the work is finished, the more excellent certainly is the work; and wherever there is a governor and a governed, there certainly is some work produced; for whatsoever is composed of many parts, which jointly become one, whether conjunct or separate, evidently show the marks of governing and governed; and this is true of every living thing in all nature; nay, even in some things which partake not of life, as in music; but this probably would be a disquisition too foreign to our present purpose. Every living thing in the first place is composed of soul and body, of these the one is by nature the governor, the other the governed; now if we would know what is natural, we ought to search for it in those subjects in which nature appears most perfect, and not in those which are corrupted; we should therefore examine into a man who is most perfectly formed both in soul and body, in whom this is evident, for in the depraved and vicious the body seems [1254b] to rule rather than the soul, on account of their being corrupt and contrary to nature. We may then, as we affirm, perceive in an animal the first principles of herile and political government; for the soul governs the body as the master governs his slave; the mind governs the appetite with a political or a kingly power, which shows that it is both natural and advantageous that the body should be governed by the soul, and the pathetic part by the mind, and that part which is possessed of reason; but to have no ruling power, or an improper one, is hurtful to all; and this holds true not only of man, but of other animals also, for tame animals are naturally better than wild ones, and it is advantageous that both should be under subjection to man; for this is productive of their common safety: so is it naturally with the male and the female; the one is superior, the other inferior; the one governs, the other is governed; and the same rule must necessarily hold good with respect to all mankind. Those men therefore who are as much inferior to others as the body is to the soul, are to be thus disposed of, as the proper use of them is their bodies, in which their excellence consists; and if what I have said be true, they are slaves by nature, and it is advantageous to them to be always under government. He then is by nature formed a slave who is qualified to become the chattel of another person, and on that account is so, and who has just reason enough to know that there is such a faculty, without being indued with the use of it; for other animals have no perception of reason, but are entirely guided by appetite, and indeed they vary very little in their use from each other; for the advantage which we receive, both from slaves and tame animals, arises from their bodily strength administering to our necessities; for it is the intention of nature to make the bodies of slaves and freemen different from each other, that the one should be robust for their necessary purposes, the others erect, useless indeed for what slaves are employed in, but fit for civil life, which is divided into the duties of war and peace; though these rules do not always take place, for slaves have sometimes the bodies of freemen, sometimes the souls; if then it is evident that if some bodies are as much more excellent than others as the statues of the gods excel the human form, every one will allow that the inferior ought to be slaves to the superior; and if this is true with respect to the body, it is still juster to determine in the same manner, when we consider the soul; though it is not so easy to perceive the beauty of [1255a] the soul as it is of the body. Since then some men are slaves by nature, and others are freemen, it is clear that where slavery is advantageous to any one, then it is just to make him a slave.

CHAPTER VI

But it is not difficult to perceive that those who maintain the contrary opinion have some reason on their side; for a man may become a slave two different ways; for he may be so by law also, and this law is a certain compact, by which whatsoever is taken in battle is adjudged to be the property of the conquerors: but many persons who are conversant in law call in question this pretended right, and say that it would be hard that a man should be compelled by violence to be the slave and subject of another who had the power to compel him, and was his superior in strength; and upon this subject, even of those who are wise, some think one way and some another; but the cause of this doubt and variety of opinions arises from hence, that great abilities, when accompanied with proper means, are generally able to succeed by force: for victory is always owing to a superiority in some advantageous circumstances; so that it seems that force never prevails but in consequence of great abilities. But still the dispute concerning the justice of it remains; for some persons think, that justice consists in benevolence, others think it just that the powerful should govern: in the midst of these contrary opinions, there are no reasons sufficient to convince us, that the right of being master and governor ought not to be placed with those who have the greatest abilities. Some persons, entirely resting upon the right which the law gives (for that which is legal is in some respects just), insist upon it that slavery occasioned by war is just, not that they say it is wholly so, for it may happen that the principle upon which the wars were commenced is unjust; moreover no one will say that a man who is unworthily in slavery is therefore a slave; for if so, men of the noblest families might happen to be slaves, and the descendants of slaves, if they should chance to be taken prisoners in war and sold: to avoid this difficulty they say that such persons should not be called slaves, but barbarians only should; but when they say this, they do nothing more than inquire who is a slave by nature, which was what we at first said; for we must acknowledge that there are some persons who, wherever they are, must necessarily be slaves, but others in no situation; thus also it is with those of noble descent: it is not only in their own country that they are Esteemed as such, but everywhere, but the barbarians are respected on this account at home only; as if nobility and freedom were of two sorts, the one universal, the other not so. Thus says the Helen of Theodectes:

"Who dares reproach me with the name of slave? When from the   immortal gods, on either side, I draw my lineage."

Those who express sentiments like these, shew only that they distinguish the slave and the freeman, the noble and the ignoble from each other by their virtues and their [1255b] vices; for they think it reasonable, that as a man begets a man, and a beast a beast, so from a good man, a good man should be descended; and this is what nature desires to do, but frequently cannot accomplish it. It is evident then that this doubt has some reason in it, and that these persons are not slaves, and those freemen, by the appointment of nature; and also that in some instances it is sufficiently clear, that it is advantageous to both parties for this man to be a slave, and that to be a master, and that it is right and just, that some should be governed, and others govern, in the manner that nature intended; of which sort of government is that which a master exercises over a slave. But to govern ill is disadvantageous to both; for the same thing is useful to the part and to the whole, to the body and to the soul; but the slave is as it were a part of the master, as if he were an animated part of his body, though separate. For which reason a mutual utility and friendship may subsist between the master and the slave, I mean when they are placed by nature in that relation to each other, for the contrary takes place amongst those who are reduced to slavery by the law, or by conquest.

...

CHAPTER XII

There are then three parts of domestic government, the masters, of which we have already treated, the fathers, and the husbands; now the government of the wife and children should both be that of free persons, but not the

[I259b] same; for the wife should be treated as a citizen of a free state, the children should be under kingly power; for the male is by nature superior to the female, except when something happens contrary to the usual course of nature, as is the elder and perfect to the younger and imperfect. Now in the generality of free states, the governors and the governed alternately change place; for an equality without any preference is what nature chooses; however, when one governs and another is governed, she endeavours that there should be a distinction between them in forms, expressions, and honours; according to what Amasis said of his laver. This then should be the established rule between the man and the woman. The government of children should be kingly; for the power of the father over the child is founded in affection and seniority, which is a species of kingly government; for which reason Homer very properly calls Jupiter "the father of gods and men," who was king of both these; for nature requires that a king should be of the same species with those whom he governs, though superior in some particulars, as is the case between the elder and the younger, the father and the son.

CHAPTER XIII

It is evident then that in the due government of a family, greater attention should be paid to the several members of it and their virtues than to the possessions or riches of it; and greater to the freemen than the slaves: but here some one may doubt whether there is any other virtue in a slave than his organic services, and of higher estimation than these, as temperance, fortitude, justice, and such-like habits, or whether they possess only bodily qualities: each side of the question has its difficulties; for if they possess these virtues, wherein do they differ from freemen? and that they do not, since they are men, and partakers of reason, is absurd. Nearly the same inquiry may be made concerning a woman and a child, whether these also have their proper virtues; whether a woman ought to be temperate, brave, and just, and whether a child is temperate or no; and indeed this inquiry ought to be general, whether the virtues of those who, by

nature, either govern or are governed, are the same or different; for if it is necessary that both of them should partake of the fair and good, why is it also necessary that, without exception, the one should govern, the other always be governed? for this cannot arise from their possessing these qualities in different degrees; for to govern, and to be governed, are things different in species, but more or less are not. And yet it is wonderful that one party ought to have them, and the other not; for if he who is to govern should not be temperate and just, how can he govern well? or if he is to be governed, how can he be governed well? for he who is intemperate [1260a] and a coward will never do what he ought: it is evident then that both parties ought to be virtuous; but there is a difference between them, as there is between those who by nature command and who by nature obey, and this originates in the soul; for in this nature has planted the governing and submitting principle, the virtues of which we say are different, as are those of a rational and an irrational being. It is plain then that the same principle may be extended farther, and that there are in nature a variety of things which govern and are governed; for a freeman is governed in a different manner from a slave, a male from a female, and a man from a child: and all these have parts of mind within them, but in a different manner. Thus a slave can have no power of determination, a woman but a weak one, a child an imperfect one. Thus also must it necessarily be with respect to moral virtues; all must be supposed to possess them, but not in the same manner, but as is best suited to every one's employment; on which account he who is to govern ought to be perfect in moral virtue, for his business is entirely that of an architect, and reason is the architect; while others want only that portion of it which may be sufficient for their station; from whence it is evident, that although moral virtue is common to all those we have spoken of, yet the temperance of a man and a woman are not the same, nor their courage, nor their justice, though Socrates thought otherwise; for the courage of the man consists in commanding, the woman's in obeying; and the same is true in other particulars: and this will be evident to those who will examine different virtues separately; for those who use general terms deceive themselves when they say, that virtue consists in a good disposition of mind, or doing what is right, or something of this sort. They do much better who enumerate the different virtues as Georgias did, than those who thus define them; and as Sophocles speaks of a woman, we think of all persons, that their 'virtues should be applicable to their characters, for says he,

"Silence is a woman's ornament,"

but it is not a man's; and as a child is incomplete, it is evident that his virtue is not to be referred to himself in his present situation, but to that in which he will be complete, and his preceptor. In like manner the virtue of a slave is to be referred to his master; for we laid it down as a maxim, that the use of a slave was to employ him in what you wanted; so that it is clear enough that few virtues are wanted in his station, only that he may not neglect his work through idleness or fear: some person may question if what I have said is true, whether virtue is not necessary for artificers in their calling, for they often through idleness neglect their work, but the difference between them is very great; for a slave is connected with you for life, but the artificer not so nearly: as near therefore as the artificer approaches to the situation of a slave, just so much ought he to have of the virtues of one; for a mean artificer is to a certain point a slave; but then a slave is one of those things which are by nature what they are, but this is not true [1260b] of a shoemaker, or any other artist. It is evident then that a slave ought to be trained to those virtues which are proper for his situation by his master; and not by him who has the power of a master, to teach him any particular art. Those therefore are in the wrong who would deprive slaves of reason, and say that they have only to follow their orders; for slaves want more instruction than children, and thus we determine this matter. It is necessary, I am sensible, for every one who treats upon government, to enter particularly into the relations of husband and wife, and of parent and child, and to show what are the virtues of each and their respective connections with each other; what is right and what is wrong; and how the one ought to be followed, and the other avoided. Since then every family is part of a city, and each of those individuals is part of a family, and the virtue of the parts ought to correspond to the virtue of the whole; it is necessary, that both the wives and children of the community should be instructed correspondent to the nature thereof, if it is of consequence to the virtue of the state, that the wives and children therein should be virtuous, and of consequence it certainly is, for the wives are one half of the free persons; and of the children the succeeding citizens are to be formed. As then we have determined these points, we will leave the rest to be spoken to in another place, as if the subject was now finished; and beginning again anew, first consider the sentiments of those who have treated of the most perfect forms of government.

BOOK II

CHAPTER I

Since then we propose to inquire what civil society is of all others best for those who have it in their power to live entirely as they wish, it is necessary to examine into the polity of those states which are allowed to be well governed; and if there should be any others which some persons have described, and which appear properly regulated, to note what is right and useful in them; and when we point out wherein they have failed, let not this be imputed to an affectation of wisdom, for it is because there are great defects in all those which are already established, that I have been induced to undertake this work. We will begin with that part of the subject which naturally presents itself first to our consideration. The members of every state must of necessity have all things in common, or some things common, and not others, or nothing at all common. To have nothing in common is evidently impossible, for society itself is one species of [1261a] community; and the first thing necessary thereunto is a common place of habitation, namely the city, which must be one, and this every citizen must have a share in. But in a government which is to be well founded, will it be best to admit of a community in everything which is capable thereof, or only in some particulars, but in others not? for it is possible that the citizens may have their wives, and children, and goods in common, as in Plato's Commonwealth; for in that Socrates affirms that all these particulars ought to be so. Which then shall we prefer? the custom which is already established, or the laws which are proposed in that treatise?

CHAPTER II

Now as a community of wives is attended with many other difficulties, so neither does the cause for which he would frame his government in this manner seem agreeable to reason, nor is it capable of producing that end which he has proposed, and for which he says it ought to take place; nor has he given any particular directions for putting it in practice. Now I also am willing to agree with Socrates in the principle which he proceeds upon, and admit that the city ought to be one as much as possible; and yet it is evident that if it is contracted too much, it will be no longer a city, for that necessarily supposes a multitude; so that if we proceed in this manner, we shall reduce a city to a family, and a family to a single person: for we admit that a family is one in a greater degree than a city, and a single person than a family; so that if this end could be obtained, it should never be put in practice, as it would annihilate the city; for a city does not only consist of a large number of inhabitants, but there must also be different sorts; for were they all alike, there could be no city; for a confederacy and a city are two different things; for a confederacy is valuable from its numbers, although all those who compose it are men of the same calling; for this is entered into for the sake of mutual defence, as we add an additional weight to make the scale go down. The same distinction prevails between a city and a nation when the people are not collected into separate villages, but live as the Arcadians. Now those things in which a city should be one are of different sorts, and in preserving an alternate reciprocation of power between these, the safety thereof consists (as I have already mentioned in my treatise on

Morals), for amongst freemen and equals this is absolutely necessary; for all cannot govern at the same time, but either by the year, or according to some other regulation or time, by which means every one in his turn will be in office; as if the shoemakers and carpenters should exchange occupations, and not always be employed in the same calling. But as it is evidently better, that these should continue to exercise their respective trades; so also in civil society, where it is possible, it would be better that the government should continue in the same hands; but where it [1261b] is not (as nature has made all men equal, and therefore it is just, be the administration good or bad, that all should partake of it), there it is best to observe a rotation, and let those who are their equals by turns submit to those who are at that time magistrates, as they will, in their turns, alternately be governors and governed, as if they were different men: by the same method different persons will execute different offices. From hence it is evident, that a city cannot be one in the manner that some persons propose; and that what has been said to be the greatest good which it could enjoy, is absolutely its destruction, which cannot be: for the good of anything is that which preserves it. For another reason also it is clear, that it is not for the best to endeavour to make a city too much one, because a family is more sufficient in itself than a single person, a city than a family; and indeed Plato supposes that a city owes its existence to that sufficiency in themselves which the members of it enjoy. If then this sufficiency is so desirable, the less the city is one the better.

CHAPTER III

But admitting that it is most advantageous for a city to be one as much as possible, it does not seem to follow that this will take place by permitting all at once to say this is mine, and this is not mine (though this is what Socrates regards as a proof that a city is entirely one), for the word All is used in two senses; if it means each individual, what Socrates proposes will nearly take place; for each person will say, this is his own son, and his own wife, and his own property, and of everything else that may happen to belong to him, that it is his own. But those who have their wives and children in common will not say so, but all will say so, though not as individuals; therefore, to use the word all is evidently a fallacious mode of speech; for this word is sometimes used distributively, and sometimes collectively, on account of its double meaning, and is the cause of inconclusive syllogisms in reasoning. Therefore for all persons to say the same thing was their own, using the word all in its distributive sense, would be well, but is impossible: in its collective sense it would by no means contribute to the concord of the state. Besides, there would be another inconvenience attending this proposal, for what is common to many is taken least care of; for all men regard more what is their own than what others share with them in, to which they pay less attention than is incumbent on every one: let me add also, that every one is more negligent of what another is to see to, as well as himself, than of his own private business; as in a family one is often worse served by many servants than by a few. Let each citizen then in the state have a thousand children, but let none of them be considered as the children of that individual, but let the relation of father and child be common to them all, and they will all be neglected. Besides, in consequence of this, [1262a] whenever any citizen behaved well or ill, every person, be the number what it would, might say, this is my son, or this man's or that; and in this manner would they speak, and thus would they doubt of the whole thousand, or of whatever number the city consisted; and it would be uncertain to whom each child belonged, and when it was born, who was to take care of it: and which do you think is better, for every one to say this is mine, while they may apply it equally to two thousand or ten thousand; or as we say, this is mine in our present forms of government, where one man calls another his son, another calls that same person his brother, another nephew, or some other relation, either by blood or marriage, and first extends his care to him and his, while another regards him as one of the same parish and the same tribe; and it is better for any one to be a nephew in his private capacity than a son after that manner. Besides, it will be

impossible to prevent some persons from suspecting that they are brothers and sisters, fathers and mothers to each other; for, from the mutual likeness there is between the sire and the offspring, they will necessarily conclude in what relation they stand to each other, which circumstance, we are informed by those writers who describe different parts of the world, does sometimes happen; for in Upper Africa there are wives in common who yet deliver their children to their respective fathers, being guided by their likeness to them. There are also some mares and cows which naturally bring forth their young so like the male, that we can easily distinguish by which of them they were impregnated: such was the mare called Just, in Pharsalia.

CHAPTER IV

Besides, those who contrive this plan of community cannot easily avoid the following evils; namely, blows, murders involuntary or voluntary, quarrels, and reproaches, all which it would be impious indeed to be guilty of towards our fathers and mothers, or those who are nearly related to us; though not to those who are not connected to us by any tie of affinity: and certainly these mischiefs must necessarily happen oftener amongst those who do not know how they are connected to each other than those who do; and when they do happen, if it is among the first of these, they admit of a legal expiation, but amongst the latter that cannot be done. It is also absurd for those who promote a community of children to forbid those who love each other from indulging themselves in the last excesses of that passion, while they do not restrain them from the passion itself, or those intercourses which are of all things most improper, between a Father and a son, a brother and a brother, and indeed the thing itself is most absurd. It is also ridiculous to prevent this intercourse between the nearest relations, for no other reason than the violence of the pleasure, while they think that the relation of father and daughter, the brother and sister, is of no consequence at all. It seems also more advantageous for the state, that the husbandmen should have their wives and children in common than the military, for there will be less affection [1262b] among them in that case than when otherwise; for such persons ought to be under subjection, that they may obey the laws, and not seek after innovations. Upon the whole, the consequences of such a law as this would be directly contrary to those things which good laws ought to establish, and which Socrates endeavoured to establish by his regulations concerning women and children: for we think that friendship is the greatest good which can happen to any city, as nothing so much prevents seditions: and amity in a city is what Socrates commends above all things, which appears to be, as indeed he says, the effect of friendship; as we learn from Aristophanes in the Erotics, who says, that those who love one another from the excess of that passion, desire to breathe the same soul, and from being two to be blended into one: from whence it would necessarily follow, that both or one of them must be destroyed. But now in a city which admits of this community, the tie of friendship must, from that very cause, be extremely weak, when no father can say, this is my son; or son, this is my father; for as a very little of what is sweet, being mixed with a great deal of water is imperceptible after the mixture, so must all family connections, and the names they go by, be necessarily disregarded in such a community, it being then by no means necessary that the father should have any regard for him he called a son, or the brothers for those they call brothers. There are two things which principally inspire mankind with care and love of their offspring, knowing it is their own, and what ought to be the object of their affection, neither of which can take place in this sort of community. As for exchanging the children of the artificers and husbandmen with those of the military, and theirs reciprocally with these, it will occasion great confusion in whatever manner it shall be done; for of necessity, those who carry the children must know from whom they took and to whom they gave them; and by this means those evils which I have already mentioned will necessarily be the more likely to happen, as blows, incestuous love, murders, and the like; for those who are given from their own parents to other citizens, the military, for instance, will not call them brothers,

sons, fathers, or mothers. The same thing would happen to those of the military who were placed among the other citizens; so that by this means every one would be in fear how to act in consequence of consanguinity. And thus let us determine concerning a community of wives and children.

CHAPTER V

We proceed next to consider in what manner property should be regulated in a state which is formed after the most perfect mode of government, whether it should be common or not; for this may be considered as a separate question from what had been determined concerning [1263a] wives and children; I mean, whether it is better that these should be held separate, as they now everywhere are, or that not only possessions but also the usufruct of them should be in common; or that the soil should have a particular owner, but that the produce should be brought together and used as one common stock, as some nations at present do; or on the contrary, should the soil be common, and should it also be cultivated in common, while the produce is divided amongst the individuals for their particular use, which is said to be practised by some barbarians; or shall both the soil and the fruit be common? When the business of the husbandman devolves not on the citizen, the matter is much easier settled; but when those labour together who have a common right of possession, this may occasion several difficulties; for there may not be an equal proportion between their labour and what they consume; and those who labour hard and have but a small proportion of the produce, will certainly complain of those who take a large share of it and do but little for that. Upon the whole, as a community between man and man so entire as to include everything possible, and thus to have all things that man can possess in common, is very difficult, so is it particularly so with respect to property; and this is evident from that community which takes place between those who go out to settle a colony; for they frequently have disputes with each other upon the most common occasions, and come to blows upon trifles: we find, too, that we oftenest correct those slaves who are generally employed in the common offices of the family: a community of property then has these and other inconveniences attending it.

But the manner of life which is now established, more particularly when embellished with good morals and a system of equal laws, is far superior to it, for it will have the advantage of both; by both I mean properties being common, and divided also; for in some respects it ought to be in a manner common, but upon the whole private: for every man's attention being employed on his own particular concerns, will prevent mutual complaints against each other; nay, by this means industry will be increased, as each person will labour to improve his own private property; and it will then be, that from a principle of virtue they will mutually perform good offices to each other, according to the proverb, "All things are common amongst friends;" and in some cities there are traces of this custom to be seen, so that it is not impracticable, and particularly in those which are best governed; some things are by this means in a manner common, and others might be so; for there, every person enjoying his own private property, some things he assists his friend with, others are considered as in common; as in Lacedaemon, where they use each other's slaves, as if they were, so to speak, their own, as they do their horses and dogs, or even any provision they may want in a journey.

It is evident then that it is best to have property private, but to make the use of it common; but how the citizens are to be brought to it is the particular [1263b] business of the legislator. And also with respect to pleasure, it is unspeakable how advantageous it is, that a man should think he has something which he may call his own; for it is by no means to no purpose, that each person should have an affection for himself, for that is natural, and yet to be a self-lover is justly censured; for we mean by that, not one that simply loves himself, but one that loves himself more than he ought; in like manner we blame a money-lover, and yet both money and self is what all men love. Besides, it is very pleasing to us to

oblige and assist our friends and companions, as well as those whom we are connected with by the rights of hospitality; and this cannot be done without the establishment of private property, which cannot take place with those who make a city too much one; besides, they prevent every opportunity of exercising two principal virtues, modesty and liberality. Modesty with respect to the female sex, for this virtue requires you to abstain from her who is another's; liberality, which depends upon private property, for without that no one can appear liberal, or do any generous action; for liberality consists in imparting to others what is our own.

This system of polity does indeed recommend itself by its good appearance and specious pretences to humanity; and when first proposed to any one, must give him great pleasure, as he will conclude it to be a wonderful bond of friendship, connecting all to all; particularly when any one censures the evils which are now to be found in society, as arising from properties not being common, I mean the disputes which happen between man and man, upon their different contracts with each other; those judgments which are passed in court in consequence of fraud, and perjury, and flattering the rich, none of which arise from properties being private, but from the vices of mankind. Besides, those who live in one general community, and have all things in common, oftener dispute with each other than those who have their property separate; from the very small number indeed of those who have their property in common, compared with those where it is appropriated, the instances of their quarrels are but few. It is also but right to mention, not only the inconveniences they are preserved from who live in a communion of goods, but also the advantages they are deprived of; for when the whole comes to be considered, this manner of life will be found impracticable.

We must suppose, then, that Socrates's mistake arose from the principle he set out with being false; we admit, indeed, that both a family and a city ought to be one in some particulars, but not entirely; for there is a point beyond which if a city proceeds in reducing itself to one, it will be no longer a city.

There is also another point at which it will still continue to be a city, but it will approach so near to not being one, that it will be worse than none; as if any one should reduce the voices of those who sing in concert to one, or a verse to a foot. But the people ought to be made one, and a community, as I have already said, by education; as property at Lacedaemon, and their public tables at Crete, were made common by their legislators. But yet, whosoever shall introduce any education, and think thereby to make his city excellent and respectable, will be absurd, while he expects to form it by such regulations, and not by manners, philosophy, and laws. And whoever [1264a] would establish a government upon a community of goods, ought to know that he should consult the experience of many years, which would plainly enough inform him whether such a scheme is useful; for almost all things have already been found out, but some have been neglected, and others which have been known have not been put in practice. But this would be most evident, if any one could see such a government really established: for it would be impossible to frame such a city without dividing and separating it into its distinct parts, as public tables, wards, and tribes; so that here the laws will do nothing more than forbid the military to engage in agriculture, which is what the Lacedaemonians are at present endeavouring to do.

Nor has Socrates told us (nor is it easy to say) what plan of government should be pursued with respect to the individuals in the state where there is a community of goods established; for though the majority of his citizens will in general consist of a multitude of persons of different occupations, of those he has determined nothing; whether the property of the husbandman ought to be in common, or whether each person should have his share to himself; and also, whether their wives and children ought to be in common: for if all things are to be alike common to all, where will be the difference between them and the military, or what would they get by submitting to their government? and upon what principles would

they do it, unless they should establish the wise practice of the Cretans? for they, allowing everything else to their slaves, forbid them only gymnastic exercises and the use of arms. And if they are not, but these should be in the same situation with respect to their property which they are in other cities, what sort of a community will there be? in one city there must of necessity be two, and those contrary to each other; for he makes the military the guardians of the state, and the husbandman, artisans, and others, citizens; and all those quarrels, accusations, and things of the like sort, which he says are the bane of other cities, will be found in his also: notwithstanding Socrates says they will not want many laws in consequence of their education, but such only as may be necessary for regulating the streets, the markets, and the like, while at the same time it is the education of the military only that he has taken any care of. Besides, he makes the husbandmen masters of property upon paying a tribute; but this would be likely to make them far more troublesome and high-spirited than the Helots, the Penestise, or the slaves which others employ; nor has he ever determined whether it is necessary to give any attention to them in these particulars, nor thought of what is connected therewith, their polity, their education, their laws; besides, it is of no little consequence, nor is it easy to determine, how these should be framed so as to preserve the community of the military.

Besides, if he makes the wives common, while the property [1264b] continues separate, who shall manage the domestic concerns with the same care which the man bestows upon his fields? nor will the inconvenience be remedied by making property as well as wives common; and it is absurd to draw a comparison from the brute creation, and say, that the same principle should regulate the connection of a man and a woman which regulates theirs amongst whom there is no family association.

It is also very hazardous to settle the magistracy as Socrates has done; for he would have persons of the same rank always in office, which becomes the cause of sedition even amongst those who are of no account, but more particularly amongst those who are of a courageous and warlike disposition; it is indeed evidently necessary that he should frame his community in this manner; for that golden particle which God has mixed up in the soul of man flies not from one to the other, but always continues with the same; for he says, that some of our species have gold, and others silver, blended in their composition from the moment of their birth: but those who are to be husbandmen and artists, brass and iron; besides, though he deprives the military of happiness, he says, that the legislator ought to make all the citizens happy; but it is impossible that the whole city can be happy, without all, or the greater, or some part of it be happy. For happiness is not like that numerical equality which arises from certain numbers when added together, although neither of them may separately contain it; for happiness cannot be thus added together, but must exist in every individual, as some properties belong to every integral; and if the military are not happy, who else are so? for the artisans are not, nor the multitude of those who are employed in inferior offices. The state which Socrates has described has all these defects, and others which are not of less consequence.

CHAPTER VI

It is also nearly the same in the treatise upon Laws which was writ afterwards, for which reason it will be proper in this place to consider briefly what he has there said upon government, for Socrates has thoroughly settled but very few parts of it; as for instance, in what manner the community of wives and children ought to be regulated, how property should be established, and government conducted.

Now he divides the inhabitants into two parts, husbandmen and soldiers, and from these he select a third part who are to be senators and govern the city; but he has not said whether or no the husbandman and artificer shall have any or what share in the government, or whether they shall have arms, and join with the others in war, or not. He thinks also that the women ought to go to war, and have the same education as the soldiers; as to other particulars, he has filled his treatise with matter foreign to the purpose; and

with respect to education, he has only said what that of the guards ought to be.

[1265a] As to his book of Laws, laws are the principal thing which that contains, for he has there said but little concerning government; and this government, which he was so desirous of framing in such a manner as to impart to its members a more entire community of goods than is to be found in other cities, he almost brings round again to be the same as that other government which he had first proposed; for except the community of wives and goods, he has framed both his governments alike, for the education of the citizens is to be the same in both; they are in both to live without any servile employ, and their common tables are to be the same, excepting that in that he says the women should have common tables, and that there should be a thousand men-at-arms, in this, that there should be five thousand.

All the discourses of Socrates are masterly, noble, new, and inquisitive; but that they are all true it may probably be too much to say. For now with respect to the number just spoken of, it must be acknowledged that he would want the country of Babylonia for them, or some one like it, of an immeasurable extent, to support five thousand idle persons, besides a much greater number of women and servants. Every one, it is true, may frame an hypothesis as he pleases, but yet it ought to be possible. It has been said, that a legislator should have two things in view when he frames his laws, the country and the people. He will also do well, if he has some regard to the neighbouring states, if he intends that his community should maintain any political intercourse with them, for it is not only necessary that they should understand that practice of war which is adapted to their own country, but to others also; for admitting that any one chooses not this life either in public or private, yet there is not the less occasion for their being formidable to their enemies, not only when they invade their country, but also when they retire out of it.

It may also be considered whether the quantity of each person's property may not be settled in a different manner from what he has done it in, by making it more determinate; for he says, that every one ought to have enough whereon to live moderately, as if any one had said to live well, which is the most comprehensive expression. Besides, a man may live moderately and miserably at the same time; he had therefore better have proposed, that they should live both moderately and liberally; for unless these two conspire, luxury will come in on the one hand, or wretchedness on the other, since these two modes of living are the only ones applicable to the employment of our substance; for we cannot say with respect to a man's fortune, that he is mild or courageous, but we may say that he is prudent and liberal, which are the only qualities connected therewith.

It is also absurd to render property equal, and not to provide for the increasing number of the citizens; but to leave that circumstance uncertain, as if it would regulate itself according to the number of women who [1265b] should happen to be childless, let that be what it would because this seems to take place in other cities; but the case would not be the same in such a state which he proposes and those which now actually unite; for in these no one actually wants, as the property is divided amongst the whole community, be their numbers what they will; but as it could not then be divided, the supernumeraries, whether they were many or few, would have nothing at all. But it is more necessary than even to regulate property, to take care that the increase of the people should not exceed a certain number; and in determining that, to take into consideration those children who will die, and also those women who will be barren; and to neglect this, as is done in several cities, is to bring certain poverty on the citizens; and poverty is the cause of sedition and evil. Now Phidon the Corinthian, one of the oldest legislators, thought the families and the number of the citizens should continue the same; although it should happen that all should have allotments at the first, disproportionate to their numbers.

In Plato's Laws it is however different; we shall mention hereafter what we think would be best in these particulars. He has also neglected in that treatise to point out how the governors are to be distinguished from the governed; for he says, that as of one sort of wool the warp ought to be made, and of another the woof, so ought some to govern, and others to be governed. But since he admits, that all their property may be increased fivefold, why should he not allow the same increase to the country? he ought also to consider whether his allotment of the houses will be useful to the community, for he appoints two houses to each person, separate from each other; but it is inconvenient for a person to inhabit two houses. Now he is desirous to have his whole plan of government neither a democracy nor an oligarchy, but something between both, which he calls a polity, for it is to be composed of men-at-arms. If Plato intended to frame a state in which more than in any other everything should be common, he has certainly given it a right name; but if he intended it to be the next in perfection to that which he had already framed, it is not so; for perhaps some persons will give the preference to the Lacedaemonian form of government, or some other which may more completely have attained to the aristocratic form.

Some persons say, that the most perfect government should be composed of all others blended together, for which reason they commend that of Lacedaemon; for they say, that this is composed of an oligarchy, a monarchy, and a democracy, their kings representing the monarchical part, the senate the oligarchical; and, that in the ephori may be found the democratical, as these are taken from the people. But some say, that in the ephori is absolute power, and that it is their common meal and daily course of life, in which the democratical form is represented. It is also said in this treatise of [1266a] Laws, that the best form of government must, be one composed of a democracy and a tyranny; though such a mixture no one else would ever allow to be any government at all, or if it is, the worst possible; those propose what is much better who blend many governments together; for the most perfect is that which is formed of many parts. But now in this government of Plato's there are no traces of a monarchy, only of an oligarchy and democracy; though he seems to choose that it should rather incline to an oligarchy, as is evident from the appointment of the magistrates; for to choose them by lot is common to both; but that a man of fortune must necessarily be a member of the assembly, or to elect the magistrates, or take part in the management of public affairs, while others are passed over, makes the state incline to an oligarchy; as does the endeavouring that the greater part of the rich may be in office, and that the rank of their appointments may correspond with their fortunes.

The same principle prevails also in the choice of their senate; the manner of electing which is favourable also to an oligarchy; for all are obliged to vote for those who are senators of the first class, afterwards they vote for the same number out of the second, and then out of the third; but this compulsion to vote at the election of senators does not extend to the third and fourth classes and the first and second class only are obliged to vote for the fourth. By this means he says he shall necessarily have an equal number of each rank, but he is mistaken—for the majority will always consist of those of the first rank, and the most considerable people; and for this reason, that many of the commonalty not being obliged to it, will not attend the elections. From hence it is evident, that such a state will not consist of a democracy and a monarchy, and this will be further proved by what we shall say when we come particularly to consider this form of government.

There will also great danger arise from the manner of electing the senate, when those who are elected themselves are afterwards to elect others; for by this means, if a certain number choose to combine together, though not very considerable, the election will always fall according to their pleasure. Such are the things which Plato proposes concerning government in his book of Laws.

...

BOOK III

CHAPTER I

Every one who inquires into the nature of government, and what are its different forms, should make this almost his first question, What is a city? For upon this there is a dispute: for some persons say the city did this or that, while others say, not the city, but the oligarchy, or the tyranny. We see that the city is the only object which both the politician and legislator have in view in all they do: but government is a certain ordering of those who inhabit a city. As a city is a collective body, and, like other wholes, composed of many parts, it is evident our first inquiry must be, what a citizen is: for a city is a certain number of citizens. So that we must consider whom we ought to call citizen, and who is one; for this is often doubtful: for every one will not allow that this character is applicable to the same person; for that man who would be a citizen in a republic would very often not be one in an oligarchy. We do not include in this inquiry many of those who acquire this appellation out of the ordinary way, as honorary persons, for instance, but those only who have a natural right to it.

Now it is not residence which constitutes a man a citizen; for in this sojourners and slaves are upon an equality with him; nor will it be sufficient for this purpose, that you have the privilege of the laws, and may plead or be impleaded, for this all those of different nations, between whom there is a mutual agreement for that purpose, are allowed; although it very often happens, that sojourners have not a perfect right therein without the protection of a patron, to whom they are obliged to apply, which shows that their share in the community is incomplete. In like manner, with respect to boys who are not yet enrolled, or old men who are past war, we admit that they are in some respects citizens, but not completely so, but with some exceptions, for these are not yet arrived to years of maturity, and those are past service; nor is there any difference between them. But what we mean is sufficiently intelligible and clear, we want a complete citizen, one in whom there is no deficiency to be corrected to make him so. As to those who are banished, or infamous, there may be the same objections made and the same answer given. There is nothing that more characterises a complete citizen than having a share in the judicial and executive part of the government.

With respect to offices, some are fixed to a particular time, so that no person is, on any account, permitted to fill them twice; or else not till some certain period has intervened; others are not fixed, as a juryman's, and a member of the general assembly: but probably some one may say these are not offices, nor have the citizens in these capacities any share in the government; though surely it is ridiculous to say that those who have the principal power in the state bear no office in it. But this objection is of no weight, for it is only a dispute about words; as there is no general term which can be applied both to the office of a juryman and a member of the assembly. For the sake of distinction, suppose we call it an indeterminate office: but I lay it down as a maxim, that those are citizens who could exercise it. Such then is the description of a citizen who comes nearest to what all those who are called citizens are. Every one also should know, that of the component parts of those things which differ from each other in species, after the first or second remove, those which follow have either nothing at all or very little common to each.

Now we see that governments differ from each other in their form, and that some of them are defective, others [1275b] as excellent as possible: for it is evident, that those which have many deficiencies and degeneracies in them must be far inferior to those which are without such faults. What I mean by degeneracies will be hereafter explained. Hence it is clear that the office of a citizen must differ as governments do from each other: for which reason he who is called a citizen has, in a democracy, every privilege which that station supposes. In other forms of government he may enjoy them; but not necessarily: for in some states the people have no power; nor have they any general assembly, but a few select men.

The trial also of different causes is allotted to different persons; as at Lacedaemon all disputes concerning contracts are brought before some of the ephori: the senate are the judges in cases of murder, and so on; some being to be heard by one magistrate, others by another: and thus at Carthage certain magistrates determine all causes. But our former description of a citizen will admit of correction; for in some governments the office of a juryman and a member of the

general assembly is not an indeterminate one; but there are particular persons appointed for these purposes, some or all of the citizens being appointed jurymen or members of the general assembly, and this either for all causes and all public business whatsoever, or else for some particular one: and this may be sufficient to show what a citizen is; for he who has a right to a share in the judicial and executive part of government in any city, him we call a citizen of that place; and a city, in one word, is a collective body of such persons sufficient in themselves to all the purposes of life.

CHAPTER II

In common use they define a citizen to be one who is sprung from citizens on both sides, not on the father's or the mother's only. Others carry the matter still further, and inquire how many of his ancestors have been citizens, as his grandfather, great-grandfather, etc., but some persons have questioned how the first of the family could prove themselves citizens, according to this popular and careless definition. Gorgias of Leontium, partly entertaining the same doubt, and partly in jest, says, that as a mortar is made by a mortar-maker, so a citizen is made by a citizen-maker, and a Larisssean by a Larisssean-maker. This is indeed a very simple account of the matter; for if citizens are so, according to this definition, it will be impossible to apply it to the first founders or first inhabitants of states, who cannot possibly claim in right either of their father or mother. It is probably a matter of still more difficulty to determine their rights as citizens who are admitted to their freedom after any revolution in the state. As, for instance, at Athens, after the expulsion of the tyrants, when Clisthenes enrolled many foreigners and city-slaves amongst the tribes; and the doubt with respect to them was, not whether they were citizens or no, but whether they were legally so or not. Though indeed some persons may have this further [1276a] doubt, whether a citizen can be a citizen when he is illegally made; as if an illegal citizen, and one who is no citizen at all, were in the same predicament: but since we see some persons govern unjustly, whom yet we admit to govern, though not justly, and the definition of a citizen is one who exercises certain offices, for such a one we have defined a citizen to be, it is evident, that a citizen illegally created yet continues to be a citizen, but whether justly or unjustly so belongs to the former inquiry.

CHAPTER III

It has also been doubted what was and what was not the act of the city; as, for instance, when a democracy arises out of an aristocracy or a tyranny; for some persons then refuse to fulfil their contracts; as if the right to receive the money was in the tyrant and not in the state, and many other things of the same nature; as if any covenant was founded for violence and not for the common good. So in like manner, if anything is done by those who have the management of public affairs where a democracy is established, their actions are to be considered as the actions of the state, as well as in the oligarchy or tyranny.

And here it seems very proper to consider this question, When shall we say that a city is the same, and when shall we say that it is different?

It is but a superficial mode of examining into this question to begin with the place and the people; for it may happen that these may be divided from that, or that some one of them may live in one place, and some in another (but this question may be regarded as no very knotty one; for, as a city may acquire that appellation on many accounts, it may be solved many ways); and in like manner, when men inhabit one common place, when shall we say that they inhabit the same city, or that the city is the same? for it does not depend upon the walls; for I can suppose Peloponnesus itself surrounded with a wall, as Babylon was, and every other place, which rather encircles many nations than one city, and that they say was taken three days when some of the inhabitants knew nothing of it: but we shall find a proper time to determine this question; for the extent of a city, how large it should be, and whether it should consist of more than one people, these are particulars that the politician should by no means be unacquainted with. This, too, is a matter of inquiry, whether we shall say that a city is the same while it is inhabited by the

same race of men, though some of them are perpetually dying, others coming into the world, as we say that a river or a fountain is the same, though the waters are continually changing; or when a revolution takes place shall we [1276b] say the men are the same, but the city is different: for if a city is a community, it is a community of citizens; but if the mode of government should alter, and become of another sort, it would seem a necessary consequence that the city is not the same; as we regard the tragic chorus as different from the comic, though it may probably consist of the same performers: thus every other community or composition is said to be different if the species of composition is different; as in music the same hands produce different harmony, as the Doric and Phrygian. If this is true, it is evident, that when we speak of a city as being the same we refer to the government there established; and this, whether it is called by the same name or any other, or inhabited by the same men or different. But whether or no it is right to dissolve the community when the constitution is altered is another question.

CHAPTER IV

What has been said, it follows that we should consider whether the same virtues which constitute a good man make a valuable citizen, or different; and if a particular inquiry is necessary for this matter we must first give a general description of the virtues of a good citizen; for as a sailor is one of those who make up a community, so is a citizen, although the province of one sailor may be different from another's (for one is a rower, another a steersman, a third a boatswain, and so on, each having their several appointments), it is evident that the most accurate description of any one good sailor must refer to his peculiar abilities, yet there are some things in which the same description may be applied to the whole crew, as the safety of the ship is the common business of all of them, for this is the general centre of all their cares: so also with respect to citizens, although they may in a few particulars be very different, yet there is one care common to them all, the safety of the community, for the community of the citizens composes the state; for which reason the virtue of a citizen has necessarily a reference to the state. But if there are different sorts of governments, it is evident that those actions which constitute the virtue of an excellent citizen in one community will not constitute it in another; wherefore the virtue of such a one cannot be perfect: but we say, a man is good when his virtues are perfect; from whence it follows, that an excellent citizen does not possess that virtue which constitutes a good man. Those who are any ways doubtful concerning this question may be convinced of the truth of it by examining into the best formed states: for, if it is impossible that a city should consist entirely of excellent citizens (while it is necessary that every one should do well in his calling, in which consists his excellence, as it is impossible that all the citizens should have the same [1277a] qualifications) it is impossible that the virtue of a citizen and a good man should be the same; for all should possess the virtue of an excellent citizen: for from hence necessarily arise the perfection of the city: but that every one should possess the virtue of a good man is impossible without all the citizens in a well-regulated state were necessarily virtuous. Besides, as a city is composed of dissimilar parts, as an animal is of life and body; the soul of reason and appetite; a family of a man and his wife—property of a master and a slave; in the same manner, as a city is composed of all these and many other very different parts, it necessarily follows that the virtue of all the citizens cannot be the same; as the business of him who leads the band is different from the other dancers. From all which proofs it is evident that the virtues of a citizen cannot be one and the same. But do we never find those virtues united which constitute a good man and excellent citizen? for we say, such a one is an excellent magistrate and a prudent and good man; but prudence is a necessary qualification for all those who engage in public affairs. Nay, some persons affirm that the education of those who are intended to command should, from the beginning, be different from other citizens, as the children of kings are generally instructed in riding and warlike exercises; and thus Euripides says:

"... No showy arts Be mine, but teach me what the state requires."

As if those who are to rule were to have an education peculiar to themselves. But if we allow, that the virtues of a good man and a good magistrate may be the same, and a citizen is one who obeys the magistrate, it follows that the virtue of the one cannot in general be the same as the virtue of the other, although it may be true of some particular citizen; for the virtue of the magistrate must be different from the virtue of the citizen. For which reason Jason declared that was he deprived of his kingdom he should pine away with regret, as not knowing how to live a private man. But it is a great recommendation to know how to command as well as to obey; and to do both these things well is the virtue of an accomplished citizen. If then the virtue of a good man consists only in being able to command, but the virtue of a good citizen renders him equally fit for the one as well as the other, the commendation of both of them is not the same. It appears, then, that both he who commands and he who obeys should each of them learn their separate business: but that the citizen should be master of and take part in both these, as any one may easily perceive; in a family government there is no occasion for the master to know how to perform the necessary offices, but rather to enjoy the labour of others; for to do the other is a servile part. I mean by the other, the common family business of the slave.

There are many sorts of slaves; for their employments are various: of these the handicraftsmen are one, who, as their name imports, get their living by the labour of their hands, and amongst these all mechanics are included; [1277b] for which reasons such workmen, in some states, were not formerly admitted into any share in the government; till at length democracies were established: it is not therefore proper for any man of honour, or any citizen, or any one who engages in public affairs, to learn these servile employments without they have occasion for them for their own use; for without this was observed the distinction between a master and a slave would be lost. But there is a government of another sort, in which men govern those who are their equals in rank, and freemen, which we call a political government, in which men learn to command by first submitting to obey, as a good general of horse, or a commander-in-chief, must acquire a knowledge of their duty by having been long under the command of another, and the like in every appointment in the army: for well is it said, no one knows how to command who has not himself been under command of another. The virtues of those are indeed different, but a good citizen must necessarily be endowed with them; he ought also to know in what manner freemen ought to govern, as well as be governed: and this, too, is the duty of a good man. And if the temperance and justice of him who commands is different from his who, though a freeman, is under command, it is evident that the virtues of a good citizen cannot be the same as justice, for instance but must be of a different species in these two different situations, as the temperance and courage of a man and a woman are different from each other; for a man would appear a coward who had only that courage which would be graceful in a woman, and a woman would be thought a talker who should take as large a part in the conversation as would become a man of consequence.

The domestic employments of each of them are also different; it is the man's business to acquire subsistence, the woman's to take care of it. But direction and knowledge of public affairs is a virtue peculiar to those who govern, while all others seem to be equally requisite for both parties; but with this the governed have no concern, it is theirs to entertain just notions: they indeed are like flute-makers, while those who govern are the musicians who play on them. And thus much to show whether the virtue of a good man and an excellent citizen is the same, or if it is different, and also how far it is the same, and how far different.

CHAPTER V

But with respect to citizens there is a doubt remaining, whether those only are truly so who are allowed to share in the government, or whether the mechanics also are to be considered

as such? for if those who are not permitted to rule are to be reckoned among them, it is impossible that the virtue of all the citizens should be the same, for these also are citizens; and if none of them are admitted to be citizens, where shall they be ranked? for they are neither [1278a] sojourners nor foreigners? or shall we say that there will no inconvenience arise from their not being citizens, as they are neither slaves nor freedmen: for this is certainly true, that all those are not citizens who are necessary to the existence of a city, as boys are not citizens in the same manner that men are, for those are perfectly so, the others under some conditions; for they are citizens, though imperfect ones: for in former times among some people the mechanics were either slaves or foreigners, for which reason many of them are so now: and indeed the best regulated states will not permit a mechanic to be a citizen; but if it be allowed them, we cannot then attribute the virtue we have described to every citizen or freeman, but to those only who are disengaged from servile offices. Now those who are employed by one person in them are slaves; those who do them for money are mechanics and hired servants: hence it is evident on the least reflection what is their situation, for what I have said is fully explained by appearances. Since the number of communities is very great, it follows necessarily that there will be many different sorts of citizens, particularly of those who are governed by others, so that in one state it may be necessary to admit mechanics and hired servants to be citizens, but in others it may be impossible; as particularly in an aristocracy, where honours are bestowed on virtue and dignity: for it is impossible for one who lives the life of a mechanic or hired servant to acquire the practice of virtue. In an oligarchy also hired servants are not admitted to be citizens; because there a man's right to bear any office is regulated by his fortune; but mechanics are, for many citizens are very rich.

There was a law at Thebes that no one could have a share in the government till he had been ten years out of trade. In many states the law invites strangers to accept the freedom of the city; and in some democracies the son of a free-woman is himself free. The same is also observed in many others with respect to natural children; but it is through want of citizens regularly born that they admit such: for these laws are always made in consequence of a scarcity of inhabitants; so, as their numbers increase, they first deprive the children of a male or female slave of this privilege, next the child of a free-woman, and last of all they will admit none but those whose fathers and mothers were both free.

That there are many sorts of citizens, and that he may be said to be as completely who shares the honours of the state, is evident from what has been already said. Thus Achilles, in Homer, complains of Agamemnon's treating him like an unhonoured stranger; for a stranger or sojourner is one who does not partake of the honours of the state: and whenever the right to the freedom of the city is kept obscure, it is for the sake of the inhabitants. [1278b] From what has been said it is plain whether the virtue of a good man and an excellent citizen is the same or different: and we find that in some states it is the same, in others not; and also that this is not true of each citizen, but of those only who take the lead, or are capable of taking the lead, in public affairs, either alone or in conjunction with others.

CHAPTER VI

Having established these points, we proceed next to consider whether one form of government only should be established, or more than one; and if more, how many, and of what sort, and what are the differences between them. The form of government is the ordering and regulating of the city, and all the offices in it, particularly those wherein the supreme power is lodged; and this power is always possessed by the administration; but the administration itself is that particular form of government which is established in any state: thus in a democracy the supreme power is lodged in the whole people; on the contrary, in an oligarchy it is in the hands of a few. We say then, that the form of government in these states is different, and we shall find the same thing hold good in others. Let us first determine for whose sake a city is established;

and point out the different species of rule which man may submit to in social life.

I have already mentioned in my treatise on the management of a family, and the power of the master, that man is an animal naturally formed for society, and that therefore, when he does not want any foreign assistance, he will of his own accord desire to live with others; not but that mutual advantage induces them to it, as far as it enables each person to live more agreeably; and this is indeed the great object not only to all in general, but also to each individual: but it is not merely matter of choice, but they join in society also, even that they may be able to live, which probably is not without some share of merit, and they also support civil society, even for the sake of preserving life, without they are grievously overwhelmed with the miseries of it: for it is very evident that men will endure many calamities for the sake of living, as being something naturally sweet and desirable. It is easy to point out the different modes of government, and we have already settled them in our exoteric discourses. The power of the master, though by nature equally serviceable, both to the master and to the slave, yet nevertheless has for its object the benefit of the master, while the benefit of the slave arises accidentally; for if the slave is destroyed, the power of the master is at an end: but the authority which a man has over his wife, and children, and his family, which we call domestic government, is either for the benefit of those who are under subjection, or else for the common benefit of the whole: but its particular object is the benefit of the governed, as we see in other arts; in physic, for instance, and the gymnastic exercises, wherein, if any benefit [1279a] arise to the master, it is accidental; for nothing forbids the master of the exercises from sometimes being himself one of those who exercises, as the steersman is always one of the sailors; but both the master of the exercises and the steersman consider the good of those who are under their government. Whatever good may happen to the steersman when he is a sailor, or to the master of the exercises when he himself makes one at the games, is not intentional, or the object of their power; thus in all political governments which are established to preserve and defend the equality of the citizens it is held right to rule by turns. Formerly, as was natural, every one expected that each of his fellow-citizens should in his turn serve the public, and thus administer to his private good, as he himself when in office had done for others; but now every one is desirous of being continually in power, that he may enjoy the advantage which he makes of public business and being in office; as if places were a never-failing remedy for every complaint, and were on that account so eagerly sought after.

It is evident, then, that all those governments which have a common good in view are rightly established and strictly just, but those who have in view only the good of the rulers are all founded on wrong principles, and are widely different from what a government ought to be, for they are tyranny over slaves, whereas a city is a community of freemen.

CHAPTER VII

Having established these particulars, we come to consider next the different number of governments which there are, and what they are; and first, what are their excellencies: for when we have determined this, their defects will be evident enough.

It is evident that every form of government or administration, for the words are of the same import, must contain a supreme power over the whole state, and this supreme power must necessarily be in the hands of one person, or a few, or many; and when either of these apply their power for the common good, such states are well governed; but when the interest of the one, the few, or the many who enjoy this power is alone consulted, then ill; for you must either affirm that those who make up the community are not citizens, or else let these share in the advantages of government. We usually call a state which is governed by one person for the common good, a kingdom; one that is governed by more than one, but by a few only, an aristocracy; either because the government is in the hands of the most worthy citizens, or because it is the best form for the city and its inhabitants. When the citizens at large govern for the public good, it is

called a state; which is also a common name for all other governments, and these distinctions are consonant to reason; for it will not be difficult to find one person, or a very few, of very distinguished abilities, but almost impossible to meet with the majority [1279b] of a people eminent for every virtue; but if there is one common to a whole nation it is valour; for this is created and supported by numbers: for which reason in such a state the profession of arms will always have the greatest share in the government.

Now the corruptions attending each of these governments are these; a kingdom may degenerate into a tyranny, an aristocracy into an oligarchy, and a state into a democracy. Now a tyranny is a monarchy where the good of one man only is the object of government, an oligarchy considers only the rich, and a democracy only the poor; but neither of them have a common good in view.

CHAPTER VIII

It will be necessary to enlarge a little more upon the nature of each of these states, which is not without some difficulty, for he who would enter into a philosophical inquiry into the principles of them, and not content himself with a superficial view of their outward conduct, must pass over and omit nothing, but explain the true spirit of each of them. A tyranny then is, as has been said, a monarchy, where one person has an absolute and despotic power over the whole community and every member therein: an oligarchy, where the supreme power of the state is lodged with the rich: a democracy, on the contrary, is where those have it who are worth little or nothing. But the first difficulty that arises from the distinctions which we have laid down is this, should it happen that the majority of the inhabitants who possess the power of the state (for this is a democracy) should be rich, the question is, how does this agree with what we have said? The same difficulty occurs, should it ever happen that the poor compose a smaller part of the people than the rich, but from their superior abilities acquire the supreme power; for this is what they call an oligarchy; it should seem then that our definition of the different states was not correct: nay, moreover, could any one suppose that the majority of the people were poor, and the minority rich, and then describe the state in this manner, that an oligarchy was a government in which the rich, being few in number, possessed the supreme power, and that a democracy was a state in which the poor, being many in number, possessed it, still there will be another difficulty; for what name shall we give to those states we have been describing? I mean, that in which the greater number are rich, and that in which the lesser number are poor (where each of these possess the supreme power), if there are no other states than those we have described. It seems therefore evident to reason, that whether the supreme power is vested in the hands of many or few may be a matter of accident; but that it is clear enough, that when it is in the hands of the few, it will be a government of the rich; when in the hands of the many, it will be a government of the poor; since in all countries there are many poor and few rich: it is not therefore the cause that has been already assigned (namely, the number of people in power) that makes the difference between the two governments; but an oligarchy and democracy differ in this from each other, in the poverty of those who govern in the one, and the riches 1280a of those who govern in the other; for when the government is in the hands of the rich, be they few or be they more, it is an oligarchy; when it is in the hands of the poor, it is a democracy: but, as we have already said, the one will be always few, the other numerous, but both will enjoy liberty; and from the claims of wealth and liberty will arise continual disputes with each other for the lead in public affairs.

CHAPTER IX

Let us first determine what are the proper limits of an oligarchy and a democracy, and what is just in each of these states; for all men have some natural inclination to justice; but they proceed therein only to a certain degree; nor can they universally point out what is absolutely just; as, for instance, what is equal appears just, and is so; but not to all; only among those who are equals: and what is unequal appears just, and is so; but not to all, only amongst those who are unequals; which circumstance some people neglect, and therefore judge ill; the reason for which is, they judge for themselves, and every one almost is the worst judge in his own cause. Since then justice has reference to persons, the same distinctions must be made with respect to persons which are made with respect to things, in the manner that I have already described in my Ethics.

As to the equality of the things, these they agree in; but their dispute is concerning the equality of the persons, and chiefly for the reason above assigned; because they judge ill in their own cause; and also because each party thinks, that if they admit what is right in some particulars, they have done justice on the whole: thus, for instance, if some persons are unequal in riches, they suppose them unequal in the whole; or, on the contrary, if they are equal in liberty, they suppose them equal in the whole: but what is absolutely just they omit; for if civil society was founded for the sake of preserving and increasing property, every one's right in the city would be equal to his fortune; and then the reasoning of those who insist upon an oligarchy would be valid; for it would not be right that he who contributed one mina should have an equal share in the hundred along with him who brought in all the rest, either of the original money or what was afterwards acquired.

Nor was civil society founded merely to preserve the lives of its members; but that they might live well: for otherwise a state might be composed of slaves, or the animal creation: but this is not so; for these have no share in the happiness of it; nor do they live after their own choice; nor is it an alliance mutually to defend each other from injuries, or for a commercial intercourse: for then the Tyrrhenians and Carthaginians, and all other nations between whom treaties of commerce subsist, would be citizens of one city; for they have articles to regulate their exports and imports, and engagements for mutual protection, and alliances for mutual defence; but [1280b] yet they have not all the same magistrates established among them, but they are different among the different people; nor does the one take any care, that the morals of the other should be as they ought, or that none of those who have entered into the common agreements should be unjust, or in any degree vicious, only that they do not injure any member of the confederacy. But whosoever endeavours to establish wholesome laws in a state, attends to the virtues and the vices of each individual who composes it; from whence it is evident, that the first care of him who would found a city, truly deserving that name, and not nominally so, must be to have his citizens virtuous; for otherwise it is merely an alliance for self-defence; differing from those of the same cast which are made between different people only in place: for law is an agreement and a pledge, as the sophist Lycophron says, between the citizens of their intending to do justice to each other, though not sufficient to make all the citizens just and good: and that this is faact is evident, for could any one bring different places together, as, for instance, enclose Megara and Corinth in a wall, yet they would not be one city, not even if the inhabitants intermarried with each other, though this inter-community contributes much to make a place one city. Besides, could we suppose a set of people to live separate from each other, but within such a distance as would admit of an intercourse, and that there were laws subsisting between each party, to prevent their injuring one another in their mutual dealings, supposing one a carpenter, another a husbandman, shoemaker, and the like, and that their numbers were ten thousand, still all that they would have together in common would be a tariff for trade, or an alliance for mutual defence, but not the same city. And why? not because their mutual intercourse is not near enough, for even if persons so situated should come to one place, and every one should live in his own house as in his native city, and there should be alliances subsisting between each party to mutually assist and prevent any injury being done to the other, still they would not be admitted to be a city by those who think correctly, if they preserved the same customs when they were together as when they were separate.

It is evident, then, that a city is not a community of place; nor established for the sake of mutual safety or traffic with each other; but that these things are the necessary consequences of a city, although they may all exist where there is no city: but a city is a society of people joining together with their families and their children to live agreeably for the sake of having their lives as happy and as independent as possible: and for this purpose it is necessary that they should live in one place and intermarry with each other: hence in all cities there are family-meetings, clubs, sacrifices, and public entertainments to promote friendship; for a love of sociability is friendship itself; so that the end then for which a city is established is, that the inhabitants of it may live happy, and these things are conducive to that end: for it is a community of families and villages for the sake of a perfect independent life; that is, as we have already said, for the sake of living well and happily. It is not therefore founded for the purpose of men's merely [1281a] living together, but for their living as men ought; for which reason those who contribute most to this end deserve to have greater power in the city than those who are their equals in family and freedom, but their inferiors in civil virtue, or those who excel them in wealth but are below them in worth. It is evident from what has been said, that in all disputes upon government each party says something that is just.

CHAPTER X

It may also be a doubt where the supreme power ought to be lodged. Shall it be with the majority, or the wealthy, with a number of proper persons, or one better than the rest, or with a tyrant? But whichever of these we prefer some difficulty will arise. For what? shall the poor have it because they are the majority? they may then divide among themselves, what belongs to the rich: nor is this unjust; because truly it has been so judged by the supreme power. But what avails it to point out what is the height of injustice if this is not? Again, if the many seize into their own hands everything which belongs to the few, it is evident that the city will be at an end. But virtue will never destroy what is virtuous; nor can what is right be the ruin of the state: therefore such a law can never be right, nor can the acts of a tyrant ever be wrong, for of necessity they must all be just; for he, from his unlimited power, compels every one to obey his command, as the multitude oppress the rich. Is it right then that the rich, the few, should have the supreme power? and what if they be guilty of the same rapine and plunder the possessions of the majority, that will be as right as the other: but that all things of this sort are wrong and unjust is evident. Well then, these of the better sort shall have it: but must not then all the other citizens live unhonoured, without sharing the offices of the city; for the offices of a city are its honours, and if one set of men are always in power, it is evident that the rest must be without honour. Well then, let it be with one person of all others the fittest for it: but by this means the power will be still more contracted, and a greater number than before continue unhonoured. But some one may say, that it is wrong to let man have the supreme power and not the law, as his soul is subject to so many passions. But if this law appoints an aristocracy, or a democracy, how will it help us in our present doubts? for those things will happen which we have already mentioned.

CHAPTER XI

Other particulars we will consider separately; but it seems proper to prove, that the supreme power ought to be lodged with the many, rather than with those of the better sort, who are few; and also to explain what doubts (and probably just ones) may arise: now, though not one individual of the many may himself be fit for the supreme power, yet when these many are joined together, it does not follow but they may be better qualified for it than those; and this not separately, but as a collective body; as the public suppers exceed those which are given at one person's private expense: for, as they are many, each person brings in his share of virtue and wisdom; and thus, coming together, they are like one man made up of a multitude, with many feet, many hands, and many intelligences: thus is it with respect to the manners and understandings of the multitude taken together; for which reason the public are the best judges of music and

poetry; for some understand one part, some another, and all collectively the whole; and in this particular men of consequence differ from each of the many; as they say those who are beautiful do from those who are not so, and as fine pictures excel any natural objects, by collecting the several beautiful parts which were dispersed among different originals into one, although the separate parts, as the eye or any other, might be handsomer than in the picture.

But if this distinction is to be made between every people and every general assembly, and some few men of consequence, it may be doubtful whether it is true; nay, it is clear enough that, with respect to a few, it is not; since the same conclusion might be applied even to brutes: and indeed wherein do some men differ from brutes? Not but that nothing prevents what I have said being true of the people in some states. The doubt then which we have lately proposed, with all its consequences, may be settled in this manner; it is necessary that the freemen who compose the bulk of the people should have absolute power in some things; but as they are neither men of property, nor act uniformly upon principles of virtue, it is not safe to trust them with the first offices in the state, both on account of their iniquity and their ignorance; from the one of which they will do what is wrong, from the other they will mistake: and yet it is dangerous to allow them no power or share in the government; for when there are many poor people who are incapable of acquiring the honours of their country, the state must necessarily have many enemies in it; let them then be permitted to vote in the public assemblies and to determine causes; for which reason Socrates, and some other legislators, gave them the power of electing the officers of the state, and also of inquiring into their conduct when they came out of office, and only prevented their being magistrates by themselves; for the multitude when they are collected together have all of them sufficient understanding for these purposes, and, mixing among those of higher rank, are serviceable to the city, as some things, which alone are improper for food, when mixed with others make the whole more wholesome than a few of them would be.

But there is a difficulty attending this form of government, for it seems, that the person who himself was capable of curing any one who was then sick, must be the best judge whom to employ as a physician; but such a one must be himself a physician; and the same holds true in every other practice and art: and as a physician ought [1282a] to give an account of his practice to a physician, so ought it to be in other arts: those whose business is physic may be divided into three sorts, the first of these is he who makes up the medicines; the second prescribes, and is to the other as the architect is to the mason; the third is he who understands the science, but never practises it: now these three distinctions may be found in those who understand all other arts; nor have we less opinion of their judgment who are only instructed in the principles of the art than of those who practise it: and with respect to elections the same method of proceeding seems right; for to elect a proper person in any science is the business of those who are skilful therein; as in geometry, of geometricians; in steering, of steersmen: but if some individuals should know something of particular arts and works, they do not know more than the professors of them: so that even upon this principle neither the election of magistrates, nor the censure of their conduct, should be entrusted to the many.

But probably all that has been here said may not be right; for, to resume the argument I lately used, if the people are not very brutal indeed, although we allow that each individual knows less of these affairs than those who have given particular attention to them, yet when they come together they will know them better, or at least not worse; besides, in some particular arts it is not the workman only who is the best judge; namely, in those the works of which are understood by those who do not profess them: thus he who builds a house is not the only judge of it, for the master of the family who inhabits it is a better; thus also a steersman is a better judge of a tiller than he who made it; and he who gives an entertainment than the cook. What has been said seems a sufficient solution of this difficulty; but there is another that follows: for it seems absurd that the power of the state should be lodged with those who are but of indifferent morals, instead of those who are of excellent characters. Now the power of election and censure are of the utmost consequence, and this, as has been said, in some states they entrust to the people; for the general assembly is the supreme court of all, and they have a voice in this, and deliberate in all public affairs, and try all causes, without any objection to the meanness of their circumstances, and at any age: but their treasurers, generals, and other great officers of state are taken from men of great fortune and worth. This difficulty also may be solved upon the same principle; and here too they may be right, for the power is not in the man who is member of the assembly, or council, but the assembly itself, and the council, and the people, of which each individual of the whole community are the parts, I mean as senator, adviser, or judge; for which reason it is very right, that the many should have the greatest powers in their own hands; for the people, the council, and the judges are composed of them, and the property of all these collectively is more than the property of any person or a few who fill the great offices of the state: and thus I determine these points.

The first question that we stated shows plainly, that the supreme power should be lodged in laws duly made and that the magistrate or magistrates, either one or more, should be authorised to determine those cases which the laws cannot particularly speak to, as it is impossible for them, in general language, to explain themselves upon everything that may arise: but what these laws are which are established upon the best foundations has not been yet explained, but still remains a matter of some question: but the laws of every state will necessarily be like every state, either trifling or excellent, just or unjust; for it is evident, that the laws must be framed correspondent to the constitution of the government; and, if so, it is plain, that a well-formed government will have good laws, a bad one, bad ones.

CHAPTER XII
Since in every art and science the end aimed at is always good, so particularly in this, which is

the most excellent of all, the founding of civil society, the good wherein aimed at is justice; for it is this which is for the benefit of all. Now, it is the common opinion, that justice is a certain equality; and in this point all the philosophers are agreed when they treat of morals: for they say what is just, and to whom; and that equals ought to receive equal: but we should know how we are to determine what things are equal and what unequal; and in this there is some difficulty, which calls for the philosophy of the politician. Some persons will probably say, that the employments of the state ought to be given according to every particular excellence of each citizen, if there is no other difference between them and the rest of the community, but they are in every respect else alike: for justice attributes different things to persons differing from each other in their character, according to their respective merits. But if this is admitted to be true, complexion, or height, or any such advantage will be a claim for a greater share of the public rights. But that this is evidently absurd is clear from other arts and sciences; for with respect to musicians who play on the flute together, the best flute is not given to him who is of the best family, for he will play never the better for that, but the best instrument ought to be given to him who is the best artist.

If what is now said does not make this clear, we will explain it still further: if there should be any one, a very excellent player on the flute, but very deficient in family and beauty, though each of them are more valuable endowments than a skill in music, and excel this art in a higher degree than that player excels others, yet the best flutes ought to be given to him; for the superiority [1283a] in beauty and fortune should have a reference to the business in hand; but these have none. Moreover, according to this reasoning, every possible excellence might come in comparison with every other; for if bodily strength might dispute the point with riches or liberty, even any bodily strength might do it; so that if one person excelled in size more than another did in virtue, and his size was to qualify him to take place of the other's virtue, everything must then admit of a comparison with each other;

for if such a size is greater than virtue by so much, it is evident another must be equal to it: but, since this is impossible, it is plain that it would be contrary to common sense to dispute a right to any office in the state from every superiority whatsoever: for if one person is slow and the other swift, neither is the one better qualified nor the other worse on that account, though in the gymnastic races a difference in these particulars would gain the prize; but a pretension to the offices of the state should be founded on a superiority in those qualifications which are useful to it: for which reason those of family, independency, and fortune, with great propriety, contend with each other for them; for these are the fit persons to fill them: for a city can no more consist of all poor men than it can of all slaves But if such persons are requisite, it is evident that those also who are just and valiant are equally so; for without justice and valour no state can be supported, the former being necessary for its existence, the latter for its happiness.

CHAPTER XIII

It seems, then, requisite for the establishment of a state, that all, or at least many of these particulars should be well canvassed and inquired into; and that virtue and education may most justly claim the right of being considered as the necessary means of making the citizens happy, as we have already said. As those who are equal in one particular are not therefore equal in all, and those who are unequal in one particular are not therefore unequal in all, it follows that all those governments which are established upon a principle which supposes they are, are erroneous.

We have already said, that all the members of the community will dispute with each other for the offices of the state; and in some particulars justly, but not so in general; the rich, for instance, because they have the greatest landed property, and the ultimate right to the soil is vested in the community; and also because their fidelity is in general most to be depended on. The freemen and men of family will dispute the point with each other, as nearly on an equality; for these latter have a right to a higher regard as citizens than obscure persons, for honourable descent is everywhere of great esteem: nor is it an improper conclusion, that the descendants of men of worth will be men of worth themselves; for noble birth is the fountain of virtue to men of family: for the same reason also we justly say, that virtue has a right to put in her pretensions. Justice, for instance, is a virtue, and so necessary to society, that all others must yield her the precedence.

Let us now see what the many have to urge on their side against the few; and they may say, that if, when collectively taken, they are compared with them, they are stronger, richer, and better than they are. But should it ever happen that all these should inhabit the [1283b] same city, I mean the good, the rich, the noble, as well as the many, such as usually make up the community, I ask, will there then be any reason to dispute concerning who shall govern, or will there not? for in every community which we have mentioned there is no dispute where the supreme power should be placed; for as these differ from each other, so do those in whom that is placed; for in one state the rich enjoy it, in others the meritorious, and thus each according to their separate manners. Let us however consider what is to be done when all these happen at the same time to inhabit the same city. If the virtuous should be very few in number, how then shall we act? shall we prefer the virtuous on account of their abilities, if they are capable of governing the city? or should they be so many as almost entirely to compose the state?

There is also a doubt concerning the pretensions of all those who claim the honours of government: for those who found them either on fortune or family have nothing which they can justly say in their defence; since it is evident upon their principle, that if any one person can be found richer than all the rest, the right of governing all these will be justly vested in this one person. In the same manner, one man who is of the best family will claim it from those who dispute the point upon family merit: and probably in an aristocracy the same dispute might arise on the score of virtue, if there is one man better than all the other men of worth who are in the same community; it seems just, by the same reasoning, that he should enjoy the supreme power. And upon this principle also, while the many suppose they ought to have the supreme command, as being more powerful than the few, if one or more than one, though a small number should be found stronger than themselves, these ought rather to have it than they.

All these things seem to make it plain, that none of these principles are justly founded on which these persons would establish their right to the supreme power; and that all men whatsoever ought to obey them: for with respect to those who claim it as due to their virtue or their fortune, they might have justly some objection to make; for nothing hinders but that it may sometimes happen, that the many may be better or richer than the few, not as individuals, but in their collective capacity.

As to the doubt which some persons have proposed and objected, we may answer it in this manner; it is this, whether a legislator, who would establish the most perfect system of laws, should calculate them for the use of the better part of the citizens, or the many, in the circumstances we have already mentioned? The rectitude of anything consists in its equality; that therefore which is equally right will be advantageous to the whole state, and to every member of it in common.

Now, in general, a citizen is one who both shares in the government and also in his turn submits to be governed; [1284a] their condition, it is true, is different in different states: the best is that in which a man is enabled to choose and to persevere in a course of virtue during his whole life, both in his public and private state. But should there be one person, or a very few, eminent for an uncommon degree of virtue, though not enough to make up a civil state, so that the virtue of the many, or their political abilities, should be too inferior to come in comparison with theirs, if more than one; or if but one, with his only; such are not to be considered as part of the city; for it would be doing them injustice to rate them on a level with those who are so far their inferiors in virtue and political abilities, that they appear to them like a god amongst men. From whence it is evident, that a system of laws must be calculated for those who are equal to each other in nature and power. Such men, therefore, are not the object of law; for they are themselves a law: and it would be ridiculous in any one to endeavour to include them in the penalties of a law: for probably they might say what Antisthenes tells us the lions did to the hares when they demanded to be admitted to an equal share with them in the government. And it is on this account that democratic states have established the ostracism; for an equality seems the principal object of their government. For which reason they compel all those who are very eminent for their power, their fortune, their friendships, or any other cause which may give them too great weight in the government, to submit to the ostracism, and leave the city for a stated time; as the fabulous histories relate the Argonauts served Hercules, for they refused to take him with them in the ship Argo on account of his superior valour. For which reason those who hate a tyranny and find fault with the advice which Periander gave to Thrasybulus, must not think there was nothing to be said in its defence; for the story goes, that Periander said nothing to the messenger in answer to the business he was consulted about, but striking off those ears of corn which were higher than the rest, reduced the whole crop to a level; so that the messenger, without knowing the cause of what was done, related the fact to Thrasybulus, who understood by it that he must take off all the principal men in the city. Nor is this serviceable to tyrants only; nor is it tyrants only who do it; for the same thing is practised both in oligarchies and democracies: for the ostracism has in a manner nearly the same power, by restraining and banishing those who are too great; and what is done in one city is done also by those who have the supreme power in separate states; as the Athenians with respect to the Samians, the Chians, and the Lesbians; for when they suddenly acquired the superiority over all Greece, they brought the other states into subjection, contrary to the treaties which subsisted between them. The King of Persia also very often reduces the Medes and Babylonians when they assume upon their former power: [1284b] and this is a principle which all governments whatsoever keep in their eye; even those which are best administered, as well as those which are not, do it; these for the sake of private utility, the others for the public good.

The same thing is to be perceived in the other arts and sciences; for a painter would not represent an animal with a foot disproportionally large, though he had drawn it remarkably beautiful; nor would the shipwright make the prow or any other part of the vessel larger than it ought to be; nor will the master of the band permit any who sings louder and better than the rest to sing in concert with them. There is therefore no reason that a monarch should not act in agreement with free states, to support his own power, if they do the same thing for the benefit of their respective communities; upon which account when there is any acknowledged difference in the power of the citizens, the reason upon which the ostracism is founded will be politically just; but it is better for the legislator so to establish his state at the beginning as not to want this remedy: but if in course of time such an inconvenience should arise, to endeavour to amend it by some such correction. Not that this was the use it was put to: for many did not regard the benefit of their respective communities, but made the ostracism a weapon in the hand of sedition.

It is evident, then, that in corrupt governments it is partly just and useful to the individual, though probably it is as clear that it is not entirely just: for in a well-governed state there may be great doubts about the use of it, not on account of the pre-eminence which one may have in strength, riches, or connection: but when the pre-eminence is virtue, what then is to be done? for it seems not right to turn out and banish such a one; neither does it seem right to govern him, for that would be like desiring to share the power with Jupiter and to govern him: nothing then remains but what indeed seems natural, and that is for all persons quietly to submit to the government of those who are thus eminently virtuous, and let them be perpetually kings in the separate states.

...

CHAPTER XV

...

Now the first thing which presents itself to our consideration is this, whether it is best to be governed by a good man, or by good laws? Those who prefer a kingly government think that laws can only speak a general language, but cannot adapt themselves to particular circumstances; for which reason it is absurd in any science to follow written rule; and even in Egypt the physician was allowed to alter the mode of cure which the law prescribed to him, after the fourth day; but if he did it sooner it was at his own peril: from whence it is evident, on the very same account, that a government of written laws is not the best; and yet general reasoning is necessary to all those who are to govern, and it will be much more perfect in those who are entirely free from passions than in those to whom they are natural. But now this is a quality which laws possess; while the other is natural to the human soul. But some one will say in answer to this, that man will be a better judge of particulars. It will be necessary, then, for a king to be a lawgiver, and that his laws should be published, but that those should have no authority which are absurd, as those which are not, should. But whether is it better for the community that those things which cannot possibly come under the cognisance of the law either at all or properly should be under the government of every worthy citizen, as the present method is, when the public community, in their general assemblies, act as judges and counsellors, where all their determinations are upon particular cases, for one individual, be he who he will, will be found, upon comparison, inferior to a whole people taken collectively: but this is what a city is, as a public entertainment is better than one man's portion: for this reason the multitude judge of many things better than any one single person. They are also less liable to corruption from their numbers, as water is from its quantity: besides, the judgment of an individual must necessarily be perverted if he is overcome by anger or any other passion; but it would be hard indeed if the whole community should be misled by anger. Moreover, let the people be free, and they will do nothing but in conformity to the law, except only in those cases which the law cannot speak to. But though what I am going to propose may not easily be met with, yet if the majority of the state should happen to be good men, should they prefer one uncorrupt governor or many equally good, is it not evident that they should choose the many? But there may be divisions among [1286b] these which cannot happen when there is but one. In answer to this it may be replied that all their souls will be as much animated with virtue as this one man's.

If then a government of many, and all of them good men, compose an aristocracy, and the government of one a kingly power, it is evident that the people should rather choose the first than the last; and this whether the state is powerful or not, if many such persons so alike can be met with: and for this reason probable it was, that the first governments were generally monarchies; because it was difficult to find a number of persons eminently virtuous, more particularly as the world was then divided into small communities; besides, kings were appointed in return for the benefits they had conferred on mankind; but such actions are peculiar to good men: but when many persons equal in virtue appeared at the time, they brooked not a superiority, but sought after an equality and established a free state; but after this, when they degenerated, they made a property of the public; which probably gave rise to oligarchies; for they made wealth meritorious, and the honours of government were reserved for the rich: and these afterwards turned to tyrannies and these in their turn gave rise to democracies; for the power of the tyrants continually decreasing, on account of their rapacious avarice, the people grew powerful enough to frame and establish democracies: and as cities after that happened to increase, probably it was not easy for them to be under any other government than a democracy. But if any person prefers a kingly government in a state, what is to be done with the king's children? Is the family also to reign? But should they have such children as some persons usually have, it will be very detrimental. It may be said, that then the king who has it in his power will never permit such children to succeed to his kingdom. But it is not easy to trust to that; for it is very hard and requires greater virtue than is to be met with in human nature. There is also a doubt concerning the power with which a king should be entrusted: whether he should be allowed force sufficient to compel those who do not choose to be obedient to the laws, and how he is to support his government? for if he is to govern according to law and do nothing of his own will which is contrary thereunto, at the same time it will be necessary to protect that power with which he guards the law, This matter however may not be very difficult to determine; for he ought to have a proper power, and such a one is that which will be sufficient to make the king superior to any one person or even a large part of the community, but inferior to the whole, as the ancients always appointed guards for that person whom they created aesumnetes or tyrant; and some one advised the Syracusians, when Dionysius asked for guards, to allow him such.

CHAPTER XVI

[1287a] We will next consider the absolute monarch that we have just mentioned, who does everything according to his own will: for a king governing under the direction of laws which he is obliged to follow does not of himself create any particular species of government, as we have already said: for in every state whatsoever, either aristocracy or democracy, it is easy to appoint a general for life; and there are many who entrust the administration of affairs to one person only; such is the government at Dyrrachium, and nearly the same at Opus. As for an absolute monarchy as it is called, that is to say, when the whole state is wholly subject to the will of one person, namely the king, it seems to many that it is unnatural that one man should have the entire rule over his fellow-citizens when the state consists of equals: for nature requires that the same right and the same rank should necessarily take place amongst all those who are equal by nature: for as it would be hurtful to the body for those who are of different constitutions to observe the same regimen, either of diet or clothing, so is it with respect to the honours of the state as hurtful, that those who are equal in merit should be unequal in rank; for which reason it is as much a man's duty to submit to command as to assume it, and this also by rotation; for this is law, for order is law; and it is more proper that law should govern than any one of the citizens: upon the same principle, if it is advantageous to place the supreme power in some particular persons, they should be appointed to be only guardians, and the servants of the laws, for the supreme power must be placed somewhere; but they say, that it is unjust that where all are equal one person should continually enjoy it. But it seems unlikely that man should be able to adjust that which the law cannot determine; it may be replied, that the law having laid down the best rules possible, leaves the adjustment and application of particulars to the discretion of the magistrate; besides, it allows anything to be altered which experience proves may be better established. Moreover, he who would place the supreme power in mind, would place it in God and the laws; but he who entrusts man with it, gives it to a wild beast, for such his appetites sometimes make him; for passion influences those who are in power, even the very best of men: for which reason law is reason without desire.

The instance taken from the arts seems fallacious: wherein it is said to be wrong for a sick person to apply for a remedy to books, but that it would be far more eligible to employ those who are skilful in physic; for these do nothing contrary to reason from motives of friendship but earn their money by curing the sick, whereas those who have the management of public affairs do many things through hatred or favour. And, as a proof of what we have advanced, it may be observed, that whenever a sick person suspects that his physician has been persuaded by his enemies to be guilty of any foul practice to him in his profession, he then rather chooses to apply to books for his cure: and not only this [1287b] but even physicians themselves when they are ill call in other physicians: and those who teach others the gymnastic exercises, exercise with those of the same profession, as being incapable from self-partiality to form a proper judgment of what concerns themselves. From whence it is evident, that those who seek for what is just, seek for a mean; now law is a mean. Moreover; the moral law is far superior and conversant with far superior objects than the written law; for the supreme magistrate is safer to be trusted to than the one, though he is inferior to the other. But as it is impossible that one person should have an eye to everything himself, it will be necessary that the supreme magistrate should employ several subordinate ones under him; why then should not this be done at first, instead of appointing one person in this manner? Besides, if, according to what has been already said, the man of worth is on that account fit to govern, two men of worth are certainly better than one: as, for instance, in Homer, "Let two together go:" and also Agamemnon's wish; "Were ten such faithful counsel mine!" Not but that there are even now some particular magistrates invested with supreme power to decide, as judges, those things which the law cannot, as being one of those cases which comes not properly under its jurisdiction; for of those which can there is no doubt: since then laws comprehend some things, but not all, it is necessary to enquire and consider which of the two is preferable, that the best man or the best law should govern; for to reduce every subject which can come under the deliberation of man into a law is impossible.

No one then denies, that it is necessary that there should be some person to decide those cases which cannot come under the cognisance of a written law: but we say, that it is better to have many than one; for though every one who decides according to the principles of the law decides justly; yet surely it seems absurd to suppose, that one person can see better with two eyes, and hear better with two ears, or do better with two hands and two feet, than many can do with many: for we see that absolute monarchs now furnish themselves with many eyes and ears and hands and feet; for they entrust those who are friends to them and their government with part of their power; for if they are not friends to the monarch, they will not do what he chooses; but if they are friends to him, they are friends also to his government: but a friend is an equal and like his

friend: if then he thinks that such should govern, he thinks that his equal also should govern. These are nearly the objections which are usually made to a kingly power.

...

CHAPTER XVIII

Since then we have said that there are three sorts of regular governments, and of these the best must necessarily be that which is administered by the best men (and this must be that which happens to have one man, or one family, or a number of persons excelling all the rest in virtue, who are able to govern and be governed in such a manner as will make life most agreeable, and we have already shown that the virtue of a good man and of a citizen in the most perfect government will be the same), it is evident, that in the same manner, and for those very qualities which would procure a man the character of good, any one would say, that the government of a state was a well-established aristocracy or kingdom; so that it will be found to be education and [1288b] morals that are almost the whole which go to make a good man, and the same qualities will make a good citizen or good king.

These particulars being treated of, we will now proceed to consider what sort of government is best, how it naturally arises, and how it is established; for it is necessary to make a proper inquiry concerning this.

BOOK IV

CHAPTER I

In every art and science which is not conversant in parts but in some one genus in which it is complete, it is the business of that art alone to determine what is fitted to its particular genus; as what particular exercise is fitted to a certain particular body, and suits it best: for that body which is formed by nature the most perfect and superior to others necessarily requires the best exercise-and also of what one kind that must be which will suit the generality; and this is the business of the gymnastic arts: and although any one should not desire to acquire an exact knowledge and skill in these exercises, yet it is not, on that account, the less necessary that he who professes to be a master and instruct the youth in them should be perfect therein: and we see that this is what equally befalls the healing, shipbuilding, cloth-making, and indeed all other arts; so that it evidently belongs to the same art to find out what kind of government is best, and would of all others be most correspondent to our wish, while it received no molestation from without: and what particular species of it is adapted to particular persons; for there are many who probably are incapable of enjoying the best form: so that the legislator, and he who is truly a politician, ought to be acquainted not only with that which is most perfect imaginable, but also that which is the best suited to any given circumstances. There is, moreover, a third sort, an imaginary one, and he ought, if such a one should be presented to his consideration, to be able to discern what sort of one it would be at the beginning; and, when once established, what would be the proper means to preserve it a long time. I mean, for instance, if a state should happen not to have the best form of government, or be deficient in what was necessary, or not receive every advantage possible, but something less. And, besides all this, it is necessary to know what sort of government is best fitting for all cities: for most of those writers who have treated this subject, however speciously they may handle other parts of it, have failed in describing the practical parts: for it is not enough to be able to perceive what is best without it is what can be put in practice. It should also be simple, and easy for all to attain to. But some seek only the most subtile forms of government. Others again, choosing [1289a] rather to treat of what is common, censure those under which they live, and extol the excellence of a particular state, as the Lacedaemonian, or some other: but every legislator ought to establish such a form of government as from the present state and disposition of the people who are to receive it they will most readily submit to and persuade the community to partake of: for it is not a business of less trouble to correct the mistakes of an established government than to form a new one;

as it is as difficult to recover what we have forgot as to learn anything afresh. He, therefore, who aspires to the character of a legislator, ought, besides all we have already said, to be able to correct the mistakes of a government already established, as we have before mentioned. But this is impossible to be done by him who does not know how many different forms of government there are: some persons think that there is only one species both of democracy and oligarchy; but this is not true: so that every one should be acquainted with the difference of these governments, how great they are, and whence they arise; and should have equal knowledge to perceive what laws are best, and what are most suitable to each particular government: for all laws are, and ought to be, framed agreeable to the state that is to be governed by them, and not the state to the laws: for government is a certain ordering in a state which particularly respects the magistrates in what manner they shall be regulated, and where the supreme power shall be placed; and what shall be the final object which each community shall have in view; but the laws are something different from what regulates and expresses the form of the constitution-it is their office to direct the conduct of the magistrate in the execution of his office and the punishment of offenders. From whence it is evident, that the founders of laws should attend both to the number and the different sorts of government; for it is impossible that the same laws should be calculated for all sorts of oligarchies and all sorts of democracies, for of both these governments there are many species, not one only.

CHAPTER II

Since, then, according to our first method in treating of the different forms of government, we have divided those which are regular into three sorts, the kingly, the aristocratical, the free states, and shown the three excesses which these are liable to: the kingly, of becoming tyrannical; the aristocratical, oligarchical; and the free state, democratical: and as we have already treated of the aristocratical and kingly; for to enter into an inquiry what sort of government is best is the same thing as to treat of these two expressly; for each of them desires to be established upon the principles of virtue: and as, moreover, we have already determined wherein a kingly power and an aristocracy differ from each other, and when a state may be said to be governed by a king, it now remains that we examine into a free state, and also these other governments, an oligarchy, a democracy, and a [1289b] tyranny; and it is evident of these three excesses which must be the worst of all, and which next to it; for, of course, the excesses of the best and most holy must be the worst; for it must necessarily happen either that the name of king only will remain, or else that the king will assume more power than belongs to him, from whence tyranny will arise, the worst excess imaginable, a government the most contrary possible to a free state. The excess next hurtful is an oligarchy; for an aristocracy differs much from this sort of government: that which is least so is a democracy. This subject has been already treated of by one of those writers who have gone before me, though his sentiments are not the same as mine: for he thought, that of all excellent constitutions, as a good oligarchy or the like, a democracy was the worst, but of all bad ones, the best.

Now I affirm, that all these states have, without exception, fallen into excess; and also that he should not have said that one oligarchy was better than another, but that it was not quite so bad. But this question we shall not enter into at present. We shall first inquire how many different sorts of free states there are; since there are many species of democracies and oligarchies; and which of them is the most comprehensive, and most desirable after the best form of government; or if there is any other like an aristocracy, well established; and also which of these is best adapted to most cities, and which of them is preferable for particular persons: for, probably, some may suit better with an oligarchy than a democracy, and others better with a democracy than an oligarchy; and afterwards in what manner any one ought to proceed who desires to establish either of these states, I mean every species of democracy, and also of oligarchy. And to conclude, when we shall have briefly gone through everything that is necessary, we will

endeavour to point out the sources of corruption, and stability, in government, as well those which are common to all as those which are peculiar to each state, and from what causes they chiefly arise.

...

CHAPTER VIII

It now remains for us to treat of that government which is particularly called a free state, and also of a tyranny; and the reason for my choosing to place that free state here is, because this, as well as those aristocracies already mentioned, although they do not seem excesses, yet, to speak true, they have all departed from what a perfect government is. Nay, they are deviations both of them equally from other forms, as I said at the beginning. It is proper to mention a tyranny the last of all governments, for it is of all others the least like one: but as my intention is to treat of all governments in general, for this reason that also, as I have said, will be taken into consideration in its proper place.

I shall now inquire into a free state and show what it is; and we shall the better understand its positive nature as we have already described an oligarchy and a democracy; for a free state is indeed nothing more than a mixture of them, and it has been usual to call those which incline most to a democracy, a free state; those which incline most to an oligarchy, an aristocracy, because those who are rich are generally men of family and education; besides, they enjoy those things which others are often guilty of crimes to procure: for which reason they are regarded as men of worth and honour and note.

Since, then, it is the genius of an aristocracy to allot the larger part of the government to the best citizens, they therefore say, that an oligarchy is chiefly composed of those men who are worthy and honourable: now it [1294a] seems impossible that where the government is in the hands of the good, there the laws should not be good, but bad; or, on the contrary, that where the government is in the hands of the bad, there the laws should be good; nor is a government well constituted because the laws are, without at the same time care is taken that they are observed;

for to enforce obedience to the laws which it makes is one proof of a good constitution in the state-another is, to have laws well calculated for those who are to abide by them; for if they are improper they must be obeyed: and this may be done two ways, either by their being the best relative to the particular state, or the best absolutely. An aristocracy seems most likely to confer the honours of the state on the virtuous; for virtue is the object of an aristocracy, riches of an oligarchy, and liberty of a democracy; for what is approved of by the majority will prevail in all or in each of these three different states; and that which seems good to most of those who compose the community will prevail: for what is called a state prevails in many communities, which aim at a mixture of rich and poor, riches and liberty: as for the rich, they are usually supposed to take the place of the worthy and honourable. As there are three things which claim an equal rank in the state, freedom, riches, and virtue (for as for the fourth, rank, it is an attendant on two of the others, for virtue and riches are the origin of family), it is evident, that the conjuncture of the rich and the poor make up a free state; but that all three tend to an aristocracy more than any other, except that which is truly so, which holds the first rank.

We have already seen that there are governments different from a monarchy, a democracy, and an oligarchy; and what they are, and wherein they differ from each other; and also aristocracies and states properly so called, which are derived from them; and it is evident that these are not much unlike each other.

...

CHAPTER XI

We proceed now to inquire what form of government and what manner of life is best for communities in general, not adapting it to that superior virtue which is above the reach of the vulgar, or that education which every advantage of nature and fortune only can furnish, nor to those imaginary plans which may be formed at pleasure; but to that mode of life which the greater part of mankind can attain to, and that government which most cities may establish: for

as to those aristocracies which we have now mentioned, they are either too perfect for a state to support, or one so nearly alike to that state we now going to inquire into, that we shall treat of them both as one.

The opinions which we form upon these subjects must depend upon one common principle: for if what I have said in my treatise on Morals is true, a happy life must arise from an uninterrupted course of virtue; and if virtue consists in a certain medium, the middle life must certainly be the happiest; which medium is attainable [1295b] by every one. The boundaries of virtue and vice in the state must also necessarily be the same as in a private person; for the form of government is the life of the city. In every city the people are divided into three sorts; the very rich, the very poor, and those who are between them. If this is universally admitted, that the mean is best, it is evident that even in point of fortune mediocrity is to be preferred; for that state is most submissive to reason; for those who are very handsome, or very strong, or very noble, or very rich; or, on the contrary; those who are very poor, or very weak, or very mean, with difficulty obey it; for the one are capricious and greatly flagitious, the other rascally and mean, the crimes of each arising from their different excesses: nor will they go through the different offices of the state; which is detrimental to it: besides, those who excel in strength, in riches, or friends, or the like, neither know how nor are willing to submit to command: and this begins at home when they are boys; for there they are brought up too delicately to be accustomed to obey their preceptors: as for the very poor, their general and excessive want of what the rich enjoy reduces them to a state too mean: so that the one know not how to command, but to be commanded as slaves, the others know not how to submit to any command, nor to command themselves but with despotic power.

A city composed of such men must therefore consist of slaves and masters, not freemen; where one party must hate, and the other despise, where there could be no possibility of friendship or political community: for community supposes affection; for we do not even on the road associate with our enemies. It is also the genius of a city to be composed as much as possible of equals; which will be most so when the inhabitants are in the middle state: from whence it follows, that that city must be best framed which is composed of those whom we say are naturally its proper members. It is men of this station also who will be best assured of safety and protection; for they will neither covet what belongs to others, as the poor do; nor will others covet what is theirs, as the poor do what belongs to the rich; and thus, without plotting against any one, or having any one plot against them, they will live free from danger: for which reason Phocylides wisely wishes for the middle state, as being most productive of happiness. It is plain, then, that the most perfect political community must be amongst those who are in the middle rank, and those states are best instituted wherein these are a larger and more respectable part, if possible, than both the other; or, if that cannot be, at least than either of them separate; so that being thrown into the balance it may prevent either scale from preponderating.

It is therefore the greatest happiness which the citizens can enjoy to possess a moderate and convenient fortune; for when some possess too much, and others nothing at [1296a] all, the government must either be in the hands of the meanest rabble or else a pure oligarchy; or, from the excesses of both, a tyranny; for this arises from a headstrong democracy or an oligarchy, but very seldom when the members of the community are nearly on an equality with each other. We will assign a reason for this when we come to treat of the alterations which different states are likely to undergo. The middle state is therefore best, as being least liable to those seditions and insurrections which disturb the community; and for the same reason extensive governments are least liable to these inconveniences; for there those in a middle state are very numerous, whereas in small ones it is easy to pass to the two extremes, so as hardly to have any in a medium remaining, but the one half rich, the other poor: and from the same principle it is that democracies are more firmly established and of longer continuance than oligarchies; but

even in those when there is a want of a proper number of men of middling fortune, the poor extend their power too far, abuses arise, and the government is soon at an end.

We ought to consider as a proof of what I now advance, that the best lawgivers themselves were those in the middle rank of life, amongst whom was Solon, as is evident from his poems, and Lycurgus, for he was not a king, and Charondas, and indeed most others. What has been said will show us why of so many free states some have changed to democracies, others to oligarchies: for whenever the number of those in the middle state has been too small, those who were the more numerous, whether the rich or the poor, always overpowered them and assumed to themselves the administration of public affairs; from hence arose either a democracy or an oligarchy. Moreover, when in consequence of their disputes and quarrels with each other, either the rich get the better of the poor, or the poor of the rich, neither of them will establish a free state; but, as the record of their victory, one which inclines to their own principles, and form either a democracy or an oligarchy.

Those who made conquests in Greece, having all of them an eye to the respective forms of government in their own cities, established either democracies or oligarchies, not considering what was serviceable to the state, but what was similar to their own; for which reason a government has never been established where the supreme power has been placed amongst those of the middling rank, or very seldom; and, amongst a few, one man only of those who have yet been conquerors has been persuaded to give the preference to this order of [1296b] men: it is indeed an established custom with the inhabitants of most cities not to desire an equality, but either to aspire to govern, or when they are conquered, to submit.

Thus we have shown what the best state is, and why. It will not be difficult to perceive of the many states which there are, for we have seen that there are various forms both of democracies and oligarchies, to which we should give the first place, to which the second, and in the same manner the next also; and to observe what are the particular excellences and defects of each, after we have first described the best possible; for that must be the best which is nearest to this, that worst which is most distant from the medium, without any one has a particular plan of his own which he judges by. I mean by this, that it may happen, that although one form of government may be better than another, yet there is no reason to prevent another from being preferable thereunto in particular circumstances and for particular purposes.

CHAPTER XII

After what has been said, it follows that we should now show what particular form of government is most suitable for particular persons; first laying this down as a general maxim, that that party which desires to support the actual administration of the state ought always to be superior to that which would alter it. Every city is made up of quality and quantity: by quality I mean liberty, riches, education, and family, and by quantity its relative populousness: now it may happen that quality may exist in one of those parts of which the city is composed, and quantity in another; thus the number of the ignoble may be greater than the number of those of family, the number of the poor than that of the rich; but not so that the quantity of the one shall overbalance the quality of the other; those must be properly adjusted to each other; for where the number of the poor exceeds the proportion we have mentioned, there a democracy will rise up, and if the husbandry should have more power than others, it will be a democracy of husbandmen; and the democracy will be a particular species according to that class of men which may happen to be most numerous: thus, should these be the husbandmen, it will be of these, and the best; if of mechanics and those who hire themselves out, the worst possible: in the same manner it may be of any other set between these two. But when the rich and the noble prevail more by their quality than they are deficient in quantity, there an oligarchy ensues; and this oligarchy may be of different species, according to the nature of the prevailing party. Every legislator in framing his constitution ought

to have a particular regard to those in the middle rank of life; and if he intends an oligarchy, these should be the object of his laws; if a democracy, to these they should be entrusted; and whenever their number exceeds that of the two others, or at least one of them, they give [1297a] stability to the constitution; for there is no fear that the rich and the poor should agree to conspire together against them, for neither of these will choose to serve the other. If any one would choose to fix the administration on the widest basis, he will find none preferable to this; for to rule by turns is what the rich and the poor will not submit to, on account of their hatred to each other. It is, moreover, allowed that an arbitrator is the most proper person for both parties to trust to; now this arbitrator is the middle rank.

Those who would establish aristocratical governments are mistaken not only in giving too much power to the rich, but also in deceiving the common people; for at last, instead of an imaginary good, they must feel a real evil, for the encroachments of the rich are more destructive to the state than those of the poor.

...

BOOK V

CHAPTER I

We have now gone through those particulars we proposed to speak of; it remains that we next consider from what causes and how alterations in government arise, and of what nature they are, and to what the destruction of each state is owing; and also to what form any form of polity is most likely to shift into, and what are the means to be used for the general preservation of governments, as well as what are applicable to any particular state; and also of the remedies which are to be applied either to all in general, or to any one considered separately, when they are in a state of corruption: and here we ought first to lay down this principle, that there are many governments, all of which approve of what is just and what is analogically equal; and yet have failed from attaining thereunto, as we have already mentioned; thus democracies have arisen from supposing that those who are equal in one thing are so in every other circumstance; as, because they are equal in liberty, they are equal in everything else; and oligarchies, from supposing that those who are unequal in one thing are unequal in all; that when men are so in point of fortune, that inequality extends to everything else. Hence it follows, that those who in some respects are equal with others think it right to endeavour to partake of an equality with them in everything; and those who are superior to others endeavour to get still more; and it is this more which is the inequality: thus most states, though they have some notion of what is just, yet are almost totally wrong; and, upon this account, when either party has not that share in the administration which answers to his expectations, he becomes seditious: but those who of all others have the greatest right to be so are the last that are; namely, those who excel in virtue; for they alone can be called generally superior. There are, too, some persons of distinguished families who, because they are so, disdain to be on an equality with others, for those esteem themselves noble who boast of their ancestors' merit and fortune: these, to speak truth, are the origin and fountain from whence seditions arise. The alterations which men may propose to make in governments are two; for either they may change the state already established into some other, as when they propose to erect an oligarchy where there is a democracy; or a democracy, or free state, where there is an oligarchy, or an aristocracy from these, or those from that; or else, when they have no objection to the established government, which they like very well, but choose to have the sole management in it themselves; either in the hands of a few or one only. They will also raise commotions concerning the degree in which they would have the established power; as if, for instance, the government is an oligarchy, to have it more purely so, and in the same manner if it is a democracy, or else to have it less so; and, in like manner, whatever may be the nature of the government, either to extend or contract its powers; or else to make some alterations in some parts of it; as to establish or abolish a particular magistracy, as some persons say Lysander

endeavoured to abolish the kingly power in Sparta; and Pausanias that of the ephori. Thus in Epidamnus there was an alteration in one part of the constitution, for instead of the philarchi they established a senate. It is also necessary for all the magistrates at Athens; to attend in the court of the Helisea when any new magistrate is created: the power of the archon also in that state partakes of the nature of an oligarchy: inequality is always the occasion of sedition, but not when those who are unequal are treated in a different manner correspondent to that inequality. Thus kingly power is unequal when exercised over equals. Upon the whole, those who aim after an equality are the cause of seditions. Equality is twofold, either in number or value. Equality in number is when two things contain the same parts or the same quantity; equality in value is by proportion as two exceeds one, and three two by the same number-thus by proportion four exceeds two, and two one in the same degree, for two is the same part of four that one is of two; that is to say, half. Now, all agree in what is absolutely and simply just; but, as we have already said they dispute concerning proportionate value; for some persons, if they are equal in one respect, think themselves equal in all; others, if they are superior in one thing, think they may claim the superiority in all; from whence chiefly arise two sorts of governments, a democracy and an oligarchy; for nobility and virtue are to be found only [1302a] amongst a few; the contrary amongst the many; there being in no place a hundred of the first to be met with, but enough of the last everywhere. But to establish a government entirely upon either of these equalities is wrong, and this the example of those so established makes evident, for none of them have been stable; and for this reason, that it is impossible that whatever is wrong at the first and in its principles should not at last meet with a bad end: for which reason in some things an equality of numbers ought to take place, in others an equality in value. However, a democracy is safer and less liable to sedition than an oligarchy; for in this latter it may arise from two causes, for either the few in power may conspire against each other or against the people; but in a democracy only one; namely, against the few who aim at exclusive power; but there is no instance worth speaking of, of a sedition of the people against themselves. Moreover, a government composed of men of moderate fortunes comes much nearer to a democracy than an oligarchy, and is the safest of all such states.

CHAPTER II

Since we are inquiring into the causes of seditions and revolutions in governments, we must begin entirely with the first principles from whence they arise. Now these, so to speak, are nearly three in number; which we must first distinguish in general from each other, and endeavour to show in what situation people are who begin a sedition; and for what causes; and thirdly, what are the beginnings of political troubles and mutual quarrels with each other. Now that cause which of all others most universally inclines men to desire to bring about a change in government is that which I have already mentioned; for those who aim at equality will be ever ready for sedition, if they see those whom they esteem their equals possess more than they do, as well as those also who are not content with equality but aim at superiority, if they think that while they deserve more than, they have only equal with, or less than, their inferiors. Now, what they aim at may be either just or unjust; just, when those who are inferior are seditious, that they may be equal; unjust, when those who are equal are so, that they may be superior. These, then, are the situations in which men will be seditious: the causes for which they will be so are profit and honour; and their contrary: for, to avoid dishonour or loss of fortune by mulcts, either on their own account or their friends, they will raise a commotion in the state. The original causes which dispose men to the things which I have mentioned are, taken in one manner, seven in number, in another they are more; two of which are the same with those that have been already mentioned: but influencing in a different manner; for profit and honour sharpen men against each other; not to get the possession of them for themselves (which was what I just now supposed), but when they see others, some

justly, others [1302b] unjustly, engrossing them. The other causes are haughtiness, fear, eminence, contempt, disproportionate increase in some part of the state. There are also other things which in a different manner will occasion revolutions in governments; as election intrigues, neglect, want of numbers, a too great dissimilarity of circumstances.

...

CHAPTER VIII

We are now to consider upon what the preservation of governments in general and of each state in particular depends; and, in the first place, it is evident that if we are right in the causes we have assigned for their destruction, we know also the means of their preservation; for things contrary produce contraries: but destruction and preservation are contrary to each other. In well-tempered governments it requires as much care as anything whatsoever, that nothing be done contrary to law: and this ought chiefly to be attended to in matters of small consequence; for an illegality that approaches insensibly, approaches secretly, as in a family small expenses continually repeated consume a man's income; for the understanding is deceived thereby, as by this false argument; if every part is little, then the whole is little: now, this in one sense is true, in another is false, for the whole and all the parts together are large, though made up of small parts. The first therefore of anything is what the state ought to guard against. In the next place, no credit ought to be given to those who endeavour to deceive the people with false pretences; for they will be [1308a] confuted by facts. The different ways in which they will attempt to do this have been already mentioned. You may often perceive both aristocracies and oligarchies continuing firm, not from the stability of their forms of government, but from the wise conduct of the magistrates, both towards those who have a part in the management of public affairs, and those also who have not: towards those who have not, by never injuring them; and also introducing those who are of most consequence amongst them into office; nor disgracing those who are desirous of honour; or encroaching on the property of individuals; towards those who have, by behaving to each other upon an equality; for that equality which the favourers of a democracy desire to have established in the state is not only just, but convenient also, amongst those who are of the same rank: for which reason, if the administration is in the hands of many, those rules which are established in democracies will be very useful; as to let no one continue in office longer than six months: that all those who are of the same rank may have their turn; for between these there is a sort of democracy: for which reason demagogues are most likely to arise up amongst them, as we have already mentioned: besides, by this means both aristocracies and democracies will be the less liable to be corrupted into dynasties, because it will not be so easy for those who are magistrates for a little to do as much mischief as they could in a long time: for it is from hence that tyrannies arise in democracies and oligarchies; for either those who are most powerful in each state establish a tyranny, as the demagogues in the one, the dynasties in the other, or the chief magistrates who have been long in power. Governments are sometimes preserved not only by having the means of their corruption at a great distance, but also by its being very near them; for those who are alarmed at some impending evil keep a stricter hand over the state; for which reason it is necessary for those who have the guardianship of the constitution to be able to awaken the fears of the people, that they may preserve it, and not like a night-guard to be remiss in protecting the state, but to make the distant danger appear at hand. Great care ought also to be used to endeavour to restrain the quarrels and disputes of the nobles by laws, as well as to prevent those who are not already engaged in them from taking a part therein; for to perceive an evil at its very first approach is not the lot of every one, but of the politician. To prevent any alteration taking place in an oligarchy or free state on account of the census, if that happens to continue the same while the quantity of money is increased, it will be useful to take a general account of the whole amount of it in former times, to compare it with the present, and to do this every year in those cities where the census is yearly, [1308b] in larger communities once in three or five years; and if the whole should be found much larger or much less than it was at the time when the census was first established in the state, let there be a law either to extend or contract it, doing both these according to its increase or decrease; if it increases making the census larger, if it decreases smaller: and if this latter is not done in oligarchies and free states, you will have a dynasty arise in the one, an oligarchy in the other: if the former is not, free states will be changed into democracies, and oligarchies into free states or democracies. It is a general maxim in democracies, oligarchies, monarchies, and indeed in all governments, not to let any one acquire a rank far superior to the rest of the community, but rather to endeavour to confer moderate honours for a continuance than great ones for a short time; for these latter spoil men, for it is not every one who can bear prosperity: but if this rule is not observed, let not those honours which were conferred all at once be all at once taken away, but rather by degrees. But, above all things, let this regulation be made by the law, that no one shall have too much power, either by means of his fortune or friends; but if he has, for his excess therein, let it be contrived that he shall quit the country. Now, as many persons promote innovations, that they may enjoy their own particular manner of living, there ought to be a particular officer to inspect the manners of every one, and see that these are not contrary to the genius of the state in which he lives, whether it may be an oligarchy, a democracy, or any other form of government; and, for the same reason, those should be guarded against who are most prosperous in the city: the means of doing which is by appointing those who are otherwise to the business and the offices of the state. I mean, to oppose men of account to the common people, the poor to the rich, and to blend both these into one body, and to increase the numbers of those who are in the middle rank; and this will prevent those seditions which arise from an inequality of condition. But above all, in every state it is necessary, both by the laws and every other method possible, to prevent those who are employed by the public from being venal, and this particularly in an oligarchy; for then the people will not be so much displeased from seeing themselves excluded from a share in the government (nay, they will rather be glad to have leisure to attend their private affairs) as at suspecting that the officers of the state steal the public money, then indeed they are afflicted with double concern, both because they are deprived of the honours of the state, and pillaged by those who enjoy them. There is one method of blending together a democracy and an aristocracy, [1309a] if office brought no profit; by which means both the rich and the poor will enjoy what they desire; for to admit all to a share in the government is democratical; that the rich should be in office is aristocratical. This must be done by letting no public employment whatsoever be attended with any emolument; for the poor will not desire to be in office when they can get nothing by it, but had rather attend to their own affairs: but the rich will choose it, as they want nothing of the community. Thus the poor will increase their fortunes by being wholly employed in their own concerns; and the principal part of the people will not be governed by the lower sort. To prevent the exchequer from being defrauded, let all public money be delivered out openly in the face of the whole city, and let copies of the accounts be deposited in the different wards tribes, and divisions. But, as the magistrates are to execute their offices without any advantages, the law ought to provide proper honours for those who execute them well. In democracies also it is necessary that the rich should be protected, by not permitting their lands to be divided, nor even the produce of them, which in some states is done unperceivably. It would be also better if the people would prevent them when they offer to exhibit a number of unnecessary and yet expensive public entertainments of plays, music, processions, and the like. In an oligarchy it is necessary to take great care of the poor, and allot them public employments which are gainful; and, if any of the rich insult them, to let their punishment be severer than if they insulted one of their own rank; and to let estates pass by affinity, and not gift: nor to permit any person to

have more than one; for by this means property will be more equally divided, and the greater part of the poor get into better circumstances. It is also serviceable in a democracy and an oligarchy to allot those who take no part in public affairs an equality or a preference in other things; the rich in a democracy, to the poor in an oligarchy: but still all the principal offices in the state to be filled only by those who are best qualified to discharge them.

CHAPTER IX

There are three qualifications necessary for those who fill the first departments in government; first of all, an affection for the established constitution; second place, abilities every way completely equal to the business of their office; in the third, virtue and justice correspondent to the nature of that particular state they are placed in; for if justice is not the same in all states, it is evident that there must be different species thereof. There may be some doubt, when all these qualifications do not in the same persons, in what manner the choice shall be made; as for instance, suppose that one person is an accomplished general, but a bad man and no friend to the [1309b] constitution; another is just and a friend to it, which shall one prefer? we should then consider of two qualities, which of them the generality possess in a greater degree, which in a less; for which reason in the choice of a general we should regard his courage more than his virtue as the more uncommon quality; as there are fewer capable of conducting an army than there are good men: but, to protect the state or manage the finances, the contrary rule should be followed; for these require greater virtue than the generality are possessed of, but only that knowledge which is common to all. It may be asked, if a man has abilities equal to his appointment in the state, and is affectionate to the constitution, what occasion is there for being virtuous, since these two things alone are sufficient to enable him to be useful to the public? it is, because those who possess those qualities are often deficient in prudence; for, as they often neglect their own affairs, though they know them and love themselves, so nothing will prevent their serving the public in the same manner. In short, whatsoever the laws contain which we allow to be useful to the state contributes to its preservation: but its first and principal support is (as has been often insisted upon) to have the number of those who desire to preserve it greater than those who wish to destroy it. Above all things that ought not to be forgotten which many governments now corrupted neglect; namely, to preserve a mean. For many things seemingly favourable to a democracy destroy a democracy, and many things seemingly favourable to an oligarchy destroy an oligarchy. Those who think this the only virtue extend it to excess, not considering that as a nose which varies a little from perfect straightness, either towards a hook nose or a flat one, may yet be beautiful and agreeable to look at; but if this particularity is extended beyond measure, first of all the properties of the part is lost, but at last it can hardly be admitted to be a nose at all, on account of the excess of the rise or sinking: thus it is with other parts of the human body; so also the same thing is true with respect to states; for both an oligarchy and a democracy may something vary from their most perfect form and yet be well constituted; but if any one endeavours to extend either of them too far, at first he will make the government the worse for it, but at last there will be no government at all remaining. The lawgiver and the politician therefore should know well what preserves and what destroys a democracy or an oligarchy, for neither the one nor the other can possibly continue without rich and poor: but that whenever an entire equality of circumstances [1310a] prevails, the state must necessarily become of another form; so that those who destroy these laws, which authorise an inequality in property, destroy the government. It is also an error in democracies for the demagogues to endeavour to make the common people superior to the laws; and thus by setting them at variance with the rich, dividing one city into two; whereas they ought rather to speak in favour of the rich. In oligarchies, on the contrary, it is wrong to support those who are in administration against the people. The oaths also which they take in an oligarchy ought to be contrary to what they now are; for, at present, in some places they swear, "I will be adverse to the common people, and contrive all I can against them;" whereas they ought rather to suppose and pretend the contrary; expressing in their oaths, that they will not injure the people. But of all things which I have mentioned, that which contributes most to preserve the state is, what is now most despised, to educate your children for the state; for the most useful laws, and most approved by every statesman, will be of no service if the citizens are not accustomed to and brought up in the principles of the constitution; of a democracy, if that is by law established; of an oligarchy, if that is; for if there are bad morals in one man, there are in the city. But to educate a child fit for the state, it must not be done in the manner which would please either those who have the power in an oligarchy or those who desire a democracy, but so as they may be able to conduct either of these forms of governments. But now the children of the magistrates in an oligarchy are brought up too delicately, and the children of the poor hardy with exercise and labour; so that they are both desirous of and able to promote innovations. In democracies of the purest form they pursue a method which is contrary to their welfare; the reason of which is, that they define liberty wrong: now, there are two things which seem to be the objects of a democracy, that the people in general should possess the supreme power, and all enjoy freedom; for that which is just seems to be equal, and what the people think equal, that is a law: now, their freedom and equality consists in every one's doing what they please: that is in such a democracy every one may live as he likes; "as his inclination guides," in the words of Euripides: but this is wrong, for no one ought to think it slavery to live in subjection to government, but protection. Thus I have mentioned the causes of corruption in different states, and the means of their preservation.

...

BOOK VII

CHAPTER I

He who proposes to make that inquiry which is necessary concerning what government is best, ought first to determine what manner of living is most eligible; for while this remains uncertain it will also be equally uncertain what government is best: for, provided no unexpected accidents interfere, it is highly probable, that those who enjoy the best government will live the most happily according to their circumstances; he ought, therefore, first to know what manner of life is most desirable for all; and afterwards whether this life is the same to the man and the citizen, or different. As I imagine that I have already sufficiently shown what sort of life is best in my popular discourses on that subject, I think I may very properly repeat the same here; as most certainly no one ever called in question the propriety of one of the divisions; namely, that as what is good, relative to man, may be divided into three sorts, what is external, what appertains to the body, and what to the soul, it is evident that all these must conspire to make a man happy: for no one would say that a man was happy who had no fortitude, no temperance, no justice, no prudence; but was afraid of the flies that flew round him: nor would abstain from the meanest theft if he was either hungry or dry, or would murder his dearest friend for a farthing; and also was in every particular as wanting in his understanding as an infant or an idiot. These truths are so evident that all must agree to them; though some may dispute about the quantity and the degree: for they may think, that a very little virtue is sufficient for happiness; but for riches, property, power, honour, and all such things, they endeavour to increase them without bounds: but to such we reply, that it is easy to prove from what experience teaches us in these cases, that these external goods produce not virtue, but virtue them. As to a happy life, whether it is to be found in pleasure or virtue or both, certain it is, that those whose morals are most pure, and whose understandings are best cultivated, will enjoy more of it, although their fortune is but moderate than those do who own an exuberance

of wealth, are deficient in those; and this utility any one who reflects may easily convince himself of; for whatsoever is external has its boundary, as a machine, and whatsoever is useful in its excess is either necessarily hurtful, or at best useless to the possessor; but every good quality of the soul the higher it is in degree, so much the more useful it is, if it is permitted on this subject to use the word useful as well as noble. It is also very evident, that the accidents of each subject take place of each other, as the subjects themselves, of which we allow they are accidents, differ from each other in value; so that if the soul is more noble than any outward possession, as the body, both in itself and with respect to us, it must be admitted of course that the best accidents of each must follow the same analogy. Besides, it is for the sake of the soul that these things are desirable; and it is on this account that wise men should desire them, not the soul for them. Let us therefore be well assured, that every one enjoys as much happiness as he possesses virtue and wisdom, and acts according to their dictates; since for this we have the example of GOD Himself, *who is completely happy, not from any external good, but in Himself, and because such is His nature. For good fortune is something different from happiness, as every good which depends not on the mind is owing to chance or fortune; but it is not from fortune that any one is wise and just: hence it follows, that that city is happiest which is the best and acts best: for no one can do well who acts not well; nor can the deeds either of man or city be praiseworthy without virtue and wisdom; for whatsoever is just, or wise, or prudent in a man, the same things are just, wise, and prudent in a city.*

Thus much by way of introduction; for I could not but just touch upon this subject, though I could not go through a complete investigation of it, as it properly belongs to another question: let us at present suppose so much, that a man's happiest life, both as an individual and as a citizen, is a life of virtue, accompanied with those enjoyments which virtue usually procures. If [1324a] there are any who are not convinced by what I have said, their doubts shall be answered hereafter, at present we shall proceed according to our intended method.

CHAPTER II

It now remains for us to say whether the happiness of any individual man and the city is the same or different: but this also is evident; for whosoever supposes that riches will make a person happy, must place the happiness of the city in riches if it possesses them; those who prefer a life which enjoys a tyrannic power over others will also think, that the city which has many others under its command is most happy: thus also if any one approves a man for his virtue, he will think the most worthy city the happiest: but here there are two particulars which require consideration, one of which is, whether it is the most eligible life to be a member of the community and enjoy the rights of a citizen, or whether to live as a stranger, without interfering in public affairs; and also what form of government is to be preferred, and what disposition of the state is best; whether the whole community should be eligible to a share in the administration, or only the greater part, and some only: as this, therefore, is a subject of political examination and speculation, and not what concerns the individual, and the first of these is what we are at present engaged in, the one of these I am not obliged to speak to, the other is the proper business of my present design. It is evident that government must be the best which is so established, that every one therein may have it in his power to act virtuously and live happily: but some, who admit that a life of virtue is most eligible, still doubt which is preferable a public life of active virtue, or one entirely disengaged from what is without and spent in contemplation; which some say is the only one worthy of a philosopher; and one of these two different modes of life both now and formerly seem to have been chosen by all those who were the most virtuous men; I mean the public or philosophic. And yet it is of no little consequence on which side the truth lies; for a man of sense must naturally incline to the better choice; both as an individual and a citizen. Some think that a tyrannic government over those near us is the greatest injustice; but that a political one is not unjust: but that still is a restraint on the pleasures and tranquillity of life. Others hold the quite contrary opinion, and think that a public and active life is the only life for man: for that private persons have no opportunity of practising any one virtue, more than they have who are engaged in public life the management of the [1324b] state. These are their sentiments; others say, that a tyrannical and despotical mode of government is the only happy one; for even amongst some free states the object of their laws seems to be to tyrannise over their neighbours: so that the generality of political institutions, wheresoever dispersed, if they have any one common object in view, have all of them this, to conquer and govern. It is evident, both from the laws of the Lacedaemonians and Cretans, as well as by the manner in which they educated their children, that all which they had in view was to make them soldiers: besides, among all nations, those who have power enough and reduce others to servitude are honoured on that account; as were the Scythians, Persians, Thracians, and Gauls: with some there are laws to heighten the virtue of courage; thus they tell us that at Carthage they allowed every person to wear as many rings for distinction as he had served campaigns. There was also a law in Macedonia, that a man who had not himself killed an enemy should be obliged to wear a halter; among the Scythians, at a festival, none were permitted to drink out of the cup was carried about who had not done the same thing. Among the Iberians, a warlike nation, they fixed as many columns upon a man's tomb as he had slain enemies: and among different nations different things of this sort prevail, some of them established by law, others by custom. Probably it may seem too absurd to those who are willing to take this subject into their consideration to inquire whether it is the business of a legislator to be able to point out by what means a state may govern and tyrannise over its neighbours, whether they will, or will not: for how can that belong either to the politician or legislator which is unlawful? for that cannot be lawful which is done not only justly, but unjustly also: for a conquest may be unjustly made. But we see nothing of this in the arts: for it is the business neither of the physician nor the pilot to use either persuasion or force, the one to his patients, the other to his passengers: and yet many seem to think a despotic government is a political one, and what they would not allow to be just or proper, if exercised over themselves, they will not blush to exercise over others; for they endeavour to be wisely governed themselves, but think it of no consequence whether others are so or not: but a despotic power is absurd, except only where nature has framed the one party for dominion, the other for subordination; and therefore no one ought to assume it over all in general, but those only which are the proper objects thereof: thus no one should hunt men either for food or sacrifice, but what is fit for those purposes, and these are wild animals which are eatable.

Now a city which is well governed might be very [1325a] happy in itself while it enjoyed a good system of laws, although it should happen to be so situated as to have no connection with any other state, though its constitution should not be framed for war or conquest; for it would then have no occasion for these. It is evident therefore that the business of war is to be considered as commendable, not as a final end, but as the means of procuring it. It is the duty of a good legislator to examine carefully into his state; and the nature of the people, and how they may partake of every intercourse, of a good life, and of the happiness which results from it: and in this respect some laws and customs differ from others. It is also the duty of a legislator, if he has any neighbouring states to consider in what manner he shall oppose each of them, or what good offices he shall show them. But what should be the final end of the best governments will be considered hereafter.

CHAPTER III

We will now speak to those who, while they agree that a life of virtue is most eligible, yet differ in the use of it addressing ourselves to both these parties; for there are some who disapprove of all political governments, and think that the life of one who is really free is different from the life of a citizen, and of all others most eligible: others again think that the citizen is the best; and that it is impossible for him who does nothing to be well employed; but that virtuous activity and happiness are the same thing. Now both parties

in some particulars say what is right, in others what is wrong, thus, that the life of a freeman is better than the life of a slave is true, for a slave, as a slave, is employed in nothing honourable; for the common servile employments which he is commanded to perform have nothing virtuous in them; but, on the other hand, it is not true that a submission to all sorts of governments is slavery; for the government of freemen differs not more from the government of slaves than slavery and freedom differ from each other in their nature; and how they do has been already mentioned. To prefer doing of nothing to virtuous activity is also wrong, for happiness consists in action, and many noble ends are produced by the actions of the just and wise. From what we have already determined on this subject, some one probably may think, that supreme power is of all things best, as that will enable a man to command very many useful services from others; so that he who can obtain this ought not to give it up to another, but rather to seize it: and, for this purpose, the father should have no attention or regard for the son, or the son for the father, or friend for friend; for what is best is most eligible: but to be a member of the community and be in felicity is best. What these persons advance might probably be true, if the supreme good was certainly theirs who plunder and use violence to others: but it is [1325b] most unlikely that it should be so; for it is a mere supposition: for it does not follow that their actions are honourable who thus assume the supreme power over others, without they were by nature as superior to them as a man to a woman, a father to a child, a master to a slave: so that he who so far forsakes the paths of virtue can never return back from whence he departed from them: for amongst equals whatever is fair and just ought to be reciprocal; for this is equal and right; but that equals should not partake of what is equal, or like to like, is contrary to nature: but whatever is contrary to nature is not right; therefore, if there is any one superior to the rest of the community in virtue and abilities for active life, him it is proper to follow, him it is right to obey, but the one alone will not do, but must be joined to the other also: and, if we are right in what we have now said, it follows that happiness consists in virtuous activity, and that both with respect to the community as well as the individual an active life is the happiest: not that an active life must necessarily refer to other persons, as some think, or that those studies alone are practical which are pursued to teach others what to do; for those are much more so whose final object is in themselves, and to improve the judgment and understanding of the man; for virtuous activity has an end, therefore is something practical; nay, those who contrive the plan which others follow are more particularly said to act, and are superior to the workmen who execute their designs. But it is not necessary that states which choose to have no intercourse with others should remain inactive; for the several members thereof may have mutual intercourse with each other; for there are many opportunities for this among the different citizens; the same thing is true of every individual: for, was it otherwise, neither could the Deity nor the universe be perfect; to neither of whom can anything external separately exist. Hence it is evident that that very same life which is happy for each individual is happy also for the state and every member of it.

...

CHAPTER XIII

We will now show of what numbers and of what sort of people a government ought to consist, that the state may be happy and well administered. As there are two particulars on which the excellence and perfection of everything depend, one of these is, that the object and end proposed should be proper; the other, that the means to accomplish it should be adapted to that purpose; for it may happen that these may either agree or disagree with each other; for the end we propose may be good, but in taking the means to obtain it we may err; at other times we may have the right and proper means in our power, but the end may be bad, and sometimes we may mistake in both; as in the art of medicine the physician does not sometimes know in what situation the body ought to be, to be healthy; nor what to do to procure the end he aims at. In every art and science, therefore, we should be master of this

knowledge, namely, the proper end, and the means to obtain it. Now it is evident that all persons are desirous to live well and be happy; but that some have the means thereof in their own power, others not; and this either through nature [1332a] or fortune; for many ingredients are necessary to a happy life; but fewer to those who are of a good than to those who are of a bad disposition. There are others who continually have the means of happiness in their own power, but do not rightly apply them. Since we propose to inquire what government is best, namely, that by which a state may be best administered, and that state is best administered where the people are the happiest, it is evident that happiness is a thing we should not be unacquainted with. Now, I have already said in my treatise on Morals (if I may here make any use of what I have there shown), that happiness consists in the energy and perfect practice of virtue; and this not relatively, but simply; I mean by relatively, what is necessary in some certain circumstances; by simply, what is good and fair in itself: of the first sort are just punishments, and restraints in a just cause; for they arise from virtue and are necessary, and on that account are virtuous; though it is more desirable that neither any state nor any individual should stand in need of them; but those actions which are intended either to procure honour or wealth are simply good; the others eligible only to remove an evil; these, on the contrary, are the foundation and means of relative good. A worthy man indeed will bear poverty, disease, and other unfortunate accidents with a noble mind; but happiness consists in the contrary to these (now we have already determined in our treatise on Morals, that he is a man of worth who considers what is good because it is virtuous as what is simply good; it is evident, therefore, that all the actions of such a one must be worthy and simply good): this has led some persons to conclude, that the cause of happiness was external goods; which would be as if any one should suppose that the playing well upon the lyre was owing to the instrument, and not to the art. It necessarily follows from what has been said, that some things should be ready at hand and others procured by the legislator; for which reason in founding a city we earnestly wish that there may be plenty of those things which are supposed to be under the dominion of fortune (for some things we admit her to be mistress over); but for a state to be worthy and great is not only the work of fortune but of knowledge and judgment also. But for a state to be worthy it is necessary that those citizens which are in the administration should be worthy also; but as in our city every citizen is to be so, we must consider how this may be accomplished; for if this is what every one could be, and not some individuals only, it would be more desirable; for then it would follow, that what might be done by one might be done by all. Men are worthy and good three ways; by nature, by custom, by reason. In the first place, a man ought to be born a man, and not any other animal; that is to say, he ought to have both a body and soul; but it avails not to be only born [1332b] with some things, for custom makes great alterations; for there are some things in nature capable of alteration either way which are fixed by custom, either for the better or the worse. Now, other animals live chiefly a life of nature; and in very few things according to custom; but man lives according to reason also, which he alone is endowed with; wherefore he ought to make all these accord with each other; for if men followed reason, and were persuaded that it was best to obey her, they would act in many respects contrary to nature and custom. What men ought naturally to be, to make good members of a community, I have already determined; the rest of this discourse therefore shall be upon education; for some things are acquired by habit, others by hearing them.

CHAPTER XIV

As every political community consists of those who govern and of those who are governed, let us consider whether during the continuance of their lives they ought to be the same persons or different; for it is evident that the mode of education should be adapted to this distinction. Now, if one man differed from another as much, as we believe, the gods and heroes differ from men: in the first place, being far their superiors in body; and, secondly, in the soul: so that the superiority of the governors over the governed might be evident beyond a doubt, it is certain that it would be better for the one always to govern, the other always to be governed: but, as this is not easy to obtain, and kings are not so superior to those they govern as Scylax informs us they are in India, it is evident that for many reasons it is necessary that all in their turns should both govern and be governed: for it is just that those who are equal should have everything alike; and it is difficult for a state to continue which is founded in injustice; for all those in the country who are desirous of innovation will apply themselves to those who are under the government of the rest, and such will be their numbers in the state, that it will be impossible for the magistrates to get the better of them. But that the governors ought to excel the governed is beyond a doubt; the legislator therefore ought to consider how this shall be, and how it may be contrived that all shall have their equal share in the administration. Now, with respect to this it will be first said, that nature herself has directed us in our choice, laying down the selfsame thing when she has made some young, others old: the first of whom it becomes to obey, the latter to command; for no one when he is young is offended at his being under government, or thinks himself too good for it; more especially when he considers that he himself shall receive the same honours which he pays when he shall arrive at a proper age. In some respects it must be acknowledged that the governors and the governed are the same, in others they are different; it is therefore necessary that their education should be in [1333a] some respect the same, in others different: as they say, that he will be a good governor who has first learnt to obey. Now of governments, as we have already said, some are instituted for the sake of him who commands; others for him who obeys: of the first sort is that of the master over the servant; of the latter, that of freemen over each other. Now some things which are commanded differ from others; not in the business, but in the end proposed thereby: for which reason many works, even of a servile nature, are not disgraceful for young freemen to perform; for many things which are ordered to be done are not honourable or dishonourable so much in their own nature as in the end which is proposed, and the reason for which they are undertaken. Since then we have determined, that the virtue of a good citizen and good governor is the same as of a good man; and that every one before he commands should have first obeyed, it is the business of the legislator to consider how his citizens may be good men, what education is necessary to that purpose, and what is the final object of a good life. The soul of man may be divided into two parts; that which has reason in itself, and that which hath not, but is capable of obeying its dictates: and according to the virtues of these two parts a man is said to be good: but of those virtues which are the ends, it will not be difficult for those to determine who adopt the division I have already given; for the inferior is always for the sake of the superior; and this is equally evident both in the works of art as well as in those of nature; but that is superior which has reason. Reason itself also is divided into two parts, in the manner we usually divide it; the theoretic and the practical; which division therefore seems necessary for this part also: the same analogy holds good with respect to actions; of which those which are of a superior nature ought always to be chosen by those who have it in their power; for that is always most eligible to every one which will procure the best ends. Now life is divided into labour and rest, war and peace; and of what we do the objects are partly necessary and useful, partly noble: and we should give the same preference to these that we do to the different parts of the soul and its actions, as war to procure peace; labour, rest; and the useful, the noble. The politician, therefore, who composes a body of laws ought to extend his views to everything; the different parts of the soul and their actions; more particularly to those things which are of a superior nature and ends; and, in the same manner, to the lives of men and their different actions.

They ought to be fitted both for labour and war, but rather [1333b] for rest and peace; and also to do what is necessary and useful, but rather what is fair and noble. It is to those objects that the education of the children ought to tend, and

of all the youths who want instruction. All the Grecian states which now seem best governed, and the legislators who founded those states, appear not to have framed their polity with a view to the best end, or to every virtue, in their laws and education; but eagerly to have attended to what is useful and productive of gain: and nearly of the same opinion with these are some persons who have written lately, who, by praising the Lacedaemonian state, show they approve of the intention of the legislator in making war and victory the end of his government. But how contrary to reason this is, is easily proved by argument, and has already been proved by facts (but as the generality of men desire to have an extensive command, that they may have everything desirable in the greater abundance; so Thibron and others who have written on that state seem to approve of their legislator for having procured them an extensive command by continually enuring them to all sorts of dangers and hardships): for it is evident, since the Lacedemonians have now no hope that the supreme power will be in their own hand, that neither are they happy nor was their legislator wise. This also is ridiculous, that while they preserved an obedience to their laws, and no one opposed their being governed by them, they lost the means of being honourable: but these people understand not rightly what sort of government it is which ought to reflect honour on the legislator; for a government of freemen is nobler than despotic power, and more consonant to virtue. Moreover, neither should a city be thought happy, nor should a legislator be commended, because he has so trained the people as to conquer their neighbours; for in this there is a great inconvenience: since it is evident that upon this principle every citizen who can will endeavour to procure the supreme power in his own city; which crime the Lacedaemonians accuse Pausanias of, though he enjoyed such great honours.

Such reasoning and such laws are neither political, useful nor true: but a legislator ought to instil those laws on the minds of men which are most useful for them, both in their public and private capacities. The rendering a people fit for war, that they may enslave their inferiors ought not to be the care of the legislator; but that they may not themselves be reduced to slavery by others. In [1334a] the next place, he should take care that the object of his government is the safety of those who are under it, and not a despotism over all: in the third place, that those only are slaves who are fit to be only so. Reason indeed concurs with experience in showing that all the attention which the legislator pays to the business of war, and all other rules which he lays down, should have for their object rest and peace; since most of those states (which we usually see) are preserved by war; but, after they have acquired a supreme power over those around them, are ruined; for during peace, like a sword, they lose their brightness: the fault of which lies in the legislator, who never taught them how to be at rest.

CHAPTER XV

As there is one end common to a man both as an individual and a citizen, it is evident that a good man and a good citizen must have the same object in view; it is evident that all the virtues which lead to rest are necessary; for, as we have often said, the end of war is peace, of labour, rest; but those virtues whose object is rest, and those also whose object is labour, are necessary for a liberal life and rest; for we want a supply of many necessary things that we may be at rest. A city therefore ought to be temperate, brave, and patient; for, according to the proverb, "Rest is not for slaves;" but those who cannot bravely face danger are the slaves of those who attack them. Bravery, therefore, and patience are necessary for labour, philosophy for rest, and temperance and justice in both; but these chiefly in time of peace and rest; for war obliges men to be just and temperate; but the enjoyment of pleasure, with the rest of peace, is more apt to produce insolence; those indeed who are easy in their circumstances, and enjoy everything that can make them happy, have great occasion for the virtues of temperance and justice. Thus if there are, as the poets tell us, any inhabitants in the happy isles, to these a higher degree of philosophy, temperance, and justice will be necessary, as they live at their ease in the full plenty of every sensual pleasure. It is evident, therefore, that these virtues are necessary in every state that would be happy or worthy; for he who is worthless can never enjoy real good, much less is he qualified to be at rest; but can appear good only by labour and being at war, but in peace and at rest the meanest of creatures. For which reason virtue should not be cultivated as the Lacedaemonians did; for they did not differ from others in their opinion concerning the supreme good, but in [1334b] imagining this good was to be procured by a particular virtue; but since there are greater goods than those of war, it is evident that the enjoyment of those which are valuable in themselves should be desired, rather than those virtues which are useful in war; but how and by what means this is to be acquired is now to be considered. We have already assigned three causes on which it will depend; nature, custom, and reason, arid shown what sort of men nature must produce for this purpose; it remains then that we determine which we shall first begin by in education, reason or custom, for these ought always to preserve the most entire harmony with each other; for it may happen that reason may err from the end proposed, and be corrected by custom. In the first place, it is evident that in this as in other things, its beginning or production arises from some principle, and its end also arises from another principle, which is itself an end. Now, with us, reason and intelligence are the end of nature; our production, therefore, and our manners ought to be accommodated to both these. In the next place, as the soul and the body are two distinct things, so also we see that the soul is divided into two parts, the reasoning and not-reasoning, with their habits which are two in number, one belonging to each, namely appetite and intelligence; and as the body is in production before the soul, so is the not-reasoning part of the soul before the reasoning; and this is evident; for anger, will and desire are to be seen in children nearly as soon as they are born; but reason and intelligence spring up as they grow to maturity. The body, therefore, necessarily demands our care before the soul; next the appetites for the sake of the mind; the body for the sake of the soul.

Chapter 5: Roman Politics

Comprehension questions you should be able to answer after reading this chapter:

1. According to the Stoics, what sorts of things are "up to us?" What things are not? Why should we focus on the things that are up to us?

2. What do the Stoics mean by each of the following? representation, judgment, assent.

3. Why do they believe we should not "add to appearances?"

4. What are "externals?" Why is their value "indifferent?" In what way are some "indifferents" nevertheless to be "preferred?"

5. What does it mean to "act under reserve?"

6. What stoic ideas influenced Cicero's own philosophy?

7. Explain the role that Reason plays in Cicero's understanding of the universal "kinship" of humanity

8. What are the moral requirements concerning war, for Cicero?

9. Explain his version of "hegemonic leadership."

10. Explain the relationship between natural law and human laws, according to Cicero.

11. What does Cicero mean by a "Republic" (res publica)?

12. Why does Cicero favor a "mixed" constitution?

13. Briefly describe Cicero's influence during the Renaissance and Enlightenment.

Thus far, we have considered political philosophy only from the ancient Greek perspective. Greek philosophy did not remain only in Greece, however. Philosophy found its way to the Roman Empire, and one of the persons most responsible for disseminating Greek philosophy to educated Romans was Marcus Tullius Cicero (106 BCE – 43 BCE).

Cicero was not merely a "fan" of Greek philosophy who shared his interests with others. He was a careful thinker and a skilled writer who translated Greek thought into the Roman (Latin) language not only in the literal sense of translation, but also to the extent that he coined new Latin vocabulary to help elucidate difficult philosophical concepts. He helped bring ancient Greek thought to the Romans, and then helped to bring both Greek and Roman philosophy to the rest of Europe, somewhat in the Middle Ages—but especially in the Renaissance.

Cicero was a gifted writer, speaker, and transmitter of ideas, in general, but he was no mere theorist. Cicero was an actual politician in his time, rising to the role of Consul (and helping to put down a *coup d'etat* during his tenure!).

We will spend a bit more attention on Cicero's biographical history than we have (or will) on other philosophers in this book—if for no other reason than Cicero's personal life was so fascinating! After a brief review of some of his major life events and accomplishments, we will consider the philosophical training he received, and the foundations upon which his own musings are built. This will manifest as a brief overview of basic Stoic principles. We will then consider Cicero's own positions on political philosophy, specifically, as built on its stoic foundation. Then, we will conclude with a consideration of Cicero's significant impact on the political philosophy that was to follow him.

Cicero's Life

Cicero was born into the "equestrian" order of Roman society in 106 BCE. Cicero achieved public offices at or near the minimum age for each: quaestor (age 31, 76 BCE), aedile (age 37), praetor (age 40, 66 BCE), and consul (age 43, 63 BCE).

That he rose to become consul (joint head of state) is an even more impressive testimony to his talents, given that the patrician class dominated politics. Nobody without senators in their family lineage had been made a consul in the last 30 years, prior to Cicero. In his capacity as consul, he uncovered and prevented a conspiracy by Cataline, and generated some controversy and trouble for himself later when he ordered the execution of some of the conspirators without a trial.

His oratory skill and political talents caught the eye of Julius Caesar, who (in 60 BCE) invited Cicero to be the 4th member of his "partnership" with Pompey and Marcus Licinius Crassus. Cicero declined the offer to join what would become the First Triumvirate due to his concern that it would undermine the Republic.

Cicero briefly fled into exile in 58 BCE when a political enemy (Publius Clodius, a tribune and supporter of Julius Caesar) sought his execution in response to Cicero's own summary execution of rebels during his consulship. His property was confiscated and his house was destroyed. His exile was overturned by a nearly unanimous vote of the Roman senate just a year later, at the request of Pompey, and he was granted amnesty in exchange for being "persuaded" to collaborate with the Triumvirate.

In 52 BCE, Consular elections were suspended, the Senate house was burned down, and Pompey became the sole (instead of joint) Consul—using the need for security and order to justify his de facto dictatorship. When the partnership between Caesar and Pompey unraveled, Cicero supported Pompey—seeing him as the defender of the traditional Roman republic, but making an enemy of Caesar at the same time.

Even though Cicero had joined Pompey in his military campaign against Caesar, Caesar pardoned him after his defeat of Pompey (48 BCE), and Cicero shifted his strategy to trying to promote the revival of the republic from within Caesar's dictatorship. Caesar, however, was reappointed dictator for an "indefinite period," and then for a period of 10 years in 46 BCE.[89]

Over the next several years, Caesar instituted numerous political changes that increased and reinforced his personal power, including granting himself veto power over the Senate, granting himself the power to personally appoint new senators (always loyal to himself, of course!), and imposing term limits on governors (to reduce the power of other generals who might prove to be potential political rivals). In February, 44 BCE, Caesar was appointed "dictator for life." Roughly a month later, he was assassinated on the Ides of March (March 15th).

Cicero had not, himself, participated in the conspiracy or assassination. However, Marcus Junius Brutus allegedly called out Cicero's name, bloodstained dagger in hand, and asked him to restore the Republic, and Cicero's own endorsement of the assassination was unmistakable.

> Yet come one, come all, the Ides of March are a consolation. Our heroes most splendidly and gloriously achieved everything that lay within their power.[90]

> How I wish you had invited me to that superb banquet on the Ides of March![91]

> For Heaven will bear witness that Rome—that any nation throughout the whole world—has never seen a greater act than theirs. There has never been an achievement more glorious—more

[89] Note that, historically, the term limit for a dictatorship was a mere 6 months!
[90] Letter to Atticus, April 9th or 10th, 44 BCE.

[91] Letter to Gaius Trebonius, February 2nd, 43 BCE

greatly deserving of renown for all eternity.[92]

In the political instability that followed the assassination, a power struggle broke out between the assassins (led by Brutus and Cassius) and "loyalists" to Caesar (led by Mark Antony and Octavian). Cicero was a political leader—and found himself in direct opposition to Mark Antony. Cicero was the spokesman for the Senate, and Antony was a consul and the unofficial executor of Caesar's will. Cicero tried to manipulate Octavian into opposing Antony, but ultimately failed.

Cicero wrote and spoke publicly against Antony in a series of speeches called the "Phillipics"—actions and writing that ultimately cost him his life. In 43 BCE, Antony, Octavian, and Lepidus formed the Second Triumvirate. They issued proscriptions against Roman citizens, including Cicero (and his brother and nephew).

Cicero was assassinated on December 7th, 43 BCE. Antony then displayed Cicero's severed head and hands (the ones that wrote the Phillipics) in the Roman Forum in a final act of humiliation.

The Second Triumvirate was short-lived, however, with Antony and Octavian soon turning on each other. Octavian proved victorious, solidifying his power and becoming the first Roman Emperor, Augustus.

Not many philosophers can rival Cicero's world-historic status! Beyond his wisdom and talents, he was an associate, at times, friend, and at other times rival, of some of the most famous and powerful (and notorious) politicians to ever grace the world's stage. Cicero was no mere theoretician, imaging how certain political principles might apply in various hypothetical scenarios. Instead, he spoke of the decay of republicanism and the rise of tyranny as a first hand witness, and wrote of resisting tyranny and affirming the rights of all as someone who was literally doing so—even at the eventual cost of his own life.

With the basic elements of his life story in

place, we will now turn to his intellectual history, so as to better situate his political thought.

Cicero's Education

Cicero was exposed to, and educated in, a variety of philosophical schools, making him familiar with every major system at the time. He was familiar with Epicureanism, though he rejected it. He appreciated the Peripatetics (Aristotle's school), and sent his own son to study under that system in Greece. He was heavily influenced by two stoic teachers, Posidonius and Diodotus. The influence of stoicism on Cicero is unmistakable, as we shall see. Despite that influence, however, Cicero did not label himself a stoic, but rather claimed a different affiliation: "I, however, belong to the New Academy, which allows wide latitude to adopt any theory supported by probability."[93]

With regard to the Academy (Plato's school), he studied under both Philo of Larissa (160-80 BCE) and Antiochus of Ascalon (130-68 BCE). These two attempted to blend stoic thought in a harmonious way with the Academy, rejecting the unyielding skepticism of earlier incarnations of the Academy, and replacing it with a moderate skepticism; not total suspension of judgment in all cases, but provisional assent to what seems "probable"—while remaining open to contrary arguments. In this way, stoic principles could be affirmed (so long as they seemed probable), as could good ideas from Aristotle, Epicurus, etc.

Because of its undeniable influence on Cicero's political thought, we will focus on Stoicism. Stoicism was named for a porch. That's right. The word "stoicism" comes from "stoa," meaning a covered walkway (similar to the *peripatoi* from which Aristotle's followers acquired their name). Specifically, the "stoa" at the Agora in Athens is where the philosophers later to be named "stoics" would loiter and lecture.

Stoicism can be divided into two rough periods: First, there was the (Greek) "theoretical" period of its founder Zeno of Citium in Cyprus

---

[92] Second Philippic against Antony.

[93] *On Duties*, 2.

(344 –262 BCE, as well as his successors: Cleanthes (330 – 230 BCE) and Chrysippus (279 – 206 BCE)(all dates are approximate). Then, there was the (Roman) "therapeutic" period represented by Seneca (4 BCE–65 CE), Musonius Rufus (20-101 CE[94]), Epictetus (55–135 CE) and the Emperor Marcus Aurelius (121–180 CE).

Early Stoicism was heavily theoretical, abstract, detailed, and painstakingly developed. The Stoic system may be divided into three disciplines: logic, "physics," and "ethics." Although Aristotle is often credited for his development of what we now call "logic," a strong case can be made that the Stoics were more important and influential in this field. They developed what we now call "propositional logic," tests for validity, and several rules of inference including *modus ponens* and *modus tollens*. They also developed careful analyses of concepts, and language in general—all of which was intended to be put to use in their pursuit of *eudaimonia*.

The second category ("physics") involves the Stoic understanding of the cosmos and how it operates. The two most central ideas (for our purposes) from this category are the Stoic concepts of Fate and Freedom.

The Stoics believed that "God," or "Zeus" (or Nature, or Fate, depending on which Stoic is writing) is immanent throughout the cosmos. To avoid confusing their concept of the divine with the Judeo-Christian concept, I will hereafter use the term "Fate."

The physical universe is Fate's "body." Fate is identical with the cosmos. This view is often referred to as "pantheism." Fate is recognized not only as the "body" (to which the cosmos is identical), but also as the "logos" (eternal Reason) that moves and governs all the operations of the universe and the unfolding of history. All events, therefore, are manifestations of Fate's "will." Moreover, Fate was thought to be perfectly rational. As such, all events transpire in accordance with perfect Reason. This assumption allows the Stoics to go from mere determinism, to "Providence." All that happens is fated to happen, but all that happens is for the best, and couldn't have turned out any better way.

Although the transition from this Stoic concept of Fate to the western theistic (e.g., Christian, Muslim, or Jewish) concept of Providence is an easy transition to make (and an appealing one, for some contemporary Stoics), we must be careful not to impose contemporary views of the divine onto the ancient Stoics. Fate, unlike the Judeo-Christian God, is identical to creation, but is not its transcendent Creator. And, while Fate is perfectly rational (and therefore a mind), Fate is not "personal" in the way the Judeo-Christian God is thought to be, nor is Fate responsive to human needs or prayers. All events occur (and will occur) as they *must* occur, according to the perfectly rational will of Fate. Praying that events might turn out a certain way is a futile effort—if your hope is to bring about an event that is contrary to the will of Fate. Instead, the Stoics thought we should attempt to align our own will with Fate.

Because *all* events are the manifestation of Fate's will, human events are no exception. All the events in your life, and all the actions you take, are fated to occur exactly as they do, and could not have turned out any other way. Nevertheless, Stoics believed that there is something different and special about human beings, and a sense in which we are "free" and accountable for our actions, even though all events are the product of Fate. It is generally recognized that the Stoics (specifically, Chrysippus) were the first "compatibilists" with regard to determinism and free will. That is to say that the Stoics believed that all events are determined (fated) to occur exactly as they do, but there is, nevertheless, a sense in which we are "free"—and that freedom (and responsibility) is "compatible" with determinism (Fate).

Contemporary compatibilists identify free actions (i.e., those for which we may rightfully be held responsible) as being the effects of internal causes. An easier way to think about this is to ask, of any action you take, "did I do it because I wanted to?" If the answer is yes, you acted on an internal cause (i.e., something about *you*). If the answer is no, you likely acted on an external cause (i.e., something "outside" of you).

For an obvious example, consider the difference between murder and suicide. Imagine that a person is standing on a balcony, twenty stories up in a tall building. Imagine that this person falls from that balcony to his death below. Now consider two different versions of that story. In one, the person is seriously depressed and wants to end his life. As a result, he leaps over the balcony. In the other version, he is simply admiring the view when another person (for some reason) rushes up behind him and tosses him over the edge. In the first case, the cause was "internal" (the man's own desire to die). In the second, the cause was "external" (the shove from the murderer). Note that we interpret these events very differently, even though the physical descriptions are quite similar (i.e., a body falling to its death). The first example is an example of suicide, and we say (with however much sympathy and compassion we might be able to generate) that it is his own fault that he's dead. He's responsible for his actions. The second example is an example of murder, and we do not claim that it's his own fault that he's dead. Instead, the responsibility is found with the person who pushed him. Why there? Because the murderer is the one who was acting from an internal cause (in this case, apparently, a desire to kill).

Although the Stoics didn't describe their compatibilism in exactly the same way, their system involves the same basic idea: we are responsible for our actions when those actions stem from something about us, as opposed to something wholly external to ourselves. To use the Stoic vocabulary, "externals" can be "initiating causes" (antecedent causes), but are not "principle causes."

Their most famous example used to illustrate this was that of a cylinder rolling down a hill. To make it a bit more visually appealing, instead of a cylinder, think of a tire. If you are standing atop the hill with that tire, and you give it a shove, you have provided the "initiating cause." However, that tire isn't going to roll down the hill unless it

has a shape that is conducive to rolling. The "principle cause," therefore, of the tire rolling down the hill is its own shape. After all, you could provide the same initiating cause to an anvil and that anvil won't roll down the hill! Because not all objects will respond to the initiating cause in the same way, the "responsibility" for the event lies in the primary cause, rather than the initiating cause—though, to be sure, the event wouldn't have taken place if not for that initiating cause.

Now, apply this same kind of reasoning to people, and our own behavior. Events that occur around us serve as initiating causes for events. However, to the extent that our own actions are the result of ourselves (as a principle cause), we are responsible for those actions.

As an example, consider two politicians both being offered an identical bribe by the same lobbyist. One politician accepts the bribe, the offer refuses. Both experienced the same initiating cause (the bribe), but their reactions were different. Wherein is to be found the difference? In *them*, of course! There is something about the one that makes him susceptible to bribes, and something about the other that makes him resistant. Their actions, therefore, are attributable to themselves, as principle causes, rather than the bribes, as initiating causes.

Just to be clear, compatibilists (include Stoics) acknowledge that the sort of person we are (i.e., our nature as a principle cause) is also the product of Fate—in other words, the sort of person we are, just like everything else in the cosmos, is the will of Fate, and couldn't have been any other way. Nevertheless, when it comes to personal responsibility, what we seek (according to compatibilists) is *not* some ability to somehow defy Fate (or causal determinism, in less "spiritualized" versions of compatibilism), but simply the ability to be able to trace our actions back to our own character, as opposed to something wholly external to us. We blame someone for having an extra million dollars in her bank account when it's the result of accepting a bribe. We don't blame that person if it was the result of an error in a bank computer. The first example can be traced back to her character, the second cannot.

The Roman Stoic, Epictetus, famously delineates those things that are "up to us" from those that are not in the very first paragraph of the *Enchiridion*.

> There are things which are within our power, and there are things which are beyond our power. Within our power are opinion, aim, desire, aversion, and, in one word, whatever affairs are our own. Beyond our power are body, property, reputation, office, and, in one word, whatever are not properly our own affairs.

Notice that those few things "within our power" are all "internal," all mental activities stemming from the sort of person we are: "opinion, aim, desire, aversion." Notice also that those things described as being "beyond our power" are all "external" to us: body, property, reputation, office. You might immediately wonder how your own body is listed as being beyond your power. After all, it seems obvious that one can control one's body to make it do as we wish. Tell that to someone with cerebral palsy, or a broken leg, or arthritis, or who is suffering from a stroke, or in the midst of a heart attack, or who is pinned underneath the rubble of a collapsed building.

You can "will" any number of things, but whether or not those things come to be depends upon the cooperation of things not under your control—including the operations of your own body.

You might wonder how "property" is not under your control. After all, your property is *your* property, to dispose of as you see fit—unless someone steals it. Or it's destroyed in an earthquake, or eaten by termites. "But isn't my reputation under my own control?" No. Your reputation is always the product of your actions and the judgments of others. Those judgments are not under your control. Your behavior might be interpreted as "confidence" by one person and "arrogance" by another. What if the person judging you is racially biased, or sexist?

To summarize, (orthodox) Stoics believed that all events are fated to occur exactly as they do by virtue of the perfectly rational will of Fate. Nevertheless, there is a sense in which we are responsible for our actions, and our proper focus should be on those things that are "up to us" rather than those that are not. Recognizing this, and regulating our mental life on that basis, leads us to the final category of Stoic theory: "ethics."

This final category has a misleading name. Most of us, today, when we think of "ethics," think either of a list of moral commandments ("thou shalts" and "thou shalt nots") or else a formalized study of moral concepts. Stoic ethics didn't so much address moral rules governing our behavior with others (though such things were certainly derived from their system) as it addressed an understanding of how best to achieve *eudaimonia* ("happiness"—understood by the Stoics as tranquility). Stoicism was more "self-help" than "ethics" (as most understand the term today).

"Ethics" involved the proper use of what is "up to us"—namely, the judgments we make concerning events as they transpire. According to orthodox Stoicism, given Fate, whatever happens was fated to occur, and could not have turned out any other way. Similarly, whatever *will* happen is also the unavoidable will of Fate. What is up to us is the extent to which we align our will with Fate. What is at stake is our own tranquility.

The Stoics offered what would become a famous analogy to illustrate our relationship to Fate. Imagine a dog leashed to a cart (or, today, a slow-moving car). The dog is being pulled, and will be pulled, in whatever direction the cart (or car) goes. Resistance is futile. The cart (or car) *will* "win." In other words, the dog is going to end up wherever he is taken. Now consider the difference between the dog that is being dragged, and the one that is happily following the cart. Both end up at the same destination, but one has a miserable trip. So too with us, and Fate.

Our lives will transpire however Fate wills them to unfold. There is nothing we can do about *that*. What is up to us, however, is whether we align our will with Fate and walk, or get dragged. It makes no difference to Fate, but it makes a lot of difference to us. Needless to say, our lives will be much more pleasant if we avoid getting dragged.

Why is it that so many of us get "dragged" along by Fate? Largely because of an improper use of our faculties of "assent" and "desire." Similar to Epicureanism, Stoicism claims that we suffer from false beliefs (judgments) and improper desires. To understand the process by which we form false judgments, we need to understand how the Stoics thought we formed judgments in the first place. Our minds process information in three steps.

1) Representation: It receives the images (impressions) that come through our bodily sensations.

2) Judgment: It develops an inner discourse that constitutes our judgment about things. The minds "tells itself" what a given impression *is*.

3) Assent: It forms desires and impulses to action based upon our judgments about a thing. It gives "assent" to the representation by acting upon it in a certain way.

Imagine that someone returns to a parking lot to discover her car has been keyed. As might be typical, she gets very upset. What has happened here? First, she received an "impression"—namely, the sight of her car with a scratch across its paint. Then, she has a (presumably quick) "conversation" with herself in which she interprets that impression. Judging from her reaction, it's obvious that she formed some sort of negative judgment in response to that impression. "Someone keyed my car? This sucks!" She then "assents" to that judgment by virtue of her actions (e.g., swearing, physiological responses such as an increased pulse rate or a headache, throwing her purse down, etc.).

One of Epictetus' most famous saying is that people "are disturbed not by things, but by the views which they take of things." In other words, things and events are not good or bad, in themselves. They take on the quality of good or bad by virtue of the judgments that we *add* to them. The controversial rejection of emotion attributed to Stoicism stems from this.

Emotions are thought to be our "assent" to judgments. When we cry in response to an event, we have assented to the judgment that there is something bad about what happened. When we fume in anger, that anger *is* our assent to the judgment that some event is worthy of our anger. Traditional Stoics believe that that is simply not true. If I get angry at the sight of my keyed car, my anger is my assent to the judgment that it's a bad thing that my car has been keyed.

Stoics believe that we should not "add" to appearances, but accept them as they are presented to us. As Epictetus says, "Right from the start, get into the habit of saying to every harsh appearance, 'You are an appearance, and not the only way of seeing the thing that appears.' Then examine it and test it by the yardsticks you have."

Being angry that my car was keyed implies that I have added a judgment ("this is bad") to an appearance (the literal sight of my car, now with an irregular line through the paint). There is nothing inherently bad about a car with a line scratched through its paint. What makes it bad is my own belief that it is bad. If I don't add that judgment to the appearance, I won't be angered by the sight of it, and my tranquility will be preserved.

"But it is a bad thing that your car got keyed!" you might respond. "Now it's worth less, and it doesn't look as good, and you'll have to pay to get the paint fixed, or at least fix it yourself, and that will be a hassle. Some jerk vandalized your property, and he didn't have that right."

So, I should give him control over my soul, in addition to control over my paint job? According to Stoicism, externals are not up to me. My car is an external. I can't control whether or not it remains in pristine condition. At best, the appearance of my car is something over which I have some, but not total, control. For example, I might make it a point to park it only in "good" areas, with ample lighting, and in so doing try to reduce the risk of vandalism. Even then, the best I can achieve is risk reduction, not risk elimination. In an obvious, common-sense, sort of way I am not in control of the other 7 billion (or so) people in the world. If someone wants to key my car, there is no way I can guarantee it won't happen unless I don't have a car—in which case the person could just vandalize other of my property instead.

Stoicism holds that externals (my car) are not under my control, but my response to events is (at least in the sense that it's based on my character). A vandal has sufficient power to damage my car, but that vandal doesn't have sufficient power to make me upset. I must give him that power. Again we can appeal to Epictetus: "For another cannot hurt you, unless you please. You will then be hurt when you consent to be hurt." When a vandal damages my car, he damages an external—something that was never under my control to begin with. When I become upset at the vandalism, I have let the vandal damage my virtue. "If a person had delivered up your body to some passer-by, you would certainly be angry. And do you feel no shame in delivering up your own mind to any reviler, to be disconcerted and confounded?"

Remember that the primary function of philosophy, of all these efforts, according to Stoicism, is *eudaimonia*—happiness, understood as a state of tranquility that we can achieve when we live "according to Nature." We live according to Nature when we are governed by Reason, when we employ what is up to us (our judgments) properly, by recognizing what is up to us and what is not, and by aligning our will with that of "Fate" with regard to those things not up to us. If your goal is something different, their advice and strategies are unlikely to make much sense. If, for example, your goal in life is to maintain a car with an unblemished surface, you will probably not agree with their advice. Good luck with that. Vandals are numerous—as are branches, rocks tossed by other cars, birds, wind and other erosive elements, etc. If your happiness is based on whether or not you can keep your car sufficiently pretty, you are setting yourself up for a lifetime of challenge and frustration. If, on the other hand, you prefer tranquility to an impeccably painted car, then the Stoic strategy might be right for you.

In addition to regulating our assent to appearances, we ought to regulate our desires.

Given the Stoic belief in Fate, the proper use of desire is to desire whatever is fated to occur. As Epictetus says, "Demand not that events should happen as you wish; but wish them to happen as they do happen, and you will go on well."

We have already discussed the Stoic notions of freedom and Fate above. If you accept the doctrine of Fate, the Stoic advice seems like common sense. If there is a conflict between your desires, and reality, there are only two ways to resolve that conflict: either change reality, or change your desires. But, given the Stoic doctrine of Fate, it is not within our power to change reality. Events will transpire as they have been fated to transpire. So, the only remedy within my power is to change my desires instead.

What should I desire? Whatever it is that actually transpires! If I "embrace fate" and desire things to happen as they do, in fact, happen, then my desires will always be satisfied, and I will never be frustrated.

At this point, some of you might rightly be wondering if this strategy doesn't just amount to paralysis in the face of life. "Desire what happens?" How does anyone *do* anything, then? It's not as if, when I get sick, I can just wait to see what happens so I know which outcome (recovery, or death) to desire.

The Stoic strategy is far from paralysis. According to Stoicism, "externals" have no true value. Only that which is up to us (our own virtue) has any value. All other things (all externals) are, strictly speaking, "indifferent." Cars are indifferent, having no value (positive or negative). This is why a proper Stoic will not be disturbed if his car gets scratched. It had no value to begin with! All "things" in our lives (e.g., clothes, furniture, phones, etc.) are indifferent, in this sense. More controversially, even such things as friends, health, and reputation, in that they are externals, are likewise "indifferent."

That being said, some externals, while being "indifferent," are nevertheless "preferred." Things that are "preferred" are those things that are consistent with our nature as rational animals and that are generally conducive to flourishing (though not necessary for it). Eating, for example, is "preferred" over starving. Being healthy is preferred to being sick. Being financially secure is preferable to desperate poverty. Having good friends is preferable to being lonely. Having a good reputation is preferable to being slandered.

With regard to things that are preferred, in this sense, it is appropriate for us to pursue them—though we should recognize that they remain "indifferent," remember that our happiness does not depend on them, and "embrace Fate" with regard to them.

How does a Stoic do this? By acting "under reserve." Stoics, like everyone else, have to make plans, have to make decisions, have to actually live their lives. Yet, Stoics are supposed to desire that things happen as they are fated to happen. A Stoic reconciles these demands by forming conditional desires in the following general form: "I want X, if Fate permits" (where "X" is something to be preferred).

Before delving into this notion in greater detail, please note the obvious similarity between "acting under reserve" and the Muslim and Christian notion of "God willing." Muslims will often say, of some future event they intend, "insha'Allah" (God willing). "And never say of anything, 'I shall do such and such thing tomorrow. Except (with the saying): 'If God wills!'"[95] In the Christian New Testament, we find the same idea: "Now listen, you who say, 'Today or tomorrow we will go to this or that city, spend a year there, carry on business and make money.' Why, you do not even know what will happen tomorrow. What is your life? You are a mist that appears for a little while and then vanishes. Instead, you ought to say, 'If it is the Lord's will, we will live and do this or that.'"[96]

What the Muslim, Christian, and Stoic systems have in common in this respect is that each recognizes a power far greater that controls what transpires, and each recognizes the value of aligning your own will with that power. A Stoic, then, will pursue preferable things, but recognize that those things are not under her control (at least not fully), and will also recognize that not even those things have true value. Health is

preferable to sickness, and I will pursue it as such. I will even desire health—if Fate permits (or, God willing). If I find myself sick instead of healthy, I will pursue recovery and desire it—if Fate permits. Whatever happens, sickness or health, recovery or decline, is beyond my control, and none of those outcomes is a prerequisite for the only thing of true value: virtue. I can be virtuous (by regulating my assent, and aligning my will with Nature) whether I am sick or healthy—though it's preferable to be healthy.

So, there is no need to think that Stoics must curl up into a fetal position, awaiting Fate and unsure of what they should desire. They will live and choose in ways outwardly similar to everyone else. They will pursue friendship and health, prosperity and love. When they do so, however, they recognize what is up to them, and what it not, and they regulate their desire so as to desire only what Fate permits. They guard themselves from attachment to "indifferents," and they discipline themselves in ways that preserve and promote their own tranquility in the face of whatever Fate has in store.

Some key stoic ideas from this preceding section that will find prominence in Cicero's writing include:

- The "divine spark" of Reason within all persons
- The claim that only virtue has intrinsic worth
- The view that Fate/Providence/Reason governs the cosmos
- The value of disciplining one's judgments and emotions

Cicero's Ideas

I want to begin this section with a brief excerpt from one of Cicero's letters to his friend, Atticus, written on March 12th, 49 BCE:

Should one stay in one's country even if it is under totalitarian rule?

---

[95]Surat Al Kahf (18):23-24.
[96]James 4:13-15.

Is it justifiable to use any means to get rid of such rule, even if they endanger the whole fabric of the state? Secondly, do precautions have to be taken to prevent the liberator from becoming an autocrat himself?

If one's country is being tyrannized, what are the arguments in favour of helping it by verbal means and when occasion arises, rather than by war?

Is it statesmanlike, when one's country is under a tyranny, to retire to some other place and remain inactive there, or ought one to brave any danger in order to liberate it? . . .

Ought one, even if not approving of war as a means of abolishing tyranny, to join up with the right-minded party in the struggle against it?

In this personal letter, Cicero is outlining some of the iconic "problems" of political philosophy that thinkers have grappled with for thousands of years, and that continue to this day. When is rebellion justifiable? When is war (rather than mere speech) warranted? Is it a violation of one's duty to one's country to flee the country and preserve oneself rather than stay, resist, and risk persecution?

These musings of Cicero are all the more powerful when we remember that, for him, they were not merely hypothetical questions! He was writing and thinking about these things before, during, and after the "tyranny" of Julius Caesar, and in the context of his own participation in the power struggle that followed.

Our present treatment of Cicero's thought will begin with his (Stoic) understanding of human nature, and the Law of Nature that accompanies it. We will then see how this feeds into his defense of "republican" forms of government,[97] as well as particular policies.

Cicero (like the stoics) believed that all humans are rational, by Nature. This rational soul is the "divine" and immortal element implanted in us all by "God," the "divine spark" or Reason establishing our kinship with each other and with God.[98] As such, we all belong to the common "family" of Humanity itself.[99] Our shared capacity for reason grants us each the additional capacity for moral judgment, and for the cultivation of virtue. "Virtue is the same in humans and gods, for they partake in moral perfection."[100] These capacities can be corrupted by false beliefs and bad habits, but this means they can also be developed as well. "There is no person of any nation who cannot reach virtue with the aid of a guide."[101]

This kind of cosmopolitanism might seem commonsensical to modern ears, but it's difficult to overstate just how radical this kind of thinking was, at the time. Greeks thought of anyone "non-Greek" as "barbarians." Aristotle argued that some people are "natural slaves." Even during the time of the Republic (to say nothing of the Empire), Rome had a vast slave population, and a vast non-citizen population with few, if any, rights. People who were "other" by virtue of their ethnicity, language, religion, citizenship, or nationality were generally regarded as inferior. This notion that *all* people, regardless of national origin, ethnicity, language, or culture was part of the same cosmic family, that each person has some baseline level of moral value, and that we each have duties to each other—even to those "others" who live "over there" was a

---

[97] Not to be confused with the contemporary Republican party in the United States!

[98] *Republic*, 3.1a. Make no mistake about it, Cicero certainly did not have the Judeo-Christian God in mind! Indeed, Cicero died several decades before Jesus of Nazareth was even born. The "God" that

he has in mind is the Stoic notion of God, understood as the supremely rational "Logos" that governs all the operations of Nature.

[99] *Laws*, 1.23

[100] Ibid., 1.25

[101] Ibid., 1.30

philosophically and politically revolutionary idea.

Although cosmopolitan in theory, this does not prevent loyalty to one's own nation or family. Our personal resources and capabilities are less than the needs of all the people in the world, so obligations will vary based on circumstances and the degree of relationships we have with others.[102] Because of our shared kinship with all persons, we have minimal obligations of "decency" to all of humanity, but greater obligations to our own family and country. Our most primary obligations, understandably, are to our own nation, parents, children, and spouse. A secondary tier of obligations would be the rest of one's family. Finally, all the rest of humanity resides in a third tier of obligation.

What this amounts to is a recognition that it is acceptable to prioritize our own national and personal responsibilities.

> That does not mean that we are bound to sacrifice our own vital interests to other people. On the contrary, in so far as we can serve our interests without harming anyone else, we should do so. Chrysippus puts the point with his usual aptness: 'A man running a race in the stadium ought to try his best and exert himself to the utmost in order to win. In no circumstances, however, should he trip up his competitors or impede them with his hand.' The same applies to the struggle of life. Anyone may fairly seek his own advantage, but no one has a right to do so at another's expense.[103]

That being said, we do, nevertheless have responsibilities that cross international borders, and there are limits to what is permissible in our treatment of other nations. "The same thing is established not only in nature, that is in the law of nations, but also in the laws of individual peoples, through which the political community of individual states is maintained: one is not allowed to harm another for the sake of one's advantage."[104]

Indeed, it is possible to infer what Cicero might have thought of the issue of illegal immigration, in this context. "Wrong is likewise done by those who ban and eject foreigners from their cities, . . . True, non-citizens are not entitled to the same rights as citizens . . . . But the exclusion of aliens from the city's amenities is completely opposed to natural human relations."[105] From Cicero's perspective, we have moral obligations to citizens and non-citizens alike due to our shared humanity. In today's terminology, all persons have moral standing regardless of their legal documentation—though he also acknowledges that it is fair for citizens to have more privileges than non-citizens.

In Cicero's time, Rome was a powerful nation that exerted influence over many other lands— and that fact only became more prominent with the growth of the Roman Empire. Today, the United States wields tremendous political, economic, cultural, and military influence across the globe.

"Hegemonic leadership," traditionally, referred to actions taken by a powerful State (e.g., Sparta, or Rome) out of self-interest, but which provided benefits to other States (e.g., security). Today, hegemony tends to refer to the domination by a single powerful nation (e.g., the United States), from a self-appointed mission to defend "the world" against "rogue nations," to preserve peace and economic stability, etc. Cicero, in the context of Roman hegemony, claimed that fear inspires hate, and hegemony by fear was ultimately self-destructive. "Fear is but a poor safeguard of lasting power; while affection, on the other hand, may be trusted to keep it safe for ever."[106]

---

[102] *On Duties*, 1.59

[103] Ibid., 3.42

[104] Ibid., 3.23

[105] Ibid., 3.46

[106] Ibid., 2.23. Contrast that idea with Machiavelli's, over a thousand years later: "Upon this a question arises: whether it be better to be loved than feared or feared than loved? It may be answered that one should wish to be both, but,

Cicero recognized that power tends to corrupt, however, and when one State wields immense hegemonic power "it is difficult to preserve the spirit of fairness which is absolutely essential for justice."[107] Seemingly benevolent hegemony can degenerate into international-scale tyranny. But, no power is so strong as to be able to rule, by fear, indefinitely.[108] A lasting and just hegemony must be based not on military power and intimidation, but by moral worth, and moral leadership that will earn the admiration and respect of other states.[109]

This idea, while ancient, is not necessarily outdated. In a speech by President Obama made in June, 2009, he said: "Democracy, rule of law, freedom of speech, freedom of religion - those are not simply principles of the West to be hoisted on these countries, but rather what I believe to be universal principles that they can embrace and affirm as part of their national identity, . . . The United States' job is not to lecture, but to encourage, to lift up what we consider to be the values that ultimately will work not just for our country, but for the - the aspirations of a lot of people."[110]

Cicero and President Obama seem to have a couple points in common on this issue. In the first place, both speak from the perspective of a State that is powerful and influential on the global stage. Secondly, they both speak of universal values, transcending borders—and both believe

that their respective nations are best served when they lead by example, rather than merely proclaiming and preaching, let alone bullying.

Sometimes, however, no matter how benevolent and enlightened a nation might try to be, conflict with other nations proves unavoidable, and war results. What moral principles govern the waging and conduct of war?

Cicero is sometimes considered the father of "just war theory." Just war theory is usually divided into two categories: *jus ad bellum* and *jus in bello* [roughly, "right to war" and "right in war" (or "laws in war"), respectively].

Jus ad bellum considerations govern when it is morally permissible to go to war in the first place. According to Cicero (and most just war theorists since him), war (the use of force) is morally permissible only as a last resort. "We must resort to force only in case we may not avail ourselves of discussion."[111] This is an extension of his moral philosophy, in general, according to which a good man is one who helps all whom he can and harms nobody, unless provoked by wrong.[112] In other words, only wars of self-defense are morally justifiable.

With regard to *jus in bello*, there are moral restraints during the conduct of the war as well. "In undertaking, waging, and ending wars both justice and good faith should be as strong as possible, and there should be official interpreters

---

because it is difficult to unite them in one person, is much safer to be feared than loved, when, of the two, either must be dispensed with. Because this is to be asserted in general of men, that they are ungrateful, fickle, false, cowardly, covetous, and as long as you succeed they are yours entirely; they will offer you their blood, property, life and children, as is said above, when the need is far distant; but when it approaches they turn against you. And that prince who, relying entirely on their promises, has neglected other precautions, is ruined; because friendships that are obtained by payments, and not by greatness or nobility of mind, may indeed be earned, but they are not secured, and in time of need cannot be relied

upon; and men have less scruple in offending one who is beloved than one who is feared, for love is preserved by the link of obligation which, owing to the baseness of men, is broken at every opportunity for their advantage; but fear preserves you by a dread of punishment which never fails."—The Prince, Chapter 27.

[107] Ibid.,1.64

[108] Ibid., 2.25-2.26

[109] Ibid., 2.31

[110] http://www.telegraph.co.uk/news/worldnews/barackobama/5426465/Barack-Obama-says-US-must-lead-by-example.html

[111] Ibid.,, 1.34-1.35

[112] Ibid., 3.76

of them."[113] A formal declaration of war is required. "No war is just, unless it is entered upon after an official demand for satisfaction has been submitted or warning has been given and a formal declaration made."[114] Cruelty is to be limited (*On Duties*, 3.46), promises to enemies are to be kept (*On Duties*, 1.40), and enemies who surrender are to be spared (*On Duties*, 1.35).

In case it's not obvious why Cicero thought that even one's enemies have rights, and are people to whom we have moral obligations, remind yourself of his starting premise: all persons share in reason, all people have some measure of moral value, and a natural law governs all people, regardless of political lines drawn on a map. "There is only one justice which constitutes the bond among humans, and which is established by one law, which is the right reason in commands and prohibitions."[115] This natural law can't be overruled by any human decree, nor any considerations of convenience or self-interest. The natural law is the foundation and judge of all human laws, whether domestic or international.

> We can distinguish good from bad laws by the standard of nature.[116]

> There is one, single, justice. It binds together human society and has been established by one, single, law.[117]

> Law in the proper sense is right reason in harmony with nature. It is spread through the whole human community, unchanging and eternal, calling people to their duty by its commands and deterring them from wrong-doing by its prohibitions. . . . This law cannot be countermanded, nor can it be in any way amended, nor can it be totally rescinded. We cannot be exempted from this law by

any decree of the Senate or the people; nor do we need anyone to else to expound or explain it. There will not be one such law in Rome and another in Athens, one now and another in the future, but all people at all times will be embraced by a single and eternal and unchangeable law; and there will be, as it were, one lord and master of us all—the god who is the author, proposer, and interpreter of that law.[118]

Human laws that fail to conform to the standard provided by natural law are not, properly speaking, "laws" at all!

> If ignorant unqualified people prescribe a lethal, instead of a healing, treatment, that treatment cannot properly be called 'medical.' In a community a law of just any kind will not be a law, even if the people (in spite of its harmful character) have accepted it. Therefore law means drawing a distinction between just and unjust, formulated in accordance with that most ancient and important of all things—nature; by her, human laws are guided in punishing the wicked and defending and protecting the good.[119]

Going back to the nature (*physis*) v. custom (*nomos*) debate initiated by the sophists several chapters ago, Cicero clearly comes down on the side of nature—a position that will endear him to Christian "natural law" theorists in the Medieval period to come. And yet, if there is allegedly "one single law for all humanity," why are there so many different opinions, customs, and human laws? How do we explain all the cultural differences, variations in laws across geographic location and time, and all the differences in opinion even within the same community? How do we explain how same-sex marriage can be

---

[113] *Laws*, 2.34
[114] *Republic*, 3.35
[115] *Laws*, 1.42
[116] Ibid., 1.44

[117] Ibid., 1.42
[118] *Republic*, 3.33
[119] *Laws*, 2.13

celebrated by a majority of the population in some countries, today, while homosexuals are being executed in brutal fashion in other parts of the world? Prescient thinker that he was, Cicero had an answer for that conundrum, as well.

> Yet we are confused by the variety and variability of men's opinions; and because the same disagreement does not occur in regard to the senses. We think the senses are reliable by nature whereas we brand as illusory those ideas that vary from one person to another and do not always remain consistent within the same person. This distinction is far from the truth. In the case of our senses, no parent or nurse or teacher or poet or stage-show distorts them, nor does popular opinion lead them astray. For our minds, however, all kinds of traps are laid, either by the people just mentioned, who on receiving young untrained minds stain them and twist them as they please, or else by that power which lurks within, entwined with every one of our senses, namely pleasure, which masquerades as goodness but is in fact the mother of all ills. Seduced by her charms, our minds fail to see clearly enough the things that are naturally good, because those things lack the sweetness and the exciting itch of pleasure.[120]

Think of it this way: most of us are not skeptics of relativists with respect to basic claims about perceptible things. As an example, most people are pretty darn confident that elephants are larger than house flies—and anyone who claims otherwise is either doing something odd with language, or else likely adopting an insincere philosophical pose for the sake of being contrary. Because sense-testimony is generally conducive to agreement, we imagine that empirical matters

are factual, objective. However, when it comes to moral judgments, there is a variety of views.

Some people think that abortion is acceptable, and others think it is murder. Some people believe it's wrong to eat meat, and others worship at the altar of bacon. Same-sex marriage is now a constitutional right in the United States, but homosexuals are executed by being thrown off of buildings in ISIS-controlled parts of Syria.[121] We are taught one thing by our parents, perhaps another by teachers, perhaps another by friends, still another by our church, and yet another by the media and pop culture. This dizzying influx of contrary moral messages can cause us to conclude that there is no moral "truth" at all—only opinion.

What's more, Cicero points out that we can be "charmed" by pleasure into thinking that certain actions, because they are pleasurable, are also therefore "good"—while our senses generally provide no such ulterior motive.

For all these reasons, Cicero explains how people can come to the *false* conclusion that there is no objective moral law. However, Cicero is confident that there is, that, because we are social beings, unjust acts are contrary to our natural fellowship, and true laws, therefore, are intended to maintain social order and harmony.

Given his views on human nature and natural law, what sort of political system does Cicero recommend? Ultimately, he doesn't travel far from either Plato or Aristotle, in that he, like they, advocates a "polity," or "mixed" constitution. A notable difference, of course, is that while Plato imagines an ideal Republic, and Aristotle likewise envisions a polity built "from scratch" in the *Laws*, Cicero models his own "ideal" state off of the actual Roman Republic that he tried so desperately to preserve and resurrect.

The Republic ("*res publica*") means "commonwealth," or the "common good." Technically, any form of government with a shared sense of justice and common interest could be called a "republic," in a broad sense, but

---

[120] *Laws*, 1.47

[121] http://www.nydailynews.com/news/world/isis-militants-throw-gay-man-building-death-article-1.2041416

for Cicero, a specifically "republican" form of government is a government of the whole people, by the whole people, and for the benefit of all the people.[122]

Like both Plato and Aristotle, Cicero discusses how the three major types of governments are prone to degeneration (monarchy into tyranny, aristocracy into oligarchy, and democracy into anarchic mob rule), even specifically referencing and summarizing Plato's own account.[123] In theory, mixed (balanced) constitution can prevent concentration (and abuse) of power.[124] The "defects" of each major government type are as follows:

- Monarchy: the rest of the population has too small a role in legislation/debate
- Aristocracy: the masses have too little liberty
- Democracy: "equality" is *unequal* since merit is not recognized and rewarded

The best government will be a harmonious mix of all three of the other types—one in which no faction has "too much" power. As the actual Roman Republic was fading before him, Cicero wrote of the undue influence that wealth can have within a political community.

> But they maintain that this ideal state has been ruined by people who cannot think straight—people who, knowing nothing about worth (which resides in a few, and is discerned and assessed by a few), imagine that aristocrats are those with large fortunes and possessions or those who belong to famous families. When, as a result of this vulgar misconception, a few with money, not worth, have gained control of the state, those leaders seize

the name of 'aristocrats' with their teeth, though lacking any right to it in fact. Money, name, and property, if divorced from good sense and skill in living one's life and directing the lives of others, lapse into total degradation and supercilious insolence. And indeed there is no more degenerate kind of state than that in which the richest are supposed to be the best. But what can be more splendid than a state governed by worth, where the man who gives orders to others is not the servant of greed, where the leader himself has embraced all the values which he preaches and recommends to his citizens, where he imposes no laws on the people which he does not obey himself, but rather presents his own life to his fellows as a code of conduct?[125]

Offices should not be assigned based on wealth (nor on mob rule, for that matter!), but (ideally) the "best" persons will be awarded office, and those who obtain them will legislate or rule for the good of all, with each class balanced in power and influence. This intended balance of power is not merely defensive, for the sake of stability, but reflects the normative ideal that all segments of the Republic *should* be represented and cared for. When this fails to be the case, the State ceases to be a "republic" (*res publica*) at all.[126]

As previously intimated, in Cicero's own time, the Republic was one in name only (e.g., there was the dictatorship of Pompey, followed by the dictatorship and proto-imperial rule of Gaius Julius Caesar). Cicero's writings aimed to produce a return to republicanism. In the *Roman Republic*, Consuls (joint heads of state) represent the monarchical element, the Senators represent the aristocratic element, and the Tribunes and

---

[122] It is impossible not to hear echoes of this in final line of Abraham Lincoln's famous Gettysburg Address: "that we here highly resolve that these dead shall not have died in vain—that this nation, under God, shall have a new birth of freedom—and that government of the people, by

the people, for the people, shall not perish from the earth."
[123] *Republic*, 1.65-1.68
[124] Ibid., 1.69
[125] Ibid., 1.51-1.53
[126] Ibid., 3.43-3.45

popular assemblies represent the democratic element. When each class is virtuous, and performs its function for the good of all, the Republic itself will be virtuous, and politically stable.

His "republican" ideal is not applicable only to the actual Roman Republic, of course. In principle, it can be generalized and applied to any suitably arranged State. W. Julian Korab-Karpowicz usefully outlines several political and moral values that are fundamental to Cicero's "republican" government:[127]

- Legitimacy based on justice and service: the government is a trustee of the people, and its function is to care for the welfare of the people, as opposed to any particular faction of the people. (*On Duties*, 1.85)
- Limited and divided political power: a reasoned balance produces harmony and cooperation among social groups is needed. (*On Duties*, 2.69a)
- Freedom and responsibility: citizens have both the right and the duty to become knowledgeable and skillful so that they can be useful to society, and also free to express their opinion and participate in politics. (*Republic* 1.33 and *Laws* 3.27)
- Justice and cooperation: benefit (both individual and national) shouldn't be pursued if doing so harms others, and the common benefit should be pursued by means of just cooperation. (*On Duties*, 2.18)
- Leadership and loyalty: Leaders should be prudent and just, and this will inspire loyalty from the people and the Republic's allies abroad. (*Republic* 5.5 and *Laws* 3.5)
- Rationality and knowledge: All humans are gifted with reason, and should cultivate it to pursue practical and moral wisdom. Knowledge and wisdom are the result of

proper education and training. (*Republic* 1.29)
- Human fellowship: common history, cultural traditions, and bonds of worship create strong bonds of fellowship. (*On Duties*, 1.55)
- Openness to other cultures: All humans are gifted with Reason, creating a common kinship that transcends geographical, national, and ethnic (etc.) barriers. (*On Duties*, 3.47)
- Moderation and peace: the well-being of society can be best served through moderate policies, and promoting and preserving peace. (*Republic* 2.26, *On Duties*, 1.35)

Cicero's Influence

Cicero's defense of "republicanism" was profoundly influential in the medieval period, and into the Renaissance and Enlightenment—inspiring Aquinas, Machiavelli, Montesquieu, and American "Founding Fathers" (e.g., John Adams, Thomas Jefferson, and James Madison). Indeed, traces (or at least analogues) of it can be seen in the U.S. government. The Supreme Court and Senate plausibly represent the "aristocratic" element, the President/executive branch the "monarchical" element, and the House of Representatives the "democratic" element

Aristotle wrote about the *Polis*—a kind of city-state that was already going "extinct" even at the time of his writing. Cicero, too, seemed to be writing of a kind of government (i.e., a Republic) that would make way for Imperial rule, only to be followed by the feudal system that would dominate Europe for centuries more. It wouldn't be until the Renaissance, over a thousand years later, that Cicero would be rediscovered, and discover a resurgence of popularity and influence.

Due in part to Petrarch's enthusiasm, the Italian Renaissance could be said to be a revival of Cicero—and only through him, of classical

---

[127] *On the History of Political Philosophy: Great Thinkers from Thucydides and Locke*, by W. Julian Korab-Karpowicz. Pearson, 2012.

studies, in general. Cicero's ideal of a well-rounded citizen, skilled in language, responsible to his community, cultivated and refined in taste, became the ideal of the "renaissance man" amongst the Italian upper class.

Cicero's influence peaked in the 18th century, manifesting in such important figures as Locke, Hume, and Montesquieu. Cicero was so influential during the Renaissance that his *De Officiis*" (*On Duties*) was the first classical work to be printed after the invention of the printing press.[128] Voltaire said of *On Duties:* "No one will ever write anything more wise, more true, or more useful. From now on, those whose ambition it is to give men instruction, to provide them with precepts, will be charlatans if they want to rise above you, or will all be your imitators."[129]

His influence did not end in the Renaissance, however, but continued on into the Enlightenment. As mentioned, he also inspired the "Founding Fathers" of America, with John Adams quoting Cicero numerous times in *his Preface on Government* (1786), and saying of him, "As all the ages of the world have not produced a greater statesman and philosopher united than Cicero, his authority should have great weight."[130] Thomas Jefferson also referenced the *Tusculan Disputations* in his own writings, and found a place in the *Declaration of Independence* for natural law and inalienable rights.

In the Middle Ages, Cicero would not "disappear," but his influence would wane, just as that of Greece and Rome, in general. Christian Europe would inherit *something* from ancient philosophy (Plato, through Augustine, and Aristotle, through Aquinas), but political philosophy would take a decidedly Christian turn for the next thousand years, or so. It is to this period of the history of political philosophy that we turn in our next chapter.

---

[128] For comparison, *On Duties* was first published in 1465. The *Gutenberg Bible* was printed in 1455.
[129] "Note to Cicero," 1771.

[130] Mortimer Sellars, *American Republicanism: Roman Ideology in the United States*, NYU Press, 1994.

Although it is tempting to provide some primary texts from Cicero himself (either "The Republic," or "On Duties," for example), I have decided instead to offer numerous suitable quotations/excerpts from Cicero and those sources (and others) throughout the chapter, and provide a stoic source at the end of the chapter, instead. As discussed previously in this chapter, much of Cicero's philosophical impact on political thought derives from his adoption of certain stoic themes, most notably their emphasis on universal reason, and the "cosmopolitanism" that follows from that. The following work from Epictetus, "The Enchiridion" is provided in its entirety. It provides a brief and helpful survey of key stoic themes, especially those that were emphasized in the Roman period of stoicism. Epictetus (55 CE – 135 CE) was a former "house slave" of Epaphroditos—a secretary to the Emperor Nero. Indeed, we don't know "Epictetus'" real name, as Epictetus (epíktetos/(ἐπίκτητος) literally means "acquired" in Latin—undoubtedly a reference to his slave status. His owner allowed him to study philosophy under the Stoic Musonius Rufus. He was freed after Nero's death in 68 CE, and began to teach philosophy in Rome, but migrated to Nicopolis in Greece after the Emperor Domitian banished philosophers from Rome in 93 CE. That both a slave (Epictetus) and a Roman Emperor (Marcus Aurelius) would both be devoted to stoicism is a testimony to its broad appeal.

Epictetus: *The Enchiridion*

("The Manual" Or "The Handbook" of Epictetus)
Translated by Thomas Wentworth Higginson.
[http://www.davemckay.co.uk/philosophy/epictetus/epictetus.php?name=enchiridion.higginson]

I.

There are things which are within our power, and there are things which are beyond our power. Within our power are opinion, aim, desire, aversion, and, in one word, whatever affairs are our own. Beyond our power are body, property, reputation, office, and, in one word, whatever are not properly our own affairs.

Now, the things within our power are by nature free, unrestricted, unhindered; but those beyond our power are weak, dependent, restricted, alien. Remember, then, that if you attribute freedom to things by nature dependent, and take what belongs to others for you own, you will be hindered, you will lament, you will be disturbed, you will find fault both with gods and men. But if you take for your own only that which is your own, and view what belongs to others just as it really is, then no one will ever compel you, no one will restrict you, you will find fault with no one, you will accuse no one, you will do nothing against your will; no one will hurt you, you will not have an enemy, nor will you suffer any harm.

Aiming therefore at such great things, remember that you must not allow yourself any inclination, however slight, towards the attainment of the others; but that you must entirely quit some of them, and for the present postpone the rest. But if you would have these, and possess power and wealth likewise, you may miss the latter in seeking the former; and you will certainly fail of that by which alone happiness and freedom are procured.

Seek at once, therefore, to be able to say to every unpleasing semblance, "You are but a semblance and by no means the real thing." And then examine it by those rules which you have; and first and chiefly, by this: whether it concerns the things which are within our own power, or those which are not; and if it concerns anything beyond our power, be prepared to say that it is nothing to you.

II.

Remember that desire demands the attainment of that of which you are desirous; and aversion demands the avoidance of that to which you are averse; that he who fails of the object of his desires is disappointed; and he who incurs the object of his aversion is wretched. If, then, you shun only those undesirable things which you can control, you will never incur anything you shun;

but if you shun sickness, or death, or poverty, you will run the risk of wretchedness. Remove [the habit of] aversion, then, from all things that are not within our power, and apply it to things undesirable, which are within our power. But for the present altogether restrain desire; for if you desire any of the things not within our own power, you must necessarily be disappointed; and you are not yet secure of those which are within our power, and so are legitimate objects of desire. Where it is practically necessary for you to pursue or avoid anything, do even this with discretion, and gentleness, and moderation.

III.

With regard to whatever objects either delight the mind, or contribute to use, or are tenderly beloved, remind yourself of what nature they are, beginning with the merest trifles: if you have a favorite cup, that it is but a cup of which you are fond, – for thus, if it is broken, you can bear it; if you embrace your child, or your wife, that you embrace a mortal, – and thus, if either of them dies, you can bear it.

IV.

When you set about any action, remind yourself of what nature the action is. If you are going to bathe, represent to yourself the incidents usual in the bath, – some persons pouring out, others pushing in, others scolding, others pilfering. And thus you will more safely go about this action, if you say to yourself, "I will now go to bathe, and keep my own will in harmony with nature." And so with regard to every other action. For thus, if any impediment arises in bathing, you will be able to say, "It was not only to bathe that I desired, but to keep my will in harmony with nature; and I shall not keep it thus, if I am out of humor at things that happen."

V.

Men are disturbed not by things, but by the views which they take of things. Thus death is nothing terrible, else it would have appeared so to Socrates. But the terror consists in our notion of death, that it is terrible. When, therefore, we are hindered, or disturbed, or grieved, let us

never impute it to others, but to ourselves; that is, to our own views. It is the action of an uninstructed person to reproach others for his own misfortunes; of one entering upon instruction, to reproach himself; and of one perfectly instructed, to reproach neither others or himself.

VI.

Be not elated at any excellence not your own. If a horse should be elated, and say, "I am handsome," it might be endurable. But when you are elated, and say, "I have a handsome horse," know that you are elated only on the merit of the horse. What then is your own? The use of phenomena of existence. So that when you are in harmony with nature in this respect, you will be elated with some reason; for you will be elated at some good of your own.

VII.

As in a voyage, when the ship is at anchor, if you go on shore to get water, you may amuse yourself with picking up a shell-fish or a truffle in your way, but your thoughts ought to be bent towards the ship, and perpetually attentive, lest the captain should call, and then you must leave all these things, that you may not have to be carried on board the vessel, bound like a sheep; thus likewise in life, if, instead of a truffle or shell-fish, such a thing as a wife or a child be granted you, there is not objection; but if the captain calls, run to the ship, leave all these things, and never look behind. But if you are old, never go far from the ship, lest you should be missing when called for.

VIII.

Demand not that events should happen as you wish; but wish them to happen as they do happen, and you will go on well.

IX.

Sickness is an impediment to the body, but not to the will, unless itself pleases. Lameness is an impediment to the leg, but not to the will; and say this to yourself with regard to everything that happens. For you will find it to be an impediment to something else, but not truly to yourself.

X.

Upon every accident, remember to turn towards yourself and inquire what faculty you have for its use. If you encounter a handsome person, you will find continence the faculty needed; if pain, then fortitude; if reviling, then patience. And when thus habituated, the phenomena of existence will not overwhelm you.

XI.

Never say of anything, "I have lost it;" but, "I have restored it." Has your child died? It is restored. Has your wife died? She is restored. Has your estate been taken away? That likewise is restored. "But it was a bad man who took it." What is it to you by whose hands he who gave it has demanded it again? While he permits you to possess it, hold it as something not your own; as do travellers at an inn.

XII.

If you would improve, lay aside such reasonings as these: "If I neglect my affairs, I shall not have a maintenance; if I do not punish my servant, he will be good for nothing." For it were better to die of hunger, exempt from grief and fear, than to live in affluence with perturbation; and it is better that your servant should be bad than you unhappy.

Begin therefore with little things. Is a little oil spilt or a little wine stolen? Say to yourself, "This is the price paid for peace and tranquillity; and nothing is to be had for nothing." And when you call your servant, consider that it is possible he may not come at your call; or, if he does, that he may not do what you wish. But it is not at all desirable for him, and very undesirable for you, that it should be in his power to cause you any disturbance.

XIII.

If you would improve, be content to be thought foolish and dull with regard to externals. Do not desire to be thought to know anything; and though you should appear to others to be

somebody, distrust yourself. For be assured, it is not easy at once to keep your will in harmony with nature, and to secure externals; but while you are absorbed in the one, you must of necessity neglect the other.

XIV.

If you wish your children and your wife and your friends to live forever, you are foolish; for you wish things to be in your power which are not so; and what belongs to others to be your own. So likewise, if you wish your servant to be without fault, you are foolish; for you wish vice not to be vice, but something else. But if you wish not to be disappointed in your desires, that is in your own power. Exercise, therefore, what is in your power. A man's master is he who is able to confer or remove whatever that man seeks or shuns. Whoever then would be free, let him wish for nothing, let him decline nothing, which depends on others; else he must necessarily be a slave.

XV.

Remember that you must behave as at a banquet. Is anything brought round to you? Put out your hand, and take a moderate share. Does it pass by you? Do not stop it. Is it not come yet? Do not yearn in desire towards it, but wait till it reaches you. So with regard to children, wife, office, riches; and you will some time or other be worthy to feast with the gods. And if you do not so much as take the things which are set before you, but are able even to forego them, then you will not only be worthy to feast with the gods, but to rule with them also. For, by thus doing, Diogenes and Heraclitus, and others like them, deservedly became divine, and were so recognized.

XVI.

When you see any one weeping for grief, either that his son has gone abroad, or that he has suffered in his affairs, take care not to be overcome by the apparent evil; but discriminate, and be ready to say, "What hurts this man is not this occurrence itself, – for another man might not be hurt by it, – but the view he chooses to take of it." As far as conversation goes, however, do not disdain to accommodate yourself to him, and if need be, to groan with him. Take heed, however, not to groan inwardly too.

XVII.

Remember that you are an actor in a drama of such sort as the author chooses, – if short, then in a short one; if long, then in a long one. If it be his pleasure that you should enact a poor man, see that you act it well; or a cripple, or a ruler, or a private citizen. For this is your business, to act well the given part; but to choose it, belongs to another.

XVIII.

When a raven happens to croak unluckily, be not overcome by appearances, but discriminate, and say, – "Nothing is portended to *me*; but either to my paltry body, or property, or reputation, or children, or wife. But to *me* all portents are lucky, if I will. For whatsoever happens, it belongs to me to derive advantage therefrom."

XIX.

You can be unconquerable, if you enter into no combat in which it is not in your own power to conquer. When, therefore, you see any one eminent in honors or power, or high esteem on any other account, take heed not to be bewildered by appearances and to pronounce him happy; for if the essence of good consists in things within our own power, there will be no room for envy or emulation. But, for your part, do not desire to be a general, or a senator, or a consul, but to be free; and the only way to this is a disregard of things which lie not within our own power.

XX.

Remember that it is not he who gives abuse or blows who affronts; but the view we take of these things as insulting. When, therefore, any one provokes you, be assured that it is your own opinion which provokes you. Try, therefore, in the first place, not to be bewildered by appearances. For if you once gain time and respite, you will more easily command yourself.

XXI.

Let death and exile, and all other things which appear terrible, be daily before your eyes, but death chiefly; and you will never entertain any abject thought, not too eagerly covet anything.

XXII.

If you have an earnest desire towards philosophy, prepare yourself from the very first to have the multitude laugh and sneer, and say, "He is returned to us a philosopher all at once;" and "Whence this supercilious look?" Now, for your part, do not have a supercilious look indeed; but keep steadily to those things which appear best to you, as one appointed by God to this particular station. For remember that, if you are persistent, those very persons who at first ridiculed will afterwards admire you. But if you are conquered by them, you will incur a double ridicule.

XXIII.

If you ever happen to turn your attention to externals, for the pleasure of any one, be assured that you have ruined your scheme of life. Be contented, then, in everything, with being a philosopher; and if you with to seem so likewise to any one, appear so to yourself, and it will suffice you.

XXIV.

Let not such considerations as these distress you: "I shall live in discredit, and be nobody anywhere." For if discredit be an evil, you can no more be involved in any evil through another, than in baseness. Is it any business of yours, then, to get power, or to be admitted to an entertainment? By no means. How, then, after all, is this discredit? And how is it true that you will be nobody anywhere; when you ought to be somebody in those things only which are within your own power, in which you may be of the greatest consequence? "But my friends will be unassisted." What do you mean by unassisted? They will not have money from you; nor will you make them Roman citizens. Who told you, then, that these are among the things within our own power, and not rather the affair of others? And who can give to another the things which he has not? "Well, but get them, then, that we too may have a share." If I can get them with the preservation of my own honor and fidelity and self-respect, show me the way, and I will get them; but if you require me to lose my own proper good, that you may gain what is no good, consider how unreasonable and foolish you are. Besides, which would you rather have, a sum of money, or a faithful and honorable friend? Rather assist me, then, to gain this character, than require me to do those things by which I may lose it. Well, but my country, say you, as far as depends upon me, will be unassisted. Here, again, what assistance is this you mean? It will not have porticoes nor baths of your providing? And what signifies that? Why, neither does a smith provide it with shoes, or a shoemaker with arms. It is enough if every one fully performs his own proper business. And were you to supply it with another faithful and honorable citizen, would not he be of use to it? Yes. Therefore neither are you yourself useless to it. "What place, then," say you, "shall I hold in the state?" Whatever you can hold with the preservation of your fidelity and honor. But if, by desiring to be useful to that, you lose these, how can you serve your country, when you have become faithless and shameless?

XXV.

Is any one preferred before you at an entertainment, or in courtesies, or in confidential conversation? If these things are good, you ought to rejoice that he has them; and if they are evil, do not be grieved that you have them not. And remember that you cannot be permitted to rival others in externals, without using the same means to obtain them. For how can he who will not haunt the door of any man, will not attend him, will not praise him, have an equal share with him who does these things? You are unjust, then, and unreasonable, if you are unwilling to pay the price for which these things are sold, and would have them for nothing. For how much are lettuces sold? An obolus, for instance. If another, then, paying an obolus, takes the lettuces, and you, not paying it, go without them, do not imagine that he has gained any advantage over you. For as he has

the lettuces, so you have the obolus which you did not give. So, in the present case, you have not been invited to such a person's entertainment, because you have not paid him the price for which a supper is sold. It is sold for praise; it is sold for attendance. Give him, then, the value, if it be for your advantage. But if you would at the same time not pay the one, and yet receive the other, you are unreasonable, and foolish. Have you nothing, then, in place of the supper? Yes, indeed, you have: not to praise him whom you do not like to praise; not to bear the insolence of his lackeys.

XXVI.

The will of Nature may be learned from things upon which we are all agreed. As, when our neighbor's boy has broken a cup, or the like, we are ready at once to say, "These are casualties that will happen;" be assured, then, that when your own cup is likewise broken, you ought to be affected just as when another's cup was broken. Now apply this to greater things. Is the child or wife of another dead? There is no one who would not say, "This is an accident of mortality." But if any one's own child happens to die, it is immediately, "Alas! how wretched am I!" It should be always remembered how we are affected on hearing the same thing concerning others.

XXVII.

As a mark is not set up for the sake of missing the aim, so neither does the nature of evil exist in the world.

XXVIII.

If a person had delivered up your body to some passer-by, you would certainly be angry. And do you feel no shame in delivering up your own mind to any reviler, to be disconcerted and confounded?

XXIX.

In every affair consider what precedes and follows, and then undertake it. Otherwise you will begin with spirit indeed, careless of the consequences, and when these are developed, you will shamefully desist. "I would conquer at the Olympic games." But consider what precedes and follows, and then, if it be for your advantage, engage in the affair. You must conform to rules, submit to a diet, refrain from dainties; exercise your body, whether you choose it or not, at a stated hour, in heat and cold; you must drink no cold water, and sometimes no wine, – in a word, you must give yourself up to your trainer as to a physician. Then, in the combat, you may be thrown into a ditch, dislocate your arm, turn your ankle, swallow abundance of dust, receive stripes [for negligence], and, after all, lose the victory. When you have reckoned up all this, if your inclination still holds, set about the combat. Otherwise, take notice, you will behave like children who sometimes play wrestlers, sometimes gladiators, sometimes blow a trumpet, and sometimes act a tragedy, when they have seen and admired these shows. Thus you too will be at one time a wrestler, at another a gladiator; now a philosopher, now an orator; but nothing in earnest. Like an ape you mimic all you see, and one thing after another is sure to please you, but is out of favor as soon as it becomes familiar. For you have never entered upon anything considerately, nor after having surveyed and tested the whole matter; but carelessly, and with a half-way zeal. Thus some, when they have seen a philosopher, and heard a man speaking like Euphrates, – though indeed who can speak like him? – have a mind to be philosophers too. Consider first, man, what the matter is, and what your own nature is able to bear. If you would be a wrestler, consider your shoulders, your back, your thighs; for different persons are made for different things. Do you think that you can act as you do, and be a philosopher; that you can eat, drink, be angry, be discontented, as you are now? You must watch, you must labor, you must get the better of certain appetites; must quit your acquaintance, be despised by your servant, be laughed at by those you meet; come off worse than others in everything, – in offices, in honors, before tribunals. When you have fully considered all these things, approach, if you please; if, by parting with them, you have a mind to purchase serenity, freedom, and tranquillity. If not, do not come hither; do not, like children, be now a philosopher, then a publican, then an orator, and then one of Caesar's officers. These things are not consistent. You must be one man either good or bad. You must cultivate either your own Reason or else externals, apply yourself either to things within or without you; that is, be either a philosopher, or one of the mob.

XXX.

Duties are universally measured by relations. Is a certain man your father? In this are implied, taking care of him; submitting to him in all things; patiently receiving his reproaches, his correction. But he is a bad father. Is your natural tie, then, to a *good* father? No, but to a father. Is a brother unjust? Well, preserve your own just relation towards him. Consider not what *he* does, but what *you* are to do, to keep your own will in state conformable to nature. For another cannot hurt you, unless you please. You will then be hurt when you consent to be hurt. In this manner, therefore, if you accustom yourself to contemplate the relations of neighbor, citizen, commander, you can deduce from each the corresponding duties.

XXXI.

Be assured that the essential property of piety towards the gods lies in this, to form right opinions concerning them, as existing, and as governing the universe justly and well. And fix yourself in this resolution, to obey them, and yield to them, and willingly follow them amidst all events, as being ruled by the most perfect wisdom. For thus you will never find fault with the gods, nor accuse them of neglecting you. And it is not possible for this to be effected any other way than by withdrawing yourself from things which are not within our own power, and by making good or evil to consist only in those which are. For if you suppose any of the things to be either good or evil, it is inevitable that, when you are disappointed of what you wish, or incur what you would avoid, you should reproach and blame their authors. For every creature is naturally formed to flee and abhor things that appear hurtful, and that which causes them; and to pursue and admire those which appear beneficial, and that which causes them. It is impractical, then, that one who supposes himself to be hurt should rejoice in the person who, as he thinks, hurts him; just as it is impossible to rejoice in the hurt itself. Hence, also, a father is reviled by his son, when he does not impart the things which seem to be good; and this made Polynices and Eteocles mutually enemies, that empire seemed good to both. On this account the husbandman reviles the gods; the sailor, the merchant, or those who have lost wife or child. For where our interest is, there too is piety directed. So that whoever is careful to regulate his desires and aversions as he ought is thus made careful of piety likewise. But it also becomes incumbent on every one to offer libations and sacrifices and first-fruits, according to the customs of his country, purely, and not heedlessly nor negligently; nor avariciously, nor yet extravagantly.

XXXII.

When you have recourse to divination, remember that you know not what the event will be, and you come to learn it of the diviner; but of what nature it is you knew before coming; at least, if you are of philosophic mind. For if it is among the things not within our power, it can by no means be either good or evil. Do not, therefore, bring with you to the diviner either desire or aversion, – else you will approach him trembling, – but first clearly understand that every event is indifferent, and nothing to *you*, of whatever sort it may be; for it will be in your power to make a right use of it, and this no one can hinder. Then come with confidence to the gods as your counsellors; and afterwards, when any counsel is given you, remember what counsellors you have assumed, and whose advice you will neglect, if you disobey. Come to divination, as Socrates prescribed, in cases of which the whole consideration relates to the event, and in which no opportunities are afforded by reason, or any other art, to discover the matter in view. When, therefore, it is our duty to share the danger of a friend or of our country, we ought not to consult

the oracle as to whether we shall share it with them or not. For though the diviner should forewarn you that the auspices are unfavorable, this means no more than that either death or mutilation or exile is portended. But we have reason within us; and it directs, even with these hazards, to stand by our friend and country. Attend, therefore, to the greater diviner, the Pythian god, who once cast out of the temple him who neglected to save his friend.

XXXIII.

Begin by prescribing to yourself some character and demeanor, such as you may preserve both alone and in company.

Be mostly silent; or speak merely what is needful, and in few words. We may, however, enter sparingly into discourse sometimes, when occasion calls for it; but let it not run on any of the common subjects, as gladiators, or horse-races, or athletic champions, or food, or drink, – the vulgar topics of conversation; and especially not on men, so as either to blame, or praise, or make comparisons. If you are able, then, by your own conversation, bring over that of your company to proper subjects; but if you happen to find yourself among strangers, be silent.

Let not your laughter be loud, frequent, or abundant.

Avoid taking oaths, if possible, altogether; at any rate, so far as you are able.

Avoid public and vulgar entertainments; but if ever an occasion calls you to them, keep your attention upon the stretch, that you may not imperceptibly slide into vulgarity. For be assured that if a person be ever so pure himself, yet, if his companion be corrupted, he who converses with him will be corrupted likewise.

Provide things relating to the body no farther than absolute need requires; as meat, drink, clothing, house, retinue. But cut off everything that looks towards show and luxury.

Before marriage, guard yourself with all your ability from unlawful intercourse with women; yet be not uncharitable or severe to those who are led into this, not frequently boast that you yourself do otherwise.

If any one tells you that such a person speaks ill of you, do not make excuses about what is said of you, but answer: "He was ignorant of my other faults, else he would not have mentioned these alone."

It is not necessary for you to appear often at public spectacles; but if ever there is a proper occasion for you to be there, do not appear more solicitous for any other than for yourself; that is, wish things to be only just as they are, and only the best man to win: for thus nothing will go against you. But abstain entirely from acclamations and derision and violent emotions. And when you come away, do not discourse a great deal on what has passed, and what contributes nothing to your own amendment. For it would appear by such discourse that you were dazzled by the show.

Be not prompt or ready to attend private recitations; but if you do attend, preserve your gravity and dignity, and yet avoid making yourself disagreeable.

When you are going to confer with any one, and especially with one who seems your superior, represent to yourself how Socrates or Zeno would behave in such a case, and you will not be at a loss to meet properly whatever may occur.

When you are going before any one in power, fancy to yourself that you may not find him at home, that you may be shut out, that the doors may not be opened to you, that he may not notice you. If, with all this, it be your duty to go, bear what happens, and never say to yourself, "It was not worth so much." For this is vulgar, and like a man bewildered by externals.

In society, avoid a frequent and excessive mention of your own actions and dangers. For however agreeable it may be to yourself to allude to risks you have run, it is not equally agreeable to others to hear your adventures. Avoid likewise an endeavor to excite laughter. For this may readily slide you into vulgarity, and, besides, may be apt to lower you in the esteem of your acquaintance. Approaches to indecent discourse are likewise dangerous. Therefore when anything of this sort happens, use the first fit opportunity to rebuke him who makes advances that way; or,

at least, by silence and blushing and a serious look, show yourself to be displeased by such talk.

XXXIV.

If you are dazzled by the semblance of any promised pleasure; guard yourself against being bewildered by it; but let the affair wait your leisure, and procure yourself some delay. Then bring to your mind both points of time, – that in which you shall enjoy the pleasure, and that in which you will repent and reproach yourself, after you have enjoyed it, – and set before you, in opposition to these, how you will rejoice and applaud yourself, if you abstain. And even though it should appear to you a seasonable gratification, take heed that its enticements and allurements and seductions may not subdue you; but set in opposition to this, how much better it is to be conscious of having gained so great a victory.

XXXV.

When you do anything from a clear judgment that it ought to be done, never shrink from being seen to do it, even though the world should misunderstand it; for if you are not acting rightly, shun the action itself; if you are, why fear those who wrongly censure you?

XXXVI.

As the proposition, *either it is day, or it is night*, has much force in a disjunctive argument, but none at all in a conjunctive one; so, at a feast, to choose the largest share is very suitable to the bodily appetite, but utterly inconsistent with the social spirit of the entertainment. Remember, then, when you eat with another, not only the value to the body of those things which are set before you, but also the value of proper courtesy toward your host.

XXXVII.

If you have assumed any character beyond your strength, you have both demeaned yourself ill that, and quitted one which you might have supported.

XXXVIII.

As in walking you take care not to tread upon a nail, or turn your foot, so likewise take care not to hurt the ruling faculty of your mind. And if we were to guard against this in every action, we should enter upon action more safely.

XXXIX.

The body is to every one the proper measure of its possessions, as the foot is of the shoe. If, therefore, you stop at this, you will keep the measure; but if you move beyond it, you must necessarily be carried forward, as down a precipice; as in the case of a shoe, if you go beyond its fitness to the foot, it comes first to be gilded, then purple, and then studded with jewels. For to that which once exceeds the fit measure there is no bound.

XL.

Women from fourteen years old are flattered by men with the title of mistresses. Therefore, perceiving that they are regarded only as qualified to give men pleasure, they begin to adorn themselves, and in that to place all their hopes. It is worth while, therefore, to try that they may perceive themselves honored only so far as they appear beautiful in their demeanor, and modestly virtuous.

XLI.

It is a mark of want of intellect, to spend much time in things relating to the body; as to be immoderate in exercises, in eating and drinking, and in the discharge of other animal functions. These things should be done incidentally and our main strength be applied to our reason.

XLII.

When any person does ill by you, or speaks ill of you, remember that he acts or speaks from an impression that it is right for him to do so. Now, it is not possible that he should follow what appears right to you, but only what appears so to himself. Therefore, if he judges from false appearances, he is the person hurt; since he too is the person deceived. For if any one takes a true proposition to be false, the proposition is not hurt, but only the man is deceived. Setting out,

then, from these principles, you will meekly bear with a person who reviles you; for you will say upon every occasion, "It seemed so to him."

XLIII.

Everything has two handles: one by which it may be borne, another by which it cannot. If your brother acts unjustly, do not lay hold on the affair by the handle of his injustice, for by that it cannot be borne; but rather by the opposite, that he is your brother, that he was brought up with you; and thus you will lay hold on it as it is to be borne.

XLIV.

These reasonings have no logical connection: "I am richer than you; therefore I am superior." "I am more eloquent than you; therefore I am your superior." The true logical connection is rather this: "I am richer than you; therefore my possessions must exceed yours." "I am more eloquent than you; therefore my style must surpass yours." But you, after all, consist neither in property nor in style.

XLV.

Does any one bathe hastily? Do not say that he does it ill, but hastily. Does any one drink much wine? Do not say that he does ill, but that he drinks a great deal. For unless you perfectly understand his motives, how should you know if he acts ill? Thus you will not risk yielding to any appearances but such as you fully comprehend.

XLVI.

Never proclaim yourself a philosopher; nor make much talk among the ignorant about your principles, but show them by actions. Thus, at an entertainment, do not discourse how people ought to eat; but eat as you ought. For remember that thus Socrates also universally avoided all ostentation. And when persons came to him, and desired to be introduced by him to philosophers, he took them and introduced them; so well did he bear being overlooked. So if ever there should be among the ignorant any discussion of principles, be for the most part silent. For there is great danger in hastily throwing out what is undigested. And if any one tells you that you know nothing, and you are not nettled at it, then you may be sure that you have really entered on your work. For sheep do not hastily throw up the grass, to show the shepherds how much they have eaten; but, inwardly digesting their food, they produce it outwardly in wool and milk. Thus, therefore, do you not make an exhibition before the ignorant of your principles; but of the actions to which their digestion gives rise.

XLVII.

When you have learned to nourish your body frugally, do not pique yourself upon it; nor, if you drink water, be saying upon every occasion, "I drink water." But first consider how much more frugal are the poor than we, and how much more patient of hardship. If at any time you would inure yourself by exercise to labor and privation, for your own sake and not for the public, do not attempt great feats; but when you are violently thirsty, just rinse your mouth with water, and tell nobody.

XLVIII.

The condition and characteristic of a vulgar person is that he never looks for either help or harm from himself, but only from externals. The condition and characteristic of a philosopher is that he looks to himself for all help or harm. The marks of a proficient are that he censures no one, praises no one, blames no one, accuses no one; says nothing concerning himself as being anybody, or knowing anything. When he is in any instance hindered or restrained, he accuses himself; and if he is praised, he smiles to himself at the person who praises him; and if he is censured, he makes no defence. But he goes about with the caution of a convalescent, careful of interference with anything that is doing well, but not yet quite secure. He restrains desire; he transfers his aversion to those things only which thwart the proper use of our own will; he employs his energies moderately in all directions; if he appears stupid or ignorant, he does not care; and, in a word, he keeps watch over himself as over an enemy and one in ambush.

XLIX.

When any one shows himself vain, on being able to understand and interpret the works of Chrysippus, say to yourself: "Unless Chrysippus had written obscurely, this person would have had nothing to be vain of. But what do I desire? To understand Nature, and follow her. I ask, then, who interprets her; and hearing that Chrysippus does, I have recourse to him. I do not understand his writings. I seek, therefore, one to interpret *them*." So far there is nothing to value myself upon. And when I find an interpreter, what remains is to make use of his instructions. This alone is the valuable thing. But if I admire merely the interpretation, what do I become more than a grammarian, instead of a philosopher, except, indeed, that instead of Homer I interpret Chrysippus? When any one, therefore, desires me to read Chrysippus to him, I rather blush, when I cannot exhibit actions that are harmonious and consonant with his discourse.

L.

Whatever rules you have adopted, abide by them as laws, and as if you would be impious to transgress them; and do not regard what any one says of you, for this, after all, is no concern of yours.

LI.

How long, then, will you delay to demand of yourself the noblest improvements, and in no instance to transgress the judgments of reason? You have received the philosophic principles with which you ought to be conversant; and you have been conversant with them. For what other master, then, do you wait as an excuse for this delay in self-reformation? You are no longer a boy, but a grown man. If, therefore, you will be negligent and slothful, and always add procrastination to procrastination, purpose to purpose, and fix day after day in which you will attend to yourself, you will insensibly continue to accomplish nothing, and, living and dying, remain of vulgar mind. This instant, then, think yourself worthy of living as a noun grown up and a proficient. Let whatever appears to be the best, be to you an inviolable law. And if any instance of pain or pleasure, glory or disgrace, be set before you, remember that now is the combat, now the Olympiad comes on, nor can it be put off; and that by one failure and defeat honor may be lost – or won. Thus Socrates became perfect, improving himself by everything, following reason alone. And though you are not yet a Socrates, you ought, however, to live as one seeking to be a Socrates.

LII.

The first and the most necessary topic in philosophy is the practical application of principles, as, *We ought not to lie*; the second is that of demonstrations, as, *Why it is that we ought not to lie*; the third, that which gives strength and logical connection to the other two, as, *Why this is a demonstration*. For what is demonstration? What is a consequence; what a contradiction; what truth; what falsehood? The third point is then necessary on account of the second; and the second on account of the first. But the most necessary, and that whereon we ought to rest, is the first. But we do just the contrary. For we spend all our time on the third point, and employ all our diligence about that, and entirely neglect the first. Therefore, at the same time that we lie, we are very ready to show how it is demonstrated that lying is wrong.

LIII.

Upon all occasions we ought to have these maxims ready at hand: –
"Conduct me, Zeus, and thou, O Destiny,
Wherever your decrees have fixed my lot.
I follow cheerfully; and, did I not,
Wicked and wretched, I must follow still."[1]
"Whoe'er yields properly to Fate is deemed
Wise among men, and knows the laws of Heaven."[2]
And this third: –
"O Crito, if it thus pleases the gods, thus let it be.
Anytus and Melitus may kill me indeed; but hurt me they cannot."[3]

----

[1] Cleanthes, *Hymn to Zeus*, quoted by Seneca, Epistle 107.
[2] Euripides, Fragment 965 Nauck.

[3] Plato, *Crito* 43d; *Apology* 30c–d.

Chapter 6: Medieval Politics

Comprehension questions you should be able to answer after reading this chapter:

1. Why does Augustine reject the "optimism" of ancient political philosophy?

2. Why does Augustine think that it doesn't matter all that much under what political system a citizen or subject lives?

3. What does Augustine mean by the "Two Cities?" What are they, and who are the citizens of each?

4. What are the restraints on human laws and rulers, according to Augustine?

5. What is meant by *jus ad bello* and *jus in bello*? What requirements are associated with each of those two categories?

6. For Aquinas, what is the difference between "felicity" and "beatitude?" How does this difference relate to the proper roles for the Church and the State?

7. What does Aquinas mean by each of the following? Eternal Law, Natural Law, Human Law, Synderesis, Conscience.

8. What is a "conclusion" from the natural law? What is a "determination" from the natural law?

9. What is the "Law of Nations?"

10. Why does Aquinas think that kings should resist becoming tyrants?

11. What are the functions of human laws (and punishment)?

12. Explain Aquinas' position on private property. Are there any (moral) limits on wealth?

13. How is Aquinas' approach to political philosophy different from Augustine's?

Our last chapter ended with Cicero, and, historically, the birth of the Roman Empire once Octavian became "Augustus." As mentioned, the influence of classical political philosophers did not disappear entirely during the Middle Ages. Indeed, the first thinker we will consider mentions Cicero by name numerous times. However, the tone of political philosophy, and the basic assumptions guiding it, changes in a profound way during this period, as illustrated by the "political philosophy" of St. Augustine.

Saint Augustine

Augustine is a very difficult "political philosopher" to explain or study, in part because Augustine would have been unlikely to consider himself as having done "political philosophy!" Indeed, he has no particular work or essay which especially lends itself to gleaning his vision of politics. Instead, one must hunt for hints and themes throughout his massive theological work, *The City of God*.[131]

---

[131] For that reason, I have not included any primary source texts from Augustine, beyond the quotations found throughout the first section of this chapter. For those who would like to read *The City of God*, you may find a public domain version

Augustine was born in 354 CE in Numidia—a North African province of the Roman Empire. At the age of 19, Augustine read Cicero's *Hortensius* and developed his love of philosophy. This led him to read, among many other things, the Bible—though he was not initially impressed! Instead, he drifted into Manichaeism and was associated with that school of thought for a decade.[132] Over this time, he also studied Skepticism and Neo-Platonism. Eventually, he began to study the Bible again, and was influenced by Bishop Ambrose of Milan. After experiencing a seemingly miraculous event [hearing what sounded like a child's voice repeating "*tolle lege*" ("pick it up and read it")], he opened the Epistles of Paul to a random page and was drawn to *Romans* 13:13-14 ("Let us walk honestly as in a day, not in revelry and drunkenness, not in debauchery and licentiousness, not in quarreling and jealousy."). He eventually converted to Christianity himself, and was baptized by Bishop Ambrose on Easter in 387.

Upon his conversion, Augustine abandoned his old life for the sake of his new life, breaking with his Manichaean past and ultimately founding a monastery and school in Hippo (North Africa). He was ordained a priest in 391, an auxiliary bishop in 395, and was appointed Bishop of Hippo in 396—a position he would fill until his death, 34 years later.

This was a time of political and theological unrest for the Roman Empire. The Emperor Constantine converted to Christianity in 312 CE, and moved the capital of the Empire to Constantinople (named after himself) in 330. Although Christianity was now the dominant religion of the Empire, there were still many pagans, many of them from influential families. Indeed, it was not until 392, that the Emperor Theodosius commanded that formal public worship of pagan gods (the "gods of Rome")

would end.

The Goths invaded and plundered Greece in 395, and then turned to Italy in 401-403. Other barbarian tribes invaded Gaul and Spain. Within the church, heresies were popping up—and Augustine first turned his writings to attack the views of the heretics, including his own former Manichaeism, as well as Pelagianism.[133]

In 410, Rome itself was sacked by the Goth invaders—something that hadn't happened for 800 years. Some of the Roman elite began to suggest that the gods of Rome were punishing the Empire for abandoning them—that the plight of Rome was the fault of Christianity. This allegation inspired the writing of Augustine's hugely influential *City of God*, within which he would not only defend Christianity against that charge, but also offer a withering criticism of the "virtues" of the Roman Republic (a topic we will turn to later).

Augustine died in 430. In 432 Vandals conquered and burned Hippo. After conquering Carthage in 439, they set their sights on Rome. In 476, a Germanic chieftan (Odaecer) toppled the last Roman Emperor (Augustulus Romulus). The "Eternal Empire" was divided amongst barbarian tribes, and the so-called Dark Ages began.

For roughly 500 years after the sack of Rome, various armies of barbarian invaders devastated Europe. With the fall of the Roman Empire, strong national powers (in the West) disappeared, replaced by small kingdoms and local governing. Self-supporting villages, dominated by agriculture, became the foundation for the feudal system in which lords (members of the noble class, including royalty) who typically had some land would offer some of that land (and a pledge of protection) to vassals, in exchange for loyalty, taxes, and service (including military conscription).

In an interesting twist, the barbarian invaders who were responsible for the collapse of the empire and this new geopolitical landscape,

---

of it at the following URL: http://oll. libertyfund.org/titles/2053

[132] A religion founded in the 3rd century, CE, by the Persian Mani that offered a thoroughly dualistic understanding of reality, including a vision of an

eternal battle between (equal) forces of good and evil, light and darkness.

[133] A "heresy" that, among other things, denied the doctrine of Original Sin.

ultimately converted to Christianity. Though the barbarians had disrupted the overarching political authority of the Roman Empire, it was eventually replaced with the overarching religious authority of the Christian Church. Across Europe, a new notion of cultural unity developed: "Christendom."

Within the context of the feudal system, a new vision would emerge of Christian society jointly governed by two governments: one secular (King), and one spiritual (Pope). The pope was superior to the king in spiritual matters, while the king was superior to the pope in temporal (lay) matters. The pope and the church needs the support and protection of the king and his resources, but the king needs salvation.

Augustine's lifetime saw the end of the Roman Empire, and the beginning of the new medieval world in Europe. Augustine himself is generally regarded as the first Christian philosopher, and a "bridge" between the ancient and medieval worlds.

Augustine was classically trained and educated, and although he held that Christianity was the one, true faith, and that pagan philosophies were all misguided to varying degrees, he did respect the Platonist school, crediting Plato with, in effect, having the right general idea of God and virtue, but missing the mark due to his lack of access to Revelation. Aristotle, too, conceived of God as the "Unmoved Mover," and the Stoics regarded God as a divine mind governing all of Nature.

As Augustine described them, "They were ignorant of the end to which all these [truths] were to be referred and the standard by which they were to be assessed."[134] There is precedent for giving ancient (pagan) philosophers partial credit for their insights. The Apostle Paul wrote that "They know the truth about God because he has made it obvious to them. For ever since the world was created, people have seen the earth and sky. Through everything God made, they can clearly see his invisible qualities—his eternal power and divine nature."[135]

Although Augustine is considered a "bridge" between the ancient (pagan) and medieval (Christian) worlds, his own approach to politics is also very much a rejection of much that was taken for granted by ancient philosophers.

The tradition of political philosophy as exemplified by such persons as Plato, Aristotle, and Cicero was one in which all parties took for granted that political society is natural for humans, and that we can only fulfill our potential within a political community. Although there was disagreement as to how best to do so, "everyone" agreed that the function of the State was to mold its citizens into the virtuous persons that they potentially are. Without too much exaggeration, politics was a means of "perfecting" (as much as is possible) the members of a community—even if only a small subset of that population (e.g., the "aristocrats") might fully actualize their potential.

The optimism of the Classical tradition is rejected by Augustine as naïve. Because of the Fall of Man, humans are incapable of "perfecting" themselves or even of achieving genuine and lasting happiness without the assistance of God. As a Christian, he accepted the doctrine of original sin, according to which all persons are spiritually depraved and disposed to sinfulness. All persons have fallen away from God and righteousness, and require salvation and God's grace in order to be better and to do better.

Because of our sinful nature, humans are naturally predisposed to misbehave. Left to our own devices, we will pursue our own desires, even at the expense of others. The State (and the threat of punishment) is necessary to restrain our behavior. Rather than being the natural means by which humans can be "perfected" within a community (as had been the vision of Plato, Aristotle, and Cicero), the State, for Augustine, is the necessary consequence of sin, and exists primarily to preserve order.

As we saw in the previous chapter, Cicero offered the historic Roman Republic as a model for a polity, and lamented its decline into what was a "republic" in name only. Augustine denies that a true Republic ever existed at all. Without

---

[134] Augustine, *City of God*, 18.41

[135] *Romans*, 1.19-1.20

God, there is no true justice, and instead people will pursue their own desires and possibly cloak it in the mantle of virtue. The shared values and vision of the common good that allegedly bound the members of the Ancient Republic together was really merely a "common agreement on the objects of their love"[136], and therefore, "there never was a Roman commonwealth."[137]

Justice is not truly possible in this world, though some communities come closer to it than others. Justice is not merely "giving to each their due," as was the commonly accepted definition in the ancient world. Instead, Augustine conceives justice as "love serving God only, and therefore ruling well all else." This provides the basis for his criticism of Cicero's idealized Roman Republic. Because the Romans never loved God, they were incapable of ever producing a genuine "republic" or "commonwealth," or ever being truly just. Indeed, without the true justice that starts with the love of God, he dismisses all States (even the Roman Republic) as mere gangs. "And what are kingdoms but gangs of criminals on a large scale? What are criminal gangs but petty kingdoms?"

Though actual earthly States will never be ideal, they do, nevertheless, serve a divine purpose: they maintain order and prevent excessive violence by the threat of punishment. With regard to crime and punishment, Augustine thinks that rulers are always authorized to punish "sins against nature" (e.g., murder), and also justified in punishing "sins against custom" (e.g., punishing tax evaders), so long as those customs do not themselves contradict God's commandments (e.g., punishing someone for worshipping God!).

The idealistic Statecraft of ancient philosophers was misguided, according to Augustine, not only because of the existence of sin, but because it's basic aim is futile. By seeking a kind of "salvation" in this life ("perfecting" citizens within their political community), ancient philosophers neglected the only salvation

that exists and matters: eternal salvation. Moreover, against the backdrop of eternity, any human life—and even the life of an entire community, such as Rome, or the United States—is a mere "speck."

Augustine's pessimism (or possibly realism, depending on your perspective) is not to be confused with a different breed of pessimism/realism that would find eloquent voice in later thinkers, such as Hobbes and Machiavelli.

Augustine believes that politics is incapable of "saving" humanity, but his solution is not to eliminate moral considerations from the political sphere altogether, as a result. Instead, he shifts the source of moral improvement and salvation from politics to the God who "gives instructions for the promotion of the highest morality and the reproof of wickedness."[138] To grant such power and authority to political institutions, instead, is a form of idolatry.[139]

Because of his belief that the State (and politics) is incapable of "saving" persons, and that our proper priority should be Eternity, rather than this life, Augustine thought that it mattered little under what sort of political system a citizen of the "City of God" lived. Unlike his predecessors, he didn't advocate for any particular governmental type (e.g., monarchy, oligarchy, democracy, mixed polity, etc.), but thought that Christians should adapt and live according to the values of the Church no matter where they might reside.

This is not to say that he is completely indifferent to earthly laws, nor that there is no limits to what a Christian citizen should accept from their secular rulers. The primary goal of the State is to prevent and resolve conflicts. So long as it does this, there need be no conflict between the Christian and the State. They are free to follow the advice of Jesus himself to "Render therefore

---

[136] *City of God*, 19.24
[137] Ibid., 19.21
[138] Ibid., 2.25

[139] An interesting article on contemporary political "idolatry" in U.S. politics may be found here: http://www.huffingtonpost.com/jim-wallis/the-idolatry-of-politics_b_1475132.html

unto Caesar the things which are Caesar's; and unto God the things that are God's."[140]

However, what the Christian may not (morally) do is cooperate with any legislation that prevents them from worshipping, nor any that compels them to do impious or immoral things (e.g., a Christian has moral grounds to refuse to worship the Emperor of Rome as a deity).[141] Within such limits, though, the Christian citizen or subject should be obedient.

> Let every person be subject to the governing authorities. For there is no authority except from God, and those that exist have been instituted by God. Therefore whoever resists the authorities resists what God has appointed, and those who resist will incur judgment. For rulers are not a terror to good conduct, but to bad. Would you have no fear of the one who is in authority? Then do what is good, and you will receive his approval, for he is God's servant for your good. But if you do wrong, be afraid, for he does not bear the sword in vain. For he is the servant of God, an avenger who carries out God's wrath on the wrongdoer. Therefore one must be in subjection, not only to avoid God's wrath but also for the sake of conscience. For because of this you also pay taxes, for the authorities are ministers of God, attending to this very thing. Pay to all what is owed to them: taxes to whom taxes are owed, revenue to whom revenue is owed, respect to whom respect is owed, honor to whom honor is owed.[142]

Augustine grants to earthly rulers much leeway with regard to their laws and policies. They are free to enact whatever laws they wish, so long as they don't conflict with God's laws, and citizens (including Christian citizens) have a duty to obey those laws (so long as they don't conflict with God's laws), regardless of the moral qualities of their ruler, with no right to rebel or to civil disobedience.

While rejecting the idealistic perfectionism of ancient political philosophy, Augustine offers an alternative (Christian) model based off of his vision of "two cities," governed by two different objects of love. There is "the self-love that reaches the point of contempt for God," and "the love of God carried as far as contempt of self."[143]

The "Earthly City" aims at human glory, while the citizens of the "City of God" aim at glorifying God. The former is focused on the life of the "Flesh;" the latter on things of the "Spirit." In the Earthly City, people focus on the pleasures of earthly life, and the rewards and honors of this life. In the City of God, earthly goods are correctly regarded as being, ultimately, "worthless," and people are unattached to them, viewing themselves as though they were pilgrims journeying through a foreign land.[144]

It is important to note that Augustine is not describing two literal cities, or even two literal *kinds* of cities. Instead, he's describing different ways of life, different worldviews, and different perspectives. Within any actual community (e.g., Rome, Athens, Los Angeles, etc.) residents of both "cities" will be found, often living right next door to each other. Some Romans (or Angelinos) will be residents of the "Earthly City," and others will be residents of the "City of God"—it depends entirely on their faith (or lack thereof), the condition of their soul, and their fundamental value orientation in life.

The "City of God" can be found everywhere, or nowhere. Not even a specifically Christian theocracy would be identical to the City of God. Citizenship in the City of God is determined at the individual level, not at the institutional level— and certainly not established by lines on a map. It is a universal community of believers living in any and all nations who have set their hearts on God, and are "citizens" by God's Grace.

It is because of the non-political, non-geographical nature of the City of God that

---

[140] *Matthew*, 22.21
[141] *City of God*, 5.17
[142] *Romans*, 13:1-7

[143] *City of God*, 14.28
[144] Ibid., 19.17

Augustine is so "hands off" with regard to actual political systems, and laws—with the only limit being that the "laws of man" not clash with the laws of God. There is even a place for war, within this framework.

Although Jesus is called the "Prince of Peace," Augustine was not a strict pacifist. He thought that Christians had a moral duty to seek and promote peace, but did allow that some use of violence (even war) can be justifiable. Acknowledging that it would be a great injustice if an unjust power conquered and ruled over just people, wars of self—defense, to repel an aggressor, are morally justifiable.[145] Christians, however, are morally entitled to refuse to fight in an unjust war.

Since Augustine is credited with being the first Christian philosopher, he is also credited with being the first Christian "just war theorist"—though his ideas are quite similar to those espoused by Cicero, before him.

As described in the previous chapter, just war theory is generally broken down into two components: *jus ad bello* and *jus in bello*. The former refers to the conditions necessary for a morally justifiable war in the first place, and the latter refers to morally justifiable conduct while waging war. With regard to *jus ad bello*, Augustine claims the following conditions must be met:

- Just cause: self-defense against an external invasion, to avenge unjust injuries, to punish nations for failing to make amends for their unjust actions, to come to the defense of allies unjustly attacked, to gain the return of something wrongfully taken, to obey a divine command to go to war (which, practically speaking would be determined and issued by the head of State).

- Right will: intending the restoration of peace, taking no delight in violence, not seeking conquest for its own sake or for its spoils, and seeing war only as a necessity.

- Declared: by a competent authority, publicly, and only as a last resort.

With regard to *jus in bello*:

- Proportional response: with violence constrained by what is necessary, militarily.

- Discriminating: between combatants and non-combatants (e.g., women, children, elderly, clergy, etc.).

- Observing good faith: with the enemy (e.g., honoring promises/treaties, avoiding treachery, etc.).

War, while permissible (and perhaps unavoidable, given humanity's "fallen" nature), is nevertheless subject to moral constraints.

The transition in Europe from paganism to Christianity had significant impact on culture and philosophy, as evidenced by Augustine. However, his voice was not the sole Christian approach to political philosophy in the Middle Ages. Nearly a thousand years later, another Saint and brilliant Christian philosopher would offer a very different approach to political philosophy. Much as Augustine drew upon classical philosophy in the person of Plato, so too would Saint Thomas Aquinas draw upon antiquity as well—but with a preference for Aristotle, and arguing to a very different conclusion.

St. Thomas Aquinas

Saint Thomas Aquinas was born in either 1224 or 1225 CE. His education began at an early age, when, at age 5, he was placed in a Benedictine monastery to receive his elementary and religious education. In 1239, he enrolled at the University of Naples to study Liberal Arts. While there, he was exposed to Aristotle's writings, and came into contact with members of the Dominican Order—an order to which he declared his intention to join at the age of 19.

---

[145] Ibid., 4.15

In what sounds like the plot of a movie, he was actually kidnapped by his own family and held for one year while they tried to dissuade him from joining the order! After his eventual release, he went to Paris and studied under the renowned Scholastic philosopher, St. Albert the Great. He earned his bachelor's degree in 1248, and was ordained a priest at the age of 25.

Aquinas' brilliance was such that he was alleged to be capable of dictating multiple treatises to multiple scribes simultaneously! One of those treatises was begun in 1266, his *Summa Theologica*. His talent and wisdom attracted notice, and he became an advisor to Popes Alexander IV and Urban IV.

Aquinas died on March 7th, 1272, at the age of 50. He was canonized in 1323, and proclaimed "Doctor of the Church" in 1567.

Although Aquinas was a prolific writer, and a comprehensive philosopher and theologian, our focus in this book is political philosophy, and so we must set aside the vast majority of Aquinas' contributions to both philosophy and theology for the sake of that focus. As was the case with Augustine, Aquinas did not produce a particular work, obviously devoted to political philosophy, within which we may find his clearly stated political views. Instead, his political thoughts are dispersed throughout his many written works, especially the *Summa Theologica*.

It is somewhat accurate (though admittedly oversimplified) to state that Aquinas offered an adaptation of the political philosophy of Aristotle that we already covered in a previous chapter, modified and supplemented to fit a Christian worldview. In fairness, it would be both uncharitable and inaccurate to suggest that he *merely* "Christianized" Aristotle. Aquinas draws on other sources of inspiration as well, including Plato, and Cicero—particularly the Stoic notion of natural law. Nevertheless, his debt to Aristotle is undeniable, going so far as to refer to Aristotle simply as "*The* Philosopher!"

Aristotle's works had been "lost" the West since the 6th century CE, but had made their way East to Syria and Persia, where they were translated into Arabic. When the Arab world expanded all the way to Spain, and certainly as a result of the Crusades, Europeans came into contact with Arab learning, and the Arabic translations of Aristotle. They were first translated from Arabic into Latin, and eventually original Greek texts were found and translated straight to Latin without Arabic as an intermediary.

Thanks to Aquinas' heavy, systematic, and sympathetic use of Aristotle, the Catholic Church moved away from Platonism (which had been adopted, in part, due to Augustine's influence) and towards a harmonizing of Aristotle and Christian doctrine. When we delve into the particulars of Aquinas' views, the similarity to Aristotle will be fairly obvious.

This is not to say their views are identical, of course. Where Aquinas differs from Aristotle is obvious: Christianity! Aristotle did not assume that there exists a universal human community with one supreme Lawgiver as its creator and Lord. In addition, Aquinas recognizes an "end" that can't be addressed even by the best possible regime. Politics, while natural for us, is not capable of addressing our *super*natural end.

Humans achieve full perfection only in Heaven (if at all). Our imperfect happiness attainable on Earth he calls "felicity," while our perfect happiness attainable only in the afterlife is called "beatitude." The Church (not the State) is needed to guide us towards *that* end. The State can help, in that good regimes and good laws can help citizens be more virtuous—which can prepare us to be receptive to Grace, and the virtues of Faith, Hope, and (Christian) Charity.

For Aristotle, there was no meaningful distinction between civic life and religious life. Participation in religious observances was not a private matter concerning one's soul, but another aspect of being a good citizen of the *polis*. Aquinas, however, while recognizing the value of both Church and State, tries to separate and protect the authority of each within their own proper sphere. "Just as the leader or ruler has chief authority in the city, so does the Pope in those things which pertain to God."[146]

> Spiritual and secular power are both derived from the Divine power, and so secular power is subject to spiritual power insofar as this is ordered by God: that is, in those things which pertain to the salvation of the soul. In such matters, then, the spiritual power is to be obeyed before the secular. But in those things which pertain to the civil good, the secular power should be obeyed before the spiritual, according to Matthew 22:21: 'Render to Caesar the things that are Caesar's.'[147]

The Church holds complete authority over spiritual matters, but is limited in secular authority—except if a secular ruler or law intrudes upon spiritual matters: "The secular power is subject to the spiritual, even as the body is subject to the soul. Consequently the judgment is not usurped if the spiritual authority interferes in those temporal matters that are subject to the spiritual authority or which have been committed to the spiritual by the temporal authority."[148]

Despite his recognition and appreciation of the secular sphere, there is no mistaking the fact that Aquinas places ultimate authority with the church, and that he believes kings, just like everyone else, are equally in need of the guidance and sacraments it offers.

> Now the same judgment is to be formed about the end of society as a whole as about the end of one man. If, therefore, the ultimate end of man were some good that existed in himself, then the ultimate end of the multitude to be governed would likewise be for the multitude to acquire such good, and persevere in its possession. If such an ultimate end either of an individual man or a multitude were a corporeal one, namely, life and health of body, to govern would then be a physician's charge. If that ultimate end were an abundance of wealth, then knowledge of economics would have the last word in the community's government. If the good of the knowledge of truth were of such a kind that the multitude might attain to it, the king would have to be a teacher. It is, however, clear that the end of a multitude gathered together is to live virtuously. For men form a group for the purpose of living well together, a thing which the individual man living alone could not attain, and good life is virtuous life. Therefore, virtuous life is the end for which men gather together....

> Yet through virtuous living man is further ordained to a higher end, which consists in the enjoyment of God, as we have said above. Consequently, since society must have the same end as the individual man, it is not the ultimate end of an assembled multitude to live virtuously, but through virtuous living to attain to the possession of God....

> Thus, in order that spiritual things might be distinguished from earthly things, the ministry of this kingdom has been entrusted not to earthly kings but to priests, and most of all to the chief priest, the successor of St. Peter, the Vicar of Christ, the Roman Pontiff. To him all the kings of the Christian People are to be subject as to our Lord Jesus Christ Himself. For those to whom pertains the care of intermediate ends should be subject to him to whom pertains the care

---

[146] Commentary on the Epistle to the Hebrews, V.1

[147] Scripta super libros sententiarum II, Dist.44, quaest.3

[148] *Summa Theologica*, II-II, 6-.6

of the ultimate end, and be directed by his rule.[149]

Given the focus of this book, we shall have to set aside Aquinas' thorough and influential treatment of our "supernatural ends," set our feet firmly on the Earth, and focus on our natural ends, as understood via Aquinas' interpretation of the natural law.

Natural Law

In his discussion of law, we find a rare occasion when Aquinas sounds more like Plato, than Aristotle.

"Law" is a sort of rational pattern analogous to Plato's Forms. In human laws, the idea the ruler has in his mind as to what his subjects should be is "law." God is the supreme Law-Giver. The rational pattern within God's mind supplies the Eternal Law, which "is nothing but the rational pattern of the Divine wisdom considered as directing all actions and motions."[150]

Most things are governed by the Eternal Law without the possibility of disobedience. For example, most things in the universe simply "obey" the laws of nature. Imagine the absurdity of a rock "rebelling" against the pull of gravity, or an acorn defiantly growing into a zebra, rather than an oak tree! Humans, however, complicate the Eternal Law by virtue of our free will.

> Wherefore, since all things subject to Divine providence are ruled and measured by the eternal law, as was stated above (Article [1]); it is evident that all things partake somewhat of the eternal law, in so far as, namely, from its being imprinted on them, they derive their respective inclinations to their proper acts and ends. Now among all others, the rational creature is subject to Divine providence in the most excellent way, in so far as it partakes of a share of providence, by being provident both for

itself and for others. Wherefore it has a share of the Eternal Reason, whereby it has a natural inclination to its proper act and end: and this participation of the eternal law in the rational creature is called the natural law.[151]

Because human subjection to the Eternal Law is different, Aquinas calls it being under the "Natural Law"—but "The Natural Law is nothing else than the rational creature's participation of the Eternal Law." That is, the natural law is simply the eternal law as it is applied to humans.

The natural law guides humans via natural inclinations toward the natural perfection to which God intends us. This includes, among other things, moral instruction.

Aquinas calls the natural knowledge humans have instructing fundamental moral requirements of our human nature "Synderesis."

> Now it is clear that, as the speculative reason argues about speculative things, so that practical reason argues about practical things. Therefore we must have, bestowed on us by nature, not only speculative principles, but also practical principles. Now the first speculative principles bestowed on us by nature do not belong to a special power, but to a special habit, which is called "the understanding of principles," as the Philosopher explains (Ethic. vi, 6). Wherefore the first practical principles, bestowed on us by nature, do not belong to a special power, but to a special natural habit, which we call "synderesis." Whence "synderesis" is said to incite to good, and to murmur at evil, inasmuch as through first principles we proceed to discover, and judge of what we have discovered.[152]

A more familiar term, "conscience," he defines as an act of applying synderesis to concrete situations.

---

[149] *De Regimine Principum*, Book 1, chapter 15
[150] *Summa Theologica*, I-II, 93.1.

[151] Ibid., I-II, 91.2
[152] Ibid., I, 79.12

For conscience, according to the very nature of the word, implies the relation of knowledge to something: for conscience may be resolved into "cum alio scientia," i.e. knowledge applied to an individual case. . . . Wherefore, properly speaking, conscience denominates an act. But since habit is a principle of act, sometimes the name conscience is given to the first natural habit---namely, 'synderesis': thus Jerome calls 'synderesis' conscience (Gloss. Ezech. 1:6); Basil [*Hom. in princ. Proverb.], the "natural power of judgment," and Damascene [*De Fide Orth. iv. 22] says that it is the "law of our intellect." For it is customary for causes and effects to be called after one another.[153]

For example, by synderesis we understand that adultery is morally wrong, but by conscience we understand that having sex with a particular woman who is not my wife is a case of adultery. The natural knowledge of our moral requirements as supplied by synderesis is universal, unchangeable, and can't be "abolished from the hearts of men."[154] With this notion of a universal moral code applying to all humans, regardless of race or nationality, Aquinas is drawing more from the Stoics than Aristotle.

What, exactly, is the instruction provided by means of synderesis? The first moral precept of the natural law is that "good is to be done and pursued and evils is to be avoided."[155] Aquinas does not bother to prove this. Instead, he claims that this precept of practical reason is analogous to the law of non-contradiction for speculative reason: neither can be demonstrated (proven), but both are principles without which reasoning to conclusions (logical, or moral, respectively) is impossible.

If we accept that good is to be pursued, and evil avoided, how do we know what qualifies as good or evil? Aquinas thinks that our natural inclinations provide a rudimentary guide to "natural goods." For example, our natural inclination to self-preservation, avoidance of pain, pursuit of pleasure, reproduction and care of our offspring, living within a community, etc., are indicators of natural goods.

These inclinations are not infallible, of course. They can (and often are) corrupted by sin, so we are not merely to act on any inclination we happen to have! Instead, we need to recognize the "natural purpose" of the inclination, and then act on it only insofar as that purpose is respected. For example, according to Aquinas (and the official Natural Law doctrine of the Catholic Church), our sexual inclination has a "natural purpose" of reproduction. Therefore, the only proper way to act on that inclination is one which "respects" its purpose: reproduction. Not surprisingly, then, Aquinas (and the Catholic Church) are opposed to homosexual activities, masturbation, oral sex, the use of contraception—and any sexual activity that can't (feasibly) result in conception. Accordingly, Aquinas specifies that all inclinations belong to the natural law only insofar as they are "ruled by reason."[156] We experience inclinations, but must test them with Reason to determine whether it is right to indulge and pursue them.

Although the natural law provides basic moral guidelines for human life, it does not provide specific guidance. For example, it is "natural" that those who commit crimes but should be punished, but what nature does not reveal to us is what exact punishment is appropriate based on the crime. Human law is needed to flesh out the details.

The first function of human law is to provide the details (understandably) left out by natural law. The second function of human law is to enforce the specific interpretation of natural law that is expressed in human law. In some cases, human laws are so close to what is offered by natural law that we find them existing "universally" in all human communities. To use Aquinas' vocabulary, some human laws

---

153 Ibid., I, 79.13
154 Ibid., I-II, 94.4-94.6

155 Ibid., I-II, 94.2
156 Ibid., I-II, 94.2

constitute "conclusions" from natural law. These pertain to matters about which natural law offers clear guidance (e.g., murder is wrong). Aquinas refers to these "conclusions" as the "law of nations," as they are (or ought to be) found in all nations, given that all humans have the same nature, and are subject to the same natural law. Indeed, a human law that opposes natural law is no longer properly "law" at all.

> As Augustine says (De Lib. Arb. i, 5) "that which is not just seems to be no law at all": wherefore the force of a law depends on the extent of its justice. Now in human affairs a thing is said to be just, from being right, according to the rule of reason. But the first rule of reason is the law of nature, as is clear from what has been stated above (Q[91], A[2], ad 2). Consequently every human law has just so much of the nature of law, as it is derived from the law of nature. But if in any point it deflects from the law of nature, it is no longer a law but a perversion of law.[157]

Other human laws involve much longer chains of reasoning to link them back to natural law, and so might be specific to certain communities only.   These laws constitute "determinations" from natural law, and these pertain to the particular details/applications that are based in the conclusions from natural law.

> Some things are therefore derived from the general principles of the natural law, by way of conclusions; e.g. that "one must not kill" may be derived as a conclusion from the principle that "one should do harm to no man": while some are derived therefrom by way of determination; e.g. the law of nature has it that the evil-doer should be punished; but that he be punished in this or that way, is a determination of the law of nature.[158]

Aquinas offers his own analogy to try to clarify the relationship between conclusions and determinations of natural law. As all houses have certain essential elements (e.g., having a foundation, a roof, etc.), but may have particular details added to them that may vary from house to house (e.g., whether the house is built from brick or wood, whether the roof is tile or shingle, how many windows it has, etc.), so too will human laws be based on general natural law principles (e.g., murder is a criminal offense), but varying with regard to details (e.g., punishing murder with execution as opposed to life imprisonment).

In addition to the guidance offered by both human laws and the natural law, Divine Law is needed, because human laws can be made in error (e.g., unjust laws), because human laws can't direct the soul (the intentions) of the citizen—but only his outward acts (i.e., a human law might cause someone to abstain from adultery from the threat of punishment, but that person can still commit adultery "in his heart."), and because human law is imperfect in its ability to punish or forbid all evil deeds. The Divine Law regulates and punishes us as sinners, not criminals. There might be actions which are not illegal, but are nevertheless sinful.

> Wherefore laws imposed on men should also be in keeping with their condition, for, as Isidore says (Etym. v, 21), law should be "possible both according to nature, and according to the customs of the country." Now possibility or faculty of action is due to an interior habit or disposition: since the same thing is not possible to one who has not a virtuous habit, as is possible to one who has. Thus the same is not possible to a child as to a full-grown man: for which reason the law for children is not the same as for adults, since many things are permitted to children, which in an adult are punished by law or at any rate are open to blame. In like manner many things are permissible

---

[157] Ibid., I-II, 95.2

[158] Ibid., I-II, 95.2

to men not perfect in virtue, which would be intolerable in a virtuous man.

Now human law is framed for a number of human beings, the majority of whom are not perfect in virtue. Wherefore human laws do not forbid all vices, from which the virtuous abstain, but only the more grievous vices, from which it is possible for the majority to abstain; and chiefly those that are to the hurt of others, without the prohibition of which human society could not be maintained: thus human law prohibits murder, theft and such like.[159]

Law and punishment can prevent wrongdoing, first by fear of punishment, and eventually (possibly) by shaping moral character so that citizens willingly do what is right, not from fear, but from virtue.

. . . man has a natural aptitude for virtue; but the perfection of virtue must be acquired by man by means of some kind of training. Thus we observe that man is helped by industry in his necessities, for instance, in food and clothing. . . . Now it is difficult to see how man could suffice for himself in the matter of this training: since the perfection of virtue consists chiefly in withdrawing man from undue pleasures, to which above all man is inclined, and especially the young, who are more capable of being trained. Consequently a man needs to receive this training from another, whereby to arrive at the perfection of virtue. And as to those young people who are inclined to acts of virtue, by their good natural disposition, or by custom, or rather by the gift of God, paternal training suffices, which is by admonitions. But since some are found to be depraved, and prone to vice, and not easily amenable to words, it was necessary for such to be restrained from

evil by force and fear, in order that, at least, they might desist from evil-doing, and leave others in peace, and that they themselves, by being habituated in this way, might be brought to do willingly what hitherto they did from fear, and thus become virtuous. Now this kind of training, which compels through fear of punishment, is the discipline of laws. Therefore in order that man might have peace and virtue, it was necessary for laws to be framed: for, as the Philosopher says (Polit. i, 2), "as man is the most noble of animals if he be perfect in virtue, so is he the lowest of all, if he be severed from law and righteousness"; because man can use his reason to devise means of satisfying his lusts and evil passions, which other animals are unable to do.[160]

Human laws therefore serve two important ends: peace/order, and instilling virtue. Aquinas (in agreement with Aristotle) claims that one of the natural goods to which we are all inclined is to live in a community. Being part of a civil society is an aspect of our human nature—not an artificial construct, nor a mere "contract."

The Value of Civil Society

In contrast to the social contract tradition, which finds ultimate authority in the humans who form the contract in the first place, Aquinas (following Aristotle) claims that humans are naturally social/political beings, and therefore the foundation/origin of society is the God who created us in the first place, endowing us with the particular natures we possess. Moreover, authority has its origin in God, rather than "man." This is not to be confused with some sort of endorsement of the "divine right" of kings. Aquinas is not claiming that particular rulers are given their authority by God Himself, but rather that the very existence of authority at all comes from God via the natural law.

Aquinas is a sharp contrast to Augustine. Augustine (like Plato) has his eyes firmly in a

[159] Ibid., I-II, 96.2

[160] Ibid., I-II, 95.1

transcendent "other" world. This Earthly world is Fallen, sinful, destructive, and temporary. Politics is necessary to restrain the worst excesses of our sinful behavior, but it is not "good." Indeed, Augustine thought that the need for politics runs counter to God's original intentions for humans, and is now needed only because of the Fall of Man. "God did not intend that His rational creature, made in His own image, should have lordship over any but irrational creatures: not man over man, but man over the beasts."[161]

Aquinas, though, accepting Aristotle's claim that humans are naturally social and political animals, has a much more positive view of politics. Politics is not a corrective measure necessary because of the Fallen world. He agrees, of course, that our highest good can only be achieved with God in Heaven, but he sees value in the present goods available here on Earth as well. Political rulership ("dominion"), though established by human law, arises from the natural law, and can be perfectly consistent with the divine law.

> If, then, it is natural for man to live in the society of many, it is necessary that there exist among men some means by which the group may be governed. For where there are many men together and each one is looking after his own interest, the multitude would be broken up and scattered unless there were also an agency to take care of what appertains to the commonweal. In like manner, the body of a man or any other animal would disintegrate unless there were a general ruling force within the body which watches over the common good of all members. With this in mind, Solomon says [Eccl. 4:9]: "Where there is no governor, the people shall fall."[162]

The achievement of earthly wellbeing requires political community, and government.

This government does not exist solely to restrain and coerce by force and fear (as claimed by Augustine), but can and should be something benevolent, serving to fulfill our human nature.

With Aquinas, politics and authority is now associated with the "good" Creation of God, rather than as a consequence of sin, as developed by Augustine. Politics is no longer a necessary evil, but a natural expression of our human nature, and a legitimate means by which we can facilitate virtue and promote the common good. The very purpose of civil authority is to direct its citizens towards the common good. Where Augustine deviated sharply from classical political theory, Aquinas reclaims it—situating it within a Christian worldview.

As previously mentioned, Aquinas (in his *Commentary on the Politics*) reiterates Aristotle's argument that, from our capacity for speech, our political/social nature is demonstrated (since, by means of speech, humans alone can deliberate on the nature of good and evil, justice and injustice, and pursue a common understanding of virtue). In addition to whatever else we are, other roles we adopt, all humans are "naturally" citizens—requiring participation in a political society. Political society not only provides safety and economic benefits, but it enhances the moral and intellectual lives of the humans within it.

Within a community, individual interests can be set aside for the same of the common good. "The common good is the end of each individual member of a community, just as the good of the whole is the end of each part."[163] Living in a political community does not serve merely the negative function of restraining vice, but is intended to serve the positive function of promoting virtue.

> For an individual man to lead a good life two things are required. The first and most important is to act in a virtuous manner (for virtue is that by which one lives well); the second, which is

---

[161] Augustine, *City of God*, 19:15.
[162] Aquinas, *De Regimine Principum*, book 1 chapter 1.

[163] *Summa Theologica*, II-II, 58.9

secondary and instrumental, is a sufficiency of those bodily goods who se use is necessary for virtuous life. Yet the unity of man is brought about by nature, while the unity of multitude, which we call peace, must be procured through the efforts of the ruler. Therefore, to establish virtuous living in a multitude three things are necessary. First of all, that the multitude be established in the unity of peace. Second, that the multitude thus united in the bond of peace, be directed to acting well. For just as a man can do nothing well unless unity within his members be presupposed, so a multitude of men lacking the unity of peace will be hindered from virtuous action by the fact that it is fighting against itself. In the third place, it is necessary that there be at hand a sufficient supply of the things required for proper living, procured by the ruler's efforts.[164]

While it is true that the State exists to establish and secure peace, it also exists to direct its members to "acting well." Do not think Aquinas is speaking merely of laws and punishments to inhibit criminal behavior. He also indicates another -function of the State: procuring a "sufficient supply of the things required for proper living."

Aquinas, like Aristotle before him, sees the State as a necessary means by which we can pursue the life proper to a human being. Since we can only fulfill our full human potential as citizens, it not only matters that we live in a State, but what *kind* of State. In contrast to Augustine, who argued that it mattered little (ultimately) what particular form of government under which we lived (since, the "City of God" transcends all national and political boundaries), Aquinas argues that only in the "best regime" can good citizens and good human beings coincide.

Aquinas uses Aristotle's method of classifying types of government based on who rules, and for whose sake—with the same

(familiar) six possibilities: Monarchy (Tyranny), Aristocracy (Oligarchy), and Polity/Republic (Democracy).

Among those, Aquinas claims that monarchy is the best of those kinds of State, and tries to demonstrate this by way of analogy, using Nature as a guide. The body is ruled by one agency (the soul), rather than a few, or many—and Nature itself is ruled by one, supreme God.

However, the potential for corruption (leading to tyranny) makes monarchy dangerous. As regards "tyranny," Augustine claimed that all authority (even that of a tyrant) is derived from God, with tyrants serving to punish sinners and test the faith of believers. Christians subject to a tyrant should realize that such is what sinners (such as themselves!) deserve, use it as an opportunity to grow in faith and look to Heaven, and endure as best they can—so long as the tyrant doesn't require the Christian to disobey God (e.g., by worshipping an idol). In that case, the Christian should disobey, and prepare to be a martyr.

Aquinas, though, thinks that kings exist not simply to punish and test, but to promote the common good. Those who promote their own interests at the expense of the public interest are tyrants (following Aristotle's classification). Such a tyrant, far from being an instrument of God's will, is actually betraying the purpose for which God appointed him in the first place.

Aquinas makes a concerted effort to demonstrate that tyranny isn't even in the best interests of the tyrant. The true happiness of a king is not to be found in mere power or earthly riches.

Now it is manifest that all earthly things are beneath the human mind. But happiness is the last perfection and the perfect good of man, which all men desire to reach. Therefore there is no earthly thing which could make man happy, nor is any earthly thing a sufficient reward for a king. For, as Augustine" says, "we do not call Christian princes happy merely

---

[164] *De Regimine Principum*, Book 1, chapter 16.

because they have reigned a long time, or because after a peaceful death they have left their sons to rule, or because they subdued the enemies of the state, or because they were able to guard against or to suppress citizens who rose up against them. Rather do we call them happy if they rule justly, if they prefer to rule their passions rather than nations, and if they do all things not for the love of vainglory but for the love of eternal happiness. Such Christian emperors we say are happy, now in hope, afterwards in very fact when that which we await shall come to pass.[165]

If true happiness can only be supplied by God, should God grant eternal happiness, then the king should be motivated to please God by ruling justly. Even at the earthly level, Aquinas claims that kings (like everyone else in the world) value and desire friendship, but that tyrants have no real friends.

First of all, among all worldly things there is nothing which seems worthy to be preferred to friendship. Friendship unites good men and preserves and promotes virtue. Friendship is needed by all men in whatsoever occupations they engage. In prosperity it does not thrust itself unwanted upon us, nor does it desert us in adversity. It is what brings with it the greatest delight, to such an extent that all that pleases is changed to weariness when friends are absent, and all difficult things are made easy and as nothing by love. There is no tyrant so cruel that friendship does not bring him pleasure.[166]

Moreover, those kings who become tyrants because they think it better secures their rule are just plain mistaken. What follows is a lengthy quotation, worthy of being provided, at length, if for no other reason than the contrast it will

provide with Machiavellian thinking in our next chapter.

The consequence of this love is that the government of good kings is stable, because their subjects do not refuse to expose themselves to any danger whatsoever on behalf of such kings. An example of this is to be seen in Julius Caesar who, as Suetonius relates [Divus Iulius 67], loved his soldiers to such an extent that when he heard that some of them were slaughtered, "he refused to cut either hair or beard until he had taken vengeance." In this way, he made his soldiers most loyal to himself as well as most valiant, so that many, on being taken prisoner, refused to accept their lives when offered them on the condition that they serve against Caesar. Octavianus Augustus, also, who was most moderate in his use of power, was so loved by his subjects that some of them "on their deathbeds provided in their wills a thank-offering to be paid by the immolation of animals, so grateful were they that the emperor's life outlasted their own" [Suetonius, Divus Augustus 59]. Therefore it is no easy task to shake the government of a prince whom the people so unanimously love. This is why Solomon says (Prov 29:14): "The king that judges the poor in justice, his throne shall be established forever."

The government of tyrants, on the other hand, cannot last long because it is hateful to the multitude, and what is against the wishes of the multitude cannot be long preserved. For a man can hardly pass through this present life without suffering some adversities, and in the time of his adversity occasion cannot be lacking to rise against the tyrant; and when there is an opportunity there will not be lacking at least one of the

---

165 Ibid., Book 1, chapter 9.

166 Ibid., Book 1, chapter 11.

multitude to use it. Then the people will fervently favour the insurgent, and what is attempted with the sympathy of the multitude will not easily fail of its effects. It can thus scarcely come to pass that the government of a tyrant will endure for a long time.

This is very clear, too, if we consider the means by which a tyrannical government is upheld. It is not upheld by love, since there is little or no bond of friendship between the subject multitude and the tyrant, as is evident from what we have said. On the other hand, tyrants cannot rely on the loyalty of their subjects, for such a degree of virtue is not found among the generality of men, that they should be restrained by the virtue of fidelity from throwing off the yoke of unmerited servitude, if they are able to do so. Nor would it perhaps be a violation of fidelity at all, according to the opinion of many,' to frustrate the wickedness of tyrants by any means whatsoever. It remains, then, that the government of a tyrant is maintained by fear alone and consequently they strive with all their might to be feared by their subjects. Fear, however, is a weak support. Those who are kept down by fear will rise against their rulers if the opportunity ever occurs when they can hope to do it with impunity, and they will rebel against their rulers all the more furiously the more they have been kept in subjection against their will by fear alone, just as water confined under pressure flows with greater impetus when it finds an outlet. That very fear itself is not without danger, because many become desperate from excessive fear, and despair of safety

impels a man boldly to dare anything. Therefore the government of a tyrant cannot be of long duration.[167]

Tyrants will lack friends, and those rulers who rule by fear rather than love will not win the support of their subjects. They might be too cowed by fear to rise up against him, but they will also be reluctant to defend or support him. In addition, should the king meet with any "adversity," they might notice the vulnerability and be quick to seize the opportunity to overthrow him.[168]

If his defense of monarchy (and arguments against tyranny) happens to fall on deaf ears, he is prepared to concede that, while monarchy might be the "best" regime, in principle, it might not be the best in *practice*. As a practical concession, then, he proposes a mixed government, somewhat similar to Aristotle's proposal, but using ancient Israel as a model.

Moses represents the monarchical element, the council of 72 elders represents the aristocratic element, and the "able men" chosen from "all the people" represents the democratic element.[169] The "ideal" Roman Republic of Cicero (so thoroughly critiqued by Augustine) is replaced with an ideal (similarly) mixed regime rooted in Scripture.

> Two points are to be observed concerning the right ordering of rulers in a state or nation. One is that all should take some share in the government: for this form of constitution ensures peace among the people, commends itself to all, and is most enduring, as stated in Polit. ii, 6. The other point is to be observed in respect of the kinds of government, or the different ways in which the constitutions are established. For whereas these differ in kind, as the Philosopher states (Polit. iii,

---

[167] Ibid., Book 1, chapter 11.
[168] Keep Aquinas' arguments here in mind when you encounter Machiavelli, in the next chapter, arguing the opposite: that it is better to be feared than to be loved (if one must choose).

[169] "But select capable men from all the people-- men who fear God, trustworthy men who hate dishonest gain--and appoint them as officials over thousands, hundreds, fifties and tens." (Exodus, 18:21)

5), nevertheless the first place is held by the "kingdom," where the power of government is vested in one; and "aristocracy," which signifies government by the best, where the power of government is vested in a few. Accordingly, the best form of government is in a state or kingdom, where one is given the power to preside over all; while under him are others having governing powers: and yet a government of this kind is shared by all, both because all are eligible to govern, and because the rules are chosen by all. For this is the best form of polity, being partly kingdom, since there is one at the head of all; partly aristocracy, in so far as a number of persons are set in authority; partly democracy, i.e. government by the people, in so far as the rulers can be chosen from the people, and the people have the right to choose their rulers.

Such was the form of government established by the Divine Law. For Moses and his successors governed the people in such a way that each of them was ruler over all; so that there was a kind of kingdom. Moreover, seventy-two men were chosen, who were elders in virtue: for it is written (Dt. 1:15): "I took out of your tribes wise and honorable, and appointed them rulers": so that there was an element of aristocracy. But it was a democratical government in so far as the rulers were chosen from all the people; for it is written (Ex. 18:21): "Provide out of all the people wise [Vulg.: 'able'] men," etc.; and, again, in so far as they were chosen by the people; wherefore it is written (Dt. 1:13): "Let me have from among you wise [Vulg.: 'able'] men," etc. Consequently it is evident that the ordering of the rulers was well provided for by the Law.[170]

As a reminder, Aquinas claimed that the natural law provides various natural inclinations towards natural goods, of which one was living in community with others. Another natural inclination, is self-preservation. Given that we are naturally inclined to self-preservation, earthly happiness, and living within a community, it is appropriate for us to seek to acquire the material means to promote those ends.

For imperfect happiness, such as can be had in this life, external goods are necessary, not as belonging to the essence of happiness, but by serving as instruments to happiness, which consists in an operation of virtue, as stated in Ethic. i, 13. For man needs in this life, the necessaries of the body, both for the operation of contemplative virtue, and for the operation of active virtue, for which latter he needs also many other things by means of which to perform its operations.

On the other hand, such goods as these are nowise necessary for perfect Happiness, which consists in seeing God. The reason of this is that all suchlike external goods are requisite either for the support of the animal body; or for certain operations which belong to human life, which we perform by means of the animal body: whereas that perfect Happiness which consists in seeing God, will be either in the soul separated from the body, or in the soul united to the body then no longer animal but spiritual. Consequently these external goods are nowise necessary for that Happiness, since they are ordained to the animal life. And since, in this life, the felicity of contemplation, as being more Godlike, approaches nearer than that of action to the likeness of that perfect Happiness, therefore it stands in less need of these goods of the body as stated in Ethic. x, 8.[171]

---

[170] *Summa Theologica*, I-II, 105.1

[171] Ibid., I-II, 4.7

Property

"Property" is natural for human beings, and based in natural law—though no particular institution of property is dictated by natural law. Nevertheless, Aquinas does advocate for private property for three reasons:

> First because every man is more careful to procure what is for himself alone than that which is common to many or to all: since each one would shirk the labor and leave to another that which concerns the community, as happens where there is a great number of servants. Secondly, because human affairs are conducted in more orderly fashion if each man is charged with taking care of some particular thing himself, whereas there would be confusion if everyone had to look after any one thing indeterminately. Thirdly, because a more peaceful state is ensured to man if each one is contented with his own. Hence it is to be observed that quarrels arise more frequently where there is no division of the things possessed.[172]

Private property causes us to manage natural resources better, since humans naturally care more for what is their own, rather than what is held in common (e.g., think of how much more "sanitary" most people are in their own bathroom, as opposed to a public bathroom at a gas station, for example). That extra care isn't merely because we are sinful and depraved, but because we are limited in our perspective and capacities. We can't care for all things equally well, and without property laws usage of resources would be ambiguous, and more conflict would occur. There is very much a limit to property, however.

Following Aristotle, Aquinas thinks we (naturally) are entitled to as much property as needed to meet our earthly needs. Anything in excess of that admittedly ambiguous "need" is owed (morally speaking) to the poor—those whose needs are not yet met.[173] Although he endorses private property, he also would endorse something like "progressive taxation" today.

> Now according to the natural order established by Divine Providence, inferior things are ordained for the purpose of succoring man's needs by their means. Wherefore the division and appropriation of things which are based on human law, do not preclude the fact that man's needs have to be remedied by means of these very things. Hence whatever certain people have in superabundance is due, by natural law, to the purpose of succoring the poor. For this reason Ambrose [*Loc. cit., A[2], OBJ[3]] says, and his words are embodied in the Decretals (Dist. xlvii, can. Sicut ii): "It is the hungry man's bread that you withhold, the naked man's cloak that you store away, the money that you bury in the earth is the price of the poor man's ransom and freedom."

> Since, however, there are many who are in need, while it is impossible for all to be succored by means of the same thing, each one is entrusted with the stewardship of his own things, so that out of them he may come to the aid of those who are in need. Nevertheless, if the need be so manifest and urgent, that it is evident that the present need must be remedied by whatever means be at hand (for instance when a person is in some imminent danger, and there is no other possible remedy), then it is lawful for a

---

[172] Ibid., II-II, 66.2

[173] As an illustration, Aquinas would presumably be against Floyd "Money" Mayweather spending $4.8 million on a single car (the Koenigsegg CCXR Trevita—of which only two exist in the world),

when other humans literally starve to death as a result of their poverty.

http://www.cnn.com/2015/08/27/sport/floyd-mayweather-4-8-million-car/index.html

man to succor his own need by means of another's property, by taking it either openly or secretly: nor is this properly speaking theft or robbery.[174]

Note the numerous ideas contained above: private property is acceptable and good, and, practically speaking, each person should be the managers of their own property/wealth. However, wealth in "excess" of one's needs is "naturally" due/owed to the poor—and given desperate enough need, the poor taking excess from the wealthy (should they refuse to donate it) isn't even, properly speaking, "theft!"

In fairness, Aquinas is not describing some sort of "communist" redistribution of wealth until no one has "excess" and everyone has the exact same standard of living. Instead, he's talking about an admittedly ambiguous minimum standard of living needed to prevent someone from being "hungry" or "naked"—and the "redistribution of wealth" requires a need that is "manifest and urgent," an "imminent danger" with "no other possible remedy." Really, what Aquinas seems to be describing is a regulated system of private property in which individuals have the freedom to own property, pursue profit, and acquire wealth, but with the understanding that their property may be "regulated" when the common welfare, the interest of the whole community, is at stake.

Conclusion

The "Fall of Rome" arguably led to the end of an era of political philosophy in the West. The optimism and perfectionism displayed by philosophers as Plato, Aristotle, and Cicero gave way, in the Dark and Middle Ages, to an admittedly more pessimistic (or realistic, depending on one's perspective) approach to politics such as that advanced by Augustine.

The ascendancy of Christianity as a worldview quite understandably led Christian philosophers to place their hope in the "world to come" rather than this "fallen" world.

With Aquinas, however, some of the "optimism" of ancient political philosophy was recovered. By synthesizing Aristotelian and Stoic philosophy with Christian doctrine, Aquinas was able to keep his eyes on "Heaven," while affirming the value of politics as both consistent with our nature, and necessary for the fullest (Earthly) expression of that nature.

Aquinas inspired a variety of political thinkers including Richard Hooker (who influenced John Locke with regard to natural law), to Martin Luther King Jr., who cited Aquinas' notion of unjust laws being invalid in his "Letter from a Birmingham Jail[175]—not to mention, of course, the profound influence of Aquinas' development of natural law on the official doctrine of the Catholic Church, resulting in numerous specific policy positions (e.g., opposition to birth control and abortion) even to this day.

While the cultural and intellectual domination of Christianity would continue for several more centuries, the next major period of political philosophy will actually hearken back to Augustine's pessimistic/realistic view of human nature, and the limited role of politics as necessary for restraining our worst (natural) tendencies. Such views will find voice in the infamous Niccolò Machiavelli, and Thomas Hobbes.

---

[174] Summa Theologica, II-II, 66.7

[175] "How does one determine whether a law is just or unjust? A just law is a man-made code that squares with the moral law or the law of God. An unjust law is a code that is out of harmony with the moral law. To put it in the terms of St. Thomas Aquinas: An unjust law is a human law that is not rooted in eternal law and natural law. Any law that uplifts human personality is just. Any law that degrades human personality is unjust. All segregation statutes are unjust because segregation distorts the soul and damages the personality. It gives the segregator a false sense of superiority and the segregated a false sense of inferiority." (Martin Luther King Jr., "Letter from a Birmingham Jail.")

St. Thomas Aquinas was a hugely influential philosopher and theologian. His brilliant adaptation of Aristotle to Christian theology provided a philosophical complement to revealed religion, and set the foundation for Christian natural law theory. His massive magnum opus, the Summa Theologica, is far too lengthy, and contains arguments far too irrelevant to be included, in entirety. Instead, just a very few excerpts have been provided. These excerpts concern the natural law, and human law.

St. Thomas Aquinas: *Summa Theologica*

Translated by The Fathers of the English Dominican Province [1947]
Treatise on Law: Questions 92, 94, 95, and 96...
Of the Effects of Law (Two Articles)
[http://sacred-texts.com/chr/aquinas/summa/index.htm]

We must now consider the effects of law; under which head there are two points of inquiry:

(1) Whether an effect of law is to make men good?

(2) Whether the effects of law are to command, to forbid, to permit, and to punish, as the Jurist states?

Whether an effect of law is to make men good?

Objection 1: It seems that it is not an effect of law to make men good. For men are good through virtue, since virtue, as stated in Ethic. ii, 6 is "that which makes its subject good." But virtue is in man from God alone, because He it is Who "works it in us without us," as we stated above (Q[55], A[4]) in giving the definition of virtue. Therefore the law does not make men good.

Objection 2: Further, Law does not profit a man unless he obeys it. But the very fact that a man obeys a law is due to his being good. Therefore in man goodness is presupposed to the law. Therefore the law does not make men good.

Objection 3: Further, Law is ordained to the common good, as stated above (Q[90], A[2]). But some behave well in things regarding the community, who behave ill in things regarding themselves. Therefore it is not the business of the law to make men good.

Objection 4: Further, some laws are tyrannical, as the Philosopher says (Polit. iii, 6). But a tyrant does not intend the good of his subjects, but considers only his own profit. Therefore law does not make men good.

On the contrary, The Philosopher says (Ethic. ii, 1) that the "intention of every lawgiver is to make good citizens."

I answer that, as stated above (Q[90], A[1], ad 2; AA[3],4), a law is nothing else than a dictate of reason in the ruler by whom his subjects are governed. Now the virtue of any subordinate thing consists in its being well subordinated to that by which it is regulated: thus we see that the virtue of the irascible and concupiscible faculties consists in their being obedient to reason; and accordingly "the virtue of every subject consists in his being well subjected to his ruler," as the Philosopher says (Polit. i). But every law aims at being obeyed by those who are subject to it. Consequently it is evident that the proper effect of law is to lead its subjects to their proper virtue: and since virtue is "that which makes its subject good," it follows that the proper effect of law is to make those to whom it is given, good, either simply or in some particular respect. For if the intention of the lawgiver is fixed on true good, which is the common good regulated according to Divine justice, it follows that the effect of the law is to make men good simply. If, however, the intention of the lawgiver is fixed on that which is not simply good, but useful or pleasurable to himself, or in opposition to Divine justice; then the law does not make men good simply, but in respect to that particular government. In this way good is found even in things that are bad of themselves: thus a man is called a good robber, because he works in a way that is adapted to his end.

Reply to Objection 1: Virtue is twofold, as explained above (Q[63], A[2]), viz. acquired and infused. Now the fact of being accustomed to an action contributes to both, but in different ways; for it causes the acquired virtue; while it disposes to infused virtue, and preserves and fosters it when it already exists. And since law is given for the purpose of directing human acts; as far as human acts conduce to virtue, so far does law make men good. Wherefore the Philosopher says in the second book of the Politics (Ethic. ii) that "lawgivers make men good by habituating them to good works."

Reply to Objection 2: It is not always through perfect goodness of virtue that one obeys the law, but sometimes it is through fear of punishment, and sometimes from the mere dictates of reason, which is a beginning of virtue, as stated above (Q[63], A[1]).

Reply to Objection 3: The goodness of any part is considered in comparison with the whole; hence Augustine says (Confess. iii) that "unseemly is the part that harmonizes not with the whole." Since then every man is a part of the state, it is impossible that a man be good, unless he be well proportionate to the common good: nor can the whole be well consistent unless its parts be proportionate to it. Consequently the common good of the state cannot flourish, unless the citizens be virtuous, at least those whose business it is to govern. But it is enough for the good of the community, that the other citizens be so far virtuous that they obey the commands of their rulers. Hence the Philosopher says (Polit. ii, 2) that "the virtue of a sovereign is the same as that of a good man, but the virtue of any common citizen is not the same as that of a good man."

Reply to Objection 4: A tyrannical law, through not being according to reason, is not a law, absolutely speaking, but rather a perversion of law; and yet in so far as it is something in the nature of a law, it aims at the citizens' being good. For all it has in the nature of a law consists in its being an ordinance made by a superior to his subjects, and aims at being obeyed by them, which is to make them good, not simply, but with respect to that particular government.

Whether the acts of law are suitably assigned?

Objection 1: It would seem that the acts of law are not suitably assigned as consisting in "command," "prohibition," "permission" and "punishment." For "every law is a general precept," as the jurist states. But command and precept are the same. Therefore the other three are superfluous.

Objection 2: Further, the effect of a law is to induce its subjects to be good, as stated above (A[1]). But counsel aims at a higher good than a command does. Therefore it belongs to law to counsel rather than to command.

Objection 3: Further, just as punishment stirs a man to good deeds, so does reward. Therefore if to punish is reckoned an effect of law, so also is to reward.

Objection 4: Further, the intention of a lawgiver is to make men good, as stated above (A[1]). But he that obeys the law, merely through fear of being punished, is not good: because "although a good deed may be done through servile fear, i.e. fear of punishment, it is not done well," as Augustine says (Contra duas Epist. Pelag. ii). Therefore punishment is not a proper effect of law.

On the contrary, Isidore says (Etym. v, 19): "Every law either permits something, as: 'A brave man may demand his reward'": or forbids something, as: "No man may ask a consecrated virgin in marriage": or punishes, as: "Let him that commits a murder be put to death."

I answer that, Just as an assertion is a dictate of reason asserting something, so is a law a dictate of reason, commanding something. Now it is proper to reason to lead from one thing to another. Wherefore just as, in demonstrative sciences, the reason leads us from certain principles to assent to the conclusion, so it induces us by some means to assent to the precept of the law.

Now the precepts of law are concerned with human acts, in which the law directs, as stated above (Q[90], AA[1],2; Q[91], A[4]). Again there are three kinds of human acts: for, as stated above (Q[18], A[8]), some acts are good generically, viz. acts of virtue; and in respect of these the act of the law is a precept or command, for "the law commands all acts of virtue" (Ethic. v, 1). Some acts are evil generically, viz. acts of vice, and in respect of these the law forbids. Some acts are generically indifferent, and in respect of these the law permits; and all acts that are either not distinctly good or not distinctly bad may be called indifferent. And it is the fear of punishment that law makes use of in order to ensure obedience: in which respect punishment is an effect of law.

Reply to Objection 1: Just as to cease from evil is a kind of good, so a prohibition is a kind of precept: and accordingly, taking precept in a wide sense, every law is a kind of precept.

Reply to Objection 2: To advise is not a proper act of law, but may be within the competency even of a private person, who cannot make a law. Wherefore too the Apostle, after giving a certain counsel (1 Cor. 7:12) says: "I speak, not the Lord." Consequently it is not reckoned as an effect of law.

Reply to Objection 3: To reward may also pertain to anyone: but to punish pertains to none but the framer of the law, by whose authority the pain is inflicted. Wherefore to reward is not reckoned an effect of law, but only to punish.

Reply to Objection 4: From becoming accustomed to avoid evil and fulfill what is good, through fear of punishment, one is sometimes led on to do so likewise, with delight and of one's own accord. Accordingly, law, even by punishing, leads men on to being good.

...

OF THE NATURAL LAW (SIX ARTICLES)

We must now consider the natural law; concerning which there are six points of inquiry:

(1) What is the natural law?

(2) What are the precepts of the natural law?

(3) Whether all acts of virtue are prescribed by the natural law?

(4) Whether the natural law is the same in all?

(5) Whether it is changeable?

(6) Whether it can be abolished from the heart of man?

Whether the natural law is a habit?

Objection 1: It would seem that the natural law is a habit. Because, as the Philosopher says (Ethic. ii, 5), "there are three things in the soul: power, habit, and passion." But the natural law is not one of the soul's powers: nor is it one of the passions; as we may see by going through them one by one. Therefore the natural law is a habit.

Objection 2: Further, Basil [*Damascene, De Fide Orth. iv, 22] says that the conscience or "synderesis is the law of our mind"; which can only apply to the natural law. But the "synderesis" is a habit, as was shown in the FP, Q[79], A[12]. Therefore the natural law is a habit.

Objection 3: Further, the natural law abides in man always, as will be shown further on (A[6]). But man's reason, which the law regards, does not always think about the natural law. Therefore the natural law is not an act, but a habit.

On the contrary, Augustine says (De Bono Conjug. xxi) that "a habit is that whereby something is done when necessary." But such is not the natural law: since it is in infants and in the damned who cannot act by it. Therefore the natural law is not a habit.

I answer that, A thing may be called a habit in two ways. First, properly and essentially: and thus the natural law is not a habit. For it has been stated above (Q[90], A[1], ad 2) that the natural law is something appointed by reason, just as a proposition is a work of reason. Now that which a man does is not the same as that whereby he does it: for he makes a becoming speech by the habit of grammar. Since then a habit is that by which we act, a law cannot be a habit properly and essentially.

Secondly, the term habit may be applied to that which we hold by a habit: thus faith may mean that which we hold by faith. And accordingly, since the precepts of the natural law are sometimes considered by reason actually, while sometimes they are in the reason only habitually, in this way the natural law may be called a habit. Thus, in speculative matters, the indemonstrable principles are not the habit itself whereby we hold those principles, but are the principles the habit of which we possess.

Reply to Objection 1: The Philosopher proposes there to discover the genus of virtue;

and since it is evident that virtue is a principle of action, he mentions only those things which are principles of human acts, viz. powers, habits and passions. But there are other things in the soul besides these three: there are acts; thus "to will" is in the one that wills; again, things known are in the knower; moreover its own natural properties are in the soul, such as immortality and the like.

Reply to Objection 2: "Synderesis" is said to be the law of our mind, because it is a habit containing the precepts of the natural law, which are the first principles of human actions.

Reply to Objection 3: This argument proves that the natural law is held habitually; and this is granted.

To the argument advanced in the contrary sense we reply that sometimes a man is unable to make use of that which is in him habitually, on account of some impediment: thus, on account of sleep, a man is unable to use the habit of science. In like manner, through the deficiency of his age, a child cannot use the habit of understanding of principles, or the natural law, which is in him habitually.

Whether the natural law contains several precepts, or only one?

Objection 1: It would seem that the natural law contains, not several precepts, but one only. For law is a kind of precept, as stated above (Q[92], A[2]). If therefore there were many precepts of the natural law, it would follow that there are also many natural laws.

Objection 2: Further, the natural law is consequent to human nature. But human nature, as a whole, is one; though, as to its parts, it is manifold. Therefore, either there is but one precept of the law of nature, on account of the unity of nature as a whole; or there are many, by reason of the number of parts of human nature. The result would be that even things relating to the inclination of the concupiscible faculty belong to the natural law.

Objection 3: Further, law is something pertaining to reason, as stated above (Q[90], A[1]). Now reason is but one in man. Therefore there is only one precept of the natural law.

On the contrary, The precepts of the natural law in man stand in relation to practical matters, as the first principles to matters of demonstration. But there are several first indemonstrable principles. Therefore there are also several precepts of the natural law.

I answer that, As stated above (Q[91], A[3]), the precepts of the natural law are to the practical reason, what the first principles of demonstrations are to the speculative reason; because both are self-evident principles. Now a thing is said to be self-evident in two ways: first, in itself; secondly, in relation to us. Any proposition is said to be self-evident in itself, if its predicate is contained in the notion of the subject: although, to one who knows not the definition of the subject, it happens that such a proposition is not self-evident. For instance, this proposition, "Man is a rational being," is, in its very nature, self-evident, since who says "man," says "a rational being": and yet to one who knows not what a man is, this proposition is not self-evident. Hence it is that, as Boethius says (De Hebdom.), certain axioms or propositions are universally self-evident to all; and such are those propositions whose terms are known to all, as, "Every whole is greater than its part," and, "Things equal to one and the same are equal to one another." But some propositions are self-evident only to the wise, who understand the meaning of the terms of such propositions: thus to one who understands that an angel is not a body, it is self-evident that an angel is not circumscriptively in a place: but this is not evident to the unlearned, for they cannot grasp it.

Now a certain order is to be found in those things that are apprehended universally. For that which, before aught else, falls under apprehension, is "being," the notion of which is included in all things whatsoever a man apprehends. Wherefore the first indemonstrable principle is that "the same thing cannot be affirmed and denied at the same time," which is based on the notion of "being" and "not-being": and on this principle all others are based, as is stated in Metaph. iv, text. 9. Now as "being" is the first thing that falls under the apprehension simply, so "good" is the first thing that falls under the apprehension of the practical reason, which is directed to action: since every agent acts for an end under the aspect of good. Consequently the first principle of practical reason is one founded on the notion of good, viz. that "good is that which all things seek after." Hence this is the first precept of law, that "good is to be done and pursued, and evil is to be avoided." All other precepts of the natural law are based upon this: so that whatever the practical reason naturally apprehends as man's good (or evil) belongs to the precepts of the natural law as something to be done or avoided.

Since, however, good has the nature of an end, and evil, the nature of a contrary, hence it is that all those things to which man has a natural inclination, are naturally apprehended by reason as being good, and consequently as objects of pursuit, and their contraries as evil, and objects of avoidance. Wherefore according to the order of natural inclinations, is the order of the precepts of the natural law. Because in man there is first of all an inclination to good in accordance with the nature which he has in common with all substances: inasmuch as every substance seeks the preservation of its own being, according to its nature: and by reason of this inclination, whatever is a means of preserving human life, and of warding off its obstacles, belongs to the natural law. Secondly, there is in man an inclination to things that pertain to him more specially, according to that nature which he has in common with other animals: and in virtue of this inclination, those things are said to belong to the natural law, "which nature has taught to all animals" [*Pandect. Just. I, tit. i], such as sexual intercourse, education of offspring and so forth. Thirdly, there is in man an inclination to good, according to the nature of his reason, which nature is proper to him: thus man has a natural inclination to know the truth about God, and to live in society: and in this respect, whatever pertains to this inclination belongs to the natural law; for instance, to shun ignorance, to avoid offending those among whom one has to live, and other such things regarding the above inclination.

Reply to Objection 1: All these precepts of the law of nature have the character of one natural law, inasmuch as they flow from one first precept.

Reply to Objection 2: All the inclinations of any parts whatsoever of human nature, e.g. of the concupiscible and irascible parts, in so far as they are ruled by reason, belong to the natural law, and are reduced to one first precept, as stated above: so that the precepts of the natural law are many in themselves, but are based on one common foundation.

Reply to Objection 3: Although reason is one in itself, yet it directs all things regarding man; so that whatever can be ruled by reason, is contained under the law of reason.

Whether all acts of virtue are prescribed by the natural law?

Objection 1: It would seem that not all acts of virtue are prescribed by the natural law. Because, as stated above (Q[90], A[2]) it is essential to a law that it be ordained to the common good. But some acts of virtue are ordained to the private good of the individual, as is evident especially in regards to acts of temperance. Therefore not all acts of virtue are the subject of natural law.

Objection 2: Further, every sin is opposed to some virtuous act. If therefore all acts of virtue are prescribed by the natural law, it seems to follow that all sins are against nature: whereas this applies to certain special sins.

Objection 3: Further, those things which are according to nature are common to all. But acts of virtue are not common to all: since a thing is virtuous in one, and vicious in another. Therefore not all acts of virtue are prescribed by the natural law.

On the contrary, Damascene says (De Fide Orth. iii, 4) that "virtues are natural." Therefore virtuous acts also are a subject of the natural law.

I answer that, We may speak of virtuous acts in two ways: first, under the aspect of virtuous; secondly, as such and such acts considered in their proper species. If then we speak of acts of virtue, considered as virtuous, thus all virtuous acts belong to the natural law. For it has been stated (A[2]) that to the natural law belongs everything to which a man is inclined according to his nature. Now each thing is inclined naturally to an operation that is suitable to it according to its form: thus fire is inclined to give heat.

Wherefore, since the rational soul is the proper form of man, there is in every man a natural inclination to act according to reason: and this is to act according to virtue. Consequently, considered thus, all acts of virtue are prescribed by the natural law: since each one's reason naturally dictates to him to act virtuously. But if we speak of virtuous acts, considered in themselves, i.e. in their proper species, thus not all virtuous acts are prescribed by the natural law: for many things are done virtuously, to which nature does not incline at first; but which, through the inquiry of reason, have been found by men to be conducive to well-living.

Reply to Objection 1: Temperance is about the natural concupiscences of food, drink and sexual matters, which are indeed ordained to the natural common good, just as other matters of law are ordained to the moral common good.

Reply to Objection 2: By human nature we may mean either that which is proper to man--- and in this sense all sins, as being against reason, are also against nature, as Damascene states (De Fide Orth. ii, 30): or we may mean that nature which is common to man and other animals; and in this sense, certain special sins are said to be against nature; thus contrary to sexual intercourse, which is natural to all animals, is unisexual lust, which has received the special name of the unnatural crime.

Reply to Objection 3: This argument considers acts in themselves. For it is owing to the various conditions of men, that certain acts are virtuous for some, as being proportionate and becoming to them, while they are vicious for others, as being out of proportion to them.

Whether the natural law is the same in all men?

Objection 1: It would seem that the natural law is not the same in all. For it is stated in the Decretals (Dist. i) that "the natural law is that which is contained in the Law and the Gospel." But this is not common to all men; because, as it is written (Rom. 10:16), "all do not obey the gospel." Therefore the natural law is not the same in all men.

Objection 2: Further, "Things which are according to the law are said to be just," as stated in Ethic. v. But it is stated in the same book that nothing is so universally just as not to be subject to change in regard to some men. Therefore even the natural law is not the same in all men.

Objection 3: Further, as stated above (AA[2],3), to the natural law belongs everything to which a man is inclined according to his nature. Now different men are naturally inclined to different things; some to the desire of pleasures, others to the desire of honors, and other men to other things. Therefore there is not one natural law for all.

On the contrary, Isidore says (Etym. v, 4): "The natural law is common to all nations."

I answer that, As stated above (AA[2],3), to the natural law belongs those things to which a man is inclined naturally: and among these it is proper to man to be inclined to act according to reason. Now the process of reason is from the common to the proper, as stated in Phys. i. The speculative reason, however, is differently situated in this matter, from the practical reason. For, since the speculative reason is busied chiefly with the necessary things, which cannot be otherwise than they are, its proper conclusions, like the universal principles, contain the truth without fail. The practical reason, on the other hand, is busied with contingent matters, about which human actions are concerned: and consequently, although there is necessity in the general principles, the more we descend to matters of detail, the more frequently we encounter defects. Accordingly then in speculative matters truth is the same in all men, both as to principles and as to conclusions: although the truth is not known to all as regards the conclusions, but only as regards the principles which are called common notions. But in matters of action, truth or practical rectitude is not the same for all, as to matters of detail, but only as to the general principles: and where there is the same rectitude in matters of detail, it is not equally known to all.

It is therefore evident that, as regards the general principles whether of speculative or of practical reason, truth or rectitude is the same for all, and is equally known by all. As to the proper conclusions of the speculative reason, the truth is the same for all, but is not equally known to all: thus it is true for all that the three angles of a triangle are together equal to two right angles, although it is not known to all. But as to the proper conclusions of the practical reason, neither is the truth or rectitude the same for all, nor, where it is the same, is it equally known by all. Thus it is right and true for all to act according to reason: and from this principle it follows as a proper conclusion, that goods entrusted to another should be restored to their owner. Now this is true for the majority of cases: but it may happen in a particular case that it would be injurious, and therefore unreasonable, to restore goods held in trust; for instance, if they are claimed for the purpose of fighting against one's country. And this principle will be found to fail the more, according as we descend further into detail, e.g. if one were to say that goods held in trust should be restored with such and such a guarantee, or in such and such a way; because the greater the number of conditions added, the greater the number of ways in which the principle may fail, so that it be not right to restore or not to restore.

Consequently we must say that the natural law, as to general principles, is the same for all, both as to rectitude and as to knowledge. But as to certain matters of detail, which are conclusions, as it were, of those general principles, it is the same for all in the majority of cases, both as to rectitude and as to knowledge; and yet in some few cases it may fail, both as to rectitude, by reason of certain obstacles (just as natures subject to generation and corruption fail in some few cases on account of some obstacle), and as to knowledge, since in some the reason is perverted by passion, or evil habit, or an evil disposition of nature; thus formerly, theft, although it is expressly contrary to the natural law, was not considered wrong among the Germans, as Julius Caesar relates (De Bello Gall. vi).

Reply to Objection 1: The meaning of the sentence quoted is not that whatever is contained in the Law and the Gospel belongs to the natural law, since they contain many things that are above nature; but that whatever belongs to the natural law is fully contained in them. Wherefore Gratian, after saying that "the natural law is what is contained in the Law and the Gospel," adds at once, by way of example, "by which everyone is commanded to do to others as he would be done by."

Reply to Objection 2: The saying of the Philosopher is to be understood of things that are naturally just, not as general principles, but as conclusions drawn from them, having rectitude in the majority of cases, but failing in a few.

Reply to Objection 3: As, in man, reason rules and commands the other powers, so all the natural inclinations belonging to the other powers must needs be directed according to reason. Wherefore it is universally right for all men, that all their inclinations should be directed according to reason.

Whether the natural law can be changed?

Objection 1: It would seem that the natural law can be changed. Because on Ecclus. 17:9, "He gave them instructions, and the law of life," the gloss says: "He wished the law of the letter to be written, in order to correct the law of nature." But that which is corrected is changed. Therefore the natural law can be changed.

Objection 2: Further, the slaying of the innocent, adultery, and theft are against the natural law. But we find these things changed by God: as when God commanded Abraham to slay his innocent son (Gn. 22:2); and when he ordered the Jews to borrow and purloin the vessels of the Egyptians (Ex. 12:35); and when He commanded Osee to take to himself "a wife of fornications" (Osee 1:2). Therefore the natural law can be changed.

Objection 3: Further, Isidore says (Etym. 5:4) that "the possession of all things in common, and universal freedom, are matters of natural law." But these things are seen to be changed by human laws. Therefore it seems that the natural law is subject to change.

On the contrary, It is said in the Decretals (Dist. v): "The natural law dates from the creation of the rational creature. It does not vary according to time, but remains unchangeable."

I answer that, A change in the natural law may be understood in two ways. First, by way of addition. In this sense nothing hinders the natural law from being changed: since many things for the benefit of human life have been added over and above the natural law, both by the Divine law and by human laws.

Secondly, a change in the natural law may be understood by way of subtraction, so that what previously was according to the natural law, ceases to be so. In this sense, the natural law is altogether unchangeable in its first principles: but in its secondary principles, which, as we have said (A[4]), are certain detailed proximate conclusions drawn from the first principles, the natural law is not changed so that what it prescribes be not right in most cases. But it may be changed in some particular cases of rare occurrence, through some special causes hindering the observance of such precepts, as stated above (A[4]).

Reply to Objection 1: The written law is said to be given for the correction of the natural law, either because it supplies what was wanting to the natural law; or because the natural law was perverted in the hearts of some men, as to certain matters, so that they esteemed those things good which are naturally evil; which perversion stood in need of correction.

Reply to Objection 2: All men alike, both guilty and innocent, die the death of nature: which death of nature is inflicted by the power of God on account of original sin, according to 1 Kings 2:6: "The Lord killeth and maketh alive." Consequently, by the command of God, death can be inflicted on any man, guilty or innocent, without any injustice whatever. In like manner adultery is intercourse with another's wife; who is allotted to him by the law emanating from God. Consequently intercourse with any woman, by the command of God, is neither adultery nor fornication. The same applies to theft, which is the taking of another's property. For whatever is taken by the command of God, to Whom all things belong, is not taken against the will of its owner, whereas it is in this that theft consists. Nor is it only in human things, that whatever is commanded by God is right; but also in natural things, whatever is done by God, is, in some way, natural, as stated in the FP, Q[105], A[6], ad 1.

Reply to Objection 3: A thing is said to belong to the natural law in two ways. First, because nature inclines thereto: e.g. that one should not do harm to another. Secondly, because nature did not bring in the contrary: thus we might say that for man to be naked is of the natural law, because nature did not give him clothes, but art invented them. In this sense, "the possession of all things in common and universal freedom" are said to be of the natural law, because, to wit, the distinction of possessions and slavery were not brought in by nature, but devised by human reason for the benefit of human life. Accordingly the law of nature was not changed in this respect, except by addition.

Whether the law of nature can be abolished from the heart of man?

Objection 1: It would seem that the natural law can be abolished from the heart of man. Because on Rom. 2:14, "When the Gentiles who have not the law," etc. a gloss says that "the law of righteousness, which sin had blotted out, is graven on the heart of man when he is restored by grace." But the law of righteousness is the law of nature. Therefore the law of nature can be blotted out.

Objection 2: Further, the law of grace is more efficacious than the law of nature. But the law of grace is blotted out by sin. Much more therefore can the law of nature be blotted out.

Objection 3: Further, that which is established by law is made just. But many things are enacted by men, which are contrary to the law of nature. Therefore the law of nature can be abolished from the heart of man.

On the contrary, Augustine says (Confess. ii): "Thy law is written in the hearts of men, which iniquity itself effaces not." But the law which is written in men's hearts is the natural law. Therefore the natural law cannot be blotted out.

I answer that, As stated above (AA[4],5), there belong to the natural law, first, certain most general precepts, that are known to all; and secondly, certain secondary and more detailed precepts, which are, as it were, conclusions following closely from first principles. As to those general principles, the natural law, in the abstract, can nowise be blotted out from men's hearts. But it is blotted out in the case of a particular action, in so far as reason is hindered from applying the general principle to a particular point of practice, on account of concupiscence or some other passion, as stated above (Q[77], A[2]). But as to the other, i.e. the secondary precepts, the natural law can be blotted out from the human heart, either by evil persuasions, just as in speculative matters errors occur in respect of necessary conclusions; or by vicious customs and corrupt habits, as among some men, theft, and even unnatural vices, as the Apostle states (Rom. i), were not esteemed sinful.

Reply to Objection 1: Sin blots out the law of nature in particular cases, not universally, except perchance in regard to the secondary precepts of the natural law, in the way stated above.

Reply to Objection 2: Although grace is more efficacious than nature, yet nature is more essential to man, and therefore more enduring.

Reply to Objection 3: This argument is true of the secondary precepts of the natural law, against which some legislators have framed certain enactments which are unjust.

...

OF HUMAN LAW (FOUR ARTICLES)

We must now consider human law; and (1) this law considered in itself; (2) its power; (3) its mutability. Under the first head there are four points of inquiry:

(1) Its utility.
(2) Its origin.
(3) Its quality.
(4) Its division.

Whether it was useful for laws to be framed by men?

Objection 1: It would seem that it was not useful for laws to be framed by men. Because the purpose of every law is that man be made good thereby, as stated above (Q[92], A[1]). But men are more to be induced to be good willingly by means of admonitions, than against their will, by means of laws. Therefore there was no need to frame laws.

Objection 2: Further, As the Philosopher says (Ethic. v, 4), "men have recourse to a judge as to animate justice." But animate justice is better than inanimate justice, which contained in laws. Therefore it would have been better for the execution of justice to be entrusted to the decision of judges, than to frame laws in addition.

Objection 3: Further, every law is framed for the direction of human actions, as is evident from what has been stated above (Q[90], AA[1],2). But since human actions are about singulars, which are infinite in number, matter pertaining to the direction of human actions cannot be taken into sufficient consideration except by a wise man, who looks into each one of them. Therefore it would have been better for human acts to be directed by the judgment of wise men, than by the framing of laws. Therefore there was no need of human laws.

On the contrary, Isidore says (Etym. v, 20): "Laws were made that in fear thereof human audacity might be held in check, that innocence might be safeguarded in the midst of wickedness, and that the dread of punishment might prevent the wicked from doing harm." But these things are most necessary to mankind. Therefore it was necessary that human laws should be made.

I answer that, As stated above (Q[63], A[1]; Q[94], A[3]), man has a natural aptitude for virtue; but the perfection of virtue must be acquired by man by means of some kind of training. Thus we observe that man is helped by industry in his necessities, for instance, in food and clothing. Certain beginnings of these he has from nature, viz. his reason and his hands; but he has not the full complement, as other animals have, to whom nature has given sufficiency of clothing and food. Now it is difficult to see how man could suffice for himself in the matter of this training: since the perfection of virtue consists chiefly in withdrawing man from undue pleasures, to which above all man is inclined, and especially the young, who are more capable of being trained. Consequently a man needs to receive this training from another, whereby to arrive at the perfection of virtue. And as to those young people who are inclined to acts of virtue, by their good natural disposition, or by custom, or rather by the gift of God, paternal training suffices, which is by admonitions. But since some are found to be depraved, and prone to vice, and not easily amenable to words, it was necessary for such to be restrained from evil by force and fear, in order that, at least, they might desist from evil-doing, and leave others in peace, and that they themselves, by being habituated in this way, might be brought to do willingly what hitherto they did from fear, and thus become virtuous. Now this kind of training, which compels through fear of punishment, is the discipline of laws. Therefore in order that man might have peace and virtue, it was necessary for laws to be framed: for, as the Philosopher says (Polit. i, 2), "as man is the most noble of animals if he be perfect in virtue, so is he the lowest of all, if he be severed from law and righteousness"; because man can use his reason to devise means of satisfying his lusts and evil passions, which other animals are unable to do.

Reply to Objection 1: Men who are well disposed are led willingly to virtue by being admonished better than by coercion: but men who are evilly disposed are not led to virtue unless they are compelled.

Reply to Objection 2: As the Philosopher says (Rhet. i, 1), "it is better that all things be regulated by law, than left to be decided by judges": and this for three reasons. First, because it is easier to find a few wise men competent to frame right laws, than to find the many who would be necessary to judge aright of each single case. Secondly, because those who make laws consider long beforehand what laws to make; whereas judgment on each single case has to be pronounced as soon as it arises: and it is easier for man to see what is right, by taking many instances into consideration, than by considering one solitary fact. Thirdly, because lawgivers judge in the abstract and of future events; whereas those who sit in judgment of things present, towards which they are affected by love, hatred, or some kind of cupidity; wherefore their judgment is perverted.

Since then the animated justice of the judge is not found in every man, and since it can be deflected, therefore it was necessary, whenever possible, for the law to determine how to judge, and for very few matters to be left to the decision of men.

Reply to Objection 3: Certain individual facts which cannot be covered by the law "have necessarily to be committed to judges," as the Philosopher says in the same passage: for instance, "concerning something that has happened or not happened," and the like.

Whether every human law is derived from the natural law?

Objection 1: It would seem that not every human law is derived from the natural law. For the Philosopher says (Ethic. v, 7) that "the legal just is that which originally was a matter of indifference." But those things which arise from the natural law are not matters of indifference. Therefore the enactments of human laws are not derived from the natural law.

Objection 2: Further, positive law is contrasted with natural law, as stated by Isidore (Etym. v, 4) and the Philosopher (Ethic. v, 7). But those things which flow as conclusions from the general principles of the natural law belong to the natural law, as stated above (Q[94], A[4]). Therefore that which is established by human law does not belong to the natural law.

Objection 3: Further, the law of nature is the same for all; since the Philosopher says (Ethic. v, 7) that "the natural just is that which is equally valid everywhere." If therefore human laws were derived from the natural law, it would follow that they too are the same for all: which is clearly false.

Objection 4: Further, it is possible to give a reason for things which are derived from the natural law. But "it is not possible to give the reason for all the legal enactments of the lawgivers," as the jurist says [*Pandect. Justin. lib. i, ff, tit. iii, v; De Leg. et Senat.]. Therefore not all human laws are derived from the natural law.

On the contrary, Tully says (Rhet. ii): "Things which emanated from nature and were approved by custom, were sanctioned by fear and reverence for the laws."

I answer that, As Augustine says (De Lib. Arb. i, 5) "that which is not just seems to be no law at all": wherefore the force of a law depends on the extent of its justice. Now in human affairs a thing is said to be just, from being right, according to the rule of reason. But the first rule of reason is the law of nature, as is clear from what has been stated above (Q[91], A[2], ad 2). Consequently every human law has just so much of the nature of law, as it is derived from the law of nature. But if in any point it deflects from the law of nature, it is no longer a law but a perversion of law.

But it must be noted that something may be derived from the natural law in two ways: first, as a conclusion from premises, secondly, by way of determination of certain generalities. The first way is like to that by which, in sciences, demonstrated conclusions are drawn from the principles: while the second mode is likened to that whereby, in the arts, general forms are particularized as to details: thus the craftsman needs to determine the general form of a house to some particular shape. Some things are therefore derived from the general principles of the natural law, by way of conclusions; e.g. that "one must not kill" may be derived as a conclusion from the principle that "one should do harm to no man": while some are derived therefrom by way of determination; e.g. the law of nature has it that the evil-doer should be punished; but that he be punished in this or that way, is a determination of the law of nature.

Accordingly both modes of derivation are found in the human law. But those things which are derived in the first way, are contained in human law not as emanating therefrom exclusively, but have some force from the natural law also. But those things which are derived in the second way, have no other force than that of human law.

Reply to Objection 1: The Philosopher is speaking of those enactments which are by way of determination or specification of the precepts of the natural law.

Reply to Objection 2: This argument avails for those things that are derived from the natural law, by way of conclusions.

Reply to Objection 3: The general principles of the natural law cannot be applied to all men in the same way on account of the great variety of human affairs: and hence arises the diversity of positive laws among various people.

Reply to Objection 4: These words of the Jurist are to be understood as referring to decisions of rulers in determining particular

points of the natural law: on which determinations the judgment of expert and prudent men is based as on its principles; in so far, to wit, as they see at once what is the best thing to decide.

Hence the Philosopher says (Ethic. vi, 11) that in such matters, "we ought to pay as much attention to the undemonstrated sayings and opinions of persons who surpass us in experience, age and prudence, as to their demonstrations."

Whether Isidore's description of the quality of positive law is appropriate?

Objection 1: It would seem that Isidore's description of the quality of positive law is not appropriate, when he says (Etym. v, 21): "Law shall be virtuous, just, possible to nature, according to the custom of the country, suitable to place and time, necessary, useful; clearly expressed, lest by its obscurity it lead to misunderstanding; framed for no private benefit, but for the common good." Because he had previously expressed the quality of law in three conditions, saying that "law is anything founded on reason, provided that it foster religion, be helpful to discipline, and further the common weal." Therefore it was needless to add any further conditions to these.

Objection 2: Further, Justice is included in honesty, as Tully says (De Offic. vii). Therefore after saying "honest" it was superfluous to add "just."

Objection 3: Further, written law is condivided with custom, according to Isidore (Etym. ii, 10). Therefore it should not be stated in the definition of law that it is "according to the custom of the country."

Objection 4: Further, a thing may be necessary in two ways. It may be necessary simply, because it cannot be otherwise: and that which is necessary in this way, is not subject to human judgment, wherefore human law is not concerned with necessity of this kind. Again a thing may be necessary for an end: and this necessity is the same as usefulness. Therefore it is superfluous to say both "necessary" and "useful."

On the contrary, stands the authority of Isidore.

I answer that, Whenever a thing is for an end, its form must be determined proportionately to that end; as the form of a saw is such as to be suitable for cutting (Phys. ii, text. 88). Again, everything that is ruled and measured must have a form proportionate to its rule and measure. Now both these conditions are verified of human law: since it is both something ordained to an end; and is a rule or measure ruled or measured by a higher measure. And this higher measure is twofold, viz. the Divine law and the natural law, as explained above (A[2]; Q[93], A[3]). Now the end of human law is to be useful to man, as the jurist states [*Pandect. Justin. lib. xxv, ff., tit. iii; De Leg. et Senat.]. Wherefore Isidore in determining the nature of law, lays down, at first, three conditions; viz. that it "foster religion," inasmuch as it is proportionate to the Divine law; that it be "helpful to discipline," inasmuch as it is proportionate to the nature law; and that it "further the common weal," inasmuch as it is proportionate to the utility of mankind.

All the other conditions mentioned by him are reduced to these three. For it is called virtuous because it fosters religion. And when he goes on to say that it should be "just, possible to nature, according to the customs of the country, adapted to place and time," he implies that it should be helpful to discipline. For human discipline depends on first on the order of reason, to which he refers by saying "just": secondly, it depends on the ability of the agent; because discipline should be adapted to each one according to his ability, taking also into account the ability of nature (for the same burdens should be not laid on children as adults); and should be according to human customs; since man cannot live alone in society, paying no heed to others: thirdly, it depends on certain circumstances, in respect of which he says, "adapted to place and time." The remaining words, "necessary, useful," etc. mean that law should further the common weal: so that "necessity" refers to the removal of evils; "usefulness" to the attainment of good; "clearness of expression," to the need of preventing any harm ensuing from the law itself.

And since, as stated above (Q[90], A[2]), law is ordained to the common good, this is expressed in the last part of the description.

This suffices for the Replies to the Objections.

Whether Isidore's division of human laws is appropriate?

Objection 1: It would seem that Isidore wrongly divided human statutes or human law (Etym. v, 4, seqq.). For under this law he includes the "law of nations," so called, because, as he says, "nearly all nations use it." But as he says, "natural law is that which is common to all nations." Therefore the law of nations is not contained under positive human law, but rather under natural law.

Objection 2: Further, those laws which have the same force, seem to differ not formally but only materially. But "statutes, decrees of the commonalty, senatorial decrees," and the like which he mentions (Etym. v, 9), all have the same force. Therefore they do not differ, except materially. But art takes no notice of such a distinction: since it may go on to infinity. Therefore this division of human laws is not appropriate.

Objection 3: Further, just as, in the state, there are princes, priests and soldiers, so are there other human offices. Therefore it seems that, as this division includes "military law," and "public law," referring to priests and magistrates; so also it should include other laws pertaining to other offices of the state.

Objection 4: Further, those things that are accidental should be passed over. But it is accidental to law that it be framed by this or that man. Therefore it is unreasonable to divide laws according to the names of lawgivers, so that one be called the "Cornelian" law, another the "Falcidian" law, etc.

On the contrary, The authority of Isidore (OBJ[1]) suffices.

I answer that, A thing can of itself be divided in respect of something contained in the notion of that thing. Thus a soul either rational or irrational is contained in the notion of animal: and therefore animal is divided properly and of itself in respect of its being rational or irrational; but not in the point of its being white or black, which are entirely beside the notion of animal. Now, in the notion of human law, many things are contained, in respect of any of which human law can be divided properly and of itself. For in the first place it belongs to the notion of human law, to be derived from the law of nature, as explained above (A[2]). In this respect positive law is divided into the "law of nations" and "civil law," according to the two ways in which something may be derived from the law of nature, as stated above (A[2]). Because, to the law of nations belong those things which are derived from the law of nature, as conclusions from premises, e.g. just buyings and sellings, and the like, without which men cannot live together, which is a point of the law of nature, since man is by nature a social animal, as is proved in Polit. i, 2. But those things which are derived from the law of nature by way of particular determination, belong to the civil law, according as each state decides on what is best for itself.

Secondly, it belongs to the notion of human law, to be ordained to the common good of the state. In this respect human law may be divided according to the different kinds of men who work in a special way for the common good: e.g. priests, by praying to God for the people; princes, by governing the people; soldiers, by fighting for the safety of the people. Wherefore certain special kinds of law are adapted to these men.

Thirdly, it belongs to the notion of human law, to be framed by that one who governs the community of the state, as shown above (Q[90], A[3]). In this respect, there are various human laws according to the various forms of government. Of these, according to the Philosopher (Polit. iii, 10) one is "monarchy," i.e. when the state is governed by one; and then we have "Royal Ordinances." Another form is "aristocracy," i.e. government by the best men or men of highest rank; and then we have the "Authoritative legal opinions" [Responsa Prudentum] and "Decrees of the Senate" [Senatus consulta]. Another form is "oligarchy," i.e. government by a few rich and powerful men; and then we have "Praetorian," also called "Honorary," law. Another form of government is that of the people, which is called "democracy,"

and there we have "Decrees of the commonalty" [Plebiscita]. There is also tyrannical government, which is altogether corrupt, which, therefore, has no corresponding law. Finally, there is a form of government made up of all these, and which is the best: and in this respect we have law sanctioned by the "Lords and Commons," as stated by Isidore (Etym. v, 4, seqq.).

Fourthly, it belongs to the notion of human law to direct human actions. In this respect, according to the various matters of which the law treats, there are various kinds of laws, which are sometimes named after their authors: thus we have the "Lex Julia" about adultery, the "Lex Cornelia" concerning assassins, and so on, differentiated in this way, not on account of the authors, but on account of the matters to which they refer.

Reply to Objection 1: The law of nations is indeed, in some way, natural to man, in so far as he is a reasonable being, because it is derived from the natural law by way of a conclusion that is not very remote from its premises. Wherefore men easily agreed thereto. Nevertheless it is distinct from the natural law, especially it is distinct from the natural law which is common to all animals.

The Replies to the other Objections are evident from what has been said.

OF THE POWER OF HUMAN LAW (SIX ARTICLES)

We must now consider the power of human law. Under this head there are six points of inquiry:

(1) Whether human law should be framed for the community?

(2) Whether human law should repress all vices?

(3) Whether human law is competent to direct all acts of virtue?

(4) Whether it binds man in conscience?

(5) Whether all men are subject to human law?

(6) Whether those who are under the law may act beside the letter of the law?

Whether human law should be framed for the community rather than for the individual?

Objection 1: It would seem that human law should be framed not for the community, but rather for the individual. For the Philosopher says (Ethic. v, 7) that "the legal just . . . includes all particular acts of legislation . . . and all those matters which are the subject of decrees," which are also individual matters, since decrees are framed about individual actions. Therefore law is framed not only for the community, but also for the individual.

Objection 2: Further, law is the director of human acts, as stated above (Q[90], AA[1],2). But human acts are about individual matters. Therefore human laws should be framed, not for the community, but rather for the individual.

Objection 3: Further, law is a rule and measure of human acts, as stated above (Q[90], AA[1],2). But a measure should be most certain, as stated in Metaph. x. Since therefore in human acts no general proposition can be so certain as not to fail in some individual cases, it seems that laws should be framed not in general but for individual cases.

On the contrary, The jurist says (Pandect. Justin. lib. i, tit. iii, art. ii; De legibus, etc.) that "laws should be made to suit the majority of instances; and they are not framed according to what may possibly happen in an individual case."

I answer that, Whatever is for an end should be proportionate to that end. Now the end of law is the common good; because, as Isidore says (Etym. v, 21) that "law should be framed, not for any private benefit, but for the common good of all the citizens." Hence human laws should be proportionate to the common good. Now the common good comprises many things. Wherefore law should take account of many things, as to persons, as to matters, and as to times. Because the community of the state is composed of many persons; and its good is procured by many actions; nor is it established to endure for only a short time, but to last for all time by the citizens succeeding one another, as Augustine says (De Civ. Dei ii, 21; xxii, 6).

Reply to Objection 1: The Philosopher (Ethic. v, 7) divides the legal just, i.e. positive law, into three parts. For some things are laid down simply in a general way: and these are the general

laws. Of these he says that "the legal is that which originally was a matter of indifference, but which, when enacted, is so no longer": as the fixing of the ransom of a captive. Some things affect the community in one respect, and individuals in another. These are called "privileges," i.e. "private laws," as it were, because they regard private persons, although their power extends to many matters; and in regard to these, he adds, "and further, all particular acts of legislation." Other matters are legal, not through being laws, but through being applications of general laws to particular cases: such are decrees which have the force of law; and in regard to these, he adds "all matters subject to decrees."

Reply to Objection 2: A principle of direction should be applicable to many; wherefore (Metaph. x, text. 4) the Philosopher says that all things belonging to one genus, are measured by one, which is the principle in that genus. For if there were as many rules or measures as there are things measured or ruled, they would cease to be of use, since their use consists in being applicable to many things. Hence law would be of no use, if it did not extend further than to one single act. Because the decrees than to one single act. Because the decrees of prudent men are made for the purpose of directing individual actions; whereas law is a general precept, as stated above (Q[92], A[2], OBJ[2]).

Reply to Objection 3: "We must not seek the same degree of certainty in all things" (Ethic. i, 3). Consequently in contingent matters, such as natural and human things, it is enough for a thing to be certain, as being true in the greater number of instances, though at times and less frequently it fail.

Whether it belongs to the human law to repress all vices?

Objection 1: It would seem that it belongs to human law to repress all vices. For Isidore says (Etym. v, 20) that "laws were made in order that, in fear thereof, man's audacity might be held in check." But it would not be held in check sufficiently, unless all evils were repressed by law. Therefore human laws should repress all evils.

Objection 2: Further, the intention of the lawgiver is to make the citizens virtuous. But a man cannot be virtuous unless he forbear from all kinds of vice. Therefore it belongs to human law to repress all vices.

Objection 3: Further, human law is derived from the natural law, as stated above (Q[95], A[2]). But all vices are contrary to the law of nature. Therefore human law should repress all vices.

On the contrary, We read in De Lib. Arb. i, 5: "It seems to me that the law which is written for the governing of the people rightly permits these things, and that Divine providence punishes them." But Divine providence punishes nothing but vices. Therefore human law rightly allows some vices, by not repressing them.

I answer that, As stated above (Q[90], AA[1],2), law is framed as a rule or measure of human acts. Now a measure should be homogeneous with that which it measures, as stated in Metaph. x, text. 3,4, since different things are measured by different measures. Wherefore laws imposed on men should also be in keeping with their condition, for, as Isidore says (Etym. v, 21), law should be "possible both according to nature, and according to the customs of the country." Now possibility or faculty of action is due to an interior habit or disposition: since the same thing is not possible to one who has not a virtuous habit, as is possible to one who has. Thus the same is not possible to a child as to a full-grown man: for which reason the law for children is not the same as for adults, since many things are permitted to children, which in an adult are punished by law or at any rate are open to blame. In like manner many things are permissible to men not perfect in virtue, which would be intolerable in a virtuous man.

Now human law is framed for a number of human beings, the majority of whom are not perfect in virtue. Wherefore human laws do not forbid all vices, from which the virtuous abstain, but only the more grievous vices, from which it is possible for the majority to abstain; and chiefly those that are to the hurt of others, without the prohibition of which human society could not be maintained: thus human law prohibits murder, theft and such like.

Reply to Objection 1: Audacity seems to refer to the assailing of others. Consequently it belongs to those sins chiefly whereby one's neighbor is injured: and these sins are forbidden by human law, as stated.

Reply to Objection 2: The purpose of human law is to lead men to virtue, not suddenly, but gradually. Wherefore it does not lay upon the multitude of imperfect men the burdens of those who are already virtuous, viz. that they should abstain from all evil. Otherwise these imperfect ones, being unable to bear such precepts, would break out into yet greater evils: thus it is written (Ps. 30:33): "He that violently bloweth his nose, bringeth out blood"; and (Mat. 9:17) that if "new wine," i.e. precepts of a perfect life, "is put into old bottles," i.e. into imperfect men, "the bottles break, and the wine runneth out," i.e. the precepts are despised, and those men, from contempt, break into evils worse still.

Reply to Objection 3: The natural law is a participation in us of the eternal law: while human law falls short of the eternal law. Now Augustine says (De Lib. Arb. i, 5): "The law which is framed for the government of states, allows and leaves unpunished many things that are punished by Divine providence. Nor, if this law does not attempt to do everything, is this a reason why it should be blamed for what it does." Wherefore, too, human law does not prohibit everything that is forbidden by the natural law.

Whether human law prescribes acts of all the virtues?

Objection 1: It would seem that human law does not prescribe acts of all the virtues. For vicious acts are contrary to acts of virtue. But human law does not prohibit all vices, as stated above (A[2]). Therefore neither does it prescribe all acts of virtue.

Objection 2: Further, a virtuous act proceeds from a virtue. But virtue is the end of law; so that whatever is from a virtue, cannot come under a precept of law. Therefore human law does not prescribe all acts of virtue.

Objection 3: Further, law is ordained to the common good, as stated above (Q[90], A[2]). But some acts of virtue are ordained, not to the common good, but to private good. Therefore the law does not prescribe all acts of virtue.

On the contrary, The Philosopher says (Ethic. v, 1) that the law "prescribes the performance of the acts of a brave man ... and the acts of the temperate man . . . and the acts of the meek man: and in like manner as regards the other virtues and vices, prescribing the former, forbidding the latter."

I answer that, The species of virtues are distinguished by their objects, as explained above (Q[54], A[2]; Q[60], A[1]; Q[62], A[2]). Now all the objects of virtues can be referred either to the private good of an individual, or to the common good of the multitude: thus matters of fortitude may be achieved either for the safety of the state, or for upholding the rights of a friend, and in like manner with the other virtues. But law, as stated above (Q[90], A[2]) is ordained to the common good. Wherefore there is no virtue whose acts cannot be prescribed by the law. Nevertheless human law does not prescribe concerning all the acts of every virtue: but only in regard to those that are ordainable to the common good---either immediately, as when certain things are done directly for the common good---or mediately, as when a lawgiver prescribes certain things pertaining to good order, whereby the citizens are directed in the upholding of the common good of justice and peace.

Reply to Objection 1: Human law does not forbid all vicious acts, by the obligation of a precept, as neither does it prescribe all acts of virtue. But it forbids certain acts of each vice, just as it prescribes some acts of each virtue.

Reply to Objection 2: An act is said to be an act of virtue in two ways. First, from the fact that a man does something virtuous; thus the act of justice is to do what is right, and an act of fortitude is to do brave things: and in this way law prescribes certain acts of virtue. Secondly an act of virtue is when a man does a virtuous thing in a way in which a virtuous man does it. Such an act always proceeds from virtue: and it does not come under a precept of law, but is the end at which every lawgiver aims.

Reply to Objection 3: There is no virtue whose act is not ordainable to the common good, as stated above, either mediately or immediately.

Whether human law binds a man in conscience?

Objection 1: It would seem that human law does not bind man in conscience. For an inferior power has no jurisdiction in a court of higher power. But the power of man, which frames human law, is beneath the Divine power. Therefore human law cannot impose its precept in a Divine court, such as is the court of conscience.

Objection 2: Further, the judgment of conscience depends chiefly on the commandments of God. But sometimes God's commandments are made void by human laws, according to Mat. 15:6: "You have made void the commandment of God for your tradition." Therefore human law does not bind a man in conscience.

Objection 3: Further, human laws often bring loss of character and injury on man, according to Is. 10:1 et seqq.: "Woe to them that make wicked laws, and when they write, write injustice; to oppress the poor in judgment, and do violence to the cause of the humble of My people." But it is lawful for anyone to avoid oppression and violence. Therefore human laws do not bind man in conscience.

On the contrary, It is written (1 Pet. 2:19): "This is thankworthy, if for conscience . . . a man endure sorrows, suffering wrongfully."

I answer that, Laws framed by man are either just or unjust. If they be just, they have the power of binding in conscience, from the eternal law whence they are derived, according to Prov. 8:15: "By Me kings reign, and lawgivers decree just things." Now laws are said to be just, both from the end, when, to wit, they are ordained to the common good---and from their author, that is to say, when the law that is made does not exceed the power of the lawgiver---and from their form, when, to wit, burdens are laid on the subjects, according to an equality of proportion and with a view to the common good. For, since one man is a part of the community, each man in all that he is and has, belongs to the community; just as a part, in all that it is, belongs to the whole; wherefore nature inflicts a loss on the part, in order to save the whole: so that on this account, such laws as these, which impose proportionate burdens, are just and binding in conscience, and are legal laws.

On the other hand laws may be unjust in two ways: first, by being contrary to human good, through being opposed to the things mentioned above---either in respect of the end, as when an authority imposes on his subjects burdensome laws, conducive, not to the common good, but rather to his own cupidity or vainglory---or in respect of the author, as when a man makes a law that goes beyond the power committed to him---or in respect of the form, as when burdens are imposed unequally on the community, although with a view to the common good. The like are acts of violence rather than laws; because, as Augustine says (De Lib. Arb. i, 5), "a law that is not just, seems to be no law at all." Wherefore such laws do not bind in conscience, except perhaps in order to avoid scandal or disturbance, for which cause a man should even yield his right, according to Matt. 5:40, 41: "If a man . . . take away thy coat, let go thy cloak also unto him; and whosoever will force thee one mile, go with him other two."

Secondly, laws may be unjust through being opposed to the Divine good: such are the laws of tyrants inducing to idolatry, or to anything else contrary to the Divine law: and laws of this kind must nowise be observed, because, as stated in Acts 5:29, "we ought to obey God rather than man."

Reply to Objection 1: As the Apostle says (Rom. 13:1, 2), all human power is from God . . . "therefore he that resisteth the power," in matters that are within its scope, "resisteth the ordinance of God"; so that he becomes guilty according to his conscience.

Reply to Objection 2: This argument is true of laws that are contrary to the commandments of God, which is beyond the scope of (human) power. Wherefore in such matters human law should not be obeyed.

Reply to Objection 3: This argument is true of a law that inflicts unjust hurt on its subjects. The power that man holds from God does not extend to this: wherefore neither in such matters

is man bound to obey the law, provided he avoid giving scandal or inflicting a more grievous hurt.

Whether all are subject to the law?

Objection 1: It would seem that not all are subject to the law. For those alone are subject to a law for whom a law is made. But the Apostle says (1 Tim. 1:9): "The law is not made for the just man." Therefore the just are not subject to the law.

Objection 2: Further, Pope Urban says [*Decretals. caus. xix, qu. 2]: "He that is guided by a private law need not for any reason be bound by the public law." Now all spiritual men are led by the private law of the Holy Ghost, for they are the sons of God, of whom it is said (Rom. 8:14): "Whosoever are led by the Spirit of God, they are the sons of God." Therefor e not all men are subject to human law.

Objection 3: Further, the jurist says [*Pandect. Justin. i, ff., tit. 3, De Leg. et Senat.] that "the sovereign is exempt from the laws." But he that is exempt from the law is not bound thereby. Therefore not all are subject to the law.

On the contrary, The Apostle says (Rom. 13:1): "Let every soul be subject to the higher powers." But subjection to a power seems to imply subjection to the laws framed by that power. Therefore all men should be subject to human law.

I answer that, As stated above (Q[90], AA[1],2; A[3], ad 2), the notion of law contains two things: first, that it is a rule of human acts; secondly, that it has coercive power. Wherefore a man may be subject to law in two ways. First, as the regulated is subject to the regulator: and, in this way, whoever is subject to a power, is subject to the law framed by that power. But it may happen in two ways that one is not subject to a power. In one way, by being altogether free from its authority: hence the subjects of one city or kingdom are not bound by the laws of the sovereign of another city or kingdom, since they are not subject to his authority. In another way, by being under a yet higher law; thus the subject of a proconsul should be ruled by his command, but not in those matters in which the subject receives his orders from the emperor: for in these matters, he is not bound by the mandate of the lower authority, since he is directed by that of a higher. In this way, one who is simply subject to a law, may not be a subject thereto in certain matters, in respect of which he is ruled by a higher law.

Secondly, a man is said to be subject to a law as the coerced is subject to the coercer. In this way the virtuous and righteous are not subject to the law, but only the wicked. Because coercion and violence are contrary to the will: but the will of the good is in harmony with the law, whereas the will of the wicked is discordant from it. Wherefore in this sense the good are not subject to the law, but only the wicked.

Reply to Objection 1: This argument is true of subjection by way of coercion: for, in this way, "the law is not made for the just men": because "they are a law to themselves," since they "show the work of the law written in their hearts," as the Apostle says (Rom. 2:14, 15). Consequently the law does not enforce itself upon them as it does on the wicked.

Reply to Objection 2: The law of the Holy Ghost is above all law framed by man: and therefore spiritual men, in so far as they are led by the law of the Holy Ghost, are not subject to the law in those matters that are inconsistent with the guidance of the Holy Ghost. Nevertheless the very fact that spiritual men are subject to law, is due to the leading of the Holy Ghost, according to 1 Pet. 2:13: "Be ye subject . . . to every human creature for God's sake."

Reply to Objection 3: The sovereign is said to be "exempt from the law," as to its coercive power; since, properly speaking, no man is coerced by himself, and law has no coercive power save from the authority of the sovereign. Thus then is the sovereign said to be exempt from the law, because none is competent to pass sentence on him, if he acts against the law. Wherefore on Ps. 50:6: "To Thee only have I sinned," a gloss says that "there is no man who can judge the deeds of a king." But as to the directive force of law, the sovereign is subject to the law by his own will, according to the statement (Extra, De Constit. cap. Cum omnes) that "whatever law a man makes for another, he should keep himself. And a wise authority

[*Dionysius Cato, Dist. de Moribus] says: 'Obey the law that thou makest thyself.'" Moreover the Lord reproaches those who "say and do not"; and who "bind heavy burdens and lay them on men's shoulders, but with a finger of their own they will not move them" (Matt. 23:3, 4). Hence, in the judgment of God, the sovereign is not exempt from the law, as to its directive force; but he should fulfil it to his own free-will and not of constraint. Again the sovereign is above the law, in so far as, when it is expedient, he can change the law, and dispense in it according to time and place.

Whether he who is under a law may act beside the letter of the law?

Objection 1: It seems that he who is subject to a law may not act beside the letter of the law. For Augustine says (De Vera Relig. 31): "Although men judge about temporal laws when they make them, yet when once they are made they must pass judgment not on them, but according to them." But if anyone disregard the letter of the law, saying that he observes the intention of the lawgiver, he seems to pass judgment on the law. Therefore it is not right for one who is under the law to disregard the letter of the law, in order to observe the intention of the lawgiver.

Objection 2: Further, he alone is competent to interpret the law who can make the law. But those who are subject to the law cannot make the law. Therefore they have no right to interpret the intention of the lawgiver, but should always act according to the letter of the law.

Objection 3: Further, every wise man knows how to explain his intention by words. But those who framed the laws should be reckoned wise: for Wisdom says (Prov. 8:15): "By Me kings reign, and lawgivers decree just things." Therefore we should not judge of the intention of the lawgiver otherwise than by the words of the law.

On the contrary, Hilary says (De Trin. iv): "The meaning of what is said is according to the motive for saying it: because things are not subject to speech, but speech to things." Therefore we should take account of the motive of the lawgiver, rather than of his very words.

I answer that, As stated above (A[4]), every law is directed to the common weal of men, and derives the force and nature of law accordingly. Hence the jurist says [*Pandect. Justin. lib. i, ff., tit. 3, De Leg. et Senat.]: "By no reason of law, or favor of equity, is it allowable for us to interpret harshly, and render burdensome, those useful measures which have been enacted for the welfare of man." Now it happens often that the observance of some point of law conduces to the common weal in the majority of instances, and yet, in some cases, is very hurtful. Since then the lawgiver cannot have in view every single case, he shapes the law according to what happens most frequently, by directing his attention to the common good. Wherefore if a case arise wherein the observance of that law would be hurtful to the general welfare, it should not be observed. For instance, suppose that in a besieged city it be an established law that the gates of the city are to be kept closed, this is good for public welfare as a general rule: but, it were to happen that the enemy are in pursuit of certain citizens, who are defenders of the city, it would be a great loss to the city, if the gates were not opened to them: and so in that case the gates ought to be opened, contrary to the letter of the law, in order to maintain the common weal, which the lawgiver had in view.

Nevertheless it must be noted, that if the observance of the law according to the letter does not involve any sudden risk needing instant remedy, it is not competent for everyone to expound what is useful and what is not useful to the state: those alone can do this who are in authority, and who, on account of such like cases, have the power to dispense from the laws. If, however, the peril be so sudden as not to allow of the delay involved by referring the matter to authority, the mere necessity brings with it a dispensation, since necessity knows no law.

Reply to Objection 1: He who in a case of necessity acts beside the letter of the law, does not judge the law; but of a particular case in which he sees that the letter of the law is not to be observed.

Reply to Objection 2: He who follows the intention of the lawgiver, does not interpret the law simply; but in a case in which it is evident, by reason of the manifest harm, that the lawgiver

intended otherwise. For if it be a matter of doubt, he must either act according to the letter of the law, or consult those in power.

Reply to Objection 3: No man is so wise as to be able to take account of every single case; wherefore he is not able sufficiently to express in words all those things that are suitable for the end he has in view. And even if a lawgiver were able to take all the cases into consideration, he ought not to mention them all, in order to avoid confusion: but should frame the law according to that which is of most common occurrence.

Chapter 7: Political "Realism"

Comprehension questions you should be able to answer after reading this chapter:

1. Why does Machiavelli focus on historical examples of politics?

2. What does Machiavelli mean by each of the following terms? Virtú, Fortuna, Necessitá.

3. Why does Machiavelli think that a Prince should not always be virtuous/good?

4. What does Machiavelli mean when he says a successful Prince must possess the properties of both the fox and the lion?

5. Why does Machiavelli think it is better to be feared, than to be loved (if one must choose)?

6. What is the "State of Nature," according to Hobbes? What are its features? What is it like?

7. What does it mean to say that Hobbes is a "nominalist" with regard to concepts like "justice" and "(moral) goodness?"

8. What does Hobbes mean by a "law of nature?" What are the first three laws of nature, according to Hobbes?

9. What is a "social contract?" What is the purpose of forming a social contract? Why does Hobbes think the State of Nature would inspire us to want to form a social contract?

10. What is a "sovereign," and why does Hobbes think we need one?

11. Why does Hobbes think the power of the sovereign must be absolute?

12. Why does Hobbes think that it is impossible for the sovereign to act unjustly?

Machiavelli

While the previous chapter focused on the shift from classical political theory to medieval (Christian) political thinking, this chapter focuses on the beginning of "modern" political philosophy.

Niccolò di Bernardo dei Machiavelli (henceforth, just Machiavelli) was born in Florence on May 3rd, 1469 –roughly two hundred and twenty five years after the death of Aquinas. Florence had ostensibly been a Republic, but had been ruled by the Medici family (autocratically) since 1434.

Florence was the center of the European Renaissance. A Platonic academy was established in 1462 by Marsilio Ficino, and the city was home to both Michelangelo and Leonardo da Vinci. There flourished a culture of humanism at the time, stressing rationalism and individualism, rejecting much medieval thought, including Augustine's emphasis on our "Fallen" nature. The humanists at the time were optimistic about the human potential for excellence and improvement.

In 1494, there was a regime change in Florence, with the Medici's being expelled. The City was first ruled by a strict Dominican priest named Girolamo Savonarola. Under his leadership, the "Renaissance" was forced to flee to Venice. Savonarola was eventually excommunicated due to his criticism of the Pope, and ultimately arrested and executed.

In 1498, one of Machiavelli's old teachers (Marcello Adriani) was appointed Chancellor of Florence, and Machiavelli was appointed Second Chancellor and Secretary to the Council of Ten for War. This Council was a group of magistrates who were tasked with diplomatic negotiations as well as supervising the military during war. He received this appointment at the ripe old age of 29!

Machiavelli spent 14 years as a diplomat to other Italian city-states, to the Court of Louis XII in France, and the Court of Maximillian I in Germany. He was influenced by his time in France, as well as by his four-month mission to the Court of the Duke of Romagna: Cesara Borgia (also the son of Pope Alexander IV).

The Medici's were eventually restored to power by means of Pope Julius II on September 14th, 1512. Machiavelli was dismissed from office, and falsely accused of conspiring against the Medicis in an attempt to restore Florence to a Republic. He was arrested and tortured for 22 days before being released and ultimately being granted amnesty—but his political career was over at the age of 43.

He turned to writing, and his works include (among others) *The Prince*, and the *Discourses on the First Ten Books of Titus Livy*[176] (hereafter called the *Discourses*), published after his death (June 21st, 1527) in 1531 and 1532, respectively. In 1559, *The Prince* was put on the recently created Index of Prohibited Books by the Vatican, and he was villain-ized in political treatises and by no less a dramatist than William Shakespeare![177]And yet, the inscription on his tomb in Florence reads: "No eulogy would be adequate to praise so great a name."

Just what did this infamous Machiavelli write, that would make him so praiseworthy, but also be called the Apostle of the Devil?

Method

Methodologically, Machiavelli saw himself as breaking with both the ancient and medieval political traditions, focusing on what is realistic rather than idealistic, from what is and what works rather than what ought to be.

> It remains now to see what ought to be the rules of conduct for a prince towards subject and friends. And as I know that many have written on this point, I expect I shall be considered presumptuous in mentioning it again, especially as in discussing it I shall depart from the methods of other people. But, it being my intention to write a thing which shall be useful to him who apprehends it, it appears to me more appropriate to follow up the real truth of the matter than the imagination of it; for many have pictured republics and principalities which in fact have never been known or seen, because how one lives is so far distant from how one ought to live, that he who neglects what is done for what ought to be done, sooner effects his ruin than his preservation; for a man who wishes to act entirely up to his professions of virtue soon meets with what destroys him among so much that is evil.[178]

Machiavelli is usually considered the first "modern" political philosopher, and sometimes even the first political scientist. Indeed, in the introduction to his Discourses, he says that his intention is "to open a new route which has not yet been followed by anyone." Part of the reason for this sense of "newness" was due to his belief that politics is better understood by studying the history of actual States and rulers than by means of abstract theorizing.[179]

---

[176] While the full text of the Prince is provided at the end of this chapter, the Discourses may be found at the following URL: https://en.wikisource.org/wiki/Discourses_on_Livy

[177] In the *Merry Wives of Windsor*, a character asks: "Am I politic? am I subtle? am I a Machiavel?"

[178] Machiavelli, *The Prince*, Chapter 15.

[179] Although Machiavelli has the advantage of much more history to draw upon, his approach is not entirely new; Aristotle, after all, studied 158

Prudent men usually say (and not by chance or without merit) that whoever wants to see what is to be, considers what has been; for all the things of the world in every time have had the very resemblance as those of ancient times. This arises because they are done by men who have been, and will always have, the same passions, and of necessity they must result in the same effects.[180]

The *Discourses* is an extended commentary on Roman history and tactics. On the assumption that human nature is unchanging, the lessons of history are applicable "today." Therefore, politicians "today" (whether in his own time, or ours) should model the behavior of (historically) great politicians.

Drawing upon ancient political writings, he acknowledges that all states go through the cycles set down by ancient political philosophers: Monarchy turns to Tyranny, Aristocracy to Oligarchy, and Polity to mob rule ("Democracy")—and sometimes back again. Even the best-planned State, with rulers of the best intentions, are subject to these cycles. War is part of the cycle of politics as well. Even "peaceful" nations will be attacked and must be prepared to defend themselves. This means that all successful States must have "good laws and good armies."[181] Pacifism is unrealistic, as other States will see it as weakness

...it is impossible that a Republic succeeds in remaining quiet and enjoy its liberty and her limited confines; for even if she does not molest others, she will be molested: and from being molested there will arise the will and desire for conquest: and even if she should not have any outside enemies, she would find some at home, as it appears necessary to occur to all great Cities.[182]

Since war and other calamities are inevitable, a good ruler (hereafter referred to as "The Prince," using Machiavelli's terminology), is one who is prepared to weather whatever storms come his way, keeping both the State, and his rule of it, secure. Such practical consideration is a sharp departure from both the ancient and Christian traditions, by virtue of it separating morality from politics.

For thousands of years, political writings for (or about) rulers had been exhortations to virtue. Indeed, an entire genre of literature developed in antiquity, and flourished in the Middle Ages and Renaissance, called the "Mirror of Princes." The Roman stoic Seneca wrote one ("On Mercy"), as did Aquinas ("On Kingship: To the King of Cyprus"). In each case, these works encouraged rulers to be virtuous, and to rule in ways consistent with their own high moral standards. Machiavelli will offer very different advice, and even shifts talk from "virtue" to *virtú*.

Virtú & Fortuna

This terminological shift which might initially seem like a mere play on words is actually of great significance. *Virtú* is not to be confused with "virtue," as traditionally conceived. *Virtú* does not refer to moral character, or specific morally-good character traits, but rather to the qualities a leader needs to maintain the state (and his own rule!). These might include such traits as firmness of purpose, foresight, being able to "read" people, fortitude in the face of adversity, etc. If a single word is needed, "vitality" might be our best choice.

Of lesser importance, but still noteworthy, is his notion of *Necessitá*. *Necessitá* refers to the means to compel human beings to "be good." This can be something like an external threat that unites the people under a common cause [e.g., the (temporary) solidarity observed in the USA after 9-11], or it can be the coercive power of laws, as "Laws can make [people] good."[183]

---

existing constitutions in his time to inform his own views on politics.
[180] Machiavelli, *The Discourses*, III,xliii.

[181] *The Prince*, Chp. 12.
[182] *Discourses*, II.xix.
[183] Ibid.,, I.iii.

A final key term for Machiavelli is *Fortuna*. Political stability is threatened by both human weakness and corruption, and as well by *Fortuna*.

Fortuna, translated as "Fortune," is understood as unpredictable (usually harmful!) circumstances. He describes her[184] as "one of our destructive rivers which, when it is angry, turns the plains into lakes, throws down the trees and buildings, takes earth from one spot, puts it in another; everyone flees before the flood; everyone yields to its fury and nowhere can repel it." [185]

She is a mysterious and destructive "force of nature" which can be resisted only by the prior development of *virtú,* and its wise application in response to whatever challenges *fortuna* brings. *Virtú* supplies the ability to respond to Fortune at any time and in any way that is necessary. *Virtú* is the ability to overcome, and even benefit, from the fickle, shifting *Fortuna*. This also involves what might be considered morally-questionable tactics and strategies.

Machiavelli urges that a successful ruler must know how not to be good. "Hence it is necessary for a prince wishing to hold his own to know how to do wrong, and to make use of it or not according to necessity."[186]

Amoral (or immoral?) Politics

As mentioned previously, in 1559, all of Machiavelli's works were put on the "Index of Prohibited Books"—a list of books banned by the Catholic Church for heresy or immorality. He was posthumously accused of being inspired by the Devil! But, why the "diabolical" reputation? First, consider a few choice quotations (and then we will put them into proper context, and perhaps save Machiavelli's reputation—at least a little):

- "Taking everything into account, one will discover that some qualities that appear to be virtue, if the prince pursues them, will end in his destruction; while other qualities that

look like vices, if he pursues them, will result in his safety and well-being."
- "[The Prince] needs not be concerned [with public opinion] if he acquires a reputation for those vices without which he would be unlikely to save the state."
- "It is not necessary for a prince to have all the above-mentioned qualities [viz,. virtues], but it is very necessary for him to appear to have them."
- "Injuries must be committed all at once...benefits should be bestowed little by little"
- "A prince must have no other objective, no other thought, nor take up any profession but that of war, its methods and its discipline"
- "for a man who strives after goodness in all his acts is sure to come to ruin"
- "A prince, therefore, must be indifferent to the charge of cruelty"
- "Disorders harm the entire citizenry, while executions...harm only a few"
- "About the generality of men: they are ungrateful, fickle, dissembling, anxious to flee danger, and covetous of gain"
- "Anyone compelled to choose will find greater security in being feared than in being loved"
- "Means of law, and by means of force. The first belongs properly to man, the second to animals; but since the first is often insufficient, it is necessary to resort to the second"
- "A wise prince cannot and should not keep his pledge when it is against his interest to do so"
- "It is often necessary to act against mercy, against faith, against humanity"
- "All men are wicked and will act wickedly whenever they have the chance to do so"

---

[184] Yes, he thinks of *Fortuna* as female...
[185] *The Prince*, chapter 25.

[186] Ibid., chapter 15.

While some of those quotations are, indeed, provocative, we must understand that Machiavelli is not advocating evil for evil's sake, nor even in all circumstances. He is, first of all, presupposing that the subjects of the Prince are "bad"—as he thought was the case in his own Florence. "And I will presuppose a City very corrupt, where such difficulties come to rise very fast, as there are found there neither laws or institutions that should be enough to check a general corruption."[187] The admittedly ruthless tactics that might be necessary (at times) to control an unstable and corrupted State are not necessarily suitable for a stable Republic with good citizens. "Different institutions and ways of living must be instituted for a bad subject than for a good one."[188]

Machiavelli's guiding norm is self-preservation for the individual (including the ruler), and for the State. Even "immoral" actions can be justifiable for the good of the State. He justifies this by means of a Roman anecdote:

> The Consul and the Roman army (as mentioned above) were besieged by the Samnites, who had proposed the most ignominious conditions to the Romans, which were to put them under the yoke, and to send them back to Rome disarmed; the Consuls were astonished and the entire army was in despair because of this; but L. Lentulus, the Roman legate said, that it did not appear he should avoid any procedure in order to save the country, for as the life of Rome depended on the life of that army, it appeared to him it should be saved in whatever way, and that the country is well defended in whatever way it is defended, either with ignominy or with glory; for by saving that army, Rome would in time wipe out that ignominy; but by not saving it, even though they should die most gloriously, Rome and its liberty would be lost. Which thing merits to be noted and observed by

any citizen who finds himself counselling his country; for where the entire safety of the country is to be decided, there ought not to exist any consideration of what is just or unjust, nor what is merciful or cruel, nor what is praiseworthy or ignominious; rather, ahead of every other consideration, that proceeding ought to be followed which will save the life of the country and maintain its liberty.[189]

Simply put, this is a case of the ends justifying the means. The "ends" of peace, security, stability, strength, and preserving the State, justify whatever "means" are required to secure those ends, including cruelty, lies, terrorism, treachery, etc. It is not that rulers should embrace "evil," but that their political decisions should not be based on whether their action will be judged good or evil. They should do whatever is necessary, given the circumstances.

In politics, traditional virtues don't serve the same role as they do in private morality. Traditional virtues are admirable, but no ruler can exhibit them all, all of the time, without coming to ruin, "for a man who wishes to act entirely up to his professions of virtue soon meets with what destroys him among so much that is evil."[190]

"Liberality," for example, from a ruler will likely mean higher taxes on his subjects in order to fund his "generosity". But, these higher taxes are likely to breed resentment from the very subjects to whom he is trying to be generous. Paradoxically, then, a "miser" can be "generous" by not taking so much from his subjects. Similarly, "mercy" might result in increased license and criminality in the population, bringing more harm to the community. "Cruelty," perhaps ironically, might be more "merciful" in the long run.

---

[187] *Discourses,* I.xviii.
[188] Ibid., I,xviii.

[189] Ibid., III. xli.
[190] *The Prince,* chapter 15.

While it is not important for a Prince to possess traditional virtues, it is important for him to *appear* to have them.[191]

Every one admits how praiseworthy it is in a prince to keep faith, and to live with integrity and not with craft. Nevertheless our experience has been that those princes who have done great things have held good faith of little account, and have known how to circumvent the intellect of men by craft, and in the end have overcome those who have relied on their word. You must know there are two ways of contesting, the one by the law, the other by force; the first method is proper to men, the second to beasts; but because the first is frequently not sufficient, it is necessary to have recourse to the second. Therefore it is necessary for a prince to understand how to avail himself of the beast and the man. This has been figuratively taught to princes by ancient writers, who describe how Achilles and many other princes of old were given to the Centaur Chiron to nurse, who brought them up in his discipline; which means solely that, as they had for a teacher one who was half beast and half man, so it is necessary for a prince to know how to make use of both natures, and that one without the other is not durable. A prince, therefore, being compelled knowingly to adopt the beast, ought to choose the fox and the lion; because the lion cannot defend himself against snares and the fox cannot defend himself against wolves. Therefore, it is necessary to be a fox to discover the snares and a lion to terrify the wolves. Those who rely simply on the lion do not understand what they are about. Therefore a wise lord cannot, nor ought he to, keep faith when such observance may be turned against him, and when the reasons that caused him to

pledge it exist no longer. If men were entirely good this precept would not hold, but because they are bad, and will not keep faith with you, you too are not bound to observe it with them. Nor will there ever be wanting to a prince legitimate reasons to excuse this non-observance. Of this endless modern examples could be given, showing how many treaties and engagements have been made void and of no effect through the faithlessness of princes; and he who has known best how to employ the fox has succeeded best.[192]

As he states in the quotation above, there are different ways to compel people to behave in the ways you want them to. Most generally, the two options are law and force. While the rule of law is proper for "men," sometimes law is insufficient, and a Prince must resort to force (the method proper to "beasts"). This means that a successful Prince must be skilled in the use of both methods.

Machiavelli represents the method of "beasts" with both the fox and the lion. The lion is powerful and bold, but not clever. The fox is clever, but not strong. A Prince who is all "lion" will not see "snares" (conspiracies and other political dangers) before it is too late, and a Prince who is all "fox," though able to detect the dangers, won't be sufficiently powerful to defend against them. "Therefore, it is necessary to be a fox to discover the snares and a lion to terrify the wolves."

Fear and Love

The Prince must be able to "terrify the wolves." Among the most famous positions attributed to Machiavelli is that it is better for a Prince to be feared, than loved. The source of this claim is worth quoting at length:

. . . I say that every prince ought to desire to be considered clement and not cruel. Nevertheless he ought to take care not to

---

[191] A position reminiscent of that offered by Adeimantus in Plato's *Republic*. . .

[192] *The Prince*, chapter 18.

misuse this clemency. Cesare Borgia was considered cruel; notwithstanding, his cruelty reconciled the Romagna, unified it, and restored it to peace and loyalty. And if this be rightly considered, he will be seen to have been much more merciful than the Florentine people, who, to avoid a reputation for cruelty, permitted Pistoia to be destroyed.

Therefore a prince, so long as he keeps his subjects united and loyal, ought not to mind the reproach of cruelty; because with a few examples he will be more merciful than those who, through too much mercy, allow disorders to arise, from which follow murders or robberies; for these are wont to injure the whole people, whilst those executions which originate with a prince offend the individual only....

Upon this a question arises: whether it be better to be loved than feared or feared than loved? It may be answered that one should wish to be both, but, because it is difficult to unite them in one person, it is much safer to be feared than loved, when, of the two, either must be dispensed with. Because this is to be asserted in general of men, that they are ungrateful, fickle, false, cowardly, covetous, and as long as you succeed they are yours entirely; they will offer you their blood, property, life, and children, as is said above, when the need is far distant; but when it approaches they turn against you. And that prince who, relying entirely on their promises, has neglected other precautions, is ruined; because friendships that are obtained by payments, and not by greatness or nobility of mind, may indeed be earned, but they are not secured, and in time of need cannot be relied upon; and men have less scruple in offending one who is beloved than one who is feared, for love is preserved by the link of obligation which,

owing to the baseness of men, is broken at every opportunity for their advantage; but fear preserves you by a dread of punishment which never fails.

Nevertheless a prince ought to inspire fear in such a way that, if he does not win love, he avoids hatred; because he can endure very well being feared whilst he is not hated, ...[193]

Machiavelli's actual position here is subtle. He is certainly not suggesting that a Prince be some sort of tyrannical sociopath, instilling terror in the hearts of his subjects! "Cruelty" and violence are tools, just as mercy and clemency are tools. Each has its own proper use, in the right context. A Prince that is not fearsome enough will "allow disorders to arise, from which follow murders or robberies." Their State will become disordered, and not only will the Prince risk losing control of his State, but the people are likely to suffer more as well. Disorder and criminality "are wont to injure the whole people, whilst those executions which originate with a prince offend the individual only."

Ultimately, he claims that it is best for a Prince to be both feared *and* loved—perhaps analogous to a parent who is loved by his or her child, but whose authority is also respected and not questioned. However, he recognizes that, "because it is difficult to unite them in one person, it is much safer to be feared than loved, when, of the two, either must be dispensed with." This is because of his admittedly low view of most people. "Because this is to be asserted in general of men, that they are ungrateful, fickle, false, cowardly, covetous, and as long as you succeed they are yours entirely; they will offer you their blood, property, life, and children, as is said above, when the need is far distant; but when it approaches they turn against you."

People are fickle, and so are their affections. When times are good, the subjects will love their Prince. But, in the face of adversity or struggle, their love quickly evaporates. A contemporary

---

[193] Ibid., chapter 27.

expression might capture this tendency: "What have you done for me *lately*?"

If a Prince relies solely on love, his rule is bound to be precarious, since love is so fragile and fleeting. Fear, on the other hand, "never fails." That being said, a Prince should not inspire so much fear that he becomes *hated*, for that, too, will result in a precarious reign.

Machiavelli's Influence

Until Machiavelli, politics was part of ethics. Virtue was thought necessary for political life. With the cultural ascendancy of Christianity, this wasn't overturned but synthesized with the Christian worldview. As of Machiavelli, however, a new option for political theory was possible: expediency. "Realism." Machiavelli's somewhat mechanistic/scientific, and admittedly pessimistic, view of human nature called for a new approach to the "science" of governing humans. This new approach remains influential to this day, but found its first major influence in the political thought of Thomas Hobbes, to whom we now turn.

Hobbes

If there is a challenger for Machiavelli's title of "Founder of Modern Political Philosophy," that challenger is Thomas Hobbes.[194]

Hobbes was born in Westport England, on April 5th, 1588. He was brilliant, even as a child—learning Latin, Greek, French, and Italian, in addition to his own native English. He translated Euripides' "Medea" from Greek to Latin at the age of fourteen, and then entered Oxford University

at the age of fifteen. After receiving his bachelor's degree five years later in 1608, he was invited to join the Cavendish household (headed by William Cavendish, the Earl of Devonshire) as a tutor. He remained connected to the family for decades, often living with them, and remaining a bachelor his entire life.

In addition to his work with the Cavendish family, he also served as a tutor to King Charles II of France, and acted as secretary for Sir Francis Bacon from 1618-1622. Between 1634 and 1637 he met Galileo Galilei, Rene Descartes, and Pierre Gassendi. Hobbes contributed some criticisms of Descartes' work, to which Descartes offered replies. It is said that their relationship was cool, if not outright acrimonious.[195]

The political context in which we must understand Hobbes' life and thought is one of change and anxiety. The Tudor dynasty ended with Queen Elizabeth's death in 1603. Her cousin James became the first "Stuart" ruler, and embraced the notion of the "divine right" of kings. Accordingly, he tried to rule without the approval of parliament. When James died in 1625, his son Charles I soon found himself at war with both France and Spain. To fund these wars, Charles imposed taxes without parliamentary consent. Hobbes, acting as secretary to the Earl of Devonshire, helped collect these taxes. Eventually, the Civil War of 1642-1646 broke out in protest of these taxes (as well as some religious issues). The King lost the civil war, was executed, and the monarchy was abolished. The Republic of Oliver Cromwell was established, and Hobbes (fearing persecution due to the essay he had written in support of the Royalist position) fled

---

[194] Although Hobbes might rightfully belong to the "Enlightenment" period addressed in our next chapter, rather than the Renaissance, I pair him with Machiavelli for thematic reasons.

[195] Descartes wrote the following about Hobbes in a letter to Marsenne (1641): "Having now had time to read the last piece by Englishman [Hobbes], I find complete confirmation of the opinion of him that I expressed to you two weeks ago. I think it would be best for me to have

nothing more to do with him, and thus to refrain from answering him. If his temperament is what I think it is, it will be hard for us to exchange views without becoming enemies. It's better for us both to leave things where they are. Please don't tell him any more than you have to of what you know of my unpublished views, because I'm pretty sure that this is someone who is looking to acquire a reputation at my expense, and by sharp practice."

from England to France, where he stayed until 1651.

Hobbes eventually returned to England and "made peace" with the Commonwealth by agreeing to take an oath of Loyalty (the "Engagement Oath"). He immediately generated controversy, though, with the publication of his *Leviathan* in that same year.

Amazingly, Hobbes works managed to anger just about every faction in England. He angered Parliament because, even though he technically endorsed the idea that government is made legitimate by the consent of the governed, he also claimed that this consent entails absolute monarchy. He angered the Royalists because, even though he advocated for absolute monarchy, he denied the divine right of kings. He angered the Church by his materialist worldview, and undeniably heretical (if not outright atheistic) claims about God, miracles, revelation, and the Bible.[196]

Nevertheless, Hobbes managed to die an old man, at the age of 91, on December 3rd, 1679. His reputation as an alleged atheist followed him even after his death. *Leviathan* was publicly burned at Oxford on June 21st, 1683, and all of his works were placed on the Vatican's Index of Prohibited Books (joining Machiavelli's!) in 1703.

Overall, Hobbes experienced a country that was always insecure, always at the brink of civil war and calamity. Peace and security were constantly in jeopardy, he thought, because of the greater demand from the growing middle class, and even farmers, for liberty and political participation. The cultural trend was to regard the authority of the Bible (and the Church), and even one's own conscience, as being above that of the king and his agents—or at least comparable. The result of all this "liberty" was instability, and the promise of strife and misery.

Method

Like other scholars of his time, Hobbes saw no distinction between philosophy and science, and he drew political implications from the discoveries of science, rejecting the claims and insights of classical political philosophy as unscientific. Such views were not based on deductive reasoning, but merely their own experience. "In these westerne parts of the world, we are made to receive our opinions concerning the Institution, and Rights of Common-wealths, from Aristotle, Cicero, and other men, Greeks and Romanes, that living under Popular States, derived those Rights, not from the Principles of Nature, but transcribed them into their books, out of the Practice of their own Common-wealths."[197]

Unlike nearly the entire tradition before him, who believed that the State is natural, and that existing States would conform (more, or less, or not at all) to that natural ideal, Hobbes flatly denies any pre-existing "ideal." Hobbes was convinced that political philosophy should be just as scientifically-based as geometry, astronomy, and "natural philosophy." "The science of making and maintaining commonwealths has definite and infallible rules, as does arithmetic and geometry."[198] To that end, Hobbes embraced a radical "nominalism," framing both geometry and political science as disciplines which start from arbitrary/conventional definitions, which then deduce conclusions on the basis of those definitions.[199]

He also rejected any "teleological" accounts of human nature or politics, denying any natural "ends" to which we incline and towards which we should act. Instead, he interprets politics mathematically, and mechanically, in terms of causes and effects. "A final cause has no place but

---

[196] For example, not only does he claim that humans are entirely material, but he also insisted that God must be a material (corporeal) being as well, describing God as a "corporeal spirit." As a result of all this, his book was debated by a committee in the House of Commons in 1666 as a possible item of criminal heresy!

[197] *Leviathan*, XXI.
[198] Ibid., XX.
[199] For example, we stipulate what a triangle is (e.g., a 3-side plane figure), and then deduce more information by building on that definition (e.g., that the interior angles of a triangle add up to 180 degrees).

in such things as have sense and will; and this also I shall prove hereafter to be an efficient cause." In the introduction to *Leviathan*, he proposes: "For what is the heart but a spring; and the nerves, but so many strings, and the joints, but so many wheels, giving the motion to the whole body, such as was intended by the artificer?"

The State of Nature

Although Hobbes rejected both teleological views of human nature, as well as natural law approaches, in general, this certainly didn't mean that he rejected the idea that humans had a "nature"—he just interpreted this nature in purely mechanical fashion. Like any machine, the human machine requires a source of "animation." The "passions" are that source. While the objects of our passion may vary, the same general passions (e.g., desire, fear, hope) drive all human behavior, in a mechanically-necessary (causally determined) fashion. Pleasure, for example, is "nothing really but motion about the heart, as conception is nothing but motion in the head."

These passions will play a critical role in his understanding of the motivational foundations of civil society: "The Passions that encline men to Peace, are Feare of Death; Desire of such things as are necessary to commodious living; and a Hope by their Industry to obtain them."[200]

Humans are equally driven by passions, but are equal in other important respects as well. Hobbes claimed that we are all (roughly) equal both physically and mentally. "Nature hath made men so equall, in the faculties of body, and mind; as that though there bee found one man sometimes manifestly stronger in body, or of quicker mind then another; yet when all is reckoned together, the difference between man, and man, is not so considerable, as that one man can thereupon claim to himselfe any benefit, to which another may not pretend, as well as he. For as to the strength of body, the weakest has strength enough to kill the strongest, either by secret machination, or by confederacy with

others, that are in the same danger with himselfe."[201]

This is an admittedly ominous sort of equality. In effect, it is an equality of vulnerability, of fear, and of danger. Even though some people are physically stronger than others, even the strongest among us is still flesh and bone, equally mortal, and can be overcome by physically weaker foes through cleverness or strength of numbers. Therefore, this basic "equality" will be, for Hobbes, a source of tension and conflict. Conflict is the "natural" state for humanity—in the absence of political society.

This absence of political society is a key assumption driving this notion of the "State of Nature." The State of Nature is a state of anarchy. It may be conceived as either a pre-political environment, or the condition that obtains when a government loses control over its populace. "It may peradventure be thought, there was never such a time, nor condition of warre as this; and I believe it was never generally so, over all the world: but there are many places, where they live so now. For the savage people in many places of America, except the government of small Families, the concord whereof dependeth on naturall lust, have no government at all; and live at this day in that brutish manner, as I said before. Howsoever, it may be perceived what manner of life there would be, where there were no common Power to feare; by the manner of life, which men that have formerly lived under a peacefull government, use to degenerate into, in a civill Warre."[202]

The State of Nature, then, is the hypothetical state of existence we would experience in the absence of any governing authority. It is a state of literal anarchy, of basic (physical and intellectual) equality, and a state of absolute freedom. There are literally no restrictions on behavior, beyond what is physically impossible for us to achieve. No laws, no rules—not even notions of right or wrong, justice or injustice. In the State of Nature, every person has a right to anything deemed necessary for self-preservation.

---

[200] *Leviathan*, XIII.
[201] Ibid., XIII.

[202] Ibid., XIII.

To this warre of every man against every man, this also is consequent; that nothing can be Unjust. The notions of Right and Wrong, Justice and Injustice have there no place. Where there is no common Power, there is no Law: where no Law, no Injustice. Force, and Fraud, are in warre the two Cardinall vertues. Justice, and Injustice are none of the Faculties neither of the Body, nor Mind. If they were, they might be in a man that were alone in the world, as well as his Senses, and Passions. They are Qualities, that relate to men in Society, not in Solitude. It is consequent also to the same condition, that there be no Propriety, no Dominion, no Mine and Thine distinct; but onely that to be every mans that he can get; and for so long, as he can keep it.[203]

Similarly, in the next section of *Leviathan*:

And because the condition of Man, (as hath been declared in the precedent Chapter) is a condition of Warre of every one against every one; in which case every one is governed by his own Reason; and there is nothing he can make use of, that may not be a help unto him, in preserving his life against his enemyes; It followeth, that in such a condition, every man has a Right to every thing; even to one anothers body. And therefore, as long as this naturall Right of every man to every thing endureth, there can be no security to any man, (how strong or wise soever he be,) of living out the time, which Nature ordinarily alloweth men to live.[204]

As a "nominalist," Hobbes denies the independent reality of such concepts as "justice." "A name or appellation therefore is the voice of man, arbitrarily imposed, for a mark to bring to his mind some conception concerning the thing on which it is imposed."[205] In the State of Nature, as mentioned, "the notions of right and wrong, justice and injustice, have there no place." Those terms acquire meaning only within the State, as specified by the sovereign. Indeed, justice is merely a name used to classify an idea. Good and evil are mere words, "ever used with relation to the person that useth them: there being nothing simply and absolutely so; nor any common rule of good and evil, to be taken from the nature of the objects themselves." What is "just" (as we will see) is determined by the will of the sovereign (whatever the sovereign *names* "just"), and is expressed in the laws of his State.

Even the difference between monarchy and tyranny is subjective. Those who dislike monarchy call it tyranny, those who dislike aristocracy call it oligarchy, and those who dislike polity (democracy) call it mob-rule or anarchy. "There be other names of Government, in the Histories, and books of Policy; as Tyranny, and Oligarchy: But they are not the names of other Formes of Government, but of the same Formes misliked. For they that are discontented under Monarchy, call it Tyranny; and they that are displeased with Aristocracy, called it Oligarchy: so also, they which find themselves grieved under a Democracy, call it Anarchy, (which signifies want of Government;) and yet I think no man believes, that want of Government, is any new kind of Government: nor by the same reason ought they to believe, that the Government is of one kind, when they like it, and another, when they mislike it, or are oppressed by the Governours."[206]

If you've read previous chapters in this book, you recognize those familiar categories of governments: monarchy / tyranny, aristocracy / oligarchy, and democracy (or polity)/anarchy. Hobbes rejects any meaningful distinction between those pairs. He also, importantly, rejects the classical idea of man as a naturally political

---

[203] Ibid., XIII.
[204] Ibid., XIV.

[205] *Elements of Law*, 5.2-3
[206] *Leviathan*, XIX.

animal –"which axiom, though received by most, is most certainly false."[207]

It is neither from our nature, nor in fulfillment of our nature, that we form political communities. It is self-interest alone that brings us into community with others. For Hobbes, humans are all equally driven by passions, egoistically motivated, lacking any innate notion of right or wrong, and fundamentally anti-social. Humans are power-seekers, and subject to a "perpetual and restless desire of power after power, that ceases only in death."[208] All other goods (e.g., wealth, knowledge, reputation, etc.) are valued because they facilitate acquiring power. Even happiness itself is conceived as a "continual satisfaction of desire, from one object to another."[209] Reason, then, is no longer the instrument by which we determine what is morally right and wrong. It is, instead, the practical instrument by which we determine which specific course of action will best satisfy our passions.

The combination of our being driven by our amoral passions, and the anarchy of the environment in the State of Nature, diminishes any hope of cooperation, and promotes conflict. This is why the State of Nature was described as "a war of every man against every man."[210] Our primary, driving motivations are competition, "diffidence" (fear, suspicion), and "glory."[211] Without external constraints on our behavior, our passions will drive us to "invade" one another for personal gain. Under these perilous conditions, "war" is more advantageous than "peace." Even those who are satisfied with their lot in life are fools to pursue peace in the State of Nature, as they "would not be able, long time, by standing only on their defense, to subsist."[212] Recalling our presupposed basic physical and intellectual equality, Hobbes envisions conflict and insecurity.

From this equality of ability, ariseth equality of hope in the attaining of our Ends. And therefore if any two men desire the same thing, which neverthelesse they cannot both enjoy, they become enemies; and in the way to their End, (which is principally their owne conservation, and sometimes their delectation only,) endeavour to destroy, or subdue one an other. And from hence it comes to passe, that where an Invader hath no more to feare, than an other mans single power; if one plant, sow, build, or possesse a convenient Seat, others may probably be expected to come prepared with forces united, to dispossesse, and deprive him, not only of the fruit of his labour, but also of his life, or liberty. And the Invader again is in the like danger of another.[213]

If you are continually fearful for your safety, think about how that will impact your behavior. The fruits of civilization, such as education, invention, science, technology, art, and recreation, all require that a certain basic level of security has been achieved. If you are fearful that you might die if you leave your home, you're unlikely to go to school, or take a piano lesson, or play some basketball. If the fruits of your labors aren't secured by property laws and police protection, you'll be unlikely to try to amass much wealth, because anything you can't keep with you at all times is so likely to be stolen as to not be worth the effort it will take to obtain it in the first place.

Imagine that we're in the State of Nature, and I spend the day gathering nuts and berries. You hide in the bushes, watching. At the end of the day, I return home to my shelter that I spent several days building, to enjoy my dinner of nuts and berries. You sneak up behind me, hit me over the head with a branch you collected, and steal

---

[207] Hobbes, *De Cive*, 1.2

[208] *Leviathan*, XI.

[209] Ibid., XI.

[210] Ibid., XII.

[211] Ibid., XIII.

[212] Ibid., XIII. Note the similarity to Machiavelli with regard to the safety of "peaceful" States!

[213] Ibid., XIII.

my nuts, berries, and shelter. What, exactly, was the point of my investing all that effort in building a shelter, and gathering food? Instead, it would make much more sense for me to live a bare, subsistence kind of life—never bothering to acquire more than I can use at that very moment, and always looking over my shoulder in case you (or anyone else) is plotting against me.

Such a world will have no industries or universities, no artistic achievements or great accomplishments of humanity. In order to enjoy any of those things, we need to feel safe. In order to feel safe, we need to be protected. Since no one is so powerful as to be able to protect himself against anyone and everyone (in whatever number), we can't manage this alone. Hobbes' mechanistic account of human motivation and behavior leaves no room for moral "choice." To change behavior, the conditions promoting those behaviors must be changed—and that means leaving the State of Nature.

The very same self-interested passions that drive us to war in the State of Nature drive us to civil society. Humans are machines moved by means of two basic drives: desire for power, and fear of death. The desire for power produces our problems in the state of nature. The fear of death inspires the social contract. "The Passions that encline men to Peace, are Feare of Death; Desire of such things as are necessary to commodious living; and a Hope by their Industry to obtain them. And Reason suggesteth convenient Articles of Peace, upon which men may be drawn to agreement."[214]

In addition to these basic drives, Hobbes proposes that there are "Laws of Nature"—though he means something very different by this term, than did those who came before him. By "law of nature" he means some sort of prudential rule, dictated and determined by reason, which promotes self-preservation. "A LAW OF NATURE, (Lex Naturalis,) is a Precept, or generall Rule, found out by Reason, by which a man is forbidden to do, that, which is destructive of his life, or taketh away the means of preserving the same;

and to omit, that, by which he thinketh it may be best preserved."[215]

Specifically, reason prescribes "That every man, ought to endeavour Peace, as farre as he has hope of obtaining it; and when he cannot obtain it, that he may seek, and use, all helps, and advantages of Warre."[216] Following from this precept is the first "Law of Nature," to seek peace. "The first, and Fundamentall Law of Nature; which is, 'To seek Peace, and follow it.'"

The second Law of Nature follows from the first. "From this Fundamentall Law of Nature, by which men are commanded to endeavour Peace, is derived this second Law; 'That a man be willing, when others are so too, as farre-forth, as for Peace, and defence of himselfe he shall think it necessary, to lay down this right to all things; and be contented with so much liberty against other men, as he would allow other men against himselfe.'"[217] This mutual transfer of rights (to "everything") is a social contract.

The Social Contract

Contract approaches weren't entirely new—not even in Hobbes' time. Glaucon, in the *Republic*, offered one well before Hobbes, and both presuppose the same basic motivation: egoism. All such approaches make politics a matter of *nomos* (convention) rather than *physis* (nature). It is conceivable that humans not be in community with each other. Indeed, this hypothetical scenario is precisely what we imagine when we consider the State of Nature.

As parties to the contract, in exchange for the promise of peace and security, we agree amongst ourselves to limit our behavior so long as others will, too. In other words, I will agree not to kill you, so long as you agree not to kill me. I'll agree not to steal your stuff, so long as you agree to the same.

The only right never surrendered in this way is our basic right of self-defense. The whole point if surrendering rights in the SON is for the sake of self-preservation. "Whensoever a man

---

[214] Ibid., XIII.
[215] Ibid., XIV.

[216] Ibid., XIV.
[217] Ibid., XIV.

Transferreth his Right, or Renounceth it; it is either in consideration of some Right reciprocally transferred to himselfe; or for some other good he hopeth for thereby. For it is a voluntary act: and of the voluntary acts of every man, the object is some Good To Himselfe. And therefore there be some Rights, which no man can be understood by any words, or other signes, to have abandoned, or transferred. As first a man cannot lay down the right of resisting them, that assault him by force, to take away his life; because he cannot be understood to ayme thereby, at any Good to himselfe."[218] To surrender the right to self-preservation for the sake of self-preservation, makes no sense, of course.

With regard to all of the freedom we surrender, and all the promises we make, the third law of nature is that we *honor* whatever contracts we make. "From that law of Nature, by which we are obliged to transferre to another, such Rights, as being retained, hinder the peace of Mankind, there followeth a Third; which is this, That Men Performe Their Covenants Made: without which, Covenants are in vain, and but Empty words; and the Right of all men to all things remaining, wee are still in the condition of Warre."[219]

Self-interest drives us into the social contract, but doesn't guarantee that we'll honor it. For some, short-term advantage will blind them to long-term self-interest, and such foolish contract-breakers risk forcing us all back into the State of Nature. A coercive power (the "Sovereign") is needed to enforce the social contract, since "covenants without the sword are but words."[220]

This is but the natural conclusion that reason leads us to, according to Hobbes. It is our fear of death that gets is to accept rules in the first place. Only fear of death (as punishment) can get us to obey those rules. If we want the peace promised by the rules, we must implicitly will the rules (and their enforcement) as well. The sovereign must

apply enough fear of punishment to overpower any other passion for criminal gain.

The Sovereign

The social contract tradition denies the "divine right" of kings, and claims that the State (and sovereign) derive their authority from the consent of the governed. Obviously, not every State is formed by the explicit forging of a contract. Some people are conquered and subjected to a sovereign. For Hobbes, that doesn't matter. When we form a contract, it is driven by fear of one another. When we submit to a conqueror, we are driven by fear of the conqueror. Either way, the cause is the same, as is the motivation. So long as we "submit," there is at least implicit "consent."[221]

While not divine ordained, the sovereign is, nevertheless, absolute, "or else there is no sovereignty at all."[222] Rights transferred to the sovereign are henceforth non-transferable, and unlimited in application. The sovereign's purpose is to preserve the State and enforce the social contract, and may do "whatever he shall think necessary to be done" for that purpose.[223]

Sovereignty can't be divided. For Hobbes, there is value in limited power, no security in "checks and balances." Given human nature, the power of the sovereign must be greater than that of any other person, or collection of them. "If there be no power erected, or not great enough for our security, every man will rely, and may lawfully rely, on his own strength and art for caution against all other men."[224] As power-seekers, all individuals and factions will seek to

---

218 Ibid., XIV.
219 Ibid., XV.
220 Ibid., XVII.
221 Ibid., XX.

222 Ibid., XX.
223 Ibid., XVIII.
224 Ibid., XVII.

acquire more power, if granted any at all—thereby chipping away at the strength and effectiveness of the sovereign. For the same reason, he denies independent authority for the church, and would make the sovereign the head of both church and State.

This emphasis on undivided sovereignty is driven by a fear of civil war, which he regarded as more dangerous than even foreign enemies. This fear of factions and emphasis on unity was nothing new. It goes all the back to and through the writings of Cicero, Aristotle, and Plato, as well. In Antiquity, unity was sought and promoted by means of crafting the best kind of State, and instilling virtue in the rulers and citizens. For Hobbes, this is all misguided both in the sense of being ineffective (factionalism is better prevented by concentrating all power in one place!), and in the sense of having misunderstood the true nature of "justice."

The sovereign must be absolute. All authority rests with, and ends with, the sovereign. The liberty of the subject is understood as just whatever is not forbidden by law.

Law is simply "the word of him that by right hath command over others," so the law is simply whatever the sovereign decrees. Nor is there any such thing as an unjust law. "Since therefore it belongs to kings to discern good and evil, wicked are those, though usual, sayings, that he only is King who does righteously, and that kings must not be obeyed unless they command us just things." Instead, "Legitimate kings therefore make the things they command just, by commanding them, and which they forbid, unjust, by forbidding them. But private men, while they assume to themselves the knowledge of good and evil, desire to be even as kings; which cannot be with the safety of the commonweal."[225] To say that a law is "unjust" can only mean that the sovereign has replaced an old law with a new one.

Given the "absoluteness" of his power, there is no right to rebel against the sovereign, of course. The only time subjects are released from their obligation of obedience to the sovereign is if the sovereign is literally incapable of fulfilling his enforcement function, either because he has been overthrown (or slain), or because he has abdicated his authority.

Thus far we have considered only the unlimited authority of the sovereign, but this authority does come with some obligation on the sovereign's part. The obligations of the ruler are ostensibly simple: "all the duties of the ruler are contained in this one sentence, 'the safety of the people is the supreme law.'"[226] We may derive from this basic obligation four particular themes:

1. Defense of the subjects against foreign threats.
2. Keeping internal peace and security.
3. "Enriching" the public "as much as consistent with public security."
4. Granting "harmless liberties"—harmless because they don't undermine peace or security.

These "harmless liberties" reveal the nature of subjects under their absolute sovereign. The subjects have surrendered all political power and rights to the sovereign, and have ceased to be "political." What remains is economic activity: producing, selling, and buying. This might be an early anticipation of the citizen (or subject) as "consumer."

The Sovereign's primary responsibility is to enforce the "social contract" we've created, and he (or she) does so by punishment, and the threat of punishment. We can still choose to break the contract, but if we do, and we get caught, we're going to be punished. Presumably, the threat of that punishment is enough to inspire most of us to obey the contract most of the time. As a result, we enjoy peace, safety, and security (in theory). As a result of that, we can feel more confident in our possessions and work to acquire more wealth and more things, we can bother to pursue education, we can bother with science and technology and art, and we can bother to pursue and enjoy hobbies and recreational activities. Society flourishes, and our own life satisfaction increases.

---

[225] *De Cive*, 12.1

[226] Ibid., 13.2

International Politics

Finally, let us give brief consideration to international politics, as it involves only a basic extension of Hobbes views on the individual State. States are in their own "macro" State of Nature with respect to each other, just as individuals were. There are no international norms, morals, justice or injustice, either. Just as individuals are driven by self-interest and retain the right of self-preservation, so too do sovereigns and States. "Every sovereign hath the same right, in procuring the safety of his people, that any particular man can have, in procuring the safety of his own body."[227]

He in no way, however, glorified or promoted war, since what we all seek is peace. Reason recommends peace for States as well! Nor does he recommend some sort of "one world government" to do for international stability what the Sovereign does for his subjects. The driving motivation isn't the same, in Hobbes' view.

Although States may be suspicious of each other, and even go to war against each other, it doesn't render the lives of their subjects comparable to that they would be in the State of Natutre. "Because [the rulers] uphold thereby the industry of their subjects, there does not follow from it that misery which accompanies the misery of individual men."[228]

Conclusion

In this chapter we saw two thinkers who departed from the classical and Christian assumptions that preceded them. Both Machiavelli and Hobbes took a "realistic" view (or "pessimistic" view, depending on one's perspective) on human nature, and the not-always polite and pleasant necessities of politics.

In the next chapter, optimism and confidence in the possibility of human improvement within well-founded political communities returns, as we shift to Enlightenment thinkers such as John

Locke and the "Founding Fathers" of the U.S. political system.

---

[227] *Leviathan*, XXX.

[228] Ibid., XIII.

Niccolò Machiavelli (1469-1527) marks a dramatic turning point in the history of Western political philosophy. He departs from the classical political tradition by emphasizing Virtú over "virtue." His "realistic" approach to politics would make him infamous, but inspire not only Thomas Hobbes, whom we also considered in this chapter, but also contemporary political thinking that focuses on what is possible and practical in the political realm, rather than what might be "ideal." What follows is his most famous work, The Prince, in entirety. Within, you will encounter his use of historical examples, familiar terms such as Virtú, and his infamous treatment on whether it is better for a Prince to be loved, or feared.

Niccolò Machiavelli: *The Prince*

Translated by W. K. Marriott
Dedication: To the Magnificent Lorenzo Di Piero De' Medici:
[http://www.gutenberg.org/cache/epub/1232/pg1232.txt]

Those who strive to obtain the good graces of a prince are accustomed to come before him with such things as they hold most precious, or in which they see him take most delight; whence one often sees horses, arms, cloth of gold, precious stones, and similar ornaments presented to princes, worthy of their greatness.

Desiring therefore to present myself to your Magnificence with some testimony of my devotion towards you, I have not found among my possessions anything which I hold more dear than, or value so much as, the knowledge of the actions of great men, acquired by long experience in contemporary affairs, and a continual study of antiquity; which, having reflected upon it with great and prolonged diligence, I now send, digested into a little volume, to your Magnificence.

And although I may consider this work unworthy of your countenance, nevertheless I trust much to your benignity that it may be acceptable, seeing that it is not possible for me to make a better gift than to offer you the opportunity of understanding in the shortest time all that I have learnt in so many years, and with so many troubles and dangers; which work I have not embellished with swelling or magnificent words, nor stuffed with rounded periods, nor with any extrinsic allurements or adornments whatever, with which so many are accustomed to embellish their works; for I have wished either that no honour should be given it,

or else that the truth of the matter and the weightiness of the theme shall make it acceptable.

Nor do I hold with those who regard it as a presumption if a man of low and humble condition dare to discuss and settle the concerns of princes; because, just as those who draw landscapes place themselves below in the plain to contemplate the nature of the mountains and of lofty places, and in order to contemplate the plains place themselves upon high mountains, even so to understand the nature of the people it needs to be a prince, and to understand that of princes it needs to be of the people.

Take then, your Magnificence, this little gift in the spirit in which I send it; wherein, if it be diligently read and considered by you, you will learn my extreme desire that you should attain that greatness which fortune and your other attributes promise. And if your Magnificence from the summit of your greatness will sometimes turn your eyes to these lower regions, you will see how unmeritedly I suffer a great and continued malignity of fortune.

THE PRINCE

CHAPTER I -- HOW MANY KINDS OF PRINCIPALITIES THERE ARE, AND BY WHAT MEANS THEY ARE ACQUIRED

All states, all powers, that have held and hold

rule over men have been and are either republics or principalities.

Principalities are either hereditary, in which the family has been long established; or they are new.

The new are either entirely new, as was Milan to Francesco Sforza, or they are, as it were, members annexed to the hereditary state of the prince who has acquired them, as was the kingdom of Naples to that of the King of Spain.

Such dominions thus acquired are either accustomed to live under a prince, or to live in freedom; and are acquired either by the arms of the prince himself, or of others, or else by fortune or by ability.

CHAPTER II -- CONCERNING HEREDITARY PRINCIPALITIES

I will leave out all discussion on republics, inasmuch as in another place I have written of them at length, and will address myself only to principalities. In doing so I will keep to the order indicated above, and discuss how such principalities are to be ruled and preserved.

I say at once there are fewer difficulties in holding hereditary states, and those long accustomed to the family of their prince, than new ones; for it is sufficient only not to transgress the customs of his ancestors, and to deal prudently with circumstances as they arise, for a prince of average powers to maintain himself in his state, unless he be deprived of it by some extraordinary and excessive force; and if he should be so deprived of it, whenever anything sinister happens to the usurper, he will regain it.

We have in Italy, for example, the Duke of Ferrara, who could not have withstood the attacks of the Venetians in '84, nor those of Pope Julius in '10, unless he had been long established in his dominions. For the hereditary prince has less cause and less necessity to offend; hence it happens that he will be more loved; and unless extraordinary vices cause him to be hated, it is reasonable to expect that his subjects will be naturally well disposed towards him; and in the antiquity and duration of his rule the memories

and motives that make for change are lost, for one change always leaves the toothing for another.

CHAPTER III -- CONCERNING MIXED PRINCIPALITIES

But the difficulties occur in a new principality. And firstly, if it be not entirely new, but is, as it were, a member of a state which, taken collectively, may be called composite, the changes arise chiefly from an inherent difficulty which there is in all new principalities; for men change their rulers willingly, hoping to better themselves, and this hope induces them to take up arms against him who rules: wherein they are deceived, because they afterwards find by experience they have gone from bad to worse. This follows also on another natural and common necessity, which always causes a new prince to burden those who have submitted to him with his soldiery and with infinite other hardships which he must put upon his new acquisition.

In this way you have enemies in all those whom you have injured in seizing that principality, and you are not able to keep those friends who put you there because of your not being able to satisfy them in the way they expected, and you cannot take strong measures against them, feeling bound to them. For, although one may be very strong in armed forces, yet in entering a province one has always need of the goodwill of the natives.

For these reasons Louis the Twelfth, King of France, quickly occupied Milan, and as quickly lost it; and to turn him out the first time it only needed Lodovico's own forces; because those who had opened the gates to him, finding themselves deceived in their hopes of future benefit, would not endure the ill-treatment of the new prince. It is very true that, after acquiring rebellious provinces a second time, they are not so lightly lost afterwards, because the prince, with little reluctance, takes the opportunity of the rebellion to punish the delinquents, to clear out the suspects, and to strengthen himself in the weakest places. Thus to cause France to lose Milan the first time it was enough for the Duke Lodovico to raise insurrections on the borders;

but to cause him to lose it a second time it was necessary to bring the whole world against him, and that his armies should be defeated and driven out of Italy; which followed from the causes above mentioned.

Nevertheless Milan was taken from France both the first and the second time. The general reasons for the first have been discussed; it remains to name those for the second, and to see what resources he had, and what any one in his situation would have had for maintaining himself more securely in his acquisition than did the King of France.

Now I say that those dominions which, when acquired, are added to an ancient state by him who acquires them, are either of the same country and language, or they are not. When they are, it is easier to hold them, especially when they have not been accustomed to self-government; and to hold them securely it is enough to have destroyed the family of the prince who was ruling them; because the two peoples, preserving in other things the old conditions, and not being unlike in customs, will live quietly together, as one has seen in Brittany, Burgundy, Gascony, and Normandy, which have been bound to France for so long a time: and, although there may be some difference in language, nevertheless the customs are alike, and the people will easily be able to get on amongst themselves. He who has annexed them, if he wishes to hold them, has only to bear in mind two considerations: the one, that the family of their former lord is extinguished; the other, that neither their laws nor their taxes are altered, so that in a very short time they will become entirely one body with the old principality.

But when states are acquired in a country differing in language, customs, or laws, there are difficulties, and good fortune and great energy are needed to hold them, and one of the greatest and most real helps would be that he who has acquired them should go and reside there.

This would make his position more secure and durable, as it has made that of the Turk in Greece, who, notwithstanding all the other measures taken by him for holding that state, if he had not settled there, would not have been able to keep it. Because, if one is on the spot, disorders are seen as they spring up, and one can quickly remedy them; but if one is not at hand, they are heard of only when they are great, and then one can no longer remedy them. Besides this, the country is not pillaged by your officials; the subjects are satisfied by prompt recourse to the prince; thus, wishing to be good, they have more cause to love him, and wishing to be otherwise, to fear him. He who would attack that state from the outside must have the utmost caution; as long as the prince resides there it can only be wrested from him with the greatest difficulty.

The other and better course is to send colonies to one or two places, which may be as keys to that state, for it is necessary either to do this or else to keep there a great number of cavalry and infantry. A prince does not spend much on colonies, for with little or no expense he can send them out and keep them there, and he offends a minority only of the citizens from whom he takes lands and houses to give them to the new inhabitants; and those whom he offends, remaining poor and scattered, are never able to injure him; whilst the rest being uninjured are easily kept quiet, and at the same time are anxious not to err for fear it should happen to them as it has to those who have been despoiled. In conclusion, I say that these colonies are not costly, they are more faithful, they injure less, and the injured, as has been said, being poor and scattered, cannot hurt. Upon this, one has to remark that men ought either to be well treated or crushed, because they can avenge themselves of lighter injuries, of more serious ones they cannot; therefore the injury that is to be done to a man ought to be of such a kind that one does not stand in fear of revenge.

But in maintaining armed men there in place of colonies one spends much more, having to consume on the garrison all the income from the state, so that the acquisition turns into a loss, and many more are exasperated, because the whole state is injured; through the shifting of the garrison up and down all become acquainted with hardship, and all become hostile, and they are enemies who, whilst beaten on their own ground, are yet able to do hurt. For every reason, therefore, such guards are as useless as a colony is useful.

Again, the prince who holds a country differing in the above respects ought to make himself the head and defender of his less powerful neighbours, and to weaken the more powerful amongst them, taking care that no foreigner as powerful as himself shall, by any accident, get a footing there; for it will always happen that such a one will be introduced by those who are discontented, either through excess of ambition or through fear, as one has seen already. The Romans were brought into Greece by the Aetolians; and in every other country where they obtained a footing they were brought in by the inhabitants. And the usual course of affairs is that, as soon as a powerful foreigner enters a country, all the subject states are drawn to him, moved by the hatred which they feel against the ruling power. So that in respect to those subject states he has not to take any trouble to gain them over to himself, for the whole of them quickly rally to the state which he has acquired there. He has only to take care that they do not get hold of too much power and too much authority, and then with his own forces, and with their goodwill, he can easily keep down the more powerful of them, so as to remain entirely master in the country. And he who does not properly manage this business will soon lose what he has acquired, and whilst he does hold it he will have endless difficulties and troubles.

The Romans, in the countries which they annexed, observed closely these measures; they sent colonies and maintained friendly relations with the minor powers, without increasing their strength; they kept down the greater, and did not allow any strong foreign powers to gain authority.

Greece appears to me sufficient for an example. The Achaeans and Aetolians were kept friendly by them, the kingdom of Macedonia was humbled, Antiochus was driven out; yet the merits of the Achaeans and Aetolians never secured for them permission to increase their power, nor did the persuasions of Philip ever induce the Romans to be his friends without first humbling him, nor did the influence of Antiochus

make them agree that he should retain any lordship over the country. Because the Romans did in these instances what all prudent princes ought to do, who have to regard not only present troubles, but also future ones, for which they must prepare with every energy, because, when foreseen, it is easy to remedy them; but if you wait until they approach, the medicine is no longer in time because the malady has become incurable; for it happens in this, as the physicians say it happens in hectic fever, that in the beginning of the malady it is easy to cure but difficult to detect, but in the course of time, not having been either detected or treated in the beginning, it becomes easy to detect but difficult to cure. This it happens in affairs of state, for when the evils that arise have been foreseen (which it is only given to a wise man to see), they can be quickly redressed, but when, through not having been foreseen, they have been permitted to grow in a way that every one can see them, there is no longer a remedy. Therefore, the Romans, foreseeing troubles, dealt with them at once, and, even to avoid a war, would not let them come to a head, for they knew that war is not to be avoided, but is only to be put off to the advantage of others; moreover they wished to fight with Philip and Antiochus in Greece so as not to have to do it in Italy; they could have avoided both, but this they did not wish; nor did that ever please them which is for ever in the mouths of the wise ones of our time:--Let us enjoy the benefits of the time--but rather the benefits of their own valour and prudence, for time drives everything before it, and is able to bring with it good as well as evil, and evil as well as good.

But let us turn to France and inquire whether she has done any of the things mentioned. I will speak of Louis (and not of Charles) as the one whose conduct is the better to be observed, he having held possession of Italy for the longest period; and you will see that he has done the opposite to those things which ought to be done to retain a state composed of divers elements.

King Louis was brought into Italy by the ambition of the Venetians, who desired to obtain half the state of Lombardy by his intervention. I will not blame the course taken by the king, because, wishing to get a foothold in Italy, and having no friends there--seeing rather that every door was shut to him owing to the conduct of Charles--he was forced to accept those friendships which he could get, and he would have succeeded very quickly in his design if in other matters he had not made some mistakes. The king, however, having acquired Lombardy, regained at once the authority which Charles had lost: Genoa yielded; the Florentines became his friends; the Marquess of Mantua, the Duke of Ferrara, the Bentivogli, my lady of Forli, the Lords of Faenza, of Pesaro, of Rimini, of Camerino, of Piombino, the Lucchese, the Pisans, the Sienese--everybody made advances to him to become his friend. Then could the Venetians realize the rashness of the course taken by them, which, in order that they might secure two towns in Lombardy, had made the king master of two-thirds of Italy.

Let any one now consider with what little difficulty the king could have maintained his position in Italy had he observed the rules above laid down, and kept all his friends secure and protected; for although they were numerous they were both weak and timid, some afraid of the Church, some of the Venetians, and thus they would always have been forced to stand in with him, and by their means he could easily have made himself secure against those who remained powerful. But he was no sooner in Milan than he did the contrary by assisting Pope Alexander to occupy the Romagna. It never occurred to him that by this action he was weakening himself, depriving himself of friends and of those who had thrown themselves into his lap, whilst he aggrandized the Church by adding much temporal power to the spiritual, thus giving it greater authority. And having committed this prime error, he was obliged to follow it up, so much so that, to put an end to the ambition of Alexander, and to prevent his becoming the master of Tuscany, he was himself forced to come into Italy.

And as if it were not enough to have aggrandized the Church, and deprived himself of friends, he, wishing to have the kingdom of Naples, divides it with the King of Spain, and

where he was the prime arbiter in Italy he takes an associate, so that the ambitious of that country and the malcontents of his own should have somewhere to shelter; and whereas he could have left in the kingdom his own pensioner as king, he drove him out, to put one there who was able to drive him, Louis, out in turn.

The wish to acquire is in truth very natural and common, and men always do so when they can, and for this they will be praised not blamed; but when they cannot do so, yet wish to do so by any means, then there is folly and blame. Therefore, if France could have attacked Naples with her own forces she ought to have done so; if she could not, then she ought not to have divided it. And if the partition which she made with the Venetians in Lombardy was justified by the excuse that by it she got a foothold in Italy, this other partition merited blame, for it had not the excuse of that necessity.

Therefore Louis made these five errors: he destroyed the minor powers, he increased the strength of one of the greater powers in Italy, he brought in a foreign power, he did not settle in the country, he did not send colonies. Which errors, had he lived, were not enough to injure him had he not made a sixth by taking away their dominions from the Venetians; because, had he not aggrandized the Church, nor brought Spain into Italy, it would have been very reasonable and necessary to humble them; but having first taken these steps, he ought never to have consented to their ruin, for they, being powerful, would always have kept off others from designs on Lombardy, to which the Venetians would never have consented except to become masters themselves there; also because the others would not wish to take Lombardy from France in order to give it to the Venetians, and to run counter to both they would not have had the courage.

And if any one should say: "King Louis yielded the Romagna to Alexander and the kingdom to Spain to avoid war," I answer for the reasons given above that a blunder ought never to be perpetrated to avoid war, because it is not to be avoided, but is only deferred to your disadvantage. And if another should allege the pledge which the king had given to the Pope that he would assist him in the enterprise, in exchange for the dissolution of his marriage and for the cap to Rouen, to that I reply what I shall write later on concerning the faith of princes, and how it ought to be kept.

Thus King Louis lost Lombardy by not having followed any of the conditions observed by those who have taken possession of countries and wished to retain them. Nor is there any miracle in this, but much that is reasonable and quite natural. And on these matters I spoke at Nantes with Rouen, when Valentino, as Cesare Borgia, the son of Pope Alexander, was usually called, occupied the Romagna, and on Cardinal Rouen observing to me that the Italians did not understand war, I replied to him that the French did not understand statecraft, meaning that otherwise they would not have allowed the Church to reach such greatness. And in fact it has been seen that the greatness of the Church and of Spain in Italy has been caused by France, and her ruin may be attributed to them. From this a general rule is drawn which never or rarely fails: that he who is the cause of another becoming powerful is ruined; because that predominancy has been brought about either by astuteness or else by force, and both are distrusted by him who has been raised to power.

CHAPTER IV -- WHY THE KINGDOM OF DARIUS, CONQUERED BY ALEXANDER, DID NOT REBEL AGAINST THE SUCCESSORS OF ALEXANDER AT HIS DEATH

Considering the difficulties which men have had to hold to a newly acquired state, some might wonder how, seeing that Alexander the Great became the master of Asia in a few years, and died whilst it was scarcely settled (whence it might appear reasonable that the whole empire would have rebelled), nevertheless his successors maintained themselves, and had to meet no other difficulty than that which arose among themselves from their own ambitions.

I answer that the principalities of which one has record are found to be governed in two different ways; either by a prince, with a body of servants, who assist him to govern the kingdom as ministers by his favour and permission; or by a prince and barons, who hold that dignity by antiquity of blood and not by the grace of the prince. Such barons have states and their own subjects, who recognize them as lords and hold them in natural affection. Those states that are governed by a prince and his servants hold their prince in more consideration, because in all the country there is no one who is recognized as superior to him, and if they yield obedience to another they do it as to a minister and official, and they do not bear him any particular affection.

The examples of these two governments in our time are the Turk and the King of France. The entire monarchy of the Turk is governed by one lord, the others are his servants; and, dividing his kingdom into sanjaks, he sends there different administrators, and shifts and changes them as he chooses. But the King of France is placed in the midst of an ancient body of lords, acknowledged by their own subjects, and beloved by them; they have their own prerogatives, nor can the king take these away except at his peril. Therefore, he who considers both of these states will recognize great difficulties in seizing the state of the Turk, but, once it is conquered, great ease in holding it. The causes of the difficulties in seizing the kingdom of the Turk are that the usurper cannot be called in by the princes of the kingdom, nor can he hope to be assisted in his designs by the revolt of those whom the lord has around him. This arises from the reasons given above; for his ministers, being all slaves and bondmen, can only be corrupted with great difficulty, and one can expect little advantage from them when they have been corrupted, as they cannot carry the people with them, for the reasons assigned.

Hence, he who attacks the Turk must bear in mind that he will find him united, and he will have to rely more on his own strength than on the revolt of others; but, if once the Turk has been conquered, and routed in the field in such a way that he cannot replace his armies, there is nothing to fear but the family of this prince, and, this being exterminated, there remains no one to fear, the others having no credit with the people; and as the conqueror did not rely on them before his victory, so he ought not to fear them after it.

The contrary happens in kingdoms governed like that of France, because one can easily enter there by gaining over some baron of the kingdom, for one always finds malcontents and such as desire a change. Such men, for the reasons given, can open the way into the state and render the victory easy; but if you wish to hold it afterwards, you meet with infinite Difficulties, both from those who have assisted you and from those you have crushed. Nor is it enough for you to have exterminated the family of the prince, because the lords that remain make themselves the heads of fresh movements against you, and as you are unable either to satisfy or exterminate them, that state is lost whenever time brings the opportunity.

Now if you will consider what was the nature of the government of Darius, you will find it similar to the kingdom of the Turk, and therefore it was only necessary for Alexander, first to overthrow him in the field, and then to take the country from him. After which victory, Darius being killed, the state remained secure to Alexander, for the above reasons. And if his successors had been united they would have enjoyed it securely and at their ease, for there were no tumults raised in the kingdom except those they provoked themselves.

But it is impossible to hold with such tranquillity states constituted like that of France. Hence arose those frequent rebellions against the Romans in Spain, France, and Greece, owing to the many principalities there were in these states, of which, as long as the memory of them endured, the Romans always held an insecure possession; but with the power and long continuance of the empire the memory of them passed away, and the Romans then became secure possessors. And when fighting afterwards amongst themselves, each one was able to attach to himself his own parts of the country, according to the authority he had assumed there; and the family of the former lord being exterminated, none other than the Romans were acknowledged.

When these things are remembered no one will marvel at the ease with which Alexander held the Empire of Asia, or at the difficulties which others have had to keep an acquisition, such as Pyrrhus and many more; this is not occasioned by the little or abundance of ability in the conqueror, but by the want of uniformity in the subject state.

CHAPTER V -- CONCERNING THE WAY TO GOVERN CITIES OR PRINCIPALITIES WHICH LIVED UNDER THEIR OWN LAWS BEFORE THEY WERE ANNEXED

Whenever those states which have been acquired as stated have been accustomed to live under their own laws and in freedom, there are three courses for those who wish to hold them: the first is to ruin them, the next is to reside there in person, the third is to permit them to live under their own laws, drawing a tribute, and establishing within it an oligarchy which will keep it friendly to you. Because such a government, being created by the prince, knows that it cannot stand without his friendship and interest, and does it utmost to support him; and therefore he who would keep a city accustomed to freedom will hold it more easily by the means of its own citizens than in any other way.

There are, for example, the Spartans and the Romans. The Spartans held Athens and Thebes, establishing there an oligarchy, nevertheless they lost them. The Romans, in order to hold Capua, Carthage, and Numantia, dismantled them, and did not lose them. They wished to hold Greece as the Spartans held it, making it free and permitting its laws, and did not succeed. So to hold it they were compelled to dismantle many cities in the country, for in truth there is no safe way to retain them otherwise than by ruining them. And he who becomes master of a city accustomed to freedom and does not destroy it, may expect to be destroyed by it, for in rebellion it has always the watchword of liberty and its ancient privileges as a rallying point, which neither time nor benefits will ever cause it to forget. And whatever you may do or provide against, they never forget that name or their privileges unless they are disunited or dispersed, but at every chance they immediately rally to them, as Pisa after the hundred years she had been held in bondage by the Florentines.

But when cities or countries are accustomed to live under a prince, and his family is exterminated, they, being on the one hand accustomed to obey and on the other hand not having the old prince, cannot agree in making one from amongst themselves, and they do not know how to govern themselves. For this reason they are very slow to take up arms, and a prince can gain them to himself and secure them much more easily. But in republics there is more vitality, greater hatred, and more desire for vengeance, which will never permit them to allow the memory of their former liberty to rest; so that the safest way is to destroy them or to reside there.

CHAPTER VI -- CONCERNING NEW PRINCIPALITIES WHICH ARE ACQUIRED BY ONE'S OWN ARMS AND ABILITY

Let no one be surprised if, in speaking of entirely new principalities as I shall do, I adduce the highest examples both of prince and of state; because men, walking almost always in paths beaten by others, and following by imitation their deeds, are yet unable to keep entirely to the ways of others or attain to the power of those they imitate. A wise man ought always to follow the paths beaten by great men, and to imitate those who have been supreme, so that if his ability does not equal theirs, at least it will savour of it. Let him act like the clever archers who, designing to hit the mark which yet appears too far distant, and knowing the limits to which the strength of their bow attains, take aim much higher than the mark, not to reach by their strength or arrow to so great a height, but to be able with the aid of so high an aim to hit the mark they wish to reach.

I say, therefore, that in entirely new principalities, where there is a new prince, more or less difficulty is found in keeping them, accordingly as there is more or less ability in him who has acquired the state. Now, as the fact of becoming a prince from a private station presupposes either ability or fortune, it is clear that one or other of these things will mitigate in some degree many difficulties. Nevertheless, he who has relied least on fortune is established the strongest. Further, it facilitates matters when the prince, having no other state, is compelled to reside there in person.

But to come to those who, by their own ability and not through fortune, have risen to be princes, I say that Moses, Cyrus, Romulus, Theseus, and such like are the most excellent examples. And although one may not discuss Moses, he having been a mere executor of the will of God, yet he ought to be admired, if only for that favour which made him worthy to speak with God. But in considering Cyrus and others who have acquired or founded kingdoms, all will be found admirable; and if their particular deeds and conduct shall be considered, they will not be found inferior to those of Moses, although he had so great a preceptor. And in examining their actions and lives one cannot see that they owed anything to fortune beyond opportunity, which brought them the material to mould into the form which seemed best to them. Without that opportunity their powers of mind would have been extinguished, and without those powers the opportunity would have come in vain.

It was necessary, therefore, to Moses that he should find the people of Israel in Egypt enslaved and oppressed by the Egyptians, in order that they should be disposed to follow him so as to be delivered out of bondage. It was necessary that Romulus should not remain in Alba, and that he should be abandoned at his birth, in order that he should become King of Rome and founder of the fatherland. It was necessary that Cyrus should find the Persians discontented with the government of the Medes, and the Medes soft and effeminate through their long peace. Theseus could not have shown his ability had he not found the Athenians dispersed. These opportunities, therefore, made those men fortunate, and their high ability enabled them to recognize the opportunity whereby their country was ennobled and made famous.

Those who by valorous ways become princes, like these men, acquire a principality with difficulty, but they keep it with ease. The difficulties they have in acquiring it rise in part from the new rules and methods which they are forced to introduce to establish their government and its security. And it ought to be remembered that there is nothing more difficult to take in hand, more perilous to conduct, or more uncertain in its success, than to take the lead in the introduction of a new order of things, because the innovator has for enemies all those who have done well under the old conditions, and lukewarm defenders in those who may do well under the new. This coolness arises partly from fear of the opponents, who have the laws on their side, and partly from the incredulity of men, who do not readily believe in new things until they have had a long experience of them. Thus it happens that whenever those who are hostile have the opportunity to attack they do it like partisans, whilst the others defend lukewarmly, in such wise that the prince is endangered along with them.

It is necessary, therefore, if we desire to discuss this matter thoroughly, to inquire whether these innovators can rely on themselves or have to depend on others: that is to say, whether, to consummate their enterprise, have they to use prayers or can they use force? In the first instance they always succeed badly, and never compass anything; but when they can rely on themselves and use force, then they are rarely endangered. Hence it is that all armed prophets have conquered, and the unarmed ones have been destroyed. Besides the reasons mentioned, the nature of the people is variable, and whilst it is easy to persuade them, it is difficult to fix them in that persuasion. And thus it is necessary to take such measures that, when they believe no longer, it may be possible to make them believe by force.

If Moses, Cyrus, Theseus, and Romulus had been unarmed they could not have enforced their constitutions for long--as happened in our time to Fra Girolamo Savonarola, who was ruined with his new order of things immediately the multitude believed in him no longer, and he had no means of keeping steadfast those who believed or of making the unbelievers to believe. Therefore such as these have great difficulties in consummating their enterprise, for all their dangers are in the ascent, yet with ability they will overcome them; but when these are overcome, and those who envied them their success are exterminated, they will begin to be respected, and they will continue afterwards powerful, secure, honoured, and happy.

To these great examples I wish to add a lesser one; still it bears some resemblance to them, and I wish it to suffice me for all of a like kind: it is Hiero the Syracusan. This man rose from a private station to be Prince of Syracuse, nor did he, either, owe anything to fortune but opportunity; for the Syracusans, being oppressed, chose him for their captain, afterwards he was rewarded by being made their prince. He was of so great ability, even as a private Citizen, that one who writes of him says he wanted nothing but a kingdom to be a king. This man abolished the old soldiery, organized the new, gave up old alliances, made new ones; and as he had his own soldiers and allies, on such foundations he was able to build any edifice: thus, whilst he had endured much trouble in acquiring, he had but little in keeping.

CHAPTER VII -- CONCERNING NEW PRINCIPALITIES WHICH ARE ACQUIRED EITHER BY THE ARMS OF OTHERS OR BY GOOD FORTUNE

Those who solely by good fortune become princes from being private citizens have little trouble in rising, but much in keeping atop; they have not any difficulties on the way up, because they fly, but they have many when they reach the summit. Such are those to whom some state is given either for money or by the favour of him who bestows it; as happened to many in Greece, in the cities of Ionia and of the Hellespont, where princes were made by Darius, in order that they might hold the cities both for his security and his glory; as also were those emperors who, by the corruption of the soldiers, from being citizens came to empire. Such stand simply elevated upon the goodwill and the fortune of him who has elevated them--two most inconstant and unstable things. Neither have they the knowledge requisite for the position; because, unless they are men of great worth and ability, it is not reasonable to expect that they should know how to command, having always lived in a private condition; besides, they cannot hold it because they have not forces which they can keep friendly and faithful.

States that rise unexpectedly, then, like all other things in nature which are born and grow rapidly, cannot leave their foundations and correspondencies fixed in such a way that the first storm will not overthrow them; unless, as is said, those who unexpectedly become princes are men of so much ability that they know they have to be prepared at once to hold that which fortune has thrown into their laps, and that those foundations, which others have laid BEFORE they became princes, they must lay AFTERWARDS.

Concerning these two methods of rising to be a prince by ability or fortune, I wish to adduce two examples within our own recollection, and these are Francesco Sforza and Cesare Borgia. Francesco, by proper means and with great ability, from being a private person rose to be Duke of Milan, and that which he had acquired with a thousand anxieties he kept with little trouble. On the other hand, Cesare Borgia, called by the people Duke Valentino, acquired his state during the ascendancy of his father, and on its decline he lost it, notwithstanding that he had taken every measure and done all that ought to be done by a wise and able man to fix firmly his roots in the states which the arms and fortunes of others had bestowed on him.

Because, as is stated above, he who has not first laid his foundations may be able with great ability to lay them afterwards, but they will be laid with trouble to the architect and danger to the building. If, therefore, all the steps taken by the duke be considered, it will be seen that he laid solid foundations for his future power, and I do not consider it superfluous to discuss them, because I do not know what better precepts to give a new prince than the example of his actions; and if his dispositions were of no avail, that was not his fault, but the extraordinary and extreme malignity of fortune.

Alexander the Sixth, in wishing to aggrandize the duke, his son, had many immediate and prospective difficulties. Firstly, he did not see his way to make him master of any state that was not a state of the Church; and if he was willing to rob the Church he knew that the Duke of Milan and

the Venetians would not consent, because Faenza and Rimini were already under the protection of the Venetians. Besides this, he saw the arms of Italy, especially those by which he might have been assisted, in hands that would fear the aggrandizement of the Pope, namely, the Orsini and the Colonnesi and their following. It behoved him, therefore, to upset this state of affairs and embroil the powers, so as to make himself securely master of part of their states. This was easy for him to do, because he found the Venetians, moved by other reasons, inclined to bring back the French into Italy; he would not only not oppose this, but he would render it more easy by dissolving the former marriage of King Louis. Therefore the king came into Italy with the assistance of the Venetians and the consent of Alexander. He was no sooner in Milan than the Pope had soldiers from him for the attempt on the Romagna, which yielded to him on the reputation of the king. The duke, therefore, having acquired the Romagna and beaten the Colonnesi, while wishing to hold that and to advance further, was hindered by two things: the one, his forces did not appear loyal to him, the other, the goodwill of France: that is to say, he feared that the forces of the Orsini, which he was using, would not stand to him, that not only might they hinder him from winning more, but might themselves seize what he had won, and that the king might also do the same. Of the Orsini he had a warning when, after taking Faenza and attacking Bologna, he saw them go very unwillingly to that attack. And as to the king, he learned his mind when he himself, after taking the Duchy of Urbino, attacked Tuscany, and the king made him desist from that undertaking; hence the duke decided to depend no more upon the arms and the luck of others.

For the first thing he weakened the Orsini and Colonnesi parties in Rome, by gaining to himself all their adherents who were gentlemen, making them his gentlemen, giving them good pay, and, according to their rank, honouring them with office and command in such a way that in a few months all attachment to the factions was destroyed and turned entirely to the duke. After this he awaited an opportunity to crush the Orsini, having scattered the adherents of the

Colonna house. This came to him soon and he used it well; for the Orsini, perceiving at length that the aggrandizement of the duke and the Church was ruin to them, called a meeting of the Magione in Perugia. From this sprung the rebellion at Urbino and the tumults in the Romagna, with endless dangers to the duke, all of which he overcame with the help of the French. Having restored his authority, not to leave it at risk by trusting either to the French or other outside forces, he had recourse to his wiles, and he knew so well how to conceal his mind that, by the mediation of Signor Pagolo--whom the duke did not fail to secure with all kinds of attention, giving him money, apparel, and horses--the Orsini were reconciled, so that their simplicity brought them into his power at Sinigalia Having exterminated the leaders, and turned their partisans into his friends, the duke laid sufficiently good foundations to his power, having all the Romagna and the Duchy of Urbino; and the people now beginning to appreciate their prosperity, he gained them all over to himself. And as this point is worthy of notice, and to be imitated by others, I am not willing to leave it out.

When the duke occupied the Romagna he found it under the rule of weak masters, who rather plundered their subjects than ruled them, and gave them more cause for disunion than for union, so that the country was full of robbery, quarrels, and every kind of violence; and so, wishing to bring back peace and obedience to authority, he considered it necessary to give it a good governor. Thereupon he promoted Messer Ramiro d'Orco, a swift and cruel man, to whom he gave the fullest power. This man in a short time restored peace and unity with the greatest success. Afterwards the duke considered that it was not advisable to confer such excessive authority, for he had no doubt but that he would become odious, so he set up a court of judgment in the country, under a most excellent president, wherein all cities had their advocates. And because he knew that the past severity had caused some hatred against himself, so, to clear himself in the minds of the people, and gain them entirely to himself, he desired to show that, if any cruelty had been practised, it had not originated

with him, but in the natural sternness of the minister. Under this pretence he took Ramiro, and one morning caused him to be executed and left on the piazza at Cesena with the block and a bloody knife at his side. The barbarity of this spectacle caused the people to be at once satisfied and dismayed.

But let us return whence we started. I say that the duke, finding himself now sufficiently powerful and partly secured from immediate dangers by having armed himself in his own way, and having in a great measure crushed those forces in his vicinity that could injure him if he wished to proceed with his conquest, had next to consider France, for he knew that the king, who too late was aware of his mistake, would not support him. And from this time he began to seek new alliances and to temporize with France in the expedition which she was making towards the kingdom of Naples against the Spaniards who were besieging Gaeta. It was his intention to secure himself against them, and this he would have quickly accomplished had Alexander lived.

Such was his line of action as to present affairs. But as to the future he had to fear, in the first place, that a new successor to the Church might not be friendly to him and might seek to take from him that which Alexander had given him, so he decided to act in four ways. Firstly, by exterminating the families of those lords whom he had despoiled, so as to take away that pretext from the Pope. Secondly, by winning to himself all the gentlemen of Rome, so as to be able to curb the Pope with their aid, as has been observed. Thirdly, by converting the college more to himself. Fourthly, by acquiring so much power before the Pope should die that he could by his own measures resist the first shock. Of these four things, at the death of Alexander, he had accomplished three. For he had killed as many of the dispossessed lords as he could lay hands on, and few had escaped; he had won over the Roman gentlemen, and he had the most numerous party in the college. And as to any fresh acquisition, he intended to become master of Tuscany, for he already possessed Perugia and Piombino, and Pisa was under his protection. And as he had no longer to study France (for the French were already driven out of the kingdom of Naples by the Spaniards, and in this way both were compelled to buy his goodwill), he pounced down upon Pisa. After this, Lucca and Siena yielded at once, partly through hatred and partly through fear of the Florentines; and the Florentines would have had no remedy had he continued to prosper, as he was prospering the year that Alexander died, for he had acquired so much power and reputation that he would have stood by himself, and no longer have depended on the luck and the forces of others, but solely on his own power and ability.

But Alexander died five years after he had first drawn the sword. He left the duke with the state of Romagna alone consolidated, with the rest in the air, between two most powerful hostile armies, and sick unto death. Yet there were in the duke such boldness and ability, and he knew so well how men are to be won or lost, and so firm were the foundations which in so short a time he had laid, that if he had not had those armies on his back, or if he had been in good health, he would have overcome all difficulties. And it is seen that his foundations were good, for the Romagna awaited him for more than a month. In Rome, although but half alive, he remained secure; and whilst the Baglioni, the Vitelli, and the Orsini might come to Rome, they could not effect anything against him. If he could not have made Pope him whom he wished, at least the one whom he did not wish would not have been elected. But if he had been in sound health at the death of Alexander, everything would have been different to him. On the day that Julius the Second was elected, he told me that he had thought of everything that might occur at the death of his father, and had provided a remedy for all, except that he had never anticipated that, when the death did happen, he himself would be on the point to die.

When all the actions of the duke are recalled, I do not know how to blame him, but rather it appears to be, as I have said, that I ought to offer him for imitation to all those who, by the fortune or the arms of others, are raised to government. Because he, having a lofty spirit and far-reaching aims, could not have regulated his conduct

otherwise, and only the shortness of the life of Alexander and his own sickness frustrated his designs. Therefore, he who considers it necessary to secure himself in his new principality, to win friends, to overcome either by force or fraud, to make himself beloved and feared by the people, to be followed and revered by the soldiers, to exterminate those who have power or reason to hurt him, to change the old order of things for new, to be severe and gracious, magnanimous and liberal, to destroy a disloyal soldiery and to create new, to maintain friendship with kings and princes in such a way that they must help him with zeal and offend with caution, cannot find a more lively example than the actions of this man.

Only can he be blamed for the election of Julius the Second, in whom he made a bad choice, because, as is said, not being able to elect a Pope to his own mind, he could have hindered any other from being elected Pope; and he ought never to have consented to the election of any cardinal whom he had injured or who had cause to fear him if they became pontiffs. For men injure either from fear or hatred. Those whom he had injured, amongst others, were San Pietro ad Vincula, Colonna, San Giorgio, and Ascanio. The rest, in becoming Pope, had to fear him, Rouen and the Spaniards excepted; the latter from their relationship and obligations, the former from his influence, the kingdom of France having relations with him. Therefore, above everything, the duke ought to have created a Spaniard Pope, and, failing him, he ought to have consented to Rouen and not San Pietro ad Vincula. He who believes that new benefits will cause great personages to forget old injuries is deceived. Therefore, the duke erred in his choice, and it was the cause of his ultimate ruin.

CHAPTER VIII -- CONCERNING THOSE WHO HAVE OBTAINED A PRINCIPALITY BY WICKEDNESS

Although a prince may rise from a private station in two ways, neither of which can be entirely attributed to fortune or genius, yet it is manifest to me that I must not be silent on them, although one could be more copiously treated when I discuss republics. These methods are when, either by some wicked or nefarious ways, one ascends to the principality, or when by the favour of his fellow-citizens a private person becomes the prince of his country. And speaking of the first method, it will be illustrated by two examples--one ancient, the other modern--and without entering further into the subject, I consider these two examples will suffice those who may be compelled to follow them.

Agathocles, the Sicilian, became King of Syracuse not only from a private but from a low and abject position. This man, the son of a potter, through all the changes in his fortunes always led an infamous life. Nevertheless, he accompanied his infamies with so much ability of mind and body that, having devoted himself to the military profession, he rose through its ranks to be Praetor of Syracuse. Being established in that position, and having deliberately resolved to make himself prince and to seize by violence, without obligation to others, that which had been conceded to him by assent, he came to an understanding for this purpose with Amilcar, the Carthaginian, who, with his army, was fighting in Sicily. One morning he assembled the people and the senate of Syracuse, as if he had to discuss with them things relating to the Republic, and at a given signal the soldiers killed all the senators and the richest of the people; these dead, he seized and held the princedom of that city without any civil commotion. And although he was twice routed by the Carthaginians, and ultimately besieged, yet not only was he able to defend his city, but leaving part of his men for its defence, with the others he attacked Africa, and in a short time raised the siege of Syracuse. The Carthaginians, reduced to extreme necessity, were compelled to come to terms with Agathocles, and, leaving Sicily to him, had to be content with the possession of Africa.

Therefore, he who considers the actions and the genius of this man will see nothing, or little, which can be attributed to fortune, inasmuch as he attained pre-eminence, as is shown above, not by the favour of any one, but step by step in the military profession, which steps were gained with a thousand troubles and perils, and were

afterwards boldly held by him with many hazardous dangers. Yet it cannot be called talent to slay fellow-citizens, to deceive friends, to be without faith, without mercy, without religion; such methods may gain empire, but not glory. Still, if the courage of Agathocles in entering into and extricating himself from dangers be considered, together with his greatness of mind in enduring and overcoming hardships, it cannot be seen why he should be esteemed less than the most notable captain. Nevertheless, his barbarous cruelty and inhumanity with infinite wickedness do not permit him to be celebrated among the most excellent men. What he achieved cannot be attributed either to fortune or genius.

In our times, during the rule of Alexander the Sixth, Oliverotto da Fermo, having been left an orphan many years before, was brought up by his maternal uncle, Giovanni Fogliani, and in the early days of his youth sent to fight under Pagolo Vitelli, that, being trained under his discipline, he might attain some high position in the military profession. After Pagolo died, he fought under his brother Vitellozzo, and in a very short time, being endowed with wit and a vigorous body and mind, he became the first man in his profession. But it appearing a paltry thing to serve under others, he resolved, with the aid of some citizens of Fermo, to whom the slavery of their country was dearer than its liberty, and with the help of the Vitelleschi, to seize Fermo. So he wrote to Giovanni Fogliani that, having been away from home for many years, he wished to visit him and his city, and in some measure to look upon his patrimony; and although he had not laboured to acquire anything except honour, yet, in order that the citizens should see he had not spent his time in vain, he desired to come honourably, so would be accompanied by one hundred horsemen, his friends and retainers; and he entreated Giovanni to arrange that he should be received honourably by the Fermians, all of which would be not only to his honour, but also to that of Giovanni himself, who had brought him up.

Giovanni, therefore, did not fail in any attentions due to his nephew, and he caused him to be honourably received by the Fermians, and he lodged him in his own house, where, having passed some days, and having arranged what was necessary for his wicked designs, Oliverotto gave a solemn banquet to which he invited Giovanni Fogliani and the chiefs of Fermo. When the viands and all the other entertainments that are usual in such banquets were finished, Oliverotto artfully began certain grave discourses, speaking of the greatness of Pope Alexander and his son Cesare, and of their enterprises, to which discourse Giovanni and others answered; but he rose at once, saying that such matters ought to be discussed in a more private place, and he betook himself to a chamber, whither Giovanni and the rest of the citizens went in after him. No sooner were they seated than soldiers issued from secret places and slaughtered Giovanni and the rest. After these murders Oliverotto, mounted on horseback, rode up and down the town and besieged the chief magistrate in the palace, so that in fear the people were forced to obey him, and to form a government, of which he made himself the prince. He killed all the malcontents who were able to injure him, and strengthened himself with new civil and military ordinances, in such a way that, in the year during which he held the principality, not only was he secure in the city of Fermo, but he had become formidable to all his neighbours. And his destruction would have been as difficult as that of Agathocles if he had not allowed himself to be overreached by Cesare Borgia, who took him with the Orsini and Vitelli at Sinigalia, as was stated above. Thus one year after he had committed this parricide, he was strangled, together with Vitellozzo, whom he had made his leader in valour and wickedness.

Some may wonder how it can happen that Agathocles, and his like, after infinite treacheries and cruelties, should live for long secure in his country, and defend himself from external enemies, and never be conspired against by his own citizens; seeing that many others, by means of cruelty, have never been able even in peaceful times to hold the state, still less in the doubtful times of war. I believe that this follows from severities being badly or properly used. Those may be called properly used, if of evil it is possible to speak well, that are applied at one blow and are necessary to one's security, and that are not

persisted in afterwards unless they can be turned to the advantage of the subjects. The badly employed are those which, notwithstanding they may be few in the commencement, multiply with time rather than decrease. Those who practise the first system are able, by aid of God or man, to mitigate in some degree their rule, as Agathocles did. It is impossible for those who follow the other to maintain themselves.

Hence it is to be remarked that, in seizing a state, the usurper ought to examine closely into all those injuries which it is necessary for him to inflict, and to do them all at one stroke so as not to have to repeat them daily; and thus by not unsettling men he will be able to reassure them, and win them to himself by benefits. He who does otherwise, either from timidity or evil advice, is always compelled to keep the knife in his hand; neither can he rely on his subjects, nor can they attach themselves to him, owing to their continued and repeated wrongs. For injuries ought to be done all at one time, so that, being tasted less, they offend less; benefits ought to be given little by little, so that the flavour of them may last longer.

And above all things, a prince ought to live amongst his people in such a way that no unexpected circumstances, whether of good or evil, shall make him change; because if the necessity for this comes in troubled times, you are too late for harsh measures; and mild ones will not help you, for they will be considered as forced from you, and no one will be under any obligation to you for them.

CHAPTER IX -- CONCERNING A CIVIL PRINCIPALITY

But coming to the other point--where a leading citizen becomes the prince of his country, not by wickedness or any intolerable violence, but by the favour of his fellow citizens--this may be called a civil principality: nor is genius or fortune altogether necessary to attain to it, but rather a happy shrewdness. I say then that such a principality is obtained either by the favour of the people or by the favour of the nobles. Because in all cities these two distinct parties are found, and from this it arises that the people do not wish to be ruled nor oppressed by the nobles, and the nobles wish to rule and oppress the people; and from these two opposite desires there arises in cities one of three results, either a principality, self-government, or anarchy.

A principality is created either by the people or by the nobles, accordingly as one or other of them has the opportunity; for the nobles, seeing they cannot withstand the people, begin to cry up the reputation of one of themselves, and they make him a prince, so that under his shadow they can give vent to their ambitions. The people, finding they cannot resist the nobles, also cry up the reputation of one of themselves, and make him a prince so as to be defended by his authority. He who obtains sovereignty by the assistance of the nobles maintains himself with more difficulty than he who comes to it by the aid of the people, because the former finds himself with many around him who consider themselves his equals, and because of this he can neither rule nor manage them to his liking. But he who reaches sovereignty by popular favour finds himself alone, and has none around him, or few, who are not prepared to obey him.

Besides this, one cannot by fair dealing, and without injury to others, satisfy the nobles, but you can satisfy the people, for their object is more righteous than that of the nobles, the latter wishing to oppress, while the former only desire not to be oppressed. It is to be added also that a prince can never secure himself against a hostile people, because of their being too many, whilst from the nobles he can secure himself, as they are few in number. The worst that a prince may expect from a hostile people is to be abandoned by them; but from hostile nobles he has not only to fear abandonment, but also that they will rise against him; for they, being in these affairs more far-seeing and astute, always come forward in time to save themselves, and to obtain favours from him whom they expect to prevail. Further, the prince is compelled to live always with the same people, but he can do well without the same nobles, being able to make and unmake them daily, and to give or take away authority when it pleases him.

Therefore, to make this point clearer, I say that the nobles ought to be looked at mainly in two ways: that is to say, they either shape their course in such a way as binds them entirely to your fortune, or they do not. Those who so bind themselves, and are not rapacious, ought to be honoured and loved; those who do not bind themselves may be dealt with in two ways; they may fail to do this through pusillanimity and a natural want of courage, in which case you ought to make use of them, especially of those who are of good counsel; and thus, whilst in prosperity you honour them, in adversity you do not have to fear them. But when for their own ambitious ends they shun binding themselves, it is a token that they are giving more thought to themselves than to you, and a prince ought to guard against such, and to fear them as if they were open enemies, because in adversity they always help to ruin him.

Therefore, one who becomes a prince through the favour of the people ought to keep them friendly, and this he can easily do seeing they only ask not to be oppressed by him. But one who, in opposition to the people, becomes a prince by the favour of the nobles, ought, above everything, to seek to win the people over to himself, and this he may easily do if he takes them under his protection. Because men, when they receive good from him of whom they were expecting evil, are bound more closely to their benefactor; thus the people quickly become more devoted to him than if he had been raised to the principality by their favours; and the prince can win their affections in many ways, but as these vary according to the circumstances one cannot give fixed rules, so I omit them; but, I repeat, it is necessary for a prince to have the people friendly, otherwise he has no security in adversity.

Nabis, Prince of the Spartans, sustained the attack of all Greece, and of a victorious Roman army, and against them he defended his country and his government; and for the overcoming of this peril it was only necessary for him to make himself secure against a few, but this would not have been sufficient had the people been hostile. And do not let any one impugn this statement with the trite proverb that "He who builds on the people, builds on the mud," for this is true when a private citizen makes a foundation there, and persuades himself that the people will free him when he is oppressed by his enemies or by the magistrates; wherein he would find himself very often deceived, as happened to the Gracchi in Rome and to Messer Giorgio Scali in Florence. But granted a prince who has established himself as above, who can command, and is a man of courage, undismayed in adversity, who does not fail in other qualifications, and who, by his resolution and energy, keeps the whole people encouraged--such a one will never find himself deceived in them, and it will be shown that he has laid his foundations well

These principalities are liable to danger when they are passing from the civil to the absolute order of government, for such princes either rule personally or through magistrates. In the latter case their government is weaker and more insecure, because it rests entirely on the goodwill of those citizens who are raised to the magistracy, and who, especially in troubled times, can destroy the government with great ease, either by intrigue or open defiance; and the prince has not the chance amid tumults to exercise absolute authority, because the citizens and subjects, accustomed to receive orders from magistrates, are not of a mind to obey him amid these confusions, and there will always be in doubtful times a scarcity of men whom he can trust. For such a prince cannot rely upon what he observes in quiet times, when citizens have need of the state, because then every one agrees with him; they all promise, and when death is far distant they all wish to die for him; but in troubled times, when the state has need of its citizens, then he finds but few. And so much the more is this experiment dangerous, inasmuch as it can only be tried once. Therefore a wise prince ought to adopt such a course that his citizens will always in every sort and kind of circumstance have need of the state and of him, and then he will always find them faithful.

CHAPTER X -- CONCERNING THE WAY IN WHICH THE STRENGTH OF ALL

PRINCIPALITIES OUGHT TO BE MEASURED

It is necessary to consider another point in examining the character of these principalities: that is, whether a prince has such power that, in case of need, he can support himself with his own resources, or whether he has always need of the assistance of others. And to make this quite clear I say that I consider those who are able to support themselves by their own resources who can, either by abundance of men or money, raise a sufficient army to join battle against any one who comes to attack them; and I consider those always to have need of others who cannot show themselves against the enemy in the field, but are forced to defend themselves by sheltering behind walls. The first case has been discussed, but we will speak of it again should it recur. In the second case one can say nothing except to encourage such princes to provision and fortify their towns, and not on any account to defend the country. And whoever shall fortify his town well, and shall have managed the other concerns of his subjects in the way stated above, and to be often repeated, will never be attacked without great caution, for men are always adverse to enterprises where difficulties can be seen, and it will be seen not to be an easy thing to attack one who has his town well fortified, and is not hated by his people.

The cities of Germany are absolutely free, they own but little country around them, and they yield obedience to the emperor when it suits them, nor do they fear this or any other power they may have near them, because they are fortified in such a way that every one thinks the taking of them by assault would be tedious and difficult, seeing they have proper ditches and walls, they have sufficient artillery, and they always keep in public depots enough for one year's eating, drinking, and firing. And beyond this, to keep the people quiet and without loss to the state, they always have the means of giving work to the community in those labours that are the life and strength of the city, and on the pursuit of which the people are supported; they also hold military exercises in repute, and moreover have many ordinances to uphold them.

Therefore, a prince who has a strong city, and had not made himself odious, will not be attacked, or if any one should attack he will only be driven off with disgrace; again, because that the affairs of this world are so changeable, it is almost impossible to keep an army a whole year in the field without being interfered with. And whoever should reply: If the people have property outside the city, and see it burnt, they will not remain patient, and the long siege and self-interest will make them forget their prince; to this I answer that a powerful and courageous prince will overcome all such difficulties by giving at one time hope to his subjects that the evil will not be for long, at another time fear of the cruelty of the enemy, then preserving himself adroitly from those subjects who seem to him to be too bold.

Further, the enemy would naturally on his arrival at once burn and ruin the country at the time when the spirits of the people are still hot and ready for the defence; and, therefore, so much the less ought the prince to hesitate; because after a time, when spirits have cooled, the damage is already done, the ills are incurred, and there is no longer any remedy; and therefore they are so much the more ready to unite with their prince, he appearing to be under obligations to them now that their houses have been burnt and their possessions ruined in his defence. For it is the nature of men to be bound by the benefits they confer as much as by those they receive. Therefore, if everything is well considered, it will not be difficult for a wise prince to keep the minds of his citizens steadfast from first to last, when he does not fail to support and defend them.

CHAPTER XI -- CONCERNING ECCLESIASTICAL PRINCIPALITIES

It only remains now to speak of ecclesiastical principalities, touching which all difficulties are prior to getting possession, because they are acquired either by capacity or good fortune, and they can be held without either; for they are sustained by the ancient ordinances of religion, which are so all-powerful, and of such a character that the principalities may be held no matter how their princes behave and live. These princes alone have states and do not defend them; and they have subjects and do not rule them; and the states, although unguarded, are not taken from them, and the subjects, although not ruled, do not

care, and they have neither the desire nor the ability to alienate themselves. Such principalities only are secure and happy. But being upheld by powers, to which the human mind cannot reach, I shall speak no more of them, because, being exalted and maintained by God, it would be the act of a presumptuous and rash man to discuss them.

Nevertheless, if any one should ask of me how comes it that the Church has attained such greatness in temporal power, seeing that from Alexander backwards the Italian potentates (not only those who have been called potentates, but every baron and lord, though the smallest) have valued the temporal power very slightly--yet now a king of France trembles before it, and it has been able to drive him from Italy, and to ruin the Venetians--although this may be very manifest, it does not appear to me superfluous to recall it in some measure to memory.

Before Charles, King of France, passed into Italy, this country was under the dominion of the Pope, the Venetians, the King of Naples, the Duke of Milan, and the Florentines. These potentates had two principal anxieties: the one, that no foreigner should enter Italy under arms; the other, that none of themselves should seize more territory. Those about whom there was the most anxiety were the Pope and the Venetians. To restrain the Venetians the union of all the others was necessary, as it was for the defence of Ferrara; and to keep down the Pope they made use of the barons of Rome, who, being divided into two factions, Orsini and Colonnesi, had always a pretext for disorder, and, standing with arms in their hands under the eyes of the Pontiff, kept the pontificate weak and powerless. And although there might arise sometimes a courageous pope, such as Sixtus, yet neither fortune nor wisdom could rid him of these annoyances. And the short life of a pope is also a cause of weakness; for in the ten years, which is the average life of a pope, he can with difficulty lower one of the factions; and if, so to speak, one people should almost destroy the Colonnesi, another would arise hostile to the Orsini, who would support their opponents, and yet would not have time to ruin the Orsini. This was the reason why the temporal powers of the pope were little esteemed in Italy.

Alexander the Sixth arose afterwards, who of all the pontiffs that have ever been showed how a pope with both money and arms was able to prevail; and through the instrumentality of the Duke Valentino, and by reason of the entry of the French, he brought about all those things which I have discussed above in the actions of the duke. And although his intention was not to aggrandize the Church, but the duke, nevertheless, what he did contributed to the greatness of the Church, which, after his death and the ruin of the duke, became the heir to all his labours.

Pope Julius came afterwards and found the Church strong, possessing all the Romagna, the barons of Rome reduced to impotence, and, through the chastisements of Alexander, the factions wiped out; he also found the way open to accumulate money in a manner such as had never been practised before Alexander's time. Such things Julius not only followed, but improved upon, and he intended to gain Bologna, to ruin the Venetians, and to drive the French out of Italy. All of these enterprises prospered with him, and so much the more to his credit, inasmuch as he did everything to strengthen the Church and not any private person. He kept also the Orsini and Colonnesi factions within the bounds in which he found them; and although there was among them some mind to make disturbance, nevertheless he held two things firm: the one, the greatness of the Church, with which he terrified them; and the other, not allowing them to have their own cardinals, who caused the disorders among them. For whenever these factions have their cardinals they do not remain quiet for long, because cardinals foster the factions in Rome and out of it, and the barons are compelled to support them, and thus from the ambitions of prelates arise disorders and tumults among the barons. For these reasons his Holiness Pope Leo found the pontificate most powerful, and it is to be hoped that, if others made it great in arms, he will make it still greater and more venerated by his goodness and infinite other virtues.

CHAPTER XII -- HOW MANY KINDS OF SOLDIERY THERE ARE, AND CONCERNING MERCENARIES

Having discoursed particularly on the characteristics of such principalities as in the beginning I proposed to discuss, and having considered in some degree the causes of their being good or bad, and having shown the methods by which many have sought to acquire them and to hold them, it now remains for me to discuss generally the means of offence and defence which belong to each of them.

We have seen above how necessary it is for a prince to have his foundations well laid, otherwise it follows of necessity he will go to ruin. The chief foundations of all states, new as well as old or composite, are good laws and good arms; and as there cannot be good laws where the state is not well armed, it follows that where they are well armed they have good laws. I shall leave the laws out of the discussion and shall speak of the arms.

I say, therefore, that the arms with which a prince defends his state are either his own, or they are mercenaries, auxiliaries, or mixed. Mercenaries and auxiliaries are useless and dangerous; and if one holds his state based on these arms, he will stand neither firm nor safe; for they are disunited, ambitious, and without discipline, unfaithful, valiant before friends, cowardly before enemies; they have neither the fear of God nor fidelity to men, and destruction is deferred only so long as the attack is; for in peace one is robbed by them, and in war by the enemy. The fact is, they have no other attraction or reason for keeping the field than a trifle of stipend, which is not sufficient to make them willing to die for you. They are ready enough to be your soldiers whilst you do not make war, but if war comes they take themselves off or run from the foe; which I should have little trouble to prove, for the ruin of Italy has been caused by nothing else than by resting all her hopes for many years on mercenaries, and although they formerly made some display and appeared valiant amongst themselves, yet when the foreigners came they showed what they were.

Thus it was that Charles, King of France, was allowed to seize Italy with chalk in hand; and he who told us that our sins were the cause of it told the truth, but they were not the sins he imagined, but those which I have related. And as they were the sins of princes, it is the princes who have also suffered the penalty.

I wish to demonstrate further the infelicity of these arms. The mercenary captains are either capable men or they are not; if they are, you cannot trust them, because they always aspire to their own greatness, either by oppressing you, who are their master, or others contrary to your intentions; but if the captain is not skillful, you are ruined in the usual way.

And if it be urged that whoever is armed will act in the same way, whether mercenary or not, I reply that when arms have to be resorted to, either by a prince or a republic, then the prince ought to go in person and perform the duty of a captain; the republic has to send its citizens, and when one is sent who does not turn out satisfactorily, it ought to recall him, and when one is worthy, to hold him by the laws so that he does not leave the command. And experience has shown princes and republics, single-handed, making the greatest progress, and mercenaries doing nothing except damage; and it is more difficult to bring a republic, armed with its own arms, under the sway of one of its citizens than it is to bring one armed with foreign arms. Rome and Sparta stood for many ages armed and free. The Switzers are completely armed and quite free.

Of ancient mercenaries, for example, there are the Carthaginians, who were oppressed by their mercenary soldiers after the first war with the Romans, although the Carthaginians had their own citizens for captains. After the death of Epaminondas, Philip of Macedon was made captain of their soldiers by the Thebans, and after victory he took away their liberty.

Duke Filippo being dead, the Milanese enlisted Francesco Sforza against the Venetians, and he, having overcome the enemy at Caravaggio, allied himself with them to crush the Milanese, his masters. His father, Sforza, having been engaged by Queen Johanna of Naples, left her unprotected, so that she was forced to throw herself into the arms of the King of Aragon, in order to save her kingdom. And if the Venetians and Florentines formerly extended their dominions by these arms, and yet their captains did not make themselves princes, but have defended them, I reply that the Florentines in this case have been favoured by chance, for of the able captains, of whom they might have stood in fear, some have not conquered, some have been opposed, and others have turned their ambitions elsewhere. One who did not conquer was Giovanni Acuto, and since he did not conquer his fidelity cannot be proved; but every one will acknowledge that, had he conquered, the Florentines would have stood at his discretion. Sforza had the Bracceschi always against him, so they watched each other. Francesco turned his ambition to Lombardy; Braccio against the Church and the kingdom of Naples. But let us come to that which happened a short while ago. The Florentines appointed as their captain Pagolo Vitelli, a most prudent man, who from a private position had risen to the greatest renown. If this man had taken Pisa, nobody can deny that it would have been proper for the Florentines to keep in with him, for if he became the soldier of their enemies they had no means of resisting, and if they held to him they must obey him. The Venetians, if their achievements are considered, will be seen to have acted safely and gloriously so long as they sent to war their own men, when with armed gentlemen and plebians they did valiantly. This was before they turned to enterprises on land, but when they began to fight on land they forsook this virtue and followed the custom of Italy. And in the beginning of their expansion on land, through not having much territory, and because of their great reputation, they had not much to fear from their captains; but when they expanded, as under Carmignuola, they had a taste of this mistake; for, having found him a most valiant man (they beat the Duke of Milan under his leadership), and, on the other hand, knowing how lukewarm he was in the war, they feared they would no longer conquer under him, and for this reason they were not willing, nor were they able, to let him go; and so, not to lose again that which they had acquired, they were compelled, in order to secure themselves, to murder him. They had afterwards for their captains Bartolomeo da Bergamo, Roberto da San Severino, the count of Pitigliano, and the like, under whom they had to dread loss and not gain, as happened afterwards at Vaila, where in one battle they lost that which in eight hundred years they had acquired with so much trouble. Because from such arms conquests come but slowly, long delayed and inconsiderable, but the losses sudden and portentous.

And as with these examples I have reached Italy, which has been ruled for many years by mercenaries, I wish to discuss them more seriously, in order that, having seen their rise and progress, one may be better prepared to counteract them. You must understand that the empire has recently come to be repudiated in Italy, that the Pope has acquired more temporal power, and that Italy has been divided up into more states, for the reason that many of the great cities took up arms against their nobles, who, formerly favoured by the emperor, were oppressing them, whilst the Church was favouring them so as to gain authority in temporal power: in many others their citizens became princes. From this it came to pass that Italy fell partly into the hands of the Church and of republics, and, the Church consisting of priests and the republic of citizens unaccustomed to arms, both commenced to enlist foreigners.

The first who gave renown to this soldiery was Alberigo da Conio, the Romagnian. From the school of this man sprang, among others, Braccio and Sforza, who in their time were the arbiters of Italy. After these came all the other captains who till now have directed the arms of Italy; and the end of all their valour has been, that she has been overrun by Charles, robbed by Louis, ravaged by Ferdinand, and insulted by the Switzers. The principle that has guided them has been, first, to lower the credit of infantry so that they might increase their own. They did this because, subsisting on their pay and without territory, they were unable to support many soldiers, and a few infantry did not give them any authority; so they were led to employ cavalry, with a moderate

force of which they were maintained and honoured; and affairs were brought to such a pass that, in an army of twenty thousand soldiers, there were not to be found two thousand foot soldiers. They had, besides this, used every art to lessen fatigue and danger to themselves and their soldiers, not killing in the fray, but taking prisoners and liberating without ransom. They did not attack towns at night, nor did the garrisons of the towns attack encampments at night; they did not surround the camp either with stockade or ditch, nor did they campaign in the winter. All these things were permitted by their military rules, and devised by them to avoid, as I have said, both fatigue and dangers; thus they have brought Italy to slavery and contempt.

CHAPTER XIII -- CONCERNING AUXILIARIES, MIXED SOLDIERY, AND ONE'S OWN

Auxiliaries, which are the other useless arm, are employed when a prince is called in with his forces to aid and defend, as was done by Pope Julius in the most recent times; for he, having, in the enterprise against Ferrara, had poor proof of his mercenaries, turned to auxiliaries, and stipulated with Ferdinand, King of Spain, for his assistance with men and arms. These arms may be useful and good in themselves, but for him who calls them in they are always disadvantageous; for losing, one is undone, and winning, one is their captive.

And although ancient histories may be full of examples, I do not wish to leave this recent one of Pope Julius the Second, the peril of which cannot fail to be perceived; for he, wishing to get Ferrara, threw himself entirely into the hands of the foreigner. But his good fortune brought about a third event, so that he did not reap the fruit of his rash choice; because, having his auxiliaries routed at Ravenna, and the Switzers having risen and driven out the conquerors (against all expectation, both his and others), it so came to pass that he did not become prisoner to his enemies, they having fled, nor to his auxiliaries, he having conquered by other arms than theirs.

The Florentines, being entirely without arms, sent ten thousand Frenchmen to take Pisa, whereby they ran more danger than at any other time of their troubles.

The Emperor of Constantinople, to oppose his neighbours, sent ten thousand Turks into Greece, who, on the war being finished, were not willing to quit; this was the beginning of the servitude of Greece to the infidels.

Therefore, let him who has no desire to conquer make use of these arms, for they are much more hazardous than mercenaries, because with them the ruin is ready made; they are all united, all yield obedience to others; but with mercenaries, when they have conquered, more time and better opportunities are needed to injure you; they are not all of one community, they are found and paid by you, and a third party, which you have made their head, is not able all at once to assume enough authority to injure you. In conclusion, in mercenaries dastardy is most dangerous; in auxiliaries, valour. The wise prince, therefore, has always avoided these arms and turned to his own; and has been willing rather to lose with them than to conquer with the others, not deeming that a real victory which is gained with the arms of others.

I shall never hesitate to cite Cesare Borgia and his actions. This duke entered the Romagna with auxiliaries, taking there only French soldiers, and with them he captured Imola and Forli; but afterwards, such forces not appearing to him reliable, he turned to mercenaries, discerning less danger in them, and enlisted the Orsini and Vitelli; whom presently, on handling and finding them doubtful, unfaithful, and dangerous, he destroyed and turned to his own men. And the difference between one and the other of these forces can easily be seen when one considers the difference there was in the reputation of the duke, when he had the French, when he had the Orsini and Vitelli, and when he relied on his own soldiers, on whose fidelity he could always count and found it ever increasing; he was never esteemed more highly than when every one saw that he was complete master of his own forces.

I was not intending to go beyond Italian and recent examples, but I am unwilling to leave out Hiero, the Syracusan, he being one of those I have named above. This man, as I have said, made head of the army by the Syracusans, soon found out that a mercenary soldiery, constituted like our Italian condottieri, was of no use; and it appearing to him that he could neither keep them not let them go, he had them all cut to pieces, and afterwards made war with his own forces and not with aliens.

I wish also to recall to memory an instance from the Old Testament applicable to this subject. David offered himself to Saul to fight with Goliath, the Philistine champion, and, to give him courage, Saul armed him with his own weapons; which David rejected as soon as he had them on his back, saying he could make no use of them, and that he wished to meet the enemy with his sling and his knife. In conclusion, the arms of others either fall from your back, or they weigh you down, or they bind you fast.

Charles the Seventh, the father of King Louis the Eleventh, having by good fortune and valour liberated France from the English, recognized the necessity of being armed with forces of his own, and he established in his kingdom ordinances concerning men-at-arms and infantry. Afterwards his son, King Louis, abolished the infantry and began to enlist the Switzers, which mistake, followed by others, is, as is now seen, a source of peril to that kingdom; because, having raised the reputation of the Switzers, he has entirely diminished the value of his own arms, for he has destroyed the infantry altogether; and his men-at-arms he has subordinated to others, for, being as they are so accustomed to fight along with Switzers, it does not appear that they can now conquer without them. Hence it arises that the French cannot stand against the Switzers, and without the Switzers they do not come off well against others. The armies of the French have thus become mixed, partly mercenary and partly national, both of which arms together are much better than mercenaries alone or auxiliaries alone, but much inferior to one's own forces. And this example proves it, for the kingdom of France would be unconquerable if the ordinance of Charles had been enlarged or maintained.

But the scanty wisdom of man, on entering into an affair which looks well at first, cannot discern the poison that is hidden in it, as I have said above of hectic fevers. Therefore, if he who rules a principality cannot recognize evils until they are upon him, he is not truly wise; and this insight is given to few. And if the first disaster to the Roman Empire should be examined, it will be found to have commenced only with the enlisting of the Goths; because from that time the vigour of the Roman Empire began to decline, and all that valour which had raised it passed away to others.

I conclude, therefore, that no principality is secure without having its own forces; on the contrary, it is entirely dependent on good fortune, not having the valour which in adversity would defend it. And it has always been the opinion and judgment of wise men that nothing can be so uncertain or unstable as fame or power not founded on its own strength. And one's own forces are those which are composed either of subjects, citizens, or dependents; all others are mercenaries or auxiliaries. And the way to make ready one's own forces will be easily found if the rules suggested by me shall be reflected upon, and if one will consider how Philip, the father of Alexander the Great, and many republics and princes have armed and organized themselves, to which rules I entirely commit myself.

CHAPTER XIV -- THAT WHICH CONCERNS A PRINCE ON THE SUBJECT OF THE ART OF WAR

A prince ought to have no other aim or thought, nor select anything else for his study, than war and its rules and discipline; for this is the sole art that belongs to him who rules, and it is of such force that it not only upholds those who are born princes, but it often enables men to rise from a private station to that rank. And, on the contrary, it is seen that when princes have thought more of ease than of arms they have lost their states. And the first cause of your losing it is to neglect this art; and what enables you to acquire a state is to be master of the art. Francesco Sforza, through being martial, from a private person became Duke of Milan; and the sons, through avoiding the hardships and troubles of arms, from dukes became private persons. For among other evils which being

unarmed brings you, it causes you to be despised, and this is one of those ignominies against which a prince ought to guard himself, as is shown later on. Because there is nothing proportionate between the armed and the unarmed; and it is not reasonable that he who is armed should yield obedience willingly to him who is unarmed, or that the unarmed man should be secure among armed servants. Because, there being in the one disdain and in the other suspicion, it is not possible for them to work well together. And therefore a prince who does not understand the art of war, over and above the other misfortunes already mentioned, cannot be respected by his soldiers, nor can he rely on them.

He ought never, therefore, to have out of his thoughts this subject of war, and in peace he should addict himself more to its exercise than in war; this he can do in two ways, the one by action, the other by study.

As regards action, he ought above all things to keep his men well organized and drilled, to follow incessantly the chase, by which he accustoms his body to hardships, and learns something of the nature of localities, and gets to find out how the mountains rise, how the valleys open out, how the plains lie, and to understand the nature of rivers and marshes, and in all this to take the greatest care. Which knowledge is useful in two ways. Firstly, he learns to know his country, and is better able to undertake its defence; afterwards, by means of the knowledge and observation of that locality, he understands with ease any other which it may be necessary for him to study hereafter; because the hills, valleys, and plains, and rivers and marshes that are, for instance, in Tuscany, have a certain resemblance to those of other countries, so that with a knowledge of the aspect of one country one can easily arrive at a knowledge of others. And the prince that lacks this skill lacks the essential which it is desirable that a captain should possess, for it teaches him to surprise his enemy, to select quarters, to lead armies, to array the battle, to besiege towns to advantage.

Philopoemen, Prince of the Achaeans, among other praises which writers have bestowed on him, is commended because in time of peace he never had anything in his mind but the rules of war; and when he was in the country with friends, he often stopped and reasoned with them: "If the enemy should be upon that hill, and we should find ourselves here with our army, with whom would be the advantage? How should one best advance to meet him, keeping the ranks? If we should wish to retreat, how ought we to pursue?" And he would set forth to them, as he went, all the chances that could befall an army; he would listen to their opinion and state his, confirming it with reasons, so that by these continual discussions there could never arise, in time of war, any unexpected circumstances that he could not deal with.

But to exercise the intellect the prince should read histories, and study there the actions of illustrious men, to see how they have borne themselves in war, to examine the causes of their victories and defeat, so as to avoid the latter and imitate the former; and above all do as an illustrious man did, who took as an exemplar one who had been praised and famous before him, and whose achievements and deeds he always kept in his mind, as it is said Alexander the Great imitated Achilles, Caesar Alexander, Scipio Cyrus. And whoever reads the life of Cyrus, written by Xenophon, will recognize afterwards in the life of Scipio how that imitation was his glory, and how in chastity, affability, humanity, and liberality Scipio conformed to those things which have been written of Cyrus by Xenophon. A wise prince ought to observe some such rules, and never in peaceful times stand idle, but increase his resources with industry in such a way that they may be available to him in adversity, so that if fortune chances it may find him prepared to resist her blows.

CHAPTER XV -- CONCERNING THINGS FOR WHICH MEN, AND ESPECIALLY PRINCES, ARE PRAISED OR BLAMED

It remains now to see what ought to be the rules of conduct for a prince towards subject and friends. And as I know that many have written on this point, I expect I shall be considered presumptuous in mentioning it again, especially as in discussing it I shall depart from the methods of other people. But, it being my intention to write a thing which shall be useful to him who apprehends it, it appears to me more appropriate to follow up the real truth of the matter than the imagination of it; for many have pictured republics and principalities which in fact have never been known or seen, because how one lives is so far distant from how one ought to live, that he who neglects what is done for what ought to be done, sooner effects his ruin than his preservation; for a man who wishes to act entirely up to his professions of virtue soon meets with what destroys him among so much that is evil.

Hence it is necessary for a prince wishing to hold his own to know how to do wrong, and to make use of it or not according to necessity. Therefore, putting on one side imaginary things concerning a prince, and discussing those which are real, I say that all men when they are spoken of, and chiefly princes for being more highly placed, are remarkable for some of those qualities which bring them either blame or praise; and thus it is that one is reputed liberal, another miserly, using a Tuscan term (because an avaricious person in our language is still he who desires to possess by robbery, whilst we call one miserly who deprives himself too much of the use of his own); one is reputed generous, one rapacious; one cruel, one compassionate; one faithless, another faithful; one effeminate and cowardly, another bold and brave; one affable, another haughty; one lascivious, another chaste; one sincere, another cunning; one hard, another easy; one grave, another frivolous; one religious, another unbelieving, and the like. And I know that every one will confess that it would be most praiseworthy in a prince to exhibit all the above qualities that are considered good; but because they can neither be entirely possessed nor observed, for human conditions do not permit it, it is necessary for him to be sufficiently prudent that he may know how to avoid the reproach of those vices which would lose him his state; and also to keep himself, if it be possible, from those which would not lose him it; but this not being possible, he may with less hesitation abandon himself to them. And again, he need not make himself uneasy at incurring a reproach for those vices without which the state can only be saved with difficulty, for if everything is considered carefully, it will be found that something which looks like virtue, if followed, would be his ruin; whilst something else, which looks like vice, yet followed brings him security and prosperity.

CHAPTER XVI -- CONCERNING LIBERALITY AND MEANNESS

Commencing then with the first of the above-named characteristics, I say that it would be well to be reputed liberal. Nevertheless, liberality exercised in a way that does not bring you the reputation for it, injures you; for if one exercises it honestly and as it should be exercised, it may not become known, and you will not avoid the reproach of its opposite. Therefore, any one wishing to maintain among men the name of liberal is obliged to avoid no attribute of magnificence; so that a prince thus inclined will consume in such acts all his property, and will be compelled in the end, if he wish to maintain the name of liberal, to unduly weigh down his people, and tax them, and do everything he can to get money. This will soon make him odious to his subjects, and becoming poor he will be little valued by any one; thus, with his liberality, having offended many and rewarded few, he is affected by the very first trouble and imperilled by whatever may be the first danger; recognizing this himself, and wishing to draw back from it, he runs at once into the reproach of being miserly.

Therefore, a prince, not being able to exercise this virtue of liberality in such a way that it is recognized, except to his cost, if he is wise he ought not to fear the reputation of being mean, for in time he will come to be more considered than if liberal, seeing that with his economy his revenues are enough, that he can defend himself against all attacks, and is able to engage in enterprises without burdening his people; thus it comes to pass that he exercises liberality towards all from whom he does not take, who are numberless, and meanness towards those to whom he does not give, who are few.

We have not seen great things done in our time except by those who have been considered mean; the rest have failed. Pope Julius the Second was assisted in reaching the papacy by a reputation for liberality, yet he did not strive afterwards to keep it up, when he made war on the King of France; and he made many wars without imposing any extraordinary tax on his subjects, for he supplied his additional expenses out of his long thriftiness. The present King of Spain would not have undertaken or conquered in so many enterprises if he had been reputed liberal. A prince, therefore, provided that he has not to rob his subjects, that he can defend himself, that he does not become poor and abject, that he is not forced to become rapacious, ought to hold of little account a reputation for being mean, for it is one of those vices which will enable him to govern.

And if any one should say: Caesar obtained empire by liberality, and many others have reached the highest positions by having been liberal, and by being considered so, I answer: Either you are a prince in fact, or in a way to become one. In the first case this liberality is dangerous, in the second it is very necessary to be considered liberal; and Caesar was one of those who wished to become pre-eminent in Rome; but if he had survived after becoming so, and had not moderated his expenses, he would have destroyed his government. And if any one should reply: Many have been princes, and have done great things with armies, who have been considered very liberal, I reply: Either a prince spends that which is his own or his subjects' or else that of others. In the first case he ought to be sparing, in the second he ought not to neglect any opportunity for liberality. And to the prince who goes forth with his army, supporting it by pillage, sack, and extortion, handling that which belongs to others, this liberality is necessary, otherwise he would not be followed by soldiers. And of that which is neither yours nor your subjects' you can be a ready giver, as were Cyrus, Caesar, and

Alexander; because it does not take away your reputation if you squander that of others, but adds to it; it is only squandering your own that injures you.

And there is nothing wastes so rapidly as liberality, for even whilst you exercise it you lose the power to do so, and so become either poor or despised, or else, in avoiding poverty, rapacious and hated. And a prince should guard himself, above all things, against being despised and hated; and liberality leads you to both. Therefore it is wiser to have a reputation for meanness which brings reproach without hatred, than to be compelled through seeking a reputation for liberality to incur a name for rapacity which begets reproach with hatred.

CHAPTER XVII -- CONCERNING CRUELTY AND CLEMENCY, AND WHETHER IT IS BETTER TO BE LOVED THAN FEARED

Coming now to the other qualities mentioned above, I say that every prince ought to desire to be considered clement and not cruel. Nevertheless he ought to take care not to misuse this clemency. Cesare Borgia was considered cruel; notwithstanding, his cruelty reconciled the Romagna, unified it, and restored it to peace and loyalty. And if this be rightly considered, he will be seen to have been much more merciful than the Florentine people, who, to avoid a reputation for cruelty, permitted Pistoia to be destroyed. Therefore a prince, so long as he keeps his subjects united and loyal, ought not to mind the reproach of cruelty; because with a few examples he will be more merciful than those who, through too much mercy, allow disorders to arise, from which follow murders or robberies; for these are wont to injure the whole people, whilst those executions which originate with a prince offend the individual only.

And of all princes, it is impossible for the new prince to avoid the imputation of cruelty, owing to new states being full of dangers. Hence Virgil, through the mouth of Dido, excuses the inhumanity of her reign owing to its being new, saying:

"Res dura, et regni novitas me talia cogunt

Moliri, et late fines custode tueri."[229]

Nevertheless he ought to be slow to believe and to act, nor should he himself show fear, but proceed in a temperate manner with prudence and humanity, so that too much confidence may not make him incautious and too much distrust render him intolerable.

Upon this a question arises: whether it be better to be loved than feared or feared than loved? It may be answered that one should wish to be both, but, because it is difficult to unite them in one person, it is much safer to be feared than loved, when, of the two, either must be dispensed with. Because this is to be asserted in general of men, that they are ungrateful, fickle, false, cowardly, covetous, and as long as you succeed they are yours entirely; they will offer you their blood, property, life, and children, as is said above, when the need is far distant; but when it approaches they turn against you. And that prince who, relying entirely on their promises, has neglected other precautions, is ruined; because friendships that are obtained by payments, and not by greatness or nobility of mind, may indeed be earned, but they are not secured, and in time of need cannot be relied upon; and men have less scruple in offending one who is beloved than one who is feared, for love is preserved by the link of obligation which, owing to the baseness of men, is broken at every opportunity for their advantage; but fear preserves you by a dread of punishment which never fails.

Nevertheless a prince ought to inspire fear in such a way that, if he does not win love, he avoids hatred; because he can endure very well being feared whilst he is not hated, which will always be as long as he abstains from the property of his citizens and subjects and from their women. But when it is necessary for him to proceed against the life of someone, he must do it on proper justification and for manifest cause, but above all things he must keep his hands off the property of others, because men more quickly forget the

---

[229] against my will, my fate
A throne unsettled, and an infant state,

Bid me defend my realms with all my pow'rs,
And guard with these severities my shores.

death of their father than the loss of their patrimony. Besides, pretexts for taking away the property are never wanting; for he who has once begun to live by robbery will always find pretexts for seizing what belongs to others; but reasons for taking life, on the contrary, are more difficult to find and sooner lapse. But when a prince is with his army, and has under control a multitude of soldiers, then it is quite necessary for him to disregard the reputation of cruelty, for without it he would never hold his army united or disposed to its duties.

Among the wonderful deeds of Hannibal this one is enumerated: that having led an enormous army, composed of many various races of men, to fight in foreign lands, no dissensions arose either among them or against the prince, whether in his bad or in his good fortune. This arose from nothing else than his inhuman cruelty, which, with his boundless valour, made him revered and terrible in the sight of his soldiers, but without that cruelty, his other virtues were not sufficient to produce this effect. And short-sighted writers admire his deeds from one point of view and from another condemn the principal cause of them. That it is true his other virtues would not have been sufficient for him may be proved by the case of Scipio, that most excellent man, not only of his own times but within the memory of man, against whom, nevertheless, his army rebelled in Spain; this arose from nothing but his too great forbearance, which gave his soldiers more license than is consistent with military discipline. For this he was upbraided in the Senate by Fabius Maximus, and called the corrupter of the Roman soldiery. The Locrians were laid waste by a legate of Scipio, yet they were not avenged by him, nor was the insolence of the legate punished, owing entirely to his easy nature. Insomuch that someone in the Senate, wishing to excuse him, said there were many men who knew much better how not to err than to correct the errors of others. This disposition, if he had been continued in the command, would have destroyed in time the fame and glory of Scipio; but, he being under the control of the Senate, this injurious characteristic not only concealed itself, but contributed to his glory.

Returning to the question of being feared or loved, I come to the conclusion that, men loving according to their own will and fearing according to that of the prince, a wise prince should establish himself on that which is in his own control and not in that of others; he must endeavour only to avoid hatred, as is noted.

CHAPTER XVIII -- CONCERNING THE WAY IN WHICH PRINCES SHOULD KEEP FAITH

Every one admits how praiseworthy it is in a prince to keep faith, and to live with integrity and not with craft. Nevertheless our experience has been that those princes who have done great things have held good faith of little account, and have known how to circumvent the intellect of men by craft, and in the end have overcome those who have relied on their word. You must know there are two ways of contesting, the one by the law, the other by force; the first method is proper to men, the second to beasts; but because the first is frequently not sufficient, it is necessary to have recourse to the second. Therefore it is necessary for a prince to understand how to avail himself of the beast and the man. This has been figuratively taught to princes by ancient writers, who describe how Achilles and many other princes of old were given to the Centaur Chiron to nurse, who brought them up in his discipline; which means solely that, as they had for a teacher one who was half beast and half man, so it is necessary for a prince to know how to make use of both natures, and that one without the other is not durable. A prince, therefore, being compelled knowingly to adopt the beast, ought to choose the fox and the lion; because the lion cannot defend himself against snares and the fox cannot defend himself against wolves. Therefore, it is necessary to be a fox to discover the snares and a lion to terrify the wolves. Those who rely simply on the lion do not understand what they are about. Therefore a wise lord cannot, nor ought he to, keep faith when such observance may be turned against him, and when the reasons that caused him to pledge it exist no longer. If men were entirely good this precept would not hold, but because they are bad, and will not keep faith with you, you too are not bound to observe it with them. Nor will there ever be wanting to a prince legitimate reasons to excuse this non-observance. Of this endless modern examples could be given, showing how many treaties and engagements have been made void and of no effect through the faithlessness of princes; and he who has known best how to employ the fox has succeeded best.

But it is necessary to know well how to disguise this characteristic, and to be a great pretender and dissembler; and men are so simple, and so subject to present necessities, that he who seeks to deceive will always find someone who will allow himself to be deceived. One recent example I cannot pass over in silence. Alexander the Sixth did nothing else but deceive men, nor ever thought of doing otherwise, and he always found victims; for there never was a man who had greater power in asserting, or who with greater oaths would affirm a thing, yet would observe it less; nevertheless his deceits always succeeded according to his wishes, because he well understood this side of mankind.

> Alexander never did what he said,
> Cesare never said what he did.--Italian Proverb.

Therefore it is unnecessary for a prince to have all the good qualities I have enumerated, but it is very necessary to appear to have them. And I shall dare to say this also, that to have them and always to observe them is injurious, and that to appear to have them is useful; to appear merciful, faithful, humane, religious, upright, and to be so, but with a mind so framed that should you require not to be so, you may be able and know how to change to the opposite.

And you have to understand this, that a prince, especially a new one, cannot observe all those things for which men are esteemed, being often forced, in order to maintain the state, to act contrary to fidelity, friendship, humanity, and religion. Therefore it is necessary for him to have a mind ready to turn itself accordingly as the winds and variations of fortune force it, yet, as I have said above, not to diverge from the good if he can avoid doing so, but, if compelled, then to know how to set about it.

For this reason a prince ought to take care that he never lets anything slip from his lips that is not replete with the above-named five qualities, that he may appear to him who sees and hears him altogether merciful, faithful, humane, upright, and religious. There is nothing more necessary to appear to have than this last quality, inasmuch as men judge generally more by the eye than by the hand, because it belongs to everybody to see you, to few to come in touch with you. Every one sees what you appear to be, few really know what you are, and those few dare not oppose themselves to the opinion of the many, who have the majesty of the state to defend them; and in the actions of all men, and especially of princes, which it is not prudent to challenge, one judges by the result.

For that reason, let a prince have the credit of conquering and holding his state, the means will always be considered honest, and he will be praised by everybody; because the vulgar are always taken by what a thing seems to be and by what comes of it; and in the world there are only the vulgar, for the few find a place there only when the many have no ground to rest on.

One prince of the present time, whom it is not well to name, never preaches anything else but peace and good faith, and to both he is most hostile, and either, if he had kept it, would have deprived him of reputation and kingdom many a time.

CHAPTER XIX -- THAT ONE SHOULD AVOID BEING DESPISED AND HATED

Now, concerning the characteristics of which mention is made above, I have spoken of the more important ones, the others I wish to discuss briefly under this generality, that the prince must consider, as has been in part said before, how to avoid those things which will make him hated or contemptible; and as often as he shall have succeeded he will have fulfilled his part, and he need not fear any danger in other reproaches.

It makes him hated above all things, as I have said, to be rapacious, and to be a violator of the property and women of his subjects, from both of which he must abstain. And when neither their property nor their honor is touched, the majority of men live content, and he has only to contend with the ambition of a few, whom he can curb with ease in many ways.

It makes him contemptible to be considered fickle, frivolous, effeminate, mean-spirited, irresolute, from all of which a prince should guard himself as from a rock; and he should endeavour to show in his actions greatness, courage, gravity, and fortitude; and in his private dealings with his subjects let him show that his judgments are irrevocable, and maintain himself in such reputation that no one can hope either to deceive him or to get round him.

That prince is highly esteemed who conveys this impression of himself, and he who is highly esteemed is not easily conspired against; for, provided it is well known that he is an excellent man and revered by his people, he can only be attacked with difficulty. For this reason a prince ought to have two fears, one from within, on account of his subjects, the other from without, on account of external powers. From the latter he is defended by being well armed and having good allies, and if he is well armed he will have good friends, and affairs will always remain quiet within when they are quiet without, unless they should have been already disturbed by conspiracy; and even should affairs outside be disturbed, if he has carried out his preparations and has lived as I have said, as long as he does not despair, he will resist every attack, as I said Nabis the Spartan did.

But concerning his subjects, when affairs outside are disturbed he has only to fear that they will conspire secretly, from which a prince can easily secure himself by avoiding being hated and despised, and by keeping the people satisfied with him, which it is most necessary for him to accomplish, as I said above at length. And one of the most efficacious remedies that a prince can have against conspiracies is not to be hated and despised by the people, for he who conspires against a prince always expects to please them by his removal; but when the conspirator can only look forward to offending them, he will not have the courage to take such a course, for the difficulties that confront a conspirator are

infinite. And as experience shows, many have been the conspiracies, but few have been successful; because he who conspires cannot act alone, nor can he take a companion except from those whom he believes to be malcontents, and as soon as you have opened your mind to a malcontent you have given him the material with which to content himself, for by denouncing you he can look for every advantage; so that, seeing the gain from this course to be assured, and seeing the other to be doubtful and full of dangers, he must be a very rare friend, or a thoroughly obstinate enemy of the prince, to keep faith with you.

And, to reduce the matter into a small compass, I say that, on the side of the conspirator, there is nothing but fear, jealousy, prospect of punishment to terrify him; but on the side of the prince there is the majesty of the principality, the laws, the protection of friends and the state to defend him; so that, adding to all these things the popular goodwill, it is impossible that any one should be so rash as to conspire. For whereas in general the conspirator has to fear before the execution of his plot, in this case he has also to fear the sequel to the crime; because on account of it he has the people for an enemy, and thus cannot hope for any escape.

Endless examples could be given on this subject, but I will be content with one, brought to pass within the memory of our fathers. Messer Annibale Bentivogli, who was prince in Bologna (grandfather of the present Annibale), having been murdered by the Canneschi, who had conspired against him, not one of his family survived but Messer Giovanni, who was in childhood: immediately after his assassination the people rose and murdered all the Canneschi. This sprung from the popular goodwill which the house of Bentivogli enjoyed in those days in Bologna; which was so great that, although none remained there after the death of Annibale who was able to rule the state, the Bolognese, having information that there was one of the Bentivogli family in Florence, who up to that time had been considered the son of a blacksmith, sent to Florence for him and gave him the government of their city, and it was ruled by him until Messer Giovanni came in due course to the government.

For this reason I consider that a prince ought to reckon conspiracies of little account when his people hold him in esteem; but when it is hostile to him, and bears hatred towards him, he ought to fear everything and everybody. And well-ordered states and wise princes have taken every care not to drive the nobles to desperation, and to keep the people satisfied and contented, for this is one of the most important objects a prince can have.

Among the best ordered and governed kingdoms of our times is France, and in it are found many good institutions on which depend the liberty and security of the king; of these the first is the parliament and its authority, because he who founded the kingdom, knowing the ambition of the nobility and their boldness, considered that a bit to their mouths would be necessary to hold them in; and, on the other side, knowing the hatred of the people, founded in fear, against the nobles, he wished to protect them, yet he was not anxious for this to be the particular care of the king; therefore, to take away the reproach which he would be liable to from the nobles for favouring the people, and from the people for favouring the nobles, he set up an arbiter, who should be one who could beat down the great and favour the lesser without reproach to the king. Neither could you have a better or a more prudent arrangement, or a greater source of security to the king and kingdom. From this one can draw another important conclusion, that princes ought to leave affairs of reproach to the management of others, and keep those of grace in their own hands. And further, I consider that a prince ought to cherish the nobles, but not so as to make himself hated by the people.

It may appear, perhaps, to some who have examined the lives and deaths of the Roman emperors that many of them would be an example contrary to my opinion, seeing that some of them lived nobly and showed great qualities of soul, nevertheless they have lost their empire or have been killed by subjects who have conspired against them. Wishing, therefore, to answer these objections, I will recall the characters of some of the emperors, and will show that the causes of their ruin were not different to those alleged by me; at the same time I will only submit for consideration those things that are noteworthy to him who studies the affairs of those times.

It seems to me sufficient to take all those emperors who succeeded to the empire from Marcus the philosopher down to Maximinus; they were Marcus and his son Commodus, Pertinax, Julian, Severus and his son Antoninus Caracalla, Macrinus, Heliogabalus, Alexander, and Maximinus.

There is first to note that, whereas in other principalities the ambition of the nobles and the insolence of the people only have to be contended with, the Roman emperors had a third difficulty in having to put up with the cruelty and avarice of their soldiers, a matter so beset with difficulties that it was the ruin of many; for it was a hard thing to give satisfaction both to soldiers and people; because the people loved peace, and for this reason they loved the unaspiring prince, whilst the soldiers loved the warlike prince who was bold, cruel, and rapacious, which qualities they were quite willing he should exercise upon the people, so that they could get double pay and give vent to their own greed and cruelty. Hence it arose that those emperors were always overthrown who, either by birth or training, had no great authority, and most of them, especially those who came new to the principality, recognizing the difficulty of these two opposing humours, were inclined to give satisfaction to the soldiers, caring little about injuring the people. Which course was necessary, because, as princes cannot help being hated by someone, they ought, in the first place, to avoid being hated by every one, and when they cannot compass this, they ought to endeavour with the utmost diligence to avoid the hatred of the most powerful. Therefore, those emperors who through inexperience had need of special favour adhered more readily to the soldiers than to the people; a course which turned out advantageous to them or not, accordingly as the prince knew how to maintain authority over them.

From these causes it arose that Marcus, Pertinax, and Alexander, being all men of modest life, lovers of justice, enemies to cruelty, humane, and benignant, came to a sad end except Marcus; he alone lived and died honoured, because he had succeeded to the throne by hereditary title, and owed nothing either to the soldiers or the people; and afterwards, being possessed of many virtues which made him respected, he always kept both orders in their places whilst he lived, and was neither hated nor despised.

But Pertinax was created emperor against the wishes of the soldiers, who, being accustomed to live licentiously under Commodus, could not endure the honest life to which Pertinax wished to reduce them; thus, having given cause for hatred, to which hatred there was added contempt for his old age, he was overthrown at the very beginning of his administration. And here it should be noted that hatred is acquired as much by good works as by bad ones, therefore, as I said before, a prince wishing to keep his state is very often forced to do evil; for when that body is corrupt whom you think you have need of to maintain yourself—it may be either the people or the soldiers or the nobles--you have to submit to its humours and to gratify them, and then good works will do you harm.

But let us come to Alexander, who was a man of such great goodness, that among the other praises which are accorded him is this, that in the fourteen years he held the empire no one was ever put to death by him unjudged; nevertheless, being considered effeminate and a man who allowed himself to be governed by his mother, he became despised, the army conspired against him, and murdered him.

Turning now to the opposite characters of Commodus, Severus, Antoninus Caracalla, and Maximinus, you will find them all cruel and rapacious-men who, to satisfy their soldiers, did not hesitate to commit every kind of iniquity against the people; and all, except Severus, came to a bad end; but in Severus there was so much valour that, keeping the soldiers friendly, although the people were oppressed by him, he reigned successfully; for his valour made him so much admired in the sight of the soldiers and

people that the latter were kept in a way astonished and awed and the former respectful and satisfied. And because the actions of this man, as a new prince, were great, I wish to show briefly that he knew well how to counterfeit the fox and the lion, which natures, as I said above, it is necessary for a prince to imitate.

Knowing the sloth of the Emperor Julian, he persuaded the army in Sclavonia, of which he was captain, that it would be right to go to Rome and avenge the death of Pertinax, who had been killed by the praetorian soldiers; and under this pretext, without appearing to aspire to the throne, he moved the army on Rome, and reached Italy before it was known that he had started. On his arrival at Rome, the Senate, through fear, elected him emperor and killed Julian. After this there remained for Severus, who wished to make himself master of the whole empire, two difficulties; one in Asia, where Niger, head of the Asiatic army, had caused himself to be proclaimed emperor; the other in the west where Albinus was, who also aspired to the throne. And as he considered it dangerous to declare himself hostile to both, he decided to attack Niger and to deceive Albinus. To the latter he wrote that, being elected emperor by the Senate, he was willing to share that dignity with him and sent him the title of Caesar; and, moreover, that the Senate had made Albinus his colleague; which things were accepted by Albinus as true. But after Severus had conquered and killed Niger, and settled oriental affairs, he returned to Rome and complained to the Senate that Albinus, little recognizing the benefits that he had received from him, had by treachery sought to murder him, and for this ingratitude he was compelled to punish him. Afterwards he sought him out in France, and took from him his government and life. He who will, therefore, carefully examine the actions of this man will find him a most valiant lion and a most cunning fox; he will find him feared and respected by every one, and not hated by the army; and it need not be wondered at that he, a new man, was able to hold the empire so well, because his supreme renown always protected him from that hatred which the people might have conceived against him for his violence.

But his son Antoninus was a most eminent man, and had very excellent qualities, which made him admirable in the sight of the people and acceptable to the soldiers, for he was a warlike man, most enduring of fatigue, a despiser of all delicate food and other luxuries, which caused him to be beloved by the armies. Nevertheless, his ferocity and cruelties were so great and so unheard of that, after endless single murders, he killed a large number of the people of Rome and all those of Alexandria. He became hated by the whole world, and also feared by those he had around him, to such an extent that he was murdered in the midst of his army by a centurion. And here it must be noted that such-like deaths, which are deliberately inflicted with a resolved and desperate courage, cannot be avoided by princes, because any one who does not fear to die can inflict them; but a prince may fear them the less because they are very rare; he has only to be careful not to do any grave injury to those whom he employs or has around him in the service of the state.

Antoninus had not taken this care, but had contumeliously killed a brother of that centurion, whom also he daily threatened, yet retained in his bodyguard; which, as it turned out, was a rash thing to do, and proved the emperor's ruin.

But let us come to Commodus, to whom it should have been very easy to hold the empire, for, being the son of Marcus, he had inherited it, and he had only to follow in the footsteps of his father to please his people and soldiers; but, being by nature cruel and brutal, he gave himself up to amusing the soldiers and corrupting them, so that he might indulge his rapacity upon the people; on the other hand, not maintaining his dignity, often descending to the theatre to compete with gladiators, and doing other vile things, little worthy of the imperial majesty, he fell into contempt with the soldiers, and being hated by one party and despised by the other, he was conspired against and was killed.

It remains to discuss the character of Maximinus. He was a very warlike man, and the armies, being disgusted with the effeminacy of Alexander, of whom I have already spoken, killed him and elected Maximinus to the throne. This he did not possess for long, for two things made him hated and despised; the one, his having kept sheep in Thrace, which brought him into contempt (it being well known to all, and considered a great indignity by every one), and the other, his having at the accession to his dominions deferred going to Rome and taking possession of the imperial seat; he had also gained a reputation for the utmost ferocity by having, through his prefects in Rome and elsewhere in the empire, practised many cruelties, so that the whole world was moved to anger at the meanness of his birth and to fear at his barbarity. First Africa rebelled, then the Senate with all the people of Rome, and all Italy conspired against him, to which may be added his own army; this latter, besieging Aquileia and meeting with difficulties in taking it, were disgusted with his cruelties, and fearing him less when they found so many against him, murdered him.

I do not wish to discuss Heliogabalus, Macrinus, or Julian, who, being thoroughly contemptible, were quickly wiped out; but I will bring this discourse to a conclusion by saying that princes in our times have this difficulty of giving inordinate satisfaction to their soldiers in a far less degree, because, notwithstanding one has to give them some indulgence, that is soon done; none of these princes have armies that are veterans in the governance and administration of provinces, as were the armies of the Roman Empire; and whereas it was then more necessary to give satisfaction to the soldiers than to the people, it is now more necessary to all princes, except the Turk and the Soldan, to satisfy the people rather the soldiers, because the people are the more powerful.

From the above I have excepted the Turk, who always keeps round him twelve thousand infantry and fifteen thousand cavalry on which depend the security and strength of the kingdom, and it is necessary that, putting aside every consideration for the people, he should keep them his friends. The kingdom of the Soldan is similar; being entirely in the hands of soldiers, it follows again that, without regard to the people, he must keep them his friends. But you must note that the state of the Soldan is unlike all other principalities, for the reason that it is like the Christian pontificate, which cannot be called either an hereditary or a newly formed principality; because the sons of the old prince are not the heirs, but he who is elected to that position by those who have authority, and the sons remain only noblemen. And this being an ancient custom, it cannot be called a new principality, because there are none of those difficulties in it that are met with in new ones; for although the prince is new, the constitution of the state is old, and it is framed so as to receive him as if he were its hereditary lord.

But returning to the subject of our discourse, I say that whoever will consider it will acknowledge that either hatred or contempt has been fatal to the above-named emperors, and it will be recognized also how it happened that, a number of them acting in one way and a number in another, only one in each way came to a happy end and the rest to unhappy ones. Because it would have been useless and dangerous for Pertinax and Alexander, being new princes, to imitate Marcus, who was heir to the principality; and likewise it would have been utterly destructive to Caracalla, Commodus, and Maximinus to have imitated Severus, they not having sufficient valour to enable them to tread in his footsteps. Therefore a prince, new to the principality, cannot imitate the actions of Marcus, nor, again, is it necessary to follow those of Severus, but he ought to take from Severus those parts which are necessary to found his state, and from Marcus those which are proper and glorious to keep a state that may already be stable and firm.

CHAPTER XX -- ARE FORTRESSES, AND MANY OTHER THINGS TO WHICH PRINCES OFTEN RESORT, ADVANTAGEOUS OR HURTFUL?

1. Some princes, so as to hold securely the state, have disarmed their subjects; others have kept their subject towns distracted by factions; others have fostered enmities against themselves; others have laid themselves out to gain over those whom they distrusted in the beginning of their governments; some have built fortresses; some have overthrown and destroyed them. And although one cannot give a final judgment on all of these things unless one possesses the particulars of those states in which a decision has to be made, nevertheless I will speak as comprehensively as the matter of itself will admit.

2. There never was a new prince who has disarmed his subjects; rather when he has found them disarmed he has always armed them, because, by arming them, those arms become yours, those men who were distrusted become faithful, and those who were faithful are kept so, and your subjects become your adherents. And whereas all subjects cannot be armed, yet when those whom you do arm are benefited, the others can be handled more freely, and this difference in their treatment, which they quite understand, makes the former your dependents, and the latter, considering it to be necessary that those who have the most danger and service should have the most reward, excuse you. But when you disarm them, you at once offend them by showing that you distrust them, either for cowardice or for want of loyalty, and either of these opinions breeds hatred against you. And because you cannot remain unarmed, it follows that you turn to mercenaries, which are of the character already shown; even if they should be good they would not be sufficient to defend you against powerful enemies and distrusted subjects. Therefore, as I have said, a new prince in a new principality has always distributed arms. Histories are full of examples. But when a prince acquires a new state, which he adds as a province to his old one, then it is necessary to disarm the men of that state, except those who have been his adherents in acquiring it; and these again, with time and opportunity, should be rendered soft and effeminate; and matters should be managed in such a way that all the armed men in the state shall be your own soldiers who in your old state were living near you.

3. Our forefathers, and those who were reckoned wise, were accustomed to say that it was necessary to hold Pistoia by factions and Pisa by fortresses; and with this idea they fostered quarrels in some of their tributary towns so as to

keep possession of them the more easily. This may have been well enough in those times when Italy was in a way balanced, but I do not believe that it can be accepted as a precept for to-day, because I do not believe that factions can ever be of use; rather it is certain that when the enemy comes upon you in divided cities you are quickly lost, because the weakest party will always assist the outside forces and the other will not be able to resist. The Venetians, moved, as I believe, by the above reasons, fostered the Guelph and Ghibelline factions in their tributary cities; and although they never allowed them to come to bloodshed, yet they nursed these disputes amongst them, so that the citizens, distracted by their differences, should not unite against them. Which, as we saw, did not afterwards turn out as expected, because, after the rout at Vaila, one party at once took courage and seized the state. Such methods argue, therefore, weakness in the prince, because these factions will never be permitted in a vigorous principality; such methods for enabling one the more easily to manage subjects are only useful in times of peace, but if war comes this policy proves fallacious.

4. Without doubt princes become great when they overcome the difficulties and obstacles by which they are confronted, and therefore fortune, especially when she desires to make a new prince great, who has a greater necessity to earn renown than an hereditary one, causes enemies to arise and form designs against him, in order that he may have the opportunity of overcoming them, and by them to mount higher, as by a ladder which his enemies have raised. For this reason many consider that a wise prince, when he has the opportunity, ought with craft to foster some animosity against himself, so that, having crushed it, his renown may rise higher.

5. Princes, especially new ones, have found more fidelity and assistance in those men who in the beginning of their rule were distrusted than among those who in the beginning were trusted. Pandolfo Petrucci, Prince of Siena, ruled his state more by those who had been distrusted than by others. But on this question one cannot speak generally, for it varies so much with the individual; I will only say this, that those men who

at the commencement of a princedom have been hostile, if they are of a description to need assistance to support themselves, can always be gained over with the greatest ease, and they will be tightly held to serve the prince with fidelity, inasmuch as they know it to be very necessary for them to cancel by deeds the bad impression which he had formed of them; and thus the prince always extracts more profit from them than from those who, serving him in too much security, may neglect his affairs. And since the matter demands it, I must not fail to warn a prince, who by means of secret favours has acquired a new state, that he must well consider the reasons which induced those to favour him who did so; and if it be not a natural affection towards him, but only discontent with their government, then he will only keep them friendly with great trouble and difficulty, for it will be impossible to satisfy them. And weighing well the reasons for this in those examples which can be taken from ancient and modern affairs, we shall find that it is easier for the prince to make friends of those men who were contented under the former government, and are therefore his enemies, than of those who, being discontented with it, were favourable to him and encouraged him to seize it.

6. It has been a custom with princes, in order to hold their states more securely, to build fortresses that may serve as a bridle and bit to those who might design to work against them, and as a place of refuge from a first attack. I praise this system because it has been made use of formerly. Notwithstanding that, Messer Nicolo Vitelli in our times has been seen to demolish two fortresses in Citta di Castello so that he might keep that state; Guido Ubaldo, Duke of Urbino, on returning to his dominion, whence he had been driven by Cesare Borgia, razed to the foundations all the fortresses in that province, and considered that without them it would be more difficult to lose it; the Bentivogli returning to Bologna came to a similar decision. Fortresses, therefore, are useful or not according to circumstances; if they do you good in one way they injure you in another. And this question can be reasoned thus: the prince who has more to fear from the people than from foreigners ought to build fortresses,

but he who has more to fear from foreigners than from the people ought to leave them alone. The castle of Milan, built by Francesco Sforza, has made, and will make, more trouble for the house of Sforza than any other disorder in the state. For this reason the best possible fortress is--not to be hated by the people, because, although you may hold the fortresses, yet they will not save you if the people hate you, for there will never be wanting foreigners to assist a people who have taken arms against you. It has not been seen in our times that such fortresses have been of use to any prince, unless to the Countess of Forli, when the Count Girolamo, her consort, was killed; for by that means she was able to withstand the popular attack and wait for assistance from Milan, and thus recover her state; and the posture of affairs was such at that time that the foreigners could not assist the people. But fortresses were of little value to her afterwards when Cesare Borgia attacked her, and when the people, her enemy, were allied with foreigners. Therefore, it would have been safer for her, both then and before, not to have been hated by the people than to have had the fortresses. All these things considered then, I shall praise him who builds fortresses as well as him who does not, and I shall blame whoever, trusting in them, cares little about being hated by the people.

CHAPTER XXI -- HOW A PRINCE SHOULD CONDUCT HIMSELF SO AS TO GAIN RENOWN

Nothing makes a prince so much esteemed as great enterprises and setting a fine example. We have in our time Ferdinand of Aragon, the present King of Spain. He can almost be called a new prince, because he has risen, by fame and glory, from being an insignificant king to be the foremost king in Christendom; and if you will consider his deeds you will find them all great and some of them extraordinary. In the beginning of his reign he attacked Granada, and this enterprise was the foundation of his dominions. He did this quietly at first and without any fear of hindrance, for he held the minds of the barons of Castile occupied in thinking of the war and not anticipating any innovations; thus they did not perceive that by these means he was acquiring power and authority over them. He was able with the money of the Church and of the people to sustain his armies, and by that long war to lay the foundation for the military skill which has since distinguished him. Further, always using religion as a plea, so as to undertake greater schemes, he devoted himself with pious cruelty to driving out and clearing his kingdom of the Moors; nor could there be a more admirable example, nor one more rare. Under this same cloak he assailed Africa, he came down on Italy, he has finally attacked France; and thus his achievements and designs have always been great, and have kept the minds of his people in suspense and admiration and occupied with the issue of them. And his actions have arisen in such a way, one out of the other, that men have never been given time to work steadily against him.

Again, it much assists a prince to set unusual examples in internal affairs, similar to those which are related of Messer Bernabo da Milano, who, when he had the opportunity, by any one in civil life doing some extraordinary thing, either good or bad, would take some method of rewarding or punishing him, which would be much spoken about. And a prince ought, above all things, always endeavour in every action to gain for himself the reputation of being a great and remarkable man.

A prince is also respected when he is either a true friend or a downright enemy, that is to say, when, without any reservation, he declares himself in favour of one party against the other; which course will always be more advantageous than standing neutral; because if two of your powerful neighbours come to blows, they are of such a character that, if one of them conquers, you have either to fear him or not. In either case it will always be more advantageous for you to declare yourself and to make war strenuously; because, in the first case, if you do not declare yourself, you will invariably fall a prey to the conqueror, to the pleasure and satisfaction of him who has been conquered, and you will have no reasons to offer, nor anything to protect or to shelter you. Because he who conquers does not want doubtful friends who will not aid him in the time of trial; and he who loses will not harbour you because you did not willingly, sword in hand, court his fate.

Antiochus went into Greece, being sent for by the Aetolians to drive out the Romans. He sent envoys to the Achaeans, who were friends of the Romans, exhorting them to remain neutral; and on the other hand the Romans urged them to take up arms. This question came to be discussed in the council of the Achaeans, where the legate of Antiochus urged them to stand neutral. To this the Roman legate answered: "As for that which has been said, that it is better and more advantageous for your state not to interfere in our war, nothing can be more erroneous; because by not interfering you will be left, without favour or consideration, the guerdon of the conqueror." Thus it will always happen that he who is not your friend will demand your neutrality, whilst he who is your friend will entreat you to declare yourself with arms. And irresolute princes, to avoid present dangers, generally follow the neutral path, and are generally ruined. But when a prince declares himself gallantly in favour of one side, if the party with whom he allies himself conquers, although the victor may be powerful and may have him at his mercy, yet he is indebted to him, and there is established a bond of amity; and men are never so shameless as to become a monument of ingratitude by oppressing you. Victories after all are never so complete that the victor must not show some regard, especially to justice. But if he with whom you ally yourself loses, you may be sheltered by him, and whilst he is able he may aid you, and you become companions on a fortune that may rise again.

In the second case, when those who fight are of such a character that you have no anxiety as to who may conquer, so much the more is it greater prudence to be allied, because you assist at the destruction of one by the aid of another who, if he had been wise, would have saved him; and conquering, as it is impossible that he should not do with your assistance, he remains at your discretion. And here it is to be noted that a prince ought to take care never to make an alliance with one more powerful than himself for the purposes of attacking others, unless necessity compels him,

as is said above; because if he conquers you are at his discretion, and princes ought to avoid as much as possible being at the discretion of any one. The Venetians joined with France against the Duke of Milan, and this alliance, which caused their ruin, could have been avoided. But when it cannot be avoided, as happened to the Florentines when the Pope and Spain sent armies to attack Lombardy, then in such a case, for the above reasons, the prince ought to favour one of the parties.

Never let any Government imagine that it can choose perfectly safe courses; rather let it expect to have to take very doubtful ones, because it is found in ordinary affairs that one never seeks to avoid one trouble without running into another; but prudence consists in knowing how to distinguish the character of troubles, and for choice to take the lesser evil.

A prince ought also to show himself a patron of ability, and to honour the proficient in every art. At the same time he should encourage his citizens to practise their callings peaceably, both in commerce and agriculture, and in every other following, so that the one should not be deterred from improving his possessions for fear lest they be taken away from him or another from opening up trade for fear of taxes; but the prince ought to offer rewards to whoever wishes to do these things and designs in any way to honour his city or state.

Further, he ought to entertain the people with festivals and spectacles at convenient seasons of the year; and as every city is divided into guilds or into societies, he ought to hold such bodies in esteem, and associate with them sometimes, and show himself an example of courtesy and liberality; nevertheless, always maintaining the majesty of his rank, for this he must never consent to abate in anything.

CHAPTER XXII -- CONCERNING THE SECRETARIES OF PRINCES

The choice of servants is of no little importance to a prince, and they are good or not according to the discrimination of the prince. And the first opinion which one forms of a prince, and of his understanding, is by observing the men he has around him; and when they are capable and faithful he may always be considered wise, because he has known how to recognize the capable and to keep them faithful. But when they are otherwise one cannot form a good opinion of him, for the prime error which he made was in choosing them.

There were none who knew Messer Antonio da Venafro as the servant of Pandolfo Petrucci, Prince of Siena, who would not consider Pandolfo to be a very clever man in having Venafro for his servant. Because there are three classes of intellects: one which comprehends by itself; another which appreciates what others comprehended; and a third which neither comprehends by itself nor by the showing of others; the first is the most excellent, the second is good, the third is useless. Therefore, it follows necessarily that, if Pandolfo was not in the first rank, he was in the second, for whenever one has judgment to know good and bad when it is said and done, although he himself may not have the initiative, yet he can recognize the good and the bad in his servant, and the one he can praise and the other correct; thus the servant cannot hope to deceive him, and is kept honest.

But to enable a prince to form an opinion of his servant there is one test which never fails; when you see the servant thinking more of his own interests than of yours, and seeking inwardly his own profit in everything, such a man will never make a good servant, nor will you ever be able to trust him; because he who has the state of another in his hands ought never to think of himself, but always of his prince, and never pay any attention to matters in which the prince is not concerned.

On the other hand, to keep his servant honest the prince ought to study him, honouring him, enriching him, doing him kindnesses, sharing with him the honours and cares; and at the same time let him see that he cannot stand alone, so that many honours may not make him desire more, many riches make him wish for more, and that many cares may make him dread chances. When, therefore, servants, and princes towards servants, are thus disposed, they can trust each

other, but when it is otherwise, the end will always be disastrous for either one or the other.

CHAPTER XXIII -- HOW FLATTERERS SHOULD BE AVOIDED

I do not wish to leave out an important branch of this subject, for it is a danger from which princes are with difficulty preserved, unless they are very careful and discriminating. It is that of flatterers, of whom courts are full, because men are so self-complacent in their own affairs, and in a way so deceived in them, that they are preserved with difficulty from this pest, and if they wish to defend themselves they run the danger of falling into contempt. Because there is no other way of guarding oneself from flatterers except letting men understand that to tell you the truth does not offend you; but when every one may tell you the truth, respect for you abates.

Therefore a wise prince ought to hold a third course by choosing the wise men in his state, and giving to them only the liberty of speaking the truth to him, and then only of those things of which he inquires, and of none others; but he ought to question them upon everything, and listen to their opinions, and afterwards form his own conclusions. With these councillors, separately and collectively, he ought to carry himself in such a way that each of them should know that, the more freely he shall speak, the more he shall be preferred; outside of these, he should listen to no one, pursue the thing resolved on, and be steadfast in his resolutions. He who does otherwise is either overthrown by flatterers, or is so often changed by varying opinions that he falls into contempt.

I wish on this subject to adduce a modern example. Fra Luca, the man of affairs to Maximilian, the present emperor, speaking of his majesty, said: He consulted with no one, yet never got his own way in anything. This arose because of his following a practice the opposite to the above; for the emperor is a secretive man--he does not communicate his designs to any one, nor does he receive opinions on them. But as in carrying them into effect they become revealed and known, they are at once obstructed by those men whom he has around him, and he, being pliant, is diverted from them. Hence it follows that those things he does one day he undoes the next, and no one ever understands what he wishes or intends to do, and no one can rely on his resolutions.

A prince, therefore, ought always to take counsel, but only when he wishes and not when others wish; he ought rather to discourage every one from offering advice unless he asks it; but, however, he ought to be a constant inquirer, and afterwards a patient listener concerning the things of which he inquired; also, on learning that any one, on any consideration, has not told him the truth, he should let his anger be felt.

And if there are some who think that a prince who conveys an impression of his wisdom is not so through his own ability, but through the good advisers that he has around him, beyond doubt they are deceived, because this is an axiom which never fails: that a prince who is not wise himself will never take good advice, unless by chance he has yielded his affairs entirely to one person who happens to be a very prudent man. In this case indeed he may be well governed, but it would not be for long, because such a governor would in a short time take away his state from him.

But if a prince who is not inexperienced should take counsel from more than one he will never get united counsels, nor will he know how to unite them. Each of the counsellors will think of his own interests, and the prince will not know how to control them or to see through them. And they are not to found otherwise, because men will always prove untrue to you unless they are kept honest by constraint. Therefore it must be inferred that good counsels, whencesoever they come, are born of the wisdom of the prince, and not the wisdom of the prince from good counsels.

CHAPTER XXIV -- WHY THE PRINCES OF ITALY HAVE LOST THEIR STATES

The previous suggestions, carefully observed, will enable a new prince to appear well established, and render him at once more secure and fixed in the state than if he had been long seated there. For the actions of a new prince are more narrowly observed than those of an hereditary one, and when they are seen to be able they gain more men and bind far tighter than ancient blood; because men are attracted more by the present than by the past, and when they find the present good they enjoy it and seek no further; they will also make the utmost defence of a prince if he fails them not in other things. Thus it will be a double glory for him to have established a new principality, and adorned and strengthened it with good laws, good arms, good allies, and with a good example; so will it be a double disgrace to him who, born a prince, shall lose his state by want of wisdom.

And if those seigniors are considered who have lost their states in Italy in our times, such as the King of Naples, the Duke of Milan, and others, there will be found in them, firstly, one common defect in regard to arms from the causes which have been discussed at length; in the next place, some one of them will be seen, either to have had the people hostile, or if he has had the people friendly, he has not known how to secure the nobles. In the absence of these defects states that have power enough to keep an army in the field cannot be lost.

Philip of Macedon, not the father of Alexander the Great, but he who was conquered by Titus Quintius, had not much territory compared to the greatness of the Romans and of Greece who attacked him, yet being a warlike man who knew how to attract the people and secure the nobles, he sustained the war against his enemies for many years, and if in the end he lost the dominion of some cities, nevertheless he retained the kingdom.

Therefore, do not let our princes accuse fortune for the loss of their principalities after so many years' possession, but rather their own sloth, because in quiet times they never thought there could be a change (it is a common defect in man not to make any provision in the calm against the tempest), and when afterwards the bad times came they thought of flight and not of defending themselves, and they hoped that the people, disgusted with the insolence of the conquerors, would recall them. This course, when others fail, may be good, but it is very bad to have neglected all other expedients for that, since you would never wish to fall because you trusted to be able to find someone later on to restore you. This again either does not happen, or, if it does, it will not be for your security, because that deliverance is of no avail which does not depend upon yourself; those only are reliable, certain, and durable that depend on yourself and your valour.

CHAPTER XXV -- WHAT FORTUNE CAN EFFECT IN HUMAN AFFAIRS AND HOW TO WITHSTAND HER

It is not unknown to me how many men have had, and still have, the opinion that the affairs of the world are in such wise governed by fortune and by God that men with their wisdom cannot direct them and that no one can even help them; and because of this they would have us believe that it is not necessary to labour much in affairs, but to let chance govern them. This opinion has been more credited in our times because of the great changes in affairs which have been seen, and may still be seen, every day, beyond all human conjecture. Sometimes pondering over this, I am in some degree inclined to their opinion. Nevertheless, not to extinguish our free will, I hold it to be true that Fortune is the arbiter of one-half of our actions, but that she still leaves us to direct the other half, or perhaps a little less.

I compare her to one of those raging rivers, which when in flood overflows the plains, sweeping away trees and buildings, bearing away the soil from place to place; everything flies before it, all yield to its violence, without being able in any way to withstand it; and yet, though its nature be such, it does not follow therefore that men, when the weather becomes fair, shall not make provision, both with defences and barriers, in such a manner that, rising again, the waters may pass away by canal, and their force be neither so unrestrained nor so dangerous. So it happens with fortune, who shows her power where valour has not prepared to resist her, and thither she turns her forces where she knows that barriers and defences have not been raised to constrain her.

And if you will consider Italy, which is the seat of these changes, and which has given to them their impulse, you will see it to be an open country without barriers and without any defence. For if it had been defended by proper valour, as are Germany, Spain, and France, either this invasion would not have made the great changes it has made or it would not have come at all. And this I consider enough to say concerning resistance to fortune in general.

But confining myself more to the particular, I say that a prince may be seen happy to-day and ruined to-morrow without having shown any change of disposition or character. This, I believe, arises firstly from causes that have already been discussed at length, namely, that the prince who relies entirely on fortune is lost when it changes. I believe also that he will be successful who directs his actions according to the spirit of the times, and that he whose actions do not accord with the times will not be successful. Because men are seen, in affairs that lead to the end which every man has before him, namely, glory and riches, to get there by various methods; one with caution, another with haste; one by force, another by skill; one by patience, another by its opposite; and each one succeeds in reaching the goal by a different method. One can also see of two cautious men the one attain his end, the other fail; and similarly, two men by different observances are equally successful, the one being cautious, the other impetuous; all this arises from nothing else than whether or not they conform in their methods to the spirit of the times. This follows from what I have said, that two men working differently bring about the same effect, and of two working similarly, one attains his object and the other does not.

Changes in estate also issue from this, for if, to one who governs himself with caution and patience, times and affairs converge in such a way that his administration is successful, his fortune is made; but if times and affairs change, he is ruined if he does not change his course of action. But a man is not often found sufficiently circumspect to know how to accommodate himself to the change, both because he cannot deviate from what nature inclines him to do, and also because, having always prospered by acting in one way, he cannot be persuaded that it is well to leave it; and, therefore, the cautious man, when it is time to turn adventurous, does not know how to do it, hence he is ruined; but had he changed his conduct with the times fortune would not have changed.

Pope Julius the Second went to work impetuously in all his affairs, and found the times and circumstances conform so well to that line of action that he always met with success. Consider his first enterprise against Bologna, Messer Giovanni Bentivogli being still alive. The Venetians were not agreeable to it, nor was the King of Spain, and he had the enterprise still under discussion with the King of France; nevertheless he personally entered upon the expedition with his accustomed boldness and energy, a move which made Spain and the Venetians stand irresolute and passive, the latter from fear, the former from desire to recover the kingdom of Naples; on the other hand, he drew after him the King of France, because that king, having observed the movement, and desiring to make the Pope his friend so as to humble the Venetians, found it impossible to refuse him. Therefore Julius with his impetuous action accomplished what no other pontiff with simple human wisdom could have done; for if he had waited in Rome until he could get away, with his plans arranged and everything fixed, as any other pontiff would have done, he would never have succeeded. Because the King of France would have made a thousand excuses, and the others would have raised a thousand fears.

I will leave his other actions alone, as they were all alike, and they all succeeded, for the shortness of his life did not let him experience the contrary; but if circumstances had arisen which required him to go cautiously, his ruin would have followed, because he would never have deviated from those ways to which nature inclined him.

I conclude, therefore that, fortune being changeful and mankind steadfast in their ways, so long as the two are in agreement men are successful, but unsuccessful when they fall out. For my part I consider that it is better to be adventurous than cautious, because fortune is a woman, and if you wish to keep her under it is necessary to beat and ill-use her; and it is seen that she allows herself to be mastered by the adventurous rather than by those who go to work more coldly. She is, therefore, always, woman-like, a lover of young men, because they are less cautious, more violent, and with more audacity command her.

CHAPTER XXVI -- AN EXHORTATION TO LIBERATE ITALY FROM THE BARBARIANS

Having carefully considered the subject of the above discourses, and wondering within myself whether the present times were propitious to a new prince, and whether there were elements that would give an opportunity to a wise and virtuous one to introduce a new order of things which would do honour to him and good to the people of this country, it appears to me that so many things concur to favour a new prince that I never knew a time more fit than the present.

And if, as I said, it was necessary that the people of Israel should be captive so as to make manifest the ability of Moses; that the Persians should be oppressed by the Medes so as to discover the greatness of the soul of Cyrus; and that the Athenians should be dispersed to illustrate the capabilities of Theseus: then at the present time, in order to discover the virtue of an Italian spirit, it was necessary that Italy should be reduced to the extremity that she is now in, that she should be more enslaved than the Hebrews, more oppressed than the Persians, more scattered than the Athenians; without head, without order, beaten, despoiled, torn, overrun; and to have endured every kind of desolation.

Although lately some spark may have been shown by one, which made us think he was ordained by God for our redemption, nevertheless it was afterwards seen, in the height of his career, that fortune rejected him; so that Italy, left as without life, waits for him who shall yet heal her wounds and put an end to the ravaging and plundering of Lombardy, to the swindling and taxing of the kingdom and of Tuscany, and cleanse those sores that for long have festered. It is seen how she entreats God to send someone who shall deliver her from these wrongs and barbarous insolencies. It is seen also that she is ready and willing to follow a banner if only someone will raise it.

Nor is there to be seen at present one in whom she can place more hope than in your illustrious house, with its valour and fortune, favoured by God and by the Church of which it is now the chief, and which could be made the head of this redemption. This will not be difficult if you will recall to yourself the actions and lives of the men I have named. And although they were great and wonderful men, yet they were men, and each one of them had no more opportunity than the present offers, for their enterprises were neither more just nor easier than this, nor was God more their friend than He is yours.

With us there is great justice, because that war is just which is necessary, and arms are hallowed when there is no other hope but in them. Here there is the greatest willingness, and where the willingness is great the difficulties cannot be great if you will only follow those men to whom I have directed your attention. Further than this, how extraordinarily the ways of God have been manifested beyond example: the sea is divided, a cloud has led the way, the rock has poured forth water, it has rained manna, everything has contributed to your greatness; you ought to do the rest. God is not willing to do everything, and thus take away our free will and that share of glory which belongs to us.

And it is not to be wondered at if none of the above-named Italians have been able to accomplish all that is expected from your illustrious house; and if in so many revolutions in Italy, and in so many campaigns, it has always appeared as if military virtue were exhausted, this has happened because the old order of things was not good, and none of us have known how to find a new one. And nothing honours a man more than to establish new laws and new ordinances when he himself was newly risen. Such things when they are well founded and dignified will make him revered and admired, and in Italy there are not wanting opportunities to bring such into use in every form.

Here there is great valour in the limbs whilst it fails in the head. Look attentively at the duels and the hand-to-hand combats, how superior the Italians are in strength, dexterity, and subtlety. But when it comes to armies they do not bear comparison, and this springs entirely from the insufficiency of the leaders, since those who are capable are not obedient, and each one seems to himself to know, there having never been any one so distinguished above the rest, either by valour or fortune, that others would yield to him. Hence it is that for so long a time, and during so much fighting in the past twenty years, whenever there has been an army wholly Italian, it has always given a poor account of itself; the first witness to this is Il Taro, afterwards Allesandria, Capua, Genoa, Vaila, Bologna, Mestri

If, therefore, your illustrious house wishes to follow these remarkable men who have redeemed their country, it is necessary before all things, as a true foundation for every enterprise, to be provided with your own forces, because there can be no more faithful, truer, or better soldiers. And although singly they are good, altogether they will be much better when they find themselves commanded by their prince, honoured by him, and maintained at his expense. Therefore it is necessary to be prepared with such arms, so that you can be defended against foreigners by Italian valour.

And although Swiss and Spanish infantry may be considered very formidable, nevertheless there is a defect in both, by reason of which a third order would not only be able to oppose them, but might be relied upon to overthrow them. For the Spaniards cannot resist cavalry, and the Switzers are afraid of infantry whenever they encounter them in close combat. Owing to this, as has been and may again be seen, the Spaniards are unable to resist French cavalry, and the Switzers are overthrown by Spanish infantry. And although a complete proof of this latter cannot be shown, nevertheless there was some evidence of it at the battle of Ravenna, when the Spanish infantry were confronted by German battalions, who follow the same tactics as the Swiss; when the Spaniards, by agility of body and with the aid of their shields, got in under the pikes of the Germans and stood out of danger, able to attack, while the Germans stood helpless, and, if the cavalry had not dashed up, all would have been over with them. It is possible, therefore, knowing the defects of both these infantries, to invent a new one, which will resist cavalry and not be afraid of infantry; this need not create a new order of arms, but a variation upon the old. And these are the kind of improvements which confer reputation and power upon a new prince.

This opportunity, therefore, ought not to be allowed to pass for letting Italy at last see her liberator appear. Nor can one express the love with which he would be received in all those provinces which have suffered so much from these foreign scourings, with what thirst for revenge, with what stubborn faith, with what devotion, with what tears. What door would be closed to him? Who would refuse obedience to him? What envy would hinder him? What Italian would refuse him homage? To all of us this barbarous dominion stinks. Let, therefore, your illustrious house take up this charge with that courage and hope with which all just enterprises are undertaken, so that under its standard our native country may be ennobled, and under its auspices may be verified that saying of Petrarch:

> Virtu contro al Furore
> Prendera l'arme, e fia il combatter corto:
> Che l'antico valore
> Negli italici cuor non e ancor morto.

> Virtue against fury shall advance the fight,
> And it i' th' combat soon shall put to flight:
> For the old Roman valour is not dead,
> Nor in th' Italians' brests extinguished.

Edward Dacre, 1640.

Thomas Hobbes (5 April 1588 – 4 December 1679) was a prominent philosopher, political theorist, and historian (among his other talents). His ideas were very influential for other social contract theorists, and political philosophers in general. Though he supported absolute monarchy, his ideas contributed to those developed by the writers of the U.S. Constitution and the Declaration of Independence. In this selection from "Leviathan," Hobbes describes the hypothetical "state of nature." Among the more important features of the state of nature are our basic physical and mental equality, and the lack of any sort of governing authority. This equality, coupled with anarchy, results in unacceptably high insecurity and misery. The antidote to this is a social contract that will provide order and rules of conduct, and the "sovereign" (government) who will enforce that contract. He also discusses the role of the sovereign, and the absolute extent of his power.

Thomas Hobbes: *Leviathan*

Chapter XIII.
Of the Naturall Condition of Mankind, as Concerning Their Felicity, and Misery
[http://www.gutenberg.org/files/3207/3207-h/3207-h.htm]

Nature hath made men so equall, in the faculties of body, and mind; as that though there bee found one man sometimes manifestly stronger in body, or of quicker mind then another; yet when all is reckoned together, the difference between man, and man, is not so considerable, as that one man can thereupon claim to himselfe any benefit, to which another may not pretend, as well as he. For as to the strength of body, the weakest has strength enough to kill the strongest, either by secret machination, or by confederacy with others, that are in the same danger with himselfe.

And as to the faculties of the mind, (setting aside the arts grounded upon words, and especially that skill of proceeding upon generall, and infallible rules, called Science; which very few have, and but in few things; as being not a native faculty, born with us; nor attained, (as Prudence,) while we look after somewhat els,) I find yet a greater equality amongst men, than that of strength. For Prudence, is but Experience; which equall time, equally bestowes on all men, in those things they equally apply themselves unto. That which may perhaps make such equality incredible, is but a vain conceipt of ones owne wisdome, which almost all men think they have in a greater degree, than the Vulgar; that is, than all men but themselves, and a few others, whom by Fame, or for concurring with themselves, they approve. For such is the nature of men, that howsoever they may acknowledge many others to be more witty, or more eloquent, or more learned; Yet they will hardly believe there be many so wise as themselves: For they see their own wit at hand, and other mens at a distance. But this proveth rather that men are in that point equall, than unequall. For there is not ordinarily a greater signe of the equall distribution of any thing, than that every man is contented with his share.

From Equality Proceeds Diffidence
From this equality of ability, ariseth equality of hope in the attaining of our Ends. And therefore if any two men desire the same thing, which neverthelesse they cannot both enjoy, they become enemies; and in the way to their End, (which is principally their owne conservation, and sometimes their delectation only,) endeavour to destroy, or subdue one an other. And from hence it comes to passe, that where an Invader hath no more to feare, than an other mans single power; if one plant, sow, build, or possesse a convenient Seat, others may probably be expected to come prepared with forces united, to dispossesse, and deprive him, not only of the fruit of his labour, but also of his life, or liberty. And the Invader again is in the like danger of another.

From Diffidence Warre

And from this diffidence of one another, there is no way for any man to secure himselfe, so reasonable, as Anticipation; that is, by force, or wiles, to master the persons of all men he can, so long, till he see no other power great enough to endanger him: And this is no more than his own conservation requireth, and is generally allowed. Also because there be some, that taking pleasure in contemplating their own power in the acts of conquest, which they pursue farther than their security requires; if others, that otherwise would be glad to be at ease within modest bounds, should not by invasion increase their power, they would not be able, long time, by standing only on their defence, to subsist. And by consequence, such augmentation of dominion over men, being necessary to a mans conservation, it ought to be allowed him.

Againe, men have no pleasure, (but on the contrary a great deale of griefe) in keeping company, where there is no power able to over-awe them all. For every man looketh that his companion should value him, at the same rate he sets upon himselfe: And upon all signes of contempt, or undervaluing, naturally endeavours, as far as he dares (which amongst them that have no common power, to keep them in quiet, is far enough to make them destroy each other,) to extort a greater value from his contemners, by dommage; and from others, by the example.

So that in the nature of man, we find three principall causes of quarrel. First, Competition; Secondly, Diffidence; Thirdly, Glory.

The first, maketh men invade for Gain; the second, for Safety; and the third, for Reputation. The first use Violence, to make themselves Masters of other mens persons, wives, children, and cattell; the second, to defend them; the third, for trifles, as a word, a smile, a different opinion, and any other signe of undervalue, either direct in their Persons, or by reflexion in their Kindred, their Friends, their Nation, their Profession, or their Name.

Out Of Civil States,

There Is Always Warre Of Every One Against Every One

Hereby it is manifest, that during the time men live without a common Power to keep them all in awe, they are in that condition which is called Warre; and such a warre, as is of every man, against every man. For WARRE, consisteth not in Battell onely, or the act of fighting; but in a tract of time, wherein the Will to contend by Battell is sufficiently known: and therefore the notion of Time, is to be considered in the nature of Warre; as it is in the nature of Weather. For as the nature of Foule weather, lyeth not in a showre or two of rain; but in an inclination thereto of many dayes together: So the nature of War, consisteth not in actuall fighting; but in the known disposition thereto, during all the time there is no assurance to the contrary. All other time is PEACE.

The Incommodites Of Such A War

Whatsoever therefore is consequent to a time of Warre, where every man is Enemy to every man; the same is consequent to the time, wherein men live without other security, than what their own strength, and their own invention shall furnish them withall. In such condition, there is no place for Industry; because the fruit thereof is uncertain; and consequently no Culture of the Earth; no Navigation, nor use of the commodities that may be imported by Sea; no commodious Building; no Instruments of moving, and removing such things as require much force; no Knowledge of the face of the Earth; no account of Time; no Arts; no Letters; no Society; and which is worst of all, continuall feare, and danger of violent death; And the life of man, solitary, poore, nasty, brutish, and short.

It may seem strange to some man, that has not well weighed these things; that Nature should thus dissociate, and render men apt to invade, and destroy one another: and he may therefore, not trusting to this Inference, made from the Passions, desire perhaps to have the same confirmed by Experience.

Let him therefore consider with himselfe, when taking a journey, he armes himselfe, and seeks to go well accompanied; when going to sleep, he locks his dores; when even in his house he locks his chests; and this when he knows there bee Lawes, and publike Officers, armed, to revenge all injuries shall bee done him; what opinion he has of his fellow subjects, when he rides armed; of his fellow Citizens, when he locks his dores; and of his children, and servants, when he locks his chests. Does he not there as much accuse mankind by his actions, as I do by my words? But neither of us accuse mans nature in it. The Desires, and other Passions of man, are in themselves no Sin. No more are the Actions, that proceed from those Passions, till they know a Law that forbids them; which till Lawes be made they cannot know: nor can any Law be made, till they have agreed upon the Person that shall make it.

It may peradventure be thought, there was never such a time, nor condition of warre as this; and I believe it was never generally so, over all the world: but there are many places, where they live so now. For the savage people in many places of America, except the government of small Families, the concord whereof dependeth on naturall lust, have no government at all; and live at this day in that brutish manner, as I said before. Howsoever, it may be perceived what manner of life there would be, where there were no common Power to feare; by the manner of life, which men that have formerly lived under a peacefull government, use to degenerate into, in a civill Warre.

But though there had never been any time, wherein particular men were in a condition of warre one against another; yet in all times, Kings, and persons of Soveraigne authority, because of their Independency, are in continuall jealousies, and in the state and posture of Gladiators; having their weapons pointing, and their eyes fixed on one another; that is, their Forts, Garrisons, and Guns upon the Frontiers of their Kingdomes; and continuall Spyes upon their neighbours; which is a posture of War. But because they uphold thereby, the Industry of their Subjects; there does not follow from it, that misery, which accompanies the Liberty of particular men.

In Such A Warre, Nothing Is Unjust

To this warre of every man against every man, this also is consequent; that nothing can be Unjust. The notions of Right and Wrong, Justice and Injustice have there no place. Where there is no common Power, there is no Law: where no Law, no Injustice. Force, and Fraud, are in warre the two Cardinall vertues. Justice, and Injustice are none of the Faculties neither of the Body, nor Mind. If they were, they might be in a man that were alone in the world, as well as his Senses, and Passions. They are Qualities, that relate to men in Society, not in Solitude. It is consequent also to the same condition, that there be no Propriety, no Dominion, no Mine and Thine distinct; but onely that to be every mans that he can get; and for so long, as he can keep it. And thus much for the ill condition, which man by meer Nature is actually placed in; though with a possibility to come out of it, consisting partly in the Passions, partly in his Reason.

The Passions That Incline Men To Peace

The Passions that encline men to Peace, are Feare of Death; Desire of such things as are necessary to commodious living; and a Hope by their Industry to obtain them. And Reason suggesteth convenient Articles of Peace, upon which men may be drawn to agreement. These Articles, are they, which otherwise are called the Lawes of Nature: whereof I shall speak more particularly, in the two following Chapters.

CHAPTER XIV. OF THE FIRST AND SECOND NATURALL LAWES, AND OF CONTRACTS

Right Of Nature What

The RIGHT OF NATURE, which Writers commonly call Jus Naturale, is the Liberty each man hath, to use his own power, as he will himselfe, for the preservation of his own Nature; that is to say, of his own Life; and consequently, of doing any thing, which in his own Judgement, and Reason, hee shall conceive to be the aptest means thereunto.

Liberty What

By LIBERTY, is understood, according to the proper signification of the word, the absence of externall Impediments: which Impediments, may oft take away part of a mans power to do what hee would; but cannot hinder him from using the power left him, according as his judgement, and reason shall dictate to him.

A Law Of Nature What

A LAW OF NATURE, (Lex Naturalis,) is a Precept, or generall Rule, found out by Reason, by which a man is forbidden to do, that, which is destructive of his life, or taketh away the means of preserving the same; and to omit, that, by which he thinketh it may be best preserved. For though they that speak of this subject, use to confound Jus, and Lex, Right and Law; yet they ought to be distinguished; because RIGHT, consisteth in liberty to do, or to forbeare; Whereas LAW, determineth, and bindeth to one of them: so that Law, and Right, differ as much, as Obligation, and Liberty; which in one and the same matter are inconsistent.

Naturally Every Man Has Right To Everything

And because the condition of Man, (as hath been declared in the precedent Chapter) is a condition of Warre of every one against every one; in which case every one is governed by his own Reason; and there is nothing he can make use of, that may not be a help unto him, in preserving his life against his enemyes; It followeth, that in such a condition, every man has a Right to every thing; even to one anothers body. And therefore, as long as this naturall Right of every man to every thing endureth, there can be no security to any man, (how strong or wise soever he be,) of living out the time, which Nature ordinarily alloweth men to live.

The Fundamental Law Of Nature

And consequently it is a precept, or generall rule of Reason, "That every man, ought to endeavour Peace, as farre as he has hope of obtaining it; and when he cannot obtain it, that he may seek, and use, all helps, and advantages of Warre." The first branch, of which Rule, containeth the first, and Fundamentall Law of Nature; which is, "To seek Peace, and follow it." The Second, the summe of the Right of Nature; which is, "By all means we can, to defend our selves."

The Second Law Of Nature

From this Fundamentall Law of Nature, by which men are commanded to endeavour Peace, is derived this second Law; "That a man be willing, when others are so too, as farre-forth, as for Peace, and defence of himselfe he shall think it necessary, to lay down this right to all things; and be contented with so much liberty against other men, as he would allow other men against himselfe." For as long as every man holdeth this Right, of doing any thing he liketh; so long are all men in the condition of Warre. But if other men will not lay down their Right, as well as he; then there is no Reason for any one, to devest himselfe of his: For that were to expose himselfe to Prey, (which no man is bound to) rather than to dispose himselfe to Peace. This is that Law of the Gospell; "Whatsoever you require that others should do to you, that do ye to them." And that Law of all men, "Quod tibi feiri non vis, alteri ne feceris."

What it is to lay down a Right

To Lay Downe a mans Right to any thing, is to Devest himselfe of the Liberty, of hindring another of the benefit of his own Right to the same. For he that renounceth, or passeth away his Right, giveth not to any other man a Right which he had not before; because there is nothing to which every man had not Right by Nature: but onely standeth out of his way, that he may enjoy his own originall Right, without hindrance from him; not without hindrance from another. So that the effect which redoundeth to one man, by another mans defect of Right, is but so much diminution of impediments to the use of his own Right originall.

Renouncing (or) Transferring Right What; Obligation Duty Justice

Right is layd aside, either by simply Renouncing it; or by Transferring it to another.

By Simply RENOUNCING; when he cares not to whom the benefit thereof redoundeth. By TRANSFERRING; when he intendeth the benefit thereof to some certain person, or persons. And when a man hath in either manner abandoned, or granted away his Right; then is he said to be OBLIGED, or BOUND, not to hinder those, to whom such Right is granted, or abandoned, from the benefit of it: and that he Ought, and it his DUTY, not to make voyd that voluntary act of his own: and that such hindrance is INJUSTICE, and INJURY, as being Sine Jure; the Right being before renounced, or transferred. So that Injury, or Injustice, in the controversies of the world, is somewhat like to that, which in the disputations of Scholers is called Absurdity. For as it is there called an Absurdity, to contradict what one maintained in the Beginning: so in the world, it is called Injustice, and Injury, voluntarily to undo that, which from the beginning he had voluntarily done. The way by which a man either simply Renounceth, or Transferreth his Right, is a Declaration, or Signification, by some voluntary and sufficient signe, or signes, that he doth so Renounce, or Transferre; or hath so Renounced, or Transferred the same, to him that accepteth it. And these Signes are either Words onely, or Actions onely; or (as it happeneth most often) both Words and Actions. And the same are the BONDS, by which men are bound, and obliged: Bonds, that have their strength, not from their own Nature, (for nothing is more easily broken then a mans word,) but from Feare of some evill consequence upon the rupture.

Not All Rights Are Alienable

Whensoever a man Transferreth his Right, or Renounceth it; it is either in consideration of some Right reciprocally transferred to himselfe; or for some other good he hopeth for thereby. For it is a voluntary act: and of the voluntary acts of every man, the object is some Good To Himselfe. And therefore there be some Rights, which no man can be understood by any words, or other signes, to have abandoned, or transferred. As first a man cannot lay down the right of resisting them, that assault him by force, to take away his life; because he cannot be understood to ayme

thereby, at any Good to himselfe. The same may be sayd of Wounds, and Chayns, and Imprisonment; both because there is no benefit consequent to such patience; as there is to the patience of suffering another to be wounded, or imprisoned: as also because a man cannot tell, when he seeth men proceed against him by violence, whether they intend his death or not. And lastly the motive, and end for which this renouncing, and transferring or Right is introduced, is nothing else but the security of a mans person, in his life, and in the means of so preserving life, as not to be weary of it. And therefore if a man by words, or other signes, seem to despoyle himselfe of the End, for which those signes were intended; he is not to be understood as if he meant it, or that it was his will; but that he was ignorant of how such words and actions were to be interpreted.

Contract What

The mutuall transferring of Right, is that which men call CONTRACT.

There is difference, between transferring of Right to the Thing; and transferring, or tradition, that is, delivery of the Thing it selfe. For the Thing may be delivered together with the Translation of the Right; as in buying and selling with ready mony; or exchange of goods, or lands: and it may be delivered some time after.

Covenant What

Again, one of the Contractors, may deliver the Thing contracted for on his part, and leave the other to perform his part at some determinate time after, and in the mean time be trusted; and then the Contract on his part, is called PACT, or COVENANT: Or both parts may contract now, to performe hereafter: in which cases, he that is to performe in time to come, being trusted, his performance is called Keeping Of Promise, or Faith; and the fayling of performance (if it be voluntary) Violation Of Faith.

Free-gift

When the transferring of Right, is not mutuall; but one of the parties transferreth, in hope to gain thereby friendship, or service from another, or from his friends; or in hope to gain the reputation of Charity, or Magnanimity; or to deliver his mind from the pain of compassion; or in hope of reward in heaven; This is not Contract, but GIFT, FREEGIFT, GRACE: which words signifie one and the same thing.

Signes Of Contract Expresse

Signes of Contract, are either Expresse, or By Inference. Expresse, are words spoken with understanding of what they signifie; And such words are either of the time Present, or Past; as, I Give, I Grant, I Have Given, I Have Granted, I Will That This Be Yours: Or of the future; as, I Will Give, I Will Grant; which words of the future, are called Promise.

Signes Of Contract By Inference

Signes by Inference, are sometimes the consequence of Words; sometimes the consequence of Silence; sometimes the consequence of Actions; sometimes the consequence of Forbearing an Action: and generally a signe by Inference, of any Contract, is whatsoever sufficiently argues the will of the Contractor.

Free Gift Passeth By Words Of The Present Or Past

Words alone, if they be of the time to come, and contain a bare promise, are an insufficient signe of a Free-gift and therefore not obligatory. For if they be of the time to Come, as, To Morrow I Will Give, they are a signe I have not given yet, and consequently that my right is not transferred, but remaineth till I transferre it by some other Act. But if the words be of the time Present, or Past, as, "I have given, or do give to be delivered to morrow," then is my to morrows Right given away to day; and that by the vertue of the words, though there were no other argument of my will. And there is a great difference in the signification of these words, Volos Hoc Tuum Esse Cras, and Cros Dabo; that is between "I will that this be thine to morrow," and, "I will give it to thee to morrow:" For the word I Will, in the former manner of speech, signifies an act of the will Present; but in the later, it signifies a promise of

an act of the will to Come: and therefore the former words, being of the Present, transferre a future right; the later, that be of the Future, transferre nothing. But if there be other signes of the Will to transferre a Right, besides Words; then, though the gift be Free, yet may the Right be understood to passe by words of the future: as if a man propound a Prize to him that comes first to the end of a race, The gift is Free; and though the words be of the Future, yet the Right passeth: for if he would not have his words so be understood, he should not have let them runne.

Signes Of Contract Are Words Both Of The Past, Present, and Future

In Contracts, the right passeth, not onely where the words are of the time Present, or Past; but also where they are of the Future; because all Contract is mutuall translation, or change of Right; and therefore he that promiseth onely, because he hath already received the benefit for which he promiseth, is to be understood as if he intended the Right should passe: for unlesse he had been content to have his words so understood, the other would not have performed his part first. And for that cause, in buying, and selling, and other acts of Contract, A Promise is equivalent to a Covenant; and therefore obligatory.

Merit What

He that performeth first in the case of a Contract, is said to MERIT that which he is to receive by the performance of the other; and he hath it as Due. Also when a Prize is propounded to many, which is to be given to him onely that winneth; or mony is thrown amongst many, to be enjoyed by them that catch it; though this be a Free Gift; yet so to Win, or so to Catch, is to Merit, and to have it as DUE. For the Right is transferred in the Propounding of the Prize, and in throwing down the mony; though it be not determined to whom, but by the Event of the contention. But there is between these two sorts of Merit, this difference, that In Contract, I Merit by vertue of my own power, and the Contractors need; but in this case of Free Gift, I am enabled to Merit onely by the benignity of the Giver; In Contract, I merit at The Contractors hand that hee should depart with his right; In this case of gift, I Merit not that the giver should part with his right; but that when he has parted with it, it should be mine, rather than anothers. And this I think to be the meaning of that distinction of the Schooles, between Meritum Congrui, and Meritum Condigni. For God Almighty, having promised Paradise to those men (hoodwinkt with carnall desires,) that can walk through this world according to the Precepts, and Limits prescribed by him; they say, he that shall so walk, shall Merit Paradise Ex Congruo. But because no man can demand a right to it, by his own Righteousnesse, or any other power in himselfe, but by the Free Grace of God onely; they say, no man can Merit Paradise Ex Condigno. This I say, I think is the meaning of that distinction; but because Disputers do not agree upon the signification of their own termes of Art, longer than it serves their turn; I will not affirme any thing of their meaning: onely this I say; when a gift is given indefinitely, as a prize to be contended for, he that winneth Meriteth, and may claime the Prize as Due.

Covenants Of Mutuall Trust, When Invalid

If a Covenant be made, wherein neither of the parties performe presently, but trust one another; in the condition of meer Nature, (which is a condition of Warre of every man against every man,) upon any reasonable suspition, it is Voyd; But if there be a common Power set over them bothe, with right and force sufficient to compell performance; it is not Voyd. For he that performeth first, has no assurance the other will performe after; because the bonds of words are too weak to bridle mens ambition, avarice, anger, and other Passions, without the feare of some coerceive Power; which in the condition of meer Nature, where all men are equall, and judges of the justnesse of their own fears cannot possibly be supposed. And therefore he which performeth first, does but betray himselfe to his enemy; contrary to the Right (he can never abandon) of defending his life, and means of living.

But in a civill estate, where there is a Power set up to constrain those that would otherwise violate their faith, that feare is no more reasonable; and for that cause, he which by the Covenant is to perform first, is obliged so to do.

The cause of Feare, which maketh such a Covenant invalid, must be always something arising after the Covenant made; as some new fact, or other signe of the Will not to performe; else it cannot make the Covenant Voyd. For that which could not hinder a man from promising, ought not to be admitted as a hindrance of performing.

Right To The End, Containeth Right To The Means

He that transferreth any Right, transferreth the Means of enjoying it, as farre as lyeth in his power. As he that selleth Land, is understood to transferre the Herbage, and whatsoever growes upon it; Nor can he that sells a Mill turn away the Stream that drives it. And they that give to a man The Right of government in Soveraignty, are understood to give him the right of levying mony to maintain Souldiers; and of appointing Magistrates for the administration of Justice.

No Covenant With Beasts

To make Covenant with bruit Beasts, is impossible; because not understanding our speech, they understand not, nor accept of any translation of Right; nor can translate any Right to another; and without mutuall acceptation, there is no Covenant.

Nor With God Without Speciall Revelation

To make Covenant with God, is impossible, but by Mediation of such as God speaketh to, either by Revelation supernaturall, or by his Lieutenants that govern under him, and in his Name; For otherwise we know not whether our Covenants be accepted, or not. And therefore they that Vow any thing contrary to any law of Nature, Vow in vain; as being a thing unjust to pay such Vow. And if it be a thing commanded by the Law of Nature, it is not the Vow, but the Law that binds them.

No Covenant, But Of Possible And Future

The matter, or subject of a Covenant, is always something that falleth under deliberation; (For to Covenant, is an act of the Will; that is to say an act, and the last act, of deliberation;) and is therefore alwayes understood to be something to come; and which is judged Possible for him that Covenanteth, to performe.

And therefore, to promise that which is known to be Impossible, is no Covenant. But if that prove impossible afterwards, which before was thought possible, the Covenant is valid, and bindeth, (though not to the thing it selfe,) yet to the value; or, if that also be impossible, to the unfeigned endeavour of performing as much as is possible; for to more no man can be obliged.

Covenants How Made Voyd

Men are freed of their Covenants two wayes; by Performing; or by being Forgiven. For Performance, is the naturall end of obligation; and Forgivenesse, the restitution of liberty; as being a retransferring of that Right, in which the obligation consisted.

Covenants Extorted By Feare Are Valide

Covenants entred into by fear, in the condition of meer Nature, are obligatory. For example, if I Covenant to pay a ransome, or service for my life, to an enemy; I am bound by it. For it is a Contract, wherein one receiveth the benefit of life; the other is to receive mony, or service for it; and consequently, where no other Law (as in the condition, of meer Nature) forbiddeth the performance, the Covenant is valid. Therefore Prisoners of warre, if trusted with the payment of their Ransome, are obliged to pay it; And if a weaker Prince, make a disadvantageous peace with a stronger, for feare; he is bound to keep it; unlesse (as hath been sayd before) there ariseth some new, and just cause of feare, to renew the war. And even in Commonwealths, if I be forced to redeem my selfe from a Theefe by promising him mony, I am bound to pay it, till the Civill Law discharge me. For whatsoever I may lawfully do without Obligation, the same I may lawfully Covenant to do through feare: and what I lawfully Covenant, I cannot lawfully break.

The Former Covenant To One, Makes Voyd The Later To Another

A former Covenant, makes voyd a later. For a man that hath passed away his Right to one man to day, hath it not to passe to morrow to another: and therefore the later promise passeth no Right, but is null.

A Mans Covenant Not To Defend Himselfe, Is Voyd

A Covenant not to defend my selfe from force, by force, is alwayes voyd. For (as I have shewed before) no man can transferre, or lay down his Right to save himselfe from Death, Wounds, and Imprisonment, (the avoyding whereof is the onely End of laying down any Right,) and therefore the promise of not resisting force, in no Covenant transferreth any right; nor is obliging. For though a man may Covenant thus, "Unlesse I do so, or so, kill me;" he cannot Covenant thus "Unless I do so, or so, I will not resist you, when you come to kill me." For man by nature chooseth the lesser evill, which is danger of death in resisting; rather than the greater, which is certain and present death in not resisting. And this is granted to be true by all men, in that they lead Criminals to Execution, and Prison, with armed men, notwithstanding that such Criminals have consented to the Law, by which they are condemned.

No Man Obliged To Accuse Himselfe

A Covenant to accuse ones Selfe, without assurance of pardon, is likewise invalide. For in the condition of Nature, where every man is Judge, there is no place for Accusation: and in the Civill State, the Accusation is followed with Punishment; which being Force, a man is not obliged not to resist. The same is also true, of the Accusation of those, by whose Condemnation a man falls into misery; as of a Father, Wife, or Benefactor. For the Testimony of such an Accuser, if it be not willingly given, is praesumed to be corrupted by Nature; and therefore not to be received: and where a mans Testimony is not to be credited, his not bound to give it. Also Accusations upon Torture, are not to be reputed as Testimonies. For Torture is to be used but as means of conjecture, and light, in the further examination, and search of truth; and what is in that case confessed, tendeth to the ease of him that is Tortured; not to the informing of the Torturers: and therefore ought not to have the credit of a sufficient Testimony: for whether he deliver himselfe by true, or false Accusation, he does it by the Right of preserving his own life.

The End Of An Oath; The Forme Of As Oath

The force of Words, being (as I have formerly noted) too weak to hold men to the performance of their Covenants; there are in mans nature, but two imaginable helps to strengthen it. And those are either a Feare of the consequence of breaking their word; or a Glory, or Pride in appearing not to need to breake it. This later is a Generosity too rarely found to be presumed on, especially in the pursuers of Wealth, Command, or sensuall Pleasure; which are the greatest part of Mankind. The Passion to be reckoned upon, is Fear; whereof there be two very generall Objects: one, the Power of Spirits Invisible; the other, the Power of those men they shall therein Offend. Of these two, though the former be the greater Power, yet the feare of the later is commonly the greater Feare. The Feare of the former is in every man, his own Religion: which hath place in the nature of man before Civill Society. The later hath not so; at least not place enough, to keep men to their promises; because in the condition of meer Nature, the inequality of Power is not discerned, but by the event of Battell. So that before the time of Civill Society, or in the interruption thereof by Warre, there is nothing can strengthen a Covenant of Peace agreed on, against the temptations of Avarice, Ambition, Lust, or other strong desire, but the feare of that Invisible Power, which they every one Worship as God; and Feare as a Revenger of their perfidy. All therefore that can be done between two men not subject to Civill Power, is to put one another to swear by the God he feareth: Which Swearing or OATH, is a Forme Of Speech, Added To A Promise; By Which He That Promiseth, Signifieth, That Unlesse He Performe, He Renounceth The Mercy Of His God, Or Calleth To Him For Vengeance On Himselfe. Such was the Heathen Forme, "Let Jupiter kill me else, as I kill this Beast." So is our Forme, "I shall do thus, and thus, so help me God."

And this, with the Rites and Ceremonies, which every one useth in his own Religion, that the feare of breaking faith might be the greater.

No Oath, But By God

By this it appears, that an Oath taken according to any other Forme, or Rite, then his, that sweareth, is in vain; and no Oath: And there is no Swearing by any thing which the Swearer thinks not God. For though men have sometimes used to swear by their Kings, for feare, or flattery; yet they would have it thereby understood, they attributed to them Divine honour. And that Swearing unnecessarily by God, is but prophaning of his name: and Swearing by other things, as men do in common discourse, is not Swearing, but an impious Custome, gotten by too much vehemence of talking.

An Oath Addes Nothing To The Obligation

It appears also, that the Oath addes nothing to the Obligation. For a Covenant, if lawfull, binds in the sight of God, without the Oath, as much as with it; if unlawfull, bindeth not at all; though it be confirmed with an Oath.

CHAPTER XV. OF OTHER LAWES OF NATURE

The Third Law Of Nature, Justice

From that law of Nature, by which we are obliged to transferre to another, such Rights, as being retained, hinder the peace of Mankind, there followeth a Third; which is this, That Men Performe Their Covenants Made: without which, Covenants are in vain, and but Empty words; and the Right of all men to all things remaining, wee are still in the condition of Warre.

Justice And Injustice What

And in this law of Nature, consisteth the Fountain and Originall of JUSTICE. For where no Covenant hath preceded, there hath no Right been transferred, and every man has right to every thing; and consequently, no action can be Unjust. But when a Covenant is made, then to break it is Unjust: And the definition of INJUSTICE, is no other than The Not Performance

Of Covenant. And whatsoever is not Unjust, is Just.

Justice And Propriety Begin With The Constitution of Common-wealth But because Covenants of mutuall trust, where there is a feare of not performance on either part, (as hath been said in the former Chapter,) are invalid; though the Originall of Justice be the making of Covenants; yet Injustice actually there can be none, till the cause of such feare be taken away; which while men are in the naturall condition of Warre, cannot be done. Therefore before the names of Just, and Unjust can have place, there must be some coercive Power, to compell men equally to the performance of their Covenants, by the terrour of some punishment, greater than the benefit they expect by the breach of their Covenant; and to make good that Propriety, which by mutuall Contract men acquire, in recompence of the universall Right they abandon: and such power there is none before the erection of a Common-wealth. And this is also to be gathered out of the ordinary definition of Justice in the Schooles: For they say, that "Justice is the constant Will of giving to every man his own." And therefore where there is no Own, that is, no Propriety, there is no Injustice; and where there is no coerceive Power erected, that is, where there is no Common-wealth, there is no Propriety; all men having Right to all things: Therefore where there is no Common-wealth, there nothing is Unjust. So that the nature of Justice, consisteth in keeping of valid Covenants: but the Validity of Covenants begins not but with the Constitution of a Civill Power, sufficient to compell men to keep them: And then it is also that Propriety begins.

Justice Not Contrary To Reason
The Foole hath sayd in his heart, there is no such thing as Justice; and sometimes also with his tongue; seriously alleaging, that every mans conservation, and contentment, being committed to his own care, there could be no reason, why every man might not do what he thought conduced thereunto; and therefore also to make, or not make; keep, or not keep Covenants, was not against Reason, when it conduced to ones

benefit. He does not therein deny, that there be Covenants; and that they are sometimes broken, sometimes kept; and that such breach of them may be called Injustice, and the observance of them Justice: but he questioneth, whether Injustice, taking away the feare of God, (for the same Foole hath said in his heart there is no God,) may not sometimes stand with that Reason, which dictateth to every man his own good; and particularly then, when it conduceth to such a benefit, as shall put a man in a condition, to neglect not onely the dispraise, and revilings, but also the power of other men. The Kingdome of God is gotten by violence; but what if it could be gotten by unjust violence? were it against Reason so to get it, when it is impossible to receive hurt by it? and if it be not against Reason, it is not against Justice; or else Justice is not to be approved for good. From such reasoning as this, Succesfull wickednesse hath obtained the Name of Vertue; and some that in all other things have disallowed the violation of Faith; yet have allowed it, when it is for the getting of a Kingdome. And the Heathen that believed, that Saturn was deposed by his son Jupiter, believed neverthelesse the same Jupiter to be the avenger of Injustice: Somewhat like to a piece of Law in Cokes Commentaries on Litleton; where he sayes, If the right Heire of the Crown be attainted of Treason; yet the Crown shall descend to him, and Eo Instante the Atteynder be voyd; From which instances a man will be very prone to inferre; that when the Heire apparent of a Kingdome, shall kill him that is in possession, though his father; you may call it Injustice, or by what other name you will; yet it can never be against Reason, seeing all the voluntary actions of men tend to the benefit of themselves; and those actions are most Reasonable, that conduce most to their ends. This specious reasoning is nevertheless false.

For the question is not of promises mutuall, where there is no security of performance on either side; as when there is no Civill Power erected over the parties promising; for such promises are no Covenants: But either where one of the parties has performed already; or where there is a Power to make him performe; there is the question whether it be against reason, that is, against the benefit of the other to performe, or not. And I say it is not against reason. For the manifestation whereof, we are to consider; First, that when a man doth a thing, which notwithstanding any thing can be foreseen, and reckoned on, tendeth to his own destruction, howsoever some accident which he could not expect, arriving may turne it to his benefit; yet such events do not make it reasonably or wisely done. Secondly, that in a condition of Warre, wherein every man to every man, for want of a common Power to keep them all in awe, is an Enemy, there is no man can hope by his own strength, or wit, to defend himselfe from destruction, without the help of Confederates; where every one expects the same defence by the Confederation, that any one else does: and therefore he which declares he thinks it reason to deceive those that help him, can in reason expect no other means of safety, than what can be had from his own single Power. He therefore that breaketh his Covenant, and consequently declareth that he thinks he may with reason do so, cannot be received into any Society, that unite themselves for Peace and defence, but by the errour of them that receive him; nor when he is received, be retayned in it, without seeing the danger of their errour; which errours a man cannot reasonably reckon upon as the means of his security; and therefore if he be left, or cast out of Society, he perisheth; and if he live in Society, it is by the errours of other men, which he could not foresee, nor reckon upon; and consequently against the reason of his preservation; and so, as all men that contribute not to his destruction, forbear him onely out of ignorance of what is good for themselves.

As for the Instance of gaining the secure and perpetuall felicity of Heaven, by any way; it is frivolous: there being but one way imaginable; and that is not breaking, but keeping of Covenant.

And for the other Instance of attaining Soveraignty by Rebellion; it is manifest, that though the event follow, yet because it cannot reasonably be expected, but rather the contrary; and because by gaining it so, others are taught to gain the same in like manner, the attempt thereof is against reason. Justice therefore, that is to say,

Keeping of Covenant, is a Rule of Reason, by which we are forbidden to do any thing destructive to our life; and consequently a Law of Nature.

There be some that proceed further; and will not have the Law of Nature, to be those Rules which conduce to the preservation of mans life on earth; but to the attaining of an eternall felicity after death; to which they think the breach of Covenant may conduce; and consequently be just and reasonable; (such are they that think it a work of merit to kill, or depose, or rebell against, the Soveraigne Power constituted over them by their own consent.) But because there is no naturall knowledge of mans estate after death; much lesse of the reward that is then to be given to breach of Faith; but onely a beliefe grounded upon other mens saying, that they know it supernaturally, or that they know those, that knew them, that knew others, that knew it supernaturally; Breach of Faith cannot be called a Precept of Reason, or Nature.

Covenants Not Discharged By The Vice Of The Person To Whom Made

Others, that allow for a Law of Nature, the keeping of Faith, do neverthelesse make exception of certain persons; as Heretiques, and such as use not to performe their Covenant to others: And this also is against reason. For if any fault of a man, be sufficient to discharge our Covenant made; the same ought in reason to have been sufficient to have hindred the making of it.

Justice Of Men, And Justice Of Actions What

The names of Just, and Unjust, when they are attributed to Men, signifie one thing; and when they are attributed to Actions, another. When they are attributed to Men, they signifie Conformity, or Inconformity of Manners, to Reason. But when they are attributed to Actions, they signifie the Conformity, or Inconformity to Reason, not of Manners, or manner of life, but of particular Actions. A Just man therefore, is he that taketh all the care he can, that his Actions may be all Just: and an Unjust man, is he that neglecteth it. And such men are more often in our Language stiled by the names of Righteous, and

Unrighteous; then Just, and Unjust; though the meaning be the same.

Therefore a Righteous man, does not lose that Title, by one, or a few unjust Actions, that proceed from sudden Passion, or mistake of Things, or Persons: nor does an Unrighteous man, lose his character, for such Actions, as he does, of forbeares to do, for feare: because his Will is not framed by the Justice, but by the apparant benefit of what he is to do. That which gives to humane Actions the relish of Justice, is a certain Noblenesse or Gallantnesse of courage, (rarely found,) by which a man scorns to be beholding for the contentment of his life, to fraud, or breach of promise. This Justice of the Manners, is that which is meant, where Justice is called a Vertue; and Injustice a Vice.

But the Justice of Actions denominates men, not Just, but Guiltlesse; and the Injustice of the same, (which is also called Injury,) gives them but the name of Guilty.

Justice Of Manners, And Justice Of Actions

Again, the Injustice of Manners, is the disposition, or aptitude to do Injurie; and is Injustice before it proceed to Act; and without supposing any individuall person injured. But the Injustice of an Action, (that is to say Injury,) supposeth an individuall person Injured; namely him, to whom the Covenant was made: And therefore many times the injury is received by one man, when the dammage redoundeth to another. As when The Master commandeth his servant to give mony to a stranger; if it be not done, the Injury is done to the Master, whom he had before Covenanted to obey; but the dammage redoundeth to the stranger, to whom he had no Obligation; and therefore could not Injure him. And so also in Common-wealths, private men may remit to one another their debts; but not robberies or other violences, whereby they are endammaged; because the detaining of Debt, is an Injury to themselves; but Robbery and Violence, are Injuries to the Person of the Common-wealth.

Nothing Done To A Man, By His Own Consent Can Be Injury

Whatsoever is done to a man, conformable to his own Will signified to the doer, is no Injury to him. For if he that doeth it, hath not passed away his originall right to do what he please, by some Antecedent Covenant, there is no breach of Covenant; and therefore no Injury done him. And if he have; then his Will to have it done being signified, is a release of that Covenant; and so again there is no Injury done him.

Justice Commutative, And Distributive

Justice of Actions, is by Writers divided into Commutative, and Distributive; and the former they say consisteth in proportion Arithmeticall; the later in proportion Geometricall. Commutative therefore, they place in the equality of value of the things contracted for; And Distributive, in the distribution of equall benefit, to men of equall merit. As if it were Injustice to sell dearer than we buy; or to give more to a man than he merits. The value of all things contracted for, is measured by the Appetite of the Contractors: and therefore the just value, is that which they be contented to give.

And Merit (besides that which is by Covenant, where the performance on one part, meriteth the performance of the other part, and falls under Justice Commutative, not Distributive,) is not due by Justice; but is rewarded of Grace onely. And therefore this distinction, in the sense wherein it useth to be expounded, is not right. To speak properly, Commutative Justice, is the Justice of a Contractor; that is, a Performance of Covenant, in Buying, and Selling; Hiring, and Letting to Hire; Lending, and Borrowing; Exchanging, Bartering, and other acts of Contract.

And Distributive Justice, the Justice of an Arbitrator; that is to say, the act of defining what is Just. Wherein, (being trusted by them that make him Arbitrator,) if he performe his Trust, he is said to distribute to every man his own: and his is indeed Just Distribution, and may be called (though improperly) Distributive Justice; but more properly Equity; which also is a Law of Nature, as shall be shewn in due place.

The Fourth Law Of Nature, Gratitude

As Justice dependeth on Antecedent Covenant; so does Gratitude depend on Antecedent Grace; that is to say, Antecedent Free-gift: and is the fourth Law of Nature; which may be conceived in this Forme, "That a man which receiveth Benefit from another of meer Grace, Endeavour that he which giveth it, have no reasonable cause to repent him of his good will." For no man giveth, but with intention of Good to himselfe; because Gift is Voluntary; and of all Voluntary Acts, the Object is to every man his own Good; of which if men see they shall be frustrated, there will be no beginning of benevolence, or trust; nor consequently of mutuall help; nor of reconciliation of one man to another; and therefore they are to remain still in the condition of War; which is contrary to the first and Fundamentall Law of Nature, which commandeth men to Seek Peace. The breach of this Law, is called Ingratitude; and hath the same relation to Grace, that Injustice hath to Obligation by Covenant.

The Fifth, Mutuall accommodation, or Compleasance

A fifth Law of Nature, is COMPLEASANCE; that is to say, "That every man strive to accommodate himselfe to the rest." For the understanding whereof, we may consider, that there is in mens aptnesse to Society; a diversity of Nature, rising from their diversity of Affections; not unlike to that we see in stones brought together for building of an Aedifice. For as that stone which by the asperity, and irregularity of Figure, takes more room from others, than it selfe fills; and for the hardnesse, cannot be easily made plain, and thereby hindereth the building, is by the builders cast away as unprofitable, and troublesome: so also, a man that by asperity of Nature, will strive to retain those things which to himselfe are superfluous, and to others necessary; and for the stubbornness of his Passions, cannot be corrected, is to be left, or cast out of Society, as combersome thereunto. For seeing every man, not onely by Right, but also by necessity of Nature, is supposed to endeavour all he can, to obtain that which is necessary for his conservation; He that shall oppose himselfe against it, for things superfluous, is guilty of the warre that thereupon is to follow; and therefore doth that, which is contrary to the fundamentall Law of Nature, which commandeth To Seek Peace. The observers of this Law, may be called SOCIABLE, (the Latines call them Commodi;) The contrary, Stubborn, Insociable, Froward, Intractable.

The Sixth, Facility To Pardon

A sixth Law of Nature is this, "That upon caution of the Future time, a man ought to pardon the offences past of them that repenting, desire it." For PARDON, is nothing but granting of Peace; which though granted to them that persevere in their hostility, be not Peace, but Feare; yet not granted to them that give caution of the Future time, is signe of an aversion to Peace; and therefore contrary to the Law of Nature.

The Seventh, That In Revenges, Men Respect Onely The Future Good

A seventh is, " That in Revenges, (that is, retribution of evil for evil,) Men look not at the greatnesse of the evill past, but the greatnesse of the good to follow." Whereby we are forbidden to inflict punishment with any other designe, than for correction of the offender, or direction of others. For this Law is consequent to the next before it, that commandeth Pardon, upon security of the Future Time. Besides, Revenge without respect to the Example, and profit to come, is a triumph, or glorying in the hurt of another, tending to no end; (for the End is always somewhat to Come;) and glorying to no end, is vain-glory, and contrary to reason; and to hurt without reason, tendeth to the introduction of Warre; which is against the Law of Nature; and is commonly stiled by the name of Cruelty.

The Eighth, Against Contumely

And because all signes of hatred, or contempt, provoke to fight; insomuch as most men choose rather to hazard their life, than not to be revenged; we may in the eighth place, for a Law of Nature set down this Precept, "That no man by deed, word, countenance, or gesture, declare Hatred, or Contempt of another." The breach of which Law, is commonly called Contumely.

The Ninth, Against Pride

The question who is the better man, has no place in the condition of meer Nature; where, (as has been shewn before,) all men are equall. The inequallity that now is, has been introduced by the Lawes civill. I know that Aristotle in the first booke of his Politiques, for a foundation of his doctrine, maketh men by Nature, some more worthy to Command, meaning the wiser sort (such as he thought himselfe to be for his Philosophy;) others to Serve, (meaning those that had strong bodies, but were not Philosophers as he;) as if Master and Servant were not introduced by consent of men, but by difference of Wit; which is not only against reason; but also against experience. For there are very few so foolish, that had not rather governe themselves, than be governed by others: Nor when the wise in their own conceit, contend by force, with them who distrust their owne wisdome, do they alwaies, or often, or almost at any time, get the Victory. If Nature therefore have made men equall, that equalitie is to be acknowledged; or if Nature have made men unequall; yet because men that think themselves equall, will not enter into conditions of Peace, but upon Equall termes, such equalitie must be admitted. And therefore for the ninth Law of Nature, I put this, "That every man acknowledge other for his Equall by Nature." The breach of this Precept is Pride.

The Tenth Against Arrogance

On this law, dependeth another, "That at the entrance into conditions of Peace, no man require to reserve to himselfe any Right, which he is not content should be reserved to every one of the rest." As it is necessary for all men that seek peace, to lay down certaine Rights of Nature; that is to say, not to have libertie to do all they list: so is it necessarie for mans life, to retaine some; as right to governe their owne bodies; enjoy aire, water, motion, waies to go from place to place; and all things else without which a man cannot live, or not live well. If in this case, at the making

of Peace, men require for themselves, that which they would not have to be granted to others, they do contrary to the precedent law, that commandeth the acknowledgement of naturall equalitie, and therefore also against the law of Nature. The observers of this law, are those we call Modest, and the breakers Arrogant Men. The Greeks call the violation of this law pleonexia; that is, a desire of more than their share.

The Eleventh Equity

Also "If a man be trusted to judge between man and man," it is a precept of the Law of Nature, "that he deale Equally between them." For without that, the Controversies of men cannot be determined but by Warre. He therefore that is partiall in judgment, doth what in him lies, to deterre men from the use of Judges, and Arbitrators; and consequently, (against the fundamentall Lawe of Nature) is the cause of Warre.

The observance of this law, from the equall distribution to each man, of that which in reason belongeth to him, is called EQUITY, and (as I have sayd before) distributive justice: the violation, Acception Of Persons, Prosopolepsia.

The Twelfth, Equall Use Of Things Common

And from this followeth another law, "That such things as cannot be divided, be enjoyed in Common, if it can be; and if the quantity of the thing permit, without Stint; otherwise Proportionably to the number of them that have Right." For otherwise the distribution is Unequall, and contrary to Equitie.

The Thirteenth, Of Lot

But some things there be, that can neither be divided, nor enjoyed in common. Then, The Law of Nature, which prescribeth Equity, requireth, "That the Entire Right; or else, (making the use alternate,) the First Possession, be determined by Lot." For equall distribution, is of the Law of Nature; and other means of equall distribution cannot be imagined.

The Fourteenth, Of Primogeniture, And First Seising

Of Lots there be two sorts, Arbitrary, and Naturall. Arbitrary, is that which is agreed on by the Competitors; Naturall, is either Primogeniture, (which the Greek calls Kleronomia, which signifies, Given by Lot;) or First Seisure.

And therefore those things which cannot be enjoyed in common, nor divided, ought to be adjudged to the First Possessor; and is some cases to the First-Borne, as acquired by Lot.

The Fifteenth, Of Mediators

It is also a Law of Nature, "That all men that mediate Peace, be allowed safe Conduct." For the Law that commandeth Peace, as the End, commandeth Intercession, as the Means; and to Intercession the Means is safe Conduct.

The Sixteenth, Of Submission To Arbitrement

And because, though men be never so willing to observe these Lawes, there may neverthelesse arise questions concerning a mans action; First, whether it were done, or not done; Secondly (if done) whether against the Law, or not against the Law; the former whereof, is called a question Of Fact; the later a question Of Right; therefore unlesse the parties to the question, Covenant mutually to stand to the sentence of another, they are as farre from Peace as ever. This other, to whose Sentence they submit, is called an ARBITRATOR. And therefore it is of the Law of Nature, "That they that are at controversie, submit their Right to the judgement of an Arbitrator."

The Seventeenth, No Man Is His Own Judge

And seeing every man is presumed to do all things in order to his own benefit, no man is a fit Arbitrator in his own cause: and if he were never so fit; yet Equity allowing to each party equall benefit, if one be admitted to be Judge, the other is to be admitted also; & so the controversie, that is, the cause of War, remains, against the Law of Nature.

The Eighteenth, No Man To Be Judge, That Has In Him Cause Of Partiality

For the same reason no man in any Cause ought to be received for Arbitrator, to whom greater profit, or honour, or pleasure apparently ariseth out of the victory of one party, than of the other: for he hath taken (though an unavoydable bribe, yet) a bribe; and no man can be obliged to trust him. And thus also the controversie, and the condition of War remaineth, contrary to the Law of Nature.

The Nineteenth, Of Witnesse

And in a controversie of Fact, the Judge being to give no more credit to one, than to the other, (if there be no other Arguments) must give credit to a third; or to a third and fourth; or more: For else the question is undecided, and left to force, contrary to the Law of Nature.

These are the Lawes of Nature, dictating Peace, for a means of the conservation of men in multitudes; and which onely concern the doctrine of Civill Society. There be other things tending to the destruction of particular men; as Drunkenness, and all other parts of Intemperance; which may therefore also be reckoned amongst those things which the Law of Nature hath forbidden; but are not necessary to be mentioned, nor are pertinent enough to this place.

A Rule, By Which The Laws Of Nature May Easily Be Examined

And though this may seem too subtile a deduction of the Lawes of Nature, to be taken notice of by all men; whereof the most part are too busie in getting food, and the rest too negligent to understand; yet to leave all men unexcusable, they have been contracted into one easie sum, intelligible even to the meanest capacity; and that is, "Do not that to another, which thou wouldest not have done to thy selfe;" which sheweth him, that he has no more to do in learning the Lawes of Nature, but, when weighing the actions of other men with his own, they seem too heavy, to put them into the other part of the ballance, and his own into their place, that his own passions, and selfe-love, may adde nothing to the weight; and then there is none of these

Lawes of Nature that will not appear unto him very reasonable.

The Lawes Of Nature Oblige In Conscience Alwayes,

But In Effect Then Onely When There Is Security The Lawes of Nature oblige In Foro Interno; that is to say, they bind to a desire they should take place: but In Foro Externo; that is, to the putting them in act, not alwayes. For he that should be modest, and tractable, and performe all he promises, in such time, and place, where no man els should do so, should but make himselfe a prey to others, and procure his own certain ruine, contrary to the ground of all Lawes of Nature, which tend to Natures preservation. And again, he that shall observe the same Lawes towards him, observes them not himselfe, seeketh not Peace, but War; & consequently the destruction of his Nature by Violence.

And whatsoever Lawes bind In Foro Interno, may be broken, not onely by a fact contrary to the Law but also by a fact according to it, in case a man think it contrary. For though his Action in this case, be according to the Law; which where the Obligation is In Foro Interno, is a breach.

The Laws Of Nature Are Eternal;

The Lawes of Nature are Immutable and Eternall, For Injustice, Ingratitude, Arrogance, Pride, Iniquity, Acception of persons, and the rest, can never be made lawfull. For it can never be that Warre shall preserve life, and Peace destroy it.

And Yet Easie

The same Lawes, because they oblige onely to a desire, and endeavour, I mean an unfeigned and constant endeavour, are easie to be observed. For in that they require nothing but endeavour; he that endeavoureth their performance, fulfilleth them; and he that fulfilleth the Law, is Just.

The Science Of These Lawes, Is The True Moral Philosophy

And the Science of them, is the true and onely Moral Philosophy. For Morall Philosophy is nothing else but the Science of what is Good, and Evill, in the conversation, and Society of mankind. Good, and Evill, are names that signifie our Appetites, and Aversions; which in different tempers, customes, and doctrines of men, are different: And divers men, differ not onely in their Judgement, on the senses of what is pleasant, and unpleasant to the tast, smell, hearing, touch, and sight; but also of what is conformable, or disagreeable to Reason, in the actions of common life. Nay, the same man, in divers times, differs from himselfe; and one time praiseth, that is, calleth Good, what another time he dispraiseth, and calleth Evil: From whence arise Disputes, Controversies, and at last War.

And therefore so long as man is in the condition of meer Nature, (which is a condition of War,) as private Appetite is the measure of Good, and Evill: and consequently all men agree on this, that Peace is Good, and therefore also the way, or means of Peace, which (as I have shewed before) are Justice, Gratitude, Modesty, Equity, Mercy, & the rest of the Laws of Nature, are good; that is to say, Morall Vertues; and their contrarie Vices, Evill. Now the science of Vertue and Vice, is Morall Philosophie; and therfore the true Doctrine of the Lawes of Nature, is the true Morall Philosophie. But the Writers of Morall Philosophie, though they acknowledge the same Vertues and Vices; Yet not seeing wherein consisted their Goodnesse; nor that they come to be praised, as the meanes of peaceable, sociable, and comfortable living; place them in a mediocrity of passions: as if not the Cause, but the Degree of daring, made Fortitude; or not the Cause, but the Quantity of a gift, made Liberality.

These dictates of Reason, men use to call by the name of Lawes; but improperly: for they are but Conclusions, or Theoremes concerning what conduceth to the conservation and defence of themselves; whereas Law, properly is the word of him, that by right hath command over others. But yet if we consider the same Theoremes, as delivered in the word of God, that by right commandeth all things; then are they properly called Lawes.

...

PART II. OF COMMON-WEALTH

CHAPTER XVII. OF THE CAUSES, GENERATION, AND DEFINITION OF A COMMON-WEALTH

The End Of Common-wealth, Particular Security

The finall Cause, End, or Designe of men, (who naturally love Liberty, and Dominion over others,) in the introduction of that restraint upon themselves, (in which wee see them live in Common-wealths,) is the foresight of their own preservation, and of a more contented life thereby; that is to say, of getting themselves out from that miserable condition of Warre, which is necessarily consequent (as hath been shewn) to the naturall Passions of men, when there is no visible Power to keep them in awe, and tye them by feare of punishment to the performance of their Covenants, and observation of these Lawes of Nature set down in the fourteenth and fifteenth Chapters.

Which Is Not To Be Had From The Law Of Nature:

For the Lawes of Nature (as Justice, Equity, Modesty, Mercy, and (in summe) Doing To Others, As Wee Would Be Done To,) if themselves, without the terrour of some Power, to cause them to be observed, are contrary to our naturall Passions, that carry us to Partiality, Pride, Revenge, and the like. And Covenants, without the Sword, are but Words, and of no strength to secure a man at all. Therefore notwithstanding the Lawes of Nature, (which every one hath then kept, when he has the will to keep them, when he can do it safely,) if there be no Power erected, or not great enough for our security; every man will and may lawfully rely on his own strength and art, for caution against all other men. And in all places, where men have lived by small Families, to robbe and spoyle one another, has been a Trade, and so farre from being reputed against the Law of Nature, that the greater spoyles they gained, the greater was their honour; and men observed no other Lawes therein, but the Lawes of Honour; that is, to abstain from cruelty, leaving to men their lives, and instruments of husbandry. And as small Familyes did then; so now do Cities and Kingdomes which are but greater Families (for their own security) enlarge their Dominions, upon all pretences of danger, and fear of Invasion, or assistance that may be given to Invaders, endeavour as much as they can, to subdue, or weaken their neighbours, by open force, and secret arts, for want of other Caution, justly; and are rememdbred for it in after ages with honour.

Nor From The Conjunction Of A Few Men Or Familyes

Nor is it the joyning together of a small number of men, that gives them this security; because in small numbers, small additions on the one side or the other, make the advantage of strength so great, as is sufficient to carry the Victory; and therefore gives encouragement to an Invasion. The Multitude sufficient to confide in for our Security, is not determined by any certain number, but by comparison with the Enemy we feare; and is then sufficient, when the odds of the Enemy is not of so visible and conspicuous moment, to determine the event of warre, as to move him to attempt.

Nor From A Great Multitude, Unlesse Directed By One Judgement

And be there never so great a Multitude; yet if their actions be directed according to their particular judgements, and particular appetites, they can expect thereby no defence, nor protection, neither against a Common enemy, nor against the injuries of one another. For being distracted in opinions concerning the best use and application of their strength, they do not help, but hinder one another; and reduce their strength by mutuall opposition to nothing: whereby they are easily, not onely subdued by a very few that agree together; but also when there is no common enemy, they make warre upon each other, for their particular interests. For if we could suppose a great Multitude of men to consent in the observation of Justice, and other Lawes of Nature, without a common Power to keep them all in awe; we might as well suppose all Man-kind to do the same; and then there neither would be nor need to be any Civill Government, or Common-wealth at all; because there would be Peace without subjection.

And That Continually

Nor is it enough for the security, which men desire should last all the time of their life, that they be governed, and directed by one judgement, for a limited time; as in one Battell, or one Warre. For though they obtain a Victory by their unanimous endeavour against a forraign enemy; yet afterwards, when either they have no common enemy, or he that by one part is held for an enemy, is by another part held for a friend, they must needs by the difference of their interests dissolve, and fall again into a Warre amongst themselves.

Why Certain Creatures Without Reason, Or Speech, Do Neverthelesse Live In Society, Without Any Coercive Power

It is true, that certain living creatures, as Bees, and Ants, live sociably one with another, (which are therefore by Aristotle numbred amongst Politicall creatures;) and yet have no other direction, than their particular judgements and appetites; nor speech, whereby one of them can signifie to another, what he thinks expedient for the common benefit: and therefore some man may perhaps desire to know, why Man-kind cannot do the same. To which I answer,

First, that men are continually in competition for Honour and Dignity, which these creatures are not; and consequently amongst men there ariseth on that ground, Envy and Hatred, and finally Warre; but amongst these not so.

Secondly, that amongst these creatures, the Common good differeth not from the Private; and being by nature enclined to their private, they procure thereby the common benefit. But man, whose Joy consisteth in comparing himselfe with other men, can relish nothing but what is eminent.

Thirdly, that these creatures, having not (as man) the use of reason, do not see, nor think they see any fault, in the administration of their common businesse: whereas amongst men, there are very many, that thinke themselves wiser, and abler to govern the Publique, better than the rest; and these strive to reforme and innovate, one this way, another that way; and thereby bring it into Distraction and Civill warre.

Fourthly, that these creatures, though they have some use of voice, in making knowne to one another their desires, and other affections; yet they want that art of words, by which some men can represent to others, that which is Good, in the likenesse of Evill; and Evill, in the likenesse of Good; and augment, or diminish the apparent greatnesse of Good and Evill; discontenting men, and troubling their Peace at their pleasure.

Fiftly, irrationall creatures cannot distinguish betweene Injury, and Dammage; and therefore as long as they be at ease, they are not offended with their fellowes: whereas Man is then most troublesome, when he is most at ease: for then it is that he loves to shew his Wisdome, and controule the Actions of them that governe the Common-wealth.

Lastly, the agreement of these creatures is Naturall; that of men, is by Covenant only, which is Artificiall: and therefore it is no wonder if there be somewhat else required (besides Covenant) to make their Agreement constant and lasting; which is a Common Power, to keep them in awe, and to direct their actions to the Common Benefit.

The Generation Of A Common-wealth

The only way to erect such a Common Power, as may be able to defend them from the invasion of Forraigners, and the injuries of one another, and thereby to secure them in such sort, as that by their owne industrie, and by the fruites of the Earth, they may nourish themselves and live contentedly; is, to conferre all their power and strength upon one Man, or upon one Assembly of men, that may reduce all their Wills, by plurality of voices, unto one Will: which is as much as to say, to appoint one man, or Assembly of men, to beare their Person; and every one to owne, and acknowledge himselfe to be Author of whatsoever he that so beareth their Person, shall Act, or cause to be Acted, in those things which concerne the Common Peace and Safetie; and therein to submit their Wills, every one to his Will, and their Judgements, to his Judgment. This is more than Consent, or Concord; it is a reall Unitie of them all, in one and the same Person, made by Covenant of every man with every man, in such manner, as if every man should say to every man, "I Authorise and give up my Right of Governing my selfe, to this Man, or to this Assembly of men, on this condition, that thou give up thy Right to him, and Authorise all his Actions in like manner." This done, the Multitude so united in one Person, is called a COMMON-WEALTH, in latine CIVITAS. This is the Generation of that great *LEVIATHAN*, or rather (to speake more reverently) of that Mortall God, to which wee owe under the Immortall God, our peace and defence. For by this Authoritie, given him by every particular man in the Common-Wealth, he hath the use of so much Power and Strength conferred on him, that by terror thereof, he is inabled to forme the wills of them all, to Peace at home, and mutuall ayd against their enemies abroad.

The Definition Of A Common-wealth
And in him consisteth the Essence of the Common-wealth; which (to define it,) is "One Person, of whose Acts a great Multitude, by mutuall Covenants one with another, have made themselves every one the Author, to the end he may use the strength and means of them all, as he shall think expedient, for their Peace and Common Defence."

Soveraigne, And Subject, What
And he that carryeth this Person, as called SOVERAIGNE, and said to have Soveraigne Power; and every one besides, his SUBJECT.

The attaining to this Soveraigne Power, is by two wayes. One, by Naturall force; as when a man maketh his children, to submit themselves, and their children to his government, as being able to destroy them if they refuse, or by Warre subdueth his enemies to his will, giving them their lives on that condition. The other, is when men agree amongst themselves, to submit to some Man, or Assembly of men, voluntarily, on confidence to be protected by him against all others. This later, may be called a Politicall Common-wealth, or

Common-wealth by Institution; and the former, a Common-wealth by Acquisition. And first, I shall speak of a Common-wealth by Institution.

CHAPTER XVIII. OF THE RIGHTS OF SOVERAIGNES BY INSTITUTION

The Act Of Instituting A Common-wealth, What
A Common-wealth is said to be Instituted, when a Multitude of men do Agree, and Covenant, Every One With Every One, that to whatsoever Man, or Assembly Of Men, shall be given by the major part, the Right to Present the Person of them all, (that is to say, to be their Representative;) every one, as well he that Voted For It, as he that Voted Against It, shall Authorise all the Actions and Judgements, of that Man, or Assembly of men, in the same manner, as if they were his own, to the end, to live peaceably amongst themselves, and be protected against other men.

The Consequences To Such Institution, Are

I. The Subjects Cannot Change The Forme Of Government

From this Institution of a Common-wealth are derived all the Rights, and Facultyes of him, or them, on whom the Soveraigne Power is conferred by the consent of the People assembled.
First, because they Covenant, it is to be understood, they are not obliged by former Covenant to any thing repugnant hereunto. And Consequently they that have already Instituted a Common-wealth, being thereby bound by Covenant, to own the Actions, and Judgements of one, cannot lawfully make a new Covenant, amongst themselves, to be obedient to any other, in any thing whatsoever, without his permission. And therefore, they that are subjects to a Monarch, cannot without his leave cast off Monarchy, and return to the confusion of a disunited Multitude; nor transferre their Person from him that beareth it, to another Man, or other Assembly of men: for they are bound, every man

to every man, to Own, and be reputed Author of all, that he that already is their Soveraigne, shall do, and judge fit to be done: so that any one man dissenting, all the rest should break their Covenant made to that man, which is injustice: and they have also every man given the Soveraignty to him that beareth their Person; and therefore if they depose him, they take from him that which is his own, and so again it is injustice. Besides, if he that attempteth to depose his Soveraign, be killed, or punished by him for such attempt, he is author of his own punishment, as being by the Institution, Author of all his Soveraign shall do: And because it is injustice for a man to do any thing, for which he may be punished by his own authority, he is also upon that title, unjust. And whereas some men have pretended for their disobedience to their Soveraign, a new Covenant, made, not with men, but with God; this also is unjust: for there is no Covenant with God, but by mediation of some body that representeth Gods Person; which none doth but Gods Lieutenant, who hath the Soveraignty under God. But this pretence of Covenant with God, is so evident a lye, even in the pretenders own consciences, that it is not onely an act of an unjust, but also of a vile, and unmanly disposition.

2. Soveraigne Power Cannot Be Forfeited

Secondly, Because the Right of bearing the Person of them all, is given to him they make Soveraigne, by Covenant onely of one to another, and not of him to any of them; there can happen no breach of Covenant on the part of the Soveraigne; and consequently none of his Subjects, by any pretence of forfeiture, can be freed from his Subjection. That he which is made Soveraigne maketh no Covenant with his Subjects beforehand, is manifest; because either he must make it with the whole multitude, as one party to the Covenant; or he must make a severall Covenant with every man. With the whole, as one party, it is impossible; because as yet they are not one Person: and if he make so many severall Covenants as there be men, those Covenants after he hath the Soveraignty are voyd, because what act soever can be pretended by any one of them

for breach thereof, is the act both of himselfe, and of all the rest, because done in the Person, and by the Right of every one of them in particular. Besides, if any one, or more of them, pretend a breach of the Covenant made by the Soveraigne at his Institution; and others, or one other of his Subjects, or himselfe alone, pretend there was no such breach, there is in this case, no Judge to decide the controversie: it returns therefore to the Sword again; and every man recovereth the right of Protecting himselfe by his own strength, contrary to the designe they had in the Institution. It is therefore in vain to grant Soveraignty by way of precedent Covenant. The opinion that any Monarch receiveth his Power by Covenant, that is to say on Condition, proceedeth from want of understanding this easie truth, that Covenants being but words, and breath, have no force to oblige, contain, constrain, or protect any man, but what it has from the publique Sword; that is, from the untyed hands of that Man, or Assembly of men that hath the Soveraignty, and whose actions are avouched by them all, and performed by the strength of them all, in him united. But when an Assembly of men is made Soveraigne; then no man imagineth any such Covenant to have past in the Institution; for no man is so dull as to say, for example, the People of Rome, made a Covenant with the Romans, to hold the Soveraignty on such or such conditions; which not performed, the Romans might lawfully depose the Roman People. That men see not the reason to be alike in a Monarchy, and in a Popular Government, proceedeth from the ambition of some, that are kinder to the government of an Assembly, whereof they may hope to participate, than of Monarchy, which they despair to enjoy.

3. No Man Can Without Injustice Protest Against The Institution Of The Soveraigne Declared By The Major Part. Thirdly, because the major part hath by consenting voices declared a Soveraigne; he that dissented must now consent with the rest; that is, be contented to avow all the actions he shall do, or else justly be destroyed by the rest. For if he voluntarily entered into the Congregation of them that were assembled, he sufficiently declared thereby his will (and

therefore tacitely covenanted) to stand to what the major part should ordayne: and therefore if he refuse to stand thereto, or make Protestation against any of their Decrees, he does contrary to his Covenant, and therfore unjustly. And whether he be of the Congregation, or not; and whether his consent be asked, or not, he must either submit to their decrees, or be left in the condition of warre he was in before; wherein he might without injustice be destroyed by any man whatsoever.

4. The Soveraigns Actions Cannot Be Justly Accused By The Subject Fourthly, because every Subject is by this Institution Author of all the Actions, and Judgements of the Soveraigne Instituted; it followes, that whatsoever he doth, it can be no injury to any of his Subjects; nor ought he to be by any of them accused of Injustice. For he that doth any thing by authority from another, doth therein no injury to him by whose authority he acteth: But by this Institution of a Common-wealth, every particular man is Author of all the Soveraigne doth; and consequently he that complaineth of injury from his Soveraigne, complaineth of that whereof he himselfe is Author; and therefore ought not to accuse any man but himselfe; no nor himselfe of injury; because to do injury to ones selfe, is impossible. It is true that they that have Soveraigne power, may commit Iniquity; but not Injustice, or Injury in the proper signification.

5. What Soever The Soveraigne Doth, Is Unpunishable By The Subject

Fiftly, and consequently to that which was sayd last, no man that hath Soveraigne power can justly be put to death, or otherwise in any manner by his Subjects punished. For seeing every Subject is author of the actions of his Soveraigne; he punisheth another, for the actions committed by himselfe.

6. The Soveraigne Is Judge Of What Is Necessary For The Peace And Defence Of His Subjects

And because the End of this Institution, is the Peace and Defence of them all; and whosoever has right to the End, has right to the Means; it belongeth of Right, to whatsoever Man, or Assembly that hath the Soveraignty, to be Judge both of the meanes of Peace and Defence; and also of the hindrances, and disturbances of the same; and to do whatsoever he shall think necessary to be done, both beforehand, for the preserving of Peace and Security, by prevention of discord at home and Hostility from abroad; and, when Peace and Security are lost, for the recovery of the same. And therefore,

And Judge Of What Doctrines Are Fit To Be Taught Them

Sixtly, it is annexed to the Soveraignty, to be Judge of what Opinions and Doctrines are averse, and what conducing to Peace; and consequently, on what occasions, how farre, and what, men are to be trusted withall, in speaking to Multitudes of people; and who shall examine the Doctrines of all bookes before they be published. For the Actions of men proceed from their Opinions; and in the wel governing of Opinions, consisteth the well governing of mens Actions, in order to their Peace, and Concord. And though in matter of Doctrine, nothing ought to be regarded but the Truth; yet this is not repugnant to regulating of the same by Peace. For Doctrine Repugnant to Peace, can no more be True, than Peace and Concord can be against the Law of Nature. It is true, that in a Common-wealth, where by the negligence, or unskilfullnesse of Governours, and Teachers, false Doctrines are by time generally received; the contrary Truths may be generally offensive; Yet the most sudden, and rough busling in of a new Truth, that can be, does never breake the Peace, but onely somtimes awake the Warre. For those men that are so remissely governed, that they dare take up Armes, to defend, or introduce an Opinion, are still in Warre; and their condition not Peace, but only a Cessation of Armes for feare of one another; and they live as it were, in the procincts of battaile continually. It belongeth therefore to him that hath the Soveraign Power, to be Judge, or constitute all Judges of Opinions and Doctrines, as a thing necessary to Peace, thereby to prevent Discord and Civill Warre.

7. The Right Of Making Rules, Whereby The Subject May Every Man Know What Is So His Owne, As No Other Subject Can Without Injustice Take It From Him

Seventhly, is annexed to the Soveraigntie, the whole power of prescribing the Rules, whereby every man may know, what Goods he may enjoy and what Actions he may doe, without being molested by any of his fellow Subjects: And this is it men Call Propriety. For before constitution of Soveraign Power (as hath already been shewn) all men had right to all things; which necessarily causeth Warre: and therefore this Proprietie, being necessary to Peace, and depending on Soveraign Power, is the Act of the Power, in order to the publique peace. These Rules of Propriety (or Meum and Tuum) and of Good, Evill, Lawfull and Unlawfull in the actions of subjects, are the Civill Lawes, that is to say, the lawes of each Commonwealth in particular; though the name of Civill Law be now restrained to the antient Civill Lawes of the City of Rome; which being the head of a great part of the World, her Lawes at that time were in these parts the Civill Law.

8. To Him Also Belongeth The Right Of All Judicature And Decision Of Controversies:

Eightly, is annexed to the Soveraigntie, the Right of Judicature; that is to say, of hearing and deciding all Controversies, which may arise concerning Law, either Civill, or naturall, or concerning Fact. For without the decision of Controversies, there is no protection of one Subject, against the injuries of another; the Lawes concerning Meum and Tuum are in vaine; and to every man remaineth, from the naturall and necessary appetite of his own conservation, the right of protecting himselfe by his private strength, which is the condition of Warre; and contrary to the end for which every Common-wealth is instituted.

9. And Of Making War, And Peace, As He Shall Think Best:

Ninthly, is annexed to the Soveraignty, the Right of making Warre, and Peace with other Nations, and Common-wealths; that is to say, of Judging when it is for the publique good, and how

great forces are to be assembled, armed, and payd for that end; and to levy mony upon the Subjects, to defray the expenses thereof. For the Power by which the people are to be defended, consisteth in their Armies; and the strength of an Army, in the union of their strength under one Command; which Command the Soveraign Instituted, therefore hath; because the command of the Militia, without other Institution, maketh him that hath it Soveraign. And therefore whosoever is made Generall of an Army, he that hath the Soveraign Power is always Generallissimo.

10. And Of Choosing All Counsellours, And Ministers, Both Of Peace, And Warre:

Tenthly, is annexed to the Soveraignty, the choosing of all Councellours, Ministers, Magistrates, and Officers, both in peace, and War. For seeing the Soveraign is charged with the End, which is the common Peace and Defence; he is understood to have Power to use such Means, as he shall think most fit for his discharge.

11. And Of Rewarding, And Punishing, And That (Where No Former Law hath Determined The Measure Of It) Arbitrary:

Eleventhly, to the Soveraign is committed the Power of Rewarding with riches, or honour; and of Punishing with corporall, or pecuniary punishment, or with ignominy every Subject according to the Lawe he hath formerly made; or if there be no Law made, according as he shall judge most to conduce to the encouraging of men to serve the Common-wealth, or deterring of them from doing dis-service to the same.

12. And Of Honour And Order

Lastly, considering what values men are naturally apt to set upon themselves; what respect they look for from others; and how little they value other men; from whence continually arise amongst them, Emulation, Quarrells, Factions, and at last Warre, to the destroying of one another, and diminution of their strength against a Common Enemy; It is necessary that there be Lawes of Honour, and a publique rate of the worth of such men as have deserved, or are able to deserve well of the Common-wealth; and that there be force in the hands of some or other, to put those Lawes in execution. But it hath already been shown, that not onely the whole Militia, or forces of the Common-wealth; but also the Judicature of all Controversies, is annexed to the Soveraignty. To the Soveraign therefore it belongeth also to give titles of Honour; and to appoint what Order of place, and dignity, each man shall hold; and what signes of respect, in publique or private meetings, they shall give to one another.

These Rights Are Indivisible

These are the Rights, which make the Essence of Soveraignty; and which are the markes, whereby a man may discern in what Man, or Assembly of men, the Soveraign Power is placed, and resideth. For these are incommunicable, and inseparable. The Power to coyn Mony; to dispose of the estate and persons of Infant heires; to have praeemption in Markets; and all other Statute Praerogatives, may be transferred by the Soveraign; and yet the Power to protect his Subject be retained. But if he transferre the Militia, he retains the Judicature in vain, for want of execution of the Lawes; Or if he grant away the Power of raising Mony; the Militia is in vain: or if he give away the government of doctrines, men will be frighted into rebellion with the feare of Spirits. And so if we consider any one of the said Rights, we shall presently see, that the holding of all the rest, will produce no effect, in the conservation of Peace and Justice, the end for which all Common-wealths are Instituted. And this division is it, whereof it is said, "A kingdome divided in it selfe cannot stand:" For unlesse this division precede, division into opposite Armies can never happen. If there had not first been an opinion received of the greatest part of England, that these Powers were divided between the King, and the Lords, and the House of Commons, the people had never been divided, and fallen into this Civill Warre; first between those that disagreed in Politiques; and after between the Dissenters about the liberty of Religion; which have so instructed men in this point of Soveraign Right, that there be few now (in England,) that do not see, that these Rights are inseparable, and

will be so generally acknowledged, at the next return of Peace; and so continue, till their miseries are forgotten; and no longer, except the vulgar be better taught than they have hetherto been.

And Can By No Grant Passe Away Without Direct Renouncing Of The Soveraign Power

And because they are essentiall and inseparable Rights, it follows necessarily, that in whatsoever, words any of them seem to be granted away, yet if the Soveraign Power it selfe be not in direct termes renounced, and the name of Soveraign no more given by the Grantees to him that Grants them, the Grant is voyd: for when he has granted all he can, if we grant back the Soveraignty, all is restored, as inseparably annexed thereunto.

The Power And Honour Of Subjects Vanisheth In The Presence Of The Power Soveraign

This great Authority being indivisible, and inseparably annexed to the Soveraignty, there is little ground for the opinion of them, that say of Soveraign Kings, though they be Singulis Majores, of greater Power than every one of their Subjects, yet they be Universis Minores, of lesse power than them all together. For if by All Together, they mean not the collective body as one person, then All Together, and Every One, signifie the same; and the speech is absurd. But if by All Together, they understand them as one Person (which person the Soveraign bears,) then the power of all together, is the same with the Soveraigns power; and so again the speech is absurd; which absurdity they see well enough, when the Soveraignty is in an Assembly of the people; but in a Monarch they see it not; and yet the power of Soveraignty is the same in whomsoever it be placed.

And as the Power, so also the Honour of the Soveraign, ought to be greater, than that of any, or all the Subjects. For in the Soveraignty is the fountain of Honour. The dignities of Lord, Earle, Duke, and Prince are his Creatures. As in the presence of the Master, the Servants are equall, and without any honour at all; So are the Subjects, in the presence of the Soveraign. And though they shine some more, some lesse, when they are out of his sight; yet in his presence, they shine no more than the Starres in presence of the Sun.

Soveraigne Power Not Hurtfull As The Want Of It, And The Hurt Proceeds For The Greatest Part From Not Submitting Readily, To A Lesse

But a man may here object, that the Condition of Subjects is very miserable; as being obnoxious to the lusts, and other irregular passions of him, or them that have so unlimited a Power in their hands. And commonly they that live under a Monarch, think it the fault of Monarchy; and they that live under the government of Democracy, or other Soveraign Assembly, attribute all the inconvenience to that forme of Common-wealth; whereas the Power in all formes, if they be perfect enough to protect them, is the same; not considering that the estate of Man can never be without some incommodity or other; and that the greatest, that in any forme of Government can possibly happen to the people in generall, is scarce sensible, in respect of the miseries, and horrible calamities, that accompany a Civill Warre; or that dissolute condition of masterlesse men, without subjection to Lawes, and a coercive Power to tye their hands from rapine, and revenge: nor considering that the greatest pressure of Soveraign Governours, proceedeth not from any delight, or profit they can expect in the dammage, or weakening of their subjects, in whose vigor, consisteth their own selves, that unwillingly contributing to their own defence, make it necessary for their Governours to draw from them what they can in time of Peace, that they may have means on any emergent occasion, or sudden need, to resist, or take advantage on their Enemies. For all men are by nature provided of notable multiplying glasses, (that is their Passions and Self-love,) through which, every little payment appeareth a great grievance; but are destitute of those prospective glasses, (namely Morall and Civill Science,) to see a farre off the miseries that hang over them, and cannot without such payments be avoyded.

Chapter 8: Politics in the Enlightenment

Comprehension questions you should be able to answer after reading this chapter:

1. Describe how Locke's version of the state of nature differs from Hobbes' (as presented in the previous chapter).

2. What is the "law of nature," according to Locke?

3. According to Locke, what is the difference between the state of nature and a state of war?

4. What are the "inconveniences" of the state of nature?

5. Explain the origin of property, according to Locke. What are the limits of property, in the state of nature?

6. How does the introduction of money change the limits of property, and how does this contribute towards our leaving the state of nature?

7. Why does Locke reject Hobbes' absolute monarchy?

8. When, if ever, does Locke think that citizens have a right to rebel against their ruler?

9. According to Locke, what is a "church?" What is a "commonwealth" (State)?

10. Why does Locke think the State (ruler) has no right to use State power for the sake of religious goals?

11. Why does he think the Church has no right to use State power for the sake of those goals either? What methods of enforcing their own dogma and rituals do churches rightfully have at their disposal, according to Locke?

12. What are the limits of tolerable behavior, in the name of religion, for Locke?

13. What kinds of religions/worldviews are not entitled to toleration, according to Locke?

The Age of Enlightenment lasted (roughly) from the 1620s to the 1780s, and was a time of massive intellectual and cultural change in Europe. Notable philosophers and scientists from this period include Francis Bacon (1562–1626), René Descartes (1596–1650), John Locke (1632–1704), Baruch Spinoza (1632–77), Voltaire (1694–1778), David Hume (1711–76), Immanuel Kant (1724–1804), Cesare Beccaria (1738–94), and Sir Isaac Newton (1642–1727).

This period was also a time of tumultuous political change, with monarchies across Europe changing hands or even disappearing, civil wars, religious conflict, and much political thinking and experimentation.

This chapter will not even pretend to do justice to the rich resources of this Age, but will humbly focus on just one figure: John Locke

Locke's Background

John Locke was born on August 29th, 1632. Locke's father (also named John) was a cavalryman on the side of Parliament during the English Civil War. John Sr.'s commander was Alexander Popham, who, in addition to his military office, was also a member of Parliament. Popham sponsored Locke Jr., and secured his placement at the prestigious Westminster School in London.

The century in which Locke lived was both eventful and chaotic. Conflicts erupted between

Parliament and the Monarchy, and between Catholics, Anglicans, and other Protestants. Civil War engulfed England in the 1640s, and when King Charles I was defeated and executed (on January 30th, 1649), it took place on scaffolding erected in front of the Banqueting House nearby the Westminster School. The headmaster of that school was Dr. Richard Busby (a Royalist), and he prevented the students from watching. Locke would have been just 17, at the time.

England then experimented with the abolishment of the Monarchy, the House of Lords, and even the Anglican Church, replacing the government with the "Protectorate" of Oliver Cromwell—which was first, ostensibly, a republic, but then became, in effect, a military dictatorship.

After Cromwell's death, his Protectorate died with him, replaced by the restored monarchy of Charles II—and the return of the House of Lords and Anglican Church, in addition to the Monarchy. This period ended in 1688 with the Glorious Revolution, and the replacement of James II with William of Orange and his wife, Mary. These latter events will be reconsidered later, in light of Locke's personal involvement with them, but we will first step back and consider Locke, the scientist and medical doctor, before turning to Locke, the political theorist and operative.

Locke went to Oxford at the age of 20, where he studied medicine as well as the "classics." His scientific mentor was none other than Robert Boyle (known for "Boyle's Law"), a "mechanical" philosopher who entertained an atomistic/corpuscular worldview, and interpreted the world in terms of matter in motion. Locke, Boyle, and Isaac Newton were all founding members of the English Royal Society in 1668. As a young doctor, Locke worked, for a time, with Dr. David Thomas, and it was through him that he met Lord Ashley Shaftesbury.

Anthony Ashley Cooper, 1st Earl of Shaftesbury (hereafter referred to as "Shaftesbury") was a wealthy and politically influential man who happened to have a potentially-fatal liver condition. In 1666 he sought a pharmaceutical remedy from Dr. David

Thomas, but the medicine was delivered by Locke. The two men hit it off, and within a year Locke had been invited to take up residence with the Ashley family as Shaftesbury's personal physician, and eventual advisor. While serving as his physician, Locke directed an astonishing surgery to remove an abscess on his liver—saving his life in the process. Keep in mind that this surgery was performed in the late 17th century!

Locke's loyalty and service was rewarded. He was given "offices" and various "secretaryships," including that of the Associated Proprietors of the colony of the Carolinas. In that capacity, Locke was involved in the writing of the constitution of the Carolinas. As a result of his association with Shaftesbury, in general, Locke found himself in the heart of English politics in the 1670s and 1680s.

Shaftesbury was politically "versatile." He had initially sided with Charles I in the Civil War, but eventually changed sides and joined the Parliamentarians. He then supported Cromwell, but was part of the Convention Parliament that invited Charles II to return to England (thereby restoring the monarchy) after Cromwell's death. He worked for Charles II from 1660-1673, rising to the position of Lord Chancellor of the Realm (second highest ranking officer of the State, second only to the Lord High Steward, and presiding officer of the House of Lords) in 1672, and Locke became his secretary in that capacity. Shaftesbury was promoted to an Earldom in 1672. His anti-Catholic views eventually led to his dismissal, however, given that Charles' brother (James) was Catholic.

Shaftesbury formed the "Country Party" to criticize and oppose the King, and to prevent James from someday succeeding to the throne. From this group, the first two "modern" political parties (the Whigs and Tories) evolved. He eventually conspired to overthrow Charles, and even marched on Parliament with a force of men in 1681, but was imprisoned and charged with treason. A sympathetic jury acquitted him, and he fled to Holland in exile. Locke followed soon thereafter. Locke would remain abroad from 1683 to 1689.

Charles II died in 1685, and his brother James took the throne. Anti-Catholic sentiment reached critical mass when his wife became pregnant with a Catholic heir. Protestant leaders conspired to bring William of Orange (the husband, and cousin, of James' daughter, Mary) from Holland, to claim the throne for himself. Locke made his return to England onboard the royal yacht, no less, escorting Princess (and soon to be Queen) Mary to join her husband.

In 1689, Locked published *An Essay Concerning Human Understanding*, as well as both the *Two Treatises on Government* and his first *Letter on Toleration* (though both of the latter were published anonymously). After more than a decade more of writing and political engagement, Locke died on the 28th of October, 1704.

Locke's impact on both philosophy and politics was seismic. Given the focus of this book, we will have to neglect much of his philosophical system, and pay attention solely to his political philosophy.

Locke's early works were much more conservative ("Hobbesian" at times!) than the later writings for which he would become famous. Those later writings shifted to a much more "libertarian" mentality, and reveal "kernels" of ideas now associated with classical liberalism: emphasis on private property ownership, minimal government, distrust of the use of coercion by authorities, and tolerance for diverse worldviews. We will begin with an idea that Locke shared with Hobbes—though interpreted very differently: the State of Nature.

The State of Nature

Similar to Hobbes, Locke thought all persons were "equal" in the State of Nature—but by this he means that we have similar faculties by virtue of being (equally) God's creations. The State of Nature is a state of equality in that there is no natural superior or inferior therein. The State of Nature can be conceived as a purely hypothetical state, though Locke described the "inland, vacant places of America" as an example of the State of Nature manifested in reality.[230]

The significance of Locke's assumption that all persons are God's creations shouldn't be underestimated, as it is the basis for several of his key political premises. God created all persons, and we are, in effect, his "property." People are sent into the world,

> by his order and about his business, they are his property whose workmanship they are, made to last during his, not another's pleasure: and being furnished with like faculties, sharing all in one community of nature, there cannot be supposed any subordination among us, that may authorize us to destroy one another, as if we were made for one another's uses, as the inferior ranks of creatures are for ours. . . . he has no liberty to destroy himself, or so much as any creature in his possession, yet when some nobler use than its bare possession calls for it.[231]

God creates us all as equals, and intends for us to survive (at least until God wills that we die). Since God intends our survival, God also wills the means necessary for it: life, liberty, health, and property. We, therefore, have natural (God-given) rights to these things, and in the State of Nature we have these rights equally. I have no right to infringe upon another's natural rights, nor does anyone else have the right to infringe upon my own. This conclusion is interpreted as the "law of nature."

> The state of nature has a law of nature to govern it, which obliges everyone: and reason which is that law, teaches all mankind who will but consult it, that being all equal and independent, no one ought to harm another in his life, health, liberty or possessions....[232]

---

[230] Locke, *Two Treatises on Government*, 2nd Book, 5.36.

[231] Ibid,. 2.6.
[232] Ibid., 2.6.

Already, we have some important differences between Hobbes' and Locke's visions of the State of Nature. For Hobbes, the state of nature is amoral anarchy. But, for Locke, even in the State of Nature, there is a law of nature, discernible by Reason, which provides moral guidance and moral limits on behavior. The State of Nature is not defined in terms of chaos and violence, but rather by virtue of the lack of a common authority to settle disputes. "Men living according to reason, without a common superior on earth, to judge between them, is properly the state of nature."[233] This is distinct from both civil society (where a government, serving as that common superior, exists) and a state of war, where men don't even abide by the law of reason.

In a clear reference (and critique) of Hobbes, Locke distinguishes between the State of Nature, and a state of war:

And here we have the plain difference between the state of nature and the state of war, which however some men have confounded, are as far distant, as a state of peace, good will, mutual assistance and preservation, and a state of enmity, malice, violence and mutual destruction, are one from another. Men living together according to reason, without a common superior on earth, with authority to judge between them, is properly the state of nature. But force, or a declared design of force, upon the person of another, where there is no common superior on earth to appeal to for relief, is the state of war: and it is the want of such an appeal gives a man the right of war even against an aggressor, tho' he be in society and a fellow subject. Thus a thief, whom I cannot harm, but by appeal to the law, for having stolen all that I am worth, I may kill, when he sets on me to rob me but of my horse or coat; because the law, which was made for my preservation, where it cannot interpose to secure my life from

present force, which, if lost, is capable of no reparation, permits me my own defence, and the right of war, a liberty to kill the aggressor, because the aggressor allows not time to appeal to our common judge, nor the decision of the law, for remedy in a case where the mischief may be irreparable. Want of a common judge with authority, puts all men in a state of nature: force without right, upon a man's person, makes a state of war, both where there is, and is not, a common judge.[234]

This means that the State of Nature is not a "war of all against all," as Hobbes conceived. For Hobbes, people flee the State of Nature out of necessity. For Locke, they do so out of *convenience*. They "unite into a community for their comfortable, safe, and peaceable living one amongst another, in a secure enjoyment of their properties."[235]

Even in this less nightmarish version of the State of Nature, there will still be those who violate the natural law and harm others, and so put themselves in a "state of war." In the State of Nature, there are no civil laws, nor police or judges. Victims must enforce their own rights, therefore, against any who violate them. In such cases, "everyone" has a right to punish the offender, but this sort of vigilante justice is both dangerous and prone to biased judgment. We might not be able successfully to do so (against a powerful criminal, for example), and we might punish more severely than the crime warrants, given that it is "personal" for us, if we were the victim. It is better that there be written laws, and impartial judges to execute and enforce them.[236] These issues and difficulties concerning punishment constitute much of the "inconveniences" of the State of Nature.

The great and chief end, therefore, of men's uniting into common-wealths, and putting themselves under government, is the preservation of their property. To

[233] Ibid., 2.19.
[234] Ibid., 3.19.

[235] Ibid., 8.95.
[236] Ibid., 9.124-9.126.

which in the state of nature there are many things wanting.

First, There wants an established, settled, known law, received and allowed by common consent to be the standard of right and wrong, and the common measure to decide all controversies between them: for though the law of nature be plain and intelligible to all rational creatures; yet men being biassed by their interest, as well as ignorant for want of study of it, are not apt to allow of it as a law binding to them in the application of it to their particular cases.

Secondly, In the state of nature there wants a known and indifferent judge, with authority to determine all differences according to the established law: for every one in that state being both judge and executioner of the law of nature, men being partial to themselves, passion and revenge is very apt to carry them too far, and with too much heat, in their own cases; as well as negligence, and unconcernedness, to make them too remiss in other men's.

Thirdly, In the state of nature there often wants power to back and support the sentence when right, and to give it due execution. They who by any injustice offended, will seldom fail, where they are able, by force to make good their injustice; such resistance many times makes the punishment dangerous, and frequently destructive, to those who attempt it.[237]

In summary, the State of Nature is lacking in several important ways:

1. The lack of a known, settled law and a common measure of that law.
2. The lack of a known and indifferent judge to interpret and apply the law.
3. The lack of sufficient power to enforce the law.

To address these "inconveniences," individuals consent to give up their right to personally judge and punish offenders, which brings them into civil society.

Man being born, as has been proved, with a title to perfect freedom, and an uncontrolled enjoyment of all the rights and privileges of the law of nature, equally with any other man, or number of men in the world, hath by nature a power, not only to preserve his property, that is, his life, liberty and estate, against the injuries and attempts of other men; but to judge of, and punish the breaches of that law in others, as he is persuaded the offence deserves, even with death itself, in crimes where the heinousness of the fact, in his opinion, requires it. But because no political society can be, nor subsist, without having in itself the power to preserve the property, and in order thereunto, punish the offences of all those of that society; there, and there only is political society, where every one of the members hath quitted this natural power, resigned it up into the hands of the community in all cases that exclude him not from appealing for protection to the law established by it. And thus all private judgment of every particular member being excluded, the community comes to be umpire, by settled standing rules, indifferent, and the same to all parties; and by men having authority from the community, for the execution of those rules, decides all the differences that may happen between any members of that society concerning any matter of right; and punishes those offences which any member hath committed against the society, with such penalties as the law has

---

[237] Ibid.

established: whereby it is easy to discern, who are, and who are not, in political society together. Those who are united into one body, and have a common established law and judicature to appeal to, with authority to decide controversies between them, and punish offenders, are in civil society one with another: but those who have no such common appeal, I mean on earth, are still in the state of nature, each being, where there is no other, judge for himself, and executioner; which is, as I have before shewed it, the perfect state of nature.

And thus the common-wealth comes by a power to set down what punishment shall belong to the several transgressions which they think worthy of it, committed amongst the members of that society, (which is the power of making laws) as well as it has the power to punish any injury done unto any of its members, by any one that is not of it, (which is the power of war and peace;) and all this for the preservation of the property of all the members of that society, as far as is possible. But though every man who has entered into civil society, and is become a member of any commonwealth, has thereby quitted his power to punish offences, against the law of nature, in prosecution of his own private judgment, yet with the judgment of offences, which he has given up to the legislative in all cases, where he can appeal to the magistrate, he has given a right to the common-wealth to employ his force, for the execution of the judgments of the common-wealth, whenever he shall be called to it; which indeed are his own judgments, they being made by himself, or his representative. And herein we have the original of the legislative and executive power of civil society, which is

to judge by standing laws, how far offences are to be punished, when committed within the common-wealth; and also to determine, by occasional judgments founded on the present circumstances of the fact, how far injuries from without are to be vindicated; and in both these to employ all the force of all the members, when there shall be need.

Wherever therefore any number of men are so united into one society, as to quit every one his executive power of the law of nature, and to resign it to the public, there and there only is a political, or civil society.[238]

Men consent to surrender their natural right to personally punish those who offend against the natural law, investing it in an impartial "executive," and, in so doing, have created a social contract. This is not our only incentive to leave behind the State of Nature, however. Much more so than Hobbes did, Locke focuses on the role of property in the formation of civil society. It is not only issues of punishment, but also issues of property that inspire us to leave the State of Nature and form a social contract.

Property

Locke's development of a philosophy of property was both original and systematic. He begins by recurring to the natural law, according to which all persons have a right to life and self-preservation. Consequently, we have a right to use natural resources for that end. By default, these resources are available to all.

The first instance of "property" is that everyone has a "property in his own person: this no body has any right to but himself."[239] Therefore, we are, by nature, free (as opposed to the property of another person). Our labor is also our own. "The labor of the body, and the work of his hands, we may say, are properly his."[240]

---

[238] Ibid., 7.87-7.89.
[239] Ibid., 5.27.

[240] Ibid.

Our own labor creates *additional* property when it mixes with resources. For example, the labor of extending my hand to pick an apple from the tree makes that resource (the apple) my property. An exception to this, for Locke, involved hired labor. Hired labor is not self-directed, so is not "labor," properly speaking, but "work."

> The turfs that my servant has cut,... where I have a right to them in common with others, become my property.[241]

To continue with our apple example: if I hire some workers to pick apples for me, the mere fact that it was their own effort that picked the apple doesn't make the apples their own property. Because I directed their work, and paid them to do so, they are "laboring" on my behalf, so the apples are still mine, as though I had picked them myself.

The initial acquisition of property in the State of Nature does not require the consent of others.

> And will any one say, he had no right to those acorns or apples, he thus appropriated, because he had not the consent of all mankind to make them his? Was it a robbery thus to assume to himself what belonged to all in common? If such a consent as that was necessary, man had starved, notwithstanding the plenty God had given him.[242]

Such "universal consent," is both impractical and impossible. Although we do not require the consent of others to claim property through our labor, there is a natural limit on what we may claim. Since everyone in the State of Nature has an equal right to self-preservation, the "natural" limit on property is what we can use without it "spoiling."

> "As much as anyone can make use of to any advantage of life before it spoils, so much by his labor he may fix a property in; whatever

is beyond this, is more than his share, and belongs to others."[243]

These limitations change, however, with the introduction of money.

> ...before the desire of having more than one needed had altered the intrinsic value of things, which depends only on their usefulness to the life of man; or had agreed, that a little piece of yellow metal, which would keep without wasting or decay, should be worth a great piece of flesh, or a whole heap of corn; though men had a right to appropriate by their labor, each one of himself, as much of the things of nature, as he could use; yet this could not be much, nor as to the prejudice of others, where the same plenty was left to those who could use the same industry.[244]

And:

> ...if he would give his nuts for a piece of metal, pleased with its color, or exchange his sheep for shells, or wool for a sparkling pebble or diamond, and keep those by him all his life, he invaded not the right of others, he might heap up as much of these durable things as he pleased; the exceeding of the bounds of his property not lying in the largeness of his possessions, but the perishing of anything useless in it.[245]

Once people consent to the use of money, one can acquire property that does not ever spoil. Inequalities result, and many are "no longer strict observers of equity and justice."[246]

> But since gold and silver, being little useful to the life of man in proportion to

---

241 Ibid., 5.28.
242 Ibid.
243 Ibid., 5.31.

244 Ibid., 5.37.
245 Ibid., 5.146.
246 Ibid., 9.123.

food, raiment, and carriage, has its value only from the consent of men, whereof labour yet makes, in great part, the measure, it is plain, that men have agreed to a disproportionate and unequal possession of the earth, they having, by a tacit and voluntary consent, found out a way how a man may fairly possess more land than he himself can use the product of, by receiving in exchange for the overplus gold and silver, which may be hoarded up without injury to any one; these metals not spoiling or decaying in the hands of the possessor. This partage of things in an inequality of private possessions, men have made practicable out of the bounds of society, and without compact, only by putting a value on gold and silver, and tacitly agreeing in the use of money: for in governments, the laws regulate the right of property, and the possession of land is determined by positive constitutions.[247]

These inequalities are the result of the "tacit and voluntary consent" to use money, but the inequalities produce difficulties all the same. Increasing population, scarcity of resources and land, and growing disputes over property cause people to reach a point where the "inconveniences" of living without written laws and impartial judges is too great, so they enter political society "for the mutual preservation of their lives, liberties, and estates."[248]

The State of Nature, therefore, has two stages. The first is one of perfect equality, both in terms of equal faculties as well as equal rights to the resources procured by our own labor. With the acceptance of currency, a second stage of the State of Nature emerges in which there are "disproportionate and unequal" possessions.[249]

The Social Contract

We see now that the "inconveniences" of the State of Nature arise because of conflict produced by those who might disobey the natural law and seek to harm others in the first place, but also because of the inequalities and resource conflicts that take place once property (and especially money) is introduced to a community. To remedy these inconveniences, there needs to be codified, written laws, and impartial judges to interpret them and punish offenders, as well as laws to clarify property rights, and to settle whatever property disputes might arise.

By the consent of the majority, the general direction and features of the State will be chosen.

> Every man, by consenting with others to make one body politic under one government, puts himself under an obligation . . . to submit to the determination of the majority.[250]

Simple majority consent must be sufficient for these purposes, since universal consent is practically impossible to gain (just as it was with regard to the acquisition of property in the state of nature).

An important difference between Hobbes and Locke is that, for Hobbes, people surrender *all* rights and power to the sovereign, who then rules (one hopes!) for their benefit. For Locke, the people form a civil society which is distinct from the State (i.e., the government), and which "retains supreme power."[251]

The State is empowered to act on behalf of the people, but the people never surrender their own power. Legitimate government is constitutionally limited, and exists by the consent of the governed. To remain legitimate, the government must rely on *continuing* consent of the people.

---

[247] Ibid., 5.50.
[248] Ibid., 9.123.
[249] Ibid., 5.50.

[250] Ibid., 8.97.
[251] Ibid., 13.149.

The absolute monarchy advocated by Hobbes is *worse* than the State of Nature, according to Locke.

> To think that men are so foolish that they take care to avoid what mischiefs may be done them by Pole-Cats, or Foxes, but are content, nay think it safety, to be devoured by lions.[252]

In other words, if, in the State of Nature, we are fearful of the power of other individuals, and what they might do with it, given their power-seeking and self-interested nature, how does it make sense to invest *all* that power into a single individual, who is just as power-seeking and self-interested as the rest of us, without retaining any ability to defend ourselves against the very likely abuse of that power? Such a change of state (i.e., from the State of Nature to Hobbes' absolute monarchy) would be irrational.

> But though men, when they enter into society, give up the equality, liberty, and executive power they had in the state of nature, into the hands of the society, to be so far disposed of by the legislative, as the good of the society shall require; yet it being only with an intention in every one the better to preserve himself, his liberty and property; (for no rational creature can be supposed to change his condition with an intention to be worse).[253]

In contrast to the "Leviathan" offered by Hobbes, Locke's government/State is "minimal." It does not exist to make men "better" (as envisioned throughout the classical and medieval-Christian periods), but exists for the practical benefit of being able to better settle disputes as they arise, and to protect the life and property of the citizens, whose own virtue and good is their own problem.

The basic purpose of the government is to promote the "peace, safety, and public good of the people."[254] A legitimate government preserves, as much as possible, the rights of life, liberty, health, and property of its citizens, and punishes those who violate them. If it fails to do so, or exceeds its authority, it abuses its power. To minimize the risk of abuse, power is to be limited and divided between legislative and executive branches. A government who violates the rights of citizens puts itself in a "state of war" against them, acting, in effect, as a large and powerful criminal. Citizens retain their right of self-defense, and their right to punish such an offender.

Rebellion

Locke argued that the people retain the right to rebel and form a new government if their current ruler becomes a tyrant. Indeed, a tyrant who can act against the people (who have no possibility of appeal or relief) has placed himself back in the State of Nature.

> For he being supposed to have all, both legislative and executive power in himself alone, there is no judge to be found, no appeal lies open to any one, who may fairly, and indifferently, and with authority decide, and from whose decision relief and redress may be expected of any injury or inconviency, that may be suffered from the prince, or by his order: so that such a man, however intitled, Czar, or Grand Seignior, or how you please, is as much in the state of nature, with all under his dominion, as he is with the rest of mankind: for where-ever any two men are, who have no standing rule, and common judge to appeal to on earth, for the determination of controversies of right betwixt them, there they are still in the state of nature, and under all the inconveniencies of it, with only this woful difference to the subject, or rather slave of an absolute

---

[252] Ibid., 7.93.
[253] Ibid., 9.31.

[254] Ibid.

prince: that whereas, in the ordinary state of nature, he has a liberty to judge of his right, and according to the best of his power, to maintain it; now, whenever his property is invaded by the will and order of his monarch, he has not only no appeal, as those in society ought to have, but as if he were degraded from the common state of rational creatures, is denied a liberty to judge of, or to defend his right; and so is exposed to all the misery and inconveniencies, that a man can fear from one, who being in the unrestrained state of nature, is yet corrupted with flattery, and armed with power.[255]

"Law" is not merely whatever the sovereign wills, in contrast to what Hobbes maintained.

Thus the law of nature stands as an eternal rule to all men, legislators as well as others. The rules that they make for other men's actions, must, as well as their own and other men's actions, be conformable to the law of nature, i.e. to the will of God, of which that is a declaration, and the fundamental law of nature being the preservation of mankind, no human sanction can be good, or valid against it.[256]

Our natural rights to life, liberty, and property are inalienable. No ruler has the right to deprive us of them except as punishment for violating the natural law itself. The natural law existed in the state of nature, and it is not suspended in civil society just because a ruler says so. We form a contract with each other for the conveniences that civil society offers, but we also form a covenant with the ruler, whose job it is to enforce that contract and promote the public good. Should a ruler break his or her end of the bargain, we are entitled to break ours in response.

Separation of Church and State

One of the ways in which a ruler might overstep his legitimate bounds concerns the treatment of religious groups. Literal wars between Catholics and Protestants had taken place in Locke's lifetime, and the "Glorious Revolution" was fought, arguably, to prevent a Catholic monarchy from taking hold (again) in England.

Despite the fact that his patron (Shaftesbury) was very much a part of the anti-Catholic movement, and despite his own "blind spots" (as we will soon see), Locke advocated a very progressive notion of religious tolerance, for his time.

In his *First Letter on Toleration*[257], Locke proceeds in systematic fashion, modeling good "analytic" philosophy for generations of philosophers to come. He begins by defining first the "State," and then the "Church."

The commonwealth seems to me to be a society of men constituted only for the procuring, preserving, and advancing their own civil interests.

Civil interest I call life, liberty, health, and indolency of body; and the possession of outward things, such as money, lands, houses, furniture, and the like.

It is the duty of the civil magistrate, by the impartial execution of equal laws, to secure unto all the people in general, and to every one of his subjects in particular, the just possession of these things belonging to this life.

The State (or "commonwealth") exists for the sake of protecting and advancing our "civil interests." Those civil interests include life,

---

[255] Ibid., 7.91.
[256] Ibid., 11.135.
[257] All of the quotations in this subsection are taken from the Locke's *First Letter Concerning*

Toleration (1689), which appears at the end of this chapter.

health, freedom from pain, and the acquisition and security of material possessions.

The duty of the ruler is to impartially enforce equal laws whose ends are precisely those civil interests. Notice that nowhere among the duties of the ruler does Locke mention the care of other people's souls. The following section of the *Letter* is worth quoting at length (with some editing, for the sake of *less* length):

> First, because the care of souls is not committed to the civil magistrate, any more than to other men. It is not committed unto him, I say, by God; because it appears not that God has ever given any such authority to one man over another, as to compel any one to his religion. Nor can any such power be vested in the magistrate by the consent of the people; because no man can so far abandon the care of his own salvation, as blindly to leave it to the choice of any other, whether prince or subject, to prescribe to him what faith or worship he shall embrace. . . .

> In the second place, the care of souls cannot belong to the civil magistrate, because his power consists only in outward force: but true and saving religion consists in the inward persuasion of the mind, without which nothing can be acceptable to God. . . .

> In the third place, the care of the salvation of men's souls cannot belong to the magistrate; because, though the rigour of laws and the force of penalties were capable to convince and change men's minds, yet would not that help at all to the salvation of their souls. For, there being but one truth, one way to heaven; what hopes is there that more men would be led into it, if they had no other rule to follow but the religion of the court, and were put under a necessity to quit the light of their own reason, to oppose the dictates of their own consciences, and

> blindly to resign up themselves to the will of their governors, and to the religion which either ignorance, ambition, or superstition had chanced to establish in the countries where they were born? In the variety and contradiction of opinions in religion, wherein the princes of the world are as much divided as in their secular interests, the narrow way would be much straitened; one country alone would be in the right, and all the rest of the world put under an obligation of following their princes in the ways that lead to destruction: and that which heightens the absurdity, and very ill suits the notion of a deity, men would owe their eternal happiness or misery to the places of their nativity.

> These considerations, to omit many others that might have been urged to the same purpose, seem unto me sufficient to conclude, that all the power of civil government relates only to men's civil interests, is confined to the care of the things of this world, and hath nothing to do with the world to come.

To summarize: the ruler does not have authority over people's salvation from God, because, in Locke's Protestant interpretation of God, God has granted to no human such authority over any other human. Nor does the ruler have such authority from the consent of the governed, since salvation is a strictly personal matter, and can't be handed over to someone else's care, regardless of what someone might want.

In addition, the ruler can only command outward conformity in the form of actions, but salvation concerns the "inward" workings of the soul.

Finally, if people were to put their salvation in the care of the ruler, rather than their own conscientious and rational care, they would be completely at the mercy of the beliefs of that ruler, and the contingency of birth alone would determine the eternal fate of their souls. After all, rulers across the globe and throughout history have held to a variety of religious views, and if there is only "one true faith," most of them must have been mistaken.

> Neither the right, nor the art of ruling, does necessarily carry along with it the certain knowledge of other things; and least of all of the true religion; for if it were so, how could it come to pass that the lords of the earth should differ so vastly as they do in religious matters?

Any subject left to the mercies of their ruler's belief system, rather than their own conscience and Reason, could face eternal (and infernal) consequences! The ruler has no right or duty to care for anyone's salvation but his own.

Of course, the ruler has the same right as any other person to offer personal opinion, and to encourage (by argument) that others embrace the "one true faith."

> In teaching, instructing, and redressing the erroneous by reason, he may certainly do what becomes any good man to do. Magistracy does not oblige him to put off either humanity or christianity. But it is one thing to persuade, another to command; one thing to press with arguments, another with penalties. . . . Every man has commission to admonish, exhort, convince another of errour, and by reasoning to draw him into truth: but to give laws, receive obedience, and compel with the sword, belongs to none but the magistrate. And upon this ground I affirm, that the magistrate's power extends not to the establishing of any article of faith, or forms of worship, by the force of his laws. For laws are of no force at all without penalties, and penalties in this case are absolutely impertinent; because they are not proper to convince the mind. Neither the profession of any articles of faith, nor the conformity to any outward form of worship, as has been already said, can be available to the salvation of souls, unless the truth of the

> one, and the acceptableness of the other unto God, be thoroughly believed by those that so profess and practise. But penalties are no ways capable to produce such belief. It is only light and evidence that can work a change in men's opinions; and that light can in no manner proceed from corporal sufferings, or any other outward penalties.

The ruler is unique in that only the ruler is authorized to use force to compel people's behavior, in general. All the rest of us must make do with our best attempts at persuasion. With regard to religious matters, though, Locke thinks that coercion is not only an illegitimate use of State power, but is also ineffective. He claims that no forced (and therefore insincere) confessions of faith, or performance of religious ritual, could ever "work" as far as God and salvation is concerned. To enforce doctrine by the threat of punishment will necessarily fail at its ostensible purpose. Indeed, Locke suspects that most instances of religious persecution are much more about the Earthly power of those doing the persecuting, than any genuine concern for the souls of those being persecuted!

> Where they have not the power to carry on persecution, and to become masters, there they desire to live upon fair terms and preach up toleration. When they are not strengthened with the civil power, then they can bear most patiently, and unmovedly, the contagion of idolatry, superstition, and heresy in their neighbourhood; of which, on other occasions, the interest of religion makes them to be extremely apprehensive.

Having defined the State, and delineated the proper limits of the ruler of that State, Locke then turns to defining the Church.

> Let us now consider what a church is. A church then I take to be a voluntary society of men, joining themselves together of their own accord in order to

the public worshipping of God, in such a manner as they judge acceptable to him, and effectual to the salvation of their souls. . . .

The end of a religious society, as has already been said, is the public worship of God, and by means thereof the acquisition of eternal life. All discipline ought therefore to tend to that end, and all ecclesiastical laws to be thereunto confined. Nothing ought, nor can be transacted in this society, relating to the possession of civil and worldly goods. No force is here to be made use of, upon any occasion whatsoever: for force belongs wholly to the civil magistrate, and the possession of all outward goods is subject to his jurisdiction.

But it may be asked, by what means then shall ecclesiastical laws be established, if they must be thus destitute of all compulsive power? I answer, they must be established by means suitable to the nature of such things, whereof the external profession and observation, if not proceeding from a thorough conviction and approbation of the mind, is altogether useless and unprofitable. The arms by which the members of this society are to be kept within their duty, are exhortations, admonitions, and advice. If by these means the offenders will not be reclaimed, and the erroneous convinced, there remains nothing farther to be done, but that such stubborn and obstinate persons, who give no ground to hope for their reformation, should be cast out and separated from the society. This is the last and utmost force of ecclesiastical authority: no other punishment can thereby be inflicted, than that the relation ceasing between the body and the member which is cut off, the person so condemned ceases to be a part of that church.

A church is a voluntary association of people who get together to worship God, according to their own determination of how best to do that, for the sake of their souls' salvation. The activity of the church is public worship, and its purpose is to gain eternal life. Therefore, the proper domain of the church is the form of its own public worship, and the doctrine and rituals its members determine best serve their goal of salvation. What is not within the proper domain of the church is *anything else*.

Even within their proper domain, the only legitimate means the Church has of promoting and enforcing its vision are "exhortations, admonitions, and advice."

If a church member stubbornly refuses to "do it right" within that church, the membership or leaders of that church may educate, encourage, or criticize as much as they please—and if none of that works they may eject the person from his voluntary membership to that association. What the church may not do, however, is use force to compel obedience and orthodoxy. Only the State ruler has the right to compel by force—and not even the ruler has that right in the domain of religious belief and practice.

The limitation on punishing or compelling persons for religious reasons extends beyond the activities of the church itself, and out into the broader community.

> no private person has any right in any manner to prejudice another person in his civil enjoyments, because he is of another church or religion. All the rights and franchises that belong to him as a man, or as a denison, are inviolably to be preserved to him. These are not the business of religion. No violence nor injury is to be offered him, whether he be christian or pagan. Nay, we must not content ourselves with the narrow measures of bare justice: charity, bounty, and liberality must be added to it. This the Gospel enjoins, this reason directs, and this that natural fellowship we are born into requires of us. If any man err from the right way, it is his own misfortune, no

injury to thee: nor therefore art thou to punish him in the things of this life, because thou supposest he will be miserable in that which is to come.

If a person professes the "wrong" faith, or even no faith at all, neither any church, nor any private citizen, has the right to deny that person the enjoyment of his own rights as a result.

If his soul is doomed to the fires of Hell, that's his problem, not mine (or yours). If I am truly concerned for his eternal well-being, I am free to speak with him, and offer my very best arguments for why he should change his ways or his beliefs, but I have no right to compel him by force, or to deny him the same rights that everyone else has (e.g., the right to own property, to vote in elections, etc.).

In private domestic affairs, in the management of estates, in the conservation of bodily health, every man may consider what suits his own conveniency, and follow what course he likes best. No man complains of the ill management of his neighbour's affairs. No man is angry with another for an errour committed in sowing his land, or in marrying his daughter. No-body corrects a spendthrift for consuming his substance in taverns. Let any man pull down, or build, or make whatsoever expences he pleases, no-body murmurs, no-body controls him; he has his liberty. But if any man do not frequent the church, if he do not there conform his behaviour exactly to the accustomed ceremonies, or if he brings not his children to be initiated in the sacred mysteries of this or the other congregation; this immediately causes an uproar, and the neighbourhood is filled with noise and clamour. Every one is ready to be the avenger of so great a crime. And the zealots hardly have patience to refrain from violence and rapine, so long till the cause be heard, and the poor man be, according to form,

condemned to the loss of liberty, goods or life. . . .

The care therefore of every man's soul belongs unto himself, and is to be left unto himself. But what if he neglect the care of his soul? I answer, what if he neglect the care of his health, or of his estate; which things are nearlier related to the government of the magistrate than the other? Will the magistrate provide by an express law, that such an one shall not become poor or sick? Laws provide, as much as is possible, that the goods and health of subjects be not injured by the fraud or violence of others; they do not guard them from the negligence or ill-husbandry of the possessors themselves. No man can be forced to be rich or healthful, whether he will or no. Nay God himself will not save men against their wills.

Here Locke points out the painful inconsistency demonstrated by the religiously intolerant. For the most part, most of us are willing to "live and let live," and let people suffer from their own mistakes, if they make them. The "zealots" (of Locke's time, at least) weren't trying to use the coercive power of the State to intervene when private farmers planted poorly on their own farms, or to stop a bad marriage arrangement made by parents, or to stop someone from spending too much of his own money on alcohol or other "questionable" expenses. And yet, some seem to think it appropriate to enlist the coercive power of the State to force someone to attend a particular church, or to say a prayer, or to "do it right" (however "right" is to be conceived by the persecutors!).

In response to the defense that some people neglect the care of their souls, Locke asks about those who neglect the care of their health or finances?

Would we use the power of the State to compel people to eat a healthier diet? To exercise more regularly? To drink less soda? Would they threaten punishment if someone fails to maintain a family budget, or save sufficiently for college or retirement? To the contrary, Locke proposes a "negative" view of laws. Laws *protect from*, as opposed to *providing for*.

> Laws provide, as much as is possible, that the goods and health of subjects be not injured by the fraud or violence of others; they do not guard them from the negligence or ill-husbandry of the possessors themselves. No man can be forced to be rich or healthful, whether he will or no. Nay God himself will not save men against their wills.

Here, the "libertarian" strain of Locke is clear. It is not the proper role of the government to guarantee positive outcomes for citizens, or to protect them from their own poor life choices, as if the government "knows best." Not even God can save us from our own bad choices, according to Locke!

Instead, the government is to be limited in its application of coercive force to that which is necessary to protect citizens in their lives and property from others. This is no less so just because the topic has changed to religious matters.

In addition, Locke observes that those who seek to use the power of the State to compel observance of some religious requirement are usually selective as to which requirements are enforced, and the mere fact that some behavior is a "sin" doesn't entail that the power of the State should be used against it anyway.

But idolatry, say some, is a sin, and therefore not to be tolerated. If they said it were therefore to be avoided, the inference were good. But it does not follow, that because it is a sin it ought therefore to be punished by the magistrate. For it does not belong unto the magistrate to make use of his sword in punishing every thing, indifferently, that he takes to be a sin against God. Covetousness, uncharitableness, idleness, and many other things are sins, by the consent of all men, which yet no man ever said were to be punished by the magistrate. The reason is, because they are not prejudicial to other men's rights, nor do they break the public peace of societies. Nay, even the sins of lying and perjury are no where punishable by laws; unless in certain cases, in which the real turpitude of the thing and the offence against God, are not considered, but only the injury done unto men's neighbours, and to the commonwealth. And what if in another country, to a mahometan or a pagan prince, the christian religion seem false and offensive to God; may not the christians for the same reason, and after the same manner, be extirpated there?

Some contemporary Christians believe homosexuality to be sinful behavior, and would use the law to forbid homosexual behavior, or at least to allow discrimination against homosexuals because of the "sinfulness" of their behavior.[258] However, very rarely do those same churches (or church members) seek to use the power of the State to enforce other elements of

---

[258] Jack Phillips, the owner of Masterpiece Cakeshop in Lakewood, Colorado, refused to bake a cake for a couple (David Mullins and Charlie Craig) for their same-sex wedding celebration because of his religious beliefs. The store's policy was to deny service to customers who wished to order baked goods to celebrate a same-sex couple's wedding. http://aclu-co.org/court-rules-bakery-illegally-discriminated-against-

gay-couple/ On 8-13-15, the Colorado Court of Appeals ruled that the bakery had unlawfully discriminated against the couple. Their attorney, Annna Harmon, replied that "the right to speak freely, to think uniquely, and to live according to our faith is the bedrock of this country." http://www.theguardian.com/us-news/2015/jul/04/oregon-bakery-same-sex-marriage-lawsuit

their own religion, such as punishing adultery, or permitting discrimination against those who have been divorced and remarried.[259]

The Church and State have very different spheres of influence. Religious matters are private, whereas the State's interests are very much public. The "Church itself is a thing absolutely separate and distinct from the commonwealth. The boundaries on both sides are fixed and immovable." The theme that emerges is familiar to the contemporary reader: *a separation of church and state.*

> if each of them would contain itself within its own bounds, the one attending to the worldly welfare of the commonwealth, the other to the salvation of souls, it is impossible that any discord should ever have happened between them.

Neither Church nor State should interfere with one another's affairs. This is not to say, however, that *any* behavior can be justified by cloaking it in the rituals and vocabulary of a religion.

> You will say, by this rule, if some congregations should have a mind to sacrifice infants, or, as the primitive christians were falsely accused, lustfully pollute themselves in promiscuous uncleanness, or practise any other such heinous enormities, is the magistrate obliged to tolerate them, because they are committed in a religious assembly? I answer, No. These things are not lawful in the ordinary course of life, nor in any private house; and therefore neither are they so in the worship of God, or in any religious meeting.

Very simply, if something is (legitimately) illegal in the civil society, it remains illegal even if it happens inside a "church."

Murder is illegal. Calling it a "sacrifice" doesn't somehow transform the act into something legal. If, odd as it might sound, a "religion" developed in which acts of stealing were called sacraments, those "sacraments" would not be tolerated, even in Locke's tolerant vision, because stealing is illegal.

> By this we see what difference there is between the church and the commonwealth. Whatsoever is lawful in the commonwealth, cannot be prohibited by the magistrate in the church. Whatsoever is permitted unto any of his subjects for their ordinary use, neither can nor ought to be forbidden by him to any sect of people for their religious uses. If any man may lawfully take bread or wine, either sitting or kneeling, in his own house, the law ought not to abridge him of the same liberty in his religious worship; though in the church the use of bread and wine be very different, and be there applied to the mysteries of faith, and rites of divine worship. But those things that are prejudicial to the commonwealth of a people in their ordinary use, and are therefore forbidden by laws, those things ought not to be permitted to churches in their sacred rites. Only the magistrate ought always to be very careful that he do not misuse his authority, to the oppression of any church under pretence of public good.

Locke's example of bread and wine is interesting, here, as it alludes to the persecution of Catholics—something his own patron, Shaftesbury, advocated!

---

[259] A notable exception to this is the Westboro Baptist Church, who, while focusing on homosexuality, also speaks out against gambling, drinking, divorce, pornography, and a whole host of other "sinful" behavior. They even criticized Kim Davis (see a later footnote) for opposing same-sex marriage licenses, while not repenting of her own multiple divorces and marriages. http://www.huffingtonpost.com/entry/kim-davis-westboro-baptist-church_55eef2c2e4b002d5c0769a82

Taking communion (bread and wine) is the signature component of a Catholic Mass. To ban communion is, of course, to interfere with the rituals of the Catholic Church. By Locke's reasoning, the State would have no right to do so, since taking communion is, in effect, eating bread and drinking wine—and that is not illegal in the broader community.

Just in case an overly clever ruler thought to ban *everyone* from eating bread and wine, in combination, so as to avoid "bigotry" but still, in effect, to prevent Catholic Mass, Locke simply urges that "the magistrate ought always to be very careful that he do not misuse his authority, to the oppression of any church under pretence of public good."

On the positive side, anything that is legal for one faith, ought to be so for any other.

> Thus if solemn assemblies, observations of festivals, public worship, be permitted to any one sort of professors; all these things ought to be permitted to the presbyterians, independents, anabaptists, arminians, quakers, and others, with the same liberty. Nay, if we may openly speak the truth, and as becomes one man to another, neither pagan, nor mahometan, nor jew, ought to be excluded from the civil rights of the commonwealth, because of his religion.

And,

> Further, the magistrate ought not to forbid the preaching or professing of any speculative opinions in any church, because they have no manner of relation to the civil rights of the subjects. If a roman catholic believe that to be really the body of Christ, which another man calls bread, he does no injury thereby to his neighbour. If a jew does not believe the New Testament to be the word of God, he does not thereby alter any thing in

men's civil rights. If a heathen doubt of both Testaments, he is not therefore to be punished as a pernicious citizen. The power of the magistrate, and the estates of the people, may be equally secure, whether any man believe these things or no. I readily grant, that these opinions are false and absurd. But the business of laws is not to provide for the truth of opinions, but for the safety and security of the commonwealth, and of every particular man's goods and person.

The scope of Locke's toleration is made clearer, in the above quotation. Although toleration is to be extended very broadly, to nearly any religion, toleration is not to be confused with agreement or acceptance.

It is inevitable that each one of us will believe that some of the things believed by people of other faiths (or of all faiths, if one is an atheist) are false, or even "stupid." A Protestant might think it "silly" for a Catholic to believe in the doctrine of transubstantiation (according to which the bread and wine are "really" the body and blood of Christ), and a Jew might think it false that Jesus was the Messiah, and a Wiccan might think it "stupid" that Muslims believe it's morally wrong to drink alcohol, etc.[260] Locke himself, in the very passage above, claims the views of both Catholics and Jews are "false and absurd!"

Absurd or not; true or not; he still thinks that the law should have nothing to say on the matter, since "the business of laws is not to provide for the truth of opinions, but for the safety and security of the commonwealth, and of every particular man's goods and person."

As mentioned, tolerance is not identical to acceptance or agreement—and nor is tolerance without limit.

> No opinions contrary to human society, or to those moral rules which are necessary to the preservation of civil society, are to be tolerated by the magistrate. . . . That

---

[260] Please note that I am not actually attributing any of those claims to any of those religious

traditions. I'm merely proposing hypothetical examples.

church can have no right to be tolerated by the magistrate, which is constituted upon such a bottom, that all those who enter into it, do thereby ipso facto deliver themselves up to the protection and service of another prince. For by this means the magistrate would give way to the settling of a foreign jurisdiction in his own country, and suffer his own people to be listed, as it were, for soldiers against his own government. Nor does the frivolous and fallacious distinction between the court and the church afford any remedy to this inconvenience; especially when both the one and the other are equally subject to the absolute authority of the same person; who has not only power to persuade the members of his church to whatsoever he lists, either as purely religious, or as in order thereunto; but can also enjoin it them on pain of eternal fire. . . . Lastly, Those are not at all to be tolerated who deny the being of God. Promises, covenants, and oaths, which are the bonds of human society, can have no hold upon an atheist.

Any religion for which the practice requires illegal acts (e.g., murder, theft) does not enjoy "toleration." Nor does any church which does not recognize the supremacy of the secular authority in civil matters.

This helps to explain (though not necessarily does it justify) the anti-Catholic sentiment in Locke's time—and that extended well into the 20th century in the United States. If one believes that Catholics are obliged to obey the Pope, even if the Pope commands actions that violate the

laws of one's own country, then, by virtue of voluntary religious affiliation, Catholics are implicitly swearing allegiance to a "foreign power." This was one of the fears in England, and, much more recently and closer to home, one of the fears surrounding the election of John F. Kennedy (the first Catholic President) in the United States.

Even more contemporary, if a particular interpretation of Islam involves swearing allegiance to a "Caliph," regardless of national origin or citizenship, then any Muslim who does so, similarly, is acknowledging that he (or she) is the subject of a "foreign power" as well.[261]

Such faiths are not entitled to toleration, for "by this means the magistrate would give way to the settling of a foreign jurisdiction in his own country, and suffer his own people to be listed, as it were, for soldiers against his own government."[262] Finally, and perhaps controversially, atheists are not to be tolerated either, on the assumption that they lack the fear of God (and eternal punishment), and therefore can't be trusted to keep promises or hold faith with others.

Thus far, we have considered the limits of the church, and of the State, but what of the individual believer? What if the ruler tries to compel a person of faith to do something against his or her beliefs?

But some may ask, "What if the magistrate should enjoin any thing by his authority, that appears unlawful to the conscience of a private person?" I answer, that if government be faithfully administered, and the counsels of the magistrate be indeed directed to the public good, this

[261] This is not a merely hypothetical scenario. In 2014, Abu Bakr al-Baghdadi, the head of ISIS, declared himself Caliph, and demanded that all Muslims, worldwide, declare obeisance to him. http://www.slate.com/articles/news_and_politics/war_stories/2014/07/iraq_isis_leader_abu_bakr_al_baghdadi_names_himself_caliph.html
[262] This actually arose as a controversial campaign issue in 2015, when Republican

Presidential candidate Ben Carson stated that "I would not advocate that we put a Muslim in charge of this nation. I absolutely would not agree with that," because Islam is "inconsistent with the values and principles of America." http://www.cnn.com/2015/09/20/politics/ben-carson-muslim-president-2016/index.html

will seldom happen. But if perhaps it do so fall out, I say, that such a private person is to abstain from the actions that he judges unlawful; and he is to undergo the punishment, which is not unlawful for him to bear; for the private judgment of any person concerning a law enacted in political matters, for the public good, does not take away the obligation of that law, nor deserve a dispensation. But if the law indeed be concerning things that lie not within the verge of the magistrate's authority; as for example, that the people, or any party amongst them, should be compelled to embrace a strange religion, and join in the worship and ceremonies of another church; men are not in these cases obliged by that law, against their consciences; for the political society is instituted for no other end, but only to secure every man's possession of the things of this life. The care of each man's soul, and of the things of heaven, which neither does belong to the commonwealth, nor can be subjected to it, is left entirely to every man's self.

This is an admittedly complicated and nuanced issue. For Locke, if the ruler keeps within the proper bounds of legitimate government, and does not attempt to intrude upon the proper domain of the church, then this issue shouldn't really arise. If an individual thinks that some law is contrary to their conscience, then they may choose to disobey, of course—in which case they should be prepared to accept the lawful punishment that is due them![263]

If the law is legitimate, and truly enacted for the public good, an individual's pangs of conscience do not somehow negate the legitimacy of that law. On the other hand, if the law is truly unjust with regard to the proper domain of religion (e.g., a law requiring attendance at a particular church), then there is no obligation to obey that law, and, if pressed enough, the "faithful" have a right to rebel against the ruler who has unlawfully overstepped his bounds.

Conclusion

Although Locke rejects much of Hobbes' work, he implicitly accepts and incorporates some of the same ideas. Humans do not engage in politics for the sake of virtue (in contrast to Ancient and Medieval political models), nor are they naturally predisposed to form political communities for the sake of fulfilling their potential. Instead, they form political communities for "convenience."

People are interpreted as individualistic, rational agents, who (with some guidance from reason and the natural law, perhaps), pursue their own self-interest in general, including their decision to form a political community in the first place.

Locke's emphasis on the role of the State in protecting property shifts the citizen from a person seeking to develop virtue, to a consumer seeking to acquire property and pursue her own vision of happiness.

Locke was undeniably a profoundly influential Enlightenment thinker. His writings influenced Voltaire and Rousseau, as well as the American Revolutionaries, and his ideas are

---

[263] In 2015, Kim Davis, a county clerk for Rowan County, Kentucky, made national headlines, and attracted the attention of Republican Presidential candidate Mike Huckabee, for refusing to issue marriage licenses to same-sex couples, despite the Supreme Court ruling in Obergefell v. Hodges (2015) declaring that the States must recognize same-sex marriages. She refused to issue marriage licenses (a major function of her job, as

an elected county clerk) to same-sex couples because she believed it to be a violation of her religion. "To issue a marriage license which conflicts with God's definition of marriage, with my name affixed to the certificate, would violate my conscience. It is not a light issue for me. It is a heaven or hell decision." http://www.cnn.com/2015/09/04/us/kentucky-clerk-kim-davis/index.html

unmistakably found in the U.S. Declaration of Independence, as we will consider in the next chapter.

John Locke (1632-1704) was a profound influential philosopher, in general. The following selections focus on his political writings, and include selections from the 2nd book of the Two Treatises on Government, as well his entire First Letter on Toleration. The selections from the Two Treatises discuss the state of nature, our motivation to form a civil society, the origin of property, rule by consent of the governed, and the permissibility of rebellion. The Letter on Toleration is devoted to a detailed argument advocating religious toleration (within limits).

John Locke: *Two Treatises of Government*

1690
Preface...of Civil-Government
Book II
[http://oregonstate.edu/instruct/phl302/texts/locke/locke2/locke2nd-a.html]

Chapter. II.
Of the State of Nature

Sect. 4. TO understand political power right, and derive it from its original, we must consider, what state all men are naturally in, and that is, a state of perfect freedom to order their actions, and dispose of their possessions and persons, as they think fit, within the bounds of the law of nature, without asking leave, or depending upon the will of any other man.

A state also of equality, wherein all the power and jurisdiction is reciprocal, no one having more than another; there being nothing more evident, than that creatures of the same species and rank, promiscuously born to all the same advantages of nature, and the use of the same faculties, should also be equal one amongst another without subordination or subjection, unless the lord and master of them all should, by any manifest declaration of his will, set one above another, and confer on him, by an evident and clear appointment, an undoubted right to dominion and sovereignty.

Sect. 5. This equality of men by nature, the judicious Hooker looks upon as so evident in itself, and beyond all question, that he makes it the foundation of that obligation to mutual love amongst men, on which he builds the duties they owe one another, and from whence he derives the great maxims of justice and charity. His words are,

The like natural inducement hath brought men to know that it is no less their duty, to love others than themselves; for seeing those things which are equal, must needs all have one measure; if I cannot but wish to receive good, even as much at every man's hands, as any man can wish unto his own soul, how should I look to have any part of my desire herein satisfied, unless myself be careful to satisfy the like desire, which is undoubtedly in other men, being of one and the same nature? To have any thing offered them repugnant to this desire, must needs in all respects grieve them as much as me; so that if I do harm, I must look to suffer, there being no reason that others should shew greater measure of love to me, than they have by me shewed unto them: my desire therefore to be loved of my equals in nature as much as possible may be, imposeth upon me a natural duty of bearing to them-ward fully the like affection; from which relation of equality between ourselves and them that are as ourselves, what several rules and canons natural reason hath drawn, for direction of life, no man is ignorant, Eccl. Pol. Lib. 1.

Sect. 6. But though this be a state of liberty, yet it is not a state of licence: though man in that state have an uncontroulable liberty to dispose of his person or possessions, yet he has not liberty to destroy himself, or so much as any creature in his possession, but where some nobler use than its bare preservation calls for it. The state of nature has a law of nature to govern it, which obliges every one: and reason, which is that law, teaches all mankind, who will but consult it, that being all equal and independent, no one ought to harm another in his life, health, liberty, or possessions: for men being all the workmanship of one omnipotent, and infinitely wise maker; all the servants of one sovereign master, sent into the world by his order, and about his business; they are his property, whose workmanship they are, made to last during his, not one another's pleasure: and being furnished with like faculties, sharing all in one community of nature, there cannot be supposed any such subordination among us, that may authorize us to destroy one another, as if we were made for one another's uses, as the inferior ranks of creatures are for our's. Every one, as he is bound to preserve himself, and not to quit his station wilfully, so by the like reason, when his own preservation comes not in competition, ought he, as much as he can, to preserve the rest of mankind, and may not, unless it be to do justice on an offender, take away, or impair the life, or what tends to the preservation of the life, the liberty, health, limb, or goods of another.

Sect. 7. And that all men may be restrained from invading others rights, and from doing hurt to one another, and the law of nature be observed, which willeth the peace and preservation of all mankind, the execution of the law of nature is, in that state, put into every man's hands, whereby every one has a right to punish the transgressors of that law to such a degree, as may hinder its violation: for the law of nature would, as all other laws that concern men in this world 'be in vain, if there were no body that in the state of nature had a power to execute that law, and thereby preserve the innocent and restrain offenders. And if any one in the state of nature may punish another for any evil he has done, every one may do so: for in that state of perfect equality, where naturally there is no superiority or jurisdiction of one over another, what any may do in prosecution of that law, every one must needs have a right to do.

Sect. 8. And thus, in the state of nature, one man comes by a power over another; but yet no absolute or arbitrary power, to use a criminal, when he has got him in his hands, according to the passionate heats, or boundless extravagancy of his own will; but only to retribute to him, so far as calm reason and conscience dictate, what is proportionate to his transgression, which is so much as may serve for reparation and restraint: for these two are the only reasons, why one man may lawfully do harm to another, which is that we call punishment. In transgressing the law of nature, the offender declares himself to live by another rule than that of reason and common equity, which is that measure God has set to the actions of men, for their mutual security; and so he becomes dangerous to mankind, the tye, which is to secure them from injury and violence, being slighted and broken by him. Which being a trespass against the whole species, and the peace and safety of it, provided for by the law of nature, every man upon this score, by the right he hath to preserve mankind in general, may restrain, or where it is necessary, destroy things noxious to them, and so may bring such evil on any one, who hath transgressed that law, as may make him repent the doing of it, and thereby deter him, and by his example others, from doing the like mischief. And in the case, and upon this ground, EVERY MAN HATH A RIGHT TO PUNISH THE OFFENDER, AND BE EXECUTIONER OF THE LAW OF NATURE.

Sect. 9. I doubt not but this will seem a very strange doctrine to some men: but before they condemn it, I desire them to resolve me, by what right any prince or state can put to death, or punish an alien, for any crime he commits in their country. It is certain their laws, by virtue of any sanction they receive from the promulgated will of the legislative, reach not a stranger: they speak not to him, nor, if they did, is he bound to hearken to them. The legislative authority, by which they are in force over the subjects of that commonwealth, hath no power over him. Those who have the supreme power of making laws in England, France or Holland, are to an Indian, but like the rest of the world, men without authority: and therefore, if by the law of nature every man hath not a power to punish offences against it, as he soberly judges the case to require, I see not how the magistrates of any community can punish an alien of another country; since, in reference to him, they can have no more power than what every man naturally may have over another.

Sect, 10. Besides the crime which consists in violating the law, and varying from the right rule of reason, whereby a man so far becomes degenerate, and declares himself to quit the principles of human nature, and to be a noxious creature, there is commonly injury done to some person or other, and some other man receives damage by his transgression: in which case he who hath received any damage, has, besides the right of punishment common to him with other men, a particular right to seek reparation from him that has done it: and any other person, who finds it just, may also join with him that is injured, and assist him in recovering from the offender so much as may make satisfaction for the harm he has suffered.

Sect. 11. From these two distinct rights, the one of punishing the crime for restraint, and preventing the like offence, which right of punishing is in every body; the other of taking reparation, which belongs only to the injured party, comes it to pass that the magistrate, who by being magistrate hath the common right of punishing put into his hands, can often, where the public good demands not the execution of the law, remit the punishment of criminal offences by his own authority, but yet cannot remit the satisfaction due to any private man for the damage he has received. That, he who has suffered the damage has a right to demand in his own name, and he alone can remit: the damnified person has this power of appropriating to himself the goods or service of the offender, by right of self-preservation, as every man has a power to punish the crime, to prevent its being committed again, by the right he has of preserving all mankind, and doing all reasonable things he can in order to that end: and thus it is, that every man, in the state of nature, has a power to kill a murderer, both to deter others from doing the like injury, which no reparation can compensate, by the example of the punishment that attends it from every body, and also to secure men from the attempts of a criminal, who having renounced reason, the common rule and measure God hath

given to mankind, hath, by the unjust violence and slaughter he hath committed upon one, declared war against all mankind, and therefore may be destroyed as a lion or a tyger, one of those wild savage beasts, with whom men can have no society nor security: and upon this is grounded that great law of nature, Whoso sheddeth man's blood, by man shall his blood be shed. And Cain was so fully convinced, that every one had a right to destroy such a criminal, that after the murder of his brother, he cries out, Every one that findeth me, shall slay me; so plain was it writ in the hearts of all mankind.

Sect. 12. By the same reason may a man in the state of nature punish the lesser breaches of that law. It will perhaps be demanded, with death? I answer, each transgression may be punished to that degree, and with so much severity, as will suffice to make it an ill bargain to the offender, give him cause to repent, and terrify others from doing the like. Every offence, that can be committed in the state of nature, may in the state of nature be also punished equally, and as far forth as it may, in a commonwealth: for though it would be besides my present purpose, to enter here into the particulars of the law of nature, or its measures of punishment; yet, it is certain there is such a law, and that too, as intelligible and plain to a rational creature, and a studier of that law, as the positive laws of commonwealths; nay, possibly plainer; as much as reason is easier to be understood, than the fancies and intricate contrivances of men, following contrary and hidden interests put into words; for so truly are a great part of the municipal laws of countries, which are only so far right, as they are founded on the law of nature, by which they are to be regulated and interpreted.

Sect. 13. To this strange doctrine, viz. That in the state of nature every one has the executive power of the law of nature, I doubt not but it will be objected, that it is unreasonable for men to be judges in their own cases, that self-love will make men partial to themselves and their friends: and on the other side, that ill nature, passion and revenge will carry them too far in punishing others; and hence nothing but confusion and disorder will follow, and that therefore God hath certainly appointed government to restrain the partiality and violence of men. I easily grant, that civil government is the proper remedy for the inconveniencies of the state of nature, which must certainly be great, where men may be judges in their own case, since it is easy to be imagined, that he who was so unjust as to do his brother an injury, will scarce be so just as to condemn himself for it: but I shall desire those who make this objection, to remember, that absolute monarchs are but men; and if government is to be the remedy of those evils, which necessarily follow from men's being judges in their own cases, and the state of nature is therefore not to be endured, I desire to know what kind of government that is, and how much better it is than the state of nature, where one man, commanding a multitude, has the liberty to be judge in his own case, and may do to all his subjects whatever he pleases, without the least liberty to any one to question or controul those who execute his pleasure? and in whatsoever he doth, whether led by reason, mistake or passion, must be submitted to? much better it is in the state of nature, wherein men are not bound to submit to the unjust will of another: and if he that judges, judges amiss in his own, or any other case, he is answerable for it to the rest of mankind.

Sect. 14. It is often asked as a mighty objection, where are, or ever were there any men in such a state of nature? To which it may suffice as an answer at present, that since all princes and rulers of independent governments all through the world, are in a state of nature, it is plain the world never was, nor ever will be, without numbers of men in that state. I have named all governors of independent communities, whether they are, or are not, in league with others: for it is not every compact that puts an end to the state of nature between men, but only this one of agreeing together mutually to enter into one community, and make one body politic; other promises, and compacts, men may make one with another, and yet still be in the state of nature. The promises and bargains for truck, &c. between the two men in the desert island, mentioned by Garcilasso de la Vega, in his history of Peru; or between a Swiss and an Indian, in the woods of

America, are binding to them, though they are perfectly in a state of nature, in reference to one another: for truth and keeping of faith belongs to men, as men, and not as members of society.

Sect. 15. To those that say, there were never any men in the state of nature, I will not only oppose the authority of the judicious Hooker, Eccl. Pol. lib. i. sect. 10, where he says,

The laws which have been hitherto mentioned, i.e. the laws of nature, do bind men absolutely, even as they are men, although they have never any settled fellowship, never any solemn agreement amongst themselves what to do, or not to do: but forasmuch as we are not by ourselves sufficient to furnish ourselves with competent store of things, needful for such a life as our nature doth desire, a life fit for the dignity of man; therefore to supply those defects and imperfections which are in us, as living single and solely by ourselves, we are naturally induced to seek communion and fellowship with others: this was the cause of men's uniting themselves at first in politic societies.

But I moreover affirm, that all men are naturally in that state, and remain so, till by their own consents they make themselves members of some politic society; and I doubt not in the sequel of this discourse, to make it very clear.

CHAPTER. III.
OF THE STATE OF WAR.

Sect. 16. THE state of war is a state of enmity and destruction: and therefore declaring by word or action, not a passionate and hasty, but a sedate settled design upon another man's life, puts him in a state of war with him against whom he has declared such an intention, and so has exposed his life to the other's power to be taken away by him, or any one that joins with him in his defence, and espouses his quarrel; it being reasonable and just, I should have a right to destroy that which threatens me with destruction: for, by the fundamental law of nature, man being to be preserved as much as possible, when all cannot be preserved, the safety of the innocent is to be preferred: and one may destroy a man who makes war upon him, or has discovered an enmity to his being, for the same reason that he may kill a wolf or a lion; because such men are not under the ties of the commonlaw of reason, have no other rule, but that of force and violence, and so may be treated as beasts of prey, those dangerous and noxious creatures, that will be sure to destroy him whenever he falls into their power.

Sect. 17. And hence it is, that he who attempts to get another man into his absolute power, does thereby put himself into a state of war with him; it being to be understood as a declaration of a design upon his life: for I have reason to conclude, that he who would get me into his power without my consent, would use me as he pleased when he had got me there, and destroy me too when he had a fancy to it; for no body can desire to have me in his absolute power, unless it be to compel me by force to that which is against the right of my freedom, i.e. make me a slave. To be free from such force is the only security of my preservation; and reason bids me look on him, as an enemy to my preservation, who would take away that freedom which is the fence to it; so that he who makes an attempt to enslave me, thereby puts himself into a state of war with me. He that, in the state of nature, would take away the freedom that belongs to any one in that state, must necessarily be supposed to have a design to take away every thing else, that freedom being the foundation of all the rest; as he that, in the state of society, would take away the freedom belonging to those of that society or commonwealth, must be supposed to design to take away from them every thing else, and so be looked on as in a state of war.

Sect. 18. This makes it lawful for a man to kill a thief, who has not in the least hurt him, nor declared any design upon his life, any farther than, by the use of force, so to get him in his power, as to take away his money, or what he pleases, from him; because using force, where he has no right, to get me into his power, let his pretence be what it will, I have no reason to suppose, that he, who would take away my liberty, would not, when he had me in his power, take away every thing else. And therefore it is lawful for me to treat him as one who has put himself into a state of war with me, i.e. kill him if I can; for to that hazard does he justly expose

himself, whoever introduces a state of war, and is aggressor in it.

Sect. 19. And here we have the plain difference between the state of nature and the state of war, which however some men have confounded, are as far distant, as a state of peace, good will, mutual assistance and preservation, and a state of enmity, malice, violence and mutual destruction, are one from another. Men living together according to reason, without a common superior on earth, with authority to judge between them, is properly the state of nature. But force, or a declared design of force, upon the person of another, where there is no common superior on earth to appeal to for relief, is the state of war: and it is the want of such an appeal gives a man the right of war even against an aggressor, tho' he be in society and a fellow subject. Thus a thief, whom I cannot harm, but by appeal to the law, for having stolen all that I am worth, I may kill, when he sets on me to rob me but of my horse or coat; because the law, which was made for my preservation, where it cannot interpose to secure my life from present force, which, if lost, is capable of no reparation, permits me my own defence, and the right of war, a liberty to kill the aggressor, because the aggressor allows not time to appeal to our common judge, nor the decision of the law, for remedy in a case where the mischief may be irreparable. Want of a common judge with authority, puts all men in a state of nature: force without right, upon a man's person, makes a state of war, both where there is, and is not, a common judge.

Sect. 20. But when the actual force is over, the state of war ceases between those that are in society, and are equally on both sides subjected to the fair determination of the law; because then there lies open the remedy of appeal for the past injury, and to prevent future harm: but where no such appeal is, as in the state of nature, for want of positive laws, and judges with authority to appeal to, the state of war once begun, continues, with a right to the innocent party to destroy the other whenever he can, until the aggressor offers peace, and desires reconciliation on such terms as may repair any wrongs he has already done, and secure the innocent for the future; nay, where an appeal to the law, and constituted judges, lies open, but the remedy is denied by a manifest perverting of justice, and a barefaced wresting of the laws to protect or indemnify the violence or injuries of some men, or party of men, there it is hard to imagine any thing but a state of war: for wherever violence is used, and injury done, though by hands appointed to administer justice, it is still violence and injury, however coloured with the name, pretences, or forms of law, the end whereof being to protect and redress the innocent, by an unbiassed application of it, to all who are under it; wherever that is not bona fide done, war is made upon the sufferers, who having no appeal on earth to right them, they are left to the only remedy in such cases, an appeal to heaven.

Sect. 21. To avoid this state of war (wherein there is no appeal but to heaven, and wherein every the least difference is apt to end, where there is no authority to decide between the contenders) is one great reason of men's putting themselves into society, and quitting the state of nature: for where there is an authority, a power on earth, from which relief can be had by appeal, there the continuance of the state of war is excluded, and the controversy is decided by that power. Had there been any such court, any superior jurisdiction on earth, to determine the right between Jephtha and the Ammonites, they had never come to a state of war: but we see he was forced to appeal to heaven. The Lord the Judge (says he) be judge this day between the children of Israel and the children of Ammon, Judg. xi. 27. and then prosecuting, and relying on his appeal, he leads out his army to battle: and therefore in such controversies, where the question is put, who shall be judge? It cannot be meant, who shall decide the controversy; every one knows what Jephtha here tells us, that the Lord the Judge shall judge. Where there is no judge on earth, the appeal lies to God in heaven. That question then cannot mean, who shall judge, whether another hath put himself in a state of war with me, and whether I may, as Jephtha did, appeal to heaven in it? of that I myself can only be judge in my own conscience, as I will answer it, at the great day, to the supreme judge of all men.

...
CHAPTER. V.
OF PROPERTY.

Sect. 25. Whether we consider natural reason, which tells us, that men, being once born, have a right to their preservation, and consequently to meat and drink, and such other things as nature affords for their subsistence: or revelation, which gives us an account of those grants God made of the world to Adam, and to Noah, and his sons, it is very clear, that God, as king David says, Psal. cxv. 16. has given the earth to the children of men; given it to mankind in common. But this being supposed, it seems to some a very great difficulty, how any one should ever come to have a property in any thing: I will not content myself to answer, that if it be difficult to make out property, upon a supposition that God gave the world to Adam, and his posterity in common, it is impossible that any man, but one universal monarch, should have any property upon a supposition, that God gave the world to Adam, and his heirs in succession, exclusive of all the rest of his posterity. But I shall endeavour to shew, how men might come to have a property in several parts of that which God gave to mankind in common, and that without any express compact of all the commoners.

Sect. 26. God, who hath given the world to men in common, hath also given them reason to make use of it to the best advantage of life, and convenience. The earth, and all that is therein, is given to men for the support and comfort of their being. And tho' all the fruits it naturally produces, and beasts it feeds, belong to mankind in common, as they are produced by the spontaneous hand of nature; and no body has originally a private dominion, exclusive of the rest of mankind, in any of them, as they are thus in their natural state: yet being given for the use of men, there must of necessity be a means to appropriate them some way or other, before they can be of any use, or at all beneficial to any particular man. The fruit, or venison, which nourishes the wild Indian, who knows no enclosure, and is still a tenant in common, must be his, and so his, i.e. a part of him, that another can no longer have any right to it, before it can do him any good for the support of his life.

Sect. 27. Though the earth, and all inferior creatures, be common to all men, yet every man has a property in his own person: this no body has any right to but himself. The labour of his body, and the work of his hands, we may say, are properly his. Whatsoever then he removes out of the state that nature hath provided, and left it in, he hath mixed his labour with, and joined to it something that is his own, and thereby makes it his property. It being by him removed from the common state nature hath placed it in, it hath by this labour something annexed to it, that excludes the common right of other men: for this labour being the unquestionable property of the labourer, no man but he can have a right to what that is once joined to, at least where there is enough, and as good, left in common for others.

Sect. 28. He that is nourished by the acorns he picked up under an oak, or the apples he gathered from the trees in the wood, has certainly appropriated them to himself. No body can deny but the nourishment is his. I ask then, when did they begin to be his? when he digested? or when he eat? or when he boiled? or when he brought them home? or when he picked them up? and it is plain, if the first gathering made them not his, nothing else could. That labour put a distinction between them and common: that added something to them more than nature, the common mother of all, had done; and so they became his private right. And will any one say, he had no right to those acorns or apples, he thus appropriated, because he had not the consent of all mankind to make them his? Was it a robbery thus to assume to himself what belonged to all in common? If such a consent as that was necessary, man had starved, notwithstanding the plenty God had given him. We see in commons, which remain so by compact, that it is the taking any part of what is common, and removing it out of the state nature leaves it in, which begins the property; without which the common is of no use. And the taking of this or that part, does not depend on the express consent of all the commoners. Thus the grass my horse has bit; the turfs my servant has cut; and the ore I have digged in any place, where

I have a right to them in common with others, become my property, without the assignation or consent of any body. The labour that was mine, removing them out of that common state they were in, hath fixed my property in them.

Sect. 29. By making an explicit consent of every commoner, necessary to any one's appropriating to himself any part of what is given in common, children or servants could not cut the meat, which their father or master had provided for them in common, without assigning to every one his peculiar part. Though the water running in the fountain be every one's, yet who can doubt, but that in the pitcher is his only who drew it out? His labour hath taken it out of the hands of nature, where it was common, and belonged equally to all her children, and hath thereby appropriated it to himself.

Sect. 30. Thus this law of reason makes the deer that Indian's who hath killed it; it is allowed to be his goods, who hath bestowed his labour upon it, though before it was the common right of every one. And amongst those who are counted the civilized part of mankind, who have made and multiplied positive laws to determine property, this original law of nature, for the beginning of property, in what was before common, still takes place; and by virtue thereof, what fish any one catches in the ocean, that great and still remaining common of mankind; or what ambergrise any one takes up here, is by the labour that removes it out of that common state nature left it in, made his property, who takes that pains about it. And even amongst us, the hare that any one is hunting, is thought his who pursues her during the chase: for being a beast that is still looked upon as common, and no man's private possession; whoever has employed so much labour about any of that kind, as to find and pursue her, has thereby removed her from the state of nature, wherein she was common, and hath begun a property.

Sect. 31. It will perhaps be objected to this, that if gathering the acorns, or other fruits of the earth, &c. makes a right to them, then any one may ingross as much as he will. To which I answer, Not so. The same law of nature, that does by this means give us property, does also bound that property too. God has given us all things richly, 1 Tim. vi. 12. is the voice of reason confirmed by inspiration. But how far has he given it us? To enjoy. As much as any one can make use of to any advantage of life before it spoils, so much he may by his Tabour fix a property in: whatever is beyond this, is more than his share, and belongs to others. Nothing was made by God for man to spoil or destroy. And thus, considering the plenty of natural provisions there was a long time in the world, and the few spenders; and to how small a part of that provision the industry of one man could extend itself, and ingross it to the prejudice of others; especially keeping within the bounds, set by reason, of what might serve for his use; there could be then little room for quarrels or contentions about property so established.

Sect. 32. But the chief matter of property being now not the fruits of the earth, and the beasts that subsist on it, but the earth itself; as that which takes in and carries with it all the rest; I think it is plain, that property in that too is acquired as the former. As much land as a man tills, plants, improves, cultivates, and can use the product of, so much is his property. He by his labour does, as it were, inclose it from the common. Nor will it invalidate his right, to say every body else has an equal title to it; and therefore he cannot appropriate, he cannot inclose, without the consent of all his fellow-commoners, all mankind. God, when he gave the world in common to all mankind, commanded man also to labour, and the penury of his condition required it of him. God and his reason commanded him to subdue the earth, i.e. improve it for the benefit of life, and therein lay out something upon it that was his own, his labour. He that in obedience to this command of God, subdued, tilled and sowed any part of it, thereby annexed to it something that was his property, which another had no title to, nor could without injury take from him.

Sect. 33. Nor was this appropriation of any parcel of land, by improving it, any prejudice to any other man, since there was still enough, and as good left; and more than the yet unprovided could use. So that, in effect, there was never the

less left for others because of his enclosure for himself: for he that leaves as much as another can make use of, does as good as take nothing at all. No body could think himself injured by the drinking of another man, though he took a good draught, who had a whole river of the same water left him to quench his thirst: and the case of land and water, where there is enough of both, is perfectly the same.

Sect. 34. God gave the world to men in common; but since he gave it them for their benefit, and the greatest conveniencies of life they were capable to draw from it, it cannot be supposed he meant it should always remain common and uncultivated. He gave it to the use of the industrious and rational, (and labour was to be his title to it;) not to the fancy or covetousness of the quarrelsome and contentious. He that had as good left for his improvement, as was already taken up, needed not complain, ought not to meddle with what was already improved by another's labour: if he did, it is plain he desired the benefit of another's pains, which he had no right to, and not the ground which God had given him in common with others to labour on, and whereof there was as good left, as that already possessed, and more than he knew what to do with, or his industry could reach to.

Sect. 35. It is true, in land that is common in England, or any other country, where there is plenty of people under government, who have money and commerce, no one can inclose or appropriate any part, without the consent of all his fellow-commoners; because this is left common by compact, i.e. by the law of the land, which is not to be violated. And though it be common, in respect of some men, it is not so to all mankind; but is the joint property of this country, or this parish. Besides, the remainder, after such enclosure, would not be as good to the rest of the commoners, as the whole was when they could all make use of the whole; whereas in the beginning and first peopling of the great common of the world, it was quite otherwise. The law man was under, was rather for appropriating. God commanded, and his wants forced him to labour. That was his property which could not be taken from him where-ever he had fixed it. And hence subduing or cultivating the earth, and having dominion, we see are joined together. The one gave title to the other. So that God, by commanding to subdue, gave authority so far to appropriate: and the condition of human life, which requires labour and materials to work on, necessarily introduces private possessions.

Sect. 36. The measure of property nature has well set by the extent of men's labour and the conveniencies of life: no man's labour could subdue, or appropriate all; nor could his enjoyment consume more than a small part; so that it was impossible for any man, this way, to intrench upon the right of another, or acquire to himself a property, to the prejudice of his neighbour, who would still have room for as good, and as large a possession (after the other had taken out his) as before it was appropriated. This measure did confine every man's possession to a very moderate proportion, and such as he might appropriate to himself, without injury to any body, in the first ages of the world, when men were more in danger to be lost, by wandering from their company, in the then vast wilderness of the earth, than to be straitened for want of room to plant in. And the same measure may be allowed still without prejudice to any body, as full as the world seems: for supposing a man, or family, in the state they were at first peopling of the world by the children of Adam, or Noah; let him plant in some inland, vacant places of America, we shall find that the possessions he could make himself, upon the measures we have given, would not be very large, nor, even to this day, prejudice the rest of mankind, or give them reason to complain, or think themselves injured by this man's incroachment, though the race of men have now spread themselves to all the corners of the world, and do infinitely exceed the small number was at the beginning. Nay, the extent of ground is of so little value, without labour, that I have heard it affirmed, that in Spain itself a man may be permitted to plough, sow and reap, without being disturbed, upon land he has no other title to, but only his making use of it. But, on the contrary, the inhabitants think themselves beholden to him, who, by his industry on neglected, and consequently waste land, has increased the stock of corn, which they wanted. But be this as it will, which I lay no stress on; this I dare boldly affirm, that the same rule of propriety, (viz.) that every man should have as much as he could make use of, would hold still in the world, without straitening any body; since there is land enough in the world to suffice double the inhabitants, had not the invention of money, and the tacit agreement of men to put a value on it, introduced (by consent) larger possessions, and a right to them; which, how it has done, I shall by and by shew more at large.

Sect. 37. This is certain, that in the beginning, before the desire of having more than man needed had altered the intrinsic value of things, which depends only on their usefulness to the life of man; or had agreed, that a little piece of yellow metal, which would keep without wasting or decay, should be worth a great piece of flesh, or a whole heap of corn; though men had a right to appropriate, by their labour, each one of himself, as much of the things of nature, as he could use: yet this could not be much, nor to the prejudice of others, where the same plenty was still left to those who would use the same industry. To which let me add, that he who appropriates land to himself by his labour, does not lessen, but increase the common stock of mankind: for the provisions serving to the support of human life, produced by one acre of inclosed and cultivated land, are (to speak much within compass) ten times more than those which are yielded by an acre of land of an equal richness lying waste in common. And therefore he that incloses land, and has a greater plenty of the conveniencies of life from ten acres, than he could have from an hundred left to nature, may truly be said to give ninety acres to mankind: for his labour now supplies him with provisions out of ten acres, which were but the product of an hundred lying in common. I have here rated the improved land very low, in making its product but as ten to one, when it is much nearer an hundred to one: for I ask, whether in the wild woods and uncultivated waste of America, left to nature, without any improvement, tillage or husbandry, a thousand acres yield the needy and wretched inhabitants as many conveniencies of life, as ten acres of equally fertile land do in Devonshire, where they are well cultivated?

Before the appropriation of land, he who gathered as much of the wild fruit, killed, caught, or tamed, as many of the beasts, as he could; he that so imployed his pains about any of the spontaneous products of nature, as any way to alter them from the state which nature put them in, by placing any of his labour on them, did thereby acquire a propriety in them: but if they perished, in his possession, without their due use; if the fruits rotted, or the venison putrified, before he could spend it, he offended against the common law of nature, and was liable to be punished; he invaded his neighbour's share, for he had no right, farther than his use called for any of them, and they might serve to afford him conveniencies of life.

Sect. 38. The same measures governed the possession of land too: whatsoever he tilled and reaped, laid up and made use of, before it spoiled, that was his peculiar right; whatsoever he enclosed, and could feed, and make use of, the cattle and product was also his. But if either the grass of his enclosure rotted on the ground, or the fruit of his planting perished without gathering, and laying up, this part of the earth, notwithstanding his enclosure, was still to be looked on as waste, and might be the possession of any other. Thus, at the beginning, Cain might take as much ground as he could till, and make it his own land, and yet leave enough to Abel's sheep to feed on; a few acres would serve for both their possessions. But as families increased, and industry inlarged their stocks, their possessions inlarged with the need of them; but yet it was commonly without any fixed property in the ground they made use of, till they incorporated, settled themselves together, and built cities; and then, by consent, they came in time, to set out the bounds of their distinct territories, and agree on limits between them and their neighbours; and by laws within themselves, settled the properties of those of the same society: for we see, that in that part of the world which was first inhabited, and therefore like to be best peopled, even as low down as Abraham's time, they wandered with their flocks, and their herds, which was their

substance, freely up and down; and this Abraham did, in a country where he was a stranger. Whence it is plain, that at least a great part of the land lay in common; that the inhabitants valued it not, nor claimed property in any more than they made use of. But when there was not room enough in the same place, for their herds to feed together, they by consent, as Abraham and Lot did, Gen. xiii. 5. separated and inlarged their pasture, where it best liked them. And for the same reason Esau went from his father, and his brother, and planted in mount Seir, Gen. xxxvi. 6.

Sect. 39. And thus, without supposing any private dominion, and property in Adam, over all the world, exclusive of all other men, which can no way be proved, nor any one's property be made out from it; but supposing the world given, as it was, to the children of men in common, we see how labour could make men distinct titles to several parcels of it, for their private uses; wherein there could be no doubt of right, no room for quarrel.

Sect. 40. Nor is it so strange, as perhaps before consideration it may appear, that the property of labour should be able to over-balance the community of land: for it is labour indeed that puts the difference of value on every thing; and let any one consider what the difference is between an acre of land planted with tobacco or sugar, sown with wheat or barley, and an acre of the same land lying in common, without any husbandry upon it, and he will find, that the improvement of labour makes the far greater part of the value. I think it will be but a very modest computation to say, that of the products of the earth useful to the life of man nine tenths are the effects of labour: nay, if we will rightly estimate things as they come to our use, and cast up the several expences about them, what in them is purely owing to nature, and what to labour, we shall find, that in most of them ninety-nine hundredths are wholly to be put on the account of labour.

Sect. 41. There cannot be a clearer demonstration of any thing, than several nations of the Americans are of this, who are rich in land, and poor in all the comforts of life; whom nature having furnished as liberally as any other people, with the materials of plenty, i.e. a fruitful soil, apt to produce in abundance, what might serve for food, raiment, and delight; yet for want of improving it by labour, have not one hundredth part of the conveniencies we enjoy: and a king of a large and fruitful territory there, feeds, lodges, and is clad worse than a day-labourer in England.

Sect. 42. To make this a little clearer, let us but trace some of the ordinary provisions of life, through their several progresses, before they come to our use, and see how much they receive of their value from human industry. Bread, wine and cloth, are things of daily use, and great plenty; yet notwithstanding, acorns, water and leaves, or skins, must be our bread, drink and cloathing, did not labour furnish us with these more useful commodities: for whatever bread is more worth than acorns, wine than water, and cloth or silk, than leaves, skins or moss, that is wholly owing to labour and industry; the one of these being the food and raiment which unassisted nature furnishes us with; the other, provisions which our industry and pains prepare for us, which how much they exceed the other in value, when any one hath computed, he will then see how much labour makes the far greatest part of the value of things we enjoy in this world: and the ground which produces the materials, is scarce to be reckoned in, as any, or at most, but a very small part of it; so little, that even amongst us, land that is left wholly to nature, that hath no improvement of pasturage, tillage, or planting, is called, as indeed it is, waste; and we shall find the benefit of it amount to little more than nothing.

This shews how much numbers of men are to be preferred to largeness of dominions; and that the increase of lands, and the right employing of them, is the great art of government: and that prince, who shall be so wise and godlike, as by established laws of liberty to secure protection and encouragement to the honest industry of mankind, against the oppression of power and narrowness of party, will quickly be too hard for his neighbours: but this by the by.

To return to the argument in hand.

Sect. 43. An acre of land, that bears here twenty bushels of wheat, and another in America, which, with the same husbandry, would do the like, are, without doubt, of the same natural intrinsic value: but yet the benefit mankind receives from the one in a year, is worth 5l. and from the other possibly not worth a penny, if all the profit an Indian received from it were to be valued, and sold here; at least, I may truly say, not one thousandth. It is labour then which puts the greatest part of value upon land, without which it would scarcely be worth any thing: it is to that we owe the greatest part of all its useful products; for all that the straw, bran, bread, of that acre of wheat, is more worth than the product of an acre of as good land, which lies waste, is all the effect of labour: for it is not barely the plough-man's pains, the reaper's and thresher's toil, and the baker's sweat, is to be counted into the bread we eat; the labour of those who broke the oxen, who digged and wrought the iron and stones, who felled and framed the timber employed about the plough, mill, oven, or any other utensils, which are a vast number, requisite to this corn, from its being feed to be sown to its being made bread, must all be charged on the account of labour, and received as an effect of that: nature and the earth furnished only the almost worthless materials, as in themselves. It would be a strange catalogue of things, that industry provided and made use of, about every loaf of bread, before it came to our use, if we could trace them; iron, wood, leather, bark, timber, stone, bricks, coals, lime, cloth, dying drugs, pitch, tar, masts, ropes, and all the materials made use of in the ship, that brought any of the commodities made use of by any of the workmen, to any part of the work; all which it would be almost impossible, at least too long, to reckon up.

Sect. 44. From all which it is evident, that though the things of nature are given in common, yet man, by being master of himself, and proprietor of his own person, and the actions or labour of it, had still in himself the great foundation of property; and that, which made up the great part of what he applied to the support or comfort of his being, when invention and arts had improved the conveniencies of life, was perfectly his own, and did not belong in common to others.

Sect. 45. Thus labour, in the beginning, gave a right of property, wherever any one was pleased to employ it upon what was common, which remained a long while the far greater part, and is yet more than mankind makes use of. Men, at first, for the most part, contented themselves with what unassisted nature offered to their necessities: and though afterwards, in some parts of the world, (where the increase of people and stock, with the use of money, had made land scarce, and so of some value) the several communities settled the bounds of their distinct territories, and by laws within themselves regulated the properties of the private men of their society, and so, by compact and agreement, settled the property which labour and industry began; and the leagues that have been made between several states and kingdoms, either expresly or tacitly disowning all claim and right to the land in the others possession, have, by common consent, given up their pretences to their natural common right, which originally they had to those countries, and so have, by positive agreement, settled a property amongst themselves, in distinct parts and parcels of the earth; yet there are still great tracts of ground to be found, which (the inhabitants thereof not having joined with the rest of mankind, in the consent of the use of their common money) lie waste, and are more than the people who dwell on it do, or can make use of, and so still lie in common; tho' this can scarce happen amongst that part of mankind that have consented to the use of money.

Sect. 46. The greatest part of things really useful to the life of man, and such as the necessity of subsisting made the first commoners of the world look after, as it doth the Americans now, are generally things of short duration; such as, if they are not consumed by use, will decay and perish of themselves: gold, silver and diamonds, are things that fancy or agreement hath put the value on, more than real use, and the necessary support of life. Now of those good things which nature hath provided in common, every one had a right (as hath been said) to as much as he could use, and property in all that he could effect with his labour; all that his industry could extend to, to

alter from the state nature had put it in, was his. He that gathered a hundred bushels of acorns or apples, had thereby a property in them, they were his goods as soon as gathered. He was only to look, that he used them before they spoiled, else he took more than his share, and robbed others. And indeed it was a foolish thing, as well as dishonest, to hoard up more than he could make use of. If he gave away a part to any body else, so that it perished not uselesly in his possession, these he also made use of. And if he also bartered away plums, that would have rotted in a week, for nuts that would last good for his eating a whole year, he did no injury; he wasted not the common stock; destroyed no part of the portion of goods that belonged to others, so long as nothing perished uselesly in his hands. Again, if he would give his nuts for a piece of metal, pleased with its colour; or exchange his sheep for shells, or wool for a sparkling pebble or a diamond, and keep those by him all his life he invaded not the right of others, he might heap up as much of these durable things as he pleased; the exceeding of the bounds of his just property not lying in the largeness of his possession, but the perishing of any thing uselesly in it.

Sect. 47. And thus came in the use of money, some lasting thing that men might keep without spoiling, and that by mutual consent men would take in exchange for the truly useful, but perishable supports of life.

Sect. 48. And as different degrees of industry were apt to give men possessions in different proportions, so this invention of money gave them the opportunity to continue and enlarge them: for supposing an island, separate from all possible commerce with the rest of the world, wherein there were but an hundred families, but there were sheep, horses and cows, with other useful animals, wholsome fruits, and land enough for corn for a hundred thousand times as many, but nothing in the island, either because of its commonness, or perishableness, fit to supply the place of money; what reason could any one have there to enlarge his possessions beyond the use of his family, and a plentiful supply to its consumption, either in what their own industry produced, or they could barter for like perishable, useful commodities, with others? Where there is not some thing, both lasting and scarce, and so valuable to be hoarded up, there men will not be apt to enlarge their possessions of land, were it never so rich, never so free for them to take: for I ask, what would a man value ten thousand, or an hundred thousand acres of excellent land, ready cultivated, and well stocked too with cattle, in the middle of the inland parts of America, where he had no hopes of commerce with other parts of the world, to draw money to him by the sale of the product? It would not be worth the enclosing, and we should see him give up again to the wild common of nature, whatever was more than would supply the conveniencies of life to be had there for him and his family.

Sect. 49. Thus in the beginning all the world was America, and more so than that is now; for no such thing as money was any where known. Find out something that hath the use and value of money amongst his neighbours, you shall see the same man will begin presently to enlarge his possessions.

Sect. 50. But since gold and silver, being little useful to the life of man in proportion to food, raiment, and carriage, has its value only from the consent of men, whereof labour yet makes, in great part, the measure, it is plain, that men have agreed to a disproportionate and unequal possession of the earth, they having, by a tacit and voluntary consent, found out, a way how a man may fairly possess more land than he himself can use the product of, by receiving in exchange for the overplus gold and silver, which may be hoarded up without injury to any one; these metals not spoiling or decaying in the hands of the possessor. This partage of things in an inequality of private possessions, men have made practicable out of the bounds of society, and without compact, only by putting a value on gold and silver, and tacitly agreeing in the use of money: for in governments, the laws regulate the right of property, and the possession of land is determined by positive constitutions.

Sect. 51. And thus, I think, it is very easy to conceive, without any difficulty, how labour could at first begin a title of property in the common things of nature, and how the spending it upon

our uses bounded it. So that there could then be no reason of quarrelling about title, nor any doubt about the largeness of possession it gave. Right and conveniency went together; for as a man had a right to all he could employ his labour upon, so he had no temptation to labour for more than he could make use of. This left no room for controversy about the title, nor for encroachment on the right of others; what portion a man carved to himself, was easily seen; and it was useless, as well as dishonest, to carve himself too much, or take more than he needed.

...

CHAPTER. VII.
OF POLITICAL OR CIVIL SOCIETY.

...

Sect. 87. Man being born, as has been proved, with a title to perfect freedom, and an uncontrouled enjoyment of all the rights and privileges of the law of nature, equally with any other man, or number of men in the world, hath by nature a power, not only to preserve his property, that is, his life, liberty and estate, against the injuries and attempts of other men; but to judge of, and punish the breaches of that law in others, as he is persuaded the offence deserves, even with death itself, in crimes where the heinousness of the fact, in his opinion, requires it. But because no political society can be, nor subsist, without having in itself the power to preserve the property, and in order thereunto, punish the offences of all those of that society; there, and there only is political society, where every one of the members hath quitted this natural power, resigned it up into the hands of the community in all cases that exclude him not from appealing for protection to the law established by it. And thus all private judgment of every particular member being excluded, the community comes to be umpire, by settled standing rules, indifferent, and the same to all parties; and by men having authority from the community, for the execution of those rules, decides all the differences that may happen between any members of that society concerning any matter of right; and punishes those offences which any member hath committed against the society, with such penalties as the law has established: whereby it is easy to discern, who are, and who are not, in political society together. Those who are united into one body, and have a common established law and judicature to appeal to, with authority to decide controversies between them, and punish offenders, are in civil society one with another: but those who have no such common appeal, I mean on earth, are still in the state of nature, each being, where there is no other, judge for himself, and executioner; which is, as I have before shewed it, the perfect state of nature.

Sect. 88. And thus the commonwealth comes by a power to set down what punishment shall belong to the several transgressions which they think worthy of it, committed amongst the members of that society, (which is the power of making laws) as well as it has the power to punish any injury done unto any of its members, by any one that is not of it, (which is the power of war and peace;) and all this for the preservation of the property of all the members of that society, as far as is possible. But though every man who has entered into civil society, and is become a member of any commonwealth, has thereby quitted his power to punish offences, against the law of nature, in prosecution of his own private judgment, yet with the judgment of offences, which he has given up to the legislative in all cases, where he can appeal to the magistrate, he has given a right to the commonwealth to employ his force, for the execution of the judgments of the commonwealth, whenever he shall be called to it; which indeed are his own judgments, they being made by himself, or his representative. And herein we have the original of the legislative and executive power of civil society, which is to judge by standing laws, how far offences are to be punished, when committed within the commonwealth; and also to determine, by occasional judgments founded on the present circumstances of the fact, how far injuries from without are to be vindicated; and in both these to employ all the force of all the members, when there shall be need.

Sect. 89. Where-ever therefore any number of men are so united into one society, as to quit every one his executive power of the law of nature, and to resign it to the public, there and there only is a political, or civil society. And this is done, where-ever any number of men, in the state of nature, enter into society to make one people, one body politic, under one supreme government; or else when any one joins himself to, and incorporates with any government already made: for hereby he authorizes the society, or which is all one, the legislative thereof, to make laws for him, as the public good of the society shall require; to the execution whereof, his own assistance (as to his own decrees) is due. And this puts men out of a state of nature into that of a commonwealth, by setting up a judge on earth, with authority to determine all the controversies, and redress the injuries that may happen to any member of the commonwealth; which judge is the legislative, or magistrates appointed by it. And where-ever there are any number of men, however associated, that have no such decisive power to appeal to, there they are still in the state of nature.

Sect. 90. Hence it is evident, that absolute monarchy, which by some men is counted the only government in the world, is indeed inconsistent with civil society, and so can be no form of civil-government at all: for the end of civil society, being to avoid, and remedy those inconveniencies of the state of nature, which necessarily follow from every man's being judge in his own case, by setting up a known authority, to which every one of that society may appeal upon any injury received, or controversy that may arise, and which every one of the society ought to obey;* where-ever any persons are, who have not such an authority to appeal to, for the decision of any difference between them, there those persons are still in the state of nature; and so is every absolute prince, in respect of those who are under his dominion.

(*The public power of all society is above every soul contained in the same society; and the principal use of that power is, to give laws unto all that are under it, which laws in such cases we must obey, unless there be reason shewed which may necessarily inforce, that the law of reason, or of God, doth enjoin the contrary, Hook. Eccl. Pol. l. i. sect. 16.)

Sect. 91. For he being supposed to have all, both legislative and executive power in himself alone, there is no judge to be found, no appeal lies open to any one, who may fairly, and indifferently, and with authority decide, and from whose decision relief and redress may be expected of any injury or inconviency, that may be suffered from the prince, or by his order: so that such a man, however intitled, Czar, or Grand Seignior, or how you please, is as much in the state of nature, with all under his dominion, as he is with therest of mankind: for where-ever any two men are, who have no standing rule, and common judge to appeal to on earth, for the determination of controversies of right betwixt them, there they are still in the state of* nature, and under all the inconveniencies of it, with only this woful difference to the subject, or rather slave of an absolute prince: that whereas, in the ordinary state of nature, he has a liberty to judge of his right, and according to the best of his power, to maintain it; now, whenever his property is invaded by the will and order of his monarch, he has not only no appeal, as those in society ought to have, but as if he were degraded from the common state of rational creatures, is denied a liberty to judge of, or to defend his right; and so is exposed to all the misery and inconveniencies, that a man can fear from one, who being in the unrestrained state of nature, is yet corrupted with flattery, and armed with power.

(*To take away all such mutual grievances, injuries and wrongs, i.e. such as attend men in the state of nature, there was no way but only by growing into composition and agreement amongst themselves, by ordaining some kind of government public, and by yielding themselves subject thereunto, that unto whom they granted authority to rule and govern, by them the peace, tranquillity and happy estate of the rest might be procured. Men always knew that where force and injury was offered, they might be defenders of themselves; they knew that however men may seek their own commodity, yet if this were done with injury unto others, it was not to be suffered, but by all men, and all good means to be withstood. Finally, they knew that no man might

in reason take upon him to determine his own right, and according to his own determination proceed in maintenance thereof, in as much as every man is towards himself, and them whom he greatly affects, partial; and therefore that strifes and troubles would be endless, except they gave their common consent, all to be ordered by some, whom they should agree upon, without which consent there would be no reason that one man should take upon him to be lord or judge over another, Hooker's Eccl. Pol. l. i. sect. 10.)

Sect. 92. For he that thinks absolute power purifies men's blood, and corrects the baseness of human nature, need read but the history of this, or any other age, to be convinced of the contrary. He that would have been insolent and injurious in the woods of America, would not probably be much better in a throne; where perhaps learning and religion shall be found out to justify all that he shall do to his subjects, and the sword presently silence all those that dare question it: for what the protection of absolute monarchy is, what kind of fathers of their countries it makes princes to be and to what a degree of happiness and security it carries civil society, where this sort of government is grown to perfection, he that will look into the late relation of Ceylon, may easily see.

Sect. 93. In absolute monarchies indeed, as well as other governments of the world, the subjects have an appeal to the law, and judges to decide any controversies, and restrain any violence that may happen betwixt the subjects themselves, one amongst another. This every one thinks necessary, and believes he deserves to be thought a declared enemy to society and mankind, who should go about to take it away. But whether this be from a true love of mankind and society, and such a charity as we owe all one to another, there is reason to doubt: for this is no more than what every man, who loves his own power, profit, or greatness, may and naturally must do, keep those animals from hurting, or destroying one another, who labour and drudge only for his pleasure and advantage; and so are taken care of, not out of any love the master has for them, but love of himself, and the profit they bring him: for if it be asked, what security, what fence is there, in such a state, against the violence and oppression of this absolute ruler? the very question can scarce be borne. They are ready to tell you, that it deserves death only to ask after safety. Betwixt subject and subject, they will grant, there must be measures, laws and judges, for their mutual peace and security: but as for the ruler, he ought to be absolute, and is above all such circumstances; because he has power to do more hurt and wrong, it is right when he does it. To ask how you may be guarded from harm, or injury, on that side where the strongest hand is to do it, is presently the voice of faction and rebellion: as if when men quitting the state of nature entered into society, they agreed that all of them but one, should be under the restraint of laws, but that he should still retain all the liberty of the state of nature, increased with power, and made licentious by impunity. This is to think, that men are so foolish, that they take care to avoid what mischiefs may be done them by pole-cats, or foxes; but are content, nay, think it safety, to be devoured by lions.

Sect. 94. But whatever flatterers may talk to amuse people's understandings, it hinders not men from feeling; and when they perceive, that any man, in what station soever, is out of the bounds of the civil society which they are of, and that they have no appeal on earth against any harm they may receive from him, they are apt to think themselves in the state of nature, in respect of him whom they find to be so; and to take care, as soon as they can, to have that safety and security in civil society, for which it was first instituted, and for which only they entered into it. And therefore, though perhaps at first, (as shall be shewed more at large hereafter in the following part of this discourse) some one good and excellent man having got a pre-eminency amongst the rest, had this deference paid to his goodness and virtue, as to a kind of natural authority, that the chief rule, with arbitration of their differences, by a tacit consent devolved into his hands, without any other caution, but the assurance they had of his uprightness and wisdom; yet when time, giving authority, and (as some men would persuade us) sacredness of customs, which the negligent, and unforeseeing

innocence of the first ages began, had brought in successors of another stamp, the people finding their properties not secure under the government, as then it was, (whereas government has no other end but the preservation of* property) could never be safe nor at rest, nor think themselves in civil society, till the legislature was placed in collective bodies of men, call them senate, parliament, or what you please. By which means every single person became subject, equally with other the meanest men, to those laws, which he himself, as part of the legislative, had established; nor could any one, by his own authority; avoid the force of the law, when once made; nor by any pretence of superiority plead exemption, thereby to license his own, or the miscarriages of any of his dependents.** No man in civil society can be exempted from the laws of it: for if any man may do what he thinks fit, and there be no appeal on earth, for redress or security against any harm he shall do; I ask, whether he be not perfectly still in the state of nature, and so can be no part or member of that civil society; unless any one will say, the state of nature and civil society are one and the same thing, which I have never yet found any one so great a patron of anarchy as to affirm.

(*At the first, when some certain kind of regiment was once appointed, it may be that nothing was then farther thought upon for the manner of goveming, but all permitted unto their wisdom and discretion, which were to rule, till by experience they found this for all parts very inconvenient, so as the thing which they had devised for a remedy, did indeed but increase the sore, which it should have cured. They saw, that to live by one man's will, became the cause of all men's misery. This constrained them to come unto laws, wherein all men might see their duty beforehand, and know the penalties of transgressing them. Hooker's Eccl. Pol. l. i. sect. 10.)

(**Civil law being the act of the whole body politic, doth therefore over-rule each several part of the same body. Hooker, ibid.)

CHAPTER. VIII.
OF THE BEGINNING OF POLITICAL SOCIETIES.

Sect. 95. MEN being, as has been said, by nature, all free, equal, and independent, no one can be put out of this estate, and subjected to the political power of another, without his own consent. The only way whereby any one divests himself of his natural liberty, and puts on the bonds of civil society, is by agreeing with other men to join and unite into a community for their comfortable, safe, and peaceable living one amongst another, in a secure enjoyment of their properties, and a greater security against any, that are not of it. This any number of men may do, because it injures not the freedom of the rest; they are left as they were in the liberty of the state of nature. When any number of men have so consented to make one community or government, they are thereby presently incorporated, and make one body politic, wherein the majority have a right to act and conclude the rest.

Sect. 96. For when any number of men have, by the consent of every individual, made a community, they have thereby made that community one body, with a power to act as one body, which is only by the will and determination of the majority: for that which acts any community, being only the consent of the individuals of it, and it being necessary to that which is one body to move one way; it is necessary the body should move that way whither the greater force carries it, which is the consent of the majority: or else it is impossible it should act or continue one body, one community, which the consent of every individual that united into it, agreed that it should; and so every one is bound by that consent to be concluded by the majority. And therefore we see, that in assemblies, impowered to act by positive laws, where no number is set by that positive law which impowers them, the act of the majority passes for the act of the whole, and of course determines, as having, by the law of nature and reason, the power of the whole.

Sect. 97. And thus every man, by consenting with others to make one body politic under one government, puts himself under an obligation, to every one of that society, to submit to the determination of the majority, and to be concluded by it; or else this original compact, whereby he with others incorporates into one society, would signify nothing, and be no compact, if he be left free, and under no other ties than he was in before in the state of nature. For what appearance would there be of any compact? what new engagement if he were no farther tied by any decrees of the society, than he himself thought fit, and did actually consent to? This would be still as great a liberty, as he himself had before his compact, or any one else in the state of nature hath, who may submit himself, and consent to any acts of it if he thinks fit.

Sect. 98. For if the consent of the majority shall not, in reason, be received as the act of the whole, and conclude every individual; nothing but the consent of every individual can make any thing to be the act of the whole: but such a consent is next to impossible ever to be had, if we consider the infirmities of health, and avocations of business, which in a number, though much less than that of a commonwealth, will necessarily keep many away from the public assembly. To which if we add the variety of opinions, and contrariety of interests, which unavoidably happen in all collections of men, the coming into society upon such terms would be only like Cato's coming into the theatre, only to go out again. Such a constitution as this would make the mighty Leviathan of a shorter duration, than the feeblest creatures, and not let it outlast the day it was born in: which cannot be supposed, till we can think, that rational creatures should desire and constitute societies only to be dissolved: for where the majority cannot conclude the rest, there they cannot act as one body, and consequently will be immediately dissolved again.

Sect. 99. Whosoever therefore out of a state of nature unite into a community, must be understood to give up all the power, necessary to the ends for which they unite into society, to the majority of the community, unless they expresly agreed in any number greater than the majority. And this is done by barely agreeing to unite into one political society, which is all the compact that is, or needs be, between the individuals, that enter into, or make up a commonwealth. And thus that, which begins and actually constitutes any political society, is nothing but the consent of any number of freemen capable of a majority to unite and incorporate into such a society. And this is that, and that only, which did, or could give beginning to any lawful government in the world.

...

Sect. 119. Every man being, as has been shewed, naturally free, and nothing being able to put him into subjection to any earthly power, but only his own consent; it is to be considered, what shall be understood to be a sufficient declaration of a man's consent, to make him subject to the laws of any government. There is a common distinction of an express and a tacit consent, which will concern our present case. No body doubts but an express consent, of any man entering into any society, makes him a perfect member of that society, a subject of that government. The difficulty is, what ought to be looked upon as a tacit consent, and how far it binds, i.e. how far any one shall be looked on to have consented, and thereby submitted to any government, where he has made no expressions of it at all. And to this I say, that every man, that hath any possessions, or enjoyment, of any part of the dominions of any government, doth thereby give his tacit consent, and is as far forth obliged to obedience to the laws of that government, during such enjoyment, as any one under it; whether this his possession be of land, to him and his heirs for ever, or a lodging only for a week; or whether it be barely travelling freely on the highway; and in effect, it reaches as far as the very being of any one within the territories of that government.

Sect. 120. To understand this the better, it is fit to consider, that every man, when he at first incorporates himself into any commonwealth, he, by his uniting himself thereunto, annexed also, and submits to the community, those possessions, which he has, or shall acquire, that do not already belong to any other government: for it would be a direct contradiction, for any one to enter into society with others for the securing and regulating of property; and yet to suppose his land, whose property is to be regulated by the laws of the society, should be exempt from the jurisdiction of that government, to which he himself, the proprietor of the land, is a subject. By the same act therefore, whereby any one unites his person, which was before free, to any commonwealth, by the same he unites his possessions, which were before free, to it also; and they become, both of them, person and possession, subject to the government and dominion of that commonwealth, as long as it hath a being. Whoever therefore, from thenceforth, by inheritance, purchase, permission, or otherways, enjoys any part of the land, so annexed to, and under the government of that commonwealth, must take it with the condition it is under; that is, of submitting to the government of the commonwealth, under whose jurisdiction it is, as far forth as any subject of it.

Sect. 121. But since the government has a direct jurisdiction only over the land, and reaches the possessor of it, (before he has actually incorporated himself in the society) only as he dwells upon, and enjoys that; the obligation any one is under, by virtue of such enjoyment, to submit to the government, begins and ends with the enjoyment; so that whenever the owner, who has given nothing but such a tacit consent to the government, will, by donation, sale, or otherwise, quit the said possession, he is at liberty to go and incorporate himself into any other commonwealth; or to agree with others to begin a new one, in vacuis locis, in any part of the world, they can find free and unpossessed: whereas he, that has once, by actual agreement, and any express declaration, given his consent to be of any commonwealth, is perpetually and indispensably obliged to be, and remain unalterably a subject to it, and can never be again in the liberty of the state of nature; unless, by any calamity, the government he was under comes to be dissolved; or else by some public act cuts him off from being any longer a member of it.

Sect. 122. But submitting to the laws of any country, living quietly, and enjoying privileges and protection under them, makes not a man a member of that society: this is only a local protection and homage due to and from all those, who, not being in a state of war, come within the territories belonging to any government, to all parts whereof the force of its laws extends. But this no more makes a man a member of that society, a perpetual subject of that commonwealth, than it would make a man a subject to another, in whose family he found it convenient to abide for some time; though, whilst he continued in it, he were obliged to comply with the laws, and submit to the government he found there. And thus we see, that foreigners, by living all their lives under another government, and enjoying the privileges and protection of it, though they are bound, even in conscience, to submit to its administration, as far forth as any denison; yet do not thereby come to be subjects or members of that commonwealth. Nothing can make any man so, but his actually entering into it by positive engagement, and express promise and compact. This is that, which I think, concerning the beginning of political societies, and that consent which makes any one a member of any commonwealth.

CHAPTER. IX.
OF THE ENDS OF POLITICAL SOCIETY AND GOVERNMENT.

Sect. 123. IF man in the state of nature be so free, as has been said; if he be absolute lord of his own person and possessions, equal to the greatest, and subject to no body, why will he part with his freedom? why will he give up this empire, and subject himself to the dominion and controul of any other power? To which it is obvious to answer, that though in the state of nature he hath such a right, yet the enjoyment of it is very uncertain, and constantly exposed to the invasion of others: for all being kings as much as he, every man his equal, and the greater part no strict observers of equity and justice, the enjoyment of the property he has in this state is very unsafe, very unsecure. This makes him willing to quit a condition, which, however free, is full of fears and continual dangers: and it is not without reason, that he seeks out, and is willing to join in society with others, who are already united, or have a mind to unite, for the mutual preservation of their lives, liberties and estates, which I call by the general name, property.

Sect. 124. The great and chief end, therefore, of men's uniting into commonwealths, and putting themselves under government, is the preservation of their property. To which in the state of nature there are many things wanting.

First, There wants an established, settled, known law, received and allowed by common consent to be the standard of right and wrong, and the common measure to decide all controversies between them: for though the law of nature be plain and intelligible to all rational creatures; yet men being biassed by their interest, as well as ignorant for want of study of it, are not apt to allow of it as a law binding to them in the application of it to their particular cases.

Sect. 125. Secondly, In the state of nature there wants a known and indifferent judge, with authority to determine all differences according to the established law: for every one in that state being both judge and executioner of the law of nature, men being partial to themselves, passion and revenge is very apt to carry them too far, and with too much heat, in their own cases; as well as negligence, and unconcernedness, to make them too remiss in other men's.

Sect. 126. Thirdly, In the state of nature there often wants power to back and support the sentence when right, and to give it due execution, They who by any injustice offended, will seldom fail, where they are able, by force to make good their injustice; such resistance many times makes the punishment dangerous, and frequently destructive, to those who attempt it.

Sect. 127. Thus mankind, notwithstanding all the privileges of the state of nature, being but in an ill condition, while they remain in it, are quickly driven into society. Hence it comes to pass, that we seldom find any number of men live any time together in this state. The inconveniencies that they are therein exposed to, by the irregular and uncertain exercise of the power every man has of punishing the transgressions of others, make them take sanctuary under the established laws of government, and therein seek the preservation of their property. It is this makes them so willingly give up every one his single power of punishing, to be exercised by such alone, as shall be appointed to it amongst them; and by such rules as the community, or those authorized by them to that purpose, shall agree on. And in this we have the original right and rise of both the legislative and executive power, as well as of the governments and societies themselves.

Sect. 128. For in the state of nature, to omit the liberty he has of innocent delights, a man has two powers.

The first is to do whatsoever he thinks fit for the preservation of himself, and others within the permission of the law of nature: by which law, common to them all, he and all the rest of mankind are one community, make up one society, distinct from all other creatures. And were it not for the corruption and vitiousness of degenerate men, there would be no need of any other; no necessity that men should separate from this great and natural community, and by positive agreements combine into smaller and divided associations.

The other power a man has in the state of nature, is the power to punish the crimes committed against that law. Both these he gives up, when he joins in a private, if I may so call it, or particular politic society, and incorporates into any commonwealth, separate from the rest of mankind.

Sect. 129. The first power, viz. of doing whatsoever he thought for the preservation of himself, and the rest of mankind, he gives up to be regulated by laws made by the society, so far forth as the preservation of himself, and the rest of that society shall require; which laws of the society in many things confine the liberty he had by the law of nature.

Sect. 130. Secondly, The power of punishing he wholly gives up, and engages his natural force, (which he might before employ in the execution of the law of nature, by his own single authority, as he thought fit) to assist the executive power of the society, as the law thereof shall require: for being now in a new state, wherein he is to enjoy many conveniencies, from the labour, assistance, and society of others in the same community, as well as protection from its whole strength; he is to part also with as much of his natural liberty, in providing for himself, as the good, prosperity, and safety of the society shall require; which is not

only necessary, but just, since the other members of the society do the like.

Sect. 131. But though men, when they enter into society, give up the equality, liberty, and executive power they had in the state of nature, into the hands of the society, to be so far disposed of by the legislative, as the good of the society shall require; yet it being only with an intention in every one the better to preserve himself, his liberty and property; (for no rational creature can be supposed to change his condition with an intention to be worse) the power of the society, or legislative constituted by them, can never be supposed to extend farther, than the common good; but is obliged to secure every one's property, by providing against those three defects above mentioned, that made the state of nature so unsafe and uneasy. And so whoever has the legislative or supreme power of any commonwealth, is bound to govern by established standing laws, promulgated and known to the people, and not by extemporary decrees; by indifferent and upright judges, who are to decide controversies by those laws; and to employ the force of the community at home, only in the execution of such laws, or abroad to prevent or redress foreign injuries, and secure the community from inroads and invasion. And all this to be directed to no other end, but the peace, safety, and public good of the people.

...

CHAPTER. XIX.
OF THE DISSOLUTION OF GOVERNMENT.

...

Sect. 222. The reason why men enter into society, is the preservation of their property; and the end why they chuse and authorize a legislative, is, that there may be laws made, and rules set, as guards and fences to the properties of all the members of the society, to limit the power, and moderate the dominion, of every part and member of the society: for since it can never be supposed to be the will of the society, that the legislative should have a power to destroy that which every one designs to secure, by entering into society, and for which the people submitted themselves to legislators of their own making; whenever the legislators endeavour to take away, and destroy the property of the people, or to reduce them to slavery under arbitrary power, they put themselves into a state of war with the people, who are thereupon absolved from any farther obedience, and are left to the common refuge, which God hath provided for all men, against force and violence. Whensoever therefore the legislative shall transgress this fundamental rule of society; and either by ambition, fear, folly or corruption, endeavour to grasp themselves, or put into the hands of any other, an absolute power over the lives, liberties, and estates of the people; by this breach of trust they forfeit the power the people had put into their hands for quite contrary ends, and it devolves to the people, who have a right to resume their original liberty, and, by the establishment of a new legislative, (such as they shall think fit) provide for their own safety and security, which is the end for which they are in society. What I have said here, concerning the legislative in general, holds true also concerning the supreme executor, who having a double trust put in him, both to have a part in the legislative, and the supreme execution of the law, acts against both, when he goes about to set up his own arbitrary will as the law of the society. He acts also contrary to his trust, when he either employs the force, treasure, and offices of the society, to corrupt the representatives, and gain them to his purposes; or openly preengages the electors, and prescribes to their choice, such, whom he has, by sollicitations, threats, promises, or otherwise, won to his designs; and employs them to bring in such, who have promised beforehand what to vote, and what to enact. Thus to regulate candidates and electors, and new-model the ways of election, what is it but to cut up the government by the roots, and poison the very fountain of public security? for the people having reserved to themselves the choice of their representatives, as the fence to their properties, could do it for no other end, but that they might always be freely chosen, and so chosen, freely act, and advise, as the necessity of the commonwealth, and the public good should, upon examination, and mature debate, be judged to require. This, those who give their votes before they hear the debate, and have weighed the reasons on all sides, are not capable of doing. To prepare such an assembly as this, and endeavour to set up the declared abettors of his own will, for the true representatives of the people, and the law-makers of the society, is certainly as great a breach of trust, and as perfect a declaration of a design to subvert the government, as is possible to be met with. To which, if one shall add rewards and punishments visibly employed to the same end, and all the arts of perverted law made use of, to take off and destroy all that stand in the way of such a design, and will not comply and consent to betray the liberties of their country, it will be past doubt what is doing. What power they ought to have in the society, who thus employ it contrary to the trust went along with it in its first institution, is easy to determine; and one cannot but see, that he, who has once attempted any such thing as this, cannot any longer be trusted.

Sect. 223. To this perhaps it will be said, that the people being ignorant, and always discontented, to lay the foundation of government in the unsteady opinion and uncertain humour of the people, is to expose it to certain ruin; and no government will be able long to subsist, if the people may set up a new legislative, whenever they take offence at the old one. To this I answer, Quite the contrary. People are not so easily got out of their old forms, as some are apt to suggest. They are hardly to be prevailed with to amend the acknowledged faults in the frame they have been accustomed to. And if there be any original defects, or adventitious ones introduced by time, or corruption; it is not an easy thing to get them changed, even when all the world sees there is an opportunity for it. This slowness and aversion in the people to quit their old constitutions, has, in the many revolutions which have been seen in this kingdom, in this and former ages, still kept us to, or, after some interval of fruitless attempts, still brought us back again to our old legislative of king, lords and commons: and whatever provocations have made the crown be taken from some of our princes heads, they never carried the people so far as to place it in another line.

Sect. 224. But it will be said, this hypothesis lays a ferment for frequent rebellion. To which I answer,

First, No more than any other hypothesis: for when the people are made miserable, and find themselves exposed to the ill usage of arbitrary power, cry up their governors, as much as you will, for sons of Jupiter; let them be sacred and divine, descended, or authorized from heaven; give them out for whom or what you please, the same will happen. The people generally ill treated, and contrary to right, will be ready upon any occasion to ease themselves of a burden that sits heavy upon them. They will wish, and seek for the opportunity, which in the change, weakness and accidents of human affairs, seldom delays long to offer itself. He must have lived but a little while in the world, who has not seen examples of this in his time; and he must have read very little, who cannot produce examples of it in all sorts of governments in the world.

Sect. 225. Secondly, I answer, such revolutions happen not upon every little mismanagement in public affairs. Great mistakes in the ruling part, many wrong and inconvenient laws, and all the slips of human frailty, will be born by the people without mutiny or murmur. But if a long train of abuses, prevarications and artifices, all tending the same way, make the design visible to the people, and they cannot but feel what they lie under, and see whither they are going; it is not to be wondered, that they should then rouze themselves, and endeavour to put the rule into such hands which may secure to them the ends for which government was at first erected; and without which, ancient names, and specious forms, are so far from being better, that they are much worse, than the state of nature, or pure anarchy; the inconveniencies being all as great and as near, but the remedy farther off and more difficult.

Sect. 226. Thirdly, I answer, that this doctrine of a power in the people of providing for their safety a-new, by a new legislative, when their legislators have acted contrary to their trust, by invading their property, is the best fence against rebellion, and the probablest means to hinder it: for rebellion being an opposition, not to persons, but authority, which is founded only in the constitutions and laws of the government; those, whoever they be, who by force break through, and by force justify their violation of them, are truly and properly rebels: for when men, by entering into society and civil-government, have excluded force, and introduced laws for the preservation of property, peace, and unity amongst themselves, those who set up force again in opposition to the laws, do rebellare, that is, bring back again the state of war, and are properly rebels: which they who are in power, (by the pretence they have to authority, the temptation of force they have in their hands, and the flattery of those about them) being likeliest to do; the properest way to prevent the evil, is to shew them the danger and injustice of it, who are under the greatest temptation to run into it.

Sect. 227. In both the fore-mentioned cases, when either the legislative is changed, or the legislators act contrary to the end for which they were constituted; those who are guilty are guilty of rebellion: for if any one by force takes away the established legislative of any society, and the laws by them made, pursuant to their trust, he thereby takes away the umpirage, which every one had consented to, for a peaceable decision of all their controversies, and a bar to the state of war amongst them. They, who remove, or change the legislative, take away this decisive power, which no body can have, but by the appointment and consent of the people; and so destroying the authority which the people did, and no body else can set up, and introducing a power which the people hath not authorized, they actually introduce a state of war, which is that of force without authority: and thus, by removing the legislative established by the society, (in whose decisions the people acquiesced and united, as to that of their own will) they untie the knot, and expose the people a-new to the state of war, And if those, who by force take away the legislative, are rebels, the legislators themselves, as has been shewn, can be no less esteemed so; when they, who were set up for the protection, and preservation of the people, their liberties and properties, shall by force invade and endeavour to take them away; and so they putting themselves into a state of war with those who made them the protectors and guardians of their peace, are, properly, and with the greatest aggravation, rebellantes, rebels.

Sect. 228. But if they, who say it lays a foundation for rebellion, mean that it may occasion civil wars, or intestine broils, to tell the people they are absolved from obedience when illegal attempts are made upon their liberties or properties, and may oppose the unlawful violence of those who were their magistrates, when they invade their properties contrary to the trust put in them; and that therefore this doctrine is not to be allowed, being so destructive to the peace of the world: they may as well say, upon the same ground, that honest men may not oppose robbers or pirates, because this may occasion disorder or bloodshed. If any mischief come in such cases, it is not to be charged upon him who defends his own right, but on him that invades his neighbours. If the innocent honest man must quietly quit all he has, for peace sake, to him who will lay violent hands upon it, I desire it may be considered, what a kind of peace there will be in the world, which consists only in violence and rapine; and which is to be maintained only for the benefit of robbers and oppressors. Who would not think it an admirable peace betwix the mighty and the mean, when the lamb, without resistance, yielded his throat to be torn by the imperious wolf? Polyphemus's den gives us a perfect pattern of such a peace, and such a government, wherein Ulysses and his companions had nothing to do, but quietly to suffer themselves to be devoured. And no doubt Ulysses, who was a prudent man, preached up passive obedience, and exhorted them to a quiet submission, by representing to them of what concernment peace was to mankind; and by shewing the inconveniences might happen, if they should offer to resist Polyphemus, who had now the power over them.

...

Sect. 240. Here, it is like, the common question will be made, Who shall be judge, whether the prince or legislative act contrary to their trust? This, perhaps, ill-affected and factious men may spread amongst the people, when the prince only makes use of his due prerogative. To this I reply, The people shall be judge; for who shall be judge whether his trustee or deputy acts well, and according to the trust reposed in him, but he who deputes him, and must, by having deputed him, have still a power to discard him, when he fails in his trust? If this be reasonable in particular cases of private men, why should it be otherwise in that of the greatest moment, where the welfare of millions is concerned, and also where the evil, if not prevented, is greater, and the redress very difficult, dear, and dangerous?

Sect. 241. But farther, this question, (Who shall be judge?) cannot mean, that there is no judge at all: for where there is no judicature on earth, to decide controversies amongst men, God in heaven is judge. He alone, it is true, is judge of the right. But every man is judge for himself, as in all other cases, so in this, whether another hath put himself into a state of war with him, and whether he should appeal to the Supreme Judge, as Jeptha did.

Sect. 242. If a controversy arise betwixt a prince and some of the people, in a matter where the law is silent, or doubtful, and the thing be of great consequence, I should think the proper umpire, in such a case, should be the body of the people: for in cases where the prince hath a trust reposed in him, and is dispensed from the common ordinary rules of the law; there, if any men find themselves aggrieved, and think the prince acts contrary to, or beyond that trust, who so proper to judge as the body of the people, (who, at first, lodged that trust in him) how far they meant it should extend? But if the prince, or whoever they be in the administration, decline that way of determination, the appeal then lies no where but to heaven; force between either persons, who have no known superior on earth, or which permits no appeal to a judge on earth, being properly a state of war, wherein the appeal lies only to heaven; and in that state the injured party must judge for himself, when he will think fit to make use of that appeal, and put himself upon it.

Sect. 243. To conclude, The power that every individual gave the society, when he entered into it, can never revert to the individuals again, as long as the society lasts, but will always remain in the community; because without this there can be no community, no commonwealth, which is contrary to the original agreement: so also when the society hath placed the legislative in any assembly of men, to continue in them and their successors, with direction and authority for providing such successors, the legislative can never revert to the people whilst that government lasts; because having provided a legislative with power to continue for ever, they have given up their political power to the legislative, and cannot resume it. But if they have set limits to the duration of their legislative, and made this supreme power in any person, or assembly, only temporary; or else, when by the miscarriages of those in authority, it is forfeited; upon the forfeiture, or at the determination of the time set, it reverts to the society, and the people have a right to act as supreme, and continue the legislative in themselves; or erect a new form, or under the old form place it in new hands, as they think good.

FINIS.

John Locke: *A Letter Concerning Toleration*

1689
Translated by William Popple
www.Constitution.org/jl/tolerati.htm

Honoured Sir,

Since you are pleased to inquire what are my thoughts about the mutual toleration of christians in their different professions of religion, I must needs answer you freely, that I esteem that toleration to be the chief characteristical mark of the true church. For whatsoever some people boast of the antiquity of places and names, or of the pomp of their outward worship; others, of the reformation of their discipline; all of the orthodoxy of their faith, for every one is orthodox to himself: these things, and all others of this nature, are much rather marks of men's striving for power and empire over one another, than of the church of Christ. Let any one have ever so true a claim to all these things, yet if he be destitute of charity, meekness, and goodwill in general towards all mankind, even to those that are not christians, he is certainly yet short of being a true christian himself. "The kings of the gentiles exercise lordship over them," said our Saviour to his disciples, "but ye shall not be so," Luke xxii. 25, 26. The business of true religion is quite another thing. It is not instituted in order to the erecting an external pomp, nor to the obtaining of ecclesiastical dominion, nor to the exercising of compulsive force; but to the regulating of men's lives according to the rules of virtue and piety. Whosoever will list himself under the banner of Christ, must, in the first place and above all things, make war upon his own lusts and vices. It is in vain for any man to usurp the name of christian, without holiness of life, purity of manners, and benignity and meekness of spirit. "Let every one that nameth the name of Christ, depart from iniquity." 2 Tim. ii. 19. "Thou, when thou art converted, strengthen thy brethren," said our Lord to Peter, Luke xxii. 32. It would indeed be very hard for one that appears careless about his own salvation, to persuade me that he were extremely concerned for mine. For it is impossible that those should sincerely and heartily apply themselves to make other people christians, who have not really embraced the christian religion in their own hearts. If the gospel and the apostles may be credited, no man can be a christian without charity, and without that faith which works, not by force, but by love. Now I appeal to the consciences of those that persecute, torment, destroy, and kill other men upon pretence of religion, whether they do it out of friendship and kindness towards them, or no: and I shall then indeed, and not till then, believe they do so, when I shall see those fiery zealots correcting, in the same manner, their friends and familiar acquaintance, for the manifest sins they commit against the precepts of the gospel; when I shall see them prosecute with fire and sword the members of their own communion that are tainted with enormous vices, and without amendment are in danger of eternal perdition; and when I shall see them thus express their love and desire of the salvation of their souls, by the infliction of torments, and exercise of all manner of cruelties. For if it be out of a principle of charity, as they pretend, and love to men's souls, that they deprive them of their estates, maim them with corporal punishments, starve and torment them in noisome prisons, and in the end even take away their lives; I say, if all this be done merely to make men christians, and procure their salvation, why then do they suffer "whoredom, fraud, malice, and such like enormities," which, according to the apostle, Rom. i. manifestly relish of heathenish corruption, to predominate so much and abound amongst their flocks and people? These, and such like things, are certainly more contrary to the glory of God, to the purity of the church, and to the salvation of souls, than any conscientious dissent from ecclesiastical decision, or separation from public worship, whilst accompanied with innocency of life. Why then does this burning zeal for God, for the church, and for the salvation of souls; burning, I say literally, with fire and faggot; pass by those moral vices and wickednesses, without any chastisement, which are acknowledged by all men to be diametrically opposite to the profession of christianity; and bend all its nerves either to the introducing of ceremonies, or to the establishment of opinions, which for the most part are about nice and intricate matters, that exceed the capacity of ordinary understandings? Which of the parties contending about these things is in the right, which of them is guilty of schism or heresy, whether those that domineer or those that suffer, will then at last be manifest, when the cause of their separation comes to be judged of. He certainly that follows Christ, embraces his doctrine, and bears his yoke, though he forsake both father and mother, separate from the public assemblies and ceremonies of his country, or whomsoever, or whatsoever else he relinquishes, will not then be judged an heretic.

Now, though the divisions that are among sects should be allowed to be ever so obstructive of the salvation of souls; yet nevertheless "adultery, fornication, uncleanness, lasciviousness, idolatry, and such like things, cannot be denied to be works of the flesh;" concerning which the apostle has expressly declared, that "they who do them shall not inherit the kingdom of God." Gal. v. 21. Whosoever therefore is sincerely solicitous about the kingdom of God, and thinks it his duty to endeavour the enlargement of it amongst men, ought to apply himself with no less care and industry to the rooting out of these immoralities than to the extirpation of sects. But if any one do otherwise, and whilst he is cruel and implacable towards those that differ from him in opinion, he be indulgent to such iniquities and immoralities as are unbecoming the name of a christian, let such a one talk ever so much of the church, he plainly demonstrates by his actions, that it is another kingdom he aims at, and not the advancement of the kingdom of God.

That any man should think fit to cause another man, whose salvation he heartily desires, to expire in torments, and that even in an unconverted state, would, I confess, seem very strange to me, and, I think, to any other also. But nobody, surely, will ever believe that such a carriage can proceed from charity, love or goodwill. If any one maintain that men ought to be compelled by fire and sword to profess certain doctrines, and conform to this or that exterior worship, without any regard had unto their morals; if any one endeavour to convert those that are erroneous unto the faith, by forcing them to profess things that they do not believe, and allowing them to practise things that the gospel does not permit; it cannot be doubted indeed, that such a one is desirous to have a numerous assembly joined in the same profession with himself; but that he principally intends by those means to compose a truly christian church, is altogether incredible. It is not therefore to be wondered at, if those who do not really contend for the advancement of the true religion, and of the church of Christ, make use of arms that do not belong to the christian warfare. If, like the captain of our salvation, they sincerely desired the good of souls, they would tread in the steps and follow the perfect example of that prince of peace, who sent out his soldiers to the subduing of nations, and gathering them into his church, not armed with the sword, or other instruments of force, but prepared with the gospel of peace, and with the exemplary holiness of their conversation. This was his method. Though if infidels were to be converted by force, if those that are either blind or obstinate were to be drawn off from their errors by armed soldiers, we know very well that it was much more easy for him to do it with armies of heavenly legions, than for any son of the church, how potent soever, with all his dragoons.

The toleration of those that differ from others in matters of religion, is so agreeable to the gospel of Jesus Christ, and to the genuine reason of mankind, that it seems monstrous for men to be so blind, as not to perceive the necessity and advantage of it, in so clear a light. I will not here tax the pride and ambition of some, the passion and uncharitable zeal of others. These are faults from which human affairs can perhaps scarce ever be perfectly freed; but yet such as nobody will bear the plain imputation of, without covering them with some specious colour; and so pretend to commendation, whilst they are carried away by their own irregular passions. But however, that some may not colour their spirit of persecution and unchristian cruelty, with a pretence of care of the public weal, and observation of the laws; and that others, under pretence of religion, may not seek impunity for their libertinism and licentiousness; in a word, that none may impose either upon himself or others, by the pretences of loyalty and obedience to the prince, or of tenderness and sincerity in the worship of God; I esteem it above all things necessary to distinguish exactly the business of civil government from that of religion, and to settle the just bounds that lie between the one and the other. If this be not done, there can be no end put to the controversies that will be always arising between those that have, or at least pretend to have, on the one side, a concernment for the interest of men's souls, and, on the other side, a care of the commonwealth.

The commonwealth seems to me to be a society of men constituted only for the procuring, preserving, and advancing their own civil interests.

Civil interest I call life, liberty, health, and indolency of body; and the possession of outward things, such as money, lands, houses, furniture, and the like.

It is the duty of the civil magistrate, by the impartial execution of equal laws, to secure unto all the people in general, and to every one of his subjects in particular, the just possession of these things belonging to this life. If any one presume to violate the laws of public justice and equity, established for the preservation of these things, his presumption is to be checked by the fear of punishment, consisting in the deprivation or diminution of those civil interests, or goods, which otherwise he might and ought to enjoy. But seeing no man does willingly suffer himself to be punished by the deprivation of any part of his goods, and much less of his liberty or life, therefore is the magistrate armed with the force and strength of all his subjects, in order to the

punishment of those that violate any other man's rights.

Now that the whole jurisdiction of the magistrate reaches only to these civil concernments; and that all civil power, right, and dominion, is bounded and confined to the only care of promoting these things; and that it neither can nor ought in any manner to be extended to the salvation of souls; these following considerations seem unto me abundantly to demonstrate.

First, Because the care of souls is not committed to the civil magistrate, any more than to other men. It is not committed unto him, I say, by God; because it appears not that God has ever given any such authority to one man over another, as to compel any one to his religion. Nor can any such power be vested in the magistrate by the consent of the people; because no man can so far abandon the care of his own salvation, as blindly to leave it to the choice of any other, whether prince or subject, to prescribe to him what faith or worship he shall embrace. For no man can, if he would, conform his faith to the dictates of another. All the life and power of true religion consists in the inward and full persuasion of the mind; and faith is not faith, without believing. Whatever profession we make, to whatever outward worship we conform, if we are not fully satisfied in our own mind that the one is true, and the other well-pleasing unto God, such profession and such practice, far from being any furtherance, are indeed great obstacles to our salvation. For in this manner, instead of expiating other sins by the exercise of religion, I say in offering thus unto God Almighty such a worship as we esteem to be displeasing unto him, we add unto the number of our other sins, those also of hypocrisy, and contempt of his Divine Majesty.

In the second place, The care of souls cannot belong to the civil magistrate, because his power consists only in outward force: but true and saving religion consists in the inward persuasion of the mind, without which nothing can be acceptable to God. And such is the nature of the understanding, that it cannot be compelled to the belief of any thing by outward force. Confiscation of estate, imprisonment, torments, nothing of that nature can have any such efficacy as to make men change the inward judgment that they have framed of things.

It may indeed be alleged, that the magistrate may make use of arguments, and thereby draw the heterodox into the way of truth, and procure their salvation. I grant it; but this is common to him with other men. In teaching, instructing, and redressing the erroneous by reason, he may certainly do what becomes any good man to do. Magistracy does not oblige him to put off either humanity or christianity. But it is one thing to persuade, another to command; one thing to press with arguments, another with penalties. This the civil power alone has a right to do; to the other, good-will is authority enough. Every man has commission to admonish, exhort, convince another of errour, and by reasoning to draw him into truth: but to give laws, receive obedience, and compel with the sword, belongs to none but the magistrate. And upon this ground I affirm, that the magistrate's power extends not to the establishing of any article of faith, or forms of worship, by the force of his laws. For laws are of no force at all without penalties, and penalties in this case are absolutely impertinent; because they are not proper to convince the mind. Neither the profession of any articles of faith, nor the conformity to any outward form of worship, as has been already said, can be available to the salvation of souls, unless the truth of the one, and the acceptableness of the other unto God, be thoroughly believed by those that so profess and practise. But penalties are no ways capable to produce such belief. It is only light and evidence that can work a change in men's opinions; and that light can in no manner proceed from corporal sufferings, or any other outward penalties.

In the third place, The care of the salvation of men's souls cannot belong to the magistrate; because, though the rigour of laws and the force of penalties were capable to convince and change men's minds, yet would not that help at all to the salvation of their souls. For, there being but one truth, one way to heaven; what hopes is there that more men would be led into it, if they had no other rule to follow but the religion of the court,

and were put under a necessity to quit the light of their own reason, to oppose the dictates of their own consciences, and blindly to resign up themselves to the will of their governors, and to the religion which either ignorance, ambition, or superstition had chanced to establish in the countries where they were born? In the variety and contradiction of opinions in religion, wherein the princes of the world are as much divided as in their secular interests, the narrow way would be much straitened; one country alone would be in the right, and all the rest of the world put under an obligation of following their princes in the ways that lead to destruction: and that which heightens the absurdity, and very ill suits the notion of a deity, men would owe their eternal happiness or misery to the places of their nativity.

These considerations, to omit many others that might have been urged to the same purpose, seem unto me sufficient to conclude, that all the power of civil government relates only to men's civil interests, is confined to the care of the things of this world, and hath nothing to do with the world to come.

Let us now consider what a church is. A church then I take to be a voluntary society of men, joining themselves together of their own accord in order to the public worshipping of God, in such a manner as they judge acceptable to him, and effectual to the salvation of their souls.

I say, it is a free and voluntary society. Nobody is born a member of any church; otherwise the religion of parents would descend unto children, by the same right of inheritance as their temporal estates, and every one would hold his faith by the same tenure he does his lands; than which nothing can be imagined more absurd. Thus therefore that matter stands. No man by nature is bound unto any particular church or sect, but every one joins himself voluntarily to that society in which he believes he has found that profession and worship which is truly acceptable to God. The hopes of salvation, as it was the only cause of his entrance into that communion, so it can be the only reason of his stay there. For if afterwards he discover any thing either erroneous in the doctrine, or incongruous in the worship of that society to which he has joined himself, why should it not be as free for him to go out as it was to enter? No member of a religious society can be tried with any other bonds but what proceed from the certain expectation of eternal life. A church then is a society of members voluntarily uniting to this end.

It follows now that we consider what is the power of this church, and unto what laws it is subject.

Forasmuch as no society, how free soever, or upon whatsoever slight occasion instituted (whether of philosophers for learning, of merchants for commerce, or of men of leisure for mutual conversation and discourse,) no church or company, I say, can in the least subsist and hold together, but will presently dissolve and break to pieces, unless it be regulated by some laws, and the members all consent to observe some order. Place and time of meeting must be agreed on; rules for admitting and excluding members must be established: distinction of officers, and putting things into a regular course, and such like, cannot be omitted. But since the joining together of several members into this church-society, as has already been demonstrated, is absolutely free and spontaneous, it necessarily follows, that the right of making its laws can belong to none but the society itself, or at least, which is the same thing, to those whom the society by common consent has authorised thereunto.

Some perhaps may object, that no such society can be said to be a true church, unless it have in it a bishop, or presbyter, with ruling authority derived from the very apostles, and continued down unto the present time by an uninterrupted succession.

To these I answer. In the first place, Let them show me the edict by which Christ has imposed that law upon his church. And let not any man think me impertinent, if, in a thing of this consequence, I require that the terms of that edict be very express and positive.—For the promise he has made us, that "wheresoever two or three are gathered together in his name, he will be in the midst of them," Matth. xviii. 20. seems to imply the contrary. Whether such an assembly want any thing necessary to a true church, pray do you consider. Certain I am, that nothing can be there wanting unto the salvation of souls, which is sufficient for our purpose.

Next, pray observe how great have always been the divisions amongst even those who lay so much stress upon the divine institution, and continued succession of a certain order of rulers in the church. Now their very dissension unavoidably puts us upon a necessity of deliberating, and consequently allows a liberty of choosing that, which upon consideration we prefer.

And, in the last place, I consent that these men have a ruler of their church, established by such a long series of succession as they judge necessary, provided I may have liberty at the same time to join myself to that society, in which I am persuaded those things are to be found which are necessary to the salvation of my soul. In this manner ecclesiastical liberty will be preserved on all sides, and no man will have a legislator imposed upon him, but whom himself has chosen.

But since men are so solicitous about the true church, I would only ask them here by the way, if it be not more agreeable to the Church of Christ to make the conditions of her communion consist in such things, and such things only, as the Holy Spirit has in the Holy Scriptures declared, in express words, to be necessary to salvation? I ask, I say, whether this be not more agreeable to the church of Christ, than for men to impose their own inventions and interpretations upon others, as if they were of divine authority; and to establish by ecclesiastical laws, as absolutely necessary to the profession of Christianity, such things as the Holy Scriptures do either not mention, or at lest not expressly command? Whosoever requires those things in order to ecclesiastical communion, which Christ does not require in order to life eternal, he may perhaps indeed constitute a society accommodated to his own opinion, and his own advantage; but how that can be called the church of Christ, which is established upon laws that are not his, and which excludes such persons from its communion, as he will one day receive into the kingdom of heaven, I understand not. But this being not a proper place to inquire into the marks of the true church, I will only mind those that contend so earnestly for the decrees of their own society, and that cry out continually the churoh, the church, with as much noise, and perhaps upon the same principle, as the Ephesian silversmiths did for their Diana; this, I say, I desire to mind them of, that the Gospel frequently declares, that the true disciples of Christ must suffer persecution; but that the church of Christ should persecute others, and force others by fire and sword to embrace her faith and doctrine, I could never yet find in any of the books of the New Testament.

The end of a religious society, as has already been said, is the public worship of God, and by means thereof the acquisition of eternal life. All discipline ought therefore to tend to that end, and all ecclesiastical laws to be thereunto confined. Nothing ought, nor can be transacted in this society, relating to the possession of civil and worldly goods. No force is here to be made use of, upon any occasion whatsoever: for force belongs wholly to the civil magistrate, and the possession of all outward goods is subject to his jurisdiction.

But it may be asked, by what means then shall ecclesiastical laws be established, if they must be thus destitute of all compulsive power? I answer, they must be established by means suitable to the nature of such things, whereof the external profession and observation, if not proceeding from a thorough conviction and approbation of the mind, is altogether useless and unprofitable. The arms by which the members of this society are to be kept within their duty, are exhortations, admonitions, and advice. If by these means the offenders will not be reclaimed, and the erroneous convinced, there remains nothing farther to be done, but that such stubborn and obstinate persons, who give no ground to hope for their reformation, should be cast out and separated from the society. This is the last and utmost force of ecclesiastical authority: no other punishment can thereby be inflicted, than that the relation ceasing between the body and the member which is cut off, the person so condemned ceases to be a part of that church.

These things being thus determined, let us inquire in the next place, how far the duty of Toleration extends, and what is required from every one by it.

And first, I hold, that no church is bound by the duty of Toleration to retain any such person in her bosom, as after admonition continues obstinately to offend against the laws of the society. For these being the condition of communion, and the bond of society, if the breach of them were permitted without any animadversion, the society would immediately be thereby dissolved. But nevertheless in all such cases care is to be taken that the sentence of excommunication, and the execution thereof, carry with it no rough usage, of word or action, whereby the ejected person may any ways be damnified in body or estate. For all force, as has often been said, belongs only to the magistrate, nor ought any private persons, at any time, to use force; unless it be in self-defence against unjust violence. Excommunication neither does nor can deprive the excommunicated person of any of those civil goods that he formerly possessed. All those things belong to the civil government, and are under the magistrate's protection. The whole force of excommunication consists only in this, that the resolution of the society in that respect being declared, the union that was between the body and some member, comes thereby to be dissolved; and that relation ceasing, the participation of some certain things which the society communicated to its members, and unto which no man has any civil right, comes also to cease. For there is no civil injury done unto the excommunicated person by the church minister's refusing him that bread and wine, in the celebration of the Lord's supper, which was not bought with his, but other men's money.

Secondly: no private person has any right in any manner to prejudice another person in his civil enjoyments, because he is of another church or religion. All the rights and franchises that belong to him as a man, or as a denison, are inviolably to be preserved to him. These are not the business of religion. No violence nor injury is to be offered him, whether he be christian or pagan. Nay, we must not content ourselves with the narrow measures of bare justice: charity, bounty, and liberality must be added to it. This the Gospel enjoins, this reason directs, and this that natural fellowship we are born into requires of us. If any man err from the right way, it is his own misfortune, no injury to thee: nor therefore art thou to punish him in the things of this life, because thou supposest he will be miserable in that which is to come.

What I say concerning the mutual toleration of private persons differing from one another in religion, I understand also of particular churches; which stand as it were in the same relation to each other as private persons among themselves; nor has any one of them any manner of jurisdiction over any other, no not even when the civil magistrate, as it sometimes happens, comes to be of this or the other communion. For the civil government can give no new right to the church, nor the church to the civil government. So that whether the magistrate join himself to any church, or separate from it, the church remains always as it was before, a free and voluntary society. It neither acquires the power of the sword by the magistrate's coming to it, nor does it lose the right of instruction and excommunication by his going from it. This is the fundamental and immutable right of a spontaneous society, that it has to remove any of its members who transgress the rules of its institution: but it cannot, by the accession of any new members, acquire any right of jurisdiction over those that are not joined with it. And therefore peace, equity, and friendship, are always mutually to be observed by particular churches, in the same manner as by private persons, without any pretence of superiority or jurisdiction over one another.

That the thing may be made yet clearer by an example; let us suppose two churches, the one of arminians, the other of calvinists, residing in the city of Constantinople. Will any one say, that either of these churches has right to deprive the members of the other of their estates and liberty, as we see practised elsewhere, because of their differing from it in some doctrines or ceremonies; whilst the Turks in the mean while silently stand by, and laugh to see with what inhuman cruelty

christians thus rage against christians? But if one of these churches hath this power of treating the other ill, I ask which of them it is to whom that power belongs, and by what right? It will be answered, undoubtedly, that it is the orthodox church which has the right of authority over the erroneous or heretical. This is, in great and specious words, to say just nothing at all. For every church is orthodox to itself; to others, erroneous or heretical. Whatsoever any church believes, it believes to be true; and the contrary thereunto it pronounces to be errour. So that the controversy between these churches about the truth of their doctrines, and the purity of their worship, is on both sides equal; nor is there any judge, either at Constantinople, or elsewhere upon earth, by whose sentence it can be determined. The decision of that question belongs only to the Supreme Judge of all men, to whom also alone belongs the punishment of the erroneous. In the mean while, let those men consider how heinously they sin, who, adding injustice, if not their errour, yet certainly to their pride, do rashly and arrogantly take upon them to misuse the servants of another master, who are not at all accountable to them.

Nay, further: if it could be manifest which of these two dissenting churches were in the right way, there would not accrue thereby unto the orthodox any right of destroying the other. For churches have neither any jurisdiction in worldly matters, nor are fire and sword any proper instruments wherewith to convince men's minds of errour, and inform them of the truth. Let us suppose, nevertheless, that the civil magistrate is inclined to favour one of them, and to put his sword into their hands, that, by his consent, they might chastise the dissenters as they pleased. Will any man say, that any right can be derived unto a christian church, over its brethren, from a Turkish emperor? An infidel, who has himself no authority to punish christians for the articles of their faith, cannot confer such an authority upon any society of christians, nor give unto them a right which he has not himself. This would be the case at Constantinople. And the reason of the thing is the same in any christian kingdom. The civil power is the same in every place: nor can that power, in the hands of a christian prince, confer any greater authority upon the church, than in the hands of a heathen; which is to say, just none at all.

Nevertheless, it is worthy to be observed, and lamented, that the most violent of these defenders of the truth, the opposers of errour, the exclaimers against schism, do hardly ever let loose this their zeal for God, with which they are so warmed and inflamed, unless where they have the civil magistrate on their side. But so soon as ever court-favour has given them the better end of the staff, and they begin to feel themselves the stronger; then presently peace and charity are to be laid aside: otherwise, they are religiously to be observed. Where they have not the power to carry on persecution, and to become masters, there they desire to live upon fair terms and preach up toleration. When they are not strengthened with the civil power, then they can bear most patiently, and unmovedly, the contagion of idolatry, superstition, and heresy in their neighbourhood; of which, on other occasions, the interest of religion makes them to be extremely apprehensive. They do not forwardly attack those errours which are in fashion at court, or are countenanced by the government. Here they can be content to spare their arguments: which yet, with their leave, is the only right method of propagating truth; which has no such way of prevailing, as when strong arguments and good reason are joined with the softness of civility and good usage.

No-body therefore, in fine, neither single persons, nor churches, nay, nor even commonwealths, have any just title to invade the civil rights and worldly goods of each other, upon pretence of religion. Those that are of another opinion, would do well to consider with themselves how pernicious a seed of discord and war, how powerful a provocation to endless hatreds, rapines, and slaughters, they thereby furnish unto mankind. No peace and security, no not so much as common friendship, can ever be established or preserved amongst men, so long as this opinion prevails "that dominion is founded in grace, and that religion is to be propagated by force of arms.

In the third place: Let us see what the duty of toleration requires from those who are distinguished from the rest of mankind, from the laity, as they please to call us, by some ecclesiastical character and office; whether they be bishops, priests, presbyters, ministers, or however else dignified or distinguished. It is not my business to enquire here into the original of the power or dignity of the clergy. This only I say, that whencesoever their authority be sprung, since it is ecclesiastical, it ought to be confined within the bounds of the church, nor can it in any manner be extended to civil affairs; because the church itself is a thing absolutely separate and distinct from the commonwealth. The boundaries on both sides are fixed and immoveable. He jumbles heaven and earth together, the things most remote and opposite, who mixes these societies, which are, in their original, end, business, and in every thing, perfectly distinct, and infinitely different from each other. No man therefore, with whatsoever ecclesiastical office he be dignified, can deprive another man that is not of his church and faith, either of liberty, or of any part of his worldly goods, upon the account of that difference which is between them in religion. For whatsoever is not lawful to the whole church cannot by any ecclesiastical right, become lawful to any of its members.

But this is not all. It is not enough that ecclesiastical men abstain from violence and rapine, and all manner of persecution. He that pretends to be a successor of the apostles, and takes upon him the office of teaching, is obliged also to admonish his hearers of the duties of peace and good-will towards all men; as well towards the erroneous as the orthodox; towards those that differ from them in faith and worship, as well as towards those that agree with them therein: and he ought industriously to exhort all men, whether private persons or magistrates, if any such there be in his church, to charity, meekness, and toleration; and diligently endeavour to allay and temper all that heat, and unreasonable averseness of mind, which either any man's fiery zeal for his own sect, or the craft of others, has kindled against dissenters. I will not undertake to represent how happy and how great would be the fruit, both in church and state, if the pulpits every-where sounded with this doctrine of peace and toleration; lest I should seem to reflect too severely upon those men whose dignity I desire not to detract from, nor would have it diminished either by others or themselves. But this I say, that thus it ought to be. And if any one that professes himself to be a minister of the word of God, a preacher of the gospel of peace, teach otherwise; he either understands not, or neglects the business of his calling, and shall one day give account thereof unto the Prince of Peace. If christians are to be admonished that they abstain from all manner of revenge, even after repeated provocations and multiplied injuries; how much more ought they who suffer nothing, who have had no harm done them, to forbear violence, and abstain from all manner of ill usage towards those from whom they have received none? This caution and temper they ought certainly to use towards those who mind only their own business, and are solicitous for nothing but that, whatever men think of them, they may worship God in that manner which they are persuaded is acceptable to him, and in which they have the strongest hopes of eternal salvation. In private domestic affairs, in the management of estates, in the conservation of bodily health, every man may consider what suits his own conveniency, and follow what course he likes best. No man complains of the ill management of his neighbour's affairs. No man is angry with another for an errour committed in sowing his land, or in marrying his daughter. No-body corrects a spendthrift for consuming his substance in taverns. Let any man pull down, or build, or make whatsoever expences he pleases, no-body murmurs, no-body controls him; he has his liberty. But if any man do not frequent the church, if he do not there conform his behaviour exactly to the accustomed ceremonies, or if he brings not his children to be initiated in the sacred mysteries of this or the other congregation; this immediately causes an uproar, and the neighbourhood is filled with noise and clamour. Every one is ready to be the avenger of so great a crime. And the zealots hardly have patience to

refrain from violence and rapine, so long till the cause be heard, and the poor man be, according to form, condemned to the loss of liberty, goods or life. Oh that our ecclesiastical orators, of every sect, would apply themselves, with all the strength of argument that they are able, to the confounding of men's errours! But let them spare their persons. Let them not supply their want of reasons with the instruments of force, which belong to another jurisdiction, and do ill become a churchman's hands. Let them not call in the magistrate's authority to the aid of their eloquence, or learning; lest perhaps, whilst they pretend only love for the truth, this their intemperate zeal, breathing nothing but fire and sword, betray their ambition, and show that what they desire is temporal dominion. For it will be very difficult to persuade men of sense, that he, who with dry eyes, and satisfaction of mind, can deliver his brother unto the executioner, to be burnt alive, does sincerely and heartily concern himself to save that brother from the flames of hell in the world to come.

In the last place. Let us now consider what is the magistrate's duty in the business of toleration: which is certainly very considerable.

We have already proved that the care of souls does not belong to the magistrate: not a magisterial care, I mean, if I may so call it, which consists in prescribing by laws, and compelling by punishments. But a charitable care, which consists in teaching, admonishing, and persuading, cannot be denied unto any man. The care therefore of every man's soul belongs unto himself, and is to be left unto himself. But what if he neglect the care of his soul? I answer, what if he neglect the care of his health, or of his estate; which things are nearlier related to the government of the magistrate than the other? Will the magistrate provide by an express law, that such an one shall not become poor or sick? Laws provide, as much as is possible, that the goods and health of subjects be not injured by the fraud or violence of others; they do not guard them from the negligence or ill-husbandry of the possessors themselves. No man can be forced to be rich or healthful, whether he will or no. Nay God himself will not save men against their wills.

Let us suppose, however, that some prince were desirous to force his subjects to accumulate riches, or to preserve the health and strength of their bodies. Shall it be provided by law, that they must consult none but Roman physicians, and shall every one be bound to live according to their prescriptions? What shall no potion, no broth, be taken, but what is prepared either in the Vatican, suppose, or in a geneva shop? Or, to make these subjects rich, shall they all be obliged by law to become merchants, or musicians? Or, shall every one turn victualler, or smith, because there are some that maintain their families plentifully, and grow rich in those professions? But it may be said, there are a thousand ways to wealth, but one only way to heaven. It is well said indeed, especially by those that plead for compelling men into this or the other way; for if there were several ways that lead thither, there would not be so much as a pretence left for compulsion. But now, if I be marching on with my utmost vigour, in that way which, according to the sacred geography, leads straight to Jerusalem; why am I beaten and ill-used by others, because, perhaps, I wear not buskins; because my hair is not of the right cut; because, perhaps, I have not been dipt in the right fashion; because I eat flesh upon the road, or some other food which agrees with my stomach; because I avoid certain by-ways, which seem unto me to lead into briars or precipices; because, amongst the several paths that are in the same road, I choose that to walk in which seems to be the straightest and cleanest; because I avoid to keep company with some travellers that are less grave, and others that are more sour than they ought to be; or in fine, because I follow a guide that either is, or is not, cloathed in white, and crowned with a mitre? Certainly, if we consider right, we shall find that for the most part they are such frivolous things as these, that, without any prejudice to religion to the salvation of souls, if not accompanied with superstition or hypocrisy, might either be observed or omitted; I say, they are such like things as these, which breed implacable enmities among christian brethren, who are all agreed in the substantial and truly fundamental part of religion.

But let us grant unto these zealots, who condemn all things that are not of their mode, that from these circumstances arise different ends. What shall we conclude from thence? There is only one of these which is the true way to eternal happiness. But, in this great variety of ways that men follow, it is still doubted which is this right one. Now neither the care of the commonwealth, nor the right of enacting laws, does discover this way that leads to heaven more certainly to the magistrate than every private man's search and study discovers it unto himself. I have a weak body, sunk under a languishing disease, for which, I suppose, there is only one remedy, but that unknown. Does it therefore belong unto the magistrate to prescribe me a remedy, because there is but one, and because it is unknown? Because there is but one way for me to escape death, will it therefore be safe for me to do whatsoever the magistrate ordains? Those things that every man ought sincerely to inquire into himself, and by meditation, study, search, and his own endeavours, attain the knowledge of, cannot be looked upon as the peculiar profession of any one sort of men. Princes indeed are born superiour unto other men in power, but in nature equal. Neither the right, nor the art of ruling, does necessarily carry along with it the certain knowledge of other things; and least of all of the true religion; for if it were so, how could it come to pass that the lords of the earth should differ so vastly as they do in religious matters? But let us grant that it is probable the way to eternal life may be better known by a prince than by his subjects; or at least, that in this incertitude of things, the safest and most commodious way for private persons is to follow his dictates. You will say, what then? If he should bid you follow merchandize for your livelihood, would you decline that course for fear it should not succeed? I answer, I would turn merchant upon the prince's command, because in case I should have ill success in trade, he is abundantly able to make up my loss some other way. If it be true, as he pretends, that he desires I should thrive and grow rich, he can set me up again when unsuccessful voyages have broke me. But this is not the case, in the things that regard the life to come. If there I take a wrong course, if in that respect I am once undone, it is not in the magistrate's power to repair my loss, to ease my suffering, or to restore me in any measure, much less entirely to a good estate. What security can be given for the kingdom of heaven?

Perhaps some will say, that they do not suppose this infallible judgment that all men are bound to follow in the affairs of religion, to be in the civil magistrate, but in the church. What the church has determined, that the civil magistrate orders to be observed; and he provides by his authority, that nobody shall either act or believe, in the business of religion, otherwise than the church teaches; so that the judgment of those things is in the church. The magistrate himself yields obedience thereunto, and requires the like obedience from others. I answer: Who sees not how frequently the name of the church, which was so venerable in the time of the apostles, has been made use of to throw dust in people's eyes, in following ages? But however, in the present case it helps us not. The one only narrow way which leads to heaven is not better known to the magistrate than to private persons, and therefore I cannot safely take him for my guide, who may probably be as ignorant of the way as myself, and who certainly is less concerned for my salvation than I myself am. Amongst so many kings of the jews, how many of them were there whom any Israelite, thus blindly following, had not fallen into idolatry, and thereby into destruction? Yet nevertheless, you bid me be of good courage, and tell me that all is now safe and secure, because the magistrate does not now enjoin the observance of his own decrees in matters of religion, but only the decrees of the church. Of what church, I beseech you? Of that which certainly likes him best. As if he that compels me by laws and penalties to enter into this or the other church, did not interpose his own judgment in the matter. What difference is there whether he lead me himself or deliver me over to be led by others? I depend both ways upon his will, and it is he that determines both ways of my eternal state. Would an Israelite, that had worshipped Baal upon the command of his king, have been in any better condition, because somebody had told him that the king ordered nothing in religion upon his own

head, nor commanded any thing to be done by his subjects in divine worship, but what was approved by the counsel of priests, and declared to be of divine right by the doctors of the church? If the religion of any church become therefore true and saving, because the head of that sect, the prelates and priests, and those of that tribe, do all of them, with all their might, extol and praise it; what religion can ever be accounted erroneous, false and destructive? I am doubtful concerning the doctrine of the socinians, I am suspicious of the way of worship practised by the papists or lutherans; will it be ever a jot the safer for me to join either unto the one or the other of those churches, upon the magistrate's command, because he commands nothing in religion but by the authority and counsel of the doctors of that church?

But to speak the truth, we must acknowledge that the church, if a convention of clergymen, making canons, must be called by that name, is for the most part more apt to be influenced by the court, than the court by the church. How the church was under the vicissitude of orthodox and arian emperors is very well known. Or if those things be too remote, our modern English history affords us fresher examples, in the reigns of Henry VIII. Edward VI. Mary, and Elizabeth, how easily and smoothly the clergy changed their decrees, their articles of faith, their form of worship, every thing, according to the inclination of those kings and queens. Yet were those kings and queens of such different minds, in points of religion, and enjoined thereupon such different things, that no man in his wits, I had almost said none but an atheist, will presume to say that any sincere and upright worshipper of God could, with a safe conscience, obey their several decrees. To conclude, It is the same thing whether a king that prescribes laws to another man's religion pretend to do it by his own judgment, or by the ecclesiastical authority and advice of others. The decisions of church-men, whose differences and disputes are sufficiently known, cannot be any sounder, or safer than his: nor can all their suffrages joined together add any new strength unto the civil power. Though this also must be taken notice of that princes seldom have any regard to the suffrages of ecclesiastics that are not favourers of their own faith and way of worship.

But after all, the principal consideration, and which absolutely determines this controversy, is this: Although the magistrate's opinion in religion be sound, and the way that he appoints be truly evangelical, yet if I be not thoroughly persuaded thereof in my own mind, there will be no safety for me in following it. No way whatsoever that I shall walk in against the dictates of my conscience, will ever bring me to the mansions of the blessed. I may grow rich by an art that I take not delight in; I may be cured of some disease by remedies that I have not faith in; but I cannot be saved by a religion that I distrust, and by a worship that I abhor. It is in vain for an unbeliever to take up the outward show of another man's profession. Faith only, and inward sincerity, are the things that procure acceptance with God. The most likely and most approved remedy can have no effect upon the patient, if his stomach reject it as soon as taken; and you will in vain cram a medicine down a sick man's throat, which his particular constitution will be sure to turn into poison. In a word; Whatsoever may be doubtful in religion, yet this at least is certain, that no religion, which I believe not to be true, can be either true or profitable unto me. In vain therefore do princes compel their subjects to come into their church-communion, under pretence of saving their souls. If they believe, they will come of their own accord; if they believe not, their coming will nothing avail them. How great soever, in fine, may be the pretence of good-will and charity, and concern for the salvation of men's souls, men cannot be forced to be saved whether they will or no; and therefore when all is done, they must be left to their own consciences.

Having thus at length freed men from all dominion over one another in matters of religion, let us now consider what they are to do. All men know and acknowledge that God ought to be publicly worshipped. Why otherwise do they compel one another unto the public assemblies? Men therefore constituted in this liberty are to enter into some religious society, that they may meet together, not only for mutual edification,

but to own to the world that they worship God, and offer unto his divine majesty such service as they themselves are not ashamed of, and such as they think not unworthy of him, nor unacceptable to him; and finally, that by the purity of doctrine, holiness of life, and decent form of worship, they may draw others unto the love of the true religion, and perform such other things in religion as cannot be done by each private man apart.

These religious societies I call churches: and these I say the magistrate ought to tolerate. For the business of these assemblies of the people is nothing but what is lawful for every man in particular to take care of; I mean the salvation of their souls: nor in this case is there any difference between the national church, and other separated congregations.

But as in every church there are two things especially to be considered; the outward form and rites of worship, and the doctrines and articles of faith; these things must be handled each distinctly, that so the whole matter of toleration may the more clearly be understood.

Concerning outward worship, I say, in the first place, that the magistrate has no power to enforce by law either in his own church, or much less in another, the use of any rites or ceremonies whatsoever in the worship of God. And this, not only because these churches are free societies, but because whatsoever is practised in the worship of God, is only so far justifiable as it is believed by those that practise it to be acceptable unto him.—Whatsoever is not done with that assurance of faith, is neither well in itself, nor can it be acceptable to God. To impose such things therefore upon any people, contrary to their own judgment, is in effect to command them to offend God; which, considering that the end of all religion is to please him, and that liberty is essentially necessary to that end, appears to be absurd beyond expression.

But perhaps it may be concluded from hence, that I deny unto the magistrate all manner of power about indifferent things; which, if it be not granted, the whole subject matter of law-making is taken away. No, I readily grant that indifferent things, and perhaps none but such, are subjected to the legislative power. But it does not therefore follow, that the magistrate may ordain whatsoever he pleases concerning any thing that is indifferent. The public good is the rule and measure of all law-making. If a thing be not useful to the commonwealth, though it be ever so indifferent, it may not presently be established by law.

But further: Things ever so indifferent in their own nature, when they are brought into the church and worship of God, are removed out of the reach of the magistrate's jurisdiction, because in that use they have no connection at all with civil affairs. The only business of the church is the salvation of souls: and it no ways concerns the commonwealth, or any member of it, that this or the other ceremony be there made use of. Neither the use, nor the omission of any ceremonies in those religious assemblies, does either advantage or prejudice the life, liberty, or estate of any man. For example: Let it be granted, that the washing of an infant with water is in itself an indifferent thing. Let it be granted also, that if the magistrate understand such washing to be profitable to the curing or preventing of any disease that children are subject unto, and esteem the matter weighty enough to be taken care of by a law, in that case he may order it to be done. But will any one therefore say, that the magistrate has the same right to ordain by law, that all children shall be baptised by priests in the sacred font, in order to the purification of their souls? The extreme difference of these two cases is visible to every one at first sight. Or let us apply the last case to the child of a jew, and the thing will speak itself. For what hinders but a christian magistrate may have subjects that are jews? Now if we acknowledge that such an injury may not be done unto a jew, as to compel him, against his own opinion, to practise in his religion a thing that is in its nature indifferent, how can we maintain that any thing of this kind may be done to a christian?

Again: Things in their own nature indifferent, cannot, by any human authority, be made any part of the worship of God, for this very reason, because they are indifferent. For since indifferent things are not capable, by any virtue of their own,

to propitiate the Deity; no human power or authority can confer on them so much dignity and excellency as to enable them to do it. In the common affairs of life, that use of indifferent things which God has not forbidden, is free and lawful: and therefore in those things human authority has place. But it is not so in matters of religion. Things indifferent are not otherwise lawful in the worship of God than as they are instituted by God himself; and as he, by some positive command, has ordained them to be made a part of that worship which he will vouchsafe to accept of at the hands of poor sinful men. Nor when an incensed Deity shall ask us, "Who has required these or such like things at your hands?" will it be enough to answer him, that the magistrate commanded them. If civil jurisdiction extended thus far, what might not lawfully be introduced into religion? What hodge-podge of ceremonies, what superstitious inventions, built upon the magistrate's authority, might not, against conscience, be imposed upon the worshippers of God? For the greatest part of these ceremonies and superstitions consists in the religious use of such things as are in their own nature indifferent: nor are they sinful upon any other account, than because God is not the author of them. The sprinkling of water, and use of bread and wine, are both in their own nature, and in the ordinary occasions of life, altogether indifferent. Will any man therefore say that these things could have been introduced into religion, and made a part of divine worship, if not by divine institution? If any human authority or civil power could have done this, why might it not also enjoin the eating of fish, and drinking of ale, in the holy banquet, as a part of divine worship? Why not the sprinkling of the blood of beasts in churches, and expiations by water or fire, and abundance more of this kind? But these things, how indifferent soever they be in common uses, when they come to be annexed unto divine worship, without divine authority, they are as abominable to God, as the sacrifice of a dog. And why a dog so abominable? What difference is there between a dog and a goat, in respect of the divine nature, equally and infinitely distant from all affinity with matter; unless it be that God required the use of the one in his worship, and not of the other? We see therefore that indifferent things, how much soever they be under the power of the civil magistrate, yet cannot upon that pretence be introduced into religion, and imposed upon religious assemblies; because in the worship of God they wholly cease to be indifferent. He that worships God does it with design to please him and procure his favour. But that cannot be done by him, who, upon the command of another, offers unto God that which he knows will be displeasing to him, because not commanded by himself. This is not to please God, or appease his wrath, but willingly and knowingly to provoke him, by a manifest contempt; which is a thing absolutely repugnant to the nature and end of worship.

But it will here be asked: If nothing belonging to divine worship be left to human discretion, how is it then that churches themselves have the power of ordering any thing about the time and place of worship, and the like? To this I answer; that in religious worship we must distinguish between what is part of the worship itself, and what is but a circumstance. That is a part of the worship which is believed to be appointed by God, and to be well pleasing to him; and therefore that is necessary. Circumstances are such things which though in general they cannot be separated from worship, yet the particular instances or modifications of them are not determined; and therefore they are indifferent. Of this sort are the time and place of worship, the habit and posture of him that worships. These are circumstances, and perfectly indifferent, where God has not given any express command about them. For example: Amongst the Jews, the time and place of their worship, and the habits of those that officiated in it, were not mere circumstances, but a part of the worship itself; in which if any thing were defective, or different from the institution, they could not hope that it would be accepted by God. But these, to christians under the liberty of the gospel, are mere circumstances of worship which the prudence of every church may bring into such use as shall be judged most subservient to the end of order, decency, and edification. Though even under the gospel also,

those who believe the first, or the seventh day to be set apart by God, and consecrated still to his worship; to them that portion of time is not a simple circumstance, but a real part of divine worship, which can neither be changed nor neglected.

In the next place: As the magistrate has no power to impose by his laws the use of any rites and ceremonies in any church, so neither has he any power to forbid the use of such rites and ceremonies as are already received, approved, and practised by any church: because if he did so, he would destroy the church itself; the end of whose institution is only to worship God with freedom, after its own manner.

You will say, by this rule, if some congregations should have a mind to sacrifice infants, or, as the primitive christians were falsely accused, lustfully pollute themselves in promiscuous uncleanness, or practise any other such heinous enormities, is the magistrate obliged to tolerate them, because they are committed in a religious assembly? I answer, No. These things are not lawful in the ordinary course of life, nor in any private house; and therefore neither are they so in the worship of God, or in any religious meeting. But indeed if any people congregated upon account of religion, should be desirous to sacrifice a calf, I deny that that ought to be prohibited by a law. Meliboeus, whose calf it is, may lawfully kill his calf at home, and burn any part of it that he thinks fit. For no injury is thereby done to any one, no prejudice to another man's goods. And for the same reason he may kill his calf also in a religious meeting. Whether the doing so be well-pleasing to God or no, it is their part to consider that do it.—The part of the magistrate is only to take care that the commonwealth receive no prejudice, and that there be no injury done to any man either in life or estate. And thus what may be spent on a feast may be spent on a sacrifice. But if peradventure such were the state of things that the interest of the commonwealth required all slaughter of beasts should be forborn for some while, in order to the increasing of the stock of cattle, that had been destroyed by some extraordinary murrain; who sees not that the magistrate, in such a case, may forbid all his subjects to kill any calves for any use whatsoever? Only it is to be observed, that in this case the law is not made about a religious, but a political matter: nor is the sacrifice, but the slaughter of calves thereby prohibited.

By this we see what difference there is between the church and the commonwealth. Whatsoever is lawful in the commonwealth, cannot be prohibited by the magistrate in the church. Whatsoever is permitted unto any of his subjects for their ordinary use, neither can nor ought to be forbidden by him to any sect of people for their religious uses. If any man may lawfully take bread or wine, either sitting or kneeling, in his own house, the law ought not to abridge him of the same liberty in his religious worship; though in the church the use of bread and wine be very different, and be there applied to the mysteries of faith, and rites of divine worship. But those things that are prejudicial to the commonwealth of a people in their ordinary use, and are therefore forbidden by laws, those things ought not to be permitted to churches in their sacred rites. Only the magistrate ought always to be very careful that he do not misuse his authority, to the oppression of any church under pretence of public good.

It may be said, what if a church be idolatrous, is that also to be tolerated by the magistrate? In answer, I ask, what power can be given to the magistrate for the suppression of an idolatrous church, which may not, in time and place, be made use of to the ruin of an orthodox one? For it must be remembered, that the civil power is the same every where, and the religion of every prince is orthodox to himself. If therefore such a power be granted unto the civil magistrate in spirituals, as that at Geneva, for example; he may extirpate, by violence and blood, the religion which is there reputed idolatrous; by the same rule, another magistrate, in some neighbouring country, may oppress the reformed religion; and in India, the christian. The civil power can either change every thing in religion, according to the prince's pleasure, or it can change nothing. If it be once permitted to introduce any thing into religion by the means of laws and penalties, there

can be no bounds put to it; but it will in the same manner be lawful to alter every thing, according to that rule of truth which the magistrate has framed unto himself. No man whatsoever ought therefore to be deprived of his terrestrial enjoyments, upon account of his religion. Not even Americans, subjected unto a christian prince, are to be punished either in body or goods for not embracing our faith and worship. If they are persuaded that they please God in observing the rites of their own country, and that they shall obtain happiness by that means, they are to be left unto God and themselves. Let us trace this matter to the bottom. Thus it is: an inconsiderable and weak number of christians, destitute of every thing, arrive in a pagan country; these foreigners beseech the inhabitants, by the bowels of humanity, that they would succour them with the necessaries of life; those necessaries are given them, habitations are granted, and they all join together and grow up into one body of people. The christian religion by this means takes root in that country, and spreads itself; but does not suddenly grow the strongest. While things are in this condition, peace, friendship, faith, and equal justice, are preserved amongst them. At length the magistrate becomes a christian, and by that means their party becomes the most powerful. Then immediately all compacts are to be broken, all civil rights to be violated, that idolatry may be extirpated: and unless these innocent pagans, strict observers of the rules of equity and the law of nature, and no ways offending against the laws of the society, I say unless they will forsake their ancient religion, and embrace a new and strange one, they are to be turned out of the lands and possessions of their forefathers, and perhaps deprived of life itself. Then at last it appears what zeal for the church, joined with the desire of dominion, is capable to produce: and how easily the pretence of religion, and of the care of souls, serves for a cloak to covetousness, rapine, and ambition.

Now whosoever maintains that idolatry is to be rooted out of any place by laws, punishments, fire, and sword, may apply this story to himself. For the reason of the thing is equal, both in America and Europe. And neither pagans there, nor any dissenting christians here, can with any right be deprived of their worldly goods, by the predominating faction of a court-church; nor are any civil rights to be either changed or violated upon account of religion in one place more than another.

But idolatry, say some, is a sin, and therefore not to be tolerated. If they said it were therefore to be avoided, the inference were good. But it does not follow, that because it is a sin it ought therefore to be punished by the magistrate. For it does not belong unto the magistrate to make use of his sword in punishing every thing, indifferently, that he takes to be a sin against God. Covetousness, uncharitableness, idleness, and many other things are sins, by the consent of all men, which yet no man ever said were to be punished by the magistrate. The reason is, because they are not prejudicial to other men's rights, nor do they break the public peace of societies. Nay, even the sins of lying and perjury are no where punishable by laws; unless in certain cases, in which the real turpitude of the thing and the offence against God, are not considered, but only the injury done unto men's neighbours, and to the commonwealth. And what if in another country, to a mahometan or a pagan prince, the christian religion seem false and offensive to God; may not the christians for the same reason, and after the same manner, be extirpated there?

But it may be urged farther, that by the law of Moses, idolaters were to be rooted out. True indeed, by the law of Moses; but that is not obligatory to us christians. Nobody pretends that every thing, generally, enjoined by the law of Moses, ought to be practised by christians. But there is nothing more frivolous than that common distinction of moral, judicial, and ceremonial law, which men ordinarily make use of. For no positive law whatsoever can oblige any people but those to whom it is given. "Hear, O Israel," sufficiently restrains the obligation of the law of Moses only to that people. And this consideration alone is answer enough unto those that urge the authority of the law of Moses, for the inflicting of capital punishments upon idolaters.

But however, I will examine this argument a little more particularly.

The case of idolaters in respect of the jewish commonwealth, falls under a double consideration. The first is of those, who, being initiated into the Mosaical rites, and made citizens of that commonwealth, did afterwards apostatize from the worship of the God of Israel. These were proceeded against as traitors and rebels, guilty of no less than high treason; for the commonwealth of the jews, different in that from all others, was an absolute theocracy: nor was there, or could there be, any difference between that commonwealth and the church. The laws established there concerning the worship of one invisible deity, were the civil laws of that people, and a part of their political government, in which God himself was the legislator. Now if any one can show me where there is a commonwealth, at this time, constituted upon that foundation, I will acknowledge that the ecclesiastical laws do there unavoidably become a part of the civil; and that the subjects of that government both may, and ought to be kept in strict conformity with that church, by the civil power. But there is absolutely no such thing, under the gospel, as a christian commonwealth. There are, indeed, many cities and kingdoms that have embraced the faith of Christ, but they have retained their ancient forms of government; with which the law of Christ hath not at all meddled. He, indeed, hath taught men how, by faith and good works, they may attain eternal life. But he instituted no commonwealth. He prescribed unto his followers no new and peculiar form of government, nor put he the sword into any magistrate's hand, with commission to make use of it in forcing men to forsake their former religion, and receive his.

Secondly, Foreigners, and such as were strangers to the commonwealth of Israel, were not compelled by force to observe the rites of the Mosaical law. But, on the contrary, in the very same place where it is ordered "that an Israelite that was an idolater should be put to death, there it is provided that strangers should not be vexed nor oppressed," Exod. xxii. 21. I confess that the seven nations that possessed the land which was promised to the Israelites, were utterly to be cut off. But this was not singly because they were idolaters; for if that had been the reason, why were the Moabites and other nations to be spared? No; the reason is this. God being in a peculiar manner the king of the jews, he could not suffer the adoration of any other deity, which was properly an act of high treason against himself, in the land of Canaan, which was his kingdom; for such a manifest revolt could no ways consist with his dominion, which was perfectly political, in that country. All idolatry was therefore to be rooted out of the bounds of his kingdom; because it was an acknowledgment of another God, that is to say, another king, against the laws of empire. The inhabitants were also to be driven out, that the entire possession of the land might be given to the Israelites. And for the like reason the Emims and the Horims were driven out of their countries by the children of Esau and Lot; and their lands, upon the same grounds, given by God to the invaders, Deut. ii. 12. But though all idolatry was thus rooted out of the land of Canaan, yet every idolater was not brought to execution. The whole family of Rahab, the whole nation of the Gibeonites, articled with Joshua, and were allowed by treaty: and there were many captives amongst the jews, who were idolaters. David and Solomon subdued many countries without the confines of the Land of Promise, and carried their conquests as far as Euphrates. Amongst so many captives taken of so many nations reduced under their obedience, we find not one man forced into the jewish religion, and the worship of the true God, and punished for idolatry, though all of them were certainly guilty of it. If any one indeed, becoming a proselyte, desired to be made a denison of their commonwealth, he was obliged to submit unto their laws; that is, to embrace their religion. But this he did willingly, on his own accord, not by constraint. He did not unwillingly submit to show his obedience; but he sought and solicited for it, as a privilege; and as soon as he was admitted, he became subject to the laws of the commonwealth, by which all idolatry was forbidden within the borders of the land of Canaan. But that law, as I have said, did not reach to any of those regions, however subjected unto the jews that were situated without those bounds.

Thus far concerning outward worship. Let us now consider articles of faith.

The articles of religion are some of them practical, and some speculative. Now, though both sorts consist in the knowledge of truth, yet these terminate simply in the understanding, those influence the will and manners. Speculative opinions, therefore, and articles of faith, as they are called, which are required only to be believed, cannot be imposed on any church by the law of the land; for it is absurd that things should be enjoined by laws, which are not in men's power to perform; [40] and to believe this or that to be true, does not depend upon our will. But of this enough has been said already. But, will some say, let men at least profess that they believe. A sweet religion, indeed, that obliges men to dissemble, and tell lies both to God and man, for the salvation of their souls! If the magistrate thinks to save men thus, he seems to understand little of the way of salvation; and if he does it not in order to save them, why is he so solicitous about the articles of faith, as to enact them by a law?

Further, The magistrate ought not to forbid the preaching or professing of any speculative opinions in any church, because they have no manner of relation to the civil rights of the subjects. If a roman catholic believe that to be really the body of Christ, which another man calls bread, he does no injury thereby to his neighbour. If a jew does not believe the New Testament to be the word of God, he does not thereby alter any thing in men's civil rights. If a heathen doubt of both Testaments, he is not therefore to be punished as a pernicious citizen. The power of the magistrate, and the estates of the people, may be equally secure, whether any man believe these things or no. I readily grant, that these opinions are false and absurd. But the business of laws is not to provide for the truth of opinions, but for the safety and security of the commonwealth, and of every particular man's goods and person. And so it ought to be; for truth certainly would do well enough, if she were once made to shift for herself. She seldom has received, and I fear never will receive, much assistance from the power of great men, to whom she is but rarely known, and more rarely welcome. She is not taught by laws, nor has she any need of force to procure her entrance into the minds of men. Errours indeed prevail by the assistance of foreign and borrowed succours. But if truth makes not her way into the understanding by her own light, she will be but the weaker for any borrowed force violence can add to her. Thus much for speculative opinions. Let us now proceed to the practical ones.

A good life, in which consists not the least part of religion and true piety, concerns also the civil government: and in it lies the safety both of men's souls and of the commonwealth. Moral actions belong therefore to the jurisdiction both of the outward and inward court; both of the civil and domestic governor; I mean, both of the magistrate and conscience. Here therefore is great danger, lest one of these jurisdictions intrench upon the other, and discord arise betwen the keeper of the public peace and the overseers of souls. But if what has been already said concerning the limits of both these governments be rightly considered, it will easily remove all difficulty in this matter.

Every man has an immortal soul, capable of eternal happiness or misery; whose happiness depending upon his believing and doing those things in this life, which are necessary to the obtaining of God's favour, and are prescribed by God to that end. It follows from thence, first, that the observance of these things is the highest obligation that lies upon mankind, and that our utmost care, application, and diligence, ought to be exercised in the search and performance of them; because there is nothing in this world that is of any consideration in comparison with eternity. Secondly, that seeing one man does not violate the right of another, by his erroneous opinions, and undue manner of worship, nor is his perdition any prejudice to another man's affairs; therefore the care of each man's salvation belongs only to himself. But I would not have this understood, as if I meant hereby to condemn all charitable admonitions, and affectionate endeavours to reduce men from errours; which are indeed the greatest duty of a christian. Any one may employ as many exhortations and arguments as he pleases, towards the promoting of another man's salvation. But all force and compulsion are to be forborn. Nothing is to be done imperiously.—Nobody is obliged in that manner to yield obedience unto the admonitions or injunctions of another, farther than he himself is persuaded. Every man, in that, has the supreme and absolute authority of judging for himself; and the reason is, because nobody else is concerned in it, nor can receive any prejudice from his conduct therein.

But besides their souls, which are immortal, men have also their temporal lives here upon earth; the state whereof being frail and fleeting, and the duration uncertain, they have need of several outward conveniencies to the support thereof, which are to be procured or preserved by pains and industry; for those things that are necessary to the comfortable support of our lives, are not the spontaneous products of nature, nor do offer themselves fit and prepared for our use. This part, therefore, draws on another care, and necessarily gives another employment. But the pravity of mankind being such, that they had rather injuriously prey upon the fruits of other men's labours, than take pains to provide for themselves; the necessity of preserving men in the possession of what honest industry has already acquired, and also of preserving their liberty and strength, whereby they may acquire what they farther want, obliges men to enter into society with one another that by mutual assistance and joint force, they may secure unto each other their properties, in the things that contribute to the comforts and happiness of this life; leaving in the mean while to every man the care of his own eternal happiness, the attainment whereof can neither be facilitated by another man's industry, nor can the loss of it turn to another man's prejudice, nor the hope of it be forced from him by any external violence. But forasmuch as men thus entering into societies, grounded upon their mutual compacts of assistance, for the defence of their temporal goods, may nevertheless be deprived of them, either by the rapine and fraud of their fellow citizens, or by the hostile violence of foreigners: the remedy of all this evil consists in arms, riches, and multitudes of citizens; the remedy of others in laws: and the care of all things relating both to the one and the other, is committed by the society to the civil magistrate. This is the original, this is the use, and these are the bounds of the legislative, which is the supreme power in every commonwealth. I mean, that provision may be made for the security of each man's private possessions; for the peace, riches, and public commodities of the whole people, and, as much as possible, for the increase of their inward strength against foreign invasions.

These things being thus explained, it is easy to understand to what end the legislative power ought to be directed, and by what measures regulated; and that is, the temporal good and outward prosperity of the society; which is the sole reason of men's entering into society, and the only thing they seek and aim at in it; and it is also evident what liberty remains to men in reference to their eternal salvation, and that is, that every one should do what he in his conscience is persuaded to be acceptable to the Almighty, on whose good pleasure and acceptance depends his eternal happiness; for obedience is due in the first place to God, and afterwards to the laws.

But some may ask, "What if the magistrate should enjoin any thing by his authority, that appears unlawful to the conscience of a private person?" I answer, that if government be faithfully administered, and the counsels of the magistrate be indeed directed to the public good, this will seldom happen. But if perhaps it do so fall out, I say, that such a private person is to abstain from the actions that he judges unlawful; and he is to undergo the punishment, which is not unlawful for him to bear; for the private judgment of any person concerning a law enacted in political matters, for the public good, does not take away the obligation of that law, nor deserve a dispensation. But if the law indeed be concerning things that lie not within the verge of the magistrate's authority; as for example, that the people, or any party amongst them, should be compelled to embrace a strange religion, and join in the worship and ceremonies of another church; men are not in these cases obliged by that law, against their consciences; for the political society

is instituted for no other end, but only to secure every man's possession of the things of this life. The care of each man's soul, and of the things of heaven, which neither does belong to the commonwealth, nor can be subjected to it, is left entirely to every man's self. Thus the safeguard of men's lives, and of the things that belong unto this life, is the business of the commonwealth; and the preserving of those things unto their owners is the duty of the magistrate; and therefore the magistrate cannot take away these worldly things from this man, or party, and give them to that; nor change property amongst fellow-subjects, no not even by a law, for a cause that has no relation to the end of civil government; I mean for their religion; which, whether it be true or false, does no prejudice to the worldly concerns of their fellow-subjects, which are the things that only belong unto the care of the commonwealth.

"But what if the magistrate believe such a law as this to be for the public good?" I answer: as the private judgment of any particular person, if erroneous, does not exempt him from the obligation of law, so the private judgment, as I may call it, of the magistrate, does not give him any new right of imposing laws upon his subjects, which neither was in the constitution of the government granted him, nor ever was in the power of the people to grant: and least of all, if he make it his business to enrich and advance his followers and fellow-sectaries with the spoils of others. But what if the magistrate believe that he has a right to make such laws, and that they are for the public good; and his subjects believe the contrary? Who shall be judge between them? I answer, God alone; for there is no judge upon earth between the supreme magistrate and the people. God, I say, is the only judge in this case, who will retribute unto every one at the last day according to his deserts; that is, according to his sincerity and uprightness in endeavouring to promote piety, and the public weal and peace of mankind. But what shall be done in the mean while? I answer: the principal and chief care of every one ought to be of his own soul first, and, in the next place, of the public peace: though yet there are few will think it is peace there, where they see all laid waste. There are two sorts of contests amongst men: the one managed by law, the other by force; and they are of that nature, that where the one ends the other always begins. But it is not my business to inquire into the power of the magistrate in the different constitutions of nations. I only know what usually happens where controversies arise, without a judge to determine them. You will say, then the magistrate being the stronger will have his will, and carry his point. Without doubt. But the question is not here concerning the doubtfulness of the event, but the rule of right.

But to come to particulars. I say, First, No opinions contrary to human society, or to those moral rules which are necessary to the preservation of civil society, are to be tolerated by the magistrate. But of those indeed examples in any church are rare. For no sect can easily arrive to such a degree of madness, as that it should think fit to teach, for doctrines of religion, such things as manifestly undermine the foundations of society, and are therefore condemned by the judgment of all mankind: because their own interest, peace, reputation, every thing would be thereby endangered.

Another more secret evil, but more dangerous to the commonwealth, is when men arrogate to themselves, and to those of their own sect, some peculiar prerogative covered over with a specious show of deceitful words, but in effect opposite to the civil rights of the community. For example: We cannot find any sect that teaches expressly and openly, that men are not obliged to keep their promise; that princes may be dethroned by those that differ from them in religion; or that the dominion of all things belongs only to themselves. For these things, proposed thus nakedly and plainly, would soon draw on them the eye and hand of the magistrate, and awaken all the care of the commonwealth to a watchfulness against the spreading of so dangerous an evil. But nevertheless, we find those that say the same things in other words. What else do they mean, who teach that, "faith is not to be kept with heretics?" Their meaning, forsooth, is, that the privilege of breaking faith belongs unto themselves: for they declare all that are not of their communion to be heretics, or at

least may declare them so whensoever they think fit. What can be the meaning of their asserting that "kings excommunicated forfeit their crowns and kingdoms?" It is evident that they thereby arrogate unto themselves the power of deposing kings: because they challenge the power of excommunication as the peculiar right of their hierarchy. "That dominion is founded in grace," is also an assertion by which those that maintain it do plainly lay claim to the possession of all things. For they are not so wanting to themselves as not to believe, or at least as not to profess, themselves to be the truly pious and faithful. These therefore, and the like, who attribute unto the faithful, religious, and orthodox, that is, in plain terms, unto themselves, any peculiar privilege or power above other mortals, in civil concernments; or who, upon pretence of religion, do challenge any manner of authority over such as are not associated with them in their ecclesiastical communion; I say these have no right to be tolerated by the magistrate; as neither those that will not own and teach the duty of tolerating all men in matters of mere religion. For what do all these and the like doctrines signify, but that they may, and are ready upon any occasion to seize the government, and possess themselves of the estates and fortunes of their fellow-subjects; and that they only ask leave to be tolerated by the magistrates so long, until they find themselves strong enough to effect it?

Again: That church can have no right to be tolerated by the magistrate, which is constituted upon such a bottom, that all those who enter into it, do thereby ipso facto deliver themselves up to the protection and service of another prince. For by this means the magistrate would give way to the settling of a foreign jurisdiction in his own country, and suffer his own people to be listed, as it were, for soldiers against his own government. Nor does the frivolous and fallacious distinction between the court and the church afford any remedy to this inconvenience; especially when both the one and the other are equally subject to the absolute authority of the same person; who has not only power to persuade the members of his church to whatsoever he lists, either as purely religious, or as in order thereunto; but can also enjoin it them on pain of eternal fire. It is ridiculous for any one to profess himself to be a mahometan only in religion, but in every thing else a faithful subject to a christian magistrate, whilst at the same time he acknowledges himself bound to yield blind obedience to the mufti of Constantinople; who himself is entirely obedient to the Ottoman emperor, and frames the feigned oracles of that religion according to his pleasure. But this mahometan living amongst christians, would yet more apparently renounce their government, if he acknowledged the same person to be head of his church, who is the supreme magistrate in the state.

Lastly, Those are not at all to be tolerated who deny the being of God. Promises, covenants, and oaths, which are the bonds of human society, can have no hold upon an atheist. The taking away of God, though but even in thought, dissolves all. Besides also, those that by their atheism undermine and destroy all religion, can have no pretence of religion whereupon to challenge the privilege of a toleration. As for other practical opinions, though not absolutely free from all errour, yet if they do not tend to establish domination over others, or civil impunity to the church in which they are taught, there can be no reason why they should not be tolerated.

It remains that I say something concerning those assemblies, which being vulgarly called, and perhaps having sometimes been conventicles, and nurseries of factions and seditions, are thought to afford the strongest matter of objection against this doctrine of toleration. But this has not happened by any thing peculiar unto the genius of such assemblies, but by the unhappy circumstances of an oppressed or ill-settled liberty. These accusations would soon cease, if the law of toleration were once so settled, that all churches were obliged to lay down toleration as the foundation of their own liberty; and teach that liberty of conscience is every man's natural right, equally belonging to dissenters as to themselves; and that nobody ought to be compelled in matters of religion either by law or force. The establishment of this one thing would take away all ground of complaints and tumults upon account of conscience. And these causes of discontents and animosities being once removed, there would remain nothing in these assemblies that were not more peaceable, and less apt to produce disturbance of state, than in any other meetings whatsoever. But let us examine particularly the heads of these accusations.

You will say, that "assemblies and meetings endanger the public peace, and threaten the commonwealth." I answer: if this be so, why are there daily such numerous meetings in markets, and courts of judicature? Why are crowds upon the Exchange, and a concourse of people in cities suffered? You will reply; these are civil assemblies, but those we object against are ecclesiastical. I answer: it is a likely thing indeed, that such assemblies as are altogether remote from civil affairs, should be most apt to embroil them. O, but civil assemblies are composed of men that differ from one another in matters of religion; but these ecclesiastical meetings are of persons that are all of one opinion. As if an agreement in matters of religion were in effect a conspiracy against the commonwealth: or as if men would not be so much the more warmly unanimous in religion the less liberty they had of assembling. But it will be urged still, that civil assemblies are open and free for any one to enter into; whereas religious conventicles are more private, and thereby give opportunity to clandestine machinations. I answer, that this is not strictly true: for many civil assemblies are not open to every one. And if some religious meetings be private, who are they, I beseech you, that are to be blamed for it? those that desire, or those that forbid their being public? Again; you will say, that religious communion does exceedingly unite men's minds and affections to one another, and is therefore the more dangerous. But if this be so, why is not the magistrate afraid of his own church; and why does he not forbid their assemblies, as things dangerous to his government? You will say, because he himself is a part, and even the head of them. As if he were not also a part of the commonwealth, and the head of the whole people.

Let us therefore deal plainly. The magistrate is afraid of other churches, but not of his own; because he is kind and favourable to the one, but severe and cruel to the other. These he treats like children, and indulges them even to wantonness. Those he uses as slaves; and how blamelessly soever they demean themselves, recompences them no otherwise than by gallies, prisons, confiscations, and death. These he cherishes and defends: those he continually scourges and oppresses. Let him turn the tables: or let those dissenters enjoy but the same privileges in civils as his other subjects, and he will quickly find that these religious meetings will be no longer dangerous. For if men enter into seditious conspiracies, it is not religion inspires them to it in their meetings, but their sufferings and oppressions that make them willing to ease themselves. Just and moderate governments are every-where quiet, every-where safe. But oppression raises ferments, and makes men struggle to cast off an uneasy and tyrannical yoke. I know that seditions are very frequently raised upon pretence of religion. But it is as true, that, for religion, subjects are frequently ill treated, and live miserably. Believe me, the stirs that are made, proceed not from any peculiar temper of this or that church or religious society; but from the common disposition of all mankind, who, when they groan under any heavy burthen, endeavour naturally to shake off the yoke that galls their necks. Suppose this business of religion were let alone, and that there were some other distinction made between men and men, upon account of their different complexions, shapes and features, so that those who have black hair, for example, or grey eyes, should not enjoy the same privileges as other citizens; that they should not be permitted either to buy or sell, or live by their callings; that parents should not have the government and education of their own children; that they should either be excluded from the benefit of the laws, or meet with partial judges: can be it doubted but these persons, thus distinguished from others by the colour of their hair and eyes, and united together by one common persecution, would be as dangerous to the magistrate, as any others that had associated themselves merely upon the account of religion? Some enter into company for trade and profit: others, for want of business, have their clubs for claret. Neighbourhood joins some, and religion others. But there is one thing only which gathers people into seditious commotions, and that is oppression.

You will say; what, will you have people to meet at divine service against the magistrate's will? I answer; why, I pray against his will? Is it not both lawful and necessary that they should meet? Against his will, do you say? That is what I complain of. That is the very root of all the mischief. Why are assemblies less sufferable in a church than in a theatre or market? Those that meet there are not either more vicious, or more turbulent, than those that meet elsewhere. The business in that is, that they are ill used, and therefore they are not to be suffered. Take away the partiality that is used towards them in matters of common right; change the laws, take away the penalties unto which they are subjected, and all things will immediately become safe and peaceable: nay, those that are averse to the religion of the magistrate, will think themselves so much the more bound to maintain the peace of the commonwealth, as their condition is better in that place than elsewhere; and all the several separate congregations, like so many guardians of the public peace, will watch one another, that nothing may be innovated or changed in the form of the government: because they can hope for nothing better than what they already enjoy; that is, an equal condition with their fellow-subjects, under a just and moderate government. Now if that church, which agrees in religion with the prince, be esteemed the chief support of any civil government, and that for no other reason, as has already been shown, than because the prince is kind, and the laws are favourable to it; how much greater will be the security of a government, where all good subjects, of whatsoever they be, without any distinction upon account of religion, enjoying the same favour of the prince, and the same benefit of the laws, shall become the common support and guard of it; and where none will have any occasion to fear the severity of the laws, but those that do injuries to their neighbours, and offend against the civil peace!

That we may draw towards a conclusion. "The sum of all we drive at is, that every man enjoy the same rights that are granted to others." Is it permitted to worship God in the Roman manner? Let it be permitted to do it in the Geneva form also. Is it permitted to speak Latin in the market place? Let those that have a mind to it, be permitted to do it also in the church. Is it lawful for any man in his own house to kneel, stand, sit, or use any other posture; and cloath himself in white or black, in short, or in long garments? Let it not be made unlawful to eat bread, drink wine, or wash with water in the church. In a word: whatsoever things are left free by law in the common occasions of life, let them remain free unto every church in divine worship. Let no man's life, or body, or house, or estate, suffer any manner of prejudice upon these accounts. Can you allow of the presbyterian discipline? why should not the episcopal also have what they like? Ecclesiastical authority, whether it be administered by the hands of a single person, or many, is every-where the same; and neither has any jurisdiction in things civil, nor any manner of power of compulsion, nor any thing at all to do with riches and revenues.

Ecclesiastical assemblies and sermons, are justified by daily experience, and public allowance. These are allowed to people of some one persuasion: why not to all? If any thing pass in a religious meeting seditiously, and contrary to the public peace, it is to be punished in the same manner, and no otherwise than as if it had happened in a fair or market. These meetings ought not to be sanctuaries of factious and flagitious fellows: nor ought it to be less lawful for men to meet in churches than in halls: nor are one part of the subjects to be esteemed more blameable for their meeting together than others. Every one is to be accountable for his own actions; and no man is to be laid under a suspicion, or odium, for the fault of another. Those that are seditious, murderers, thieves, robbers, adulterers, slanderers, &c. of whatsoever church, whether national or not, ought to be punished and suppressed. But those

whose doctrine is peaceable, and whose manners are pure and blameless, ought to be upon equal terms with their fellow-subjects. Thus if solemn assemblies, observations of festivals, public worship, be permitted to any one sort of professors; all these things ought to be permitted to the presbyterians, independents, anabaptists, arminians, quakers, and others, with the same liberty. Nay, if we may openly speak the truth, and as becomes one man to another, neither pagan, nor mahometan, nor jew, ought to be excluded from the civil rights of the commonwealth, because of his religion. The gospel commands no such thing. The church, "which judgeth not those that are without," 1 Cor. v. 11. wants it not. And the commonwealth, which embraces indifferently all men that are honest, peaceable, and industrious, requires it not. Shall we suffer a pagan to deal and trade with us, and shall we not suffer him to pray unto and worship God? If we allow the jews to have private houses and dwellings amongst us, why should we not allow them to have synagogues? Is their doctrine more false, their worship more abominable, or is the civil peace more endangered, by their meeting in public, than in their private houses? But if these things may be granted to jews and pagans, surely the condition of any christians ought not to be worse than theirs, in a christian commonwealth.

You will say, perhaps, yes, it ought to be: because they are more inclinable to factions, tumults, and civil wars. I answer: is this the fault of the christian religion? If it be so, truly the christian religion is the worst of all religions, and ought neither to be embraced by any particular person, nor tolerated by any commonwealth. For if this be the genius, this the nature of the christian religion, to be turbulent, and destructive of the civil peace, that church itself which the magistrate indulges, will not always be innocent. But far be it from us to say any such thing of that religion, which carries the greatest opposition to covetousness, ambition, discord, contention, and all manner of inordinate desires; and is the most modest and peaceable religion that ever was. We must therefore seek another cause of those evils that are charged upon religion. And if we consider right, we shall find it consist wholly in the subject that I am treating of. It is not the diversity of opinions, which cannot be avoided; but the refusal of toleration to those that are of different opinions, which might have been granted, that has produced all the bustles and wars, that have been in the christian world, upon account of religion. The heads and leaders of the church, moved by avarice and insatiable desire of dominion, making use of the immoderate ambition of magistrates, and the credulous superstition of the giddy multitude, have incensed and animated them against those that dissent from themselves, by preaching unto them, contrary to the laws of the gospel, and to the precepts of charity, that schismatics and heretics are to be outed of their possessions, and destroyed. And thus have they mixed together, and confounded two things, that are in themselves most different, the church and the commonwealth. Now as it is very difficult for men patiently to suffer themselves to be stript of the goods which they have got by their honest industry; and contrary to all the laws of equity, both human and divine, to be delivered up for a prey to other men's violence and rapine; especially when they are otherwise altogether blameless; and that the occasion for which they are thus treated, does not at all belong to the jurisdiction of the magistrate, but entirely to the conscience of every particular man; for the conduct of which he is accountable to God only; what else can be expected, but that these men, growing weary of the evils under which they labour, should in the end think it lawful for them to resist force with force, and to defend their natural rights, which are not forfeitable upon account of religion, with arms as well as they can? That this has been hitherto the ordinary course of things, is abundantly evident in history; and that it will continue to be so hereafter, is but too apparent in reason. It cannot indeed be otherwise, so long as the principle of persecution for religion shall prevail, as it has done hitherto, with magistrate and people; and so long as those that ought to be the preachers of peace and concord, shall continue, with all their art and strength, to excite men to arms, and sound the trumpet of war. But that magistrates should thus suffer these incendiaries, and disturbers of the public peace, might justly be wondered at, if it did not appear that they have been invited by them into a participation of the spoil; and have therefore thought fit to make use of their covetousness and pride, as means whereby to increase their own power. For who does not see that these good men are indeed more ministers of the government, than ministers of the gospel; and that by flattering the ambition, and favouring the dominion of princes and men in authority, they endeavour with all their might to promote that tyranny in the commonwealth, which otherwise they should not be able to establish in the church? This is the unhappy agreement that we see between the church and the state. Whereas if each of them would contain itself within its own bounds, the one attending to the worldly welfare of the commonwealth, the other to the salvation of souls, it is impossible that any discord should ever have happened between them. "Sed pudet hæc opprobria, &c." God Almighty grant, I beseech him, that the gospel of peace may at length be preached, and that civil magistrates, growing more careful to conform their own consciences to the law of God, and less solicitous about the binding of other men's consciences by human laws, may, like fathers of their country, direct all their counsels and endeavours to promote universally the civil welfare of all their children; except only of such as are arrogant, ungovernable, and injurious to their brethren; and that all ecclesiastical men, who boast themselves to be the successors of the apostles, walking peaceably and modestly in the apostles' steps, without intermeddling with state-affairs, may apply themselves wholly to promote the salvation of souls. Farewell.

Perhaps it may not be amiss to add a few things concerning heresy and schism. A turk is not, nor can be either heretic or schismatic, to a christian: and if any man fall off from the christian faith to mahometism, he does not thereby become a heretic or a schismatic, but an apostate and an infidel. This no-body doubts of. And by this it appears that men of different religions cannot be heretics or schismatics to one another.

We are to enquire therefore, what men are of the same religion. Concerning which, it is manifest that those who have one and the same rule of faith and worship, are of the same religion, and those who have not the same rule of faith and worship, are of different religions. For since all things that belong unto that religion are contained in that rule, it follows necessarily, that those who agree in one rule are of one and the same religion: and vice versâ. Thus turks and christians are of different religions: because these take the Holy Scriptures to be the rule of their religion, and those the Koran. And for the same reason, there may be different religions also even amongst christians. The papists and the lutherans, though both of them profess faith in Christ, and are therefore called christians, yet are not both of the same religion: because these acknowledge nothing but the Holy Scriptures to be the rule and foundation of their religion; those take in also traditions and decrees of popes, and of all these together make the rule of their religion. And thus the christians of St. John, as they are called, and the christians of Geneva, are of different religions: because these also take only the scriptures; and those, I know not what traditions; for the rule of their religion.

This being settled, it follows, First, That heresy is a separation made in ecclesiastical communion between men of the same religion, for some opinions no way contained in the rule itself. And secondly, That amongst those who acknowledge nothing but the Holy Scriptures to be their rule of faith, heresy is a separation made in their christian communion, for opinions not contained in the express words of scripture.

Now this separation may be made in a twofold manner.

First, When the greater part, or, by the magistrate's patronage, the stronger part of the church separates itself from others, by excluding them out of her communion, because they will not profess their belief of certain opinions which are not to be found in the express words of scripture. For it is not the paucity of those that are separated, nor the authority of the magistrate, that can make any man guilty of heresy. But he only is an heretic who divides the church into parts, introduces names and marks of distinction, and voluntarily makes a separation because of such opinions.

Secondly, When any one separates himself from the communion of a church, because that church does not publicly profess some certain opinions which the Holy Scriptures do not expressly teach.

Both these are "heretics, because they err in fundamentals, and they err obstinately against knowledge." For when they have determined the Holy Scriptures to be the only foundation of faith, they nevertheless lay down certain propositions as fundamental, which are not in the scripture; and because others will not acknowledge these additional opinions of theirs, nor build upon them as if they were necessary and fundamental, they therefore make a separation in the church, either by withdrawing themselves from the others, or expelling the others from them. Nor does it signify any thing for them to say that their confessions and symbols are agreeable to scripture, and to the analogy of faith. For if they be conceived in the express words of scripture, there can be no question about them; because those are acknowledged by all christians to be of divine inspiration, and therefore fundamental. But if they say that the articles which they require to be professed, are consequences deduced from the scripture; it is undoubtedly well done of them to believe and profess such things as seem unto them so agreeable to the rule of faith: but it would be very ill done to obtrude those things upon others, unto whom they do not seem to be the indubitable doctrines of the scripture. And to make a separation for such things as these, which neither are nor can be fundamental, is to become heretics. For I do not think there is any man arrived to that degree of madness, as that he dare give out his consequences and interpretations of scripture as divine inspirations, and compare the articles of faith that he has framed according to his own fancy, with the authority of the scripture. I know there are some propositions so evidently agreeable to scripture, that no-body can deny them to be drawn from thence: but about those therefore than can be no difference. This only I say, that however clearly we may think this or the other doctrine to be deduced from scripture, we ought not therefore to impose it upon others, as a necessary article of faith, because we believe it to be agreeable to the rule of faith; unless we would be content also that other doctrines should be imposed upon us in the same manner; and that we should be compelled to receive and profess all the different and contradictory opinions of lutherans, calvinists, remonstrants, anabaptists, and other sects which the contrivers of symbols, systems, and confessions, are accustomed to deliver unto their followers as genuine and necessary deductions from the Holy Scripture. I cannot but wonder at the extravagant arrogance of those men who think that they themselves can explain things necessary to salvation more clearly than the Holy Ghost, the eternal and infinite wisdom of God.

Thus much concerning heresy; which word in common use is applied only to the doctrinal part of religion. Let us now consider schism, which is a crime near a-kin to it. For both these words seem unto me to signify an "ill-grounded separation in ecclesiastical communion, made about things not necessary." But since use, which is the supreme law in matter of language, has determined that heresy relates to errours in faith, and schism to those in worship or discipline, we must consider them under that distinction.

Schism then, for the same reasons that have already been alleged, is nothing else but a separation made in the communion of the church, upon account of something in divine worship, or ecclesiastical discipline, that is not any necessary part of it. Now nothing in worship or discipline can be necessary to christian communion, but what Christ our legislator, or the apostles, by inspiration of the Holy Spirit, have commanded in express words.

In a word: he that denies not any thing that the Holy Scriptures teach in express words, nor makes a separation upon occasion of any thing that is not manifestly contained in the sacred text; however he may be nick-named by any sect of christians, and declared by some or all of them, to be utterly void of true christianity; yet indeed and in truth this man cannot be either a heretic or schismatic.

These things might have been explained more largely, and more advantageously; but it is enough to have hinted at them, thus briefly, to a person of your parts.

Chapter 9: Politics at the American Founding

Comprehension questions you should be able to answer after reading this chapter:

1. What is the "moral argument" of the Declaration of Independence as formulated by Morton White?

2. Describe the influence of Locke's *Two Treatises on Government* on the Declaration of Independence.

3. What was the motivation behind the *Federalist Papers*?

4. Describe *Publius'* assumption concerning human motivation.

5. What is a "faction" and why are they seen as a threat to the community?

6. Expalin why *Publius* believes factions are inevitable.

7. What is the primary cause of factions?

8. Why does *Publius* think the effects of factions can't be constrained by "enlightened Statesmen," or "moral" or "religious" reasons?

9. What is a "Republic?" How is it different from a direct democracy?

10. How does a Republic diminish the threat of factions?

11. Why does *Publius* think the Republic should be large?

12. What is meant by "checks and balances?" How did the proposed government under the U.S. Constitution provide for both a Republic and checks and balances?

13. Why does *Publius* think the Judiciary needs to be independent of the other branches of government? How is this achieved, by the Constitution?

14. What is meant by the "supremacy" of the Supreme Court on matters of the Constitution? What is "judicial review?"

15. What is *Publius'* argument in favor of the Electoral College electing the President, instead of a direct vote?

The focus of our last chapter was John Locke. While the focus of this chapter is the political philosophy behind some profoundly significant documents concerning the founding of the United States' system of government, the connection to Locke will be made clear, at least as regards the Declaration of Independence.

The Declaration of Independence

The United States Declaration of Independence was adopted by the Second Continental Congress on July 4th, 1776. Thomas Jefferson drafted the original version, which was then edited by the Continental Congress. It offered a formal statement of Independence from Great Britain, more than one year after the actual American Revolutionary War had begun.

The structure of the Declaration of Independence is a classic philosophical argument. First, the signers declare the necessity of justifying their act of rebellion against their king. Then, they provide the moral argument that would justify their actions. Then, they provide examples to show that their own case satisfies the conditions of the argument. As Morton White formulated it:

1.   Whenever a people is treated by a government in a manner which shows that the government intends to tyrannize over them, the people have a duty to sever their connection with that government.
2.   The American people have been treated in that manner by the British government.
3.   Therefore, the American people have a duty to sever their connection with the British government.[264]

The full text of the Declaration can be found at the end of this chapter, where you may see the structure as described above. Presently, however, we will focus just on some key ideas found in the Declaration. Jefferson himself acknowledged that the ideas expressed in the Declaration were not "original."

Neither aiming at originality of principle or sentiment, nor yet copied from any particular and previous writing, it was intended to be an expression of the American mind, and to give to that expression the proper tone and spirit called for by the occasion.[265]

Immediate sources of influence included Jefferson's own preamble to the Constitution of Virginia, and George Mason's draft of the Virginia Declaration of Rights—both of which, in turn, could be traced back to the 1689 English Declaration of Rights.[266] Philosophically speaking, however, a strong case can be made for the influence of John Locke, whom Jefferson listed as one of "the three greatest men that have ever lived."[267]

The coincidence of themes found in both Locke and the United States *Declaration of Independence* is undeniable. Appeals to the laws of Nature, self-evident basic human equality, unalienable rights to life, liberty, and happiness (Declaration) or property (Locke), government by consent of the governed, and the right of the people to rebel against their ruler should he violate their rights, are made by Locke and found in the "moral argument" section of the Declaration. In the comparison table that follows, you will find selections from Locke's *Two Treatises* in the left column, and corresponding sections of the *Declaration of Independence* in the right column. I have rendered the most relevant points of comparison in bold.

---

[264] Morton White, *Philosophy, The Federalist, and the Constitution* , Oxford University Press, 1989. p. 209

[265] "TO HENRY LEE – Thomas Jefferson, The Works, vol. 12 (Correspondence and Papers 1816–1826; 1905)". The Online Library of Liberty. May 8, 1825.

[266] http://avalon.law.yale.edu/17th_century/england.asp

[267] The other two were Francis Bacon and Isaac Newton.
http://www.loc.gov/exhibits/treasures/trm033.html

John Locke Two Treatises of Government 1690 *The Second Treatise of Civil Government*	The Declaration of Independence
To understand political power right, and derive it from its original, we must consider, what state all men are naturally in, and that is, a state of perfect freedom to order their actions, and dispose of their possessions and persons, as they think fit, within the bounds of *the law of nature*, without asking leave, or depending upon the will of any other man. *A state also of equality, wherein all the power and jurisdiction is reciprocal, no one having more than another; there being nothing more evident, than that creatures of the same species and rank, promiscuously born to all the same advantages of nature, and the use of the same faculties, should also be equal one amongst another without subordination or subjection*, unless the lord and master of them all should, by any manifest declaration of his will, set one above another, and confer on him, by an evident and clear appointment, an undoubted right to dominion and sovereignty. *This equality of men by nature, the judicious Hooker looks upon as so evident in itself, and beyond all question*, that he makes it the foundation of that obligation to mutual love amongst men, on which he builds the duties they owe one another, and from whence he derives the great maxims of justice and charity. [2.4-2.5]	When in the Course of human events, it becomes necessary for one people to dissolve the political bands which have connected them with another, and to assume among the powers of the earth, the separate and equal station to which the ***Laws of Nature*** and of Nature's God entitle them, a decent respect to the opinions of mankind requires that they should declare the causes which impel them to the separation. **We hold these truths to be self-evident, that all men are created equal,**
Man being born, as has been proved, with a title to perfect freedom, and an uncontrolled enjoyment of all the rights and privileges of the law of nature, equally with any other man, or number of men in the world, hath by nature *a power, not only to preserve his property, that is, his life, liberty and estate, against the injuries and attempts of other men*; but to judge of, and punish the breaches of that law in others, as he is persuaded the offence deserves, even with death itself, in crimes where the heinousness of the fact, in his opinion, requires	that they are endowed by their Creator with certain **unalienable Rights, that among these are Life, Liberty and the pursuit of Happiness.**—

it. But *because no political society can be, nor subsist, without having in itself the power to preserve the property, and in order thereunto, punish the offences of all those of that society; there, and there only is political society, where every one of the members hath quitted this natural power, resigned it up into the hands of the community* in all cases that exclude him not from appealing for protection to the law established by it. . . . *Wherever therefore any number of men are so united into one society, as to quit every one his executive power of the law of nature, and to resign it to the public, there and there only is a political, or civil society.* [8.87-8.89]

But if the unlawful acts done by the magistrate be maintained (by the power he has got), and the remedy which is due by law, be by the same power obstructed; **yet the right of resisting, even in such manifest acts of tyranny, will not suddenly, or on slight occasions, disturb the government: for if it reach no farther than some private men's cases, though they have a right to defend themselves, and to recover by force what by unlawful force is taken from them; yet the right to do so will not easily engage them in a contest, wherein they are sure to perish; it being as impossible for one, or a few oppressed men to disturb the government, where the body of the people do not think themselves concerned in it**, as for a raving mad-man, or heady malcontent to overturn a well settled state; the people being as little apt to follow the one, as the other.
But if either these illegal acts have extended to the majority of the people; or if the mischief and oppression has lighted only on some few, but in such cases, as the precedent, and consequences seem to threaten all; and they are persuaded in their consciences, that their laws, and with them their estates, liberties, and lives are in danger, and perhaps their religion too; how they will be hindered from resisting illegal force, used against them, I cannot tell. [18.208-18.209]

To be free from such force is the only security of my

That to secure these rights, Governments are instituted among Men, deriving their just powers from the consent of the governed,

--That whenever any Form of Government becomes destructive of these ends, it is the Right of the People to alter or to abolish it, and to institute new Government, laying its foundation on such principles and organizing its powers in such form, as to them shall seem most likely to effect their Safety and Happiness. **Prudence, indeed, will dictate that Governments long established should not be changed for light and transient causes; and accordingly all experience hath shewn, that mankind are more disposed to suffer, while evils are sufferable, than to right themselves by abolishing the forms to which they are accustomed. But when a long train of abuses and usurpations, pursuing invariably the same Object evinces a design to reduce them under absolute Despotism, it is their right, it is their duty, to throw off such Government, and to provide new Guards for their future security.—**

...

preservation; and reason bids me look on him, as an enemy to my preservation, who would take away that freedom which is the fence to it; so that *he who makes an attempt to enslave me, thereby puts himself into a state of war with me*. He that, in the state of nature, would take away the freedom that belongs to any one in that state, must necessarily be supposed to have a design to take away everything else, that freedom being the foundation of all the rest; *as he that in the state of society would take away the freedom belonging to those of that society or commonwealth, must be supposed to design to take away from them every thing else, and so be looked on as in a state of war.* [3.17]

In every stage of these Oppressions We have Petitioned for Redress in the most humble terms: Our repeated Petitions have been answered only by repeated injury. **A Prince whose character is thus marked by every act which may define a Tyrant, is unfit to be the ruler of a free people. . . .**

We must, therefore, acquiesce in the necessity, which denounces our Separation, and hold them, as we hold the rest of mankind, Enemies in War, in Peace Friends. . . .

It is undeniable that Locke exerted much influence on the Founders of the U.S. political system, with his ideas of natural rights, limited government, rule by consent, separation of powers, and emphasis on private property—but this influence by Locke on the Founders was not entire nor unmatched by other ideas.

The Federalist Papers were written by Alexander Hamilton, John Jay, and James Madison, after the Constitutional Convention of 1787. Interestingly, rather than use their own names, each letter was signed *"Publius"*—indicating an intentional link with the *classical* tradition of politics. Among other things, these papers call for a return to virtue, with the expectation that elected officials will be the most virtuous and meritorious among us. Citizens show their own virtue by electing leaders of the "purest and noblest characters."

So important was virtue, that the authors regarded the celebrated "checks and balances" of the U.S. Constitution as ineffective without virtue. Madison said, in a speech delivered to the Virginia ratifying convention (June 20th, 1788):

"I have observed, that gentlemen suppose, that the general legislature will do every mischief they possibly can, and

that they will omit to do every thing good which they are authorised to do. If this were a reasonable supposition, their objections would be good. I consider it reasonable to conclude, that they will as readily do their duty, as deviate from it: Nor do I go on the grounds mentioned by gentlemen on the other side--that we are to place unlimited confidence in them, and expect nothing but the most exalted integrity and sublime virtue. But I go on this great republican principle, that the people will have virtue and intelligence to select men of virtue and wisdom. Is there no virtue among us? If there be not, we are in a wretched situation. No theoretical checks--no form of government can render us secure. To suppose that any form of government will secure liberty or happiness without any virtue in the people, is a chimerical idea. If there be sufficient virtue and intelligence in the community, it will be exercised in the selection of these men. So that we do not depend on their virtue, or put confidence in our rulers, but in the people who are to choose them."[268]

---

[268] http://press-pubs.uchicago.edu/founders/documents/v1ch13s36.html

This emphasis on virtue was not so much a rejection of the appeal of self-interest, but rather a claim that a system based on self-interest will not succeed unless the self-interest is "enlightened," and regulated by virtuous citizens. John Adams claimed that "Our Constitution was made only for a moral and religious people. It is wholly inadequate for any others."[269]

This is not to say that the writers of the *Federalist Papers* were rejecting Locke's ideas, but rather that his modern interpretation of people as self-interested consumers (with natural rights) had not *entirely* replaced the classical emphasis on virtue as being essential for both the citizenry as well as the rulers.

For the remainder of the chapter, we will consider some key ideas developed in the *Federalist Papers*—an understanding of which is essential for understanding the peculiar form of government that was created and implemented in the United States.

The *Federalist Papers*

The *Federalist Papers* were written in defense of the States' ratification of the Constitution (to replace the Articles of Confederation). The project was spearheaded by Hamilton, who wrote most of the letters (51). He recruited John Jay, who only wrote five letters, after falling ill, and James Madison, who wrote the remaining 29. Because each letter was written under the pseudonym, "*Publius*," and because the authors' intention was that the letters be treated as a coherent single project, I will simply refer to *Publius* as the author going forward. The letters initially appeared in newspapers (mostly New York publications), and were later collected and published as a single volume

While very different in format and motivation than the other works of philosophy considered in this book, the *Federalist Papers*

have always been considered a definitive explanation of the motives and principles held by the Founders of the American Constitutional system of government. Indeed, no less a figure than President Thomas Jefferson himself, said the following:

> With respect to the Federalist, . . . It [is]. . . , in my opinion, the best commentary on the principles of government which ever was written."[270]

Having already discussed the Declaration of Independence above, it's worth pointing out a basic analogy. The Declaration begins by recognizing a need to justify the proposed independence from Great Britain. The *Federalist Papers* were written to justify the ratification of the U.S. Constitution. The Declaration offers an argument based on certain premises about human nature and governing, then proceeds to show how the actions of Great Britain warrant the act of rebellion. The *Federalist Papers* offer an argument, based on certain premises about human nature and governing, for the necessity of a certain kind of government, and then proceeds to demonstrate that the U.S. Constitution creates that kind of government. The importance of *reasons* is evident in both documents. The Declaration lays out a meticulous and rigorous defense of its case, and in the first Federalist paper *Publius* urges the use of evidence and reason and cautions against emotional appeals.

> To judge from the conduct of the opposite parties, we shall be led to conclude that they will mutually hope to evince the justness of their opinions, and to increase the number of their converts by the loudness of their declamations and the bitterness of their invectives. . . . a dangerous ambition more often lurks

---

[269] Message from John Adams to the Officers of the First Brigade of the Third Division of the Militia of Massachusetts October 11, 1798. https://founders.archives.gov/documents/Adams/99-02-02-3102

[270] Letter written to James Madison, 11-18-1788. (https://founders.archives.gov/documents/Madison/01-11-02-0257)

behind the specious mask of zeal for the rights of the people than under the forbidden appearance of zeal for the firmness and efficiency of government. History will teach us that the former has been found a much more certain road to the introduction of despotism than the latter, and that of those men who have overturned the liberties of republics, the greatest number have begun their career by paying an obsequious court to the people; commencing demagogues, and ending tyrants.

A final point of analogy: The Declaration relies upon certain key premises regarding human nature and just government, including self-evident basic human equality, unalienable rights to life, liberty, and happiness, and government by consent of the governed. While the philosophy is less overt in the *Federalist Papers*, key assumptions about human nature are still present, and guide the entire project.

Publius operates from an implicitly accepted theory of human motivation. "Reason" is a relatively weak motive. Indeed, *Publius* acknowledges the vulnerability of Reason at the very outset of Paper #1:

So numerous indeed and so powerful are the causes which serve to give a false bias to the judgment, that we, upon many occasions, see wise and good men on the wrong as well as on the right side of questions of the first magnitude to society. This circumstance, if duly attended to, would furnish a lesson of moderation to those who are ever so much persuaded of their being in the right in any controversy. And a further reason for caution, in this respect, might be drawn from the reflection that we are not always sure that those who advocate the truth are influenced by purer principles than their antagonists. Ambition, avarice, personal animosity, party opposition, and many other motives not more laudable than these, are apt to operate as well upon

those who support as those who oppose the right side of a question.

All persons, on either side of any issue, are vulnerable to bias, and susceptible to greed, ambition, personal grudges, and other, less "reasonable" motivations. We cannot, therefore, rely solely (or even primarily) on Reason to guide and restrain human behavior. In Paper #10 *Publius* explicitly claims that neither "moral" nor "religious" motives can be relied upon to restrain ambitious "factions"—a term he also defines in that same paper.

By a faction, I understand a number of citizens, whether amounting to a majority or a minority of the whole, who are united and actuated by some common impulse of passion, or of interest, adversed to the rights of other citizens, or to the permanent and aggregate interests of the community.

His assumption is that both factions as well as individual politicians would defy their moral obligations, as dictated by Reason, and indulge their impulses in oppressive ways. Although the Natural Law makes clear what is right and wrong, just and unjust, people will be tempted to violate the rights of others anyway, and will do so if given the chance.

Moreover, the existence of factions, *Publius* argues, is inevitable. There will always be differences of opinion, and differences in values, among people. So, "giving to every citizen the same opinions, the same passions, and the same interests" is not a viable option. In addition, the most common and prominent cause of faction— unequal distribution of property and wealth—is also inevitable.

Those who hold and those who are without property have ever formed distinct interests in society. Those who are creditors, and those who are debtors, fall under a like discrimination. A landed interest, a manufacturing interest, a mercantile interest, a moneyed interest, with many lesser interests, grow up of necessity in civilized nations, and divide them into different classes, actuated by different sentiments and views. The regulation of these various and interfering interests forms the principal task of modern legislation, and involves the spirit of party and faction in the necessary and ordinary operations of the government.[271]

Because people have different abilities, some will acquire more than others, and economic class differences are inevitable. Some people will use the power of the State to facilitate and protect their property, and factions will inevitably develop—and this is a cause of conflict and a threat to the common good. One possible way to eliminate the cause of factions is by "destroying the liberty which is essential to its existence." In other words, if we simply took away self-determination (and submitted to an absolute monarchy, for example), the threat of factions would be removed because subjects would have no meaningful amount of power and influence to pool and deploy in the first place. However, *Publius* dismisses that "remedy" as worse than the disease."

> Liberty is to faction what air is to fire, an aliment without which it instantly expires. But it could not be less folly to abolish liberty, which is essential to political life, because it nourishes faction, than it would be to wish the annihilation of air, which is essential to animal life, because it imparts to fire its destructive agency.

Resigned that the *causes* of factions can't be removed, *Publius* shifts to considering remedies that block their *effect*. One possible remedy is to rely on "enlightened statesmen" to protect the community from divisive factions, but *Publius* dismisses this as "vain." It is naïve to think that *only* enlightened rulers will come to power, and

certainly history has shown, again and again, that rulers can be just as corrupt, foolish, or even wicked, as anyone else.

Another possible remedy is to rely on the power and influence of the majority within a community to restrain the efforts of a minority faction. The problem with this, obviously, is the scenario is which it is the majority itself who is the faction. "When a majority is included in a faction, the form of popular government, on the other hand, enables it to sacrifice to its ruling passion or interest both the public good and the rights of other citizens. To secure the public good and private rights against the danger of such a faction, and at the same time to preserve the spirit and the form of popular government, is then the great object to which our inquiries are directed."

Beyond recognizing the threat of the majority, note the significance of the specific wording of that quotation. Securing "the public good and private rights against the danger of such a faction" is "*the* great object to which our inquiries are directed."[272] *The* overarching goal/purpose of the efforts of those drafting the Constitution is to protect society against the tyranny of the majority—and the purpose of the *Federalist Papers* is to explain and justify those efforts.

Having rejected Reason, moral and religious motives, enlightened Statesmen, and the influence of the majority as viable ways to constrain factions, *Publius* finally turns to the one remedy that he thinks can actually work: "external" restraints on the effects of factions. The form of government adopted should be one that can effectively channel and counter the ambitions of both individuals and groups. In Federalist #51, *Publius* says that

> Ambition must be made to counteract ambition. The interest of the man must be connected with the constitutional rights of the place. It may be a reflection on human nature, that such devices should be necessary to control the abuses of

---

[271] #10.

[272] Emphasis added.

government. But what is government itself, but the greatest of all reflections on human nature? If men were angels, no government would be necessary. If angels were to govern men, neither external nor internal controls on government would be necessary. In framing a government which is to be administered by men over men, the great difficulty lies in this: you must first enable the government to control the governed; and in the next place oblige it to control itself. A dependence on the people is, no doubt, the primary control on the government; but experience has taught mankind the necessity of auxiliary precautions.

The "devices" that will "check" the abuses of government include the creation of a sufficiently large Republic, as well as a system of "checks and balances" within the particular structure of that republican government. We will begin with the need for a Republic, as opposed to a direct democracy. In Federalist #10, *Publius* made his case against direct democracy.

From this view of the subject it may be concluded that a pure democracy, by which I mean a society consisting of a small number of citizens, who assemble and administer the government in person, can admit of no cure for the mischiefs of faction. A common passion or interest will, in almost every case, be felt by a majority of the whole; a communication and concert result from the form of government itself; and there is nothing to check the inducements to sacrifice the weaker party or an obnoxious individual. Hence it is that such democracies have ever been spectacles of turbulence and contention; have ever been found incompatible with personal security or the rights of property; and have in general been as short in their lives as they have been violent in their deaths. Theoretic politicians, who have patronized this species of government,

have erroneously supposed that by reducing mankind to a perfect equality in their political rights, they would, at the same time, be perfectly equalized and assimilated in their possessions, their opinions, and their passions.

In direct democracies, a simple majority vote is all that is needed to create laws. Unpopular minorities can easily be sacrificed by the majority, and the few are obviously vulnerable to the many. As an alternative, *Publius* will propose a (Constitutional) Republic. In Federalist #39 he defines a Republic as "a government which derives all its powers directly or indirectly from the great body of the people, and is administered by persons holding their offices during pleasure, for a limited period, or during good behavior."

Unlike a direct democracy, in which the people personally vote on all laws, in a Republic, the people will instead vote for their representatives, who themselves will vote for laws and policies. In theory, these representatives will genuinely represent the interests of their constituents, but, will do so (argues *Publius* in Federalist #10), in an "enlightened" fashion.

The effect . . . is . . . to refine and enlarge the public views, by passing them through the medium of a chosen body of citizens, whose wisdom may best discern the true interest of their country, and whose patriotism and love of justice will be least likely to sacrifice it to temporary or partial considerations. Under such a regulation, it may well happen that the public voice, pronounced by the representatives of the people, will be more consonant to the public good than if pronounced by the people themselves, convened for the purpose.

The assumption seems to be that passions will be tempered, and actions more measured and reasonable, by creating some distance between the people and the acts of legislation. In theory, wise, educated, and responsible citizens will be the ones who win elections, and those persons will be both better informed, and have a better temperament, than the average citizen who voted for him.[273]

If you're sensing some elitism in this approach, you're correct. *Publius* was not confident that "the people" could be relied upon to rule wisely, and actively sought to check the influence of the "mob." In Federalist #55 he argues that no matter how virtuous the people might be, as individuals, they become dangerous to liberty once they become a group.

> The truth is, that in all cases a certain number at least seems to be necessary to secure the benefits of free consultation and discussion, and to guard against too easy a combination for improper purposes; as, on the other hand, the number ought at most to be kept within a certain limit, in order to avoid the confusion and intemperance of a multitude. In all very numerous assemblies, of whatever character composed, passion never fails to wrest the sceptre from reason. Had every Athenian citizen been a Socrates, every Athenian assembly would still have been a mob.

Certainly, a direct democracy would constitute a "mob," in this sense, so a Republic is recommended instead. However, republican representation, by itself, is still not sufficient to restrain the majority, since "men of factious tempers, of local prejudices, or of sinister designs, may, by intrigue, by corruption, or by other means, first obtain the suffrages, and then betray the interests, of the people."[274] This is just to acknowledge that these representatives are subject to all the same ambition and temptation as any other person, and, once in office, might betray the trust of their constituents or the public good, and promote their own interests, or that of a faction, instead.

The risk of corrupted representatives could be mitigated, according to *Publius* in Federalist #10, by increasing the *size* of the Republic not only in terms of geography, but also in terms of population. This, it was thought, would make it more likely that representatives with the most "merit" will win.

> as each representative will be chosen by a greater number of citizens in the large than in the small republic, it will be more difficult for unworthy candidates to practice with success the vicious arts by which elections are too often carried; and the suffrages of the people being more free, will be more likely to centre in men who possess the most attractive merit and the most diffusive and established characters.[275]

Here, the assumption seems to be that it will be more difficult for a person of poor qualification or shady character to be elected if his constituency is larger. Simply put, it's more difficult to fool a lot of people than a few people. A charismatic (but corrupt) politician might be able to win over his neighbors, but will have a harder time traveling the countryside and conning a sufficient number of other people as well. This assumption seems less-obvious in a world connected by television, the internet, and social media.[276]

An additional benefit of a large Republic, according to *Publius* in that same letter, is that by increasing the number of citizens, you increase the number and diversity of interests and agendas, and thereby weaken the power of individual factions.

---

[273] This is not sexist pronoun use. At the time, the representative would have certainly been male.
[274] Federalist #10.
[275] Federalist #10

[276] Politicians of all kinds can amass millions of Twitter followers today. Towards the end of the 2016 Presidential campaign, for example, Donald Trump had over 10 million Twitter followers, and Hillary Clinton over 8 million.

The smaller the society, the fewer probably will be the distinct parties and interests composing it; the fewer the distinct parties and interests, the more frequently will a majority be found of the same party; and the smaller the number of individuals composing a majority, and the smaller the compass within which they are placed, the more easily will they concert and execute their plans of oppression. Extend the sphere, and you take in a greater variety of parties and interests; you make it less probable that a majority of the whole will have a common motive to invade the rights of other citizens; or if such a common motive exists, it will be more difficult for all who feel it to discover their own strength, and to act in unison with each other.

Speaking solely of religion, as an example, the larger the population, the more likely that the population will exhibit a larger number of different religions, sects within the same religion, and diverse points of view. Even if a community overwhelmingly subscribes to a single religious tradition (e.g., Christianity), that single religion will admit of numerous different sects (e.g., Catholics, Lutherans, Evangelicals, etc.) with different interests and foci. By fragmenting "the people" into a larger number of special interest groups, the size and influence of each group is diminished, making them less dangerous to the other groups.

In a society under the forms of which the stronger faction can readily unite and oppress the weaker, anarchy may as truly be said to reign as in a state of nature, where the weaker individual is not secured against the violence of the stronger; and as, in the latter state, even the stronger individuals are prompted, by the uncertainty of their condition, to submit to a government which may protect the weak as well as themselves;

so, in the former state, will the more powerful factions or parties be gradually induced, by a like motive, to wish for a government which will protect all parties, the weaker as well as the more powerful.[277]

All of this is consistent, of course, with *Publius'* claim in this same letter that "ambition must be made to counteract ambition."

Having made a case for the necessity of a Republic, *Publius* then makes the case that the proposed Constitution is, in fact, a Republic. In Federalist #39 he lays out the specific ways in which the proposed form of government conforms to Republican principles.

On comparing the Constitution planned by the convention with the standard here fixed, we perceive at once that it is, in the most rigid sense, conformable to it. The House of Representatives, like that of one branch at least of all the State legislatures, is elected immediately by the great body of the people. The Senate, like the present Congress, and the Senate of Maryland, derives its appointment indirectly from the people. The President is indirectly derived from the choice of the people, according to the example in most of the States. Even the judges, with all other officers of the Union, will, as in the several States, be the choice, though a remote choice, of the people themselves, the duration of the appointments is equally conformable to the republican standard, and to the model of State constitutions. The House of Representatives is periodically elective, as in all the States; and for the period of two years, as in the State of South Carolina. The Senate is elective, for the period of six years; which is but one year more than the period of the Senate of Maryland, and but two more than that of the Senates of New York and Virginia. The President is to continue in

---

[277] Federalist #51.

office for the period of four years; as in New York and Delaware, the chief magistrate is elected for three years, and in South Carolina for two years. In the other States the election is annual. In several of the States, however, no constitutional provision is made for the impeachment of the chief magistrate. And in Delaware and Virginia he is not impeachable till out of office. The President of the United States is impeachable at any time during his continuance in office. The tenure by which the judges are to hold their places, is, as it unquestionably ought to be, that of good behavior. The tenure of the ministerial offices generally, will be a subject of legal regulation, conformably to the reason of the case and the example of the State constitutions.

To summarize *Publius'* case that the Constitution creates a Republic, and one that contains numerous "checks and balances:"

- The government is split into National, State, and local governments—with the ambition of each "checking" the ambitions of the others.
- Within both the State and National governments, governmental powers are separated into three branches: the Executive, Legislative, and Judicial.
- Within the legislative branch at both the National and State levels, power is further divided into two "chambers:" a House and a Senate.[278]
- At the time of the ratification, the House of Representatives would be filled by

direct elections in the States, while the Senators would be elected by their State legislators.[279]
- These elections would be staggered, with elections in the House occurring every two years, versus six in the Senate. This would prevent drastic and sudden legislative changes by preventing the entirely of the National Legislature to be subject to re-election at the same time.
- The head of the Executive branch is elected every four years, indirectly by the Electoral College, and is subject to impeachment at any time.[280]
- The Judiciary (at all levels) hold their office subject to "good behavior," for the sake of maintaining their independence from other branches and sources of influence.

Publius was dedicated to demonstrating the system of checks and balances contained in the Constitution, and the value and application of this system has been seen numerous times for nearly 250 years. Only a month into Donald Trump's Presidency, there were already dozens of articles and editorials with the phrase "checks and balances" in their headlines. The executive order that triggered these headlines was his controversial ban on immigrants from seven Muslim-majority countries (viz., Iran, Iraq, Libya, Somalia, Sudan, Syria and Yemen), as well as an indefinite ban on all refugees from Syria.[281] The "check and balance" was the immediate legal challenge to the order, and the subsequent halting of the enforcement of the order after the 9th Circuit Court of Appeals upheld a temporary restraining order. At that time, the order could be rewritten, or appealed to the U.S. Supreme Court,

---

[278] Even today, more than two centuries later, 49 out of the 50 States have bicameral legislatures—with Nebraska being the only exception.

[279] The Constitution was amended (Amendment 17) in 1913 so that Senators were elected directly by the people from their States. The amendment revised the first paragraph of Article I, section 3 of the Constitution by replacing the phrase

"chosen by the Legislature thereof" with "elected by the people thereof."

[280] The rationale for the Electoral College will be addressed at the end of the chapter.

[281] The full text of the order can be found here: https://www.nytimes.com/2017/01/27/us/politics/refugee-muslim-executive-order-trump.html

but the point remains, nonetheless: The Executive Branch acted, and another Branch (i.e., the Judiciary) "restrained" it.

President Trump is hardly the only President to have been "checked"—including in recent history. The U.S. Supreme Court, for example, blocked President Obama's executive action on immigration, as well as President George W. Bush's executive order concerning military tribunals for Guantanamo Bay prisoners.[282]

Publius addresses the role of the Judiciary in Federalist #78, with an emphasis on the need for their "independence." He acknowledges that the Judiciary is, in a sense, the least powerful branch of the government, since it has no ability to command the military (unlike the Executive), or to collect money or pass laws (unlike the Legislative).

> The judiciary, on the contrary, has no influence over either the sword or the purse; no direction either of the strength or of the wealth of the society; and can take no active resolution whatever. It may truly be said to have neither force nor will, but merely judgment; and must ultimately depend upon the aid of the executive arm even for the efficacy of its judgments.

Indeed, the only thing the Judiciary *can* do is interpret and judge the laws passed by the Legislative branch and the actions taken by the Executive—a process known as "judicial review." The authority of the Judiciary is based on a clear principle: "every act of a delegated authority, contrary to the tenor of the commission under which it is exercised, is void." What this means is that "No legislative act, therefore, contrary to the Constitution, can be valid. To deny this, would be to affirm, that the deputy is greater than his principal; that the servant is above his master; that the representatives of the people are superior to the people themselves; that men acting by virtue of powers, may do not only what

their powers do not authorize, but what they forbid."

The supremacy of the Supreme Court on matters of Constitutionality is stated clearly in the *Federalist Papers*.

> [T]he courts were designed to be an intermediate body between the people and the legislature, in order, among other things, to keep the latter within the limits assigned to their authority. The interpretation of the laws is the proper and peculiar province of the courts. A constitution is, in fact, and must be regarded by the judges as, a fundamental law. It, therefore, belongs to them to ascertain its meaning, as well as the meaning of any particular act proceeding from the legislative body. (#78)

This supremacy has also been upheld by Court precedent. The Supremacy Clause of the Constitution states that the Constitution "and the Laws of the United States which shall be made in Pursuance thereof; and all Treaties made, or which shall be made, under the Authority of the United States, shall be the supreme Law of the Land (Article 6, Clause 2)." The 1803 case of *Marbury v. Madison* established that the *Judiciary* is the arbiter of what the Constitution permits.

> It is emphatically the province and duty of the Judicial Department [the judicial branch] to say what the law is. Those who apply the rule to particular cases must, of necessity, expound and interpret that rule. If two laws conflict with each other, the Courts must decide on the operation of each.

> So, if a law [e.g., a statute or treaty] be in opposition to the Constitution, if both the law and the Constitution apply to a particular case, so that the Court must either decide that case conformably to the

---

law, disregarding the Constitution, or conformably to the Constitution, disregarding the law, the Court must determine which of these conflicting rules governs the case. This is of the very essence of judicial duty. If, then, the Courts are to regard the Constitution, and the Constitution is superior to any ordinary act of the Legislature, the Constitution, and not such ordinary act, must govern the case to which they both apply.

Those, then, who controvert the principle that the Constitution is to be considered in court as a paramount law are reduced to the necessity of maintaining that courts must close their eyes on the Constitution, and see only the law [e.g., the statute or treaty].

This doctrine would subvert the very foundation of all written constitutions.[283]

The 1958 case of *Cooper v. Aaron* cited *Marbury* as precedent and further reinforced the role of the Judiciary: ". . . the federal judiciary is supreme in the exposition of the law of the Constitution, and that principle has ever since been respected by the Court and the country as a permanent and indispensable feature of our constitutional system."[284]

Between those cases, President Abraham Lincoln said of the infamous 1857 *Dred Scot* decision (in which African-Americans were determined to be ineligible to claim citizenship, and in which "property rights" for slave owners was maintained): "We believe, as much as Judge Douglas, (perhaps more) in obedience to, and respect for the judicial department of government. We think its decisions on

Constitutional questions, when fully settled, should control, not only the particular cases decided, but the general policy of the country, subject to be disturbed only by amendments of the Constitution as provided in that instrument itself. More than this would be revolution. But we think the Dred Scott decision is erroneous. We know the court that made it, has often over-ruled its own decisions, and we shall do what we can to have it to over-rule this. We offer no resistance to it."[285]

The "check" offered by the Judiciary manifests not only by virtue of its power of judicial review. *Publius* claims that the mere existence of the judiciary will temper the acts of legislators.

But it is not with a view to infractions of the Constitution only, that the independence of the judges may be an essential safeguard against the effects of occasional ill humors in the society. These sometimes extend no farther than to the injury of the private rights of particular classes of citizens, by unjust and partial laws. Here also the firmness of the judicial magistracy is of vast importance in mitigating the severity and confining the operation of such laws. It not only serves to moderate the immediate mischiefs of those which may have been passed, but it operates as a check upon the legislative body in passing them; who, perceiving that obstacles to the success of iniquitous intention are to be expected from the scruples of the courts, are in a manner compelled, by the very motives of the injustice they meditate, to qualify their attempts. This is a circumstance calculated to have more influence upon the character of our governments, than

283

http://www.ache.org/pubs/hap_companion/Wing/MarburyMadison.pdf
284

https://www.princeton.edu/~ereading/cooperaaron.pdf

285

http://teachingamericanhistory.org/library/document/speech-on-the-dred-scott-decision/

but few may be aware of. The benefits of the integrity and moderation of the judiciary have already been felt in more States than one; and though they may have displeased those whose sinister expectations they may have disappointed, they must have commanded the esteem and applause of all the virtuous and disinterested. Considerate men, of every description, ought to prize whatever will tend to beget or fortify that temper in the courts: as no man can be sure that he may not be to-morrow the victim of a spirit of injustice, by which he may be a gainer to-day. And every man must now feel, that the inevitable tendency of such a spirit is to sap the foundations of public and private confidence, and to introduce in its stead universal distrust and distress.

The idea here is simple: if the other two branches know that their actions are subject to judicial review, and could be overturned by the Judiciary, they will make it a point to carefully craft laws or executive orders that are less likely to be challenged and overturned. The threat of being "checked" by the Courts cause the other branches to preemptively "check" themselves!

In order for the Judiciary to be effective in this role, it must be independent from the other branches. Article Two of the Constitution specifies that the President nominates judges for the Supreme Court, but with input from the Senate. "[He] shall nominate, and by and with the Advice and Consent of the Senate, shall appoint ... Judges of the supreme Court..."

Already we see the functioning of separation of powers, and checks and balances. The Executive branch nominates judges, but they must be approved by one of the houses of the Legislative branch. Once confirmed by the Senate, these judges retain their appointment for life, contingent on "good behavior."

The judicial Power of the United States, shall be vested in one supreme Court, and in such inferior Courts as the Congress may from time to time ordain and establish. The Judges, both of the supreme and inferior Courts, shall hold their Offices during good Behavior, and shall, at stated Times, receive for their Services a Compensation which shall not be diminished during their Continuance in Office.[286]

There are several things to consider here. In the first place, their lifetime appointments facilitate independence by virtue of the fact that judges can't be "fired" by the President. This is critically important since a fear of job security might motivate judges to rule in ways pleasing to their "boss" rather than in ways consistent with the Constitution. Technically, a judge may be impeached if they violate the "good behavior" clause—but this requires that articles of impeachment be approved by a majority in the House of Representatives, and that two-thirds of Senators convict the judge after a trial in the Senate.

"Impeachment" may not occur just because a judge angers or annoys a member of another branch of government. They must have committed an impeachable offense. Article two, Section 4 of the Constitution specifies that the grounds for impeachment are "Treason, Bribery, or other high Crimes and Misdemeanors."

Admittedly, "high crimes and misdemeanors" is a vague expression, and subject to interpretation, but it is difficult to remove judges from office, all the same. The Executive branch has no power to do so at all. The Legislative branch does, but it requires a majority of the House and two-thirds of the Senate to be of like-mind. It's unlikely that a sufficiently large faction of both Representatives and Senators could be united against a judge except under special circumstances.

---

[286] Article three, Section one, of the U.S. Constitution.

In the entire history of the United States thus far, the House has only initiated impeachment proceedings 62 times. Only 19 people have actually been impeached (15 federal judges, 2 Presidents, 1 cabinet secretary, and 1 Senator). Of those 19, only 8 were actually convicted and removed from office. In almost 250 years, only 8 officials (all of whom were judges) have been removed from office. It's safe to say that history has thus far confirmed that the life-tenure of judges is secure, and good grounds for their independence.

Another contribution to the independence of the Judiciary, provided by Article 3, Section 1 (cited above), is that the compensation of the judges "shall not be diminished during their Continuance in Office." Job security doesn't amount to much if another branch of government could stop paying you for doing your job. Ultimately, both their position and their salaries are guaranteed, once confirmed, barring extraordinary circumstances—both of which promote their independence and facilitate the ability of the Judiciary to serve as a "check" against the other branches.

We will now consider one final issue addressed by *Publius*, whose relevance has been highlighted recently: the role of the Electoral College in the election of the President.

In 2000, George W. Bush won the electoral vote with 271 (versus Al Gore's 266), but lost the popular vote: 50, 456, 002 to 50,999,897. Despite more people voting for Al Gore, George W. Bush was elected President. The same thing happened again in 2016, by an even larger margin.

Donald Trump received 62,979,636 votes to Hillary Clinton's 65,844,610—a difference of more than 3 million votes. Nevertheless, he was elected President by virtue of winning 306 electoral votes to Hillary Clinton's 232.[287]

The experience of two candidates losing the election despite receiving the majority of votes in the span of only 12 years has inspired some to call for the abolishment of the Electoral College.[288] California State Senator Barbara Boxer introduced a bill in November 2016 to end the Electoral College, and similar (unsuccessful) attempts had been tried in 1934, 1966, and 1979.[289]

On its surface, there seems something obviously "undemocratic" about the recipient of the majority of votes *losing* the election, and yet the Founders set it up that way on purpose. Initially, there wasn't even a popular vote at all![290]

Publius' assumption, explained in Federalist #68, was that a small number of electors could better discern the qualities of candidates than could the "people."

the people of each State shall choose a number of persons as electors, equal to the number of senators and representatives of such State in the national government, who shall assemble within the State, and vote for some fit person as President. Their votes, thus given, are to be transmitted to the seat of the national government, and the person who may happen to have a majority of the whole number of votes will be the President. But as a majority of the votes might not always happen to centre in one man, and as it might be unsafe to permit less than a majority to be conclusive, it is provided that, in such a contingency, the House of Representatives shall select out of the candidates who shall have the five

---

[287] http://www.infoplease.com/ipa/A0781450.html

[288] http://petitions.moveon.org/sign/abolish-the-electoral-6

[289] https://www.washingtonpost.com/news/the-fix/wp/2016/11/09/getting-rid-of-the-electoral-college-dream-ondemocrats/?utm_term=.500d243a187f

[290] Electors were originally chosen by State legislatures, much like National Senators. By 1836, all States except for South Carolina chose electors via Statewide popular vote instead. As of 1860, South Carolina adopted this approach as well.

highest number of votes, the man who in their opinion may be best qualified for the office.

The process of election affords a moral certainty, that the office of President will never fall to the lot of any man who is not in an eminent degree endowed with the requisite qualifications. Talents for low intrigue, and the little arts of popularity, may alone suffice to elevate a man to the first honors in a single State; but it will require other talents, and a different kind of merit, to establish him in the esteem and confidence of the whole Union, or of so considerable a portion of it as would be necessary to make him a successful candidate for the distinguished office of President of the United States. It will not be too strong to say, that there will be a constant probability of seeing the station filled by characters pre-eminent for ability and virtue.

One more time, we see an attempt to restrain the effects of factions, and a lack of confidence in the discernment of "the people." The very nature of a Republic presupposes that relatively enlightened representatives will make better decisions than their constituents, and the use of Electors to elect the President mirrors (and for the same reason) the (original) use of State Legislatures to elect Senators to the U.S. Congress. *Publius* also assumes that only persons of high character and qualification could earn the votes of a majority of electors across all the several States. A lesser candidate might be able to achieve popularity in his own State, but would be unable to wield such influence across a sufficient number of other States—or so the argument goes. As mentioned above in our discussion of the election of representatives, in general:

as each representative will be chosen by a greater number of citizens in the large than in the small republic, it will be more

difficult for unworthy candidates to practice with success the vicious arts by which elections are too often carried; and the suffrages of the people being more free, will be more likely to centre in men who possess the most attractive merit and the most diffusive and established characters.[291]

This is a bold assumption, and is by no means obviously true—at least not any longer, given the ability to communicate instantly across the entire Nation via the internet, television, and social media. Nevertheless, whether one *agrees* with the reasons or not, there were certainly reasons behind the Electoral College, and those reasons were provided by *Publius*.

Conclusion

The political philosophy that took place at the time of the founding of the American system of government was both derivative, and original. As we have seen, there is a clear line of influence from Enlightenment thinkers such as Locke, and the assumptions about human nature made by *Publius* find roots in the mechanistic psychology shared by Thomas Hobbes (and others). Even the favored form of government, a Republic, has ancient origins tracing back to Rome and the works of Cicero. Another Founder, John Adams, was explicit in his intellectual debt to Cicero.

As all the ages of the world have not produced a greater statesman and philosopher united in the same character, his authority should have great weight. His decided opinion in favour of three branches is founded on a reason that is unchangeable; the laws, which are the only posslble rule, measure, and security of justice, can be sure of protection, for any course of time, in no other form of government: and the very name of a republic implies, that the property of the people should be represented in the

---

[291] Federalist #10

legislature, and decide the rule of justice.[292]

All philosophical inheritance notwithstanding, the U.S. Constitution, and the *Federalist Papers* that defended it, also represent a fascinating experiment in which political theory is put to the test of actual governing. For all its genuine limitations, faults, and missteps, the U.S. political system, with its notion of separation of powers, constitutionally limited (representative) government, and checks and balances, has endured as a model for much of the Western world for nearly a quarter of a millennia.

The United States is known, worldwide, not only for its system of democratic government, but also for its economic system. Our next chapter will focus on the intersection of politics and economics, and we will consider the virtues of capitalism as advocated by Adam Smith and Ayn Rand.

---

[292] http://www.constitution.org/jadams/ ja1_pre.htm

The United States Declaration of Independence was adopted by the Second Continental Congress on July 4th, 1776. Thomas Jefferson drafted the original version, which was then edited by the Continental Congress. It offered a formal statement of Independence from Great Britain, more than one year after the actual American Revolutionary War had begun. The Declaration makes a moral argument in support of the legitimacy of independence from Great Britain, and references numerous ideas that can be traced back to John Locke.

The Declaration of Independence

IN CONGRESS, July 4, 1776.

The unanimous Declaration of the thirteen united States of America,

When in the Course of human events, it becomes necessary for one people to dissolve the political bands which have connected them with another, and to assume among the powers of the earth, the separate and equal station to which the Laws of Nature and of Nature's God entitle them, a decent respect to the opinions of mankind requires that they should declare the causes which impel them to the separation.

We hold these truths to be self-evident, that all men are created equal, that they are endowed by their Creator with certain unalienable Rights, that among these are Life, Liberty and the pursuit of Happiness.--That to secure these rights, Governments are instituted among Men, deriving their just powers from the consent of the governed, --That whenever any Form of Government becomes destructive of these ends, it is the Right of the People to alter or to abolish it, and to institute new Government, laying its foundation on such principles and organizing its powers in such form, as to them shall seem most likely to effect their Safety and Happiness. Prudence, indeed, will dictate that Governments long established should not be changed for light and transient causes; and accordingly all experience hath shewn, that mankind are more disposed to suffer, while evils are sufferable, than to right themselves by abolishing the forms to which they are accustomed. But when a long train of abuses and usurpations, pursuing invariably the same Object evinces a design to reduce them under absolute Despotism, it is their right, it is

their duty, to throw off such Government, and to provide new Guards for their future security.-- Such has been the patient sufferance of these Colonies; and such is now the necessity which constrains them to alter their former Systems of Government. The history of the present King of Great Britain is a history of repeated injuries and usurpations, all having in direct object the establishment of an absolute Tyranny over these States. To prove this, let Facts be submitted to a candid world.

He has refused his Assent to Laws, the most wholesome and necessary for the public good.

He has forbidden his Governors to pass Laws of immediate and pressing importance, unless suspended in their operation till his Assent should be obtained; and when so suspended, he has utterly neglected to attend to them.

He has refused to pass other Laws for the accommodation of large districts of people, unless those people would relinquish the right of Representation in the Legislature, a right inestimable to them and formidable to tyrants only.

He has called together legislative bodies at places unusual, uncomfortable, and distant from the depository of their public Records, for the sole purpose of fatiguing them into compliance with his measures.

He has dissolved Representative Houses repeatedly, for opposing with manly firmness his invasions on the rights of the people.

He has refused for a long time, after such dissolutions, to cause others to be elected; whereby the Legislative powers, incapable of Annihilation, have returned to the People at large for their exercise; the State remaining in the mean time exposed to all the dangers of invasion from without, and convulsions within.

He has endeavoured to prevent the population of these States; for that purpose obstructing the Laws for Naturalization of Foreigners; refusing to pass others to encourage their migrations hither, and raising the conditions of new Appropriations of Lands.

He has obstructed the Administration of Justice, by refusing his Assent to Laws for establishing Judiciary powers.

He has made Judges dependent on his Will alone, for the tenure of their offices, and the amount and payment of their salaries.

He has erected a multitude of New Offices, and sent hither swarms of Officers to harrass our people, and eat out their substance.

He has kept among us, in times of peace, Standing Armies without the Consent of our legislatures.

He has affected to render the Military independent of and superior to the Civil power.

He has combined with others to subject us to a jurisdiction foreign to our constitution, and unacknowledged by our laws; giving his Assent to their Acts of pretended Legislation:

For Quartering large bodies of armed troops among us:

For protecting them, by a mock Trial, from punishment for any Murders which they should commit on the Inhabitants of these States:

For cutting off our Trade with all parts of the world:

For imposing Taxes on us without our Consent:

For depriving us in many cases, of the benefits of Trial by Jury:

For transporting us beyond Seas to be tried for pretended offences

For abolishing the free System of English Laws in a neighbouring Province, establishing therein an Arbitrary government, and enlarging its Boundaries so as to render it at once an example and fit instrument for introducing the same absolute rule into these Colonies:

For taking away our Charters, abolishing our most valuable Laws, and altering fundamentally the Forms of our Governments:

For suspending our own Legislatures, and declaring themselves invested with power to legislate for us in all cases whatsoever.

He has abdicated Government here, by declaring us out of his Protection and waging War against us.

He has plundered our seas, ravaged our Coasts, burnt our towns, and destroyed the lives of our people.

He is at this time transporting large Armies of foreign Mercenaries to compleat the works of death, desolation and tyranny, already begun with circumstances of Cruelty & perfidy scarcely paralleled in the most barbarous ages, and totally unworthy the Head of a civilized nation.

He has constrained our fellow Citizens taken Captive on the high Seas to bear Arms against their Country, to become the executioners of their friends and Brethren, or to fall themselves by their Hands.

He has excited domestic insurrections amongst us, and has endeavoured to bring on the inhabitants of our frontiers, the merciless Indian

Savages, whose known rule of warfare, is an undistinguished destruction of all ages, sexes and conditions.

In every stage of these Oppressions We have Petitioned for Redress in the most humble terms: Our repeated Petitions have been answered only by repeated injury. A Prince whose character is thus marked by every act which may define a Tyrant, is unfit to be the ruler of a free people.

Nor have We been wanting in attentions to our Brittish brethren. We have warned them from time to time of attempts by their legislature to extend an unwarrantable jurisdiction over us. We have reminded them of the circumstances of our emigration and settlement here. We have appealed to their native justice and magnanimity, and we have conjured them by the ties of our common kindred to disavow these usurpations, which, would inevitably interrupt our connections and correspondence. They too have been deaf to the voice of justice and of consanguinity. We must, therefore, acquiesce in the necessity, which denounces our Separation, and hold them, as we hold the rest of mankind, Enemies in War, in Peace Friends.

We, therefore, the Representatives of the united States of America, in General Congress, Assembled, appealing to the Supreme Judge of the world for the rectitude of our intentions, do, in the Name, and by Authority of the good People of these Colonies, solemnly publish and declare, That these United Colonies are, and of Right ought to be Free and Independent States; that they are Absolved from all Allegiance to the British Crown, and that all political connection between them and the State of Great Britain, is and ought to be totally dissolved; and that as Free and Independent States, they have full Power to levy War, conclude Peace, contract Alliances, establish Commerce, and to do all other Acts and Things which Independent States may of right do. And for the support of this Declaration, with a firm reliance on the protection of divine Providence, we mutually pledge to each other our Lives, our Fortunes and our sacred Honor.

After declaring independence from Great Britain, the government of the United States first took the form of the Continental Congress (1774-1781), then the Second Continental Congress (1775-1781). The Second Continental Congress drafted the Articles of Confederation and Perpetual Union in 1777, and the Articles were ratified by all 13 original States as of 1781. In response to perceived weaknesses and inadequacies of the Articles, the Confederation Congress called a convention of State delegates in 1787. The Constitutional Convention met for four contentious months, and the final draft was submitted to the States for ratification. Two parties emerged: one supportive of ratification (the Federalists) and one opposed (the Anti-Federalists). The views of the Federalists are recorded in the Federalist Papers—some of which are included later in this chapter. The famous Bill of Rights was not originally included, but was ratified in 1791—partly to address some concerns of the Anti-Federalists.

The Constitution of the United States[293]

(Preamble)

We the People of the United States, in Order to form a more perfect Union, establish Justice, insure domestic Tranquility, provide for the common defence, promote the general Welfare, and secure the Blessings of Liberty to ourselves and our Posterity, do ordain and establish this Constitution for the United States of America.

Article I (Article 1 - Legislative)

Section 1

All legislative Powers herein granted shall be vested in a Congress of the United States, which shall consist of a Senate and House of Representatives.

Section 2

1: The House of Representatives shall be composed of Members chosen every second Year by the People of the several States, and the Electors in each State shall have the Qualifications requisite for Electors of the most numerous Branch of the State Legislature.

2: No Person shall be a Representative who shall not have attained to the Age of twenty five Years, and been seven Years a Citizen of the United States, and who shall not, when elected, be an Inhabitant of that State in which he shall be chosen.

3: Representatives and direct Taxes shall be apportioned among the several States which may be included within this Union, according to their respective Numbers, which shall be determined by adding to the whole Number of free Persons, including those bound to Service for a Term of Years, and excluding Indians not taxed, three fifths of all other Persons.2 The actual Enumeration shall be made within three Years after the first Meeting of the Congress of the United States, and within every subsequent Term of ten Years, in such Manner as they shall by Law direct. The Number of Representatives shall not exceed one for every thirty Thousand, but each State shall have at Least one Representative; and until such enumeration shall be made, the State of New Hampshire shall be entitled to chuse three, Massachusetts eight, Rhode-Island and Providence Plantations one, Connecticut five, New-York six, New Jersey four, Pennsylvania eight, Delaware one, Maryland six, Virginia ten, North Carolina five, South Carolina five, and Georgia three.

4: When vacancies happen in the Representation from any State, the Executive Authority thereof shall issue Writs of Election to fill such Vacancies.

5: The House of Representatives shall chuse their Speaker and other Officers; and shall have the sole Power of Impeachment.

Section 3

1: The Senate of the United States shall be composed of two Senators from each State, chosen by the Legislature thereof,3 for six Years; and each Senator shall have one Vote.

---

[293] http://constitutionus.com/

2: Immediately after they shall be assembled in Consequence of the first Election, they shall be divided as equally as may be into three Classes. The Seats of the Senators of the first Class shall be vacated at the Expiration of the second Year, of the second Class at the Expiration of the fourth Year, and of the third Class at the Expiration of the sixth Year, so that one third may be chosen every second Year; and if Vacancies happen by Resignation, or otherwise, during the Recess of the Legislature of any State, the Executive thereof may make temporary Appointments until the next Meeting of the Legislature, which shall then fill such Vacancies.4

3: No Person shall be a Senator who shall not have attained to the Age of thirty Years, and been nine Years a Citizen of the United States, and who shall not, when elected, be an Inhabitant of that State for which he shall be chosen.

4: The Vice President of the United States shall be President of the Senate, but shall have no Vote, unless they be equally divided.

5: The Senate shall chuse their other Officers, and also a President pro tempore, in the Absence of the Vice President, or when he shall exercise the Office of President of the United States.

6: The Senate shall have the sole Power to try all Impeachments. When sitting for that Purpose, they shall be on Oath or Affirmation. When the President of the United States is tried, the Chief Justice shall preside: And no Person shall be convicted without the Concurrence of two thirds of the Members present.

7: Judgment in Cases of impeachment shall not extend further than to removal from Office, and disqualification to hold and enjoy any Office of honor, Trust or Profit under the United States: but the Party convicted shall nevertheless be liable and subject to Indictment, Trial, Judgment and Punishment, according to Law.

Section 4

1: The Times, Places and Manner of holding Elections for Senators and Representatives, shall be prescribed in each State by the Legislature thereof; but the Congress may at any time by Law make or alter such Regulations, except as to the Places of chusing Senators.

2: The Congress shall assemble at least once in every Year, and such Meeting shall be on the first Monday in December,5 unless they shall by Law appoint a different Day.

Section 5

1: Each House shall be the Judge of the Elections, Returns and Qualifications of its own Members, and a Majority of each shall constitute a Quorum to do Business; but a smaller Number may adjourn from day to day, and may be authorized to compel the Attendance of absent Members, in such Manner, and under such Penalties as each House may provide.

2: Each House may determine the Rules of its Proceedings, punish its Members for disorderly Behaviour, and, with the Concurrence of two thirds, expel a Member.

3: Each House shall keep a Journal of its Proceedings, and from time to time publish the same, excepting such Parts as may in their Judgment require Secrecy; and the Yeas and Nays of the Members of either House on any question shall, at the Desire of one fifth of those Present, be entered on the Journal.

4: Neither House, during the Session of Congress, shall, without the Consent of the other, adjourn for more than three days, nor to any other Place than that in which the two Houses shall be sitting.

Section 6

1: The Senators and Representatives shall receive a Compensation for their Services, to be ascertained by Law, and paid out of the Treasury of the United States.6 They shall in all Cases, except Treason, Felony and Breach of the Peace, be privileged from Arrest during their Attendance at the Session of their respective Houses, and in going to and returning from the same; and for any Speech or Debate in either House, they shall not be questioned in any other Place.

2: No Senator or Representative shall, during the Time for which he was elected, be appointed to any civil Office under the Authority of the United States, which shall have been created, or the Emoluments whereof shall have been encreased during such time; and no Person holding any Office under the United States, shall be a Member of either House during his Continuance in Office.

Section 7

1: All Bills for raising Revenue shall originate in the House of Representatives; but the Senate may propose or concur with Amendments as on other Bills.

2: Every Bill which shall have passed the House of Representatives and the Senate, shall, before it become a Law, be presented to the President of the United States; If he approve he shall sign it, but if not he shall return it, with his Objections to that House in which it shall have originated, who shall enter the Objections at large on their Journal, and proceed to reconsider it. If after such Reconsideration two thirds of that House shall agree to pass the Bill, it shall be sent, together with the Objections, to the other House, by which it shall likewise be reconsidered, and if approved by two thirds of that House, it shall become a Law. But in all such Cases the Votes of both Houses shall be determined by yeas and Nays, and the Names of the Persons voting for and against the Bill shall be entered on the Journal of each House respectively. If any Bill shall not be returned by the President within ten Days (Sundays excepted) after it shall have been presented to him, the Same shall be a Law, in like Manner as if he had signed it, unless the Congress by their Adjournment prevent its Return, in which Case it shall not be a Law.

3: Every Order, Resolution, or Vote to which the Concurrence of the Senate and House of Representatives may be necessary (except on a question of Adjournment) shall be presented to the President of the United States; and before the Same shall take Effect, shall be approved by him, or being disapproved by him, shall be repassed by two thirds of the Senate and House of Representatives, according to the Rules and Limitations prescribed in the Case of a Bill.

Section 8

1: The Congress shall have Power To lay and collect Taxes, Duties, Imposts and Excises, to pay the Debts and provide for the common Defence and general Welfare of the United States; but all Duties, Imposts and Excises shall be uniform throughout the United States;

2: To borrow Money on the credit of the United States;

3: To regulate Commerce with foreign Nations, and among the several States, and with the Indian Tribes;

4: To establish an uniform Rule of Naturalization, and uniform Laws on the subject of Bankruptcies throughout the United States;

5: To coin Money, regulate the Value thereof, and of foreign Coin, and fix the Standard of Weights and Measures;

6: To provide for the Punishment of counterfeiting the Securities and current Coin of the United States;

7: To establish Post Offices and post Roads;

8: To promote the Progress of Science and useful Arts, by securing for limited Times to Authors and Inventors the exclusive Right to their respective Writings and Discoveries;

9: To constitute Tribunals inferior to the supreme Court;

10: To define and punish Piracies and Felonies committed on the high Seas, and Offences against the Law of Nations;

11: To declare War, grant Letters of Marque and Reprisal, and make Rules concerning Captures on Land and Water;

12: To raise and support Armies, but no Appropriation of Money to that Use shall be for a longer Term than two Years;

13: To provide and maintain a Navy;

14: To make Rules for the Government and Regulation of the land and naval Forces;

15: To provide for calling forth the Militia to execute the Laws of the Union, suppress Insurrections and repel Invasions;

16: To provide for organizing, arming, and disciplining, the Militia, and for governing such Part of them as may be employed in the Service of the United States, reserving to the States respectively, the Appointment of the Officers, and the Authority of training the Militia according to the discipline prescribed by Congress;

17: To exercise exclusive Legislation in all Cases whatsoever, over such District (not exceeding ten Miles square) as may, by Cession of particular States, and the Acceptance of Congress, become the Seat of the Government of the United

States, and to exercise like Authority over all Places purchased by the Consent of the Legislature of the State in which the Same shall be, for the Erection of Forts, Magazines, Arsenals, dock-Yards, and other needful Buildings;—And

18: To make all Laws which shall be necessary and proper for carrying into Execution the foregoing Powers, and all other Powers vested by this Constitution in the Government of the United States, or in any Department or Officer thereof.

Section 9

1: The Migration or Importation of such Persons as any of the States now existing shall think proper to admit, shall not be prohibited by the Congress prior to the Year one thousand eight hundred and eight, but a Tax or duty may be imposed on such Importation, not exceeding ten dollars for each Person.

2: The Privilege of the Writ of Habeas Corpus shall not be suspended, unless when in Cases of Rebellion or Invasion the public Safety may require it.

3: No Bill of Attainder or ex post facto Law shall be passed.

4: No Capitation, or other direct, Tax shall be laid, unless in Proportion to the Census or Enumeration herein before directed to be taken.7

5: No Tax or Duty shall be laid on Articles exported from any State.

6: No Preference shall be given by any Regulation of Commerce or Revenue to the Ports of one State over those of another: nor shall Vessels bound to, or from, one State, be obliged to enter, clear, or pay Duties in another.

7: No Money shall be drawn from the Treasury, but in Consequence of Appropriations made by Law; and a regular Statement and Account of the Receipts and Expenditures of all public Money shall be published from time to time.

8: No Title of Nobility shall be granted by the United States: And no Person holding any Office of Profit or Trust under them, shall, without the Consent of the Congress, accept of any present, Emolument, Office, or Title, of any kind whatever, from any King, Prince, or foreign State.

Section 10

1: No State shall enter into any Treaty, Alliance, or Confederation; grant Letters of Marque and Reprisal; coin Money; emit Bills of Credit; make any Thing but gold and silver Coin a Tender in Payment of Debts; pass any Bill of Attainder, ex post facto Law, or Law impairing the Obligation of Contracts, or grant any Title of Nobility.

2: No State shall, without the Consent of the Congress, lay any Imposts or Duties on Imports or Exports, except what may be absolutely necessary for executing it's inspection Laws: and the net Produce of all Duties and Imposts, laid by any State on Imports or Exports, shall be for the Use of the Treasury of the United States; and all such Laws shall be subject to the Revision and Controul of the Congress.

3: No State shall, without the Consent of Congress, lay any Duty of Tonnage, keep Troops, or Ships of War in time of Peace, enter into any Agreement or Compact with another State, or with a foreign Power, or engage in War, unless actually invaded, or in such imminent Danger as will not admit of delay.

Article II (Article 2 - Executive)

Section 1

1: The executive Power shall be vested in a President of the United States of America. He shall hold his Office during the Term of four Years, and, together with the Vice President, chosen for the same Term, be elected, as follows

2: Each State shall appoint, in such Manner as the Legislature thereof may direct, a Number of Electors, equal to the whole Number of Senators and Representatives to which the State may be entitled in the Congress: but no Senator or Representative, or Person holding an Office of Trust or Profit under the United States, shall be appointed an Elector.

3: The Electors shall meet in their respective States, and vote by Ballot for two Persons, of whom one at least shall not be an Inhabitant of the same State with themselves. And they shall make a List of all the Persons voted for, and of the Number of Votes for each; which List they shall sign and certify, and transmit sealed to the Seat of the Government of the United States, directed to the President of the Senate. The President of the

Senate shall, in the Presence of the Senate and House of Representatives, open all the Certificates, and the Votes shall then be counted. The Person having the greatest Number of Votes shall be the President, if such Number be a Majority of the whole Number of Electors appointed; and if there be more than one who have such Majority, and have an equal Number of Votes, then the House of Representatives shall immediately chuse by Ballot one of them for President; and if no Person have a Majority, then from the five highest on the List the said House shall in like Manner chuse the President. But in chusing the President, the Votes shall be taken by States, the Representation from each State having one Vote; A quorum for this Purpose shall consist of a Member or Members from two thirds of the States, and a Majority of all the States shall be necessary to a Choice. In every Case, after the Choice of the President, the Person having the greatest Number of Votes of the Electors shall be the Vice President. But if there should remain two or more who have equal Votes, the Senate shall chuse from them by Ballot the Vice President.8

4: The Congress may determine the Time of chusing the Electors, and the Day on which they shall give their Votes; which Day shall be the same throughout the United States.

5: No Person except a natural born Citizen, or a Citizen of the United States, at the time of the Adoption of this Constitution, shall be eligible to the Office of President; neither shall any Person be eligible to that Office who shall not have attained to the Age of thirty five Years, and been fourteen Years a Resident within the United States.

6: In Case of the Removal of the President from Office, or of his Death, Resignation, or Inability to discharge the Powers and Duties of the said Office,9 the Same shall devolve on the VicePresident, and the Congress may by Law provide for the Case of Removal, Death, Resignation or Inability, both of the President and Vice President, declaring what Officer shall then act as President, and such Officer shall act accordingly, until the Disability be removed, or a President shall be elected.

7: The President shall, at stated Times, receive for his Services, a Compensation, which shall neither be encreased nor diminished during the Period for which he shall have been elected, and he shall not receive within that Period any other Emolument from the United States, or any of them.

8: Before he enter on the Execution of his Office, he shall take the following Oath or Affirmation:—"I do solemnly swear (or affirm) that I will faithfully execute the Office of President of the United States, and will to the best of my Ability, preserve, protect and defend the Constitution of the United States."

Section 2

1: The President shall be Commander in Chief of the Army and Navy of the United States, and of the Militia of the several States, when called into the actual Service of the United States; he may require the Opinion, in writing, of the principal Officer in each of the executive Departments, upon any Subject relating to the Duties of their respective Offices, and he shall have Power to grant Reprieves and Pardons for Offences against the United States, except in Cases of Impeachment.

2: He shall have Power, by and with the Advice and Consent of the Senate, to make Treaties, provided two thirds of the Senators present concur; and he shall nominate, and by and with the Advice and Consent of the Senate, shall appoint Ambassadors, other public Ministers and Consuls, Judges of the supreme Court, and all other Officers of the United States, whose Appointments are not herein otherwise provided for, and which shall be established by Law: but the Congress may by Law vest the Appointment of such inferior Officers, as they think proper, in the President alone, in the Courts of Law, or in the Heads of Departments.

3: The President shall have Power to fill up all Vacancies that may happen during the Recess of the Senate, by granting Commissions which shall expire at the End of their next Session.

Section 3

He shall from time to time give to the Congress Information of the State of the Union, and recommend to their Consideration such

Measures as he shall judge necessary and expedient; he may, on extraordinary Occasions, convene both Houses, or either of them, and in Case of Disagreement between them, with Respect to the Time of Adjournment, he may adjourn them to such Time as he shall think proper; he shall receive Ambassadors and other public Ministers; he shall take Care that the Laws be faithfully executed, and shall Commission all the Officers of the United States.

Section 4

The President, Vice President and all civil Officers of the United States, shall be removed from Office on Impeachment for, and Conviction of, Treason, Bribery, or other high Crimes and Misdemeanors.

Article III (Article 3 - Judicial)

Section 1

The judicial Power of the United States, shall be vested in one supreme Court, and in such inferior Courts as the Congress may from time to time ordain and establish. The Judges, both of the supreme and inferior Courts, shall hold their Offices during good Behaviour, and shall, at stated Times, receive for their Services, a Compensation, which shall not be diminished during their Continuance in Office.

Section 2

1: The judicial Power shall extend to all Cases, in Law and Equity, arising under this Constitution, the Laws of the United States, and Treaties made, or which shall be made, under their Authority;—to all Cases affecting Ambassadors, other public Ministers and Consuls;—to all Cases of admiralty and maritime Jurisdiction;—to Controversies to which the United States shall be a Party;—to Controversies between two or more States;—between a State and Citizens of another State;10 —between Citizens of different States, —between Citizens of the same State claiming Lands under Grants of different States, and between a State, or the Citizens thereof, and foreign States, Citizens or Subjects.

2: In all Cases affecting Ambassadors, other public Ministers and Consuls, and those in which a State shall be Party, the supreme Court shall have original Jurisdiction. In all the other Cases before mentioned, the supreme Court shall have appellateJurisdiction, both as to Law and Fact, with such Exceptions, and under such Regulations as the Congress shall make.

3: The Trial of all Crimes, except in Cases of Impeachment, shall be by Jury; and such Trial shall be held in the State where the said Crimes shall have been committed; but when not committed within any State, the Trial shall be at such Place or Places as the Congress may by Law have directed.

Section 3

1: Treason against the United States, shall consist only in levying War against them, or in adhering to their Enemies, giving them Aid and Comfort. No Person shall be convicted of Treason unless on the Testimony of two Witnesses to the same overt Act, or on Confession in open Court.

2: The Congress shall have Power to declare the Punishment of Treason, but no Attainder of Treason shall work Corruption of Blood, or Forfeiture except during the Life of the Person attainted.

Article IV (Article 4 - States' Relations)

Section 1

Full Faith and Credit shall be given in each State to the public Acts, Records, and judicial Proceedings of every other State. And the Congress may by general Laws prescribe the Manner in which such Acts, Records and Proceedings shall be proved, and the Effect thereof.

Section 2

1: The Citizens of each State shall be entitled to all Privileges and Immunities of Citizens in the several States.

2: A Person charged in any State with Treason, Felony, or other Crime, who shall flee from Justice, and be found in another State, shall on Demand of the executive Authority of the State from which he fled, be delivered up, to be removed to the State having Jurisdiction of the Crime.

3: No Person held to Service or Labour in one State, under the Laws thereof, escaping into another, shall, in Consequence of any Law or Regulation therein, be discharged from such Service or Labour, but shall be delivered up on

Claim of the Party to whom such Service or Labour may be due.11

Section 3

1: New States may be admitted by the Congress into this Union; but no new State shall be formed or erected within the Jurisdiction of any other State; nor any State be formed by the Junction of two or more States, or Parts of States, without the Consent of the Legislatures of the States concerned as well as of the Congress.

2: The Congress shall have Power to dispose of and make all needful Rules and Regulations respecting the Territory or other Property belonging to the United States; and nothing in this Constitution shall be so construed as to Prejudice any Claims of the United States, or of any particular State.

Section 4

The United States shall guarantee to every State in this Union a Republican Form of Government, and shall protect each of them against Invasion; and on Application of the Legislature, or of the Executive (when the Legislature cannot be convened) against domestic Violence.

Article V (Article 5 - Mode of Amendment)

The Congress, whenever two thirds of both Houses shall deem it necessary, shall propose Amendments to this Constitution, or, on the Application of the Legislatures of two thirds of the several States, shall call a Convention for proposing Amendments, which, in either Case, shall be valid to all Intents and Purposes, as Part of this Constitution, when ratified by the Legislatures of three fourths of the several States, or by Conventions in three fourths thereof, as the one or the other Mode of Ratification may be proposed by the Congress; Provided that no Amendment which may be made prior to the Year One thousand eight hundred and eight shall in any Manner affect the first and fourth Clauses in the Ninth Section of the first Article; and that no State, without its Consent, shall be deprived of its equal Suffrage in the Senate.

Article VI (Article 6 - Prior Debts, National Supremacy, Oaths of Office)

1: All Debts contracted and Engagements entered into, before the Adoption of this Constitution, shall be as valid against the United States under this Constitution, as under the Confederation.

2: This Constitution, and the Laws of the United States which shall be made in Pursuance thereof; and all Treaties made, or which shall be made, under the Authority of the United States, shall be the supreme Law of the Land; and the Judges in every State shall be bound thereby, any Thing in the Constitution or Laws of any State to the Contrary notwithstanding.

3: The Senators and Representatives before mentioned, and the Members of the several State Legislatures, and all executive and judicial Officers, both of the United States and of the several States, shall be bound by Oath or Affirmation, to support this Constitution; but no religious Test shall ever be required as a Qualification to any Office or public Trust under the United States.

Article VII (Article 7 - Ratification)

The Ratification of the Conventions of nine States, shall be sufficient for the Establishment of this Constitution between the States so ratifying the Same.

The Word "the", being interlined between the seventh and eight Lines of the first Page, The Word "Thirty" being partly written on an Erazure in the fifteenth Line of the first Page. The Words "is tried" being interlined between the thirty second and thirty third Lines of the first Page and the Word "the" being interlined between the forty third and forty fourth Lines of the second Page.

done in Convention by the Unanimous Consent of the States present the Seventeenth Day of September in the Year of our Lord one thousand seven hundred and Eighty seven and of the Independence of the United States of America the Twelfth In witness whereof We have hereunto subscribed our Names,

[Signatures omitted for space considerations]

[Articles/Amendments][294]

Article [I] (Amendment 1 - Freedom of expression and religion) 13

Congress shall make no law respecting an establishment of religion, or prohibiting the free exercise thereof; or abridging the freedom of speech, or of the press; or the right of the people peaceably to assemble, and to petition the Government for a redress of grievances.

Article [II] (Amendment 2 - Bearing Arms)

A well regulated Militia, being necessary to the security of a free State, the right of the people to keep and bear Arms, shall not be infringed.

Article [III] (Amendment 3 - Quartering Soldiers)

No Soldier shall, in time of peace be quartered in any house, without the consent of the Owner, nor in time of war, but in a manner to be prescribed by law.

Article [IV] (Amendment 4 - Search and Seizure)

The right of the people to be secure in their persons, houses, papers, and effects, against unreasonable searches and seizures, shall not be violated, and no Warrants shall issue, but upon probable cause, supported by Oath or affirmation, and particularly describing the place to be searched, and the persons or things to be seized.

Article [V] (Amendment 5 - Rights of Persons)

No person shall be held to answer for a capital, or otherwise infamous crime, unless on a presentment or indictment of a Grand Jury, except in cases arising in the land or naval forces, or in the Militia, when in actual service in time of War or public danger; nor shall any person be subject for the same offence to be twice put in jeopardy of life or limb; nor shall be compelled in any criminal case to be a witness against himself, nor be deprived of life, liberty, or property, without due process of law; nor shall private property be taken for public use, without just compensation.

Article [VI] (Amendment 6 - Rights of Accused in Criminal Prosecutions)

In all criminal prosecutions, the accused shall enjoy the right to a speedy and public trial, by an impartial jury of the State and district wherein the crime shall have been committed, which district shall have been previously ascertained by law, and to be informed of the nature and cause of the accusation; to be confronted with the witnesses against him; to have compulsory process for obtaining witnesses in his favor, and to have the Assistance of Counsel for his defence.

Article [VII] (Amendment 7 - Civil Trials)

In Suits at common law, where the value in controversy shall exceed twenty dollars, the right of trial by jury shall be preserved, and no fact tried by a jury, shall be otherwise re-examined in any Court of the United States, than according to the rules of the common law.

Article [VIII] (Amendment 8 - Further Guarantees in Criminal Cases)

Excessive bail shall not be required, nor excessive fines imposed, nor cruel and unusual punishments inflicted.

Article [IX] (Amendment 9 - Unenumerated Rights)

The enumeration in the Constitution, of certain rights, shall not be construed to deny or disparage others retained by the people.

Article [X] (Amendment 10 - Reserved Powers)

The powers not delegated to the United States by the Constitution, nor prohibited by it to the States, are reserved to the States respectively, or to the people.

Attest,

John Beckley, Clerk of the House of Representatives.

Sam. A. Otis Secretary of the Senate.

Frederick Augustus Muhlenberg Speaker of the House of Representatives.

John Adams, Vice-President of the United States, and President of the Senate.

---

[294] http://constitutionus.com/#billofrights Note that some annotations have been added for the sake of clarity.

(end of the Bill of Rights)

[Article XI] (Amendment 11 - Suits Against States)

The Judicial power of the United States shall not be construed to extend to any suit in law or equity, commenced or prosecuted against one of the United States by Citizens of another State, or by Citizens or Subjects of any Foreign State. ratified #11 affects 10

[Article XII] (Amendment 12 - Election of President)

The Electors shall meet in their respective states, and vote by ballot for President and Vice-President, one of whom, at least, shall not be an inhabitant of the same state with themselves; they shall name in their ballots the person voted for as President, and in distinct ballots the person voted for as Vice-President, and they shall make distinct lists of all persons voted for as President, and of all persons voted for as Vice-President, and of the number of votes for each, which lists they shall sign and certify, and transmit sealed to the seat of the government of the United States, directed to the President of the Senate;—The President of the Senate shall, in the presence of the Senate and House of Representatives, open all the certificates and the votes shall then be counted;—The person having the greatest number of votes for President, shall be the President, if such number be a majority of the whole number of Electors appointed; and if no person have such majority, then from the persons having the highest numbers not exceeding three on the list of those voted for as President, the House of Representatives shall choose immediately, by ballot, the President. But in choosing the President, the votes shall be taken by states, the representation from each state having one vote; a quorum for this purpose shall consist of a member or members from two-thirds of the states, and a majority of all the states shall be necessary to a choice. And if the House of Representatives shall not choose a President whenever the right of choice shall devolve upon them, before the fourth day of March next following, then the Vice-President shall act as President, as in the case of the death or other constitutional disability of the President.14 —

The person having the greatest number of votes as Vice-President, shall be the Vice-President, if such number be a majority of the whole number of Electors appointed, and if no person have a majority, then from the two highest numbers on the list, the Senate shall choose the Vice-President; a quorum for the purpose shall consist of two-thirds of the whole number of Senators, and a majority of the whole number shall be necessary to a choice. But no person constitutionally ineligible to the office of President shall be eligible to that of Vice-President of the United States.   ratified #12 affects 8

Article XIII (Amendment 13 - Slavery and Involuntary Servitude)

Neither slavery nor involuntary servitude, except as a punishment for crime whereof the party shall have been duly convicted, shall exist within the United States, or any place subject to their jurisdiction. affects 11

Congress shall have power to enforce this article by appropriate legislation. ratified #13

Article XIV (Amendment 14 - Rights Guaranteed: Privileges and Immunities of Citizenship, Due Process, and Equal Protection)

1: All persons born or naturalized in the United States, and subject to the jurisdiction thereof, are citizens of the United States and of the State wherein they reside. No State shall make or enforce any law which shall abridge the privileges or immunities of citizens of the United States; nor shall any State deprive any person of life, liberty, or property, without due process of law; nor deny to any person within its jurisdiction the equal protection of the laws.

2: Representatives shall be apportioned among the several States according to their respective numbers, counting the whole number of persons in each State, excluding Indians not taxed. But when the right to vote at any election for the choice of electors for President and Vice President of the United States, Representatives in Congress, the Executive and Judicial officers of a State, or the members of the Legislature thereof, is denied to any of the male inhabitants of such State, being twenty-one years of age,15 and citizens of the United States, or in any way abridged, except for participation in rebellion, or other crime, the basis of representation therein shall be reduced in the proportion which the number of such male citizens shall bear to the whole number of male citizens twenty-one years of age in such State. affects 2

3: No person shall be a Senator or Representative in Congress, or elector of President and Vice President, or hold any office, civil or military, under the United States, or under any State, who, having previously taken an oath, as a member of Congress, or as an officer of the United States, or as a member of any State legislature, or as an executive or judicial officer of any State, to support the Constitution of the United States, shall have engaged in insurrection or rebellion against the same, or given aid or comfort to the enemies thereof. But Congress may by a vote of two-thirds of each House, remove such disability.

4: The validity of the public debt of the United States, authorized by law, including debts incurred for payment of pensions and bounties for services in suppressing insurrection or rebellion, shall not be questioned. But neither the United States nor any State shall assume or pay any debt or obligation incurred in aid of insurrection or rebellion against the United States, or any claim for the loss or emancipation of any slave; but all such debts, obligations and claims shall be held illegal and void.

5: The Congress shall have power to enforce, by appropriate legislation, the provisions of this article. ratified #14

Article XV (Amendment 15 - Rights of Citizens to Vote)

The right of citizens of the United States to vote shall not be denied or abridged by the United States or by any State on account of race, color, or previous condition of servitude.

The Congress shall have power to enforce this article by appropriate legislation.   ratified #15

Article XVI (Amendment 16 - Income Tax)

The Congress shall have power to lay and collect taxes on incomes, from whatever source derived, without apportionment among the several States, and without regard to any census or enumeration. ratified #16   affects 2

[Article XVII] (Amendment 17 - Popular Election of Senators)

1: The Senate of the United States shall be composed of two Senators from each State, elected by the people thereof, for six years; and each Senator shall have one vote. The electors in each State shall have the qualifications requisite for electors of the most numerous branch of the State legislatures. affects 3

2: When vacancies happen in the representation of any State in the Senate, the executive authority of such State shall issue writs of election to fill such vacancies: Provided, That the legislature of any State may empower the executive thereof to make temporary appointments until the people fill the vacancies by election as the legislature may direct. affects 4

3: This amendment shall not be so construed as to affect the election or term of any Senator chosen before it becomes valid as part of the Constitution. ratified #17

Article [XVIII] (Amendment 18 - Prohibition of Intoxicating Liquors)16

1: After one year from the ratification of this article the manufacture, sale, or transportation of intoxicating liquors within, the importation thereof into, or the exportation thereof from the United States and all territory subject to the jurisdiction thereof for beverage purposes is hereby prohibited.

2: The Congress and the several States shall have concurrent power to enforce this article by appropriate legislation.

3: This article shall be inoperative unless it shall have been ratified as an amendment to the Constitution by the legislatures of the several States, as provided in the Constitution, within seven years from the date of the submission hereof to the States by the Congress. ratified #18

Article [XIX] (Amendment 19 - Women's Suffrage Rights)

The right of citizens of the United States to vote shall not be denied or abridged by the United States or by any State on account of sex. affects 15

Congress shall have power to enforce this article by appropriate legislation. ratified #19

Article [XX] (Amendment 20 - Terms of President, Vice President, Members of Congress: Presidential Vacancy)

1: The terms of the President and Vice President shall end at noon on the 20th day of January, and the terms of Senators and Representatives at noon on the 3d day of January, of the years in which such terms would have ended if this article had not been ratified; and the terms of their successors shall then begin. affects 5

2: The Congress shall assemble at least once in every year, and such meeting shall begin at noon on the 3d day of January, unless they shall by law appoint a different day. affects 5

3: If, at the time fixed for the beginning of the term of the President, the President elect shall have died, the Vice President elect shall become President. If a President shall not have been chosen before the time fixed for the beginning of his term, or if the President elect shall have failed to qualify, then the Vice President elect shall act as President until a President shall have qualified; and the Congress may by law provide for the case wherein neither a President elect nor a Vice President elect shall have qualified, declaring who shall then act as President, or the manner in which one who is to act shall be selected, and such person shall act accordingly until a President or Vice President shall have qualified. affects 9 affects 14

4: The Congress may by law provide for the case of the death of any of the persons from whom the House of Representatives may choose a President whenever the right of choice shall have devolved upon them, and for the case of the death of any of the persons from whom the Senate may choose a Vice President whenever the right of choice shall have devolved upon them. affects 9

5: Sections 1 and 2 shall take effect on the 15th day of October following the ratification of this article.

6: This article shall be inoperative unless it shall have been ratified as an amendment to the Constitution by the legislatures of three-fourths of the several States within seven years from the date of its submission. ratified #20

Article [XXI] (Amendment 21 - Repeal of Eighteenth Amendment)

1: The eighteenth article of amendment to the Constitution of the United States is hereby repealed. affects 16

2: The transportation or importation into any State, Territory, or possession of the United States for delivery or use therein of intoxicating liquors, in violation of the laws thereof, is hereby prohibited.

3: This article shall be inoperative unless it shall have been ratified as an amendment to the Constitution by conventions in the several States, as provided in the Constitution, within seven years from the date of the submission hereof to the States by the Congress. ratified #21

Amendment XXII (Amendment 22 - Presidential Tenure)

1: No person shall be elected to the office of the President more than twice, and no person who has held the office of President, or acted as President, for more than two years of a term to which some other person was elected President shall be elected to the office of the President more than once. But this article shall not apply to any person holding the office of President when this article was proposed by the Congress, and shall not prevent any person who may be holding the office of President, or acting as President, during the term within which this article becomes operative from holding the office of President or acting as President during the remainder of such term.

2: This article shall be inoperative unless it shall have been ratified as an amendment to the Constitution by the legislatures of three-fourths of the several states within seven years from the date of its submission to the states by the Congress. ratified #22

Amendment XXIII (Amendment 23 - Presidential Electors for the District of Columbia)

1: The District constituting the seat of government of the United States shall appoint in such manner as the Congress may direct: A number of electors of President and Vice President equal to the whole number of Senators and Representatives in Congress to which the District would be entitled if it were a state, but in no event more than the least populous state; they shall be in addition to those appointed by the states, but they shall be considered, for the purposes of the election of President and Vice President, to be electors appointed by a state; and they shall meet in the District and perform such duties as provided by the twelfth article of amendment.

2: The Congress shall have power to enforce this article by appropriate legislation.   ratified #23

Amendment XXIV (Amendment 24 - Abolition of the Poll Tax Qualification in Federal Elections)

1. The right of citizens of the United States to vote in any primary or other election for President or Vice President, for electors for President or Vice President, or for Senator or Representative in Congress, shall not be denied or abridged by the United States or any state by reason of failure to pay any poll tax or other tax.

2. The Congress shall have power to enforce this article by appropriate legislation.   ratified #24

Amendment XXV affects 9 (Amendment 25 - Presidential Vacancy, Disability, and Inability)

1: In case of the removal of the President from office or of his death or resignation, the Vice President shall become President.

2: Whenever there is a vacancy in the office of the Vice President, the President shall nominate a Vice President who shall take office upon confirmation by a majority vote of both Houses of Congress.

3: Whenever the President transmits to the President pro tempore of the Senate and the Speaker of the House of Representatives his written declaration that he is unable to discharge the powers and duties of his office, and until he transmits to them a written declaration to the contrary, such powers and duties shall be discharged by the Vice President as Acting President.

4: Whenever the Vice President and a majority of either the principal officers of the executive departments or of such other body as Congress may by law provide, transmit to the President pro tempore of the Senate and the

Speaker of the House of Representatives their written declaration that the President is unable to discharge the powers and duties of his office, the Vice President shall immediately assume the powers and duties of the office as Acting President.

Thereafter, when the President transmits to the President pro tempore of the Senate and the Speaker of the House of Representatives his written declaration that no inability exists, he shall resume the powers and duties of his office unless the Vice President and a majority of either the principal officers of the executive department or of such other body as Congress may by law provide, transmit within four days to the President pro tempore of the Senate and the Speaker of the House of Representatives their written declaration that the President is unable to discharge the powers and duties of his office. Thereupon Congress shall decide the issue, assembling within forty-eight hours for that purpose if not in session. If the Congress, within twenty-one days after receipt of the latter written declaration, or, if Congress is not in session, within twenty-one days after Congress is required to assemble, determines by two-thirds vote of both Houses that the President is unable to discharge the powers and duties of his office, the Vice President shall continue to discharge the same as Acting President; otherwise, the President shall resume the powers and duties of his office.   ratified #25

Amendment XXVI (Amendment 26 - Reduction of Voting Age Qualification)

1: The right of citizens of the United States, who are 18 years of age or older, to vote, shall not be denied or abridged by the United States or any state on account of age. affects 15

2: The Congress shall have the power to enforce this article by appropriate legislation. ratified #26

Amendment XXVII (Amendment 27 - Congressional Pay Limitation)

No law varying the compensation for the services of the Senators and Representatives shall take effect until an election of Representatives shall have intervened.   ratified #27

The Federalist Papers are a collection of 85 letters written under the pen-name, Publius. The actual authors were Alexander Hamilton, James Madison, and John Jay. Originally appearing in newspapers (often several times each week) between October 1787 and August 1788, they were later collected and published in two volumes in 1788. Meant to justify the ratification of the proposed U.S. Constitution, they are widely regarded as the best source for the intentions of the drafters of the Constitution. Of the 85 letters, six appear below: 1, 10, 39, 51, 68, and 78. These letters address several key themes including the threat of factions, the value of republican forms of governments, the necessity of "checks and balances," the independence of the Judiciary, and the use of the Electoral College to elect the President of the United States.

The *Federalist Papers*[295]
(Numbers 1, 10, 39, 51, 68, and 78)

Federalist № 1

General Introduction

To the People of the State of New York:

After an unequivocal experience of the inefficacy of the subsisting federal government, you are called upon to deliberate on a new Constitution for the United States of America. The subject speaks its own importance; comprehending in its consequences nothing less than the existence of the union, the safety and welfare of the parts of which it is composed, the fate of an empire in many respects the most interesting in the world. It has been frequently remarked that it seems to have been reserved to the people of this country, by their conduct and example, to decide the important question, whether societies of men are really capable or not of establishing good government from reflection and choice, or whether they are forever destined to depend for their political constitutions on accident and force. If there be any truth in the remark, the crisis at which we are arrived may with propriety be regarded as the era in which that decision is to be made; and a wrong election of the part we shall act may, in this view, deserve to be considered as the general misfortune of mankind.

This idea will add the inducements of philanthropy to those of patriotism, to heighten the solicitude which all considerate and good

men must feel for the event. Happy will it be if our choice should be directed by a judicious estimate of our true interests, unperplexed and unbiased by considerations not connected with the public good. But this is a thing more ardently to be wished than seriously to be expected. The plan offered to our deliberations affects too many particular interests, innovates upon too many local institutions, not to involve in its discussion a variety of objects foreign to its merits, and of views, passions and prejudices little favorable to the discovery of truth.

Among the most formidable of the obstacles which the new Constitution will have to encounter may readily be distinguished the obvious interest of a certain class of men in every State to resist all changes which may hazard a diminution of the power, emolument, and consequence of the offices they hold under the State establishments; and the perverted ambition of another class of men, who will either hope to aggrandize themselves by the confusions of their country, or will flatter themselves with fairer prospects of elevation from the subdivision of the empire into several partial confederacies than from its union under one government.

It is not, however, my design to dwell upon observations of this nature. I am well aware that it would be disingenuous to resolve indiscriminately the opposition of any set of men (merely because their situations might subject them to suspicion) into interested or ambitious views. Candor will oblige us to admit that even

---

[295] http://federali.st/

such men may be actuated by upright intentions; and it cannot be doubted that much of the opposition which has made its appearance, or may hereafter make its appearance, will spring from sources, blameless at least, if not respectable—the honest errors of minds led astray by preconceived jealousies and fears. So numerous indeed and so powerful are the causes which serve to give a false bias to the judgment, that we, upon many occasions, see wise and good men on the wrong as well as on the right side of questions of the first magnitude to society. This circumstance, if duly attended to, would furnish a lesson of moderation to those who are ever so much persuaded of their being in the right in any controversy. And a further reason for caution, in this respect, might be drawn from the reflection that we are not always sure that those who advocate the truth are influenced by purer principles than their antagonists. Ambition, avarice, personal animosity, party opposition, and many other motives not more laudable than these, are apt to operate as well upon those who support as those who oppose the right side of a question. Were there not even these inducements to moderation, nothing could be more ill-judged than that intolerant spirit which has, at all times, characterized political parties. For in politics, as in religion, it is equally absurd to aim at making proselytes by fire and sword. Heresies in either can rarely be cured by persecution.

And yet, however just these sentiments will be allowed to be, we have already sufficient indications that it will happen in this as in all former cases of great national discussion. A torrent of angry and malignant passions will be let loose. To judge from the conduct of the opposite parties, we shall be led to conclude that they will mutually hope to evince the justness of their opinions, and to increase the number of their converts by the loudness of their declamations and the bitterness of their invectives. An enlightened zeal for the energy and efficiency of government will be stigmatized as the offspring of a temper fond of despotic power and hostile to the principles of liberty. An over-scrupulous jealousy of danger to the rights of the people, which is more commonly the fault of the head than of the heart, will be represented as mere pretense and artifice, the stale bait for popularity at the expense of the public good. It will be forgotten, on the one hand, that jealousy is the usual concomitant of love, and that the noble enthusiasm of liberty is apt to be infected with a spirit of narrow and illiberal distrust. On the other hand, it will be equally forgotten that the vigor of government is essential to the security of liberty; that, in the contemplation of a sound and well-informed judgment, their interest can never be separated; and that a dangerous ambition more often lurks behind the specious mask of zeal for the rights of the people than under the forbidden appearance of zeal for the firmness and efficiency of government. History will teach us that the former has been found a much more certain road to the introduction of despotism than the latter, and that of those men who have overturned the liberties of republics, the greatest number have begun their career by paying an obsequious court to the people; commencing demagogues, and ending tyrants.

In the course of the preceding observations, I have had an eye, my fellow-citizens, to putting you upon your guard against all attempts, from whatever quarter, to influence your decision in a matter of the utmost moment to your welfare, by any impressions other than those which may result from the evidence of truth. You will, no doubt, at the same time, have collected from the general scope of them, that they proceed from a source not unfriendly to the new Constitution. Yes, my countrymen, I own to you that, after having given it an attentive consideration, I am clearly of opinion it is your interest to adopt it. I am convinced that this is the safest course for your liberty, your dignity, and your happiness. I affect not reserves which I do not feel. I will not amuse you with an appearance of deliberation when I have decided. I frankly acknowledge to you my convictions, and I will freely lay before you the reasons on which they are founded. The consciousness of good intentions disdains ambiguity. I shall not, however, multiply professions on this head. My motives must remain in the depository of my own breast. My arguments will be open to all, and may be judged of by all. They shall at least be offered in a spirit which will not disgrace the cause of truth.

I propose, in a series of papers, to discuss the following interesting particulars:

- the utility of the union to your political prosperity

- the insufficiency of the present confederation to preserve that union

- the necessity of a government at least equally energetic with the one proposed, to the attainment of this object

- the conformity of the proposed constitution to the true principles of republican government

- its analogy to your own state constitution

- and lastly, the additional security which its adoption will afford to the preservation of that species of government, to liberty, and to property.

In the progress of this discussion I shall endeavor to give a satisfactory answer to all the objections which shall have made their appearance, that may seem to have any claim to your attention.

It may perhaps be thought superfluous to offer arguments to prove the utility of the union, a point, no doubt, deeply engraved on the hearts of the great body of the people in every State, and one, which it may be imagined, has no adversaries. But the fact is, that we already hear it whispered in the private circles of those who oppose the new Constitution, that the thirteen States are of too great extent for any general system, and that we must of necessity resort to separate confederacies of distinct portions of the whole.[1] This doctrine will, in all probability, be gradually propagated, till it has votaries enough to countenance an open avowal of it. For nothing can be more evident, to those who are able to take an enlarged view of the subject, than the alternative of an adoption of the new Constitution or a dismemberment of the Union. It will therefore be of use to begin by examining the advantages of that Union, the certain evils, and the probable dangers, to which every State will be exposed from its dissolution. This shall accordingly constitute the subject of my next address.

Publius. [Alexander Hamilton]

1.   The same idea, tracing the arguments to their consequences, is held out in several of the late publications against the new Constitution.

First published in the Saturday, October 27th, 1787 issue of the *Independent Journal.*

Federalist № 10
The Same Subject Continued
The Union as a Safeguard Against Domestic Faction and Insurrection

To the People of the State of New York:

Among the numerous advantages promised by a well constructed Union, none deserves to be more accurately developed than its tendency to break and control the violence of faction. The friend of popular governments never finds himself so much alarmed for their character and fate, as when he contemplates their propensity to this dangerous vice. He will not fail, therefore, to set a due value on any plan which, without violating the principles to which he is attached, provides a proper cure for it. The instability, injustice, and confusion introduced into the public councils, have, in truth, been the mortal diseases under which popular governments have everywhere perished; as they continue to be the favorite and fruitful topics from which the adversaries to liberty derive their most specious declamations. The valuable improvements made by the American constitutions on the popular models, both ancient and modern, cannot certainly be too much admired; but it would be an unwarrantable partiality, to contend that they have as effectually obviated the danger on this side, as was wished and expected. Complaints are everywhere heard from our most considerate and virtuous citizens, equally the friends of public and private faith, and of public and personal liberty, that our governments are too unstable, that the public good is disregarded in the conflicts of rival parties, and that measures are too often decided, not according to the rules of justice and the rights of the minor party, but by the superior force of an interested and overbearing majority. However anxiously we may wish that these complaints had no foundation, the evidence, of known facts will not permit us to deny that they are in some degree true. It will be found, indeed, on a candid review of our situation, that some of the distresses under which we labor have been erroneously charged on the operation of our governments; but it will be found, at the same time, that other causes will not alone account for many of our heaviest misfortunes; and, particularly, for that prevailing and increasing distrust of public engagements, and alarm for private rights, which are echoed from one end of the continent to the other. These must be chiefly, if not wholly, effects of the unsteadiness and injustice with which a factious spirit has tainted our public administrations.

By a faction, I understand a number of citizens, whether amounting to a majority or a minority of the whole, who are united and actuated by some common impulse of passion, or of interest, adversed to the rights of other citizens, or to the permanent and aggregate interests of the community.

There are two methods of curing the mischiefs of faction: the one, by removing its causes; the other, by controlling its effects.

There are again two methods of removing the causes of faction: the one, by destroying the liberty which is essential to its existence; the other, by giving to every citizen the same opinions, the same passions, and the same interests.

It could never be more truly said than of the first remedy, that it was worse than the disease. Liberty is to faction what air is to fire, an aliment without which it instantly expires. But it could not be less folly to abolish liberty, which is essential to political life, because it nourishes faction, than it would be to wish the annihilation of air, which is essential to animal life, because it imparts to fire its destructive agency.

The second expedient is as impracticable as the first would be unwise. As long as the reason of man continues fallible, and he is at liberty to exercise it, different opinions will be formed. As long as the connection subsists between his reason and his self-love, his opinions and his passions will have a reciprocal influence on each other; and the former will be objects to which the latter will attach themselves. The diversity in the faculties of men, from which the rights of property originate, is not less an insuperable obstacle to a uniformity of interests. The protection of these faculties is the first object of government. From the protection of different and unequal faculties of acquiring property, the possession of different degrees and kinds of property immediately results; and from the influence of these on the sentiments and views of the respective proprietors, ensues a division of the society into different interests and parties.

The latent causes of faction are thus sown in the nature of man; and we see them everywhere brought into different degrees of activity, according to the different circumstances of civil society. A zeal for different opinions concerning religion, concerning government, and many other points, as well of speculation as of practice; an attachment to different leaders ambitiously contending for pre-eminence and power; or to persons of other descriptions whose fortunes have been interesting to the human passions, have, in turn, divided mankind into parties, inflamed them with mutual animosity, and rendered them much more disposed to vex and oppress each other than to co-operate for their common good. So strong is this propensity of mankind to fall into mutual animosities, that where no substantial occasion presents itself, the most frivolous and fanciful distinctions have been sufficient to kindle their unfriendly passions and excite their most violent conflicts. But the most common and durable source of factions has been the various and unequal distribution of property. Those who hold and those who are without property have ever formed distinct interests in society. Those who are creditors, and those who are debtors, fall under a like discrimination. A landed interest, a manufacturing interest, a mercantile interest, a moneyed interest, with many lesser interests, grow up of necessity in civilized nations, and divide them into different classes, actuated by different sentiments and views. The regulation of these various and interfering interests forms the principal task of modern legislation, and involves the spirit of party and faction in the necessary and ordinary operations of the government.

No man is allowed to be a judge in his own cause, because his interest would certainly bias his judgment, and, not improbably, corrupt his integrity. With equal, nay with greater reason, a body of men are unfit to be both judges and parties at the same time; yet what are many of the most important acts of legislation, but so many judicial determinations, not indeed concerning the rights of single persons, but concerning the rights of large bodies of citizens? And what are the different classes of legislators but advocates and parties to the causes which they determine? Is a law proposed concerning private debts? It is a question to which the creditors are parties on one side and the debtors on the other. Justice ought to hold the balance between them. Yet the parties are, and must be, themselves the judges; and the most numerous party, or, in other words, the most powerful faction must be expected to prevail. Shall domestic manufactures be encouraged, and in what degree, by restrictions on foreign manufactures? are questions which would be differently decided by the landed and the manufacturing classes, and probably by neither with a sole regard to justice and the public good. The apportionment of taxes on the various descriptions of property is an act which seems to require the most exact impartiality; yet there is, perhaps, no legislative act in which greater opportunity and temptation are given to a predominant party to trample on the rules of justice. Every shilling with which they overburden the inferior number, is a shilling saved to their own pockets.

It is in vain to say that enlightened statesmen will be able to adjust these clashing interests, and render them all subservient to the public good. Enlightened statesmen will not always be at the helm. Nor, in many cases, can such an adjustment be made at all without taking into view indirect and remote considerations, which will rarely prevail over the immediate interest which one party may find in disregarding the rights of another or the good of the whole.

The inference to which we are brought is, that the causes of faction cannot be removed, and that relief is only to be sought in the means of controlling its effects.

If a faction consists of less than a majority, relief is supplied by the republican principle, which enables the majority to defeat its sinister views by regular vote. It may clog the administration, it may convulse the society; but it will be unable to execute and mask its violence under the forms of the Constitution. When a majority is included in a faction, the form of popular government, on the other hand, enables it to sacrifice to its ruling passion or interest both the public good and the rights of other citizens. To secure the public good and private rights against the danger of such a faction, and at the same time to preserve the spirit and the form of popular government, is then the great object to which our inquiries are directed. Let me add that it is the great desideratum by which this form of government can be rescued from the opprobrium under which it has so long labored, and be recommended to the esteem and adoption of mankind.

By what means is this object attainable? Evidently by one of two only. Either the existence of the same passion or interest in a majority at the same time must be prevented, or the majority, having such coexistent passion or interest, must be rendered, by their number and local situation, unable to concert and carry into effect schemes of oppression. If the impulse and the opportunity be suffered to coincide, we well know that neither moral nor religious motives can be relied on as an adequate control. They are not found to be such on the injustice and violence of individuals, and lose their efficacy in proportion to the number combined together, that is, in proportion as their efficacy becomes needful.

From this view of the subject it may be concluded that a pure democracy, by which I mean a society consisting of a small number of citizens, who assemble and administer the government in person, can admit of no cure for the mischiefs of faction. A common passion or interest will, in almost every case, be felt by a majority of the whole; a communication and concert result from the form of government itself; and there is nothing to check the inducements to sacrifice the weaker party or an obnoxious individual. Hence it is that such democracies have ever been spectacles of turbulence and contention; have ever been found incompatible with personal security or the rights of property; and have in general been as short in their lives as they have been violent in their deaths. Theoretic politicians, who have patronized this species of government, have erroneously supposed that by reducing mankind to a perfect equality in their political rights, they would, at the same time, be perfectly equalized and assimilated in their possessions, their opinions, and their passions.

A republic, by which I mean a government in which the scheme of representation takes place, opens a different prospect, and promises the cure for which we are seeking. Let us examine the points in which it varies from pure democracy, and we shall comprehend both the nature of the cure and the efficacy which it must derive from the Union.

The two great points of difference between a democracy and a republic are: first, the delegation of the government, in the latter, to a small number of citizens elected by the rest; secondly, the greater number of citizens, and greater sphere of country, over which the latter may be extended.

The effect of the first difference is, on the one hand, to refine and enlarge the public views, by passing them through the medium of a chosen body of citizens, whose wisdom may best discern the true interest of their country, and whose patriotism and love of justice will be least likely to sacrifice it to temporary or partial considerations. Under such a regulation, it may well happen that the public voice, pronounced by the representatives of the people, will be more consonant to the public good than if pronounced by the people themselves, convened for the purpose. On the other hand, the effect may be inverted. Men of factious tempers, of local prejudices, or of sinister designs, may, by intrigue, by corruption, or by other means, first obtain the suffrages, and then betray the interests, of the people. The question resulting is, whether small or extensive republics are more favorable to the election of proper guardians of the public weal; and it is clearly decided in favor of the latter by two obvious considerations:

In the first place, it is to be remarked that, however small the republic may be, the representatives must be raised to a certain number, in order to guard against the cabals of a few; and that, however large it may be, they must be limited to a certain number, in order to guard against the confusion of a multitude. Hence, the number of representatives in the two cases not being in proportion to that of the two constituents, and being proportionally greater in the small republic, it follows that, if the proportion of fit characters be not less in the large than in the small republic, the former will present a greater option, and consequently a greater probability of a fit choice.

In the next place, as each representative will be chosen by a greater number of citizens in the large than in the small republic, it will be more difficult for unworthy candidates to practice with success the vicious arts by which elections are too often carried; and the suffrages of the people being more free, will be more likely to centre in men who possess the most attractive merit and the most diffusive and established characters.

It must be confessed that in this, as in most other cases, there is a mean, on both sides of which inconveniences will be found to lie. By enlarging too much the number of electors, you render the representatives too little acquainted with all their local circumstances and lesser interests; as by reducing it too much, you render him unduly attached to these, and too little fit to comprehend and pursue great and national objects. The federal Constitution forms a happy combination in this respect; the great and aggregate interests being referred to the national, the local and particular to the State legislatures.

The other point of difference is, the greater number of citizens and extent of territory which may be brought within the compass of republican than of democratic government; and it is this circumstance principally which renders factious combinations less to be dreaded in the former than in the latter. The smaller the society, the fewer probably will be the distinct parties and interests composing it; the fewer the distinct parties and interests, the more frequently will a majority be found of the same party; and the smaller the number of individuals composing a majority, and the smaller the compass within which they are placed, the more easily will they concert and execute their plans of oppression. Extend the sphere, and you take in a greater variety of parties and interests; you make it less probable that a majority of the whole will have a common motive to invade the rights of other citizens; or if such a common motive exists, it will be more difficult for all who feel it to discover their own strength, and to act in unison with each other. Besides other impediments, it may be remarked that, where there is a consciousness of unjust or dishonorable purposes, communication is always checked by distrust in proportion to the number whose concurrence is necessary.

Hence, it clearly appears, that the same advantage which a republic has over a democracy, in controlling the effects of faction, is enjoyed by a large over a small republic,—is enjoyed by the Union over the States composing it. Does the advantage consist in the substitution of representatives whose enlightened views and virtuous sentiments render them superior to local prejudices and schemes of injustice? It will not be denied that the representation of the Union will be most likely to possess these requisite endowments. Does it consist in the greater security afforded by a greater variety of parties, against the event of any one party being able to outnumber and oppress the rest? In an equal degree does the increased variety of parties comprised within the Union, increase this security. Does it, in fine, consist in the greater obstacles opposed to the concert and accomplishment of the secret wishes of an unjust and interested majority? Here, again, the extent of the Union gives it the most palpable advantage.

The influence of factious leaders may kindle a flame within their particular States, but will be unable to spread a general conflagration through the other States. A religious sect may degenerate into a political faction in a part of the Confederacy; but the variety of sects dispersed over the entire face of it must secure the national councils against any danger from that source. A rage for paper money, for an abolition of debts, for an equal division of property, or for any other improper or wicked project, will be less apt to pervade the whole body of the Union than a particular member of it; in the same proportion as such a malady is more likely to taint a particular county or district, than an entire State.

In the extent and proper structure of the Union, therefore, we behold a republican remedy for the diseases most incident to republican government. And according to the degree of pleasure and pride we feel in being republicans, ought to be our zeal in cherishing the spirit and supporting the character of Federalists.

Publius. [James Madison]

First published in the Friday, November 23, 1787 issue of the *New York Packet.*

Federalist № 39

The Conformity of the Plan to Republican Principles

To the People of the State of New York:

The last paper having concluded the observations which were meant to introduce a candid survey of the plan of government reported by the convention, we now proceed to the execution of that part of our undertaking. The first question that offers itself is, whether the general form and aspect of the government be strictly republican. It is evident that no other form would be reconcilable with the genius of the people of America; with the fundamental principles of the Revolution; or with that honorable determination which animates every votary of freedom, to rest all our political experiments on the capacity of mankind for self-government. If the plan of the convention, therefore, be found to depart from the republican character, its advocates must abandon it as no longer defensible.

What, then, are the distinctive characters of the republican form? Were an answer to this question to be sought, not by recurring to principles, but in the application of the term by political writers, to the constitution of different States, no satisfactory one would ever be found. Holland, in which no particle of the supreme authority is derived from the people, has passed almost universally under the denomination of a republic. The same title has been bestowed on Venice, where absolute power over the great body of the people is exercised, in the most absolute manner, by a small body of hereditary nobles. Poland, which is a mixture of aristocracy and of monarchy in their worst forms, has been dignified with the same appellation. The government of England, which has one republican branch only, combined with an hereditary aristocracy and monarchy, has, with equal impropriety, been frequently placed on the list of republics. These examples, which are nearly as dissimilar to each other as to a genuine republic, show the extreme inaccuracy with which the term has been used in political disquisitions.

If we resort for a criterion to the different principles on which different forms of government are established, we may define a republic to be, or at least may bestow that name on, a government which derives all its powers directly or indirectly from the great body of the people, and is administered by persons holding their offices during pleasure, for a limited period, or during good behavior. It is essential to such a government that it be derived from the great body of the society, not from an inconsiderable proportion, or a favored class of it; otherwise a handful of tyrannical nobles, exercising their oppressions by a delegation of their powers, might aspire to the rank of republicans, and claim for their government the honorable title of republic. It is sufficient for such a government that the persons administering it be appointed, either directly or indirectly, by the people; and that they hold their appointments by either of the tenures just specified; otherwise every government in the United States, as well as every other popular government that has been or can be well organized or well executed, would be degraded from the republican character. According to the constitution of every State in the Union, some or other of the officers of government are appointed indirectly only by the people. According to most of them, the chief magistrate himself is so appointed. And according to one, this mode of appointment is extended to one of the co-ordinate branches of the legislature. According to all the constitutions, also, the tenure of the highest offices is extended to a definite period, and in many instances, both within the legislative and executive departments, to a period of years. According to the provisions of most of the constitutions, again, as well as according to the most respectable and received opinions on the subject, the members of the judiciary department are to retain their offices by the firm tenure of good behavior.

On comparing the Constitution planned by the convention with the standard here fixed, we perceive at once that it is, in the most rigid sense, conformable to it. The House of Representatives, like that of one branch at least of all the State legislatures, is elected immediately by the great body of the people. The Senate, like the present Congress, and the Senate of Maryland, derives its appointment indirectly from the people. The President is indirectly derived from the choice of the people, according to the example in most of the States. Even the judges, with all other officers of the Union, will, as in the several States, be the choice, though a remote choice, of the people themselves, the duration of the appointments is equally conformable to the republican standard, and to the model of State constitutions The House of Representatives is periodically elective, as in all the States; and for the period of two years, as in the State of South Carolina. The Senate is elective, for the period of six years; which is but one year more than the period of the Senate of Maryland, and but two more than that of the Senates of New York and Virginia. The President is to continue in office for the period of four years; as in New York and Delaware, the chief magistrate is elected for three years, and in South Carolina for two years. In the other States the election is annual. In several of the States, however, no constitutional provision is made for the impeachment of the chief magistrate. And in Delaware and Virginia he is not impeachable till out of office. The President of the United States is impeachable at any time during his continuance in office. The tenure by which the judges are to hold their places, is, as it unquestionably ought to be, that of good behavior. The tenure of the ministerial offices generally, will be a subject of legal regulation, conformably to the reason of the case and the example of the State constitutions.

Could any further proof be required of the republican complexion of this system, the most decisive one might be found in its <u>absolute prohibition of titles of nobility</u>, both under the federal and the State governments; and in its express guaranty of the republican form to each of the latter

But it was not sufficient, say the adversaries of the proposed Constitution, for the convention to adhere to the republican form. They ought, with equal care, to have preserved the federal form, which regards the Union as a confederacy of sovereign states; instead of which, they have framed a national government, which regards the Union as a consolidation of the States. And it is asked by what authority this bold and radical innovation was undertaken? The handle which has been made of this objection requires that it should be examined with some precision.

Without inquiring into the accuracy of the distinction on which the objection is founded, it will be necessary to a just estimate of its force, first, to ascertain the real character of the government in question; secondly, to inquire how far the convention were authorized to propose such a government; and thirdly, how far the duty they owed to their country could supply any defect of regular authority.

First. In order to ascertain the real character of the government, it may be considered in relation to the foundation on which it is to be established; to the sources from which its ordinary powers are to be drawn; to the operation of those powers; to the extent of them; and to the authority by which future changes in the government are to be introduced.

On examining the first relation, it appears, on one hand, that the Constitution is to be founded on the assent and ratification of the people of America, given by deputies elected for the special purpose; but, on the other, that this assent and ratification is to be given by the people, not as individuals composing one entire nation, but as composing the distinct and independent States to which they respectively belong. It is to be the assent and ratification of the several States, derived from the supreme authority in each State, the authority of the people themselves. The act, therefore, establishing the Constitution, will not be a national, but a federal act.

That it will be a federal and not a national act, as these terms are understood by the objectors; the act of the people, as forming so many independent States, not as forming one aggregate nation, is obvious from this single consideration, that it is to result neither from the decision of a majority of the people of the Union, nor from that of a majority of the States. It must result from the unanimous assent of the several States that are parties to it, differing no otherwise from their ordinary assent than in its being expressed, not by the legislative authority, but by that of the people themselves. Were the people regarded in this transaction as forming one nation, the will of the majority of the whole people of the United States would bind the minority, in the same manner as the majority in each State must bind the minority; and the will of the majority must be determined either by a comparison of the individual votes, or by considering the will of the majority of the States as evidence of the will of a majority of the people of the United States. Neither of these rules have been adopted. Each State, in ratifying the Constitution, is considered as a sovereign body, independent of all others, and only to be bound by its own voluntary act. In this relation, then, the new Constitution will, if established, be a federal, and not a national constitution.

The next relation is, to the sources from which the ordinary powers of government are to be derived. The House of Representatives will derive its powers from the people of America; and the people will be represented in the same proportion, and on the same principle, as they are in the legislature of a particular State. So far the government is national, not federal. The Senate, on the other hand, will derive its powers from the States, as political and coequal societies; and these will be represented on the principle of equality in the Senate, as they now are in the existing Congress. So far the government is federal, not national. The executive power will be derived from a very compound source. The immediate election of the President is to be made by the States in their political characters. The votes allotted to them are in a compound ratio, which considers them partly as distinct and coequal societies, partly as unequal members of the same society. The eventual election, again, is to be made by that branch of the legislature which consists of the national representatives; but in this particular act they are to be thrown into the form of individual delegations, from so many distinct and coequal bodies politic. From this aspect of the government it appears to be of a mixed character, presenting at least as many federal as national features.

The difference between a federal and national government, as it relates to the operation of the government, is supposed to consist in this, that in the former the powers operate on the political bodies composing the Confederacy, in their political capacities; in the latter, on the individual citizens composing the nation, in their individual capacities. On trying the Constitution by this criterion, it falls under the national, not the federal character; though perhaps not so completely as has been understood. In several cases, and particularly in the trial of controversies to which States may be parties, they must be viewed and proceeded against in their collective and political capacities only. So far the national countenance of the government on this side seems to be disfigured by a few federal features. But this blemish is perhaps unavoidable in any plan; and the operation of the government on the people, in their individual capacities, in its ordinary and most essential proceedings, may, on the whole, designtate it, in this relation, a national government.

But if the government be national with regard to the operation of its powers, it changes its aspect again when we contemplate it in relation to the extent of its powers. The idea of a national government involves in it, not only an authority over the individual citizens, but an indefinite supremacy over all persons and things, so far as they are objects of lawful government. Among a people consolidated into one nation, this supremacy is completely vested in the national legislature. Among communities united for particular purposes, it is vested partly in the general and partly in the municipal legislatures. In the former case, all local authorities are subordinate to the supreme; and may be controlled, directed, or abolished by it at pleasure. In the latter, the local or municipal authorities form distinct and independent portions of the supremacy, no more subject, within their respective spheres, to the general authority, than the general authority is subject to them, within its own sphere. In this relation, then, the proposed government cannot be deemed a national one; since its jurisdiction extends to certain enumerated objects only, and leaves to the several States a residuary and inviolable sovereignty over all other objects. It is true that in controversies relating to the boundary between the two jurisdictions, the tribunal which is ultimately to decide, is to be established under the general government. But this does not change the principle of the case. The decision is to be impartially made, according to the rules of the Constitution; and all the usual and most effectual precautions are taken to secure this impartiality. Some such tribunal is clearly essential to prevent an appeal to the sword and a dissolution of the compact; and that it ought to be established under the general rather than under the local governments, or, to speak more properly, that it could be safely established under the first alone, is a position not likely to be combated.

If we try the Constitution by its last relation to the authority by which amendments are to be made, we find it neither wholly national nor wholly federal. Were it wholly national, the supreme and ultimate authority would reside in the majority of the people of the Union; and this authority would be competent at all times, like that of a majority of every national society, to alter or abolish its established government. Were it wholly federal, on the other hand, the concurrence of each State in the Union would be essential to every alteration that would be binding on all. The mode provided by the plan of the convention is not founded on either of these principles. In requiring more than a majority, and principles. In requiring more than a majority, and particularly in computing the proportion by states, not by citizens, it departs from the national and advances towards the federal character; in rendering the concurrence of less than the whole number of States sufficient, it loses again the federal and partakes of the national character.

The proposed Constitution, therefore, is, in strictness, neither a national nor a federal Constitution, but a composition of both. In its foundation it is federal, not national; in the sources from which the ordinary powers of the government are drawn, it is partly federal and partly national; in the operation of these powers, it is national, not federal; in the extent of them, again, it is federal, not national; and, finally, in the authoritative mode of introducing amendments, it is neither wholly federal nor wholly national.

Publius. [James Madison]

First published in the Wednesday, January 16, 1788 issue of the *Independent Journal*.

Federalist № 51

The Structure of the Government Must Furnish the Proper Checks and Balances Between the Different Departments

To the People of the State of New York:

To what expedient, then, shall we finally resort, for maintaining in practice the necessary partition of power among the several departments, as laid down in the Constitution? The only answer that can be given is, that as all these exterior provisions are found to be inadequate, the defect must be supplied, by so contriving the interior structure of the government as that its several constituent parts may, by their mutual relations, be the means of keeping each other in their proper places. Without presuming to undertake a full development of this important idea, I will hazard a few general observations, which may perhaps place it in a clearer light, and enable us to form a more correct judgment of the principles and structure of the government planned by the convention.

In order to lay a due foundation for that separate and distinct exercise of the different powers of government, which to a certain extent is admitted on all hands to be essential to the preservation of liberty, it is evident that each department should have a will of its own; and consequently should be so constituted that the members of each should have as little agency as possible in the appointment of the members of the others. Were this principle rigorously adhered to, it would require that all the appointments for the supreme executive, legislative, and judiciary magistracies should be drawn from the same fountain of authority, the people, through channels having no communication whatever with one another. Perhaps such a plan of constructing the several departments would be less difficult in practice than it may in contemplation appear. Some difficulties, however, and some additional expense would attend the execution of it. Some deviations, therefore, from the principle must be admitted. In the constitution of the judiciary department in particular, it might be inexpedient to insist rigorously on the principle: first, because peculiar qualifications being essential in the members, the primary consideration ought to be to select that mode of choice which best secures these qualifications; secondly, because the permanent tenure by which the appointments are held in that department, must soon destroy all sense of dependence on the authority conferring them.

It is equally evident, that the members of each department should be as little dependent as possible on those of the others, for the emoluments annexed to their offices. Were the executive magistrate, or the judges, not independent of the legislature in this particular, their independence in every other would be merely nominal.

But the great security against a gradual concentration of the several powers in the same department, consists in giving to those who administer each department the necessary constitutional means and personal motives to resist encroachments of the others. The provision for defense must in this, as in all other cases, be made commensurate to the danger of attack. Ambition must be made to counteract ambition. The interest of the man must be connected with the constitutional rights of the place. It may be a reflection on human nature, that such devices should be necessary to control the abuses of government. But what is government itself, but the greatest of all reflections on human nature? If men were angels, no government would be necessary. If angels were to govern men, neither external nor internal controls on government would be necessary. In framing a government which is to be administered by men over men, the great difficulty lies in this: you must first enable the government to control the governed; and in the next place oblige it to control itself. A dependence on the people is, no doubt, the primary control on the government; but experience has taught mankind the necessity of auxiliary precautions.

This policy of supplying, by opposite and rival interests, the defect of better motives, might be traced through the whole system of human affairs, private as well as public. We see it particularly displayed in all the subordinate distributions of power, where the constant aim is to divide and arrange the several offices in such a manner as that each may be a check on the other that the private interest of every individual may be a sentinel over the public rights. These inventions of prudence cannot be less requisite in the distribution of the supreme powers of the State.

But it is not possible to give to each department an equal power of self-defense. In republican government, the legislative authority necessarily predominates. The remedy for this inconveniency is to divide the legislature into different branches; and to render them, by different modes of election and different principles of action, as little connected with each other as the nature of their common functions and their common dependence on the society will admit. It may even be necessary to guard against dangerous encroachments by still further precautions. As the weight of the legislative authority requires that it should be thus divided, the weakness of the executive may require, on the other hand, that it should be fortified. An absolute negative on the legislature appears, at first view, to be the natural defense with which the executive magistrate should be armed. But perhaps it would be neither altogether safe nor alone sufficient. On ordinary occasions it might not be exerted with the requisite firmness, and on extraordinary occasions it might be perfidiously abused. May not this defect of an absolute negative be supplied by some qualified connection between this weaker department and the weaker branch of the stronger department, by which the latter may be led to support the constitutional rights of the former, without being too much detached from the rights of its own department?

If the principles on which these observations are founded be just, as I persuade myself they are, and they be applied as a criterion to the several State constitutions, and to the federal Constitution it will be found that if the latter does not perfectly correspond with them, the former are infinitely less able to bear such a test.

There are, moreover, two considerations particularly applicable to the federal system of America, which place that system in a very interesting point of view.

First. In a single republic, all the power surrendered by the people is submitted to the administration of a single government; and the usurpations are guarded against by a division of the government into distinct and separate departments. In the compound republic of America, the power surrendered by the people is first divided between two distinct governments, and then the portion allotted to each subdivided among distinct and separate departments. Hence a double security arises to the rights of the people. The different governments will control each other, at the same time that each will be controlled by itself.

Second. It is of great importance in a republic not only to guard the society against the oppression of its rulers, but to guard one part of the society against the injustice of the other part. Different interests necessarily exist in different classes of citizens. If a majority be united by a common interest, the rights of the minority will be insecure. There are but two methods of providing against this evil: the one by creating a will in the community independent of the majority that is, of the society itself; the other, by comprehending in the society so many separate descriptions of citizens as will render an unjust combination of a majority of the whole very improbable, if not impracticable. The first method prevails in all governments possessing an hereditary or self-appointed authority. This, at best, is but a precarious security; because a power independent of the society may as well espouse the unjust views of the major, as the rightful interests of the minor party, and may possibly be turned against both parties. The second method will be exemplified in the federal republic of the United States. Whilst all authority in it will be derived from and dependent on the society, the society itself will be broken into so many parts, interests, and classes of citizens, that the rights of individuals, or of the minority, will be in little danger from interested combinations of the majority. In a free government the security for civil rights must be the same as that for religious rights. It consists in the one case in the multiplicity of interests, and in the other in the multiplicity of sects. The degree of security in both cases will depend on the number of interests and sects; and this may be presumed to depend on the extent of country and number of people comprehended under the same government. This view of the subject must particularly recommend a proper federal system to all the sincere and considerate friends of republican government, since it shows that in exact proportion as the territory of the Union may be formed into more circumscribed Confederacies, or States oppressive combinations of a majority will be facilitated: the best security, under the republican forms, for the rights of every class of citizens, will be diminished: and consequently the stability and independence of some member of the government, the only other security, must be proportionately increased. Justice is the end of government. It is the end of civil society. It ever has been and ever will be pursued until it be obtained, or until liberty be lost in the pursuit. In a society under the forms of which the stronger faction can readily unite and oppress the weaker, anarchy may as truly be said to reign as in a state of nature, where the weaker individual is not secured against the violence of the stronger; and as, in the latter state, even the stronger individuals are prompted, by the uncertainty of their condition, to submit to a government which may protect the weak as well as themselves; so, in the former state, will the more powerful factions or parties be gradually induced, by a like motive, to wish for a government which will protect all parties, the weaker as well as the more powerful. It can be little doubted that if the State of Rhode Island was separated from the Confederacy and left to itself, the insecurity of rights under the popular form of government within such narrow limits would be displayed by such reiterated oppressions of factious majorities that some power altogether independent of the people would soon be called for by the voice of the very factions whose misrule had proved the necessity of it. In the extended republic of the United States, and among the great variety of interests, parties, and sects which it embraces, a coalition of a majority of the whole society could seldom take place on any other principles than those of justice and the general good; whilst there being thus less danger to a minor from the will of a major party, there must be less pretext, also, to provide for the security of the former, by introducing into the government a will not dependent on the latter, or, in other words, a will independent of the society itself. It is no less certain than it is important, notwithstanding the contrary opinions which have been entertained, that the larger the society, provided it lie within a practical sphere, the more duly capable it will be of self-government. And happily for the republican cause, the practicable sphere may be carried to a very great extent, by a judicious modification and mixture of the federal principle.

Publius.   [Alexander   Hamilton or James Madison]

First published in the Friday, February 8, 1788 issue of the *Independent Journal*.

The Mode of Electing the President

To the People of the State of New York:

The mode of appointment of the Chief Magistrate of the United States is almost the only part of the system, of any consequence, which has escaped without severe censure, or which has received the slightest mark of approbation from its opponents. The most plausible of these, who has appeared in print, has even deigned to admit that the election of the President is pretty well guarded.1 I venture somewhat further, and hesitate not to affirm, that if the manner of it be not perfect, it is at least excellent. It unites in an eminent degree all the advantages, the union of which was to be wished for.

It was desirable that the sense of the people should operate in the choice of the person to whom so important a trust was to be confided. This end will be answered by committing the right of making it, not to any preestablished body, but to men chosen by the people for the special purpose, and at the particular conjuncture.

It was equally desirable, that the immediate election should be made by men most capable of analyzing the qualities adapted to the station, and acting under circumstances favorable to deliberation, and to a judicious combination of all the reasons and inducements which were proper to govern their choice. A small number of persons, selected by their fellow-citizens from the general mass, will be most likely to possess the information and discernment requisite to such complicated investigations. http://federali.st/68 - p3

It was also peculiarly desirable to afford as little opportunity as possible to tumult and disorder. This evil was not least to be dreaded in the election of a magistrate, who was to have so important an agency in the administration of the government as the President of the United States. But the precautions which have been so happily concerted in the system under consideration, promise an effectual security against this mischief. The choice of several, to form an intermediate body of electors, will be much less apt to convulse the community with any extraordinary or violent movements, than the choice of one who was himself to be the final object of the public wishes. And as the electors, chosen in each State, are to assemble and vote in the State in which they are chosen, this detached and divided situation will expose them much less to heats and ferments, which might be communicated from them to the people, than if they were all to be convened at one time, in one place.

Nothing was more to be desired than that every practicable obstacle should be opposed to cabal, intrigue, and corruption. These most deadly adversaries of republican government might naturally have been expected to make their approaches from more than one querter, but chiefly from the desire in foreign powers to gain an improper ascendant in our councils. How could they better gratify this, than by raising a creature of their own to the chief magistracy of the Union? But the convention have guarded against all danger of this sort, with the most provident and judicious attention. They have not made the appointment of the President to depend on any preexisting bodies of men, who might be tampered with beforehand to prostitute their votes; but they have referred it in the first instance to an immediate act of the people of America, to be exerted in the choice of persons for the temporary and sole purpose of making the appointment. And they have excluded from eligibility to this trust, all those who from situation might be suspected of too great devotion to the President in office. No senator, representative, or other person holding a place of trust or profit under the United States, can be of the numbers of the electors. Thus without corrupting the body of the people, the immediate agents in the election will at least enter upon the task free from any sinister bias. Their transient existence, and their detached situation, already taken notice of, afford a satisfactory prospect of their continuing so, to the conclusion of it. The business of corruption, when it is to embrace so considerable a number of men, requires time as well as means. Nor would it be found easy suddenly to embark them, dispersed as they would be over thirteen States, in any combinations founded upon motives, which though they could not properly be denominated corrupt, might yet be of a nature to mislead them from their duty.

Another and no less important desideratum was, that the Executive should be independent for his continuance in office on all but the people themselves. He might otherwise be tempted to sacrifice his duty to his complaisance for those whose favor was necessary to the duration of his official consequence. This advantage will also be secured, by making his re-election to depend on a special body of representatives, deputed by the society for the single purpose of making the important choice.

All these advantages will happily combine in the plan devised by the convention; which is, that the people of each State shall choose a number of persons as electors, equal to the number of senators and representatives of such State in the national government, who shall assemble within the State, and vote for some fit person as President. Their votes, thus given, are to be transmitted to the seat of the national government, and the person who may happen to have a majority of the whole number of votes will be the President. But as a majority of the votes might not always happen to centre in one man, and as it might be unsafe to permit less than a majority to be conclusive, it is provided that, in such a contingency, the House of Representatives shall select out of the candidates who shall have the five highest number of votes, the man who in their opinion may be best qualified for the office.

The process of election affords a moral certainty, that the office of President will never fall to the lot of any man who is not in an eminent degree endowed with the requisite qualifications. Talents for low intrigue, and the little arts of popularity, may alone suffice to elevate a man to the first honors in a single State; but it will require other talents, and a different kind of merit, to establish him in the esteem and confidence of the whole Union, or of so considerable a portion of it as would be necessary to make him a successful candidate for the distinguished office of President of the United States. It will not be too strong to say, that there will be a constant probability of seeing the station filled by characters pre-eminent for ability and virtue. And this will be thought no inconsiderable recommendation of the Constitution, by those who are able to estimate the share which the executive in every government must necessarily have in its good or ill administration. Though we cannot acquiesce in the political heresy of the poet who says: For forms of government let fools contest That which is best administered is best, yet we may safely pronounce, that the true test of a good government is its aptitude and tendency to produce a good administration.

The Vice-President is to be chosen in the same manner with the President; with this difference, that the Senate is to do, in respect to the former, what is to be done by the House of Representatives, in respect to the latter.

The appointment of an extraordinary person, as Vice-President, has been objected to as superfluous, if not mischievous. It has been alleged, that it would have been preferable to have authorized the Senate to elect out of their own body an officer answering that description. But two considerations seem to justify the ideas of the convention in this respect. One is, that to secure at all times the possibility of a definite resolution of the body, it is necessary that the President should have only a casting vote. And to take the senator of any State from his seat as senator, to place him in that of President of the Senate, would be to exchange, in regard to the State from which he came, a constant for a contingent vote. The other consideration is, that as the Vice-President may occasionally become a substitute for the President, in the supreme executive magistracy, all the reasons which recommend the mode of election prescribed for the one, apply with great if not with equal force to the manner of appointing the other. It is remarkable that in this, as in most other instances, the objection which is made would lie against the constitution of this State. We have a Lieutenant-Governor, chosen by the people at large, who presides in the Senate, and is the constitutional substitute for the Governor, in casualties similar to those which would authorize the Vice-President to exercise the authorities and discharge the duties of the President.

PUBLIUS. [Alexander Hamilton]

1. Vide *FEDERAL FARMER.*

First published in the Friday, March 14, 1788 issue of the *Independent Journal.*

Federalist № 78

The Judiciary Department

To the People of the State of New York:

We proceed now to an examination of the judiciary department of the proposed government.

In unfolding the defects of the existing Confederation, the utility and necessity of a federal judicature have been clearly pointed out. It is the less necessary to recapitulate the considerations there urged, as the propriety of the institution in the abstract is not disputed; the only questions which have been raised being relative to the manner of constituting it, and to its extent. To these points, therefore, our observations shall be confined.

The manner of constituting it seems to embrace these several objects: 1st. The mode of appointing the judges. 2d. The tenure by which they are to hold their places. 3d. The partition of the judiciary authority between different courts, and their relations to each other.

First. As to the mode of appointing the judges; this is the same with that of appointing the officers of the Union in general, and has been so fully discussed in the two last numbers, that nothing can be said here which would not be useless repetition. Second. As to the tenure by which the judges are to hold their places; this chiefly concerns their duration in office; the provisions for their support; the precautions for their responsibility.

According to the plan of the convention, all judges who may be appointed by the United States are to hold their offices during good behavior; which is conformable to the most approved of the State constitutions and among the rest, to that of this State. Its propriety having been drawn into question by the adversaries of that plan, is no light symptom of the rage for objection, which disorders their imaginations and judgments. The standard of good behavior for the continuance in office of the judicial magistracy, is certainly one of the most valuable of the modern improvements in the practice of government. In a monarchy it is an excellent barrier to the despotism of the prince; in a republic it is a no less excellent barrier to the encroachments and oppressions of the representative body. And it is the best expedient which can be devised in any government, to secure a steady, upright, and impartial administration of the laws.

Whoever attentively considers the different departments of power must perceive, that, in a government in which they are separated from each other, the judiciary, from the nature of its functions, will always be the least dangerous to the political rights of the Constitution; because it will be least in a capacity to annoy or injure them. The Executive not only dispenses the honors, but holds the sword of the community. The legislature not only commands the purse, but prescribes the rules by which the duties and rights of every citizen are to be regulated. The judiciary, on the contrary, has no influence over either the sword or the purse; no direction either of the strength or of the wealth of the society; and can take no active resolution whatever. It may truly be said to have neither force nor will, but merely judgment; and must ultimately depend upon the aid of the executive arm even for the efficacy of its judgments.

This simple view of the matter suggests several important consequences. It proves incontestably, that the judiciary is beyond comparison the weakest of the three departments of power[1]; that it can never attack with success either of the other two; and that all possible care is requisite to enable it to defend itself against their attacks. It equally proves, that though individual oppression may now and then proceed from the courts of justice, the general liberty of the people can never be endangered from that quarter; I mean so long as the judiciary remains truly distinct from both the legislature and the Executive. For I agree, that there is no liberty, if the power of judging be not separated from the legislative and executive powers.[2] And it proves, in the last place, that as liberty can have nothing to fear from the judiciary alone, but would have every thing to fear from its union with either of the other departments; that as all the effects of such a union must ensue from a dependence of the former on the latter, notwithstanding a nominal and apparent separation; that as, from the natural feebleness of the judiciary, it is in continual jeopardy of being overpowered, awed, or influenced by its co-ordinate branches; and that as nothing can contribute so much to its firmness and independence as permanency in office, this quality may therefore be justly regarded as an indispensable ingredient in its constitution, and, in a great measure, as the citadel of the public justice and the public security.

The complete independence of the courts of justice is peculiarly essential in a limited Constitution. By a limited Constitution, I understand one which contains certain specified exceptions to the legislative authority; such, for instance, as that it shall pass no bills of attainder, no ex-post-facto laws, and the like. Limitations of this kind can be preserved in practice no other way than through the medium of courts of justice, whose duty it must be to declare all acts contrary to the manifest tenor of the Constitution void. Without this, all the reservations of particular rights or privileges would amount to nothing.

Some perplexity respecting the rights of the courts to pronounce legislative acts void, because contrary to the Constitution, has arisen from an imagination that the doctrine would imply a superiority of the judiciary to the legislative power. It is urged that the authority which can declare the acts of another void, must necessarily be superior to the one whose acts may be declared void. As this doctrine is of great importance in all the American constitutions, a brief discussion of the ground on which it rests cannot be unacceptable.

There is no position which depends on clearer principles, than that every act of a delegated authority, contrary to the tenor of the commission under which it is exercised, is void. No legislative act, therefore, contrary to the Constitution, can be valid. To deny this, would be to affirm, that the deputy is greater than his principal; that the servant is above his master; that the representatives of the people are superior to the people themselves; that men acting by virtue of powers, may do not only what their powers do not authorize, but what they forbid.

If it be said that the legislative body are themselves the constitutional judges of their own powers, and that the construction they put upon them is conclusive upon the other departments, it may be answered, that this cannot be the natural presumption, where it is not to be collected from any particular provisions in the Constitution. It is not otherwise to be supposed, that the Constitution could intend to enable the representatives of the people to substitute their will to that of their constituents. It is far more rational to suppose, that the courts were designed to be an intermediate body between the people and the legislature, in order, among other things, to keep the latter within the limits assigned to their authority. The interpretation of the laws is the proper and peculiar province of the courts. A constitution is, in fact, and must be regarded by the judges, as a fundamental law. It therefore belongs to them to ascertain its meaning, as well as the meaning of any particular act proceeding from the legislative body. If there should happen to be an irreconcilable variance between the two, that which has the superior obligation and validity ought, of course, to be preferred; or, in other words, the Constitution ought to be preferred to the statute, the intention of the people to the intention of their agents.

Nor does this conclusion by any means suppose a superiority of the judicial to the legislative power. It only supposes that the power of the people is superior to both; and that where the will of the legislature, declared in its statutes, stands in opposition to that of the people, declared in the Constitution, the judges ought to be governed by the latter rather than the former. They ought to regulate their decisions by the fundamental laws, rather than by those which are not fundamental.

This exercise of judicial discretion, in determining between two contradictory laws, is exemplified in a familiar instance. It not uncommonly happens, that there are two statutes existing at one time, clashing in whole or in part with each other, and neither of them containing any repealing clause or expression. In such a case, it is the province of the courts to liquidate and fix their meaning and operation. So far as they can, by any fair construction, be reconciled to each other, reason and law conspire to dictate that this should be done; where this is impracticable, it becomes a matter of necessity to give effect to one, in exclusion of the other. The rule which has obtained in the courts for determining their relative validity is, that the last in order of time shall be preferred to the first. But this is a mere rule of construction, not derived from any positive law, but from the nature and reason of the thing. It is a rule not enjoined upon the courts by legislative provision, but adopted by themselves, as consonant to truth and propriety, for the direction of their conduct as interpreters of the law. They thought it reasonable, that between the interfering acts of an equal authority, that which was the last indication of its will should have the preference.

But in regard to the interfering acts of a superior and subordinate authority, of an original and derivative power, the nature and reason of the thing indicate the converse of that rule as proper to be followed. They teach us that the prior act of a superior ought to be preferred to the subsequent act of an inferior and subordinate authority; and that accordingly, whenever a particular statute contravenes the Constitution, it will be the duty of the judicial tribunals to adhere to the latter and disregard the former.

It can be of no weight to say that the courts, on the pretense of a repugnancy, may substitute their own pleasure to the constitutional intentions of the legislature. This might as well happen in the case of two contradictory statutes; or it might as well happen in every adjudication upon any single statute. The courts must declare the sense of the law; and if they should be disposed to exercise will instead of judgment, the consequence would equally be the substitution of their pleasure to that of the legislative body. The observation, if it prove any thing, would prove that there ought to be no judges distinct from that body.

If, then, the courts of justice are to be considered as the bulwarks of a limited Constitution against legislative encroachments, this consideration will afford a strong argument for the permanent tenure of judicial offices, since nothing will contribute so much as this to that independent spirit in the judges which must be essential to the faithful performance of so arduous a duty.

This independence of the judges is equally requisite to guard the Constitution and the rights of individuals from the effects of those ill humors, which the arts of designing men, or the influence of particular conjunctures, sometimes disseminate among the people themselves, and which, though they speedily give place to better information, and more deliberate reflection, have a tendency, in the meantime, to occasion dangerous innovations in the government, and serious oppressions of the minor party in the community. Though I trust the friends of the proposed Constitution will never concur with its enemies,[3] in questioning that fundamental principle of republican government, which admits the right of the people to alter or abolish the established Constitution, whenever they find it inconsistent with their happiness, yet it is not to be inferred from this principle, that the representatives of the people, whenever a momentary inclination happens to lay hold of a majority of their constituents, incompatible with the provisions in the existing Constitution, would, on that account, be justifiable in a violation of those provisions; or that the courts would be under a greater obligation to connive at infractions in this shape, than when they had proceeded wholly from the cabals of the representative body. Until the people have, by some solemn and authoritative act, annulled or changed the established form, it is binding upon themselves collectively, as well as individually; and no presumption, or even knowledge, of their sentiments, can warrant their representatives in a departure from it, prior to such an act. But it is easy to see, that it would require an uncommon portion of fortitude in the judges to do their duty as faithful guardians of the Constitution, where legislative invasions of it had been instigated by the major voice of the community.

But it is not with a view to infractions of the Constitution only, that the independence of the judges may be an essential safeguard against the effects of occasional ill humors in the society. These sometimes extend no farther than to the injury of the private rights of particular classes of citizens, by unjust and partial laws. Here also the firmness of the judicial magistracy is of vast importance in mitigating the severity and confining the operation of such laws. It not only serves to moderate the immediate mischiefs of those which may have been passed, but it operates as a check upon the legislative body in passing them; who, perceiving that obstacles to the success of iniquitous intention are to be expected from the scruples of the courts, are in a manner compelled, by the very motives of the injustice they meditate, to qualify their attempts. This is a circumstance calculated to have more influence upon the character of our governments, than but few may be aware of. The benefits of the integrity and moderation of the judiciary have already been felt in more States than one; and though they may have displeased those whose sinister expectations they may have disappointed, they must have commanded the esteem and applause of all the virtuous and disinterested. Considerate men, of every description, ought to prize whatever will tend to beget or fortify that temper in the courts: as no man can be sure that he may not be to-morrow the victim of a spirit of injustice, by which he may be a gainer to-day. And every man must now feel, that the inevitable tendency of such a spirit is to sap the foundations of public and private confidence, and to introduce in its stead universal distrust and distress.

That inflexible and uniform adherence to the rights of the Constitution, and of individuals, which we perceive to be indispensable in the courts of justice, can certainly not be expected from judges who hold their offices by a temporary commission. Periodical appointments, however regulated, or by whomsoever made, would, in some way or other, be fatal to their necessary independence. If the power of making them was committed either to the Executive or legislature, there would be danger of an improper complaisance to the branch which possessed it; if to both, there would be an unwillingness to hazard the displeasure of either; if to the people, or to persons chosen by them for the special purpose, there would be too great a disposition to consult popularity, to justify a reliance that nothing would be consulted but the Constitution and the laws.

There is yet a further and a weightier reason for the permanency of the judicial offices, which is deducible from the nature of the qualifications they require. It has been frequently remarked, with great propriety, that a voluminous code of laws is one of the inconveniences necessarily connected with the advantages of a free government. To avoid an arbitrary discretion in the courts, it is indispensable that they should be bound down by strict rules and precedents, which serve to define and point out their duty in every particular case that comes before them; and it will readily be conceived from the variety of controversies which grow out of the folly and wickedness of mankind, that the records of those precedents must unavoidably swell to a very considerable bulk, and must demand long and laborious study to acquire a competent knowledge of them. Hence it is, that there can be but few men in the society who will have sufficient skill in the laws to qualify them for the stations of judges. And making the proper deductions for the ordinary depravity of human nature, the number must be still smaller of those who unite the requisite integrity with the requisite knowledge. These considerations apprise us, that the government can have no great option between fit character; and that a temporary duration in office, which would naturally discourage such characters from quitting a lucrative line of practice to accept a seat on the bench, would have a tendency to throw the administration of justice into hands less able, and less well qualified, to conduct it with utility and dignity. In the present circumstances of this country, and in those in which it is likely to be for a long time to come, the disadvantages on this score would be greater than they may at first sight appear; but it must be confessed, that they are far inferior to those which present themselves under the other aspects of the subject.

Upon the whole, there can be no room to doubt that the convention acted wisely in copying from the models of those constitutions which have established good behavior as the tenure of their judicial offices, in point of duration; and that so far from being blamable on this account, their plan would have been inexcusably defective, if it had wanted this important feature of good government. The experience of Great Britain affords an illustrious comment on the excellence of the institution.

Publius. [Alexander Hamilton]

1. The celebrated Montesquieu, speaking of them, says: Of the three powers above mentioned, the judiciary is next to nothing. "Spirit of Laws." vol. i., page 186.

2. Idem, page 181.

3. Vide "Protest of the Minority of the Convention of Pennsylvania," Martin's Speech, etc.

First published in the Saturday, June 14, 1788 issue of the *Independent Journal.*
In CONGRESS, July 4, 1776.

Chapter 10: Politics and Economics

Comprehension questions you should be able to answer after reading this chapter:

1. Describe the role of "sympathy" in moral judgment, according to Smith.

2. What is the "impartial spectator?" What function does it serve?

3. How are general moral rules formed, according to Smith?

4. What is the "invisible hand?" What purpose does it serve? What is its source/origin?

5. What is the value of the pursuit of self-interest, for Smith?

6. How does the division of labor (and specialization) create wealth?

7. How can the division of labor dull the intellect, according to Smith? How can this be prevented?

8. Why does Smith favor a limited government?

9. What are the legitimate functions of government, for Smith?

10. How is it a *mistake* to admire the wealthy, according to Smith? Why is this envy threatening to the accuracy of our moral judgments?

11. Why does Smith think it is right for the government to provide for the poor, including, at least, universal education?

12. What (in general) is the morally right thing to do, according to Rand's ethical egoism?

13. What does Rand mean by "selfishness?"

14. According to Rand, what is a "value?" What is the "ultimate value" for humans? What makes something good or evil, given this ultimate value?

15. What is our "highest moral purpose" according to Rand?

16. Why does Rand reject "altruism?"

17. How are Smith's and Rand's views similar? How are they different?

The title of this chapter is, I must confess, a bit misleading. It's not as though a connection between political philosophy and economics emerged in, or after, the Enlightenment. Clearly, economic issues, including issues of distributive justice, regulation of wealth, and the proper role of the State in providing for the people, go all the way back to ancient political philosophy.

With that being said, I think a case can be made that politics and economics became especially entwined and "volatile" in the last couple centuries, and it is nearly impossible to formulate a clear political position, or engage in political discussion, without economic assumptions at least implicitly entering into the conversation. Contemporary American (domestic) political differences, for example, can generally be lumped into one of two categories: "social" issues (e.g., abortion, sexuality, race relations, etc.), and "economic issues" (e.g., taxes, social welfare programs, the national debt, etc.).

The two polarizing economic systems in the West for the last century, at least, have been capitalism and communism. For our purposes, we will focus exclusively on capitalism. This is not because communism is somehow unimportant or uninteresting, but simply because capitalism has been the central (and generally unquestioned) economic system in the United States, with communism serving more as a point of contrast, at best, or a "bogeyman," at worst.

No discussion of capitalism in a book such as thing one could neglect the man widely regarded as its philosophical "founder"—or at least its greatest proponent: Adam Smith.

Background

Adam Smith was the "Founding Father" of capitalism. He was a tireless crusader for "laissez-faire" economics, a ceaseless foe of taxation, and a firm believer in the value of wealth, and the virtues of the wealthy. He was opposed to government intervention, in general, and believed that government efforts to help the poor, especially at the expense of the wealthy, were woefully misguided and illegitimate.

Reality check: most of that preceding paragraph was much more mythology than reality! Indeed, some of it is patently and demonstrably false.

In truth, although Smith is very often quoted, he is very rarely read (even by those who quote him), and even more rarely understood. This is not to say that the myth of Adam Smith bears no resemblance to the real man at all. Smith did offer offers accounts of the division of labor, free trade, self-interest in economic transactions, and limited government intervention, pricing, and general market structures. He was not, however, primarily an economist, and the free market is just one component of his broader theory of human interaction.

Smith was born in June of 1723, in Kirkcaldy (Eastern Scotland). In 1737 he went to Glasgow College at the age of 13, and then on to Oxford University, where he was taught by Francis Hutcheson, an early leader of the "Scottish Enlightenment." More so than an economist, Smith was a philosopher. Smith held the Chair of Logic from 1751-1752, and then was appointed to Hutcheson's old chair: the Chair of Moral Philosophy.

His *Theory of Moral Sentiments* (first published in 1759) is an account of morality: how we ought to behave, and how we are to know such things. The book was well-received, including by his equally-if-not-more-famous friend David Hume.

> . . . Supposing, therefore, that you have duly prepared yourself for the worst by all these reflections, I proceed to tell you the melancholy news that your book has been very unfortunate, for the public seem disposed to applaud it extremely. It was looked for by the foolish people with some impatience; and the mob of literati are beginning already to be very loud in its praises. Three bishops called yesterday at Millar's shop in order to buy copies, and to ask questions about the author. The Bishop of Peter-borough said he had passed the evening in a company where he heard it extolled above all books in the world. You may conclude what Opinion true Philosophers will entertain of it, when these Retainers of Superstition praise it so highly.[296]

After the success of the *Theory of Moral Sentiments*, Smith was offered a lucrative tutoring position by Charles Townshend (the Chancellor of Exchequer responsible for the taxes that triggered the American Revolution!). He moved with the family to France in 1763, where he became bored. The abundance of free time gave him time to write the *Wealth of Nations*, however.

> The Duke is acquainted with no Frenchman whatever. I cannot cultivate the acquaintance of the few with whom I am acquainted, as I cannot bring them to our house, and am not always at liberty to go to theirs. The life which I led at Glasgow was a pleasurable dissipated life in comparison of that which I lead here at Present. I have begun to write a book in order to pass away the time.[297]

---

[296] Letter from Hume to Smith, April 12th, 1759.

[297] Letter from Smith to Hume, July 5th, 1764.

He eventually returned to London and continued working for Townshend until 1767. He was elected to the Royal Society at this time, and published the *Wealth of Nations* in 1776—four months before the signing of the United States Declaration of Independence. This book, too, was immediately well-received. He published nothing else of significance in his life, and died on July 17th, 1790.

Although it is tempting to leap into a discussion of Smith's economic views, this neglects the fact that his views on economics were derived, in part, from his earlier philosophical work. Moreover, this is a political philosophy textbook, not a text on economics! As such, we will first focus on his account of "sympathy" as developed in the *Theory of Moral Sentiments*, and then see how this connects to his broader political and economic theory.

Sympathy

Smith rejected any purely "self-interested" interpretation of human nature. The very first sentence of the *Theory of Moral Sentiments* makes this clear. "How selfish soever man may be supposed, there are evidently some principles in his nature, which interest him in the fortune of others, and render their happiness necessary to him, though he derives nothing from it except the pleasure of seeing it."

In contrast to selfish individualists, Smith considers people to be *social* beings. We care about others, with their happiness or unhappiness bringing us our own pleasure or pain. Smith was undoubtedly influenced by his close friend, David Hume, with regard to "sympathy." What follows is a section not from Smith, but from Hume's *Treatise on Human Nature*.

> When experience has once given us a competent knowledge of human affairs, and has taught us the proportion they bear to human passion, we perceive, that the generosity of men is very limited, and that it seldom extends beyond their

friends and family, or, at most, beyond their native country. Being thus acquainted with the nature of man, we expect not any impossibilities from him; but confine our view to that narrow circle, in which any person moves, in order to form a judgment of his moral character. When the natural tendency of his passions leads him to be serviceable and useful within his sphere, we approve of his character, and love his person, by a sympathy with the sentiments of those, who have a more particular connexion with him. We are quickly oblig'd to forget our own interest in our judgments of this kind, by reason of the perpetual contradictions, we meet with in society and conversation, from persons that are not plac'd in the same situation, and have not the same interest with ourselves. The only point of view, in which our sentiments concur with those of others, is, when we consider the tendency of any passion to the advantage or harm of those, who have any immediate connexion or intercourse with the person possess'd of it. And tho' this advantage or harm be often very remote from ourselves, yet sometimes 'tis very near us, and interests us strongly by sympathy. This concern we readily extend to other cases, that are resembling; and when these are very remote, our sympathy is proportionably weaker, and our praise or blame fainter and more doubtful. The case is here the same as in our judgments concerning external bodies. All objects seem to diminish by their distance: But tho' the appearance of objects to our senses be the original standard, by which we judge of them, yet we do not say, that they actually diminish by the distance; but correcting the appearance by reflection, arrive at a more constant and establish'd judgment concerning them. In like manner, tho' sympathy be much fainter than our concern for ourselves, and a sympathy with persons remote from us much fainter than that with persons near and contiguous; yet we neglect all these differences in our calm judgments concerning the characters of men. Besides, that we ourselves often change our situation in this particular, we every day meet with persons, who are in a different situation from ourselves, and who cou'd never converse with us on any reasonable terms, were we to remain constantly in that situation and point of view, which is peculiar to us. The intercourse of sentiments, therefore, in society and conversation, makes us form some general inalterable standard, by which we may approve or disapprove of characters and manners. And tho' the heart does not always take part with those general notions, or regulate its love and hatred by them, yet are they sufficient for discourse, and serve all our purposes in company, in the pulpit, on the theatre, and in the schools.

From these principles we may easily account for that merit, which is commonly ascrib'd to generosity, humanity, compassion, gratitude, friendship, fidelity, zeal, disinterestedness, liberality, and all those other qualities, which form the character of good and benevolent. A propensity to the tender passions makes a man agreeable and useful in all the parts of life; and gives a just direction to all his other qualities, which otherwise may become prejudicial to society. Courage and ambition, when not regulated by benevolence, are fit only to make a tyrant and public robber. 'Tis the same case with judgment and capacity, and all the qualities of that kind. They are indifferent in themselves to the interests of society, and have a tendency to the good or ill of mankind, according as they are directed by these other passions.[298]

Sympathy is, arguably, the basis for Smith's entire moral philosophy. Sympathy (according to Smith) arises when we imagine how we would feel in the circumstances of others. The "process" of sympathy is roughly as follows:

1. The observer witnesses the actions/reactions of the actor.
2. The observer imagines what it's like to be the actor in those circumstances, and imagines what he (the observer) would do in their place.
3. If the imagined reaction is similar to the observed reaction, the observer sympathizes with the actor.
4. If the imagined reaction is significantly different from the observed reaction, the observer does not sympathize. Sympathy, or its lack, is a form of moral approval or disapproval.

This process, one must note, requires imagination. Sympathy is a reaction not just to someone's experience, but their experience in a context. "Fury" might inspire compassion for the furious, if they have been horribly wronged, but unwarranted anger (given the circumstances) can actually produce the opposite effect. Similarly, we might feel sadness in a situation, even when the actor, himself, does not. Our ability to discern what an "impartial spectator" would feel in contexts drives this ability, and also helps us to be sympathetic even when our own actual feelings are lacking. For example, if we just lost a loved one, our grief might prevent us from feeling joy at a friend's good fortune—but our recognition of the appropriateness of that joy allows us to still "be happy" for that person, even if we're not (literally) feeling it (viz., happiness) ourselves.

Sympathy, however, cannot, in any sense, be regarded as a selfish principle. When I sympathize with your sorrow or your

---

[298] Hume, *A Treatise of Human Nature*, 3.3.3.2-3.3.3.4.

indignation, it may be pretended, indeed, that my emotion is founded in self-love, because it arises from bringing your case home to myself, from putting myself in your situation, and thence conceiving what I should feel in the like circumstances. But though sympathy is very properly said to arise from an imaginary change of situations with the person principally concerned, yet this imaginary change is not supposed to happen to me in my own person and character, but in that of the person with whom I sympathize. When I condole with you for the loss of your only son, in order to enter into your grief I do not consider what I, a person of such a character and profession, should suffer, if I had a son, and if that son was unfortunately to die: but I consider what I should suffer if I was really you, and I not only change circumstances with you, but I change persons and characters. My grief, therefore, is entirely upon your account, and not in the least upon my own. It is not, therefore, in the least selfish. How can that be regarded as a selfish passion, which does not arise even from the imagination of any thing that has befallen, or that relates to myself, in my own proper person and character, but which is entirely occupied about what relates to you? A man may sympathize with a woman in child-bed; though it is impossible that he should conceive himself as suffering her pains in his own proper person and character. That whole account of human nature, however, which deduces all sentiments and affections from self-love, which has made so much noise in the world, but which, so far as I know, has never yet been fully and distinctly explained, seems to me to have arisen from some confused misapprehension of the system of

sympathy.[299]

This quotation also makes it clear that Smith did not regard sympathy as egoistic. It is not a matter of imagining *myself* in similar circumstances, and thereby making it "about me," but of imagining myself as *you*.

> In order to produce this concord, as nature teaches the spectators to assume the circumstances of the person principally concerned, so she teaches this last in some measure to assume those of the spectators. As they are continually placing themselves in his situation, and thence conceiving emotions similar to what he feels; so he is as constantly placing himself in theirs, and thence conceiving some degree of that coolness about his own fortune, with which he is sensible that they will view it. As they are constantly considering what they themselves would feel, if they actually were the sufferers, so he is as constantly led to imagine in what manner he would be affected if he was only one of the spectators of his own situation. As their sympathy makes them look at it, in some measure, with his eyes, so his sympathy makes him look at it, in some measure, with theirs, especially when in their presence and acting under their observation: and as the reflected passion, which he thus conceives, is much weaker than the original one, it necessarily abates the violence of what he felt before he came into their presence, before he began to recollect in what manner they would be affected by it, and to view his situation in this candid and impartial light.[300]

Effective sympathy requires information about events and people. Without it, it's difficult for us to sympathize. There are limits to our actual capacity for sympathy, and sympathy can

---

[299] *The Moral Sentiments*, Part VI, Section iii, chapter 1.

[300] Ibid., Part I, Section i, chapter 4.

be impeded by ignorance of particular circumstances, or personal biases. Our goal should be to judge and act based on how an "impartial spectator" would.

Let us suppose that the great empire of China, with all its myriads of inhabitants, was suddenly swallowed up by an earthquake, and let us consider how a man of humanity in Europe, who had no sort of connexion with that part of the world, would be affected upon receiving intelligence of this dreadful calamity. He would, I imagine, first of all, express very strongly his sorrow for the misfortune of that unhappy people, he would make many melancholy reflections upon the precariousness of human life, and the vanity of all the labours of man, which could thus be annihilated in a moment. He would too, perhaps, if he was a man of speculation, enter into many reasonings concerning the effects which this disaster might produce upon the commerce of Europe, and the trade and business of the world in general. And when all this fine philosophy was over, when all these humane sentiments had been once fairly expressed, he would pursue his business or his pleasure, take his repose or his diversion, with the same ease and tranquillity, as if no such accident had happened. The most frivolous disaster which could befal himself would occasion a more real disturbance. If he was to lose his little finger to-morrow, he would not sleep to-night; but, provided he never saw them, he will snore with the most profound security over the ruin of a hundred millions of his brethren, and the destruction of that immense multitude seems plainly an object less interesting to him, than this paltry misfortune of his own. To prevent, therefore, this paltry misfortune to himself, would a man of humanity be willing to sacrifice the lives of a hundred millions of his brethren, provided he had never seen them? Human nature startles with horror at the thought, and the world, in its greatest depravity and corruption, never produced such a villain as could be capable of entertaining it. But what makes this difference? When our passive feelings are almost always so sordid and so selfish, how comes it that our active principles should often be so generous and so noble? When we are always so much more deeply affected by whatever concerns ourselves, than by whatever concerns other men; what is it which prompts the generous, upon all occasions, and the mean upon many, to sacrifice their own interests to the greater interests of others? It is not the soft power of humanity, it is not that feeble spark of benevolence which Nature has lighted up in the human heart, that is thus capable of counteracting the strongest impulses of self-love. It is a stronger power, a more forcible motive, which exerts itself upon such occasions. It is reason, principle, conscience, the inhabitant of the breast, the man within, the great judge and arbiter of our conduct. It is he who, whenever we are about to act so as to affect the happiness of others, calls to us, with a voice capable of astonishing the most presumptuous of our passions, that we are but one of the multitude, in no respect better than any other in it; and that when we prefer ourselves so shamefully and so blindly to others, we become the proper objects of resentment, abhorrence, and execration. It is from him only that we learn the real littleness of ourselves, and of whatever relates to ourselves, and the natural misrepresentations of self-love can be corrected only by the eye of this impartial spectator.[301]

---

[301] Ibid., Part III, Chapter 3.

This idea of the "impartial spectator" is crucial for understanding Smith's theory of moral judgment, and it is repeated throughout the *Theory of Moral Sentiments*.

When I endeavour to examine my own conduct, when I endeavour to pass sentence upon it, and either to approve or condemn it, it is evident that, in all such cases, I divide myself, as it were, into two persons; and that I, the examiner and judge, represent a different character from that other I, the person whose conduct is examined into and judged of. The first is the spectator, whose sentiments with regard to my own conduct I endeavour to enter into, by placing myself in his situation, and by considering how it would appear to me, when seen from that particular point of view. The second is the agent, the person whom I properly call myself, and of whose conduct, under the character of a spectator, I was endeavouring to form some opinion. The first is the judge; the second the person judged of. But that the judge should, in every respect, be the same with the person judged of, is as impossible, as that the cause should, in every respect, be the same with the effect."[302]

And again:

"But we admire that noble and generous resentment which governs its pursuit of the greatest injuries, not by the rage which they are apt to excite in the breast of the sufferer, but by the indignation which they naturally call forth in that of the impartial spectator; which allows no word, no gesture, to escape it beyond what this more equitable sentiment would dictate; which never, even in thought, attempts any greater vengeance, nor desires to inflict any greater

punishment, than what every indifferent person would rejoice to see executed.[303]

To sympathize with another's feelings is to implicitly approve of them, and to sympathize as we imagine an impartial spectator would, is to bestow moral approval on those feelings as well. Not every "feeling" we have is equally legitimate! Smith thinks that the feelings the impartial spectator *would* have are the ones that fit the situation. In other words, the feelings of the impartial spectator are the "correct" feelings that one *should* have in that particular situation. The feelings of the impartial spectator are the measure by which our own sentiments can be judged, indicating that some emotional responses are correct, and others are incorrect.

Because we desire the sympathy of others, we will regulate our actions to procure it. We will limit our displays of anger, and be humble in our moments of triumph—all to garner the sympathy of spectators, based on what we anticipate would seem appropriate to them. We can imagine what someone *should* feel (e.g., that the death of millions of people is far more tragic than the loss of a single finger!), and then act accordingly. Moral norms, then, express the *feelings* of the impartial spectator.

Once moral norms are identified, moral rules can be articulated in support of those norms. Moral rules are formed on the basis of our reactions to specific instances of especially disturbing actions (e.g., rape, murder). Our experience of such events is so repulsive that we, in effect, vow that we would never do such a thing—and surely the "impartial spectator" has the same revulsion, and would limit his or her actions in the same way.

It is thus that the general rules of morality are formed. They are ultimately founded upon experience of what, in particular instances, our moral faculties, our natural sense of merit and propriety, approve, or disapprove of. We do not originally approve or condemn particular actions;

---

[302] Ibid., Part III, Chapter 1.

[303] Ibid., Part I, Section i, Chapter 5.

because, upon examination, they appear to be agreeable or inconsistent with a certain general rule. The general rule, on the contrary, is formed, by finding from experience, that all actions of a certain kind, or circumstanced in a certain manner, are approved or disapproved of. To the man who first saw an inhuman murder, committed from avarice, envy, or unjust resentment, and upon one too that loved and trusted the murderer, who beheld the last agonies of the dying person, who heard him, with his expiring breath, complain more of the perfidy and ingratitude of his false friend, than of the violence which had been done to him, there could be no occasion, in order to conceive how horrible such an action was, that he should reflect, that one of the most sacred rules of conduct was what prohibited the taking away the life of an innocent person, that this was a plain violation of that rule, and consequently a very blamable action. His detestation of this crime, it is evident, would arise instantaneously and antecedent to his having formed to himself any such general rule. The general rule, on the contrary, which he might afterwards form, would be founded upon the detestation which he felt necessarily arise in his own breast, at the thought of this, and every other particular action of the same kind.[304]

These general rules give us minimal guidelines to follow, even if our own *actual* feelings haven't caught up with those of the impartial spectator. I might not personally feel revulsion at the thought of killing someone I hate, but I recognize that the impartial spectator would feel that revulsion, and so I can guide my behavior accordingly, despite my own lack of appropriate sentiment.

Although Smith's teacher, Frances Hutcheson, as well as his friend Hume, were

arguably "proto-utilitarians," Smith resisted the temptation to reduce all of morality to just an emphasis on "consequences." If anything, he said his own approach aligned more with the (virtue) approach of Aristotle.

> Virtue, according to Aristotle, consists in the habit of mediocrity according to right reason. Every particular virtue, according to him, lies in a kind of middle between two opposite vices, of which the one offends from being too much, the other from being too little affected by a particular species of objects. Thus the virtue of fortitude or courage lies in the middle between the opposite vices of cowardice and of presumptuous rashness, of which the one offends from being too much, and the other from being too little affected by the objects of fear. Thus too the virtue of frugality lies in a middle between avarice and profusion, of which the one consists in an excess, the other in a defect of the proper attention to the objects of self-interest. Magnanimity, in the same manner, lies in a middle between the excess of arrogance and the defect of pusillanimity, of which the one consists in too extravagant, the other in too weak a sentiment of our own worth and dignity. It is unnecessary to observe that this account of virtue corresponds too pretty exactly with what has been said above concerning the propriety and impropriety of conduct.[305]

Smith thought that the foundation of all virtue is "self-command," which allows us to control and restrain our passions, and feel compassion for (and empathize with) others. We develop and internalize this capacity only after experiencing the disapproval of others. This first occurs as children at play. As adults, the major sphere in which this trait is developed and displayed is the "market." As an example, try getting (and keeping) a job if you are exclusively

---

[304] Ibid., Part 3, Chapter 4.

[305] Ibid., Part VII, Section i, Chapter 2.

focused only on your own desires and gratification! "I know I'm supposed to be to work by 9 AM, but I'd prefer to sleep in later." How does that work out for you, in "real life?"

> But man has almost constant occasion for the help of his brethren, and it is in vain for him to expect it from their benevolence only. He will be more likely to prevail if he can interest their self-love in his favour, and shew them that it is for their own advantage to do for him what he requires of them. Whoever offers to another a bargain of any kind, proposes to do this. Give me that which I want, and you shall have this which you want, is the meaning of every such offer; and it is in this manner that we obtain from one another the far greater part of those good offices which we stand in need of. It is not from the benevolence of the butcher, the brewer, or the baker that we expect our dinner, but from their regard to their own interest. We address ourselves, not to their humanity, but to their self-love, and never talk to them of our own necessities, but of their advantages. Nobody but a beggar chooses to depend chiefly upon the benevolence of his fellow-citizens. Even a beggar does not depend upon it entirely. The charity of well-disposed people, indeed, supplies him with the whole fund of his subsistence. But though this principle ultimately provides him with all the necessaries of life which he has occasion for, it neither does nor can provide him with them as he has occasion for them. The greater part of his occasional wants are supplied in the same manner as those of other people, by treaty, by barter, and by purchase. With the money which one man gives him he purchases food. The old clothes which another bestows upon him he exchanges for other clothes which suit him better, or for lodging, or for food, or for money, with which he can buy either food, clothes, or lodging, as he has occasion.[306]

Market interactions, despite the common ("mythological") interpretation of Smith, are *not* about channeling the raw self-interest of others to one's own advantage, but are an interaction in which we must *subordinate* our exclusive focus on our own self-interest, and consider the "other," in order to come to an agreement.

This capacity we have for sympathy, and our ability to imagine how an impartial spectator would feel (using that to guide our own reactions and behavior), has an extraordinary origin: it is the product of the "Deity," an "invisible hand" guiding our conduct. This Deity gave humanity a surer guide to our collective well-being than Reason alone: our passions. Sympathy moves us, and then Reason can be employed to expand the scope of our sympathy.

The "invisible hand," while usually understood only in the context of the free market, is actually, therefore, a reference to the covert work of a (deistic) God intervening in human affairs for the betterment of all. The "invisible hand" thus refers to the several ways in which our "natural" pursuits (e.g., the pursuit of our self-interest, our pursuit of the sympathy of others, our pursuit of wealth, etc.) helps us, collectively. Certainly *one* of the arenas in which the invisible hand leads us is economics, but it is not the only, nor even the primary. First and foremost, it guides our sentiments and moral judgments.

Having established Smith's basic moral foundations, we will now turn to that for which he was most famous: his views on capitalism.

Economics

Smith, technically, did not actually endorse "capitalism," as that term didn't acquire widespread use until the next century. However, vocabulary notwithstanding, there is no doubt as to type of economic system he had in mind.

The Wealth of Nations (the full title being *An Inquiry into the Nature and Causes of the Wealth*

---

[306] *Wealth of Nations*, Book I, Chapter 2.

of Nations), is a lengthy book, split into five smaller books, with key themes as follows:

1. Division of labor and self-Interest
2. Stock and capital
3. An historical account of economic systems
4. The interaction between urban and rural commercial interests
5. The role of the sovereign in a market economy, and limited government

For our starting point, we will consider Smith's description of the birth of "capitalism" out of the feudal system.

> But what all the violence of the feudal institutions could never have effected, the silent and insensible operation of foreign commerce and manufactures gradually brought about. These gradually furnished the great proprietors with something for which they could exchange the whole surplus produce of their lands, and which they could consume themselves, without sharing it either with tenants or retainers. All for ourselves, and nothing for other people, seems, in every age of the world, to have been the vile maxim of the masters of mankind. As soon, therefore, as they could find a method of consuming the whole value of their rents themselves, they had no disposition to share them with any other persons. For a pair of diamond buckles, perhaps, or for something as frivolous and useless, they exchanged the maintenance, or, what is the same thing, the price of the maintenance of 1000 men for a year, and with it the whole weight and authority which it could give them. The buckles, however, were to be all their own, and no other human creature was to have any share of them; whereas, in the more ancient method of expense, they must have shared with at least 1000 people.

> With the judges that were to determine the preference, this difference was perfectly decisive; and thus, for the gratification of the most childish, the meanest, and the most sordid of all vanities they gradually bartered their whole power and authority.[307]

Both the lords and the merchants were pursuing their own self-interest. For the lords, their pursuit was for their vanity. For the merchants and craftsmen, their livelihoods and prosperity. Not surprisingly, this theme of the pursuit of self-interest is rather important, and will recur again and again throughout this chapter.

In his discussion of the different kinds of cultures and economic systems, Smith claims that civil governments, when instituted for the protection of property (as espoused by Locke, for example), actually exist to protect the interests of the wealthy against the poor!

> Among nations of hunters and shepherds, therefore, whose food consists chiefly in the flesh of those animals, everyman, by providing himself with food, provides himself with the materials of more clothing than he can wear. If there was no foreign commerce, the greater part of them would be thrown away as things of no value. . . . It is in the age of shepherds, in the second period of society, that the inequality of fortune first begins to take place, and introduces among men a degree of authority and subordination, which could not possibly exist before. It thereby introduces some degree of that civil government which is indispensably necessary for its own preservation; and it seems to do this naturally, and even independent of the consideration of that necessity. The consideration of that necessity comes, no doubt, afterwards, to contribute very much to maintain and secure that authority and subordination.

---

[307] Ibid., Book III, Chapter 4.

The rich, in particular, are necessarily interested to support that order of things, which can alone secure them in the possession of their own advantages. Men of inferior wealth combine to defend those of superior wealth in the possession of their property, in order that men of superior wealth may combine to defend them in the possession of theirs. . . . Civil government, so far as it is instituted for the security of property, is, in reality, instituted for the defence of the rich against the poor, or of those who have some property against those who have none at all.[308]

Commercial society is not "timeless" and natural, but emerged as the outcome of conflict between merchants and feudal lords—both pursuing their self-interest. Although he frames the history of capitalism in terms of the rich protecting their own interests via civil government, the overarching concern in the *Wealth of Nations* is the creation of a "universal opulence which extends itself to the lowest ranks of *all* people."[309]

Is this improvement in the circumstances of the lower ranks of the people to be regarded as an advantage, or as an inconveniency, to the society? The answer seems at first abundantly plain. Servants, labourers, and workmen of different kinds, make up the far greater part of every great political society. But what improves the circumstances of the greater part, can never be regarded as any inconveniency to the whole. No society can surely be flourishing and happy, of which the far greater part of the members are poor and miserable. It is but equity, besides, that they who feed, clothe, and lodge the whole body of the people, should have such a share of the produce

of their own labour as to be themselves tolerably well fed, clothed, and lodged.[310]

The key to improving the condition of the poor is by increasing labor productivity. The main influences on that are the "skill, dexterity, and judgment with which its labor is generally applied" (i.e., division of labor and specialization), and "the proportion between the number of those who are employed in useful labor, and that of those who are not" (i.e., unemployment rates).[311]

Many improvements have been made by the ingenuity of the makers of the machines, when to make them became the business of a peculiar trade; and some by that of those who are called philosophers, or men of speculation, whose trade it is not to do anything, but to observe everything, and who, upon that account, are often capable of combining together the powers of the most distant and dissimilar objects in the progress of society, philosophy or speculation becomes, like every other employment, the principal or sole trade and occupation of a particular class of citizens. Like every other employment, too, it is subdivided into a great number of different branches, each of which affords occupation to a peculiar tribe or class of philosophers; and this subdivision of employment in philosophy, as well as in every other business, improve dexterity, and saves time. Each individual becomes more expert in his own peculiar branch, more work is done upon the whole, and the quantity of science is considerably increased by it.[312]

A free market harnesses personal desire not just for the individual's benefit, but that of the community, as a whole. What makes the pursuit

---

[308] Ibid., Book V, Part 1 and Part 2.
[309] Ibid., Book I, Chapter 1. Emphasis added.
[310] Ibid., Book I, Chapter 8.

[311] Ibid., Introduction.
[312] Ibid., Book I, Chapter 1.

of self-interest in a free market good, and morally permissible, is the presumed fact that it benefits the *community*, and not just the individual. As a basic (and important) psychological premise, Smith argues that we all naturally seek our own betterment.

> But the principle which prompts to save, is the desire of bettering our condition; a desire which, though generally calm and dispassionate, comes with us from the womb, and never leaves us till we go into the grave. In the whole interval which separates those two moments, there is scarce, perhaps, a single instance, in which any man is so perfectly and completely satisfied with his situation, as to be without any wish of alteration or improvement of any kind.[313]

The "invisible hand" implants in us a confusion of wealth with "betterment." The capitalist will be driven by this to increase his wealth. The fruits of his labor will be (presumably) reinvested in his business so as to acquire *more* wealth. He will (presumably) invest in new and better technology, which will require not only more workers, but more specialized workers. This division of labor will increase production, and therefore increase profit, leading to economic growth and the betterment of all— once again emphasizing what is good for *all*, and not merely the individual.

> Observe the accommodation of the most common artificer or day-labourer in a civilized and thriving country, and you will perceive that the number of people, of whose industry a part, though but a small part, has been employed in procuring him this accommodation, exceeds all computation. The woollen coat, for example, which covers the day-labourer, as coarse and rough as it may appear, is the produce of the joint labour of a great multitude of workmen. The shepherd, the sorter of the wool, the

wool-comber or carder, the dyer, the scribbler, the spinner, the weaver, the fuller, the dresser, with many others, must all join their different arts in order to complete even this homely production. How many merchants and carriers, besides, must have been employed in transporting the materials from some of those workmen to others who often live in a very distant part of the country? How much commerce and navigation in particular, how many ship-builders, sailors, sail-makers, rope-makers, must have been employed in order to bring together the different drugs made use of by the dyer, which often come from the remotest corners of the world? What a variety of labour, too, is necessary in order to produce the tools of the meanest of those workmen! To say nothing of such complicated machines as the ship of the sailor, the mill of the fuller, or even the loom of the weaver, let us consider only what a variety of labour is requisite in order to form that very simple machine, the shears with which the shepherd clips the wool. The miner, the builder of the furnace for smelting the ore, the feller of the timber, the burner of the charcoal to be made use of in the smelting-house, the brickmaker, the bricklayer, the workmen who attend the furnace, the millwright, the forger, the smith, must all of them join their different arts in order to produce them. Were we to examine, in the same manner, all the different parts of his dress and household furniture, the coarse linen shirt which he wears next his skin, the shoes which cover his feet, the bed which he lies on, and all the different parts which compose it, the kitchen-grate at which he prepares his victuals, the coals which he makes use of for that purpose, dug from the bowels of the earth, and brought to him, perhaps, by a long sea and a long land-carriage, all the other utensils

---

[313] Ibid., Book II, Chapter 3.

of his kitchen, all the furniture of his table, the knives and forks, the earthen or pewter plates upon which he serves up and divides his victuals, the different hands employed in preparing his bread and his beer, the glass window which lets in the heat and the light, and keeps out the wind and the rain, with all the knowledge and art requisite for preparing that beautiful and happy invention, without which these northern parts of the world could scarce have afforded a very comfortable habitation, together with the tools of all the different workmen employed in producing those different conveniencies; if we examine, I say, all these things, and consider what a variety of labour is employed about each of them, we shall be sensible that, without the assistance and co-operation of many thousands, the very meanest person in a civilized country could not be provided, even according to, what we very falsely imagine, the easy and simple manner in which he is commonly accommodated. Compared, indeed, with the more extravagant luxury of the great, his accommodation must no doubt appear extremely simple and easy; and yet it may be true, perhaps, that the accommodation of an European prince does not always so much exceed that of an industrious and frugal peasant, as the accommodation of the latter exceeds that of many an African king, the absolute masters of the lives and liberties of ten thousand naked savages.[314]

Setting aside the needless and breathtaking racism in the quotation above (which was no doubt the product of his time and culture, as it certainly is not warranted by his philosophical system), the basic point of his fantastic anecdote is that the production (and sale) of something even as simple as a wool coat involves, and enriches, far more people than we might initially

realize. Within a market economy, even the "common day-labourer" who is but an "industrious and frugal peasant" has a lifestyle that exceeds that of "many an African king."

A more culturally sensitive way to express his idea is that even "poor" people achieve levels of comparative wealth within capitalist systems—at least as compared to their counterparts within mercantilist, feudal, or other economic systems.

Key to this enrichment and aggrandizement, of course, is competition. The value of competition for society is that individuals are driven by their desire for wealth, and competition additionally dismantles rigid class structures by allowing for social mobility. Competition attracts labor and capital when the market price is above the "natural price" (what it costs to produce the product or service), and labor and capital will move elsewhere if the market price is below the natural price.

This is another demonstration of the "invisible hand" at work. Competition turns self-interest towards socially useful goals—so long as people are free to market their labor, and competition (rather than monopolies) reign, that is.

The poor man's son, whom heaven in its anger has visited with ambition, when he begins to look around him, admires the condition of the rich. He finds the cottage of his father too small for his accommodation, and fancies he should be lodged more at his ease in a palace. He is displeased with being obliged to walk a-foot, or to endure the fatigue of riding on horseback. He sees his superiors carried about in machines, and imagines that in one of these he could travel with less inconveniency. He feels himself naturally indolent, and willing to serve himself with his own hands as little as possible; and judges, that a numerous retinue of servants would save him from a great deal of trouble. He thinks if he had

---

[314] Ibid., Book I, Chapter 1.

attained all these, he would sit still contentedly, and be quiet, enjoying himself in the thought of the happiness and tranquillity of his situation. He is enchanted with the distant idea of this felicity. It appears in his fancy like the life of some superior rank of beings, and, in order to arrive at it, he devotes himself for ever to the pursuit of wealth and greatness. To obtain the conveniencies which these afford, he submits in the first year, nay in the first month of his application, to more fatigue of body and more uneasiness of mind than he could have suffered through the whole of his life from the want of them. He studies to distinguish himself in some laborious profession. With the most unrelenting industry he labours night and day to acquire talents superior to all his competitors. He endeavours next to bring those talents into public view, and with equal assiduity solicits every opportunity of employment. For this purpose he makes his court to all mankind; he serves those whom he hates, and is obsequious to those whom he despises.

Through the whole of his life he pursues the idea of a certain artificial and elegant repose which he may never arrive at, for which he sacrifices a real tranquillity that is at all times in his power, and which, if in the extremity of old age he should at last attain to it, he will find to be in no respect preferable to that humble security and contentment which he had abandoned for it. It is then, in the last dregs of life, his body wasted with toil and diseases, his mind galled and ruffled by the memory of a thousand injuries and disappointments which he imagines he has met with from the injustice of his enemies, or from the perfidy and ingratitude of his friends, that he begins at last to find that wealth and greatness are mere trinkets of frivolous utility, no more adapted for procuring ease of body or tranquillity of mind than the tweezer-cases of the lover of toys; and like them too, more troublesome to the person who carries them about with him than all the advantages they can afford him are commodious. . . . If we consider the real satisfaction which all these things are capable of affording, by itself and separated from the beauty of that arrangement which is fitted to promote it, it will always appear in the highest degree contemptible and trifling. But we rarely view it in this abstract and philosophical light. We naturally confound it in our imagination with the order, the regular and harmonious movement of the system, the machine or oeconomy by means of which it is produced. The pleasures of wealth and greatness, when considered in this complex view, strike the imagination as something grand and beautiful and noble, of which the attainment is well worth all the toil and anxiety which we are so apt to bestow upon it.

And it is well that nature imposes upon us in this manner. It is this deception which rouses and keeps in continual motion the industry of mankind. It is this which first prompted them to cultivate the ground, to build houses, to found cities and commonwealths, and to invent and improve all the sciences and arts, which ennoble and embellish human life; which have entirely changed the whole face of the globe, have turned the rude forests of nature into agreeable and fertile plains, and made the trackless and barren ocean a new fund of subsistence, and the great high road of communication to the different nations of the earth. The earth by these labours of mankind has been obliged to redouble her natural fertility, and to maintain a greater multitude of inhabitants.[315]

---

[315] *TMS*, Part IV, Chapter 1.

Interestingly, the "invisible hand" of the Deity implants in us a desire for self-enrichment, and an envy of the wealthy. This causes us to believe that the lives of the wealthy are better and happier, and we therefore work to improve our circumstances. Although we might well eventually discover that the rich are not necessarily happier than anyone else, our original perception has fulfilled its function. Our hard work and ambition has made us productive, and has increased the wealth and usable resources around us. Land that otherwise might have been left fallow has been cultivated. Time that otherwise might have been spent at leisure has been used "productively," supplying humanity with inventions, goods, and services it otherwise would not have enjoyed.

Another (probably outdated) way in which the "invisible hand" is at work within and among us is with regard to how the rich can (could?) only consume as much as any other person. They will admittedly pick the "best" portions for themselves, but will leave the rest for others.

The rich only select from the heap what is most precious and agreeable. They consume little more than the poor, and in spite of their natural selfishness and rapacity, though they mean only their own conveniency, though the sole end which they propose from the labours of all the thousands whom they employ, be the gratification of their own vain and insatiable desires, they divide with the poor the produce of all their improvements. They are led by an invisible hand to make nearly the same distribution of the necessaries of life, which would have been made, had the earth been divided into equal portions among all its inhabitants, and thus

without intending it, without knowing it, advance the interest of the society, and afford means to the multiplication of the species. When Providence divided the earth among a few lordly masters, it neither forgot nor abandoned those who seemed to have been left out in the partition. These last too enjoy their share of all that it produces.[316]

This account might hold true if we imagine the resources of the world as if food at a table. The wealthiest among us can't eat much more than the poorest. So, although the rich might pick for their share the finest food from the table, there is still food left over for everyone else. The problem with this imagery, of course, is that modern wealth is not understood solely, or even primarily, as consumable and perishable goods. Wealth that is money, shares of stock, investment portfolios, etc., can be acquired without limit, and never "spoils"—and it is by no means obvious that the wealthy will be satisfied with merely the "best" of an equal share, leaving plenty for everyone else.![317]

Another contemporary limitation, or counter-point, to Smith is that modern economies are far from "mom and pop" tradesmen who can respond quickly to changes in demand by shifting from making horse shoes to door hinges, for example. Modern economies are driven by massive corporations, large-scale businesses with expensive operations and strategic plans that project out months, or even years into the future. Such businesses are incapable of "rapid" responses to changes in demand, or the pull of self-interest. In addition, modern technology brings "unintended consequences" such as pollution, climate change, etc. Such an application of the "invisible hand" is no longer obviously to the benefit of all . . . .

---

[316] Ibid., Book IV, Chapter 1.

[317] Globally, as of 2010, the richest 0.5 percent of the adult population held over 1/3 of the world's wealth. In the United States, as of 2015, Americans in the top 1 percent of income average

over 38 times more income than the bottom 90 percent, while the top 0.1 percent make over 184 times the income of the bottom 90 percent. http://inequality.org/income-inequality/

This brings us to an easily misunderstood aspect of Smith's philosophy: while he does, indeed, favor a limited government, as we shall see in our next section, he by no means rejects government intervention entirely. Indeed, he believes that the "sovereign" has several important functions—and that taxes should be levied to fund these functions!

Limited Government

Smith's advocacy for what we know today as "*laissez-faire*" capitalism is based on his belief that government intervention in market decisions fails to improve the outcomes of those decisions, and can do more harm than good. This is empirically verifiable, of course. Therefore, if there should be compelling evidence that some government "interference" does, in fact, produce *better* outcomes, then Smith would have endorsed such interference. For example, Smith thought that monopolies were themselves destructive to the effectiveness and efficiency of the free market. Should government intervention be required to break up monopolies, he would presumably favor it.

Occasional cases for government intervention notwithstanding, Smith was certainly more confident in the decisions of individual participants in the market than in government officials.

> But the annual revenue of every society is always precisely equal to the exchangeable value of the whole annual produce of its industry, or rather is precisely the same thing with that exchangeable value. As every individual, therefore, endeavours as much as he can, both to employ his capital in the support of domestic industry, and so to direct that industry that its produce maybe of the greatest value; every individual necessarily labours to render the annual revenue of the society as great as he can. He generally, indeed, neither intends to promote the public interest, nor knows how much he is promoting it. By preferring the support of domestic to that of foreign industry, he intends only his own security; and by directing that industry in such a manner as its produce may be of the greatest value, he intends only his own gain; and he is in this, as in many other cases, led by an invisible hand to promote an end which was no part of his intention. Nor is it always the worse for the society that it was no part of it. By pursuing his own interest, he frequently promotes that of the society more effectually than when he really intends to promote it. I have never known much good done by those who affected to trade for the public good. It is an affectation, indeed, not very common among merchants, and very few words need be employed in dissuading them from it.[318]

Knowledge is imperfect—as are people. The accumulation of experience helps correct for both of these deficiencies. We should be wary of "systems" which are at least as flawed as the individuals who devise them, and which are more resistant to reflection and adjustment based on new experience.

> The man of system, on the contrary, is apt to be very wise in his own conceit; and is often so enamoured with the supposed beauty of his own ideal plan of government, that he cannot suffer the smallest deviation from any part of it. He goes on to establish it completely and in all its parts, without any regard either to the great interests, or to the strong prejudices which may oppose it. He seems to imagine that he can arrange the different members of a great society with as much ease as the hand arranges the different pieces upon a chess-board. He does not consider that the pieces upon the chess-board have no other principle of

---

[318] *WN*, Book IV, Chapter 2.

motion besides that which the hand impresses upon them; but that, in the great chess-board of human society, every single piece has a principle of motion of its own, altogether different from that which the legislature might chuse to impress upon it. If those two principles coincide and act in the same direction, the game of human society will go on easily and harmoniously, and is very likely to be happy and successful. If they are opposite or different, the game will go on miserably, and the society must be at all times in the highest degree of disorder.[319]

One can do more damage trying to manipulate market exchanges, than by trusting in the individuals (and their own judgment) involved. Smith favored limited government, trusting in the ordinary person to discern what is best in their own circumstances, rather than entrusting politicians to "know what's best."

It is the highest impertinence and presumption, therefore, in kings and ministers to pretend to watch over the economy of private people, and to restrain their expense, either by sumptuary laws, or by prohibiting the importation of foreign luxuries. They are themselves always, and without any exception, the greatest spendthrifts in the society. Let them look well after their own expense, and they may safely trust private people with theirs. If their own extravagance does not ruin the state, that of the subject never will.[320]

In Smith's time, the cultural presumption was that the poor needed moral guidance, including laws regulating alcohol consumption, and even the wearing of "luxurious" clothing.[321] Social sanctions do a better job than government sanctions, according to Smith. The sumptuary laws, for example, were unnecessary because *most* people are sensible enough, and desirous enough of prosperity, that they wouldn't squander their rent or food money on fancy clothing.

Although Smith is wary of government "meddling," he does acknowledge several *proper* functions for the State. The three proper duties of a sovereign are to:

1. Protect citizens from external threats.
2. Protect citizens from each other (internal threats), and enforce justice.
3. Create and maintain "certain public works, and certain public institutions."

thirdly, the duty of erecting and maintaining certain public works, and certain public institutions, which it can never be for the interest of any individual, or small number of individuals to erect

---

[319] *TMS*, Part VI, Section ii, Chapter 2.
[320] *WN*, Book II, Chapter 3.
[321] An example of such a "sumptuary" law, issued by Queen Elizabeth I: "The excess of apparel and the superfluity of unnecessary foreign wares thereto belonging now of late years is grown by sufferance to such an extremity that the manifest decay of the whole realm generally is like to follow (by bringing into the realm such superfluities of silks, cloths of gold, silver, and other most vain devices of so great cost for the quantity thereof as of necessity the moneys and treasure of the realm is and must be yearly conveyed out of the same to answer the said

excess) but also particularly the wasting and undoing of a great number of young gentlemen, otherwise serviceable, and others seeking by show of apparel to be esteemed as gentlemen, who, allured by the vain show of those things, do not only consume themselves, their goods, and lands which their parents left unto them, but also run into such debts and shifts as they cannot live out of danger of laws without attempting unlawful acts, whereby they are not any ways serviceable to their country as otherwise they might be." — Statute issued at Greenwich, 15 June 1574.

and maintain; because the profit could never repay the expense to any individual, or small number of individuals, though it may frequently do much more than repay it to a great society.[322]

Consistent with "libertarian" thinking, those first two duties are protective: protecting against external and internal threats. In addition to that, though, he mentions the creation and maintenance of certain public works and public institutions.

As a possible contemporary American example, the California Community College System was officially created in 1967, though it can be traced back to the State legislature authorizing the creation of "junior colleges" in 1907 (the first of which was Fresno City College in 1910). The rationale was that it was beneficial to society that people have education beyond high school. The 1960 "Master Plan for Higher Education" originally banned tuition fees for students, promising free college education to "every student who is willing and able to benefit from attendance." Although budget deficits starting in 1978 have resulted in students paying per unit costs for courses, the community college is still heavily subsidized by tax-payer dollars—again, on the assumption that the public good is served by having more of the population with a college education. This sort of program is entirely consistent with Smith's 3rd duty of the sovereign, and not at all at odds with his alleged libertarianism.

As another example, consider public roads.

The tolls for the maintenance of a highroad cannot, with any safety, be made the property of private persons. A high-road, though entirely neglected, does not become altogether impassable, though a canal does. The proprietors of the tolls upon a high-road, therefore, might neglect altogether the repair of the road, and yet continue to levy very nearly the same tolls. It is proper, therefore, that the tolls for the maintenance of such a work should be put under the management of commissioners or trustees.[323]

Some contemporary libertarians argue that the government should provide only basic protection (i.e., police and military), and leave everything else "privatized." Privately owned and operated hospitals, fire departments, utilities, and street creation/maintenance—all for those who can afford them, of course.

Though this sort of system is presented as an idyllic "Free Market" society, clearly Smith himself would disagree! Smith argues that roads should be maintained by commissioners or trustees (i.e., *public* employees), given the risk that private owners would neglect the proper maintenance of the road in order to increase their profit. Public employees, on the other hand, who would not benefit from such profit, would have no such incentive. Beyond this concern of corruption, of course, is the practical benefit of (literally) free travel! If a relatively poor person can't afford to pay for private roads, his own travel (and trade) options are limited. This prevents him from selling his labor based on market conditions, and thereby prevents the most efficient and optimal outcomes of the market. Oddly enough, there is a "free market" justification for State control of things like road construction and maintenance.

As we have seen, many of the things that "everybody" knows about Smith have turned out to be either false, or at least more nuanced. If one believes Smith to be the "patron saint" of Capitalism, and an unapologetic advocate for the unrestricted accumulation of wealth, then one might form some very *false* conclusions about his actual system. Smith did indeed favor the accumulation of societal wealth—but for the betterment of *all*, not merely for the sake of the wealthy few.

---

[322] *WN*, Book IV, Chapter 9.

[323] Ibid., Book V, Part 3, Article 1.

Wealth and the Wealthy

Smith neither despised the poor, nor adored the rich. Indeed, the poor are not essentially different from the rich, according to Smith.

> The difference of natural talents in different men, is, in reality, much less than we are aware of; and the very different genius which appears to distinguish men of different professions, when grown up to maturity, is not upon many occasions so much the cause, as the effect of the division of labour. The difference between the most dissimilar characters, between a philosopher and a common street porter, for example, seems to arise not so much from nature, as from habit, custom, and education. When they came in to the world, and for the first six or eight years of their existence, they were, perhaps, very much alike, and neither their parents nor play-fellows could perceive any remarkable difference. About that age, or soon after, they come to be employed in very different occupations.[324]

In sharp contrast to the crudely "social Darwinist" ideas that some hold today, according to which the wealthy are so because of their inherent talent and merit, whereas the poor are so from their character flaws and incompetence, Smith is claiming that the rich and poor alike start out very similar to each other, but as they grow up, different experiences, resources, and educational opportunities cause them to be "employed in very different occupations."

Not only does Smith not advocate any sort of presumption of moral superiority in the wealthy, he explicitly argues *against* such a presumption, claiming that many *mistakenly* envy the rich, and pursue wealth at the expense of virtue.

> It is from our disposition to admire, and consequently to imitate, the rich and the great, that they are enabled to set, or to lead what is called the fashion. Their dress is the fashionable dress; the language of their conversation, the fashionable style; their air and deportment, the fashionable behaviour. Even their vices and follies are fashionable; and the greater part of men are proud to imitate and resemble them in the very qualities which dishonour and degrade them. Vain men often give themselves airs of a fashionable profligacy, which, in their hearts, they do not approve of, and of which, perhaps, they are really not guilty. They desire to be praised for what they themselves do not think praise-worthy, and are ashamed of unfashionable virtues which they sometimes practise in secret, and for which they have secretly some degree of real veneration. There are hypocrites of wealth and greatness, as well as of religion and virtue; and a vain man is as apt to pretend to be what he is not, in the one way, as a cunning man is in the other. He assumes the equipage and splendid way of living of his superiors, without considering that whatever may be praise-worthy in any of these, derives its whole merit and propriety from its suitableness to that situation and fortune which both require and can easily support the expence. Many a poor man places his glory in being thought rich, without considering that the duties (if one may call such follies by so very venerable a name) which that reputation imposes upon him, must soon reduce him to beggary, and render his situation still more unlike that of those whom he admires and imitates, than it had been originally.

> To attain to this envied situation, the candidates for fortune too frequently abandon the paths of virtue; for

---

[324] Ibid., Book I, Chapter 2.

unhappily, the road which leads to the one, and that which leads to the other, lie sometimes in very opposite directions. But the ambitious man flatters himself that, in the splendid situation to which he advances, he will have so many means of commanding the respect and admiration of mankind, and will be enabled to act with such superior propriety and grace, that the lustre of his future conduct will entirely cover, or efface, the foulness of the steps by which he arrived at that elevation. In many governments the candidates for the highest stations are above the law; and, if they can attain the object of their ambition, they have no fear of being called to account for the means by which they acquired it. They often endeavour, therefore, not only by fraud and falsehood, the ordinary and vulgar arts of intrigue and cabal; but sometimes by the perpetration of the most enormous crimes, by murder and assassination, by rebellion and civil war, to supplant and destroy those who oppose or stand in the way of their greatness. They more frequently miscarry than succeed; and commonly gain nothing but the disgraceful punishment which is due to their crimes. But, though they should be so lucky as to attain that wished-for greatness, they are always most miserably disappointed in the happiness which they expect to enjoy in it. It is not ease or pleasure, but always honour, of one kind or another, though frequently an honour very ill understood, that the ambitious man really pursues. But the honour of his exalted station appears, both in his own eyes and in those of other people, polluted and defiled by the baseness of the means through which he rose to it.[325]

Though written over 150 years ago, this could just have easily been written today.

Imitation of the wealthy achieved new heights of absurdity with the "Kylie Jenner Lip Challenge" that swept Instagram in 2015, only to be supplanted by the "Kylie Jenner 'Thighbrow' Challenge" in that same year. A young woman, known only for her wealth and status on a reality TV show ("Keeping up with the Kardashians"), became an object of imitation for countless young girls who sought to acquire the same puffy lips, and particular thigh creases. This is only an extreme example from social media, but countless more examples abound of the ways in which the wealthy set fashion trends, and how their behavior—no matter how scandalous—inspires imitation from persons who want to be "just like" their "role-models."

This envy of the wealthy, and the confusing of wealth with virtue, is problematic because it can distort our sympathies, and even the objectivity of the "impartial spectator." It skews our moral judgments by causing us to be insufficiently sympathetic to the poor, and overly sympathetic to the wealthy. The following excerpt is lengthy, but worth quoting at length.

> This disposition to admire, and almost to worship, the rich and the powerful, and to despise, or, at least, to neglect persons of poor and mean condition, though necessary both to establish and to maintain the distinction of ranks and the order of society, is, at the same time, the great and most universal cause of the corruption of our moral sentiments. That wealth and greatness are often regarded with the respect and admiration which are due only to wisdom and virtue; and that the contempt, of which vice and folly are the only proper objects, is often most unjustly bestowed upon poverty and weakness, has been the complaint of moralists in all ages.
>
> We desire both to be respectable and to be respected. We dread both to be contemptible and to be contemned. But,

---

[325] *TMS*, Part I, Section iii, Chapter 8.

upon coming into the world, we soon find that wisdom and virtue are by no means the sole objects of respect; nor vice and folly, of contempt. We frequently see the respectful attentions of the world more strongly directed towards the rich and the great, than towards the wise and the virtuous. We see frequently the vices and follies of the powerful much less despised than the poverty and weakness of the innocent. To deserve, to acquire, and to enjoy the respect and admiration of mankind, are the great objects of ambition and emulation. Two different roads are presented to us, equally leading to the attainment of this so much desired object; the one, by the study of wisdom and the practice of virtue; the other, by the acquisition of wealth and greatness. Two different characters are presented to our emulation; the one, of proud ambition and ostentatious avidity. the other, of humble modesty and equitable justice. Two different models, two different pictures, are held out to us, according to which we may fashion our own character and behaviour; the one more gaudy and glittering in its colouring; the other more correct and more exquisitely beautiful in its outline: the one forcing itself upon the notice of every wandering eye; the other, attracting the attention of scarce anybody but the most studious and careful observer. They are the wise and the virtuous chiefly, a select, though, I am afraid, but a small party, who are the real and steady admirers of wisdom and virtue. The great mob of mankind are the admirers and worshippers, and, what may seem more extraordinary, most frequently the disinterested admirers and worshippers, of wealth and greatness.

The respect which we feel for wisdom and virtue is, no doubt, different from that which we conceive for wealth and greatness; and it requires no very nice discernment to distinguish the difference.

But, notwithstanding this difference, those sentiments bear a very considerable resemblance to one another. In some particular features they are, no doubt, different, but, in the general air of the countenance, they seem to be so very nearly the same, that inattentive observers are very apt to mistake the one for the other.

In equal degrees of merit there is scarce any man who does not respect more the rich and the great, than the poor and the humble. With most men the presumption and vanity of the former are much more admired, than the real and solid merit of the latter. It is scarce agreeable to good morals, or even to good language, perhaps, to say, that mere wealth and greatness, abstracted from merit and virtue, deserve our respect. We must acknowledge, however, that they almost constantly obtain it; and that they may, therefore, be considered as, in some respects, the natural objects of it. Those exalted stations may, no doubt, be completely degraded by vice and folly. But the vice and folly must be very great, before they can operate this complete degradation. The profligacy of a man of fashion is looked upon with much less contempt and aversion, than that of a man of meaner condition. In the latter, a single transgression of the rules of temperance and propriety, is commonly more resented, than the constant and avowed contempt of them ever is in the former.

In the middling and inferior stations of life, the road to virtue and that to fortune, to such fortune, at least, as men in such stations can reasonably expect to acquire, are, happily in most cases, very nearly the same. In all the middling and inferior professions, real and solid professional abilities, joined to prudent, just, firm, and temperate conduct, can very seldom fail of success. Abilities will even sometimes prevail where the conduct is by no means correct. Either habitual imprudence, however, or injustice, or weakness, or profligacy, will always cloud, and sometimes depress altogether, the most splendid professional abilities. Men in the inferior and middling stations of life, besides, can never be great enough to be above the law, which must generally overawe them into some sort of respect for, at least, the more important rules of justice. The success of such people, too, almost always depends upon the favour and good opinion of their neighbours and equals; and without a tolerably regular conduct these can very seldom be obtained. The good old proverb, therefore, that honesty is the best policy, holds, in such situations, almost always perfectly true. In such situations, therefore, we may generally expect a considerable degree of virtue; and, fortunately for the good morals of society, these are the situations of by far the greater part of mankind.

In the superior stations of life the case is unhappily not always the same. In the courts of princes, in the drawing-rooms of the great, where success and preferment depend, not upon the esteem of intelligent and well-informed equals, but upon the fanciful and foolish favour of ignorant, presumptuous, and proud superiors; flattery and falsehood too often prevail over merit and abilities. In such societies the abilities to please, are more regarded than the abilities to serve. In quiet and peaceable times, when the storm is at a distance, the prince, or great man, wishes only to be amused, and is even apt to fancy that he has scarce any occasion for the service of any body, or that those who amuse him are sufficiently able to serve him. The external graces, the frivolous accomplishments of that

impertinent and foolish thing called a man of fashion, are commonly more admired than the solid and masculine virtues of a warrior, a statesman, a philosopher, or a legislator. All the great and awful virtues, all the virtues which can fit, either for the council, the senate, or the field, are, by the insolent and insignificant flatterers, who commonly figure the most in such corrupted societies, held in the utmost contempt and derision. When the duke of Sully was called upon by Lewis the Thirteenth, to give his advice in some great emergency, he observed the favourites and courtiers whispering to one another, and smiling at his unfashionable appearance. 'Whenever your majesty's father,' said the old warrior and statesman, 'did me the honour to consult me, he ordered the buffoons of the court to retire into the antechamber.'[326]

This breathtaking commentary on the unfair treatment, and even the unfair judgment, of the poor (and in favor of the wealthy) is shocking, given the myth of Adam Smith as the champion of the wealthy. The myth is precisely that, though: a myth.

Smith joins his voice to the "complaint of moralists in all ages" that the admiration rightfully bestowed upon wisdom and virtue is misguidedly being extended to "wealth and greatness," whereas the contempt rightfully reserved for "vice and folly" is being bestowed instead upon "poverty."

We all desire to be respected, but we soon discover that wisdom and good character are not the only means by which one can become respected, nor even the surest ways. Instead, we discover that esteem is bestowed due to wealth and celebrity, and even the *vice* of the wealthy seems to be overlooked and more easily forgiven than the "poverty and weakness of the innocent." We conclude that there are two roads to the esteem we desire: virtue, or wealth.

---

[326] Ibid., Part 1, Section 3, Chapter 3.

Virtue is difficult, and often not even noticed by any "but the most studious and careful observer." Someone has to get to know you pretty well to perceive that you are wise and good—but wealth is noticed right away! When someone pulls up in their expensive sports car at the most exclusive restaurant in town, with an entourage of well-dressed tag-alongs, and surrounded by the paparazzi, there is no mistaking their wealth and "greatness."

Even though we recognize that the respect we feel for wisdom and virtue is different from that we feel for wealth and celebrity, the feelings "bear a considerable resemblance to one another," and so are easily confused, or substituted, in our minds. While we might be willing to proclaim that the wealthy who are without virtue don't deserve our respect, we also have to acknowledge "that they almost certainly obtain it" anyway!

Interestingly, there is something advantageous, with respect to building and maintaining moral character, about being *poor*. Poor people can't get away with acting as if they were above the law (unlike the rich), but must instead regulate their behavior if they want to avoid trouble. Similarly, the success of a poor person depends much more heavily on their reputation among their peers, who tend to not be very forgiving of foolish behavior. Poorer people must therefore maintain "tolerably regular conduct." In wealthier circles, however, "flattery and falsehood too often prevail over merit and abilities," and "frivolous accomplishments . . . are commonly more admired than the solid and masculine virtues of a warrior, a statesman, a philosopher, or a legislator."

Bemoaning this false equivalence of "wealth" with "virtue" and "poverty" with "vice," Smith recommends that education is needed to correct any gaps of understanding with regard to the merits of the rich and the poor (just as education is needed to correct any misunderstanding of Smith himself!).

Government intervention for the poor

While it is mythological thinking to imagine Smith as hostile to the poor, it would be equally mythological to imagine Smith as some sort of socialist champion of the "Proletariat," in contrast. He was far from either. He did, however, explicitly argue that a legitimate and important role for the government was to intervene on behalf of the poor. Book five of the *Wealth of Nations* addresses the importance of universal education, social unity, religious toleration, and the need to regulate against the dangers of religious extremism. Our focus will be limited to what he has to say about universal education.

Although the division of labor (and subsequent specialization) is what makes possible the economic growth and general prosperity for which capitalism is known, Smith argues that, without education, the very division of labor that makes possible the economic growth that promotes the "universal opulence which extends itself to the lowest ranks of all people" can be mentally stultifying. In "primitive economies," on the other hand, the variety of tasks keeps the mind active and engaged.

> In the progress of the division of labour, the employment of the far greater part of those who live by labour, that is, of the great body of the people, comes to be confined to a few very simple operations; frequently to one or two. But the understandings of the greater part of men are necessarily formed by their ordinary employments. The man whose whole life is spent in performing a few simple operations, of which the effects, too, are perhaps always the same, or very nearly the same, has no occasion to exert his understanding, or to exercise his invention, in finding out expedients for removing difficulties which never occur. He naturally loses, therefore, the habit of such exertion, and generally becomes as stupid and ignorant as it is possible for a human creature to become. The torpor of his mind renders him not only incapable

of relishing or bearing a part in any rational conversation, but of conceiving any generous, noble, or tender sentiment, and consequently of forming any just judgment concerning many even of the ordinary duties of private life. Of the great and extensive interests of his country he is altogether incapable of judging; and unless very particular pains have been taken to render him otherwise, he is equally incapable of defending his country in war. The uniformity of his stationary life naturally corrupts the courage of his mind, and makes him regard, with abhorrence, the irregular, uncertain, and adventurous life of a soldier. It corrupts even the activity of his body, and renders him incapable of exerting his strength with vigour and perseverance in any other employment, than that to which he has been bred. His dexterity at his own particular trade seems, in this manner, to be acquired at the expense of his intellectual, social, and martial virtues. But in every improved and civilized society, this is the state into which the labouring poor, that is, the great body of the people, must necessarily fall, unless government takes some pains to prevent it.

It is otherwise in the barbarous societies, as they are commonly called, of hunters, of shepherds, and even of husbandmen in that rude state of husbandry which precedes the improvement of manufactures, and the extension of foreign commerce. In such societies, the varied occupations of every man oblige every man to exert his capacity, and to invent expedients for removing difficulties which are continually occurring. Invention is kept alive, and the mind is not suffered to fall into that drowsy stupidity, which, in a civilized society, seems to benumb the understanding of almost all the inferior ranks of people. In those barbarous

societies, as they are called, every man, it has already been observed, is a warrior. Every man, too, is in some measure a statesman, and can form a tolerable judgment concerning the interest of the society, and the conduct of those who govern it. How far their chiefs are good judges in peace, or good leaders in war, is obvious to the observation of almost every single man among them. In such a society, indeed, no man can well acquire that improved and refined understanding which a few men sometimes possess in a more civilized state. Though in a rude society there is a good deal of variety in the occupations of every individual, there is not a great deal in those of the whole society.

Every man does, or is capable of doing, almost everything which any other man does, or is capable of being. Every man has a considerable degree of knowledge, ingenuity, and invention but scarce any man has a great degree. The degree, however, which is commonly possessed, is generally sufficient for conducting the whole simple business of the society. In a civilized state, on the contrary, though there is little variety in the occupations of the greater part of individuals, there is an almost infinite variety in those of the whole society. These varied occupations present an almost infinite variety of objects to the contemplation of those few, who, being attached to no particular occupation themselves, have leisure and inclination to examine the occupations of other people. The contemplation of so great a variety of objects necessarily exercises their minds in endless comparisons and combinations, and renders their understandings, in an extraordinary degree, both acute anti comprehensive. Unless those few, however, happen to be placed in some very particular situations, their great abilities, though honourable to themselves, may contribute very little to the good government or happiness of their society. Notwithstanding the great abilities of those few, all the nobler parts of the human character may be, in a great measure, obliterated and extinguished in the great body of the people.[327]

The concern here is not difficult to imagine. Suppose a lower-skilled "blue collar" worker is trained and specializes in fulfilling a very specific function at a factory, such as taping boxes shut for shipment at the end of an assembly line. He performs the same motion (swiping a tape dispenser) again and again, hour after hour, five days (at minimum!) each week, every week of the year, for 30-40 years. Now imagine that this worker is employed in Smith's era, when workers worked longer hours, and poor workers had even fewer resources than today for recreation and mental stimulation.

> The man whose whole life is spent in performing a few simple operations, of which the effects, too, are perhaps always the same, or very nearly the same, has no occasion to exert his understanding, or to exercise his invention, in finding out expedients for removing difficulties which never occur. He naturally loses, therefore, the habit of such exertion, and generally becomes as stupid and ignorant as it is possible for a human creature to become.[328]

Such a repetitive task requires no creativity, no problem-solving. There is nothing new or stimulating. It's as though the mind is a muscle, and it atrophies from lack of stimulation. The concern isn't just that the worker might grow "bored." "The torpor of his mind renders him not only incapable of relishing or bearing a part in any rational conversation, but of conceiving any

generous, noble, or tender sentiment, and consequently of forming any just judgment concerning many even of the ordinary duties of private life. Of the great and extensive interests of his country he is altogether incapable of judging..."

Such a person loses his ability to problem-solve, in general, from lack of use; loses the ability to participate in rational conversation, and given the crucial role of the imagination in anticipating what the "impartial spectator" would do in a situation, such persons are even stunted in their capacity for correct moral judgment!

It's implausible that employers will take it upon themselves to remodel the workplace for the sake of mental stimulation. After all, it would reduce their efficiency and profits if they did so. That means that it is by education that we must combat this mental atrophy to which most of the work force is subject.

Since the poor, by virtue of being poor, are unlikely to be able to pay for private schools or tutors, it will fall to the State to provide that education at public expense. This means, of course, that taxes will have to be levied to pay for that education.

Smith did not regard taxation as theft,[329] nor even as something bad. "Every tax, however, is to the person who pays it a badge, not of slavery, but of liberty. It denotes that he is subject to government, indeed, but that, as he has some property, he cannot himself be the property of a master."[330] The very fact that someone *has* property subject to taxation means that the person has *private* property, *personal* wealth (to whatever extent). This is the mark of a citizen, not a subject or slave. Smith, while critical of government meddling, was not critical of taxation, or even "redistribution of wealth."

> When the carriages which pass over a highway or a bridge, and the lighters which sail upon a navigable canal, pay toll

---

327 *WN*, Book V, Chapter 1, Part 3, Article 1.
328 Ibid.
329 In contrast to the view espoused by Judge Andrew Napolitano:

https://reason.com/archives/2013/04/18/taxation-is-theft
330 *WN*, Book V, Chapter 2.

in proportion to their weight or their tonnage, they pay for the maintenance of those public works exactly in proportion to the wear and tear which they occasion of them. It seems scarce possible to invent a more equitable way of maintaining such works. This tax or toll, too, though it is advanced by the carrier, is finally paid by the consumer, to whom it must always be charged in the price of the goods. As the expense of carriage, however, is very much reduced by means of such public works, the goods, notwithstanding the toll, come cheaper to the consumer than they could otherwise have done, their price not being so much raised by the toll, as it is lowered by the cheapness of the carriage. The person who finally pays this tax, therefore, gains by the application more than he loses by the payment of it. His payment is exactly in proportion to his gain. It is, in reality, no more than a part of that gain which he is obliged to give up, in order to get the rest. It seems impossible to imagine a more equitable method of raising a tax. When the toll upon carriages of luxury, upon coaches, post-chaises, etc. is made somewhat higher in proportion to their weight, than upon carriages of necessary use, such as carts, waggons, etc. the indolence and vanity of the rich is made to contribute, in a very easy manner, to the relief of the poor, by rendering cheaper the transportation of heavy goods to all the different parts of the country.[331]

In fact, Smith even argues for what today would be called "progressive taxation" (i.e., taxing the wealthy at higher rates).

The necessaries of life occasion the great expense of the poor. They find it difficult to get food, and the greater part of their little revenue is spent in getting it. The

luxuries and vanities of life occasion the principal expense of the rich; and a magnificent house embellishes and sets off to the best advantage all the other luxuries and vanities which they possess. *A tax upon house-rents, therefore, would in general fall heaviest upon the rich; and in this sort of inequality there would not, perhaps, be anything very unreasonable. It is not very unreasonable that the rich should contribute to the public expense, not only in proportion to their revenue, but something more than in that proportion.*[332]

Even Smith's genuine libertarian strain is not so completely "hands off" as one might think.

A superior may, indeed, sometimes, with universal approbation, oblige those under his jurisdiction to behave, in this respect, with a certain degree of propriety to one another. The laws of all civilized nations oblige parents to maintain their children, and children to maintain their parents, and impose upon men many other duties of beneficence. The civil magistrate is entrusted with the power not only of preserving the public peace by restraining injustice, but of promoting the prosperity of the commonwealth, by establishing good discipline, and by discouraging every sort of vice and impropriety; *he may prescribe rules, therefore, which not only prohibit mutual injuries among fellow-citizens, but command mutual good offices to a certain degree.*[333]

Don't gloss over that last sentence! Smith is claiming that the legitimate application of law and coercion by the State is not merely "negative," to protect us from injuries from each other, but can, "to a certain degree," be "positive" as well—commanding "mutual good offices." In other words, to an extent, at least, it is legitimate

---

[331] Ibid., Book V, Chapter 1.
[332] Ibid., Book V, Chapter 2. Emphasis added.

[333] *TMS*, Part II, Section ii, Chapter 1. Emphasis added.

to use the State, and taxation, to provide for the needs of the poor.

The purely libertarian depiction of Smith is an inaccurate caricature that fails to acknowledge his subtleties. Indeed, much of what is commonly attributed to Smith is more accurately attributable to Ayn Rand. For that reason, the remainder of this chapter is going to skip ahead in time a good century and a half. This anachronistic treatment of Smith and Rand in the same chapter is warranted by their combined contribution to contemporary fiscal conservativism, as well as by my motive to distinguish the myth of Smith (which is more "Rand" than "Smith"), from Smith's actual views.

Ayn Rand

The Russian-born philosopher and novelist Ayn Rand entered the world as Alisa Zinov'yevna Rosenbaum in 1905. She studied philosophers such as Aristotle and Plato at Petrograd State University, but was "purged" from the University before graduating due to her "bourgeois" family background. She immigrated to the United States in 1925, and became an American citizen in 1931.

She published her first major success, *The Fountainhead*, in 1943, followed by *Atlas Shrugged* in 1957. She was politically active for generally conservative/libertarian causes until her health began to decline in the 1970s. She died on March 6th, 1982.

Although she did not use the term herself, Rand is known for being an enthusiastic proponent of "ethical egoism." Ethical egoism (hereafter, EE), appeals to self-interest as the guide for how people should behave.

Nathaniel Branden, a psychotherapist and former (long-time) associate of Ayn Rand wrote an essay entitled "Isn't Everyone Selfish?" Within it, he not only demonstrates that ethical egoism is distinct from psychological egoism (the descriptive theory claiming that all people, in fact, act from self-interest, whether they would want

to, or not), but he also argues that psychological egoism (hereafter, PE) is a confused, false theory.

In response to PE's more extravagant claim that everyone always acts selfishly (knowingly or not), because every purposeful action is motivated by some sort of value or goal desired by the agent, Branden clarifies that the selfishness (or unselfishness) of an action is determined *objectively*, not by the particular feelings of the agent performing the act. Of course it's true that every intentional action must be motivated by some "want," but whether or not the action is selfish depends on *why* the agent wants to do it.

> To equate 'motivated behavior' with 'selfish behavior' is to blank out the distinction between an elementary fact of human psychology and the phenomenon of *ethical* choice. It is to evade the central *problem* of ethics, namely: by *what* is a man to be motivated? . . . Those who assert that 'everyone is selfish' commonly intend their statement as an expression of cynicism and contempt. But the truth is that their statement pays mankind a compliment it does not deserve.[334]

Notice the interesting phrasing at the end of that quotation from Branden, though: to say that all people are selfish is to pay them a *compliment* that they *don't deserve*. Rather obviously, Brandon perceives "selfishness" as something good, something complimentary. This brings us to the basic elements of EE.

As stated, EE prescribes that we *should* pursue our own self-interest. It's important to realize that "should," in this case, is not merely a recommendation of prudence. EE is not claiming that it is shrewd, or clever, or useful to pursue your own self-interest—though it may well be so. EE is claiming that it is *morally right* to pursue your own self-interest, that the pursuit of self-interest is morally good. Indeed, the most well-known advocate of ethical egoism (Rand) entitled

---

[334] Nathaniel Branden, "Isn't Everyone Selfish?" in *The Virtue of Selfishness*, by Ayn Rand.

a collection of essays addressing this idea, *The Virtue of Selfishness.*

On its surface, this might seem to be an outrageous and provocative claim. Selfishness, after all, has traditionally been regarded as a vice. Selfish people are greedy, petty individuals. One wants a reputation for being generous and charitable, not self-centered—and yet, Rand boldly proclaims that selfishness is a *virtue.*

For some, the appeal of EE is that the pursuit of self-interest, ultimately, benefits *everyone.* It is sometimes called the "capitalist" defense of EE because it makes the same appeal as do defenders of free market ("*laissez-faire*") capitalism: by leaving people free to pursue their own self-interest, the optimal results for all involved are achieved. It is here where we have a legitimate point of contact between Rand and Smith: both appeal to the collective positive outcome of the pursuit of self-interest.

Consider a simple example: selecting a check-out line at a store. Barring unusual circumstances, I'm confident that your basic strategy when it comes to line selection is the same as mine: you select the shortest line. Why? Because it serves your self-interest to do so—just as it serves mine when I do so. I have no desire to wait in line any longer than I must, so I pick the shortest line (all else being equal), and so does everyone else. Now, it just so happens that when everyone selects the shortest line (all else being equal), the number of people in each available line becomes roughly equal, and the most efficient rate of completing transactions is achieved. Customers, as a whole, and the employees and managers, as a whole, arguably achieve maximal benefit from this outcome. But, notice that no one was deliberately trying to "maximize efficiency," or make things best for "everyone." Each one of us is pursuing what we perceive to be in our own interest, and it just so happens that when we do, the best available result for everyone is achieved.

With respect to capitalism, the basic prescription is that people should be maximally

free to pursue their own self-interest, with as little (government) interference as possible. When this occurs, the optimal result for everyone involved is achieved, whether we're talking about the prices of products, or the wage of workers, etc.

As is true of our economic interactions, so too with *all* our interactions. If we all pursue our own self-interest, we will obtain the optimal "result" for everyone involved. We might offer a formal version of this argument as follows:

1. We ought to do whatever will best promote everyone's interests.
2. The best way to promote everyone's interests is for each of us to adopt the policy of pursuing our own interests exclusively.
3. Therefore, each of us should adopt the policy of pursuing our own interests exclusively.

Whether or not this is true is an empirical matter, more so than a philosophical one—but for our purposes we can set aside the truth or falsity of this "capitalist" claim. As it turns out, this is an odd defense of EE, given that this argument is really an argument for a *different* ethical theory: utilitarianism. Utilitarians claim that the morally right thing to do is whatever will maximize "utility" for all involved, whatever will produce the best result for all involved.[335]

As it turns out, the "capitalist" argument for EE isn't really claiming that what is morally right is to pursue self-interest. Instead, it's claiming that what is morally right is to "maximize utility," and that the best way to achieve that goal is by the pursuit of self-interest. That is, our moral goal is to achieve the best result for all involved, and the *means* to achieve this is the pursuit of self-interest. The pursuit of self-interest, then, is, at best, merely instrumentally valuable.

Whether or not the pursuit of self-interest is always the best way to "maximize utility" is certainly subject to debate, and if the reason why

---

[335] The role of utilitarianism in political philosophy will be explored in another chapter.

someone endorses the pursuit of self-interest is because of this "capitalist" argument, it seems that such persons would have to acknowledge that if it could be shown that altruism could better achieve that end, then altruistic behavior would be recommended instead. This suggests that an appeal to what is "best for all involved" is not actually a very compelling endorsement of EE, after all.

Indeed, this so-called "capitalist" argument for EE bears only superficial resemblance to Smith's views. As we saw previously in this chapter, Smith did not regard the pursuit of self-interest as somehow intrinsically valuable, but only as a means to an end, with the end being collective well-being. Smith did not frame this in strictly utilitarian terms, but there's no question that what he finds good about the pursuit of self-interest is that it enriches us all. It is mutual enrichment, not self-interest, which ultimately should guide our behavior.

Rand took the value of self-interest much further, though. Rand's emphasis on self-interest is not tied, implicitly or explicitly, to some "greater good." In fact, she repeatedly rails against utilitarianism and other "altruistic" systems that sacrifice the individual for the sake of the "greater good." Instead, she advocates unapologetic *self*-interest, the pursuit of one's *own* good. "Selfishness," according to Rand, is a *virtue*.

To proclaim selfishness a virtue is both bold and controversial, but before attempting to justify this claim, it's important to clarify what is meant by it. Neither Rand, nor ethical egoists in general, propose the reckless and wanton pursuit of (so-called) "self-interest." The caricature of a sociopath flouting social conventions and ruthlessly exploiting others is just that: a caricature. Selfishness, according to Rand, is simply "concern with one's own interests." There is nothing morally good or bad about selfishness so far in that formulation.

"Selfishness" ("concern with one's own interests") is preferable, according to Rand, in contrast to its opposite: altruism. Rand understands "altruism" in a particular way (one that, admittedly, might not be agreed upon by altruists themselves). According to her understanding of "altruism," and altruistic ethical systems, any action taken for the benefit of others is good, and any action taken for one's own benefit is evil. In this way, the only standard of moral value is the beneficiary. If I'm the one performing the action, and the beneficiary is "me," then the action is morally "bad;" but, if the beneficiary is "you," then it's "good."

Rand claims that this standard of moral value makes morality our "enemy." Doing what is morally right is always something that benefits others, that causes others to gain, but that causes oneself to lose. While we might hope that we will benefit from the actions of others from time to time, just as they benefit from our own actions, this approach ultimately breeds mutual resentment rather than happiness. "Morally, their pursuit of values will be like an exchange of unwanted, unchosen Christmas presents, which neither is morally permitted to buy for himself."[336]

In contrast to this, her "Objectivist Ethics" (for us, still EE) claims that the moral agent herself should always be the beneficiary of her own actions.[337] In order to understand Rand's advocacy for the pursuit of self-interest, and to give it a fair hearing, we need to understand the premises by which she comes to her conclusion, the foundation on which she builds her ethical system.

Rand defines morality or ethics as a code of values to guide choices and actions, and it is our choices and actions that determine the purpose and course of one's life. Historically, the two major types of ethical codes in the West have been associated with "mystics" or "neo-mystics." Rand claims that "mystics" proclaim that the

---

[336] Ayn Ran, *The Virtue of Selfishness*, Introduction, p. viii.
[337] The text of her essay, "The Objectivist Ethics," is available at the following URL:

http://aynrandlexicon.com/ayn-rand-ideas/the-objectivist-ethics.html

"arbitrary, unaccountable 'will of God'" is the standard of "the good," whereas "neo-mystics" hold the "good of society" as the standard of "the good" instead.[338] The obvious candidates for "mystics" are any sort of "divine command" ethical theory, and the most obvious candidate for "neo-mystics" are utilitarians—though any system that posits a "good" other than oneself could be lumped into this "neo-mystic" camp as well.

In either case, Rand claims that some persons, claiming to be spokespersons for either God or society, are ethically entitled to interpret this "good" while everyone else is obliged to spend their lives in service to that "gang's" desires. In practice, it's not difficult to see the force of this interpretation. Religious leaders, throughout history, have been the official spokespersons of their faith, have interpreted what their deity (or deities) demand, and have then attempted to encourage (or outright compel) the faithful to obey. In secular systems, particular people (e.g., politicians) decide what is "best" for society, and then enact legislation to inspire (or compel) everyone else to play along. Rand is a fan of neither camp.

Central to understanding Rand's emphasis on self-interest is her concept of "value." A value, for Rand, is simply "that which one acts to gain and/or keep." Any meaningful concept of value presupposes alternatives (choices), and an agent capable of choosing from amongst those options, and acting in pursuit of that value.

For living organisms of all kinds (including humans), the most fundamental choice, the most basic alternative, is life or death. When a living organism fails to sustain itself, it dies. When it succeeds in sustaining itself, it lives. Rand claims that life is what makes "value" possible. Only living things are capable of choices, and only living things can pursue the objects of those choices. Accordingly, only to living things can other things be "good" or "evil/bad."

In that only living things can make choices, only living things can have goals, and engage in goal-directed action. All living livings have at least one implicit goal in common. The automatic (unintentional) function of all living organisms is the maintenance of its own life. The natural pursuit of all living things is the continuation of its own existence. This functions automatically and "unintentionally" for most living things, such as plants and most animals. That is just to say that my rosemary bush doesn't consciously *intend* to remain alive—it automatically functions in pursuit of its continued life until something kills it. This seems to be the case for most living things.

For any living thing, life depends on two factors: "fuel" (food), and the actions of its body in using that fuel properly. What determines a "proper" use of the fuel? Simply, that which is required for the organism's survival. This is not a matter of subjective preference, but is objectively determined by a thing's nature. A plant doesn't *choose* photosynthesis—not only because a plant is incapable of choice but because the plant doesn't have any other option. Although humans are capable of choice, I don't have the luxury of choosing to be "fed" by photosynthesis, as my "nature" does not allow it.[339]

For any living thing, its life is maintained only by virtue of constant self-sustaining action. The implicit goal of those actions, and their ultimate value ("that which one acts to gain/keep") is the organism's life. Life itself, then, is the *ultimate* value, the final end/goal to which all lesser goals are means, and the standard by which lesser goals are evaluated.

With this standard in place, "good" is that which furthers one's life, and "evil" is that which threatens it. Plants, of course, are incapable of cognition and moral judgment, but "good" for a plant would be things like sunlight, water, and nutrient rich soil (and the actions of the plant that pursue/promote those things), while "evil" for a plant would be things like drought, locust swarms, over-zealous gardeners, etc.

---

[338] Rand, "The Objectivist Ethics," *The Virtue of Selfishness*, 14.

[339] Despite the claims and wishes of those at www.humanphotosynthesis.com.

Humans are more sophisticated than plants, of course, but our "good" and "evil" is built upon the same foundation: the preservation and promotion of our own lives. Unlike plants, humans have a crude (but effective) capacity to become aware of what is good and evil (in its simplest form): our capacity for pleasure and pain. Pain is a warning signal to any animal, including humans, that it is pursuing the "wrong" course of action, while pleasure is a signal that it is pursuing the "right" course of action.

Pain is *usually* an indicator that the body is being damaged. Suffer enough damage, and you will die. This basic recognition signals that we should eat when hungry, remove our hands from fires, run away or fight back if we're being eaten, stop stepping on jagged rocks, etc.

Pleasure is *usually* an indicator that the body is being "nurtured" or benefitted. Physical comfort suggests safe living conditions, the pleasure of eating encourages us to sustain ourselves with "fuel"—even sexual pleasure promotes the continued life of the species itself.

Just as pain is a signal of a "wrong course of action," and pleasure is a signal of a "right course of action," happiness is an indicator of a successful state of life, while suffering is a warning signal of "failure."

As we've seen with plants, some living things automatically pursue their "good." A plant doesn't need instruction on how to absorb and convert sunlight, nor can it make a mistake and choose to try to eat nuts and berries instead. For conscious living beings, such as humans, though, our bodies can only automatically *use* fuel—we can't automatically *obtain* it. A plant can just stay in place and absorb its fuel from its environment. In contrast, if I just "stay in place" I will grow increasingly hungry and thirsty and then die.

Unlike plants and (most) non-human animals, humans have no "automatic" knowledge of how to survive, no automatic set of values, no automatic understanding of "good" and "evil," and no automatic set of goals proper to our nature, nor knowledge of how to obtain those goals. We humans must *discover* these things (e.g., which plants are nutritious, and which are poison; how to hunt and prepare meat, etc.), and

then *choose* to pursue them. Humans are *volitional*, which is to say that our intentional actions are voluntary; we must *intend* them. The faculty/capacity that directs this process of discovery and volition is *reason*. The process, itself, is *thinking*.

Rand observes that thinking is *not* automatic, but is also a choice. We must focus our consciousness, focus our thoughts, direct our minds, or else we sink to the level of an undirected "sensory-perceptual mechanism," such as that presumably exhibited by most non-human animals.

For humans, reason is an indispensable tool. Reason is our basic means of survival. We don't benefit from roots and the capacity for photosynthesis. We don't have instincts to hunt or spin webs to catch flies. Although we automatically feel hunger, and automatically digest food once it's in our bellies, we don't automatically know how to get that food into our stomachs, or even what qualifies as food to begin with! We have to use our reason and *think* our way to a full stomach. This is not anything subjective or arbitrary either. What is required for our survival is not *determined* by us, any more than it is determined by the plant, but is instead discovered by us—and whether we rightly pursue these requirements is chosen by us. As Rand says of "Man," "He is free to make the wrong choice, but not free to succeed with it." I am free to choose to eat rocks, but not free to be nourished by them.

A "successful" life, at its most basic level, is simply one that continues, one in which life is maintained. For volitional creatures like humans, this requires recognizing and pursuing goals and values proper to our survival. Ethics, as a discipline, seeks to answer these questions: what are the right goals to pursue? What are the values required for survival?

Again, for Rand, there is nothing subjective about this. "Ethics is *not* a mystic fantasy—nor a social convention—nor a dispensable subjective luxury, to be switched or discarded in any emergency. Ethics is an *objective, metaphysical necessity of man's survival*—not by the grace of the supernatural nor of your neighbors nor of your whims, but by the grace of reality and the nature of life."[340]

In determining what is necessary for our survival, though, we must remember what sort of living thing we are. Humans are *rational* animals. Since reason is our means of survival, that which is proper to the life of a *rational* being is "the good;" that which opposes/destroys it is the "evil." This is a very important point. The survival proper to the human animal is not merely what is needed to prevent organ failure, and to keep the heart beating, but what is needed to maintain a human *as a rational animal.* There might be some actions that maintain life, but at the expense of reason. In such a case, we would be surviving as an animal, but not as a person.

What *is* proper to the life of a person, as a rational animal? Everything a human needs to survive has to be discovered by his own mind, and produced by his own effort. Essential to *proper* survival, then, are thinking and productive work. Seeming exceptions to this (e.g., "looters," "robbers") are mere parasites on those who *do* the productive work, and these so-called exceptions could not survive without the work of the producers. Herein is to be found Rand's complaint against altruism (as she understands it).

"Altruism" commands that we act in service to others, that we sacrifice our own interests for the good of others. However, for Rand, this is simply *unnatural.* As a living creature, my ultimate value is the maintenance of my own life, and every other value is subordinate to (and in service of) that ultimate value. Your life is of ultimate value to you, but it is not of ultimate value to me—nor should it be. Altruism demands that we make someone else's life (indeed, *anyone* else's life) our ultimate value. That would be like asking a flower to live for the sake of a bee.

Rand advocates that each person should act for her own *rational* self-interest, her own *actual* self-interest. This is not some license to "do as

one pleases." Just as not everything one chooses to eat is necessarily nutritious and safe food, so too is it the case that not everything someone desires and pursues is in her actual self-interest. Remember, our actual (rational) self-interest is not determined by our whims, but by our nature, by the sort of living thing we are, by the values required for human survival.

"Self-interest" is not identical to "what I want," or even "what I *think* is in my self-interest. "One's own independent judgment is the means by which one must choose one's actions, but one's own judgment is not itself the moral criterion of action."[341] I might think that a poisonous plant is safe to eat, and then die from my mistake. Similarly, I might think a particular course of life is in my self-interest, but be mistaken about that as well, and sow the seeds of my own unhappiness and failure.

That we should each pursue our own self-interest doesn't entail that we must be in conflict with each other, and certainly doesn't entail that we each live our lives trying to "use" other people for our own benefit. If we recognize that life (in general) is an end in itself (i.e., our ultimate value), then this implies that every human life is therefore an end in itself, and not a mere means to another end. Each person should live for his own sake, neither sacrificing himself to others, not sacrificing others to himself. According to Rand, "to live for his own sake means that *the achievement of his own happiness is man's highest moral purpose.*"[342]

Although happiness is our highest moral purpose, happiness is not the primary *standard* of evaluation or our primary value. "Man's life" is primary, and pursuing the rational values that life requires allows one to *achieve* happiness. "Happiness can properly be the purpose of ethics, but not the standard."[343] In contrast, employing some subjective emotional standard of what "makes you happy" is to let yourself be guided by emotional whims.

---

[340] Rand, "The Objectivist Ethics," *The Virtue of Selfishness*, 23.
[341] Ayn Rand, *The Virtue of Selfishness*, Introduction, p. x.

[342] Rand, "The Objectivist Ethics," *The Virtue of Selfishness*, 27.
[343] Ibid., 29.

The subjectivist theory of ethics is, strictly speaking, not a theory, but a negation of ethics. And more: it is a negation of reality, a negation not merely of man's existence, but of *all* existence. Only the concept of a fluid, plastic, indeterminate, Heraclitean universe could permit anyone to think or to preach that man needs no *objective* principles of action—that reality gives him a blank check on values—that anything he cares to pick as the good or the evil, will do—that a man's whim is a valid moral standard, and that the only question is how to get away with it. The existential monument to *this* theory is the present state of our culture.[344]

If desire (regardless of its nature, or cause, regardless of what the desire happens to be) is primary, and the gratification of desire is taken as an ethical goal (such as "the greatest happiness for the greatest number"), then desires and interests will inevitably clash. You might desire to produce, but I might desire to steal what you have produced. If mere desire is the standard of the good, then every desire has equal moral validity. That is the origin of conflict, according to Rand. Her objectivist ethic, in contrast, entails no such conflict.

The Objectivist ethics proudly advocates and upholds *rational selfishness*—which means: the values required for man's survival *qua* man—which means: the values required for *human* survival—not the values produced by the desires, the emotions, the "aspirations," the feelings, the whims or the needs of irrational brutes, who have never outgrown the primordial practice of human sacrifices, have never discovered an industrial society and can conceive of no self-interest but that of grabbing the loot of the moment.

The Objectivist ethics holds that *human* good does not require human sacrifices and cannot be achieved by the sacrifice of anyone to anyone. It holds that the *rational* interests of men do not clash—that there is no conflict of interests among men who do not desire the unearned, who do not make sacrifices nor accept them, who deal with one another as *traders*, giving value for value.

The principle of *trade* is the only rational ethical principle for all human relationships, personal and social, private and public, spiritual and material. It is the principle of *justice*.

A trader is a man who earns what he gets and does not give or take the undeserved. He does not treat men as masters or slaves, but as independent equals. He deals with men by means of a free, voluntary, unforced, uncoerced exchange—an exchange which benefits both parties by their independent judgment. A trader does not expect to be paid for his defaults, only for his achievements. He does not switch to others the burden of his failures, and he does not mortgage his life into bondage to the failure of others.

In spiritual issues—(by 'spiritual' I mean: 'pertaining to man's consciousness')—the currency or medium of exchange is different, but the principle is the same. Love, friendship, respect, admiration are the emotional response of one man to the virtues of another, the spiritual *payment* given in exchange for the personal, selfish pleasure which one man derives from the virtues of another man's character.[345]

Rand's ideal is that all persons greet and interact with each other as equals, offering and

[344] Ibid., 34.

[345] Ibid., 31.

accepting terms of interaction that are of mutual benefit. This includes not only our obvious economic exchanges, such as offering labor to an employer in exchange for wages, but even our personal relationships are "contractual" in that sense. We are friends with someone because we find value in it, because we benefit from the continued companionship of that person. If that ceases to be true, we cease to be friends.

Contrary to the caricature of ruthless "selfishness," Rand thinks her promotion of rational self-interest is the only ethical system that honors the value of the individual, is consistent with our nature, and that avoids the "evils" of altruistic moral codes. Indeed, Rand's condemnation of altruistic systems is both persistent and harsh. A few sections from her novel, "Atlas Shrugged," demonstrate this.

> This much is true: the most selfish of all things is the independent mind that recognizes no authority higher than its own and no value higher than its judgment of truth. You are asked to sacrifice your intellectual integrity, your logic, your reason, your standard of truth-in favor of becoming a prostitute whose standard is the greatest good for the greatest number.

> If you search your code for guidance, for an answer to the question: 'What is the good?'-the only answer you will find is 'The good of others.' The good is whatever others wish, whatever you feel they feel they wish, or whatever you feel they ought to feel. 'The good of others' is a magic formula that transforms anything into gold, a formula to be recited as a guarantee of moral glory and as a fumigator for any action, even the slaughter of a continent. Your standard of virtue is not an object, not an act, not a principle, but an intention. You need no proof, no reasons, no success, you need not achieve in fact the good of others-all you need to know is that your motive was the good of others, not your own. Your

> only definition of the good is a negation: the good is the 'non-good for me.'...

> If you wish it, it's evil; if others wish it, it's good; if the motive of your action is your welfare, don't do it; if the motive is the welfare of others, then anything goes.

> As this double-jointed, double-standard morality splits you in half, so it splits mankind into two enemy camps: one is you, the other is all the rest of humanity. You are the only outcast who has no right to wish to live. You are the only servant, the rest are the masters, you are the only giver, the rest are the takers, you are the eternal debtor, the rest are the creditors never to be paid off. You must not question their right to your sacrifice, or the nature of their wishes and their needs: their right is conferred upon them by a negative, by the fact that they are 'non-you.'...

> I, who do not accept the unearned, neither in values nor in guilt, am here to ask the questions you evaded. Why is it moral to serve the happiness of others, but not your own? If enjoyment is a value, why is it moral when experienced by others, but immoral when experienced by you? If the sensation of eating a cake is a value, why is it an immoral indulgence in your stomach, but a moral goal for you to achieve in the stomach of others? Why is it immoral for you to desire, but moral for others to do so? Why is it immoral to produce a value and keep it, but moral to give it away? And if it is not moral for you to keep a value, why is it moral for others to accept it? If you are selfless and virtuous when you give it, are they not selfish and vicious when they take it? Does virtue consist of serving vice? Is the moral purpose of those who are good, self-immolation for the sake of those who are evil?...

Under a morality of sacrifice, the first value you sacrifice is morality; the next is self-esteem. When need is the standard, every man is both victim and parasite. As a victim, he must labor to fill the needs of others, leaving himself in the position of a parasite whose needs must be filled by others. He cannot approach his fellow men except in one of two disgraceful roles: he is both a beggar and a sucker.

You fear the man who has a dollar less than you, that dollar is rightfully his, he makes you feel like a moral defrauder. You hate the man who has a dollar more than you, that dollar is rightfully yours, he makes you feel that you are morally defrauded. The man below is a source of, your guilt, the man above is a source of your frustration.[346]

The writing here is rhetorically powerful, to be sure. We might formalize Rand's argument in the following way:

1. Each person has only one life to life to live.
2. If we value the individual (i.e., if the individual has moral worth), then this life is of supreme importance, as it is all one has, and all one is.
3. The ethics of altruism regards the life of the individual as something one must be ready to sacrifice for the good of others.
4. Therefore, the ethics of altruism does not take seriously the value of the individual.
5. Ethical egoism regards the individual's own life as being of ultimate value.
6. Ethical egoism is the only moral philosophy to take seriously the value of the individual.
7. Therefore, ethical egoism is the moral philosophy we ought to accept.

Now we can see the significance of Rand, and how her views have been conflated with Smith's by virtue of their shared emphasis on the value of the pursuit of self-interest. It is much more "Rand" than "Smith" that is influencing contemporary fiscal conservatism.

As an example, Congressman Paul Ryan (the Vice-Presidential candidate for the Republican Party in 2012, and the Speaker of the House as of 2017) mentioned Rand in a speech he gave in 2005. "[T]he reason I got involved in public service, by and large, if I had to credit one thinker, one person, it would be Ayn Rand. And the fight we are in here, make no mistake about it, is a fight of individualism versus collectivism." Then, in 2009, he credited her again: "what's unique about what's happening today in government, in the world, in America, is that it's as if we're living in an Ayn Rand novel right now. I think Ayn Rand did the best job of anybody to build a moral case of capitalism, and that morality of capitalism is under assault."[347]

Similarly, any policy proposals based on the view that taxation is theft, that the poor are not entitled to any assistance, that neither the rich nor the State has any obligation or responsibility to provide for the less-fortunate, that "greed is good," that selfishness is a "virtue;" right or wrong, for better or for worse, such proposals are far more accurately attributed to Rand than to Smith.

Conclusion

Using Adam Smith as our spring board, we have leapt from the 18th century all the way into the 20th century (passing over numerous important people and ideas along the way!), and have presumably found ourselves in the midst of some familiar political issues: social welfare, taxation, individual rights v. the greater good of the community, and the proper limits of government intrusion into the economy (or into our personal decisions, in general).

---

[346] Ayn Rand, *Atlas Shrugged*, 388-389.

[347] http://www.politico.com/story/2012/08/ryans-love-hate-with-ayn-rand-079597

One of the themes in this chapter, loosely associated with both capitalism and ethical egoism, is an appeal to a "greater good." Though neither Smith nor Rand were utilitarians, there are some points of contact between them and that theory, as well as some genuine points of contrast. To further develop our understanding of this contrast, our next chapter will focus on utilitarianism, and its undeniable influence and applications with regard to political thought and decision-making.

In what follows, you will find selections from both the Theory of Moral Sentiments as well as the Wealth of Nations. Both are lengthy works, and so much material has been cut for the sake of space and reasonable reading requirements. I have attempted to provide key ideas from both works. In the initial selections from The Moral Sentiments, we have Smith's account of sympathy, the impartial spectator, and the "corruption" of our moral sentiments due to unwarranted envy of the rich. We also find mentions of the infamous "invisible hand." In the selections from the Wealth of Nations, we have his discussion of the division of labor, competition, limited government intervention, as well as proper taxation and government institutions.

Adam Smith: *The Theory of Moral Sentiments*

Professor of Moral Philosophy in the University of Glasgow.
London Printed for A. Millar, in the Strand; And A. Kincaid and J. Bell in Edinburgh.
MDCCLIX
[http://web.archive.org/web/20030324040029/http://etext.lib.virginia.edu/etcbin/toccer-new2?id=SmiMora.xml&images=images/modeng&data=/texts/english/modeng/parsed&tag=public&part=all]

Part I: Of the Propriety of Action Consisting of Three Sections
  Section I: Of the Sense of Propriety
    Chap. I: Of Sympathy

How selfish soever man may be supposed, there are evidently some principles in his nature, which interest him in the fortune of others, and render their happiness necessary to him, though he derives nothing from it except the pleasure of seeing it. Of this kind is pity or compassion, the emotion which we feel for the misery of others, when we either see it, or are made to conceive it in a very lively manner. That we often derive sorrow from the sorrow of others, is a matter of fact too obvious to require any instances to prove it; for this sentiment, like all the other original passions of human nature, is by no means confined to the virtuous and humane, though they perhaps may feel it with the most exquisite sensibility. The greatest ruffian, the most hardened violator of the laws of society, is not altogether without it.

As we have no immediate experience of what other men feel, we can form no idea of the manner in which they are affected, but by conceiving what we ourselves should feel in the like situation. Though our brother is upon the rack, as long as we ourselves are at our ease, our senses will never inform us of what he suffers. They never did, and never can, carry us beyond our own person, and it is by the imagination only that we can form any conception of what are his sensations. Neither can that faculty help us to this any other way, than by representing to us what would be our own, if we were in his case. It is the impressions of our own senses only, not those of his, which our imaginations copy. By the imagination we place ourselves in his situation, we conceive ourselves enduring all the same torments, we enter as it were into his body, and become in some measure the same person with him, and thence form some idea of his sensations, and even feel something which, though weaker in degree, is not altogether unlike them. His agonies, when they are thus brought home to ourselves, when we have thus adopted and made them our own, begin at last to affect us, and we then tremble and shudder at the thought of what he feels. For as to be in pain or distress of any kind excites the most excessive sorrow, so to conceive or to imagine that we are in it, excites some degree of the same emotion, in proportion to the vivacity or dulness of the conception.

That this is the source of our fellow-feeling for the misery of others, that it is by changing places in fancy with the sufferer, that we come either to conceive or to be affected by what he feels, may be demonstrated by many obvious observations, if it should not be thought sufficiently evident of itself. When we see a stroke aimed and just ready to fall upon the leg or arm of another person, we naturally shrink and draw back our own leg or our own arm; and when it does fall, we feel it in some measure, and are hurt by it as well as the sufferer. The mob, when they are gazing at a dancer on the slack rope, naturally writhe and twist and balance their own bodies, as they see him do, and as they feel that they themselves must do if in his situation. Persons of delicate fibres and a weak constitution of body complain, that in looking on the sores and ulcers which are exposed by beggars in the streets, they are apt to feel an itching or uneasy sensation in the correspondent part of their own bodies. The horror which they conceive at the misery of those wretches affects that particular part in themselves more than any other; because that horror arises from conceiving what they themselves would suffer, if they really were the wretches whom they are looking upon, and if that particular part in themselves was actually affected in the same miserable manner. The very force of this conception is sufficient, in their feeble frames, to produce that itching or uneasy sensation complained of. Men of the most robust make, observe that in looking upon sore eyes they often feel a very sensible soreness in their own, which proceeds from the same reason; that organ being in the strongest man more delicate, than any other part of the body is in the weakest.

Neither is it those circumstances only, which create pain or sorrow, that call forth our fellow-feeling. Whatever is the passion which arises from any object in the person principally concerned, an analogous emotion springs up, at the thought of his situation, in the breast of every attentive spectator. Our joy for the deliverance of those heroes of tragedy or romance who interest us, is as sincere as our grief for their distress, and our fellow-feeling with their misery is not more real than that with their happiness. We enter into their gratitude towards those faithful friends who did not desert them in their difficulties; and we heartily go along with their resentment against

those perfidious traitors who injured, abandoned, or deceived them. In every passion of which the mind of man is susceptible, the emotions of the by-stander always correspond to hat, by bringing the case home to himself, he imagines should be the sentiments of the sufferer.

Pity and compassion are words appropriated to signify our fellow-feeling with the sorrow of others. Sympathy, though its meaning was, perhaps, originally the same, may now, however, without much impropriety, be made use of to denote our fellow-feeling with any passion whatever.

Upon some occasions sympathy may seen to arise merely from the view of a certain emotion in another person. The passions, upon some occasions, may seem to be transfused from one man to another, instantaneously and antecedent to any knowledge of what excited them in the person principally concerned. Grief and joy, for example, strongly expressed in the look and gestures of any one, at once affect the spectator with some degree of a like painful or agreeable emotion. A smiling face is, to every body that sees it, a cheerful object; as a sorrowful countenance, on the other hand, is a melancholy one.

This, however, does not hold universally, or with regard to every passion. There are some passions of which the expressions excite no sort of sympathy, but before we are acquainted with what gave occasion to them, serve rather to disgust and provoke us against them. The furious behaviour of an angry man is more likely to exasperate us against himself than against his enemies. As we are unacquainted with his provocation, we cannot bring his case home to ourselves, nor conceive any thing like the passions which it excites. But we plainly see what is the situation of those with whom he is angry, and to what violence they may be exposed from so enraged an adversary. We readily, therefore, sympathize with their fear or resentment, and are immediately disposed to take part against the man from whom they appear to be in so much danger.

If the very appearances of grief and joy inspire us with some degree of the like emotions, it is because they suggest to us the general idea of some good or bad fortune that has befallen the person in whom we observe them: and in these passions this is sufficient to have some little influence upon us. The effects of grief and joy terminate in the person who feels those emotions, of which the expressions do not, like those of resentment, suggest to us the idea of any other person for whom we are concerned, and whose interests are opposite to his. The general idea of good or bad fortune, therefore, creates some concern for the person who has met with it, but the general idea of provocation excites no sympathy with the anger of the man who has received it. Nature, it seems, teaches us to be more averse to enter into this passion, and, till informed of its cause, to be disposed rather to take part against it.

Even our sympathy with the grief or joy of another, before we are informed of the cause of either, is always extremely imperfect. General lamentations, which express nothing but the anguish of the sufferer, create rather a curiosity to inquire into his situation, along with some disposition to sympathize with him, than any actual sympathy that is very sensible. The first question which we ask is, What has befallen you? Till this be answered, though we are uneasy both from the vague idea of his misfortune, and still more from torturing ourselves with conjectures about what it may be, yet our fellow-feeling is not very considerable.

Sympathy, therefore, does not arise so much from the view of the passion, as from that of the situation which excites it. We sometimes feel for another, a passion of which he himself seems to be altogether incapable; because, when we put ourselves in his case, that passion arises in our breast from the imagination, though it does not in his from the reality. We blush for the impudence and rudeness of another, though he himself appears to have no sense of the impropriety of his own behaviour; because we

cannot help feeling with what confusion we ourselves should be covered, had we behaved in so absurd a manner.

Of all the calamities to which the condition of mortality exposes mankind, the loss of reason appears, to those who have the least spark of humanity, by far the most dreadful, and they behold that last stage of human wretchedness with deeper commiseration than any other. But the poor wretch, who is in it, laughs and sings perhaps, and is altogether insensible of his own misery. The anguish which humanity feels, therefore, at the sight of such an object, cannot be the reflection of any sentiment of the sufferer. The compassion of the spectator must arise altogether from the consideration of what he himself would feel if he was reduced to the same unhappy situation, and, what perhaps is impossible, was at the same time able to regard it with his present reason and judgment.

What are the pangs of a mother, when she hears the moanings of her infant that during the agony of disease cannot express what it feels? In her idea of what it suffers, she joins, to its real helplessness, her own consciousness of that helplessness, and her own terrors for the unknown consequences of its disorder; and out of all these, forms, for her own sorrow, the most complete image of misery and distress. The infant, however, feels only the uneasiness of the present instant, which can never be great. With regard to the future, it is perfectly secure, and in its thoughtlessness and want of foresight, possesses an antidote against fear and anxiety, the great tormentors of the human breast, from which reason and philosophy will, in vain, attempt to defend it, when it grows up to a man.

We sympathize even with the dead, and overlooking what is of real importance in their situation, that awful futurity which awaits them, we are chiefly affected by those circumstances which strike our senses, but can have no influence upon their happiness. It is miserable, we think, to be deprived of the light of the sun; to be shut out from life and conversation; to be laid in the cold grave, a prey to corruption and the reptiles of the earth; to be no more thought of in this world, but to be obliterated, in a little time, from the affections, and almost from the memory, of their dearest friends and relations. Surely, we imagine, we can never feel too much for those who have suffered so dreadful a calamity. The tribute of our fellow-feeling seems doubly due to them now, when they are in danger of being forgot by every body; and, by the vain honours which we pay to their memory, we endeavour, for our own misery, artificially to keep alive our melancholy remembrance of their misfortune. That our sympathy can afford them no consolation seems to be an addition to their calamity; and to think that all we can do is unavailing, and that, what alleviates all other distress, the regret, the love, and the lamentations of their friends, can yield no comfort to them, serves only to exasperate our sense of their misery. The happiness of the dead, however, most assuredly, is affected by none of these circumstances; nor is it the thought of these things which can ever disturb the profound security of their repose. The idea of that dreary and endless melancholy, which the fancy naturally ascribes to their condition, arises altogether from our joining to the change which has been produced upon them, our own consciousness of that change, from our putting ourselves in their situation, and from our lodging, if I may be allowed to say so, our own living souls in their inanimated bodies, and thence conceiving what would be our emotions in this case. It is from this very illusion of the imagination, that the foresight of our own dissolution is so terrible to us, and that the idea of those circumstances, which undoubtedly can give us no pain when we are dead, makes us miserable while we are alive. And from thence arises one of the most important principles in human nature, the dread of death, the great poison to the happiness, but the great restraint upon the injustice of mankind, which, while it afflicts and mortifies the individual, guards and protects the society.

. . .

Chap. III: Of the manner in which we judge of the propriety or impropriety of the affections of *other men, by their concord or dissonance with our own.*

When the original passions of the person principally concerned are in perfect concord with the sympathetic emotions of the spectator, they necessarily appear to this last just and proper, and suitable to their objects; and, on the contrary, when, upon bringing the case home to himself, he finds that they do not coincide with what he feels, they necessarily appear to him unjust and improper, and unsuitable to the causes which excite them. To approve of the passions of another, therefore, as suitable to their objects, is the same thing as to observe that we entirely sympathize with them; and not to approve of them as such, is the same thing as to observe that we do not entirely sympathize with them. The man who resents the injuries that have been done to me, and observes that I resent them precisely as he does, necessarily approves of my resentment. The man whose sympathy keeps time to my grief, cannot but admit the reasonableness of my sorrow. He who admires the same poem, or the same picture, and admires them exactly as I do, must surely allow the justness of my admiration. He who laughs at the same joke, and laughs along with me, cannot well deny the propriety of my laughter. On the contrary, the person who, upon these different occasions, either feels no such emotion as that which I feel, or feels none that bears any proportion to mine, cannot avoid disapproving my sentiments on account of their dissonance with his own. If my animosity goes beyond what the indignation of my friend can correspond to; if my grief exceeds what his most tender compassion can go along with; if my admiration is either too high or too low to tally with his own; if I laugh loud and heartily when he only smiles, or, on the contrary, only smile when he laughs loud and heartily; in all these cases, as soon as he comes from considering the object, to observe how I am affected by it, according as there is more or less disproportion between his sentiments and mine, I must incur a greater or less degree of his disapprobation: and upon all occasions his own sentiments are the standards and measures by which he judges of mine.

To approve of another man's opinions is to adopt those opinions, and to adopt them is to approve of them. If the same arguments which convince you convince me likewise, I necessarily approve of your conviction; and if they do not, I necessarily disapprove of it: neither can I possibly conceive that I should do the one without the other. To approve or disapprove, therefore, of the opinions of others is acknowledged, by every body, to mean no more than to observe their agreement or disagreement with our own. But this is equally the case with regard to our approbation or disapprobation of the sentiments or passions of others.

There are, indeed, some cases in which we seem to approve without any sympathy or correspondence of sentiments, and in which, consequently, the sentiment of approbation would seem to be different from the perception of this coincidence. A little attention, however, will convince us that even in these cases our approbation is ultimately founded upon a sympathy or correspondence of this kind. I shall give an instance in things of a very frivolous nature, because in them the judgments of mankind are less apt to be perverted by wrong systems. We may often approve of a jest, and think the laughter of the company quite just and proper, though we ourselves do not laugh, because, perhaps, we are in a grave humour, or happen to have our attention engaged with other objects. We have learned, however, from experience, what sort of pleasantry is upon most occasions capable of making us laugh, and we observe that this is one of that kind. We approve, therefore, of the laughter of the company, and feel that it is natural and suitable to its object; because, though in our present mood we cannot easily enter into it, we are sensible that upon most occasions we should very heartily join in it.

The same thing often happens with regard to all the other passions. A stranger passes by us in the street with all the marks of the deepest affliction; and we are immediately told that he has just received the news of the death of his father. It is impossible that, in this case, we should not approve of his grief. Yet it may often happen, without any defect of humanity on our part, that, so far from entering into the violence of his sorrow, we should scarce conceive the first movements of concern upon his account. Both he and his father, perhaps, are entirely unknown to us, or we happen to be employed about other things, and do not take time to picture out in our imagination the different circumstances of distress which must occur to him. We have learned, however, from experience, that such a misfortune naturally excites such a degree of sorrow, and we know that if we took time to consider his situation, fully and in all its parts, we should, without doubt, most sincerely sympathize with him. It is upon the consciousness of this conditional sympathy, that our approbation of his sorrow is founded, even in those cases in which that sympathy does not actually take place; and the general rules derived from our preceding experience of what our sentiments would commonly correspond with, correct upon this, as upon many other occasions, the impropriety of our present emotions.

The sentiment or affection of the heart from which any action proceeds, and upon which its whole virtue or vice must ultimately depend, may be considered under two different aspects, or in two different relations; first, in relation to the cause which excites it, or the motive which gives occasion to it; and secondly, in relation to the end which it proposes, or the effect which it tends to produce.

In the suitableness or unsuitableness, in the proportion or disproportion which the affection seems to bear to the cause or object which excites it, consists the propriety or impropriety, the decency or ungracefulness of the consequent action.

In the beneficial or hurtful nature of the effects which the affection aims at, or tends to produce, consists the merit or demerit of the action, the qualities by which it is entitled to reward, or is deserving of punishment.

Philosophers have, of late years, considered chiefly the tendency of affections, and have given little attention to the relation which they stand in to the cause which excites them. In common life, however, when we judge of any person's conduct, and of the sentiments which directed it, we constantly consider them under both these aspects. When we blame in another man the excesses of love, of grief, of resentment, we not only consider the ruinous effects which they tend to produce, but the little occasion which was given for them. The merit of his favourite, we say, is not so great, his misfortune is not so dreadful, his provocation is not so extraordinary, as to justify so violent a passion. We should have indulged, we say; perhaps, have approved of the violence of his emotion, had the cause been in any respect proportioned to it.

When we judge in this manner of any affection, as proportioned or disproportioned to the cause which excites it, it is scarce possible that we should make use of any other rule or canon but the correspondent affection in ourselves. If, upon bringing the case home to our own breast, we find that the sentiments which it gives occasion to, coincide and tally with our own, we necessarily approve of them as proportioned and suitable to their objects; if otherwise, we necessarily disapprove of them, as extravagant and out of proportion.

Every faculty in one man is the measure by which he judges of the like faculty in another. I judge of your sight by my sight, of your ear by my ear, of your reason by my reason, of your resentment by my resentment, of your love by my love. I neither have, nor can have, any other way of judging about them.

Chap. IV: The same subject continued

We may judge of the propriety or impropriety of the sentiments of another person by their correspondence or disagreement with

our own, upon two different occasions; either, first, when the objects which excite them are considered without any peculiar relation, either to ourselves or to the person whose sentiments we judge of; or, secondly, when they are considered as peculiarly affecting one or other of us.

1. With regard to those objects which are considered without any peculiar relation either to ourselves or to the person whose sentiments we judge of; wherever his sentiments entirely correspond with our own, we ascribe to him the qualities of taste and good judgment. The beauty of a plain, the greatness of a mountain, the ornaments of a building, the expression of a picture, the composition of a discourse, the conduct of a third person, the proportions of different quantities and numbers, the various appearances which the great machine of the universe is perpetually exhibiting, with the secret wheels and springs which product them; all the general subjects of science and taste, are what we and our companion regard as having no peculiar relation to either of us. We both look at them from the same point of view, and we have no occasion for sympathy, or for that imaginary change of situations from which it arises, in order to produce, with regard to these, the most perfect harmony of sentiments and affections. If, notwithstanding, we are often differently affected, it arises either from the different degrees of attention, which our different habits of life allow us to give easily to the several parts of those complex objects, or from the different degrees of natural acuteness in the faculty of the mind to which they are addressed.

When the sentiments of our companion coincide with our own in things of this kind, which are obvious and easy, and in which, perhaps, we never found a single person who differed from us, though we, no doubt, must approve of them, yet he seems to deserve no praise or admiration on account of them. But when they not only coincide with our own, but lead and direct our own; when in forming them he appears to have attended to many things which we had overlooked, and to have adjusted them to all the various circumstances of their objects; we not only approve of them, but wonder and are surprised at their uncommon and unexpected acuteness and comprehensiveness, and he appears to deserve a very high degree of admiration and applause. For approbation heightened by wonder and surprise, constitutes the sentiment which is properly called admiration, and of which applause is the natural expression. The decision of the man who judges that exquisite beauty is preferable to the grossest deformity, or that twice two are equal to four, must certainly be approved of by all the world, but will not, surely, be much admired. It is the acute and delicate discernment of the man of taste, who distinguishes the minute, and scarce perceptible differences of beauty and deformity; it is the comprehensive accuracy of the experienced mathematician, who unravels, with ease, the most intricate and perplexed proportions; it is the great leader in science and taste, the man who directs and conducts our own sentiments, the extent and superior justness of whose talents astonish us with wonder and surprise, who excites our admiration, and seems to deserve our applause: and upon this foundation is grounded the greater part of the praise which is bestowed upon what are called the intellectual virtues.

The utility of those qualities, it may be thought, is what first recommends them to us; and, no doubt, the consideration of this, when we come to attend to it, gives them a new value. Originally, however, we approve of another man's judgment, not as something useful, but as right, as accurate, as agreeable to truth and reality: and it is evident we attribute those qualities to it for no other reason but because we find that it agrees with our own. Taste, in the same manner, is originally approved of, not as useful, but as just, as delicate, and as precisely suited to its object. The idea of the utility of all qualities of this kind, is plainly an after-thought, and not what first recommends them to our approbation.

2. With regard to those objects, which affect in a particular manner either ourselves or the person whose sentiments we judge of, it is at once more difficult to preserve this harmony and correspondence, and at the same time, vastly more important. My companion does not naturally look upon the misfortune that has befallen me, or the injury that has been done me, from the same point of view in which I consider them. They affect me much more nearly. We do not view them from the same station, as we do a picture, or a poem, or a system of philosophy, and are, therefore, apt to be very differently affected by them. But I can much more easily overlook the want of this correspondence of sentiments with regard to such indifferent objects as concern neither me nor my companion, than with regard to what interests me so much as the misfortune that has befallen me, or the injury that has been done me. Though you despise that picture, or that poem, or even that system of philosophy, which I admire, there is little danger of our quarrelling upon that account. Neither of us can reasonably be much interested about them. They ought all of them to be matters of great indifference to us both; so that, though our opinions may be opposite, our affections may still be very nearly the same. But it is quite otherwise with regard to those objects by which either you or I are particularly affected. Though your judgments in matters of speculation, though your sentiments in matters of taste, are quite opposite to mine, I can easily overlook this opposition; and if I have any degree of temper, I may still find some entertainment in your conversation, even upon those very subjects. But if you have either no fellow-feeling for the misfortunes I have met with, or none that bears any proportion to the grief which distracts me; or if you have either no indignation at the injuries I have suffered, or none that bears any proportion to the resentment which transports me, we can no longer converse upon these subjects. We become intolerable to one another. I can neither support your company, nor you mine. You are confounded at my violence and passion, and I am enraged at your cold insensibility and want of feeling.

In all such cases, that there may be some correspondence of sentiments between the spectator and the person principally concerned, the spectator must, first of all, endeavour, as much as he can, to put himself in the situation of the other, and to bring home to himself every little circumstance of distress which can possibly occur to the sufferer. He must adopt the whole case of his companion with all its minutest incidents; and strive to render as perfect as possible, that imaginary change of situation upon which his sympathy is founded.

After all this, however, the emotions of the spectator will still be very apt to fall short of the violence of what is felt by the sufferer. Mankind, though naturally sympathetic, never conceive, for what has befallen another, that degree of passion which naturally animates the person principally concerned. That imaginary change of situation, upon which their sympathy is founded, is but momentary. The thought of their own safety, the thought that they themselves are not really the sufferers, continually intrudes itself upon them; and though it does not hinder them from conceiving a passion somewhat analogous to what is felt by the sufferer, hinders them from conceiving any thing that approaches to the same degree of violence. The person principally concerned is sensible of this, and at the same time passionately desires a more complete sympathy. He longs for that relief which nothing can afford him but the entire concord of the affections of the spectators with his own. To see the emotions of their hearts, in every respect, beat time to his own, in the violent and disagreeable passions, constitutes his sole consolation. But he can only hope to obtain this by lowering his passion to that pitch, in which the spectators are capable of going along with him. He must flatten, if I may be allowed to say so, the sharpness of its natural tone, in order to reduce it to harmony and concord with the emotions of those who are about him. What they feel, will, indeed, always be, in some respects, different from what he feels, and compassion can never be exactly the same with original sorrow; because the secret consciousness that the change of situations, from

which the sympathetic sentiment arises, is but imaginary, not only lowers it in degree, but, in some measure, varies it in kind, and gives it a quite different modification. These two sentiments, however, may, it is evident, have such a correspondence with one another, as is sufficient for the harmony of society. Though they will never be unisons, they may be concords, and this is all that is wanted or required.

In order to produce this concord, as nature teaches the spectators to assume the circumstances of the person principally concerned, so she teaches this last in some measure to assume those of the spectators. As they are continually placing themselves in his situation, and thence conceiving emotions similar to what he feels; so he is as constantly placing himself in theirs, and thence conceiving some degree of that coolness about his own fortune, with which he is sensible that they will view it. As they are constantly considering what they themselves would feel, if they actually were the sufferers, so he is as constantly led to imagine in what manner he would be affected if he was only one of the spectators of his own situation. As their sympathy makes them look at it, in some measure, with his eyes, so his sympathy makes him look at it, in some measure, with theirs, especially when in their presence and acting under their observation: and as the reflected passion, which he thus conceives, is much weaker than the original one, it necessarily abates the violence of what he felt before he came into their presence, before he began to recollect in what manner they would be affected by it, and to view his situation in this candid and impartial light.

The mind, therefore, is rarely so disturbed, but that the company of a friend will restore it to some degree of tranquillity and sedateness. The breast is, in some measure, calmed and composed the moment we come into his presence. We are immediately put in mind of the light in which he will view our situation, and we begin to view it ourselves in the same light; for the effect of sympathy is instantaneous. We expect less sympathy from a common acquaintance than from a friend: we cannot open to the former all those little circumstances which we can unfold to the latter: we assume, therefore, more tranquillity before him, and endeavour to fix our thoughts upon those general outlines of our situation which he is willing to consider. We expect still less sympathy from an assembly of strangers, and we assume, therefore, still more tranquillity before them, and always endeavour to bring down our passion to that pitch, which the particular company we are in may be expected to go along with. Nor is this only an assumed appearance: for if we are at all masters of ourselves, the presence of a mere acquaintance will really compose us, still more than that of a friend; and that of an assembly of strangers still more than that of an acquaintance.

Society and conversation, therefore, are the most powerful remedies for restoring the mind to its tranquillity, if, at any time, it has unfortunately lost it; as well as the best preservatives of that equal and happy temper, which is so necessary to self-satisfaction and enjoyment. Men of retirement and speculation, who are apt to sit brooding at home over either grief or resentment, though they may often have more humanity, more generosity, and a nicer sense of honour, yet seldom possess that equality of temper which is so common among men of the world.

. . .

Section III: Of the Effects of Prosperity and Adversity upon the Judgment of Mankind with regard to the Propriety of Action; and why it is more easy to obtain their Aprobation in the one state than in the other

. . .

Chap. II: Of the origin of Ambition, and of the distinction of Ranks

It is because mankind are disposed to sympathize more entirely with our joy than with our sorrow, that we make parade of our riches, and conceal our poverty. Nothing is so mortifying as to be obliged to expose our distress to the view of the public, and to feel, that though our situation is open to the eyes of all mankind, no mortal conceives for us the half of what we suffer. Nay, it is chiefly from this regard to the sentiments of mankind, that we pursue riches and avoid poverty. For to what purpose is all the toil and bustle of this world? what is the end of avarice and ambition, of the pursuit of wealth, of power, and preheminence? Is it to supply the necessities of nature? The wages of the meanest labourer can supply them. We see that they afford him food and clothing, the comfort of a house, and of a family. If we examined his oeconomy with rigour, we should find that he spends a great part of them upon conveniencies, which may be regarded as superfluities, and that, upon extraordinary occasions, he can give something even to vanity and distinction. What then is the cause of our aversion to his situation, and why should those who have been educated in the higher ranks of life, regard it as worse than death, to be reduced to live, even without labour, upon the same simple fare with him, to dwell under the same lowly roof, and to be clothed in the same humble. attire? Do they imagine that their stomach is better, or their sleep sounder in a palace than in a cottage? The contrary has been so often observed, and, indeed, is so very obvious, though it had never been observed, that there is nobody ignorant of it. From whence, then, arises that emulation which runs through all the different ranks of men, and what are the advantages which we propose by that great purpose of human life which we call bettering our condition? To be observed, to be attended to, to be taken notice of with sympathy, complacency, and approbation, are all the advantages which we can propose to derive from it. It is the vanity, not the ease, or the pleasure, which interests us. But vanity is always founded upon the belief of our being the object of attention and approbation. The rich man glories in his riches, because he feels that they naturally draw upon him the attention of the world, and that mankind are disposed to go along with him in all those agreeable emotions with which the advantages of his situation so readily inspire him. At the thought of this, his heart seems to swell and dilate itself within him, and he is fonder of his wealth, upon this account, than for all the other advantages it procures him. The poor man, on the contrary, is ashamed of his poverty. He feels that it either places him out of the sight of mankind, or, that if they take any notice of him, they have, however, scarce any fellow-feeling with the misery and distress which he suffers. He is mortified upon both accounts. for though to be overlooked, and to be disapproved of, are things entirely different, yet as obscurity covers us from the daylight of honour and approbation, to feel that we are taken no notice of, necessarily damps the most agreeable hope, and disappoints the most ardent desire, of human nature. The poor man goes out and comes in unheeded, and when in the midst of a crowd is in the same obscurity as if shut up in his own hovel. Those humble cares and painful attentions which occupy those in his situation, afford no amusement to the dissipated and the gay. They turn away their eyes from him, or if the extremity of his distress forces them to look at him, it is only to spurn so disagreeable an object from among them. The fortunate and the proud wonder at the insolence of human wretchedness, that it should dare to present itself before them, and with the loathsome aspect of its misery presume to disturb the serenity of their happiness. The man of rank and distinction, on the contrary, is observed by all the world. Every body is eager to look at him, and to conceive, at least by sympathy, that joy and exultation with which his circumstances naturally inspire him. His actions are the objects of the public care. Scarce a word, scarce a gesture, can fall from him that is altogether neglected. In a great assembly he is the person upon whom all direct their eyes; it is upon him that their passions seem all to wait with expectation, in order to receive that movement and direction which he shall impress upon them; and if his behaviour is not altogether absurd, he has, every moment, an opportunity of interesting mankind, and of rendering himself the object of the observation and fellow-feeling of every body about him. It is this, which, notwithstanding the restraint it imposes, notwithstanding the loss of liberty with which it is attended, renders greatness the object of envy, and compensates, in the opinion of all those mortifications which must mankind, all that toil, all that anxiety, be undergone in the pursuit of it; and what is of yet more consequence, all that

leisure, all that ease, all that careless security, which are forfeited for ever by the acquisition.

When we consider the condition of the great, in those delusive colours in which the imagination is apt to paint it. it seems to be almost the abstract idea of a perfect and happy state. It is the very state which, in all our waking dreams and idle reveries, we had sketched out to ourselves as the final object of all our desires. We feel, therefore, a peculiar sympathy with the satisfaction of those who are in it. We favour all their inclinations, and forward all their wishes. What pity, we think, that any thing should spoil and corrupt so agreeable a situation! We could even wish them immortal; and it seems hard to us, that death should at last put an end to such perfect enjoyment. It is cruel, we think, in Nature to compel them from their exalted stations to that humble, but hospitable home, which she has provided for all her children. Great King, live for ever! is the compliment, which, after the manner of eastern adulation, we should readily make them, if experience did not teach us its absurdity. Every calamity that befals them, every injury that is done them, excites in the breast of the spectator ten times more compassion and resentment than he would have felt, had the same things happened to other men. It is the misfortunes of Kings only which afford the proper subjects for tragedy. They resemble, in this respect, the misfortunes of lovers. Those two situations are the chief which interest us upon the theatre; because, in spite of all that reason and experience can tell us to the contrary, the prejudices of the imagination attach to these two states a happiness superior to any other. To disturb, or to put an end to such perfect enjoyment, seems to be the most atrocious of all injuries. The traitor who conspires against the life of his monarch, is thought a greater monster than any other murderer. All the innocent blood that was shed in the civil wars, provoked less indignation than the death of Charles I. A stranger to human nature, who saw the indifference of men about the misery of their inferiors, and the regret and indignation which they feel for the misfortunes and sufferings of those above them, would be apt to imagine, that pain must be more agonizing, and the convulsions of death more terrible to persons of higher rank, than to those of meaner stations.

Upon this disposition of mankind, to go along with all the passions of the rich and the powerful, is founded the distinction of ranks, and the order of society. Our obsequiousness to our superiors more frequently arises from our admiration for the advantages of their situation, than from any private expectations of benefit from their good-will. Their benefits can extend but to a few. but their fortunes interest almost every body. We are eager to assist them in completing a system of happiness that approaches so near to perfection; and we desire to serve them for their own sake, without any other recompense but the vanity or the honour of obliging them. Neither is our deference to their inclinations founded chiefly, or altogether, upon a regard to the utility of such submission, and to the order of society, which is best supported by it. Even when the order of society seems to require that we should oppose them, we can hardly bring ourselves to do it. That kings are the servants of the people, to be obeyed, resisted, deposed, or punished, as the public conveniency may require, is the doctrine of reason and philosophy; but it is not the doctrine of Nature. Nature would teach us to submit to them for their own sake, to tremble and bow down before their exalted station, to regard their smile as a reward sufficient to compensate any services, and to dread their displeasure, though no other evil were to follow from it, as the severest of all mortifications. To treat them in any respect as men, to reason and dispute with them upon ordinary occasions, requires such resolution, that there are few men whose magnanimity can support them in it, unless they are likewise assisted by familiarity and acquaintance. The strongest motives, the most furious passions, fear, hatred, and resentment, are scarce sufficient to balance this natural disposition to respect them: and their conduct must, either justly or unjustly, have excited the highest degree of all those passions, before the bulk of the people can be brought to oppose them with violence, or to desire to see

them either punished or deposed. Even when the people have been brought this length, they are apt to relent every moment, and easily relapse into their habitual state of deference to those whom they have been accustomed to look upon as their natural superiors. They cannot stand the mortification of their monarch. Compassion soon takes the place of resentment, they forget all past provocations, their old principles of loyalty revive, and they run to re-establish the ruined authority of their old masters, with the same violence with which they had opposed it. The death of Charles I brought about the Restoration of the royal family. Compassion for James II when he was seized by the populace in making his escape on ship-board, had almost prevented the Revolution, and made it go on more heavily than before.

Do the great seem insensible of the easy price at which they may acquire the public admiration; or do they seem to imagine that to them, as to other men, it must be the purchase either of sweat or of blood? By what important accomplishments is the young nobleman instructed to support the dignity of his rank, and to render himself worthy of that superiority over his fellow-citizens, to which the virtue of his ancestors had raised them? Is it by knowledge, by industry, by patience, by self-denial, or by virtue of any kind? As all his words, as all his motions are attended to, he learns an habitual regard to every circumstance of ordinary behaviour, and studies to perform all those small duties with the most exact propriety. As he is conscious how much he is observed, and how much mankind are disposed to favour all his inclinations, he acts, upon the most indifferent occasions, with that freedom and elevation which the thought of this naturally inspires. His air, his manner, his deportment, all mark that elegant and graceful sense of his own superiority, which those who are born to inferior stations can hardly ever arrive at. These are the arts by which he proposes to make mankind more easily submit to his authority, and to govern their inclinations according to his own pleasure: and in this he is seldom disappointed. These arts, supported by rank and preheminence, are, upon ordinary occasions, sufficient to govern the world. Lewis XIV during the greater part of his reign, was regarded, not only in France, but over all Europe, as the most perfect model of a great prince. But what were the talents and virtues by which he acquired this great reputation? Was it by the scrupulous and inflexible justice of all his undertakings, by the immense dangers and difficulties with which they were attended, or by the unwearied and unrelenting application with which he pursued them? Was it by his extensive knowledge, by his exquisite judgment, or by his heroic valour? It was by none of these qualities. But he was, first of all, the most powerful prince in Europe, and consequently held the highest rank among kings; and then, says his historian, 'he surpassed all his courtiers in the gracefulness of his shape, and the majestic beauty of his features. The sound of his voice, noble and affecting, gained those hearts which his presence intimidated. He had a step and a deportment which could suit only him and his rank, and which would have been ridiculous in any other person. The embarrassment which he occasioned to those who spoke to him, flattered that secret satisfaction with which he felt his own superiority. The old officer, who was confounded and faultered in asking him a favour, and not being able to conclude his discourse, said to him: Sir, your majesty, I hope, will believe that I do not tremble thus before your enemies: had no difficulty to obtain what he demanded.' These frivolous accomplishments, supported by his rank, and, no doubt too, by a degree of other talents and virtues, which seems, however, not to have been much above mediocrity, established this prince in the esteem of his own age, and have drawn, even from posterity, a good deal of respect for his memory. Compared with these, in his own times, and in his own presence, no other virtue, it seems, appeared to have any merit. Knowledge, industry, valour, and beneficence, trembled, were abashed, and lost all dignity before them.

But it is not by accomplishments of this kind, that the man of inferior rank must hope to distinguish himself. Politeness is so much the virtue of the great, that it will do little honour to any body but themselves. The coxcomb, who imitates their manner, and affects to be eminent by the superior propriety of his ordinary behaviour, is rewarded with a double share of contempt for his folly and presumption. Why should the man, whom nobody thinks it worth while to look at, be very anxious about the manner in which he holds up his head, or disposes of his arms while he walks through a room? He is occupied surely with a very superfluous attention, and with an attention too that marks a sense of his own importance, which no other mortal can go along with. The most perfect modesty and plainness, joined to as much negligence as is consistent with the respect due to the company, ought to be the chief characteristics of the behaviour of a private man. If ever he hopes to distinguish himself, it must be by more important virtues. He must acquire dependants to balance the dependants of the great, and he has no other fund to pay them from, but the labour of his body, and the activity of his mind. He must cultivate these therefore: he must acquire superior knowledge in his profession, and superior industry in the exercise of it. He must be patient in labour, resolute in danger, and firm in distress. These talents he must bring into public view, by the difficulty, importance, and, at the same time, good judgment of his undertakings, and by the severe and unrelenting application with which he pursues them. Probity and prudence, generosity and frankness, must characterize his behaviour upon all ordinary occasions; and he must, at the same time, be forward to engage in all those situations, in which it requires the greatest talents and virtues to act with propriety, but in which the greatest applause is to be acquired by those who can acquit themselves with honour. With what impatience does the man of spirit and ambition, who is depressed by his situation, look round for some great opportunity to distinguish himself? No circumstances, which can afford this, appear to him undesirable. He even looks forward with satisfaction to the prospect of foreign war, or civil dissension; and, with secret transport and delight, sees through all the confusion and bloodshed which attend them, the probability of those wished-for occasions presenting themselves, in which he may draw upon himself the attention and admiration of mankind. The man of rank and distinction, on the contrary, whose whole glory consists in the propriety of his ordinary behaviour, who is contented with the humble renown which this can afford him, and has no talents to acquire any other, is unwilling to embarrass himself with what can be attended either with difficulty or distress. To figure at a ball is his great triumph, and to succeed in an intrigue of gallantry, his highest exploit. He has an aversion to all public confusions, not from the love of mankind, for the great never look upon their inferiors as their fellow-creatures; nor yet from want of courage, for in that he is seldom defective; but from a consciousness that he possesses none of the virtues which are required in such situations, and that the public attention will certainly be drawn away from him by others. He may be willing to expose himself to some little danger, and to make a campaign when it happens to be the fashion. But he shudders with horror at the thought of any situation which demands the continual and long exertion of patience, industry, fortitude, and application of thought. These virtues are hardly ever to be met with in men who are born to those high stations. In all governments accordingly, even in monarchies, the highest offices are generally possessed, and the whole detail of the administration conducted, by men who were educated in the middle and inferior ranks of life, who have been carried forward by their own industry and abilities, though loaded with the jealousy, and opposed by the resentment, of all those who were born their superiors, and to whom the great, after having regarded them first with contempt, and afterwards with envy, are at last contented to truckle with the same abject meanness with which they desire that the rest of mankind should behave to themselves.

It is the loss of this easy empire over the affections of mankind which renders the fall from greatness so insupportable. When the family of the king of Macedon was led in triumph by Paulus Aemilius, their misfortunes, it is said, made them divide with their conqueror the attention of the Roman people. The sight of the royal children, whose tender age rendered them insensible of their situation, struck the spectators, amidst the public rejoicings and prosperity, with the tenderest sorrow and compassion. The king appeared next in the procession; and seemed like one confounded and astonished, and bereft of all sentiment, by the greatness of his calamities. His friends and ministers followed after him. As they moved along, they often cast their eyes upon their fallen sovereign, and always burst into tears at the sight; their whole behaviour demonstrating that they thought not of their own misfortunes, but were occupied entirely by the superior greatness of his. The generous Romans, on the contrary, beheld him with disdain and indignation, and regarded as unworthy of all compassion the man who could be so mean-spirited as to bear to live under such calamities. Yet what did those calamities amount to? According to the greater part of historians, he was to spend the remainder of his days, under the protection of a powerful and humane people, in a state which in itself should seem worthy of envy, a state of plenty, ease, leisure, and security, from which it was impossible for him even by his own folly to fall. But he was no longer to be surrounded by that admiring mob of fools, flatterers, and dependants, who had formerly been accustomed to attend upon all his motions. He was no longer to be gazed upon by multitudes, nor to have it in his power to render himself the object of their respect, their gratitude, their love, their admiration. The passions of nations were no longer to mould themselves upon his inclinations. This was that insupportable calamity which bereaved the king of all sentiment; which made his friends forget their own misfortunes; and which the Roman magnanimity could scarce conceive how any man could be so mean-spirited as to bear to survive.

'Love,' says my Lord Rochfaucault, 'is commonly succeeded by ambition; but ambition is hardly ever succeeded by love.' That passion, when once it has got entire possession of the breast, will admit neither a rival nor a successor. To those who have been accustomed to the possession, or even to the hope of public admiration, all other pleasures sicken and decay. Of all the discarded statesmen who for their own ease have studied to get the better of ambition, and to despise those honours which they could no longer arrive at, how few have been able to succeed? The greater part have spent their time in the most listless and insipid indolence, chagrined at the thoughts of their own insignificancy, incapable of being interested i n the occupations of private life, without enjoyment, except when they talked of their former greatness, and without satisfaction, except when they were employed in some vain project to recover it. Are you in earnest resolved never to barter your liberty for the lordly servitude of a court, but to live free, fearless, and independent? There seems to be one way to continue in that virtuous resolution; and perhaps but one. Never enter the place from whence so few have been able to return; never come within the circle of ambition; nor ever bring yourself into comparison with those masters of the earth who have already engrossed the attention of half mankind before you.

Of such mighty importance does it appear to be, in the imaginations of men, to stand in that situation which sets them most in the view of general sympathy and attention. And thus, place, that great object which divides the wives of aldermen, is the end of half the labours of human life; and is the cause of all the tumult and bustle, all the rapine and injustice, which avarice and ambition have introduced into this world. People of sense, it is said, indeed despise place; that is, they despise sitting at the head of the table, and are indifferent who it is that is pointed out to the company by that frivolous circumstance, which the smallest advantage is capable of overbalancing. But rank, distinction pre-eminence, no man despises, unless he is either raised very much above, or sunk very much below, the ordinary standard of human nature; unless he is either so confirmed in wisdom and real philosophy, as to be satisfied that, while the

propriety of his conduct renders him the just object of approbation, it is of little consequence though he be neither attended to, nor approved of; or so habituated to the idea of his own meanness, so sunk in slothful and sottish indifference, as entirely to have forgot the desire, and almost the very wish, for superiority.

As to become the natural object of the joyous congratulations and sympathetic attentions of mankind is, in this manner, the circumstance which gives to prosperity all its dazzling splendour; so nothing darkens so much the gloom of adversity as to feel that our misfortunes are the objects, not of the fellow-feeling, but of the contempt and aversion of our brethren. It is upon this account that the most dreadful calamities are not always those which it is most difficult to support. It is often more mortifying to appear in public under small disasters, than under great misfortunes. The first excite no sympathy; but the second, though they may excite none that approaches to the anguish of the sufferer, call forth, however, a very lively compassion. The sentiments of the spectators are, in this last case, less wide of those of the sufferer, and their imperfect fellow-feeling lends him some assistance in supporting his misery. Before a gay assembly, a gentleman would be more mortified to appear covered with filth and rags than with blood and wounds. This last situation would interest their pity; the other would provoke their laughter. The judge who orders a criminal to be set in the pillory, dishonours him more than if he had condemned him to the scaffold. The great prince, who, some years ago, caned a general officer at the head of his army, disgraced him irrecoverably. The punishment would have been much less had he shot him through the body. By the laws of honour, to strike with a cane dishonours, to strike with a sword does not, for an obvious reason. Those slighter punishments, when inflicted on a gentleman, to whom dishonour is the greatest of all evils, come to be regarded among a humane and generous people, as the most dreadful of any. With regard to persons of that rank, therefore, they are universally laid aside, and the law, while it takes their life upon many occasions, respects their honour upon almost all. To scourge a person of quality, or to set him in the pillory, upon account of any crime whatever, is a brutality of which no European government, except that of Russia, is capable.

A brave man is not rendered contemptible by being brought to the scaffold; he is, by being set in the pillory. His behaviour in the one situation may gain him universal esteem and admiration. No behaviour in the other can render him agreeable. The sympathy of the spectators supports him in the one case, and saves him from that shame, that consciousness that his misery is felt by himself only, which is of all sentiments the most unsupportable. There is no sympathy in the other; or, if there is any, it is not with his pain, which is a trifle, but with his consciousness of the want of sympathy with which this pain is attended. It is with his shame, not with his sorrow. Those who pity him, blush and hang down their heads for him. He droops in the same manner, and feels himself irrecoverably degraded by the punishment, though not by the crime. The man, on the contrary, who dies with resolution, as he is naturally regarded with the erect aspect of esteem and approbation, so he wears himself the same undaunted countenance; and, if the crime does not deprive him of the respect of others, the punishment never will. He has no suspicion that his situation is the object of contempt or derision to any body, and he can, with propriety, assume the air, not only of perfect serenity, but of triumph and exultation.

'Great dangers,' says the Cardinal de Retz, 'have their charms, because there is some glory to be got, even when we miscarry. But moderate dangers have nothing but what is horrible, because the loss of reputation always attends the want of success.' His maxim has the same foundation with what we have been just now observing with regard to punishments.

Human virtue is superior to pain, to poverty, to danger, and to death; nor does it even require its utmost efforts do despise them. But to

have its misery exposed to insult and derision, to be led in triumph, to be set up for the hand of scorn to point at, is a situation in which its constancy is much more apt to fail. Compared with the contempt of mankind, all other external evils are easily supported.

Chap. III: Of the corruption of our moral sentiments, which is occasioned by this disposition to admire the rich and the great, and to despise or neglect persons of poor and mean condition

This disposition to admire, and almost to worship, the rich and the powerful, and to despise, or, at least, to neglect persons of poor and mean condition, though necessary both to establish and to maintain the distinction of ranks and the order of society, is, at the same time, the great and most universal cause of the corruption of our moral sentiments. That wealth and greatness are often regarded with the respect and admiration which are due only to wisdom and virtue; and that the contempt, of which vice and folly are the only proper objects, is often most unjustly bestowed upon poverty and weakness, has been the complaint of moralists in all ages.

We desire both to be respectable and to be respected. We dread both to be contemptible and to be contemned. But, upon coming into the world, we soon find that wisdom and virtue are by no means the sole objects of respect; nor vice and folly, of contempt. We frequently see the respectful attentions of the world more strongly directed towards the rich and the great, than towards the wise and the virtuous. We see frequently the vices and follies of the powerful much less despised than the poverty and weakness of the innocent. To deserve, to acquire, and to enjoy the respect and admiration of mankind, are the great objects of ambition and emulation. Two different roads are presented to us, equally leading to the attainment of this so much desired object; the one, by the study of wisdom and the practice of virtue; the other, by the acquisition of wealth and greatness. Two different characters are presented to our emulation; the one, of proud ambition and ostentatious avidity. the other, of humble modesty and equitable justice. Two different models, two different pictures, are held out to us, according to which we may fashion our own character and behaviour; the one more gaudy and glittering in its colouring; the other more correct and more exquisitely beautiful in its outline: the one forcing itself upon the notice of every wandering eye; the other, attracting the attention of scarce any body but the most studious and careful observer. They are the wise and the virtuous chiefly, a select, though, I am afraid, but a small party, who are the real and steady admirers of wisdom and virtue. The great mob of mankind are the admirers and worshippers, and, what may seem more extraordinary, most frequently the disinterested admirers and worshippers, of wealth and greatness.

The respect which we feel for wisdom and virtue is, no doubt, different from that which we conceive for wealth and greatness; and it requires no very nice discernment to distinguish the difference. But, notwithstanding this difference, those sentiments bear a very considerable resemblance to one another. In some particular features they are, no doubt, different, but, in the general air of the countenance, they seem to be so very nearly the same, that inattentive observers are very apt to mistake the one for the other.

In equal degrees of merit there is scarce any man who does not respect more the rich and the great, than the poor and the humble. With most men the presumption and vanity of the former are much more admired, than the real and solid merit of the latter. It is scarce agreeable to good morals, or even to good language, perhaps, to say, that mere wealth and greatness, abstracted from merit and virtue, deserve our respect. We must acknowledge, however, that they almost constantly obtain it; and that they may, therefore, be considered as, in some respects, the natural objects of it. Those exalted stations may, no doubt, be completely degraded by vice and folly. But the vice and folly must be very great, before they can operate this complete degradation. The profligacy of a man of fashion is looked upon with

much less contempt and aversion, than that of a man of meaner condition. In the latter, a single transgression of the rules of temperance and propriety, is commonly more resented, than the constant and avowed contempt of them ever is in the former.

In the middling and inferior stations of life, the road to virtue and that to fortune, to such fortune, at least, as men in such stations can reasonably expect to acquire, are, happily in most cases, very nearly the same. In all the middling and inferior professions, real and solid professional abilities, joined to prudent, just, firm, and temperate conduct, can very seldom fail of success. Abilities will even sometimes prevail where the conduct is by no means correct. Either habitual imprudence, however, or injustice, or weakness, or profligacy, will always clouD, and sometimes Depress altogether, the most splendid professional abilities. Men in the inferior and middling stations of life, besides, can never be great enough to be above the law, which must generally overawe them into some sort of respect for, at least, the more important rules of justice. The success of such people, too, almost always depends upon the favour and good opinion of their neighbours and equals; and without a tolerably regular conduct these can very seldom be obtained. The good old proverb, therefore, That honesty is the best policy, holds, in such situations, almost always perfectly true. In such situations, therefore, we may generally expect a considerable degree of virtue; and, fortunately for the good morals of society, these are the situations of by far the greater part of mankind.

In the superior stations of life the case is unhappily not always the same. In the courts of princes, in the drawing-rooms of the great, where success and preferment depend, not upon the esteem of intelligent and well-informed equals, but upon the fanciful and foolish favour of ignorant, presumptuous, and proud superiors; flattery and falsehood too often prevail over merit and abilities. In such societies the abilities to please, are more regarded than the abilities to serve. In quiet and peaceable times, when the storm is at a distance, the prince, or great man, wishes only to be amused, and is even apt to fancy that he has scarce any occasion for the service of any body, or that those who amuse him are sufficiently able to serve him. The external graces, the frivolous accomplishments of that impertinent and foolish thing called a man of fashion, are commonly more admired than the solid and masculine virtues of a warrior, a statesman, a philosopher, or a legislator. All the great and awful virtues, all the virtues which can fit, either for the council, the senate, or the field, are, by the insolent and insignificant flatterers, who commonly figure the most in such corrupted societies, held in the utmost contempt and derision. When the duke of Sully was called upon by Lewis the Thirteenth, to give his advice in some great emergency, he observed the favourites and courtiers whispering to one another, and smiling at his unfashionable appearance. 'Whenever your majesty's father,' said the old warrior and statesman, 'did me the honour to consult me, he ordered the buffoons of the court to retire into the antechamber.'

It is from our disposition to admire, and consequently to imitate, the rich and the great, that they are enabled to set, or to lead what is called the fashion. Their dress is the fashionable dress; the language of their conversation, the fashionable style; their air and deportment, the fashionable behaviour. Even their vices and follies are fashionable; and the greater part of men are proud to imitate and resemble them in the very qualities which dishonour and degrade them. Vain men often give themselves airs of a fashionable profligacy, which, in their hearts, they do not approve of, and of which, perhaps, they are really not guilty. They desire to be praised for what they themselves do not think praise-worthy, and are ashamed of unfashionable virtues which they sometimes practise in secret, and for which they have secretly some degree of real veneration. There are hypocrites of wealth and greatness, as well as of religion and virtue; and a vain man is as apt to pretend to be what he is not, in the one way, as a cunning man is in the other. He assumes the equipage and splendid way of living of his superiors, without considering that whatever may be praise-worthy in any of these, derives its whole merit and propriety from its suitableness to that situation and fortune which both require and can easily support the expence. Many a poor man places his glory in being thought rich, without considering that the duties (if one may call such follies by so very venerable a name) which that reputation imposes upon him, must soon reduce him to beggary, and render his situation still more unlike that of those whom he admires and imitates, than it had been originally.

To attain to this envied situation, the candidates for fortune too frequently abandon the paths of virtue; for unhappily, the road which leads to the one, and that which leads to the other, lie sometimes in very opposite directions. But the ambitious man flatters himself that, in the splendid situation to which he advances, he will have so many means of commanding the respect and admiration of mankind, and will be enabled to act with such superior propriety and grace, that the lustre of his future conduct will entirely cover, or efface, the foulness of the steps by which he arrived at that elevation. In many governments the candidates for the highest stations are above the law; and, if they can attain the object of their ambition, they have no fear of being called to account for the means by which they acquired it. They often endeavour, therefore, not only by fraud and falsehood, the ordinary and vulgar arts of intrigue and cabal; but sometimes by the perpetration of the most enormous crimes, by murder and assassination, by rebellion and civil war, to supplant and destroy those who oppose or stand in the way of their greatness. They more frequently miscarry than succeed; and commonly gain nothing but the disgraceful punishment which is due to their crimes. But, though they should be so lucky as to attain that wished-for greatness, they are always most miserably disappointed in the happiness which they expect to enjoy in it. It is not ease or pleasure, but always honour, of one kind or another, though frequently an honour very ill understood, that the ambitious man really pursues. But the honour of his exalted station appears, both in his own eyes and in those of other people, polluted and defiled by the baseness of the means through which he rose to it. Though by the profusion of every liberal expence; though by excessive indulgence in every profligate pleasure, the wretched, but usual, resource of ruined characters; though by the hurry of public business, or by the prouder and more dazzling tumult of war, he may endeavour to efface, both from his own memory and from that of other people, the remembrance of what he has done; that remembrance never fails to pursue him. He invokes in vain the dark and dismal powers of forgetfulness and oblivion. He remembers himself what he has done, and that remembrance tells him that other people must likewise remember it. Amidst all the gaudy pomp of the most ostentatious greatness; amidst the venal and vile adulation of the great and of the learned; amidst the more innocent, though more foolish, acclamations of the common people; amidst all the pride of conquest and the triumph of successful war, he is still secretly pursued by the avenging furies of shame and remorse; and, while glory seems to surround him on all sides, he himself, in his own imagination, sees black and foul infamy fast pursuing him, and every moment ready to overtake him from behind. Even the great Caesar, though he had the magnanimity to dismiss his guards, could not dismiss his suspicions. The remembrance of Pharsalia still haunted and pursued him. When, at the request of the senate, he had the generosity to pardon Marcellus, he told that assembly, that he was not unaware of the designs which were carrying on against his life; but that, as he had lived long enough both for nature and for glory, he was contented to die, and therefore despised all conspiracies. He had, perhaps, lived long enough for nature. But the man who felt himself the object of such deadly resentment, from those whose favour he wished to gain, and whom he still wished to consider as his friends, had certainly lived too long for real glory; or for all the happiness which he could ever hope to enjoy in the love and esteem of his equals.

. . .

Part IV: Of the Effect of Utility upon the Sentiment of Approbation Consisting of One Section

Chap. I: Of the Beauty which the Appearance of Utility bestows upon all the Productions of Art, and of the extensive Influence of this Species of Beauty

That utility is one of the principal sources of beauty has been observed by every body, who has considered with any attention what constitutes the nature of beauty. The conveniency of a house gives pleasure to the spectator as well as its regularity, and he is as much hurt when he observes the contrary defect, as when he sees the correspondent windows of different forms, or the door not placed exactly in the middle of the building. That the fitness of any system or machine to produce the end for which it was intended, bestows a certain propriety and beauty upon the whole, and renders the very thought and contemplation of it agreeable, is so very obvious that nobody has overlooked it.

The cause too, why utility pleases, has of late been assigned by an ingenious and agreeable philosopher, who joins the greatest depth of thought to the greatest elegance of expression, and possesses the singular and happy talent of treating the abstrusest subjects not only with the most perfect perspicuity, but with the most lively eloquence. The utility of any object, according to him, pleases the master by perpetually suggesting to him the pleasure or conveniency which it is fitted to promote. Every time he looks at it, he is put in mind of this pleasure; and the object in this manner becomes a source of perpetual satisfaction and enjoyment. The spectator enters by sympathy into the sentiments of the master, and necessarily views the object under the same agreeable aspect. When we visit the palaces of the great, we cannot help conceiving the satisfaction we should enjoy if we ourselves were the masters, and were possessed of so much artful and ingeniously contrived accommodation. A similar account is given why the appearance of inconveniency should render any object disagreeable both to the owner and to the spectator.

But that this fitness, this happy contrivance of any production of art, should often be more valued, than the very end for which it was intended; and that the exact adjustment of the means for attaining any conveniency or pleasure, should frequently be more regarded, than that very conveniency or pleasure, in the attainment of which their whole merit would seem to consist, has not, so far as I know, been yet taken notice of by any body. That this however is very frequently the case, may be observed in a thousand instances, both in the most frivolous and in the most important concerns of human life.

When a person comes into his chamber, and finds the chairs all standing in the middle of the room, he is angry with his servant, and rather than see them continue in that disorder, perhaps takes the trouble himself to set them all in their places with their backs to the wall. The whole propriety of this new situation arises from its superior conveniency in leaving the floor free and disengaged. To attain this conveniency he voluntarily puts himself to more trouble than all he could have suffered from the want of it; since nothing was more easy, than to have set himself down upon one of them, which is probably what he does when his labour is over. What he w.anted therefore, it seems, was not so much this conveniency, as that arrangement of things which promotes it. Yet it is this conveniency which ultimately recommends that arrangement, and bestows upon it the whole of its propriety and beauty.

A watch, in the same manner, that falls behind above two minutes in a day, is despised by one curious in watches. He sells it perhaps for a couple of guineas, and purchases another at fifty, which will not lose above a minute in a fortnight. The sole use of watches however, is to tell us what o'clock it is, and to hinder us from breaking any engagement, or suffering any other inconveniency by our ignorance in that particular point. But the person so nice with regard to this machine, will not always be found either more scrupulously punctual than other men, or more anxiously concerned upon any other account, to know precisely what time of day it is. What interests him is not so much the attainment of this piece of knowledge, as the perfection of the machine which serves to attain it.

How many people ruin themselves by laying out money on trinkets of frivolous utility? What pleases these lovers of toys is not so much the utility, as the aptness of the machines which are fitted to promote it. All their pockets are stuffed with little conveniencies. They contrive new pockets, unknown in the clothes of other people, in order to carry a greater number. They walk about loaded with a multitude of baubles, in weight and sometimes in value not inferior to an ordinary Jew's-box, some of which may sometimes be of some little use, but all of which might at all times be very well spared, and of which the whole utility is certainly not worth the fatigue of bearing the burden.

Nor is it only with regard to such frivolous objects that our conduct is influenced by this principle; it is often the secret motive of the most serious and important pursuits of both private and public life.

The poor man's son, whom heaven in its anger has visited with ambition, when he begins to look around him, admires the condition of the rich. He finds the cottage of his father too small for his accommodation, and fancies he should be lodged more at his ease in a palace. He is displeased with being obliged to walk a-foot, or to endure the fatigue of riding on horseback. He sees his superiors carried about in machines, and imagines that in one of these he could travel with less inconveniency. He feels himself naturally indolent, and willing to serve himself with his own hands as little as possible; and judges, that a numerous retinue of servants would save him from a great deal of trouble. He thinks if he had attained all these, he would sit still contentedly, and be quiet, enjoying himself in the thought of the happiness and tranquillity of his situation. He is enchanted with the distant idea of this felicity. It appears in his fancy like the life of some superior rank of beings, and, in order to arrive at it, he devotes himself for ever to the pursuit of wealth and greatness. To obtain the conveniencies which these afford, he submits in the first year, nay in the first month of his application, to more fatigue of body and more uneasiness of mind than he could have suffered through the whole of his life from the want of them. He studies to distinguish himself in some laborious profession. With the most unrelenting industry he labours night and day to acquire talents superior to all his competitors. He endeavours next to bring those talents into public view, and with equal assiduity solicits every opportunity of employment. For this purpose he makes his court to all mankind; he serves those whom he hates, and is obsequious to those whom he despises. Through the whole of his life he pursues the idea of a certain artificial and elegant repose which he may never arrive at, for which he sacrifices a real tranquillity that is at all times in his power, and which, if in the extremity of old age he should at last attain to it, he will find to be in no respect preferable to that humble security and contentment which he had abandoned for it. It is then, in the last dregs of life, his body wasted with toil and diseases, his mind galled and ruffled by the memory of a thousand injuries and disappointments which he imagines he has met with from the injustice of his enemies, or from the perfidy and ingratitude of his friends, that he begins at last to find that wealth and greatness are mere trinkets of frivolous utility, no more adapted for procuring ease of body or tranquillity of mind than the tweezer-cases of the lover of toys; and like them too, more troublesome to the person who carries them about with him than all the advantages they can afford him are commodious. There is no other real difference between them, except that the conveniencies of the one are somewhat more observable than those of the other. The palaces, the gardens, the equipage, the retinue of the great, are objects of which the obvious conveniency strikes every body. They do not require that their masters should point out to us wherein consists their

utility. Of our own accord we readily enter into it, and by sympathy enjoy and thereby applaud the satisfaction which they are fitted to afford him. But the curiosity of a tooth-pick, of an ear-picker, of a machine for cutting the nails, or of any other trinket of the same kind, is not so obvious. Their conveniency may perhaps be equally great, but it is not so striking, and we do not so readily enter into the satisfaction of the man who possesses them. They are therefore less reasonable subjects of vanity than the magnificence of wealth and greatness; and in this consists the sole advantage of these last. They more effectually gratify that love of distinction so natural to man. To one who was to live alone in a desolate island it might be a matter of doubt, perhaps, whether a palace, or a collection of such small conveniencies as are commonly contained in a tweezer-case, would contribute most to his happiness and enjoyment. If he is to live in society, indeed, there can be no comparison, because in this, as in all other cases, we constantly pay more regard to the sentiments of the spectator, than to those of the person principally concerned, and consider rather how his situation will appear to other people, than how it will appear to himself. If we examine, however, why the spectator distinguishes with such admiration the condition of the rich and the great, we shall find that it is not so much upon account of the superior ease or pleasure which they are supposed to enjoy, as of the numberless artificial and elegant contrivances for promoting this ease or pleasure. He does not even imagine that they are really happier than other people: but he imagines that they possess more means of happiness. And it is the ingenious and artful adjustment of those means to the end for which they were intended, that is the principal source of his admiration. But in the languor of disease and the weariness of old age, the pleasures of the vain and empty distinctions of greatness disappear. To one, in this situation, they are no longer capable of recommending those toilsome pursuits in which they had formerly engaged him. In his heart he curses ambition, and vainly regrets the ease and the indolence of youth, pleasures which are fled for ever, and which he has foolishly sacrificed for what, when he has got it, can afford him no real satisfaction. In this miserable aspect does greatness appear to every man when reduced either by spleen or disease to observe with attention his own situation, and to consider what it is that is really wanting to his happiness. Power and riches appear then to be, what they are, enormous and operose machines contrived to produce a few trifling conveniencies to the body, consisting of springs the most nice and delicate, which must be kept in order with the most anxious attention, and which in spite of all our care are ready every moment to burst into pieces, and to crush in their ruins their unfortunate possessor. They are immense fabrics, which it requires the labour of a life to raise, which threaten every moment to overwhelm the person that dwells in them, and which while they stand, though they may save him from some smaller inconveniencies, can protect him from none of the severer inclemencies of the season. They keep off the summer shower, not the winter storm, but leave him always as much, and sometimes more exposed than before, to anxiety, to fear, and to sorrow; to diseases, to danger, and to death.

But though this splenetic philosophy, which in time of sickness or low spirits is familiar to every man, thus entirely depreciates those great objects of human desire, when in better health and in better humour, we never fail to regard them under a more agreeable aspect. Our imagination, which in pain and sorrow seems to be confined and cooped up within our own persons, in times of ease and prosperity expands itself to everything around us. We are then charmed with the beauty of that accommodation which reigns in the palaces and oeconomy of the great; and admire how everything is adapted to promote their ease, to prevent their wants, to gratify their wishes, and to amuse and entertain their most frivolous desires. If we consider the real satisfaction which all these things are capable of affording, by itself and separated from the beauty of that arrangement which is fitted to promote it, it will always appear in the highest degree contemptible and trifling. But we rarely view it in this abstract and philosophical light. We

naturally confound it in our imagination with the order, the regular and harmonious movement of the system, the machine or oeconomy by means of which it is produced. The pleasures of wealth and greatness, when considered in this complex view, strike the imagination as something grand and beautiful and noble, of which the attainment is well worth all the toil and anxiety which we are so apt to bestow upon it.

And it is well that nature imposes upon us in this manner. It is this deception which rouses and keeps in continual motion the industry of mankind. It is this which first prompted them to cultivate the ground, to build houses, to found cities and commonwealths, and to invent and improve all the sciences and arts, which ennoble and embellish human life; which have entirely changed the whole face of the globe, have turned the rude forests of nature into agreeable and fertile plains, and made the trackless and barren ocean a new fund of subsistence, and the great high road of communication to the different nations of the earth. The earth by these labours of mankind has been obliged to redouble her natural fertility, and to maintain a greater multitude of inhabitants. It is to no purpose, that the proud and unfeeling landlord views his extensive fields, and without a thought for the wants of his brethren, in imagination consumes himself the whole harvest that grows upon them. The homely and vulgar proverb, that the eye is larger than the belly, never was more fully verified than with regard to him. The capacity of his stomach bears no proportion to the immensity of his desires, and will receive no more than that of the meanest peasant. The rest he is obliged to distribute among those, who prepare, in the nicest manner, that little which he himself makes use of, among those who fit up the palace in which this little is to be consumed, among those who provide and keep in order all the different baubles and trinkets, which are employed in the oeconomy of greatness; all of whom thus derive from his luxury and caprice, that share of the necessaries of life, which they would in vain have expected from his humanity or his justice. The produce of the soil maintains at all times nearly that number of inhabitants which it is capable of maintaining. The rich only select from the heap what is most precious and agreeable. They consume little more than the poor, and in spite of their natural selfishness and rapacity, though they mean only their own conveniency, though the sole end which they propose from the labours of all the thousands whom they employ, be the gratification of their own vain and insatiable desires, they divide with the poor the produce of all their improvements. They are led by an invisible hand to make nearly the same distribution of the necessaries of life, which would have been made, had the earth been divided into equal portions among all its inhabitants, and thus without intending it, without knowing it, advance the interest of the society, and afford means to the multiplication of the species. When Providence divided the earth among a few lordly masters, it neither forgot nor abandoned those who seemed to have been left out in the partition. These last too enjoy their share of all that it produces. In what constitutes the real happiness of human life, they are in no respect inferior to those who would seem so much above them. In ease of body and peace of mind, all the different ranks of life are nearly upon a level, and the beggar, who suns himself by the side of the highway, possesses that security which kings are fighting for.

The same principle, the same love of system, the same regard to the beauty of order, of art and contrivance, frequently serves to recommend those institutions which tend to promote the public welfare. When a patriot exerts himself for the improvement of any part of the public police, his conduct does not always arise from pure sympathy with the happiness of those who are to reap the benefit of it. It is not commonly from a fellow-feeling with carriers and waggoners that a public-spirited man encourages the mending of high roads. When the legislature establishes premiums and other encouragements to advance the linen or woollen manufactures, its conduct seldom proceeds from pure sympathy with the wearer of cheap or fine cloth, and much less from that with the manufacturer or merchant. The perfection of police, the extension of trade and manufactures, are noble and magnificent objects. The contemplation of them pleases us, and we are interested in whatever can tend to advance them. They make part of the great system of government, and the wheels of the political machine seem to move with more harmony and ease by means of them. We take pleasure in beholding the perfection of so beautiful and grand a system, and we are uneasy till we remove any obstruction that can in the least disturb or encumber the regularity of its motions. All constitutions of government, however, are valued only in proportion as they tend to promote the happiness of those who live under them. This is their sole use and end. From a certain spirit of system, however, from a certain love of art and contrivance, we sometimes seem to value the means more than the end, and to be eager to promote the happiness of our fellow-creatures, rather from a view to perfect and improve a certain beautiful and orderly system, than from any immediate sense or feeling of what they either suffer or enjoy. There have been men of the greatest public spirit, who have shown themselves in other respects not very sensible to the feelings of humanity. And on the contrary, there have been men of the greatest humanity, who seem to have been entirely devoid of public spirit. Every man may find in the circle of his acquaintance instances both of the one kind and the other. Who had ever less humanity, or more public spirit, than the celebrated legislator of Muscovy? The social and well-natured James the First of Great Britain seems, on the contrary, to have had scarce any passion, either for the glory or the interest of his country. Would you awaken the industry of the man who seems almost dead to ambition, it will often be to no purpose to describe to him the happiness of the rich and the great; to tell him that they are generally sheltered from the sun and the rain, that they are seldom hungry, that they are seldom cold, and that they are rarely exposed to weariness, or to want of any kind. The most eloquent exhortation of this kind will have little effect upon him. If you would hope to succeed, you must describe to him the conveniency and arrangement of the different apartments in their palaces; you must explain to him the propriety of their equipages, and point out to him the number, the order, and the different offices of all their attendants. If any thing is capable of making impression upon him, this will. Yet all these things tend only to keep off the sun and the rain, to save them from hunger and cold, from want and weariness. In the same manner, if you would implant public virtue in the breast of him who seems heedless of the interest of his country, it will often be to no purpose to tell him, what superior advantages the subjects of a well-governed state enjoy; that they are better lodged, that they are better clothed, that they are better fed. These considerations will commonly make no great impression. You will be more likely to persuade, if you describe the great system of public police which procures these advantages, if you explain the connexions and dependencies of its several parts, their mutual subordination to one another, and their general subserviency to the happiness of the society; if you show how this system might be introduced into his own country, what it is that hinders it from taking place there at present, how those obstructions might be removed, and all the several wheels of the machine of government be made to move with more harmony and smoothness, without grating upon one another, or mutually retarding one another's motions. It is scarce possible that a man should listen to a discourse of this kind, and not feel himself animated to some degree of public spirit. He will, at least for the moment, feel some desire to remove those obstructions, and to put into motion so beautiful and so orderly a machine. Nothing tends so much to promote public spirit as the study of politics, of the several systems of civil government, their advantages and disadvantages, of the constitution of our own country, its situation, and interest with regard to foreign nations, its commerce, its defence, the disadvantages it labours under, the dangers to which it may be exposed, how to remove the one, and how to guard against the other. Upon this account political disquisitions, if just, and reasonable, and practicable, are of all the works of speculation the most useful. Even the weakest and the worst of them are not altogether without

their utility. They serve at least to animate the public passions of men, and rouse them to seek out the means of promoting the happiness of the society.

. . .

Adam Smith: *An Inquiry into the Nature and Causes of the Wealth of Nations*

Introduction and Plan of the Work
[http://www.gutenberg.org/cache/epub/3300/pg3300.txt]

The annual labour of every nation is the fund which originally supplies it with all the necessaries and conveniencies of life which it annually consumes, and which consist always either in the immediate produce of that labour, or in what is purchased with that produce from other nations.

According, therefore, as this produce, or what is purchased with it, bears a greater or smaller proportion to the number of those who are to consume it, the nation will be better or worse supplied with all the necessaries and conveniencies for which it has occasion.

But this proportion must in every nation be regulated by two different circumstances: first, by the skill, dexterity, and judgment with which its labour is generally applied; and, secondly, by the proportion between the number of those who are employed in useful labour, and that of those who are not so employed. Whatever be the soil, climate, or extent of territory of any particular nation, the abundance or scantiness of its annual supply must, in that particular situation, depend upon those two circumstances.

The abundance or scantiness of this supply, too, seems to depend more upon the former of those two circumstances than upon the latter. Among the savage nations of hunters and fishers, every individual who is able to work is more or less employed in useful labour, and endeavours to provide, as well as he can, the necessaries and conveniencies of life, for himself, and such of his family or tribe as are either too old, or too young, or too infirm, to go a-hunting and fishing. Such nations, however, are so miserably poor, that, from mere want, they are frequently reduced, or

at least think themselves reduced, to the necessity sometimes of directly destroying, and sometimes of abandoning their infants, their old people, and those afflicted with lingering diseases, to perish with hunger, or to be devoured by wild beasts. Among civilized and thriving nations, on the contrary, though a great number of people do not labour at all, many of whom consume the produce of ten times, frequently of a hundred times, more labour than the greater part of those who work; yet the produce of the whole labour of the society is so great, that all are often abundantly supplied; and a workman, even of the lowest and poorest order, if he is frugal and industrious, may enjoy a greater share of the necessaries and conveniencies of life than it is possible for any savage to acquire.

The causes of this improvement in the productive powers of labour, and the order according to which its produce is naturally distributed among the different ranks and conditions of men in the society, make the subject of the first book of this Inquiry.

Whatever be the actual state of the skill, dexterity, and judgment, with which labour is applied in any nation, the abundance or scantiness of its annual supply must depend, during the continuance of that state, upon the proportion between the number of those who are annually employed in useful labour, and that of those who are not so employed. The number of useful and productive labourers, it will hereafter appear, is everywhere in proportion to the quantity of capital stock which is employed in setting them to work, and to the particular way in which it is so employed. The second book, therefore, treats of the nature of capital stock, of the manner in which it is gradually accumulated, and of the different quantities of labour which it puts into motion, according to the different ways in which it is employed.

Nations tolerably well advanced as to skill, dexterity, and judgment, in the application of labour, have followed very different plans in the general conduct or direction of it; and those plans have not all been equally favourable to the greatness of its produce. The policy of some nations has given extraordinary encouragement to the industry of the country; that of others to the industry of towns. Scarce any nation has dealt equally and impartially with every sort of industry. Since the down-fall of the Roman empire, the policy of Europe has been more favourable to arts, manufactures, and commerce, the industry of towns, than to agriculture, the Industry of the country. The circumstances which seem to have introduced and established this policy are explained in the third book.

Though those different plans were, perhaps, first introduced by the private interests and prejudices of particular orders of men, without any regard to, or foresight of, their consequences upon the general welfare of the society; yet they have given occasion to very different theories of political economy; of which some magnify the importance of that industry which is carried on in towns, others of that which is carried on in the country. Those theories have had a considerable influence, not only upon the opinions of men of learning, but upon the public conduct of princes and sovereign states. I have endeavoured, in the fourth book, to explain as fully and distinctly as I can those different theories, and the principal effects which they have produced in different ages and nations.

To explain in what has consisted the revenue of the great body of the people, or what has been the nature of those funds, which, in different ages and nations, have supplied their annual consumption, is the object of these four first books. The fifth and last book treats of the revenue of the sovereign, or commonwealth. In this book I have endeavoured to shew, first, what are the nec essary expenses of the sovereign, or commonwealth; which of those expenses ought to be defrayed by the general contribution of the whole society, and which of them, by that of some particular part only, or of some particular members of it: secondly, what are the different methods in which the whole society may be made to contribute towards defraying the expenses incumbent on the whole society, and what are the principal advantages and inconveniencies of each of those methods; and, thirdly and lastly, what are the reasons and causes which have induced almost all modern governments to mortgage some part of this revenue, or to contract debts; and what have been the effects of those debts upon the real wealth, the annual produce of the land and labour of the society.

BOOK I. OF THE CAUSES OF IMPROVEMENT IN THE PRODUCTIVE POWERS OF LABOUR, AND OF THE ORDER ACCORDING TO WHICH ITS PRODUCE IS NATURALLY DISTRIBUTED AMONG THE DIFFERENT RANKS OF THE PEOPLE.

CHAPTER I. OF THE DIVISION OF LABOUR.

The greatest improvements in the productive powers of labour, and the greater part of the skill, dexterity, and judgment, with which it is anywhere directed, or applied, seem to have been the effects of the division of labour. The effects of the division of labour, in the general business of society, will be more easily understood, by considering in what manner it operates in some particular manufactures.

It is commonly supposed to be carried furthest in some very trifling ones; not perhaps that it really is carried further in them than in others of more importance: but in those trifling manufactures which are destined to supply the small wants of but a small number of people, the whole number of workmen must necessarily be small; and those employed in every different branch of the work can often be collected into the same workhouse, and placed at once under the view of the spectator.

In those great manufactures, on the contrary, which are destined to supply the great wants of the great body of the people, every different branch of the work employs so great a number of workmen, that it is impossible to collect them all into the same workhouse. We can seldom see more, at one time, than those employed in one single branch. Though in such manufactures, therefore, the work may really be divided into a much greater number of parts, than in those of a more trifling nature, the division is not near so obvious, and has accordingly been much less observed.

To take an example, therefore, from a very trifling manufacture, but one in which the division of labour has been very often taken notice of, the trade of a pin-maker: a workman not educated to this business (which the division of labour has rendered a distinct trade), nor acquainted with the use of the machinery employed in it (to the invention of which the same division of labour has probably given occasion), could scarce, perhaps, with his utmost industry, make one pin in a day, and certainly could not make twenty. But in the way in which this business is now carried on, not only the whole work is a peculiar trade, but it is divided into a number of branches, of which the greater part are likewise peculiar trades. One man draws out the wire; another straights it; a third cuts it; a fourth points it; a fifth grinds it at the top for receiving the head; to make the head requires two or three distinct operations; to put it on is a peculiar business; to whiten the pins is another; it is even a trade by itself to put them into the paper; and the important business of making a pin is, in this manner, divided into about eighteen distinct operations, which, in some manufactories, are all performed by distinct hands, though in others the same man will sometimes perform two or three of them. I have seen a small manufactory of this kind, where ten men only were employed, and where some of them consequently performed two or three distinct operations. But though they were very poor, and therefore but indifferently

accommodated with the necessary machinery, they could, when they exerted themselves, make among them about twelve pounds of pins in a day. There are in a pound upwards of four thousand pins of a middling size. Those ten persons, therefore, could make among them upwards of forty-eight thousand pins in a day. Each person, therefore, making a tenth part of forty-eight thousand pins, might be considered as making four thousand eight hundred pins in a day. But if they had all wrought separately and independently, and without any of them having been educated to this peculiar business, they certainly could not each of them have made twenty, perhaps not one pin in a day; that is, certainly, not the two hundred and fortieth, perhaps not the four thousand eight hundredth, part of what they are at present capable of performing, in consequence of a proper division and combination of their different operations.

In every other art and manufacture, the effects of the division of labour are similar to what they are in this very trifling one, though, in many of them, the labour can neither be so much subdivided, nor reduced to so great a simplicity of operation. The division of labour, however, so far as it can be introduced, occasions, in every art, a proportionable increase of the productive powers of labour. The separation of different trades and employments from one another, seems to have taken place in consequence of this advantage. This separation, too, is generally carried furthest in those countries which enjoy the highest degree of industry and improvement; what is the work of one man, in a rude state of society, being generally that of several in an improved one. In every improved society, the farmer is generally nothing but a farmer; the manufacturer, nothing but a manufacturer. The labour, too, which is necessary to produce any one complete manufacture, is almost always divided among a great number of hands. How many different trades are employed in each branch of the linen and woolen manufactures, from the growers of the flax and the wool, to the bleachers and smoothers of the linen, or to the dyers and dressers of the cloth! The nature of agriculture, indeed, does not admit of so many subdivisions of labour, nor of so complete a separation of one business from another, as manufactures. It is impossible to separate so entirely the business of the grazier from that of the corn-farmer, as the trade of the carpenter is commonly separated from that of the smith. The spinner is almost always a distinct person from the weaver; but the ploughman, the harrower, the sower of the seed, and the reaper of the corn, are often the same. The occasions for those different sorts of labour returning with the different seasons of the year, it is impossible that one man should be constantly employed in any one of them. This impossibility of making so complete and entire a separation of all the different branches of labour employed in agriculture, is perhaps the reason why the improvement of the productive powers of labour, in this art, does not always keep pace with their improvement in manufactures. The most opulent nations, indeed, generally excel all their neighbours in agriculture as well as in manufactures; but they are commonly more distinguished by their superiority in the latter than in the former. Their lands are in general better cultivated, and having more labour and expense bestowed upon them, produce more in proportion to the extent and natural fertility of the ground. But this superiority of produce is seldom much more than in proportion to the superiority of labour and expense. In agriculture, the labour of the rich country is not always much more productive than that of the poor; or, at least, it is never so much more productive, as it commonly is in manufactures. The corn of the rich country, therefore, will not always, in the same degree of goodness, come cheaper to market than that of the poor. The corn of Poland, in the same degree of goodness, is as cheap as that of France, notwithstanding the superior opulence and improvement of the latter country. The corn of France is, in the corn-provinces, fully as good, and in most years nearly about the same price with the corn of England, though, in opulence and improvement, France is perhaps inferior to England. The corn-lands of England, however, are better cultivated than those of France, and the corn-lands of France are said to be much better cultivated than those of Poland. But though the poor country, notwithstanding the inferiority of its cultivation, can, in some measure, rival the rich in the cheapness and goodness of its corn, it can pretend to no such competition in its manufactures, at least if those manufactures suit the soil, climate, and situation, of the rich country. The silks of France are better and cheaper than those of England, because the silk manufacture, at least under the present high duties upon the importation of raw silk, does not so well suit the climate of England as that of France. But the hardware and the coarse woollens of England are beyond all comparison superior to those of France, and much cheaper, too, in the same degree of goodness. In Poland there are said to be scarce any manufactures of any kind, a few of those coarser household manufactures excepted, without which no country can well subsist.

This great increase in the quantity of work, which, in consequence of the division of labour, the same number of people are capable of performing, is owing to three different circumstances; first, to the increase of dexterity in every particular workman; secondly, to the saving of the time which is commonly lost in passing from one species of work to another; and, lastly, to the invention of a great number of machines which facilitate and abridge labour, and enable one man to do the work of many.

First, the improvement of the dexterity of the workmen, necessarily increases the quantity of the work he can perform; and the division of labour, by reducing every man's business to some one simple operation, and by making this operation the sole employment of his life, necessarily increases very much the dexterity of the workman. A common smith, who, though accustomed to handle the hammer, has never been used to make nails, if, upon some particular occasion, he is obliged to attempt it, will scarce, I am assured, be able to make above two or three hundred nails in a day, and those, too, very bad ones. A smith who has been accustomed to make nails, but whose sole or principal business has not been that of a nailer, can seldom, with his utmost diligence, make more than eight hundred or a thousand nails in a day. I have seen several boys, under twenty years of age, who had never exercised any other trade but that of making nails, and who, when they exerted themselves, could make, each of them, upwards of two thousand three hundred nails in a day. The making of a nail, however, is by no means one of the simplest operations. The same person blows the bellows, stirs or mends the fire as there is occasion, heats the iron, and forges every part of the nail: in forging the head, too, he is obliged to change his tools. The different operations into which the making of a pin, or of a metal button, is subdivided, are all of them much more simple, and the dexterity of the person, of whose life it has been the sole business to perform them, is usually much greater. The rapidity with which some of the operations of those manufactures are performed, exceeds what the human hand could, by those who had never seen them, be supposed capable of acquiring.

Secondly, the advantage which is gained by saving the time commonly lost in passing from one sort of work to another, is much greater than we should at first view be apt to imagine it. It is impossible to pass very quickly from one kind of work to another, that is carried on in a different place, and with quite different tools. A country weaver, who cultivates a small farm, must loose a good deal of time in passing from his loom to the field, and from the field to his loom. When the two trades can be carried on in the same workhouse, the loss of time is, no doubt, much less. It is, even in this case, however, very considerable. A man commonly saunters a little in turning his hand from one sort of employment to another. When he first begins the new work, he is seldom very keen and hearty; his mind, as they say, does not go to it, and for some time he rather trifles than applies to good purpose. The habit of sauntering, and of indolent careless application, which is naturally, or rather necessarily, acquired by every country workman who is obliged to change his work and his tools every half hour, and to apply his hand in twenty different ways almost

every day of his life, renders him almost always slothful and lazy, and incapable of any vigorous application, even on the most pressing occasions. Independent, therefore, of his deficiency in point of dexterity, this cause alone must always reduce considerably the quantity of work which he is capable of performing.

Thirdly, and lastly, everybody must be sensible how much labour is facilitated and abridged by the application of proper machinery. It is unnecessary to give any example. I shall only observe, therefore, that the invention of all those machines by which labour is so much facilitated and abridged, seems to have been originally owing to the division of labour. Men are much more likely to discover easier and readier methods of attaining any object, when the whole attention of their minds is directed towards that single object, than when it is dissipated among a great variety of things. But, in consequence of the division of labour, the whole of every man's attention comes naturally to be directed towards some one very simple object. It is naturally to be expected, therefore, that some one or other of those who are employed in each particular branch of labour should soon find out easier and readier methods of performing their own particular work, whenever the nature of it admits of such improvement. A great part of the machines made use of in those manufactures in which labour is most subdivided, were originally the invention of common workmen, who, being each of them employed in some very simple operation, naturally turned their thoughts towards finding out easier and readier methods of performing it. Whoever has been much accustomed to visit such manufactures, must frequently have been shewn very pretty machines, which were the inventions of such workmen, in order to facilitate and quicken their own particular part of the work. In the first fire engines {this was the current designation for steam engines}, a boy was constantly employed to open and shut alternately the communication between the boiler and the cylinder, according as the piston either ascended or descended. One of those boys, who loved to play with his companions, observed that, by tying a string from the handle of the valve which opened this communication to another part of the machine, the valve would open and shut without his assistance, and leave him at liberty to divert himself with his play-fellows. One of the greatest improvements that has been made upon this machine, since it was first invented, was in this manner the discovery of a boy who wanted to save his own labour.

All the improvements in machinery, however, have by no means been the inventions of those who had occasion to use the machines. Many improvements have been made by the ingenuity of the makers of the machines, when to make them became the business of a peculiar trade; and some by that of those who are called philosophers, or men of speculation, whose trade it is not to do anything, but to observe everything, and who, upon that account, are often capable of combining ogether the powers of the most distant and dissimilar objects in the progress of society, philosophy or speculation becomes, like every other employment, the principal or sole trade and occupation of a particular class of citizens. Like every other employment, too, it is subdivided into a great number of different branches, each of which affords occupation to a peculiar tribe or class of philosophers; and this subdivision of employment in philosophy, as well as in every other business, improve dexterity, and saves time. Each individual becomes more expert in his own peculiar branch, more work is done upon the whole, and the quantity of science is considerably increased by it.

It is the great multiplication of the productions of all the different arts, in consequence of the division of labour, which occasions, in a well-governed society, that universal opulence which extends itself to the lowest ranks of the people. Every workman has a great quantity of his own work to dispose of beyond what he himself has occasion for; and every other workman being exactly in the same situation, he is enabled to exchange a great quantity of his own goods for a great quantity or,

what comes to the same thing, for the price of a great quantity of theirs. He supplies them abundantly with what they have occasion for, and they accommodate him as amply with what he has occasion for, and a general plenty diffuses itself through all the different ranks of the society.

Observe the accommodation of the most common artificer or daylabourer in a civilized and thriving country, and you will perceive that the number of people, of whose industry a part, though but a small part, has been employed in procuring him this accommodation, exceeds all computation. The woollen coat, for example, which covers the day-labourer, as coarse and rough as it may appear, is the produce of the joint labour of a great multitude of workmen. The shepherd, the sorter of the wool, the wool-comber or carder, the dyer, the scribbler, the spinner, the weaver, the fuller, the dresser, with many others, must all join their different arts in order to complete even this homely production. How many merchants and carriers, besides, must have been employed in transporting the materials from some of those workmen to others who often live in a very distant part of the country? How much commerce and navigation in particular, how many ship-builders, sailors, sail-makers, rope-makers, must have been employed in order to bring together the different drugs made use of by the dyer, which often come from the remotest corners of the world? What a variety of labour, too, is necessary in order to produce the tools of the meanest of those workmen! To say nothing of such complicated machines as the ship of the sailor, the mill of the fuller, or even the loom of the weaver, let us consider only what a variety of labour is requisite in order to form that very simple machine, the shears with which the shepherd clips the wool. The miner, the builder of the furnace for smelting the ore, the feller of the timber, the burner of the charcoal to be made use of in the smelting-house, the brickmaker, the bricklayer, the workmen who attend the furnace, the millwright, the forger, the smith, must all of them join their different arts in order to produce them. Were we to examine, in the same manner, all the different parts of his dress and household furniture, the coarse linen shirt which he wears next his skin, the shoes which cover his feet, the bed which he lies on, and all the different parts which compose it, the kitchen-grate at which he prepares his victuals, the coals which he makes use of for that purpose, dug from the bowels of the earth, and brought to him, perhaps, by a long sea and a long land-carriage, all the other utensils of his kitchen, all the furniture of his table, the knives and forks, the earthen or pewter plates upon which he serves up and divides his victuals, the different hands employed in preparing his bread and his beer, the glass window which lets in the heat and the light, and keeps out the wind and the rain, with all the knowledge and art requisite for preparing that beautiful and happy invention, without which these northern parts of the world could scarce have afforded a very comfortable habitation, together with the tools of all the different workmen employed in producing those different conveniencies; if we examine, I say, all these things, and consider what a variety of labour is employed about each of them, we shall be sensible that, without the assistance and co-operation of many thousands, the very meanest person in a civilized country could not be provided, even according to, what we very falsely imagine, the easy and simple manner in which he is commonly accommodated. Compared, indeed, with the more extravagant luxury of the great, his accommodation must no doubt appear extremely simple and easy; and yet it may be true, perhaps, that the accommodation of an European prince does not always so much exceed that of an industrious and frugal peasant, as the accommodation of the latter exceeds that of many an African king, the absolute masters of the lives and liberties of ten thousand naked savages.

CHAPTER II. OF THE PRINCIPLE WHICH GIVES OCCASION TO THE DIVISION OF LABOUR.

This division of labour, from which so many advantages are derived, is not originally the effect of any human wisdom, which foresees and intends that general opulence to which it gives

occasion. It is the necessary, though very slow and gradual, consequence of a certain propensity in human nature, which has in view no such extensive utility; the propensity to truck, barter, and exchange one thing for another.

Whether this propensity be one of those original principles in human nature, of which no further account can be given, or whether, as seems more probable, it be the necessary consequence of the faculties of reason and speech, it belongs not to our present subject to inquire. It is common to all men, and to be found in no other race of animals, which seem to know neither this nor any other species of contracts. Two greyhounds, in running down the same hare, have sometimes the appearance of acting in some sort of concert. Each turns her towards his companion, or endeavours to intercept her when his companion turns her towards himself. This, however, is not the effect of any contract, but of the accidental concurrence of their passions in the same object at that particular time. Nobody ever saw a dog make a fair and deliberate exchange of one bone for another with another dog. Nobody ever saw one animal, by its gestures and natural cries signify to another, this is mine, that yours; I am willing to give this for that. When an animal wants to obtain something either of a man, or of another animal, it has no other means of persuasion, but to gain the favour of those whose service it requires. A puppy fawns upon its dam, and a spaniel endeavours, by a thousand attractions, to engage the attention of its master who is at dinner, when it wants to be fed by him. Man sometimes uses the same arts with his brethren, and when he has no other means of engaging them to act according to his inclinations, endeavours by every servile and fawning attention to obtain their good will. He has not time, however, to do this upon every occasion. In civilized society he stands at all times in need of the co-operation and assistance of great multitudes, while his whole life is scarce sufficient to gain the friendship of a few persons. In almost every other race of animals, each individual, when it is grown up to maturity, is entirely independent, and in its natural state has occasion for the assistance of no other living creature. But man has almost constant occasion for the help of his brethren, and it is in vain for him to expect it from their benevolence only. He will be more likely to prevail if he can interest their self-love in his favour, and shew them that it is for their own advantage to do for him what he requires of them. Whoever offers to another a bargain of any kind, proposes to do this. Give me that which I want, and you shall have this which you want, is the meaning of every such offer; and it is in this manner that we obtain from one another the far greater part of those good offices which we stand in need of. It is not from the benevolence of the butcher, the brewer, or the baker that we expect our dinner, but from their regard to their own interest. We address ourselves, not to their humanity, but to their self-love, and never talk to them of our own necessities, but of their advantages.

Nobody but a beggar chooses to depend chiefly upon the benevolence of his fellow-citizens. Even a beggar does not depend upon it entirely. The charity of well-disposed people, indeed, supplies him with the whole fund of his subsistence. But though this principle ultimately provides him with all the necessaries of life which he has occasion for, it neither does nor can provide him with them as he has occasion for them. The greater part of his occasional wants are supplied in the same manner as those of other people, by treaty, by barter, and by purchase. With the money which one man gives him he purchases food. The old clothes which another bestows upon him he exchanges for other clothes which suit him better, or for lodging, or for food, or for money, with which he can buy either food, clothes, or lodging, as he has occasion.

As it is by treaty, by barter, and by purchase, that we obtain from one another the greater part of those mutual good offices which we stand in need of, so it is this same trucking disposition which originally gives occasion to the division of labour. In a tribe of hunters or shepherds, a particular person makes bows and arrows, for example, with more readiness and dexterity than

any other. He frequently exchanges them for cattle or for venison, with his companions; and he finds at last that he can, in this manner, get more cattle and venison, than if he himself went to the field to catch them. From a regard to his own interest, therefore, the making of bows and arrows grows to be his chief business, and he becomes a sort of armourer. Another excels in making the frames and covers of their little huts or moveable houses. He is accustomed to be of use in this way to his neighbours, who reward him in the same manner with cattle and with venison, till at last he finds it his interest to dedicate himself entirely to this employment, and to become a sort of house-carpenter. In the same manner a third becomes a smith or a brazier; a fourth, a tanner or dresser of hides or skins, the principal part of the clothing of savages. And thus the certainty of being able to exchange all that surplus part of the produce of his own labour, which is over and above his own consumption, for such parts of the produce of other men's labour as he may have occasion for, encourages every man to apply himself to a particular occupation, and to cultivate and bring to perfection whatever talent of genius he may possess for that particular species of business.

The difference of natural talents in different men, is, in reality, much less than we are aware of; and the very different genius which appears to distinguish men of different professions, when grown up to maturity, is not upon many occasions so much the cause, as the effect of the division of labour. The difference between the most dissimilar characters, between a philosopher and a common street porter, for example, seems to arise not so much from nature, as from habit, custom, and education. When they came in to the world, and for the first six or eight years of their existence, they were, perhaps, very much alike, and neither their parents nor play-fellows could perceive any remarkable difference. About that age, or soon after, they come to be employed in very different occupations. The difference of talents comes then to be taken notice of, and widens by degrees, till at last the vanity of the philosopher is willing to acknowledge scarce any resemblance. But without the disposition to truck, barter, and exchange, every man must have procured to himself every necessary and conveniency of life which he wanted. All must have had the same duties to perform, and the same work to do, and there could have been no such difference of employment as could alone give occasion to any great difference of talents.

As it is this disposition which forms that difference of talents, so remarkable among men of different professions, so it is this same disposition which renders that difference useful. Many tribes of animals, acknowledged to be all of the same species, derive from nature a much more remarkable distinction of genius, than what, antecedent to custom and education, appears to take place among men. By nature a philosopher is not in genius and disposition half so different from a street porter, as a mastiff is from a grey-hound, or a grey-hound from a spaniel, or this last from a shepherd's dog. Those different tribes of animals, however, though all of the same species are of scarce any use to one another. The strength of the mastiff is not in the least supported either by the swiftness of the greyhound, or by the sagacity of the spaniel, or by the docility of the shepherd's dog. The effects of those different geniuses and talents, for want of the power or disposition to barter and exchange, cannot be brought into a common stock, and do not in the least contribute to the better accommodation and conveniency of the species. Each animal is still obliged to support and defend itself, separately and independently, and derives no sort of advantage from that variety of talents with which nature has distinguished its fellows. Among men, on the contrary, the most dissimilar geniuses are of use to one another; the different produces of their respective talents, by the general disposition to truck, barter, and exchange, being brought, as it were, into a common stock, where every man may purchase whatever part of the produce of other men's talents he has occasion for.

. . .

CHAPTER V. OF THE REAL AND NOMINAL PRICE OF COMMODITIES, OR OF THEIR PRICE IN LABOUR, AND THEIR PRICE IN MONEY.

Every man is rich or poor according to the degree in which he can afford to enjoy the necessaries, conveniencies, and amusements of human life. But after the division of labour has once thoroughly taken place, it is but a very small part of these with which a man's own labour can supply him. The far greater part of them he must derive from the labour of other people, and he must be rich or poor according to the quantity of that labour which he can command, or which he can afford to purchase. The value of any commodity, therefore, to the person who possesses it, and who means not to use or consume it himself, but to exchange it for other commodities, is equal to the quantity of labour which it enables him to purchase or command. Labour therefore, is the real measure of the exchangeable value of all commodities.

The real price of everything, what everything really costs to the man who wants to acquire it, is the toil and trouble of acquiring it. What everything is really worth to the man who has acquired it and who wants to dispose of it, or exchange it for something else, is the toil and trouble which it can save to himself, and which it can impose upon other people. What is bought with money, or with goods, is purchased by labour, as much as what we acquire by the toil of our own body. That money, or those goods, indeed, save us this toil. They contain the value of a certain quantity of labour, which we exchange for what is supposed at the time to contain the value of an equal quantity. Labour was the first price, the original purchase money that was paid for all things. It was not by gold or by silver, but by labour, that all the wealth of the world was originally purchased; and its value, to those who possess it, and who want to exchange it for some new productions, is precisely equal to the quantity of labour which it can enable them to purchase or command.

Wealth, as Mr Hobbes says, is power. But the person who either acquires, or succeeds to a great fortune, does not necessarily acquire or succeed to any political power, either civil or military. His fortune may, perhaps, afford him the means of acquiring both; but the mere possession of that fortune does not necessarily convey to him either. The power which that possession immediately and directly conveys to him, is the power of purchasing a certain command over all the labour, or over all the produce of labour which is then in the market. His fortune is greater or less, precisely in proportion to the extent of this power, or to the quantity either of other men's labour, or, what is the same thing, of the produce of other men's labour, which it enables him to purchase or command. The exchangeable value of everything must always be precisely equal to the extent of this power which it conveys to its owner.

But though labour be the real measure of the exchangeable value of all commodities, it is not that by which their value is commonly estimated. It is often difficult to ascertain the proportion between two different quantities of labour. The time spent in two different sorts of work will not always alone determine this proportion. The different degrees of hardship endured, and of ingenuity exercised, must likewise be taken into account. There may be more labour in an hour's hard work, than in two hours easy business; or in an hour's application to a trade which it cost ten years labour to learn, than in a month's industry, at an ordinary and obvious employment. But it is not easy to find any accurate measure either of hardship or ingenuity. In exchanging, indeed, the different productions of different sorts of labour for one another, some allowance is commonly made for both. It is adjusted, however, not by any accurate measure, but by the higgling and bargaining of the market, according to that sort of rough equality which, though not exact, is sufficient for carrying on the business of common life.

Every commodity, besides, is more frequently exchanged for, and thereby compared with, other commodities, than with labour. It is more natural, therefore, to estimate its exchangeable value by the quantity of some other commodity, than by that of the labour which it can produce. The greater part of people, too, understand better what is meant by a quantity of a particular commodity, than by a quantity of labour. The one is a plain palpable object; the other an abstract notion, which though it can be made sufficiently intelligible, is not altogether so natural and obvious.

But when barter ceases, and money has become the common instrument of commerce, every particular commodity is more frequently exchanged for money than for any other commodity. The butcher seldom carries his beef or his mutton to the baker or the brewer, in order to exchange them for bread or for beer; but he carries them to the market, where he exchanges them for money, and afterwards exchanges that money for bread and for beer. The quantity of money which he gets for them regulates, too, the quantity of bread and beer which he can afterwards purchase. It is more natural and obvious to him, therefore, to estimate their value by the quantity of money, the commodity for which he immediately exchanges them, than by that of bread and beer, the commodities for which he can exchange them only by the intervention of another commodity; and rather to say that his butcher's meat is worth three-pence or fourpence a-pound, than that it is worth three or four pounds of bread, or three or four quarts of small beer. Hence it comes to pass, that the exchangeable value of every commodity is more frequently estimated by the quantity of money, than by the quantity either of labour or of any other commodity which can be had in exchange for it.

Gold and silver, however, like every other commodity, vary in their value; are sometimes cheaper and sometimes dearer, sometimes of easier and sometimes of more difficult purchase. The quantity of labour which any particular quantity of them can purchase or command, or the quantity of other goods which it will exchange for, depends always upon the fertility or barrenness of the mines which happen to be known about the time when such exchanges are made. The discovery of the abundant mines of America, reduced, in the sixteenth century, the value of gold and silver in Europe to about a third of what it had been before. As it cost less labour to bring those metals from the mine to the market, so, when they were brought thither, they could purchase or command less labour; and this revolution in their value, though perhaps the greatest, is by no means the only one of which history gives some account. But as a measure of quantity, such as the natural foot, fathom, or handful, which is continually varying in its own quantity, can never be an accurate measure of the quantity of other things; so a commodity which is itself continually varying in its own value, can never be an accurate measure of the value of other commodities. Equal quantities of labour, at all times and places, may be said to be of equal value to the labourer. In his ordinary state of health, strength, and spirits; in the ordinary degree of his skill and dexterity, he must always lay down the same portion of his ease, his liberty, and his happiness. The price which he pays must always be the same, whatever may be the quantity of goods which he receives in return for it. Of these, indeed, it may sometimes purchase a greater and sometimes a smaller quantity; but it is their value which varies, not that of the labour which purchases them. At all times and places, that is dear which it is difficult to come at, or which it costs much labour to acquire; and that cheap which is to be had easily, or with very little labour. Labour alone, therefore, never varying in its own value, is alone the ultimate and real standard by which the value of all commodities can at all times and places be estimated and compared. It is their real price; money is their nominal price only.

But though equal quantities of labour are always of equal value to the labourer, yet to the person who employs him they appear sometimes to be of greater, and sometimes of smaller value. He purchases them sometimes with a greater, and sometimes with a smaller quantity of goods, and to him the price of labour seems to vary like that of all other things. It appears to him dear in

the one case, and cheap in the other. In reality, however, it is the goods which are cheap in the one case, and dear in the other.

In this popular sense, therefore, labour, like commodities, may be said to have a real and a nominal price. Its real price may be said to consist in the quantity of the necessaries and conveniencies of life which are given for it; its nominal price, in the quantity of money. The labourer is rich or poor, is well or ill rewarded, in proportion to the real, not to the nominal price of his labour.

. . .

CHAPTER VIII. OF THE WAGES OF LABOUR.

The produce of labour constitutes the natural recompence or wages of labour.

In that original state of things which precedes both the appropriation of land and the accumulation of stock, the whole produce of labour belongs to the labourer. He has neither landlord nor master to share with him.

Had this state continued, the wages of labour would have augmented with all those improvements in its productive powers, to which the division of labour gives occasion. All things would gradually have become cheaper. They would have been produced by a smaller quantity of labour; and as the commodities produced by equal quantities of labour would naturally in this state of things be exchanged for one another, they would have been purchased likewise with the produce of a smaller quantity.

But though all things would have become cheaper in reality, in appearance many things might have become dearer, than before, or have been exchanged for a greater quantity of other goods. Let us suppose, for example, that in the greater part of employments the productive powers of labour had been improved to tenfold, or that a day's labour could produce ten times the quantity of work which it had done originally; but that in a particular employment they had been improved only to double, or that a day's labour could produce only twice the quantity of work which it had done before. In exchanging the produce of a day's labour in the greater part of employments for that of a day's labour in this particular one, ten times the original quantity of work in them would purchase only twice the original quantity in it. Any particular quantity in it, therefore, a pound weight, for example, would appear to be five times dearer than before. In reality, however, it would be twice as cheap. Though it required five times the quantity of other goods to purchase it, it would require only half the quantity of labour either to purchase or to produce it. The acquisition, therefore, would be twice as easy as before.

But this original state of things, in which the labourer enjoyed the whole produce of his own labour, could not last beyond the first introduction of the appropriation of land and the accumulation of stock. It was at an end, therefore, long before the most considerable improvements were made in the productive powers of labour; and it would be to no purpose to trace further what might have been its effects upon the recompence or wages of labour.

As soon as land becomes private property, the landlord demands a share of almost all the produce which the labourer can either raise or collect from it. His rent makes the first deduction from the produce of the labour which is employed upon land.

It seldom happens that the person who tills the ground has wherewithal to maintain himself till he reaps the harvest. His maintenance is generally advanced to him from the stock of a master, the farmer who employs him, and who would have no interest to employ him, unless he was to share in the produce of his labour, or unless his stock was to be replaced to him with a profit. This profit makes a second deduction from the produce of the labour which is employed upon land.

The produce of almost all other labour is liable to the like deduction of profit. In all arts and manufactures, the greater part of the workmen stand in need of a master, to advance them the materials of their work, and their wages and maintenance, till it be completed. He shares in the produce of their labour, or in the value which it adds to the materials upon which it is bestowed; and in this share consists his profit.

It sometimes happens, indeed, that a single independent workman has stock sufficient both to purchase the materials of his work, and to maintain himself till it be completed. He is both master and workman, and enjoys the whole produce of his own labour, or the whole value which it adds to the materials upon which it is bestowed. It includes what are usually two distinct revenues, belonging to two distinct persons, the profits of stock, and the wages of labour.

Such cases, however, are not very frequent; and in every part of Europe twenty workmen serve under a master for one that is independent, and the wages of labour are everywhere understood to be, what they usually are, when the labourer is one person, and the owner of the stock which employs him another.

What are the common wages of labour, depends everywhere upon the contract usually made between those two parties, whose interests are by no means the same. The workmen desire to get as much, the masters to give as little, as possible. The former are disposed to combine in order to raise, the latter in order to lower, the wages of labour.

It is not, however, difficult to foresee which of the two parties must, upon all ordinary occasions, have the advantage in the dispute, and force the other into a compliance with their terms. The masters, being fewer in number, can combine much more easily: and the law, besides, authorises, or at least does not prohibit, their combinations, while it prohibits those of the workmen. We have no acts of parliament against combining to lower the price of work, but many against combining to raise it. In all such disputes, the masters can hold out much longer. A landlord, a farmer, a master manufacturer, or merchant, though they did not employ a single workman, could generally live a year or two upon the stocks, which they have already acquired. Many workmen could not subsist a week, few could subsist a month, and scarce any a year, without employment. In the long run, the workman may be as necessary to his master as his master is to him; but the necessity is not so immediate.

We rarely hear, it has been said, of the combinations of masters, though frequently of those of workmen. But whoever imagines, upon this account, that masters rarely combine, is as ignorant of the world as of the subject. Masters are always and everywhere in a sort of tacit, but constant and uniform, combination, not to raise the wages of labour above their actual rate. To violate this combination is everywhere a most unpopular action, and a sort of reproach to a master among his neighbours and equals. We seldom, indeed, hear of this combination, because it is the usual, and, one may say, the natural state of things, which nobody ever hears of. Masters, too, sometimes enter into particular combinations to sink the wages of labour even below this rate. These are always conducted with the utmost silence and secrecy till the moment of execution; and when the workmen yield, as they sometimes do without resistance, though severely felt by them, they are never heard of by other people. Such combinations, however, are frequently resisted by a contrary defensive combination of the workmen, who sometimes, too, without any provocation of this kind, combine, of their own accord, to raise the price of their labour. Their usual pretences are, sometimes the high price of provisions, sometimes the great profit which their masters make by their work. But whether their combinations be offensive or defensive, they are always abundantly heard of. In order to bring the point to a speedy decision, they have always recourse to the loudest clamour, and sometimes to the most shocking violence and outrage. They are desperate, and act with the folly and

extravagance of desperate men, who must either starve, or frighten their masters into an immediate compliance with their demands. The masters, upon these occasions, are just as clamorous upon the other side, and never cease to call aloud for the assistance of the civil magistrate, and the rigorous execution of those laws which have been enacted with so much severity against the combination of servants, labourers, and journeymen. The workmen, accordingly, very seldom derive any advantage from the violence of those tumultuous combinations, which, partly from the interposition of the civil magistrate, partly from the superior steadiness of the masters, partly from the necessity which the greater part of the workmen are under of submitting for the sake of present subsistence, generally end in nothing but the punishment or ruin of the ringleaders.

But though, in disputes with their workmen, masters must generally have the advantage, there is, however, a certain rate, below which it seems impossible to reduce, for any considerable time, the ordinary wages even of the lowest species of labour.

A man must always live by his work, and his wages must at least be sufficient to maintain him. They must even upon most occasions be somewhat more, otherwise it would be impossible for him to bring up a family, and the race of such workmen could not last beyond the first generation. Mr Cantillon seems, upon this account, to suppose that the lowest species of common labourers must everywhere earn at least double their own maintenance, in order that, one with another, they may be enabled to bring up two children; the labour of the wife, on account of her necessary attendance on the children, being supposed no more than sufficient to provide for herself: But one half the children born, it is computed, die before the age of manhood. The poorest labourers, therefore, according to this account, must, one with another, attempt to rear at least four children, in order that two may have an equal chance of living to that age. But the necessary maintenance of four children, it is supposed, may be nearly equal to that of one man. The labour of an able-bodied slave, the same author adds, is computed to be worth double his maintenance; and that of the meanest labourer, he thinks, cannot be worth less than that of an able-bodied slave. Thus far at least seems certain, that, in order to bring up a family, the labour of the husband and wife together must, even in the lowest species of common labour, be able to earn something more than what is precisely necessary for their own maintenance; but in what proportion, whether in that above-mentioned, or many other, I shall not take upon me to determine.

There are certain circumstances, however, which sometimes give the labourers an advantage, and enable them to raise their wages considerably above this rate, evidently the lowest which is consistent with common humanity.

When in any country the demand for those who live by wages, labourers, journeymen, servants of every kind, is continually increasing; when every year furnishes employment for a greater number than had been employed the year before, the workmen have no occasion to combine in order to raise their wages. The scarcity of hands occasions a competition among masters, who bid against one another in order to get workmen, and thus voluntarily break through the natural combination of masters not to raise wages. The demand for those who live by wages, it is evident, cannot increase but in proportion to the increase of the funds which are destined to the payment of wages. These funds are of two kinds, first, the revenue which is over and above what is necessary for the maintenance; and, secondly, the stock which is over and above what is necessary for the employment of their masters.

When the landlord, annuitant, or monied man, has a greater revenue than what he judges sufficient to maintain his own family, he employs either the whole or a part of the surplus in maintaining one or more menial servants. Increase this surplus, and he will naturally increase the number of those servants.

When an independent workman, such as a weaver or shoemaker, has got more stock than what is sufficient to purchase the materials of his own work, and to maintain himself till he can dispose of it, he naturally employs one or more journeymen with the surplus, in order to make a profit by their work. Increase this surplus, and he will naturally increase the number of his journeymen.

The demand for those who live by wages, therefore, necessarily increases with the increase of the revenue and stock of every country, and cannot possibly increase without it. The increase of revenue and stock is the increase of national wealth. The demand for those who live by wages, therefore, naturally increases with the increase of national wealth, and cannot possibly increase without it.

It is not the actual greatness of national wealth, but its continual increase, which occasions a rise in the wages of labour. It is not, accordingly, in the richest countries, but in the most thriving, or in those which are growing rich the fastest, that the wages of labour are highest. England is certainly, in the present times, a much richer country than any part of North America. The wages of labour, however, are much higher in North America than in any part of England. In the province of New York, common labourers earned in 1773, before the commencement of the late disturbances, three shillings and sixpence currency, equal to two shillings sterling, a-day; ship-carpenters, ten shillings and sixpence currency, with a pint of rum, worth sixpence sterling, equal in all to six shillings and sixpence sterling; house-carpenters and bricklayers, eight shillings currency, equal to four shillings and sixpence sterling; journeymen tailors, five shillings currency, equal to about two shillings and tenpence sterling. These prices are all above the London price; and wages are said to be as high in the other colonies as in New York. The price of provisions is everywhere in North America much lower than in England. A dearth has never been known there. In the worst seasons they have always had a sufficiency for themselves, though less for exportation. If the money price of labour, therefore, be higher than it is anywhere in the mother-country, its real price, the real command of the necessaries and conveniencies of life which it conveys to the labourer, must be higher in a still greater proportion.

But though North America is not yet so rich as England, it is much more thriving, and advancing with much greater rapidity to the further acquisition of riches. The most decisive mark of the prosperity of any country is the increase of the number of its inhabitants. In Great Britain, and most other European countries, they are not supposed to double in less than five hundred years. In the British colonies in North America, it has been found that they double in twenty or five-and-twenty years. Nor in the present times is this increase principally owing to the continual importation of new inhabitants, but to the great multiplication of the species. Those who live to old age, it is said, frequently see there from fifty to a hundred, and sometimes many more, descendants from their own body. Labour is there so well rewarded, that a numerous family of children, instead of being a burden, is a source of opulence and prosperity to the parents. The labour of each child, before it can leave their house, is computed to be worth a hundred pounds clear gain to them. A young widow with four or five young children, who, among the middling or inferior ranks of people in Europe, would have so little chance for a second husband, is there frequently courted as a sort of fortune. The value of children is the greatest of all encouragements to marriage. We cannot, therefore, wonder that the people in North America should generally marry very young. Notwithstanding the great increase occasioned by such early marriages, there is a continual complaint of the scarcity of hands in North America. The demand for labourers, the funds destined for maintaining them increase, it seems, still faster than they can find labourers to employ.

Though the wealth of a country should be very great, yet if it has been long stationary, we must not expect to find the wages of labour very high in it. The funds destined for the payment of wages, the revenue and stock of its inhabitants, may be of the greatest extent; but if they have continued for several centuries of the same, or very nearly of the same extent, the number of labourers employed every year could easily supply, and even more than supply, the number wanted the following year.

There could seldom be any scarcity of hands, nor could the masters be obliged to bid against one another in order to get them. The hands, on the contrary, would, in this case, naturally multiply beyond their employment. There would be a constant scarcity of employment, and the labourers would be obliged to bid against one another in order to get it. If in such a country the wages off labour had ever been more than sufficient to maintain the labourer, and to enable him to bring up a family, the competition of the labourers and the interest of the masters would soon reduce them to the lowest rate which is consistent with common humanity. China has been long one of the richest, that is, one of the most fertile, best cultivated, most industrious, and most populous, countries in the world. It seems, however, to have been long stationary. Marco Polo, who visited it more than five hundred years ago, describes its cultivation, industry, and populousness, almost in the same terms in which they are described by travellers in the present times. It had, perhaps, even long before his time, acquired that full complement of riches which the nature of its laws and institutions permits it to acquire. The accounts of all travellers, inconsistent in many other respects, agree in the low wages of labour, and in the difficulty which a labourer finds in bringing up a family in China. If by digging the ground a whole day he can get what will purchase a small quantity of rice in the evening, he is contented. The condition of artificers is, if possible, still worse. Instead of waiting indolently in their work-houses for the calls of their customers, as in Europe, they are continually running about the streets with the tools of their respective trades, offering their services, and, as it were, begging employment. The poverty of the lower ranks of people in China far surpasses that of the most beggarly nations in Europe. In the neighbourhood of Canton, many hundred, it is commonly said, many thousand families have no habitation on the land, but live constantly in little fishing-boats upon the rivers and canals. The subsistence which they find there is so scanty, that they are eager to fish up the nastiest garbage thrown overboard from any European ship. Any carrion, the carcase of a dead dog or cat, for example, though half putrid and stinking, is as welcome to them as the most wholesome food to the people of other countries. Marriage is encouraged in China, not by the profitableness of children, but by the liberty of destroying them. In all great towns, several are every night exposed in the street, or drowned like puppies in the water. The performance of this horrid office is even said to be the avowed business by which some people earn their subsistence.

China, however, though it may, perhaps, stand still, does not seem to go backwards. Its towns are nowhere deserted by their inhabitants. The lands which had once been cultivated, are nowhere neglected. The same, or very nearly the same, annual labour, must, therefore, continue to be performed, and the funds destined for maintaining it must not, consequently, be sensibly diminished. The lowest class of labourers, therefore, notwithstanding their scanty subsistence, must some way or another make shift to continue their race so far as to keep up their usual numbers.

But it would be otherwise in a country where the funds destined for the maintenance of labour were sensibly decaying. Every year the demand for servants and labourers would, in all the different classes of employments, be less than it had been the year before. Many who had been bred in the superior classes, not being able to find employment in their own business, would be glad to seek it in the lowest. The lowest class being not only overstocked with its own workmen, but with the overflowings of all the other classes, the competition for employment would be so great in

it, as to reduce the wages of labour to the most miserable and scanty subsistence of the labourer. Many would not be able to find employment even upon these hard terms, but would either starve, or be driven to seek a subsistence, either by begging, or by the perpetration perhaps, of the greatest enormities. Want, famine, and mortality, would immediately prevail in that class, and from thence extend themselves to all the superior classes, till the number of inhabitants in the country was reduced to what could easily be maintained by the revenue and stock which remained in it, and which had escaped either the tyranny or calamity which had destroyed the rest. This, perhaps, is nearly the present state of Bengal, and of some other of the English settlements in the East Indies. In a fertile country, which had before been much depopulated, where subsistence, consequently, should not be very difficult, and where, notwithstanding, three or four hundred thousand people die of hunger in one year, we maybe assured that the funds destined for the maintenance of the labouring poor are fast decaying. The difference between the genius of the British constitution, which protects and governs North America, and that of the mercantile company which oppresses and domineers in the East Indies, cannot, perhaps, be better illustrated than by the different state of those countries.

The liberal reward of labour, therefore, as it is the necessary effect, so it is the natural symptom of increasing national wealth. The scanty maintenance of the labouring poor, on the other hand, is the natural symptom that things are at a stand, and their starving condition, that they are going fast backwards.

. . .

The real recompence of labour, the real quantity of the necessaries and conveniencies of life which it can procure to the labourer, has, during the course of the present century, increased perhaps in a still greater proportion than its money price. Not only grain has become somewhat cheaper, but many other things, from which the industrious poor derive an agreeable and wholesome variety of food, have become a great deal cheaper. Potatoes, for example, do not at present, through the greater part of the kingdom, cost half the price which they used to do thirty or forty years ago. The same thing may be said of turnips, carrots, cabbages; things which were formerly never raised but by the spade, but which are now commonly raised by the plough. All sort of garden stuff, too, has become cheaper. The greater part of the apples, and even of the onions, consumed in Great Britain, were, in the last century, imported from Flanders. The great improvements in the coarser manufactories of both linen and woollen cloth furnish the labourers with cheaper and better clothing; and those in the manufactories of the coarser metals, with cheaper and better instruments of trade, as well as with many agreeable and convenient pieces of household furniture. Soap, salt, candles, leather, and fermented liquors, have, indeed, become a good deal dearer, chiefly from the taxes which have been laid upon them. The quantity of these, however, which the labouring poor an under any necessity of consuming, is so very small, that the increase in their price does not compensate the diminution in that of so many other things. The common complaint, that luxury extends itself even to the lowest ranks of the people, and that the labouring poor will not now be contented with the same food, clothing, and lodging, which satisfied them in former times, may convince us that it is not the money price of labour only, but its real recompence, which has augmented.

Is this improvement in the circumstances of the lower ranks of the people to be regarded as an advantage, or as an inconveniency, to the society? The answer seems at first abundantly plain. Servants, labourers, and workmen of different kinds, make up the far greater part of every great political society. But what improves the circumstances of the greater part, can never be regarded as any inconveniency to the whole. No society can surely be flourishing and happy, of which the far greater part of the members are poor and miserable. It is but equity, besides, that

they who feed, clothe, and lodge the whole body of the people, should have such a share of the produce of their own labour as to be themselves tolerably well fed, clothed, and lodged.

Poverty, though it no doubt discourages, does not always prevent, marriage. It seems even to be favourable to generation. A half-starved Highland woman frequently bears more than twenty children, while a pampered fine lady is often incapable of bearing any, and is generally exhausted by two or three. Barrenness, so frequent among women of fashion, is very rare among those of inferior station. Luxury, in the fair sex, while it inflames, perhaps, the passion for enjoyment, seems always to weaken, and frequently to destroy altogether, the powers of generation.

But poverty, though it does not prevent the generation, is extremely unfavourable to the rearing of children. The tender plant is produced; but in so cold a soil, and so severe a climate, soon withers and dies. It is not uncommon, I have been frequently told, in the Highlands of Scotland, for a mother who has born twenty children not to have two alive. Several officers of great experience have assured me, that, so far from recruiting their regiment, they have never been able to supply it with drums and fifes, from all the soldiers' children that were born in it. A greater number of fine children, however, is seldom seen anywhere than about a barrack of soldiers. Very few of them, it seems, arrive at the age of thirteen or fourteen. In some places, one half the children die before they are four years of age, in many places before they are seven, and in almost all places before they are nine or ten.

This great mortality, however will everywhere be found chiefly among the children of the common people, who cannot afford to tend them with the same care as those of better station. Though their marriages are generally more fruitful than those of people of fashion, a smaller proportion of their children arrive at maturity. In foundling hospitals, and among the children brought up by parish charities, the mortality is still greater than among those of the common people.

Every species of animals naturally multiplies in proportion to the means of their subsistence, and no species can ever multiply be yond it. But in civilized society, it is only among the inferior ranks of people that the scantiness of subsistence can set limits to the further multiplication of the human species; and it can do so in no other way than by destroying a great part of the children which their fruitful marriages produce.

The liberal reward of labour, by enabling them to provide better for their children, and consequently to bring up a greater number, naturally tends to widen and extend those limits. It deserves to be remarked, too, that it necessarily does this as nearly as possible in the proportion which the demand for labour requires. If this demand is continually increasing, the reward of labour must necessarily encourage in such a manner the marriage and multiplication of labourers, as may enable them to supply that continually increasing demand by a continually increasing population. If the reward should at any time be less than what was requisite for this purpose, the deficiency of hands would soon raise it; and if it should at any time be more, their excessive multiplication would soon lower it to this necessary rate. The market would be so much understocked with labour in the one case, and so much overstocked in the other, as would soon force back its price to that proper rate which the circumstances of the society required. It is in this manner that the demand for men, like that for any other commodity, necessarily regulates the production of men, quickens it when it goes on too slowly, and stops it when it advances too fast. It is this demand which regulates and determines the state of propagation in all the different countries of the world; in North America, in Europe, and in China; which renders it rapidly progressive in the first, slow and gradual in the second, and altogether stationary in the last.

The wear and tear of a slave, it has been said, is at the expense of his master; but that of a free servant is at his own expense. The wear and tear of the latter, however, is, in reality, as much at the expense of his master as that of the former. The wages paid to journeymen and servants of every kind must be such as may enable them, one with another to continue the race of journeymen and servants, according as the increasing, diminishing, or stationary demand of the society, may happen to require. But though the wear and tear of a free servant be equally at the expense of his master, it generally costs him much less than that of a slave. The fund destined for replacing or repairing, if I may say so, the wear and tear of the slave, is commonly managed by a negligent master or careless overseer. That destined for performing the same office with regard to the freeman is managed by the freeman himself. The disorders which generally prevail in the economy of the rich, naturally introduce themselves into the management of the former; the strict frugality and parsimonious attention of the poor as naturally establish themselves in that of the latter. Under such different management, the same purpose must require very different degrees of expense to execute it. It appears, accordingly, from the experience of all ages and nations, I believe, that the work done by freemen comes cheaper in the end than that performed by slaves. It is found to do so even at Boston, New-York, and Philadelphia, where the wages of common labour are so very high.

The liberal reward of labour, therefore, as it is the effect of increasing wealth, so it is the cause of increasing population. To complain of it, is to lament over the necessary cause and effect of the greatest public prosperity.

It deserves to be remarked, perhaps, that it is in the progressive state, while the society is advancing to the further acquisition, rather than when it has acquired its full complement of riches, that the condition of the labouring poor, of the great body of the people, seems to be the happiest and the most comfortable. It is hard in the stationary, and miserable in the declining state. The progressive state is, in reality, the cheerful and the hearty state to all the different orders of the society; the stationary is dull; the declining melancholy.

The liberal reward of labour, as it encourages the propagation, so it increases the industry of the common people. The wages of labour are the encouragement of industry, which, like every other human quality, improves in proportion to the encouragement it receives. A plentiful subsistence increases the bodily strength of the labourer, and the comfortable hope of bettering his condition, and of ending his days, perhaps, in ease and plenty, animates him to exert that strength to the utmost. Where wages are high, accordingly, we shall always find the workmen more active, diligent, and expeditious, than where they are low; in England, for example, than in Scotland; in the neighbourhood of great towns, than in remote country places. Some workmen, indeed, when they can earn in four days what will maintain them through the week, will be idle the other three. This, however, is by no means the case with the greater part. Workmen, on the contrary, when they are liberally paid by the piece, are very apt to overwork themselves, and to ruin their health and constitution in a few years. A carpenter in London, and in some other places, is not supposed to last in his utmost vigour above eight years. Something of the same kind happens in many other trades, in which the workmen are paid by the piece; as they generally are in manufactures, and even in country labour, wherever wages are higher than ordinary. Almost every class of artificers is subject to some peculiar infirmity occasioned by excessive application to their peculiar species of work. Ramuzzini, an eminent Italian physician, has written a particular book concerning such diseases. We do not reckon our soldiers the most industrious set of people among us; yet when soldiers have been employed in some particular sorts of work, and liberally paid by the piece, their officers have frequently been obliged to stipulate with the undertaker, that they should not be allowed to earn above a certain sum every day, according to the rate at which they were paid. Till this stipulation was made, mutual emulation, and the desire of greater gain, frequently prompted

them to overwork themselves, and to hurt their health by excessive labour. Excessive application, during four days of the week, is frequently the real cause of the idleness of the other three, so much and so loudly complained of. Great labour, either of mind or body, continued for several days together is, in most men, naturally followed by a great desire of relaxation, which, if not restrained by force, or by some strong necessity, is almost irresistible. It is the call of nature, which requires to be relieved by some indulgence, sometimes of ease only, but sometimes too of dissipation and diversion. If it is not complied with, the consequences are often dangerous and sometimes fatal, and such as almost always, sooner or later, bring on the peculiar infirmity of the trade. If masters would always listen to the dictates of reason and humanity, they have frequently occasion rather to moderate, than to animate the application of many of their workmen. It will be found, I believe, in every sort of trade, that the man who works so moderately, as to be able to work constantly, not only preserves his health the longest, but, in the course of the year, executes the greatest quantity of work.

In cheap years it is pretended, workmen are generally more idle, and in dear times more industrious than ordinary. A plentiful subsistence, therefore, it has been concluded, relaxes, and a scanty one quickens their industry. That a little more plenty than ordinary may render some workmen idle, cannot be well doubted; but that it should have this effect upon the greater part, or that men in general should work better when they are ill fed, than when they are well fed, when they are disheartened than when they are in good spirits, when they are frequently sick than when they are generally in good health, seems not very probable. Years of dearth, it is to be observed, are generally among the common people years of sickness and mortality, which cannot fail to diminish the produce of their industry.

In years of plenty, servants frequently leave their masters, and trust their subsistence to what they can make by their own industry. But the same cheapness of provisions, by increasing the fund which is destined for the maintenance of servants, encourages masters, farmers especially, to employ a greater number. Farmers, upon such occasions, expect more profit from their corn by maintaining a few more labouring servants, than by selling it at a low price in the market. The demand for servants increases, while the number of those who offer to supply that demand diminishes. The price of labour, therefore, frequently rises in cheap years.

In years of scarcity, the difficulty and uncertainty of subsistence make all such people eager to return to service. But the high price of provisions, by diminishing the funds destined for the maintenance of servants, disposes masters rather to diminish than to increase the number of those they have. In dear years, too, poor independent workmen frequently consume the little stock with which they had used to supply themselves with the materials of their work, and are obliged to become journeymen for subsistence. More people want employment than easily get it; many are willing to take it upon lower terms than ordinary; and the wages of both servants and journeymen frequently sink in dear years.

Masters of all sorts, therefore, frequently make better bargains with their servants in dear than in cheap years, and find them more humble and dependent in the former than in the latter. They naturally, therefore, commend the former as more favourable to industry. Landlords and farmers, besides, two of the largest classes of masters, have another reason for being pleased with dear years. The rents of the one, and the profits of the other, depend very much upon the price of provisions. Nothing can be more absurd, however, than to imagine that men in general should work less when they work for themselves, than when they work for other people. A poor independent workman will generally be more industrious than even a journeyman who works by the piece. The one enjoys the whole produce of his own industry, the other shares it with his

master. The one, in his separate independent state, is less liable to the temptations of bad company, which, in large manufactories, so frequently ruin the morals of the other. The superiority of the independent workman over those servants who are hired by the month or by the year, and whose wages and maintenance are the same, whether they do much or do little, is likely to be still greater. Cheap years tend to increase the proportion of independent workmen to journeymen and servants of all kinds, and dear years to diminish it. . . .

It is because the demand for labour increases in years of sudden and extraordinary plenty, and diminishes in those of sudden and extraordinary scarcity, that the money price of labour sometimes rises in the one, and sinks in the other.

In a year of sudden and extraordinary plenty, there are funds in the hands of many of the employers of industry, sufficient to maintain and employ a greater number of industrious people than had been employed the year before; and this extraordinary number cannot always be had. Those masters, therefore, who want more workmen, bid against one another, in order to get them, which sometimes raises both the real and the money price of their labour.

The contrary of this happens in a year of sudden and extraordinary scarcity. The funds destined for employing industry are less than they had been the year before. A considerable number of people are thrown out of employment, who bid one against another, in order to get it, which sometimes lowers both the real and the money price of labour. In 1740, a year of extraordinary scarcity, many people were willing to work for bare subsistence. In the succeeding years of plenty, it was more difficult to get labourers and servants. The scarcity of a dear year, by diminishing the demand for labour, tends to lower its price, as the high price of provisions tends to raise it. The plenty of a cheap year, on the contrary, by increasing the demand, tends to raise the price of labour, as the cheapness of provisions tends to lower it. In the ordinary variations of the prices of provisions, those two opposite causes seem to counterbalance one another, which is probably, in part, the reason why the wages of labour are everywhere so much more steady and permanent than the price of provisions.

The increase in the wages of labour necessarily increases the price of many commodities, by increasing that part of it which resolves itself into wages, and so far tends to diminish their consumption, both at home and abroad. The same cause, however, which raises the wages of labour, the increase of stock, tends to increase its productive powers, and to make a smaller quantity of labour produce a greater quantity of work. The owner of the stock which employs a great number of labourers necessarily endeavours, for his own advantage, to make such a proper division and distribution of employment, that they may be enabled to produce the greatest quantity of work possible. For the same reason, he endeavours to supply them with the best machinery which either he or they can think of. What takes place among the labourers in a particular workhouse, takes place, for the same reason, among those of a great society. The greater their number, the more they naturally divide themselves into different classes and subdivisions of employments. More heads are occupied in inventing the most proper machinery for executing the work of each, and it is, therefore, more likely to be invented. There me many commodities, therefore, which, in consequence of these improvements, come to be produced by so much less labour than before, that the increase of its price is more than compensated by the diminution of its quantity.

. . .

BOOK II. OF THE NATURE, ACCUMULATION, AND EMPLOYMENT OF STOCK.

. . .

CHAPTER III. OF THE ACCUMULATION OF CAPITAL, OR OF PRODUCTIVE AND UNPRODUCTIVE LABOUR.

There is one sort of labour which adds to the value of the subject upon which it is bestowed; there is another which has no such effect. The former as it produces a value, may be called productive, the latter, unproductive labour. {Some French authors of great learning and ingenuity have used those words in a different sense. In the last chapter of the fourth book, I shall endeavour to shew that their sense is an improper one.} Thus the labour of a manufacturer adds generally to the value of the materials which he works upon, that of his own maintenance, and of his master's profit. The labour of a menial servant, on the contrary, adds to the value of nothing. Though the manufacturer has his wages advanced to him by his master, he in reality costs him no expense, the value of those wages being generally restored, together with a profit, in the improved value of the subject upon which his labour is bestowed. But the maintenance of a menial servant never is restored. A man grows rich by employing a multitude of manufacturers; he grows poor by maintaining a multitude or menial servants. The labour of the latter, however, has its value, and deserves its reward as well as that of the former. But the labour of the manufacturer fixes and realizes itself in some particular subject or vendible commodity, which lasts for some time at least after that labour is past. It is, as it were, a certain quantity of labour stocked and stored up, to be employed, if necessary, upon some other occasion. That subject, or, what is the same thing, the price of that subject, can afterwards, if necessary, put into motion a quantity of labour equal to that which had originally produced it. The labour of the menial servant, on the contrary, does not fix or realize itself in any particular subject or vendible commodity. His services generally perish in the very instant of their performance, and seldom leave any trace of value behind them, for which an equal quantity of service could afterwards be procured.

The labour of some of the most respectable orders in the society is, like that of menial servants, unproductive of any value, and does not fix or realize itself in any permanent subject, or vendible commodity, which endures after that labour is past, and for which an equal quantity of labour could afterwards be procured. The sovereign, for example, with all the officers both of justice and war who serve under him, the whole army and navy, are unproductive labourers. They are the servants of the public, and are maintained by a part of the annual produce of the industry of other people. Their service, how honourable, how useful, or how necessary soever, produces nothing for which an equal quantity of service can afterwards be procured. The protection, security, and defence, of the commonwealth, the effect of their labour this year, will not purchase its protection, security, and defence, for the year to come. In the same class must be ranked, some both of the gravest and most important, and some of the most frivolous professions; churchmen, lawyers, physicians, men of letters of all kinds; players, buffoons, musicians, opera-singers, opera-dancers, etc. The labour of the meanest of these has a certain value, regulated by the very same principles which regulate that of every other sort of labour; and that of the noblest and most useful, produces nothing which could afterwards purchase or procure an equal quantity of labour. Like the declamation of the actor, the harangue of the orator, or the tune of the musician, the work of all of them perishes in the very instant of its production.

Both productive and unproductive labourers, and those who do not labour at all, are all equally maintained by the annual produce of the land and labour of the country. This produce, how great soever, can never be infinite, but must have certain limits. According, therefore, as a smaller or greater proportion of it is in any one year employed in maintaining unproductive hands, the more in the one case, and the less in the other, will remain for the productive, and the next year's produce will be greater or smaller accordingly; the whole annual produce, if we except the spontaneous productions of the earth, being the effect of productive labour.

Though the whole annual produce of the land and labour of every country is no doubt ultimately destined for supplying the consumption of its inhabitants, and for procuring a revenue to them; yet when it first comes either from the ground, or from the hands of the productive labourers, it naturally divides itself into two parts. One of them, and frequently the largest, is, in the first place, destined for replacing a capital, or for renewing the provisions, materials, and finished work, which had been withdrawn from a capital; the other for constituting a revenue either to the owner of this capital, as the profit of his stock, or to some other person, as the rent of his land. Thus, of the produce of land, one part replaces the capital of the farmer; the other pays his profit and the rent of the landlord; and thus constitutes a revenue both to the owner of this capital, as the profits of his stock, and to some other person as the rent of his land. Of the produce of a great manufactory, in the same manner, one part, and that always the largest, replaces the capital of the undertaker of the work; the other pays his profit, and thus constitutes a revenue to the owner of this capital.

That part of the annual produce of the land and labour of any country which replaces a capital, never is immediately employed to maintain any but productive hands. It pays the wages of productive labour only. That which is immediately destined for constituting a revenue, either as profit or as rent, may maintain indifferently either productive or unproductive hands.

Whatever part of his stock a man employs as a capital, he always expects it to be replaced to him with a profit. He employs it, therefore, in maintaining productive hands only; and after having served in the function of a capital to him, it constitutes a revenue to them. Whenever he employs any part of it in maintaining unproductive hands of any kind, that part is from that moment withdrawn from his capital, and placed in his stock reserved for immediate consumption.

Unproductive labourers, and those who do not labour at all, are all maintained by revenue; either, first, by that part of the annual produce which is originally destined for constituting a revenue to some particular persons, either as the rent of land, or as the profits of stock; or, secondly, by that part which, though originally destined for replacing a capital, and for maintaining productive labourers only, yet when it comes into their hands, whatever part of it is over and above their necessary subsistence, may be employed in maintaining indifferently either productive or unproductive hands. Thus, not only the great landlord or the rich merchant, but even the common workman, if his wages are considerable, may maintain a menial servant; or he may sometimes go to a play or a puppet-show, and so contribute his share towards maintaining one set of unproductive labourers; or he may pay some taxes, and thus help to maintain another set, more honourable and useful, indeed, but equally unproductive. No part of the annual produce, however, which had been originally destined to replace a capital, is ever directed towards maintaining unproductive hands, till after it has put into motion its full complement of productive labour, or all that it could put into motion in the way in which it was employed. The workman must have earned his wages by work done, before he can employ any part of them in this manner. That part, too, is generally but a small one. It is his spare revenue only, of which productive labourers have seldom a great deal. They generally have some, however; and in the payment of taxes, the greatness of their number may compensate, in some measure, the smallness of their contribution. The rent of land and the profits of stock are everywhere, therefore, the principal sources from which unproductive hands derive their subsistence. These are the two sorts of revenue of which the owners have generally most to spare. They might oth maintain indifferently, either productive or unproductive hands. They seem, however, to have some predilection for the latter. The expense of a great lord feeds generally more idle than industrious people. The rich merchant, though with his capital he maintains industrious people only, yet by his expense, that is, by the employment of his revenue, he feeds commonly the very same sort as the great lord.

The proportion, therefore, between the productive and unproductive hands, depends very much in every country upon the proportion between that part of the annual produce, which, as soon as it comes either from the ground, or from the hands of the productive labourers, is destined for replacing a capital, and that which is destined for constituting a revenue, either as rent or as profit. This proportion is very different in rich from what it is in poor countries.

. . .

The proportion between capital and revenue, therefore, seems everywhere to regulate the proportion between industry and idleness Wherever capital predominates, industry prevails; wherever revenue, idleness. Every increase or diminution of capital, therefore, naturally tends to increase or diminish the real quantity of industry, the number of productive hands, and consequently the exchangeable value of the annual produce of the land and labour of the country, the real wealth and revenue of all its inhabitants.

Capitals are increased by parsimony, and diminished by prodigality and misconduct.

Whatever a person saves from his revenue he adds to his capital, and either employs it himself in maintaining an additional number of productive hands, or enables some other person to do so, by lending it to him for an interest, that is, for a share of the profits. As the capital of an individual can be increased only by what he saves from his annual revenue or his annual gains, so the capital of a society, which is the same with that of all the individuals who compose it, can be increased only in the same manner.

Parsimony, and not industry, is the immediate cause of the increase of capital. Industry, indeed, provides the subject which parsimony accumulates; but whatever industry might acquire, if parsimony did not save and store up, the capital would never be the greater.

Parsimony, by increasing the fund which is destined for the maintenance of productive hands, tends to increase the number of those hands whose labour adds to the value of the subject upon winch it is bestowed. It tends, therefore, to increase the exchangeable value of the annual produce of the land and labour of the country. It puts into motion an additional quantity of industry, which gives an additional value to the annual produce.

What is annually saved, is as regularly consumed as what is annually spent, and nearly in the same time too: but it is consumed by a different set of people. That portion of his revenue which a rich man annually spends, is, in most cases, consumed by idle guests and menial servants, who leave nothing behind them in return for their consumption. That portion which he annually saves, as, for the sake of the profit, it is immediately employed as a capital, is consumed in the same manner, and nearly in the same time too, but by a different set of people: by labourers, manufacturers, and artificers, who reproduce, with a profit, the value of their annual consumption. His revenue, we shall suppose, is paid him in money. Had he spent the whole, the food, clothing, and lodging, which the whole could have purchased, would have been distributed among the former set of people. By saving a part of it, as that part is, for the sake of the profit, immediately employed as a capital, either by himself or by some other person, the food, clothing, and lodging, which may be purchased with it, are necessarily reserved for the latter. The consumption is the same, but the consumers are different.

By what a frugal man annually saves, he not only affords maintenance to an additional number of productive hands, for that of the ensuing year, but like the founder of a public work-house he establishes, as it were, a perpetual fund for the maintenance of an equal number in all times to come. The perpetual allotment and destination of this fund, indeed, is not always guarded by any positive law, by any trust-right or deed of mortmain. It is always guarded, however, by a very powerful principle, the plain and evident interest of every individual to whom any

share of it shall ever belong. No part of it can ever afterwards be employed to maintain any but productive hands, without an evident loss to the person who thus perverts it from its proper destination.

The prodigal perverts it in this manner: By not confining his expense within his income, he encroaches upon his capital. Like him who perverts the revenues of some pious foundation to profane purposes, he pays the wages of idleness with those funds which the frugality of his forefathers had, as it were, consecrated to the maintenance of industry. By diminishing the funds destined for the employment of productive labour, he necessarily diminishes, so far as it depends upon him, the quantity of that labour which adds a value to the subject upon which it is bestowed, and, consequently, the value of the annual produce of the land and labour of the whole country, the real wealth and revenue of its inhabitants. If the prodigality of some were not compensated by the frugality of others, the conduct of every prodigal, by feeding the idle with the bread of the industrious, would tend not only to beggar himself, but to impoverish his country.

Though the expense of the prodigal should be altogether in home made, and no part of it in foreign commodities, its effect upon the productive funds of the society would still be the same. Every year there would still be a certain quantity of food and clothing, which ought to have maintained productive, employed in maintaining unproductive hands. Every year, therefore, there would still be some diminution in what would otherwise have been the value of the annual produce of the land and labour of the country.

This expense, it may be said, indeed, not being in foreign goods, and not occasioning any exportation of gold and silver, the same quantity of money would remain in the country as before. But if the quantity of food and clothing which were thus consumed by unproductive, had been distributed among productive hands, they would have reproduced, together with a profit, the full value of their consumption. The same quantity of money would, in this case, equally have remained in the country, and there would, besides, have been a reproduction of an equal value of consumable goods. There would have been two values instead of one.

The same quantity of money, besides, can not long remain in any country in which the value of the annual produce diminishes. The sole use of money is to circulate consumable goods. By means of it, provisions, materials, and finished work, are bought and sold, and distributed to their proper consumers. The quantity of money, therefore, which can be annually employed in any country, must be determined by the value of the consumable goods annually circulated within it. These must consist, either in the immediate produce of the land and labour of the country itself, or in something which had been purchased with some part of that produce. Their value, therefore, must diminish as the value of that produce diminishes, and along with it the quantity of money which can be employed in circulating them. But the money which, by this annual diminution of produce, is annually thrown out of domestic circulation, will not be allowed to lie idle. The interest of whoever possesses it requires that it should be employed; but having no employment at home, it will, in spite of all laws and prohibitions, be sent abroad, and employed in purchasing consumable goods, which may be of some use at home. Its annual exportation will, in this manner, continue for some time to add something to the annual consumption of the country beyond the value of its own annual produce. What in the days of its prosperity had been saved from that annual produce, and employed in purchasing gold and silver, will contribute, for some little time, to support its consumption in adversity. The exportation of gold and silver is, in this case, not the cause, but the effect of its declension, and may even, for some little time, alleviate the misery of that declension.

The quantity of money, on the contrary, must in every country naturally increase as the value of the annual produce increases. The value of the consumable goods annually circulated within the society being greater, will require a greater quantity of money to circulate them. A part of the increased produce, therefore, will naturally be employed in purchasing, wherever it is to be had, the additional quantity of gold and silver necessary for circulating the rest. The increase of those metals will, in this case, be the effect, not the cause, of the public prosperity. Gold and silver are purchased everywhere in the same manner. The food, clothing, and lodging, the revenue and maintenance, of all those whose labour or stock is employed in bringing them from the mine to the market, is the price paid for them in Peru as well as in England. The country which has this price to pay, will never belong without the quantity of those metals which it has occasion for; and no country will ever long retain a quantity which it has no occasion for.

Whatever, therefore, we may imagine the real wealth and revenue of a country to consist in, whether in the value of the annual produce of its land and labour, as plain reason seems to dictate, or in the quantity of the precious metals which circulate within it, as vulgar prejudices suppose; in either view of the matter, every prodigal appears to be a public enemy, and every frugal man a public benefactor.

The effects of misconduct are often the same as those of prodigality. Every injudicious and unsuccessful project in agriculture, mines, fisheries, trade, or manufactures, tends in the same manner to diminish the funds destined for the maintenance of productive labour. In every such project, though the capital is consumed by productive hands only, yet as, by the injudicious manner in which they are employed, they do not reproduce the full value of their consumption, there must always be some diminution in what would otherwise have been the productive funds of the society.

It can seldom happen, indeed, that the circumstances of a great nation can be much affected either by the prodigality or misconduct of individuals; the profusion or imprudence of some being always more than compensated by the frugality and good conduct of others.

With regard to profusion, the principle which prompts to expense is the passion for present enjoyment; which, though sometimes violent and very difficult to be restrained, is in general only momentary and occasional. But the principle which prompts to save, is the desire of bettering our condition; a desire which, though generally calm and dispassionate, comes with us from the womb, and never leaves us till we go into the grave. In the whole interval which separates those two moments, there is scarce, perhaps, a single instance, in which any man is so perfectly and completely satisfied with his situation, as to be without any wish of alteration or improvement of any kind. An augmentation of fortune is the means by which the greater part of men propose and wish to better their condition. It is the means the most vulgar and the most obvious; and the most likely way of augmenting their fortune, is to save and accumulate some part of what they acquire, either regularly and annually, or upon some extraordinary occasion. Though the principle of expense, therefore, prevails in almost all men upon some occasions, and in some men upon almost all occasions; yet in the greater part of men, taking the whole course of their life at an average, the principle of frugality seems not only to predominate, but to predominate very greatly.

With regard to misconduct, the number of prudent and successful undertakings is everywhere much greater than that of injudicious and unsuccessful ones. After all our complaints of the frequency of bankruptcies, the unhappy men who fall into this misfortune, make but a very small part of the whole number engaged in trade, and all other sorts of business; not much more, perhaps, than one in a thousand. Bankruptcy is, perhaps, the greatest and most humiliating calamity which can befal an innocent man. The greater part of men, therefore, are sufficiently

careful to avoid it. Some, indeed, do not avoid it; as some do not avoid the gallows.

Great nations are never impoverished by private, though they sometimes are by public prodigality and misconduct. The whole, or almost the whole public revenue is, in most countries, employed in maintaining unproductive hands. Such are the people who compose a numerous and splendid court, a great ecclesiastical establishment, great fleets and armies, who in time of peace produce nothing, and in time of war acquire nothing which can compensate the expense of maintaining them, even while the war lasts. Such people, as they themselves produce nothing, are all maintained by the produce of other men's labour. When multiplied, therefore, to an unnecessary number, they may in a particular year consume so great a share of this produce, as not to leave a sufficiency for maintaining the productive labourers, who should reproduce it next year. The next year's produce, therefore, will be less than that of the foregoing; and if the same disorder should continue, that of the third year will be still less than that of the second. Those unproductive hands who should be maintained by a part only of the spare revenue of the people, may consume so great a share of their whole revenue, and thereby oblige so great a number to encroach upon their capitals, upon the funds destined for the maintenance of productive labour, that all the frugality and good conduct of individuals may not be able to compensate the waste and degradation of produce occasioned by this violent and forced encroachment.

This frugality and good conduct, however, is, upon most occasions, it appears from experience, sufficient to compensate, not only the private prodigality and misconduct of individuals, but the public extravagance of government. The uniform, constant, and uninterrupted effort of every man to better his condition, the principle from which public and national, as well as private opulence is originally derived, is frequently powerful enough to maintain the natural progress of things towards improvement, in spite both of the extravagance of government, and of the greatest errors of administration. Like the unknown principle of animal life, it frequently restores health and vigour to the constitution, in spite not only of the disease, but of the absurd prescriptions of the doctor.

The annual produce of the land and labour of any nation can be increased in its value by no other means, but by increasing either the number of its productive labourers, or the productive powers of those labourers who had before been employed. The number of its productive labourers, it is evident, can never be much increased, but in consequence of an increase of capital, or of the funds destined for maintaining them. The productive powers of the same number of labourers cannot be increased, but in consequence either of some addition and improvement to those machines and instruments which facilitate and abridge labour, or of more proper division and distribution of employment. In either case, an additional capital is almost always required. It is by means of an additional capital only, that the undertaker of any work can either provide his workmen with better machinery, or make a more proper distribution of employment among them. When the work to be done consists of a number of parts, to keep every man constantly employed in one way, requires a much greater capital than where every man is occasionally employed in every different part of the work. When we compare, therefore, the state of a nation at two different periods, and find that the annual produce of its land and labour is evidently greater at the latter than at the former, that its lands are better cultivated, its manufactures more numerous and more flourishing, and its trade more extensive; we may be assured that its capital must have increased during the interval between those two periods, and that more must have been added to it by the good conduct of some, than had been taken from it either by the private misconduct of others, or by the public extravagance of government. But we shall find this to have been the case of almost all nations, in all tolerably quiet and peaceable times, even of those who have not enjoyed the

most prudent and parsimonious governments. To form a right judgment of it, indeed, we must compare the state of the country at periods somewhat distant from one another. The progress is frequently so gradual, that, at near periods, the improvement is not only not sensible, but, from the declension either of certain branches of industry, or of certain districts of the country, things which sometimes happen, though the country in general is in great prosperity, there frequently arises a suspicion, that the riches and industry of the whole are decaying.

. . .

The annual produce of its land and labour is undoubtedly much greater at present than it was either at the Restoration or at the Revolution. The capital, therefore, annually employed in cultivating this land, and in maintaining this labour, must likewise be much greater. In the midst of all the exactions of government, this capital has been silently and gradually accumulated by the private frugality and good conduct of individuals, by their universal, continual, and uninterrupted effort to better their own condition. It is this effort, protected by law, and allowed by liberty to exert itself in the manner that is most advantageous, which has maintained the progress of England towards opulence and improvement in almost all former times, and which, it is to be hoped, will do so in all future times. England, however, as it has never been blessed with a very parsimonious government, so parsimony has at no time been the characteristic virtue of its inhabitants. It is the highest impertinence and presumption, therefore, in kings and ministers to pretend to watch over the economy of private people, and to restrain their expense, either by sumptuary laws, or by prohibiting the importation of foreign luxuries. They are themselves always, and without any exception, the greatest spendthrifts in the society. Let them look well after their own expense, and they may safely trust private people with theirs. If their own extravagance does not ruin the state, that of the subject never will.

As frugality increases, and prodigality diminishes, the public capital, so the conduct of those whose expense just equals their revenue, without either accumulating or encroaching, neither increases nor diminishes it. Some modes of expense, however, seem to contribute more to the growth of public opulence than others.

The revenue of an individual may be spent, either in things which are consumed immediately, and in which one day's expense can neither alleviate nor support that of another; or it may be spent in things mere durable, which can therefore be accumulated, and in which every day's expense may, as he chooses, either alleviate, or support and heighten, the effect of that of the following day. A man of fortune, for example, may either spend his revenue in a profuse and sumptuous table, and in maintaining a great number of menial servants, and a multitude of dogs and horses; or, contenting himself with a frugal table, and few attendants, he may lay out the greater part of it in adorning his house or his country villa, in useful or ornamental buildings, in useful or ornamental furniture, in collecting books, statues, pictures; or in things more frivolous, jewels, baubles, ingenious trinkets of different kinds; or, what is most trifling of all, in amassing a great wardrobe of fine clothes, like the favourite and minister of a great prince who died a few years ago. Were two men of equal fortune to spend their revenue, the one chiefly in the one way, the other in the other, the magnificence of the person whose expense had been chiefly in durable commodities, would be continually increasing, every day's expense contributing something to support and heighten the effect of that of the following day; that of the other, on the contrary, would be no greater at the end of the period than at the beginning. The former too would, at the end of the period, be the richer man of the two. He would have a stock of goods of some kind or other, which, though it might not be worth all that it cost, would always be worth something. No trace or vestige of the expense of the latter would remain, and the effects of ten or twenty years' profusion would be as completely annihilated as if they had never existed.

As the one mode of expense is more favourable than the other to the opulence of an individual, so is it likewise to that of a nation. The houses, the furniture, the clothing of the rich, in a little time, become useful to the inferior and middling ranks of people. They are able to purchase them when their superiors grow weary of them; and the general accommodation of the whole people is thus gradually improved, when this mode of expense becomes universal among men of fortune.

. . .

BOOK IV. OF SYSTEMS OF POLITICAL ECONOMY.

Political economy, considered as a branch of the science of a statesman or legislator, proposes two distinct objects; first, to provide a plentiful revenue or subsistence for the people, or, more properly, to enable them to provide such a revenue or subsistence for themselves; and, secondly, to supply the state or commonwealth with a revenue sufficient for the public services. It proposes to enrich both the people and the sovereign.

The different progress of opulence in different ages and nations, has given occasion to two different systems of political economy, with regard to enriching the people. The one may be called the system of commerce, the other that of agriculture. I shall endeavour to explain both as fully and distinctly as I can, and shall begin with the system of commerce. It is the modern system, and is best understood in our own country and in our own times.

. . .

CHAPTER II. OF RESTRAINTS UPON IMPORTATION FROM FOREIGN COUNTRIES OF SUCH GOODS AS CAN BE PRODUCED AT HOME.

By restraining, either by high duties, or by absolute prohibitions, the importation of such goods from foreign countries as can be produced at home, the monopoly of the home market is more or less secured to the domestic industry employed in producing them. Thus the prohibition of importing either live cattle or salt provisions from foreign countries, secures to the graziers of Great Britain the monopoly of the home market for butcher's meat. The high duties upon the importation of corn, which, in times of moderate plenty, amount to a prohibition, give a like advantage to the growers of that commodity. The prohibition of the importation of foreign woollen is equally favourable to the woolen manufacturers. The silk manufacture, though altogether employed upon foreign materials, has lately obtained the same advantage. The linen manufacture has not yet obtained it, but is making great strides towards it. Many other sorts of manufactures have, in the same manner obtained in Great Britain, either altogether, or very nearly, a monopoly against their countrymen. The variety of goods, of which the importation into Great Britain is prohibited, either absolutely, or under certain circumstances, greatly exceeds what can easily be suspected by those who are not well acquainted with the laws of the customs.

That this monopoly of the home market frequently gives great encouragement to that particular species of industry which enjoys it, and frequently turns towards that employment a greater share of both the labour and stock of the society than would otherwise have gone to it, cannot be doubted. But whether it tends either to increase the general industry of the society, or to give it the most advantageous direction, is not, perhaps, altogether so evident.

The general industry of the society can never exceed what the capital of the society can employ. As the number of workmen that can be kept in employment by any particular person must bear a certain proportion to his capital, so the number of those that can be continually employed by all the members of a great society must bear a certain proportion to the whole capital of the society, and never can exceed that proportion. No regulation of commerce can increase the quantity of industry in any society beyond what its capital

can maintain. It can only divert a part of it into a direction into which it might not otherwise have gone; and it is by no means certain that this artificial direction is likely to be more advantageous to the society, than that into which it would have gone of its own accord.

Every individual is continually exerting himself to find out the most advantageous employment for whatever capital he can command. It is his own advantage, indeed, and not that of the society, which he has in view. But the study of his own advantage naturally, or rather necessarily, leads him to prefer that employment which is most advantageous to the society.

First, every individual endeavours to employ his capital as near home as he can, and consequently as much as he can in the support of domestic industry, provided always that he can thereby obtain the ordinary, or not a great deal less than the ordinary profits of stock.

Thus, upon equal, or nearly equal profits, every wholesale merchant naturally prefers the home trade to the foreign trade of consumption, and the foreign trade of consumption to the carrying trade. In the home trade, his capital is never so long out of his sight as it frequently is in the foreign trade of consumption. He can know better the character and situation of the persons whom he trusts; and if he should happen to be deceived, he knows better the laws of the country from which he must seek redress. In the carrying trade, the capital of the merchant is, as it were, divided between two foreign countries, and no part of it is ever necessarily brought home, or placed under his own immediate view and command. The capital which an Amsterdam merchant employs in carrying corn from Koningsberg to Lisbon, and fruit and wine from Lisbon to Koningsberg, must generally be the one half of it at Koningsberg, and the other half at Lisbon. No part of it need ever come to Amsterdam. The natural residence of such a merchant should either be at Koningsberg or Lisbon; and it can only be some very particular circumstances which can make him prefer the residence of Amsterdam. The uneasiness, however, which he feels at being separated so far from his capital, generally determines him to bring part both of the Koningsberg goods which he destines for the market of Lisbon, and of the Lisbon goods which he destines for that of Koningsberg, to Amsterdam; and though this necessarily subjects him to a double charge of loading and unloading as well as to the payment of some duties and customs, yet, for the sake of having some part of his capital always under his own view and command, he willingly submits to this extraordinary charge; and it is in this manner that every country which has any considerable share of the carrying trade, becomes always the emporium, or general market, for the goods of all the different countries whose trade it carries on.

The merchant, in order to save a second loading and unloading, endeavours always to sell in the home market, as much of the goods of all those different countries as he can; and thus, so far as he can, to convert his carrying trade into a foreign trade of consumption. A merchant, in the same manner, who is engaged in the foreign trade of consumption, when he collects goods for foreign markets, will always be glad, upon equal or nearly equal profits, to sell as great a part of them at home as he can. He saves himself the risk and trouble of exportation, when, so far as he can, he thus converts his foreign trade of consumption into a home trade. Home is in this manner the centre, if I may say so, round which the capitals of the inhabitants of every country are continually circulating, and towards which they are always tending, though, by particular causes, they may sometimes be driven off and repelled from it towards more distant employments. But a capital employed in the home trade, it has already been shown, necessarily puts into motion a greater quantity of domestic industry, and gives revenue and employment to a greater number of the inhabitants of the country, than an equal capital employed in the foreign trade of consumption; and one employed in the foreign trade of consumption has the same advantage over an equal capital employed in the carrying trade.

Upon equal, or only nearly equal profits, therefore, every individual naturally inclines to employ his capital in the manner in which it is likely to afford the greatest support to domestic industry, and to give revenue and employment to the greatest number of people of his own country.

Secondly, every individual who employs his capital in the support of domestic industry, necessarily endeavours so to direct that industry, that its produce may be of the greatest possible value.

The produce of industry is what it adds to the subject or materials upon which it is employed. In proportion as the value of this produce is great or small, so will likewise be the profits of the employer. But it is only for the sake of profit that any man employs a capital in the support of industry; and he will always, therefore, endeavour to employ it in the support of that industry of which the produce is likely to be of the greatest value, or to exchange for the greatest quantity either of money or of other goods.

But the annual revenue of every society is always precisely equal to the exchangeable value of the whole annual produce of its industry, or rather is precisely the same thing with that exchangeable value. As every individual, therefore, endeavours as much as he can, both to employ his capital in the support of domestic industry, and so to direct that industry that its produce maybe of the greatest value; every individual necessarily labours to render the annual revenue of the society as great as he can. He generally, indeed, neither intends to promote the public interest, nor knows how much he is promoting it. By preferring the support of domestic to that of foreign industry, he intends only his own security; and by directing that industry in such a manner as its produce may be of the greatest value, he intends only his own gain; and he is in this, as in many other cases, led by an invisible hand to promote an end which was no part of his intention. Nor is it always the worse for the society that it was no part of it. By pursuing his own interest, he frequently promotes that of the society more effectually than when he really intends to promote it. I have never known much good done by those who affected to trade for the public good. It is an affectation, indeed, not very common among merchants, and very few words need be employed in dissuading them from it.

What is the species of domestic industry which his capital can employ, and of which the produce is likely to be of the greatest value, every individual, it is evident, can in his local situation judge much better than any statesman or lawgiver can do for him. The statesman, who should attempt to direct private people in what manner they ought to employ their capitals, would not only load himself with a most unnecessary attention, but assume an authority which could safely be trusted, not only to no single person, but to no council or senate whatever, and which would nowhere be so dangerous as in the hands of a man who had folly and presumption enough to fancy himself fit to exercise it.

To give the monopoly of the home market to the produce of domestic industry, in any particular art or manufacture, is in some measure to direct private people in what manner they ought to employ their capitals, and must in almost all cases be either a useless or a hurtful regulation. If the produce of domestic can be brought there as cheap as that of foreign industry, the regulation is evidently useless. If it cannot, it must generally be hurtful. It is the maxim of every prudent master of a family, never to attempt to make at home what it will cost him more to make than to buy. The tailor does not attempt to make his own shoes, but buys them of the shoemaker. The shoemaker does not attempt to make his own clothes, but employs a tailor. The farmer attempts to make neither the one nor the other, but employs those different artificers. All of them find it for their interest to employ their whole industry in a way in which they have some advantage over their neighbours, and to purchase with a part of its produce, or, what is the same

thing, with the price of a part of it, whatever else they have occasion for.

What is prudence in the conduct of every private family, can scarce be folly in that of a great kingdom. If a foreign country can supply us with a commodity cheaper than we ourselves can make it, better buy it of them with some part of the produce of our own industry, employed in a way in which we have some advantage. The general industry of the country being always in proportion to the capital which employs it, will not thereby be diminished, no more than that of the abovementioned artificers; but only left to find out the way in which it can be employed with the greatest advantage. It is certainly not employed to the greatest advantage, when it is thus directed towards an object which it can buy cheaper than it can make. The value of its annual produce is certainly more or less diminished, when it is thus turned away from producing commodities evidently of more value than the commodity which it is directed to produce. According to the supposition, that commodity could be purchased from foreign countries cheaper than it can be made at home; it could therefore have been purchased with a part only of the commodities, or, what is the same thing, with a part only of the price of the commodities, which the industry employed by an equal capital would have produced at home, had it been left to follow its natural course. The industry of the country, therefore, is thus turned away from a more to a less advantageous employment; and the exchangeable value of its annual produce, instead of being increased, according to the intention of the lawgiver, must necessarily be diminished by every such regulation.

By means of such regulations, indeed, a particular manufacture may sometimes be acquired sooner than it could have been otherwise, and after a certain time may be made at home as cheap, or cheaper, than in the foreign country. But though the industry of the society may be thus carried with advantage into a particular channel sooner than it could have been otherwise, it will by no means follow that the sum-total, either of its industry, or of its revenue, can ever be augmented by any such regulation. The industry of the society can augment only in proportion as its capital augments, and its capital can augment only in proportion to what can be gradually saved out of its revenue. But the immediate effect of every such regulation is to diminish its revenue; and what diminishes its revenue is certainly not very likely to augment its capital faster than it would have augmented of its own accord, had both capital and industry been left to find out their natural employments.

Though, for want of such regulations, the society should never acquire the proposed manufacture, it would not upon that account necessarily be the poorer in anyone period of its duration. In every period of its duration its whole capital and industry might still have been employed, though upon different objects, in the manner that was most advantageous at the time. In every period its revenue might have been the greatest which its capital could afford, and both capital and revenue might have been augmented with the greatest possible rapidity.

The natural advantages which one country has over another, in producing particular commodities, are sometimes so great, that it is acknowledged by all the world to be in vain to struggle with them. By means of glasses, hot-beds, and hot-walls, very good grapes can be raised in Scotland, and very good wine, too, can be made of them, at about thirty times the expense for which at least equally good can be brought from foreign countries. Would it be a reasonable law to prohibit the importation of all foreign wines, merely to encourage the making of claret and Burgundy in Scotland? But if there would be a manifest absurdity in turning towards any employment thirty times more of the capital and industry of the country than would be necessary to purchase from foreign countries an equal quantity of the commodities wanted, there must be an absurdity, though not altogether so glaring, yet exactly of the same kind, in turning towards any such employment a thirtieth, or even a three hundredth part more of either. Whether

the advantages which one country has over another be natural or acquired, is in this respect of no consequence. As long as the one country has those advantages, and the other wants them, it will always be more advantageous for the latter rather to buy of the former than to make. It is an acquired advantage only, which one artificer has over his neighbour, who exercises another trade; and yet they both find it more advantageous to buy of one another, than to make what does not belong to their particular trades.

Merchants and manufacturers are the people who derive the greatest advantage from this monopoly of the home market. The prohibition of the importation of foreign cattle and of salt provisions, together with the high duties upon foreign corn, which in times of moderate plenty amount to a prohibition, are not near so advantageous to the graziers and farmers of Great Britain, as other regulations of the same kind are to its merchants and manufacturers. Manufactures, those of the finer kind especially, are more easily transported from one country to another than corn or cattle. It is in the fetching and carrying manufactures, accordingly, that foreign trade is chiefly employed. In manufactures, a very small advantage will enable foreigners to undersell our own workmen, even in the home market. It will require a very great one to enable them to do so in the rude produce of the soil. If the free importation of foreign manufactures were permitted, several of the home manufactures would probably suffer, and some of them perhaps go to ruin altogether, and a considerable part of the stock and industry at present employed in them, would be forced to find out some other employment. But the freest importation of the rude produce of the soil could have no such effect upon the agriculture of the country.

. . .

There seem, however, to be two cases, in which it will generally be advantageous to lay some burden upon foreign, for the encouragement of domestic industry.

The first is, when some particular sort of industry is necessary for the defence of the country. The defence of Great Britain, for example, depends very much upon the number of its sailors and shipping. The act of navigation, therefore, very properly endeavours to give the sailors and shipping of Great Britain the monopoly of the trade of their own country, in some cases, by absolute prohibitions, and in others, by heavy burdens upon the shipping of foreign countries. The following are the principal dispositions of this act.

First, All ships, of which the owners, masters, and three-fourths of the mariners, are not British subjects, are prohibited, upon pain of forfeiting ship and cargo, from trading to the British settlements and plantations, or from being employed in the coasting trade of Great Britain.

Secondly, A great variety of the most bulky articles of importation can be brought into Great Britain only, either in such ships as are above described, or in ships of the country where those goods are produced, and of which the owners, masters, and three-fourths of the mariners, are of that particular country; and when imported even in ships of this latter kind, they are subject to double aliens duty. If imported in ships of any other country, the penalty is forfeiture of ship and goods.

When this act was made, the Dutch were, what they still are, the great carriers of Europe; and by this regulation they were entirely excluded from being the carriers to Great Britain, or from importing to us the goods of any other European country.

Thirdly, A great variety of the most bulky articles of importation are prohibited from being imported, even in British ships, from any country but that in which they are produced, under pain of forfeiting ship and cargo. This regulation, too, was probably intended against the Dutch. Holland was then, as now, the great emporium for all European goods; and by this regulation,

British ships were hindered from loading in Holland the goods of any other European country.

Fourthly, Salt fish of all kinds, whale fins, whalebone, oil, and blubber, not caught by and cured on board British vessels, when imported into Great Britain, are subject to double aliens duty. The Dutch, as they are still the principal, were then the only fishers in Europe that attempted to supply foreign nations with fish. By this regulation, a very heavy burden was laid upon their supplying Great Britain.

When the act of navigation was made, though England and Holland were not actually at war, the most violent animosity subsisted between the two nations. It had begun during the government of the long parliament, which first framed this act, and it broke out soon after in the Dutch wars, during that of the Protector and of Charles II. It is not impossible, therefore, that some of the regulations of this famous act may have proceeded from national animosity. They are as wise, however, as if they had all been dictated by the most deliberate wisdom. National animosity, at that particular time, aimed at the very same object which the most deliberate wisdom would have recommended, the diminution of the naval power of Holland, the only naval power which could endanger the security of England.

The act of navigation is not favourable to foreign commerce, or to the growth of that opulence which can arise from it. The interest of a nation, in its commercial relations to foreign nations, is, like that of a merchant with regard to the different people with whom he deals, to buy as cheap, and to sell as dear as possible. But it will be most likely to buy cheap, when, by the most perfect freedom of trade, it encourages all nations to bring to it the goods which it has occasion to purchase; and, for the same reason, it will be most likely to sell dear, when its markets are thus filled with the greatest number of buyers. The act of navigation, it is true, lays no burden upon foreign ships that come to export the produce of British industry. Even the ancient aliens duty, which used to be paid upon all goods, exported as well as imported, has, by several subsequent acts, been taken off from the greater part of the articles of exportation. But if foreigners, either by prohibitions or high duties, are hindered from coming to sell, they cannot always afford to come to buy; because, coming without a cargo, they must lose the freight from their own country to Great Britain. By diminishing the number of sellers, therefore, we necessarily diminish that of buyers, and are thus likely not only to buy foreign goods dearer, but to sell our own cheaper, than if there was a more perfect freedom of trade. As defence, however, is of much more importance than opulence, the act of navigation is, perhaps, the wisest of all the commercial regulations of England.

The second case, in which it will generally be advantageous to lay some burden upon foreign for the encouragement of domestic industry, is when some tax is imposed at home upon the produce of the latter. In this case, it seems reasonable that an equal tax should be imposed upon the like produce of the former. This would not give the monopoly of the borne market to domestic industry, nor turn towards a particular employment a greater share of the stock and labour of the country, than what would naturally go to it. It would only hinder any part of what would naturally go to it from being turned away by the tax into a less natural direction, and would leave the competition between foreign and domestic industry, after the tax, as nearly as possible upon the same footing as before it. In Great Britain, when any such tax is laid upon the produce of domestic industry, it is usual, at the same time, in order to stop the clamorous complaints of our merchants and manufacturers, that they will be undersold at home, to lay a much heavier duty upon the importation of all foreign goods of the same kind.

This second limitation of the freedom of trade, according to some people, should, upon most occasions, be extended much farther than to the precise foreign commodities which could come into competition with those which had been taxed at home. When the necessaries of life have

been taxed in any country, it becomes proper, they pretend, to tax not only the like necessaries of life imported from other countries, but all sorts of foreign goods which can come into competition with any thing that is the produce of domestic industry. Subsistence, they say, becomes necessarily dearer in consequence of such taxes; and the price of labour must always rise with the price of the labourer's subsistence. Every commodity, therefore, which is the produce of domestic industry, though not immediately taxed itself, becomes dearer in consequence of such taxes, because the labour which produces it becomes so. Such taxes, therefore, are really equivalent, they say, to a tax upon every particular commodity produced at home. In order to put domestic upon the same footing with foreign industry, therefore, it becomes necessary, they think, to lay some duty upon every foreign commodity, equal to this enhancement of the price of the home commodities with which it can come into competition.

Whether taxes upon the necessaries of life, such as those in Great Britain upon soap, salt, leather, candles, etc. necessarily raise the price of labour, and consequently that of all other commodities, I shall consider hereafter, when I come to treat of taxes. Supposing, however, in the mean time, that they have this effect, and they have it undoubtedly, this general enhancement of the price of all commodities, in consequence of that labour, is a case which differs in the two following respects from that of a particular commodity, of which the price was enhanced by a particular tax immediately imposed upon it.

First, It might always be known with great exactness, how far the price of such a commodity could be enhanced by such a tax; but how far the general enhancement of the price of labour might affect that of every different commodity about which labour was employed, could never be known with any tolerable exactness. It would be impossible, therefore, to proportion, with any tolerable exactness, the tax of every foreign, to the enhancement of the price of every home commodity.

Secondly, Taxes upon the necessaries of life have nearly the same effect upon the circumstances of the people as a poor soil and a bad climate. Provisions are thereby rendered dearer, in the same manner as if it required extraordinary labour and expense to raise them. As, in the natural scarcity arising from soil and climate, it would be absurd to direct the people in what manner they ought to employ their capitals and industry, so is it likewise in the artificial scarcity arising from such taxes. To be left to accommodate, as well as they could, their industry to their situation, and to find out those employments in which, notwithstanding their unfavourable circumstances, they might have some advantage either in the home or in the foreign market, is what, in both cases, would evidently be most for their advantage. To lay a new-tax upon them, because they are already overburdened with taxes, and because they already pay too dear for the necessaries of life, to make them likewise pay too dear for the greater part of other commodities, is certainly a most absurd way of making amends.

Such taxes, when they have grown up to a certain height, are a curse equal to the barrenness of the earth, and the inclemency of the heavens, and yet it is in the richest and most industrious countries that they have been most generally imposed. No other countries could support so great a disorder. As the strongest bodies only can live and enjoy health under an unwholesome regimen, so the nations only, that in every sort of industry have the greatest natural and acquired advantages, can subsist and prosper under such taxes. Holland is the country in Europe in which they abound most, and which, from peculiar circumstances, continues to prosper, not by means of them, as has been most absurdly supposed, but in spite of them.

As there are two cases in which it will generally be advantageous to lay some burden upon foreign for the encouragement of domestic industry, so there are two others in which it may sometimes be a matter of deliberation, in the one, how far it is proper to continue the free importation of certain foreign goods; and, in the other, how far, or in what manner, it may be proper to restore that free importation, after it has been for some time interrupted.

The case in which it may sometimes be a matter of deliberation how far it is proper to continue the free importation of certain foreign goods, is when some foreign nation restrains, by high duties or prohibitions, the importation of some of our manufactures into their country. Revenge, in this case, naturally dictates retaliation, and that we should impose the like duties and prohibitions upon the importation of some or all of their manufactures into ours. Nations, accordingly, seldom fail to retaliate in this manner. The French have been particularly forward to favour their own manufactures, by restraining the importation of such foreign goods as could come into competition with them. In this consisted a great part of the policy of Mr Colbert, who, notwithstanding his great abilities, seems in this case to have been imposed upon by the sophistry of merchants and manufacturers, who are always demanding a monopoly against their countrymen. It is at present the opinion of the most intelligent men in France, that his operations of this kind have not been beneficial to his country. That minister, by the tariff of 1667, imposed very high duties upon a great number of foreign manufactures. Upon his refusing to moderate them in favour of the Dutch, they, in 1671, prohibited the importation of the wines, brandies, and manufactures of France. The war of 1672 seems to have been in part occasioned by this commercial dispute. The peace of Nimeguen put an end to it in 1678, by moderating some of those duties in favour of the Dutch, who in consequence took off their prohibition. It was about the same time that the French and English began mutually to oppress each other's industry, by the like duties and prohibitions, of which the French, however, seem to have set the first example, The spirit of hostility which has subsisted between the two nations ever since, has hitherto hindered them from being moderated on either side. In 1697, the English prohibited the importation of bone lace, the manufacture of Flanders. The government of that country, at that time under the dominion of Spain, prohibited, in return, the importation of English woollens. In 1700, the prohibition of importing bone lace into England was taken oft; upon condition that the importation of English woolens into Flanders should be put on the same footing as before.

There may be good policy in retaliations of this kind, when there is a probability that they will procure the repeal of the high duties or prohibitions complained of. The recovery of a great foreign market will generally more than compensate the transitory inconveniency of paying dearer during a short time for some sorts of goods. To judge whether such retaliations are likely to produce such an effect, does not, perhaps, belong so much to the science of a legislator, whose deliberations ought to be governed by general principles, which are always the same, as to the skill of that insidious and crafty animal vulgarly called a statesman or politician, whose councils are directed by the momentary fluctuations of affairs. When there is no probability that any such repeal can be procured, it seems a bad method of compensating the injury done to certain classes of our people, to do another injury ourselves, not only to those classes, but to almost all the other classes of them. When our neighbours prohibit some manufacture of ours, we generally prohibit, not only the same, for that alone would seldom affect them considerably, but some other manufacture of theirs.

This may, no doubt, give encouragement to some particular class of workmen among ourselves, and, by excluding some of their rivals, may enable them to raise their price in the home market. Those workmen however, who suffered by our neighbours prohibition, will not be benefited by ours. On the contrary, they, and almost all the other classes of our citizens, will thereby be obliged to pay dearer than before for certain goods. Every such law, therefore, imposes a real tax upon the whole country, not in favour of that particular class of workmen who were

injured by our neighbours prohibitions, but of some other class.

The case in which it may sometimes be a matter of deliberation, how far, or in what manner, it is proper to restore the free importation of foreign goods, after it has been for some time interrupted, is when particular manufactures, by means of high duties or prohibitions upon all foreign goods which can come into competition with them, have been so far extended as to employ a great multitude of hands. Humanity may in this case require that the freedom of trade should be restored only by slow gradations, and with a good deal of reserve and circumspection. Were those high duties and prohibitions taken away all at once, cheaper foreign goods of the same kind might be poured so fast into the home market, as to deprive all at once many thousands of our people of their ordinary employment and means of subsistence. The disorder which this would occasion might no doubt be very considerable. It would in all probability, however, be much less than is commonly imagined, for the two following reasons.

First, All those manufactures of which any part is commonly exported to other European countries without a bounty, could be very little affected by the freest importation of foreign goods. Such manufactures must be sold as cheap abroad as any other foreign goods of the same quality and kind, and consequently must be sold cheaper at home. They would still, therefore, keep possession of the home market; and though a capricious man of fashion might sometimes prefer foreign wares, merely because they were foreign, to cheaper and better goods of the same kind that were made at home, this folly could, from the nature of things, extend to so few, that it could make no sensible impression upon the general employment of the people. But a great part of all the different branches of our woollen manufacture, of our tanned leather, and of our hardware, are annually exported to other European countries without any bounty, and these are the manufactures which employ the greatest number of hands. The silk, perhaps, is the manufacture which would suffer the most by this freedom of trade, and after it the linen, though the latter much less than the former.

Secondly, Though a great number of people should, by thus restoring the freedom of trade, be thrown all at once out of their ordinary employment and common method of subsistence, it would by no means follow that they would thereby be deprived either of employment or subsistence. By the reduction of the army and navy at the end of the late war, more than 100,000 soldiers and seamen, a number equal to what is employed in the greatest manufactures, were all at once thrown out of their ordinary employment: but though they no doubt suffered some inconveniency, they were not thereby deprived of all employment and subsistence. The greater part of the seamen, it is probable, gradually betook themselves to the merchant service as they could find occasion, and in the mean time both they and the soldiers were absorbed in the great mass of the people, and employed in a great variety of occupations. Not only no great convulsion, but no sensible disorder, arose from so great a change in the situation of more than 100,000 men, all accustomed to the use of arms, and many of them to rapine and plunder. The number of vagrants was scarce anywhere sensibly increased by it; even the wages of labour were not reduced by it in any occupation, so far as I have been able to learn, except in that of seamen in the merchant service. But if we compare together the habits of a soldier and of any sort of manufacturer, we shall find that those of the latter do not tend so much to disqualify him from being employed in a new trade, as those of the former from being employed in any. The manufacturer has always been accustomed to look for his subsistence from his labour only; the soldier to expect it from his pay. Application and industry have been familiar to the one; idleness and dissipation to the other. But it is surely much easier to change the direction of industry from one sort of labour to another, than to turn idleness and dissipation to any. To the greater part of manufactures, besides,

it has already been observed, there are other collateral manufactures of so similar a nature, that a workman can easily transfer his industry from one of them to another. The greater part of such workmen, too, are occasionally employed in country labour.

The stock which employed them in a particular manufacture before, will still remain in the country, to employ an equal number of people in some other way. The capital of the country remaining the same, the demand for labour will likewise be the same, or very nearly the same, though it may be exerted in different places, and for different occupations. Soldiers and seamen, indeed, when discharged from the king's service, are at liberty to exercise any trade within any town or place of Great Britain or Ireland. Let the same natural liberty of exercising what species of industry they please, be restored to all his Majesty's subjects, in the same manner as to soldiers and seamen; that is, break down the exclusive privileges of corporations, and repeal the statute of apprenticeship, both which are really encroachments upon natural Liberty, and add to those the repeal of the law of settlements, so that a poor workman, when thrown out of employment, either in one trade or in one place, may seek for it in another trade or in another place, without the fear either of a prosecution or of a removal; and neither the public nor the individuals will suffer much more from the occasional disbanding some particular classes of manufacturers, than from that of the soldiers. Our manufacturers have no doubt great merit with their country, but they cannot have more than those who defend it with their blood, nor deserve to be treated with more delicacy.

To expect, indeed, that the freedom of trade should ever be entirely restored in Great Britain, is as absurd as to expect that an Oceana or Utopia should ever be established in it. Not only the prejudices of the public, but, what is much more unconquerable, the private interests of many individuals, irresistibly oppose it. Were the officers of the army to oppose, with the same zeal and unanimity, any reduction in the number of forces, with which master manufacturers set themselves against every law that is likely to increase the number of their rivals in the home market; were the former to animate their soldiers. In the same manner as the latter inflame their workmen, to attack with violence and outrage the proposers of any such regulation; to attempt to reduce the army would be as dangerous as it has now become to attempt to diminish, in any respect, the monopoly which our manufacturers have obtained against us. This monopoly has so much increased the number of some particular tribes of them, that, like an overgrown standing army, they have become formidable to the government, and, upon many occasions, intimidate the legislature. The member of parliament who supports every proposal for strengthening this monopoly, is sure to acquire not only the reputation of understanding trade, but great popularity and influence with an order of men whose numbers and wealth render them of great importance. If he opposes them, on the contrary, and still more, if he has authority enough to be able to thwart them, neither the most acknowledged probity, nor the highest rank, nor the greatest public services, can protect him from the most infamous abuse and detraction, from personal insults, nor sometimes from real danger, arising from the insolent outrage of furious and disappointed mono*polis*ts.

The undertaker of a great manufacture, who, by the home markets being suddenly laid open to the competition of foreigners, should be obliged to abandon his trade, would no doubt suffer very considerably. That part of his capital which had usually been employed in purchasing materials, and in paying his workmen, might, without much difficulty, perhaps, find another employment; but that part of it which was fixed in workhouses, and in the instruments of trade, could scarce be disposed of without considerable loss. The equitable regard, therefore, to his interest, requires that changes of this kind should never be introduced suddenly, but slowly, gradually, and after a very long warning. The legislature, were it possible that its deliberations could be always

directed, not by the clamorous importunity of partial interests, but by an extensive view of the general good, ought, upon this very account, perhaps, to be particularly careful, neither to establish any new monopolies of this kind, nor to extend further those which are already established. Every such regulation introduces some degree of real disorder into the constitution of the state, which it will be difficult afterwards to cure without occasioning another disorder.

How far it may be proper to impose taxes upon the importation of foreign goods, in order not to prevent their importation, but to raise a revenue for government, I shall consider hereafter when I come to treat of taxes. Taxes imposed with a view to prevent, or even to diminish importation, are evidently as destructive of the revenue of the customs as of the freedom of trade.

. . .

BOOK V. OF THE REVENUE OF THE SOVEREIGN OR COMMONWEALTH

. . .

PART II. Of the Expense of Justice

The second duty of the sovereign, that of protecting, as far as possible, every member of the society from the injustice or oppression of every other member of it, or the duty of establishing an exact administration of justice, requires two very different degrees of expense in the different periods of society.

Among nations of hunters, as there is scarce any property, or at least none that exceeds the value of two or three days labour; so there is seldom any established magistrate, or any regular administration of justice. Men who have no property, can injure one another only in their persons or reputations. But when one man kills, wounds, beats, or defames another, though he to whom the injury is done suffers, he who does it receives no benefit. It is otherwise with the injuries to property. The benefit of the person who does the injury is often equal to the loss of him who suffers it. Envy, malice, or resentment, are the only passions which can prompt one man to injure another in his person or reputation. But the greater part of men are not very frequently under the influence of those passions; and the very worst men are so only occasionally. As their gratification, too, how agreeable soever it may be to certain characters, is not attended with any real or permanent advantage, it is, in the greater part of men, commonly restrained by prudential considerations. Men may live together in society with some tolerable degree of security, though there is no civil magistrate to protect them from the injustice of those passions. But avarice and ambition in the rich, in the poor the hatred of labour and the love of present ease and enjoyment, are the passions which prompt to invade property; passions much more steady in their operation, and much more universal in their influence. Wherever there is a great property, there is great inequality. For one very rich man, there must be at least five hundred poor, and the affluence of the few supposes the indigence of the many. The affluence of the rich excites the indignation of the poor, who are often both driven by want, and prompted by envy to invade his possessions. It is only under the shelter of the civil magistrate, that the owner of that valuable property, which is acquired by the labour of many years, or perhaps of many successive generations, can sleep a single night in security. He is at all times surrounded by unknown enemies, whom, though he never provoked, he can never appease, and from whose injustice he can be protected only by the powerful arm of the civil magistrate, continually held up to chastise it. The acquisition of valuable and extensive property, therefore, necessarily requires the establishment of civil government. Where there is no property, or at least none that exceeds the value of two or three days labour, civil government is not so necessary.

Civil government supposes a certain subordination. But as the necessity of civil government gradually grows up with the acquisition of valuable property; so the principal causes, which naturally introduce subordination, gradually grow up with the growth of that valuable property.

The causes or circumstances which naturally introduce subordination, or which naturally and antecedent to any civil institution, give some men some superiority over the greater part of their brethren, seem to be four in number.

The first of those causes or circumstances, is the superiority of personal qualifications, of strength, beauty, and agility of body; of wisdom and virtue; of prudence, justice, fortitude, and moderation of mind. The qualifications of the body, unless supported by those of the mind, can give little authority in any period of society. He is a very strong man, who, by mere strength of body, can force two weak ones to obey him. The qualifications of the mind can alone give very great authority. They are however, invisible qualities; always disputable, and generally disputed. No society, whether barbarous or civilized, has ever found it convenient to settle the rules of precedency of rank and subordination, according to those invisible qualities; but according to something that is more plain and palpable.

The second of those causes or circumstances, is the superiority of age. An old man, provided his age is not so far advanced as to give suspicion of dotage, is everywhere more respected than a young man of equal rank, fortune, and abilities. Among nations of hunters, such as the native tribes of North America, age is the sole foundation of rank and precedency. Among them, father is the appellation of a superior; brother, of an equal; and son, of an inferior. In the most opulent and civilized nations, age regulates rank among those who are in every other respect equal; and among whom, therefore, there is nothing else to regulate it. Among brothers and among sisters, the eldest always takes place; and in the succession of the paternal estate, everything which cannot be divided, but must go entire to one person, such as a title of honour, is in most cases given to the eldest. Age is a plain and palpable quality, which admits of no dispute.

The third of those causes or circumstances, is the superiority of fortune. The authority of riches, however, though great in every age of society, is, perhaps, greatest in the rudest ages of society, which admits of any considerable inequality of fortune. A Tartar chief, the increase of whose flocks and herds is sufficient to maintain a thousand men, cannot well employ that increase in any other way than in maintaining a thousand men. The rude state of his society does not afford him any manufactured produce any trinkets or baubles of any kind, for which he can exchange that part of his rude produce which is over and above his own consumption. The thousand men whom he thus maintains, depending entirely upon him for their subsistence, must both obey his orders in war, and submit to his jurisdiction in peace. He is necessarily both their general and their judge, and his chieftainship is the necessary effect of the superiority of his fortune. In an opulent and civilized society, a man may possess a much greater fortune, and yet not be able to command a dozen of people. Though the produce of his estate may be sufficient to maintain, and may, perhaps, actually maintain, more than a thousand people, yet, as those people pay for everything which they get from him, as he gives scarce any thing to any body but in exchange for an equivalent, there is scarce anybody who considers himself as entirely dependent upon him, and his authority extends only over a few menial servants. The authority of fortune, however, is very great, even in an opulent and civilized society. That it is much greater than that either of age or of personal qualities, has been the constant complaint of every period of society which admitted of any considerable inequality of fortune. The first period of society, that of hunters, admits of no such inequality. Universal poverty establishes their universal equality; and the superiority, either of age or of personal qualities, are the feeble, but the sole foundations of authority and subordination. There is, therefore, little or no authority or subordination in this period of society. The second period of society, that of shepherds, admits of very great inequalities of fortune, and there is no period in which the superiority of fortune gives so great authority to those who possess it. There is no period, accordingly, in which authority and subordination are more perfectly established.

The authority of an Arabian scherif is very great; that of a Tartar khan altogether despotical.

The fourth of those causes or circumstances, is the superiority of birth. Superiority of birth supposes an ancient superiority of fortune in the family of the person who claims it. All families are equally ancient; and the ancestors of the prince, though they may be better known, cannot well be more numerous than those of the beggar. Antiquity of family means everywhere the antiquity either of wealth, or of that greatness which is commonly either founded upon wealth, or accompanied with it. Upstart greatness is everywhere less respected than ancient greatness. The hatred of usurpers, the love of the family of an ancient monarch, are in a great measure founded upon the contempt which men naturally have for the former, and upon their veneration for the latter. As a military officer submits, without reluctance, to the authority of a superior by whom he has always been commanded, but cannot bear that his inferior should be set over his head; so men easily submit to a family to whom they and their ancestors have always submitted; but are fired with indignation when another family, in whom they had never acknowledged any such superiority, assumes a dominion over them.

The distinction of birth, being subsequent to the inequality of fortune, can have no place in nations of hunters, among whom all men, being equal in fortune, must likewise be very nearly equal in birth. The son of a wise and brave man may, indeed, even among them, be somewhat more respected than a man of equal merit, who has the misfortune to be the son of a fool or a coward. The difference, however will not be very great; and there never was, I believe, a great family in the world, whose illustration was entirely derived from the inheritance of wisdom and virtue.

The distinction of birth not only may, but always does, take place among nations of shepherds. Such nations are always strangers to every sort of luxury, and great wealth can scarce ever be dissipated among them by improvident profusion. There are no nations, accordingly, who abound more in families revered and honoured on account of their descent from a long race of great and illustrious ancestors; because there are no nations among whom wealth is likely to continue longer in the same families.

Birth and fortune are evidently the two circumstances which principally set one man above another. They are the two great sources of personal distinction, and are, therefore, the principal causes which naturally establish authority and subordination among men. Among nations of shepherds, both those causes operate with their full force. The great shepherd or herdsman, respected on account of his great wealth, and of the great number of those who depend upon him for subsistence, and revered on account of the nobleness of his birth, and of the immemorial antiquity or his illustrious family, has a natural authority over all the inferior shepherds or herdsmen of his horde or clan. He can command the united force of a greater number of people than any of them. His military power is greater than that of any of them. In time of war, they are all of them naturally disposed to muster themselves under his banner, rather than under that of any other person; and his birth and fortune thus naturally procure to him some sort of executive power. By commanding, too, the united force of a greater number of people than any of them, he is best able to compel any one of them, who may have injured another, to compensate the wrong. He is the person, therefore, to whom all those who are too weak to defend themselves naturally look up for protection. It is to him that they naturally complain of the injuries which they imagine have been done to them; and his interposition, in such cases, is more easily submitted to, even by the person complained of, than that of any other person would be. His birth and fortune thus naturally procure him some sort of judicial authority.

It is in the age of shepherds, in the second period of society, that the inequality of fortune

first begins to take place, and introduces among men a degree of authority and subordination, which could not possibly exist before. It thereby introduces some degree of that civil government which is indispensably necessary for its own preservation; and it seems to do this naturally, and even independent of the consideration of that necessity. The consideration of that necessity comes, no doubt, afterwards, to contribute very much to maintain and secure that authority and subordination. The rich, in particular, are necessarily interested to support that order of things, which can alone secure them in the possession of their own advantages. Men of inferior wealth combine to defend those of superior wealth in the possession of their property, in order that men of superior wealth may combine to defend them in the possession of theirs. All the inferior shepherds and herdsmen feel, that the security of their own herds and flocks depends upon the security of those of the great shepherd or herdsman; that the maintenance of their lesser authority depends upon that of his greater authority; and that upon their subordination to him depends his power of keeping their inferiors in subordination to them. They constitute a sort of little nobility, who feel themselves interested to defend the property, and to support the authority, of their own little sovereign, in order that he may be able to defend their property, and to support their authority. Civil government, so far as it is instituted for the security of property, is, in reality, instituted for the defence of the rich against the poor, or of those who have some property against those who have none at all.

The judicial authority of such a sovereign, however, far from being a cause of expense, was, for a long time, a source of revenue to him. The persons who applied to him for justice were always willing to pay for it, and a present never failed to accompany a petition. After the authority of the sovereign, too, was thoroughly established, the person found guilty, over and above the satisfaction which he was obliged to make to the party, was like-wise forced to pay an amercement to the sovereign. He had given trouble, he had disturbed, he had broke the peace of his lord the king, and for those offences an amercement was thought due. In the Tartar governments of Asia, in the governments of Europe which were founded by the German and Scythian nations who overturned the Roman empire, the administration of justice was a considerable source of revenue, both to the sovereign, and to all the lesser chiefs or lords who exercised under him any particular jurisdiction, either over some particular tribe or clan, or over some particular territory or district. Originally, both the sovereign and the inferior chiefs used to exercise this jurisdiction in their own persons.

Afterwards, they universally found it convenient to delegate it to some substitute, bailiff, or judge. This substitute, however, was still obliged to account to his principal or constituent for the profits of the jurisdiction. Whoever reads the instructions (They are to be found in Tyrol's History of England) which were given to the judges of the circuit in the time of Henry II will see clearly that those judges were a sort of itinerant factors, sent round the country for the purpose of levying certain branches of the king's revenue. In those days, the administration of justice not only afforded a certain revenue to the sovereign, but, to procure this revenue, seems to have been one of the principal advantages which he proposed to obtain by the administration of justice.

This scheme of making the administration of justice subservient to the purposes of revenue, could scarce fail to be productive of several very gross abuses. The person who applied for justice with a large present in his hand, was likely to get something more than justice; while he who applied for it with a small one was likely to get something less. Justice, too, might frequently be delayed, in order that this present might be repeated. The amercement, besides, of the person complained of, might frequently suggest a very strong reason for finding him in the wrong, even when he had not really been so. That such abuses were far from being uncommon, the ancient history of every country in Europe bears witness.

When the sovereign or chief exercises his judicial authority in his own person, how much soever he might abuse it, it must have been scarce possible to get any redress; because there could seldom be any body powerful enough to call him to account. When he exercised it by a bailiff, indeed, redress might sometimes be had. If it was for his own benefit only, that the bailiff had been guilty of an act of injustice, the sovereign himself might not always be unwilling to punish him, or to oblige him to repair the wrong. But if it was for the benefit of his sovereign; if it was in order to make court to the person who appointed him, and who might prefer him, that he had committed any act of oppression; redress would, upon most occasions, be as impossible as if the sovereign had committed it himself. In all barbarous governments, accordingly, in all those ancient governments of Europe in particular, which were founded upon the ruins of the Roman empire, the administration of justice appears for a long time to have been extremely corrupt; far from being quite equal and impartial, even under the best monarchs, and altogether profligate under the worst.

Among nations of shepherds, where the sovereign or chief is only the greatest shepherd or herdsman of the horde or clan, he is maintained in the same manner as any of his vassals or subjects, by the increase of his own herds or flocks. Among those nations of husbandmen, who are but just come out of the shepherd state, and who are not much advanced beyond that state, such as the Greek tribes appear to have been about the time of the Trojan war, and our German and Scythian ancestors, when they first settled upon the ruins of the western empire; the sovereign or chief is, in the same manner, only the greatest landlord of the country, and is maintained in the same manner as any other landlord, by a revenue derived from his own private estate, or from what, in modern Europe, was called the demesne of the crown. His subjects, upon ordinary occasions, contribute nothing to his support, except when, in order to protect them from the oppression of some of their fellow-subjects, they stand in need of his authority. The presents which they make him upon such occasions constitute the whole ordinary revenue, the whole of the emoluments which, except, perhaps, upon some very extraordinary emergencies, he derives from his dominion over them. When Agamemnon, in Homer, offers to Achilles, for his friendship, the sovereignty of seven Greek cities, the sole advantage which he mentions as likely to be derived from it was, that the people would honour him with presents. As long as such presents, as long as the emoluments of justice, or what may be called the fees of court, constituted, in this manner, the whole ordinary revenue which the sovereign derived from his sovereignty, it could not well be expected, it could not even decently be proposed, that he should give them up altogether. It might, and it frequently was proposed, that he should regulate and ascertain them. But after they had been so regulated and ascertained, how to hinder a person who was all-powerful from extending them beyond those regulations, was still very difficult, not to say impossible. During the continuance of this state of things, therefore, the corruption of justice, naturally resulting from the arbitrary and uncertain nature of those presents, scarce admitted of any effectual remedy.

But when, from different causes, chiefly from the continually increasing expense of defending the nation against the invasion of other nations, the private estate of the sovereign had become altogether insufficient for defraying the expense of the sovereignty; and when it had become necessary that the people should, for their own security, contribute towards this expense by taxes of different kinds; it seems to have been very commonly stipulated, that no present for the administration of justice should, under any pretence, be accepted either by the sovereign, or by his bailiffs and substitutes, the judges. Those presents, it seems to have been supposed, could more easily be abolished altogether, than effectually regulated and ascertained. Fixed salaries were appointed to the judges, which were supposed to compensate to them the loss of

whatever might have been their share of the ancient emoluments of justice; as the taxes more than compensated to the sovereign the loss of his. Justice was then said to be administered gratis.

Justice, however, never was in reality administered gratis in any country. Lawyers and attorneys, at least, must always be paid by the parties; and if they were not, they would perform their duty still worse than they actually perform it. The fees annually paid to lawyers and attorneys, amount, in every court, to a much greater sum than the salaries of the judges. The circumstance of those salaries being paid by the crown, can nowhere much diminish the necessary expense of a law-suit. But it was not so much to diminish the expense, as to prevent the corruption of justice, that the judges were prohibited from receiving my present or fee from the parties.

The office of judge is in itself so very honourable, that men are willing to accept of it, though accompanied with very small emoluments. The inferior office of justice of peace, though attended with a good deal of trouble, and in most cases with no emoluments at all, is an object of ambition to the greater part of our country gentlemen. The salaries of all the different judges, high and low, together with the whole expense of the administration and execution of justice, even where it is not managed with very good economy, makes, in any civilized country, but a very inconsiderable part of the whole expense of government.

The whole expense of justice, too, might easily be defrayed by the fees of court; and, without exposing the administration of justice to any real hazard of corruption, the public revenue might thus be entirely discharged from a certain, though perhaps but a small incumbrance. It is difficult to regulate the fees of court effectually, where a person so powerful as the sovereign is to share in them and to derive any considerable part of his revenue from them. It is very easy, where the judge is the principal person who can reap any benefit from them. The law can very easily oblige the judge to respect the regulation though it might not always be able to make the sovereign respect it. Where the fees of court are precisely regulated and ascertained where they are paid all at once, at a certain period of every process, into the hands of a cashier or receiver, to be by him distributed in certain known proportions among the different judges after the process is decided and not till it is decided; there seems to be no more danger of corruption than when such fees are prohibited altogether. Those fees, without occasioning any considerable increase in the expense of a law-suit, might be rendered fully sufficient for defraying the whole expense of justice. But not being paid to the judges till the process was determined, they might be some incitement to the diligence of the court in examining and deciding it. In courts which consisted of a considerable number of judges, by proportioning the share of each judge to the number of hours and days which he had employed in examining the process, either in the court, or in a committee, by order of the court, those fees might give some encouragement to the diligence of each particular judge. Public services are never better performed, than when their reward comes only in consequence of their being performed, and is proportioned to the diligence employed in performing them. In the different parliaments of France, the fees of court (called epices and vacations) constitute the far greater part of the emoluments of the judges. After all deductions are made, the neat salary paid by the crown to a counsellor or judge in the parliament of Thoulouse, in rank and dignity the second parliament of the kingdom, amounts only to 150 livres, about £6:11s. sterling a-year. About seven years ago, that sum was in the same place the ordinary yearly wages of a common footman. The distribution of these epices, too, is according to the diligence of the judges. A diligent judge gains a comfortable, though moderate revenue, by his office; an idle one gets little more than his salary. Those parliaments are, perhaps, in many respects, not very convenient courts of justice; but they have never been accused; they seem never even to have been suspected of corruption.

The fees of court seem originally to have been the principal support of the different courts of justice in England. Each court endeavoured to draw to itself as much business as it could, and was, upon that account, willing to take cognizance of many suits which were not originally intended to fall under its jurisdiction. The court of king's bench, instituted for the trial of criminal causes only, took cognizance of civil suits; the plaintiff pretending that the defendant, in not doing him justice, had been guilty of some trespass or misdemeanour. The court of exchequer, instituted for the levying of the king's revenue, and for enforcing the payment of such debts only as were due to the king, took cognizance of all other contract debts; the plaintiff alleging that he could not pay the king, because the defendant would not pay him.

In consequence of such fictions, it came, in many cases, to depend altogether upon the parties, before what court they would choose to have their cause tried, and each court endeavoured, by superior dispatch and impartiality, to draw to itself as many causes as it could. The present admirable constitution of the courts of justice in England was, perhaps, originally, in a great measure, formed by this emulation, which anciently took place between their respective judges: each judge endeavouring to give, in his own court, the speediest and most effectual remedy which the law would admit, for every sort of injustice.

Originally, the courts of law gave damages only for breach of contract. The court of chancery, as a court of conscience, first took upon it to enforce the specific performance of agreements. When the breach of contract consisted in the non-payment of money, the damage sustained could be compensated in no other way than by ordering payment, which was equivalent to a specific performance of the agreement. In such cases, therefore, the remedy of the courts of law was sufficient. It was not so in others. When the tenant sued his lord for having unjustly outed him of his lease, the damages which he recovered were by no means equivalent to the possession of the land. Such causes, therefore, for some time, went all to the court of chancery, to the no small loss of the courts of law. It was to draw back such causes to themselves, that the courts of law are said to have invented the artificial and fictitious writ of ejectment, the most effectual remedy for an unjust outer or dispossession of land.

A stamp-duty upon the law proceedings of each particular court, to be levied by that court, and applied towards the maintenance of the judges, and other officers belonging to it, might in the same manner, afford a revenue sufficient for defraying the expense of the administration of justice, without bringing any burden upon the general revenue of the society. The judges, indeed, might in this case, be under the temptation of multiplying unnecessarily the proceedings upon every cause, in order to increase, as much as possible, the produce of such a stamp-duty. It has been the custom in modern Europe to regulate, upon most occasions, the payment of the attorneys and clerks of court according to the number of pages which they had occasion to write; the court, however, requiring that each page should contain so many lines, and each line so many words. In order to increase their payment, the attorneys and clerks have contrived to multiply words beyond all necessity, to the corruption of the law language of, I believe, every court of justice in Europe. A like temptation might, perhaps, occasion a like corruption in the form of law proceedings.

But whether the administration of justice be so contrived as to defray its own expense, or whether the judges be maintained by fixed salaries paid to them from some other fund, it does not seen necessary that the person or persons entrusted with the executive power should be charged with the management of that fund, or with the payment of those salaries. That fund might arise from the rent of landed estates, the management of each estate being entrusted to the particular court which was to be maintained by it. That fund might arise even from the interest of a sum of money, the lending out of which might, in the same manner, be entrusted to the court

which was to be maintained by it. A part, though indeed but a small part of the salary of the judges of the court of session in Scotland, arises from the interest of a sum of money. The necessary instability of such a fund seems, however, to render it an improper one for the maintenance of an institution which ought to last forever.

The separation of the judicial from the executive power, seems originally to have arisen from the increasing business of the society, in consequence of its increasing improvement. The administration of justice became so laborious and so complicated a duty, as to require the undivided attention of the person to whom it was entrusted. The person entrusted with the executive power, not having leisure to attend to the decision of private causes himself, a deputy was appointed to decide them in his stead. In the progress of the Roman greatness, the consul was too much occupied with the political affairs of the state, to attend to the administration of justice. A praetor, therefore, was appointed to administer it in his stead. In the progress of the European monarchies, which were founded upon the ruins of the Roman empire, the sovereigns and the great lords came universally to consider the administration of justice as an office both too laborious and too ignoble for them to execute in their own persons. They universally, therefore, discharged themselves of it, by appointing a deputy, bailiff or judge.

When the judicial is united to the executive power, it is scarce possible that justice should not frequently be sacrificed to what is vulgarly called politics. The persons entrusted with the great interests of the state may even without any corrupt views, sometimes imagine it necessary to sacrifice to those interests the rights of a private man. But upon the impartial administration of justice depends the liberty of every individual, the sense which he has of his own security. In order to make every individual feel himself perfectly secure in the possession of every right which belongs to him, it is not only necessary that the judicial should be separated from the executive power, but that it should be rendered as much as possible independent of that power. The judge should not be liable to be removed from his office according to the caprice of that power. The regular payment of his salary should not depend upon the good will, or even upon the good economy of that power.

PART III. Of the Expense of public Works and public Institutions.

The third and last duty of the sovereign or commonwealth, is that of erecting and maintaining those public institutions and those public works, which though they may be in the highest degree advantageous to a great society, are, however, of such a nature, that the profit could never repay the expense to any individual, or small number of individuals; and which it, therefore, cannot be expected that any individual, or small number of individuals, should erect or maintain. The performance of this duty requires, too, very different degrees of expense in the different periods of society.

After the public institutions and public works necessary for the defence of the society, and for the administration of justice, both of which have already been mentioned, the other works and institutions of this kind are chiefly for facilitating the commerce of the society, and those for promoting the instruction of the people. The institutions for instruction are of two kinds: those for the education of the youth, and those for the instruction of people of all ages. The consideration of the manner in which the expense of those different sorts of public works and institutions may be most properly defrayed will divide this third part of the present chapter into three different articles.

ARTICLE I.--Of the public Works and Institutions for facilitating the Commerce of the Society.

And, first, of those which are necessary for facilitating Commerce in general.

That the erection and maintenance of the public works which facilitate the commerce of any country, such as good roads, bridges, navigable canals, harbours, etc. must require very different degrees of expense in the different periods of society, is evident without any proof. The expense of making and maintaining the public roads of any country must evidently increase with the annual produce of the land and labour of that country, or with the quantity and weight of the goods which it becomes necessary to fetch and carry upon those roads. The strength of a bridge must be suited to the number and weight of the carriages which are likely to pass over it. The depth and the supply of water for a navigable canal must be proportioned to the number and tonnage of the lighters which are likely to carry goods upon it; the extent of a harbour, to the number of the shipping which are likely to take shelter in it.

It does not seem necessary that the expense of those public works should be defrayed from that public revenue, as it is commonly called, of which the collection and application are in most countries, assigned to the executive power. The greater part of such public works may easily be so managed, as to afford a particular revenue, sufficient for defraying their own expense without bringing any burden upon the general revenue of the society.

A highway, a bridge, a navigable canal, for example, may, in most cases, be both made add maintained by a small toll upon the carriages which make use of them; a harbour, by a moderate port-duty upon the tonnage of the shipping which load or unload in it. The coinage, another institution for facilitating commerce, in many countries, not only defrays its own expense, but affords a small revenue or a seignorage to the sovereign. The post-office, another institution for the same purpose, over and above defraying its own expense, affords, in almost all countries, a very considerable revenue to the sovereign.

When the carriages which pass over a highway or a bridge, and the lighters which sail upon a navigable canal, pay toll in proportion to their weight or their tonnage, they pay for the maintenance of those public works exactly in proportion to the wear and tear which they occasion of them. It seems scarce possible to invent a more equitable way of maintaining such works. This tax or toll, too, though it is advanced by the carrier, is finally paid by the consumer, to whom it must always be charged in the price of the goods. As the expense of carriage, however, is very much reduced by means of such public works, the goods, notwithstanding the toll, come cheaper to the consumer than they could otherwise have done, their price not being so much raised by the toll, as it is lowered by the cheapness of the carriage. The person who finally pays this tax, therefore, gains by the application more than he loses by the payment of it. His payment is exactly in proportion to his gain. It is, in reality, no more than a part of that gain which he is obliged to give up, in order to get the rest. It seems impossible to imagine a more equitable method of raising a tax. When the toll upon carriages of luxury, upon coaches, post-chaises, etc. is made somewhat higher in proportion to their weight, than upon carriages of necessary use, such as carts, waggons, etc. the indolence and vanity of the rich is made to contribute, in a very easy manner, to the relief of the poor, by rendering cheaper the transportation of heavy goods to all the different parts of the country.

When high-roads, bridges, canals, etc. are in this manner made and supported by the commerce which is carried on by means of them, they can be made only where that commerce requires them, and, consequently, where it is proper to make them. Their expense, too, their grandeur and magnificence, must be suited to what that commerce can afford to pay. They must be made, consequently, as it is proper to make them. A magnificent high-road cannot be made through a desert country, where there is little or no commerce, or merely because it happens to lead to the country villa of the intendant of the province, or to that of some great lord, to whom the intendant finds it convenient to make his court. A great bridge cannot be thrown over a

river at a place where nobody passes, or merely to embellish the view from the windows of a neighbouring palace; things which sometimes happen in countries, where works of this kind are carried on by any other revenue than that which they themselves are capable of affording.

In several different parts of Europe, the toll or lock-duty upon a canal is the property of private persons, whose private interest obliges them to keep up the canal. If it is not kept in tolerable order, the navigation necessarily ceases altogether, and, along with it, the whole profit which they can make by the tolls. If those tolls were put under the management of commissioners, who had themselves no interest in them, they might be less attentive to the maintenance of the works which produced them. The canal of Languedoc cost the king of France and the province upwards of thirteen millions of livres, which (at twenty-eight livres the mark of silver, the value of French money in the end of the last century) amounted to upwards of nine hundred thousand pounds sterling. When that great work was finished, the most likely method, it was found, of keeping it in constant repair, was to make a present of the tolls to Riquet, the engineer who planned and conducted the work.

Those tolls constitute, at present, a very large estate to the different branches of the family of that gentleman, who have, therefore, a great interest to keep the work in constant repair. But had those tolls been put under the management of commissioners, who had no such interest, they might perhaps, have been dissipated in ornamental and unnecessary expenses, while the most essential parts of the works were allowed to go to ruin.

The tolls for the maintenance of a highroad cannot, with any safety, be made the property of private persons. A high-road, though entirely neglected, does not become altogether impassable, though a canal does. The proprietors of the tolls upon a high-road, therefore, might neglect altogether the repair of the road, and yet continue to levy very nearly the same tolls. It is proper, therefore, that the tolls for the maintenance of such a work should be put under the management of commissioners or trustees.

In Great Britain, the abuses which the trustees have committed in the management of those tolls, have, in many cases, been very justly complained of. At many turnpikes, it has been said, the money levied is more than double of what is necessary for executing, in the completest manner, the work, which is often executed in a very slovenly manner, and sometimes not executed at all. The system of repairing the high-roads by tolls of this kind, it must be observed, is not of very long standing. We should not wonder, therefore, if it has not yet been brought to that degree of perfection of which it seems capable. If mean and improper persons are frequently appointed trustees; and if proper courts of inspection and account have not yet been established for controlling their conduct, and for reducing the tolls to what is barely sufficient for executing the work to be done by them; the recency of the institution both accounts and apologizes for those defects, of which, by the wisdom of parliament, the greater part may, in due time, be gradually remedied.

The money levied at the different turnpikes in Great Britain, is supposed to exceed so much what is necessary for repairing the roads, that the savings which, with proper economy, might be made from it, have been considered, even by some ministers, as a very great resource, which might, at some time or another, be applied to the exigencies of the state. Government, it has been said, by taking the management of the turnpikes into its own hands, and by employing the soldiers, who would work for a very small addition to their pay, could keep the roads in good order, at a much less expense than it can be done by trustees, who have no other workmen to employ, but such as derive their whole subsistence from their wages. A great revenue, half a million, perhaps {Since publishing the two first editions of this book, I have got good reasons to believe that all the turnpike tolls levied in Great Britain do not produce a neat revenue that amounts to half a million; a sum which, under the management of government, would not be sufficient to keep, in repair five of the principal roads in the kingdom}, it has been pretended, might in this manner be gained, without laying any new burden upon the people; and the turnpike roads might be made to contribute to the general expense of the state, in the same manner as the post-office does at present.

That a considerable revenue might be gained in this manner, I have no doubt, though probably not near so much as the projectors of this plan have supposed. The plan itself, however, seems liable to several very important objections.

First, If the tolls which are levied at the turnpikes should ever be considered as one of the resources for supplying the exigencies of the state, they would certainly be augmented as those exigencies were supposed to require. According to the policy of Great Britain, therefore, they would probably be augmented very fast. The facility with which a great revenue could be drawn from them, would probably encourage administration to recur very frequently to this resource. Though it may, perhaps, be more than doubtful whether half a million could by any economy be saved out of the present tolls, it can scarcely be doubted, but that a million might be saved out of them, if they were doubled; and perhaps two millions, if they were tripled {I have now good reason to believe that all these conjectural sums are by much too large.}. This great revenue, too, might be levied without the appointment of a single new officer to collect and receive it. But the turnpike tolls, being continually augmented in this manner, instead of facilitating the inland commerce of the country, as at present, would soon become a very great incumbrance upon it. The expense of transporting all heavy goods from one part of the country to another, would soon be so much increased, the market for all such goods, consequently, would soon be so much narrowed, that their production would be in a great measure discouraged, and the most important branches of the domestic industry of the country annihilated altogether.

Secondly, A tax upon carriages, in proportion to their weight, though a very equal tax when applied to the sole purpose of repairing the roads, is a very unequal one when applied to any other purpose, or to supply the common exigencies of the state. When it is applied to the sole purpose above mentioned, each carriage is supposed to pay exactly for the wear and tear which that carriage occasions of the roads. But when it is applied to any other purpose, each carriage is supposed to pay for more than that wear and tear, and contributes to the supply of some other exigency of the state. But as the turnpike toll raises the price of goods in proportion to their weight and not to their value, it is chiefly paid by the consumers of coarse and bulky, not by those of precious and light commodities. Whatever exigency of the state, therefore, this tax might be intended to supply, that exigency would be chiefly supplied at the expense of the poor, not of the rich; at the expense of those who are least able to supply it, not of those who are most able.

Thirdly, If government should at any time neglect the reparation of the high-roads, it would be still more difficult, than it is at present, to compel the proper application of any part of the turnpike tolls. A large revenue might thus be levied upon the people, without any part of it being applied to the only purpose to which a revenue levied in this manner ought ever to be applied. If the meanness and poverty of the trustees of turnpike roads render it sometimes difficult, at present, to oblige them to repair their wrong; their wealth and greatness would render it ten times more so in the case which is here supposed.

In France, the funds destined for the reparation of the high-roads are under the immediate direction of the executive power. Those funds consist, partly in a certain number of days labour, which the country people are in most parts of Europe obliged to give to the reparation of the highways; and partly in such a portion of the general revenue of the state as the king chooses to spare from his other expenses.

By the ancient law of France, as well as by that of most other parts of Europe, the labour of the country people was under the direction of a local or provincial magistracy, which had no immediate dependency upon the king's council. But, by the present practice, both the labour of the country people, and whatever other fund the king may choose to assign for the reparation of the high-roads in any particular province or generality, are entirely under the management of the intendant; an officer who is appointed and removed by the king's council who receives his orders from it, and is in constant correspondence with it. In the progress of despotism, the authority of the executive power gradually absorbs that of every other power in the state, and assumes to itself the management of every branch of revenue which is destined for any public purpose. In France, however, the great post-roads, the roads which make the communication between the principal towns of the kingdom, are in general kept in good order; and, in some provinces, are even a good deal superior to the greater part of the turnpike roads of England. But what we call the cross roads, that is, the far greater part of the roads in the country, are entirely neglected, and are in many places absolutely impassable for any heavy carriage. In some places it is even dangerous to travel on horseback, and mules are the only conveyance which can safely be trusted. The proud minister of an ostentatious court, may frequently take pleasure in executing a work of splendour and magnificence, such as a great highway, which is frequently seen by the principal nobility, whose applauses not only flatter his vanity, but even contribute to support his interest at court. But to execute a great number of little works, in which nothing that can be done can make any great appearance, or excite the smallest degree of admiration in any traveller, and which, in short, have nothing to recommend them but their extreme utility, is a business which appears, in every respect, too mean and paltry to merit the attention of so great a magistrate. Under such an administration therefore, such works are almost always entirely neglected.

In China, and in several other governments of Asia, the executive power charges itself both with the reparation of the high-roads, and with the maintenance of the navigable canals. In the instructions which are given to the governor of each province, those objects, it is said, are constantly recommended to him, and the judgment which the court forms of his conduct is very much regulated by the attention which he appears to have paid to this part of his instructions. This branch of public police, accordingly, is said to be very much attended to in all those countries, but particularly in China, where the high-roads, and still more the navigable canals, it is pretended, exceed very much everything of the same kind which is known in Europe. The accounts of those works, however, which have been transmitted to Europe, have generally been drawn up by weak and wondering travellers; frequently by stupid and lying missionaries. If they had been examined by more intelligent eyes, and if the accounts of them had been reported by more faithful witnesses, they would not, perhaps, appear to be so wonderful. The account which Bernier gives of some works of this kind in Indostan, falls very short of what had been reported of them by other travellers, more disposed to the marvellous than he was. It may too, perhaps, be in those countries, as it is in France, where the great roads, the great communications, which are likely to be the subjects of conversation at the court and in the capital, are attended to, and all the rest neglected. In China, besides, in Indostan, and in several other governments of Asia, the revenue of the sovereign arises almost altogether from a land tax or land rent, which rises or falls with the rise and fall of the annual produce of the land. The great interest of the sovereign, therefore, his revenue, is in such countries necessarily and immediately connected with the cultivation of the land, with the greatness of its produce, and with the value of its produce. But in order to render that produce both as great and as valuable as possible, it is necessary to procure to it as extensive a market as possible, and consequently to establish the freest, the easiest, and the least expensive communication between all the different parts of the country; which can be done only by means of the best roads and the best navigable canals. But the revenue of the sovereign does not, in any part of Europe, arise chiefly from a land tax or land rent. In all the great kingdoms of Europe, perhaps, the greater part of it may ultimately depend upon the produce of the land: but that dependency is neither so immediate nor so evident. In Europe, therefore, the sovereign does not feel himself so directly called upon to promote the increase, both in quantity and value of the produce of the land, or, by maintaining good roads and canals, to provide the most extensive market for that produce.

Though it should be true, therefore, what I apprehend is not a little doubtful, that in some parts of Asia this department of the public police is very properly managed by the executive power, there is not the least probability that, during the present state of things, it could be tolerably managed by that power in any part of Europe.

Even those public works, which are of such a nature that they cannot afford any revenue for maintaining themselves, but of which the conveniency is nearly confined to some particular place or district, are always better maintained by a local or provincial revenue, under the management of a local and provincial administration, than by the general revenue of the state, of which the executive power must always have the management. Were the streets of London to be lighted and paved at the expense of the treasury, is there any probability that they would be so well lighted and paved as they are at present, or even at so small an expense? The expense, besides, instead of being raised by a local tax upon the inhabitants of each particular street, parish, or district in London, would, in this case, be defrayed out of the general revenue of the state, and would consequently be raised by a tax upon all the inhabitants of the kingdom, of whom the greater part derive no sort of benefit from the lighting and paving of the streets of London.

The abuses which sometimes creep into the local and provincial administration of a local and provincial revenue, how enormous soever they may appear, are in reality, however, almost always very trifling in comparison of those which commonly take place in the administration and expenditure of the revenue of a great empire. They are, besides, much more easily corrected. Under the local or provincial administration of the justices of the peace in Great Britain, the six days labour which the country people are obliged to give to the reparation of the highways, is not always, perhaps, very judiciously applied, but it is scarce ever exacted with any circumstance of cruelty or oppression. In France, under the administration of the intendants, the application is not always more judicious, and the exaction is frequently the most cruel and oppressive. Such corvees, as they are called, make one of the principal instruments of tyranny by which those officers chastise any parish or communeaute, which has had the misfortune to fall under their displeasure.

. . .

Chapter 11: Utilitarianism & Politics

> *Comprehension questions you should be able to answer after reading this chapter:*
>
> 1. How do utilitarians (in general) determine what is morally right and morally wrong?
> 2. Who "counts" in the utilitarian cost-benefit analysis?
> 3. What is the "principle of utility?" What is the "greatest happiness principle?"
> 4. What is the difference between "act" utilitarianism and "rule" utilitarianism?
> 5. What is meant by the criticism of utilitarianism that it is too "artificial" and "unrealistic?" How might a utilitarian respond to this criticism?
> 6. What is meant by the criticism of utilitarianism that it allows, and even requires, "unjust" actions? How might a utilitarian respond?
> 7. What is meant by the criticism of utilitarianism that it is a "Swinish doctrine?" How does John Stuart Mill respond?
> 8. What is meant by the criticism of utilitarianism that it is too difficult to anticipate the consequences of our actions? How might a utilitarian respond?
> 9. According to Mill, what is the only justification for the use of force/coercion by the government against a person?
> 10. What is the difference between an act of commission and an act of omission?
> 11. What are Mill's three regions of human liberty?
> 12. How does Mill use utilitarianism to justify both freedom of expression and freedom of lifestyle?
> 13. What are the four advantages/reasons Mill offers in defense of free expression?

At 8:46 a.m., on September 11th, 2001, American Airlines Flight 11 was intentionally crashed into the World Trade Center's North Tower. At 9:03 a.m., it was followed by United Airlines Flight 175. At 9:37 a.m., American Airlines Flight 77 was crashed into the Pentagon. United Airlines Flight 93 is believed to have been headed to either the Capitol Building or the White House, but it never reached its intended target. Passengers on Flight 93 resisted, and the plane crashed instead in a field near Shanksville, Pennsylvania at 10:03 a.m. Had the passengers not acted, and brought the plane down themselves, it is likely that the United States Air Force would have done it for them. Consider the following excerpt from an interview with (then) U.S. Vice-President Dick Cheney.

"VICE PRES. CHENEY: Well, the--I suppose the toughest decision was this question of whether or not we would intercept incoming commercial aircraft.
"TIM RUSSERT: And you decided?
"VICE PRES. CHENEY: We decided to do it. We'd, in effect, put a flying combat air patrol up over the city; F-16s with an AWACS, which is an airborne radar system, and tanker support so they could stay up a long time...
"It doesn't do any good to put up a combat air patrol if you don't give them instructions to act, if, in fact, they feel it's appropriate.

"MR. RUSSERT: So if the United States government became aware that a hijacked commercial airline[r] was destined for the White House or the Capitol, we would take the plane down?

"VICE PRES. CHENEY: Yes. The president made the decision...that if the plane would not divert...as a last resort, our pilots were authorized to take them out. Now, people say, you know, that's a horrendous decision to make. Well, it is. You've got an airplane full of American citizens, civilians, captured by...terrorists, headed and are you going to, in fact, shoot it down, obviously, and kill all those Americans on board?" (NBC, 'Meet the Press' 16 September 2001)

The United States government was prepared to shoot down a commercial passenger jet, with 40 innocent civilians onboard. Why would the government be willing to make this decision? Why, for that matter, did the passengers on Flight 93 resist their hijackers, ultimately resulting in the premature crashing of their plane? The answer, in both cases, is quite possibly the same: "It's for the greater good."

That slogan captures the central idea of utilitarianism. Utilitarianism is usually associated with Jeremy Bentham (1748-1832), James Mill (1773-1836), and his son John Stuart Mill (1806-1873)—though early traces of utilitarian thought can be found all the way back in the writings of Epicurus (341 BCE-270 BCE).

Utilitarianism is an objective theory, which is to say that utilitarians believe that the morally right thing to do in a given situation is not merely a matter of opinion, but is a *fact*. What, specifically, will be *the* morally right thing to do brings us back to the appeal to "the greater good."

Although utilitarians will often differ with respect to the particulars of their theories, what they will all have in common is an emphasis on the consequences of our actions. For that reason,

utilitarianism is one of several theories called "consequentialist." Consequentialist theories are just what they sound like: they are theories emphasizing the consequences or outcomes of our decisions and actions.

In our everyday evaluation of actions, we will sometimes forgive someone when their actions produce undesirable consequences so long as their "heart is in the right place." Not so with utilitarians. *Intentions do not matter* (morally speaking). The only thing that matters when evaluating the moral goodness or badness of an action are the *consequences* of that action.

Although some utilitarians are interested in the satisfaction of "preferences" when considering consequences, most utilitarians (including both Bentham and Mill) focus instead on "happiness." For such a simple word, happiness is notoriously difficult to define, and utilitarians have bickered over how best to understand "happiness" for centuries. For Bentham, the founder of modern utilitarian thought, happiness was to be understood in terms of pleasure, or at least the absence of pain. Unhappiness is to be understood in terms of pain.

With pleasure as our focus, the first formulation of utilitarianism is that the morally right thing to do will be whichever action produces, as a *consequence*, the most happiness (pleasure), or the least unhappiness (pain) for all involved. Bentham labeled this the "principle of utility."

The Principle of Utility

By the principle of utility is meant that principle which approves or disapproves of every action whatsoever, according to the tendency which it appears to have to augment or diminish the happiness of the party whose interest is in question: or, what is the same thing in other words, to promote or to oppose that happiness...."[348]

---

[348] Jeremy Bentham, *An Introduction to the Principles of Morals and Legislation* (1789), Chapter 1, section 2.

John Stuart Mill provides a very similar principle that he calls the "greatest happiness principle.

The Greatest Happiness Principle

The creed which accepts as the foundation of morals utility, or the greatest happiness principle, holds that actions are right in proportion as they tend to promote happiness, wrong as they tend to produce the reverse of happiness. By 'happiness' is intended pleasure, and the absence of pain; by 'unhappiness,' pain, and the privation of pleasure.[349]

One of the appeals of this approach is how intuitively powerful—even how obvious—is its basic emphasis on pleasure and pain. We don't need any argument to justify our aversion to pain and our inclinations towards pleasure. They just

"are." I like pleasure. So do you. Why? I don't know. Maybe God made me that way. Maybe there's an evolutionary advantage in creatures acquiring sentience. Maybe pleasure and pain are "Nature's" way of guiding us with respect to actions to pursue or avoid.

Whatever the ultimate explanation happens to be, we all naturally pursue pleasure, and we all naturally avoid pain. What could be more basic, more fundamental, than the value judgments that pleasure is good and pain is bad? What could be more obvious? And, if so obvious and so universal, doesn't it make sense to think that our notion of "good" and "bad," morally speaking, would have something to do with pleasure and pain? Don't we recognize that it's "good" to promote pleasure/happiness, and "bad" to promote pain/unhappiness? Isn't there an element of pleasure or pain to be found in every act we label morally good or bad?

Exercise Break

Consider the following actions usually deemed morally wrong, or at least morally suspect. Identify how each is responsible for increasing the amount of pain/unhappiness in the world. Be creative, and don't restrict yourself to short-term thinking.

- Rape
- Child abuse
- "War Crimes"
- Smoking crack cocaine
- Politicians "selling" their support to lobbyists
- Murder
- Election fraud

---

[349] John Stuart Mill, *Utilitarianism* (1863), chapter 2. Portions of this text are included at the end of this chapter.

If you actually performed the recommended exercise, you might have been surprised to see how easy it was to identify the "pain" associated with those examples. This is certainly one of the more powerful appeals of the utilitarian approach. It just seems *obvious* that we do, in fact, care about the amount of pleasure and pain not just in our own lives, but in the lives of others— indeed, in the world in general. Very often, when we condemn the actions of another (or our own actions), one of the first explanations we can offer for our condemnation involves pain.

"Stop! That *hurts.*"

Most of the time, we treat that explanation as a morally sufficient explanation. If what you are doing is hurting someone, you should stop. If you don't, you're usually doing something morally bad.

There is room for some sophistication with this approach. For example, we recognize that actual physical pain is not the only sort of "pain" that matters.

"When you did that, it really hurt my feelings."

Usually, this sort of appeal doesn't suggest that actual physical pain resulted (though, sometimes powerful emotions do seem to produce a physical reaction in the body, including feelings of pain in the stomach, head, throat, or chest). Nevertheless, we have a concept of emotional pain that is similarly motivating. Embarrassment, a feeling of betrayal, shame, fear ... all of these, while not necessarily physically painful, are nevertheless feelings we prefer to avoid, and we describe them in terms of "hurt." Most utilitarians therefore include "emotional" pain in their considerations as well.

Another layer of sophistication that utilitarianism offers, and needs, is the recognition that we do not always categorically avoid painful experiences, nor do we invariably pursue pleasurable experiences. For example, I don't enjoy going to the dentist. It's usually an uncomfortable experience, and sometimes actually painful. But, I go anyway (at least twice

each year). As another example, I have been told that shooting heroin is an intensely pleasurable experience, but I have no intention of pursuing that pleasure—nor do most other people.

We have two easy examples of avoiding pleasure and pursuing pain. Doesn't that contradict the basic values-assumptions behind utilitarianism? Not at all. Although going to the dentist can be painful, *avoiding* the dentist can be more so. I endure a little pain to avoid the greater pain of tooth decay and gum disease. Most Americans have their children inoculated against diseases even though the needles hurt them. Are they bad utilitarians? Sadists? Of course not. They recognize that the tiny and fleeting prick of a needle is far less painful than polio. Why do we avoid the pleasure of heroin? Because we wish to avoid the greater pain that follows! Not only is heroin deadly and debilitating, but it is powerfully addictive. No one who has ever known an addict would ever claim that the use of heroin is, on balance and all things considered, a "pleasurable" activity.

What these examples and their analyses indicate is that utilitarian thought can be complicated. When calculating the consequences of our actions, we often have to look beyond the immediate experience and anticipate what the consequences will be in the future. Getting a polio vaccination might be slightly painful the moment one receives it, but it spares you from the threat of a far more painful disease later on. In receiving the shot, you are still pursuing the greater happiness.

The final layer of sophistication we'll consider, before getting into the actual application of this kind of theory, involves sentience. As you know by now, utilitarians focus on pleasure and pain. Pain is to be avoided, pleasure is to be pursued, generally speaking. It is good to promote pleasure, bad to promote pain. What's probably obvious to you is that human beings are not the only creatures capable of pleasure and pain. My cat feels pain. So do dogs, and monkeys, and buffalo, and sparrows, and cows, and lots of other creatures.

Much evidence has been gathered demonstrating that mammals, birds, reptiles and amphibians, fish, and cephalopods (such as the octopus) all have central nervous systems, all have nociceptors ("pain receptors") connected to their central nervous system, and all exhibit response to damaging stimuli similar to that of human responses. Although there is less consensus among researchers, it's at least clear that even invertebrates such as lobsters have rudimentary motor responses in response to "noxious" stimulants (e.g., being dropped in boiling water!), though whether they possess a sophisticated enough nervous system for that response to be an indicator of "pain" remains subject to debate.

Debate aside, because a great many non-human creatures can clearly experience pleasure and pain, they "count" as far as utilitarianism is concerned. If pleasure is to be pursued, and pain is to be avoided, this is so for cats and cows as well as for you and me. To ignore this and to consider only human pain is arbitrary, irrational, and "speciesist" (a phrase popularized by the utilitarian Peter Singer, who intentionally wished to conjure associations with racism and sexism). Therefore, when a utilitarian considers consequences, and seeks to maximize happiness and minimize pain (sometimes referred to simply as maximizing "utility"), she will have to consider the pleasure and pain of *every creature* capable of pleasure and pain, human and non-human alike. What's more, no one counts "more" than anyone else in this calculation. My happiness is not more valuable simply because it's mine, nor is mine more valuable simply because I'm human. Everyone's happiness counts equally, all else being equal.[350]

This has been a lengthy introduction to utilitarianism! Let's see how it actually works, in application. There are two major types of utilitarian theories: act, and rule.

Act Utilitarianism

An "act utilitarian" is a utilitarian who

believes that utility is and ought to be maximized by performing a "cost-benefit analysis" for each intended action on a case-by-case basis. That is, when trying to determine the right course of action, one ought to consider all the available options, weigh their "costs" (pains) and "benefits" (pleasures) for each sentient being involved, and select the option that produces the greatest overall "utility" (i.e., most overall pleasure or least overall pain). The goal is to bring about the "best" possible consequences, given the available options.

Bentham thought that our cost-benefit analysis should be informed by the following variables. When only one sentient being is to be effected, the utility calculation will consider each of the following with regard to pleasure and pain:

1. Intensity (how pleasurable or painful the experience will be)
2. Duration (how long the pleasure or pain will last)
3. Certainty/uncertainty (how confident we can be as to the actual experiencing of the pleasure or pain)
4. Propinquity/remoteness (how soon in time the pleasure or pain will be experienced)
5. Fecundity (the tendency of the experience to produce more of its kind—more pleasure or more pain)
6. Purity (the absence of its opposite—e.g., some pleasures are mixed with pain, while others produce only pleasure)

In the likely event that more than one creature will be affected, we add one more consideration (7): the extent (number affected). This just means that if five people are involved, we will have to consider how each of the five will be affected, pleasurably or painfully, when weighing our alternatives.

If we were to adopt Bentham's method, then whenever we find ourselves presented with a

---

[350] Note that having a lesser capacity for pleasure by virtue of being a fish, for example, would mean that all else is *not* equal.

number of options, and interested in doing the morally right thing, we ought to consider each option, and calculate the pleasure and pain generated with respect to each of the variables above. After we have done so, we identify the option with the greatest overall utility (i.e., the greatest quantity of pleasure or least quantity of pain), compared to the alternatives, and this will show us the morally right thing to do. Lest we think ourselves finished, please note that Mill would add one more level of complexity to this process: "quality" of the pleasures involved.

For Mill, not all pleasures are equal, and "quantity" is not the only relevant measure of pleasure. There are the so-called "lower" pleasures, the pleasures we have in common with many other animals. Such pleasures include the pleasures of eating, drinking, sex, sleep, etc. There are also "higher" pleasures, such as creating and appreciating art, pursuing knowledge, games of skill, etc. "Higher" pleasures are qualitatively superior to lower pleasures, and Mill believes that the mere intensity of a lower pleasure is not necessarily sufficient to make it more desirable than a less intense, but superior higher pleasure.

Much has been written on the controversial nature of Mill's hierarchy, and whether or not he can actually justify that qualitative distinction. For our purposes, though, let's just assume that there is *something* legitimate about his appeal to quality, and make it our eighth variable. To recap what must be calculated in order to establish the morally right thing to do:

1. Intensity
2. Duration
3. Certainty
4. Propinquity
5. Fecundity
6. Purity
7. Extent
8. *Quality*

Honestly, I (personally) find this to be a hopeless and fruitless method—though you are certainly not required to agree with me on this point. Bentham was brilliant, and he was certainly articulating an authentic moral insight

with what he offers, but a literal assignment of positive or negative values representing pain and pleasure (often referred to as "utils"—positive when pleasure, negative when pain), somehow modified with respect to duration, certainty, "propinquity," "fecundity," and "purity" is an abominable exercise—and a needless one. Several of the variables are painfully abstract ("purity?"), speculative at best ("certainty"), and potentially arbitrary ("intensity"—not to mention Mill's notoriously subjective "quality").

Rather than create an Excel spreadsheet with a formula in an effort to discern whether the morally right thing to do, for example, is to shoot down a hijacked passenger jet with 40 innocent passengers onboard, let's try some intuition and common sense.

Hijackers had set the precedent for what they were probably going to do with United Airlines Flight 93. Three other jets had already been flown into buildings that very morning, killing everyone onboard, and many at the target sites. There was good reason to believe that the 40 passengers were going to die anyway, as terrible as that would be to admit.

Prior to September 11th, that would *not* have been the reasonable assumption to make. Organizations have been hijacking passenger jets for political purposes for over 40 years. In the vast majority of those cases, the planes are forced to land somewhere, and negotiations begin. The passengers are either freed after the demands are met (usually the release of some "political prisoners") or the jet is raided by police or military forces. On many occasions, the hijackers were slain, and a few passengers, crew, or police/military personnel often die as well, but most of the passengers end up freed and relatively unharmed. Whether or not it was the right thing to do, it at least made sense to *consider* waiting and negotiating with the hijackers. After the first intentional crashes on 9-11, it was no longer safe to assume that the plane would land, and that it would be possible to free the passengers. What became safe for us to assume is that the jet was going to be used as a weapon, and flown into a high-profile target, killing even more people.

Assuming that to be so, it's not hard to see how the cost-benefit analysis would recommend shooting down the plane. The 40 passengers are presumed to be doomed, so their pain, as well as the pain of their friends and family members appears unavoidable. What does appear to be avoidable is additional death and misery. If the jet is shot down, at least no additional people will die—and perhaps future hijackers will have to consider that they will be unable to strike their intended targets since they will be shot down instead. Maybe this will deter similar hijackings in the future? Is anyone being made "happy?" It's probably too generous to think so. This is one of those examples where the utilitarian is looking merely to minimize unhappiness. It's a terrible dilemma, with no "good" outcome available. The best the utilitarian can hope for is the "least bad" consequence.

Notice how important it was to have a sense of history. Prior to 9-11, hijackers did not have a reputation for flying planes into buildings. Now, they do. As act utilitarians, our calculations have to adjust to reflect this. Twenty years ago, the best course of action might well have been to let the plane land, and then either negotiate or use a special forces team to raid the plane. Circumstances change. Perhaps the "shoot it down" approach only makes sense when the plane has been hijacked by members of al-Qu'aida. The simple point is this: an act utilitarian will make a determination of what will maximize happiness for all involved on a case-by-case basis. Sometimes, the right thing to do is to shoot the plane down. Other times, the right thing to do might be to negotiate. Sometimes, the right thing to do is to tell the truth. Other times, the right thing to do will be to tell a lie. Sometimes, it's wrong to steal. Other times, it might be the right thing to do.

Although reliable patterns might emerge, what makes an act utilitarian an *act* utilitarian is that she performs the cost-benefit analysis for each individual situation, and recognizes that as the "input" changes, so too will the "output."

That act utilitarianism is sensitive to circumstances is seen by some to be an asset. However, the time it takes to perform such calculations on a case-by-case basis can be seen as a liability. Some are additionally concerned that subjectivity can easily creep into our calculations. Sometimes lying is wrong, other times, it's acceptable. How interesting that most of the time I conclude that it's acceptable is when *I* am the one doing the lying! Isn't it possible that we might "tip the scales" in our own favor when performing our calculations, inflating the value of our own happiness while underestimating that of others?

Rule Utilitarianism

To address these concerns, and others, some turn to "rule utilitarianism." Like act utilitarianism, rule utilitarianism emphasizes happiness, and maximizing utility. Where it differs is with regard to when and how these calculations are performed. Rule utilitarians believe that we best maximize utility by following rules which themselves maximize utility. That might sound complicated, but it's really quite simple. Far more often than not, killing innocent people causes more pain than pleasure. Therefore, human beings decided, a very long time ago, that there ought to be a rule against killing innocent people. You would find it very challenging to find a community anywhere in the world that does not forbid murder.

Rather than having to figure things out on a case-by-case basis, rule utilitarians propose that we just follow rules such as "don't kill innocent people." It's possible that in rare, exceptional cases, it might actually maximize utility to kill an innocent person, but it's a very safe assumption that killing innocent people *usually* brings more pain than pleasure, and when it appears otherwise, there's a very good chance we're skewing our calculation to our own benefit anyway. The safe thing to do (morally speaking) is to refrain from murdering people. Theft, more often than not, inflicts more pain than pleasure. Therefore, we should follow the rule that says we shouldn't steal. So, too, with rape. So, too, with lying. And so on.

The "shortcut" provided by rule utilitarianism serves to address at least some of several well-known criticisms of utilitarianism in general. We'll now consider these criticisms, as well as how utilitarians have been known to respond.

Possible problem #1: Utilitarianism is too "artificial" and unrealistic

The basic concern behind this criticism is the claim that no one "calculates" like Bentham proposes. Morality is not a math problem, and often times we must make judgment calls with very little time in which to perform a complex calculation. Therefore, utilitarianism is an unrealistic approach to moral decision-making.

Utilitarian possible response:

Sometimes we *do* perform overt cost-benefit analyses. How many of you have ever listed (either mentally, or actually on paper, or on a spread sheet) the "pros" and "cons" of the options before you, and used that list to make your decision? Even if you rarely, if ever, do so according to the eight specific variables Bentham offers, it's probable that the notion of a cost-benefit analysis is not a new and strange idea to you. Moreover, there's no reason why many of these calculations couldn't be "unconscious," or performed at an intuitive level "instantly." It does not, for example, require very much time to conclude that choking to death the guy who cuts in front of me in line does not maximize utility! That's "easy math," to say the least. Besides, utilitarians need not be bound by Bentham's specific calculation method, and could instead adopt a much simpler, more intuitive, less quantitative approach to the cost-benefit analysis which, if adopted, side-steps much of this criticism.

Finally, with regard to the charge that we haven't enough time to calculate utility, the rule utilitarian (specifically) has a simple response. Mill says "there is ample time, namely, the whole past duration of the human species." What Mill means by this is that it's not as though humans have to figure out fresh each day what sorts of actions promote utility and which do not. Murder

is reliably bad as far as utility is concerned. Humans figured out that whole "murder is bad" thing thousands of years ago. They already "did the math" for us. We no more have to rediscover the badness of murder than we have to rediscover the hotness of fire. Much of the time, the calculations have been done, and our answers are obvious, morally speaking.

It is, for most of us, a rare thing when we encounter a true moral quandary, a situation in which it is truly unclear which course of action will promote the most happiness. In those situations, we might have to work out the problem ourselves, but most of the time, no time is needed.

Possible problem #2: Utilitarianism allows, and even demands (on occasion), what we would consider to be immoral actions.

Utilitarianism promotes the greatest good for the greatest number. It is undeniable that the individual's happiness might be outweighed, and even sacrificed, for the happiness of a greater number, or even the greater happiness of another individual. There is no shortage of "nightmare" scenarios and perverse hypothetical examples meant to illustrate that such reasoning can generate powerfully (seemingly) *immoral* outcomes. Consider the following (intentionally disturbing) examples:

- Unequal treatment and unequal rights for a minority group within a community is morally justifiable so long as the combined benefit to the majority outweighs the combined harm to the minority group.
- Targeting innocent civilians, such as the family members of suspected terrorists, is morally justifiable so long as it serves

the greater good of reducing the number of terrorist attacks.[351]

If these examples seem "counter-intuitive" to you, then you're experiencing what Bernard Williams calls an "integrity objection."

> It is absurd to demand of such a man, when the sums come in from the utility network which the projects of others have in part determined, that he should just step aside from his own project and decision and acknowledge the decision which utilitarian calculation requires. It is to alienate him in a real sense from his actions and the source of his action in his own convictions....It is thus, in the most literal sense an attack on his integrity.[352]

If utilitarianism really does allow—let alone recommend—such counter-intuitive outcomes, then to the extent such outcomes violate our moral sensibilities, utilitarianism seems suspect, as a moral theory.

Utilitarian possible response:

One quick and easy reply available to utilitarians is to point out that the critic begs the question in claiming that such outcomes would be immoral. According to utilitarianism, the morally correct thing to do is whatever action will maximize happiness. If (outrageous as this might sound) a gang-rape really does maximize happiness (unlikely though this would be!), then, *by definition* it is the morally right thing to do. If a critic wants to claim that the action is nevertheless immoral, then the critic is clearly appealing to a standard other than maximizing utility. That's fine. It just means the critic is not a utilitarian, and is defining moral rightness and

wrongness in some other way. In that case, the conflict is deep, involving fundamental premises concerning what establishes moral rightness and wrongness.

A more compelling response, however, is to once again appeal to rule utilitarianism. A rule utilitarian would likely claim that all four of the examples above are, in fact, examples of morally wrong actions. Why? Because it's likely that our examples would violate a moral rule which tends to maximize utility. For example, it might be argued that a rule guaranteeing equal rights for all within a community generally serves to maximize utility. If that is true, than discrimination and unequal treatment would violate that rule. Similarly, it could be argued that a rule forbidding the targeting of innocent civilians for military purposes maximizes utility—especially when considered on a global scale. If true, then targeting terrorists' family members would violate that rule. In summary, rule utilitarians can claim that fantastic hypothetical scenarios are likely to be irrelevant, to the extent that they don't apply to rule utilitarianism.

Possible problem #3: Utilitarianism is a "swinish doctrine"

Some think there is something low and hedonistic about such an emphasis on pleasure and pain. Perhaps animals can and should be guided by such drives, but human beings are different. We're special. We're better. To the extent that utilitarianism urges us to follow our baser inclinations, it lowers us to the level of swine. Surely human beings can be, and ought to be, guided by nobler aspirations!

---

[351] This is not merely hypothetical, but was actually proposed by then-Presidential candidate (now President) Donald Trump. "The other thing with the terrorists is you have to take out their families, when you get these terrorists, you have to take out their families. They care about their lives, don't kid yourself. When they say they don't care about their lives, you have to take out their

families."
http://www.cnn.com/2015/12/02/politics/donald-trump-terrorists-families/
[352] A sustained critique of utilitarianism is offered in Bernard Williams' *Utilitarianism: For and Against*, with J.J.C. Smart, Cambridge: Cambridge University Press, 1973.

<u>Utilitarian possible response:</u>

This sort of criticism was well known to John Stuart Mill. He defends utilitarianism against these charges by first agreeing with the critic that human beings *are* different from non-human animals, and for that reason the sorts of activities that please us will *not* be identical to those that please swine.

"Now it is an unquestionable fact that those who are equally acquainted with, and equally capable of appreciating and enjoying, both, do give a most marked preference to the manner of existence which employs their higher faculties. Few human creatures would consent to be changed into any of the lower animals, for a promise of the fullest allowance of a beast's pleasures; no intelligent human being would consent to be a fool, no instructed person would be an ignoramus, no person of feeling and conscience would be selfish and base, even though they should be persuaded that the fool, the dunce, or the rascal is better satisfied with his lot than they are with theirs. They would not resign what they possess more than he for the most complete satisfaction of all the desires which they have in common with him. If they ever fancy they would, it is only in cases of unhappiness so extreme, that to escape from it they would exchange their lot for almost any other, however undesirable in their own eyes. A being of higher faculties requires more to make him happy, is capable probably of more acute suffering, and certainly accessible to it at more points, than one of an inferior type; but in spite of these liabilities, he can never really wish to sink into what he feels to be a lower grade of existence. We may give what explanation we please of this unwillingness; ... but its most appropriate appellation is a sense of dignity, which all human beings possess in one form or other, and in some, though by no means in exact, proportion to their higher faculties, and which is so essential a part of the happiness of those in whom it is strong, that nothing which conflicts with it could be, otherwise than momentarily, an object of desire to them.... It is better to be a human being dissatisfied than a pig satisfied; better to be Socrates dissatisfied than a fool satisfied. And if the fool, or the pig, are of a different opinion, it is because they only know their own side of the question. The other party to the comparison knows both sides."[353]

Recall Mill's distinguishing of higher and lower pleasures from earlier in this chapter. Granted, we share the capacity for lower pleasures with other animals, but, unlike them (presumably), we have a capacity for the higher pleasures as well—and the higher pleasures are qualitatively superior. Mill is confident that the vast majority of us recognize this as a fact, and would never pursue a life consisting solely in experiencing lower pleasures, or even a life consisting primarily in experiencing lower pleasures.

But what about *this* guy, and the many like him? Isn't it obvious that lots of people *do* pursue "lower" pleasures, and seem to prefer them? Doesn't it seem true that, given a choice, a great

---

[353] Mill, *Utilitarianism*, Chapter 2.

many people would pick "beer and UFC" over Shakespeare in the park?

Mill has an answer to that criticism as well.

It may be objected, that many who are capable of the higher pleasures, occasionally, under the influence of temptation, postpone them to the lower. But this is quite compatible with a full appreciation of the intrinsic superiority of the higher. Men often, from infirmity of character, make their election for the nearer good, though they know it to be the less valuable; and this no less when the choice is between two bodily pleasures, than when it is between bodily and mental. They pursue sensual indulgences to the injury of health, though perfectly aware that health is the greater good. It may be further objected, that many who begin with youthful enthusiasm for everything noble, as they advance in years sink into indolence and selfishness. But I do not believe that those who undergo this very common change, voluntarily choose the lower description of pleasures in preference to the higher. I believe that before they devote themselves exclusively to the one, they have already become incapable of the other. Capacity for the nobler feelings is in most natures a very tender plant, easily killed, not only by hostile influences, but by mere want of sustenance; and in the majority of young persons it speedily dies away if the occupations to which their position in life has devoted them, and the society into which it has thrown them, are not favourable to keeping that higher capacity in exercise. Men lose their high aspirations as they lose their intellectual tastes, because they have not time or opportunity for indulging them; and they addict themselves to inferior pleasures,

not because they deliberately prefer them, but because they are either the only ones to which they have access, or the only ones which they are any longer capable of enjoying.[354]

In other words, when people seem to prefer lower pleasures to higher, there is probably an explanation rooted in the life circumstances of those persons—and this is not difficult to understand. Perhaps you work hard all day and come home tired and "brain-dead." You just don't feel like reading philosophy, so you opt for a cold beer and some relatively mindless diversion from the TV. Maybe you live in a neighborhood without a public theatre, or a library. Maybe the "higher" pleasures have never been modeled for you. Elitist though he might have been, Mill seems to be right about our general preference for activities that are mentally stimulating. In fact, psychological studies have suggested that extended passive pleasures actually become mildly *depressive* over time.[355]

Possible problem #4: It's too difficult to anticipate the consequences of our actions.

This criticism emerges from the fact that utilitarianism (like other consequentialist theories) focuses solely on the actual consequences of our actions. The problem is that it is often difficult to predict, with great accuracy, just what those consequences will be, and our actions often produce unintended consequences. This can produce bizarre and counter-intuitive judgments from utilitarians.

Suppose, for example that someone is a guest attending a party celebrating the 2nd birthday for the son of a wealthy business associate. The birthday boy begins to choke on a piece of food. The guest is the only one present who knows how to perform the Heimlich maneuver. Suppose also that the guest is a utilitarian. It seems like "easy math" to conclude that saving the boy's life will

---

[354] Ibid.

[355] Interested readers should investigate the works of Mihaly Csikszentmihalyi, a psychologist famous for his research on happiness.

maximize happiness, so the guest does so, and the boy's life is saved.

The year is 1959. The wealthy business associate is Muhammed Awad Bin Laden. The birthday boy is little Osama Bin Laden. By saving the boy's life, the guest has facilitated the unintended consequence of the formation of al-Qu'aida and the deadliest terrorist attack (as of the time of this writing) on U.S. soil. With all those things in mind, it seems clear that it was morally *wrong* to save the little boy from choking.

Some of you are probably thinking to yourself, "but that's not fair! How could the guest have possibly known that the two year old boy would grow up to be an international terrorist? It's unfair to expect the guest to work with information he couldn't possibly have."

Utilitarian possible response:

You're correct. That *would* be unfair, and there are a couple ways we can process that. One way is to reject consequentialist theories entirely. Consequences lie in the future, and the future is not perfectly known to us. Perhaps it makes more sense to focus on something better known, such as intent. The guest "meant well," and maybe that's all that really matters.

However, while it's certainly possible to just reject utilitarianism as a result of this criticism, that's not the only response available—nor is it

the most reasonable, I think. Why throw out the baby with the bath water? Rule utilitarianism is useful once more, in the face of this criticism. The plain fact is that most babies *don't* grow up to become the heads of terrorist organizations, nor do they become serial killers, or Hitler! For that matter, most don't grow up to cure cancer either. Most babies grow up to be *ordinary* people, sometimes doing good things, and sometimes doing bad things.

It would be unreasonable and even irrational to perceive a two-year-old choking to death, infer that he will become a terrorist one day, and therefore decline to help. It makes much more sense to adhere to a "rule" that says something like "try to save the lives of other people, including children, when you're able to do so." In the vast majority of cases, this will maximize utility. Sometimes, it won't—but how could you possibly know which cases those will be?

The best anyone can do, utilitarian or otherwise, is to choose the course of action which she has good reason to believe is the right thing to do. Mistakes are possible no matter which theory we adopt. Neither the fact, nor the fear, of mistakes should get in the way of our trying to do the right thing, nor be used to call into question the very project of moral understanding in the first place.

Exercise Break

For each of the following examples, use either Act or Rule utilitarian reasoning to determine what the right policy/action would be.

- Requiring all Americans to have health insurance.
- Allowing certain school employees (e.g., those who have passed background checks and who have taken gun safety/use courses) to have guns at schools (including colleges and universities).
- Deporting undocumented immigrants.
- Public funding of political campaigns.
- Banning abortion except in cases where the mother's life is in danger from the pregnancy.
- Building a wall along the U.S./Mexico border.
- Allowing the water-boarding (i.e., torture) of suspected terrorists during interrogation.

Politics

Having established the basic elements of utilitarian thought, we will now consider a more sustained and politically practical application of utilitarianism as it occurs in another of John Stuart Mill's works: *On Liberty*. In that book, it becomes obvious that utilitarianism is not merely an ethical theory confined to solving personal moral dilemmas, but a prescriptive model for decision making, in general, that explains the proper role and limits of government as well.

Mill begins *On Liberty* with a review of some of the fundamental assumptions long held about the necessity (and dangers) of the State. Reminiscent of Hobbes, he claims that "to prevent the weaker members of the community from being preyed upon by innumerable vultures, it was needful that there should be an animal of prey stronger than the rest, commissioned to keep them down."[356] For Hobbes, this demonstrated the necessity not only of a "sovereign," but one whose power was absolute. As we saw in our chapter on Locke, however, the sovereign, too, could be considered a threat— something Mill recognizes as well.

> But as the king of the vultures would be no less bent upon preying on the flock than any of the minor harpies, it was indispensable to be in a perpetual attitude of defence against his beak and claws. The aim, therefore, of patriots, was to set limits to the power which the ruler should be suffered to exercise over the community; and this limitation was what they meant by liberty.

Mill describes this attempt to secure liberty in terms of establishing certain political rights against the sovereign as well as the establishment of constitutional checks requiring the consent of the community. He seeks to establish in broader terms, though, just what is meant (or should be meant) by "liberty," and on what basis that liberty is to be justified.

In a very reader-friendly fashion, Mill explicitly states his conclusion for us in no uncertain terms, in a section worth quoting at length.

> The object of this Essay is to assert one very simple principle, as entitled to govern absolutely the dealings of society with the individual in the way of compulsion and control, whether the means used be physical force in the form of legal penalties, or the moral coercion of public opinion. That principle is, that the sole end for which mankind are warranted, individually or collectively, in interfering with the liberty of action of any of their number, is self-protection. That the only purpose for which power can be rightfully exercised over any member of a civilised community, against his will, is to prevent harm to others. His own good, either physical or moral, is not a sufficient warrant. He cannot rightfully be compelled to do or forbear because it will be better for him to do so, because it will make him happier, because, in the opinions of others, to do so would be wise, or even right. These are good reasons for remonstrating with him, or reasoning with him, or persuading him, or entreating him, but not for compelling him, or visiting him with any evil in case he do otherwise. To justify that, the conduct from which it is desired to deter him must be calculated to produce evil to some one else. The only part of the conduct of any one, for which he is amenable to society, is that which concerns others. In the part which merely concerns himself, his independence is, of right, absolute. Over himself, over his own

---

[356] All quotations in this section are from Mill's *On Liberty*, unless otherwise indicated. Selections of that work appear at the end of this chapter.

body and mind, the individual is sovereign.

With regard to the application of "force," where force could include legal compulsion or restriction, the application of fines or other punishments, or even the "moral coercion of public opinion," with regard to any interference with the liberty of a person by either another individual or the community as a whole, the only legitimate justification is "self-protection." That is, it is acceptable to use the force of law to prevent someone from harming another, as in the obvious examples of murder or rape. However, it is not justifiable to use the force of law to compel someone to do something for "his own good."

One's "own good," for Mill, is a sufficient reason to try to *persuade* or encourage someone through the use of reason, but "but not for compelling him, or visiting him with any evil in case he do otherwise." Mill is quick to add, in case it wasn't obvious, that "this doctrine is meant to apply only to human beings in the maturity of their faculties." The most obvious examples of exceptions would be children, who clearly don't (and shouldn't) enjoy the same autonomy as adults, though this reasoning would properly apply to adults as well, if they are somehow mentally incapable of self-determination, as might be the case with persons who have serious mental illness or developmental disabilities.

Exercise Break

Consider (and be prepared to discuss) each of the following laws/policies according to Mill's principle.
- Mandatory seatbelt laws.
- Mandatory motorcycle helmet laws.
- Prohibition of marijuana use.
- Prohibition of making or viewing pornography.
- Banning the sale of sugary drinks (e.g., soda).
- Mandating the purchase of Health Insurance as was the case under "Obamacare."

Mill's "hands-off" approach to the infringement of individual liberty makes him the champion of self-professed libertarians. The contemporary Libertarian party in the United States claim that "Libertarians strongly oppose any government interference into their personal, family, and business decisions. Essentially, we believe all Americans should be free to live their lives and pursue their interests as they see fit as long as they do no harm to another."[357] The connection to Mill is unmistakable, and his appeal is understandable. How, though, does Mill *justify* his vision of such limited government? Very simply: in the same way he justifies any other action or outcome.

I regard utility as the ultimate appeal on all ethical questions; but it must be utility in the largest sense, grounded on the permanent interests of man as a progressive being.

Remember: this is the same John Stuart Mill from earlier in this chapter who endorsed what we called Rule Utilitarianism. What is right or wrong, good or bad, just or unjust, is to be understood in terms of whether and to what extent those actions (or policies) maximize utility. Rather obviously, acts of violence such as rape or murder don't maximize utility for all involved, so it makes sense that we would have

---

[357] https://www.lp.org/about/

rules against them, and use the law to enforce those rules. That is a perfectly legitimate application of State coercion.

It is not only *preventing* certain actions, such as acts of violence, which are justified by appeals to utility, but also (in some cases) compelling persons *to act*.

> There are also many positive acts for the benefit of others, which he may rightfully be compelled to perform; such as, to give evidence in a court of justice; to bear his fair share in the common defence, or in any other joint work necessary to the interest of the society of which he enjoys the protection; and to perform certain acts of individual beneficence, such as saving a fellow-creature's life, or interposing to protect the defenceless against ill-usage, things which whenever it is obviously a man's duty to do, he may rightfully be made responsible to society for not doing. A person may cause evil to others not only by his actions but by his inaction, and in either case he is justly accountable to them for the injury. The latter case, it is true, requires a much more cautious exercise of compulsion than the former.

Some of this should appear as common sense, but other elements of this paragraph should dispel the illusion that Mill was some sort of radical libertarian who proposed no government coercion whatsoever. It might help to distinguish *acts of commission* from *acts of omission*. The basic difference between them is that acts of commission refer to things that we do, and acts of omission to things that we refrain from doing. Telling a lie is an act of commission. Withholding the truth is an act of omission. Forcing someone's head underwater is an act of commission. Standing by and doing nothing while someone drowns is an act of omission.

The most enthusiastic libertarians might claim that the State only has the right to restrict acts of commission, but not acts of omission. For example, it would be legitimate to criminalize

murder, but not legitimate to punish someone for "doing nothing" and allowing someone to die who could have been saved. In plainer terms, it's legitimate for the State to prevent you from hurting your neighbors, but it shouldn't force you to help them.

A clear example of this actually occurred in 2011 during one of the Republican primary debates. The following was the exchange between CNN moderator Wolf Blitzer, and candidate (and self-professed libertarian) Ron Paul.

> BLITZER: ... you're a physician, Ron Paul, so you're a doctor. You know something about this subject. Let me ask you this hypothetical question.
>
> A healthy 30-year-old young man has a good job, makes a good living, but decides, you know what? I'm not going to spend $200 or $300 a month for health insurance because I'm healthy, I don't need it. But something terrible happens, all of a sudden he needs it.
>
> Who's going to pay if he goes into a coma, for example? Who pays for that?
>
> PAUL: Well, in a society that you accept welfarism and socialism, he expects the government to take care of him.
>
> BLITZER: Well, what do you want?
>
> PAUL: But what he should do is whatever he wants to do, and assume responsibility for himself. My advice to him would have a major medical policy, but not be forced --
>
> BLITZER: But he doesn't have that. He doesn't have it, and he needs intensive care for six months. Who pays?
>
> PAUL: That's what freedom is all about, taking your own risks. This whole idea

that you have to prepare and take care of everybody --

(APPLAUSE)

BLITZER: But Congressman, are you saying that society should just let him die?

PAUL: No. I practiced medicine before we had Medicaid, in the early 1960s, when I got out of medical school. I practiced at Santa Rosa Hospital in San Antonio, and the churches took care of them. We never turned anybody away from the hospitals. (APPLAUSE)

PAUL: And we've given up on this whole concept that we might take care of ourselves and assume responsibility for ourselves. Our neighbors, our friends, our churches would do it. This whole idea, that's the reason the cost is so high. [358]

Ron Paul was confident that charities might step in to provide health services to those who needed them, but he was adamant that the government should not do so, and was equally adamant that people assume personal responsibility for their own lives and circumstances. "That's what freedom is all about, taking your own risks."

Mill is often credited with endorsing the view that the State should only protect citizens from harm, but this overlooks the clear content of the Mill quotation above. "A person may cause evil to others not only by his actions but by his inaction, and in either case he is justly accountable to them for the injury." Mill's own examples include compelling witnesses to testify in court, compelling people to defend their nation through military service, and even compelling people to save others' lives when possible!

Forcing a citizen to pay taxes is not merely "preventing harm" but positively compelling

someone to do good (on the assumption that taxes are needed to fund at least the minimal protections and services offered by the government). Forcing citizens to serve in the military is a profound intrusion into their personal liberty, but might be necessary to preserve the State itself, in times of war. Even mandating "saving a fellow-creature's life," while certainly intrusive, is considered legitimate, by Mill.

Such laws are not merely philosophical hypotheticals, by the way. They are called "duty to rescue" laws, and actually exist in several States, including California. California penal code section 152.3 says that:

152.3. (a) Any person who reasonably believes that he or she has observed the commission of any of the following offenses where the victim is a child under the age of 14 years shall notify a peace officer, as defined in Chapter 4.5 (commencing with Section 830) of Title 3 of Part 2:

(1) Murder.

(2) Rape.

(3) A violation of paragraph (1) of subdivision (b) of Section 288 of the Penal Code.

(b) This section shall not be construed to affect privileged relationships as provided by law.

(c) The duty to notify a peace officer imposed pursuant to subdivision (a) is satisfied if the notification or an attempt to provide notice is made by telephone or any other means.

(d) Failure to notify as required pursuant to subdivision (a) is a misdemeanor and is

---

[358]

http://transcripts.cnn.com/TRANSCRIPTS/1109/12/se.06.html

punishable by a fine of not more than one thousand five hundred dollars ($1,500), by imprisonment in a county jail for not more than six months, or by both that fine and imprisonment.

(e) The requirements of this section shall not apply to the following:

(1) A person who is related to either the victim or the offender, including a husband, wife, parent, child, brother, sister, grandparent, grandchild, or other person related by consanguinity or affinity.

(2) A person who fails to report based on a reasonable mistake of fact.

(3) A person who fails to report based on a reasonable fear for his or her own safety or for the safety of his or her family.[359]

Admittedly, there are a lot of "disqualifiers" in that law, but the intent is clear: to compel people to "do the right thing," if they are not sufficiently internally motivated to do so. Such laws are legitimate, to Mill—though he acknowledges that such "positive" laws require "a much more cautious exercise of compulsion."

Having established that utility is the basis for all his political ideas, and that the only legitimate use of coercion is to prevent harm (as opposed to coercion for paternalistic reasons), Mill then lays out the domain of human liberty, as he understands it.

This, then, is the appropriate region of human liberty. It comprises, first, the inward domain of consciousness; demanding liberty of conscience, in the most comprehensive sense; liberty of thought and feeling; absolute freedom of opinion and sentiment on all subjects,

practical or speculative, scientific, moral, or theological. The liberty of expressing and publishing opinions may seem to fall under a different principle, since it belongs to that part of the conduct of an individual which concerns other people; but, being almost of as much importance as the liberty of thought itself, and resting in great part on the same reasons, is practically inseparable from it. Secondly, the principle requires liberty of tastes and pursuits; of framing the plan of our life to suit our own character; of doing as we like, subject to such consequences as may follow: without impediment from our fellow-creatures, so long as what we do does not harm them, even though they should think our conduct foolish, perverse, or wrong. Thirdly, from this liberty of each individual, follows the liberty, within the same limits, of combination among individuals; freedom to unite, for any purpose not involving harm to others: the persons combining being supposed to be of full age, and not forced or deceived.

No society in which these liberties are not, on the whole, respected, is free, whatever may be its form of government; and none is completely free in which they do not exist absolute and unqualified. The only freedom which deserves the name, is that of pursuing our own good in our own way, so long as we do not attempt to deprive others of theirs, or impede their efforts to obtain it. Each is the proper guardian of his own health, whether bodily, or mental and spiritual. Mankind are greater gainers by suffering each other to live as seems good to themselves, than by compelling each to live as seems good to the rest.

Mill lists three regions of human liberty:

---

[359] http://law.onecle.com/california/penal/152.3.html

1. Conscience (including freedom of expression and opinion)
2. Lifestyle (including freedom of personal taste and life-plan)
3. Association (including freedom to form groups, political parties, etc.)

For our purposes we focus on just the first two regions—but first note the repetition of two key ideas in the last paragraph of the quotation above. He emphasizes personal autonomy when he states that the "only freedom which deserves the name, is that of pursuing our own good in our own way, so long as we do not attempt to deprive others of theirs, or impede their efforts to obtain it." That is, people should be free to live their lives as they see fit, without interference, unless interference is necessary to prevent them from harming others.

Then, he reiterates his utilitarian foundation. "Mankind are greater gainers by suffering each other to live as seems good to themselves, than by compelling each to live as seems good to the rest."

It's important not to gloss over this point.

Why should government intrude minimally in persons' lives? Why should people be allowed to live as they see fit, provided they're not harming others? Because we are "greater gainers" when we do so. In other words, this approach to governing *maximizes utility*. In fairness, though, if the justification for a "hands off" approach to governing is that it maximizes utility, then it would follow that if that were not true, and a more intrusive approach actually produced more utility, then Mill, in order to be consistent, would have to endorse *that* approach instead. It falls to him, therefore, to justify his utilitarian interpretation of his broadly libertarian approach to governing. We will see how he does so first with regard to freedom of conscience.

The U.S. Constitution was ratified in 1788. Included in that Constitution is the Bill of Rights. The first amendment states that "Congress shall make no law respecting an establishment of religion, or prohibiting the free exercise thereof; or abridging the freedom of speech, or of the press; or the right of the people peaceably to assemble, and to petition the government for a redress of grievances."[360]

Mill's *On Liberty* was published in 1859, over 80 years later. Clearly, "freedom of expression" was not invented by Mill, nor first recognized by Mill, but had, instead, been part of the philosophical landscape for some time. Mill does offer a valuable contribution, however, by offering a philosophical defense of the value of freedom of conscience and expression in terms of utility.

He starts his defense of freedom of opinion and expression in bold terms. "If all mankind minus one, were of one opinion, and only one person were of the contrary opinion, mankind would be no more justified in silencing that one person, than he, if he had the power, would be justified in silencing mankind."

Suppose that there are seven billion people in the world. If 6,999,999,999 of them all believed the same thing, and only one person out of that seven billion believed otherwise, it would be just as unjustifiable to silence that one person as it would for that one to silence the 6,999,999,999. This is an extraordinary claim! But, Mill doesn't merely assert this out of some sentimental appreciation for the minority opinion, but out of his utilitarian worldview.

Were an opinion a personal possession of no value except to the owner; if to be obstructed in the enjoyment of it were simply a private injury, it would make some difference whether the injury was inflicted only on a few persons or on many. But the peculiar evil of silencing the expression of an opinion is, that it is robbing the human race; posterity as well as the existing generation; those who dissent from the opinion, still more than those who hold it. If the opinion is right, they are deprived of the opportunity of

---

[360] https://www.billofrightsinstitute.org/founding-documents/bill-of-rights/

exchanging error for truth: if wrong, they lose, what is almost as great a benefit, the clearer perception and livelier impression of truth, produced by its collision with error.

Mill believes that a *greater good* is served by not silencing any particular point of view, even if there is clear and overwhelming consensus opposing it. Interestingly, he claims the greater harm from silencing that opinion applies to those who *disagree*. With regard to that unpopular opinion, it is either true, or it is false. If it is true, then the majority are "deprived of the opportunity of exchanging error for truth." In other words, we remain *wrong*.

An increasing number of parents in the United States believe that vaccinations are linked to autism in children, and a great many more are unsure. Of Americans surveyed, 6% think vaccines cause autism, 41% think that they do not, and 52% (a majority) are unsure.[361] Even President Trump has contributed to the vaccine-autism link. In 2015 he said "We had so many instances, people that work for me, just the other day, 2 years old, a beautiful child, went to have the vaccine and came back and a week later got a tremendous fever, got very, very sick, now is autistic."[362] Back in 2012, he tweeted "Massive combined inoculations to small children is the cause for big increase in autism."[363] This, despite the fact that only *one* study has ever linked vaccinations to autism, and that solitary study has since been discredited as fraudulent, the article was officially retracted from the science journal in which it was published, and the researcher who wrote it lost his medical license![364] Given the public health dangers of "anti-vaxxers," we might think that promoting the discredited link between vaccines and autism

should be prohibited. Mill, however, would presumably disagree.

What if, contrary to all expectations and evidence, the anti-vaxxers are actually *right*?

> First: the opinion which it is attempted to suppress by authority may possibly be true. Those who desire to suppress it, of course deny its truth; but they are not infallible. They have no authority to decide the question for all mankind, and exclude every other person from the means of judging. To refuse a hearing to an opinion, because they are sure that it is false, is to assume that their certainty is the same thing as absolute certainty. All silencing of discussion is an assumption of infallibility. Its condemnation may be allowed to rest on this common argument, not the worse for being common.

No one is infallible. Every person is capable of being mistaken, and we can be mistaken as individuals as well as in communities. Medieval communities who believed the bubonic plague was being spread by witches or Jews were *mistaken*. It's possible (however unlikely) that *there really is* a danger posed by vaccinations, in which case the safer course of action is to allow dissent.

To be clear, allowing dissent does not entail putting the dissenting voice on equal footing with the consensus view. To say that people should be allowed to express contrary opinions is just that: they are *allowed* to. It doesn't mean they should be treated as having the same credibility as the majority who disagrees. It might be consistent with Mill's theory to allow anti-vaxxers to express their perspective, but it certainly doesn't mean that we should pretend that their view has the

[361] http://www.huffingtonpost.com/2015/03/06/gallup-poll-vaccines_n_6818416.html
[362] http://www.standard.net/National/2017/01/10/Trump-asks-vaccine-skeptic-Robert-Kennedy-Jr-to-lead-commission-on-vaccine-safety-1

[363] https://twitter.com/realdonaldtrump/status/238717783007977473?lang=en
[364] http://www.publichealth.org/public-awareness/understanding-vaccines/vaccine-myths-debunked/

same standing as the overwhelming majority of every doctor and researcher who has any experience and expertise in this subject.

Some internet "experts" claim that Hillary Clinton is actually an alien reptilian shapeshifter (along with a surprising number of other celebrities and politicians!).[365] It is technically possible that these conspiracy-theorists are right, and a subversive alien invasion is underway— but it seems vastly more likely that they are either mentally-ill, or gullible, or internet trolls. We certainly shouldn't claim that it is just as likely that our world leaders are aliens as that they are not—but nor should we literally censor the conspiracy theory, no matter how bizarre or implausible it might be.

Thus far, we have considered the value of allowing free expression out of concern that the minority view might be true. It's entirely possible, though, that the view is false. Even then, Mill thinks there is value in it being expressed. Confidence in the truth of one's own claim requires a clash with opposing points of view.

> There is the greatest difference between presuming an opinion to be true, because, with every opportunity for contesting it, it has not been refuted, and assuming its truth for the purpose of not permitting its refutation. Complete liberty of contradicting and disproving our opinion, is the very condition which justifies us in assuming its truth for purposes of action; and on no other terms can a being with human faculties have any rational assurance of being right.

Consider the example of climate change deniers. The overwhelming majority of climate scientists are convinced that human activity contributes (harmfully) to global warming.[366] However, there is a minority view that either denies the extent of human-impact, or that is least

unsettled on it. Mill would already think that they should be allowed to express and explore that view, given the possibility that they might be correct, but he would also claim that the existence of this contrary view serves to sharpen and strengthen the majority view.

Those of us who subject ourselves to differing points of view run the risk of actually learning something from the process! Even if we conclude (repeatedly) that the other point of view is mistaken, the process of examining it and being challenged by it is an intellectual "workout" that strengthens our confidence in our own view and enhances our ability to defend it. Without this contrast, Mill claims our ideas can turn into "dogma."

> However unwillingly a person who has a strong opinion may admit the possibility that his opinion may be false, he ought to be moved by the consideration that however true it may be, if it is not fully, frequently, and fearlessly discussed, it will be held as a dead dogma, not a living truth.

As mentioned in the first chapter of this book, in the final speech President Obama gave as President, he warned against our increasing tendency to operate within our own ideological "bubbles."

> For too many of us, it's become safer to retreat into our own bubbles, whether in our neighborhoods or college campuses or places of worship or our social media feeds, surrounded by people who look like us and share the same political outlook and never challenge our assumptions. The rise of naked partisanship, increasing economic and regional stratification, the splintering of our media into a channel for every taste –

---

[365] http://alien-uforesearch.com/ researchdiscussion/viewtopic.php?t=3125
[366] http://www.politifact.com/virginia/ statements/2016/apr/04/don-beyer/don-

beyer-says-97-percent-scientists-believe-human/

all this makes this great sorting seem natural, even inevitable. And increasingly, we become so secure in our bubbles that we accept only information, whether true or not, that fits our opinions, instead of basing our opinions on the evidence that's out there.[367]

This isn't merely some anecdotal cautionary tale about liberals only watching MSNBC and conservatives only watching Fox News. A study published in the "Proceedings of the National Academy of Sciences of the United States of America" concluded that "selective exposure to content is the primary driver of content diffusion and generates the formation of homogeneous clusters, i.e., 'echo chambers.' Indeed, homogeneity appears to be the primary driver for the diffusion of contents and each echo chamber has its own cascade dynamics."[368]

In other words, people on Facebook mostly share news that they already agree with, that is consistent with their worldview, and they don't share information that challenges it. As the researchers put it: "users show a tendency to search for, interpret, and recall information that confirm their pre-existing beliefs."

Combine this tendency with the fact that Facebook has nearly 2 billion users (out of roughly 7 billion people on the planet), and reaches 67% of U.S. adults, and that 62% of Americans get their news mainly from social media sites such as Facebook and Twitter.[369]

A majority of Americans get their news primarily from social media, and research confirms the application of the confirmation bias to social media platforms. It should go without saying that these trends seriously compromise our ability to think critically, and to responsibly accept or reject claims. Mill described this condition with prescience more than 150 years ago.

The greatest orator, save one, of antiquity, has left it on record that he always studied his adversary's case with as great, if not with still greater, intensity than even his own. What Cicero practised as the means of forensic success, requires to be imitated by all who study any subject in order to arrive at the truth. He who knows only his own side of the case, knows little of that. His reasons may be good, and no one may have been able to refute them. But if he is equally unable to refute the reasons on the opposite side; if he does not so much as know what they are, he has no ground for preferring either opinion. The rational position for him would be suspension of judgment, and unless he contents himself with that, he is either led by authority, or adopts, like the generality of the world, the side to which he feels most inclination. Nor is it enough that he should hear the arguments of adversaries from his own teachers, presented as they state them, and accompanied by what they offer as refutations. That is not the way to do justice to the arguments, or bring them into real contact with his own mind. He must be able to hear them from persons who actually believe them; who defend them in earnest, and do their very utmost for them. He must know them in their most plausible and persuasive form; he must feel the whole force of the difficulty which the true view of the subject has to encounter and dispose of; else he will never really possess himself of the portion of truth which meets and removes that difficulty. Ninety-nine in a hundred of what are called educated men are in this condition; even of those who

[367] http://www.latimes.com/politics/la-pol-obama-farewell-speech-transcript-20170110-story.html

[368]
http://www.pnas.org/content/113/3/554.full

[369] http://www.journalism.org/2016/05/26/news-use-across-social-media-platforms-2016/?utm_content=bufferae870&utm_medium=social&utm_source=twitter.com&utm_campaign=buffer

can argue fluently for their opinions. Their conclusion may be true, but it might be false for anything they know: they have never thrown themselves into the mental position of those who think differently from them, and considered what such persons may have to say; and consequently they do not, in any proper sense of the word, know the doctrine which they themselves profess. They do not know those parts of it which explain and justify the remainder; the considerations which show that a fact which seemingly conflicts with another is reconcilable with it, or that, of two apparently strong reasons, one and not the other ought to be preferred. All that part of the truth which turns the scale, and decides the judgment of a completely informed mind, they are strangers to; nor is it ever really known, but to those who have attended equally and impartially to both sides, and endeavoured to see the reasons of both in the strongest light. So essential is this discipline to a real understanding of moral and human subjects, that if opponents of all important truths do not exist, it is indispensable to imagine them, and supply them with the strongest arguments which the most skilful devil's advocate can conjure up.

In what might come as a shocking claim, Mill suggests that if you only know your own side of a debate, rather than this causing you to be certain of your own opinion, it should instead cause you to suspend judgment! After all, if you don't know what reasons exist that are contrary to your own, how can you be confident that those hypothetical reasons are not better than yours? It's not even sufficient to hear opposing points of view from others, if those others actually agree with you. Pretending to "debate" the issue with like-minded friends isn't good enough. "He must be able to hear them from persons who actually believe them; who defend them in earnest, and do their very utmost for them."

This is what we try to do when we employ the principle of charity when evaluating arguments (as described in chapter one). Indeed, Mill even gestures at this when he says "So essential is this discipline to a real understanding of moral and human subjects, that if opponents of all important truths do not exist, it is indispensable to imagine them, and supply them with the strongest arguments which the most skilful devil's advocate can conjure up." But, there is no comparison between considering "the other side" as best you can, and actually *hearing* (or reading) the other side from people who actually sincerely believe in it.

Practically speaking, this means that if you self-identify as a liberal, you should probably turn off MSNBC and NPR and watch Fox News from time to time. Conversely, if you are conservative, that might mean turning off Rush Limbaugh and listening to Keith Olbermann for a change. If you are a person of faith, actually read some serious, credible arguments for atheism. If you are an atheist, read some serious, scholarly books or articles from people of faith. While it's possible that you might change your mind, this isn't necessarily very likely. Far more likely, but still valuable, is that you *understand* the different perspective, and thereby better understand *your own*.

Thus far, we have consider the value of free expression based on the possibility that the idea might be true, or, that even if it is false there is still value in considering alternatives. Mill reminds us that there is still a third option, as well.

We have hitherto considered only two possibilities: that the received opinion may be false, and some other opinion, consequently, true; or that, the received opinion being true, a conflict with the opposite error is essential to a clear apprehension and deep feeling of its truth. But there is a commoner case than either of these; when the conflicting doctrines, instead of being one true and the other false, share the truth between them; and the nonconforming opinion is needed to supply the remainder of the truth, of which the received doctrine embodies only a part. Popular opinions, on subjects not palpable to sense, are often true, but seldom or never the whole truth. They are a part of the truth; sometimes a greater, sometimes a smaller part, but exaggerated, distorted, and disjoined from the truths by which they ought to be accompanied and limited. Heretical opinions, on the other hand, are generally some of these suppressed and neglected truths, bursting the bonds which kept them down, and either seeking reconciliation with the truth contained in the common opinion, or fronting it as enemies, and setting themselves up, with similar exclusiveness, as the whole truth.

When dealing with simple and uncontroversial claims, truth is pretty binary. 2+2 = 4, and any contrary view is simply mistaken. It's an all-or-nothing situation. 2+2 = 4 is entirely true, and 2+2 = "anything else" is entirely false. In other cases, however—and especially when it comes to politics—it is often the case that "both sides" have something to contribute in a meaningful way. Mill makes this connection to politics explicitly clear.

In politics, again, it is almost a commonplace, that a party of order or stability, and a party of progress or reform, are both necessary elements of a healthy state of political life; until the one or the other shall have so enlarged its mental grasp as to be a party equally of order and of progress, knowing and distinguishing what is fit to be preserved from what ought to be swept away. Each of these modes of thinking derives its utility from the deficiencies of the other; but it is in a great measure the opposition of the other that keeps each within the

limits of reason and sanity. Unless opinions favourable to democracy and to aristocracy, to property and to equality, to co-operation and to competition, to luxury and to abstinence, to sociality and individuality, to liberty and discipline, and all the other standing antagonisms of practical life, are expressed with equal freedom, and enforced and defended with equal talent and energy, there is no chance of both elements obtaining their due; one scale is sure to go up and the other down. Truth, in the great practical concerns of life, is so much a question of the reconciling and combining of opposites, that very few have minds sufficiently capacious and impartial to make the adjustment with an approach to correctness, and it has to be made by the rough process of a struggle between combatants fighting under hostile banners. On any of the great open questions just enumerated, if either of the two opinions has a better claim than the other, not merely to be tolerated, but to be encouraged and countenanced, it is the one which happens at the particular time and place to be in a minority. That is the opinion which, for the time being, represents the neglected interests, the side of human well-being which is in danger of obtaining less than its share.

The Affordable Care Act ("Obamacare) was incredibly unpopular among conservatives, and the House of Representatives voted to repeal it (unsuccessfully) dozens of times. President Trump campaigned promising to "repeal and replace" the ACA, and began taking steps to do so within days of his inauguration. Interestingly, though, several of the key components of the ACA actually came from a conservative think tank: the Heritage Foundation.[370] In fact, a bill inspired by the Heritage Foundation report was introduced by Republican Senator John Chafee of Rhode

---

[370] http://www.heritage.org/research/reports/1989/a-national-health-system-for-america

Island in 1993, and that bill was co-sponsored by 18 other Republican Senators, including former Republican Presidential candidate Bob Dole. The bill called for:

- An individual mandate
- Creation of purchasing pools
- Standardized benefits
- Vouchers for the poor to buy insurance
- A ban on denying coverage based on a pre-existing condition[371]

If these ideas sound familiar to you, they should: all of them are found in the ACA, and most of them were originally considered to be "conservative" ideas.

While the idea that health care is a "right" and that certain services, such as birth control, should be provided by all insurance policies might be "liberal" ideas, the notion of personal responsibility behind the individual mandate, and the free-market appeal of "exchanges" are traditionally conservative ideas. Whether the ACA was good and successful policy is subject to honest debate, but Mill is confident that the exchange and combination of ideas often serves the greater good.

If nothing else, opposition parties are valuable in that they limit the "success" of the dominant party at the time. "Each of these modes of thinking derives its utility from the deficiencies of the other; but it is in a great measure the opposition of the other that keeps each within the limits of reason and sanity." We might imagine Mill saying that it serves a greater good that Republicans limit the efforts of Democrats, and vice versa, that the United States is better off when policy reflects a moderated compromise between the wish lists of both parties, rather than an unrestrained embodiment of either party's "perfect" society.

To summarize Mill up to this point, we can appeal to Mill himself, who helpfully reviews his argument thus far:

We have now recognised the necessity to the mental well-being of mankind (on which all their other well-being depends) of freedom of opinion, and freedom of the expression of opinion, on four distinct grounds; which we will now briefly recapitulate.

First, if any opinion is compelled to silence, that opinion may, for aught we can certainly know, be true. To deny this is to assume our own infallibility.

Secondly, though the silenced opinion be an error, it may, and very commonly does, contain a portion of truth; and since the general or prevailing opinion on any subject is rarely or never the whole truth, it is only by the collision of adverse opinions, that the remainder of the truth has any chance of being supplied.

Thirdly, even if the received opinion be not only true, but the whole truth; unless it is suffered to be, and actually is, vigorously and earnestly contested, it will, by most of those who receive it, be held in the manner of a prejudice, with little comprehension or feeling of its rational grounds. And not only this, but, **fourthly**, the meaning of the doctrine itself will be in danger of being lost, or enfeebled, and deprived of its vital effect on the character and conduct: the dogma becoming a mere formal profession, inefficacious for good, but cumbering the ground, and preventing the growth of any real and heartfelt conviction, from reason or personal experience.[372]

Having addressed Mill's defense of free opinion and expression, we can now turn to his defense for the freedom to live as one sees fit, to live a lifestyle of one's own choosing, so long as no harm is being inflicted on anyone else. He recognizes, of course, that actions are more subject to proper limitation than are ideas.

---

[371]https://www.congress.gov/bill/103rd-congress/senate-bill/1770

[372] I have added my own emphasis to this quotation.

No one pretends that actions should be as free as opinions. On the contrary, even opinions lose their immunity, when the circumstances in which they are expressed are such as to constitute their expression a positive instigation to some mischievous act. An opinion that corn-dealers are starvers of the poor, or that private property is robbery, ought to be unmolested when simply circulated through the press, but may justly incur punishment when delivered orally to an excited mob assembled before the house of a corn-dealer, or when handed about among the same mob in the form of a placard. Acts, of whatever kind, which, without justifiable cause, do harm to others, may be, and in the more important cases absolutely require to be, controlled by the unfavourable sentiments, and, when needful, by the active interference of mankind. The liberty of the individual must be thus far limited; he must not make himself a nuisance to other people. But if he refrains from molesting others in what concerns them, and merely acts according to his own inclination and judgment in things which concern himself, the same reasons which show that opinion should be free, prove also that he should be allowed, without molestation, to carry his opinions into practice at his own cost.

Several points are worth reviewing here. First, not even opinions are entirely immune to restriction. Deliberately using speech to incite a riot, for example, is not a legitimate use of one's freedom to express an opinion.

The U.S. Supreme Court case of *Schenck v. United States* established that "the most stringent protection of free speech would not protect a man falsely shouting fire in a theater and causing a panic. [...] The question in every case is whether the words used are used in such circumstances

and are of such a nature as to create a clear and present danger that they will bring about the substantive evils that Congress has a right to prevent."[373]

Decades later, the case of *Brandenburg v. Ohio* refined this ruling by stating that even speech that supports breaking the law, and even violence, is protected by the First Amendment unless it directly encourages people to immediately break the law.[374] We might imagine the difference between someone blogging about overthrowing the government, versus someone speaking to a crowd of people and encouraging them to assault the politician who is giving a speech just a few yards away.

In any event, as free as expression should be for Mill, this freedom is not unlimited, and the freedom of actions even less so. "Acts, of whatever kind, which, without justifiable cause, do harm to others, may be, and in the more important cases absolutely require to be, controlled by the unfavourable sentiments, and, when needful, by the active interference of mankind."

Any action that harms others is subject to restriction. Again, obvious cases include rape and murder. But, if someone's actions harm no one at all, or even if they only harm himself or herself, then that person should be left free to "carry his opinions into practice at his own cost."

You might think that someone is wasting their life, squandering their potential, or acting foolishly or sinfully. You might think that someone who smokes marijuana is harming themselves and their life prospects, or that someone who gives a good portion of their money to their church is a fool. You might think that homosexuality is "gross," or that monogamy and marriage are "unnatural."

Mill would say you are free to *judge* other lifestyles however you please, and it's even acceptable for you to try to convince the person to change their ways. What is not acceptable, however, is to use the power of the State to make "them" live more like you.

---

[373] https://supreme.justia.com/cases/federal/us/249/47/case.html

[374] https://supreme.justia.com/cases/federal/us/395/444/

One more time, Mill offers a utilitarian justification for his endorsement of individuality and being free to live your life as you see fit.

It is not by wearing down into uniformity all that is individual in themselves, but by cultivating it and calling it forth, within the limits imposed by the rights and interests of others, that human beings become a noble and beautiful object of contemplation; and as the works partake the character of those who do them, by the same process human life also becomes rich, diversified, and animating, furnishing more abundant aliment to high thoughts and elevating feelings, and strengthening the tie which binds every individual to the race, by making the race infinitely better worth belonging to. In proportion to the development of his individuality, each person becomes more valuable to himself, and is therefore capable of being more valuable to others. There is a greater fulness of life about his own existence, and when there is more life in the units there is more in the mass which is composed of them. As much compression as is necessary to prevent the stronger specimens of human nature from encroaching on the rights of others, cannot be dispensed with; but for this there is ample compensation even in the point of view of human development. The means of development which the individual loses by being prevented from gratifying his inclinations to the injury of others, are chiefly obtained at the expense of the development of other people. And even to himself there is a full equivalent in the better development of the social part of his nature, rendered possible by the restraint put upon the selfish part. To be held to rigid rules of justice for the sake of others, develops the feelings and capacities which have the good of others for their object. But to be restrained in things not affecting their good, by their mere displeasure, develops

nothing valuable, except such force of character as may unfold itself in resisting the restraint. If acquiesced in, it dulls and blunts the whole nature. To give any fair-play to the nature of each, it is essential that different persons should be allowed to lead different lives.

He describes cultivating individuality as a process that makes a person "noble and beautiful." Cultivating individuality makes life "rich" and makes the human race "infinitely better worth belonging to." It makes life have "greater fullness." "In proportion to the development of his individuality, each person becomes more valuable to himself, and is therefore capable of being more valuable to others." That is, developing my own individuality not only makes my own life more valuable to me, but also more valuable to others—hence the "greater good." Forced conformity, in contrast, "dulls and blunts the whole nature."

So long as we're not harming anyone else, Mill thinks we should be free to experiment with our own vision of the good life. Some of these experiments will turn out well and satisfying, and others of us might learn from those examples and emulate those lifestyles ourselves. Other experiments will turn out poorly, such as a life of opiate-addiction. Sadly, there is utility in that example as well: it might teach the rest of us not to make those same mistakes. In any event, we should be free to pursue our own good, at our own cost, and to our own benefit, so long as we're not harming anyone else in the process.

Conclusion

It's easy to see why Mill has been influential to both libertarians and liberals alike. Libertarians (and some conservatives) appreciate his vision of a small and limited government, as well as his robust protection of free speech and expression. Liberals appreciate his endorsement of individuality, and rejection of forcing people to conform to a single vision of what's right. It's important to recall, in either case, that his conclusions are informed by a coherent vision of decision-making that applies to all judgments, both ethical and political: the principle of utility. In this, we have a wonderful example of the application of philosophical theory to political practice.

Mill's defense of the classical liberal ideal of letting people live as they see fit, so long as they're not harming others, facilitates the development of a pluralistic society—one in which numerous worldviews, value systems, and political ideologies coexist.

Clearly, the American political landscape is informed by a variety of worldviews, influenced by a variety of philosophers and philosophies, and the result of all this poses a serious question: how can a political community, such as the United States, resolve those conflicts and remain stable? It is to that question that we will turn in our next chapter, by exploring the work of John Rawls, as well as his influence on President Barack Obama.

John Stuart Mill (20 May 1806 – 8 May 1873) was an important proponent of utilitarian philosophy and (classical) liberal political philosophy. Mill was a child genius, studying under both his father (James Mill) and Jeremy Bentham (the founder of modern utilitarianism). At the age of three, he was taught Greek, and, by eight, had read all of "Herodotus" (see the brief excerpt from Herodotus at the end of our chapter on cultural relativism for a sample of Herodotus—then imagine an eight year old child having read him in the original Greek). In the excerpt that follows, Mill begins with a basic statement of the "Greatest Happiness Principle," upon which he claims all moral calculations are based. Although happiness is the central motivator (and determiner) of moral action, Mill resists the criticism that utilitarianism is a "swinish" doctrine by emphasizing the qualitative distinction between "higher" and "lower" pleasures. After offering additional evidence in support of the actual use and acceptance of utilitarian cost-benefit analyses, Mill considers and attempts to respond to some of the more traditional criticisms of utilitarianism.

John Stuart Mill: *Utilitarianism*

Chapter 2 – What Utilitarianism Is

A passing remark is all that needs be given to the ignorant blunder of supposing that those who stand up for utility as the test of right and wrong, use the term in that restricted and merely colloquial sense in which utility is opposed to pleasure. An apology is due to the philosophical opponents of utilitarianism, for even the momentary appearance of confounding them with any one capable of so absurd a misconception; which is the more extraordinary, inasmuch as the contrary accusation, of referring everything to pleasure, and that too in its grossest form, is another of the common charges against utilitarianism: and, as has been pointedly remarked by an able writer, the same sort of persons, and often the very same persons, denounce the theory "as impracticably dry when the word utility precedes the word pleasure, and as too practicably voluptuous when the word pleasure precedes the word utility." Those who know anything about the matter are aware that every writer, from Epicurus to Bentham, who maintained the theory of utility, meant by it, not something to be contradistinguished from pleasure, but pleasure itself, together with exemption from pain; and instead of opposing the useful to the agreeable or the ornamental, have always declared that the useful means these, among other things. Yet the common herd, including the herd of writers, not only in

newspapers and periodicals, but in books of weight and pretension, are perpetually falling into this shallow mistake. Having caught up the word utilitarian, while knowing nothing whatever about it but its sound, they habitually express by it the rejection, or the neglect, of pleasure in some of its forms; of beauty, of ornament, or of amusement. Nor is the term thus ignorantly misapplied solely in disparagement, but occasionally in compliment; as though it implied superiority to frivolity and the mere pleasures of the moment. And this perverted use is the only one in which the word is popularly known, and the one from which the new generation are acquiring their sole notion of its meaning. Those who introduced the word, but who had for many years discontinued it as a distinctive appellation, may well feel themselves called upon to resume it, if by doing so they can hope to contribute anything towards rescuing it from this utter degradation.

The creed which accepts as the foundation of morals, Utility, or the Greatest Happiness Principle, holds that actions are right in proportion as they tend to promote happiness, wrong as they tend to produce the reverse of happiness. By happiness is intended pleasure, and the absence of pain; by unhappiness, pain, and the privation of pleasure. To give a clear view of the moral standard set up by the theory, much more requires to be said; in particular, what things it includes in the ideas of pain and pleasure; and to what extent this is left an open question. But these supplementary explanations do not affect the theory of life on which this theory of morality is grounded — namely, that pleasure, and freedom from pain, are the only things desirable as ends; and that all desirable things (which are as numerous in the utilitarian as in any other scheme) are desirable either for the pleasure inherent in themselves, or as means to the promotion of pleasure and the prevention of pain.

Now, such a theory of life excites in many minds, and among them in some of the most estimable in feeling and purpose, inveterate dislike. To suppose that life has (as they express it) no higher end than pleasure — no better and nobler object of desire and pursuit — they designate as utterly mean and grovelling; as a doctrine worthy only of swine, to whom the followers of Epicurus were, at a very early period, contemptuously likened; and modern holders of the doctrine are occasionally made the subject of equally polite comparisons by its German, French, and English assailants.

When thus attacked, the Epicureans have always answered, that it is not they, but their accusers, who represent human nature in a degrading light; since the accusation supposes human beings to be capable of no pleasures except those of which swine are capable. If this supposition were true, the charge could not be gainsaid, but would then be no longer an imputation; for if the sources of pleasure were precisely the same to human beings and to swine, the rule of life which is good enough for the one would be good enough for the other. The comparison of the Epicurean life to that of beasts is felt as degrading, precisely because a beast's pleasures do not satisfy a human being's conceptions of happiness. Human beings have faculties more elevated than the animal appetites, and when once made conscious of them, do not regard anything as happiness which does not include their gratification. I do not, indeed, consider the Epicureans to have been by any means faultless in drawing out their scheme of consequences from the utilitarian principle. To do this in any sufficient manner, many Stoic, as

well as Christian elements require to be included. But there is no known Epicurean theory of life which does not assign to the pleasures of the intellect, of the feelings and imagination, and of the moral sentiments, a much higher value as pleasures than to those of mere sensation. It must be admitted, however, that utilitarian writers in general have placed the superiority of mental over bodily pleasures chiefly in the greater permanency, safety, uncostliness, etc., of the former — that is, in their circumstantial advantages rather than in their intrinsic nature. And on all these points utilitarians have fully proved their case; but they might have taken the other, and, as it may be called, higher ground, with entire consistency. It is quite compatible with the principle of utility to recognise the fact, that some kinds of pleasure are more desirable and more valuable than others. It would be absurd that while, in estimating all other things, quality is considered as well as quantity, the estimation of pleasures should be supposed to depend on quantity alone.

If I am asked, what I mean by difference of quality in pleasures, or what makes one pleasure more valuable than another, merely as a pleasure, except its being greater in amount, there is but one possible answer. Of two pleasures, if there be one to which all or almost all who have experience of both give a decided preference, irrespective of any feeling of moral obligation to prefer it, that is the more desirable pleasure. If one of the two is, by those who are competently acquainted with both, placed so far above the other that they prefer it, even though knowing it to be attended with a greater amount of discontent, and would not resign it for any quantity of the other pleasure which their nature is capable of, we are justified in ascribing to the preferred enjoyment a superiority in quality, so far outweighing quantity as to render it, in comparison, of small account.

Now it is an unquestionable fact that those who are equally acquainted with, and equally capable of appreciating and enjoying, both, do give a most marked preference to the manner of existence which employs their higher faculties. Few human creatures would consent to be changed into any of the lower animals, for a promise of the fullest allowance of a beast's pleasures; no intelligent human being would consent to be a fool, no instructed person would be an ignoramus, no person of feeling and conscience would be selfish and base, even though they should be persuaded that the fool, the dunce, or the rascal is better satisfied with his lot than they are with theirs. They would not resign what they possess more than he for the most complete satisfaction of all the desires which they have in common with him. If they ever fancy they would, it is only in cases of unhappiness so extreme, that to escape from it they would exchange their lot for almost any other, however undesirable in their own eyes. A being of higher faculties requires more to make him happy, is capable probably of more acute suffering, and certainly accessible to it at more points, than one of an inferior type; but in spite of these liabilities, he can never really wish to sink into what he feels to be a lower grade of existence. We may give what explanation we please of this unwillingness; we may attribute it to pride, a name which is given indiscriminately to some of the most and to some of the least estimable feelings of which mankind are capable: we may refer it to the love of liberty and personal independence, an appeal to which was with the Stoics one of the most effective means for the inculcation of it; to the love of power, or to the love of excitement, both of which do really enter into and contribute to it: but its most appropriate appellation is a sense of dignity, which all human beings possess in one form or other, and in some, though by no means in exact, proportion to their higher faculties, and which is so essential a part of the happiness of those in whom it is strong, that nothing which conflicts with it could be, otherwise than momentarily, an object of desire to them. Whoever supposes that this preference takes place at a sacrifice of happiness — that the superior being, in anything like equal circumstances, is not happier than the inferior — confounds the two very different ideas, of happiness, and content. It is indisputable that the being whose capacities of enjoyment are low, has the greatest chance of having them fully satisfied;

and a highly endowed being will always feel that any happiness which he can look for, as the world is constituted, is imperfect. But he can learn to bear its imperfections, if they are at all bearable; and they will not make him envy the being who is indeed unconscious of the imperfections, but only because he feels not at all the good which those imperfections qualify. It is better to be a human being dissatisfied than a pig satisfied; better to be Socrates dissatisfied than a fool satisfied. And if the fool, or the pig, are of a different opinion, it is because they only know their own side of the question. The other party to the comparison knows both sides.

It may be objected, that many who are capable of the higher pleasures, occasionally, under the influence of temptation, postpone them to the lower. But this is quite compatible with a full appreciation of the intrinsic superiority of the higher. Men often, from infirmity of character, make their election for the nearer good, though they know it to be the less valuable; and this no less when the choice is between two bodily pleasures, than when it is between bodily and mental. They pursue sensual indulgences to the injury of health, though perfectly aware that health is the greater good. It may be further objected, that many who begin with youthful enthusiasm for everything noble, as they advance in years sink into indolence and selfishness. But I do not believe that those who undergo this very common change, voluntarily choose the lower description of pleasures in preference to the higher. I believe that before they devote themselves exclusively to the one, they have already become incapable of the other. Capacity for the nobler feelings is in most natures a very tender plant, easily killed, not only by hostile influences, but by mere want of sustenance; and in the majority of young persons it speedily dies away if the occupations to which their position in life has devoted them, and the society into which it has thrown them, are not favourable to keeping that higher capacity in exercise. Men lose their high aspirations as they lose their intellectual tastes, because they have not time or opportunity for indulging them; and they addict themselves to inferior pleasures, not because they deliberately prefer them, but because they are either the only ones to which they have access, or the only ones which they are any longer capable of enjoying. It may be questioned whether any one who has remained equally susceptible to both classes of pleasures, ever knowingly and calmly preferred the lower; though many, in all ages, have broken down in an ineffectual attempt to combine both.

From this verdict of the only competent judges, I apprehend there can be no appeal. On a question which is the best worth having of two pleasures, or which of two modes of existence is the most grateful to the feelings, apart from its moral attributes and from its consequences, the judgment of those who are qualified by knowledge of both, or, if they differ, that of the majority among them, must be admitted as final. And there needs be the less hesitation to accept this judgment respecting the quality of pleasures, since there is no other tribunal to be referred to even on the question of quantity. What means are there of determining which is the acutest of two pains, or the intensest of two pleasurable sensations, except the general suffrage of those who are familiar with both? Neither pains nor pleasures are homogeneous, and pain is always heterogeneous with pleasure. What is there to decide whether a particular pleasure is worth purchasing at the cost of a particular pain, except the feelings and judgment of the experienced? When, therefore, those feelings and judgment declare the pleasures derived from the higher faculties to be preferable in kind, apart from the question of intensity, to those of which the animal nature, disjoined from the higher faculties, is susceptible, they are entitled on this subject to the same regard.

I have dwelt on this point, as being a necessary part of a perfectly just conception of Utility or Happiness, considered as the directive rule of human conduct. But it is by no means an indispensable condition to the acceptance of the utilitarian standard; for that standard is not the agent's own greatest happiness, but the greatest amount of happiness altogether; and if it may possibly be doubted whether a noble character is always the happier for its nobleness, there can be no doubt that it makes other people happier, and that the world in general is immensely a gainer by it. Utilitarianism, therefore, could only attain its end by the general cultivation of nobleness of character, even if each individual were only benefited by the nobleness of others, and his own, so far as happiness is concerned, were a sheer deduction from the benefit. But the bare enunciation of such an absurdity as this last, renders refutation superfluous.

According to the Greatest Happiness Principle, as above explained, the ultimate end, with reference to and for the sake of which all other things are desirable (whether we are considering our own good or that of other people), is an existence exempt as far as possible from pain, and as rich as possible in enjoyments, both in point of quantity and quality; the test of quality, and the rule for measuring it against quantity, being the preference felt by those who in their opportunities of experience, to which must be added their habits of self-consciousness and self-observation, are best furnished with the means of comparison. This, being, according to the utilitarian opinion, the end of human action, is necessarily also the standard of morality; which may accordingly be defined, the rules and precepts for human conduct, by the observance of which an existence such as has been described might be, to the greatest extent possible, secured to all mankind; and not to them only, but, so far as the nature of things admits, to the whole sentient creation.

Against this doctrine, however, arises another class of objectors, who say that happiness, in any form, cannot be the rational purpose of human life and action; because, in the first place, it is unattainable: and they contemptuously ask, what right hast thou to be happy? a question which Mr Carlyle clenches by the addition, What right, a short time ago, hadst thou even to be? Next, they say, that men can do without happiness; that all noble human beings have felt this, and could not have become noble but by learning the lesson of Entsagen, or renunciation; which lesson, thoroughly learnt and submitted to, they affirm to be the beginning and necessary condition of all virtue.

The first of these objections would go to the root of the matter were it well founded; for if no happiness is to be had at all by human beings, the attainment of it cannot be the end of morality, or of any rational conduct. Though, even in that case, something might still be said for the utilitarian theory; since utility includes not solely the pursuit of happiness, but the prevention or mitigation of unhappiness; and if the former aim be chimerical, there will be all the greater scope and more imperative need for the latter, so long at least as mankind think fit to live, and do not take refuge in the simultaneous act of suicide recommended under certain conditions by Novalis. When, however, it is thus positively asserted to be impossible that human life should be happy, the assertion, if not something like a verbal quibble, is at least an exaggeration. If by happiness be meant a continuity of highly pleasurable excitement, it is evident enough that this is impossible. A state of exalted pleasure lasts only moments, or in some cases, and with some intermissions, hours or days, and is the occasional brilliant flash of enjoyment, not its permanent and steady flame. Of this the philosophers who have taught that happiness is the end of life were as fully aware as those who taunt them. The happiness which they meant was not a life of rapture; but moments of such, in an existence made up of few and transitory pains, many and various pleasures, with a decided predominance of the active over the passive, and having as the foundation of the whole, not to expect more from life than it is capable of bestowing. A life thus composed, to those who have been fortunate enough to obtain it, has always appeared worthy of the name of happiness. And such an existence is even now the lot of many, during some considerable portion of their lives. The present wretched education, and wretched social arrangements, are the only real hindrance to its being attainable by almost all.

The objectors perhaps may doubt whether human beings, if taught to consider happiness as the end of life, would be satisfied with such a moderate share of it. But great numbers of mankind have been satisfied with much less. The main constituents of a satisfied life appear to be

two, either of which by itself is often found sufficient for the purpose: tranquillity, and excitement. With much tranquillity, many find that they can be content with very little pleasure: with much excitement, many can reconcile themselves to a considerable quantity of pain. There is assuredly no inherent impossibility in enabling even the mass of mankind to unite both; since the two are so far from being incompatible that they are in natural alliance, the prolongation of either being a preparation for, and exciting a wish for, the other. It is only those in whom indolence amounts to a vice, that do not desire excitement after an interval of repose: it is only those in whom the need of excitement is a disease, that feel the tranquillity which follows excitement dull and insipid, instead of pleasurable in direct proportion to the excitement which preceded it. When people who are tolerably fortunate in their outward lot do not find in life sufficient enjoyment to make it valuable to them, the cause generally is, caring for nobody but themselves. To those who have neither public nor private affections, the excitements of life are much curtailed, and in any case dwindle in value as the time approaches when all selfish interests must be terminated by death: while those who leave after them objects of personal affection, and especially those who have also cultivated a fellow-feeling with the collective interests of mankind, retain as lively an interest in life on the eve of death as in the vigour of youth and health. Next to selfishness, the principal cause which makes life unsatisfactory is want of mental cultivation. A cultivated mind — I do not mean that of a philosopher, but any mind to which the fountains of knowledge have been opened, and which has been taught, in any tolerable degree, to exercise its faculties — finds sources of inexhaustible interest in all that surrounds it; in the objects of nature, the achievements of art, the imaginations of poetry, the incidents of history, the ways of mankind, past and present, and their prospects in the future. It is possible, indeed, to become indifferent to all this, and that too without having exhausted a thousandth part of it; but only when one has had from the beginning no moral or human interest in these things, and has sought in them only the gratification of curiosity.

Now there is absolutely no reason in the nature of things why an amount of mental culture sufficient to give an intelligent interest in these objects of contemplation, should not be the inheritance of every one born in a civilised country. As little is there an inherent necessity that any human being should be a selfish egotist, devoid of every feeling or care but those which centre in his own miserable individuality. Something far superior to this is sufficiently common even now, to give ample earnest of what the human species may be made. Genuine private affections, and a sincere interest in the public good, are possible, though in unequal degrees, to every rightly brought up human being. In a world in which there is so much to interest, so much to enjoy, and so much also to correct and improve, every one who has this moderate amount of moral and intellectual requisites is capable of an existence which may be called enviable; and unless such a person, through bad laws, or subjection to the will of others, is denied the liberty to use the sources of happiness within his reach, he will not fail to find this enviable existence, if he escape the positive evils of life, the great sources of physical and mental suffering — such as indigence, disease, and the unkindness, worthlessness, or premature loss of objects of affection. The main stress of the problem lies, therefore, in the contest with these calamities, from which it is a rare good fortune entirely to escape; which, as things now are, cannot be obviated, and often cannot be in any material degree mitigated. Yet no one whose opinion deserves a moment's consideration can doubt that most of the great positive evils of the world are in themselves removable, and will, if human affairs continue to improve, be in the end reduced within narrow limits. Poverty, in any sense implying suffering, may be completely extinguished by the wisdom of society, combined with the good sense and providence of individuals. Even that most intractable of enemies, disease, may be indefinitely reduced in dimensions by good physical and moral education, and proper control of noxious

influences; while the progress of science holds out a promise for the future of still more direct conquests over this detestable foe. And every advance in that direction relieves us from some, not only of the chances which cut short our own lives, but, what concerns us still more, which deprive us of those in whom our happiness is wrapt up. As for vicissitudes of fortune, and other disappointments connected with worldly circumstances, these are principally the effect either of gross imprudence, of ill-regulated desires, or of bad or imperfect social institutions. All the grand sources, in short, of human suffering are in a great degree, many of them almost entirely, conquerable by human care and effort; and though their removal is grievously slow — though a long succession of generations will perish in the breach before the conquest is completed, and this world becomes all that, if will and knowledge were not wanting, it might easily be made — yet every mind sufficiently intelligent and generous to bear a part, however small and unconspicuous, in the endeavour, will draw a noble enjoyment from the contest itself, which he would not for any bribe in the form of selfish indulgence consent to be without.

And this leads to the true estimation of what is said by the objectors concerning the possibility, and the obligation, of learning to do without happiness. Unquestionably it is possible to do without happiness; it is done involuntarily by nineteen-twentieths of mankind, even in those parts of our present world which are least deep in barbarism; and it often has to be done voluntarily by the hero or the martyr, for the sake of something which he prizes more than his individual happiness. But this something, what is it, unless the happiness of others, or some of the requisites of happiness? It is noble to be capable of resigning entirely one's own portion of happiness, or chances of it: but, after all, this self-sacrifice must be for some end; it is not its own end; and if we are told that its end is not happiness, but virtue, which is better than happiness, I ask, would the sacrifice be made if the hero or martyr did not believe that it would earn for others immunity from similar sacrifices? Would it be made if he thought that his renunciation of happiness for himself would produce no fruit for any of his fellow creatures, but to make their lot like his, and place them also in the condition of persons who have renounced happiness? All honour to those who can abnegate for themselves the personal enjoyment of life, when by such renunciation they contribute worthily to increase the amount of happiness in the world; but he who does it, or professes to do it, for any other purpose, is no more deserving of admiration than the ascetic mounted on his pillar. He may be an inspiriting proof of what men can do, but assuredly not an example of what they should.

Though it is only in a very imperfect state of the world's arrangements that any one can best serve the happiness of others by the absolute sacrifice of his own, yet so long as the world is in that imperfect state, I fully acknowledge that the readiness to make such a sacrifice is the highest virtue which can be found in man. I will add, that in this condition of the world, paradoxical as the assertion may be, the conscious ability to do without happiness gives the best prospect of realising such happiness as is attainable. For nothing except that consciousness can raise a person above the chances of life, by making him feel that, let fate and fortune do their worst, they have not power to subdue him: which, once felt, frees him from excess of anxiety concerning the evils of life, and enables him, like many a Stoic in the worst times of the Roman Empire, to cultivate in tranquillity the sources of satisfaction accessible to him, without concerning himself about the uncertainty of their duration, any more than about their inevitable end.

Meanwhile, let utilitarians never cease to claim the morality of self devotion as a possession which belongs by as good a right to them, as either to the Stoic or to the Transcendentalist. The utilitarian morality does recognise in human beings the power of sacrificing their own greatest good for the good of others. It only refuses to admit that the sacrifice is itself a good. A sacrifice which does not increase, or tend to increase, the sum total of happiness, it considers as wasted. The only self-renunciation which it applauds, is devotion to the happiness, or to some of the means of happiness, of others; either of mankind collectively, or of individuals within the limits imposed by the collective interests of mankind.

I must again repeat, what the assailants of utilitarianism seldom have the justice to acknowledge, that the happiness which forms the utilitarian standard of what is right in conduct, is not the agent's own happiness, but that of all concerned. As between his own happiness and that of others, utilitarianism requires him to be as strictly impartial as a disinterested and benevolent spectator. In the golden rule of Jesus of Nazareth, we read the complete spirit of the ethics of utility. To do as you would be done by, and to love your neighbour as yourself, constitute the ideal perfection of utilitarian morality. As the means of making the nearest approach to this ideal, utility would enjoin, first, that laws and social arrangements should place the happiness, or (as speaking practically it may be called) the interest, of every individual, as nearly as possible in harmony with the interest of the whole; and secondly, that education and opinion, which have so vast a power over human character, should so use that power as to establish in the mind of every individual an indissoluble association between his own happiness and the good of the whole; especially between his own happiness and the practice of such modes of conduct, negative and positive, as regard for the universal happiness prescribes; so that not only he may be unable to conceive the possibility of happiness to himself, consistently with conduct opposed to the general good, but also that a direct impulse to promote the general good may be in every individual one of the habitual motives of action, and the sentiments connected therewith may fill a large and prominent place in every human being's sentient existence. If the impugners of the utilitarian morality represented it to their own minds in this its true character, I know not what recommendation possessed by any other morality they could possibly affirm to be wanting to it; what more beautiful or more exalted developments of human nature any other ethical system can be supposed to foster, or what springs of action, not accessible to the utilitarian, such systems rely on for giving effect to their mandates.

The objectors to utilitarianism cannot always be charged with representing it in a discreditable light. On the contrary, those among them who entertain anything like a just idea of its disinterested character, sometimes find fault with its standard as being too high for humanity. They say it is exacting too much to require that people shall always act from the inducement of promoting the general interests of society. But this is to mistake the very meaning of a standard of morals, and confound the rule of action with the motive of it. It is the business of ethics to tell us what are our duties, or by what test we may know them; but no system of ethics requires that the sole motive of all we do shall be a feeling of duty; on the contrary, ninety-nine hundredths of all our actions are done from other motives, and rightly so done, if the rule of duty does not condemn them. It is the more unjust to utilitarianism that this particular misapprehension should be made a ground of objection to it, inasmuch as utilitarian moralists have gone beyond almost all others in affirming that the motive has nothing to do with the morality of the action, though much with the worth of the agent. He who saves a fellow creature from drowning does what is morally right, whether his motive be duty, or the hope of being paid for his trouble; he who betrays the friend that trusts him, is guilty of a crime, even if his object be to serve another friend to whom he is under greater obligations.[2] But to speak only of actions done from the motive of duty, and in direct obedience to principle: it is a misapprehension of the utilitarian mode of thought, to conceive it as implying that people should fix their minds upon so wide a generality as the world, or society at large. The great majority of good actions are intended not for the benefit of the world, but for that of individuals, of which the good of the world is made up; and the thoughts of the most virtuous man need not on these occasions travel beyond the particular persons concerned, except so far as is necessary to assure himself that in benefiting them he is not violating the rights, that is, the legitimate and authorised expectations, of any one else. The multiplication of happiness is, according to the utilitarian ethics, the object of virtue: the occasions on which any person (except one in a thousand) has it in his power to do this on an extended scale, in other words to be a public benefactor, are but exceptional; and on these occasions alone is he called on to consider public utility; in every other case, private utility, the interest or happiness of some few persons, is all he has to attend to. Those alone the influence of whose actions extends to society in general, need concern themselves habitually about so large an object. In the case of abstinences indeed — of things which people forbear to do from moral considerations, though the consequences in the particular case might be beneficial — it would be unworthy of an intelligent agent not to be consciously aware that the action is of a class which, if practised generally, would be generally injurious, and that this is the ground of the obligation to abstain from it. The amount of regard for the public interest implied in this recognition, is no greater than is demanded by every system of morals, for they all enjoin to abstain from whatever is manifestly pernicious to society.

The same considerations dispose of another reproach against the doctrine of utility, founded on a still grosser misconception of the purpose of a standard of morality, and of the very meaning of the words right and wrong. It is often affirmed that utilitarianism renders men cold and unsympathising; that it chills their moral feelings towards individuals; that it makes them regard only the dry and hard consideration of the consequences of actions, not taking into their moral estimate the qualities from which those actions emanate. If the assertion means that they do not allow their judgment respecting the rightness or wrongness of an action to be influenced by their opinion of the qualities of the person who does it, this is a complaint not against utilitarianism, but against having any standard of morality at all; for certainly no known ethical standard decides an action to be good or bad because it is done by a good or a bad man, still less because done by an amiable, a brave, or a benevolent man, or the contrary. These considerations are relevant, not to the estimation of actions, but of persons; and there is nothing in the utilitarian theory inconsistent with the fact that there are other things which interest us in persons besides the rightness and wrongness of their actions. The Stoics, indeed, with the paradoxical misuse of language which was part of their system, and by which they strove to raise themselves above all concern about anything but virtue, were fond of saying that he who has that has everything; that he, and only he, is rich, is beautiful, is a king. But no claim of this description is made for the virtuous man by the utilitarian doctrine. Utilitarians are quite aware that there are other desirable possessions and qualities besides virtue, and are perfectly willing to allow to all of them their full worth. They are also aware that a right action does not necessarily indicate a virtuous character, and that actions which are blamable, often proceed from qualities entitled to praise. When this is apparent in any particular case, it modifies their estimation, not certainly of the act, but of the agent. I grant that they are, notwithstanding, of opinion, that in the long run the best proof of a good character is good actions; and resolutely refuse to consider any mental disposition as good, of which the predominant tendency is to produce bad conduct. This makes them unpopular with many people; but it is an unpopularity which they must share with every one who regards the distinction between right and wrong in a serious light; and the reproach is not one which a conscientious utilitarian need be anxious to repel.

If no more be meant by the objection than that many utilitarians look on the morality of actions, as measured by the utilitarian standard, with too exclusive a regard, and do not lay sufficient stress upon the other beauties of character which go towards making a human being lovable or admirable, this may be admitted. Utilitarians who have cultivated their moral feelings, but not their sympathies nor their artistic perceptions, do fall into this mistake; and so do all other moralists under the same conditions. What can be said in excuse for other moralists is equally available for them, namely,

that, if there is to be any error, it is better that it should be on that side. As a matter of fact, we may affirm that among utilitarians as among adherents of other systems, there is every imaginable degree of rigidity and of laxity in the application of their standard: some are even puritanically rigorous, while others are as indulgent as can possibly be desired by sinner or by sentimentalist. But on the whole, a doctrine which brings prominently forward the interest that mankind have in the repression and prevention of conduct which violates the moral law, is likely to be inferior to no other in turning the sanctions of opinion against such violations. It is true, the question, What does violate the moral law? is one on which those who recognise different standards of morality are likely now and then to differ. But difference of opinion on moral questions was not first introduced into the world by utilitarianism, while that doctrine does supply, if not always an easy, at all events a tangible and intelligible mode of deciding such differences.

It may not be superfluous to notice a few more of the common misapprehensions of utilitarian ethics, even those which are so obvious and gross that it might appear impossible for any person of candour and intelligence to fall into them; since persons, even of considerable mental endowments, often give themselves so little trouble to understand the bearings of any opinion against which they entertain a prejudice, and men are in general so little conscious of this voluntary ignorance as a defect, that the vulgarest misunderstandings of ethical doctrines are continually met with in the deliberate writings of persons of the greatest pretensions both to high principle and to philosophy. We not uncommonly hear the doctrine of utility inveighed against as a godless doctrine. If it be necessary to say anything at all against so mere an assumption, we may say that the question depends upon what idea we have formed of the moral character of the Deity. If it be a true belief that God desires, above all things, the happiness of his creatures, and that this was his purpose in their creation, utility is not only not a godless doctrine, but more profoundly religious than any other. If it be meant that utilitarianism does not recognise the revealed will of God as the supreme law of morals, I answer, that a utilitarian who believes in the perfect goodness and wisdom of God, necessarily believes that whatever God has thought fit to reveal on the subject of morals, must fulfil the requirements of utility in a supreme degree. But others besides utilitarians have been of opinion that the Christian revelation was intended, and is fitted, to inform the hearts and minds of mankind with a spirit which should enable them to find for themselves what is right, and incline them to do it when found, rather than to tell them, except in a very general way, what it is; and that we need a doctrine of ethics, carefully followed out, to interpret to us the will of God. Whether this opinion is correct or not, it is superfluous here to discuss; since whatever aid religion, either natural or revealed, can afford to ethical investigation, is as open to the utilitarian moralist as to any other. He can use it as the testimony of God to the usefulness or hurtfulness of any given course of action, by as good a right as others can use it for the indication of a transcendental law, having no connection with usefulness or with happiness.

Again, Utility is often summarily stigmatised as an immoral doctrine by giving it the name of Expediency, and taking advantage of the popular use of that term to contrast it with Principle. But the Expedient, in the sense in which it is opposed to the Right, generally means that which is expedient for the particular interest of the agent himself; as when a minister sacrifices the interests of his country to keep himself in place. When it means anything better than this, it means that which is expedient for some immediate object, some temporary purpose, but which violates a rule whose observance is expedient in a much higher degree. The Expedient, in this sense, instead of being the same thing with the useful, is a branch of the hurtful. Thus, it would often be expedient, for the purpose of getting over some momentary embarrassment, or attaining some object immediately useful to ourselves or others, to tell a lie. But inasmuch as the cultivation in ourselves of a sensitive feeling on the subject of veracity, is one of the most useful, and the enfeeblement of that feeling one of

the most hurtful, things to which our conduct can be instrumental; and inasmuch as any, even unintentional, deviation from truth, does that much towards weakening the trustworthiness of human assertion, which is not only the principal support of all present social well-being, but the insufficiency of which does more than any one thing that can be named to keep back civilisation, virtue, everything on which human happiness on the largest scale depends; we feel that the violation, for a present advantage, of a rule of such transcendent expediency, is not expedient, and that he who, for the sake of a convenience to himself or to some other individual, does what depends on him to deprive mankind of the good, and inflict upon them the evil, involved in the greater or less reliance which they can place in each other's word, acts the part of one of their worst enemies. Yet that even this rule, sacred as it is, admits of possible exceptions, is acknowledged by all moralists; the chief of which is when the withholding of some fact (as of information from a malefactor, or of bad news from a person dangerously ill) would save an individual (especially an individual other than oneself) from great and unmerited evil, and when the withholding can only be effected by denial. But in order that the exception may not extend itself beyond the need, and may have the least possible effect in weakening reliance on veracity, it ought to be recognised, and, if possible, its limits defined; and if the principle of utility is good for anything, it must be good for weighing these conflicting utilities against one another, and marking out the region within which one or the other preponderates.

Again, defenders of utility often find themselves called upon to reply to such objections as this — that there is not time, previous to action, for calculating and weighing the effects of any line of conduct on the general happiness. This is exactly as if any one were to say that it is impossible to guide our conduct by Christianity, because there is not time, on every occasion on which anything has to be done, to read through the Old and New Testaments. The answer to the objection is, that there has been ample time, namely, the whole past duration of the human species. During all that time, mankind have been learning by experience the tendencies of actions; on which experience all the prudence, as well as all the morality of life, are dependent. People talk as if the commencement of this course of experience had hitherto been put off, and as if, at the moment when some man feels tempted to meddle with the property or life of another, he had to begin considering for the first time whether murder and theft are injurious to human happiness. Even then I do not think that he would find the question very puzzling; but, at all events, the matter is now done to his hand. It is truly a whimsical supposition that, if mankind were agreed in considering utility to be the test of morality, they would remain without any agreement as to what is useful, and would take no measures for having their notions on the subject taught to the young, and enforced by law and opinion. There is no difficulty in proving any ethical standard whatever to work ill, if we suppose universal idiocy to be conjoined with it; but on any hypothesis short of that, mankind must by this time have acquired positive beliefs as to the effects of some actions on their happiness; and the beliefs which have thus come down are the rules of morality for the multitude, and for the philosopher until he has succeeded in finding better. That philosophers might easily do this, even now, on many subjects; that the received code of ethics is by no means of divine right; and that mankind have still much to learn as to the effects of actions on the general happiness, I admit, or rather, earnestly maintain. The corollaries from the principle of utility, like the precepts of every practical art, admit of indefinite improvement, and, in a progressive state of the human mind, their improvement is perpetually going on. But to consider the rules of morality as improvable, is one thing; to pass over the intermediate generalisations entirely, and endeavour to test each individual action directly by the first principle, is another. It is a strange notion that the acknowledgment of a first principle is inconsistent with the admission of secondary ones. To inform a traveller respecting the place of his ultimate destination, is not to forbid the use of landmarks and direction-posts

on the way. The proposition that happiness is the end and aim of morality, does not mean that no road ought to be laid down to that goal, or that persons going thither should not be advised to take one direction rather than another. Men really ought to leave off talking a kind of nonsense on this subject, which they would neither talk nor listen to on other matters of practical concernment. Nobody argues that the art of navigation is not founded on astronomy, because sailors cannot wait to calculate the Nautical Almanack. Being rational creatures, they go to sea with it ready calculated; and all rational creatures go out upon the sea of life with their minds made up on the common questions of right and wrong, as well as on many of the far more difficult questions of wise and foolish. And this, as long as foresight is a human quality, it is to be presumed they will continue to do. Whatever we adopt as the fundamental principle of morality, we require subordinate principles to apply it by; the impossibility of doing without them, being common to all systems, can afford no argument against any one in particular; but gravely to argue as if no such secondary principles could be had, and as if mankind had remained till now, and always must remain, without drawing any general conclusions from the experience of human life, is as high a pitch, I think, as absurdity has ever reached in philosophical controversy.

The remainder of the stock arguments against utilitarianism mostly consist in laying to its charge the common infirmities of human nature, and the general difficulties which embarrass conscientious persons in shaping their course through life. We are told that a utilitarian will be apt to make his own particular case an exception to moral rules, and, when under temptation, will see a utility in the breach of a rule, greater than he will see in its observance. But is utility the only creed which is able to furnish us with excuses for evil doing, and means of cheating our own conscience? They are afforded in abundance by all doctrines which recognise as a fact in morals the existence of conflicting considerations; which all doctrines do, that have been believed by sane persons. It is not the fault of any creed, but of the complicated nature of human affairs, that rules of conduct cannot be so framed as to require no exceptions, and that hardly any kind of action can safely be laid down as either always obligatory or always condemnable. There is no ethical creed which does not temper the rigidity of its laws, by giving a certain latitude, under the moral responsibility of the agent, for accommodation to peculiarities of circumstances; and under every creed, at the opening thus made, self-deception and dishonest casuistry get in. There exists no moral system under which there do not arise unequivocal cases of conflicting obligation. These are the real difficulties, the knotty points both in the theory of ethics, and in the conscientious guidance of personal conduct. They are overcome practically, with greater or with less success, according to the intellect and virtue of the individual; but it can hardly be pretended that any one will be the less qualified for dealing with them, from possessing an ultimate standard to which conflicting rights and duties can be referred. If utility is the ultimate source of moral obligations, utility may be invoked to decide between them when their demands are incompatible. Though the application of the standard may be difficult, it is better than none at all: while in other systems, the moral laws all claiming independent authority, there is no common umpire entitled to interfere between them; their claims to precedence one over another rest on little better than sophistry, and unless determined, as they generally are, by the unacknowledged influence of considerations of utility, afford a free scope for the action of personal desires and partialities. We must remember that only in these cases of conflict between secondary principles is it requisite that first principles should be appealed to. There is no case of moral obligation in which some secondary principle is not involved; and if only one, there can seldom be any real doubt which one it is, in the mind of any person by whom the principle itself is recognized.

This selection is a portion of Mill's "On Liberty." In these excerpts, Mill reinforces his basic utilitarian foundation, and argues that the only proper use of State force to restrain an individual's behavior is for the sake of the protection of others from harm. He rejects government sanctions for the person's "own good." He also offers a spirited defense of the value of free expression, and even of personal expression and individualism. Mill's arguments find a home today in the Libertarian political party, but also in the Liberal notion that the government should not interfere in the "personal life" of citizens, as well as the Conservation preference for smaller governments.

John Stuart Mill: *On Liberty.*

...

The Walter Scott Publishing Co., Ltd.
London and Felling-on-Tyne
New York and Melbourne
http://www.gutenberg.org/ebooks/34901

...

CHAPTER I.
INTRODUCTORY.

The subject of this Essay is not the so-called Liberty of the Will, so unfortunately opposed to the misnamed doctrine of Philosophical Necessity; but Civil, or Social Liberty: the nature and limits of the power which can be legitimately exercised by society over the individual. A question seldom stated, and hardly ever discussed, in general terms, but which profoundly influences the practical controversies of the age by its latent presence, and is likely soon to make itself recognised as the vital question of the future. It is so far from being new, that in a certain sense, it has divided mankind, almost from the remotest ages; but in the stage of progress into which the more civilised portions of the species have now entered, it presents itself under new conditions, and requires a different and more fundamental treatment.

The struggle between Liberty and Authority is the most conspicuous feature in the portions of history with which we are earliest familiar, particularly in that of Greece, Rome, and England. But in old times this contest was between subjects, or some classes of subjects, and the government. By liberty, was meant protection against the tyranny of the political rulers. The rulers were conceived (except in some of the popular governments of Greece) as in a necessarily antagonistic position to the people whom they ruled. They consisted of a governing One, or a governing tribe or caste, who derived their authority from inheritance or conquest, who, at all events, did not hold it at the pleasure of the governed, and whose supremacy men did not venture, perhaps did not desire, to contest, whatever precautions might be taken against its oppressive exercise. Their power was regarded as necessary, but also as highly dangerous; as a weapon which they would attempt to use against their subjects, no less than against external enemies. To prevent the weaker members of the community from being preyed upon by innumerable vultures, it was needful that there should be an animal of prey stronger than the rest, commissioned to keep them down. But as the king of the vultures would be no less bent upon preying on the flock than any of the minor harpies, it was indispensable to be in a perpetual attitude of defence against his beak and claws. The aim, therefore, of patriots, was to set limits to the power which the ruler should be suffered to exercise over the community; and this limitation was what they meant by liberty. It was attempted in two ways. First, by obtaining a recognition of certain immunities, called political liberties or rights, which it was to be regarded as a breach of duty in the ruler to infringe, and which if he did infringe, specific resistance, or general rebellion, was held to be justifiable. A second, and generally a later expedient, was the establishment of constitutional checks; by which the consent of the community, or of a body of some sort, supposed to represent its interests, was made a necessary condition to some of the more important acts of the governing power. To the first of these modes of limitation, the ruling power, in most European countries, was compelled, more or less, to submit. It was not so with the second; and to attain this, or when already in some degree possessed, to attain it more completely, became everywhere the principal object of the lovers of liberty. And so long as mankind were content to combat one enemy by another, and to be ruled by a master, on condition of being guaranteed more or less efficaciously against his tyranny, they did not carry their aspirations beyond this point.

A time, however, came, in the progress of human affairs, when men ceased to think it a necessity of nature that their governors should be an independent power, opposed in interest to themselves. It appeared to them much better that the various magistrates of the State should be their tenants or delegates, revocable at their pleasure. In that way alone, it seemed, could they have complete security that the powers of government would never be abused to their disadvantage. By degrees, this new demand for elective and temporary rulers became the prominent object of the exertions of the popular party, wherever any such party existed; and superseded, to a considerable extent, the previous efforts to limit the power of rulers. As the struggle proceeded for making the ruling power emanate from the periodical choice of the ruled, some persons began to think that too much importance had been attached to the limitation of the power itself. *That* (it might seem) was a resource against rulers whose interests were habitually opposed to those of the people. What was now wanted was, that the rulers should be identified with the people; that their interest and will should be the interest and will of the nation. The nation did not need to be protected against its own will. There was no fear of its tyrannising over itself. Let the rulers be effectually

responsible to it, promptly removable by it, and it could afford to trust them with power of which it could itself dictate the use to be made. Their power was but the nation's own power, concentrated, and in a form convenient for exercise. This mode of thought, or rather perhaps of feeling, was common among the last generation of European liberalism, in the Continental section of which it still apparently predominates. Those who admit any limit to what a government may do, except in the case of such governments as they think ought not to exist, stand out as brilliant exceptions among the political thinkers of the Continent. A similar tone of sentiment might by this time have been prevalent in our own country, if the circumstances which for a time encouraged it, had continued unaltered.

But, in political and philosophical theories, as well as in persons, success discloses faults and infirmities which failure might have concealed from observation. The notion, that the people have no need to limit their power over themselves, might seem axiomatic, when popular government was a thing only dreamed about, or read of as having existed at some distant period of the past. Neither was that notion necessarily disturbed by such temporary aberrations as those of the French Revolution, the worst of which were the work of a usurping few, and which, in any case, belonged, not to the permanent working of popular institutions, but to a sudden and convulsive outbreak against monarchical and aristocratic despotism. In time, however, a democratic republic came to occupy a large portion of the earth's surface, and made itself felt as one of the most powerful members of the community of nations; and elective and responsible government became subject to the observations and criticisms which wait upon a great existing fact. It was now perceived that such phrases as "self-government," and "the power of the people over themselves," do not express the true state of the case. The "people" who exercise the power are not always the same people with those over whom it is exercised; and the "self-government" spoken of is not the government of each by himself, but of each by all the rest. The will of the people, moreover, practically means, the will of the most numerous or the most active *part* of the people; the majority, or those who succeed in making themselves accepted as the majority: the people, consequently, *may* desire to oppress a part of their number; and precautions are as much needed against this, as against any other abuse of power. The limitation, therefore, of the power of government over individuals, loses none of its importance when the holders of power are regularly accountable to the community, that is, to the strongest party therein. This view of things, recommending itself equally to the intelligence of thinkers and to the inclination of those important classes in European society to whose real or supposed interests democracy is adverse, has had no difficulty in establishing itself; and in political speculations "the tyranny of the majority" is now generally included among the evils against which society requires to be on its guard.

Like other tyrannies, the tyranny of the majority was at first, and is still vulgarly, held in dread, chiefly as operating through the acts of the public authorities. But reflecting persons perceived that when society is itself the tyrant—society collectively, over the separate individuals who compose it—its means of tyrannising are not restricted to the acts which it may do by the hands of its political functionaries. Society can and does execute its own mandates: and if it issues wrong mandates instead of right, or any mandates at all in things with which it ought not to meddle, it practises a social tyranny more formidable than many kinds of political oppression, since, though not usually upheld by such extreme penalties, it leaves fewer means of escape, penetrating much more deeply into the details of life, and enslaving the soul itself. Protection, therefore, against the tyranny of the magistrate is not enough: there needs protection also against the tyranny of the prevailing opinion and feeling; against the tendency of society to impose, by other means than civil penalties, its own ideas and practices as rules of conduct on those who dissent from them; to fetter the development, and, if possible, prevent the

formation, of any individuality not in harmony with its ways, and compel all characters to fashion themselves upon the model of its own. There is a limit to the legitimate interference of collective opinion with individual independence: and to find that limit, and maintain it against encroachment, is as indispensable to a good condition of human affairs, as protection against political despotism.

. . .

There is, in fact, no recognised principle by which the propriety or impropriety of government interference is customarily tested. People decide according to their personal preferences. Some, whenever they see any good to be done, or evil to be remedied, would willingly instigate the government to undertake the business; while others prefer to bear almost any amount of social evil, rather than add one to the departments of human interests amenable to governmental control. And men range themselves on one or the other side in any particular case, according to this general direction of their sentiments; or according to the degree of interest which they feel in the particular thing which it is proposed that the government should do, or according to the belief they entertain that the government would, or would not, do it in the manner they prefer; but very rarely on account of any opinion to which they consistently adhere, as to what things are fit to be done by a government. And it seems to me that in consequence of this absence of rule or principle, one side is at present as often wrong as the other; the interference of government is, with about equal frequency, improperly invoked and improperly condemned.

The object of this Essay is to assert one very simple principle, as entitled to govern absolutely the dealings of society with the individual in the way of compulsion and control, whether the means used be physical force in the form of legal penalties, or the moral coercion of public opinion. That principle is, that the sole end for which mankind are warranted, individually or collectively, in interfering with the liberty of action of any of their number, is self-protection.

That the only purpose for which power can be rightfully exercised over any member of a civilised community, against his will, is to prevent harm to others. His own good, either physical or moral, is not a sufficient warrant. He cannot rightfully be compelled to do or forbear because it will be better for him to do so, because it will make him happier, because, in the opinions of others, to do so would be wise, or even right. These are good reasons for remonstrating with him, or reasoning with him, or persuading him, or entreating him, but not for compelling him, or visiting him with any evil in case he do otherwise. To justify that, the conduct from which it is desired to deter him must be calculated to produce evil to some one else. The only part of the conduct of any one, for which he is amenable to society, is that which concerns others. In the part which merely concerns himself, his independence is, of right, absolute. Over himself, over his own body and mind, the individual is sovereign.

It is, perhaps, hardly necessary to say that this doctrine is meant to apply only to human beings in the maturity of their faculties. We are not speaking of children, or of young persons below the age which the law may fix as that of manhood or womanhood. Those who are still in a state to require being taken care of by others, must be protected against their own actions as well as against external injury. For the same reason, we may leave out of consideration those backward states of society in which the race itself may be considered as in its nonage. The early difficulties in the way of spontaneous progress are so great, that there is seldom any choice of means for overcoming them; and a ruler full of the spirit of improvement is warranted in the use of any expedients that will attain an end, perhaps otherwise unattainable. Despotism is a legitimate mode of government in dealing with barbarians, provided the end be their improvement, and the means justified by actually effecting that end. Liberty, as a principle, has no application to any state of things anterior to the time when mankind have become capable of being improved by free and equal discussion. Until then, there is nothing for them but implicit obedience to an Akbar or a Charlemagne, if they are so fortunate as to find one. But as soon as mankind have attained the capacity of being guided to their own improvement by conviction or persuasion (a period long since reached in all nations with whom we need here concern ourselves), compulsion, either in the direct form or in that of pains and penalties for non-compliance, is no longer admissible as a means to their own good, and justifiable only for the security of others.

It is proper to state that I forego any advantage which could be derived to my argument from the idea of abstract right, as a thing independent of utility. I regard utility as the ultimate appeal on all ethical questions; but it must be utility in the largest sense, grounded on the permanent interests of man as a progressive being. Those interests, I contend, authorise the subjection of individual spontaneity to external control, only in respect to those actions of each, which concern the interest of other people. If any one does an act hurtful to others, there is a *primâ facie* case for punishing him, by law, or, where legal penalties are not safely applicable, by general disapprobation. There are also many positive acts for the benefit of others, which he may rightfully be compelled to perform; such as, to give evidence in a court of justice; to bear his fair share in the common defence, or in any other joint work necessary to the interest of the society of which he enjoys the protection; and to perform certain acts of individual beneficence, such as saving a fellow-creature's life, or interposing to protect the defenceless against ill-usage, things which whenever it is obviously a man's duty to do, he may rightfully be made responsible to society for not doing. A person may cause evil to others not only by his actions but by his inaction, and in either case he is justly accountable to them for the injury. The latter case, it is true, requires a much more cautious exercise of compulsion than the former. To make any one answerable for doing evil to others, is the rule; to make him answerable for not preventing evil, is, comparatively speaking, the exception. Yet there are many cases clear enough and grave enough to justify that exception. In all things which regard the external relations of the individual, he is *de jure* amenable to those whose interests are concerned, and if need be, to society as their protector. There are often good reasons for not holding him to the responsibility; but these reasons must arise from the special expediencies of the case: either because it is a kind of case in which he is on the whole likely to act better, when left to his own discretion, than when controlled in any way in which society have it in their power to control him; or because the attempt to exercise control would produce other evils, greater than those which it would prevent. When such reasons as these preclude the enforcement of responsibility, the conscience of the agent himself should step into the vacant judgment seat, and protect those interests of others which have no external protection; judging himself all the more rigidly, because the case does not admit of his being made accountable to the judgment of his fellow-creatures.

But there is a sphere of action in which society, as distinguished from the individual, has, if any, only an indirect interest; comprehending all that portion of a person's life and conduct which affects only himself, or if it also affects others, only with their free, voluntary, and undeceived consent and participation. When I say only himself, I mean directly, and in the first instance: for whatever affects himself, may affect others *through* himself; and the objection which may be grounded on this contingency, will receive consideration in the sequel. This, then, is the appropriate region of human liberty. It comprises, first, the inward domain of consciousness; demanding liberty of conscience, in the most comprehensive sense; liberty of thought and feeling; absolute freedom of opinion and sentiment on all subjects, practical or speculative, scientific, moral, or theological. The liberty of expressing and publishing opinions may seem to fall under a different principle, since it belongs to that part of the conduct of an individual which concerns other people; but, being almost of as much importance as the liberty of thought itself, and resting in great part on the same reasons, is practically inseparable from it. Secondly, the principle requires liberty of tastes

and pursuits; of framing the plan of our life to suit our own character; of doing as we like, subject to such consequences as may follow: without impediment from our fellow-creatures, so long as what we do does not harm them, even though they should think our conduct foolish, perverse, or wrong. Thirdly, from this liberty of each individual, follows the liberty, within the same limits, of combination among individuals; freedom to unite, for any purpose not involving harm to others: the persons combining being supposed to be of full age, and not forced or deceived.

No society in which these liberties are not, on the whole, respected, is free, whatever may be its form of government; and none is completely free in which they do not exist absolute and unqualified. The only freedom which deserves the name, is that of pursuing our own good in our own way, so long as we do not attempt to deprive others of theirs, or impede their efforts to obtain it. Each is the proper guardian of his own health, whether bodily, or mental and spiritual. Mankind are greater gainers by suffering each other to live as seems good to themselves, than by compelling each to live as seems good to the rest.

. . .

CHAPTER II.
OF THE LIBERTY OF THOUGHT AND DISCUSSION.

The time, it is to be hoped, is gone by, when any defence would be necessary of the "liberty of the press" as one of the securities against corrupt or tyrannical government. No argument, we may suppose, can now be needed, against permitting a legislature or an executive, not identified in interest with the people, to prescribe opinions to them, and determine what doctrines or what arguments they shall be allowed to hear. This aspect of the question, besides, has been so often and so triumphantly enforced by preceding writers, that it need not be specially insisted on in this place. Though the law of England, on the subject of the press, is as servile to this day as it was in the time of the Tudors, there is little danger of its being actually put in force against political discussion, except during some temporary panic, when fear of insurrection drives ministers and judges from their propriety; and, speaking generally, it is not, in constitutional countries, to be apprehended that the government, whether completely responsible to the people or not, will often attempt to control the expression of opinion, except when in doing so it makes itself the organ of the general intolerance of the public. Let us suppose, therefore, that the government is entirely at one with the people, and never thinks of exerting any power of coercion unless in agreement with what it conceives to be their voice. But I deny the right of the people to exercise such coercion, either by themselves or by their government. The power itself is illegitimate. The best government has no more title to it than the worst. It is as noxious, or more noxious, when exerted in accordance with public opinion, than when in or opposition to it. If all mankind minus one, were of one opinion, and only one person were of the contrary opinion, mankind would be no more justified in silencing that one person, than he, if he had the power, would be justified in silencing mankind. Were an opinion a personal possession of no value except to the owner; if to be obstructed in the enjoyment of it were simply a private injury, it would make some difference whether the injury was inflicted only on a few persons or on many. But the peculiar evil of silencing the expression of an opinion is, that it is robbing the human race; posterity as well as the existing generation; those who dissent from the opinion, still more than those who hold it. If the opinion is right, they are deprived of the opportunity of exchanging error for truth: if wrong, they lose, what is almost as great a benefit, the clearer perception and livelier impression of truth, produced by its collision with error.

It is necessary to consider separately these two hypotheses, each of which has a distinct branch of the argument corresponding to it. We can never be sure that the opinion we are endeavouring to stifle is a false opinion; and if we were sure, stifling it would be an evil still.

First: the opinion which it is attempted to suppress by authority may possibly be true.

Those who desire to suppress it, of course deny its truth; but they are not infallible. They have no authority to decide the question for all mankind, and exclude every other person from the means of judging. To refuse a hearing to an opinion, because they are sure that it is false, is to assume that *their* certainty is the same thing as *absolute* certainty. All silencing of discussion is an assumption of infallibility. Its condemnation may be allowed to rest on this common argument, not the worse for being common.

Unfortunately for the good sense of mankind, the fact of their fallibility is far from carrying the weight in their practical judgment, which is always allowed to it in theory; for while every one well knows himself to be fallible, few think it necessary to take any precautions against their own fallibility, or admit the supposition that any opinion, of which they feel very certain, may be one of the examples of the error to which they acknowledge themselves to be liable. Absolute princes, or others who are accustomed to unlimited deference, usually feel this complete confidence in their own opinions on nearly all subjects. People more happily situated, who sometimes hear their opinions disputed, and are not wholly unused to be set right when they are wrong, place the same unbounded reliance only on such of their opinions as are shared by all who surround them, or to whom they habitually defer: for in proportion to a man's want of confidence in his own solitary judgment, does he usually repose, with implicit trust, on the infallibility of "the world" in general. And the world, to each individual, means the part of it with which he comes in contact; his party, his sect, his church, his class of society: the man may be called, by comparison, almost liberal and large-minded to whom it means anything so comprehensive as his own country or his own age. Nor is his faith in this collective authority at all shaken by his being aware that other ages, countries, sects, churches, classes, and parties have thought, and even now think, the exact reverse. He devolves upon his own world the responsibility of being in the right against the dissentient worlds of other people; and it never troubles him that mere accident has decided which of these numerous worlds is the object of his reliance, and that the same causes which make him a Churchman in London, would have made him a Buddhist or a Confucian in Pekin. Yet it is as evident in itself as any amount of argument can make it, that ages are no more infallible than individuals; every age having held many opinions which subsequent ages have deemed not only false but absurd; and it is as certain that many opinions, now general, will be rejected by future ages, as it is that many, once general, are rejected by the present.

The objection likely to be made to this argument, would probably take some such form as the following. There is no greater assumption of infallibility in forbidding the propagation of error, than in any other thing which is done by public authority on its own judgment and responsibility. Judgment is given to men that they may use it. Because it may be used erroneously, are men to be told that they ought not to use it at all? To prohibit what they think pernicious, is not claiming exemption from error, but fulfilling the duty incumbent on them, although fallible, of acting on their conscientious conviction. If we were never to act on our opinions, because those opinions may be wrong, we should leave all our interests uncared for, and all our duties unperformed. An objection which applies to all conduct, can be no valid objection to any conduct in particular. It is the duty of governments, and of individuals, to form the truest opinions they can; to form them carefully, and never impose them upon others unless they are quite sure of being right. But when they are sure (such reasoners may say), it is not conscientiousness but cowardice to shrink from acting on their opinions, and allow doctrines which they honestly think dangerous to the welfare of mankind, either in this life or in another, to be scattered abroad without restraint, because other people, in less enlightened times, have persecuted opinions now believed to be true. Let us take care, it may be said, not to make the same mistake: but governments and nations have made mistakes in other things, which are not denied to be fit subjects for the exercise of authority: they have laid on bad taxes, made unjust wars. Ought we therefore to lay on no

taxes, and, under whatever provocation, make no wars? Men, and governments, must act to the best of their ability. There is no such thing as absolute certainty, but there is assurance sufficient for the purposes of human life. We may, and must, assume our opinion to be true for the guidance of our own conduct: and it is assuming no more when we forbid bad men to pervert society by the propagation of opinions which we regard as false and pernicious.

I answer that it is assuming very much more. There is the greatest difference between presuming an opinion to be true, because, with every opportunity for contesting it, it has not been refuted, and assuming its truth for the purpose of not permitting its refutation. Complete liberty of contradicting and disproving our opinion, is the very condition which justifies us in assuming its truth for purposes of action; and on no other terms can a being with human faculties have any rational assurance of being right.

When we consider either the history of opinion, or the ordinary conduct of human life, to what is it to be ascribed that the one and the other are no worse than they are? Not certainly to the inherent force of the human understanding; for, on any matter not self-evident, there are ninety-nine persons totally incapable of judging of it, for one who is capable; and the capacity of the hundredth person is only comparative; for the majority of the eminent men of every past generation held many opinions now known to be erroneous, and did or approved numerous things which no one will now justify. Why is it, then, that there is on the whole a preponderance among mankind of rational opinions and rational conduct? If there really is this preponderance— which there must be, unless human affairs are, and have always been, in an almost desperate state—it is owing to a quality of the human mind, the source of everything respectable in man either as an intellectual or as a moral being, namely, that his errors are corrigible. He is capable of rectifying his mistakes, by discussion and experience. Not by experience alone. There must be discussion, to show how experience is to be interpreted. Wrong opinions and practices gradually yield to fact and argument: but facts and arguments, to produce any effect on the mind, must be brought before it. Very few facts are able to tell their own story, without comments to bring out their meaning. The whole strength and value, then, of human judgment, depending on the one property, that it can be set right when it is wrong, reliance can be placed on it only when the means of setting it right are kept constantly at hand. In the case of any person whose judgment is really deserving of confidence, how has it become so? Because he has kept his mind open to criticism of his opinions and conduct. Because it has been his practice to listen to all that could be said against him; to profit by as much of it as was just, and expound to himself, and upon occasion to others, the fallacy of what was fallacious. Because he has felt, that the only way in which a human being can make some approach to knowing the whole of a subject, is by hearing what can be said about it by persons of every variety of opinion, and studying all modes in which it can be looked at by every character of mind. No wise man ever acquired his wisdom in any mode but this; nor is it in the nature of human intellect to become wise in any other manner. The steady habit of correcting and completing his own opinion by collating it with those of others, so far from causing doubt and hesitation in carrying it into practice, is the only stable foundation for a just reliance on it: for, being cognisant of all that can, at least obviously, be said against him, and having taken up his position against all gainsayers—knowing that he has sought for objections and difficulties, instead of avoiding them, and has shut out no light which can be thrown upon the subject from any quarter—he has a right to think his judgment better than that of any person, or any multitude, who have not gone through a similar process.

. . .

Let us now pass to the second division of the argument, and dismissing the supposition that any of the received opinions may be false, let us assume them to be true, and examine into the worth of the manner in which they are likely to be held, when their truth is not freely and openly canvassed. However unwillingly a person who has a strong opinion may admit the possibility that his opinion may be false, he ought to be moved by the consideration that however true it may be, if it is not fully, frequently, and fearlessly discussed, it will be held as a dead dogma, not a living truth.

There is a class of persons (happily not quite so numerous as formerly) who think it enough if a person assents undoubtingly to what they think true, though he has no knowledge whatever of the grounds of the opinion, and could not make a tenable defence of it against the most superficial objections. Such persons, if they can once get their creed taught from authority, naturally think that no good, and some harm, comes of its being allowed to be questioned. Where their influence prevails, they make it nearly impossible for the received opinion to be rejected wisely and considerately, though it may still be rejected rashly and ignorantly; for to shut out discussion entirely is seldom possible, and when it once gets in, beliefs not grounded on conviction are apt to give way before the slightest semblance of an argument. Waiving, however, this possibility— assuming that the true opinion abides in the mind, but abides as a prejudice, a belief independent of, and proof against, argument— this is not the way in which truth ought to be held by a rational being. This is not knowing the truth. Truth, thus held, is but one superstition the more, accidentally clinging to the words which enunciate a truth.

If the intellect and judgment of mankind ought to be cultivated, a thing which Protestants at least do not deny, on what can these faculties be more appropriately exercised by any one, than on the things which concern him so much that it is considered necessary for him to hold opinions on them? If the cultivation of the understanding consists in one thing more than in another, it is surely in learning the grounds of one's own opinions. Whatever people believe, on subjects on which it is of the first importance to believe rightly, they ought to be able to defend against at least the common objections. But, some one may say, "Let them be *taught* the grounds of their opinions. It does not follow that opinions must be merely parroted because they are never heard controverted. Persons who learn geometry do not simply commit the theorems to memory, but understand and learn likewise the demonstrations; and it would be absurd to say that they remain ignorant of the grounds of geometrical truths, because they never hear any one deny, and attempt to disprove them." Undoubtedly: and such teaching suffices on a subject like mathematics, where there is nothing at all to be said on the wrong side of the question. The peculiarity of the evidence of mathematical truths is, that all the argument is on one side. There are no objections, and no answers to objections. But on every subject on which difference of opinion is possible, the truth depends on a balance to be struck between two sets of conflicting reasons. Even in natural philosophy, there is always some other explanation possible of the same facts; some geocentric theory instead of heliocentric, some phlogiston instead of oxygen; and it has to be shown why that other theory cannot be the true one: and until this is shown, and until we know how it is shown, we do not understand the grounds of our opinion. But when we turn to subjects infinitely more complicated, to morals, religion, politics, social relations, and the business of life, three-fourths of the arguments for every disputed opinion consist in dispelling the appearances which favour some opinion different from it. The greatest orator, save one, of antiquity, has left it on record that he always studied his adversary's case with as great, if not with still greater, intensity than even his own. What Cicero practised as the means of forensic success, requires to be imitated by all who study any subject in order to arrive at the truth. He who knows only his own side of the case, knows little of that. His reasons may be good, and no one may have been able to refute them. But if he is equally unable to refute the reasons on the opposite side; if he does not so much as know what they are, he has no ground for preferring either opinion. The rational position for him would be suspension of judgment, and unless he contents himself with that, he is either led by authority, or adopts, like the generality of the world, the side to which he

feels most inclination. Nor is it enough that he should hear the arguments of adversaries from his own teachers, presented as they state them, and accompanied by what they offer as refutations. That is not the way to do justice to the arguments, or bring them into real contact with his own mind. He must be able to hear them from persons who actually believe them; who defend them in earnest, and do their very utmost for them. He must know them in their most plausible and persuasive form; he must feel the whole force of the difficulty which the true view of the subject has to encounter and dispose of; else he will never really possess himself of the portion of truth which meets and removes that difficulty. Ninety-nine in a hundred of what are called educated men are in this condition; even of those who can argue fluently for their opinions. Their conclusion may be true, but it might be false for anything they know: they have never thrown themselves into the mental position of those who think differently from them, and considered what such persons may have to say; and consequently they do not, in any proper sense of the word, know the doctrine which they themselves profess. They do not know those parts of it which explain and justify the remainder; the considerations which show that a fact which seemingly conflicts with another is reconcilable with it, or that, of two apparently strong reasons, one and not the other ought to be preferred. All that part of the truth which turns the scale, and decides the judgment of a completely informed mind, they are strangers to; nor is it ever really known, but to those who have attended equally and impartially to both sides, and endeavoured to see the reasons of both in the strongest light. So essential is this discipline to a real understanding of moral and human subjects, that if opponents of all important truths do not exist, it is indispensable to imagine them, and supply them with the strongest arguments which the most skilful devil's advocate can conjure up.

. . .

It still remains to speak of one of the principal causes which make diversity of opinion advantageous, and will continue to do so until mankind shall have entered a stage of intellectual advancement which at present seems at an incalculable distance. We have hitherto considered only two possibilities: that the received opinion may be false, and some other opinion, consequently, true; or that, the received opinion being true, a conflict with the opposite error is essential to a clear apprehension and deep feeling of its truth. But there is a commoner case than either of these; when the conflicting doctrines, instead of being one true and the other false, share the truth between them; and the nonconforming opinion is needed to supply the remainder of the truth, of which the received doctrine embodies only a part. Popular opinions, on subjects not palpable to sense, are often true, but seldom or never the whole truth. They are a part of the truth; sometimes a greater, sometimes a smaller part, but exaggerated, distorted, and disjoined from the truths by which they ought to be accompanied and limited. Heretical opinions, on the other hand, are generally some of these suppressed and neglected truths, bursting the bonds which kept them down, and either seeking reconciliation with the truth contained in the common opinion, or fronting it as enemies, and setting themselves up, with similar exclusiveness, as the whole truth. The latter case is hitherto the most frequent, as, in the human mind, one-sidedness has always been the rule, and many-sidedness the exception. Hence, even in revolutions of opinion, one part of the truth usually sets while another rises. Even progress, which ought to superadd, for the most part only substitutes one partial and incomplete truth for another; improvement consisting chiefly in this, that the new fragment of truth is more wanted, more adapted to the needs of the time, than that which it displaces. Such being the partial character of prevailing opinions, even when resting on a true foundation; every opinion which embodies somewhat of the portion of truth which the common opinion omits, ought to be considered precious, with whatever amount of error and confusion that truth may be blended. No sober judge of human affairs will feel bound to be indignant because those who force on our notice truths which we should otherwise have overlooked, overlook some of those which we see. Rather, he will think that so long as popular truth is one-sided, it is more desirable than otherwise that unpopular truth should have one-sided asserters too; such being usually the most energetic, and the most likely to compel reluctant attention to the fragment of wisdom which they proclaim as if it were the whole.

Thus, in the eighteenth century, when nearly all the instructed, and all those of the uninstructed who were led by them, were lost in admiration of what is called civilisation, and of the marvels of modern science, literature, and philosophy, and while greatly overrating the amount of unlikeness between the men of modern and those of ancient times, indulged the belief that the whole of the difference was in their own favour; with what a salutary shock did the paradoxes of Rousseau explode like bombshells in the midst, dislocating the compact mass of one-sided opinion, and forcing its elements to recombine in a better form and with additional ingredients. Not that the current opinions were on the whole farther from the truth than Rousseau's were; on the contrary, they were nearer to it; they contained more of positive truth, and very much less of error. Nevertheless there lay in Rousseau's doctrine, and has floated down the stream of opinion along with it, a considerable amount of exactly those truths which the popular opinion wanted; and these are the deposit which was left behind when the flood subsided. The superior worth of simplicity of life, the enervating and demoralising effect of the trammels and hypocrisies of artificial society, are ideas which have never been entirely absent from cultivated minds since Rousseau wrote; and they will in time produce their due effect, though at present needing to be asserted as much as ever, and to be asserted by deeds, for words, on this subject, have nearly exhausted their power.

In politics, again, it is almost a commonplace, that a party of order or stability, and a party of progress or reform, are both necessary elements of a healthy state of political life; until the one or the other shall have so enlarged its mental grasp as to be a party equally of order and of progress, knowing and distinguishing what is fit to be preserved from what ought to be swept away. Each of these modes of thinking derives its utility from the deficiencies of the other; but it is in a great measure the opposition of the other that keeps each within the limits of reason and sanity. Unless opinions favourable to democracy and to aristocracy, to property and to equality, to co-operation and to competition, to luxury and to abstinence, to sociality and individuality, to liberty and discipline, and all the other standing antagonisms of practical life, are expressed with equal freedom, and enforced and defended with equal talent and energy, there is no chance of both elements obtaining their due; one scale is sure to go up and the other down. Truth, in the great practical concerns of life, is so much a question of the reconciling and combining of opposites, that very few have minds sufficiently capacious and impartial to make the adjustment with an approach to correctness, and it has to be made by the rough process of a struggle between combatants fighting under hostile banners. On any of the great open questions just enumerated, if either of the two opinions has a better claim than the other, not merely to be tolerated, but to be encouraged and countenanced, it is the one which happens at the particular time and place to be in a minority. That is the opinion which, for the time being, represents the neglected interests, the side of human well-being which is in danger of obtaining less than its share. I am aware that there is not, in this country, any intolerance of differences of opinion on most of these topics. They are adduced to show, by admitted and multiplied examples, the universality of the fact, that only through diversity of opinion is there, in the existing state of human intellect, a chance of fair-play to all sides of the truth. When there are persons to be found, who form an exception to the apparent unanimity of the world on any subject, even if the world is in the right, it is always probable that dissentients have something worth hearing to say for themselves, and that truth would lose something by their silence.

. . .

We have now recognised the necessity to the mental well-being of mankind (on which all their other well-being depends) of freedom of opinion, and freedom of the expression of opinion, on four distinct grounds; which we will now briefly recapitulate.

First, if any opinion is compelled to silence, that opinion may, for aught we can certainly know, be true. To deny this is to assume our own infallibility.

Secondly, though the silenced opinion be an error, it may, and very commonly does, contain a portion of truth; and since the general or prevailing opinion on any subject is rarely or never the whole truth, it is only by the collision of adverse opinions, that the remainder of the truth has any chance of being supplied.

Thirdly, even if the received opinion be not only true, but the whole truth; unless it is suffered to be, and actually is, vigorously and earnestly contested, it will, by most of those who receive it, be held in the manner of a prejudice, with little comprehension or feeling of its rational grounds. And not only this, but, fourthly, the meaning of the doctrine itself will be in danger of being lost, or enfeebled, and deprived of its vital effect on the character and conduct: the dogma becoming a mere formal profession, inefficacious for good, but cumbering the ground, and preventing the growth of any real and heartfelt conviction, from reason or personal experience.

Before quitting the subject of freedom of opinion, it is fit to take some notice of those who say, that the free expression of all opinions should be permitted, on condition that the manner be temperate, and do not pass the bounds of fair discussion. Much might be said on the impossibility of fixing where these supposed bounds are to be placed; for if the test be offence to those whose opinion is attacked, I think experience testifies that this offence is given whenever the attack is telling and powerful, and that every opponent who pushes them hard, and whom they find it difficult to answer, appears to them, if he shows any strong feeling on the subject, an intemperate opponent. But this, though an important consideration in a practical point of view, merges in a more fundamental objection. Undoubtedly the manner of asserting an opinion, even though it be a true one, may be very objectionable, and may justly incur severe censure. But the principal offences of the kind are such as it is mostly impossible, unless by accidental self-betrayal, to bring home to conviction. The gravest of them is, to argue sophistically, to suppress facts or arguments, to misstate the elements of the case, or misrepresent the opposite opinion. But all this, even to the most aggravated degree, is so continually done in perfect good faith, by persons who are not considered, and in many other respects may not deserve to be considered, ignorant or incompetent, that it is rarely possible on adequate grounds conscientiously to stamp the misrepresentation as morally culpable; and still less could law presume to interfere with this kind of controversial misconduct. With regard to what is commonly meant by intemperate discussion, namely invective, sarcasm, personality, and the like, the denunciation of these weapons would deserve more sympathy if it were ever proposed to interdict them equally to both sides; but it is only desired to restrain the employment of them against the prevailing opinion: against the unprevailing they may not only be used without general disapproval, but will be likely to obtain for him who uses them the praise of honest zeal and righteous indignation. Yet whatever mischief arises from their use, is greatest when they are employed against the comparatively defenceless; and whatever unfair advantage can be derived by any opinion from this mode of asserting it, accrues almost exclusively to received opinions. The worst offence of this kind which can be committed by a polemic, is to stigmatise those who hold the contrary opinion as bad and immoral men. To calumny of this sort, those who hold any unpopular opinion are peculiarly exposed, because they are in general few and uninfluential, and nobody but themselves feel much interest in seeing justice done them; but this weapon is, from the nature of the case, denied to those who attack a prevailing opinion: they can neither use it with safety to themselves, nor, if they could, would it do anything but recoil on their own cause. In

general, opinions contrary to those commonly received can only obtain a hearing by studied moderation of language, and the most cautious avoidance of unnecessary offence, from which they hardly ever deviate even in a slight degree without losing ground: while unmeasured vituperation employed on the side of the prevailing opinion, really does deter people from professing contrary opinions, and from listening to those who profess them. For the interest, therefore, of truth and justice, it is far more important to restrain this employment of vituperative language than the other; and, for example, if it were necessary to choose, there would be much more need to discourage offensive attacks on infidelity, than on religion. It is, however, obvious that law and authority have no business with restraining either, while opinion ought, in every instance, to determine its verdict by the circumstances of the individual case; condemning every one, on whichever side of the argument he places himself, in whose mode of advocacy either want of candour, or malignity, bigotry, or intolerance of feeling manifest themselves; but not inferring these vices from the side which a person takes, though it be the contrary side of the question to our own: and giving merited honour to every one, whatever opinion he may hold, who has calmness to see and honesty to state what his opponents and their opinions really are, exaggerating nothing to their discredit, keeping nothing back which tells, or can be supposed to tell, in their favour. This is the real morality of public discussion; and if often violated, I am happy to think that there are many controversialists who to a great extent observe it, and a still greater number who conscientiously strive towards it.

CHAPTER III.
OF INDIVIDUALITY, AS ONE OF THE ELEMENTS OF WELL-BEING.

Such being the reasons which make it imperative that human beings should be free to form opinions, and to express their opinions without reserve; and such the baneful consequences to the intellectual, and through that to the moral nature of man, unless this liberty is either conceded, or asserted in spite of prohibition; let us next examine whether the same reasons do not require that men should be free to act upon their opinions—to carry these out in their lives, without hindrance, either physical or moral, from their fellow-men, so long as it is at their own risk and peril. This last proviso is of course indispensable. No one pretends that actions should be as free as opinions. On the contrary, even opinions lose their immunity, when the circumstances in which they are expressed are such as to constitute their expression a positive instigation to some mischievous act. An opinion that corn-dealers are starvers of the poor, or that private property is robbery, ought to be unmolested when simply circulated through the press, but may justly incur punishment when delivered orally to an excited mob assembled before the house of a corn-dealer, or when handed about among the same mob in the form of a placard. Acts, of whatever kind, which, without justifiable cause, do harm to others, may be, and in the more important cases absolutely require to be, controlled by the unfavourable sentiments, and, when needful, by the active interference of mankind. The liberty of the individual must be thus far limited; he must not make himself a nuisance to other people. But if he refrains from molesting others in what concerns them, and merely acts according to his own inclination and judgment in things which concern himself, the same reasons which show that opinion should be free, prove also that he should be allowed, without molestation, to carry his opinions into practice at his own cost. That mankind are not infallible; that their truths, for the most part, are only half-truths; that unity of opinion, unless resulting from the fullest and freest comparison of opposite opinions, is not desirable, and diversity not an evil, but a good, until mankind are much more capable than at present of recognising all sides of the truth, are principles applicable to men's modes of action, not less than to their opinions. As it is useful that while mankind are imperfect there should be different opinions, so is it that there should be different experiments of living; that free scope

should be given to varieties of character, short of injury to others; and that the worth of different modes of life should be proved practically, when any one thinks fit to try them. It is desirable, in short, that in things which do not primarily concern others, individuality should assert itself. Where, not the person's own character, but the traditions or customs of other people are the rule of conduct, there is wanting one of the principal ingredients of human happiness, and quite the chief ingredient of individual and social progress.

In maintaining this principle, the greatest difficulty to be encountered does not lie in the appreciation of means towards an acknowledged end, but in the indifference of persons in general to the end itself. If it were felt that the free development of individuality is one of the leading essentials of well-being; that it is not only a co-ordinate element with all that is designated by the terms civilisation, instruction, education, culture, but is itself a necessary part and condition of all those things; there would be no danger that liberty should be under-valued, and the adjustment of the boundaries between it and social control would present no extraordinary difficulty. But the evil is, that individual spontaneity is hardly recognised by the common modes of thinking, as having any intrinsic worth, or deserving any regard on its own account. The majority, being satisfied with the ways of mankind as they now are (for it is they who make them what they are), cannot comprehend why those ways should not be good enough for everybody; and what is more, spontaneity forms no part of the ideal of the majority of moral and social reformers, but is rather looked on with jealousy, as a troublesome and perhaps rebellious obstruction to the general acceptance of what these reformers, in their own judgment, think would be best for mankind. Few persons, out of Germany, even comprehend the meaning of the doctrine which Wilhelm von Humboldt, so eminent both as a *savant* and as a politician, made the text of a treatise—that "the end of man, or that which is prescribed by the eternal or immutable dictates of reason, and not suggested by vague and transient desires, is the highest and most harmonious development of his powers to a complete and consistent whole;" that, therefore, the object "towards which every human being must ceaselessly direct his efforts, and on which especially those who design to influence their fellow-men must ever keep their eyes, is the individuality of power and development;" that for this there are two requisites, "freedom, and a variety of situations;" and that from the union of these arise "individual vigour and manifold diversity," which combine themselves in "originality."

Little, however, as people are accustomed to a doctrine like that of Von Humboldt, and surprising as it may be to them to find so high a value attached to individuality, the question, one must nevertheless think, can only be one of degree. No one's idea of excellence in conduct is that people should do absolutely nothing but copy one another. No one would assert that people ought not to put into their mode of life, and into the conduct of their concerns, any impress whatever of their own judgment, or of their own individual character. On the other hand, it would be absurd to pretend that people ought to live as if nothing whatever had been known in the world before they came into it; as if experience had as yet done nothing towards showing that one mode of existence, or of conduct, is preferable to another. Nobody denies that people should be so taught and trained in youth, as to know and benefit by the ascertained results of human experience. But it is the privilege and proper condition of a human being, arrived at the maturity of his faculties, to use and interpret experience in his own way. It is for him to find out what part of recorded experience is properly applicable to his own circumstances and character. The traditions and customs of other people are, to a certain extent, evidence of what their experience has taught *them*; presumptive evidence, and as such, have a claim to his deference: but, in the first place, their experience may be too narrow; or they may not have interpreted it rightly. Secondly, their interpretation of experience may be correct, but unsuitable to him. Customs are made for customary circumstances, and customary characters: and his circumstances or his

character may be uncustomary. Thirdly, though the customs be both good as customs, and suitable to him, yet to conform to custom, merely *as* custom, does not educate or develop in him any of the qualities which are the distinctive endowment of a human being. The human faculties of perception, judgment, discriminative feeling, mental activity, and even moral preference, are exercised only in making a choice. He who does anything because it is the custom, makes no choice. He gains no practice either in discerning or in desiring what is best. The mental and moral, like the muscular powers, are improved only by being used. The faculties are called into no exercise by doing a thing merely because others do it, no more than by believing a thing only because others believe it. If the grounds of an opinion are not conclusive to the person's own reason, his reason cannot be strengthened, but is likely to be weakened by his adopting it: and if the inducements to an act are not such as are consentaneous to his own feelings and character (where affection, or the rights of others, are not concerned), it is so much done towards rendering his feelings and character inert and torpid, instead of active and energetic.

He who lets the world, or his own portion of it, choose his plan of life for him, has no need of any other faculty than the ape-like one of imitation. He who chooses his plan for himself, employs all his faculties. He must use observation to see, reasoning and judgment to foresee, activity to gather materials for decision, discrimination to decide, and when he has decided, firmness and self-control to hold to his deliberate decision. And these qualities he requires and exercises exactly in proportion as the part of his conduct which he determines according to his own judgment and feelings is a large one. It is possible that he might be guided in some good path, and kept out of harm's way, without any of these things. But what will be his comparative worth as a human being? It really is of importance, not only what men do, but also what manner of men they are that do it. Among the works of man, which human life is rightly employed in perfecting and beautifying, the first in importance surely is man himself. Supposing it were possible to get houses built, corn grown, battles fought, causes tried, and even churches erected and prayers said, by machinery—by automatons in human form—it would be a considerable loss to exchange for these automatons even the men and women who at present inhabit the more civilised parts of the world, and who assuredly are but starved specimens of what nature can and will produce. Human nature is not a machine to be built after a model, and set to do exactly the work prescribed for it, but a tree, which requires to grow and develop itself on all sides, according to the tendency of the inward forces which make it a living thing.

. . .

It is not by wearing down into uniformity all that is individual in themselves, but by cultivating it and calling it forth, within the limits imposed by the rights and interests of others, that human beings become a noble and beautiful object of contemplation; and as the works partake the character of those who do them, by the same process human life also becomes rich, diversified, and animating, furnishing more abundant aliment to high thoughts and elevating feelings, and strengthening the tie which binds every individual to the race, by making the race infinitely better worth belonging to. In proportion to the development of his individuality, each person becomes more valuable to himself, and is therefore capable of being more valuable to others. There is a greater fulness of life about his own existence, and when there is more life in the units there is more in the mass which is composed of them. As much compression as is necessary to prevent the stronger specimens of human nature from encroaching on the rights of others, cannot be dispensed with; but for this there is ample compensation even in the point of view of human development. The means of development which the individual loses by being prevented from gratifying his inclinations to the injury of others, are chiefly obtained at the expense of the development of other people. And even to himself there is a full equivalent in the better development of the social part of his nature, rendered possible by the restraint put upon the selfish part. To be held to rigid rules of justice for the sake of others, develops the feelings and capacities which have the good of others for their object. But to be restrained in things not affecting their good, by their mere displeasure, develops nothing valuable, except such force of character as may unfold itself in resisting the restraint. If acquiesced in, it dulls and blunts the whole nature. To give any fair-play to the nature of each, it is essential that different persons should be allowed to lead different lives. In proportion as this latitude has been exercised in any age, has that age been noteworthy to posterity. Even despotism does not produce its worst effects, so long as Individuality exists under it; and whatever crushes individuality is despotism, by whatever name it may be called, and whether it professes to be enforcing the will of God or the injunctions of men.

Having said that Individuality is the same thing with development, and that it is only the cultivation of individuality which produces, or can produce, well-developed human beings, I might here close the argument: for what more or better can be said of any condition of human affairs, than that it brings human beings themselves nearer to the best thing they can be? or what worse can be said of any obstruction to good, than that it prevents this? Doubtless, however, these considerations will not suffice to convince those who most need convincing; and it is necessary further to show, that these developed human beings are of some use to the undeveloped—to point out to those who do not desire liberty, and would not avail themselves of it, that they may be in some intelligible manner rewarded for allowing other people to make use of it without hindrance.

In the first place, then, I would suggest that they might possibly learn something from them. It will not be denied by anybody, that originality is a valuable element in human affairs. There is always need of persons not only to discover new truths, and point out when what were once truths are true no longer, but also to commence new practices, and set the example of more enlightened conduct, and better taste and sense in human life. This cannot well be gainsaid by anybody who does not believe that the world has already attained perfection in all its ways and practices. It is true that this benefit is not capable of being rendered by everybody alike: there are but few persons, in comparison with the whole of mankind, whose experiments, if adopted by others, would be likely to be any improvement on established practice. But these few are the salt of the earth; without them, human life would become a stagnant pool. Not only is it they who introduce good things which did not before exist; it is they who keep the life in those which already existed. If there were nothing new to be done, would human intellect cease to be necessary? Would it be a reason why those who do the old things should forget why they are done, and do them like cattle, not like human beings? There is only too great a tendency in the best beliefs and practices to degenerate into the mechanical; and unless there were a succession of persons whose ever-recurring originality prevents the grounds of those beliefs and practices from becoming merely traditional, such dead matter would not resist the smallest shock from anything really alive, and there would be no reason why civilisation should not die out, as in the Byzantine Empire. Persons of genius, it is true, are, and are always likely to be, a small minority; but in order to have them, it is necessary to preserve the soil in which they grow. Genius can only breathe freely in an *atmosphere* of freedom. Persons of genius are, *ex vi termini*, *more* individual than any other people—less capable, consequently, of fitting themselves, without hurtful compression, into any of the small number of moulds which society provides in order to save its members the trouble of forming their own character. If from timidity they consent to be forced into one of these moulds, and to let all that part of themselves which cannot expand under the pressure remain unexpanded, society will be little the better for their genius. If they are of a strong character, and break their fetters, they become a mark for the society which has not succeeded in reducing them to commonplace, to point at with solemn warning as "wild," "erratic,"

and the like; much as if one should complain of the Niagara river for not flowing smoothly between its banks like a Dutch canal.

I insist thus emphatically on the importance of genius, and the necessity of allowing it to unfold itself freely both in thought and in practice, being well aware that no one will deny the position in theory, but knowing also that almost every one, in reality, is totally indifferent to it. People think genius a fine thing if it enables a man to write an exciting poem, or paint a picture. But in its true sense, that of originality in thought and action, though no one says that it is not a thing to be admired, nearly all, at heart, think that they can do very well without it. Unhappily this is too natural to be wondered at. Originality is the one thing which unoriginal minds cannot feel the use of. They cannot see what it is to do for them: how should they? If they could see what it would do for them, it would not be originality. The first service which originality has to render them, is that of opening their eyes: which being once fully done, they would have a chance of being themselves original. Meanwhile, recollecting that nothing was ever yet done which some one was not the first to do, and that all good things which exist are the fruits of originality, let them be modest enough to believe that there is something still left for it to accomplish, and assure themselves that they are more in need of originality, the less they are conscious of the want.

In sober truth, whatever homage may be professed, or even paid, to real or supposed mental superiority, the general tendency of things throughout the world is to render mediocrity the ascendant power among mankind. In ancient history, in the middle ages, and in a diminishing degree through the long transition from feudality to the present time, the individual was a power in himself; and if he had either great talents or a high social position, he was a considerable power. At present individuals are lost in the crowd. In politics it is almost a triviality to say that public opinion now rules the world. The only power deserving the name is that of masses, and of governments while they make themselves the organ of the tendencies and instincts of masses. This is as true in the moral and social relations of private life as in public transactions. Those whose opinions go by the name of public opinion, are not always the same sort of public: in America they are the whole white population; in England, chiefly the middle class. But they are always a mass, that is to say, collective mediocrity. And what is a still greater novelty, the mass do not now take their opinions from dignitaries in Church or State, from ostensible leaders, or from books. Their thinking is done for them by men much like themselves, addressing them or speaking in their name, on the spur of the moment, through the newspapers. I am not complaining of all this. I do not assert that anything better is compatible, as a general rule, with the present low state of the human mind. But that does not hinder the government of mediocrity from being mediocre government. No government by a democracy or a numerous aristocracy, either in its political acts or in the opinions, qualities, and tone of mind which it fosters, ever did or could rise above mediocrity, except in so far as the sovereign Many have let themselves be guided (which in their best times they always have done) by the counsels and influence of a more highly gifted and instructed One or Few. The initiation of all wise or noble things, comes and must come from individuals; generally at first from some one individual. The honour and glory of the average man is that he is capable of following that initiative; that he can respond internally to wise and noble things, and be led to them with his eyes open. I am not countenancing the sort of "hero-worship" which applauds the strong man of genius for forcibly seizing on the government of the world and making it do his bidding in spite of itself. All he can claim is, freedom to point out the way. The power of compelling others into it, is not only inconsistent with the freedom and development of all the rest, but corrupting to the strong man himself. It does seem, however, that when the opinions of masses of merely average men are everywhere become or becoming the dominant power, the counterpoise and corrective to that tendency would be, the more and more pronounced individuality of those who stand on

the higher eminences of thought. It is in these circumstances most especially, that exceptional individuals, instead of being deterred, should be encouraged in acting differently from the mass. In other times there was no advantage in their doing so, unless they acted not only differently, but better. In this age the mere example of nonconformity, the mere refusal to bend the knee to custom, is itself a service. Precisely because the tyranny of opinion is such as to make eccentricity a reproach, it is desirable, in order to break through that tyranny, that people should be eccentric. Eccentricity has always abounded when and where strength of character has abounded; and the amount of eccentricity in a society has generally been proportional to the amount of genius, mental vigour, and moral courage which it contained. That so few now dare to be eccentric, marks the chief danger of the time.

I have said that it is important to give the freest scope possible to uncustomary things, in order that it may in time appear which of these are fit to be converted into customs. But independence of action, and disregard of custom are not solely deserving of encouragement for the chance they afford that better modes of action, and customs more worthy of general adoption, may be struck out; nor is it only persons of decided mental superiority who have a just claim to carry on their lives in their own way. There is no reason that all human existences should be constructed on some one, or some small number of patterns. If a person possesses any tolerable amount of common-sense and experience, his own mode of laying out his existence is the best, not because it is the best in itself, but because it is his own mode. Human beings are not like sheep; and even sheep are not undistinguishably alike. A man cannot get a coat or a pair of boots to fit him, unless they are either made to his measure, or he has a whole warehouseful to choose from: and is it easier to fit him with a life than with a coat, or are human beings more like one another in their whole physical and spiritual conformation than in the shape of their feet? If it were only that people have diversities of taste, that is reason enough for not attempting to shape them all after one model. But different persons also require different conditions for their spiritual development; and can no more exist healthily in the same moral, than all the variety of plants can in the same physical, atmosphere and climate. The same things which are helps to one person towards the cultivation of his higher nature, are hindrances to another. The same mode of life is a healthy excitement to one, keeping all his faculties of action and enjoyment in their best order, while to another it is a distracting burthen, which suspends or crushes all internal life. Such are the differences among human beings in their sources of pleasure, their susceptibilities of pain, and the operation on them of different physical and moral agencies, that unless there is a corresponding diversity in their modes of life, they neither obtain their fair share of happiness, nor grow up to the mental, moral, and aesthetic stature of which their nature is capable. Why then should tolerance, as far as the public sentiment is concerned, extend only to tastes and modes of life which extort acquiescence by the multitude of their adherents? Nowhere (except in some monastic institutions) is diversity of taste entirely unrecognised; a person may, without blame, either like or dislike rowing, or smoking, or music, or athletic exercises, or chess, or cards, or study, because both those who like each of these things, and those who dislike them, are too numerous to be put down. But the man, and still more the woman, who can be accused either of doing "what nobody does," or of not doing "what everybody does," is the subject of as much depreciatory remark as if he or she had committed some grave moral delinquency. Persons require to possess a title, or some other badge of rank, or of the consideration of people of rank, to be able to indulge somewhat in the luxury of doing as they like without detriment to their estimation. To indulge somewhat, I repeat: for whoever allow themselves much of that indulgence, incur the risk of something worse than disparaging speeches—they are in peril of a commission *de lunatico*, and of having their property taken from them and given to their relations.

. . .

CHAPTER IV.
OF THE LIMITS TO THE AUTHORITY OF SOCIETY OVER THE INDIVIDUAL.

What, then, is the rightful limit to the sovereignty of the individual over himself? Where does the authority of society begin? How much of human life should be assigned to individuality, and how much to society?

Each will receive its proper share, if each has that which more particularly concerns it. To individuality should belong the part of life in which it is chiefly the individual that is interested; to society, the part which chiefly interests society.

Though society is not founded on a contract, and though no good purpose is answered by inventing a contract in order to deduce social obligations from it, every one who receives the protection of society owes a return for the benefit, and the fact of living in society renders it indispensable that each should be bound to observe a certain line of conduct towards the rest. This conduct consists, first, in not injuring the interests of one another; or rather certain interests which, either by express legal provision or by tacit understanding, ought to be considered as rights; and secondly, in each person's bearing his share (to be fixed on some equitable principle) of the labours and sacrifices incurred for defending the society or its members from injury and molestation. These conditions society is justified in enforcing, at all costs to those who endeavour to withhold fulfilment. Nor is this all that society may do. The acts of an individual may be hurtful to others, or wanting in due consideration for their welfare, without going the length of violating any of their constituted rights. The offender may then be justly punished by opinion though not by law. As soon as any part of a person's conduct affects prejudicially the interests of others, society has jurisdiction over it, and the question whether the general welfare will or will not be promoted by interfering with it, becomes open to discussion. But there is no room for entertaining any such question when a person's conduct affects the interests of no persons besides himself, or needs not affect them unless they like (all the persons concerned being of full age, and the ordinary amount of understanding). In all such cases there should be perfect freedom, legal and social, to do the action and stand the consequences.

It would be a great misunderstanding of this doctrine, to suppose that it is one of selfish indifference, which pretends that human beings have no business with each other's conduct in life, and that they should not concern themselves about the well-doing or well-being of one another, unless their own interest is involved. Instead of any diminution, there is need of a great increase of disinterested exertion to promote the good of others. But disinterested benevolence can find other instruments to persuade people to their good, than whips and scourges, either of the literal or the metaphorical sort. I am the last person to undervalue the self-regarding virtues; they are only second in importance, if even second, to the social. It is equally the business of education to cultivate both. But even education works by conviction and persuasion as well as by compulsion, and it is by the former only that, when the period of education is past, the self-regarding virtues should be inculcated. Human beings owe to each other help to distinguish the better from the worse, and encouragement to choose the former and avoid the latter. They should be for ever stimulating each other to increased exercise of their higher faculties, and increased direction of their feelings and aims towards wise instead of foolish, elevating instead of degrading, objects and contemplations. But neither one person, nor any number of persons, is warranted in saying to another human creature of ripe years, that he shall not do with his life for his own benefit what he chooses to do with it. He is the person most interested in his own well-being: the interest which any other person, except in cases of strong personal attachment, can have in it, is trifling, compared with that which he himself has; the interest which society has in him individually (except as to his conduct to others) is fractional, and altogether indirect: while, with respect to his own feelings and circumstances, the most ordinary man or woman has means of knowledge immeasurably

surpassing those that can be possessed by any one else. The interference of society to overrule his judgment and purposes in what only regards himself, must be grounded on general presumptions; which may be altogether wrong, and even if right, are as likely as not to be misapplied to individual cases, by persons no better acquainted with the circumstances of such cases than those are who look at them merely from without. In this department, therefore, of human affairs, Individuality has its proper field of action. In the conduct of human beings towards one another, it is necessary that general rules should for the most part be observed, in order that people may know what they have to expect; but in each person's own concerns, his individual spontaneity is entitled to free exercise. Considerations to aid his judgment, exhortations to strengthen his will, may be offered to him, even obtruded on him, by others; but he himself is the final judge. All errors which he is likely to commit against advice and warning, are far outweighed by the evil of allowing others to constrain him to what they deem his good.

I do not mean that the feelings with which a person is regarded by others, ought not to be in any way affected by his self-regarding qualities or deficiencies. This is neither possible nor desirable. If he is eminent in any of the qualities which conduce to his own good, he is, so far, a proper object of admiration. He is so much the nearer to the ideal perfection of human nature. If he is grossly deficient in those qualities, a sentiment the opposite of admiration will follow. There is a degree of folly, and a degree of what may be called (though the phrase is not unobjectionable) lowness or depravation of taste, which, though it cannot justify doing harm to the person who manifests it, renders him necessarily and properly a subject of distaste, or, in extreme cases, even of contempt: a person could not have the opposite qualities in due strength without entertaining these feelings. Though doing no wrong to any one, a person may so act as to compel us to judge him, and feel to him, as a fool, or as a being of an inferior order: and since this judgment and feeling are a fact which he would prefer to avoid, it is doing him a service to warn him of it beforehand, as of any other disagreeable consequence to which he exposes himself. It would be well, indeed, if this good office were much more freely rendered than the common notions of politeness at present permit, and if one person could honestly point out to another that he thinks him in fault, without being considered unmannerly or presuming. We have a right, also, in various ways, to act upon our unfavourable opinion of any one, not to the oppression of his individuality, but in the exercise of ours. We are not bound, for example, to seek his society; we have a right to avoid it (though not to parade the avoidance), for we have a right to choose the society most acceptable to us. We have a right, and it may be our duty, to caution others against him, if we think his example or conversation likely to have a pernicious effect on those with whom he associates. We may give others a preference over him in optional good offices, except those which tend to his improvement. In these various modes a person may suffer very severe penalties at the hands of others, for faults which directly concern only himself; but he suffers these penalties only in so far as they are the natural, and, as it were, the spontaneous consequences of the faults themselves, not because they are purposely inflicted on him for the sake of punishment. A person who shows rashness, obstinacy, self-conceit—who cannot live within moderate means—who cannot restrain himself from hurtful indulgences—who pursues animal pleasures at the expense of those of feeling and intellect—must expect to be lowered in the opinion of others, and to have a less share of their favourable sentiments; but of this he has no right to complain, unless he has merited their favour by special excellence in his social relations, and has thus established a title to their good offices, which is not affected by his demerits towards himself.

. . .

The distinction here pointed out between the part of a person's life which concerns only himself, and that which concerns others, many persons will refuse to admit. How (it may be asked) can any part of the conduct of a member

of society be a matter of indifference to the other members? No person is an entirely isolated being; it is impossible for a person to do anything seriously or permanently hurtful to himself, without mischief reaching at least to his near connections, and often far beyond them. If he injures his property, he does harm to those who directly or indirectly derived support from it, and usually diminishes, by a greater or less amount, the general resources of the community. If he deteriorates his bodily or mental faculties, he not only brings evil upon all who depended on him for any portion of their happiness, but disqualifies himself for rendering the services which he owes to his fellow-creatures generally; perhaps becomes a burthen on their affection or benevolence; and if such conduct were very frequent, hardly any offence that is committed would detract more from the general sum of good. Finally, if by his vices or follies a person does no direct harm to others, he is nevertheless (it may be said) injurious by his example; and ought to be compelled to control himself, for the sake of those whom the sight or knowledge of his conduct might corrupt or mislead.

And even (it will be added) if the consequences of misconduct could be confined to the vicious or thoughtless individual, ought society to abandon to their own guidance those who are manifestly unfit for it? If protection against themselves is confessedly due to children and persons under age, is not society equally bound to afford it to persons of mature years who are equally incapable of self-government? If gambling, or drunkenness, or incontinence, or idleness, or uncleanliness, are as injurious to happiness, and as great a hindrance to improvement, as many or most of the acts prohibited by law, why (it may be asked) should not law, so far as is consistent with practicability and social convenience, endeavour to repress these also? And as a supplement to the unavoidable imperfections of law, ought not opinion at least to organise a powerful police against these vices, and visit rigidly with social penalties those who are known to practise them? There is no question here (it may be said) about restricting individuality, or impeding the trial of

Political Philosophy

new and original experiments in living. The only things it is sought to prevent are things which have been tried and condemned from the beginning of the world until now; things which experience has shown not to be useful or suitable to any person's individuality. There must be some length of time and amount of experience, after which a moral or prudential truth may be regarded as established: and it is merely desired to prevent generation after generation from falling over the same precipice which has been fatal to their predecessors.

I fully admit that the mischief which a person does to himself, may seriously affect, both through their sympathies and their interests, those nearly connected with him, and in a minor degree, society at large. When, by conduct of this sort, a person is led to violate a distinct and assignable obligation to any other person or persons, the case is taken out of the self-regarding class, and becomes amenable to moral disapprobation in the proper sense of the term. If, for example, a man, through intemperance or extravagance, becomes unable to pay his debts, or, having undertaken the moral responsibility of a family, becomes from the same cause incapable of supporting or educating them, he is deservedly reprobated, and might be justly punished; but it is for the breach of duty to his family or creditors, not for the extravagance. If the resources which ought to have been devoted to them, had been diverted from them for the most prudent investment, the moral culpability would have been the same. George Barnwell murdered his uncle to get money for his mistress, but if he had done it to set himself up in business, he would equally have been hanged. Again, in the frequent case of a man who causes grief to his family by addiction to bad habits, he deserves reproach for his unkindness or ingratitude; but so he may for cultivating habits not in themselves vicious, if they are painful to those with whom he passes his life, or who from personal ties are dependent on him for their comfort. Whoever fails in the consideration generally due to the interests and feelings of others, not being compelled by some more imperative duty, or justified by allowable self-preference, is a subject of moral

disapprobation for that failure, but not for the cause of it, nor for the errors, merely personal to himself, which may have remotely led to it. In like manner, when a person disables himself, by conduct purely self-regarding, from the performance of some definite duty incumbent on him to the public, he is guilty of a social offence. No person ought to be punished simply for being drunk; but a soldier or a policeman should be punished for being drunk on duty. Whenever, in short, there is a definite damage, or a definite risk of damage, either to an individual or to the public, the case is taken out of the province of liberty, and placed in that of morality or law.

Chapter 12: Politics and Pluralism

Comprehension questions you should be able to answer after reading this chapter:

1. What is Rawls' "Original Position" (OP)?

2. What is the "veil of ignorance" (VOI)? Explain what is meant by "ignorance," in this context. Of what are participants "ignorant?" What is the purpose of this ignorance?

3. What are Rawls' Two Principles of Justice? (POJ)

4. What are the "basic liberties" described in the 1st POJ?

5. What are the "primary goods" in the 2nd POJ? What two conditions must be met to justify an unequal distribution of primary goods? How could an unequal distribution of primary goods be to everyone's advantage?

6. Who are the "least advantaged?" Why should we focus on them, when considering applications of the two Principles of Justice?

7. What does Rawls mean by each of the following? Reasonable pluralism, well-ordered society, overlapping consensus, comprehensive moral doctrine, public reason, stability.

8. What does it mean to be constrained by "public reason" in the context of political debates and activism?

9. According to Rawls, when it is acceptable to "resist" our institutions and laws?

10. What is the difference between a "state," and a "people?" What are the features of "Peoples?"

11. What is the difference between "liberal" people and "decent" people?

12. Why does Rawls reject a global redistribution principle under a "one world government?"

13. What is a "burdened society?" What is the "duty of assistance" to burdened societies? How and when is that duty fulfilled?

14. What is an "outlaw state?" What are Rawls' principles of "just war" with respect to outlaw states?

Having surveyed a couple thousand years' worth of political philosophy, we will now turn to a decidedly contemporary and American political philosopher: John Rawls.

Rawls was born on February 21st, 1921. Before he died in 2002, he taught at both Harvard and Oxford. He is undeniably a candidate for the most famous and important American philosopher of the 20th century. He was presented with a National Humanities Medal by President Bill Clinton in 1999, in recognition of how Rawls' work "helped a whole generation of learned Americans revive their faith in democracy itself."[375]

His most famous work is *A Theory of Justice*, first published in 1979. This book revolutionized contemporary ethical and political thought, and is now regarded as "one of the primary texts in

---

[375] *"The National Medal of the Arts and the National Humanities Medal"*. Clinton4.nara.gov. 1999-09-29.

political philosophy," according to Cambridge Dictionary of Philosophy.

At the heart of Rawls' philosophy is a 20th century version of the social contract approach—sometimes called an "enlightened" social contract. We will consider his approach to the social contract tradition in three stages:

1. his development of a "liberal political conception of justice"
2. his consideration of political stability given the fact of pluralism
3. his extension of stages one and two into the realm of international politics

Stage 1: The Original Position

As mentioned, Rawls is part of the same social contract tradition that we have studied in previous chapters; a tradition that includes such theorists as Hobbes and Locke. In each case, they had their own particular vision of State of Nature—and Rawls is no different, in that regard.

Central to understanding Rawls' interpretation of the social contract tradition is his idea of the "original position." The "original position" (hereafter referred to as the OP) is another hypothetical situation, another thought-experiment analogous to that of the State of Nature itself. The OP is the hypothetical meeting that Rawls imagines taking place when people collectively decide to leave the State of Nature and create a government under which to live.

So, imagine a meeting of all the people who will be living in that new society. They have gathered together in order to decide upon the most fundamental political questions, such as what kind of government they will have, what sorts of laws, what sorts of rights (if any), how to distribute the resources of their society, and so on. What sort of decision-making procedure could participants employ, in the OP, in order to produce a government and laws that will be just and fair, that will be agreeable to everyone in the society?

To promote fairness, Rawls imagines that participants in the OP must first pass through a "veil of ignorance" (hereafter: VOI). Imagine that

everyone must pass under a curtain before entering the meeting hall, and, when they do, this curtain temporarily suppresses all kinds of memories and information—it induces a selective "ignorance." Obviously, this is an imaginary process, but Rawls thinks it gives us insight into the requirements of justice. The image below should look somewhat familiar, as a simpler version of it was used in our previous explanation of Hobbes. There, the idea was that we emerge from the State of Nature to create a social contract, and then appoint a sovereign to enforce that contract. In the expanded version applicable to Rawls, we emerge from the State of Nature into the OP, where we will decide on the social contract and sovereign—but a key feature of the OP is that we are behind the VOI.

Behind the veil, participants are "ignorant" as concerns a variety of pieces of demographic information. These include:

- Race and ethnicity
- Gender
- Age
- Physical and mental ability or disability
- Sexual orientation
- Religious affiliation
- Socioeconomic status
- Generation (e.g., "baby boomer," "Gen X")
- Vision of the good life (i.e., personal values)

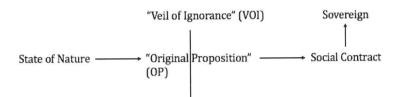

Participants are not ignorant of everything, of course. To begin with, they have *concepts* of all of those things (e.g., race, gender, religion, etc.)—they just don't know how those concepts apply to themselves, or other participants.

In addition, in order to make important political decisions, they must have other kinds of basic knowledge intact. In order to decide what sort of government to create, what sorts of tax systems to enact, etc., participants must have a rudimentary understanding of the following:

- Basic economics
- Basic political theory
- Basic science
- Basic social sciences (including psychology and sociology, and the fact that different persons have different worldviews and values)

Note the repetition of the word "basic." No one is suggesting that participants all have a Ph.D. in economics, or are professional psychologists. Instead, they are assumed to have the basic everyday understanding of the world and how it works that you and I already possess. They understand that there are different kinds of political systems (e.g., democracy, monarchy, theocracy, etc.) and have a basic understanding of how they work. They have a basic understanding of economics (e.g., supply and demand). They have a basic understanding of human psychology (e.g., motivation, behavioral tendencies, etc.).

This sort of knowledge will allow them to decide between different forms of government, and will allow them to agree upon certain approaches to social and economic policy. The value of what they *do* know is obvious, but what's the value of what they do *not* know (i.e., all that demographic information suppressed by the VOI)? If you haven't figured it out already, you'll probably be stunned by how obvious the answer is.

As Rawls puts it: the purpose of the veil of ignorance is to ensure that principles of justice are chosen such that "no one is advantaged or disadvantaged in the choice of principles by the outcome of natural chance or the contingency of social circumstances." Put another way, if you don't know who you are, you can't use that information when making your decisions. In one word, the purpose of the VOI is <u>fairness.</u>

As an example, consider the very basic question of what sort of government ("sovereign") to create/appoint. A participant in the OP suggests a dictatorship, in which one person wields all power, and everyone else has to submit to that one person's power. Keeping in mind that you don't know who you are when you step out from behind the VOI, would you agree to a dictatorship? Of course not! It's likely that the only way you would agree to a dictatorship is if you knew you were going to be the dictator. But, behind the VOI, you don't know who you are. Maybe you're the dictator, but it's much more likely that you're not.

So, what system would you agree to, then? Probably some form of democracy, since, in a democracy, (almost) everyone (in theory) has a right to participate in the political process. With a democratic political system, it doesn't matter who you are behind the VOI. If you agree to a democracy, you will have a presumably equal right to participate in basic political decision-making no matter who you happen to be.

To continue with the same example, having agreed upon "democracy," you now turn to the question of who will vote. Suppose that someone proposes that only property-owning white males will be allowed to vote.[376] Would you agree to that behind the VOI? Of course not! You don't know whether or not you own property (socioeconomic status), whether or not you're white (race/ethnicity), or whether or not you're male (gender). Suppose you agree to this, then step out from behind the VOI to discover you're an African-American woman. Now you can't vote. Pretty foolish of you, right? If you don't know your own race or ethnicity, you're not going to agree to any law or policy that privileges one race over another. So too with gender. So too with religion. Would you agree to form a State in which everyone must be Christian, if you had to make this decision behind the VOI? No way. For all you know, you're Muslim, or Hindu, or an atheist. For the very same reason, you would never agree to a social contract in which everyone was bound by Sharia law, nor one in which the exercise of religion (in general) was banned. None of those outcomes would be *fair*.

As previously stated, the primary purpose of the VOI is to ensure fairness. How do we ensure fairness? Recall that Rawls' theory is situated within the Social Contract tradition.

Here we face a difficulty for any political conception of justice that uses the idea of

a contract, whether social or otherwise. The difficulty is this: we must find some point of view, removed from and not distorted by the particular features and circumstances of the all-encompassing background framework, from which a fair agreement between free and equal persons can be reached. The original position, with the feature I have called 'the veil of ignorance,' is this point of view.[377]

The participants in the OP are not presumed to be idealists, seeking to create a utopia for all. Much more modestly, they are merely presumed to be self-interested. I want the best social contract for myself. You want the best one for yourself. And so on. How can we take that basic self-interest, and turn it towards fairness? By preventing participants from using certain (presumably politically irrelevant) pieces of information, such as race or gender, in making their decisions.

Perhaps controversially, or perhaps in a display of common-sense, Rawls thinks that the contingencies of birth are morally arbitrary. No one "deserves" to be born into a rich or poor family, into one ethnic group or another, into one sex or gender or sexual orientation, or to be more or less naturally intelligent or physically gifted, etc. These are unearned accidents of birth. Since none of us "deserves" them, none of us is entitled

---

[376] As a historical reminder: as of 1789 in the United States, the American Constitution allowed each state to determine voting requirements. In the vast majority of cases, the states allowed only white male property owners to vote. The Naturalization Act of 1790 allowed white men born outside the United States to become citizens and vote. Property requirements for white men were phased out by the states as of 1856. The 15th Amendment of the Constitution granted non-white men (including freed male slaves) the right to vote in 1870. The 19th Amendment to the U.S. Constitution granted women the right to vote in 1920. Native Americans were granted the right

to vote in 1924. The Magnuson Act of 1943 granted Chinese immigrants the right to become citizens (and therefore the right to vote). In 1966, property requirements for voting were ruled unconstitutional by the Supreme Court in the case of *Harper v. Virginia*. In 1971, the age requirement for the right to vote was reduced to age 18. As of today, it is still permissible to deny the right to vote to convicted felons, and residents of Puerto Rico are not allowed to vote in the presidential election despite being US citizens.

[377] John Rawls, "Justice as Fairness: Political not Metaphysical," *Philosophy and Public Affairs*, 14(3), 1985, p. 235.

to any benefit we might receive (or penalty we might suffer) due to the contingency of our birth.[378]

Bluntly: things like race, gender, sexual orientation, religious affiliation, socioeconomic status (etc.) shouldn't *matter* in the context of constructing a just and fair social contract, and the just and fair political, legal, and economic institutions that will govern it, or the just and fair laws that should flow from those institutions. Since those things shouldn't matter, we shouldn't take them into consideration—and the VOI

attempts to enforce that.

In theory, the only principles, laws, and policies you would agree to behind the VOI are those that you would agree to no matter who you are in society. If you would agree to them, no matter whom you are, that's a pretty good indicator that they're fair. In essence, if I don't know who I will be once I step out from behind the VOI, the contract that's best for "me" will turn out to be the contract that is best for anyone and everyone.

Test Your Understanding

For each of the following examples, evaluate whether or not you would agree to them from behind the VOI (and be able to explain why):

- Racially segregated schools
- Laws prohibiting the issuing of State marriage licenses for same-sex couples
- Laws requiring members of the clergy to perform same-sex marriage ceremonies, regardless of their theological views on homosexuality
- Laws requiring wheelchair access into buildings
- Laws protecting people against housing discrimination on the basis of mental illness
- Requiring prayers in public schools
- Allowing voluntary preyer in public schools

Using this basic approach, we could test every single policy proposal, law, and political decision by the standard of "would I agree to this behind the VOI?" However, Rawls offers us a shortcut. Rawls believed that the basic outcome of the OP and decisions made behind the VOI could be summarized by two basic <u>principles of justice</u>:

1. *Each person is to have an equal right to the most extensive scheme of equal basic liberties compatible with a similar scheme of liberties for others.*

2. *Social and economic inequalities are to be arranged so that they are both (a) reasonably expected to be to everyone's advantage and (b) attached to positions and offices open to all.*

The first principle of justice (hereafter referred to as a POJ) deals with basic rights and liberties and applies to the design of the political constitution of the society. The second POJ deals with the just distribution of what Rawls calls "primary goods" (including wealth), and therefore to the economic institutions and policies of the society.

Rawls does *not* include citizenship or nationality as items to be excluded behind the veil of ignorance. In other words, those things can and will be considered when making policy behind the veil of ignorance.

---

[378] Some of you might be wondering if citizenship status or nationality are equally contingent accidents of birth, and if they should be excluded here as well. Interestingly enough, for reasons we will explore towards the end of the chapter,

Basic Liberties

Rawls claims that participants behind the VOI would agree to equal access to, and an equal share of, certain **basic liberties**. If you are a United States citizen, or live in the U.S., or have merely heard of the U.S., you are probably familiar with the sorts of liberties he has in mind:

1. Political liberty (the right to vote and hold public office)
2. Freedom of speech and assembly
3. Liberty of conscience and thought
4. Freedom of the person (e.g., freedom from psychological oppression, physical assault, dismemberment, etc.)
5. The right to hold personal property
6. Freedom from arbitrary arrest and seizure

Certainly the idea that we have the right of free speech and the free exercise of religion is neither original nor unique to Rawls. One of the impressive things about Rawls' philosophy, though, is that he gives us a way to explain *why* we think we all do (or should) have such liberties, and why we think (for the most part), that everyone should have them equally. Moreover, his justification for such a right does not depend upon any particular (religious) worldview—unlike other social contract theorists. John Locke, for example claimed that our rights, even in the State of Nature, come by virtue of our being equally created by God. What if you are an atheist, and don't believe that anyone is created by God, equally or otherwise, because God doesn't exist?

If, on the other hand, we derive our rights based on what we would (theoretically) agree to behind the VOI, then we have a justification for that right whether your worldview is religious, or naturalistic.

Let's start with the equal right to participate in the political process (i.e., democratic self-governance). Why do we think it just that we have such a right, and that it is unjust if it is denied us? Think about what you would agree to behind the VOI. Not knowing who you are, it would be foolish of you to deny political participation to anyone on the basis of such things as race, gender, income, etc., because you might unwittingly disenfranchise yourself in the process.

So, what *would* you agree to? Who should be allowed to participate? *Everyone*—or, at least almost everyone, with few and defensible exceptions.[379] In that way, no matter who you are when you step out from behind the VOI, you have a right to self-governance. How much of a right? An equal right. In that way, no matter who you are, you have no less (nor any more) of a right than anyone else. Not only would it be foolish of you to agree to a contract where some people have rights, and others don't (while not knowing into which group you fall!), it would also be foolish of you to agree to a contract in which some people have a greater share of a right than do others (again, while not knowing into which group you fall).

As one more example, let's consider certain civil liberties pertaining to criminal trials. Some people express frustration with the fact that it costs more to execute a condemned criminal in the U.S. than to imprison him for the rest of his life.[380] How is this possible? How could a few

---

[379] Note: Some of you might be thinking that the fact that one must be 18 years old, or older, to vote in the U.S. signifies a violation of Rawls' procedure. After all, you don't know how old you are behind the VOI. However, no matter who you are behind the VOI, you probably recognize that children aren't terribly well equipped (mentally, And in terms of maturity) to vote. You are aware of basic human nature behind the VOI, after all.

Moreover, all one needs to do in order to overcome this age "discrimination" is survive to the age of 18. Unlike denying the vote on the basis of race or gender, which is nothing one can "out grow," a minimum age requirement is a temporary distinction, and could survive the scrutiny of the VOI.

[380] For example, according to the Death Penalty Information Center, if the Governor of the State of

seconds of electricity, or a single bullet, or a dose of poison, be more expensive than room and board for life? Many of you already know the answer: because of the lengthy and expensive appeals process.

It's not as if a criminal is sentenced to death and is then dragged out behind the courthouse and shot. Instead, most condemned criminals spend decades filing appeals to their conviction, and the State must pay for its own attorneys and associated fees every single time—and often must pay for the condemned person's lawyer as well. By the time a couple decades go by, the cost adds up.

"I have the solution!" you exclaim. "Eliminate all those costly appeals! If a judge or jury finds the guy guilty, and sentences him to death, drag him out of the room and shoot him. Problem solved."

And yet, we have all those appeals and "safety nets" in place to protect convicted criminals. Why would we (or should we) have all those protections in place? Go behind the VOI, and you'll find your answer. Not knowing who you are, you don't know if you're someone who has been, or ever will be, involved in the criminal justice system. It's a possibility though. Not knowing your income level, you don't know if you'll be able to afford an attorney—but you better believe you'd want one! So, behind the VOI, you would agree that everyone should have access to a lawyer, even if they can't afford to pay for one personally.

You'd want other protections in place, too. You'd want for *the State* to have to *prove* that you're guilty, instead of you having to prove that you're innocent. You'd want the State to have to present evidence against you, in public, as opposed to being able to arrest, try, and convict

you on evidence unseen (or maybe even on no evidence at all).

What about all those expensive appeals? You'd want those, too. A dirty, ugly, fact is that innocent people have been, and continue to be, convicted of crimes they did not commit. Set aside conspiracy theories and crooked cops, sometimes people just plain make a mistake, and point to the wrong guy in a police lineup, or think they remember seeing someone who they didn't really see. It happens. It happens in death penalty cases as well.

In the year 2000, Illinois Governor George Ryan (a death penalty *supporter*) put an indefinite hold on executions in his state after 13 death row inmates' convictions were overturned. Also in 2000, the most comprehensive study (at that time) of death penalty cases in the U.S. found that 2/3 of all capital sentences that were reviewed were overturned when appealed due to either errors or inappropriate conduct during the trial. Examples of problems included incompetent defense teams, evidence suppressed by police and prosecutors, misinformed jurors, and biased judges.

DNA evidence alone has resulted in the post-conviction exoneration of 350 people (so far)— and 20 of them had been sentenced to death.[381] People awaiting execution on death row have been found innocent, and released, before it was too late. It's reasonable to believe that, sometimes, it was already too late — and an innocent person was put to death.[382] Imagine that you are that innocent person, wrongfully convicted and facing execution. Wouldn't you want a right to an appeal, every reasonable chance to prove that a mistake was made, before it's too late? That's why, behind the VOI, recognizing that someday we might be the person

---

California "commuted the sentences of those remaining on death row to life without parole, it would result in an immediate savings of $170 million per year, with a savings of $5 billion over the next 20 years." (http://www.deathpenaltyinfo .org/costs-death-penalty)

[381] https://www.innocenceproject.org/exonerate/

[382] http://www.sfgate.com/crime/article/Judge-says-California-executed-man-who-6300005.php?cmpid=fb-desktop

needing those protections, we would agree to them—despite the inconvenience, annoyance, and expense, when we're not the ones having to worry about it.

We could conduct this same exercise with each of the basic liberties. Put yourself behind the VOI, and ask yourself what you would agree to, and you'll be able to figure out why each of those basic liberties makes the list and, just as importantly, why the first POJ requires that each of us has an equal share of those liberties.

Primary Goods

We now turn to the second POJ. As a reminder, according to the second POJ, "social and economic inequalities are to be arranged so that they are both (a) reasonably expected to be to everyone's advantage and (b) attached to positions and offices open to all."

The second POJ, then, concerns the just distribution of "primary goods." "Primary good" is simply a term used to signify those things which nearly all of us want, all things considered, and that we typically would rather have more of, than less. Primary goods are those things which are useful in the pursuit of a wide range of visions of the good life. Examples of primary goods include:

- the basic rights and liberties addressed in the 1st POJ
- freedom to move and choose from among a wide variety of occupations
- income and wealth
- access to educational resources
- access to health care
- the social bases of self-respect that give citizens a sense of dignity and self-worth

It's hard to find someone who doesn't want income, and the opportunity to earn it; who doesn't want access to health care or education,

and so on. A harsh fact concerning some of these primary goods, though, is that they are finite. There is not an infinite amount of wealth, or educational access, or health care to go around. A simple illustration is available if you have ever had to sit in the waiting area of an emergency room waiting for medical attention for yourself or a loved one. Many patients with only a few doctors results in a long wait. Because some primary goods are limited, it's inevitable that we come up with some method of distributing them—this is an issue with which every society must contend, and that must be addressed by any social contract.

There are many possible methods of distribution. One person could get everything. Or a few people get most, and the rest fight for the scraps. Or, (as of 2013), the wealthiest 160,000 families could own as much wealth as the poorest 145 *million* families combined.[383] Or, everyone gets an equal share—or any number of distributions in-between. Which, distribution, though, is *fair* (given Rawls' approach)? Put yourself behind the VOI, and find out.

What would you agree to behind the VOI? We might assume that a participant's default choice of distribution will be "equal" — everyone has an exactly equal share of each primary good. That would mean that we all have an equal educational opportunity, equal access to health care, an equal standard of living, and so on. Why would we agree to that? Because no matter who I am once I step out from behind the VOI, I'm no worse off than anyone else. No one else has better health care, or a better standard of living, etc. However, while this might be our default distribution, Rawls claims that we don't have to stick with the default.

There is a way in which some inequality is permissible and just. An unequal distribution of primary goods is acceptable if and only if everyone is better off by virtue of that unequal distribution than they would have been had the

---

[383] http://fortune.com/2014/10/31/inequality-wealth-income-us/

distribution been equal. How is that possible? Consider the two bar graphs.

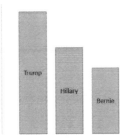

These two graphs represent the distribution of primary goods in two hypothetical communities ("left," and "right"). These are very simple communities, as each contains only three people: Trump, Hillary, and Bernie. Obviously, this is a grossly oversimplified picture, but that's all we need to illustrate the point. In the left-side community, there is an unequal distribution of primary goods. Trump has more of those goods (e.g., wealth, income, access to education, etc.) than Hillary and Bernie, and Hillary has more than Bernie. In the right-side community, there is a perfectly even distribution instead. Trump, Hillary, and Bernie each have an exactly equal share of those goods.

Although our default distribution that we would agree to behind the VOI would be the kind we see in the right-side community (i.e., a perfectly equal distribution), Rawls acknowledges that unequal distributions would be agreeable so long as they are "reasonably expected to be to everyone's advantage" and "attached to positions and offices open to all."

To be attached to positions and offices open to all simply means that it must be possible, in principle, for anyone to enjoy the greater share of the distribution. There must be genuine equality of opportunity (though not a guaranteed equality of outcome).

...fair equality of opportunity is said to require not merely that public offices and social positions be open in the formal sense, but that all should have a fair chance to attain them. To specify the idea of fair chance we say: supposing that there is a distribution of native endowments, those who have the same level of talent and ability and the same willingness to use these gifts should have the same prospects of success regardless of their social class of origin, the class into which they are born and develop until the age of reason. In all parts of society there are to be roughly the same prospects of culture and achievement for those similarly motivated and endowed.[384]

If it's possible for some people to become wealthier than others, that possibility must be open to everyone (in theory). Laws or customs that allowed only people of a particular race, or religion, or gender, for example, to attain great wealth, or to attend the best schools, would not satisfy this requirement, and would be considered unjust.

As to the first requirement, that the unequal distribution be to everyone's advantage, we can see how this is possible by comparing the two graphs. Notice that although the distribution is

---

[384] John Rawls, *Justice as Fairness: A Restatement.* Erin Kelly, ed. Cambridge: Harvard University Press 2001, pp. 43-44.

unequal in the left-side community, and some people are better off than others, every member of left-side is better off than she or he would be in right-side. Trump has a greater amount of primary goods in left-side than he does is right-side. So do Hillary and Bernie. This is important. Behind the VOI, I don't know who I am in society (e.g., Trump, Hillary, or Bernie). If I had to choose between left-side and right-side, why would I

pick left-side? Because no matter who I am in left-side, I'm better off. Even if I'm the worst off, comparatively (viz., Bernie), I still have more in left-side than I do in right-side. It makes sense, then, for me to pick left-side, no matter who I might turn out to be.

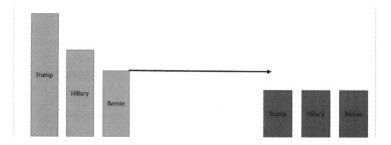

Some of you might be thinking to yourself, "Wait a minute! This is an unfair comparison. Each person is comparatively better off in left-side than in right-side because there are more primary goods to distribute in left-side." This is true. If you take the total combined area of each

bar in left-side, and compare it to the total combined area of each bar in right-side, left-side does produce a much greater overall area, representing a greater amount of primary goods to distribute. In other words, left side is a wealthier community.

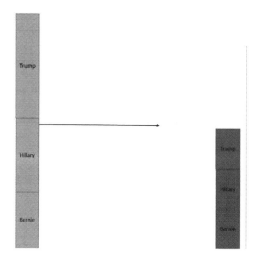

This isn't necessarily cause for suspicion, though — it's the product of a basic promise of capitalism. A key assumption behind capitalism — especially the *laissez-faire* variety — is that by allowing people to pursue wealth and luxury, the economy is stimulated and grows larger than it would be under a more egalitarian system.[385]

If I knew that no matter how hard I worked, and no matter how much I risked, I would never be any better off than my neighbor, I (allegedly) wouldn't have the incentive to work so hard or take those risks — but that hard work and risk-taking is precisely what produces economic growth and improves society.

Billionaires are far wealthier than the average citizen, but they don't just swim around in a tank of money; they use it. That use of money creates jobs, and the wealth "trickles down" to others, ultimately making everyone better off than they otherwise would have been — or so the argument goes.[386] This sort of reasoning explains how the unequal distribution in left-side makes everyone better off compared to the equal distribution found in right-side. By allowing Trump to be so much more fabulously wealthy than Bernie, it makes Bernie better off too (i.e., better off than he would have been in a perfectly equal distribution).

Rawls was profoundly critical of *actual* U.S. economic policy, and thought that our own systems of distribution did not actually satisfy this requirement, but he was open to the possibility, in principle, that unequal distributions could be justified. We need to be careful that these unequal distributions really are to everyone's advantage, though, and one way to do this is by focusing on the "least advantaged," and how they are impacted by the proposed unequal distribution. Who are these least advantaged?

...persons whose family and class origins are more disadvantaged than others, whose natural endowments (as realized) permit them to fare less well, and whose fortune and luck in the course of life turn out to be less happy, all within the normal range . . . and with the relevant measures based on social primary goods.[387]

Candidates for the "least advantaged" include (but are not limited to) the homeless, the sick, the injured, victims of natural disasters, people with physical or mental disabilities, and people belonging to groups that have traditionally been discriminated against (e.g., on the basis of race, gender, religion, etc.).

"Least advantaged" is not necessarily a permanent classification. If I get hurt at work, that can place me among the "least advantaged" for a time, but if I heal and can return to work and "normal" life, my relative disadvantage goes away.

If a group of people is discriminated against, its members may be amongst the least advantaged, but *if* circumstances *truly* change and there is no longer any stigma or harm attached to that group membership, people belonging to that group will no longer count as "least advantaged" (for that reason).

Remember, too, that we're talking about a *relative* disadvantage. If I'm blind, it's going to be more difficult for me to succeed in life than if I had use of my eyes—not impossible, of course, but *more* difficult. If I'm a woman in a society that is somewhat gender biased, it will be more difficult for me to succeed—not impossible, but certainly *more* difficult.

In an ideal (Rawlsian) world, everyone has an equal chance at a good life. In the real world, we face obstacles that shouldn't be there: discrimination, for example, or even just plain bad luck. Unequal distributions of primary goods

---

[385] An argument advanced in a previous chapter, by Adam Smith, of course.

[386] This involves important and complicated economic theories, for which there is great

debate. Take an economics class to explore this further.

[387] John Rawls, *A Theory of Justice*, revised edition. Harvard University Press, 1999. p.83.

are justifiable only if they are to everyone's advantage, and a good way to see if everyone is better off is to check with the least advantaged. If they're better off, it's a good bet that everyone else is too.

It's important to remember that society is not obliged to arrange its practices and institutions so as to guarantee a perfectly equal distribution of goods. Instead, the arrangements must be such that at least those actions and policies that result in an unequal distribution of goods bring about a state of affairs in which the least-advantaged are better off than they would have been in the absence of the action or policy.

Stage 2: Pluralism

Having established the basic foundation for Rawls' approach to the social contract tradition in terms of the original position, veil of ignorance, and two principles of justice, we will now turn to the political issue that occupied him later in his career, and which might seem especially relevant to the current U.S. political climate: the "problem" of reasonable pluralism.

Pluralism, in general, merely refers to the fact that a variety of different worldviews exist. Some worldviews are religious (e.g., Christianity, Islam, Hinduism, etc.), and some are purely naturalistic (e.g., atheism, humanism, etc.). Even within these broad categories of religious and naturalistic, there are widely differing worldviews. Anglican Christianity is quite different from Wahhabist Islam, for example. Religious and moral values range across a wide spectrum, and these values influence our political beliefs and values as well.

There is a difference, though, between mere pluralism and *reasonable* pluralism. Mere pluralism simply recognizes the plurality of views. Reasonable pluralism refers to the idea that no one worldview has an obvious monopoly on rationality. That is just to say that smart, sincere, reasonable people can be Christian, Muslim, atheists, Buddhists, etc. Such persons can be pro-life, or pro-choice; vegetarian, or

omnivores; for or against the death penalty. It is simply not the case that one worldview is "obviously" true, and anyone subscribing to any other is "crazy."

Is the existence of reasonable pluralism in Western democratic societies also the *problem* of reasonable pluralism? Can a "well-ordered society" achieve the "overlapping consensus" of reasonable "comprehensive moral doctrines" needed to achieve "stability?" Before addressing that question, it's important to identify some key vocabulary.

Well-ordered society: a society in which everyone accepts, and knows that everyone else accepts, the basic principles of justice, in which the main social and political institutions of that society satisfy those principles of justice, and in which the citizens regard their basic institutions as just and comply with their demands.

Comprehensive moral doctrine: a "worldview," including views on morality, religion, etc.

Overlapping consensus: when citizens support and obey laws and public policies for reasons internal to their own comprehensive moral doctrines, supporting the same law but for possibly different reasons.

Stability: when citizens willingly obey their society's laws and policies, even in cases of sincere disagreement.

Rawls gives serious consideration to the problem of reasonable pluralism in his book entitled *Political Liberalism*, where one of his foci is to answer the question of how it is possible for a just and stable society of free and equal citizens to exist and endure when its citizens "remain profoundly divided by reasonable religious, philosophical, and moral doctrines."[388]

Stability is an important issue because laws and policies are *coercive*. Citizens tend to accept

---

[388] John Rawls, *Political Liberalism*, p. xxxix.

coercion when they recognize that the coercion is legitimate, but resist when they think it is not. Laws forbidding murder and laws forbidding African-Americans from eating at lunch counters were, are, and should be received very differently, and afforded very different levels of respect. Acts of civil disobedience for the sake of pedophilia and acts of civil disobedience for the sake of ending segregation are (and should be) regarded with very different degrees of acceptance and respect.

Rawls' goal is to "uncover the conditions of the possibility of a reasonable public basis of justification on fundamental political questions' given the fact of 'reasonable pluralism' in a democratic culture."[389] To this end, he develops a political conception of justice that does not rely on any particular comprehensive moral doctrine for its foundation and that could, in theory, be endorsed by adherents of many different (and even competing) comprehensive moral doctrines. This political conception of justice is intended to be consistent and harmonious with various, competing, comprehensive doctrines so as to achieve the above-mentioned "overlapping consensus."

His account of justice as "fairness," involving the ideas of the original position, veil of ignorance (etc.) described earlier in this chapter is an example of just such a political conception of justice. In theory, people from a wide range of worldviews could agree upon the procedures and principles provided by his theory (or so he hoped, at least), resulting in an overlapping consensus and a stable society.

It is important to note that Rawls is asking about stability with respect to a *well-ordered* society. If a society is well-ordered, then it is a society "in which everyone accepts, and knows that everyone else accepts, the very same principles of justice"[390] As well, the main social and political institutions of that society are

believed, with good reason, to satisfy those principles. Finally, the citizens regard the society's basic institutions as just, have a normally effective sense of justice themselves, and so generally comply with their society's basic institutions.

In other words, if you live in a "well-ordered society," everyone in your society has a basic, shared sense of justice and what it requires, your government and laws are themselves just, and, as such, inspire you (and others) to obey those (just) laws and respect those (just) institutions.

The possible "problem" is that some *reasonable* comprehensive doctrines could be so at odds, in certain places, with the principles of justice and the just society that results from them, that an overlapping consensus would not be achieved, and stability would not be achieved either.

Why would pluralism represent a threat to the stability of such a society? Generally, because pluralism entails different (and sometimes competing) views of the demands of morality and what constitutes a good and right way to live— and therefore what sorts of laws and public policies might be necessary and appropriate.

The most obvious possible tensions arise from religiously-based moral doctrines, in which an adherent might believe it morally imperative that one abstain from certain behaviors (or perform others), but where such is not the belief of other fellow citizens. For example, the consumption of alcohol is forbidden by Islam on the basis of scripture—but the appeal to the Qur'an will hardly be persuasive to anyone who isn't a Muslim, and who has *no other reason* to believe drinking alcohol is morally wrong.[391] Unless the Muslim seeking to ban alcohol by means of public policy can somehow demonstrate that the "principles of justice" require the prohibition of alcohol consumption, it is entirely possible (indeed *likely*) that other

---

[389] Ibid., p. xxi.

[390] Ibid., p. 35.

[391] "You who believe! Intoxicants, gambling, al-ansāb, and al-azlām (arrows for seeking luck or

decision) are an abomination of Shaytān's (Satan's) handiwork. So avoid that in order that you may be successful."
—Qur'an, Surah 5 (al-Ma'idah), ayah 90

citizens, who subscribe to other, reasonable, comprehensive moral doctrines (i.e., nearly any other major worldview than Islam), will disagree with and resist the proposed ban on alcohol—and be *reasonable* in so doing.

It's worth taking a moment, here, to make an important point: the *truth* of Islam (or any other comprehensive moral doctrine) is *not* what is up for debate here. Islam might offer a true account of what is right and wrong, or it might not. That is beside the point.

What is at issue here is what is *reasonable* to do or require within a political context. If everyone within a society was Muslim, and shared the same core values, then it is unlikely that there would be much disagreement as regards alcohol—nor would any ban on alcohol consumption likely be controversial or seem unreasonable. But, in a great many communities (including the United States), it is simply not the case that "everyone" is *anything*: not Muslim, not

Christian, not Buddhist, not atheist. Instead, we are a mix of (mostly) reasonable and, at times, competing comprehensive moral doctrines.

To put it bluntly, if I am a Christian I would probably find it unreasonable to be denied some wine at dinner (let alone at communion!) just because my Muslim neighbor's God (in whom I don't believe) forbids it, just as if I were an atheist, I might find it unreasonable for my Christian neighbor to make homosexual activity illegal because his God (in whom I don't believe) thinks it an "abomination."[392] Making murder (i.e., the unjustified killing of an innocent person) illegal, however, is likely to find agreement across a wide variety of comprehensive moral doctrines. Not surprisingly, then, most people are "onboard" with prohibiting murder, but there would be considerable disagreement when it comes to prohibiting alcohol consumption.

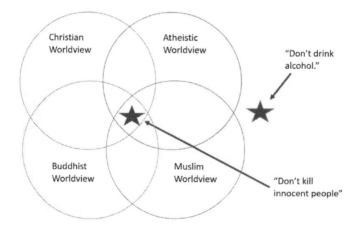

---

[392] Not all Christians believe this, of course. . . .

Given the existence of reasonable pluralism, is it even possible to achieve the overlapping consensus of reasonable comprehensive moral doctrines needed for stability? Even if citizens have deep disagreements on certain issues because of their different worldviews, can there be enough "buy-in" to achieve a stable, well-ordered society?

To explore this issue of stability in the face of pluralism, we will consider the political hot-button of abortion—considering what (little) Rawls had to say about abortion, and how the moral and political issues surrounding abortion present a "stability" issue.

First, and for the record, what did Rawls say about abortion, himself? We will consider two representative quotations from Rawls (with underlining added for emphasis):

1. Regarding the troubled question of abortion: consider the question in terms of these three important political values: the due respect for human life, the ordered reproduction of political society over time, including the family in some form, and finally the equality of women as equal citizens.. . . any reasonable balance of these three values will give a woman a duly qualified right to decide whether or not to end her pregnancy during the first trimester.. . . [A]t this early stage of pregnancy the political value of the equality of women is overriding, and this right is required to give it substance and force.[393]

2. In particular, when hotly disputed questions, such as that of abortion, arise which may lead to a stand-off between different political conceptions, citizens must vote on the question according to their complete ordering of political values. Indeed, this is a normal case: unanimity of views is not to be expected. Reasonable political

conceptions of justice do not always lead to the same conclusion; nor do citizens holding the same conception always agree on particular issues. Yet the outcome of the vote, as I said before, is to be seen as legitimate provided all government officials, supported by other reasonable citizens, of a reasonably just constitutional regime sincerely vote in accordance with the idea of public reason. This doesn't mean the outcome is true or correct, but that it is reasonable and legitimate law, binding on citizens by the majority principle.

Some may, of course, reject a legitimate decision, as Roman Catholics may reject a decision to grant a right to abortion. They may present an argument in public reason for denying it and fail to win a majority. But they need not themselves exercise the right to abortion. They can recognize the right as belonging to legitimate law enacted in accordance with legitimate political institutions and public reason, and therefore not resist it with force. Forceful resistance is unreasonable: it would mean attempting to impose by force their own comprehensive doctrine that a majority of other citizens who follow public reason, not unreasonably, do not accept. Certainly Catholics may, in line with public reason, continue to argue against the right to abortion. Reasoning is not closed once and for all in public reason any more than it is closed in any form of reasoning. Moreover, that the Catholic Church's nonpublic reason requires its members to follow its doctrine is perfectly consistent with their also honoring public   reason.

---

[393] *Political Liberalism*, footnote 32, p.243.

I do not discuss the question of abortion in itself since my concern is not with that question but rather to stress that political liberalism does not hold that the ideal of public reason should always lead to a general agreement of views, nor is it a fault that it does not. Citizens learn and profit from debate and argument, and when their arguments follow public reason, they instruct society's political culture and deepen their understanding of one another even when agreement cannot be reached.[394]

In brief, Rawls appears to believe that women have a right to make their own reproductive choices, at least within the first trimester of pregnancy—but far more important than his personal view on abortion, and far more relevant for our purposes in this chapter, is what he says about those who disagree.

...unanimity of views is not to be expected. Reasonable political conceptions of justice do not always lead to the same conclusion; nor do citizens holding the same conception always agree on particular issues. Yet the outcome of the vote, as I said before, is to be seen as legitimate provided all government officials, supported by other reasonable citizens, of a reasonably just constitutional regime sincerely vote in accordance with the idea of public reason. This doesn't mean the outcome is true or correct, but that it is reasonable and legitimate law, binding on citizens by the majority principle.[395]

It is inevitable that citizens will disagree with each other on various laws and policy issues—even important, high-stakes issues like abortion, war, the death penalty, environmental policy, etc. Nevertheless, the policy outcome might still be the result of fair and legitimate political processes (e.g., a majority vote subject to just Constitutional constraints), in which case the law or policy is reasonable and legitimate—even if not "true."[396] The hypothetical Catholics who disagree are certainly free to abstain from abortion themselves, and to continue to vote against abortion access, and preach against it at the pulpit or over the dinner table—but what they may not do is use *force* to impose their will on their fellow citizens.

Forceful resistance is unreasonable: it would mean attempting to impose by force their own comprehensive doctrine that a majority of other citizens who follow public reason, not unreasonably, do not accept.[397]

In fairness, though, just how persuasive will an appeal to "reasonableness" be? If one believes that "abortion is murder," and one's "just" society not only permits the murder of unborn babies but perhaps even subsidizes and otherwise supports it by means of health care policies, one is likely to be dismayed at the unwillingness of one's public institutions to do the "right" thing. What does this admittedly hard case tell us about pluralism and Rawls' ability to address it?

Whether or not such a scenario indicates a stability problem depends upon whether or not the pro-life activists in question are "reasonable." Rawls defines a person as <u>reasonable</u> when, among equals, *"they are ready to propose*

---

[394] Rawls, "The Idea of Public Reason Revisited," in *The Law of Peoples with "The Idea of Public Reason Revisited."* Harvard University Press, 2002, pp. 169-171.
[395] Ibid., 169.
[396] This is just to say that it could, in fact, be *true* that there is a God who forbids abortion, and

therefore laws that allow abortion are "false"—but those laws might nevertheless have been the result of just, fair, and reasonable political processes.
[397] Ibid., 170.

principles and standards as fair terms of cooperation and to abide by them willingly, given the assurance that others will likewise do so. Those norms they view as reasonable for everyone to accept and therefore as justifiable to them; and they are ready to discuss the fair terms that others propose.[398]

<u>Unreasonable</u> persons, on the other hand, *"plan to engage in cooperative schemes but are unwilling to honor, or even to propose, except as a necessary public pretense, any general principles or standards for specifying fair terms of cooperation. They are ready to violate such terms as suits their interests when circumstances allow."*

To put this in very simple, non-political terms: imagine that you and a friend both want to play a new video game, and are trying to decide who gets to go first. You agree to flip a coin and the winner of the coin toss will get to play first, and then after one hour the other person gets to play. Your friend then reveals to you the following: "Just so you know, if I win the coin toss, everything will go as planned. But, if I lose, I'm just going to beat you up, and play first anyway— oh, and you won't get a turn at all, let alone the first one." Your friend doesn't sound very reasonable! What's the point of even doing the coin toss at all, if your friend isn't going to abide by the outcome anyway? Similarly, what's the point of an election if one side intends to assassinate the opposing candidate and impose a military coup if they should happen to lose? Democracy is great, so long as "we" win—but if we lose, to hell with voting? For Rawls, "reasonable" people intend to abide by the rules, even if they "lose." "Unreasonable" people are willing to cheat and ignore the rules if they should "lose."

Returning to the example of abortion, certain sorts of responses from our activist in question would be indicative of unreasonableness.

Obvious examples would be things like bombing abortion clinics, murdering abortion providers, violent overthrow of the government or an election result, etc. Far less dramatic than any of those things is an unwillingness to honor "public reason."

Public Reason

The idea of public reason limits political discussion and deliberation primarily (and at the least) done by judges and justices, government officials (especially legislators and executives), and political candidates and their campaign spokespersons. *Ideally*, it applies to ordinary citizens as well whenever they personally deliberate upon, endorse or reject, and ultimately vote on a given policy.

> A democratic government should justify its policies solely in terms of values that every reasonable citizen can endorse, at least when matters of basic justice are at stake. And, since the policies of a democratic government are ultimately the policies of the people, ordinary citizens should, in voting or in public advocacy, also support only those positions on matters of basic justice that can be justified in this way. [399]

Or, as Rawls states in "The Idea of Public Reason Revisited":

> Our exercise of political power is proper only when we sincerely believe that the reasons we offer for our political actions—were we to state them as government officials—are sufficient, and

---

[398] Pritchard, Michael S. and Robison, Wade L (1999) "Justice and the Treatment of Animals: A Critique of Rawls," in Richardson, Henry S. and Weithman, Paul J. (ed.) *The Philosophy of Rawls: A*

Collection of Essays, New York: Garland Publishing, Inc. p. 49.

[399] Peter de Marneffe, 'Rawls' Idea of Public Reason,' *Pacific Philosophical Quarterly*, 1994, 75 (3/4), p. 233.

we also think that other citizens might reasonably accept those reasons.[400]

The central claim of **public reason** is that, when dealing with the scope of basic liberty and other matters of basic justice, citizens should take only those positions that are defendable from some liberal political conception of justice, independently of any wider comprehensive moral doctrine.

According to Rawls, if a policy addresses "fundamental issues," it must be supported by the political values of public reason. "Since the exercise of political power must be legitimate, the ideal of citizenship imposes a moral, not a legal, duty—the duty of civility—to be able to explain to one another on those fundamental questions how the principles and policies they advocate and vote for can be supported by the political values of public reason."[401]

In other words, while it is (of course) not *illegal* (in the United States) to invoke religious reasons for opposition to abortion, and, if you do, you certainly do not violate any *legal* obligations of citizenship, it is, nevertheless, a "duty of civility" to offer reasons that are not unique to any particular worldview (e.g., Christian), but that instead draw on "public reason."

The point of invoking public reasons is a recognition that we have a duty to justify our policy decisions to one another by appealing to public values and public standards, principles of reasoning and pieces of evidence that all citizens could reasonably endorse and that do not rely on controversial theories, metaphysical assumptions, or controversial evidence.[402]

To use an admittedly extreme example, imagine that a small but wealthy organization of citizens lobbies to end (and ban) all vaccination of children, and their reason for this is that they have received telepathic communications from an alien mothership warning that only unvaccinated children will be allowed to "beam up" when the ship comes to claim us and take us to our new home in another galaxy. Needless to say, very few of us will be persuaded by appeals to telepathic messages from aliens. Similarly, if People for the Ethical Treatment of Animals (PETA) lobbied to ban all animal experimentation and meat consumption because their members all claim to have been animals in one of their many past lives, they would find no allies among the majority of citizens who do not believe in reincarnation. Perhaps wisely, PETA focuses on the far less controversial claim that animals experience pain—something that we can all acknowledge, and something which (could) appeal to any and all of us.

The moral/civil "demands" of public reason do not apply to everything and every context. Rawls claims that, at minimum, public reasons should be invoked when deep, fundamental issues of justice are at stake, such as "constitutional essentials" and matters of basic justice. When political decisions concern things like who gets to vote (or whether to impose voter-ID laws), which religions are to be tolerated (or whether to provide public financial support to private church charities), who can own property, who should be assured equality of opportunity—basically, anything involving the basic liberties described earlier in this chapter—then public reasons should be provided so that, in theory,

---

[400] Rawls, "The Idea of Public Reason Revisited," in: Freeman, Samuel (ed.) *John Rawls: Collected Papers*, Cambridge: Harvard University Press, p. 578.

[401] John Rawls, *Political Liberalism*, p. 217.

[402] As an example of this at work, recall the difference from earlier in this chapter between the prohibition of murder and a prohibition of alcohol consumption. Justifying the alcohol ban

by appealing to scriptural references is far less likely to generate an overlapping consensus than would a general appeal to public health, increases in crime associated with alcohol use, etc. Justifying the ban on killing innocent people, however, is a fairly easy task. Pretty much anyone, from within any worldview, can appreciate the value of protecting innocent life.

people from across a wide variety of comprehensive moral doctrines could understand, and agree to, the reasons provided for one's policy stance.

Even when dealing with constitutional essentials and basic liberties, the demand of public reason is merely that public reasons be provided, not that non-public reasons be *excluded*. Citizens may offer *nonpublic reasons* as support for their views so long as the public reasons are themselves sufficient to render their answer to a political question "reasonable." A sufficient reason is one that is "good enough, standing on its own, to justify the position taken in public political debate."[403]

> Reasonable comprehensive doctrines, religious or non-religious, may be introduced in public political discourse at any time, provided that in due course proper political reasons—and not reasons given solely by comprehensive doctrines—are presented that are sufficient to support whatever the comprehensive doctrines introduced are said to support. This injunction to present proper political reasons I refer to as *the proviso,* and it specifies public political culture as distinct from the background culture.[404]

Thus, groups are not entirely prevented from appealing to the values from their comprehensive doctrines when promoting policies concerning fundamental issues, but they are obliged to use such values as *supplements* to their already sufficient argument that has been made under the restrictions set by the idea of public reason. A policy issue that isn't so "fundamental" (i.e.,

doesn't pertain to basic justice or constitutional essentials, such as how much public funding to provide for State parks) need not be justified by public reason at all, but Rawls says that it is nevertheless "usually highly desirable to settle political questions by invoking the values of public reason."[405] That is, while it is not required that non-essential issues be justified by public reason, it's a good and desirable thing if they are.

Why would citizens, individually or collectively, agree to abide by the limits of public reason? Rawls thinks that this is because they might recognize that it is the reasonable and morally civil thing to do. This is so because "except by endorsing a reasonable constitutional democracy, there is no other way fairly to ensure the liberty of its adherents consistent with the equal liberties of other reasonable free and equal citizens."[406]

That is, a reasonable comprehensive moral doctrine will recognize that *reasonable* political judgments cannot be overridden according to the dictates of a particular comprehensive doctrine without trampling on the rights of other free, equal, and reasonable citizens.

Those who wish to override their fellow citizens when the reasonable judgments of the majority are at odds with the values of their own doctrine are *un*reasonable because they refuse to honor the reasonable judgments arrived at by their fellow citizens through legitimate majoritarian political procedures. What could this be other than an attempt to *coerce* others into accepting one's own beliefs? In the case of our hypothetical pro-life activist, *she* believes that abortion is murder. Clearly, not everyone else does!

What might our pro-lifer do in such a situation? One option would be to attempt to

---

[403] Peter de Marneffe, "Rawls' Idea of Public Reason," *Pacific Philosophical Quarterly*, 1994, p. 230, note 12.

[404] Rawls, "The Idea of Public Reason Revisited," in: Freeman, Samuel (ed.) *John Rawls: Collected Papers*, Cambridge: Harvard University Press, p. 591.

[405] Rawls, *Political Liberalism*, p. 215.

[406] Rawls, "The Idea of Public Reason Revisited," in: Freeman, Samuel (ed.) *John Rawls: Collected Papers*, Cambridge: Harvard University Press, p. 590.

coerce others into compliance through acts of sabotage, intimidation, or civil disobedience. As an extreme example, Dr. George Tiller was shot and killed by Scott Roeder in 2009. Dr. Tiller was one of only a few doctors willing to perform late-term abortions, and Roeder publicly confessed to the killing, offering the following as his justification: "preborn children's lives were in imminent danger."[407]

However, according to Rawls, "Forceful resistance is unreasonable: it would mean attempting to impose by force their own comprehensive doctrine that a majority of other citizens who follow public reason, not unreasonably, do not accept."[408] If our pro-lifer is "reasonable," she must honor the policies and laws of her society—though she is free to use *legitimate* means to alter policies. For example, she might support Operation Rescue financially, educate herself on the merits of the pro-life position, sponsor and participate in "speak-outs" and consciousness-raising events, wear and distribute pro-life t-shirts and caps, lobby her elected representatives, and otherwise attempt to persuade her fellow citizens that abortion is wrong.

A Christian pro-lifer who adheres to the constraints of public reason will recognize that not all her fellow citizens share her theological worldview—nor even do all her fellow *Christian* citizens share her political stance on abortion. Recognizing that other (reasonable) citizens subscribe to other (reasonable) worldviews, she will not base her public opposition to abortion solely on a reference to a Bible verse—a reference that many of her fellow citizens (e.g., atheists, Hindus, Buddhists, etc.) will not accept as authoritative.[409] Instead, she will attempt to offer reasons to oppose abortion that could, in

theory, be persuasive regardless of one's particular worldview.

Given that most of us, for example, agree that someone taking our own life (in most cases) would be a bad thing, perhaps the pro-lifer could offer an argument demonstrating the basic similarity between a fetus and an adult with respect to the default value of life itself, and propose that just as (generally speaking) it would be wrong to deprive an adult of his or her life without proper justification, so too is it wrong (in general) to deprive a fetus of its life (without proper justification).[410]

This strategy does not require that the pro-lifer accept that other worldviews are equally true, nor that she abandon her own faith and convictions. It merely acknowledges that, in the public political sphere, it is "reasonable" to advocate for or against policy positions without relying solely on potentially controversial (and not universally recognized) values and beliefs.

Depending on what sorts of expectations she has, and on what sorts of activities in which she's willing to engage, our pro-lifer is either reasonable or unreasonable. If *unreasonable*, then, surprisingly enough, there is no "stability" problem. This is so because of the way Rawls defines the stability issue to begin with.

---

[407] AP: Man admits killing Kansas abortion doctor". *MSNBC*. Associated Press. November 9, 2009. Retrieved January 21, 2010.
[408] Rawls, "The Idea of Public Reason Revisited," in: Freeman, Samuel (ed.) *John Rawls: Collected Papers*, Cambridge: Harvard University Press, p. 606.

[409] For example, Job 31:15: "Did not he that made me in the womb make him? and did not one fashion us in the womb?"
[410] Please don't assume that this is my advocacy against abortion access, nor that this is the best (let alone only) way to formulate such a strategy. This example is just that: an example.

Recall that our focus is on a well-ordered society. Rawls claims a democratic society can be well-ordered by a political conception of justice as long as two conditions are met. The first is that citizens from *reasonable* comprehensive doctrines (at least) belong to the overlapping consensus. The overlapping consensus is generated by reasonable people adhering to the limits of public reason. The second condition is that "unreasonable comprehensive doctrines do not gain enough currency to undermine society's essential justice."[411]

The overlapping consensus is built from *reasonable* comprehensive doctrines. If our pro-lifer's comprehensive moral doctrine is unreasonable in the ways described above, then she is not part of the overlapping consensus in the first place. Accordingly, she is not a threat to *stability*—though she might well be a threat to the well-orderedness of the society if her comprehensive moral doctrine is both unreasonable and gains sufficient "currency."

To step away from our pro-lifer for a moment, consider the example of ISIS (or ISIL). The particular Salafist version of Islam espoused by this organization is an example of a comprehensive moral doctrine. Using Rawls' vocabulary, it is also undeniably an "unreasonable" comprehensive moral doctrine because, among other things, it opposes democracy!

Adherents to this worldview believe that their views are "the truth," that all opposing views are heretical or blasphemous, and that even voting itself is morally wrong. Clearly, sincere members of ISIS would not abide by the outcome of a fair election that doesn't go their way, if they are opposed to elections in the first place! Any societies where ISIS has gained "sufficient currency" (e.g., ISIS-controlled portions of Syria or Iraq) are simply not "well-ordered" societies governed by a liberal political conception of justice. The stability concern does not arise there because there is no well-ordered society to be stable, or unstable, in the first place.

The United States, however, is not ISIS-controlled Syria or Iraq, and a case could be made that U.S. society is well-ordered.[412] Here, though, the same as "there," well-orderedness can be threatened by "unreasonable" groups who grow too large or too influential—and this is precisely the worry behind the possible problem of pluralism. Though the analogy with ISIS might be uncomfortable and overly provocative, it's not difficult to see how the analogy can be made.

Why should we assume that a sincere pro-lifer would be persuaded by the appeal to reasonableness? Why assume that she would acknowledge that it is unreasonable to expect others to comply with the demands of *her* comprehensive moral doctrine (forcibly, if necessary) given the reality of reasonable pluralism? If our pro-lifer believes her doctrine to

---

[411]John Rawls, *Political Liberalism*, p. 39.

[412] A claim subject to debate, of course. . . .

be *true*, what force does an appeal to "reasonableness" have on her? Michael Huemer, using the example of a religious fundamentalist, argues that appeals to reasonableness will be effective only insofar as the dissident values reasonableness more than his "truth."

> If a view which entails that I should do act A is true, whereas another view which entails that I should not do A is, while false, more 'reasonable' than the first, then what must I do? *Ex hypothesi*, I should do act A—that is, act in accordance with the first view.[413]

His general point is that any value (such as "reasonableness") brought to bear on a comprehensive doctrine will be *evaluated from the viewpoint of that doctrine*. We might imagine our pro-lifer scoffing at appeals to reasonableness, if reasonableness demands that she tolerate the "murder" of unborn children. Indeed, the aforementioned Roeder posted a comment on the Operation Rescue website, claiming that Dr. "Tiller is the concentration camp 'Mengele' of our day and needs to be stopped before he and those who protect him bring judgment upon our nation."[414]

Needless to say, urging someone like Roeder to be "reasonable" might be unpersuasive, much as urging members of ISIS to be "reasonable" might be. This is *not* to suggest that people opposed to abortion are "just like members of ISIS!" This is only to point out that appeals to "reasonableness" will only be persuasive to the extent that one values reasonableness, and it's not difficult to imagine any number of comprehensive moral doctrines in which "reasonableness" is less important than "truth," or "God's will."

Be that as it may, Rawls claims that the zeal to embody the whole truth in politics is incompatible with an idea of public reason belonging to democratic citizenship. In other words, if a citizen believes that policy should conform to the dictates of her comprehensive doctrine *regardless* of what the majority of her fellow citizens (reasonably) believe, because the "truth" of her doctrine trumps the demand for "reasonableness" in political deliberation, this citizen is herself unreasonable. "When there is a plurality of reasonable doctrines, it is unreasonable or worse to want to use the sanctions of state power to correct, or to punish, those who disagree with us."[415] Such persons certainly exist, maybe even in a hypothetical well-ordered society, but in such a society, as unreasonable, they are not part of the overlapping consensus of reasonable comprehensive moral doctrines anyway.

Does this mean that it could *never* be reasonable, from a Rawlsian perspective, for a pro-lifer (or adherents of any other comprehensive moral doctrine) to insist that her values be enforced? That it is never justifiable to "act up" in defense of one's values? As it turns out, resistance *is* sometimes justifiable.

Under the principle of fairness, a person is required to "do his part as defined by the rules of an institution" given two conditions:

1. The institution is itself just (i.e., satisfies the principles of justice).
2. The person has voluntarily accepted the benefits provided by the institution.

That is, someone who benefits from a just institution is obligated to fulfill her obligations as defined by the institution. On the other hand, "it is not possible to be bound to unjust institutions, or at least to institutions which exceed the limits

---

[413] Michael Huemer, "Rawls' Problem of Stability," *Social Theory and Practice*, 22(3), p. 383.

[414] "Shooter In Kansas Physician Killing Held Extreme Beliefs". Anti-Defamation League. June

2, 2009. Archived from the original on June 8, 2009. Retrieved June 3, 2009.

[415] Rawls, *Political Liberalism*, p. 138.

of tolerable injustice."[416]

We are morally bound to *just* institutions, but *not* to those that are intolerably unjust. A society with an inadequate political conception of justice, or one in which the public institutions are not themselves just (or permit gross injustice to occur) is not one with respect to which one must necessarily be tolerant. As examples, Rawls appeals to both the abolitionist and civil rights movements.

Both slavery and racial discrimination violate the principles of justice. That such things were not only permitted, but even legislated and enforced by the political institutions of the country at the time, is indicative that our public institutions, at least with respect to those issues, were *unjust*. Both abolitionists and leaders of the civil rights movement extensively appealed to their comprehensive moral doctrines (typically, religiously-based) to provide arguments against those practices—though they certainly also appealed to the *public* (shared) values of freedom and equality. Rawls supposes that such activists "could have seen their actions as the best way to bring about a well-ordered and just society in which the ideal of public reason could eventually be honored. . . . Given those historical conditions, it was not unreasonable of them to act as they did for the sake of the ideal of public reason itself."[417]

Exactly *when* civil disobedience, inspired by our comprehensive moral doctrines, is justified is a complicated question, and beyond the scope of this chapter. With certain issues, and in certain scenarios, however, justice might not only allow, but *depend upon*, an activist doing more than simply attempting to persuade others, through the use of public reasons, to change the problematic policies. By definition, such a society is not a well-ordered society, and so our focus will have shifted from stability issues to the justice of civil disobedience, but this is nevertheless one scenario in which more aggressive measures might be appropriate.

Stage 3: International Politics

Keep in mind everything that you have learned in the previous two stages: some of it is about to get recycled.

John Rawls offers an interpretation of the social contract tradition that attempts to not only establish the bases of a just and fair constitution and political institutions, but also define the basic principles of justice that will determine the legitimacy of our laws and policies, and establish our basic liberties. This conception of justice as fairness is an example of a political conception of justice that is not dependent upon any particular comprehensive moral doctrine, but is intended to be consistent with a wide variety of them. In this way, Rawls offers an example of how an overlapping consensus of reasonable comprehensive moral doctrines can be achieved.

By justifying our policy positions within the limits of public reason, we promote and preserve the legitimacy of those policies such that, even when we "lose," we still respect the legitimacy of that outcome, and will honor the results, despite our disagreement. In this way, the well-ordered society becomes and remains stable, despite the existence of reasonable pluralism with respect to worldviews.

We will now consider what Rawls had to say about the extension of his theory into the realm of international politics. Although it might be overly simple, for our purposes I think an instructive way to understand this third stage is simply as a combination of the first two.

In the first stage, Rawls employs the idea of the original position to identify the principles of justice that he thinks individuals would agree to when constructing their society and its political institutions. At this third stage, a second "original position" will be employed with the notable exception being that instead of individuals being the participants, it will be entire "peoples."

In the second stage, Rawls considered how the pluralism of comprehensive worldviews held

---

[416] Rawls, *A Theory of Justice*. Revised Edition, p. 96.

[417] John Rawls, *Political Liberalism*, pp. 250-251.

by different individuals could be accommodated in a way that achieves political stability within their shared society. At this third stage, Rawls considers how the pluralism of dominant comprehensive worldviews held by different societies can be accommodated in a way that achieves political stability within our shared global community.

Before delving into the synthesis of these two stages however, I want to introduce a little bit of vocabulary, much as I did in the previous section.

- "States:"
  o A group of persons moved by desires to enlarge territory, or to convert other societies to its religion, or to gain power over others, or to increase its own relative economic strength resources.
  o Not to be confused with "peoples"
- "Peoples:"
  o A group of persons who have (sufficiently) in common traits such as culture, history, tradition, or sentiment.
  o They are presumed to be ruled by a common government, and attached to a common conception of what is right and what is just.
  o In most cases, this will usually correspond to the term "nation." However, this is not necessarily always the case.
  o They see themselves as free, politically independent, and equally deserving of respect.
  o They are "reasonable" to the extent they honor fair terms of cooperation with other peoples, and are willing to abide by them even at the expense of their own interests, so long as other peoples are willing to do the same.
  o They are unwilling to impose by force their own political or social ideals on other reasonable peoples.
  o Peoples may be subdivided into two types:
    ▪ Liberal peoples: peoples governed by liberal principles of justice identical to, or at least similar to, those developed in *A Theory of Justice*. ("Stage 1" of this chapter)
  ▪ Decent peoples: peoples who are *not* "just" according to the standards of liberal principles of justice.
    • The basic institutions of their society do *not* recognize reasonable pluralism, nor do they have "liberal" equality with regard to their citizens or subjects.
    • Their public institutions might be organized around a single comprehensive doctrine, probably religious in nature, and their political system might not be democratic. However, they are sufficiently well-ordered to merit equal membership in the international society.
    • They do not have aggressive foreign policies.
    • Although they are not liberal societies (in the sense of political conceptions of justice), they do secure and honor a core list of human rights, and their government, even if not a democracy, does make a sincere effort to consult with representatives of all social groups.
    • They also allow for protest, and for their citizens to emigrate to other countries.

Whereas stages one and two of our exploration of Rawls concerns individual human beings within one domestic political community, stage three will concern "peoples," within one global political community.

The (global) Original Position

For those of you paying attention, you might recall that in a footnote earlier in this chapter I mentioned that although Rawls thinks participants would be ignorant of contingent "accidents of birth" such as race, gender, ability, sexual orientation, etc. (among other traits), he did not think that nationality or citizenship status should be included among those traits of which participants are ignorant. This is a significant omission that produces significant consequences. For example, because participants at the first original position are ignorant of their socioeconomic status, they are motivated to agree to principles of justice that include restrictions on inequality with regard to primary goods. The second principle of justice, as you might recall, only allows unequal distributions if these unequal distributions are open to everyone and improve the circumstances of everyone involved more so than would have an equal distribution.

One could easily imagine, and some critics of Rawls' international theory have in fact imagined, that representatives of societies at the second original position might make similar demands, thereby introducing a global redistribution principle. Much like the second principle of justice only allows for unequal distributions of primary goods between individuals within a particular society if those unequal distributions are to everyone's advantage, someone might suppose that at this second original position representatives of societies would only agree upon unequal distributions of primary goods between entire societies if those unequal distributions were to the advantage of *all* societies.

Just as at the level of the first original position this mentality produces redistribution of wealth and a fairly robust system of social safety nets, we would anticipate that a similar approach at the global level would likewise result in substantial redistributions of wealth between nations – and yet, Rawls *rejects* this outcome.

Although Rawls does use the idea of the original position a second time to develop his international notions of justice, and although participants are "ignorant" of the relative wealth, prosperity, and power of the nation they represent, he thinks that participants would not operate as they did at the first original position—demanding that inequalities be addressed through redistribution of primary goods, if necessary. Specifically, they will not demand that national resources be redistributed to improve the lives of the least well-off nations. Although there will likely be in some cases large differences in wealth between individuals of different countries, and between countries themselves, Rawls thinks that this is not in itself objectionable. At this point, we can offer his explanation as to why.

Rawls' account that he develops in the *Law of Peoples* is constrained, by his own admission, by the need to describe a "realistic utopia." Essential to this constraint, and his claim that the principles of justice developed in the original position do not apply on a global scale, is his belief that a "world state" proposed at a global-level original position is unworkable for a variety of reasons, including cultural and communication difficulties. He claims that a world government "would either be a global despotism or else will rule over a fragile Empire torn by frequent civil strife as various regions and peoples tried to gain their political freedom and autonomy."[418]

In other words, a so-called "one world government" (within which resources might be redistributed according to some global principle of justice analogous to the second principle of justice in the first original position) is not a feasible option.[419] Beyond that though, Rawls seems to think that even if such a system were

---

[418] John Rawls, *The Law of Peoples*, Harvard University press, 1999. p. 36.

[419] His rejection of the feasibility of a so-called "one world government" has an impact on immigration policy as well. Just as Rawls does not exclude nationality behind the veil of ignorance, nor does he (to a point at least) exclude

citizenship status. This is just to say that he thinks it is reasonable (and probably inevitable) that a society would keep track of (and regulate) immigration. John Rawls argues that although national boundaries are arbitrary from a historical point of view, an important role of government is to be the "effective agent of a possible, global redistribution of primary goods would not be desirable or fair.

> If a global principle of distributive justice for the Law of Peoples is meant to apply to our world as it is with its extreme injustices, crippling poverty, and inequalities, its appeal is understandable. But if it is meant to apply continuously without end – without a target, as one might say – and the hypothetical world arrived at after the duty of assistance is fully satisfied, its appeal is questionable. In the latter hypothetical world a global principle gives what we would, I think, regard as unacceptable results.[420]

This is not to say that Rawls will claim that nations have no responsibility to assist other, less advantaged communities. Under the Law of Peoples, there is a "duty of assistance" to "burdened societies." Burdened societies "lack the political and cultural traditions, human capital, and know-how, and, often, the material and technological resources needed to be well-ordered."[421] The "duty of assistance" is structurally *dis*similar to the difference principle developed in the (original) OP, however, for a variety of reasons.

For one, the difference principle in the first original position applies continuously. Policies are to be continuously adjusted and applied to make sure that unequal distributions of primary goods are to everyone's advantage. The duty of assistance agreed to at the second original position, however, is fulfilled once the burdened society is well-ordered.

Another point of difference is that the difference principle is specifically about primary goods, while the duty of assistance might not actually involve much actual wealth. If the burdened society is not well-ordered because of technological limitations, or institutional deficiencies, then the assistance provided might more appropriately be information, technology, training, etc.

In effect, Rawls promotes a two-tiered approach to distributive justice: at the first level, which is a domestic context, there is a demand for a roughly egalitarian distribution of primary goods – with exceptions being justifiable only if they meet both conditions set out in the second principle of justice. In the international context, however, equality just requires that each person finds themselves in a well-ordered "people," and that "people" be respected within international society.

This strong distinction between domestic and international demands of justice is justified by Rawls by his claim that limitations on distributive justice are consequences of tolerating and respecting the decisions, including the economic decisions, of peoples. On the assumption that these peoples are well-ordered, they have made autonomous decisions concerning their economic policies, savings rates, population policies, etc. These decisions have consequences. He thinks it would be disrespectful of decisions made by peoples, presumably adopted for what those peoples took to be good

---

people as they take responsibility for their territory and the size of the population, as well as for maintaining the lands environmental integrity. Unless a definite agent is given responsibility for maintaining an asset and bears the responsibility and loss for not doing so, that asset tends to deteriorate." (*Law of Peoples*, 8) Moreover, of the numerous causes of immigration, Rawls thinks that several would disappear in the ideal society of liberal and decent peoples. One cause is the persecution of religious and ethnic minorities. Another is a denial of human rights. Another is political oppression. Yet another is fleeing from starvation or desperate poverty. If genuine freedom and equal justice were established, in ways consistent with or at least similar to those prescribed by the principles of justice, he thinks that than many of the causes of immigration would be eliminated. (*Law of Peoples*, 9)

[420] Ibid., 117.
[421] Ibid., 106.

reasons, to require one people to compensate another.

> I believe that the causes of the wealth of a people and the forms it takes lie in their political culture and in the religious, philosophical, and moral traditions that support the basic structure of their political and social institutions, as well as in the industriousness and cooperative talents of its members, all supported by their political virtues.... The crucial elements that make the difference are the political culture, the political virtues and civic society of the country, its members' probity and industriousness, their capacity for innovation, and much else. Crucial also is the country's population policy: it must take care that it does not overburden its lands and economy with a larger population than it can sustain.... What must be realized is that merely dispensing funds will not suffice to rectify basic political and social injustices (though money is often essential). But an emphasis on human rights may work to change ineffective regimes and the conduct of the rulers who have been callous about the well-being of their own people.[422]

The duty of assistance requires well-ordered peoples to help burdened societies eventually become members of the society of well-ordered peoples. Achieving membership is the goal. Once it is achieved, additional assistance is not required, even though the newly well-ordered society might still be economically (relatively) poor.[423]

One reason for reducing inequalities with a domestic society is to relieve the suffering and hardships of the poor. Yet this does not require that all persons be equal in wealth. In itself, it doesn't matter how great the gap between rich and poor may be. What matters are the consequences. In a liberal domestic society that gap cannot be wider than the criterion of reciprocity allows, so that the least advantaged (as the third liberal principle requires) have sufficient all-purpose means to make intelligent and effective use of their freedoms and live reasonable and worthwhile lives. If that situation exists, there is no further need to narrow the gap. Similarly in the basic structure of the Society of Peoples, once the duty of assistance is satisfied and all the peoples have a working liberal or decent government, there is again no reason to narrow the gap between the average wealth of different peoples.[424]

Rawls gives an example of two liberal (or at least "decent") peoples with roughly the same level of wealth in terms of primary goods and roughly the same population size. The first decides to industrialize and increase its rate of saving, and the second does not. The second is content with its current condition, and enjoys a more leisurely society. Decades later, the first society is twice as wealthy as the second. On the assumption that both societies are liberal or decent, and that their peoples are free, responsible, and able to make (and have made) their own decisions, should the first country be taxed to increase the wealth of the second? According to the duty of assistance, the answer is no. According to a global egalitarian principle without a target, the answer would be yes. Rawls thinks that this is unacceptable.[425]

At this point, we have only considered what Rawls is denying at the global stage. It's time to

---

[422] Ibid., 108-109.
[423] Ibid., 111.
[424] Ibid., 114.

[425] Ibid., 117. Editorial Note: it seems that this line of reasoning could work backwards, and against the basic assumptions behind *A Theory of Justice*, as well, operating as a criticism of Rawls.

backtrack and develop what he is supplying as well. With regard to international political philosophy, Rawls begins within the social contract tradition and adds to it his thought experiment of the original position (and veil of ignorance). He will extend this thought experiment by introducing a second "original position," in which representatives of "liberal peoples" make agreements with other such peoples.

At the second veil of ignorance, participants do not know the size of their territorial population, the relative strength of the people whose interests they represent, the extent of the resources, the level of their economic development, or other such information.[426] Rawls makes the connection between the original position and the issues he addressed in *Political Liberalism* clear:

> Putting people's comprehensive doctrines behind the veil of ignorance enables us to find a political conception of justice that can be the focus of an overlapping consensus and thereby serve as a public basis of justification in a society marked by the fact of reasonable pluralism.[427]

Participants at this second original position are largely and strategically "ignorant," as in the first OP—but just like in the first OP, they retain some information as well. What they *do* know is that they come from reasonably favorable

conditions such that a constitutional democracy is possible for their politically liberal society. It is also the case that their basic needs are met, though they are not necessarily "cheerful and happy."[428] In addition, such peoples have an interest in a proper sort of self-respect, as a people. This is not mere nationalism or patriotism, though there is undoubtedly some overlap. What distinguishes peoples from states in this regard is that peoples are prepared to grant the same respect and recognition to other peoples as they desire for themselves.[429]

In the first OP, Rawls thinks participants would agree (among other things) to the Two Principles of Justice. At the second OP, he comes up with a similar (lengthier) set of principles on an international scale:

1. Peoples are free and independent, and their freedom and independence are to be respected by other peoples.
2. Peoples are to observe treaties and undertakings.
3. Peoples are equal and are parties to the agreements that bind them.
4. Peoples are to observe a duty of nonintervention.
5. Peoples have the right of self-defense but no right to instigate war for reasons other than self-defense.
6. Peoples are to honor human rights.
7. Peoples are to observe certain specified restrictions in the conduct of war.

One could argue that a significant contributing factor to differences in wealth and prosperity for *individuals* is individual choice, personal responsibility, management of money and savings habits, etc. Couldn't one argue that it is unfair and unreasonable to expect other individuals to make up for the deficiencies of less responsible individuals in order to secure more equal distributions of wealth and prosperity? A critic of Rawls could generate a parallel example involving *individuals* who make informed and autonomous decisions that result in significant

differences in their share of primary goods within the community. On the assumption that these different outcomes result from those actual decisions, as opposed to the contingencies of birth that are excluded behind the veil of ignorance, is it fair to redistribute primary goods to benefit the lesser advantaged in this case, if Rawls is opposed to it at an international level?

[426] Ibid., 34 – 35.
[427] Ibid., 32.
[428] Ibid., 47.
[429] Ibid., 35.

8. Peoples have a duty to assist other peoples living under unfavorable conditions that prevent their having a just or decent political and social regime.[430]

Having established the international equivalent of the "principles of justice" (and having done so using basically the same method as employed in *A Theory of Justice*), we can now turn to the international equivalent of the issue of pluralism.

Global Pluralism

After the first OP, even after a liberal political conception of justice had been worked out, there remained the task of figuring out how people subscribing to a variety of different world views could achieve a stable, overlapping consensus. That was the work of *Political Liberalism*. In *Political Liberalism*, Rawls addresses the fact of reasonable pluralism and tries to articulate ways in which the fact of reasonable pluralism need not become the *problem* of reasonable pluralism. The *international* equivalent of this is the fact of diversity with respect to culture, religion, tradition, etc.

At neither the domestic nor international level is it reasonable to try to force policies on those who disagree by means of force itself. The political conception of justice includes an idea of toleration that operates at both the domestic and international level. We may paraphrase Rawls' argument in defense of this notion of reasonable tolerance as follows:

1. Not all reasonable persons affirm the same comprehensive doctrine.
2. Of the many reasonable comprehensive doctrines that are affirmed, not all of them can be true (as judged from within any one comprehensive doctrine).

3. It is not unreasonable of someone to affirm a reasonable comprehensive doctrine.
4. Those who affirm reasonable comprehensive doctrines that are different from our own are reasonable, just as we are reasonable in affirming our own reasonable comprehensive doctrine.
5. It is unreasonable to use political power to repress comprehensive doctrines that are reasonable yet different from your own.[431]

There is a direct and intended parallel between *Political Liberalism* and the "society of peoples" he develops in the *Law of Peoples*. In *Political Liberalism*, the proposal is that in a constitutional democratic system, comprehensive moral doctrines of "truth," or of "right," are to be replaced (in political discourse) by the idea of the "politically reasonable" addressed from one citizen to another. This involves adhering to the limits of "public reason."

In the society of peoples, public reason is likewise invoked and its principles are addressed from one peoples to another. The comprehensive moral doctrines which might be persuasive within a particular society are replaced by public reasons which could be shared by a variety of different peoples.[432]

Within a politically liberal constitutional democracy, the ideal of public reason is idealized by government officials whenever they (in their speech and conduct) follow public reason. Citizens follow public reason when they vote and act *as if* they were legislators.

At the level of peoples, the ideal of public reason is realized when executives and legislators of those peoples likewise follow the principles of the Law of Peoples and explain their reasons to other peoples in ways that could theoretically be shared. Analogously, at this level, private citizens should simply aspire in their

---

[430] Ibid., 37.
[431] Paraphrased from Ibid., 16, footnote 8.

[432] Ibid., 55.

voting and actions to act as though they were these legislators.[433]

The importance of adhering to public reason cannot be overstated as far as Rawls is concerned. His endorsement of the urgency and necessity of public reason seems especially prescient given the current climate of political discourse in the United States.

> Without citizens' allegiance to public reason and their honoring the duty of civility, divisions and hostilities between doctrines are bound in time to assert themselves, should they not already exist. Harmony and concord among doctrines and a people's affirming public reason are unhappily not a permanent condition of social life. Rather, harmony and concord depend on the vitality of the public political culture and on citizens' being devoted to and realizing the ideal of public reason. Citizens could easily fall into bitterness and resentment, once they no longer see the point of affirming an ideal of public reason and come to ignore it.[434]

In *Political Liberalism*, the goal was to generate an overlapping consensus between reasonable people from across a variety of comprehensive doctrines for the sake of establishing a stable and well-ordered society. Only "reasonable" persons could be candidates for the overlapping consensus because only reasonable persons would agree to the principle of reciprocity, according to which it is agreed that it is unreasonable to use force to exert one's

political will. Now that we have shifted to international politics, it remains to be seen who Rawls thinks can be a part of the society of peoples.

Rawls does *not* limit the society of peoples only to liberal constitutional democracies, such as those he presupposes in *Political Liberalism*. Instead, he claims that liberal societies are required to cooperate with all peoples in "good standing." To require that all societies be liberal would be to violate the requirement of appropriate toleration found in *Political Liberalism* itself.

So long as a non-liberal society's basic institutions meet certain minimum requirements, then those peoples are "decent," though not "liberal."[435] Rawls breaks up societal types into several categories, including "reasonable liberal peoples," "decent peoples" (a variety of which will be discussed below), and "burdened societies" (for whom the "duty of assistance" was discussed above). Recall that a burdened society is one whose "historical, social, and economic circumstances make their achieving a well-ordered regime, whether liberal or decent, difficult if not impossible."[436] In addition, there are "outlaw states" (who will be discussed at the end of this section).

An example of an alternative to liberal political constitutional democracies that is, nevertheless, "decent" is a "decent hierarchical society." As a hypothetical example of such a society, Rawls imagines an imaginary Muslim theocracy that he calls "Kazanistan."[437]

What makes a decent hierarchical society "decent," is that it satisfies several criteria. First, it is not aggressive, and recognizes the necessity

---

[433] Ibid., 56.

[434] Ibid., 175. It seems clear to me that the sort of cynicism and resentment that Rawls is concerned with could arise not only within the sphere of national politics, but international politics as well. It is not difficult to notice dissatisfaction among citizens with their own governments, as well as the international community, such as the United Nations.

[435] Ibid., 59-60.

[436] Ibid., 90.

[437] It is important to note that Rawls does not assume that any "decent hierarchical societies" actually exist, any more than he assumes that any genuine liberal political constitutional democracies actually exist. In both cases, ideals are presented.

of diplomacy and trade as opposed to war. Although its particular comprehensive moral doctrine (religious or otherwise) has significant influence on government and its policies, it respects the political and social values of other societies.[438]

Second, its system of law secures human rights for all of its members. These rights include the right to life (and the means of subsistence and security), liberty (including freedom from slavery, serfdom, and forced occupation, property (specifically *personal* property), and formal equality before the law.[439]

In addition, the system of law imposes moral duties and obligations that are recognized and respected by its people and which operates through political and social cooperation.

Finally, there must be a sincere and reasonable belief on the part of judges and other administrators of the legal system that the law is actually guided by a "common good" idea of justice, assigns human rights to all its members, and is upheld in good faith.[440]

An important limitation to decent hierarchical societies is that although they might have a state religion which is the ultimate authority within their own society, that authority may not be extended to relations with *other* societies. In addition, there must be a "sufficient measure of liberty of conscience and freedom of religion and thought, even if these freedoms are not as extensive nor as equal for all members of the decent society as they are in liberal societies. Although the established religion may have various privileges, is essential to the societies being decent that no religion be persecuted, or denied civic and social conditions permitting its practice in peace and without fear."[441]

Rawls allows that "reasonableness" exists along a spectrum, and is not simply binary. With regard to freedom of religion, a genuinely liberal society allows for full and equal freedom of religion, and is thus fully reasonable in that regard. A fully unreasonable society, in contrast, denies it entirely. A decent hierarchical society would be somewhere in between: allowing for some of freedom of conscience, but not full and equal expression of it.[442]

Liberal and decent peoples alike are to be respected, and can cooperate to form the overlapping consensus that generates the society of peoples, but "outlaw states" are a different matter. Outlaw states do not meet the standards of either liberal or decent societies, and as such are aggressive and dangerous. Outlaw states are the equivalent of "unreasonable" individuals with "unreasonable" comprehensive moral doctrines with regard to stability and an overlapping consensus in a particular society.

Outlaw states are likewise "unreasonable," and Rawls claims that liberal and decent societies have a right to intervene against outlaw states, when necessary.[443] This generates one of the *rare* circumstances in which Rawls thinks that war is justifiable.

According to Rawls' version of just war theory, no state has a right to go to war in pursuit of its rational, as opposed to reasonable, interests. For example, it might be in the rational interest of a society to invade a vulnerable neighbor in order to seize its wealth and resources. However, to do so is not "reasonable." Only wars of self-defense are justifiable. Such wars are waged in order to protect the basic freedom of citizens and political institutions, as opposed to in order to gain the wealth, power, territory, etc.[444] The official principles that make up his just war doctrine with regard to *jus in bello* (the conduct of war) are as follows:

(I)   The aim of a just war is just and lasting peace among peoples.

---

[438] Ibid., 64.
[439] Ibid., 65.
[440] Ibid., 66 – 67.
[441] Ibid., 74.

[442] Ibid., 74.
[443] Ibid., 81.
[444] Ibid., 91

(II) Well-Ordered peoples don't wage war against each other, but only against non-well-ordered states who threaten them.

(III) Well-Ordered peoples distinguish between the leaders of an outlaw state, its soldiers, and its civilian population. Because the outlaw state is not well-ordered, its civilian population is not responsible for the aggressive acts of their leaders. Aside from the upper ranks of officers, soldiers are also not responsible.

(IV) During the conduct of war, a well-ordered people should indicate the kind of peace and relationships they seek to obtain.

(V) War plans and strategies must be limited by the preceding principles.[445]

Conclusion

The work of John Rawls spanned decades of the 20th century. Situated within the social contract tradition, Rawls justifies his liberal political philosophy by means of the original position and the veil of ignorance, and the principles of justice that he thinks follow from them. He uses that same basic idea, along with his conclusions concerning reasonable pluralism, public reason, and the importance of an overlapping consensus, to consider not only how a particular society can be politically stable, but how numerous and diverse peoples can reasonably cooperate on the world stage.

In our next chapter, we will leave behind the lofty theories of famous philosophers, and consider the particular platforms of the major American political parties. In so doing, we can try to discern to what extent, if at all, they have been formed by the great minds we've examined thus far. Along the way, we will also consider a *non-*

philosophical interpretation of political decision-making.

Appendix: President Barack Obama and John Rawls

In this appendix, I would like to offer a concrete example of where political philosophy has concrete policy implications. Far from being a "merely theoretical" exercise, political theories can, and do, influence politicians and policies alike.

There is reason to believe that President Obama is familiar with the work of John Rawls. For one, his Columbia college roommate says so:

> Mr. Boerner recalls Mr. Obama wrapping himself in a green sleeping bag . . . to keep warm when they studied at home. They listened to reggae. Bob Marley. Peter Tosh. Talked philosophy. Theories of justice and John Rawls. Mr. Boerner recalled Mr. Obama joking that he would rather be spending his time pondering Lou Rawls, the singer.[446]

Far more compelling than an appeal to his roommate's memory, though, is a comparison of some excerpts of one of President Obama's speeches with statements written by Rawls himself, where it is clear that both Rawls and Obama are concerned with the "problem" of reasonable pluralism.[447]

> "How it is possible for a just and stable society of free and equal citizens to exist and endure when its citizens 'remain profoundly divided by reasonable religious, philosophical, and moral doctrines?'" (Rawls)

> "I answered with what has come to be the typically liberal response in such debates

---

[445] Ibid., 94 – 96.

[446] http://cityroom.blogs.nytimes.com/2009/01/20/recollections-of-obamas-ex-roommate/comment-page-2/

[447] The full transcript of the speech is available here: http://www.nytimes.com/2006/06/28/us/politics/2006obamaspeech.html?_r=0

- namely, I said that we live in a pluralistic society, that I can't impose my own religious views on another, . . ." (Obama)

Both see the value of, and need for, and "overlapping consensus" of comprehensive moral doctrines.

Overlapping consensus: wide-spread agreement on core issues involving various (and even competing) comprehensive moral doctrines— necessary for a stable, well-ordered society. (paraphrase of Rawls)

"Moreover, if we progressives shed some of these biases, we might recognize some overlapping values that both religious and secular people share when it comes to the moral and material direction of our country." (Obama—emphasis added)

Both recognize the importance of being able to articulate one's policy positions by appealing to shared values, and reasons that could, in principle, be endorsed by a wide variety of people— including even those who do not agree with one's own comprehensive moral doctrine.

Rawls: "Our exercise of political power is proper only when we sincerely believe that the reasons we offer for our political actions—were we to state them as government officials—are sufficient, and we also think that other citizens might reasonably accept those reasons."

Obama (with emphasis added): "Whatever we once were, we are no longer just a Christian nation; we are also a Jewish nation, a Muslim nation, a Buddhist nation, a Hindu nation, and a nation of nonbelievers.
And even if we did have only Christians in our midst, if we expelled every non-Christian from the United States of America, whose Christianity would we

teach in the schools? Would we go with James Dobson's, or Al Sharpton's? Which passages of Scripture should guide our public policy? . . .
This brings me to my second point. Democracy demands that the religiously motivated translate their concerns into universal, rather than religion-specific, values. It requires that their proposals be subject to argument, and amenable to reason. I may be opposed to abortion for religious reasons, but if I seek to pass a law banning the practice, I cannot simply point to the teachings of my church or evoke God's will. I have to explain why abortion violates some principle that is accessible to people of all faiths, including those with no faith at all.
Now this is going to be difficult for some who believe in the inerrancy of the Bible, as many evangelicals do. But in a pluralistic democracy, we have no choice. Politics depends on our ability to persuade each other of common aims based on a common reality. It involves the compromise, the art of what's possible. At some fundamental level, religion does not allow for compromise. It's the art of the impossible. If God has spoken, then followers are expected to live up to God's edicts, regardless of the consequences. To base one's life on such uncompromising commitments may be sublime, but to base our policy making on such commitments would be a dangerous thing. And if you doubt that, let me give you an example.
We all know the story of Abraham and Isaac. Abraham is ordered by God to offer up his only son, and without argument, he takes Isaac to the mountaintop, binds him to an altar, and raises his knife, prepared to act as God has commanded.
Of course, in the end God sends down an angel to intercede at the very last minute, and Abraham passes God's test of devotion.

But it's fair to say that if any of us leaving this church saw Abraham on a roof of a building raising his knife, we would, at the very least, call the police and expect the Department of Children and Family Services to take Isaac away from Abraham. We would do so because <u>we do not hear what Abraham hears, do not see what Abraham sees, *true as those experiences may be*. So the best we can do is act in accordance with those things that we all see, and that we all hear, be it common laws or basic reason.</u>"

While Rawls thinks that we have a moral and civil duty to one another to advocate for our policy positions by appealing to reasons subject to the limits of public reason, he also recognizes that non-public reasons may be invoked as well, as a supplement.

Rawls: "Reasonable comprehensive doctrines, religious or non-religious, may be introduced in public political discourse at any time, provided that in due course proper political reasons—and not reasons given solely by comprehensive doctrines—are presented that are sufficient to support whatever the comprehensive doctrines introduced are said to support."

Obama (with emphasis added): "But what I am suggesting is this secularists are wrong when they ask believers to leave their religion at the door before entering into the public square. Frederick Douglas, Abraham Lincoln, Williams Jennings Bryant, Dorothy Day, Martin Luther King - indeed, the majority of great reformers in American history - were not only motivated by faith, but repeatedly used religious language to argue for their cause. So <u>to say that men and women should not inject their "personal morality" into public policy debates is a practical absurdity.</u>"

Perhaps more forcefully than Rawls, President Obama recognizes the importance and value of one's comprehensive moral doctrine. However, he also clearly recognizes the importance of being able to "translate" those values into shared, overlapping values.

Democracy demands that the religiously motivated translate their concerns into universal, rather than religion-specific, values. It requires that their proposals be subject to argument, and amenable to reason. I may be opposed to abortion for religious reasons, but if I seek to pass a law banning the practice, I cannot simply point to the teachings of my church or evoke God's will. I have to explain why abortion violates some principle that is accessible to people of all faiths, including those with no faith at all. (Obama)

None of the preceding is meant to suggest that President Obama was exclusively, or even primarily, "Rawlsian" in his political theory or practice. It is, however, a clear example of where theory meets practice, and when a political philosopher can influence the decisions and strategies of actual political leaders. However theoretical political philosophy might be, we should always remember that the *point* of these theories is to ultimately find application in the actual political institutions, policies, and lives of real people.

.

Chapter 13: Politics without Philosophy?

Comprehension questions you should be able to answer after reading this chapter:

1. What is a "conceptual metaphor?"

2. Explain the "strict father" model. What are its main features and assumptions? Be sure to discuss "folk behaviorism," reward and punishment, moral strength, self-discipline, competition, self-interest, and internal and external evils.

3. Explain the "nurturant parent" model. What are its main features and assumptions? Be sure to discuss empathy, attachment, self-care, internal and external evils, and emotional maturity.

4. Using the example of federal student loans, compare and contrast conservative and liberal positions using their respective family models.

5. Describe conservative model citizens, and "demons." Do the same for liberal model citizens and "demons."

All the previous chapters have been attempts to describe the philosophical foundations of various political theories, including different visions of the State, the origin and purpose of the State, different visions of human nature, the scope and limit of laws, the nature of law itself, the value (and limits) of tolerance and pluralism, and the political significance of economic systems—among other things.

This historical survey, I hope, has been interesting—but is it useful? What if contemporary politicians and voters alike do not (or no longer) employ such rational, "philosophical" approaches to political decision-making? What if politics has been divorced from philosophy?

George Lakoff (born May 24th, 1941) is not a philosopher, but rather a "cognitive linguist." He has been a professor of linguistics at U.C. Berkeley since 1972.

> I am not a political philosopher and did not begin with any philosophical presuppositions about what I would find. Nor did I use either the intellectual tools or forms of reasoning of political philosophers. These results emerged

from empirical study using the tools of a cognitive scientist to study political worldviews. As empirical findings, they have a very different status than theoretical speculations, and so should not be confused with political philosophy—for which, incidentally, I have great respect.[448]

Lakoff was initially motivated by his own personal confusion, his recognition that he literally did not understand why conservatives supported the positions they did. At first glance, liberal and conservative policy stances might seem unusual, or even contradictory, from the outside. Conservatives, after all, tend to be very much opposed to abortion, and yet are also opposed to government programs to provide prenatal care to low-income mothers—programs proven to reduce infant mortality rates. How does this make sense? How can a conservative be so dedicated to the value of the fetus in the womb, but not support government programs that would actually increase the chance of that fetus surviving? And why would they be opposed to government programs that protect and provide for those fetuses after they are born?

---

[448] Lakoff, *Moral Politics*, 21-22.

On the other hand, how can liberals be in favor of the right to abortion (which kills "children"), but then turn around and support welfare and other government programs that benefit children? Do liberals love children, or think they should be killed? Which is it? How can liberals be in favor of government spending on AIDS research and prevention, but then be in favor of things like needle exchange programs (which could be seen as implicitly accepting behavior that increases risk of spreading HIV), as well as condoning the homosexual "lifestyle" which is associated with the spread of HIV in the first place?

Conservatives claim to be in favor of cutting spending and for small government, but then want to increase military spending, and use the government to interfere with people's sex lives. Liberals claim to be for equal opportunity, but then support "reverse discrimination" practices like affirmative action. How can these seemingly inconsistent positions (on both sides) be reconciled?

To account for these seeming contradictions, he develops a view that our political decision-making is not guided by philosophical ideals and arguments, but by *metaphors*. A "conceptual metaphor," to be specific, is "a correspondence between concepts across conceptual domains, allowing forms of reasoning and words from one domain . . . to be used in the other."[449] Metaphors, by definition, are figures of speech in which a word or phrase is applied to an object or action to which it is not literally applicable; a thing regarded as representative or symbolic of something else, especially something abstract. This latter part of the definition is most applicable for what Lakoff has in mind.

When it comes to politics, Lakoff argues that that both "conservatives" and "liberals" experience, understand, and act on political issues by virtue of how they are "framed" as metaphors—with conservatives and liberals employing different metaphors (or at least

interpreting the metaphors in importantly different ways).

A non-political example that should be quite familiar to philosophers and students of philosophy is the metaphor of argument as "war" or combat. I have often referred to philosophy conferences as "philosophical bloodsport"—and I did not intend the metaphor to be positive. Arguments are usually seen as a "zero sum" contest, in which one person "wins," and the other, necessarily, "loses." You "defend" your argument, and "attack" others'. We speak of criticisms that are "on target" as opposed to those that "miss the mark." If you search youtube for footage of debates (especially those between atheists and theists), you can find such video titles as "Professor Lawrence Krauss, Atheist, destroys idiotic Muslim in debate." Arguments are "shot down," "defeated," and "destroyed."

While it's possible that this is all just hyperbole used to express excitement, Lakoff claims that the metaphors we use color the way we experience and interpret things. When it comes to contemporary American politics, Lakoff claims that both liberals and conservatives employ the same basic, central metaphor: the political community as family. However, their respective models of the family are strikingly different, thereby causing liberals and conservatives to interpret political issues in very different ways, and causing them to offer very different solutions to the same "problems."

According to Lakoff's analysis, conservatives employ what he calls a "strict father" model of the family.

The Strict Father Model

A traditional nuclear family with the father having primary responsibility for the well-being of the household. The mother has day-to-day responsibility for the care of the house and details of raising the children. But the father has primary responsibility for setting overall family

---
449 Ibid., 63.

policy, and the mother's job is to be supportive of the father and to help carry out the father's views on what should be done. Ideally, she respects his views and supports them.

Life is seen as fundamentally difficult and the world as fundamentally dangerous. Evil is conceptualized as a force in the world, and it is the father's job to support his family and protect it from evils -- both external and internal. External evils include enemies, hardships, and temptations. Internal evils come in the form of uncontrolled desires and are as threatening as external ones. The father embodies the values needed to make one's way in the world and to support a family: he is morally strong, self-disciplined, frugal, temperate, and restrained. He sets an example by holding himself to high standards. He insists on his moral authority, commands obedience, and when he doesn't get it, metes out retribution as fairly and justly as he knows how. It is his job to protect and support his family, and he believes that safety comes out of strength.

In addition to support and protection, the father's primary duty is tell his children what is right and wrong, punish them when they do wrong, and to bring them up to be self-disciplined and self-reliant. Through self-denial, the children can build strength against internal evils. In this way, he teaches his children to be self-disciplined, industrious, polite, trustworthy, and respectful of authority.

The strict father provides nurturance and expresses his devotion to his family by supporting and protecting them, but just as importantly by setting and enforcing strict moral bounds and by inculcating self-discipline and self-reliance through hard work and self-denial. This builds character. For the strict father, strictness is a form of nurturance and love -- tough love.

The strict father is restrained in showing affection and emotion overtly, and prefers the appearance of strength and calm. He gives to charity as an expression of compassion for those less fortunate than he and as an expression of gratitude for his own good fortune.

Once his children are grown -- once they have become self-disciplined and self-reliant -- they are on their own and must succeed or fail by themselves; he does not meddle in their lives, just as he doesn't want any external authority meddling in his life.[450]

Let's work through this description, one important piece at a time. First, the very name of the model is important: strict *father*. This is a gendered model, with males being in charge. This model of the family is the "traditional" (patriarchal, hetero-normative) model, with one male and one female, in which the male is the head of the household. The mother has an important role to play as well, of course, but hers is a support role, whereas his is a leadership role.

With leadership comes responsibility. The primary responsibility of the father is to protect and provide for his family—and this is necessary because the world is seen as a dangerous, competitive place with limited resources. Evil is a real force in the universe, and not merely a matter of "misunderstanding" or different perspectives. Given this binary view of good and evil, the world is filled with genuine threats. Some of them are

---

450 George Lakoff, " Metaphor, Morality, and Politics, Or, Why Conservatives Have Left Liberals in the Dust." 1995. *Social Research* 62(3):177-213

external threats, such as criminals (thieves, rapists, murderers, pedophiles, terrorists, etc.), but other threats are internal: primarily uncontrolled desires and moral weakness.

In order to defend against internal and external threats alike, the father (and mother) must be "strong," and he must teach and train his children to be strong as well, so that they can resist evil and defend their own families when they are adults. Some of this teaching might be literally instructional, such as talking to children about morality and character, but this instruction is primarily in the form of discipline and punishment. Children must learn to obey the (just) commands of their parents (primarily their father), not only because the commands are issued for a good reason, but also because obedience is itself a necessary trait to acquire in life.

When children disobey, and behave badly, they must be punished so they learn that there are negative consequences for undesirable behavior, and so that they will be trained to behave differently in the future. This punishment is for their own good. Over time, they will internalize the discipline, gain control over themselves, and be able to act properly without the threat of punishment—but it is naïve to think that this will happen all on its own, in the absence of consistent discipline and punishment for violating the rules. It is only by acquiring self-discipline that children can become strong enough to resist "internal" threats as adults.

Once the children have grown, they are adults responsible for their own behavior. The parents will still love them, but will not meddle in their lives, as it is no longer their place to do so. Grown children can be prepared for the challenges of adult life, but they must be allowed to sink, or swim, on their own.

Strict Father Politics

Using Lakoff's interpretation of these family metaphors, he proposes that conservative politics can be understood in terms of the following moral categories:

1. Promoting Strict Father morality in general.
2. Promoting self-discipline, responsibility, and self-reliance.
3. Upholding the Morality of Reward and Punishment
4. Protecting moral people from external evils.
5. Upholding the Moral Order.

First, there is the promotion of the strict father moral worldview, in general. This includes the promotion and reinforcement of metaphors of moral strength, moral boundaries, and moral authority. Remember: the distinction between good and evil is real, grounded in reality, and corresponding to genuine evil (and goodness). It is imperative that one be strong enough to resist and defeat evil. Strict moral boundaries must be maintained, so that evil (people, or ideas) can't infiltrate the community (or mind) and undermine it from within. Just as criminals or terrorists might sneak in through a crack in the defenses, so too can moral weakness creep into one's character by a lapse of self-discipline. For these reasons, the moral rules that identify what is morally right and wrong must be respected and obeyed, and those in authority, whose job it is to teach and enforce these rules, should be obeyed as well.

Not surprisingly, there is an authoritarian strain in strict father politics, and authority figures command respect—as do those who literally protect us from danger, such as the military and police. The strict father model recognizes and reveres legitimate moral authority—but resents illegitimate authority as "meddling." Fathers know what's best for their own families, and don't need the "nanny state" meddling in their homes and interfering, as if the government knows better. By extension, local authorities know better how to deal with local issues (than does the Federal government)—which helps to explain conservatives' emphasis on "State's Rights."

Second, there is the promotion of self-discipline, personal responsibility, and self-reliance. All of these qualities require (and show) moral strength. Only those who are self-disciplined will be strong enough to resist temptations, and be responsible adult citizens. By taking responsibility for one's actions and one's life, the citizen becomes self-reliant, and capable of surviving and succeeding in the dangerous, competitive world. Any actions that promote and reinforce personal responsibility and self-reliance, then, will fit with this model, while those that seem to undermine those qualities will be opposed.

Thirdly, and relatedly, there is the upholding of the morality of reward and punishment. According to the strict father model, all people are governed by "folk behaviorism"—which is just to say that we act for the sake of obtaining rewards and avoiding punishment. "People, left to their own devices, tend simply to satisfy their desires. But, people will make themselves do things they don't want to do in order to get rewards; they will refrain from doing things they do want to do in order to avoid punishment."[451]

Young children will not automatically do the right thing (as they would have no notion of what that is, without first being taught!), nor will they automatically obey their parents (once they have been taught), without some incentive to do so: punishment for disobedience. Adults are no different. When we obtain rewards for certain actions, we are motivated to perform them, and when we are punished for other actions, we are motivated to avoid them. Self-interest is what drives us, in either case.

In the real-world, resources are scarce, and we are in competition with others for those scarce resources. Obtaining those resources is rewarding, and so we are motivated to develop those qualities which will help us obtain those rewards (e.g., self-discipline, a good work ethic, personal responsibility, etc.). If the reward can be obtained without those qualities, the motivation to obtain them dissolves. Giving someone a so-called "free lunch" is ultimately harmful to them, as it undermines the natural system in which rewards only come to those who have earned them by virtue of their talent, hard work, and self-discipline. Rewards given to those who haven't earned them via competition are immoral, and remove the incentive to become self-disciplined and obey authority (and rules, in general). If the recipient never acquires those traits and that self-discipline, they will be unable to compete should their "meal ticket" ever stop with the handouts!

Competition is necessary and good. It creates incentive to develop your talents, and to work hard. Given the scarcity and gritty reality of life, competition prepares us to survive and succeed in the real world. But, even if there was no scarcity, and there were more than enough "things" for everyone, competition would still be a good thing (and necessary) because it promotes the self-discipline needed to make plans, make commitments, and carry them out. Even a basic plan of life for oneself requires the ability to make decisions and then act in pursuit of that plan. All the material resources in the world won't do you any good if you don't have enough focus and willpower to make use of them.

If competition is good, then the outcomes of competition are good as well. In a competition, some people "win," and others "lose." Not everyone can finish first. This means that a hierarchy will emerge, with the most successful competitors at the top. They deserve to be there, and to reap the rewards of winning. "Losers" don't deserve the rewards of "winners"—not if the competition is to retain any meaning.

Everyone is equally motivated by reward and punishment, all equally motivated by the pursuit of self-interest. This pursuit is a good thing, though, since the collective pursuit of individual self-interest is thought to maximize the well-being of all involved. This folk interpretation of Adam Smith explains conservatives' devotion to free-market capitalism. Competition and the pursuit of self-interest is morally good. Systems that interfere with this (such as socialism or

---

[451] Moral Politics, 67.

communism), are immoral systems in that they interfere with this maximization of well-being, unjustifiably (and presumably ineffectively) meddle in the private pursuit of self-interest by individuals, and undermine the moral values of competition, hard work, and self-discipline.

A particular application of this moral value of upholding the morality of reward and punishment is preventing interference with the pursuit of self-interest by self-disciplined, self-reliant people. Someone who is self-disciplined, and works hard in pursuit of his own self-interest, while playing by the rules of society, is "doing it right." Such persons are behaving as they are supposed to. To put obstacles in their path, or to help other, less-worthy people "win" instead, is to rig the system. That is unfair, immoral, and undermines the whole system of reward and punishment. Not surprisingly, then, conservatives will generally be opposed to policies which interfere with business (e.g., "excess" regulations), or that "punish" success (e.g., taxes), as well as policies that allows others to "cheat" or provide an "unfair advantage" (e.g., affirmative action).

The idea of the "American Dream" fits perfectly with the strict father worldview. American is a land of opportunity. Anyone with the self-discipline to work hard and follow the rules can, and will, climb the ladder of success and live the American dream. Therefore, anyone who has not succeeded either lacks talent or hasn't worked hard—either way, they don't deserve the success of a hard-working and talented person. If the person hasn't worked hard, then he is lazy, and doesn't deserve success. If he is a hard-worker, but is untalented, then it's only fair that he doesn't enjoy the same success as the more-talented. After all, in a race, you can push yourself as hard as you can, but if someone else is just more athletic than you, that person will win the race, despite your hard work—and they *should*. At the societal level, then, the poor deserve their poverty (they have "earned" it), and the rich deserve their success and prosperity (as they have earned it). The rich are, therefore, not merely wealthier than others, but morally better

than others—at least with regard to the moral virtues of talent and hard work.

The strict father emphasis on strength and self-discipline can help us to understand stereotypically conservative positions on various policies. Why are conservatives (generally) opposed to welfare? Because it gives people something for "nothing," removes their incentive to work—and even does so at the expense of "winners" (i.e., those who do work and pay their taxes). Why are conservatives opposed to giving free condoms to teenagers, even though doing so is proven to reduce teen pregnancy and STD infections? Because teenagers should have (or acquire) the self-discipline to refrain from sex— and if they don't they have to face the consequences. Otherwise, they will never learn their lesson and grow stronger.

Fourthly, we have the morality of protecting moral people from external evils. Since protection from external evils is a fundamental part of strict father morality, protective actions are moral and inhibiting them is immoral. Not surprisingly, conservatives tend to be in favor of large, powerful militaries, and supporters of the police. In addition, they tend to favor gun-rights and gun-ownership.

Finally, we have the moral value of upholding the "moral order" itself. This moral order refers back to the family model, in which there is a clear (gendered) hierarchy, presumed hetero-normativity, and unquestioned obedience on the part of children. "Father knows best," in this model—and with religious (usually Christian) variations of this model, God is placed at the very top of the hierarchy. What this means is that policies or movements that defy or disrupt this order are seen as deviant and dangerous. Feminism, acceptance of homosexuality as a morally legitimate alternative to heterosexuality, atheism/humanism/Islam/religious pluralism, immigrants with different cultural norms and speaking different languages . . . all these things (and others) can be seen as subversive forces from which the family (and community) needs protection.

To summarize:

Conservatives believe in individual responsibility alone, not social responsibility. They don't think government should help its citizens. That is, they don't think citizens should help each other. The part of government they want to cut is not the military (we have over 800 military bases around the world), not government subsidies to corporations, not the aspect of government that fits their worldview. They want to cut the part that helps people. Why? Because that violates individual responsibility.

But where does that view of individual responsibility alone come from? The way to understand the conservative moral system is to consider a strict father family. The father is The Decider, the ultimate moral authority in the family. His authority must not be challenged. His job is to protect the family, to support the family (by winning competitions in the marketplace), and to teach his kids right from wrong by disciplining them physically when they do wrong. The use of force is necessary and required. Only then will children develop the internal discipline to become moral beings. And only with such discipline will they be able to prosper. And what of people who are not prosperous? They don't have discipline, and without discipline they cannot be moral, so they deserve their poverty. The good people are hence the prosperous people. Helping others takes away their discipline, and hence makes them both unable to prosper on their own and function morally.

The market itself is seen in this way. The slogan, "Let the market decide" assumes the market itself is The Decider. The market is seen as both natural (since it is assumed that people naturally seek their self-interest) and moral (if everyone seeks their own profit, the profit of all will be maximized by the invisible hand). As the ultimate moral authority, there should be no power higher than the market that might go against market values. Thus the government can spend money to protect the market and promote market values, but should not rule over it either through (1) regulation, (2) taxation, (3) unions and worker rights, (4) environmental protection or food safety laws, and (5) tort cases. Moreover, government should not do public service. The market has service industries for that. Thus, it would be wrong for the government to provide health care, education, public broadcasting, public parks, and so on. The very idea of these things is at odds with the conservative moral system. No one should be paying for anyone else. It is individual responsibility in all arenas. Taxation is thus seen as taking money away from those who have earned it and giving it to people who don't deserve it. Taxation cannot be seen as providing the necessities of life, a civilized society, and as necessary for business to prosper.

In conservative family life, the strict father rules. Fathers and husbands should have control over reproduction; hence, parental and spousal notification laws and opposition to abortion. In conservative religion, God is seen as the strict father, the Lord, who rewards and punishes according to individual responsibility in following his Biblical word.

Above all, the authority of conservatism itself must be maintained. The country should be ruled by conservative values, and progressive values are seen as evil. Science should NOT have authority over the market, and so the science of global warming and evolution must be denied. Facts that are inconsistent with the authority of conservatism must be ignored or denied or explained away. To protect and extend conservative values themselves, the devil's own means can be used against conservatism's immoral enemies, whether lies, intimidation, torture, or even death, say, for women's doctors.

Freedom is defined as being your own strict father — with individual not social responsibility, and without any government authority telling you what you can and cannot do. To defend that freedom as an individual, you will of course need a gun.[452]

Liberals, in contrast, while still employing a family metaphor, envision the "nurturant parent" model instead.

The Nurturant Parent Model

The family is of either one or two parents. Two are generally preferable, but not always possible.

The primal experience behind this model is one of being cared for and cared about, having one's desires for loving interactions met, living as happily as possible, and deriving meaning from one's community and from caring for and about others.

People are realized in and through their "secure attachments": through their positive relationships to others, through their contribution to their community, and through the ways in which they develop their potential and find joy in life. Work is a means toward these ends, and it is through work that these forms of meaning are realized. All of this requires strength and self-discipline, which are

fostered by the constant support of, and attachment to, those who love and care about you.

Protection is a form of caring, and protection from external dangers takes up a significant part of the nurturant parent's attention. The world is filled with evils that can harm a child, and it is the nurturant parent's duty to be ward them off.

Crime and drugs are, of course, significant, but so are less obvious dangers: cigarettes, cars without seat belts, dangerous toys, inflammable clothing, pollution, asbestos, lead paint, pesticides in food, diseases, unscrupulous businessmen, and so on. Protection of innocent and helpless children from such evils is a major part of a nurturant parent's job.

Children are taught self-discipline in the service of nurturance: to take care of themselves, to deal with existing hardships, to be responsible to others, and to realize their potential. Children are also taught self-nurturance: the intrinsic value of emotional connection with others, of health, of education, of art, of communion with the natural world, and of being able to take care of oneself. In addition to learning the discipline required for responsibility and self-nurturance, it is important that children have a childhood, that they learn to develop their imaginations, and that they just plain have fun.

Through empathizing and interacting positively with their children, parents develop close bonds with children and teach them empathy and responsibility

452 http://georgelakoff.com/2011/02/19/what-conservatives-really-want/

towards others and toward society. Nurturant parents view the family as a community in which children have commitments and responsibilities that grow out of empathy for others. The obedience of children comes out of love and respect for parents, not out of fear of punishment. When children do wrong, nurturant parents choose restitution over retribution whenever possible as a form of justice. Retribution is reserved for those who harm their children.

The pursuit of self-interest is shaped by these values: anything inconsistent with these values is not in one's self-interest. Pursuing self-interest, so understood, is a means for fulfilling the values of the model.[453]

Let's work through this description, one important piece at a time, as well. Once again, the name of the model is telling: "nurturant parent" is gender-neutral, and not even hetero-normative. What is essential is merely that the parent be "nurturant," and this could presumably be the case with any combination of male or female parents, singly or in groups.

In contrast to the discipline-focused strict father approach, the nurturant parent model uses nurturance to develop in children both self-nurturance (the ability to care for oneself) as well as the ability to care for others. This model rejects the "folk behaviorism" of the strict father model, and doesn't accept that children (or people in general) learn primarily via rewards and punishment. Instead, the emphasis is on attachment.

If a child develops a secure and loving "attachment" to her parents, they will model that nurturing behavior themselves. From that secure attachment, they will try to anticipate their parents' expectations, and will be motivated to

please them—not from fear of punishment, but from a desire to make happy someone you love. By way of analogy, if you are in a deeply loving romantic relationship, you (presumably) want your partner to be happy, and it makes you feel good when your actions are pleasing to them. You try to anticipate what will make them happy (or upset), and you probably do your best to make them happy. This is presumably not merely (or even primarily) because you're afraid they will break up with you if you don't, but because of the empathy you have for them. In a way, their happiness becomes your own. It is true, of course, that if you continually disappoint them, they might leave you, and you might experience that as a "punishment," but, if your actions are truly driven primarily by that fear of punishment, how much do you actually *love* that person?

When parents love and nurture their children, the children develop the capacity to become loving and nurturing themselves. Confident in their own worth, they have self-esteem, and are less likely to act out against others to compensate for their own sense of inadequacy (e.g., the stereotypical interpretation of bullies as lacking in self-esteem, and trying to gain it at the expense of others). Well-nurtured parents develop self-discipline as well, but not from fear. As children become more capable of caring for themselves and others (requiring self-discipline, of course), this pleases their parents, and the behavior is reinforced

Rather than focusing on strength and discipline, this model focuses on the experiencing of caring and being cared for. This is not to say that strength and self-discipline are unimportant—just that these qualities develop from the experience of unconditional love and consistent care, rather than discipline and the fear of punishment. Children who are well cared for learn to care for themselves, and to be empathetic—and therefore are motivated to care for others as well.

---

[453] George Lakoff, " Metaphor, Morality, and Politics, Or, Why Conservatives Have Left Liberals in the Dust." 1995. *Social Research* 62(3):177-213

When morality is understood in terms of empathy rather than strength, the strict "good-evil" dichotomy fades away. People with different values are not necessarily "evil," and it is virtuous to be able to empathize with others and see things from their own point of view. Even when people, regrettably, harm others (such as criminal behavior, or even acts of terrorism), it is too simplistic to dismiss such persons as irredeemably "evil." Surely there are causes for hurtful behavior. Mental illness? In that case, we should try to provide better mental health care for that person, and the community in general. Addiction? In that case, we should help people to overcome their addictions, perhaps by providing rehabilitation services. Poverty or oppression? Maybe some criminal acts are symptoms of broader societal problems, and we should try to address those "macro" issues so that fewer people are led to make poor life choices. Even the most despicable acts of terrorism might have roots in poverty and foreign policy issues. This is not to justify the behavior, but to try to understand it so that we are able to prevent such horrible acts rather than merely punishing those who commit them.

With regard to "internal evils," the nurturant parent model doesn't look to temptation and weakness of will as an explanation, but to such traits as selfishness, lack of social responsibility, arrogance, self-righteousness, insensitivity—and other traits associated with a lack of empathy.

Nurturant parents also believe that the world is filled with dangers from which the child needs protecting, but rather than focusing solely on "bad people" (who are often the products of bad childhoods, destructive social and economic circumstances, and a lack of being loved and appreciated) as the source danger in the world, they consider also the dangers of such things as pollution, poverty, second-hand smoke, unsafe food sources or consumer products, and "unscrupulous business practices."

The children of nurturant parents are not considered impertinent for asking questions. Blind obedience to authority is neither expected, nor desired. Children are to be encouraged to ask questions, so that they can understand why some behaviors are loving, and others are not. In this way, their empathy increases with understanding, and their own capacity for nurturance increases as well.

As adults, they are self-confident and emotionally mature. They practice self-care, which enables them to "be there" for others, when needed. As an empathetic person, they will recognize the connections between persons, and the value of all individuals, and seeks to make the community more caring and responsive to the needs of others. Cooperation, rather than competition, is emphasized; as is interdependence over hierarchy. It is not the case that if one person "wins," another must "lose." Sometimes, we can all have our needs met, and be happy.

Although children grow up to become adults, they never cease to be your "child"—and nurturant parents will continue to support and care for their children regardless of their age.

Nurturant Parent Politics

In contrast to the moral categories in the strict father model, we have the following moral categories for liberal politics, according to Lakoff:

1. Empathetic behavior and promoting fairness.
2. Helping those who cannot help themselves.
3. Protecting those who cannot protect themselves.
4. Promoting fulfillment in life.
5. Nurturing and strengthening oneself in order to do the above.

First, we have the moral value of empathy. While strength is the focus of the strict father model, empathy is the focus for the nurturant parent. To care for another one must be able to empathize with them, to be moved and motivated by the other person's fear, pain, or joy. Those who can't empathize at all are considered psychopaths!

Empathy is thought to be essential for notions of fairness and reciprocity. When a child does something unkind to another child, we might ask them how they would feel if that had been done to them, instead. For adults, we might appeal to the Golden Rule, or urge someone not to judge until they have "walked a mile in the other person's shoes." The assumption is that if you can identify with the other person, and imagine their needs, suffering, or happiness as your own, you will motivated for them to be treated fairly—just as you would want to be treated fairly!

The more capable we are of empathy, the more likely we will be to be concerned with others' lives, and to help those in need. This brings us to the *second* moral value: helping those who cannot help themselves.

Parents are naturally moved, by love, to care for their children who, for many years, are not capable of caring for themselves. A loving parent doesn't demand some sort of payment from her infant in exchange for food, protection, affection, and care! Because of our empathy for others, their suffering becomes our own (in a sense), and this can motivate us to help others in need. I could be that homeless person on the street, and I would want someone to take a moment and offer me some kindness, and maybe some food. In different circumstances, I could have been one of those Syrian refugees fleeing from ISIS, and would want my fellow humans to offer me some kindness and care.

The *third* moral value, very much related to the second, is protecting those who cannot protect themselves. Just as a nurturant parent will protect his child from dangers (which include not only "strangers," but also things like lead in paint, unsafe child car seats, climate change, polluted water supplies, etc.), so too should we protect anyone who needs it from dangers, to the extent that we can. If we can empathize with a woman in an abusive relationship, we would want to protect her from that violence, and we would be moved to protect the Syrian refugees, and we would be moved to protect people

threatened by a natural disaster, or from crippling poverty, etc.

Fourthly, nurturant parents recognize that being a loving parent isn't only about protecting from danger and providing the necessities of life. A nurturant parent doesn't merely want her child to survive, but to thrive. This means promoting fulfillment in life. If you empathize with others, you recognize that they have hopes and dreams just like we do, they have potential that can be realized (possibly with some help), and an intrinsic worth—just like ourselves. Nurturant parents try to help their children flourish as individuals by promoting their education, enriching hobbies, creative expression, meaningful work, healthy relationships, etc. Adults deserve no less.

Finally, being a nurturing parent requires empathy for oneself as well! To care for others, one must also care for oneself. This means taking action to remain healthy, rested, and cared-for.

The Two Models Applied and Compared

Clearly, these contrasting models reveal two different parenting models. The first emphasizes "tough love," and sees the role of the parent as protector and moral instructor so that the child may grow into a successful adult. The second emphasizes healthy attachment (achieved by continuous nurturance), so that the child may grow into an emotionally mature and empathetic adult, equipped to care for others in return. We can now apply these family models to the State, in an effort to understand the differences between conservative and liberal worldviews, and policy stances. As an example, we will consider federally-funded college loans.

The official Democratic party platform for the 2012 campaign season says this about student loans (emphasis added):

> To help keep college within reach for every student, Democrats took on banks to reform our student loan program, saving more than $60 billion by removing

the banks acting as middlemen <u>so we can better and more directly invest in students. To make college affordable for students of all backgrounds and confront the loan burden our students shoulder,</u> we doubled our investment in Pell Grant scholarships and created the American Opportunity Tax Credit worth up to $10,000 over four years of college, and we're creating avenues for students to manage their federal student loans so that their payments can be only 10 percent of what they make each month.

The official Republican party platform for the 2012 campaign season, in contrast, says the following about student loans (emphasis added):

Federal student aid is on an unsustainable path, and efforts should be taken to <u>provide families with greater transparency and the information they need to make prudent choices about a student's future:</u> completion rates, repayment rates, future earnings, and other factors that may affect their decisions. <u>The federal government should not be in the business of originating student loans; however, it should serve as an insurance guarantor for the private sector as they offer loans to students.</u>

Republicans are officially against (originating) federal student loans, whereas Democrats support it. What explains this difference? Lakoff thinks he knows the answer.

From a "liberal" perspective, federal student loans are a good and worthy cause. It helps those who can't help themselves (i.e., to pay for college). It promotes fulfillment in life since education is fulfilling in itself, and a higher education allows access to more fulfilling work. It strengthens the community by producing a better-educated citizenry and ultimately bringing in more tax money. It makes access to college more fair since the opportunity to go to college will not be dependent upon the contingencies of

birth (i.e., how wealthy is the family into which you were born?). Finally, and perhaps most importantly, it is empathetic behavior. If someone is talented enough to get accepted into a college, and wants to attend, but is being held back by financial struggles, it is simply the nurturing thing to do to help them.

From a "conservative" perspective, however, this is a bad idea. Since loan recipients are dependent upon the loan, federal loan programs create dependency on the government rather than promoting self-reliance. Since not everyone has access to the loans, because they are based on financial need, they are unfair, and interfere with the free market. After all, private lending institutions, like any other commercial interest, will be driven by competition and market demands, so long as they are not interfered with. The government hand-picking some people to receive loans on the basis of their perceived "need" rather than by what the market will bear interferes with what would otherwise be the fair pursuit of self-interest. Moreover, since the loans are subsidized by the government, they are ultimately provided by tax-payer dollars. Since all the risk is borne by the government in the event a student defaults on the loan, it is tax-payer dollars that will be lost, rather than private lending institutions. Private lenders, of course, wary of losing their money, carefully screen to whom they lend money, so as to minimize that risk. "Riskier" clients either don't get loans at all, or else pay higher interest rates to account for their "riskiness." Not so with federal loans. But, since the program takes money earned by one group and, through taxation, gives it to another group, it is unfair and penalizes the pursuit of self-interest by taking money from someone who has earned it and giving it to someone who hasn't.

Admittedly, the Republic platform doesn't claim that *no* student loans should be available, but that it should be handled by the "private sector." Notice, though, that on this issue the official position of the Republican party is not entirely consistent with the strict father model. It claims that, while the federal government should not be providing student loans, it "should serve as an insurance guarantor for the private sector as they offer loans to students." Perhaps the assumption is that access to college education is a worthy enough goal that private lenders should be encouraged in their lending, by virtue of the government guaranteeing the loans? In any event, this is a nice illustration that neither of the major political parties are presumed to be 100% compliant and consistent with their respective family models.

Moving on to other examples, with regard to social and economic forces, liberals and conservatives tend to have striking different interpretations. Liberals tend to recognize that some people are "trapped" by their circumstances (e.g., poverty, racism, sexism, high crime neighborhoods, lack of resources, poorly funded schools, etc.), and a nurturing parent (or nurturing government) should be motivated by empathy to help those people. If social and economic forces are the problem, the solution must address those forces!

Conservatives, on the other hand, believing in the "American dream" and its meritocracy, deny the strength of economic and social forces. Anyone with sufficient talent and self-discipline can (and will) succeed. The solution is not to provide "handouts" and short-circuit the true path to success, but, instead, to emphasize personal responsibility and hard work.

With the regard abortion, one might wonder how conservatives can be "pro-life" but against providing subsidized pre-natal care, or food assistance to poor parents. There is no necessary inconsistency, if one believes that the fetus is innocent, and abortion is, therefore, murder—and categorically evil. That being said, if someone isn't prepared to deal with the predictable consequences of sex (i.e., pregnancy), that person shouldn't be having sex in the first place. If someone is too poor to care for their children, they shouldn't have them! They should have sufficient will-power to abstain from sex, or at least use reliable birth control. Providing free services to poor parents only subsidizes their weakness and reinforces it.

From the liberal perspective, nurturant parents see the pregnant girl or woman as being "in trouble" and therefore in need of help. The anxiety and possible guilt or shame she is experiencing from the unintended pregnancy is "punishment" enough—she certainly doesn't need to be scolded on top of it. If she is seeking an abortion, she has concluded she isn't ready to be a mother yet, or else doesn't think she can handle a child (or another one). If that is the case, she is in no position to properly care for the child, once it is born, and her self-care would suggest that she not have to endure the pregnancy either.

This sort of comparison and analysis is possible, in principle, with each and every point of political contention in the United States today. The same family models that allow us to predict (and understand) conservative and liberal stances on various policy issues also allows us to generalize and identify, for each, their respective "heroes" and "villains."

Model Citizens and "Demons"

"Conservative" model citizens have conservative values, act to support those values, are self- disciplined and self-reliant, generally uphold the morality of reward and punishment, work to protect moral citizens, and act in support of the moral order. Those who best exemplify those traits are successful, wealthy, law-abiding, conservative businessmen who support a strong military and a strict criminal justice system, and are against government regulation and things like affirmative action.

They are our role-models, the people whom all Americans should emulate. Such people deserve to be rewarded and respected because they succeeded through hard work and have earned whatever they have through their own self-discipline. Therefore, they deserve to *keep* what they have earned.

Through their own success and wealth they create jobs, which they "give" to other citizens. Even simply by investing their money to maximize their earnings, they become philanthropists who "give" jobs to others and thereby "create wealth" for others. Their successful pursuit of self-interest helps many others as well.

If such persons are conservative model citizens, their opposites (whom Lakoff terms conservative "demons") are against conservative values (e.g., Strict Father morality, in general). This includes feminists, gays, and other "deviants" who defy the very assumptions of the Strict Father family. Other "demons" are the advocates of multiculturalism, who reject the primacy of the Strict Father model and who deny American "exceptionalism," postmodern humanists who deny the existence of any absolute values, and progressive "egalitarians" who are against hierarchy, in general.

There are many such "demons" in the United States. They include people whose lack of self-discipline has led to a lack of self-reliance. This would include unwed mothers on welfare, since their lack of sexual self-control has led to their dependence on the state. It also includes unemployed drug users, whose weakness has led to drug addiction, which has itself led to their being unable to support themselves. It additionally includes any able-bodied people on welfare. Such persons can work, but don't. Given this land of opportunity, this means they are lazy and are willing to be a burden to others.

Other sorts of "demons" are the so-called protectors of the "public good." This will include environmentalists, consumer advocates, advocates of affirmative action, and advocates of government-supported universal health care ("Obamacare!")—all of whom want the government to interfere with the pursuit of self-interest and thus constrain the business activities of the conservatives' "model citizens."

Yet another type of "demon" opposes law and order, and a strong military. This includes antiwar protesters, advocates of prisoners' rights, opponents of police brutality, and those pushing for "gun-control." People who would restrict access to guns are not only trampling on the 2nd Amendment, but are trying to take guns away from those who need them to protect themselves and their families both from

criminals and from possible government tyranny. Of all these "demons," abortion doctors might be the worst, since they directly kill the most innocent people of all: unborn babies.

Once again, in sharp contrast, "liberals" have a very different image of a model citizen. Liberal model citizens are those who are empathetic, help the disadvantaged, protect those who need it, promote and exemplify fulfillment in life, and who take proper care of themselves so that they can do all those things!

Such persons are those who live a socially responsible life, such as socially responsible professionals; environmental, consumer, and minority rights advocates, as well as union organizers. Such persons also include doctors, and social workers who devote their lives to helping the poor and the elderly, as well as peace advocates, educators, artists, and those in the healing professions, in general.

Lakoff claims that liberals have their own "demons." Liberal "demons" are mean-spirited, selfish, and unfair people who have no empathy and show no sense of social responsibility. Right at the top of this list are wealthy corporations and business persons who care only about profit, and use their power and political influence to pursue it, at all costs.

Other liberal "demons" are those who ignore, harm, or exploit the disadvantaged. Companies or politicians who "bust" unions are an example of such "demons," as are large agricultural firms that exploit farm workers by exposing them to poor working conditions for low pay. Also included here would be those who oppose providing health care or other necessary services to the needy.

Another kind of "demon" is one who hurts either people or the environment itself. This will include not only criminals, but also "out-of-control" police who use brutal tactics. It also includes polluters, those who make unsafe products or engage in consumer fraud, and large companies that make extensive profits from government subsidies by contributing to politicians and their campaigns.

Finally, additional liberal "demons" include those who are opposed to publicly supporting education, art, and research, as well as other personal (and culturally) enriching activities.

Conclusion

Lakoff's approach is a sharp departure from everything else we have done and considered in this book. Rather than offering an argument for what the State *should* do, or what sorts of policy stances we should have, he offers an explanation for the opinions we form, and the actions we take, not in terms of philosophical arguments, but contrasting family metaphors.[454]

If Lakoff is right, most of us don't vote from well-considered philosophical positions, nor are we responsive to arguments. Instead, we interpret political situations and "arguments" through the lens of our dominant family model. In that case, a more effective means of political persuasion than rational argument would be an informed and intentional use of metaphor— something Lakoff thinks explains how Ronald Reagan won over so many traditionally democratic voters in the 1980s, ushering in the "Reagan Revolution."

Rather than taking a stance on whether Lakoff's approach, or that of traditional political theorists, is correct, I propose that we attempt to understand both. On the one hand, there is rhetoric, psychology, and an understanding of how emotions are triggered (or even manipulated). On the other hand, there are coherent world views, in which one hopes to construct (or at least operate from) consistent premises that inform political conclusions.

Perhaps these are skill sets belonging to two different kinds of politicians? One is the domain of the charismatic leader (or advisor) who can swing votes and "get things done." The other is the domain of the traditional "statesman," who

can conceive of the proper aims and actions of the State in the first place. There is no question that this book has focused more on the latter, than the former.

Hyperlinks to the official party platforms of the two "Major" parties (and their two most credible competitors) are provided below. If you are reading this book in a traditional printed format, the URL for each is thankfully short, and can easily be typed into your web browser.

I encourage you to read them with both kinds of lenses in place. With one lens, look for the telltale signs of either the "strict father" or "nurturant parent" models. With the other, look for traces of influence from any of the several substantial political thinkers and their ideas we have explored in the previous chapters. To what extent are these ideas used in coherent and consistent fashion?

Both approaches should be informative.

2016 Party Platforms

Democrat Party:
http://www.presidency.ucsb.edu/papers_pdf/117717.pdf

Green Party:
http://www.gp.org/platform

Libertarian Party:
https://www.lp.org/platform/

Republican Party:
https://www.gop.com/the-2016-republican-party-platform/

---

[454] In fairness, at the end of *Moral Politics*, Lakoff does advocate for the superiority of the Nurturant Parent model, and is active in promoting liberal causes and politicians. Most of his book (and all of our use of it), though, is limited to the descriptive, rather than the prescriptive.

Chapter 14: Special Topics: White Nationalism?

> *Comprehension questions you should be able to answer after reading this chapter:*
>
> 1. What is "white nationalism?
>
> 2. What is a "race realist?"
>
> 3. What is an "ethno-state?"
>
> 4. What are some of the political goals of contemporary white nationalists such as Richard Spencer and Jared Taylor?
>
> 5. According to Hitler, what is the proper relationship between "race" and the State?
>
> 6. What are some of the educational reforms proposed by Hitler? What ultimate purpose do these reforms (and government in general) serve?
>
> 7. Explain how Supreme Court decisions such as Dred Scott, Ozawa, and Thind can be used as evidence for the social-construction of race.
>
> 8. What is the difference between "racialism" and "racism?" What do they have in common?
>
> 9. What is the "popular account" of race?
>
> 10. What is the difference between "race" and a "racialized group," as described by Blum?
>
> 11. Explain why it would be relevant in the context of a white nationalism if "race" were a social construct (as opposed to a biological "essence")?
>
> 12. What does Nietzsche mean by the *Übermensch*? Explain why this is not necessarily a reference to the Aryan "master race".
>
> 13. What is the "artistic" interpretation of the "will to power"? How can it be seen as a refutation of the "Nazi" totalitarian/political interpretation of the will to power?

I did not enjoy researching or writing this chapter. The subject matter is "ugly." Just to put all cards on the table: I'm "white."[455] I am not, however, anything resembling a white supremacist or a white nationalist. I generally try to refrain from editorializing in my chapters, but this chapter will be an exception to that general rule.

I am opposed to white supremacist/white nationalist ideologies (and, frankly, any *other* race-based ideologies as well) for both moral reasons as well as epistemic reasons. That is to say that I think such ideologies are both morally misguided and intellectually bankrupt. What they are not, however, are mere historical curiosities—just one more relic in a pile of bad and dangerous ideas.

Unfortunately, white supremacy/ nationalism has been rebranded and is enjoying a resurgence and relevance. It has found a home in the "alt-right" movement, and spokespersons for, and sympathizers of, this movement have become increasing accepted into "mainstream" political consideration and discourse.

---

[455] Although, exactly that *means* is complicated – as will be evident later in the chapter.

While this iteration of their ideology is new, the ideology itself is not. It can be traced back rather easily to the worldview of the Nazi party, and the words of none other than Adolf Hitler. What was true about this ideology then is equally true now: it is based on multiple mistakes. For our purposes we will consider only two of those mistakes:

1. A mistaken understanding of Nietzsche.
2. A mistaken understanding of race.

We will begin this chapter with a brief treatment of contemporary white nationalism as expressed by some of its more prominent spokespersons (Jared Taylor and Richard Spencer). We will then trace those ideas back to the "philosophy" of Hitler. We will consider the alleged contributions of Nietzsche to the Nazi ideology as well as their assumptions about race. We will conclude by demonstrating that Nietzsche (for all his merits and flaws) was demonstrably opposed to race-based notions of supremacy and openly critical of German nationalism, and that the basic assumptions about race that are fundamental to this ideology have no grounding in science.

White Nationalism

"White nationalism" can, with some controversy, be taken as a euphemism for white supremacy. The basic position of white supremacy is, I suspect, self-explanatory: the belief that there is such a thing as the "white" race, and that that race is superior to other (non-white) races.

Traditionally, white supremacy has been associated with Nazism, neo-Nazis, the Ku Klux Klan, and various other hate groups. Today, some people associated with white nationalism use other terms to describe themselves: "alt-right," "identitarians," or "race realists."

Whatever the name, the political goal is basically the same: the establishment of a white "ethno-state," where "white culture" is celebrated, and the "perils" of multiculturalism are avoided by virtue of segregation.

White nationalism has manifested in increasing numbers of rallies and protests, including the "Unite the Right" rally that occurred in August, 2017 in Charlottesville, Virginia. The protest was ostensibly over the pending removal of a statue of Robert E Lee from Emancipation Park. As the Confederate general, Lee is a symbol for white supremacists/nationalists and the removal of his statue was seen as another example of the attack on "white culture." One of the organizers of the event, Nathan Damigo, said that one of the purposes of the rally was to unify the white nationalist movement in the United States.[456] Protesters consisted of a mix of white supremacists, white nationalists, neo-Nazis, militia members, and Klansmen. They displayed Confederate flags, swastikas, semi-automatic rifles, and some chanted racist and anti-Semitic slogans during their march. The rally was especially controversial due to the violent confrontation between the protesters, and counter protesters. Dozens of people were injured, and one woman was killed, when one of the white supremacists intentionally rammed his car into a crowd of counter protesters. Further controversy was generated when President Trump commented on the rally:

> I think there is blame on both sides. You look at both sides. I think there is blame on both sides. I have no doubt about it. You don't have doubt about it either. If you reported it accurately, you would say that the neo-Nazis started this thing. They showed up in Charlottesville. Excuse me. They didn't put themselves down as neo-Nazis. You had some very bad people in that group. You also had some very fine

---

[456]

http://www.modbee.com/news/article167213427.html

people on both sides. You had people in that group -- excuse me, excuse me. I saw the same pictures as you did. You had people in that group that were there to protest the taking down, of to them, a very, very important statue and the renaming of a park from Robert E. Lee to another name.

George Washington was a slave owner. Was George Washington a slave owner? So will George Washington now lose his status? Are we going to take down -- excuse me. Are we going to take down statues to George Washington? How about Thomas Jefferson? What do you think of Thomas Jefferson? You like him. Good. Are we going to take down his statue? He was a major slave owner. Are we going to take down his statue? It is fine. You are changing history and culture.

You had people and I'm not talking about the neo-Nazis and the white nationalists. They should be condemned totally. You had many people in that group other than neo-Nazis and white nationalists. The press has treated them absolutely unfairly. Now, in the other group also, you had some fine people but you also had troublemakers and you see them come with the black outfits and with the helmets and with the baseball bats. You had a lot of bad people in the other group too.[457]

In President Trump's defense, he does attempt to make a distinction between white nationalists and some "very fine people" that were involved (on the same side) of the same protest. However, his defense of the cultural value of the Robert E Lee statue, his analogy to George Washington and Thomas Jefferson, and his statement about "changing history and culture" seem to suggest a solidarity with those who are claiming that "white culture" is under attack. It is certainly the case that some of the more prominent members of the white supremacists/nationalist movement interpreted his words to be very favorable to their cause.[458]

David Duke
@DrDavidDuke

Follow

Thank you President Trump for your honesty & courage to tell the truth about #Charlottesville & condemn the leftist terrorists in BLM/Antifa

NBC News @NBCNews
President Trump: "George Washington was a slave owner... Are we gonna take down statues to George Washington? How about Thomas Jefferson?"
1:04

1:45 PM - 15 Aug 2017

---

[457] https://www.vox.com/2017/8/15/16154028/trump-press-conference-transcript-charlottesville
[458] David Duke is the former "grand Wizard" of the Ku Klux Klan and a globally recognized representative of the white supremacist movement, and Richard Spencer is a leader of the "alt – right" and will be featured in greater detail later in this chapter.

For a variety of reasons, the white nationalist movement (or alt-right) has made its way into mainstream media coverage and political discourse.   Although it is far from being a mainstream political movement, it cannot and should not be ignored. To put it bluntly: we have seen this sort of thing before, historically speaking. Then, as now, such ideas were dangerous.

The *Turner Diaries* was written over 40 years ago by William Luther Pierce. It is a work of dystopian fiction depicting a white nationalist revolution (fictionally begun on 9-16-1991) in the United States, and culminating in an overthrow of the government, a campaign of global genocide against non-white people, and the institution of a white supremacist State. The revolutionary work is carried out by an organization of loose "cells" called The Order. One of the more chilling and memorable portions of the revolution is called the "day of rope."

Today has been the Day of the Rope — a grim and bloody day, but an unavoidable one. Tonight, from tens of thousands of lampposts, power poles, and trees throughout this vast metropolitan area the grisly forms hang. Even the street signs at intersections have been pressed into service, and at practically every street corner I passed this evening on my way to HQ there was a dangling corpse, four at every intersection. Hanging from a single overpass only about a mile from here is a group of about 30, each with an identical placard around its neck bearing the printed legend, "I betrayed my race."

Two or three of that group had been decked out in academic robes before they were strung up, and the whole batch are apparently faculty members from the nearby UCLA campus. ...The first thing I saw in the moonlight was the placard with its legend in large, block letters: "I defiled my race." Above the placard leered the horribly bloated, purplish face of a young woman, her eyes wide open and bulging, her mouth agape.

Finally I could make out the thin, vertical line of rope disappearing into the branches above. I shuddered and quickly went on my way. There are many thousands of hanging female corpses like that in this city tonight, all wearing identical placards around their necks. They are the White women who were married to or living with Blacks, with Jews, or with other non-White males. There are also a number of men wearing the I-defiled-my-race placard, but the women easily outnumber them seven or eight to one. On the other hand, about ninety per cent of the corpses with the I-betrayed-my-race placards are men, and overall the sexes seem to be roughly balanced.

Those wearing the latter placards are the politicians, the lawyers, the businessmen, the TV newscasters, the newspaper reporters and editors, the judges, the teachers, the school officials, the "civic leaders", the bureaucrats, the preachers, and all the others who, for reasons of career or status or votes or whatever, helped promote or implement the System's racial program.[459]

The problem with the *Turner Diaries* is that it's not just a case of troubling fiction: it has had real-world consequences, inspiring dozens of armed robberies and more than 200 murders in the decades since its publication.[460] Oklahoma City Bomber Timothy McVeigh was inspired by the book. Indeed, characters in the book blow up a federal building using a truck filled with explosives and fertilizer!

An actual white nationalist gang calling itself "The Order," in direct reference to the novel, murdered three people and committed robberies back in 1983. Some members referred to the Diaries as their "bible." One member of this gang (David Lane) became a writer himself (while in prison). One of his works is entitled the "White Genocide Manifesto." The manifesto equates "integration" with white genocide. He later condensed his views into a slogan now known in white supremacist/nationalist circles as "The 14 Words:" "We must secure the existence of our people and a future for white children." Other contemporary white nationalists have continued this theme of framing "race-mixing" and multiculturalism as "white genocide."

In the remainder of this section, I will provide a brief overview of two of the more prominent figures of the *contemporary* white nationalist movement, Richard Spencer and Jared Taylor, before considering their more infamous predecessor.

Richard Spencer

Richard Spencer (May 11, 1978 --) is the president of the National Policy Institute, which is widely regarded as a white supremacists think tank.[461] Spencer rejects that label and calls himself an "identitarian" instead. The problem with this rejection is that his words demonstrate a pattern in which he clearly *does* think that "white" peoples are superior to non-white peoples. Consider, for example, when President Trump stirred up controversy by referring disparagingly to Haiti, El Salvador, and African countries (in general).

Why are we having all these people from shithole countries come here?[462]

---

[459] The fact that I wrote this chapter, not to mention that I am married to an African-American woman, would certainly qualify me as a "race traitor," in this scenario.

[460] https://www.theatlantic.com/politics/archive/2016/09/how-the-turner-diaries-changed-white-nationalism/500039/

[461] https://nationalpolicy.institute/

[462] https://www.washingtonpost.com/politics/trump-attacks-protections-for-immigrants-from-shithole-countries-in-oval-office-meeting/2018/01/11/bfc0725c-f711-11e7-91af31ac729add94_story.html?tid=a_mcntx&utm_term=.cdbec1eef048

It is worth pointing out that, at the same time, President Trump proposed immigrants from Norway as a preferable alternative. Norway is 83% Norwegian, and 8.3% (other) European, leaving just less than 9% of its population "non-European."[463] In fairness, Norway is consistently ranked among the top 5 "happiest" countries,[464] and scores considerably better than the United States with respect to crime rates,[465] so there are legitimately "good" things to say about Norwegians that ostensibly have nothing to do with race. In context, however, suggesting that the USA recruit more Norwegian immigrants immediately after calling "black" (Haiti; all of Africa) and brown (El Salvador) countries "shit holes" certainly raises the idea that race is a factor—and Spencer enthusiastically agreed.

Richard ▇▇ Spencer
@RichardBSpencer

Follow

I must come to the defense of #Haiti! It's a potentially beautiful and productive country. The problem is that it's filled with shithole people. If the French dominated, they could make it great again. #MakeHaitiGreatAgain

8:14 PM - 11 Jan 2018

While Twitter is hardly the vehicle for nuanced philosophical discourse, the basic point here is obvious. Haitians (who are black) are "shithole people." The French (who are white—at least "traditionally," and in all the ways that count according to Spencer) would make Haiti "great again." It's impossible to *not* detect the supremacist tone here. When countries are ruled by white people, they are great. When they are ruled by non-white people (or, at least, specifically, black people), they are "shitholes."

Spencer claims to have created the term "alt-right" to represent a movement about "white identity." While he had been known in various corners of the Internet for years, he achieved national mainstream prominence when a video of him speaking at a National Policy Institute conference just after 2016 election of President Trump went viral. Most noteworthy was him proclaiming "hail Trump, hail our people, hail victory!" In response, several members of the audience gave the Nazi salute.[466]

It's hard to believe that the specific use of the word "hail," in the phrase "hail Trump" (rather close to "heil Hitler"), and the Nazi salute in response show no connection to Hitler and the Nazis. Indeed, like many white nationalists, Spencer embraces the notion of an essential culture/"spirit" of a people that is quite similar to the notion of a "Volk" that we find in Hitler.

The political outcome that Spencer and his followers seek is the creation of a distinct and separate "white Christian ethno-state," with distinct geographic borders, populated with people of European descent (as understood to be fair skinned people who populated Europe several hundred years ago). The process by which this outcome is to be achieved is the cultivation of ethnic pride for white people and

[463] https://www.indexmundi.com/norway/demographics_profile.html
[464] http://worldhappiness.report/ed/2018/
[465] http://www.nationmaster.com/country-info/compare/Norway/United-States/Crime

[466] Bradner, Eric (November 22, 2016). "Alt-right leader: 'Hail Trump! Hail our people! Hail victory!'". CNN

the promotion of government policies that promote and protect that new white racial consciousness.

Practically speaking, this will mean the mainstream acceptance of "white pride," the dismantling of programs that allegedly promote the welfare and success of non-white persons in the United States over those of white people, a radical change in immigration policies to favor immigrants from predominately white countries and to exclude (or even deport) non-white immigrants, etc.

In an essay, entitled "Race: Stalking the Wild Taboo", Spencer explains achievement, wealth, and (apparent) intelligence differences between the races as follows:

> Perhaps the most important single environmental difference faced by these early humans was that much of the Eurasian landmass turns cold for several months of the year, and food is scarce during this time. It required intelligence, resourcefulness, foresight, and an ability to delay gratification (that is, impulse control), for ancient hunter-gatherers to survive cold winters. People with these qualities were more successful raising children than those who lacked them, so humans in more northerly areas gradually became more intelligent and future-oriented than those who remained in the tropics. The higher intelligence and lower crime rates of Whites and East Asians as compared with Africans may be due in large part to the selective pressure of cold winters.[467]

Here, he is drawing on the work of Richard Lynn.[468] The basic idea behind Lynn's theory is

that "when early peoples migrated from equatorial East Africa into the more northern latitudes of North Africa, South Asia, Europe and Northeast Asia they encountered progressively more cognitively demanding environments that required greater intelligence, including the need to hunt large animals, build fires and shelters and make clothes. The colder the winter temperatures and the more northerly the environment, the higher were the IQs that evolved."[469]

Basically, white people come from colder places than black or brown people, and therefore their ancestors were forced (by evolution) to be "smarter" in order to survive. This theoretical explanation for these alleged differences in IQ is not only controversial among scientists, but also seems challenged by common sense and a cursory understanding of history.[470]

The accepted understanding of the evolution of humanity is that all humans alive today are descendants of African ancestors. "H. heidelbergensis" is thought to be the likely ancestor of both modern humans and Neanderthals, and is thought to have migrated from Africa approximately 500,000 years ago. Still within Africa, Homo sapiens diverged roughly 300,000 years ago, and is thought to have migrated roughly 70,000 years ago. Modern humans are thought to have spread across Europe only 40,000 years ago, with migration to the Americas roughly 20,000 years ago.

According to the "cold-weather" theory, the colder temperatures of Europe should have triggered more intelligent humans while those in the warmer climates of Africa and the Middle East, being less intellectually challenged by their environment, would develop less impressive IQ scores. Oddly enough, when we consider the birth of civilization itself, the communities we associate with the development of politics,

[467] (https://nationalpolicy.institute/2017/10/05/race-stalking-the-wild-taboo/

[468] Richard Lynn, Race Differences in Intelligence: An Evolutionary Analysis, 2nd Revised Edition, Washington Summit Publishers, 2015.

[469] https://www.amren.com/news/2016 /07/richard-lynn-on-race-differences-in-intelligence/

[470] https://www.psychologytoday.com /blog/unique-everybody-else/201211/cold-winters-and-the-evolution-intelligence

religion, mathematics, literacy, early science, philosophy, medicine, etc.; they all come from those conspicuously *warm* climates: Babylonia (1895 BCE–619 BCE). Persian Empire (6th century BCE). Ancient Egypt (3150 BCE – 332 BCE). Ancient Greece (480 – 146 BCE).The Roman Republic and Empire (509 BCE – 395 CE).[471]

Their intellectually "superior" counterparts in northern Europe, despite their allegedly genetically superior IQ and tens of thousands of years' worth of evolutionary advantage, were, comparatively speaking, illiterate barbarians during the same time periods. This, in addition to the fact that the civilization of China (with a wide-ranging climate) had been established in the 21st century BCE!

Spencer draws upon another contemporary white nationalist, Jared Taylor, in his echoing of the claim that it is "natural" to prefer members of the same race, citing him specifically in an essay sub-section entitled "The Preference for One's Own."[472] We will now turn to Taylor himself.

Jared Taylor

Samuel Jared Taylor (September 15, 1951 –) is another white nationalist/supremacist. He is the founder and editor of a white supremacist magazine entitled "American Renaissance."[473] He is an author and publisher, and the former director of the National Policy Institute (a white nationalist "think tank" based in Virginia, now run by the aforementioned Richard Spencer). A key premise in Taylor's worldview is the idea of "*race realism.*"

What we call race realism is what was considered common sense until perhaps the 1950s. It is a body of views that was so taken for granted it had no name, but it

can be summarized as follows: That race is an important aspect of individual and group identity, that different races build different societies that reflect their natures, and that it is entirely normal for whites (or for people of any other race) to want to be the majority race in their own homeland.[474]

Taylor believes in and argues for an essentialist notion of race, according to which real, meaningful, and enduring differences between peoples is accounted for by their race. He claims that recognition of these "facts" was, until relatively recently, accepted as obvious and common sense by all people, and is presently accepted and promoted by all people with the notable exception of "whites."

People of all races generally prefer the company of people like themselves. Racial diversity is a source of conflict, not strength. Non-whites, especially blacks and Hispanics, nurture a strong sense of racial pride and solidarity. Whites have little sense of racial solidarity, and most whites strongly condemn any signs of it.[475]

He further argues that the recognition of distinct races, and preferring one's own, is natural, inevitable, and entirely appropriate.

Racial identity comes naturally to all non-white groups. It comes naturally because it is good, normal, and healthy to feel kinship for people like oneself. Despite the fashionable view that race is a socially created illusion, race is a biological reality. All people of the same race are

---

[471] All dates are approximate and very much subject to debate.

[472] https://nationalpolicy.institute/2017/ 10/05/race-stalking-the-wild-taboo/

[473] https://www.amren.com/

[474] https://www.amren.com/about/issues/

[475] Jared Taylor, *White Identity. Racial Consciousness in the 21st Century*. New Century Foundation. 2011, 201.

more closely related genetically than they are to anyone of a different race, and this helps explain racial solidarity.

Families are close for the same reason. Parents love their children, not because they are the smartest, best-looking, most talented children on earth. They love them because they are genetically close to them. They love them because they are a family.

Most people have similar feelings about race. Their race is the largest extended family to which they feel an instinctive kinship. Like members of a family, members of a race do not need objective reasons to prefer their own group; they prefer it because it is theirs (though they may well imagine themselves as having many fine, partly imaginary qualities).

These mystic preferences need not imply hostility towards others. Parents may have great affection for the children of others, but their own children come first. Likewise, affection often crosses racial lines, but the deeper loyalties of most people are to their own group—their extended family.[476]

Notice that Taylor explicitly claims that race is "reality" and it is biological rather than socially constructed—a point I will attempt to refute later in this chapter. In addition, he claims that racial preferences need not imply hostility towards other races, it is natural/normal/healthy/good to prefer people of one's own race.

Despite making it a point to say that these preferences need not imply hostility, there is ample hostility throughout Taylor's writings. I have provided a replica of the table of contents from his book, *White Identity. Racial Consciousness in the 21st Century*. I do this so that

you may see the themes and subcategories he addresses in the book.

---

[476] Ibid., 204.

Chapters 1 – 4 attempt to argue for the natural and objective reality of segregation and racial preference and for the failure of attempts to integrate and to ignore this "reality." Chapters 5 – 7 offer his account of how non-whites embrace their own racial identity and consciousness, and advocate for "their own kind." Chapter 8 provides a thorough (and not terribly surprising) demonstration of the rampant racist assumptions that many white people (including presidents, politicians, and business leaders) exhibited and expressed for most of the history of the United States. He provides this history presumably in an attempt to demonstrate the "naturalness" of racial bias. In the final chapter (chapter 9) he offers a painstaking account of the "crisis" that is developing as a result of multiculturalism and increasing numbers of non-white people living in the United States.

Again, despite his claim that racial preference "need not imply hostility" towards other races, it's difficult to see how the depiction of a "crisis" for white people and white culture brought about by other races would not engender hostility, particularly when the crisis is described in terms of increasing national poverty rates (caused by non-white people), a deteriorating public school system (caused by non-white people), the loss of jobs for white people (caused by non-white people), increased crime and violence (caused by non-white people), the deterioration of our medical system (caused by non-white people), increased political corruption (caused by non-white people), and the loss of a distinctive and valued "white culture" (caused by non-white people).

Here is a very small sample from the many statistics and anecdotes that Taylor cites:

- Fourteen-year-old James Tokarski was one of a handful of whites attending Bailly Middle School in Gary, Indiana, in 2006. Black students called him "whitey" and "white trash" and repeatedly beat him up. They knocked him unconscious twice. The school offered James a "lunch buddy," to be with him whenever he was not in class, but his parents took him out of Bailly. The mother of another white student said it was typical for whites to be called "whitey" or "white boy," and to get passes to eat lunch in the library rather than face hostile blacks in the lunch room.[477]

- Some people claim that all population groups commit crimes at the same rates, and that racial differences in incarceration rates reflect police and justice system bias. This view is wrong. The US Department of Justice carefully tracks murder, which is the violent crime for which racial data on victim and perpetrator are most complete. In 2005, the department noted that blacks were six times more likely than whites to be victims of murder and seven times more likely to commit murder. . . There are practically no crimes blacks and Hispanics do not commit at higher rates than whites, whether it is larceny, car theft, drug offenses, burglary, rape, or alcohol offenses. Even for white collar crimes—fraud, racketeering, bribery/conflict of interest, embezzlement— blacks are incarcerated at three to five times the white rate, and Hispanics at about twice the white rate.[478]

- It is sobering to visit the websites for the FBI and various state police agencies and look at the photographs of the "most wanted" criminals. There is a huge preponderance of blacks and Hispanics, and sometimes not a single picture of a white criminal.[479]

- Small towns south of Los Angeles, such as South Gate, Lynwood, Bell Gardens, Maywood, Huntington Park, and Vernon were once white suburbs but have become largely Hispanic. They have also become notorious for thieving, bribe-taking politicians. Mayors, city council members, and treasurers have paraded off to jail.[480]

- The United States is now a nation that can produce headlines such as these: Baby Dies in Bucket of Mom's Vomit; 99-Year-Old Woman Among Rapist's Victims; Mom Allegedly Microwaves Baby; Town Stunned As 8-Year-Old Charged in Two Killings; Woman Accused of Using Infant as Car Down Payment; L.A. Police Say Killing of 3-Year-Old in Gang Attack Was Intentional; North Dade Baby Shower Turns Deadly as Gunfight

---

[477] Ibid., 179.
[478] Ibid., 181 – 182.

[479] Ibid., 184.
[480] Ibid., 186.

Breaks Out; Mother, Daughter and Granddaughter Teamed Up for Attack; Boston Police Say 7-Year-Old Shot 8-Year-Old Dead; Florida Woman Starves Children and Throws Dead Baby into Garbage Can; Parents Fight Over Which Gang Toddler Should Join; Mayhem Erupts Throughout City After Appeal to End Violence.

The people in these stories are about evenly split between blacks and Hispanics. As America's population changes, headlines like these will become more common.[481]

His point is not subtle: the differences between the white race and other races amount to differences between what is good and what is bad, what is superior and what is inferior. No one could possibly think that he is not projecting some sort of negative judgment on non-white people when he paints such a vivid picture of crime, violence, corruption, moral decay, and an "otherness" that is building to a "crisis" for white people. Indeed, one of his explicit goals is to "awaken" white people to racial consciousness so that they can actively fight against such dire trends as those he points out.

- All other groups take it for granted that they have a right to speak out in their own interests. Only whites have lost this conviction.[482]

- If whites permit themselves to become a minority population, they will lose their civilization, their heritage, and even their existence as a distinct people.[483]

- The number of Hispanics is growing very quickly in this country, and Hispanics are ecstatic about this. It means their language,

their culture, their physical type, their heritage, their aspirations are all gaining ground and could eventually dominate the United States. Hispanics want this very much, and they consistently try to change laws and policies to increase their numbers, and benefit their people. This is considered a sign of healthy collective pride.

- But if whites tried to delay their dispossession, if whites proposed steps to maintain their majority status, that would be hate and bigotry. Why? The processes are perfectly symmetrical. The percentage of Hispanics increases as the percentage of whites decreases. Why is it right for Hispanics to celebrate their gains but wrong for whites to regret their losses?

- I make no secret of my view on this. My ancestors have been white for tens of thousands of years. My children are white and I want my grandchildren to be white. I like the culture of Europe, I prefer the society that whites create. What's wrong with that?[484]

- At what point would it be legitimate for whites to act in their own group interests? When they become a minority? When they are no more than 30 percent of the population? Ten percent? Or must they never be allowed to take any action to ensure that the land in which they live reflects their values, their culture, their manners, their traditions, and honors the achievements of their ancestors? If whites do not cherish and defend these things, no one else will do it for them. If whites do not rekindle some sense of their collective interests they will be pushed

[481] Ibid., 200.

[482] https://www.amren.com/about/issues/

[483] https://www.amren.com/about/issues/

[484] https://www.amren.com/features/2015/04/white-survival-beyond-left-and-right/

aside by people who have a very clear sense of their interests. Eventually, whites will come to understand that to dismantle and even demonize white racial consciousness while other races cultivate racial consciousness is a fatal form of unilateral disarmament.

- For their very survival as a distinct people with a distinct culture, whites must recognize something all others take for granted: that race is a fundamental part of individual and group identity. Any society based on the assumption that race can be wished or legislated away ensures for itself an endless agony of pretense, conflict, and failure. For 60 years, we have wished and legislated in vain. In so doing, by opening the United States to peoples from every corner of the world, we have created agonizing problems for future generations. As surely as the Communists were mistaken in their hopes of remaking human nature, so have been the proponents of diversity and multi-culturalism.[485]

Given the "crisis" and "agonizing problems" produced by multiculturalism and growing populations of non-white people, Taylor advocates a variety of specific political policies in response:

- End immigration ("it is not in the interests of whites to be displaced by others.")
- Recognize that "when whites prefer to live, work, and go to school with people of their own race that it is no different from anyone else wanting to do these things. Whites—and others—should have legal means to preserve local majorities if that is their preference." This, presumably, amounts to a demand for the reintroduction of legal segregation on the basis of race as well as the right to discriminate on the basis of race, in housing, the workplace, and education – in other words, the undoing of the Civil Rights Movement of the 1960s.
- "End the current propaganda about the advantages of diversity, for it only justifies [white] dispossession."[486]

In addition, while he does not appear to advocate for any laws specifically forbidding "miscegenation," he does describe it as the means by which to eliminate "whites." Indeed, interracial relationships (that include white people) are sometimes literally described as "white genocide."

[485] Taylor, 205.   [486] Ibid., 205.

For most of American history, miscegenation was the ultimate nightmare for whites. . . . Of course, widespread miscegenation would not eliminate race; it would eliminate whites. Whites are no more than 17 percent of the world's population and are having perhaps seven percent of the world's children. No one is proposing large-scale intermarriage for Africa or Asia. Nor would mixing eliminate discrimination. Blacks, South Americans, and Asians discriminate among themselves on the basis of skin tone even when they are the same race. . . . The revolution in thinking among today's whites leaves no grounds to argue against their own displacement through immigration or disappearance through intermarriage. . . . All non-whites celebrate their growing numbers and influence—just as whites once did. Whites—not only in America but around the world —cheerfully contemplate their disappearance as a distinct people.[487]

While the intensity and tone of someone like Taylor (and his sympathizers) might be "elevated," the basic themes and concerns have penetrated to mainstream media coverage. In 2018, *National Geographic* dedicated an entire issue to matters of race (calling it literally "The Race Issue"). One of their articles was entitled "As America Changes, Some Anxious Whites Feel Left Behind."[488]

While always a part of American politics, race seemed to have an enhanced prominence in the 2016 presidential election. "The biggest difference between the two parties is the urban-rural divide. That gap widened. Politically, that translates into race and identity as the main political dividing line. Rural and exurban America is very white, and generally inward-looking. Urban America is very diverse and cosmopolitan. . . . In 1992, a majority of the voters in both parties were white Christian. Today, the GOP has essentially become a party of white Christians, while Democrats rely on a coalition of religiously, racially and ethnically diverse voters."[489]

---

[487] Ibid., 151 – 165.
[488] https://www.nationalgeographic.com/ magazine/2018/04/race-rising-anxiety-white-america/

[489] https://www.nbcnews.com/politics/ white-house/how-2016-election-exposed-america-s-racial-cultural-divides-n682306

Clearly, the phenomenon of white nationalism raises many issues, including epistemological, moral, and political. The policies advocated by white nationalists such as Spencer and Taylor are, quite frankly, frightening. These policies, however, do not emerge from a vacuum. Instead, they emerge from a worldview that presupposes certain key premises. Among these are "race realism," the dependency relationship between race and culture, and the critique of certain cultures/races in terms of degeneration and superiority/inferiority.

I will first demonstrate the philosophical foundations of their movement as it is found in the writings of Hitler.[490] Then, in the remainder of the chapter, I will attempt to demonstrate that the white nationalist worldview rests upon a very shaky foundation. I will do this primarily by demonstrating that their understanding of race (and Hitler's as well) is simply misinformed. I will also attempt to demonstrate that the appreciation for Nietzsche shared by both the Nazis and contemporary white nationalists is equally misinformed.

Hitler

Adolf Hitler (20 April 1889 – 30 April 1945) was an Austrian-born German politician and the leader of the National Socialist German Workers Party (Nazi party). He was the totalitarian leader of Germany from 1933 to 1945. He gained popular support by promoting German nationalism, anti-Semitism, anti-capitalism, and anti-communism. Under his rule, Nazi forces engaged in the systematic murder of as many as 17 million civilians, an estimated six million of whom were Jews.

There should have been nothing surprising about the policies Hitler pursued once he acquired power. He had made no secret of his values, beliefs, and ambitions – detailing them a decade prior to taking power in his lengthy book, *Mein Kampf* ("my struggle"). In that work, he details his understanding of race, culture, and the proper role and purpose of the state.

Hitler (like many from his time, and even today) believed that "race" was real. The current name for this is "race realism." He states that, among the most "patent principles of Nature's rule" is "the inner segregation of the species of all living beings on this earth."[491] Moreover, in addition to being real, race is relevant—indeed, it is the *most* relevant aspect of a person. As you presumably already know, Hitler also believed that the various races of humanity were not equal. At the apex of humanity (according to Hitler) is the Aryan race.

> Everything we admire on this earth today – science and art, technology and inventions – is only the creative product of a few peoples and originally perhaps of one race. On them depends the existence of this whole culture. If they perish, the beauty of this earth will sink into the grave with them.

> All the human culture, all the results of art, science, and technology that we see

---

[490] To be clear, I'm not claiming that there is a direct link between the writings of Hitler and the ideas of Richard Spencer and Jared Taylor specifically, as though they sat down one day, read "*Mein Kampf*" and then developed their worldviews in direct response. It is entirely possible that independent ideas informed both Hitler and contemporary white nationalists. Do not think of this section as intellectual biography. But what I think can be demonstrated, however, is the similarity and overlap of ideas.

[491] *Mein Kampf*, volume 1, chapter XI: nation and race. All references from this section of the chapter are from this book, unless otherwise indicated. Note that I make extensive use of quotation in this chapter, rather than supplying a larger block of text from the original source at the end of the chapter, as I do in other chapters. This is on purpose. I have no intention of pursuing copyright permissions from whoever might have the rights to that work.

before us today, are almost exclusively the creative product of the Aryan. This very fact admits of the not unfounded inference that he alone was the founder of all higher humanity, therefore representing the prototype of all that we understand by the word 'man.' ... Exclude him – and perhaps after a few thousand years darkness will again ascend on the earth, human culture will pass, and the world turned to a desert.[492]

With his assumptions of the existence of distinct races, and a natural hierarchy among those races, he vehemently opposed any sort of "race-mixing."

Any crossing of two beings not exactly the same level produces a medium between the level of the two parents. This means: the offspring will probably stand higher than the racially lower parent, but not as high as the higher one. Consequently, it will later succumb in the struggle against the higher level. Such mating is contrary to the will of Nature for a higher breeding of all life. The precondition for this does not lie in associating superior and inferior, but in a total victory of the former. The stronger must dominate not blend with the weaker, thus sacrificing his own greatness. Only the born weakling condemn this as cruel, but he after all is only a weak and limited man; for if this law did not prevail, any conceivable higher development of organic living beings would be unthinkable.[493]

He not only proposed keeping the races "pure" by avoiding race mixture, but an active and deliberate "breeding program" was an essential element of his political program, as we will see in

a later section. For Hitler, race and politics are and *must* be connected. Indeed, he claimed that race was the very foundation of the (proper) state!

If we try to penetrate to the inner meaning of the word *völkisch* we arrive at the following conclusions: the current political conception of the world is that the State, though it possesses a creative force which can build up civilizations, has nothing in common with the concept of race as the foundation of the State. The State is considered rather as something which has resulted from economic necessity, or, at best, the natural outcome of the play of political forces and impulses. Such a conception of the foundations of the State, together with all its logical consequences, not only ignores the primordial racial forces that underlie the State, but it also leads to a policy in which the importance of the individual is minimized. If it be denied that races differ from one another in their powers of cultural creativeness, then the same erroneous notion must necessarily influence our estimation of the value of the individual. The assumption that all races are alike leads to the assumption that nations and individuals are equal to one another.[494]

In contrast to his race-based concept of the State, he distinguishes several other (flawed and misguided) variants.

Those who hold that the State is a more or less voluntary association of men who have agreed to set up and obey a ruling authority.[495]

---

[492] Ibid.
[493] Ibid.

[494] Volume 2, Chapter I: Philosophy and Party.
[495] Ibid.

This is a generic "social contract" model of the State—the very type considered in several other chapters of this book, and promoted by political theorists such as Hobbes, Locke, Rousseau, and Rawls, among others.

> Those who hold that "the State exists to promote the good of its subjects....Moreover, in this view the first duty laid upon the State is to guarantee the economic well-being of the individual citizens.[496]

This second category is even more general than his depiction of the social contract tradition. It could include anything from utilitarian justifications of the State, to more communitarian models such as Aristotle's *Polis*, and others. It seems that the States in this category have in common that they are thought to exist to promote the "good" of those subject to them, and Hitler assumes that some sort of economic good is the foremost good to be pursued.

Hitler thinks both these models are getting it wrong. The "correct" justification for the State is "a means for the realization of tendencies that arise from a policy of power, on the part of a people who are ethnically homogenous and speak the same language."[497]

In contemporary alt-Right vocabulary, he is promoting the idea of an "ethno-state." An ethno-state is simply a political entity populated by, and run in the interest of, a particular ethnic group. For contemporary white nationalists like Richard Spencer and Jared Taylor, the ethno-state they long for is a "white Eurocentric" ethno-state. For Hitler, it was a State by and for the German "volk."

> The State is only a means to an end. Its end and its purpose is to preserve and promote a community of human beings who are physically as well as spiritually kindred. Above all, it must preserve the existence of the race, thereby providing the indispensable condition for the free development of all the forces dormant in this race. A great part of these faculties will always have to be employed in the first place to maintain the physical existence of the race, and only a small portion will be free to work in the field of intellectual progress. But, as a matter of fact, the one is always the necessary counterpart to the other.
>
> Those States which do not serve this purpose have no justification for their existence. They are monstrosities. The fact they do exist is no more of a justification than the successful raids carried out by band of pirates can be considered a justification of piracy....
>
> The State is only the vessel and the race is what it contains. The vessel can have a meaning only if it preserves and safeguards the contents. Otherwise it is worthless.
>
> Hence the supreme purpose of the folkish State is to guard and preserve those original racial elements which, through their work in the cultural field, create that beauty and dignity which are characteristics of a higher mankind. We, as Aryans, can consider the State only as a living organism of a people, an organism which does not merely maintain the existence of a people, but functions in such a way as to lead people to a position of supreme liberty by the progressive development of the intellectual and cultural faculties.[498]

This "volkstadt" is not identical to a culture, and he insisted that the two notions not be confused. The point (for Hitler) is not to have

---

[496] Ibid.
[497] Ibid.

[498] Ibid.

"people" speaking German, listening to Wagner, dancing polkas, and eating schnitzel. Not just any "people" will do, and the fact that non-German people might adopt and emulate German cultural traditions signified nothing.

> What they mostly meant by Germanization was a process of forcing other people to speak the German language. But it is almost inconceivable how such a mistake could be made as to think that a Negro or Chinaman will become a German because he has learned the German language and is willing to speak German for the future, and even to cast his vote for a German political party. Our bourgeois nationalists could never clearly see that such a process of Germanization is in reality de-Germanization; for even if all the outstanding and visible differences between the various peoples could be bridged over and finally wiped out by the use of a common language, that would produce a process of bastardization which in this case would not signify Germanization but the annihilation of the German element. In the course of history does happen only too often that a conquering race succeeded by external force in compelling the people whom they subjected to speak the tongue of the conqueror and that after 1000 years their language was spoken by another people and thus the conqueror finally turned out to be the conquered.

> What makes a people, to be more correct, a race, is not language but blood. Therefore it would be justifiable to speak of Germanization only if that process could change the blood of the people who would be subjected to it, which is obviously impossible. A change would be possible only by a mixture of blood, but in

this case the quality of the superior race would be debased. The final result of such a mixture would be that precisely those qualities would be destroyed which had enabled the conquering race to achieve victory over and inferior people. It is especially the cultural creativeness which disappears when the superior race center mixes with an inferior one, even though the resultant mongrel race should excel a thousandfold in speaking the language of the race that once had been superior."

> A profound truth is that the capacity for creating cultural values is essentially based on the racial element and that, in accordance with this fact, the paramount purpose of the State is to preserve and improve the race; for this is an indispensable condition of all progress in human civilization.[499]

Every aspect of the State will be governed by an appeal to race, its promotion, and its preservation. This is nowhere as obvious as in Hitler's views on public education.

> If we consider it the first duty of the State to serve and promote the general welfare of the people, by preserving and encouraging the development of the best racial elements, the logical consequences of this task not be limited to measures concerning the birth of the infant members of the race and nation but that the State will also have to adopt educational means for making each citizen a worthy factor in the further propagation of the racial stock.

> Just as, in general, the racial quality is the preliminary condition for the mental efficiency of any given human material, the training of the individual will first of all have to be directed towards the

---

[499] Ibid.

development of sound bodily health. For the general rule is that a strong and healthy mind is found only in a strong and healthy body. The fact that men of genius or sometimes not robust in health and stature, or even a basically healthy constitution, is no proof against the principle I have enunciated. These cases are only exceptions which, as everywhere else, prove the rule. But when the bulk of a nation is composed of physical degenerates it is rare for a great spirit to arise from such a miserable motley. ...

The State that is grounded on the racial principle and is alive to the significance of this truth will first of all have to base its educational work not on the mere imparting of knowledge but rather on physical training and development of healthy bodies. The cultivation of the intellectual facilities comes only in the second place. And here again is character which has to be developed first of all, strength of will and decision. And the educational system ought to foster the spirit of readiness to accept responsibilities gladly. Formal instruction in the sciences must be considered last in importance. Accordingly the State which is grounded on the racial idea must start with the principle that a person whose formal education in the sciences is relatively small but was physically sound and robust, of a steadfast and honest character, ready and able to make decisions and endowed with strength of will, is a more useful member of the national community than a weakling who was scholarly and refined. A nation composed of learned men who are physical weaklings, hesitant about decisions of the will, and timid pacifists, is not capable of assuring even its own

existence on this earth. In the bitter struggle which decides the destiny of man it is very rare that an individual has succumbed because he lacked learning. Those who fail are they who try to ignore these consequences and are too fainthearted about putting them into effect. There must be a certain balance between mind and body. An ill-kept body is not made a more beautiful sight by the indwelling of a radiant spirit. We should not be acting justly if we were to bestow the highest intellectual training on those who are physically deformed and crippled, who lack decision and are weak willed and cowardly. What has made the Greek ideal of beauty immortal is the wonderful union of a splendid physical beauty with nobility of mind and spirit.[500]

Note the heightened emphasis on physical fitness, and the proposed reduction in the curriculum of science. Formal instruction in the sciences "must be considered last in importance." This is far removed from our contemporary emphasis on STEM (Science, Technology, Engineering, and Math) training, and the trend of reducing or even eliminating physical education requirements.

Under Hitler's vision, "character" is developed "first of all," and he states this in terms of strength of will.

Loyalty, self-sacrifice and discretion are virtues which a great nation must possess. And the teaching and development of these in the school is a more important matter than many other things now included in the curriculum. To make the children give up habits of complaining and whining and howling when they are hurt, etc., also belongs to this part of the training. If the educational system fails to teach the child at an early age to endure pain and injury without

---

[500] Ibid.

complaining we cannot be surprised if at a later age, when the boy has grown to be the man and is, for example, in the trenches, the Postal Service is used for nothing else than to send home letters of weeping and complaint. If our youths, during their years in the primary schools, had had their minds crammed with a little less knowledge, and if instead they had been better taught how to be masters of themselves, it would have served us well during the years 1914 – 1918.[501]

Character training occurs in the context of physical training, including mandatory boxing and rigorous fitness training. This increased emphasis on physical training comes at the expense of more traditional academic subjects—all of which will be instituted and run by the State.

The formal imparting of knowledge, which constitutes the chief work of our educational system today, will be taken over by the People's State with only few modifications. These modifications must be made in three branches.

First of all, the brains of the young people must not generally be burdened with subjects of which 95% are useless to them and are therefore forgotten again. The curriculum of the primary and secondary schools presents an odd mixture at the present time. In many branches of study the subject matter to be learned has become so enormous that only a very small fraction of it can be remembered later on, and indeed only a very small fraction of this whole mass of knowledge can be used. On the other hand, what is learned is insufficient for anybody who wishes to specialize in any certain branch for the purpose of earning his daily bread. Take, for example, the average civil

servant who is passed through the Gymnasium or High School, and ask them at the age of 30 or 40 how much he has retained the knowledge that was crammed into him with so much pains. . . .[502]

All along, the central focus of this new education program is race.

The whole organization of education and training which the People's State is to build up must take as its crowning task the work of instilling into the hearts and brains of the youth entrusted to it the racial instinct and understanding of the racial idea. No boy or girl must leave school without having obtained a clear insight into the meaning of racial purity and the importance of maintaining the racial blood unadulterated. Thus the first indispensable condition for the preservation of our race will have been established and thus the future cultural progress of our people will be assured."[503]

Even with regard to particular subjects, such as history, race takes center stage.

It is the business of the People's State to arrange for the writing of a world history in which the race problem will occupy a dominant position.[504]

The training of boys does not end once they complete their primary education. He also envisions mandatory military service for all boys, unless they are physically unfit to serve. Already physically fit and "strong in character" from their school days, their training could focus specifically on military skills and matters. After a man

[501] Ibid.
[502] Ibid.
[503] Ibid.
[504] Ibid.

completes military training, will be given two certifications:

1. Diploma of citizenship, permitting participation in public affairs.
2. Certification of fitness for marriage (based on physical health)

Note the significance of this: in order to be "certified" to participate in politics, and even to marry and have children, a man must have served in the military to the satisfaction of the State. As for girls, "in the education of the girl the final goal always to be kept in mind is that she is one day to be a mother."[505]

One final core principle governing Hitler's ideal State (for the purposes of our focus) is found in the lengthy quotation below (and worth quoting at length, with emphasis added). You might find it hauntingly familiar, if you have read previous chapters of this book.

> It will be the task of the People's State so to organize and administer its educational system that the existing intellectual class will be constantly furnished with supply of fresh blood from beneath. From the bulk of the nation the State must sift out with careful scrutiny those persons who are endowed with natural talents and see that they are employed in the service of the community. For neither the State itself nor the various departments of State exist to furnish revenues for members of a special class, but to fulfill the tasks allotted to them. This will be possible, however, only if the State trains individuals specially for these offices. Such individuals must have the necessary fundamental capabilities and willpower. The principal does not hold true only in regard to the civil service but also in regard to all those who are to take part in

the intellectual and moral leadership of the people, no matter in what sphere they may be employed. The greatness of a people is partly dependent on the condition that it must succeed in training the best brains for those branches of the public service for which they show a special natural aptitude and in placing them in the offices where they can do their best work for the good of the community. If two nations of equal strength and quality engage in a mutual conflict that nation will come up us which has entrusted its intellectual and moral leadership to its best talents and that nation will go under whose government represents only a common food trough for privilege groups or classes and where the inner talents of its individual members are not availed of.

> Of course such a reform seems impossible in the world as it is today. The objection will at once be raised that it is too much to expect from the favorite son of a highly placed civil servant, for instance, the he shall work with his hands simply because somebody else whose parents belong to the working class seems more capable for a job in the civil service. That argument may be valid as long as manual work is looked upon in the same way as it is looked upon today. Hence the People's State will have to take up an attitude towards the appreciation of manual labor which will be fundamentally different from that which now exists. If necessary, it will have to organize a persistent system of teaching which will aim at abolishing the present day stupid habit of looking down on physical labor as an occupation to be ashamed of.

> The individual will have to be valued, not by the class of work he does but by the

---

[505] Ibid.

way in which he does it and by its usefulness to the community.... On the ideal or abstract plans all workmen become equal the moment each strives to do his best in his own field, no matter what that field may be. It is on this that a man's value must be estimated, and not on the amount of recompense received.

In a reasonably directed State care must be taken that each individual is given the kind of work which corresponds to his capabilities. In other words, people will be trained for the positions indicated by their natural endowments: but these endowments are faculties are innate and cannot be acquired by any amount of training, being a gift from Nature and not merited by men. Therefore, the way in which men are generally esteemed by their fellow citizens must not be according to the kind of work they do, because that has been more or less assigned to the individual. Seeing that the kind of work in which the individual is employed is to be accounted to his inborn gifts and resultant training which has received from the community, it will have to be judged by the way in which he performs this work entrusted to him by the community. For the work which the individual performs is not the purpose of his existence, but only a means. His real purpose in life is to better himself and raise himself to a higher level as a human being; but this he can only do in and through the community whose cultural life he shares. And this community must always exist on the foundations on which the State is based. He ought to contribute to the conservation of those foundations. Nature determines the form of this contribution. It is the duty of the individual to return to the community, zealously and honestly, what the

community has given him. He who does this deserves the highest respect and esteem....

The present epoch is working out its own ruin. It introduces universal suffrage, chatters about equal rights but can find no foundation for this equality. It considers the material wage as the expression of a man's value and thus destroys the basis of the noblest kind of equality that can exist. For equality cannot and does not depend on the work a man does, but only on the manner in which each one does the particular work allotted to him. Thus alone will mere natural chance be set aside in determining the work of a man and thus only does the individual become the artificer of his own social worth.[506]

One basic theme here is that the community takes priority over the individual. Another is that individuals are "naturally" suited to fulfill different functions within a community, and the community is best served if persons fulfill the role for which they are best suited—even if their personal preference would be to do something else. Moreover, there is honor to be found in any occupation/role, so long as one performs at his or her best, in service to the community.

Sound familiar? If not, reread the Plato chapter in this book, especially the section on the Principle of Specialization!

This is a "totalitarian" vision, no doubt, but, in a gesture that makes me admittedly uncomfortable, I want to highlight an idea from Hitler that is not in any obvious way evil or horrifying: valuing honest labor, of any kind, and not being "elitist" about certain kinds of work. In his proposed system, horrifying though it would be in other respects, one goal is to change cultural norms so that "blue collar" jobs, including manual labor, are no longer looked down upon as somehow inferior, degrading, worthy only of

---

[506] Ibid. Underlining added for emphasis.

"stupid" people, etc. Another goal is the simultaneous dismantling of the prestige that comes merely from occupying a conventionally "respected" role such as scientist, doctor, lawyer, etc. People will be esteemed based on how hard and capably they work, regardless of the particular kind of work. In theory, someone who works hard and well at mowing lawns would be just as esteemed as a similarly hard working lawyer, and *more* esteemed than a lawyer who "phones it in."

Not to overdo the comparison, but Hitler's similarity to Plato does not end with the Principle of Specialization. They also share in common a rejection of democracy.

> Hence the People's State must mercilessly expurgate from all the leading circles in the government of the country the parliamentarian principle, according to which decisive power through the majority vote is invested in the multitude. . . . There are no decisions made by the majority vote, but only by responsible persons. And the word 'council' is once more restored to its original meaning. Every man in a position of responsibility will have councillors at his side, but the decision is made by that individual person alone. . . . No vote will be taken in the chambers or Senate. They are to be organizations for work and not voting machines. The individual members will have consultive votes but no right of decision will be attached thereto. The right of decision belongs exclusively to the president, who must be entirely responsible for the matter under discussion.[507]

In summary, Hitler advances a political philosophy that rejects democracy in favor of the totalitarian rule of a "charismatic" individual. He advocates significant educational and social reform, and all of this for the sake of the only

legitimate purpose of the State (in his estimation): the preservation and promotion of the ("Master") race.

Obviously, a key premise for any ideology promoting racial supremacy, whether Hitler's or that of contemporary white nationalism, is the existence of race itself. Indeed, as stated, for Hitler, the preservation and promotion of race was the fundamental purpose of the State. Moreover, not just any concept of race will do. Within these ideologies, race has to do quite a lot of "work." It has to be something that is biologically real, and transmitted across generations through reproduction. Otherwise, Hitler's obsession with eugenics and racial purity, and contemporary white nationalists' anxiety about "white genocide," makes little sense. Race has to be something that is not identical to culture; race and ethnicity must signify fundamentally different things. Moreover, race has to not only be an aspect of one's identity, but an *essential* aspect. That is, one's race must be not only something "real," but among the most important elements of who you are – if not *the* most important element. As it turns out, however, "race" isn't so simple and "genetic" as racial supremacists might believe.

Race?

If someone were to ask you your race, the answer probably comes to your mind instantly. "White" (or Caucasian). "Black" (or perhaps African-American). Latino. Chicano. Hispanic. Asian. Chinese. Indian. Native American. Mixed....

We think and speak as though these terms are fixed and clear, when that is, in fact, far from the case. We will begin by considering some important vocabulary, both as they are commonly used, as well as in more philosophically "precise" terms. We will also consider a variety of perspectives, for the sake of balance.

Let us begin, then, with the "everyday" meanings of race and ethnicity. In common usage,

---

[507] Ibid.

these are often muddled, or treated as though interchangeable. Indeed, we can try to dodge our own confusion as to the exact meaning of those terms by the use of the combined term "race/ethnicity!"

Although interpretations vary, for our purposes we will say that "race," as the term is *commonly* used, refers to a biological type of human being (e.g., the "white race," the "black race," etc.). Whereas ethnicity refers to learned cultural behaviors that are often *associated* with a certain ancestry and physical appearance.

Race has been presumed to be biologically transmitted, whereas ethnicity is thought to be culturally transmitted. In use, both "Irish" and "Scottish" people might be considered members of the "white race," though of different ancestry and cultural heritage. Similarly, in common usage, anyone with a Spanish surname and descended from a Spanish-speaking people might be considered ethnically Hispanic, including Spaniards—though Spaniards would not be "Latinos," since they don't come from "Latin America." To further complicate matters, there is also the consideration of nationality, since Hispanic/Latino people from Mexico are distinct from those hailing from El Salvador.

Rather than trying to parse the nuances of various ethnic distinctions, I would like to address a more foundational (and possibly more controversial) issue: the nature of race itself. Although the view I'm about to present has become increasingly accepted, especially among biologists, anthropologists, and sociologists, it might nevertheless come as a surprise to some of you: "race," as a biological concept, is a *fiction*—a "*social construct*" created and perpetuated in cultures but not existing in nature. The evidence for this "socially constructed" interpretation of race is both ample, and, I think, compelling. Let's begin with some history.

The history of the meaning of "race" reveals just how mercurial the concept has been. In ancient Greece and Rome, race referred to group membership in terms of one's ancestral place and culture. The Greeks, for example, were a "race." The Greeks recognized physical differences amongst people (e.g., the darker skin of Africans, the lighter skin of Northern Europeans, etc.), but did not presume superiority or inferiority on such bases (though they did regard their own *culture* (Greece) as superior!).

In the Middle Ages, race referred more to one's "lineage," as in personal family ancestry, or a people of common origin and history. For example, there was the Anglo-Saxon "race" (i.e., "Germanic" people who came to inhabit what is now England and Wales), the Norman "race" (i.e., the descendants of Viking raiders who populated the region of Normandy in what is now France), and the Teutons (i.e., descendants of "Germanic" tribes).

When European powers turned to conquest, colonization, and slavery, racial thinking began to develop as a rationale for these actions—though race was *still* not a biological concept. As of the 17th century, race referred more to a culture or civilization in a particular area. The French, for example, would have been considered a "race."

The 18th century saw race in terms of religious and cultural divisions. Throughout these centuries, for example, Native Americans and Africans were regarded first as "heathens" (and therefore "inferior"—but because they weren't Christians, not because of their biology). Then, they became "savages" (and therefore "inferior," but because they were "uncivilized," not because of their biology).

With the spread of slavery, neither religion nor culture was sufficient to justify differential treatment, since both could be overcome by conversion or education. An educated, Christian African would no longer be a "heathen" or a "savage." What could justify his continued enslavement? To remain viable, differential treatment (including enslavement) had to be founded on something permanent and unchangeable.

The focus on Africans for the slave population was practical, rather than rooted in racial ideology (at least initially). Of the various groups of people who had been used for cheap (or slave) labor in the "New World," Africans proved most suitable. Poor Europeans were insufficient in number, and could easily blend in with the population of free persons if they escaped slavery. Native Americans could escape and seek refuge with other (free) tribes, and were vulnerable to European diseases anyway. Africans, in contrast, were easily identifiable thanks to their skin color, stood out amongst European settlers, were accustomed to the heat prevalent in the Southern American colonies and Caribbean (unlike European workers, for example), had no local groups to which they could escape (unlike Native Americans), and were generally unfamiliar with the territory.

Africans would need to be classified as a distinct (and "inferior") race to justify their enslavement, and to allow the pretense of consistency when the United States of America emerged from the Declaration of Independence and the Constitutional Convention. The highest legal authority in the United States shamefully sealed the status of "Blacks" in the *Dred Scott v. Sandford* of 1857.

> . . . It is difficult at this day to realize the state of public opinion in relation to that unfortunate race which prevailed in the civilized and enlightened portions of the world at the time of the Declaration of Independence and when the Constitution of the United States was framed and adopted. But the public history of every European nation displays it in a manner too plain to be mistaken.

> They had for more than a century before been regarded as beings of an inferior order, and altogether unfit to associate with the white race either in social or political relations, and so far inferior that they had no rights which the white man was bound to respect, and that the negro might justly and lawfully be reduced to slavery for his benefit. He was bought and

sold, and treated as an ordinary article of merchandise and traffic whenever a profit could be made by it. This opinion was at that time fixed and universal in the civilized portion of the white race. It was regarded as an axiom in morals as well as in politics which no one thought of disputing or supposed to be open to dispute, and men in every grade and position in society daily and habitually acted upon it in their private pursuits, as well as in matters of public concern, without doubting for a moment the correctness of this opinion.[508]

Note that while the ruling ostensibly applies only to slaves and their descendants, the rationale for the ruling refers to the "unfortunate race" (i.e., "Blacks") who are "so far inferior that they had no rights which the white man was bound to respect."

The Dred Scott case not only established that escaped slaves had no rights of citizens, but that the very "race" of people of whom those slaves belong are inherently inferior and without any rights at all! This was not the last time the Supreme Court validated unmistakably racist ideas, nor even the last time the Supreme Court helped to define race itself, as we shall see a little later in this section.

By the late 18th and early 19th centuries, race had emerged as a biological concept, alongside the development of modern biological science and classification methods. Linnaeus (1701-1778) was the founder of modern taxonomy, and applied his thinking to humans as well as other animals. He identified four distinct kinds of humans, and believed them to have been created distinctly/differently by God: Asiaticus, Europaeus, Africanus, and Americanus. These four groups were "natural kinds" by which all actual humans could be sorted and understood.

---

[508] *Dred Scott v. Sandford.* Full text available here: http://teachingamericanhistory.org/library/document/dred-scott-v-sandford/

Despite the obvious ability to interbreed with members of the other "kinds," Linnaeus thought of these kinds as "species-like"—implying natural, permanent, and important differences between them. His typological descriptions of each included not only physical traits, but mental and personality traits as well. According to his stereotypes, Asiaticus is ruled by emotion and ritual, whereas Europaeus is ruled by laws and intelligence; Americanus is ruled by custom and superstition, whereas Africanus is ruled by caprice and whim. Conveniently enough, it was his *own* "kind" that was governed by reason and law, whereas all other "races" were naturally governed by mere opinion and whatever passing fancy caught their attention.

An alternative to Linnaeus developed even in his own time. Louis Leclerc developed a classification system that didn't claim inherent (and inherited) natural differences, but instead focused on different cultural conditions. "Those marks which distinguish men who inhabit different regions of the Earth are not original, but purely superficial."[509]

Linnaeus' approach prevailed, though, and its legacy included a biological basis for race, assuming significant and immutable differences, as well as the confusion of cultural factors for innate (biological) factors to account for differences in communities.

By the mid-19th century, race was firmly accepted in terms of biological groupings of human beings (e.g., "Negroid," "Caucasoid," "Mongoloid") who shared inherited physical, mental, and moral traits that are different from those of other races.

It can't be overlooked that race, as a biological concept, was developed by American scientists during the periods of both slavery and segregation, and was instrumental in the justification of both practices. Racial classification made a big difference in one's legal status in the United States. In 1790, Congress'

first act was to restrict naturalized citizenship to "free white persons" only. Blacks were included in 1870 (after the Civil War, of course), but East Asians and Filipinos had to wait until 1952! Considerations of the naturalness and immutability of race found also their way into interpretations of law, as the Supreme Court once again offered its "enlightened" opinions on the issue.

Takao Ozawa was born in Japan in 1875, but moved to California in 1894, where he attended UC Berkeley. He moved to what was then the "territory" of Hawaii, and applied for naturalization in 1914. The U.S. District Attorney of Hawaii opposed his application on the grounds that Ozawa was of the Japanese race, and therefore not a white person. Ozawa fought this judgment for eight years, with his case ultimately reaching the Supreme Court. Among several arguments he offered, one was literal: his skin color was "white."

Although he was of Japanese ancestry, his skin color was literally the same pinkish color as that of "white" people. Therefore, he was a white person. The Court rejected his logic.

> Manifestly, the test [of race] afforded by the mere color of the skin of each individual is impracticable as that differs greatly among persons of the same race, even among Anglo-Saxons, ranging by imperceptible gradations from the fair blond to the swarthy brunette, the latter being darker than many of the lighter hued persons of the brown or yellow races.[510]

Here, the Court accepts and asserts that skin color does *not* reliably correlate with racial identity. However, rather than rejecting racial classification in biological terms, the "experts," anthropologists, and scientists of the time resorted to continually shifting standards to

---

[509] Audrey Smedly, *Race in North America: Origin and Evolution of a Worldview*. 2nd ed. 1993. p.165.

[510] *Ozawa v. United States.*

maintain their racial groupings. So would the Court.

Rejecting Ozawa's claim based on skin color, the Court ruled that "the words 'white person' are synonymous with the words 'a person of the Caucasian race.'" However, just three months later, the Court rejected its very own equivalence of "white" and "Caucasian" in *United States v. Thind*.

Bhagat Singh Thind came to the United States from India on July 4th, 1913. Importantly, anthropologists of that era had classified Asian Indians as "Caucasians" rather than "Mongolians." Thind seized on this and applied for naturalization on the grounds that he was Caucasian, and therefore a "white person."

The Ninth Circuit Court of Appeals asked, "Is a high caste Hindu of full Indian blood, born at Amrit Sar, Punjab, India, a white person?" Note already the conflation of religion (Hindu) with "race," the assumption that "race" is something carried by blood, and even that something like place of birth is somehow relevant to whether someone is "white."

The Court accepted that Thind was Caucasian. "It may be true that the blond Scandinavian and the brown Hindu have a common ancestor in the dim reaches of antiquity, but the average man knows perfectly well that there are unmistakable and profound differences between them today." The Court then argued that the word "Caucasian" is "at best a conventional term." "What we now hold is that the words 'free white persons' are words of common speech, to be interpreted in accordance with the understanding of the common man, synonymous with the word 'Caucasian' only as that word is popularly understood."

In *Ozawa*, the Court rejected literal "whiteness" in the sense of pinkish skin, in favor of a "scientific" classification, in order to exclude a person of Japanese ancestry from being considered "white." In *Thind*, just three months later, the *same Court* abandoned "science" altogether, appealing to the "understanding of the common man" to exclude someone from India from being considered "white."

The mental gymnastics performed by the Justices to preserve racial preferences is breathtaking, but we can't ignore the fact that these decisions had profound life-impacting results. Neither East Asians nor Asian Indians, nor, indeed, anyone who wasn't "white"—as understood by the "common man"—could be or could become citizens. Not only did this ostracize and limit the rights of such persons, these decisions even *stripped away* the citizenship of at least 65 Asian Indians to whom it had previously been granted. One such person was Vaisho Das Bagai.

Vaisho had renounced his British citizenship to become an American. With his American citizenship stripped away, he became a citizen of no country at all. Because he was not a citizen (any longer), he was no longer allowed to own property in California, and was forced to sell his home and general store. The U.S. Government even refused to grant him a passport to visit his family in India. He committed suicide in 1928, and sent one of his suicide notes to the San Francisco Examiner:

> I came to America thinking, dreaming and hoping to make this land my home. Sold my properties and brought more than twenty-five thousand dollars (gold) to this country, established myself and tried my very best to give my children the best American education.

> In year 1921 the Federal court at San Francisco accepted me as a naturalized citizen of the United States and issued to my name the final certificate, giving therein the name and description of my wife and three sons. In last 12 or 13 years we all made ourselves as much Americanized as possible.

> But they now come to me and say, I am no longer an American citizen. They will not permit me to buy my home and, lo, they even shall not issue me a passport to go

back to India. Now what am I? What have I made of myself and my children?

We cannot exercise our rights, we cannot leave this country. Humility and insults, who is responsible for all this? Myself and American government.

I do not choose to live the life of an interned person; yes, I am in a free country and can move about where and when I wish inside the country. Is life worth living in a gilded cage? Obstacles this way, blockades that way, and the bridges burnt behind.[511]

Although both the effect of, and very probably the intent behind, the Court decisions was racist, that racism was predicated on deeply held (and arguably *false*) premises. Those premises, however, were (and are) *widely believed*.

The *"popular account"* of race, for the last 150 years or so, is that races are real, naturally occurring, and more stable/real/natural than contingent human groupings such as nationality or religion. Many would agree, for example, that "France" is a contingent historical artifact that didn't always exist, didn't have to exist, and could

cease to exist (e.g., if Hitler had won the Second World War).

So too with religion. Scientology hasn't always existed, and very few people (if any) still worship the ancient Egyptian pantheon (e.g., Isis and Osiris). Races, on the other hand, are generally regarded as older, inevitable, immutable, and more "natural."

The racial assumptions that emerged from the 18th and 19th centuries, which were adopted by people like Hitler, and which continue to be employed by contemporary white nationalists such as Spencer and Taylor, included profound (and damaging) ideas:

- All humans fall into one, and only one, distinct, natural, fixed race.[512]
- These races are presumed to differ (essentially) in significant physical, mental, and moral qualities.
- Every member of a race is thought to possess their races "essence," and this essence is transmitted to one's children.
- There are physical indicators that allegedly correlate with race membership, and that provide mental "shortcuts." For example, dark skin and curly hair indicates that someone is "Black," which also means

---

[511]   http://www.aiisf.org/stories-by-author/876-bridges-burnt-behind-the-story-of-vaishno-das-bagai

[512] The racism inherent to racial essentialism (originally, at least) is evident in the "one drop rule." Historically, in the United States, one was "white" if they had no "black" ancestry anywhere in the family lineage. Even "one drop" of "black" meant that you were not "white." The assumptions lurking behind the "one-drop" rule are hardly ancient history, by the way. In March of 2016, a 6-year old girl was taken from her ("white") foster parents in Santa Clarita, California, after having lived with them for four years. Her biological parents had lost custody of her after a child abuse investigation. Her mother also had substance abuse issues, and her father

had a criminal record. She was removed from foster care, though, because she is "1.5% Choctaw," and a 1978 federal law was invoked (The Indian Child Welfare Act, designed to prevent large numbers of native American children to be adopted away from their tribal heritage and placed in non-Native American households). Although this child had never actually been exposed to any Native American culture, the mere "fact" that she was 1.5% Choctaw meant she was "Native American" under federal law, and therefore subject to the Indian Child Welfare Act.
http://m.nydailynews.com/news/national/girl-6-foster-family-native-american-law-article-1.2572704

(according to *racist stereotypes*) that that person is lazy.

- A natural hierarchy is thought to exist based on the "natural superiority" of some races over others. Although the precise number of races and their relative placement varies, in the United States it has always been the assumption that "whites" were at the top and "blacks" were at the bottom.

The belief that there are distinct, natural races, and that each race has its own particular "essence" that is transmitted by biological means, is known as "racialism."[513] This is not to be confused with racism! Racism certainly includes racialist beliefs, but adds to them notions of superiority/ inferiority, negative stereotypes, and moral judgments. In other words, racism is value-laden, whereas racialism is value-neutral.

- **Racialism**: beliefs and actions presupposing the existence of *biologically-transmitted racial "essences."*[514]
- **Racism**: *negative* value judgments and actions based on racialist assumptions.[515]

White nationalists are necessarily racialists, in that they explicitly espouse "race realism," but they also tend overwhelmingly to be racist as well, given their obvious disdain for "non-whites." Arguably, *most* Americans today are "racialists," whether they realize it or not, and whether or not they are additionally *racists*. This

is so despite the clear evidence for the social construction of race (as seen by our survey of history and Supreme Court rulings above), and despite the lack of evidence for *biologically-based* races or racial essentialism.

To put it plainly, there is no genetic basis for racial classification. There are no general racial characteristics that are shared by all members of the same "race," nor any genes shared by all such members. 85.4% of genetic differences between humans occur *within* a population ("race"), with roughly 85% of all human genetic variation found in a random sample of two people from the *same* tribal/ethnic group, from the same region. Genetic differences between people of different "races" are only marginally greater than that of two people from the same "race." Even the study of diseases that are more prevalent in certain "races" (e.g., sickle cell anemia in "Blacks") is based on *social definitions of race*. Nor is there any "race" found in or transmitted by blood. Although we might say that someone has "Native American blood" in them, there are only four major blood types (A, B, AB, and O), that can be additionally "positive" or "negative"—but none of these correspond to racial membership.

It's worth noting that only some patterns of physical features have acquired any racial significance. We don't regard height (e.g., "over seven feet tall," or "under five feet tall") as a signifier of racial membership, nor do we regard being a "redhead" as indicative of one's race. Not even skin color reliably picks out a particular group of people (e.g., some Australian Aborigines

---

[513] Note: this term is used by different people in different ways. I offer a specific definition of this term in this section, and it is that specific definition that is presupposed for the remainder of this chapter.

[514] This is not to be confused with ethnicism or ethnocentrism, both of which concern ethnicity, which refers to *learned cultural behaviors and norms*, as distinct from biologically-transmitted traits.

[515] There is also what is known as "institutional racism," which, in general, is racism expressed

and practices by social and political institutions, as distinct from racism by individuals. Institutional racism can be conscious and intentional, such as segregation laws, or unconscious and racist in its effects, rather than intentions, such as disparate minimum prison sentences for crack and powder cocaine. Institutional racism can be both a product and a source of embedded racist cultural practices within our social structure. This then creates barriers and privileges based on race through socio-political institutions.

are darker in complexion than many African-Americans, but are not regarded as "black"—at least not by Americans).

Simply put, which physical differences or similarities "count" has been historically arbitrary. Again and again, the pattern was the same: "races" were first defined based on socio-cultural conventions, and then physical means of classification were selected based on their usefulness in discriminating between the already-created socially constructed groups.

If race were truly and merely a matter of physical features, there could be no distinction between "looking white" (for example) and actually *being* white. To "appear white" just would mean that one *is* white, if personal appearance were all that mattered. And yet, for centuries there has been a meaningful notion of "passing" in the United States. . . .

Although it might seem like I'm belaboring the point, establishing the lack of a genetic basis for race is *important* because, without genetic carriers, racial traits can't be biologically *inherited*. Children might model behavior exhibited by their parents, but this doesn't entail anything resembling genetic destiny. "Lazy" parents might inspire laziness in *any* child, including an adopted child from another "race." Moreover, such learned behaviors could include a fondness for cloth napkins as much as "laziness"—neither of which is biological nor essentialist. If this is correct, there is no genetically-based "master race" that can be preserved through Hitler's most ambitious eugenics programs, nor is some genetically-based "whiteness" subject to "genocide" when "race-mixing" occurs, no matter how much white nationalists cry otherwise.

Although races seemingly don't exist as biological entities, they do have existence of a certain kind. There exists what Lawrence Blum calls *"racialized groups."*[516] Blum describes *"racialization"* as the:

treating of groups as if there were inherent and immutable differences between them; *as if* certain somatic characteristics marked the presence of significant characteristics of mind, emotion, and character; and *as if* some were of greater worth than others.[517]

Racialized groups can shift over time. The "Irish" used to be a "race," but are now an "ethnicity." To say that races are "social constructions," that there are not "races" in the sense of biological kinds but that instead there are "racialized" groups, is *not* to deny "race" any kind of existence at all! Nations are "social constructions," as is the State of California, but both are "real." Neither the USA nor California, however, have existed or will exist "naturally" and immutably throughout time. Nor is it the case that someone born in California necessarily and immutably inherits any particular physical, intellectual, social, or moral traits as a result of the particular State in which they are born!

Analogously, "races," as biological groupings, don't exist as natural artifacts—but racialized groups are real, treated as real, and *experienced* as real by their members. Members of racialized groups are often treated in similar ways, and thus often share similar experiences (e.g., being followed in stores, being asked if they speak English, being asked "where are you from?", etc.). This shared experience can contribute to someone adopting a group identity, and this self-identification can further contribute to the members' "racialization." Accordingly, we can recognize the lived experiences of people who have most certainly been treated as though their race is something "real" and determinant, while recognizing that race, is a biological/genetic concept is generally discredited.

To the extent that any worldview requires "race realism" in this biological sense, that worldview is unwarranted. In other words, when it comes to race, both Hitler and contemporary

---

[516] Lawrence Blum, *I'm not a Racist, But. . . The Moral Quandary of Race*. 2002.

[517] Blum, 147

white nationalists are simply mistaken. Another shared error involves the belief that Nietzsche was somehow a philosophical forefather and source of intellectual support for such worldviews.

Nietzsche

> I know my fate. One day my name will be associated with the memory of something tremendous—a crisis without equal on earth, the most profound collision of conscience, a decision that was conjured against everything that had been believed, demanded, hallowed so far. I am no man, I am dynamite.[518]

Friedrich Wilhelm Nietzsche (15 October 1844 – 25 August 1900) was a German philosopher notorious for what he wrote, for what people *think* he wrote, for the influence he has had on philosophy, and for the (often unjustified) influence he has had on various cultural and political movements.

He was born in the small German town of Röcken bei Lützen, located in a rural farmland area southwest of Leipzig, on October 15, 1844. His father was the town minister, and his grandfathers were also Lutheran ministers. When Nietzsche was 4 years old, his father died from a "brain ailment," and Nietzsche's infant brother died just a few months later.

Nietzsche entered the University of Bonn in 1864 as a theology and philology student. He attended lectures by the classics scholar Friedrich Wilhelm Ritschl (1806-1876). Ritschl was clearly impressed by the young Nietzsche, eventually writing a glowing recommendation of Nietzsche for a position on the classical philology faculty at the University of Basel.

However many young talents I have seen develop under my eyes for thirty-nine years now, never yet have I known a young man, or tried to help one along in my field as best I could, who was so mature as early and as young as this Nietzsche. His Museum articles he wrote in the second and third year of his triennium. He is the first from whom I have ever accepted any contribution at all while he was still a student. If--God grant--he lives long enough, I prophesy that he will one day stand in the front rank of German philology. He is now twenty-four years old: strong, vigorous, healthy, courageous physically and morally, so constituted as to impress those of a similar nature. On top of that, he possesses the enviable gift of presenting ideas, talking freely, as calmly as he speaks skillfully and clearly. He is the idol and, without wishing it, the leader of the whole younger generation of philologists here in Leipzig who--and they are rather numerous--cannot wait to hear him as a lecturer. You will say, I describe a phenomenon. Well, that is just what he is--and at the same time pleasant and modest. Also a gifted musician, which is irrelevant here.[519]

Nietzsche was offered the position and he began teaching there in May, 1869, at the modest age of 24! His writings, over the span of his career, covered a wide variety of topics: art, philology, history, religion, tragedy, culture, and science. He is known for his "perspectivism," his "genealogical" critique of both religion and Christian moral values, his theory of "master" and "slave" morality, his existentialist response to the alleged "death of God," his idea of the "eternal

---

[518]Friedrich Nietzsche, "*Ecce Homo*," in *The Portable Nietzsche*. Edited and Translated by Walter Kaufmann. New York. Penguin Books, 1982. "Why I am a Destiny," section 1.

[519] Nietzsche's recommendation letter from Ritschl.

recurrence," and the "*übermensch*," and the "will to power" (among other things).

Nietzsche served as a hospital attendant during the Franco-Prussian War (1870-71). He witnessed the horrors of war, contracted diphtheria and dysentery, and would suffer from a variety of health problems for the rest of his life. Migraine headaches, vision problems, and vomited precipitated his resignation from his teaching position in June, 1879.

In Turin (Italy), on the morning of January 3, 1889, Nietzsche experienced a mental breakdown which would leave him mentally incompetent for the rest of his life. One theory is that this was the result of syphilis;[520] another is that it was an effect of his use of chloral hydrate as a sedative; and yet another is that he suffered from a genetic disorder inherited from his father.

After a brief stay in a "sanatorium," his mother took him home and cared for him for the next seven years. After his mother died in 1897, his care was taken over by his sister, Elizabeth. She and her husband Bernhard Förster had been working to establish an Aryan, anti-Semitic German colony in Paraguay called "New Germany" ("Nueva Germania").

Having spent over a decade in a mentally incapacitated state, Nietzsche died on August 25, 1900, prior to his 56th birthday, from pneumonia in combination with a stroke.

After his death, his sister Elizabeth became the curator and editor of his manuscripts. She edited and reframed his unpublished writings to fit her own German nationalist ideology, despite the fact that his actual views were explicitly and undeniably opposed to both anti-Semitism and nationalism. Due to her efforts, his work became associated with fascism and Nazism.

- **Why does Nietzsche matter, in a chapter about white nationalism?**

Although I think the connection is misguided and unfair, it is undeniable that the Nazis considered Nietzsche a sympathetic fore-runner, and there is direct evidence that Hitler himself was both familiar with Nietzsche's work, and had a very high regard for him.

In the Great Hall of the Linz Library are the busts of Kant, Schopenhauer and Nietzsche, the greatest of our thinkers, in comparison with whom the British, the French and the Americans have nothing to offer. His complete refutation of the teachings which were a heritage from the Middle Ages, and of the dogmatic philosophy of the Church, is the greatest of the services which Kant has rendered to us. It is on the foundation of Kant's theory of knowledge that Schopenhauer built the edifice of his philosophy, and it is Schopenhauer who annihilated the pragmatism of Hegel. I carried Schopenhauer's works with me throughout the whole of the First World War. From him I learned a great deal. Schopenhauer's pessimism, which springs partly, I think, from his own line of philosophical thought and partly from subjective feeling and the experiences of his own personal life, has been far surpassed by Nietzsche.[521]

Nietzsche's sister went out of her way to encourage Hitler and the Nazis to appropriate her brother's work, not only by her selective and misleading editing of his notes, and outright

---

[520] Though this theory is now largely thought to be   discredited: http://www.leonardsax.com/Nietzsche.pdf

[521] H.R. Trevor-Roper, *Hitler's Table Talk 1941-1944, His Private Conversations*, Enigma Books, 2000, pp. 546-547. From a conversation recorded May 16, 1944.

forgeries of passages he never wrote, but by direct contact. There is a famous photograph from 1934 depicting her welcoming Hitler when he came to visit the Nietzsche archives. She later gave him Nietzsche's personal walking stick as a gift.[522]

This association was reinforced by hostile sources as well. In some writings, Nietzsche was nearly (personally) blamed for the occurrence of World War II itself!

> The Second World War was a war of insanity. Such a catastrophe can of course not develop solely out of the writings of one disturbed philosopher. . . . But the formulas employed by the perpetrators of the war, and the moral and philosophical justifications which they employed— these were given the "Powers of Darkness" by the lonely thinker of Sils-Maria and Turin.[523]

This (hyperbolic) association is not merely a *historical* curiosity. *Contemporary* white supremacists/nationalists continue to point to Nietzsche as an inspiration.[524] In an interview from 2017, Richard Spencer explicitly credits Nietzsche for his intellectual "awakening." "You could say I was red-pilled by Nietzsche."[525]

Specifically citing Nietzsche's "On the Genealogy of Morals," Spencer claims that his moral universe was "shattered" by Nietzsche's systematic dismantling of taken for granted moral and religious truths. This undermining of traditional values helps to explain the difficulty of placing Spencer into contemporary conservative "boxes." Unlike many conservatives, he is not bothered by gay marriage or abortion – in fact he favors abortion to the extent that it reduces the number of ethnic minorities that are born. "Smart people are not using abortion as birth control ... It is the unintelligent and blacks and Hispanics who use abortion as birth control. . . This can be something that can be a great boon for our people, our race."[526]

The original Nazis embraced Nietzsche because they (mistakenly) thought he endorsed their anti-Semitism, nationalism, and supremacist ideology. Contemporary white nationalists embrace Nietzsche in part through sharing some ideological "ancestry" with the Nazis, but also because they think Nietzsche's critique of "herd morality" and advocacy for a "master morality" applies to them and their causes. We will now consider (very briefly) Nietzsche's *actual* views, based on the works he wrote, edited, and published himself.

---

[522] http://sauer-thompson.com/conversations/archives/elis1933.jpg

[523] Lange-Eichbaum W. Nietzsche: *Krankheit und Wirkung*. Hamburg: Lettenbauer, 1947. p. 89.

[524] https://www.nationalaffairs.com/publications/detail/answering-the-alt-right

[525] https://www.theatlantic.com/magazine/archive/2017/06/his-kampf/524505/ Note: "red pill" is a slang term derived from a reference to

the film "The Matrix." It refers to being awakened to reality, and abandoning a world of illusions.

[526] https://www.theatlantic.com/magazine/archive/2017/06/his-kampf/524505/

- **"Was Nietzsche a proto-Nazi/national Socialist?"**

Far from it. In the fifth book of "the Gay science," Nietzsche denounces "nationalism and race hatred" as a "scabies of the heart and blood poisoning." He could not have been more explicit with respect to his views of German nationalism, specifically:

One pays heavily for coming to power: power *makes stupid*. The Germans, once called the people of thinkers – do they still think it all today? The Germans are now bored with the spirit, the Germans now mistrust the spirit....*Deutschland, Deutschland über alles*, I fear that was the end of German philosophy.[527]

- **"Was Nietzsche an anti-Semite?"**

Not at all. Although he did offer a scathing criticism of what we would consider "Judeo-Christian" values, he was not an anti-Semite. There is ample evidence for this. For example, the composer Richard Wagner was a one-time idol for Nietzsche, but he eventually broke with him in dramatic and public fashion precisely because of Wagner's anti-Semitism. In fact, Nietzsche devoted a lengthy essay ("Nietzsche contra Wagner"), and an entire book ("The Case of Wagner"), to his disillusionment with his former friend.

With regard to his sister, their relationship was strained to say the least. A significant source of his eventual contempt for her was her choice of husbands: Bernhard Förster, a prominent leader of the German anti-Semitic movement. Bernhard immigrated to Paraguay after a public scandal involving his abuse of Jewish streetcar

passengers. He founded a "Teutonic" colony that he named Nueva Germania. This activity, and her involvement in it, infuriated Nietzsche.

One of the greatest stupidities you have committed – for yourself and for me! Your association with an anti-Semitic chief expresses a foreignness to *my* whole way of life which fills me ever again with ire or melancholy. . . . It is a matter of honor to me to be absolutely clean and unequivocal regarding anti-Semitism, namely *opposed*, as I am in my writings. I have been persecuted in recent times with letters and anti-Semitic correspondence sheets; my disgust with this party (which would like all too well the advantage of my name!) is as *outspoken* as possible, but the relation to Förster, as well as the aftereffect of my former anti-Semitic publisher Schmeitzner, always brings the adherence of this disagreeable party back to the idea that I must after all belong to them . . . Above all it arouses mistrust against my character, as if I publicly condemned something which I favored secretly – and that I am unable to do anything against it, that the name of Zarathustra is used in every anti-Semitic correspondence sheets, has almost made me almost sick several times.[528]

You have gone over to my antipodes . . I will not conceal that I consider this engagement an insult – or a stupidity which will harm you as much as me.[529]

I have not yet laid eyes on my brother-in-law Herr Dr. Förster . . . That suited me excellently just that way.[530]

---

[527] Friedrich Nietzsche, "Twilight of the Idols," in *The Portable Nietzsche*. Edited and Translated by Walter Kaufmann. New York. Penguin Books, 1982. "What the Germans Lack," 1.

[528] Friedrich Nietzsche, *Gesammelte Briefe* ("notes"), V, 1909. #479. (Letter to his sister.)
[529] Ibid., Letter #377.
[530] Ibid., #418.

In reference to anti-Semites, generally, Nietzsche wrote: "you see, because of this species of men I could not go to Paraguay: I'm so happy that they voluntarily exiled themselves from Europe. For even if I should be a bad German – in any case I'm a *very good European*."[531]

Even in his own time, anti-Semites had begun to claim him as a kindred spirit, and this was something he found "laughable"—not laughable in that it was somehow insignificant to him, but laughable in that he could have been so thoroughly misunderstood.

> I have somehow something like 'influence.'. . . In the anti-Semitic correspondence. . . My name is mentioned almost in every issue. Zarathustra, 'the divine man,' has charmed the anti-Semites; there is a special anti-Semitic interpretation of it which made me laugh very much.[532]

There is ample evidence that Nietzsche was not anti-Semitic, and none (taken in appropriate context) to indicate that he was. Even if he wasn't an anti-Semite, he could still have been a white supremacist, of course. The contemporary white supremacist Jared Taylor, for example, is conspicuously *not* anti-Semitic. "I don't think that Jews are the enemy in the way that some people do."[533] Although white supremacy and anti-Semitism offer come as a package deal, this need not necessarily be the case.

Having established that Nietzsche was not an anti-Semite, we will now (independently) establish that he was not a white supremacist either.

- ## "Was Nietzsche a white (Aryan) supremacist?"

Once again, no.

The most often quoted (out of context) writing from Nietzsche in support of an Aryan interpretation is his reference to the "blonde beast." The "Aryan" reading of this quotation becomes far more challenging, however, given a fuller and more representative context.

> How much respect a noble man has for his enemies! – and a respect of that sort is a bridge to love . . . For he insists on having his enemy to himself, as a mark of distinction, indeed he will tolerate as enemies none other than such as have nothing to be despised and a great deal to be honoured! Against this, imagine 'the enemy' as conceived of by the man of *ressentiment* – and here we have his deed, his creation: he has conceived of the 'evil enemy', 'the evil one' as a basic idea to which he now thinks up a copy and counterpart, the 'good one' – himself! . . .

> Exactly the opposite is true of the noble one who conceives of the basic idea 'good' by himself, in advance and spontaneously, and only then creates a notion of 'bad'! This 'bad' of noble origin and that 'evil' from the cauldron of unassuaged hatred – the first is an afterthought, an aside, a complementary colour, whilst the other is the original, the beginning, the actual deed in the conception of slave morality – how different are the two words 'bad' and 'evil', although both seem to be the opposite for the same concept, 'good'! But it is not the same concept 'good'; on the contrary, one should ask who is actually evil in the sense of the morality of

---

[531] Ibid., #443.

[532] Ibid., #460.

[533] https://www.splcenter.org/fightinghate/intelligence-report/2006/schism-over-anti-semitism-divides-key-white-nationalist-group-american-renaissance

ressentiment. The stern reply is: precisely the 'good' person of the other morality, the noble, powerful, dominating one, but re-touched, re-interpreted and reviewed through the poisonous eye of ressentiment. Here there is one point we would be the last to deny: anyone who came to know these 'good men' as enemies came to know nothing but 'evil enemies', and the same people who are so strongly held in check by custom, respect, habit, gratitude and even more through spying on one another and through peer group jealousy, who, on the other hand, behave towards one another by showing such resourcefulness in consideration, self-control, delicacy, loyalty, pride and friendship, – they are not much better than uncaged beasts of prey in the world outside where the strange, the foreign, begin. There they enjoy freedom from every social constraint, in the wilderness they compensate for the tension which is caused by being closed in and fenced in by the peace of the community for so long, they return to the innocent conscience of the wild beast, as exultant monsters, who perhaps go away having committed a hideous succession of murder, arson, rape and torture, in a mood of bravado and spiritual equilibrium as though they had simply played a student's prank, convinced that poets will now have something to sing about and celebrate for quite some time. *At the centre of all these noble races we cannot fail to see the beast of prey, the magnificent blond beast avidly prowling round for spoil and victory; this hidden centre needs release from time to time, the beast must out again, must return to the wild: – Roman, Arabian, Germanic, Japanese nobility, Homeric heroes,*

Scandinavian Vikings – in this requirement they are all alike.[534]

It is a curious interpretation indeed to think that Nietzsche is referring specifically to so-called Aryans, when he explicitly points to non-Aryan people (e.g. Roman, Arabian, and Japanese), refers to noble races in the plural, and says of them with respect to this quality that they are "all alike."

In other words, he did not endorse "Aryans" as a "master race," and he certainly did not believe in German supremacy.

> The Poles I considered the most gifted and gallant among the Slavic people; and the giftedness of the Slavs seem greater to me than that of the Germans – yes, I thought that the Germans it entered the line of gifted nations only through a strong mixture with Slavic blood.[535]

Far from endorsing the pursuit of racial "purity," he explicitly advocated for *mixing* the races.

> Maxim: to have intercourse with nobody who has any share in the mendacious race swindle.[536]

> Where races are mixed, there is the source of great cultures.[537]

Yet another quotation that advocates the blending of races simultaneously negates the anti-Semitic interpretation of Nietzsche—a convenient "two for the price of one" rebuttal.

> The whole problem of the *Jews* exists only in nation states, for here their energy and higher intelligence, their accumulated

[534] Friedrich Nietzsche, *On the Genealogy of Morals*. Translated by Douglas Smith. Oxford. Oxford University Press, 1996. First essay, sections 10 and 11. Emphasis added.

[535] Nietzsche, *Gesammelte Werke*, volume XI, p. 300.
[536] Ibid., volume XVI, p. 374.
[537] Ibid., p. 373.

capital of spirit and will, gathered from generation to generation through a long schooling and suffering, it's become so preponderant as to arouse mass envy and hatred. In almost all contemporary nations, therefore – in direct proportion to the degree to which they act up nationalistically—the literary obscenity of leading the Jews to slaughter as scapegoats of every conceivable public and internal misfortune is spreading. As soon it is no longer a matter of preserving nations, but of producing the strongest possible European mixed-race, the Jew is just as useful and desirable an ingredient as any other national remnant.[538]

In the quest for "the strongest possible European mixed-race," Jews are "just as useful and desirable an ingredient." Not exactly the words of someone in favor of separation and racial purity, nor of someone who thought Jewish people were somehow lesser.

This is not to say that Nietzsche somehow possessed an accurate and progression notion of race. Nietzsche believed in the "Lamarckian" interpretation of evolution according to which offspring inherit the characteristics (including acquired characteristics) of their parents. According to this model, qualities acquired by parents over their lives can actually be passed down, biologically, to their children.

One cannot erase out of the soul of a man what his ancestors have done most easily and often.... It is not at all possible that a man should *not* have in his body the qualities and preferences of his parents and ancestors—whatever appearances may say against this. This is the problem of race.[539]

As a simple example, this model would suggest that if a parent lifted weights and became very strong and fit, their children would be born stronger and fit as well. We now know that this model isn't accurate, and genetic inheritance just doesn't work that way—but this view does help to explain his stance on the value of "race mixing." He advocated "mixed races" so as to cultivate the most diverse and advantageous mix of characteristics.

Importantly, although he seemed to think that characteristics would be transmitted biologically, he was not advocating some sort of eugenics program, in which people of exceptional physical traits breed with each other to produce "superior" babies. Instead, his focus was on culture. His understanding of a people (*Volk*) is based not on race/blood but on shared experience. "When men have lived together for a long time under similar conditions (of climate, soil, danger, needs, and work), then there *comes to be* ... a people."[540] With this cultural emphasis, the elevation of humankind, for Nietzsche, was to be found in art, religion, and philosophy – not "race."

We have seen that Nietzsche did not actually advocate anti-Semitism, Nationalism, or (Aryan) racial supremacy. He did write extensively about the "will to power," however, as well as the *Übermensch*. These certainly sound like macho appeals to strength/power, and the so-called "superman" or "overman" certainly seems ripe for placement into an ideology of "supremacy." In the remainder of this section, therefore, we will consider what Nietzsche meant by the will to power, how it applies to the *Übermensch*, and the sort of "mastery" he had in mind.

---

[538] Friedrich Nietzsche, *Human, All Too Human. A Book for Free Spirits*, translated by RJ Hollingdale (Cambridge: Cambridge University Press, 1996), section I, 475.

[539] Friedrich Nietzsche, *Beyond Good and Evil*. Translated by Walter Kaufmann. New York. Vintage Books, 1989. # 264.

[540] Ibid., # 268.

• What is the "will to power?"

You should become master over yourself, master also over your virtues. Formerly *they* were your masters; but they must be only your instruments besides other instruments.[541]

The will to power (hereafter abbreviated as WTP) is not mentioned by name in any officially published work until it is proclaimed by his signature creation, "Zarathustra." Prior to *Thus Spoke Zarathustra*, Nietzsche mentions the WTP in unpublished notes of the late 1870s.

In his early notes and works, Nietzsche considers the WTP to be one of two primary psychological drives (the second drive being fear). From this and other discussions, it becomes clear that Nietzsche's *initial* conception of the power sought by the WTP was political or physical – achieved via social success, making friends, being influential, etc.[542] What's more, Nietzsche's early discussions of power were often *critical* of this drive. "Who among you would renounce power, knowing and having learned that power is evil?"[543]

Power is denounced as "evil" because the pursuit of it – still considered the pursuit of worldly power – comes at the expense of personal integrity and individual autonomy. Nietzsche had not yet expanded his conception of power into the all-encompassing drive it would later become

With *Human, All Too Human*, Nietzsche's efforts become clearly focused on psychological forces. One example lies in human knowledge

acquisition. Humans do not merely passively receive information from their environment. We might argue over the degree of participation humans have, but the notion that humans *do* participate in the learning process seems indisputable.

Humans gather and organize sense data. Out of a chaotic stream of impressions, we construct (or at least filter) a comprehensible (diluted) set of data within which we can operate. We inevitably attempt to make sense of our environment, to give form to it, to impose structures, and, most tellingly, to conform it to our needs.[544] In this way, Nietzsche argues that philosophers especially exhibit strong WTP. Hitler attempted to conquer the world with his army, but Hegel attempted to subdue the entire cosmos with his philosophical system. To proclaim that the course of history has culminated in one's own theory is a transparent flexing of one's "muscle!"

The gathering, structuring, and production of knowledge, is but one example of the expression of WTP. As has been stated, Nietzsche attempted to explain *all* human behavior as such expressions. As Kaufman notes, an important development in Nietzsche's thought occurs in *Daybreak*, where he recognizes that the Greeks "value the feeling for power more highly than any kind of utility or good name."[545] His acknowledgment that the people for whom he had great respect also pursued power helped him to develop his idea that not only do *all* people pursue power, but that power can be pursued in different – and praiseworthy – ways. Among the most praiseworthy is the development of *self-*

---

[541] *Human, All Too Human*, preface, #6.

[542] Walter Kaufmann, *Nietzsche: Philosopher, Psychologist, Antichrist*, fourth edition. (Princeton: Princeton University Press, 1974), 180.

[543] Nietzsche, "Richard Wagner in Bayreuth" in *Untimely Meditations*, translated by RJ Hollingdale (Cambridge: Cambridge University Press, 1983), section 11.

[544] Bernd Magnus, *Nietzsche's Existential Imperative* (Bloomington: Indiana University Press, 1978), 25.

[545] Nietzsche, *Daybreak*, translated by RJ Hollingdale. Ed. Maudemarie Clark and Brian Leiter (Cambridge: Cambridge University Press, 1997), section 360.

mastery. Consider the first published mention of the WTP in *Thus Spoke Zarathustra*.

> A tablet of good hangs over every people. Behold it is the table of their overcomings; behold, it is the voice of their will to power.
> Praiseworthy is whatever seems difficult to a people; whatever seems indispensable and difficult is called good; and whatever liberates even out of the deepest need, the rarest, the most difficult – that they call holy.[546]

It is important to note that in this first official public proclamation of the WTP, it is already conceived in terms of *self*-overcoming. Through their "overcomings" a people inspire the "awe and envy of their neighbors."[547]

Interpreters differ on how power should be measured. Kaufmann argues that Nietzsche measures WTP quantitatively. "The quantitative degree of power is the measure of value."[548] That is, there is some identifiable "quanta" of power and the more one has, the more powerful one is. Unfortunately, all the warrior imagery Nietzsche employs may mislead his readers. Alexander Nehamas has researched *Beyond Good and Evil* and, of the hundred plus names that appear within, 90% are "writers and artists, not *führers* and Homeric heroes."[549] Kaufmann argues that Nietzsche's condemnation of tyrannical power is explicit, that "tyranny over others is not part of Nietzsche's vision."[550] Even prior to Zarathustra, Nietzsche envisions a scale of power with a barbarian at the bottom and an ascetic, who triumphs "over himself," at the top.[551]

We are still on our knees before *strength* – after the ancient custom of slaves – and yet when the degree of *worthiness to be revered* is fixed, only the *degree of rationality and strength* is decisive: we must assess to what extent precisely strength has been overcome by something higher, and the service of which it now stands as means an instrument![552]

In contrast to Kaufmann, Golomb argues that Nietzsche is better interpreted as promoting *qualitative* measures of power. That is, the kind of power employed by the artist (positive power) is qualitatively different (and more viable) than that exhibited by a thug (negative power). The distinction is that obtained between constructive and destructive power. It is a common theory within the psychological community that domestic batterers attempt to dominate their partners because they feel a lack of power over their own lives and situations. This frustration is given direct and primitive release through violence. This is "negative power" – a power to oppress/destroy. Contrast this behavior with that of a similarly frustrated artist. Rage wells up within him as well. However, rather than releasing these energies in a violent outburst, he takes hold of that energy, transforms it, and *uses* it for something desirable and productive: a work of art. His passions are channeled into artistic expression. He has mastered his drives and, in so doing, achieved a level of mastery over himself. This is "positive" power – a power to transform/create. The difference between these two is not simply a difference of degree but is also a difference in kind. Some manifestations of power are "higher" than others. Mastering

---

[546] Nietzsche, "Thus Spoke Zarathustra," in *The Portable Nietzsche*, translated and edited by Walter Kaufmann (New York: Penguin Books, 1976), section 15, p. 170.

[547] Ibid. section 15, p. 170

[548] Kaufman, 199.

[549] Robert C. Solomon, "Introduction: Reading Nietzsche," in *Reading Nietzsche*, edited by Robert Solomon and Kathleen Marie Higgins (Oxford: Oxford University Press, 1988): 6.

[550] Kaufman, 316.

[551] *Daybreak*, section 113, p. 113.

[552] Ibid., section 548, p. 549.

(overcoming) oneself is perhaps the greatest of all displays of power and an essential aspect of the present interpretation of the WTP.

This is not to say that Nietzsche claimed that WTP is expressed *solely* as a drive to overcome oneself. The striving for power is more fundamental than its target. "Where I found the living, there I found will to power, and even in the will of those who serve I found the will to be master."[553] The WTP is in all of us with variance arising only in its expression – and we can already see what expressions Nietzsche favors: self-mastery and authenticity. The person that best expresses power, that is most truly powerful, is the person who looks inward and disciplines herself to greatness. This kind of person is one of Nietzsche's "superior men." Ideally, this kind of person would be the *Übermensch* (Overman).

• The Übermensch

The Overman is the symbol of what someone will become when he conquers himself.[554] How does this kind of powerful person arise? The use of reason is indispensable. The powerful person is the rational person who subjects even her most cherished beliefs to scrutiny and he will surrender them if they can't withstand it.[555] This emphasis on reason gives further support for the position that the kind of powerful character that interested Nietzsche was not a thug or a warlord but was someone with a great mind capable of exerting much power (over himself).

> Rationality,... Gives men mastery over himself;... Reason is the "highest" manifestation of the will to power, in the distinct sense that through rationality it can realize its objective most fully.... In human affairs too, Nietzsche points out,

reason gives men greater power than sheer bodily strength. Foresight and patience, and above all, "great self – mastery"....[556]

> ... If his reason is strong enough, he will naturally control his passions. He is, without being ostentatious, an ascetic – insofar as he does not yield to his impulses – but instead of extirpating them he masters and employs them.[557]

The self-knowledge necessary for this self-overcoming is not easy to come by. "Everybody is farthest away – from himself; all who try the reins know this to their chagrin and the maxim 'know thyself!' Addressed to human beings by a god, is almost malicious."[558] Self-knowledge is not only difficult, but unsettling – and perhaps not suited for everyone. It appears that some people "must look at themselves only from a distance in order to find themselves at all tolerable or attractive and invigorating. Self-knowledge is strictly inadvisable for them."[559]

Rejecting both "Platonism" and Christianity alike, Nietzsche believed that because not all people are fundamentally the same, it is absurd to suppose that the same values (or models for life) are appropriate for all people. There are no absolute moral rules or standards, no single blueprint for humanity to which we should all aspire.

This is not to say that Nietzsche was some sort of amoral anarchist, let alone some sort of immoral sociopath. It is not "morality" that he wants to challenge so much as the belief that moralities have an unconditioned, universal validity. Although there is no one set of behaviors valid for all persons, there are moralities that are *conditionally* valid. They are validated on the

---

[553] *Thus Spoke Zarathustra*, section II. 12, p. 226.
[554] Karl Jaspers, *Nietzsche: An Introduction to the Understanding of His Philosophical Activity*, translated by Charles F Wallraff and Frederick J Schmitz (Baltimore: Johns Hopkins *University Press, 1997), p. 128.*

[555] Kaufman, 244.
[556] Ibid., 230
[557] Ibid., 234.
[558] *The Gay Science*, section 335.
[559] Ibid., section 15.

basis of their ability to "enhance life," given a certain person's own particular constitution—and we do not all have equally "robust" constitutions, according to Nietzsche.

In contrast to "herd morality" and mediocrity, Nietzsche encourages the capable few, the elite, to overcome and master themselves, to achieve their potential and to become the "justification" for mankind. Such a genuinely original and creative person "transvalues" traditional morals, and adopts her own "good" and "evil."

For Nietzsche, the "good" or noble person is someone whose "will to power" is channeled creatively, someone who looks at herself as an artwork in progress, who takes control of herself and masters herself. This artistic metaphor is pervasive in Nietzsche's writings.

> It is only as an aesthetic phenomenon that existence and the world are eternally justified.[560]

> To 'give style' to one's character--a great and rare art! It is practiced by those who survey all the strengths and weaknesses of their nature and fit them into an artistic plan until every one of them appears as art and reason and even weaknesses delight the eye.[561]

Nietzsche's "heroes" and role-models tended to be artists, rather than warrior or politicians. In references to the writer, Goethe, he says:

> He did not retire from life but put himself in the midst of it; he was not fainthearted but took as much as possible upon himself, over himself, into himself. What he wanted was *totality;* . . . he disciplined himself to wholeness, he *created* himself.[562]

What makes great persons *great* is their power to channel and transform their own inner drive (their "will to power').

> Once you suffered passions and called them evil. But now you have only your virtues left: they grew out of your passions. . . . Once you had wild dogs in your cellar, but in the end they turned into birds and lovely singers.[563]

The lovely and poetic imagery Nietzsche uses here portrays someone transforming their inner drive and passions, something they once regarded as "evil," into something beautiful: "birds and lovely singers."

For Nietzsche, part of what it is to be "good" (according to his own taste, of course!) is to not take life for granted, to not simply go along with the "herd," and to make of yourself a work of art. For those up to the challenge, *authenticity* should be one's goal—not that he believes very many are capable of this achievement! Most of us allow ourselves to be defined by others, and unthinkingly play out that assigned role.

Authenticity comes in two general stages, for those up to the task. The first is when we liberate ourselves from conditioning, rationalizations, illusions, and masks. This is a "negative" stage where one "hammers" one's "idols." It is important to note, though, that hammers are used for both destruction *and* construction; they destroy, but they also build.

After having broken our "tablets" of value, we freely assimilate values and norms consistent with our own nature in the second stage. This is the "positive" stage where we rebuild ourselves, and in which Nietzsche encourages those who can, the few, the "free spirits," to "become who we are."

> Be yourself! All you are now doing, thinking, desiring is not you yourself. . . . We are responsible to ourselves for our

---

[560] Nietzsche, *The Birth of Tragedy*, section 5.
[561] Nietzsche, *The Gay Science*, section 290.

[562] Nietzsche, *Twilight of the Idols*, section 49.
[563] Nietzsche, *Thus Spoke Zarathustra*, section I:5.

own existence; consequently, we want to be the true helmsman of this existence and refuse to allow our existence to resemble a mindless act of chance. One has to take a somewhat bold and dangerous line with this existence: especially as, whatever happens, we are bound to lose it. . . . There exists in the world a single path along which no one can go except you: whither does it lead? Do not ask, go along it.[564]

The greatest and rarest of such "free spirits" could be considered the *Übermensch*. This "Superman" ("Overman" is a more accurate translation—and one that doesn't conjure up images of spandex and capes!) would be the pinnacle of self-mastery, strong, confident, free— even a replacement for "God" (since Nietzsche believed that "God is dead.").

The "Overman" is also someone mentally strong enough to affirm the "Eternal Recurrence" of the same.

The greatest weight.-- What, if some day or night a demon were to steal after you into your loneliest loneliness and say to you: "This life as you now live it and have lived it, you will have to live once more and innumerable times more; and there will be nothing new in it, but every pain and every joy and every thought and sigh and everything unutterably small or great in your life will have to return to you, all in the same succession and sequence - even this spider and this moonlight between the trees, and even this moment and I myself. The eternal hourglass of existence is turned upside down again and again, and you with it, speck of dust!"

Would you not throw yourself down and gnash your teeth and curse the demon who spoke thus?... Or how well disposed would you have to become to yourself and to life to crave nothing more fervently than this ultimate eternal confirmation and seal?[565]

The idea of the eternal recurrence is actually an ancient idea, finding a home in Stoic cosmology, for example. Nietzsche's version, however, is best interpreted as an "existential imperative" rather than a cosmological hypothesis.

The question is simply this: given a chance, would you do <u>everything</u> in your life, all over again, exactly the same—all the pains, frustrations, and losses, as well as the triumphs and happy moments—and would you will to do so <u>forever.</u> Finally, could you will that this be so, and be *joyful* in the willing? To do so is to truly "embrace Fate"—what Nietzsche called *"Amor Fati."* The ability to do so is also, he thought, a profoundly *rare* thing, and anyone capable of doing so has truly executed a beautiful work-of-art self.

A person, in self – overcoming, is self – creating. For Nietzsche, *if* a particular person has risen "above" the animals, it is because that person has cultivated her nature. We are all suspended between two worlds and two selves. On the one hand, we have the world as it is given to us; on the other, there is the world as we create it. On the one hand, we have our empirical self, shaped and molded by prevailing social forces and customs; on the other, we have the self that we create for ourselves. "In man, *creature* and *creator* are united."[566] Also, "man is a rope, tied between beast and Overman – a rope over an abyss."[567] The suggested ethic is one of self – realization, posed within a full awareness and acceptance that the majority persons never do

---

[564] Friedrich Nietzsche, *"Untimely Meditations.* Translated by R.J. Hollingdale. Cambridge University Press, 1983. "Schopenhauer as Educator," section 1.
[565] Nietzsche, *The Gay Science*, section 341.

[566] Nietzsche, *Beyond Good and Evil.* Section 225, p. 154.
[567] Nietzsche, "Thus Spoke Zarathustra," section I:4, p. 126.

realize themselves and are ever resigned to exist in the "herd." "We, however, *want to become those we are* – human beings who are new, unique, incomparable, who give themselves laws, who create themselves."[568]

> If will to power is formed – giving, shaping, articulation, then the *Übermensch* forms and shapes the will to power which he himself is. It is not a question of mastering others, of overcoming the herd by overpowering it. The herd to be overcome is the herd in ourselves. Mastery and overcoming are to be understood as self – mastery and self – overcoming primarily....And since giving form to one's life in this instance cannot be a question of conforming to the format given by others, the *Übermensch* is self-forming...[569]

Conclusion

There is no question that Nietzsche was a radical and provocative philosopher. His writing style is challenging, and this invites numerous interpretations – and misinterpretations. Among the most pernicious of those misinterpretations is that Nietzsche was somehow the intellectual grandfather of Nazi ideology. This is demonstrably false, as I hope has been shown in this chapter. Nietzsche explicitly rejected anti-Semitism, German Nationalism, and notions of racial purity. The *Übermensch*, in his estimation, is far better expressed as a self-mastering free spirit than a totalitarian regime.

While white nationalism might be dismissed as a fringe movement, but it should be considered, understood, and philosophically resisted in the same way that Muslim-majority countries would be wise to monitor Isis sympathizers. Although the particular ideologies are different, of course, the threat can be framed in language that should be familiar if you have read the chapter on Rawls in this book. Fringe groups are not part of a well ordered society, and they represent a threat to stability if they grow large enough, and influential enough.

It would be quite uncharitable to suggest that the Trump victory of 2016 was the result of white nationalism – and that is certainly not my contention. However, issues raised by white nationalist groups, and anxieties they express, have undoubtedly worked their way into the political process and it had an impact on recent elections. A 2017 study of white working-class voters revealed the following trends:

- Nearly two-thirds (65%) of white working-class Americans believe American culture and way of life has deteriorated since the 1950s.
- Nearly half (48%) of white working-class Americans say, "things have changed so much that I often feel like a stranger in my own country."
- Nearly seven in ten (68%) white working-class Americans believe the American way of life needs to be protected from foreign influence.
- Nearly seven in ten (68%) white working-class Americans—along with a majority (55%) of the public overall—believe the U.S. is in danger of losing its culture and identity.
- More than six in ten (62%) white working-class Americans believe the growing number of newcomers from other countries threatens American culture.
- More than half (52%) of white working-class Americans believe discrimination against whites has become as big a problem as discrimination against blacks and other minorities. Nearly six in ten (59%) white working-class seniors (age 65 and older) believe it is.
- Six in ten (60%) white working-class Americans say because things have gotten so

---

[568] Nietzsche, *The Gay Science*, section 335, p. 266

[569] Magnus, 34.

far off track, we need a strong leader who is willing to break the rules.

- Nearly two-thirds (64%) of white working-class Americans have an authoritarian orientation, including 37% who are classified as "high authoritarian."[570]

Consider those numbers and now place them in the context of some other demographic trends. For the 2016 presidential election, white working-class voters are estimated to have been 44.8% of those who voted.[571] It is predicted that the United States will become "minority white" as of 2045.[572] Supposing that that is true, there are still decades remaining in which the white working-class will make up a sizable percentage of voters, and it seems reasonable to predict that if a significant percentage of them are already feeling anxiety about changing demographic and cultural trends, that anxiety will increase as their "minority status" ceases to be paranoia and becomes reality. The fears and complaints currently marinating and amplifying in the white nationalist movement could certainly become more widespread, and the threat to stability and a well-ordered society would increase as a result. Given the fact that a clear majority of white working-class voters *currently* exhibit authoritarian traits and think we need a "strong leader who is willing to break the rules," the inclusion of Hitler in this chapter might be disturbingly apt.

---

[570] Jones, Robert P., Daniel Cox, and Rachel Lienesch. "Beyond Economics: Fears of Cultural Displacement Pushed the White Working Class to Trump | PRRI/*The Atlantic* Report." PRRI. 2017. Available at: https://www.prri.org/research/white-working-class-attitudes-economy-trade-immigration-election-donald-trump/

[571] https://www.americanprogress.org/issues/democracy/reports/2017/11/01/441926/voter-trends-in-2016/
[572] https://www.brookings.edu/blog/the-avenue/2018/03/14/the-us-will-become-minority-white-in-2045-census-projects/

NOTES

NOTES

NOTES

NOTES